"To some degree, preachers have always had to take on the mantle of the minor prophets. It is a task that is vital in our day, and it is laden with challenges. How does the preacher denounce the sins of their age in a clear and compelling way? How can they hold out grace while remaining unrelenting about sin and its consequences? Preachers could use some help facing these questions. Paul House and Stephen Coleman provide answers. And these answers are the best kind, for they are pastoral and proclamatory in nature. The contemporary preacher should, can, and must preach the Minor Prophets. House and Coleman are helpful companions in fulfilling the call to proclaim the whole council of God."

> **Jeremy Meeks,** Director, The Chicago Course on Preaching; author, *Amos* (Matthias Bible Guides)

"In this masterful exploration of the Minor Prophets, authors Paul House and Stephen Coleman skillfully weave together profound scholarship and pastoral insight to illuminate the timeless relevance of these often-overlooked texts. Each chapter guides readers through prophetic clarion calls with clarity and conviction underscored by relevant New Testament connections and practical application. This work is a must-read that makes ancient truths accessible and transformative for those seeking to know God more deeply, seek his face more completely, and understand his enduring call to justice, mercy, transformation, and faithful living more fully."

> **Robert Smith Jr.,** Distinguished Professor of Divinity, Beeson Divinity School, Samford University; author, *Doctrine that Dances*; *The Oasis of God*; and *Exalting Jesus in Joshua*

"The Minor Prophets are life-giving and relevant in every age, including—or perhaps especially—in our own time. Yet preaching them faithfully comes with unique challenges. This excellent and important volume from House and Coleman will guide and encourage pastors to open these words from God to his people with confidence, clarity, and conviction."

> **James A. Johnston,** Senior Pastor, Camelback Bible Church, Paradise Valley, Arizona

"The Minor Prophets have posed numerous challenges for pastors for many centuries, often resulting in their neglect in the preaching ministry of the church. This volume provides a handsome resource that unravels these difficulties. It offers a treasure chest of literary, historical, and theological materials, while keeping in mind that these books are for the church (1 Pet. 1:11). For any pastor seeking to enrich God's people with the teachings of the Minor Prophets, this volume is indispensable."

> **Peter Lee,** Professor of Old Testament, Reformed Theological Seminary

"There are few commentary series more consistently faithful and pastorally helpful than the Preaching the Word series. This volume on the Minor Prophets is no exception. Paul House and Stephen Coleman prove to be reliable and wise guides through these often-neglected books. With clarity and conviction, they demonstrate that the unified message of the Twelve is one of divine confrontation and mercy: the Lord calls his people to account for their sin, summons them to repentance, and offers hope of forgiveness and restoration to the repentant. This volume will equip pastors to preach these prophetic books with both theological depth and pastoral warmth and help them to see and savor our holy and merciful God in their private devotions."

**Juan R. Sanchez,** Senior Pastor, High Pointe Baptist Church, Austin, Texas; coauthor, *Reaching Your Child's Heart*

"In *The Minor Prophets: Seek the Lord and Live*, Paul House and Stephen Coleman have provided the church a rich resource of biblical exposition, theological reflection, and practical application. Not only do the authors faithfully explicate the prophetic message, but they also powerfully capture the prophetic voice in its evocative and imaginative power. Though often overlooked by preachers today, these books contain much that the church needs to hear, and this volume will serve pastors and students of the word in relating the message of the Minor Prophets to the challenges, sins, and hopes of God's people today. This commentary is a timely and enduring gift to those who preach, teach, and love the whole counsel of God."

**Benyamin F. Intan,** President and Professor of Christian Ethics, International Reformed Evangelical Seminary, Jakarta, Indonesia

"The Minor Prophets are strange territory to most Christians (with the exception of Messianic texts at Christmas time and a few passages about social ills that have come to the fore recently). They are forbidding to most preachers, and it is deeply gratifying to see these efforts by highly qualified scholars who are also faithful preachers. All of us can learn something of our craft here!"

**C. John Collins,** Professor of Old Testament, Covenant Theological Seminary

# THE MINOR PROPHETS

# PREACHING THE WORD
Edited by R. Kent Hughes

*Genesis* | R. Kent Hughes
*Exodus* | Philip Graham Ryken
*Leviticus* | Kenneth A. Mathews
*Numbers* | Iain M. Duguid
*Deuteronomy* | Ajith Fernando
*Joshua* | David Jackman
*Judges and Ruth* | Barry G. Webb
*1 Samuel* | John Woodhouse
*2 Samuel* | John Woodhouse
*1 Kings* | John Woodhouse
*Ezra, Nehemiah, and Esther* | Wallace P. Benn
*Job* | Christopher Ash
*The Psalms (Volumes 1 & 2)* | James Johnston
*Proverbs* | Raymond C. Ortlund Jr.
*Ecclesiastes* | Philip Graham Ryken
*Song of Solomon* | Douglas Sean O'Donnell
*Isaiah* | Raymond C. Ortlund Jr.
*Jeremiah and Lamentations* | R. Kent Hughes
*Daniel* | Rodney D. Stortz
*The Minor Prophets* | Paul R. House and Stephen M. Coleman
*Matthew* | Douglas Sean O'Donnell
*Mark* | R. Kent Hughes
*Luke* | R. Kent Hughes
*John* | R. Kent Hughes
*Acts* | R. Kent Hughes
*Romans* | R. Kent Hughes
*1 Corinthians* | Stephen T. Um
*2 Corinthians* | R. Kent Hughes
*Galatians* | Todd Wilson
*Ephesians* | R. Kent Hughes
*Philippians, Colossians, and Philemon* | R. Kent Hughes
*1–2 Thessalonians* | James H. Grant Jr.
*1–2 Timothy and Titus* | R. Kent Hughes and Bryan Chapell
*Hebrews* | R. Kent Hughes
*James* | R. Kent Hughes
*1–2 Peter and Jude* | David R. Helm
*1–3 John* | David L. Allen
*Revelation* | James M. Hamilton Jr.
*The Sermon on the Mount* | R. Kent Hughes

((( PREACHING *the* WORD )))

# THE MINOR PROPHETS

## SEEK THE LORD *and* LIVE

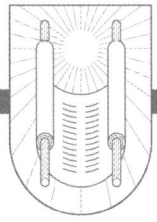

PAUL R. HOUSE AND
STEPHEN M. COLEMAN

R. Kent Hughes
*Series Editor*

WHEATON, ILLINOIS

The Minor Prophets: Seek the Lord and Live
© 2026 by Paul R. House and Stephen M. Coleman
Published by Crossway
   1300 Crescent Street
   Wheaton, Illinois 60187
All rights reserved. No part of this publication may be reproduced, stored in a retrieval system, or transmitted in any form by any means, electronic, mechanical, photocopy, recording, or otherwise, without the prior permission of the publisher, except as provided for by USA copyright law. Crossway® is a registered trademark in the United States of America.

Cover design: Jon McGrath, Simplicated Studio

Cover image: Adam Greene, illustrator

First printing 2026

Printed in the United States of America

Unless otherwise indicated, Scripture quotations are from the ESV® Bible (The Holy Bible, English Standard Version®), © 2001 by Crossway, a publishing ministry of Good News Publishers. Used by permission. All rights reserved. The ESV text may not be quoted in any publication made available to the public by a Creative Commons license. The ESV may not be translated in whole or in part into any other language.

Scripture quotations marked AT are the author's translation.

Scripture quotations designated JPS are from The Holy Scriptures (Old Testament), originally published by the Jewish Publication Society in 1917. Electronic text copyright © 1995–1998 by Larry Nelson (Box 1681, Cathedral City, CA 92235). All rights reserved. Used by permission.

Scripture quotations marked NIV are taken from the Holy Bible, New International Version®, NIV®. Copyright © 1973, 1978, 1984, 2011 by Biblica, Inc.™ Used by permission of Zondervan. All rights reserved worldwide. www.zondervan.com. The "NIV" and "New International Version" are trademarks registered in the United States Patent and Trademark Office by Biblica, Inc.™

All emphases in Scripture quotations have been added by the authors.

Hardcover ISBN: 978-1-4335-6401-7
Epub ISBN: 978-1-4335-6404-8
PDF ISBN: 978-1-4335-6402-4

---

**Library of Congress Cataloging-in-Publication Data**

Names: House, Paul R., 1958- author. | Coleman, Stephen M., 1980- author.
Title: The Minor Prophets: seek the Lord and live / Paul R. House and Stephen M. Coleman.
Description: Wheaton, Illinois: Crossway, [2025] | Series: Preaching the Word | Includes bibliographical references and index.
Identifiers: LCCN 2024048995 (print) | LCCN 2024048996 (ebook) | ISBN 9781433564017 (hardcover) | ISBN 9781433564024 (pdf) | ISBN 9781433564048 (epub)
Subjects: LCSH: Bible. Minor Prophets—Commentaries.
Classification: LCC BS1560 .H67 2025 (print) | LCC BS1560 (ebook) | DDC 224/.907—dc23/eng/20250219
LC record available at https://lccn.loc.gov/2024048995
LC ebook record available at https://lccn.loc.gov/2024048996

---

Crossway is a publishing ministry of Good News Publishers.

| VP | | 35 | 34 | 33 | 32 | 31 | 30 | 29 | 28 | 27 | 26 |
|----|----|----|----|----|----|----|----|----|----|----|----|
| 15 | 14 | 13 | 12 | 11 | 10 | 9 | 8 | 7 | 6 | 5 | 4 | 3 | 2 | 1 |

To the Homestead and Deeper Life Classes at Briarwood Presbyterian Church, Birmingham, Alabama.
—Paul R. House

To my father, Michael Coleman, with gratitude for your faithfulness to Christ, to Christ's church, and to your family.
—Stephen M. Coleman

*Seek the* LORD *and live,*
*lest he break out like fire . . .*

AMOS 5:6a

# Contents

| | |
|---|---|
| *A Word to Those Who Preach the Word* | xi |
| *Preface by Paul R. House* | 1 |
| *Preface by Stephen M. Coleman* | 3 |

## HOSEA (Paul R. House)

| | | |
|---|---|---|
| 1 | God's Enduring Love for Israel (1:1—2:1) | 7 |
| 2 | God's Disciplining Love (2:2–23) | 17 |
| 3 | Go Love Again: God's Determined Love for Israel (3) | 25 |
| 4 | Like People, Like Priest: God's Lawsuit against Israel (4) | 31 |
| 5 | Earnest Seeking of God (5) | 39 |
| 6 | Real Repentance and Foolish Rebellion (6—7) | 47 |
| 7 | The Vulture, the Whirlwind, and the Fire (8) | 55 |
| 8 | Leaving Harvest Joy Behind (9) | 63 |
| 9 | Time to Seek God, Time to Sow Righteousness (10) | 69 |
| 10 | "How Can I Give You Up, O Ephraim?" (11:1–11) | 77 |
| 11 | Idols, Money, and Prophets: A Family Story (11:12—12:14) | 85 |
| 12 | Ransom from Death (13) | 93 |
| 13 | Repentance, Healing, Fruitfulness, and Wisdom (14) | 101 |

## JOEL (Paul R. House)

| | | |
|---|---|---|
| 14 | A Plague for the Ages (1) | 111 |
| 15 | Even Now, Seek the Lord (2:1–17) | 119 |
| 16 | When God Answers Prayer (2:18–27) | 127 |
| 17 | God's Spirit for God's People (2:28–32) | 135 |
| 18 | When God Roars from Zion (3) | 143 |

## AMOS (Paul R. House)

| | | |
|---|---|---|
| 19 | The Shepherd, the King, and the Lion (1:1, 2; 7:10–17) | 151 |
| 20 | God's Authority and the Nations' Sins (1:3—2:3) | 159 |
| 21 | Israel and Judah Have Sinned (2:4–16) | 169 |
| 22 | Privilege, Responsibility, and Consequences (3) | 177 |
| 23 | You Did Not Return to Me (4) | 183 |
| 24 | Seek the Lord and Live (5:1–17) | 191 |
| 25 | Let Justice Roll Down (5:18–27) | 199 |
| 26 | Undisturbed by Injustice (6) | 207 |
| 27 | No More Delaying of Judgment (7) | 215 |
| 28 | The Ending Has Begun (8) | 223 |
| 29 | The Household of Jacob, the Booth of David, and the Remnant of Edom (9) | 229 |

## OBADIAH (Paul R. House)

| | | |
|---|---|---|
| 30 | Brothers, Bystanders, and Betrayers (1–11) | 239 |
| 31 | The Kingdom Shall Be the Lord's (12–21) | 249 |

## JONAH (Stephen M. Coleman)

| | | |
|---|---|---|
| 32 | Running from God (1:1–6) | 259 |
| 33 | Divine Pursuit (1:7–16) | 269 |
| 34 | Prayer from the Depths (1:17—2:10) | 281 |
| 35 | Portraits of Repentance (3:1—4:1) | 291 |
| 36 | Lessons in Compassion (4:2–11) | 303 |

## MICAH (Stephen M. Coleman)

| | | |
|---|---|---|
| 37 | Judgment Is Coming (1) | 317 |
| 38 | One Word of Truth (2) | 331 |
| 39 | God's Mountain Ruined and Raised (3:1—4:7) | 345 |
| 40 | Road to Glory (4:8—5:15) | 359 |

| | | |
|---|---|---|
| 41 | And to Walk Humbly with Thy God (6:1–8) | 375 |
| 42 | Lamenting in Hope (6:9—7:7) | 387 |
| 43 | A Liturgy of Hope (7:8–20) | 399 |

## NAHUM (Stephen M. Coleman)

| | | |
|---|---|---|
| 44 | A Stronghold in the Day of Trouble (1:1–8) | 413 |
| 45 | The Exalted Will Fall, and the Fallen Will Be Exalted (1:9—2:2) | 427 |
| 46 | God's Victory over the Pride of Man (2:3–13) | 439 |
| 47 | He Put Them to Open Shame (3:1–7) | 451 |
| 48 | A History Lesson (3:8–13) | 461 |
| 49 | And Death Shall Be No More (3:14–19) | 471 |

## HABAKKUK (Paul R. House)

| | | |
|---|---|---|
| 50 | Seeking God in Troubling Times (1:1–11) | 485 |
| 51 | Praying in Troubling Times (1:12—2:5) | 495 |
| 52 | God's Answer to Troubling People (2:6–20) | 505 |
| 53 | Rejoicing during Troubling Times (3) | 513 |

## ZEPHANIAH (Paul R. House)

| | | |
|---|---|---|
| 54 | God Won't Be Used: Renewal and Its Limits (1:1 and 2 Chronicles 34—35) | 523 |
| 55 | The Great Day of the Lord Is Near (1:2–18) | 531 |
| 56 | Gather to Seek the Lord (2) | 539 |
| 57 | A Singing God (3) | 547 |

## HAGGAI (Stephen M. Coleman)

| | | |
|---|---|---|
| 58 | Work, for the Lord Is with You (1:1–15a) | 557 |
| 59 | Future Glories (1:15b—2:9) | 569 |
| 60 | Defiled People, Divine Blessing (2:10–19) | 579 |
| 61 | Christ Victorious (2:20–23) | 589 |

## ZECHARIAH (Stephen M. Coleman)

| | | |
|---|---|---|
| 62 | Breaking with the Past (1:1–6) | 601 |
| 63 | How Long, O Lord? (1:7–17) | 611 |
| 64 | Glorious Things of Thee Are Spoken (1:18—2:13) | 623 |
| 65 | Clothed in Righteousness (3) | 637 |
| 66 | A Day of Small Things (4) | 647 |
| 67 | Thy Kingdom Come (5:1—6:8) | 659 |
| 68 | Behold, Your Priest-King! (6:9–15) | 669 |
| 69 | Mourning into Dancing, Fasting into Feasting (7—8) | 679 |
| 70 | The Return of the King (9) | 693 |
| 71 | The Work of the Good Shepherd (10) | 705 |
| 72 | Death Shall Be Their Shepherd (11) | 717 |
| 73 | By Thy Transforming Power (12—13) | 729 |
| 74 | On That Day . . . (14) | 741 |

## MALACHI (Stephen M. Coleman)

| | | |
|---|---|---|
| 75 | Questioning God's Love (1:1–5) | 757 |
| 76 | Our Great High Priest (1:6—2:9) | 769 |
| 77 | Created for Faithfulness (2:10–16) | 781 |
| 78 | A Consuming and Purifying Fire (2:17—3:5) | 793 |
| 79 | Putting the Lord to the Test (3:6–12) | 805 |
| 80 | When Faith Shall Be Sight (3:13—4:6) | 817 |

| | |
|---|---|
| *Acknowledgments* | 829 |
| *Notes* | 831 |
| *Scripture Index* | 917 |
| *General Index* | 961 |
| *Index of Sermon Illustrations* | 975 |

# A Word to Those Who Preach the Word

There are times when I am preaching that I have especially sensed the pleasure of God. I usually become aware of it through the unnatural silence. The ever-present coughing ceases, and the pews stop creaking, bringing an almost physical quiet to the sanctuary—through which my words sail like arrows. I experience a heightened eloquence, so that the cadence and volume of my voice intensify the truth I am preaching.

There is nothing quite like it—the Holy Spirit filling one's sails, the sense of his pleasure, and the awareness that something is happening among one's hearers. This experience is, of course, not unique, for thousands of preachers have similar experiences, even greater ones.

What has happened when this takes place? How do we account for this sense of his smile? The answer for me has come from the ancient rhetorical categories of *logos*, *ethos*, and *pathos*.

The first reason for his smile is the *logos*—in terms of preaching, God's Word. This means that as we stand before God's people to proclaim his Word, we have done our homework. We have exegeted the passage, mined the significance of its words in their context, and applied sound hermeneutical principles in interpreting the text so that we understand what its words meant to its hearers. And it means that we have labored long until we can express in a sentence what the theme of the text is—so that our outline springs from the text. Then our preparation will be such that as we preach, we will not be preaching our own thoughts about God's Word, but God's actual Word, his *logos*. This is fundamental to pleasing him in preaching.

The second element in knowing God's smile in preaching is *ethos*—what you are as a person. There is a danger endemic to preaching, which is having your hands and heart cauterized by holy things. Phillips Brooks illustrated it by the analogy of a train conductor who comes to believe that he has been to the places he announces because of his long and loud heralding of them. And that is why Brooks insisted that preaching must be "the bringing of truth through personality." Though we can never perfectly embody the truth we preach, we must be subject to it, long for it, and make it as much a part of our ethos as possible. As the Puritan William Ames said, "Next to the Scriptures, nothing makes a sermon more to pierce, than when it comes out of the inward affection of the heart without any affectation." When a preacher's *ethos* backs up his *logos*, there will be the pleasure of God.

Last, there is *pathos*—personal passion and conviction. David Hume, the Scottish philosopher and skeptic, was once challenged as he was seen going to hear George Whitefield preach: "I thought you do not believe in the gospel." Hume replied," I don't, but he does." Just so! When a preacher believes what he preaches, there will be passion. And this belief and requisite passion will know the smile of God.

The pleasure of God is a matter of *logos* (the Word), *ethos* (what you are), and *pathos* (your passion). As you preach the Word may you experience his smile—the Holy Spirit in your sails.

R. Kent Hughes

# Preface

Paul R. House

Preaching God's Word is a tremendous privilege and a serious responsibility. This task has been part of my vocation for more than fifty years. I truly wish that I had preached better, and I have not stopped trying to improve. I write this brief preface so that readers will know what I have tried to do. They can judge whether what I have done matches my goals or fits their needs. My sermons in this book seek to explain Old Testament prophetic texts in the context of Christian worship to help others know, love, and serve God the Father, Son, and Holy Spirit.

## Explaining Old Testament Texts

Since 1986 my preaching has occurred alongside my role as an Old Testament teacher. In effect, I have been a bivocational preacher, albeit one with a job related to the content of my preaching. Many invitations to preach that I receive come with a request that I speak on an Old Testament passage. Over time I have probably preached five or ten times more sermons on the Old Testament than on the New Testament. Thus, I have come to feel a deep kinship with the first Christians, who evangelized and discipled from the Hebrew Bible.

In general, Old Testament passages are longer and less familiar to hearers than their average New Testament counterparts. Therefore, I tend to cover about a chapter per sermon. I also find it necessary to explain more details, to do what my friend Phillip Jensen calls "explicatory preaching." Sometimes I struggle to show how the details fit the whole. Sometimes I explain too much or too little. Since most people know next to nothing about the Old Testament, I hopefully keep at it in the spirit of how Jesus and the apostles did similar work.

## In the Context of Christian Worship

Sermons are a key component in Christian worship services. They are not, however, the only component. Prayers, songs, Bible readings, offerings, and exchanges of greetings are likewise vital parts of our gatherings. Sermons do not have to contain everything in the Christian faith. Put another way, they should mainly contain the part of Christian faith that is *in the sermon passage*. This fact is worth noting if one desires to preach what texts say, not what preachers want them to say or what current preaching trends claim they should say. Every passage fits into the whole of the Christian story. Not every text tells the whole story. Inserting any portion of the story into a text as if it were in the text harms good Biblical reading and understanding.

Our worship services ought to tell the big Christian story. Sermons help our prayers, readings, singing, and greetings to do that. I hope that my sermons have done that. Since readers do not have copies of the order of worship in which I preached these sermons, I ask you to believe that the full gospel was included in our services.

## For Knowing, Loving, and Serving God

Sermons foster people's relationship with God. As I have preached these sermons, I have become ever more aware that the prophets wrote from a deep relationship with him. They knew God's character and how he governs the world and provides for his people. They testified of God's enduring love. They served God in normal and extreme circumstances. Their words strove to bring others into a closer relationship with their Lord. Sermons that hew closely to these texts have the same goals.

My sermons in this volume have a strong corrective and exhortative tone. I believe that this tendency is in keeping with the prophets' ministries. I think that it also fits Paul's words about preaching in 2 Timothy 4:2: "Preach the word; be ready in season and out of season; reprove, rebuke, and exhort, with complete patience and teaching." All correction is meant to bring hearers closer to God.

Illustrations can help facilitate knowing, loving, and serving God. They are not for entertainment. I have used illustrations sparingly in these sermons' written form, preferring to focus on explication. In person, I use more illustrations, ones fitting the congregation I address. As with all written sermons, the audience for these sermons is wider than the original one. I especially hope that these sermons will help pastors preach and enrich people who read them devotionally.

## Conclusion

As I write these words, I anticipate preaching tomorrow. I am praying for other preachers. I am also praying that hearers and readers of sermons will receive Christ, walk with him, serve him, and rejoice in him until the day when God sings with us in the new heavens and earth (Isaiah 65:17–25; Zephaniah 3:14–20).

# Preface

Stephen M. Coleman

It is often (and correctly) noted that there is nothing minor about the minor prophets. Their corpus contains some of the greatest literature in the history of the world. *Jonah*, for instance, is considered by many as the finest short story ever written. Nahum, to name another, is rightly regarded as a poet of singular genius. Preaching through this corpus, I was time and again struck by the immense cognitive and aesthetic power of these ancient figures, and I found myself often trying (and often failing) to convey something of their prophetic voice in my own sermons.

However, much more than literary giants, these prophets were towering figures because they functioned as mouthpieces of the living God. As such, they delivered powerful messages of judgment and salvation, ruin and restoration to God's covenant people. As any reader will quickly observe, their oracles are often difficult, obscure, and bewildering. The ancient Near Eastern context feels foreign to our modern experience, and Israel's life seems quite distant from our daily lives. However, though much is different, much is also the same. We see in these books (scrolls?) that the same sins that plagued the hearts of ancient Israel continue to beset our own hearts today. Their struggles with doubt, discouragement, and at times despair resonate in our experiences as we too struggle to trust God and to understand his ways in the world. Thankfully, our connection with our forefathers and foremothers goes deeper than shared sin, as the hope of Israel announced by these prophets remains our hope today—namely, "the sufferings of Christ and the subsequent glories" (1 Peter 1:11). Though inhabitants of a foreign and distant world, these messengers of God continue to serve his people today as they announce the penalty-paying substitute for God's people under the old covenant and the new. For this reason it has been a unique joy for me to work through the Minor Prophets with a view to expounding their message for Christ's Church today.

In keeping with the vision of the Preaching the Word series, the commentary that follows has been adapted from sermons written for and, for the most part, preached, in a variety of church contexts. My goal in these sermons is basically fourfold: 1) to exposit the message of the text as given in its original context, 2) to situate the text within its larger redemptive historical context, 3) to show how it finds its fulfillment in the Christ who stands at the center of Scripture (Luke 24:25–27), and 4) to tease out some implications of the text for Christian life and worship. Whether or not I accomplished these goals is, of course, for the reader to decide. To whatever extent I have accomplished them, however, may God receive all the glory and may his church be blessed through these efforts.

Though a fuller, though by no means exhaustive, acknowledgment of individuals and churches who have supported and contributed to this work may be found at the end of this volume, here at the beginning I would like to mention just one: I wish to thank my father, Michael Coleman, whose forty years of pastoral ministry modeled for me (and many others) how to shepherd Christ's flock faithfully both in and out of the pulpit. Thank you, Dad, for your faithfulness to Christ, to Christ's Church, and to your family. It is with love and gratitude that I dedicate my portion of this commentary to you.

# HOSEA

*By Paul R. House*

# 1

# God's Enduring Love for Israel

HOSEA 1:1—2:1

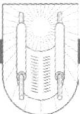

THE BIBLE TELLS US many things about God's character. For instance, in Exodus 34:6, 7 God states that he is "merciful and gracious, slow to anger, and abounding in steadfast love and faithfulness, keeping steadfast love for thousands, forgiving iniquity and transgression and sin, but who will by no means clear the guilty." First John 4:7, 8 summarizes all these traits and how we are to respond to them when it says, "Beloved, let us love one another, for love is from God, and whoever loves has been born of God and knows God. Anyone who does not love does not know God, because God is love." John teaches that since God is love, we must love him and love one another. By stressing these twin themes, John agrees with Moses (see Leviticus 19:18; Deuteronomy 6:4–9) and Jesus (see Mark 12:28–32). Though simple in concept, we all know these truths are hard to understand and hard to practice in daily life.

The book of Hosea is about God and his love. In Hosea, God endures horrible unfaithfulness on Israel's part. Yet his love is not controlled by circumstances or dependent on human faithfulness. In Hosea, God's love is as permanent and determined as God himself, and this love transforms people. God's love stands and stays when Israel tries to run and hide. It is a tenacious love, and it addresses sin. When a person accepts God's love, God binds that person to himself in an unbreakable relationship. He never lets them go.

Hosea 1:1—2:1 introduces us to God's enduring and life-changing love. God shows his love for Israel by calling a faithful prophet who will minister to them in turbulent times (1:1). This prophet lives what God has experienced with unfaithful Israel. Thus he endures pain like God's (1:2–9). This prophet declares God's tenacious love for Israel and Judah, claiming that God's covenant love can transform even the most hardened sinner (1:10—2:1). Hosea's opening verses remind us that because of God's love, the future may always be bright. God will set apart a people for relationship with him, and we can be part of these people who share his love.

### God's Faithful Prophet for Turbulent Times (1:1)

There are no easy times in human history. Jesus promised that in this world we would have tribulation (John 16:33), and we certainly do. Some eras are easier to navigate than others. But since the first humans sinned in the garden of Eden there never has been a golden age free of troubles. Still, certain times are worse than others. Times when major changes in political, social, economic, and religious arenas happen are especially challenging. Hosea lived in such times. During his ministry his people went from political and material security and prosperity to utter collapse.

The book of Hosea opens with this word: "The word of the Lord that came to Hosea, the son of Beeri, in the days of Uzziah, Jotham, Ahaz, and Hezekiah, kings of Judah, and in the days of Jeroboam the son of Joash, king of Israel." This verse informs us that what follows is from Yahweh and is given through Hosea. It also indicates that about 760–710 B.C. is the historical setting the book addresses. Finally, it invites us to recall Israel's relationship with God during these years.

It is always good when beginning a prophetic book to remember these books' extraordinary nature. Hosea does not speak on his own authority. Rather, "the word of the Lord came" to him. Like all faithful Biblical prophets, he is God's messenger. He is sent by God, the great King, to declare God's will to God's subjects. Yet these words are also Hosea's. They reflect Hosea's times, personality, and individual gifts. Thus, this book is not exactly like any other prophet's.

Because it is from God, we should take this book very seriously. We can learn the proper attitude to the prophetic books from the Apostle Peter. He reminds us that he and his missionary team did not tell "cleverly devised myths when we made known . . . the power and coming of our Lord Jesus Christ" (2 Peter 1:16). Rather, Peter gave eyewitness testimony of life with Jesus. He shared what he saw and heard when he and other apostles were with Jesus on the Mount of Transfiguration (2 Peter 1:16–18; see Matthew 17:1–8).

Peter adds that we have something "more fully confirmed" (2 Peter 1:19). What could be "more fully confirmed" than a word from Heaven that he heard with his own ears? What is more confirmed is "the prophetic word . . . to which you will do well to pay attention as to a lamp shining in a dark place, until the day dawns and the morning star rises in your hearts" (1:19). What makes the prophetic word so special, so certain, so deserving of trust? Because, he explains, "no prophecy was ever produced by the will of man, but men spoke from God as they were carried along by the Holy Spirit" (v. 21).

When we read Hosea, we take in the words of a man carried along by the Holy Spirit. We can trust these words to guide and shape us into the people God created us to be (Romans 12:1, 2). We can trust these words to change our stubborn wills and make us obedient to Christ. This transformation can only take place as we humble ourselves before God's Word. In his kindness he gives us his word about his love through Hosea. We are wise if we will receive this book, then, not as Hosea's opinions and experiences but as God's very words to us at this moment in our lives (Hosea 14:9).

Hosea appears nowhere else in the Bible. We know nothing about his parents except his father's name. We do not know how Hosea became a prophet. But it is safe to conclude from the book that Hosea was absolutely dedicated to God, completely faithful to his family, fearless in his presentation of God's word, and very creative in his speaking and writing. He held nothing back. He used all his gifts in God's service.

Hosea 1:1 lists four kings of Judah. Uzziah died c. 742–740 B.C., and Hezekiah began ruling by 715 B.C., making the book's time frame 750–710 B.C. or so. Uzziah, Jotham, and Hezekiah followed the Lord. But Ahaz worshiped idols. He was one of the least faithful rulers ever to defile David's throne. During Uzziah's reign, Judah had peace and prosperity. This was mainly due to no large, powerful nation being able to dominate smaller countries like Judah. Later, during Ahaz's and Hezekiah's days, neighboring nations and the mighty Assyrian Empire constantly oppressed Judah.

Given the book's contents, Hosea probably lived and ministered in the kingdom of Israel. Jeroboam II is the only king of Israel that verse 1 lists. He ruled Israel as coregent with his father Jehoash from 793–782 B.C. He then ruled on his own c. 782–752 B.C. Second Kings 14:24 states, "He did what was evil in the sight of the LORD." In particular, "He did not depart from all the sins of Jeroboam the son of Nebat, which he made Israel to sin." Verses 24–29 reveal that Jeroboam II sinned the same way his namesake, Jeroboam I, did two centuries earlier. What were these sins?

Jeroboam I (930–909 B.C.) was the new nation of Israel's first king. Israel seceded from Judah in 930 B.C. when Solomon died. Solomon sinned against God in his old age by worshiping idols, so God decided to take ten tribes away from him (1 Kings 11:1—12:24). Though God made him king, Jeroboam I feared that his people would worship in Jerusalem and would then want to reunite with Judah. His answer was to begin a new religion (1 Kings 12:25–33).

This maverick faith claimed to worship the same God as before. Yet it disobeyed much that God had revealed to Moses. It allowed non-Levites to become priests, used images of God, and set up worship centers in Dan and Bethel to rival Jerusalem. It became the state religion in Israel. The author of 1 and 2 Kings considered Jeroboam I the prime example of bad leadership for starting it (1 Kings 15:26, 34).

Mixing true faith with false faith eventually opened the door for other religions to enter the land. In particular, many Israelites eventually worshiped Baal. The most famous Baal worshiper in Israelite history was Jezebel, wife of King Ahab (c. 869–850 B.C.). Baal worshipers considered Baal the god of fertility. They believed Baal made land fertile by giving seasonable rain. They thought Baal also made women and animals fertile. Baal's followers engaged in sexual acts with "sacred" male or female prostitutes to show their commitment to him and to honor his power to provide fertility. Israel's economy was based on agriculture. Animals and crops were how people made a living. In other words, worshiping Baal amounted to worshiping sex and money. Baal worship was especially vile in God's sight, as Hosea stresses repeatedly.

This deadly combination of improper worship of God and worship of other gods made it difficult for faithful followers of God to live in Israel. The troubles the faithful prophets Elijah and Elisha endured make this point quite plain (see 1 Kings 17—2 Kings 13). These sins led God to punish Israel by sending Assyria against them. By 732 B.C. Assyria made Israel a satellite nation in its empire. By 722 B.C. Assyria had destroyed Samaria, Israel's capital. Each time, Assyria took captives.

Hosea warned that these things would occur, but the people did not listen. One reason they did not listen was that the nation was wealthy during Jeroboam II's reign. Also, there were few wars. Everything seemed fine. The people probably thought Hosea was a crank. *If God is so angry*, they thought, *then why are we doing so well?* They may even have ignored Hosea altogether. After all, if Baal is the most powerful god, why listen to a lesser god's messenger? Hosea certainly had his work cut out for him. Religious pluralism and secular materialism are hardly new challenges for God's servants. Hosea faced these, and we do as well.

God despised what he saw in Israel. Turbulent times followed easy times, and Hosea ministered during both times. We need to remember that God may not be pleased with what he sees in our land. Faithfulness to him, not good financial times, determines his pleasure with us. Faithful Christian service requires us to follow Hosea's example. We must share God's message even if the world around us sees no problem with the way they are living. All who turn away from God and his offer of salvation in Christ will have turbulent times. These troubles may not come in this life. They will certainly come when unbelievers stand before God to give an account of what they have done with Christ in this life (2 Corinthians 5:10).

## God's Unfaithful People (1:2–9)

God sometimes commanded prophets to act out a message. This was abnormal. Prophets usually wrote or spoke God's message. These acts were deadly serious, not religious skits. Symbolic acts usually meant judgment was imminent. Time was up. Only repentance could stop punishment from coming.

These symbolic acts could be humiliating. They could seem almost cruel. For example, Isaiah went naked and barefoot for three years to warn the people that exile and loss were coming soon (Isaiah 20:1–6). God commanded Jeremiah not to marry to show the people that normal life was about to end (Jeremiah 16:1–4). Horrible times were on the horizon. Repentance was in order.

What God asked Hosea to act out exceeded all these in difficulty and sacrifice. His symbolic acts included his wife, his children, and his message. His whole life was involved. His witness showed Israel it was way past time to repent. In fact, judgment was near.

We all want a happy and normal home. God commanded Hosea to take on one of the unhappiest marriages one can imagine. At the very start of his ministry, God told Hosea to take "a wife of whoredom" and have "children of whoredom" (Hosea 1:2a). This extreme act symbolized the fact that "the land commits great whoredom by forsaking the Lord" (v. 2b). In absolute obedience Hosea went and married Gomer, a woman involved in some form of whoredom (v. 3).

People are fascinated with Gomer's lifestyle before and after she married Hosea. Scholars have suggested several possibilities.[1] They propose that perhaps she was not yet engaged in whoredom before marrying. Perhaps she was not sexually impure, only religiously impure, as the Israelites were at this time. Perhaps the story is a parable. Hosea may not have literally endured what the text describes. Perhaps Gomer was a prostitute in the Baal cult before she and Hosea married. People today are fascinated with sexual escapades and sex scandals, so we may be more interested in this discussion than we are in other Old Testament scholarly debates.

All these suggestions are relevant, and the issue is significant.

In response, God deals with concrete situations in all the prophetic symbolic-act passages. The acts demonstrate something happening in real life. Since the Hosea account is so straightforward, with no hint that what follows is an allegory, it is best to think that Gomer was a real woman with a real past that included real sexual activity that God deplores. This sexual activity may have been in service to Baal or not. Regardless, she acted in a way that God forbids.

God showed grace to her, however, by telling a man of Hosea's level of commitment to marry her. Hosea did not hold Gomer's previous life against her. The couple began marriage with a clean slate. Hosea did not treat his wife differently because of her past. He mirrored God's grace to her. With God, one's past does not determine one's identity. Jesus showed this when he spoke with the woman at the well (John 4:1–25), another woman with a troubled sexual past.

At first all went well in the marriage. Soon Gomer "conceived and bore him [Hosea] a son" (Hosea 1:3). God instructed Hosea to give the boy a symbolic name, Jezreel (v. 4). Little Jezreel was not the only prophet's son given a name that helped his father's ministry. A few years later, Isaiah gave his sons the symbolic names Maher-shalal-hashbaz and Shear-yashuv (Isaiah 7:1; 8:3). Isaiah's kids probably thought Jezreel was a pretty simple name for a prophet's son!

In Hebrew, Jezreel means "God sows." The Valley of Jezreel was where Gideon defeated the Midianites (Judges 7). It was also where Ahab and Jezebel had a palace and where they killed Naboth to take his adjoining property (1 Kings 21). It was the place where Jehu killed the kings of Israel and Judah and took possession of Israel's throne (2 Kings 9—10).[2] God explained why this name was given and what message the boy would carry with him all his life when he said, "In just a little while I will punish the house of Jehu for the blood of Jezreel, and I will put an end to the kingdom of the house of Israel" (Hosea 1:4b). For good measure he added, "On that day I will break the bow of Israel in the Valley of Jezreel" (v. 5). The boy's name meant that God would soon destroy Israel's royal house and its subjects. His name declared that a kingdom bathed in blood cannot endure and that a nation that approves of such governments will be punished.

The family story continues. Gomer conceives again. This time she has a daughter (v. 6a). Again, God orders a symbolic name. She will be called "No Mercy," for God has determined he will no longer "have mercy on the house of Israel, to forgive them at all" (v. 6b). God has been letting Israel's sins go unpunished. He has been bearing with their breaking of the covenant they made with him when he delivered them from Egypt (Exodus 20:1–17). He has shown compassion by giving them time to repent (cf. Exodus 34:6, 7). However, time will soon expire. Repentance must become their top priority.

God is ready to judge Israel, but he has decided not to punish Judah yet (Hosea 1:7). Remember that Assyria defeated Israel in 732 B.C. and again in 722 B.C. In 722 B.C. Assyria conquered Samaria, Israel's capital, and finished Israel as a viable nation with its own government. Though Judah also sinned repeatedly, God allowed them to exist until 587 B.C. when Babylon destroyed Jerusalem. God was patient with both countries. He was patient with Judah longer. Sadly, as the minor prophets reveal, Judah did nothing with this extra time. Instead, they followed in Israel's footsteps.

Hosea's family grows again. Another son is born (v. 8). God orders Hosea to name him "Not My People," a name that conveys illegitimacy. God chooses this name to declare to Israel, "You are not my people, and I am not your God" (v. 9). Israel has not been God's people because they have served other gods. They have broken their covenant's most basic command: "You shall have no other gods before me" (Exodus 20:3). Gomer may already have been similarly unfaithful to Hosea. Only when Jezreel was born does the text state that Gomer bore "him [Hosea]" a child (Hosea 1:3). Perhaps Gomer conceived the next two children with another man. Regardless, she later abandons Hosea and the children. Israel had certainly committed spiritual adultery time and time again by worshiping other gods. The third child's name reveals God's response to this betrayal.

What a family! Its very existence shows human love, human hope, human failure, and God's divine word. It also presents God's message to the world. As the book goes on, the prophet will declare Israel's murderous ways, Israel's callous disregard for God's mercy, and Israel's decision to reject God as God. Hosea will plead with the people to come home to their husband, to God. His heart and God's heart, his words and God's words, are one. Marital adultery is terrible, but spiritual adultery is even worse, for it has eternal, unchangeable consequences. It separates people from God and thus from mercy.

## God's Enduring Love for His People (1:10—2:1)

God's love for his covenant people endures through all sorts of sin and corruption. This is true at the individual and corporate levels. Though believers must not take God's kindness for granted, he holds us in his hand no matter what happens (John 10:28, 29). He did not renounce Simon Peter for denying Jesus (21:15–19). God did not disown the Galatians for their confused theology. He did not reject the Corinthians for their divisiveness and their terrible treatment of Paul. God keeps all his promises to those he redeems, for he made these promises based on his own character. His word and grace never depend on us. They are based on his covenant faithfulness. This faithfulness includes keeping his promise to Abraham of a large family, to David of a great kingdom, and to Moses of mercy for Israel.

In c. 2000 B.C. God delivered Abraham from idol worship in Mesopotamia (Joshua 24:2, 3). He called Abraham to follow him, and he made specific promises to him. God promised Abraham protection, land, fame, and many descendants (Genesis 12:1–9). When Abraham believed God's promise of a child when having a child seemed impossible, God counted his faith as righteousness (Genesis 15:1–6). God kept his promise. Six hundred years later, Abraham had so many descendants that Egypt was afraid of them (Exodus 1:7–10).

God will judge Israel in Hosea's time, but judgment is not the end of the story. Even after defeat and exile, God will see to it that "the number of the children of Israel shall be like the sand of the sea, which cannot be measured or numbered" (Hosea 1:10a). God will always maintain a number of Israelites who trust in him. These numbers will swell in part because "in the place where it was said to them, 'You are not my people,' it shall be said to them, 'Children of the living God' " (v. 10b). This means that Israelites will trust God in places where they will live outside Israel, which will in turn lead to Gentiles also trusting God. Paul quotes this verse in Romans 9:26 in a section devoted to explaining how Jewish and Gentile believers are both part of God's people. Paul indicates that Gentiles will swell the number of faithful ones, but there will always be Jews who trust in Christ.

God does not lie. His promises have no expiration date. Abraham will have Israelite and non-Israelite descendants until the world ends.

In c. 1000 B.C. God made special promises to David. He had taken David from being the shepherd of sheep to being the shepherd of Israel. When David desired to build God a house, a temple, God responded by promising to give him a house, a dynasty on Israel's throne. He promised David an eternal kingdom (2 Samuel 7:1–17). Every messianic passage afterward builds on this promise.

Hosea 1:11 reflects God's promise to David. Israel was divided from Judah in Hosea's day. Each nation had its own king. Hosea states that such will not always be the case. He proclaims that someday Israel will have one leader. When Jesus chose twelve disciples to minister in northern and southern Israel, he clearly began a new Israel with old Israelites. He kept God's promise to David (see Matthew 1:1–17; Romans 1:3, 4) by being the King promised long ago. He proved he was Messiah through his ministry (see Matthew 11:1–6), death, resurrection, and ascension. He sent his disciples to the ends of the earth to extend his kingdom. As the gospel is sown, there is a great harvest. As Hosea wrote in verse 11, "Great will be the day of Jezreel [sowing]." Great indeed!

God promised Moses that he would always be gracious, compassionate, and loyal (Exodus 34:6, 7). He would be Israel's God, and they would be his people (Deuteronomy 7:6). Because God keeps his word, he shows compassion to people who have been judged. He takes back people who have not acted like they are his people. Hosea foresees that when God gathers his people around one leader, the people will be his again. The family will be restored. God cannot act contrary to his own character. This means there is hope—even for Israel, even for Hosea's family, even for us. God does not change; hope remains even when all seems lost.

## Conclusion

This chapter introduces Hosea's message. God has spoken (Hosea 1:1). Rejecting God is like committing adultery against our Creator (vv. 2–9). Our sin pollutes the people around us. He will judge sins great and small. But he will see to it that some people follow him. He forgives those who turn to him (1:10—2:1). His promises never fail. We need not remain in our sins.

We can receive this restoration the same way as in Hosea's day. We can believe God's word, repent, and walk with God. The promised King has come. He has united the faithful ones in Israel. Gentiles have begun entering the kingdom. God's people are sowing God's word around the world. All who trust in Jesus, the One promised in 1:11, receive the forgiveness and reconciliation 1:10—2:1 promises.

God's love reaches out today. People with a past like Gomer's can find grace. People who have simply stepped away from God for a time can find grace. We can be part of God's people. We can find mercy. God's love is strong enough to take us back, take us in, and take us home.

# 2

# God's Disciplining Love

HOSEA 2:2–23

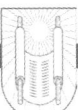

THE WHOLE BIBLE IS TRUE, but no part seems truer to me than Hebrews 12:11: "For the moment all discipline seems painful rather than pleasant, but later it yields the peaceful fruit of righteousness to those who have been trained by it."

Any sort of discipline, whether spiritual or otherwise, hardly ever feels pleasant to me, at least at first. For me the word *discipline* brings basketball and track practices to mind. It reminds me of hours spent learning Greek and Hebrew. It reminds me of writing my first college essays, when I worked and reworked sentences for hours just to make them actual paragraphs. The word *discipline* conjures up memories of late-night hours spent honing lectures when I was a young teacher. Most of all, it brings back memories of well-deserved punishments from my parents. I am not a big fan of discipline. Are you?

But I am a big fan of winning basketball games and track meets. I am extremely grateful to know some Hebrew and Greek. Writing good sentences and paragraphs makes me glad. Delivering a good lecture makes the preparation worthwhile. I have to admit that my parents' approach to raising children has helped make me a decent human being, at least on my best days. I am a big fan of the results of discipline, "the peaceful fruit" of discipline.

The best forms of discipline are born from love. Coaches and teachers are more popular in the short term if they have low standards. Kids often consider lenient parents "cool." It is easier to let people get by with anything they want to do, but this is not love at work. Love leads people to take the harder path. Love makes parents shape kids. Love drives teachers to help students reach

17

their potential. Love can inspire spouses to forgive much and to expect much. Love does the hard work that real life requires.

Hosea 2:2–23 describes love that disciplines and restores. In this passage, Gomer has clearly not been faithful to Hosea. She has not cared properly for her children. In fact, she has deserted the family. Hosea has many reasons to invoke Deuteronomy 24:1–4 and end the marriage. Yet this is not what he does, for this is not how God treats Israel who has sinned more often and for a longer time than Gomer has. Hosea reaches out to Gomer, yet with a strong and disciplining love that can cleanse and reconcile. This is also how God reaches out to Israel, and to us. Hosea and God show their love. They indict sin (Hosea 2:2–5), they punish sin to discipline and restore the offender (vv. 6–13), and they make plans for future renewed relationship (vv. 14–23). This love includes faith and hope, to be sure, but it also includes discipline. This brand of discipline restores relationships and remakes human beings.

### God's Indictment of Israel's Sin (2:2–5)

The prophets often present their messages as indictments in court cases (see Isaiah 3:13; Jeremiah 2:9; Micah 6:1, 2). In such instances they portray God bringing evidence against Israel or the nations for some form of covenant-breaking. In Hosea 2:2–5, the lawsuit is particularly tragic, for it involves an entire family in Hosea's case and an entire nation in God's case. It involves children pleading with their mother (v. 2), a husband considering serious action against his wife (v. 3), and a father wondering what to do with children that are not his own (vv. 4, 5).

Family troubles are hard on everyone. In many ways they are hardest on children, in part because kids have the least power, experience, and perspective. At their best, adults try to keep children out of harm's way in such times. Thus for Hosea to tell the children, "Contend[1] with your mother, contend—for she is not my wife, and I am not her husband" (v. 2), he must be at the end of his rope. Duane Garrett has noted that the Hebrew word I have translated as "contend" (*riv*) can also be translated as "plead," "rebuke," "find fault with," or "denounce."[2] The word usually appears in a context of a very negative statement about a person. Legal overtones are typically involved.

Hosea asks his children to reach out to their mother. He asks them to state that she has not been what a wife should be. In effect, God asks the same of his children and friends, the prophets. They must cry out and tell Israel that she has not been faithful to God. They must play the role of children asked to do the impossible—exercise authority over their mother.

It is important to understand the nature of this literature. The language is highly symbolic. It compares a terrible family situation to a terrible religious situation. This passage does not sanction using children to admonish a straying spouse. It certainly does not command us to do so. Instead, this verse plucks at our heartstrings. It tries to make us sad that things could come to such a state. If we are treating God or our own families badly, then it spurs us to seek God's way back to the right way of life.

In 2:3, Hosea states what he will do if Gomer does not change her behavior. He will feel compelled to take decisive disciplinary action. Instead of providing clothing for her, he will "strip her naked." Instead of providing food, drink, and financial security for her, he will "make her like a wilderness, and make her like a parched land." She cannot have his support and act however she wishes. He will not enable her sinful behavior.

These images remind us of the Bible's story of God's covenant provision for Israel throughout her history. He redeemed Israel from slavery. He fed and clothed her in the desert for forty years, bearing with her sins all along. He gave her the promised land, and this made her contented and faithful for a while. Yet later she rebelled again and again, and he sent her away from the land to teach her not to break her covenant vows. Still, he never gave up on her, and he protected her faithful children. Finally, he sent his Son to Israel to provide forgiveness for sins and reconciliation with him. Many believed, and they shared the good news with the world. Yet some refused to believe.

The story continues as the Church continues Christ's work on earth. It is important for each Christian, each church, and each denomination to ask how the story is going today. Are we walking with God, or have we left Christ, our first love (Revelation 2:1–7)? If the latter, we can expect God's discipline, not because he hates us but because he wants us back.

The imagery shifts a bit in Hosea 2:4, 5. Hosea is perplexed about what to do with the children, with his daughter No Mercy and his son Not My People. In a play on the first child's name, he states that he will have "no mercy" on these children "because they are children of whoredom . . . she who conceived them has acted shamefully" (vv. 4, 5a). He acts as if these are not his biological children. It is as if his wife left him with children that he thought were his, but he finds out they are not.

He reveals that his wife has gone after lovers and enjoyed the gifts she thought they gave her (v. 5b).

When Israel's adults went after other gods, they raised children who also worshiped idols. They did not follow Hosea and the other prophets' way of life; they followed the practices of those who worshiped Baal or other idols.

Such children are not what they should be. Their mother has led them to be like her. To protect the children, Hosea must keep them. He must take on and care for children who are not his own. He must show the sort of grace God shows to the citizens of Israel in Hosea's day.

As I have stated already, Hosea has a strong case for divorce. He has evidence that his wife has cheated and had children by her lovers instead of her husband. She has left Hosea with children that should not technically be his responsibility. Like God does repeatedly in history, however, the prophet takes another path. He does what is necessary to effect reconciliation. What he does is the subject of the next section of the book.

### Discipline for Renewal (2:6–13)

Hosea determines to cut off Gomer's access to her lovers (vv. 6, 7), her access to his financial support (vv. 8, 9), and her access to pagan temples (vv. 10–13). As the passage continues, it becomes clear that he sees these as first steps to reconciliation. He does not view them simply as a means of punishment or of shaming her. Renewed relationship is the goal. All along he wants to hear her say, "I will go and return to my first husband, for it was better for me then than now" (v. 7). Such reconciliation is always God's desire. He takes no delight in judging people, but he takes great pleasure in redeeming them.

In verses 6, 7 Hosea speaks as if Gomer is in a garden, which probably represents her home and marriage. She has been leaving the garden to pursue her lovers. Therefore, Hosea proposes to plant a hedge and build a wall that will keep her in the garden. She will not be able to get out on the old paths that lead her away from her family. As will become apparent, this means Gomer will lose her husband's monetary support. For Israel this means God will not protect them from their enemies. He will compress their borders. Foreign armies will take their land. They will not be able to get to the worship sites for Baal they are used to visiting.

Again the goal is to restore relationship. Despite all she has done, Hosea wants his wife back. He longs for her to say that it was better with him than with other men (v. 7). Today's talk-show counselors might find this pathetic or decide that Hosea is codependent in a dysfunctional relationship. This is not the case, for he knows exactly what he is doing. So does God. He does not need Israel's love to survive. He does not thrive on desperate circumstances. He acts in selfless love for Israel. He is filled to overflowing with grace. Love is reason enough for him to do what he does.

Verses 8, 9 present Gomer as unaware of how her needs have been met. She chases after her lovers, oblivious to the fact that Hosea provided for her all along. Thomas McComiskey has noted, "Israel did not acknowledge Yahweh as the source of her material blessing. It seemed obvious to many that one should seek fertile fields and abundant harvest from the fertility god. The wealth they had accrued from Yahweh's hand was used in the service of Baal."[3] Israel was as clueless as Gomer. The people considered Baal the giver of agricultural wealth and daily sustenance. They bought into Baalism's beliefs and practices. They took what God gave them and offered it to a false god (v. 8).

God's response is to withhold his grain, wine, wool, and flax (v. 9). In an agricultural community, this can only mean that the people will face economic hard times. The cause could be bad weather that inhibits the growth of crops, invasion by a foreign army that interrupts harvesting, or the partial or full collapse of their economic system. This threat echoes Deuteronomy 28:15–19, where Moses warned Israel that ongoing disobedience would lead God to cut off their normal food supply. God's goal was not simply punitive. His goal was to use means to awaken the people to their need to return to their God, the true giver of life.

We Americans should understand this passage quite well. We love our money. Sometimes we do not even realize we love money because materialism is so pervasive in our land. I am often asked if God uses financial privation to get people to return to him or to turn to him for the first time. The answer is that he does. God will get our attention so that we will flee from idols.

I do not have a simple formula that shows when God is doing this; the Bible offers no such thing. But it may be good for us to consider hard financial times as an opportunity to ask God to search our hearts and teach us of any wicked ways in us (Psalm 19:12–14). The purpose of this type of discipline is the same as any other: to bring us back to a right, loving relationship with God through Jesus Christ. If we think our needs are met outside of God's kindness, then losing cash may lead us to a better understanding of reality in Christ. If so, we will be the better for it.

Hosea 2:10–13 portrays Gomer as a party girl with many lovers. Apparently the lovers do not know about one another, for God says he will "uncover her lewdness in the sight of her lovers" (v. 10). They will see her shameful ways and repudiate her.[4] This will have the effect of ending the parties they have celebrated with her.

These parties were religious in nature. They included feasts, new moons, and Sabbaths (v. 11). In fact, they were days spent reveling specifically in Baal worship (v. 13), with all the sensuality associated with that religion. All this stopped during 733–732 B.C. when Israel's allies that worshiped Baal fell to Assyria's armies. These allies could no longer help Israel fend off her attackers. Furthermore, Baal could not save Israel. Israel was naked to the world, and all the pagan religious feasting ceased.

These verses describe a sad end to Gomer's and Israel's loose lifestyle. Her adultery, idolatry, and pleasure-seeking ended swiftly and violently. Shame followed shame. Yet it must be recalled that God brought this disaster to provide an opportunity for renewal. As long as Israel chased after other gods, there could be no relationship with the one true God. Unless God uses means to bring people determined to stray from him to their senses, there could be no redemption. God is merciful, even when he punishes.

## Plans for a Restored Relationship (2:14-23)

The Bible stresses that God is a great planner. For instance, Ephesians 1:3–14 states that before time began, God planned to redeem people from sin through the work of his Son, Jesus. Hosea 2:14–23 emphasizes the same divine, long-term planning. Having stripped Israel of her idols, God plans to renew and restore Israel to relationship with him. He will reach his redemptive goal. He will woo the people (vv. 14, 15), betroth himself to them (vv. 16–20), and have mercy on them yet again (vv. 21–23).

God is always gracious and compassionate (Exodus 34:6, 7). He always operates out of love for others (1 John 4:7, 8). He draws people to himself. He makes promises to those who enter into a saving relationship with him. Hosea stresses these truths about God by comparing God's love to a husband's love for a wife.

Having gotten Israel's attention by taking away her support, God says in Hosea 2:14 that he will now speak tenderly to his spouse. A. A. Macintosh has written that the word translated in the ESV as "allure" "is used [in the Old Testament] of deceit (1 Kgs 22:20ff; Jer 20:7; Ezek 14:9) and, between the sexes, of seduction and enticement (Exod 22:15; Judg 14:15; 16:5). The usage here is striking."[5] God will speak kindly, lovingly, even enticingly to Israel. As a result, she will come to her senses. She will respond positively and lovingly to God as she did when she followed him out of Egypt during Moses's time, according to Hosea 2:15. When she follows, her situation will go from one of living in the Valley of Trouble to one of living in the Valley of Hope. God will restore all he has taken away.

Israel chose to follow God at the time of the exodus. Hosea asserts that she will do so again. God will convince Israel to follow him. She will follow him, and this following will be like marriage, and Israel will call God her husband (2:16). When the Israelites served Baal, they married themselves to that idol. When they return to God, however, they will be married to him.

God will strike the family name of Baal from Israel (v. 17). The Bible often uses marital language to describe believers' relations with God (see Ephesians 5:22–33; Revelation 21:1, 2). This beautiful comparison gives great dignity to Christian marriage.

Christian marriage is not simply a solid contractual arrangement that helps a secular society order its affairs. It is a covenant relationship. That is, it is anchored in God's person and God's standards. Such is the case here in Hosea. This new marital relationship between God and Israel includes a new covenant (Hosea 2:18). This new covenant will benefit Israel, of course, but it will also benefit all of creation. Whatever has been devastated by God when he disciplines Israel will be healed. Wars and the weapons of war will no longer exist. Everything on the earth and in the heavens will bring benefit.

Isaiah calls this restoration "new heavens and a new earth" (see Isaiah 65:17–25; Revelation 21:1–4).

Hosea calls it betrothal (2:19). In ancient times, betrothal meant a great deal more than what Westerners now typically think of when they become engaged. A betrothal was a solemn promise that expected fulfillment. It included ironclad pledges. Here God makes such pledges to repenting Israel. This betrothal will last "forever" (Hosea 2:19).

The betrothal includes complete integrity on God's part. He declares his love in "righteousness," "justice," "steadfast love," "mercy," and "faithfulness" (vv. 19, 20a). This means God promises to act correctly in all situations, to judge rightly at all times, to stay loyal in every instance, and to maintain the relationship no matter what comes. These are very strong vows. They are even better than our "for better or worse" vows. Nothing will break his love. Israel can count on it.

This betrothal also includes love and faithfulness on Israel's part. Because of what God will do and because of the promises he makes, Israel will "know the Lord" (v. 20b). Israel will have a deep and wholehearted relationship with God. This relationship will include knowing God with heart, soul, mind, and strength (see Deuteronomy 6:4–9; Mark 12:28–32). It will be everything a marriage is supposed to be. God's grace will create and sustain the relationship.

These verses are Hosea's version of what Jeremiah 31:31–34 and Hebrews 8:8–12 describe as "a new covenant." God will begin afresh with Israel. He will forgive her sins, make her pure, and make her faithful. This restored relationship will result in great benefits for the whole world, not just Israel. Redemption will break out all over the globe. Israel will become the kingdom of priests and the holy nation that Exodus 19:5, 6 and 1 Peter 2:9, 10 envisioned. Twenty-seven centuries after Hosea lived, we see the truth of what he promised. Jesus Christ redeemed and called Israelite disciples, who took his message to the ends of the earth. All creation has benefited from God's great gift of a new covenant in Christ's blood (Luke 22:20). God has kept all his betrothal promises.

The chapter ends by reminding us of the names of Hosea's children. When God restores creation, the land will declare itself sown with God's love. Thus, it will declare itself "Jezreel" (Hosea 1:4, 5; 2:21, 22), for God will have sown it and made it grow. When God restores, he will have mercy on No Mercy (1:6, 7; 2:23). When God restores, he will make people who were Not My People (1:9) to be his people (2:23). All of sin's negative effects will be removed by grace through faith shown by repentance.

## Conclusion

Discipline is indeed hard. It takes away things we have come to love, even if they are things that are not good for us. But God's discipline always has the potential to restore, refresh, and reconcile. Gomer and Hosea's marriage seemed irretrievably broken. Israel and God's relationship seemed hopeless. God's grace surmounts all these obstacles. Just as Gomer and Israel repented of serving other gods and returned to the One who truly loved them, so we can return to God. He is the One who has created, supported, and loved us. He is the One who merits our love and faithfulness. If we wake up and return to the One who truly loves us, he will receive us. He will give salvation to those who are yet in sin, and he will bring back into full fellowship believers who have strayed from their covenant vows. God's grace is this powerful and this necessary.

# 3

# Go Love Again: God's Determined Love for Israel

## HOSEA 3

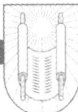

IN HIS NOVEL *SIMON'S NIGHT*, Jon Hassler portrays the life and struggles of Simon Shea, a retired English teacher living in Minnesota.¹ Shea thinks his life, or at least his mind, is nearing its end. So he checks himself into a boarding home for aged persons. Simon fears that he will soon no longer be able to think, write, and converse as he has for more than seven decades. He has stopped hoping to love again, for his wife ran off with one of his colleagues years ago. Due to his Roman Catholic roots, he has chosen not to divorce her, though she urged him to do so, no longer believing in marriage herself.

As the story unfolds, Shea learns that he was too hasty in his decision to leave his own home. His mind was not as far gone as he had feared. Friends young and old help him see himself more clearly. To the surprise of all, Shea's wife also returns to town, simply wishing to see him before they both die. Shea has never stopped loving her and has never stopped considering her his wife. He invites her home, and she accepts. Love begins again, despite all that has transpired. Shea can love again. His long-suffering patience has been rewarded.

Most of us have known real-life cases of what looked like hopelessly shattered homes put back together. I certainly have seen such miracles happen. What strikes me about all the happy endings that come to mind is that each one took great grace, great courage, and great humility. Not one couple's story was easy. They came away victorious yet hardly unscathed.

Hosea 1—2 has recounted God's strenuous calling for Hosea. Commanded to marry an adulterous woman, the prophet complies. He has children with his wife, Gomer. She eventually leaves him. This story parallels God's relationship with Israel. He has married Israel through his covenants with Abraham, Moses, and David. He has protected and provided for Israel. Yet the people have left him for other gods. Nonetheless, he has planned to bring Israel back to the marriage. He will woo, win, and betroth Israel again.

Hosea 3 provides a living picture of what God will do for Israel. As before, this living example comes through the real-life family of Hosea, Gomer, and their children. God has decided to go and love Israel again. Therefore, he calls on Hosea to go and love Gomer again. The grace that God and Hosea show provides a stunning portrayal of divine love and human love that is best seen in the life, death, resurrection, and ascension of Jesus Christ. This chapter requires Hosea to love again (v. 1), wait again (vv. 2, 3), and hope again (vv. 4, 5). His actions disclose good news. God still loves Israel. He will buy them back from self-imposed slavery, and they will seek him again.

## Go Love Again (3:1)

When we are young, we often think that love cannot be quenched. We consider it eternal and unending. Though we see the love of others cool and die out, we do not think our love can possibly be like that.

Such sentiments do not do justice to the nature of love—they are immature at best. They fail to see that love is a commitment made by choice. They fail to understand that love must come by grace. We cannot make someone love us. They must gift us with their love.

Such immature feelings likewise fail to grasp that love can be rekindled as one finds the wisdom and power to begin again. Most of all, they fail to respect the hard work love requires. Love is joyous work but work nonetheless. When God asks Hosea to love Gomer again, he is asking Hosea to show character that usually only God demonstrates. He is asking Hosea to do a rare, dangerous, and beautiful thing.

In Hosea 1—2, what God asks his servant to do mirrors what God experiences with Israel. Having endured desertion and having absorbed God's word for the future (2:2–23), Hosea hears from God once more. The prophet recounts that "the LORD said to me, 'Go again, love a woman who is loved by another man and is an adulteress' " (3:1a). Scholars have discussed this command at great length. Some believe that the text speaks only figuratively here, concluding God would not order a prophet to marry such a woman.[2] Others think the lack of a name here means Hosea married a woman other than

Gomer this time.³ Still others surmise that Gomer is the woman in 3:1–5, just as in 1:2–9.⁴

The third option seems most likely to me. No second wife's name appears. The events described in 3:2, 3 coincide with what 2:2–25 describes. Perhaps most significantly, God does not redeem a new partner. Hosea's situation parallels his. As 3:1b states, "The LORD loves the children of Israel, though they turn to other gods and love cakes of raisins."

Both Israel and Gomer have deserted their spouse. They have broken their covenant marital bonds. Gomer has sought lovers, thinking they will supply all her needs (2:5). Israel has gone after other gods and their supposed gifts, which is what "cakes of raisins" signify.⁵ Both have loved someone they should not. Both have treated their husband's love as expendable.

This betrayal serves to highlight the enormity of what God and Hosea are prepared to do. God will love Israel again even though the people have not cherished and believed in him enough to keep the first two of the Ten Commandments. Hosea will love Gomer again even though she has been with another unnamed man.

Such love reveals God's character and Hosea's. Their love exemplifies grace, forgiveness, perseverance, self-sacrifice, humility, and respect for ultimate concerns. It offers high standards for all relationships, especially with God and with our spouses. Christ's death for sinners came from this divine love. The willingness of Ruth, Jeremiah, Paul, and John to place their lives on the line for others grows out of God's example and God's empowering Spirit.

## Go Betroth Again (3:2–4)

In Hosea 2:19, 20 God pledged to betroth Israel forever. This betrothal was part of the restored relationship, and it preceded the full marriage imagery in 2:19, 20. Hosea 3:2–4 reflects these betrothal promises. As Stuart explains, betrothal "refers to the ancient Israelite practice of settling the marriage contractually by the groom's payment of the bride-price to the bride's father. This was the final step in the courtship process, virtually equivalent in legal status to the wedding ceremony. After the betrothal, cohabitation would follow at an arranged time."⁶ Presumably, Hosea would have made any such necessary arrangements when he married Gomer.

Now he has to pay again. To be able to take her as his wife again, he must buy her, perhaps from the man 3:1 mentions. He pays fifteen pieces of silver and a bit of barley (v. 2). The text does not divulge whether this is a high or low price or whether there were other bidders.⁷ What seems clear is that this would have been a hard, humbling experience for Hosea and for Gomer. At the same time, it made a fresh start possible. A second bride price means a second chance for them.

This second betrothal also includes a second decision about when full marriage will resume. Hosea tells her what they will do: "You must dwell as mine for many days. You shall not play the whore, or belong to another man; so will I also be to you" (v. 3). In other words, they will not have full marital relations immediately. After some time passes they will, but not yet. The betrothal means they are starting over, not simply picking up where they left off.

Hosea explains that this time of waiting has special significance. Once again, his marriage mirrors God's relationship with Israel. Hosea knows that "the children of Israel shall dwell many days without king or prince, without sacrifice or pillar, without ephod or household gods" (v. 4). In coming days the northern kingdom will lack a government ("king"; "prince"). It will lack a functioning worship center and priesthood. Thus it will lack the typical things that make a kingdom look like a kingdom. These "many days" begin when Assyria strikes Israel in 732, 722, 720, 701, and 671 B.C. Over a sixty-year period, this mighty empire leaves Israel with none of the trappings of a functioning nation.

But Israel still had who it needed most. Yahweh, their covenant God, had not left them. His love remained. He still claimed them, no matter what the circumstances looked like. As with Hosea and Gomer's betrothal, God's relationship with Israel would blossom into full reality in due time. Long after Hosea's death, Jeremiah harbored similar hopes (Jeremiah 3:16–18), as did Zechariah (Zechariah 10:6, 7). Like God himself, the prophets never gave up on the dream of all Israel reunited and worshiping the Lord. Time passes and dreams can fade, but God's promises never fail.

### Go Hope Again (3:5)

Looking far ahead, Hosea sees what God's love, kindness, and power will do. He offers no specific timeline. He gives no revealing details. He simply states, "Afterward the children of Israel shall return and seek the Lord their God, and David their king, and they shall come in fear to the Lord and to his goodness in the latter days" (Hosea 3:5). Knowing that such is the case, Hosea can hope again. His ministry will not be in vain. His marriage, which has been such a painful symbol of God's love for Israel, has not been for nothing. It stands as a marker of future blessing. This hope will be realized in several ways.

First, Israel will return to the Lord. The word translated as "return" literally means "turn around." It is often translated as "repent," and that meaning is implicit here. Israel will come to its senses and turn back from its rebellious course of action. A fundamental change in perspective and behavior will happen. God's people will be back on track with God.

Second, Israel will "seek" God. There will be urgency in their desire for him. They will hunger for a right relationship with the Lord, their personal God, who delivered them from idolatry and slavery through the exodus. No longer will other gods satisfy them. They will pursue and find the living God who has sought them for so long.

Third, Israel will seek "David their king."[8] The phrase reflects the biblical prophets' belief that someday Israel and Judah would reunite as one people under one king (see Isaiah 7:17; 9:1–7; 11:1–9; Jeremiah 3:6–18; 23:1–8; 30:9; Ezekiel 34:23, 24; 37:24, 25). This development will put an end to the division that occurred when Solomon died in 930 B.C. (1 Kings 11:26—12:24). It also reflects messianic theology. Isaiah, Jeremiah, and Ezekiel all looked to a Davidic descendant to unite the people, rule the people, and save the people. New Testament writers considered Jesus this rightful Davidic descendant (see Matthew 1:1–17; Luke 3:23–38; Romans 1:3, 4). Jesus's ministry fulfilled this promise. He ministered in Galilee and Samaria—both parts of Israel. He chose twelve disciples, not ten or two. He reunited Israel and called them to his side, which was the side of their King.

Fourth, they will "come in fear to the LORD and to his goodness" (Hosea 3:5). In this case, "fear" means deep penitence[9] along with the normal meaning of "awe" and "respect." Israel will "tremble their way back to God."[10] Yet this motivation is not all that will draw them. God's "goodness" includes his integrity, kindness, and faithfulness on behalf of his people.[11] As Hosea 2:2–23 has already stated, Israel will understand that God has been their good provider all along.

These promises occurred in history, especially in the person and work of Jesus, the Christ. People from all twelve tribes of Israel returned to Palestine during the days of Zerubbabel, Ezra, and Nehemiah (c. 538–450 B.C.). Many sought God and waited for the Messiah. As was noted already, when Jesus came, he gathered followers from both north and south. Israel at last had unity and a king. Indeed, these were "latter days," or "later days," from Hosea's standpoint. He saw and believed, and he asks us to do the same.

## Conclusion

Hosea's family situation now fades from the book. We read no more about Gomer and the children. But God's family situation remains prominent. He continues to bear with Israel, yet he will not do so forever. He will cut off the nation because they will not repent. He will leave them without king or support for some time. Their sin will be extremely costly. God will hold them accountable.

He will also redeem them. He will see to it that some from Israel will trust him, seek him, fear him, and love him. Despite all that has happened, he will love them again and again. He will buy them and betroth them by the work of Jesus. Thus they will hope again.

Hosea confessed his faith in God's absolute determination to redeem faithful Israelites. His faith and God's love seem incredible to us. However, it is the same love and faith that redeems seemingly hopeless sinners today. God's incredible love calls us to faith and hope. If we believe and seek God, he will take us back, even if we have fallen into lifestyles worse than Gomer's.

# 4

# Like People, Like Priest: God's Lawsuit against Israel

HOSEA 4

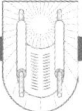

CHAUCER'S *CANTERBURY TALES* displays the author's marvelous understanding of human beings. It is amazing how, after 700 years, the stories still ring true for us. We strive valiantly to be like the knight as we hear his tale, yet we know few are like him. We smile knowingly—at least to ourselves—as we read the Wife of Bath spin her tales of lust. She reminds us of someone we knew in our hometown. Or we somehow recall someone who reminds us of the Clerk of Oxford, the student who studies all day and spends his spare cash on books. Maybe the person lived in our dorm at college. All these characters continue to come to life as we "go on pilgrimage."

Sadly, we also recognize a less famous character, the Pardoner. He is a preacher who bilks the public. He sells pardons from sin by coercing people, laying guilt on them, and manipulating them. Apparently he feels no qualms at all about what he does. In fact, he brags about how easily he gets gullible people to give him money. He is a predatory priest. Even the constantly gracious Host of the tales loses patience with him.

People have never liked lying, greedy, proud ministers. Even unbelievers think religious phonies have no place in the Church. Sadly, we recognize the Pardoner. Someone comes to mind when we read this tale, and we are not necessarily being uncharitable.

There are worse people in ministry than the Pardoner. Year after year we hear of pastors who fail morally. Sex scandals ranging from adultery to pedophilia have rocked the Church. Pastors who preach for the money and who seek to entertain the people (to give them what they want) are not hard to find. Faithful persons often toil for the Lord in obscurity while celebrity priests gain notoriety. Jesus once said about attention-seeking religious leaders, "They have received their reward" (Matthew 6:2). This is a stunning reminder to seek rewards that exceed our time on earth.

Israel certainly had predator priests like the Pardoner in Hosea's day. Like the Pardoner, they worked for the money. Like entertainment-oriented pastors, they gave the people what they wanted. Like the lascivious pastor, they enjoyed pleasure and immorality. Such priests were deadly to the people's souls. Tragically, after a while, the people wanted such priests. They did not share Chaucer's disdain for such so-called ministers. Like their priests, Israel wallowed in what Hosea describes as "a spirit of whoredom" (Hosea 4:12).

Hosea 4 addresses such priests and the people who support them. Here the Lord presents his critique of Israel's culture of whoredom in the form of a lawsuit. Israel has broken their covenant commitments to God. So God brings them before the bar of judgment to state their infidelity. He announces his lawsuit and why he brings it in 4:1–3, indicts the priests in 4:4–11, and concludes by indicting the people in 4:12–19. At the end of the passage, he notes that Israel is probably too far gone to save. Nonetheless he makes the effort. Once again he offers grace by giving his frank assessment of the people's spiritual condition.

### The Lord's Lawsuit (4:1–3)

Like a great king, God summons his people. They must listen to his convicting words about how they have walked away from him. This lawsuit has a plaintiff (v. 1a), offers an accusation (vv. 1b, 2), and describes the results of the people's actions (v. 3). The situation is dire, for Israel gives God little reason to continue the covenant. Israel does not sense their peril. Therefore, these verses are kind in their intent, though harsh in their tone. Hosea's goal is to wake the people from their moral slumber.

In verse 1, Hosea calls the people together and demands, "Hear the word of the LORD, O children of Israel." This command reminds us of Deuteronomy 6:4–9, where Moses called Israel to hear and love their God. The plaintiff in this suit has redeemed Israel from slavery in Egypt. He has forgiven their sins and guided them through his teaching. He has given them the air they breathe, the food they eat, and the land they live on (Hosea 2:8–23). They have a special mission: to take his glory to the nations (Exodus 19:4–6; 1 Peter 2:9, 10). This is no normal plaintiff. This is the one person Israel should honor and obey. God merits that reverence.

The prophet gathers them because "the LORD has a controversy with the inhabitants of the land" (Hosea 4:1). This "controversy," or "indictment," is that there is no evidence of covenant-keeping on the people's part. There is "no faithfulness," the sort of ongoing integrity of character that means they can be trusted.[1] There is no "steadfast love," the sort of loyalty to a covenant partner that goes beyond minimum expectations.[2] There is "no knowledge of God in the land." Here, as everywhere in Hosea, "knowledge" means the full range of mental and spiritual commitments that make a dedicated relationship.[3] The people fail to demonstrate any of the personal traits that one values in a strong, covenantal relationship. In short, they are nothing like God, who displays all these qualities.[4]

Israel's lack of moral character is evident. In verse 2, Hosea lists five of the Ten Commandments they have broken.[5] There is "swearing," which probably refers to cursing someone in God's name (the third commandment; see Exodus 20:7). There is "lying" (Hosea 4:2), the bearing of false witness against one's neighbor (the ninth commandment; see Exodus 20:16). There is "murder" (Hosea 4:2), the premeditated taking of life (commandment six; see Exodus 20:13). There is "stealing" (Hosea 4:2), the taking of others' property (commandment eight; see Exodus 20:15). There is "adultery" (Hosea 4:2), both spiritual and physical, as Hosea knows all too well (commandment seven; see Exodus 20:14). Such behaviors "break all bounds" that God has set for his people and for mankind. As a result of all this immorality, there is terrible violence: "Bloodshed follows bloodshed." An immoral society almost inevitably becomes a violent society—one in which physical brutality becomes a tool for getting what one wants. Clearly these sins mean Israel is no longer living like God's people.[6]

Because the people are living this way, Hosea 4:3 says that "the land mourns." Its inhabitants "languish." The animals God created suffer, perhaps because of a drought that has ravaged the land.[7] This suffering is not surprising. Leviticus 26:19, 20 and Deuteronomy 28:23, 24 state that God will discipline disobedient Israel by withholding rain. In an agricultural society like Israel's, the loss of crops and animals might awaken the people to repentance and renewal. Hosea declares then that God calls his people back to the covenant by sending threatened consequences. They are under God's discipline, yet they do not seem to care.

God uses all the means at his disposal to convict believers and unbelievers of sin. As Creator of the world, these resources include the natural order. He can make it rain or not. He can give food and water or not. We cannot know today if a particular disaster is sent specifically because of particular sins at a particular time. But we can ask ourselves in light of natural disasters if we have turned to the One who made the world. Eternity lies on the other side of droughts, tornadoes, tsunamis, and floods. Wise persons will see such wonders and make certain of their relationship with God and rededicate themselves to his service.

### God's Indictment of the Priests (4:4–11)

Israel must bear responsibility for their actions—they have chosen to sin. Nonetheless, they have had help turning away from God. These verses indicate that their priests have rejected knowledge of God (Hosea 4:4–6). They have ministered for greed, not for God (vv. 7, 8). Therefore, they will share the punishment God has set for the people (vv. 9–11).

Before anyone can answer his indictment of the people, God shifts his attention to the priests. In verse 4 he singles them out for special condemnation, declaring, "With you is my contention, O priest." They have special responsibility for the nation's spiritual decay because priests were supposed to teach the people God's ways (see Deuteronomy 33:8–11; Malachi 2:1–9). They were to set an example of service and justice.[8] They were to intercede for the people in prayer, and they were to help people offer proper sacrifices in the proper spirit to God (see Malachi 1:6–14). They were to possess and share "knowledge of God" (Hosea 4:1) in the fullest sense of that phrase. They were to teach the people the content of the faith and how to live out that content in their daily lives. They were to teach God's people how to be "a kingdom of priests and a holy nation" (Exodus 19:6) that declares God's glory to the nations (see Exodus 19:4–6; 1 Peter 2:9, 10).

When I was a teenager and felt a call to preach, my father gave me a study Bible. He said that the most valuable thing I could offer the people was explaining God's Word to them. But the priests of Hosea's day didn't have anyone to give them that advice, or they ignored it. The priests failed in every task God gave them. Hosea makes this plain by stating that the priest stumbles by day and the prophet stumbles by night (4:5). They have lost their way. They cannot find God themselves; they certainly cannot lead someone else to him. According to verses 5, 6a their actions contribute to their people's and their country's (their mother's) destruction. They have rejected knowledge of God in their own lives, and God will reject them (v. 6b).

What have these priests done to deserve such condemnation? First Kings 12:25–33 states that Israel's religion failed from the start. When Jeroboam I (930–909 B.C.) became Israel's first king, he set up a new religion.[9] This religion claimed to serve the covenant God of Israel. Yet it allowed priests from outside the tribe of Levi. It allowed the use of images in worship. It included dangerous components of un-Biblical religions. By Hosea's time it had long included aspects of Baal worship. There were probably priests who fought these trends, but the religion failed to stay true to God's standards. As a result, they did not know God, so they broke God's commandments, as Hosea 4:1–3 has already noted. These priests used God's name but did not teach God's ways. They held worship services but not in the manner God required. They taught ethical standards but not those God had revealed. Their ministries could not succeed by God's definition of "success."

It is prudent to ask how well those of us in ministry have avoided these priests' mistakes. Have we rejected knowledge of God by embracing false doctrine? Have we cast off Biblical truth in our effort to be scholarly or relevant? Have we replaced God's standards for those of our culture? Have we forgotten God's Word due to a lack of study? Do we care about notoriety more than we should? Have we led to the salvation and spiritual growth of our people, or have we contributed to their destruction? Faithful ministers need not fear or be overly introspective on the subject. Unfaithful ministers, on the other hand, should consider seriously God's judgment of these priests and repent.

Greed is a human problem, and ministers are human beings. Greed is particularly prevalent in ministry, however, when people go into ministry because they think it pays well. It is also prevalent when ministers use churches as stepping-stones to more prominent, better-paying positions. Hosea 4:7 describes Israel's priesthood as increasing. Duane Garrett explains that this verse "apparently refers to the fact that during a time of prosperity the number of people free to enter a religious vocation increases. Israel experienced such prosperity under Jeroboam II, and no doubt many considered the increased number of priests, their increased power, and the increased interest in formal worship to be signs of spiritual vitality. To the contrary, Hosea retorts, the more religious leadership the nation had the worse they became."[10] More priests led to more sin, for many of them had covetous motives.

The fact that their main problem was greed becomes more apparent in 4:8. God says these priests "feed on the sin of my people" (v. 8a). They benefit personally from the sin offerings the people bring. Like Eli's sons, who took for themselves the best parts of the animals brought as sacrifices (1 Samuel 2:12–17), they abuse God's system for forgiveness. They treat the worship of God as a scam and the people like suckers. They are happy when the people do the wrong thing rather than doing what is right (Hosea 4:8b). James Luther Mays observed that this passage shows the "priests have changed the cult into a way for them to make a living instead of a way for Yahweh's elect people to live before him."[11]

Ministers deserve to make a decent wage for the work they do. In fact, the Apostle Paul asserts that elders who labor in preaching and teaching merit "double honor" or double salary (1 Timothy 5:17). Yet Paul is determined to avoid charges of teaching solely for money. He takes pains to refute the idea that a ministry's value is evident by how much the minister can get for it. This is why he refused to take money from the Corinthians (see 2 Corinthians 11:7–15).

Ministry is not about money. Pastors who insist on a salary that buys the best cars, the best clothes, the best haircuts, and the best homes are not acting in a Biblical manner. Perhaps they are unaware of the Bible's teachings on the matter. If they know what the Bible teaches, they risk the condemnation Hosea declared on the priests of his day.

Hosea is saying that the priests lead the people to be as bad as they are. God will punish both for the way they are living. Hosea 4:9 reads, "It shall be like people, like priest; I will punish them for their ways and repay them for their deeds." The priests only seem to care about getting paid. God will indeed pay them but not in the coin they expect. Verse 10 states that God will see to it that they will "eat, but not be satisfied" and will "play the whore, but not multiply." The strong wine they desire will take away their understanding, according to verse 11. The things they crave will become God's means of punishing them. The sensual rituals and feasting associated with their worship of false gods will lead to God's punishing them for their covenant infidelity.[12]

This punishment occurred at various points in history. God sent Assyria to defeat Israel a number of times, including 738, 732, 722, 713, 701, and 670 B.C. Each instance happened because of Israel's failure to return to God (see 2 Kings 17:1–23). By the time Assyria was finished with Israel, the nation's kings, officials, priests, and people were all devastated. The priests were decimated, and their alternative religions ended forever. God's payment for their sinful deeds came as promised.

### God's Indictment of the People (4:12–19)

Though the priests are leading the people astray, the people seem very happy to go along. They do not want anything else; they especially do not want the Lord. The people seek guidance from other gods (Hosea 4:12, 13), practice immorality as part of the worship of other gods (v. 14), lead other nations astray (v. 15), and will suffer the consequences of their stubborn, sinful choices (vv. 16–19).

God is disgusted with Israel's choices. Having rejected him, his word, and his prophets, they seek information about the future from other so-called deities. This seeking includes what seem to us to be odd practices. Verse 12a reveals that they "inquire of a piece of wood, and their walking staff gives them oracles." This phrase probably means at least two things. First, it means the people sought help from idols, which were usually wooden images overlaid with gold or another precious metal. Second, it means they used some ritual associated with wood, such as throwing sticks or arrows in the air and taking direction from interpretations of how they landed.[13] Local priests or prophets probably led this activity. Only a "spirit of whoredom," a tendency to reject God in favor of an idol, could lead Israel to act this way (4:12b).

Of course, those who ask for guidance from another god also offer sacrifices to that other god. In Israel's case, verse 13 says they do this in various local shrines, not in Jerusalem. Israel pursues their worship in these places because "their shade is good" (v. 13), which probably means it is pleasant to them to offer sacrifice in these settings. Their worship centers on their wishes and wants, not on their actual need of God. Such worship is, once again, spiritual adultery.

There are always unintended consequences of false worship. According to verse 14, young people have grown sexually lax because of what they have been taught. Young women "play the whore" and "commit adultery." These are terrible sins, yet God says he will not punish them as if they have done their husbands wrong since they learned adultery from their leaders. In other words, they saw men going to sacred prostitutes or perhaps losing self-control because of drunken rituals, and they committed sexual immorality in daily life. They did with people outside so-called worship services what they saw their elders doing in such services. Just as children may learn to lie, act hypocritically, fight others, and engage in other bad behaviors they see in church, so these women acted out what they observed in the false worship of their day.

It was not enough for Israel to harm their own people. They also led other nations away from God. They tempted Judah to follow their example. In verse 15, God strongly cautions Judah against falling prey to Israel's way of life. Judah shared a religious history with their northern kinsmen. This history was rich with places, and two of them figure in this verse. Both now featured corrupt worship sites just across Israel's southern border.

First, they tempted Judah to come to Gilgal, where Joshua had led the people (Joshua 5:7–12), where some of the Saul stories began to unfold (1 Samuel 11:14, 15), and where Elisha and his disciples stayed (2 Kings 4:38).[14] Second, they lured Judah to attend worship at Beth-aven (Hosea 4:15), which means "house of iniquity." This is the name Hosea gives to Bethel, which means "house of God." Bethel is where Abraham camped (Genesis 12:8) and Jacob had his vision of the ladder to Heaven (Genesis 28:11–19).[15] However, by Hosea's time, Gilgal and Bethel were places where false worship occurred.

One of the most prevalent features of sin is that it refuses to be lonely. It seeks out companions. It draws others into its web. Knowingly or not, Israel tried to make Judah as unfaithful to God as they were.

God was very patient with Israel. By Hosea's time, the majority of the people had already strayed from God's standards for two centuries. Israel has been like a repeat offender offered probation many times. But God's patience will not last forever. Israel cannot be as stubborn as a strong heifer and enjoy the green pastures of the promised land (Hosea 4:16). Israel has shown God that they do not want HIM in their lives, so God has decided to leave them alone (v. 17). They have loved the sensual rituals associated with other religions (v. 18), but such religious exercises will not help them when God judges (v. 19). Shame awaits them. Hosea warns that God is about to pronounce sentence. He will not shield them much longer.

### Conclusion

Greedy, self-serving, predatory priests are a curse to any nation. God holds the people who speak in his name accountable. At the same time, people often get the sort of minister they desire. Tragically it is often the case that the people and the priests share the same despicable traits. The ministers are no more lustful and money-hungry than the people.

It is time for us to look in the mirror. What sort of ministers are we? Why are we in ministry? Do we work for God, for the people, or for ourselves? What sorts of people attend our services? Do they want to serve God, or do they want him to serve them? God will not give us the luxury of not answering these questions. How we answer them determines whether we are his people or people of a lesser god, regardless of what we may pretend to be.

# 5

# Earnest Seeking of God

HOSEA 5

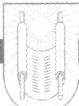

HOSEA CONTINUES TO PRESENT God's case against the priests, leaders, and people of Israel (see Hosea 4:1–19). As before, he calls on them to "hear" God's charges (compare 4:1 and 5:1). He declares their actions indefensible (compare 4:2, 3 and 5:1, 2). He stresses that only God can heal their sins and protect them from national collapse (compare 4:4–19 and 5:3–15). In this chapter, however, the prophet goes deeper. He gets to the heart of Israel's problems in 5:1–14. He then concludes in 5:15 that only those who "earnestly seek" God will have his help in the coming days. The word translated as "earnestly" indicates a focused, committed searching, like a person looking for food or necessary help.[1] It precludes a superficial, so-called seeking.

Seeking the Lord is a key theme in the Minor Prophets, as we learned in Hosea 2:7; 3.[2] The word "seek" denotes a persistent, regular, self-demanding inquiring of God and his will. In the ancient world, people often sought to know God and to find his will by consulting a prophet or a priest at a shrine.[3] In the Biblical context, seeking God requires wanting no other god and no other way of life. It includes finding God's will through Scripture, prayer, and ethical living. Seeking God and his ways is the essence of Christian faith. As Jesus declared in Matthew 6:33, "Seek first the kingdom of God and his righteousness." While we hope that whole churches and communities will seek the Lord, a lone individual may do so, as Hosea learned through hard experience.

This chapter has three parts. Each one focuses on one of the groups that 5:1a identifies. Each one shows why 5:15 states that earnest seeking of God is what Hosea's people need most. In 5:1, the prophet calls the priests, people, and government officials to hear what God says to them. He addresses the "house of the king." Without hearing God and accepting his instruction, his "discipline" (v. 2), the people fail to seek him earnestly. In 5:3–7, Hosea focuses on the activities that bad priests have taught the people. Practicing false religion makes it impossible for the Israelites to seek the Lord properly. In 5:8–15, Hosea describes how the "house of Israel" (v. 1) has made one bad political decision after another, which includes opposing Judah in some manner. As I have already said, verse 15 closes the section with the declaration that only a true, earnest seeking of God will bring them the help they need.

Seeking God is wholesome, life-giving, loyal, and wise. It is a good, right, and true thing to do on its own. However, we should never forget that the greatest thing about seeking God is that we find him. We get to have a relationship with the One who loves us the most. Hosea had a deep and good relationship with God, and he wanted all who read or heard his words to have that as well. Let us learn what he knew.

### Hearing God and Accepting His Discipline (5:1, 2)

In verse 1, Hosea calls listeners to "hear" God's judicial decision[4] ("the judgment") regarding them. This verdict relates to every category of person in Israel—her priests, her people, and her leaders (v. 1a). The priests and royal officials were supposed to foster justice and obedience to God, according to 4:6. For their part, the people were to act as "a kingdom of priests" declaring God's glory to the world (see Exodus 19:5, 6; 1 Peter 2:9, 10). Every category of person has failed in their duties, though there were faithful individuals such as Hosea in the land. Overall, the people have not fulfilled their assigned responsibilities.

Having introduced all three categories, Hosea focuses on "the house of the king" in 5:1b, 2. The phrase includes the whole government, not just the monarch and his direct relatives. Hosea claims that the officials "have been a snare at Mizpah and a net spread upon Tabor" (v. 1b). Mizpah and Tabor were attractive wooded areas where hunters often set snares for birds. They were also centers of idol worship.[5] Attractive places with important worship centers were perfect places for people to plot against the government.[6] Hosea depicts the leaders as human traps. Israel has become a dangerous place. The officials look lovely and peaceful on the outside, but on the inside they are full of deadly plans. In short, they are deceitful and dangerous. They are a threat to kings that displease them.

God gets more specific in 5:2, where he explains that "the revolters have gone deep into slaughter." After Jeroboam II died c. 752 B.C., no less than four kings were slain by rivals before Assyria ended Israel's monarchy in 722

B.C. (see 2 Kings 15:8–21). The king's supporters were also likely killed. God promises that he will "discipline" the rebels (Hosea 5:2). This means that the true king will impose order on the miscreant nation. A. A. Macintosh says that discipline "denotes both instruction and chastisement . . . to inculcate obedience and wisdom."[7] God disciplines to restore relationship with human beings, not simply to punish.

As we learned when we studied Hosea 4:1, those who "hear" God's call will obey what he says (compare Deuteronomy 6:4–9); they are stirred to action. Likewise, those who accept his chastisement are on the road to wisdom; they will learn to act in the right manner. Taken together, hearing and accepting would put them in a position to seek God honestly and earnestly.

We need to be like those people. We have access to the Bible and to generations of Christian witness. We can embrace a fresh openness to listening to God and to following faithful examples. We can search our own hearts for where we have revolted against God and our neighbors. But whatever we find, let us accept God's gracious correction. However hard to manage, this openness to God will lead to the honest and earnest seeking that we need.

### An Exclusive Commitment to God (5:3–7)

Hosea now turns to religious activities most associated with priests. He observes that the Israelites need to return to the exclusive relationship they had with God before they started worshiping other deities. But he indicates that returning will not be simple or easy. The problem is not just that the priests and their people have failed to return to God. Their actions indicate that they are in no condition to return to God (5:3, 4a). Their hearts, minds, and activities reveal that they do not know God and that they do not know how to seek him (vv. 4b–7). Seeking God requires an exclusive commitment to him, as the first of the Ten Commandments makes plain (Exodus 20:3).

The prophet knows all this about the people because, according to Hosea 5:3, God can gaze into their hearts, where motivations and desires give birth to actions. In their hearts he sees unfaithfulness ("played the whore") and defilement. God sees hearts unwilling to be faithful to him and thus unable to receive his healing from sin.

Indeed, verse 4 says that God discerns "the spirit of whoredom," of unfaithfulness, gripping their hearts. This spirit, this driving influence, corrupts them. Therefore, they cannot repent and return to God. They need new wishes, new desires, and new deeds, and only God can give these. What they are doing now keeps them from doing what is right. All this proves they simply do not know God. They do not understand the nature of a relationship with God.

He sets the terms of the relationship; they do not. He offers grace to sinners who truly repent, not to people who just want his help to keep living as they have been.

Their actions keep God from treating them as his special people because they are not living like they are his people. They fail to see the danger of rejecting God's word and thus making their hearts hard, their eyes glazed over, and their ears closed. When they refuse to repent on God's terms, the very offer of grace becomes the occasion for further hardening.[8]

"The spirit of whoredom" has its roots in the fact that they are filled with "pride," according to verse 5. Here the word "pride" reflects "a nationalistic arrogance, a heedless sense of self-importance, and a related stubbornness of will."[9] His people do not think they need God's word to make their choices. They do not seek God's permission to make their decisions. They do not pursue God's guidance in any way.

Yet they change their minds temporarily when trouble comes. When they "stumble" in their chosen political path, taking Judah down with them (v. 5), then they take "flocks and herds" and "go to seek the LORD," according to verse 6. Then they seek God in the sense that they want his help, just in case he can help. But they do not find him, for "he has withdrawn from them" (v. 6) because of their faithlessness and their idolatry, according to verse 7. Like Samson after Delilah cut his hair (Judges 16:20), the priests do not know that God has left them to their own choices. They cannot pick and choose when they will serve the Lord. He does not exist to support them despite their unfaithful ways.

This passage is a strong warning about presuming God owes us help. In *Why Does God Allow War?* Martyn Lloyd-Jones notes how World War II-era Britain demanded to know how God could allow Germany to oppress them.[10] Though people gave God no thought in good times, in their arrogance and ignorance they felt free to expect God to deliver them from trouble.[11] Though the nation lived as they pleased, Lloyd-Jones reasons, they expected a holy God to aid them.[12] He then asks, "What if war has come because we were not fit for peace, because we did not deserve peace, because we by our disobedience and godlessness and sinfulness had so utterly abused the blessing of peace?"[13] He concludes by asserting that war, like all trials, comes so that people may seek, know, depend upon, and glorify God.[14] In short, Lloyd-Jones describes his nation like Hosea described his. Both nations presume they can gain God's help regardless of how they live. Both are doomed to disappointment, for only true repentance that turns from sin to God meets with God's favor.

People do not change. Godless people still demand to know why God allows suffering clearly caused by human sin. People still want God's help with no strings attached. Even Christians sometimes live as if we think God is required to bail us out of every bad situation regardless of the state of our hearts and our relationship with him. God owes us nothing, for he has already given us everything. We cannot come to him until we bow to his sovereignty in our lives. A superficial response will not do. God deserves full commitment, nothing less.

## Earnest Seeking of God (5:8–15)

In this final section, Hosea deals with political matters that relate to both Israel and Judah, the whole "house of Israel" (5:1). Though it is impossible to know for certain, 5:8–15 likely addresses events near the year 732 B.C.[15] Assyria was the dominant power of the day. Its strong monarch, Tiglath-Pileser III (c. 745–727 B.C.), was building a vast empire. In c. 734 B.C., Israel and Syria became part of a coalition of smaller nations that sought to withstand Assyrian oppression. Judah refused to join the group, so Israel and Syria invaded their neighbor (see 2 Kings 16:5, 6; Isaiah 7:1–9). Judah's ruler, Ahaz, called on Assyria for help, and the Assyrian army crushed Israel and Syria (see 2 Kings 16:7–9). Then, to gain Israel's throne, Hoshea (c. 732–722 B.C.) swore allegiance to Assyria (see 2 Kings 15:27–30; 17:1–6). So it was that Judah gladly became a satellite nation in the Assyrian Empire, and Israel was forced to bow unwillingly to Assyria. Both Judah and Israel now served Assyria, a nation not known for its gentleness to its servant countries. Indeed, the prophet Isaiah declared at this time that Judah had brought a terrible foe into its life (Isaiah 7:17–25).

Hosea 5:8 presents God's servant as a watchman during a crisis.[16] Hosea calls out for someone to blow a trumpet so that three cities may get ready for a military invasion. Gibeah, Ramah, and Beth-aven were cities in the old tribal region of Benjamin that were affiliated with Judah by this time.[17] What seems clear in verse 9 is that these cities' woes prefigure a more widespread invasion that includes Ephraim, the major tribe in Israel that perhaps stands for the whole nation here. War is on the horizon for both Judah and Israel. It is time to sound the alarm.

The blowing of the horn leads Judah's leaders to act in verse 10. They decide to redraw old boundary lines, which probably refers to them giving land to Assyria. In short, their first response is to appease the great power. This strategy will not work. God intends to pour out his wrath on Judah and Israel. Assyria will not be satisfied until they control both Judah and Israel, a goal they will achieve by 722 B.C.

Verse 11 states that Israel (Ephraim) will experience Assyria's oppression and crushing military might first. This is indeed how things happened. Having invaded Judah in 733–732 B.C., the Israelites felt the sting of defeat soon after. Verse 12 shows that God is determined to punish both Judah and Israel, even if it takes years. Moths and dry rot work slowly, but they work. Little by little the Lord punished Israel and Judah. This imagery most likely relates to the gradual loss of land that each nation endured before Assyria finally dominated them.

Verses 13, 14 state what happened after Assyria gained control of Judah and Israel. Rather than seeing their sickness and wounds as reasons to turn to God, Judah and Israel combated one another by seeking help from Assyria, the very source of their woes (v. 13). Though Judah and Israel thought their problem was one another, their chief problem was God, who was tearing the two like a lion tearing its prey (v. 14). They thought they needed to seek help from Assyria when they needed to seek God.

Verse 15 states what God is about to do and what Israel needs to do. He is about to "return" to his place, for they refuse to "return" to him (compare v. 4). God will leave them to "the ravages of history."[18] But he will not go so far away that he cannot hear or see.[19] He will be able to see if they "acknowledge their guilt" (v. 15) for forsaking him and seek his "face," his presence, presumably in prayer and thoughtful listening to good instruction from a faithful priest or prophet. He will be able to see if they "earnestly seek" him and hungrily see him when "their distress" presses them to do so. When they seek him in this manner, the Lord will return to them. He will be present among them and work for them. His going away can thus become the beginning of their salvation. For this to happen, however, the people must reverse their behavior from the false seeking of God that we saw in 5:4–6, to the true seeking of God that we find here (v. 15).

Seeking God is not a slogan or a program. It is a way of life. It amounts to an ongoing, authentic relationship with him. As with any authentic relationship, it includes a heart for the other person as well as conversation, companionship, and commitment. Pretense and falseness have no place in an authentic relationship. I am glad to remind us that God wants a relationship with us. The greatest proof of that desire is the sending of his Son to live on earth with us, as John 1:1–18 and 3:14–17 declare. It is a joy and an honor to be able to seek God and find him and to have him seek and find us.

## Conclusion

This chapter reveals that Israel's rebellion against God surfaced in all areas of their nation's life. Israel collectively revolted against God, but also against their political leaders. They replaced God with false gods and their kings with new leaders. When new kings and new gods did not solve their problems, they replaced them by turning to Assyria. In short, they were as disloyal to their leaders as they were to God. Thus they stumbled from one political blunder to another. Hosea warned that their pride, rebellion, and disloyalty would lead to worse things, indeed to destruction.

As the chapter has unfolded, we have gained a clearer picture of what seeking God means. In Hosea 5:1, 2 seeking God requires openness to seeking God. This openness requires hearing God and accepting his discipline. In 5:3–7 seeking God requires an honest and exclusive commitment to God that encompasses the whole person. In 5:8–15 seeking God requires an earnest desire to find God that mirrors his determination to weed out wickedness. This dawning awareness of the necessity and goodness of seeking God leaves us with great hope. If God was willing to receive Israel back after such massive unfaithfulness, then he is willing to receive us.

# 6

# Real Repentance and Foolish Rebellion

HOSEA 6—7

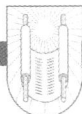

HOSEA 1—5 HAS MADE THE CASE for Israel's need to repent. God has claimed that Israel has acted like an adulterous spouse by turning to other gods. Israel has spurned the Lord, the God who delivered them from Egypt and has blessed them for centuries. Priests, prophets, rulers, and citizens of the land are all at fault. What is more, Judah has joined Israel in this adultery. Because Israel has rejected God, they seek help from political change and from foreign alliances. It seems that they will try anything except returning to God. In fact, 5:4 states that they cannot return to the Lord in their current condition. They have to make up their minds to serve God alone. It is time for real repentance.

Hosea 6 begins with Hosea explaining what real repentance looks like (vv. 1–3). The passage ends with God stating his frustrations with Israel's foolish rebellion (7:11–16). In between, the text reveals how Israel's and Judah's actions prove their lack of repentance (6:4—7:10). Sadly, the people never take the necessary steps to return to the Lord, their covenant partner and redeemer.

Repentance is absolutely essential to our walk with God. We cannot be saved from our sin in the first place if we do not confess that we are sinners and turn from our sin to God. Only when we turn *from* our sin and *to* Jesus can we find forgiveness and eternal life. This life-changing turning to God is the first and most important repenting we will ever do. But it is not the *last* repenting we will ever do. First John 1:5–10 declares that we sin regularly and that we need to keep repenting. Our fellowship with God depends on it. Thus we never stop needing to turn from sin and turn to God. The good news is that when we repent, God forgives and receives us. He never turns away from real repentance, only from phony repentance—the kind the Israelites offer in this passage. It is vital to our spiritual health to know the difference.

## Real Repentance (6:1–3)

In Hosea 4:1 and 5:1 the prophet calls the people to "hear" God's indictment of their actions. Now he calls on them to gather and "return to the LORD" (6:1). Surely they have heard and experienced enough already to answer this summons quickly. Their nation is coming apart at the seams, according to 5:8–14. God is leaving them to their own devices, according to 5:15. They have every reason, then, to obey immediately. These three verses explain how true repentance proceeds from conviction of sin to healing from sin to protection from sin.

After calling the people together (6:1a), Hosea advises that they repent. As we have already seen, repentance means turning from sin to God. The word basically conveys the sense that the people have been going in the wrong direction. They are on a faithless and destructive path. It is crucial that they turn around and go *back* to God, who saved them from bondage and made them his covenant people to minister to the nations (see Exodus 19:5, 6). Returning to him is the only way out of the political messes they have gotten themselves into (Hosea 5). More importantly, it is the only way to heal their souls.

Hosea next tells them that God has "torn" them (6:1b). That is, he has brought about circumstances calculated to show them their sins. These include political and social problems of all sorts. They also include natural deprivations that agricultural disasters have caused (2:1–13). These problems have not simply been punishments. God intends them to convict the people of their sins and to compel thoughtful repentance.

This point becomes clear when Hosea states that God has turned and struck, yet will heal and bandage (6:1c). In short, God has disciplined them *so that* he can heal them. He has never stopped loving them. He has never ceased to have compassion, mercy, and covenant loyalty toward them (see Exodus 34:6, 7). His goal has always been to awaken them and restore them. God acts toward them exactly as he promised he would in Leviticus 26:40–45 and Deuteronomy 30:1–10. Renewal remains God's reason for striking his sinful people. Accepting his discipline and turning to him is the first step in real repentance.

The second step is for God to raise them up so they can live in his presence. Only God can raise up a people as spiritually dead as Israel (see Ezekiel 37:1–14; Ephesians 2:1–10). Hosea declares, "After two days he will revive us; on the third day he will raise us up" (Hosea 6:2). The phrase likely means quickly and in a manner that is like other great deeds God has done on the third day.[1] God can raise the lifeless nation. This promise reminds us of God raising Jesus from the dead. In fact, this verse may stand behind 1 Corinthians 15:4. New Testament writers at times indicated that what happened to Israel happened to Jesus (see Matthew 2:15). If God can raise Israel on the third day, then he can raise Jesus on the third day.

God does not raise Israel to sin again. Rather, he raises them to "live before him" (Hosea 6:2b). This phrase means "to live for him in his world as he directs."[2] It often indicates proper obedience and worship when it occurs in the Old Testament (Psalm 24:4–6; 27:8). When God takes Israel from death to life, he will also take them from unfaithfulness to obedience.

Thus raised, the people will know the Lord, according to Hosea 6:3. Indeed, they will pursue hard after him (v. 3b). Once they are headed in the right direction, nothing will stop them from closely following their life-giving Lord. As they pursue him, they will receive refreshment akin to regular rain throughout the growing season (v. 3c). God's nurturing will be as constant as sunrise and sunset. His people will find that he meets all their needs.

I think verse 3 is beautiful. It is like 2:14–23, where God promises to woo, win, and provide for Israel. God's response to repentance is always lovely. He takes people as they are, as if they never sinned and as if they will never sin again. Therefore, every time his people repent, they receive a down payment on what they will experience forever in the kingdom of God. The beauty of forgiveness follows close on the heels of repentance.

How real is our repentance? We do not have to engage in obsessive self-examination and self-criticism to find out. In fact, we can easily mistake sorrowful self-loathing for repentance. Sadly, this type of sorrow may be just another form of self-reliance. The depth of our sorrow is not the key to real repentance. Rather, real repentance means turning to and walking with God. It accepts God as the goal and his gifts as what we need.

Israel did not seek this goal and did not want what God offered. In contrast, those who want Christ do not want sin. They will struggle daily with sin, as we all experience, but they continue the battle because they want Christ.

Thankfully the power to repent does not come from us. God gives us his Word and his Spirit to bring us to repentance. He gives healing and life to sustain us in the war against sin. He has taken away the penalty of sin and opened the way of life. In short, he raises us up and gives us life, as both Hosea 6:2, 3 and Ephesians 2:5, 6 attest.

### Refusing to Repent (6:4—7:10)

Hosea's instruction in repentance fails. Silence results. He has no takers. Perhaps the people think they are already doing what is necessary. If so, then the Lord's comments in 6:4—7:10 set them straight. They may think they have repented, but they are wrong. God declares that they merely play at repenting. They only pretend to change. God states in 6:4–11 that no matter what he did, Israel and Judah kept rebelling. In 7:1–10, he claims he would have healed them, but they sinned even more. Now they face a woe-filled future, for they return to their sins and their plans, but not to him (7:11–16). Playing at repentance proves to be a very dangerous game.

God begins the section by asking, "What shall I do with you, O Ephraim? What shall I do with you, O Judah?" (6:4a). Israel and Judah are an exasperating bunch. God has been perfectly faithful to them. Yet he says, "Your [covenant loyalty[3]] is like a morning cloud, like the dew that goes early away" (6:4b). Unlike his covenant love, theirs evaporates every morning. It disappears as surely as dew does when the sun grows hot. Their loyalty has no staying power.

God desired covenant loyalty from Israel and Judah (6:6a). He wanted them to know him personally and intimately (6:6b). Loyalty in relationship matters most to God (see Matthew 9:13; 12:7). Sacrifices are only viable when they represent love, faith, and repentance. Otherwise, sacrifices have no purpose. This text reveals that the people killed animals, but they did not seek God. Therefore, they did not offer valid sacrifices. This is why he sent the prophets to speak just and good words (Hosea 6:5). God warned Judah and Israel through prophets like Elijah, Elisha, Hosea, Amos, and Isaiah. A few people turned to God. Most did not.

Most wallowed in unfaithfulness. God mentions three places as examples. In Adam they "[overflowed the boundaries of] the covenant,"[4] probably by worshiping false gods, or at least worshiping at an unapproved shrine (Hosea 6:7). Adam was where the Jordan River stood up while Israel crossed on dry ground (Joshua 3:16, 17). Now it has become a place that overflows the boundaries of the covenant. In Gilead evildoers have shed blood and left their tracks in it (Hosea 6:8). Gilead is the name of a region and the name of a specific town (Judges 10:17; 12:7). It is the place where Laban met with Jacob (Genesis 31:25), so it is a spot where God spared Jacob's life. But now it is a murderous, unsparing place. In Shechem the false priests (see Hosea 4—5:1) are like robbers lying in wait (6:9). They kill people's relationship with God by what they do and teach. Shechem was where Levi, the father of Israel's priests, and

Simeon avenged their sister Dinah's rape. Though their sister deserved justice, the way they avenged her amounted to murder. It was a deceitful plan (Genesis 34). Shechem's priests are no less deadly. They kill unsuspecting souls.

In short, Israel has sinned greatly. Instead of repenting, they commit acts of violence and idolatry. Their covenant infidelity amounts to spiritual "whoredom" and uncleanness (Hosea 6:10). As for Judah, verse 11 says they are no better, as 6:4 has already stated. Therefore, Judah can expect a harvest of judgment (see Jeremiah 51:33; Joel 3:13).[5] They have acted like Israel, so they will face punishment like Israel's. To summarize, then, Hosea 6:4–11 shows that God's people show no covenant loyalty and no knowledge of God. They offer sacrifices but show no signs of a torn heart. They ignore the prophets and mistreat one another. Hard times do not change them.

Worse yet, good times do not lead them to true repentance either. When God changed their circumstances ("restore[d] the fortunes"), they did not change their actions (6:11b—7:1a). When he healed Israel's social and political wounds, the people did not use their restored health to serve God. Rather, the capital city of Samaria engaged in deceit (7:1b). Given some relief from God's discipline, the people continued with business as usual. They gave no thought to correcting their ways or to the fact that God could see them (v. 2).

Their political activities particularly reveal their wickedness. Their evil and treachery please their king and make their rulers happy (v. 3). This verse probably reflects the constant political unrest in Israel. Kings were toppled often in the last two decades of the nation's existence.[6] The officials that came to power were of course happy. Their followers had won the day.

God takes a dim view of these revolts. He describes the revolters' character and deeds in a series of negative metaphors. In 7:4 God calls the people political "adulterers." Then he compares them to "a heated oven." This oven smolders overnight while the baker is busy making dough. In 7:5 God mentions the king and princes getting drunk on "the day of our king." This day could be a coronation day or any other special occasion. These revelers are in no condition to defend themselves. Third, in 7:6, 7 God returns to the oven image. The people are now compared to an oven whose fire has been stoked again. Their anger smoldered, then blazed hot. When stirred, its flames consumed Israel's leaders. All this has happened without God's approval. Neither king nor people have called on God (v. 7b). They go their own way, and the land descends into chaos.

These rebels think they are very smart. No doubt they are convinced they have saved their country. In 7:8–10 God claims the opposite. He asserts that "Ephraim [Israel] mixes himself with the peoples" (v. 8a). This phrase means they have made alliances with bad allies. Verse 11 mentions Egypt and Assyria as two of these. After 733 B.C. every king of Israel had to have Assyria's approval to stay in power. Those wishing freedom from Assyria tended to ask Egypt for aid. This situation left Israel scorched on one side and uncooked on the other (v. 8b). Instead of being wise, the constant rebellions were a half-baked way of governing. It led to a no-win situation. It led to other nations draining Israel's strength (v. 9). It was nothing but sheer, stupid "pride" (v. 10a). Nonetheless the people refused to return to God (v. 10b). They did not repent. Instead, they kept playing at politics and playing at religion.

These verses reveal the self-deceiving nature of rebellion and pride. It may seem trendy and intellectually bright to question God, to expect religion to conform to current cultural trends, and to change political leaders. In the United States at least, it seems that whatever and whoever is new and puts action first is good. But rebellion for its own sake can be the result. Neglect of God and rebellion against his word can become common. Religion can look good from a distance yet be half-baked and good for nothing. Human pride does not produce good religion (6:4–6), good societies (6:7—7:2), or secure government (7:3–10). It produces chaos and stupidity. It produces people who ruin their nation and their lives and do not know any better (v. 9).

Things do not have to be this way.

### The High Cost of Refusing to Repent (7:11–16)

Israel's refusal to repent will lead to even more terrible results. Once again God will discipline the people so that they might return to him. He cannot just let them continue their self-destructive behavior. He must intervene. Sadly, this will mean hardship for hard-hearted Israel and Judah. God will have to trap them like a bird (7:11–13) and send them back to Egypt (vv. 14–16). Their foolish rebellion, lying lips, and love of idols leave him little choice.

Verse 9 has stated that proud Israel is unaware of how self-defeating their actions are. Now verse 11 compares the nation to "a dove, silly and without sense." Israel flits back and forth between Assyria and Egypt, trying to get what they need to stay alive. God warns that he is setting a snare for the silly dove; he will bring Israel down like one brings "down the birds of the heavens" (7:12). In fact, Assyria and Egypt are the net God will use to catch and discipline them. As James Luther Mays has written, "In their very search for help they fly into the real danger that threatens them."[7] Eventually Egypt will not help Israel, thus leaving them in Assyria's hands (see 2 Kings 17:4).[8]

This situation saddens God. He announces woe and destruction on Israel, but he would prefer to redeem them (Hosea 7:13). God's heart always tends to mercy (Exodus 34:6, 7). Judgment is his "strange" act, not his normal one (Isaiah 28:21). He does not judge "from his heart" (Lamentations 3:33). Yet he will not clear the guilty (Exodus 34:6, 7). Thus he must discipline Israel for their constant lies about God and to God (Hosea 7:13). Israel cannot claim that the Lord is their God and rebel against him. They cannot worship him and other gods and be righteous covenant partners. Israel is living by lies, and a truthful God will respond.

This truthful God can see the people's hearts. He recognizes that "they do not cry to me from the heart" though "they wail upon their beds" (v. 14a). The people seem moved to pray, though not because they want a renewed relationship with God. Instead, they cry out because they are lacking "grain and wine" (v. 14b). When disciplined, all they see is the discipline, not the reason for the discipline. They see religion as a way to get things. If God does not provide what they demand, then they will seek another deity. Turning from their sins is simply out of the question.

Israel's ongoing rebellion is unreasonable. God is the One who "trained and strengthened" Israel (v. 15). He called Abraham, redeemed Israel from slavery, gave them land, and protected them. Everything they have has come from God. Yet they forget him. They cast him off like they cast off kings that displease them.

This section concludes with God again raising the matter of returning to him. He notes that Israel often turns or returns to something. They just do not return to "higher things"[9] (v. 16); in other words, to God. Thus they are left to lower things. They are left to do battle in their own strength. Or they are reduced to hoping Egypt will help them against Assyria. God, who knows all things, sees that Egypt laughs at Israel's folly. Egypt will not help, though they will be happy to take Israel's money before Assyria conquers Israel. When this defeat occurs, it will be because of Israel's rebellion. Indeed, 2 Kings 17:1–23 states that Assyria's conquest of Israel in 722 B.C. happened due to Israel's refusal to return to God.

I was a teenager when the famous Watergate hearings were held. New revelations about wrongdoing in the highest levels of government came out daily, or at least it seemed that way. Each new shocking development revealed that these officials had many chances to turn back. They made their eventual fall worse by failing to come clean. At one poignant moment Senator Ervin, head of the investigating committee, quoted Galatians 6:7: "Be not deceived; God is not mocked: for whatsoever a man soweth, that shall he also reap" (KJV). The lack of repentance, coupled with the crimes themselves, led the nation's leaders and the nation itself into dark times.

Israel's leaders and people were as inept as the Nixon administration. One sin led to another. One revolt led to another. One disciplining act by God led to another. Sadly there was never one act of repentance that led to another. All acts of repentance seemed to die at birth. Refusing help and refusing to heed the warnings, the people headed foolishly into the dark and forbidding abyss of unnecessary defeat. God was not mocked. They reaped what they sowed.

## Conclusion

God has given us Hosea's writings so that we might avoid Israel's mistakes. We do not have to suffer their fate. God speaks to us today through his Word, his people, and most fully in his Son. If we turn to God from sin and trust in Jesus, then we can be changed. God can raise us from spiritual death right now. If we have trusted Christ but have rebelled against God, then we can also turn back to God and be received back into fellowship with him. He would have forgiven and restored a faithless, foolish, and bloodthirsty people. Surely that means he will receive us when we turn back to him. He will do so even if we have walked sin's road for some time. Are we ready for real repentance, or are we determined to be half-baked rebels?

# 7

# The Vulture, the Whirlwind, and the Fire

HOSEA 8

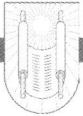

BY NOW HOSEA HAS MADE certain things crystal clear. He has declared that Israel's covenant-breaking amounts to spiritual adultery. He has noted that Israel's rulers, priests, and people all share in the nation's sin and guilt. He has stated that Israel has refused to repent, despite their protests otherwise. He has laid bare the nation's rebellious spirit that leads to political intrigue and spiritual decay. In clear and creative language, he has warned that the person and nation that refuses to repent decides to die. Despite all the people's failures, however, God also promises that he loves Israel. God stands ready to forgive those who repent. Though Israel has sinned for a long time, there is still time to return to God, their covenant-maker. But time has grown short. Hosea presents an emergency message.

In Hosea 8:1, the prophet returns to an image he used in 5:8. He announces it is time to blow a trumpet. This act signifies that trouble is near. It is time to take defensive action; the nation is at risk. God is about to judge by allowing the nations Israel has courted and betrayed to defeat them. As before, Hosea uses very picturesque language to present his message. He writes of a vulture circling over Israel (v. 1), of Israel sowing the wind and reaping the whirlwind (8:7), and of a fire kindling in Israel's cities that will destroy their defenses (8:14). Time has grown short. The people must stop pretending that they know and serve God (v. 2). They must stop offering insincere sacrifices (v. 13). They must return to God, his word (v. 12), and his mission for them in the world. Otherwise, the vulture, the whirlwind, and the fire will consume them.

Charles Simeon warned that in every age, people claim to know God and yet trust in lesser things.[1] We can place trust in our Christian heritage, our nation's power, our religious observances, and in professions of faith that our lifestyles betray.[2] Simeon warns that God can use many means to judge sin in the world and in the Church: "There are other enemies that may pursue both the world and the Church of God: for most assuredly the wrath of God shall follow and overtake sin, whether it be found in the openly profane, or in the professors of the Gospel of Christ."[3] Sin will always be discovered; so we must practice repentance and obedience if we truly have come to Christ.[4] Hosea describes human traits that never change. He also describes God's unchanging ways. We must turn to God or face the manifestation of the vulture, the whirlwind, and the fire in our own lives.

## A Vulture Circling over Israel (8:1–3)

These verses provide an introduction for the whole chapter. The prophet declares a crisis and explains why it has arisen in 8:1. He again states the self-deceived people's reaction to his message in 8:2. Finally he hands down God's decision on what the people have done and its results in 8:3. Overall he portrays Israel like a person unaware that a predator lurks nearby. Though they are in danger every moment, Israel is unwilling and thus unable to recognize their perilous situation.

The passage begins with a hurried command to blow a trumpet about a circling bird.[5] The Hebrew phrase is brief and chaotic.[6] The verse's form follows its message. The verse conveys danger, speed, and urgency. There is no time to waste. A large predator looms overhead. As the chapter unfolds, it becomes clear that either Assyria or Egypt is the likeliest candidate for the bird's identity.

The second half of verse 1 explains why the vulture has been drawn to Israel. It has come "because they have transgressed my covenant and rebelled against my law." The word the ESV translates as "transgressed" is also found in 6:7. It indicates that Israel has passed beyond the bounds the covenant has set. As in previous chapters, rebellion is behind the covenant-breaking. From Adam and Eve onward, rebellion against God reveals itself as disobedience to God's word. Such disobedience always prompts God to discipline his people (see Leviticus 26:14–45; Deuteronomy 27—28; Hebrews 12:3–11). His love requires this response (Hebrews 12:3–17).

Despite their guilt, God hears no words of repentance from Israel. Rather he hears only their cry: "My God, we—Israel—know you" (Hosea 8:2). This is precisely the opposite of what 4:4–6; 5:4; and 6:3 say. At this point, Israel clearly does not know the Lord. As long as they treat him as a national heritage and as one god among many, they do not know him at all. This means the people have "spurned the good" (8:3a), which refers both to God and to the help he gives. This was the meaning in 2:8. Since they reject the good, they can expect the bad. In this case, the bad is an "enemy" that will "pursue them" (8:3b). It is the "vulture" from 8:1.

As swiftly as a predator flies, Hosea has connected this chapter to what he has already declared. Though stated through a new vivid image, the message has not changed. God's people do not know him. They show this by committing covenant adultery. They will learn soon that God will not allow the behavior to continue. He rules nature and history. He will use both to judge his people so that some will return to him.

## Sowing the Wind and Reaping the Whirlwind (8:4–10)

Little by little Israel has gone about the process of self-destruction. It has not been just one thing that has brought them to this point. It has been several ongoing acts of disobedience. The nation has been under indictment since 4:1. More charges and penalties are added now. Hosea continues to share these words in hopes that the people will change. But he surely knows things do not look good at this stage. The section has two major parts. In 8:4–6 the prophet describes idolatry and its results. In 8:7–10 he notes Israel's seeking help from Assyria and declares how this scheme will play out.

God makes two charges in 8:4–6. The first is not new: Israel has chosen kings whom God did not approve (8:4a; see 7:3–7). As Douglas Stuart writes, "The Israelites have arrogated to themselves the right to install or depose kings (cf. 7:3–7). Yahweh alone determines who can be king either by charismatic gifts or by direct revelation through a prophet. He *gives* kings to the nations (e.g., 1 Kings 19:15, 16); they do not decide who their kings will be."[7] Or at least they should not do so. God knew what his people needed in the way of leadership. He provided the right person in David and others. At this point, Israel has not ignored God's recommendation—they have not even sought his opinion. His will is not even a factor in their thinking. This is what God means when he states, "They set up princes, but I knew it not" (Hosea 8:4) Though they did not consult God in the choice of a king, the people seem to expect God's support. God will not be bound by their choices.

The second charge is also not new. The Lord asserts that Israel has "made idols for their own destruction" out of "their silver and gold" (v. 4). Just as they made their own kings, so have they made their own gods. Israel has donated liberally to the expenses related to making metal gods of silver and gold. Verse 5 mentions in particular an idol in the form of a calf identified with Samaria, the capital city. This idol represents the mixing of Biblical faith and Canaanite religion.[8] A calf represented strength and fertility in the ancient world. Thus both Aaron (see Exodus 32:3, 4) and Jeroboam I (c. 930–909 B.C.) "could envisage a calf as an acceptable divine symbol in Israel."[9] Indeed, Aaron and Jeroboam seemed to claim that the calves they made actually represented Yahweh, the covenant God of Israel.

Even if this were true, God does not sanction this connecting of the ancient symbol and himself. The first two of the Ten Commandments deny Israel the right to worship any other god or to make an image of God (Exodus 20:3, 4). In Hosea 8:6, God gives the reason for these prohibitions: "A craftsman made it [the idol]; it is not God." Making and bowing down to images stirs God's anger (v. 5). This is true not just because idolatry breaks Israel's covenant with God but also because idols are not real; they do not represent real gods. God's anger comes in part because idol worship involves people in self-worship, which is really no worship at all. Idolatry destroys people, so God will act against it. The way that Israel is practicing religion, based as it is on idols and lies, will end. God will break the calf and the nation that serves it into pieces (v. 6).

The Bible denounces idolatry so often because it is a constant temptation. Though worshiping anything other than God is foolish (see Isaiah 44:9–20; Jeremiah 10), human beings engage in idolatry all the time. I do not just mean that some non-Christian religions believe in many gods and use images of them in worship. That is true, but idolatry exists elsewhere. It exists in America in many forms, most of which are attached to the love of money.

Americans have become accustomed to wealth and ease. We oppose anything that threatens these, specifically anything that threatens our own wealth and ease. Thus many people judge every public proposal based solely on its effects on them. We think very seldom about others or about the community as a whole. We worry most when our own bank accounts and retirements are threatened, not when God's work suffers or when injustice reigns. Our spending habits often have more to do with obeying advertisements than with obeying God and reflecting his priorities. Even Christians are lured into these patterns, often without realizing it. As Paul warns, "The love of money is a root of all kinds of evils" (1 Timothy 6:10). He also commanded, "Put to death . . . covetousness, which is idolatry" (Colossians 3:5).

One could extend the list to include sex, fame, and power. It is no secret that America is a sex-saturated society. Television programs, the Internet, and magazines are filled with sexual imagery advertising everything from cosmetics to burgers to tires. Our society loves celebrities, whether movie stars or pastors with large crowds live and via video on off-campus sites. Those with big numbers of followers gain power. It becomes easy to adopt the patterns of the sexy, well-known, and powerful in every realm of life.

These are all idols of our own making. They are idols we choose to our own destruction. Because he loves us, God will take them from us.

Idolatry has unexpected results. Israel has forgotten God. They have turned to other gods. Consequently, they lose their ability to think clearly and to make sound decisions. According to Hosea 8:8–10, they make bad alliances. They try to hire Assyria to help them, as if they could control Assyria like one can control a hired lover (v. 9). Little do they know how much this lover will cost them. They will soon "writhe because of the tribute," the money Assyria will charge for their help (v. 10). When Israel cannot pay, Assyria will take over their land. Israel has already become like other nations Assyria has "swallowed up" (v. 8). Sadly, God's people are not aware of the consequences of their actions.

Hosea uses an arresting image to summarize idolatry and its results: "They sow the wind, but[10] they shall reap the whirlwind" (v. 7a). Without intending to do so, "Israel sows the seed of futility and so shall reap the harvest of destruction."[11] Israel thought they planted a gentle wind, but they reaped a tornado or a hurricane. Bringing Assyria into their lives will bring them destruction. Idolatry has so clouded their minds that they fall into a nasty political-military trap. Sadly they set the trap themselves. The whirlwind eventually swept through Israel and scattered the people around the ancient world (see 2 Kings 17:1–6). Idolatry was the beginning of this disastrous storm (see 2 Kings 17:7–23).

No nation steeped in idolatry can expect to avoid these storms. God must judge idolatry due to his holiness and his love. Like Hosea, part of the Church's task is to sound the alarm against worshiping idols. We must sound the alarm clearly and kindly, but we must sound it. This prophetic word may or may not be heard; the results belong to God. Our job is to be faithful messengers. God may indeed use us to keep people from reaping the whirlwind. Only time can tell.

### A Fire Will Destroy (8:11–14)

God's indictment continues. He has already commented on Israel's broken relationship with him (Hosea 8:1–3) and ill-conceived foreign entanglements (8:7–10). He has used imagery from the animal kingdom (v. 1) and the natural world (v. 7) to describe Israel's gloomy future. Now God directs his attention to Israel's worship practices. Of course, these are related to what 8:1–10 has covered. God also chooses a final striking image to portray the future. This time God uses a metaphor drawn from warfare: he will send fire against Israel's military strongholds. The fire will consume Israel's defenses. Israel inches ever closer to final disaster. Failing to observe the vulture and notice the whirlwind, the fire will finish them. That is, it will do so unless they repent.

Verse 11 is hard to understand at first glance. In Hebrew it "is a terse elliptical saying with a repetitive vocabulary."[12] It probably conveys "sarcasm, and it represents a thought complementary to 4:7–8."[13] It may mean one of the following options. First, it may indicate that as the people felt increased political pressure, they built more altars to the gods they already worshiped.[14] Second, it may mean they added altars to gods they had not worshiped previously.[15] Third, it may mean they raised new altars to God, yet had no intention of living as he directed.[16] Given what follows in 8:12, 13 the last possibility may be correct. Regardless, they are simply doing more of the same things God has already denounced. This is like trying to become a better musician or athlete by practicing bad habits more hours each day. The more altars Israel added, the more sin they had the chance to commit.

Going to worship for the wrong reason and with the same negative results is fruitless. God states that even if he wrote "laws by the ten thousands" (v. 12), the people would not understand or obey them. The implication is that 10,000 altars and 10,000 Bibles are no solution to sin where no repentance exists. Those who do not obey God's word cannot worship correctly. The reverse is also true. Those who do not worship God as he directs, or who worship other gods, cannot obey God's word (see 4:1–6). Disobedience and spiritual ignorance go hand in hand. The number of worship sites and copies of Scripture are not the ultimate test of a right relationship with God,[17] nor is the number of sacrifices Israel offers. The people place plenty of meat on the altar, and these make a fine meal (8:13). Yet without an exclusive faith commitment to God shown by clear, faithful obedience, all the religious rituals in the world are of no use. God "does not accept them" (v. 13).

Repentance motivated by faith for the purpose of obedience causes God to forget sin. That is, because of his promise based on his grace, he chooses to forgive. But the opposite is also true. He remembers rebellion and the way people twist his word when no repentance and no proper sacrifice exist (v. 13b). He will punish such sin. In this instance, Hosea 8:13b states that Israel "shall return to Egypt." Douglas Stuart has commented that going back to Egypt means going back into slavery defined by another nation. Unlike the situation in Exodus 1, however, this time Israel volunteers for slavery.[18] They do so by paying Egypt and in turn, Assyria, vast sums of money for protection. They do so by becoming vassal states. Mainly they do so by trusting in secondary powers rather than God, the primary source of all help. Thus they sin, and as Paul writes, obeying sin makes people slaves of sin (Romans 6:16).

Ultimately what lies behind Israel's false worship? The answer is that "Israel has forgotten his Maker" (Hosea 8:14a). This is basically what 4:1–6 outlines in greater detail. Forgetting God leads to disobeying his word, which leads to false worship. Soon people do not even know God. Sadly they do not even know that they do not know God. They mistakenly think that all the altar-building, temple-building, sacrificing, and ritual meals create a relationship with God. These activities make them think they are worshiping when they truly don't know him at all.

While Israel has been building altars, Judah has been constructing "fortified cities" (8:14b). It seems that each nation deals with trouble in its own way. For many people, gathering weapons makes more sense than multiplying sanctuaries. But in a way, Judah is even farther from God than Israel. At least Israel recognizes that there are factors beyond human control, however misguided their religious efforts. Judah trusts in soldiers, towers, and weapons. Judah trusts in its army's ability to kill. God's response is clear and to the point. He will make certain that other nations' fires of war destroy the strongholds of Judah (v. 14b). Amos uses this same phrasing when he promises judgment to several countries in Amos 1—2. God will assert his control over Judah. Neither altars nor weapons can take God's place. They are simply idols of a different size and shape.

If building altars and strongholds were snares to Israel and Judah, what must they be for the United States and other countries today? It is hard to think of a more outwardly Christian nation than the United States. And it is difficult to think of a more outwardly Christian part of the United States than Alabama, where I currently live. In my one-and-a-half mile drive to the freeway, I pass five churches, an extension branch of a Christian college, and at least one Christian day-care center. Once I'm on the freeway I can see at least another four or five churches before I exit; then I pass at least two more churches before I park at the Christian university where I teach. There are at least three other church-related colleges and universities in our city. Twenty-five percent of Alabama's population claims membership in the Southern Baptist denomination alone. Multiple Christian radio stations and the nation's best-known Catholic television station broadcast from Alabama. If altars and Bibles could save, then surely Alabama would be redeemed.

While there are many, many benefits of living near so many Christian enterprises, Alabama proves Hosea's point. We have all these signs of Christianity, but we still have atheists. We still have prejudice between the many races and socioeconomic classes that live here. We still have about 100 murders per year in our largest city. We still struggle to welcome the immigrant, care for the unborn and fatherless, protect widows and single mothers, and generally love our neighbor. We still have God-talk without godliness. We still love money, and we're definitely willing to designate a large portion of public funds to pay for college football. We still love our guns and perhaps trust them for our safety more than we trust God. I could extend the list, but you get the point. Altars and weapons do not free us from sin any more than they did for Israel and Judah. Only God does that through the blood of his Son, the right sacrifice for all our sins.

On the positive side, God has changed lives by the thousands in Alabama. Persons are changed by the Spirit's power when they turn to God in Christ. Racial reconciliation results. Prisoners in maximum security facilities come to faith and become new persons. Marriages are healed. Covetousness turns to generosity. Obedience follows faith. Those who turn to God in Christ find the proper way to worship and obey him. People who truly know God become covenant-keepers saved by grace who confess their sin. They cannot help it. God works these changes in them.

## Conclusion

Hosea 8 presents old truths in new ways. Covenant-breaking is pictured as a vulture preying on Israel. Political scheming is described as sowing the wind and reaping the whirlwind. Trusting in altars and weapons is portrayed as a consuming fire. Remembering that God is the Creator and the Covenant-maker is the solution to all that ails Israel and Judah. Like Israel, we must decide if we will embrace the solution or the punishments.

We may experience the vulture, the tornado, and the fire. Or we may return to our Maker, who is also our Savior. Within a few years, Israel was ruined. Decades later, Judah was as well. Let us not presume we have more time. Let us come to God before judgment falls. The bird is circling, and the fire is sparking into flame. Will we sow faith and obedience or reap the whirlwind?

# 8

# Leaving Harvest Joy Behind

## HOSEA 9

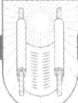

HOSEA HAS ALREADY PROVEN to be an engaging and imaginative writer with a convicting message. So far he has compared God's relationship with Israel to a very rocky marriage (1—3). He has described Israel's religious and political leaders as dangerous snares (4—5). He has likened Israel's spiritual unfaithfulness to fading clouds and half-baked bread (6—7). He has compared future political disaster to a vulture, a whirlwind, and a devouring flame (8). Now he combines images drawn from religious rituals, agriculture, and human birth to warn Israel of coming judgment. With harvesttime and harvest festivals as a backdrop, he now claims that Israel can expect no joy in the future. They can only expect woe.

In 9:1–6, Hosea warns that the Israelites will no longer rejoice on feast days. In 9:7–9, he asserts that days of punishment have arrived. In 9:10–17, he declares that his people shall bear no fruit. Unless they repent, they can expect a barren life lived in exile. His sober warnings ring true today.

## No Joy on Feast Days (9:1–6)

Feast days and harvest festivals have been linked throughout human history. Communities built on agriculture have every reason to celebrate the ingathering of crops well-planted and well-tended. Such celebrations often include giving thanks to the God or gods the community worships. After all, farmers can only till, plant, and cultivate; they cannot make the skies rain or make plants grow. The harvest must come from a higher power who thereby earns praise and gratitude. People show their gratitude by observing appropriate religious rituals related to that higher power. For example, in the United States, the Thanksgiving holiday was initially a feast linked to divine provision. The connection between harvest season and Thanksgiving has lessened as the United States has become urbanized. Nonetheless, many Americans remember the connection.

Israel had its own traditional harvest festivals and feasts. One of these was the Feast of Booths (or Tabernacles), which occurred in autumn (see Exodus 23:16; Leviticus 23:33–43; Deuteronomy 16:13–17).[1] Like so many other aspects of Biblical faith in Old Testament times, it was easy for feasts to get corrupted. In particular, it was easy to mix a harvest observance with practices drawn from Baalism. After all, Baal was considered the god of fertility by Israel's neighbors, as we learned in Hosea 2. Baal worshipers thought that Baal made people, land, and animals fertile. As the populations mixed, portions of Baalism were added to this traditional Israelite celebration.

Hosea 9:1–6 indicates that Israel had indeed included at least some foreign aspects in its festivals. Though harvest season was a time of celebration, Hosea 9 declares, "Rejoice not, O Israel! Exult not like the peoples" (9:1a) They are denied this celebrating because they "have played the whore" by "forsaking . . . God" (v. 1b). Israel has abandoned God much like Gomer abandoned Hosea in the book's first two chapters. They have become like Baalism's sacred prostitutes, sleeping with those who come to the fall festival. They have loved money and ease, and they credit other gods with providing what God alone can give. This spiritual whoredom also has a political aspect. Israel has chosen to seek help from other nations and, by extension, from their gods.

Their rejoicing will stop because their whoredom will not get them what they need. According to verse 2, God will make sure their allies fail to give them grain and wine. In fact, verse 3 asserts that the people will soon enough not be around to see if the land is productive or not. Israel cannot stay in their land if they continue to commit idolatry. As 7:11b has indicated, some Israelites will go to Egypt. Others will go to Assyria. The ones going to Egypt will flee Assyria's invading armies in 732 and 722 B.C. These people will become refugees. The ones going to Assyria will be taken into exile as Assyria conquers Israel. These people will lose their freedom. Clearly there will be no rejoicing at harvest festival then. Spiritual and political unfaithfulness will have led to loss of harvest and loss of land.

Things will go badly for them in the places where they go, according to Hosea 9:3, 4. James L. Mays wrote, "When the celebrants end up in foreign lands, the cult will end. They will offer no libations (Num.15:1–12; Ex. 29:40; Lev. 23:13). Sacrifice will cease because there will be no shrines to Yahweh. . . . Eating unclean food in an unclean land, they will be ineligible for the worship of Yahweh (Deut. 26:14)."[2] Even if sacrifices were to continue, the people would have none to give, "for their bread shall be for their hunger only" (Hosea 9:4). Hosea asks, "What will you do on the day of the appointed festival?" (v. 5). The answer is that they will have fled, some of them to Egypt (v. 6a). Once Israel is in Egypt, the Egyptians will swallow up their wealth as surely as thistles will swallow up their former homeland (v. 6b). Fleeing from one bad scene will simply usher Israel into another. In such conditions, rejoicing over a harvest will be far from their minds. If they think of the past, it will be to mourn what has been lost.

This section invites us to think carefully about the high cost of corrupted faith in at least two areas. First, it warns us to count the cost of mixing pure and false doctrine. For instance, Israel thought they could worship God and also venerate other deities. They thought they could be married to the living God and yet sleep with Baal's prostitutes. Today we may think we can worship Jesus as Lord while mistreating others to advance our careers and greedily guard our bank accounts. We cannot. Second, it warns us not to mix the world's values into our worship practices. Israel turned the Feast of Booths from a time of recalling God's provision to one of worshiping the provisions. Today we might divide churches over music preferences, preach on topics taken from secular life, and turn worship services into sheer entertainment. The result may please participants, but the result does not please God.

### The Days of Punishment Have Come (9:7–14)

Hosea continues to reveal why the people will leave festivals behind. As I have already stated, Israel had probably mixed aspects of fertility worship into the Feast of Booths. Fertility gods supposedly helped female fertility. Thus people behind these gods ensured numerous children and animals, which made the local agricultural economy hum. Nothing could be worse than a low birth rate when there was a high death rate among surviving children. This section warns that the people's actions are leading to fewer births and to early deaths of existing children. The parents' actions endanger the children.

The prophet speaks quite plainly in verse 7. Time is up: "The days of punishment have come; the days of recompense have come; Israel shall know it" (v. 7a).[3] The word translated as "know" often means "experience" in the Old Testament. Thus Israel will experience judgment. Why? In part because they prefer lies over truth. Hosea writes, "The prophet is a fool; the man of the spirit is mad" (v. 7b). He may mean that this is the people's opinion of faithful prophets like Hosea. If so, the people believe this because of their "great iniquity and great hatred" (v. 7c). This phrase could also mean that their great sinfulness and hatred drive a good prophet mad, or that their sinful actions show that they will only accept prophetic messages that are madness in God's eyes. In other words, foolish prophets are exactly what this wicked nation wants. Though it is hard to be dogmatic on this point, I think the last option is best. Over time their sin has driven them to listen to only the worst kind of prophets.

This interpretation fits verses 8, 9. A prophet is supposed to be God's "watchman" (v. 8). Prophets guard and warn the people when trouble is on the horizon. Israel does not want a good watchman like Hosea. Rather they set snares for such a man. They want him dead. Such is their "hatred" for the good prophet, even "in the house of his God" (v. 8). These people have grown vicious. They are like the mob in the days of Gibeah that committed the "heinous crime that is recorded in Judges 19. The rape, murder, and subsequent dismemberment of the concubine in this account"[4] parallels Israel's murderous intentions against God's prophet. These people deserve foolish prophets. They certainly prefer them, for they want all the good ones dead.

God only offers grace for so long. Eventually he judges sin. God is patient with sinners (Exodus 34:6, 7). At times we mistake his long-suffering for indifference (see Zephaniah 1:12; 2 Peter 3:1–10). Israel ignored God's grace and soon learned that God will "not clear the guilty" (Exodus 34:7). Because he loves us, he cannot let soul-killing sin continue. Because he is holy, he will eventually remove sin from the earth (2 Peter 3:11–13).

God offers grace through his servants. People have always persecuted these servants in small or large ways. Hosea, Amos, Isaiah, Jeremiah, and other prophets knew what it was like to suffer for sharing God's truth. Throughout history faithful believers, pastors, and missionaries have faced extreme pressures around the world. Though they seem fools to those who rebel against God, they share the true wisdom that comes from God alone (1 Corinthians 1:18–31).

## Israel Shall Bear No Fruit (9:10–17)

In 9:10–17 Hosea reminds us of other episodes in Israel's story. In 9:10 he goes clear back to the beginning. God compares his initial calling of Israel to finding fresh fruit in the wilderness (v. 10a). Israel had a good beginning. The future seemed bright. Yet after the exodus, the people sinned in the desert. Reflecting on the incident described in Numbers 25, God asserts, "They came to Baal-Peor and consecrated themselves to the thing of shame, and became detestable like the thing they loved" (Hosea 9:10b). They worshiped a fertility god in Moses's day, and they worship one in

Hosea's time. What began as a fresh and beautiful life with God became vile and depraved.

The results of their worship will be the opposite of what they expect. Fertility worship should obviously lead to fertility. Yet because fertility gods are not really gods, this does not happen. Punishment happens instead. God eventually sends Israel into exile. The people ultimately "fly away like a bird" (v. 11a) to another land. Without God's blessing there is "no birth, no pregnancy, no conception!" (v. 11b). Even the children already born will languish (v. 12a). Departing from God to serve idols costs the people everything they hold dear—their faith, their families, their homes, and their freedom. Such will be the sad ending of a story that began with God delivering Israel from slavery.

God returns to Israel's history in 9:13–15. This time he begins with Israel's separation from Judah when Solomon died in 930 B.C. Once again Hosea describes a lovely scene. Ephraim, the name Hosea often uses for Israel, was like a tree planted in a good field (v. 13a). This image means that Israel was blessed with excellent natural resources and many other advantages. Sadly, Israel will leave this lovely land behind. Worse yet, Israel will go to a deadly place (v. 13b), a place where mothers will suffer miscarriages and offer "dry breasts" to babies due to the terrible conditions they will encounter (v. 14).

God again emphasizes how seeking fertility deities will end in the loss of life. The rituals practiced in Gilgal will lead God to "drive" the worshipers from the land, according to 9:15. The passage does not specify what these practices were. However, other texts list Gilgal as a place where improper worship occurred (see 4:15; 12:11; Amos 4:4, 5). In this context it is likely that some form of Baal worship happened there.[5] Since God specifically condemns Israel's political leaders ("princes") in Hosea 9:15, it is likely that they particularly supported this shrine.

Regardless, their deeds at Gilgal were wicked enough that God says, "There I began to hate them" (v. 15). This phrase means that God decided to stop treating Israel with covenant love. He would "hate" them in the sense that he would no longer choose them[6] as special persons he would protect. Malachi 1:2, 3 also uses the Hebrew words translated into English as "love" and "hate" in this way. God will treat Israel in a manner described by Hosea's daughter's name in Hosea 1:6. That is, the Lord will have no compassion (*lo ruhamah*) for them[7] at this time. He will "drive" them from his house (9:15). He will exile them from the land.

Every element of fertility will share in this terrible barrenness. Ephraim's roots will dry up, and its trees will "bear no fruit" (v. 16a). Children born to them will die (v. 16b). Because they have not listened to God and his prophets

(v. 17a; see vv. 7, 8), they will go from place to place, never finding a home (v. 17b). Having chosen fertility rituals, they will ironically leave harvest festivals behind. Having chosen to trust in foreign allies rather than in God, they will live in places not their own. Having chosen to trust in Baal to give them children and animals, they will have neither.

God warned Israel of these results long before Hosea's time. Moses told the people in Leviticus 26:14–39 and Deuteronomy 28:15–68 of the dangers associated with long-term rebellion against God. He warned of crop failure, loss of land, and loss of life. These things need never have happened. That they did shows the terrible grip unbelief has on people and the terrible price it extracts.

Conclusion

Every day we see the cost sin demands from people's bodies and souls. Alcoholism, drug addiction, prostitution, oppression, injustice, covetousness, and corruption are but a small sampling of death-dealing sins in our society. We cannot worship pleasure and think there will be no drunkenness, adultery, sex slavery, or gluttony. We cannot worship money and consumption and think there will be no stealing, bribery, or mistreatment of the land. We cannot worship sex and ease and think there will be no abortions, divorces, or sexual abuse. Societies that fail to grasp these truths die. They die slowly and painfully.

God's Word teaches that his people do not have to live this way no matter how others choose to live. God calls on all people to repent, as he did in Hosea's day. From where we sit today, we know that God has sent his Son to save us from our sins. We know that God promises to restore believers who stray from his ways (see 1 John 1:9, 10). We know that we do not have to leave harvest joy behind. We do not have to live barren lives.

We can choose to reject joy and fruitfulness, but such a terrible decision is not our fate. It is simply our fault. Let us choose the right path. Let us seek God and live.

# 9

# Time to Seek God, Time to Sow Righteousness

HOSEA 10

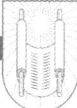

HOSEA 9 WARNS THE ISRAELITES that continued devotion to fertility gods will not yield crops, animals, and children. In fact, the opposite will occur. All good gifts come from God, the Creator and provider (see James 1:17; Genesis 1—2). When Israel rejects God, they reject him as their provider. They no longer receive the benefits of being his covenant people, for he withdraws his resources to make them come to their senses (see Leviticus 26:14–45; Deuteronomy 28:15–68; 30:1–10; Hosea 2). Because he loves them, he cannot support them in their sinful ways. Having left him behind, Israel can expect to leave fruitful harvests behind also.

Now Hosea surveys the wreck Israel has made of life, and he hopes for better things. He returns to their history and notes how they have turned to other gods (10:1, 2). Then he describes Israel's loss of their king and its ramifications (vv. 3–10). Assyria has come into the land. Israel no longer enjoys political autonomy. Yet Hosea remains unfailingly hopeful. He encourages the people that this political defeat could lead to good. If they will seek God and plan to practice righteousness, then they can enjoy God's harvests again (vv. 11, 12).[1] So far they have planted wickedness and have reaped loss (vv. 13–15). Though hopeful, Hosea has no illusions. He recognizes that Israel will have to change drastically and quickly for positive things to happen.

God's grace never rests. Even amid terrible situations caused by sin, he reaches out to sinners. Israel had rejected God. They had served idols. They had embraced immorality. Their moral decline had led to political decline.

Assyria was in the process of turning Israel into one of their provinces. These were bleak times indeed. Yet Hosea claims that though the people's hearts have been corrupted (vv. 1, 2), and though they lost their government (vv. 3–10), they can still turn to God (vv. 11–15). There remains time to seek God, plant righteousness, and reap God's covenant love and loyalty (v. 12).

This message is the heart of God's gospel. Time grows short every day for every sinner. Death awaits us all as surely as it awaited Israel's people and freedom. We must hear and obey God's gracious, urgent call. Only when we realize it is always time to seek God and always time to practice righteousness will we escape sin's present and future devastation.

### Israel's Corrupt Heart and Corrupt Gifts (10:1, 2)

As in chapter 9, Hosea returns to Israel's past to explain their present circumstances. He notes that "Israel is a luxuriant vine that yields its fruit" (10:1a). Israel had many financial advantages. It had a lot of fine land. This was no small thing in an economy based on agriculture. Israel was also located on the main trade road between Egypt in the south and great northern lands such as Babylon and Assyria. Furthermore, Israel bordered the sea and could conduct trade with other countries through Tyre and other ports. Hosea and Amos indicate that Israel was quite wealthy overall, which archaeological evidence confirms.[2] God gave Israel many resources, just as he promised in Leviticus 26:3–13 and Deuteronomy 28:1–14. Affluence was not—and is not—evil in and of itself. Money may be honestly earned and spent according to God's standards.

Israel ignored these standards, for they ignored God. They took the resources God granted them and invested them in idolatry. Like Gomer, the people were looking out for what they thought were their best interests (see Hosea 2:5–13). As their riches mounted, they built more altars. The more their land improved, the more they built "pillars," which were expensive memorials at religious sites. These could have been erected to honor God, but most likely they were dedicated to other gods (10:1b). James L. Mays explains their thinking when he writes, "This co-ordination of welfare [wealth] and cult shows that Israel saw a functional relation between the two; the development of cultic sanctuaries was simply turning part of the profit back into the business. Altars and pillars were the holy machinery which produced the prosperity—a typically Canaanite understanding of cult."[3] Thus the people simply considered giving to religious causes good business.

Unfortunately for them, God knows the human heart. In this case, according to verse 2, God knows that "their heart is false." The word translated as "false" in the ESV can also mean "divided"[4] or "smooth."[5] McComiskey observes that the word "describes deceptive speech" in Proverbs 5:3, "a lying tongue" in Proverbs 26:28, and "flattering prophecy" in Ezekiel 12:24.[6] None of these options speaks well of Israel. The people are not what they seem. They outwardly worship God or some other gods. Inwardly they simply love money and use religion to get more of it.

God sees the altars and knows the hearts. He will tear down the former and expose the latter. Judgment is coming on the people, their altars, and their pillars (Hosea 10:2b). God has not been fooled. He has been patient with their foolishness. But everything they have built up by misusing God's money will soon come crashing down.

These two pungent verses should probe our consciences. What is in our heart? Why do we practice our religion—yes, our Christian religion? We live in a money-motivated, consumer-driven culture. Many of our American churches are luxurious. Many of them are as spacious as shopping centers and as well-equipped as spas. We often market our churches the same way some businesses market their goods. What is in our hearts that would motivate us to spend so much money on ourselves? It is possible that we wish to minister effectively. It is also possible that we build expensive things because our hearts value them most.

What if we did not have these things or the other things that make our lives comfortable and enjoyable? Would we turn away from God? We should ask ourselves if we give to God because we want a good return on our gift or if we rightly give God what already belongs to him. None of us has pure motives all the time. Still, examining our hearts might lead us to cleanse our desires more fully. It might lead us to change before God finds it necessary to take sterner measures to change us.

## Israel's Mounting Losses (10:3–10)

It is hard to determine how long Hosea has been ministering by this point in the book. We know that he began before Assyria defeated Israel decisively in 732 B.C. and finally in 722 B.C. Yet how long he labored before those days is unclear. Regardless, these great disasters have now arrived. God has begun his threatened days of destruction.

Sadly, these verses show that even the loss of their government and their idols does not move most of the people to repent. No matter how terrified they become, they do not turn to God. Instead, they brag about how they will recover. Unbelief fueled by lust for money is an unbelievably stubborn thing. Their losses just keep mounting.

Israel has no king at this point (v. 3a). It may be that verse 3 reflects the situation in Israel in 732 B.C. At that time Assyria supported Hoshea, who rebelled against Pekah (see 2 Kings 15:29–31). Assyria had invaded the land and forced Israel to accept status as a satellite nation in the Assyrian Empire. Thus the people may not have considered Hoshea a real king. The verse could also relate to what occurred in 722 B.C. By then, Hoshea rebelled against Assyria, who then invaded Israel again and this time put an end to Israel's monarchy (see 2 Kings 17:1–6). At that point Israel literally had no king. And they never had another.

Tough times often lead to tough talk. The people state that it is no big thing that they have no king. After all, they ask, "What could he do for us?" (Hosea 10:3b). They have had so many kings by now—all of them ineffective against Assyria—that they may have considered all kings worthless. Surely they can make it just as well without a king! Israel has even haughtier words for Hosea about God. With great bravado they declare, "We do not fear the LORD" (v. 3a). Hosea has declared that God has brought their troubles on them to get them to repent. If so, they are unafraid. They likely think that a deity who does not defeat Assyria is no good to them. After all, they think religion exists to give them what they want.

Hosea bluntly asserts, "They utter mere words" (v. 4a). Their statements are just hot air. Their real problem is that the covenants they make are also hot air. They make their covenants with God and others using "vain oaths."[7] Their deeds invalidate their oaths. Because their words are as false as their hearts (v. 2), "judgment springs up like poisonous weeds in the furrows of the field" (v. 4b). Judgment naturally grows out of the seeds of lies and pride.

Hosea adds in verses 5, 6 that the people are actually afraid despite their bold talk. They are trembling and mourning over the loss of their cult and their calf-shaped[8] idols. In 10:5, Hosea locates this false worship at "Beth-aven," which means "house of evil." This is most likely Bethel, which means "house of God." Because Israel worships idols at Bethel, they have turned "the house of God" into "the house of evil."

There were similar idols at Samaria, according to 8:5. When Samaria fell to Assyria in 722 B.C., the rituals practiced there ended. As was their habit, the Assyrians "carried to Assyria" (10:6a) Samaria's idols. When they sacked a city, they took that city's gods/idols away in full view of the city's people. Their point was that these gods could not protect the place from Assyria's armies. Their goal was to produce fear.

It is easy to see how defeat caused shame for and mourning by the defeated. It is Samaria's and Bethel's turn to lose their pride and their gods. Once they rejoiced, but now they mourn. All their bold talk was just that—only talk.

But this is not all. When the capital city fell, the monarchy also fell. Verse 7 says that Samaria's king was swept away "like a twig on the face of the waters." Their king was as powerless as their gods. Every source they trusted in failed. Thousands of Israelites were swept away into exile along with the king (2 Kings 17:6). Hosea 10:8 adds that in their absence, "Thorn and thistle shall grow up on their altars." The people will be so miserable that "they shall say to the mountains, 'Cover us,' and to the hills, 'Fall on us' " (10:8b). There will be no tough talk then, just a terrible crying out for death.[9]

All this comes as the natural result of a long national addiction to sin. Indeed since "the days of Gibeah" (v. 9), when the people raped and murdered a woman (Judges 19:22–30), the people have sinned.[10] They have been lustful, violent, and proud of their sins. As promised in Leviticus 26:14–39 and Deuteronomy 28:15–68, God will not let such sin pass unnoticed. He states quite matter-of-factly in Hosea 10:10a, "When I please, I will discipline them." How will he do so? He continues: "Nations shall be gathered against them when they are bound up for their double iniquity" (v. 10b). God rules all peoples. He is quite able to send troops to punish his straying people, and he does so. Assyria is his instrument of discipline.[11]

Brash talk is no substitute for confession and repentance. Sometimes our sins so blind us that we cannot see reality. Israel lost their king, capital city, and worship sites, yet did not confess their sin. They just bragged that they could stand it and bounce back.

All my life I have heard people foolishly say they are not afraid of God. I have heard people say they want to go to Hell, for that is where their friends will be. I have seen commercials that make Hell look like a cool, hip place, somewhat like a popular nightclub. All this talk is just talk. When God judges, no one laughs. In this life they cry out for relief, even when death approaches. In eternity they will cry out with no hope of relief. Having laughed at God in life, they will not do so after death. They will face an eternity in judgment, while thorns and thistles grow over their idols on earth. These are stout words, I know, but time grows shorter for us all. It is time to confess and repent, not to brag and wait to see what happens next.

### Time to Seek God, Time to Sow Righteousness (10:11–15)

Hosea begins this last section by recalling happier days before turning to a call for repentance from past sins. In 10:11a, the prophet offers yet another image drawn from agrarian life: "Ephraim was a trained calf that loved to thresh, and I spared her fair neck." Derek Kidner explains that "threshing was a comparatively light task, made pleasant by the fact that the creature was unmuzzled and free to eat (Dt 25:4) as it pulled the threshing-sledge over the gathered corn."[12] In other words, God treated Israel well. He gave them good land, strong leadership, and many benefits as his covenant people (see Leviticus 26:1–13; Deuteronomy 28:1–14). God spared Israel when he could have let other nations ravage their lands.

All this will change. Now Israel and Judah have a new situation. God will "put Ephraim to the yoke" (Hosea 10:11b). Israel will be harnessed and used to break up ("harrow") ground for planting (v. 11b). This will be harder work done by an animal unused to such labors. There will be less freedom and no eating during the working. Oxen, not calves, usually did such work. One wonders how the favored calf will survive the extra exertion.

Yet God has a positive purpose for putting Israel to harder work. He wants the people to awaken. They must plow and sow seeds. So they may as well plant what is good for them. They may as well sow "righteousness" so they can reap steadfast, covenantal love (v. 12a). "Righteousness" here amounts to doing the right thing, which is to return to God. This repentance from sin and turning to God is what the covenant people should do. Repentance will demonstrate covenant-based love. When God sees the seeds of repentance planted, he will "rain righteousness" on them (v. 12b). He will reconcile, restore, and help them. Their righteousness ultimately comes from God, for they would not even know to repent had he not reached out to them.

In short, the prophet declares that it is "time [for them] to seek the LORD." They have sought fake gods; now it is time to seek the Lord. They have sought help from Egypt, but now it is time to seek the Lord. They have sought comfort in bragging, but now it is time to seek the Lord. They have found no security in the places where they have looked. But if they seek God by repentance and prayer, they will find the strength and hope they so desperately need.

Hosea continues his planting and harvesting imagery in verses 13–15. Thus far Israel has "plowed wickedness,"[13] "reaped injustice," and "eaten the fruit of lies" (v. 13a). Their farming methods have left them eating poisonous food. They have sought lies, planted lies, and eaten lies. It is no wonder the whole nation is spiritually and politically sick.

In particular, the people have placed their trust in their own way of doing things "and in the multitude of [their] warriors" (v. 13b). They trusted their plans, not God's. Their plan was to guarantee security by building up their armed forces. Trusting in weapons has been considered the smart way to operate since nations began. However, those who live by the sword die by the sword, as Jesus told Peter in Matthew 26:52. Because Israel trusts in their ability to make war, they will get to see how strong they are. God will send overwhelming force against them. Their "fortresses shall be destroyed" (Hosea 10:14a). Mothers and children will die (v. 14b), as is the case in nearly every war. Assyria will rout Israel.

Hosea cites an example of such a lopsided defeat, but the particulars of how "Shalman destroyed Beth-arbel on the day of battle" (v. 14b) are not known at this time.[14] He clearly thought his people would know the reference. Their plans will fail. This failure will extend beyond the people to the palace. Because the kings have trusted in and perpetrated lies, Hosea declares, "At dawn the king of Israel shall be utterly cut off" (v. 15b). The monarchy ended in 722 B.C. and was never restored.

Hosea portrays a devastating scene. The people have trusted in their own ways, their own lies, and they will suffer the consequences. From the king to the average citizen, they have put their hopes in military might. They have turned to the priests and worship centers that affirmed their plans. All the while God called on them to turn to him and find grace and help in their time of need. In love he offered them righteousness and covenant blessings. In love he sent his servant Hosea. They stubbornly cling to their pride and consequent self-deceit. Eventually God gives them what they want. They want death, and they shall have it. They could have planted righteousness and harvested life. Things could have turned out so differently.

These verses offer a clear alternative for all people. Every person and every nation should turn to God through Christ. All should give up their sinful, self-defeating plans and trust in God alone. He has sent his Son to the world to save the world (John 3:14–17). All nations may come to God through the Son.

But many of us who are Christians live as if we agree with the Israelites. By that I mean we trust in our nation's military, political leaders, and economic geniuses. We profess faith in Christ, but we anchor our hopes for our security in a military budget. Hosea learned that God alone rules history and armies in history. He found security in God while his nation collapsed around him. We must agree with him if we are to have a viable witness to a watching world. We must seek God and sow righteousness if we are to have the peace that Christ gives (John 16:33), the peace that surpasses merely human comprehension (Philippians 4:4–7).

## Conclusion

Hosea's perseverance is impressive. He has ministered faithfully for a long time. He has done so despite meager results. His character thereby mirrors God's, as it has throughout the book. God has loved Israel without reservation. Even in the nation's last hours he reaches out to them with love-saturated grace. Even now he sends his prophet with truthful, helpful words. These words transcend barriers of time and place. They speak to us now (see 1 Corinthians 10:1–13). Even now, if our actions have brought all we hold dear to an end, God reaches out. May each of us in our own area of need cry out to him before we cry out to the mountains, "Fall on us" (Hosea 10:8).

# 10

# "How Can I Give You Up, O Ephraim?"

HOSEA 11:1–11

GOD IS UNENDINGLY CREATIVE, and he often uses extremely gifted people. The book of Hosea has confirmed these two principles repeatedly. Through his prophet Hosea, the Lord has compared his relationship with Israel in several ways. He has likened it to a faithful spouse married to a perpetually straying one. He has compared himself to a faithful farmer who has planted good seeds but has seen those seeds spring up into useless plants. He has presented Israel as a snare to others (5:1), a fading morning cloud (6:4), bad bread from an overheated oven (7:4), and a luxuriant vine used as an excuse to build altars to idols (10:1). Throughout the book, God has noted Israel's tendency to commit spiritual adultery. Each image was meant to sting—not to hurt the people's feelings but to shake them into repentance. So far nothing has worked. All these remarkable metaphors have fallen on hard hearts, closed minds, and decaying souls.

Now God returns to family imagery. This time he chooses a paternal metaphor. He portrays himself as a good and caring father. He declares that he has loved Israel from the beginning (11:1). But the more he did for Israel, the more Israel rebelled (v. 2). Israel has been determined to reject this father, so the father will not save the son from the consequences of his actions (vv. 3–7). One could not blame such a good and mistreated father if he turned away. After all, a good parent cannot bail out a child forever! Parents sometimes must exercise tough love. Eventually children must face the consequences of their poor choices.

Yet Hosea has already shown us that the living God is not a normal husband or farmer. He has capacities we human beings cannot match or even fathom. God will not only seek his adulterous wife, he will find, purchase, and win her (2—3). God gives crops to feed his people again and again even though they give credit to other deities. They deserve death, yet he gives life. His power and patience are equally amazing.

God gave promises to Noah, Abraham, Moses, and David, and he will keep them. Since he cannot lie, he cannot quit. Like his mercy, his endurance endures forever. Thus he is not a normal father either. He will not let this child go so easily. In fact, he will not let Israel go at all. His compassion will stir him to restore Israel, this most prodigal of sons (11:8–10). Israel will "come trembling . . . like doves" (v. 11), but they will come. God's love is massively greater than Israel's sin. He will always find his people.

Hosea has often used Israel's past to criticize its present deeds. He does so again here. This time he begins by telling the history as God nurturing a child who does not return that love in 11:1–4. Then he declares the consequence of rebellion that we have come to expect: Israel will lose their cherished land (vv. 5–7). They will be exiled. However, as Hosea 2, 3, and 6:1–3 have already hinted, exile is not the last chapter in the story. He promises that God will bring some Israelites back to the land, where they will serve him (11:8–11). God will not give up on his people. This is the major theme of Hosea and the major theme of the Bible. It is the gospel of God.

## The Rejected Father (11:1–4)

Parents and grandparents have such high hopes when babies are born. We pray that the next generation will embody our best features and avoid our worst ones. We look forward to joyous events, and we put bad things that could happen way in the back of our minds. No decent parent wants the child to fail, and no parent hopes to fail as a parent. No decent parent hopes to raise an ungrateful, hateful, self-absorbed child. As these verses show, God got exactly the sort of child no parent wants. God got a foolish and heartless child.

Hosea 11 begins with Israel's time in Egypt. Verse 1 describes Israel as a child that God loved and called. This image reminds us of God's command to Moses in Exodus 4:22, 23: "Then you shall say to Pharaoh, 'Thus says the LORD, Israel is my firstborn son, and I say to you, "Let my son go that he may serve me." If you refuse to let him go, behold, I will kill your firstborn son.'" Of course Pharaoh refused. Thus he suffered sad consequences for this terrible decision. God indeed set Israel free through signs, wonders, and plagues. He did for his people what they could not do for themselves.

Israel was happy enough to be called out of slavery. Yet when God called them to serve him alone and live as "a kingdom of priests and a holy nation" (Exodus 19:5, 6), they ran from his call. They ran from him to worship Baal once they were established in Canaan. As Hosea 11:2 notes, "They kept sacrificing to the Baals and burning offerings to idols." Israel abandoned their Father, the One who loved them the most. It is worth repeating that passages like 11:1, 2 describe the majority of the Israelites. There were always some faithful persons, such as Elijah and Elisha. In fact, when Elijah felt quite alone in his faith, God told him there were 7,000 other faithful ones (1 Kings 19:9–18). Still, even a faithful minority is a minority.

Hosea 11:3, 4 expresses God's anguish and Israel's callous disregard of their father's kindness. God "taught Ephraim to walk" (Hosea 11:3a). This phrase likely refers to God establishing the northern kingdom after Solomon died. God carried them "by their arms" when the people were too tired to walk. Without God's help, the nation would have fallen to foreign armies much sooner.

I remember seeing a commercial where a father holds up a young child so that the boy can dunk a basketball. The child turns in delight to the father and says, "I did it!" Just as the child overlooks the father's help in "his" accomplishment, the Israelites refuse to see God at work among them. The people "did not know"—they did not grasp—that God had "healed" them time and time again (v. 3b). Eventually their hearts became so hard they did not even feel his love or see his goodness. They did not recognize that he bound himself to them with "bands of love" (v. 4a). They did not recall that he eased "the yoke" of slavery they labored under in Egypt (v. 4b). They did not remember how he "fed them" while they were in Egypt, as well as afterward in the desert and in Canaan. God bent low to meet them on their level to fill their needs. They took him for granted and ran from his voice.

These verses tell a heart-wrenching tale. Many good parents know what it is like to have rebellious and selfish children. Certainly every parent has endured some measure of disrespect and bad conduct from their kids. Many good children recognize when they have been wrong and change their behavior, or at least sincerely apologize for it later. Many others choose to live their entire lives in opposition to or in neglect of the Christian spiritual heritage that their parents worked hard to pass on to them. These parents almost always continue to love their children. Still, the barriers between them cause great pain.

If this is the case with us human parents, how much more does God hurt when his people reject him? God has created us. He has fed and clothed us. Whatever good things we have come from his hand. He teaches, shapes, and disciplines us. Any good character traits we have ultimately come from him. When anyone rebels against him, it pains him. When those who are Christians do so, it hurts him even more. Our faithlessness against God is as cruel as it is stupid.

God's sorrow does not diminish his power. It does not make him unable or unwilling to rule the world according to his purposes. Indeed, it shows how great he is to put up with our thoughtlessness and still maintain his character. Regardless, such sin certainly shows how low we can sink, how foolish we can be, and how much we need to repent and come back to the One who has always loved us.

Jesus Christ shows us the proper way to respond to God's voice. Matthew 2:15 cites Hosea 11:1 when describing Jesus's early life. Matthew notes that the holy family's time in Egypt "was to fulfill" Hosea's statement about God calling Israel out of Egypt. Scholars have proposed several options for what Matthew means.[1] In the context of Hosea 11:1–4, I think Matthew means that Jesus came out of Egypt after Herod died and then he obeyed and loved his Father always. He did not commit the sins verse 2 describes. He fulfilled 11:1–4 in that he did what God wanted all along. Thus he pleased the Father through his life, death, and resurrection. He always came when God called him.

As we place our trust in Christ, he shows us how to be his disciples. Our faith in Christ and our obedience to him pleases God the Father. Jesus shows us how to be proper sons and daughters of our heavenly Father, who frees and provides for his children.

## The Exiled Child (11:5–7)

By now we know what comes next in the passage. We have learned that judgment follows stubborn, resilient sin as surely as night follows day. We have also discovered that God warns that judgment is coming to give the people a chance to change. So it comes as no surprise when this section declares where Israel is headed, how they will go there, and why they must take this awful journey.

Verses 1–4 have highlighted Israel's deliverance from Egypt. Previous passages have noted Israel's recent interest in making treaties with Egypt (such as 7:11–16) and the folly of this course of action. Now in 11:5, God reveals that the people will not go to live in Egypt as they did before in Joseph's time. Then Egypt helped Israel. Now Israel has turned to Egypt for support against Assyria (9:3), but Egypt will be no help when help counts most. When the great battles end in 732 and 722 B.C., "Assyria shall be their king" (Hosea 11:5). This means that Israel is headed for defeat. Worse yet, thousands of

Israelites will go into exile to the vast reaches of the Assyrian Empire. Many will not be treated gently. When the Assyrians took captives, they were often brutal. For example, they put fishhooks in people's upper lips, fitted a small rope through the hook, linked the captives together, and marched them away.[2] It was a hard march, not unlike the one the Japanese army inflicted on Allied soldiers in World War II or the one the United States government imposed on native Americans in the nineteenth century. Where Israel is going, they can be sure that pain, loss, and death will be constant companions.

Verse 6 states how Assyria will overcome Israel. The enemy will wage war "against their cities, consume the bars of their gates, and devour them." When the Assyrians raised the sword against a place, they were patient. For instance, they laid siege to Samaria, the capital of Israel, from 724–722 B.C. Eventually Samaria ran out of food, water, and ammunition. Once Assyria breached a city's defense, they killed soldiers, impaled people on spikes, boiled people in hot liquid, took many captives, and left a frightened and starving populace behind.[3] These disasters came upon Israel "because of their own counsels" (11:6), which recommended trusting in Egypt as the best way to withstand Assyria. Israel fell due to Assyria's might and because of their own miscalculations.

Verse 7 stresses that the ultimate reason Israel fell to Assyria was their stubborn refusal to hear God's word. The people were "bent on turning away from" God. Chapters 6 and 7 demonstrated Israel's insincerity toward God. Their prayers are mere words. Israel has no intention of repenting when they pray for God's help. Thus when they cry out to God once the Assyrians arrive, the Lord will not answer them. The enemy will knock Israel down, and God "shall not raise them up at all" (11:7). He will finally let them suffer the consequences of their false spirituality and bad political decisions.

In short, God will do what no parent wants to do: he will not rescue his child from a terrible situation. To compare Hosea 11:5–7 to situations we understand today, he will not bail his son out of jail this time. He will not give his reckless child any more money. He will not force his son into a drug rehab program one more time while the son loudly proclaims that he does not have a problem. He will put his grown, addicted son out of the house, and he will change the locks. This is a horrible scene. It is so sad that it has come to this. It tears at our hearts. It tears at God's too. But as any parent in a similar situation knows, God does this for a reason. He does this to set Israel right. Clearly God's love includes severe mercy and tough love.

Many of us have experienced God's discipline. As Hebrews 12:3–17 indicates, we rarely appreciate this correction. But quite honestly, there have been times in my life that it took tough love on God's part to get me to turn back to him. I have also seen some Christians run from God for years before hard things bring them home to God. Hosea 11:5–7 and Hebrews 12:3–17 remind us that God disciplines us because he loves us. He disciplines us to remind us we are his children. God loves us enough to risk our anger at him to heal our souls, to reconcile us to him.

### The Restoring Father (11:8–11)

In Exodus 34:6, 7 God explains his character to Moses. The first two things he says are that he is "merciful and gracious." The word translated as "merciful" refers to the kind of love a good mother has for her child (see 1 Kings 3:26). God has this sort of love for his people. The final thing God says about himself in the Exodus passage is that he does not "clear the guilty." This means that he does not let his compassion wipe out his justice, and he does not judge in a heartless manner. This means God always has a reason for judging, and this reason has something to do with compassion and mercy. Hosea 11:8–11 demonstrates how God perfectly balances these different character traits. These verses depict God as a just and restoring father.

In Hosea 11:8, God asks four related questions and describes the emotions he feels for Israel. He wonders how he can "give up" and "hand over" Israel (v. 8a). These words describe the giving up and handing over to enemies in other Old Testament passages.[4] He then ponders how he can possibly make Israel "like Admah" and "like Zeboiim" (v. 8a). These two small places were allies of Sodom and Gomorrah. They were probably destroyed alongside Sodom and Gomorrah (see Genesis 14:2, 8; 19:25). Mays observed, "To be like Admah and Zeboiim is to exist only as a memory of swift and final calamity."[5] It is to exist only as a nearly unknown friend of very wicked places. So God asks if he should make Israel a mere footnote in the history of the destruction of more famous places.

Certainly God could do so. After all, he is the Lord of history. Also, Israel has hardly merited a better future. But God's heart is "overthrown"[6] at the thought (see Hosea 11:8b). The word translated as "overthrown" also appears in Genesis 19:25, where we read that God overthrows Sodom and Gomorrah and presumably Admah and Zeboiim. Furthermore God's "compassion grows warm and tender" (Hosea 11:8b). His compassion lets him know when his justice has been fulfilled. The father's heart turns to his child, as is always true of good fathers.

Thus God declares he will not "execute" his "burning anger" (v. 9a), which probably means he will not pour out all the wrath he could rightly dispense. He promises he "will not again destroy Ephraim" (v. 9a). Their defeat by Assyria is enough. He will not continue to judge them until they no longer exist. That is what human rulers, such as the rulers of Assyria, did in the ancient world. That is what human rulers try to do today. But he is "God and not a man" (v. 9b).[7] In fact, he is "the Holy One in [their] midst" (v. 9b). God is set apart from human beings. He does not act as they do in that he does not overstep proper bounds when he judges. Therefore, he will not destroy Israel. His child will live, and the child will come home.

Verses 10, 11 reveal how this homecoming will occur. As 11:5 indicates, Israel will be scattered throughout the Assyrian Empire. Now Hosea says they will come when God calls them (v. 10a). This is a complete reversal of Israel running away from his call in 11:1, 2. God's call will come in a strange form, the roar of a lion (v. 10a). The word translated as "lion" usually occurs in passages that "depict the ravaging wrath of Yahweh."[8] When he roars, "his children shall come trembling from the west; they shall come trembling like birds from Egypt, and like doves from the land of Assyria" (vv. 10b, 11a). They will come from every direction to which they have been scattered. Perhaps they tremble at the roar. If so, they will see that God roars against their captors, not against them. His roaring leads them "to their homes" (v. 11b). Their father is a lion; he has the power to defeat all their opponents. His lair is their home.

This deliverance comes after much pain. God restores his people *because of* judgment, not *from* judgment. Judgment has done its job, for the people come when God roars. Sadly, perhaps only judgment could do this job, for until then the people rebelled against God's written and spoken word. Still, the good news is that at long last the children come home. The sinful son has returned to the father's side. I do not know if Jesus had this text in mind when he told the parable of the prodigal son (Luke 15:11–32), but the two stories are certainly similar. Pain plays a strong role in producing reconciliation in both cases.

Hosea 11:1–11 serves as an excellent summary of the message of the Old Testament's prophetic literature.[9] The text highlights God's relationship with Israel, then describes sin, judgment, and renewal. These are the prophets' most-used themes. Each theme flows from God's character. He redeems and forgives because he is gracious, compassionate, and merciful (Exodus 34:6, 7). He judges sin to effect repentance and renewal because he will not clear the guilty (Exodus 34:7) or fail to bless all peoples through Abraham's family (Genesis 12:1–9). His character provides the storyline for the history of his straying people.

Of course, Jesus reflects and shares his Father's character. When Jesus sees the people living like sheep without a shepherd, he has compassion on them and urges prayer for more shepherds (Matthew 9:35–38). When Jesus told the rich young man to sell all he had and follow him, it was because Jesus loved him (Mark 10:17–22). When Jesus went to the cross, it was to lay down his life for his friends (John 15:13), people he loved and loves still. This love for us came from the love the Father and Jesus shared (John 17:20–23, 26). This love for us came to us because God loves the world so much (John 3:16). This loving God is the restoring father of Hosea 11:1–11. His love has not changed. It has simply grown more apparent and more amazing as history has unfolded. God's love remains, as always, unstoppable.

## Conclusion

Hosea 11:1–11 presents God's gospel to us. It shows God at work. He redeems, reconciles, and renews sinners. His love recaptures rebellious hearts. It never hesitates, never fails, and never stops. God's character calls us all to follow his Son, who always obeyed the Father. Those who come to the Father may tremble as they follow his voice, but they follow nonetheless. May each of us each day come to the restoring Father, the One who has carried us all our days.

# 11

# Idols, Money, and Prophets: A Family Story

HOSEA 11:12—12:14

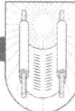

DURING A RECENT VISIT in Illinois, I asked my wife's father to tell me more about his ancestors. He confessed that he did now know much about them. "Once," he said, "I asked my grandmother to tell me about previous generations. She just looked at me and said, 'Honey, you don't want to know.'"

Many of us may share her desire to shield our grandchildren from what we consider sordid family stories. Others of us want the whole story told. The Bible seems to take this latter view. It holds back very few secrets about our spiritual ancestors. Hosea 11:12—12:14 not only follows this pattern of full disclosure, but it uses Jacob's failures as a warning to readers.

As we have seen, Hosea is steeped in Biblical history. He has used his people's family story to make several points. This time he uses the life story of Jacob, the father of the nation's twelve tribes, as a cautionary tale. The stories Hosea chooses indict his people on charges of idolatry, love of money, and ignoring God's word. They are reliving the mistakes their patriarch made, and once again the prophet hauls them into court to face God's charges. His goal is to get them to repent and thus change their own story. He wants them to give up their idols and coveting even at this late hour of their national history. In short, he wants them to act as Jacob did. Jacob waited a very long time to get right with God, but he did it. If their patriarch came to his senses, then they can as well.

## Jacob and the Idols (11:12—12:6)

Hosea 11:12—12:1[1] has long baffled interpreters. These verses are certainly in accord with previous statements about the people, yet they do not fit easily with either 11:1–11 or 12:2–14. Though it is impossible to know for sure, I think these verses provide a conclusion to 11:1–11 and an introduction to 12:2–14. Therefore, these verses are a sort of bridge. On the one hand, they explain why 11:1–11 declares that God will send Israel into exile. Israel is currently deceitful (v. 12). The people claim to serve God, but they do not. In fact, "they multiply falsehood and violence" in their land (12:1). They reject God's promise of help in favor of alliances with Egypt and Assyria. Thus they must go from the land. On the other hand, these verses lead into the indictment found in 12:2–14. Israel continues to act as they have in the past. God's word will keep convicting them.

As in 4:1, in 12:2 Hosea announces that God has a case against his people. This one relates to Judah and Jacob,[2] in short, to all of Jacob's descendants. It addresses "his ways" and "his deeds" and pledges to "punish" him for these. Hosea again uses the patriarch as a symbol of his current, living descendants. Through this creative means, the prophet will illustrate Israel's sin.

What was Jacob like? What were his ways and deeds? Hosea 12:3, 4 indicates that in his early years he was a greedy, grasping, and competitive man. He was combative and hard-nosed. At birth he grabbed his older twin brother Esau's heel (v. 3). Apparently he was trying to be the firstborn. Eventually he grasped his brother's rights and privileges as the oldest child (Genesis 25:19–34; 27:1–19). This did him little good, for his brother threatened to kill him (27:41). This threat led Jacob to flee from his family and his homeland, the only venues where his privileges had any value (Genesis 28:1–5). He then spent many years under the thumb of his father-in-law Laban (Genesis 29—30). He battled Laban mentally and financially for years and finally got free of him (Genesis 31). Clearly Jacob was a fighter.

Unfortunately he also fought God. As Hosea puts it in 12:3, "In his manhood he strove with God." This striving was a way of life with Jacob. He was unkind to his brother and deceitful to his father (Genesis 27:1–40). When God first revealed himself to Jacob at Bethel, the patriarch tried to make a deal with God. He promised to serve God if God brought him home safely (Genesis 28:10–22). But the striving Hosea has in mind likely refers to Genesis 32:28 one of the few places in Scripture where the word appears. Frightened that his brother will kill him, Jacob strives with God all night. Indeed, he "strove [or wrestled] with the angel and [endured]" (Hosea 12:4).[3] He endured, all the time crying for mercy, which God gave. God protected him from his brother.

Jacob walked with a limp the rest of his life due to a hip injury that he received during the wrestling (Genesis 32:31, 32). He endured to do the work that God wanted him to do all along: serve God and continue the covenant work God began with Abraham (see 25:19–26; 28:10–17). God won this contest, not Jacob.[4] When Jacob cried out, God graciously answered him.

Still basing his message on Jacob's life, Hosea now turns to the people as a whole in 12:4b. He asserts, "He found us[5] at Bethel, and there God spoke with us." When God met with Jacob at Bethel and continued the covenant with Abraham, all of Jacob's descendants were there. God offered the covenant to them then. This image is similar to believers today considering Jesus's initiating of the new covenant in his blood in Luke 22:20 as applying to us. Hosea 12:5 says that at Bethel "the LORD, the God of hosts" revealed himself to Jacob and thus to all of them. God continued his covenant with Abraham and Isaac with Jacob, and he continues the same covenant with Jacob's descendants in Hosea's day.

Since these things are true, the people need to follow Jacob's positive example. Hosea 12:6 says, Return unto your God,[6] just as Jacob turned to God for help when he feared Esau. The people face terrible times. Like Jacob, they have every reason to turn to the Lord. But they cannot turn to God if they have no intention of living for him. Hosea 5:6, 7 has already made this point. Rather they must "hold fast to" (or "guard") covenant[7] "love and justice" (12:6). Doing so requires them to "wait continually" for God. Here *waiting* means seeking God's will and giving him time to enact his will. The people must endure as Jacob did. They must be as changed as Jacob was after his long night of striving was over.

How do we know that Jacob was changed? How do we know he became loyal to God? After he limped off to face a new day, Jacob stopped trying to deceive his brother. He met Esau in an honest manner (Genesis 33:1–11), and Esau forgave him. Furthermore, in Genesis 35:1–15 Jacob returned to Bethel, where God had first given him covenant promises. There, to honor God's help in his time of distress, Jacob buried "the foreign gods" his family had collected (Genesis 35:1, 2, 4). I think Hosea has this last scene in mind when he exhorts the people to turn to God and keep the covenant in 12:6. The people have worshiped idols, often at Bethel (see 10:5–15). They must now recall how God met them through Jacob at Bethel, and they must turn aside from idols as Jacob did at Bethel. If they do so, God will aid them, just as he helped Jacob.

Even if we love our ancestors, it is important to avoid their mistakes. This is especially true as we consider their walk with God. My own grandfathers remind me of Jacob in that they were also farmers who waited many years before they surrendered to God. They suffered many kinds of physical, financial, and emotional losses as they stubbornly rebelled against God. This part of their lives was a cautionary tale to their descendants, including me. Yet when they gave their lives to God, it took. They forged ahead with God, growing in him in their own ways until they met him face-to-face. Their enduring witness of keeping faith with God challenges and encourages me to this day.

Each of us needs to imitate our spiritual ancestor Jacob's post-wrestling witness. He was not a flawless man, but he was a changed man. Christ can do the same in and for us.

### Ephraim and His Money (12:7-9)

The family story continues. As we have already seen, the saga includes some devious dealings on Jacob's part. Many of these dealings related to getting money by deceitful means. Hosea now highlights this past lust for money and applies it to his own day. Yet he focuses on Ephraim rather than on Jacob.

Ephraim was an ancestor associated with the northern kingdom, for this tribe was the largest in Israel. Therefore, several Old Testament passages use the name as a synonym for the ten tribes that separated from Judah and Benjamin when Solomon died in 930 B.C. Thus the mention of Ephraim here probably intends to make readers think about the beginnings of the northern kingdom. More specifically, Hosea wants readers to know that the northern kingdom was riddled with greed from its earliest days.

Hosea 12:7 begins with a word that can either mean "Canaan," the place where Ephraim lived, or "a merchant," the trade Hosea is about to attack. In Canaan, the Israelites took up the business practices of the people they met there. They used "false balances" when they traded. They did so because they enjoyed oppressing others. Cheating people pleased them.

Verse 8 reveals why they like deceiving their customers so much. Simply put, it makes them rich. Love for money trumps concern for morality. When confronted, Ephraim says, "They cannot find in me iniquity or sin." In other words, "You have nothing on me. You cannot prove any charges against me." He is greedy, he cheats people to get money, and he gets away with it. Or so he thinks.

God sees what Ephraim has done, according to verse 9. God has known Ephraim since he lived in Egypt, long before the northern kingdom was established. God was the One who gave the people land, homes, and businesses in Canaan. He can just as easily make them "dwell in tents" again as they did before they got to Canaan, and as they still do on "appointed feast" days such as the Feast of Booths. Ephraim did not get the land by cheating others, but they can certainly leave the land by doing so. God can make them as poor as their ancestors were when they first arrived in Canaan.

Family stories often begin with tales of how the first generation came to the country with very little. Sometimes it seems the initial family members get poorer every time the story is told! The tale usually continues with accounts of hard work and eventual success. It is rare that anyone says, "We were very poor, but then Great-Grandpa started committing fraud," or "Our people were poor until we figured out how to sell illegal drugs to kids" or "Our ancestors had little money, but then we got into prostitution and pornography." We leave out the nastier details. But Hosea does not leave them out here. He tells the whole disturbing story. Ephraim has been crooked from the start, and his descendants follow his example.

We probably should not continue on without stating the obvious. Every ethical portion of the Bible opposes the sort of business practices Ephraim exhibits. The issue is not whether we get caught cheating people. The issue is not fearing the loss of what we have if God does not like what we do. The issue is obeying what God commands. The issue is treating others with justice and love (see Leviticus 19:18; Micah 6:8; Mark 12:28–34). This is the example we should set for coming generations.

### God and His Prophets (12:10–14)

Hosea presses on with the family story as God continues to speak. Now he raises a matter that is common in the Bible (see 2 Kings 17:13, 14; Jeremiah 1:17–19; Matthew 5:11, 12). He mentions his servants the prophets and decries how Israel has ignored and rejected them. God sent prophets out of kindness, not out of spite. He sent them to warn and heal the people. Their rejection of these faithful ones is yet another ugly chapter in Israel's history.

Hosea 12:10 asserts that God called, equipped, and sent faithful prophets. Northern Israel was where Elijah, Elisha, Amos, Hosea, and many other good prophets ministered. It is likely that Hosea was not the only God-sent prophet in this era.[8] Israel had every chance to hear God's word and respond.

Therefore, the "iniquity in Gilead" and numerous altars in Gilgal that verse 11 mentions are completely inexcusable. It is unclear exactly what iniquity Gilead committed, but Hosea mentions it here and in 6:8. His first readers probably knew precisely what he meant. Gilgal's piling up of sacrifices was almost certainly done to other gods or done without sincerity to God (12:11).

The whole of Hosea leads to this conclusion. Despite all that God's prophets said and did, they could not stem the rising tide of the people's sins.

In 12:12, 13 Hosea turns to illustrations from Jacob's life and from the exodus. Because of "Jacob's devious actions, family tensions were such that he fled to an area settled by his mother's family in Aram, today the country of (northern) Syria."[9] Once there, he kept sheep for his father-in-law Laban in exchange for marrying Rachel and Leah (v. 12). This was hardly a happy period in Jacob's life, for Laban treated him worse than Jacob had treated his brother Esau. Jacob's wives competed for his affections and used their children as pawns in their family power games. Jacob struggled to outwit Laban. Left to his own ways, Israel's patriarch suffered in a foreign land.

With no connecting bridge, Hosea switches to the exodus story. He reminds readers that it was through a prophet, Moses, that God led Israel out of Egypt (v. 13). Moses also "guarded" Israel in that he led the people through the desert to the promised land. Again Hosea's point is that true prophets have been God's gift to Israel. Without them, the people are as vulnerable as Jacob in Aram and the Israelites in Egypt.

Ephraim has understood none of this. Instead he has provoked God to anger, according to 12:14. He has done so by rejecting the covenant God gave through his prophet Moses. He has sinned against God and neighbor and offered sacrifices God did not sanction, as 12:11 has already revealed. Ephraim has done so since breaking with Judah two centuries earlier. Ephraim has rejected Moses, Elijah, and Elisha. Now he has rejected Hosea. Ephraim takes no correction and accepts no help. Worse yet, he kills the prophets that God sends. Thus God "will leave his bloodguilt on him and will repay him for his disgraceful deeds" (v. 14). This chapter of the family story will be unpleasant indeed.

## Conclusion

After Hosea 12 you can see the wisdom of my father-in-law's grandmother. Sometimes it is hard to hear the whole family story. Sometimes "Honey, you don't want to know." But we do know Jacob's winding and often disturbing family story. We know it includes much sin and some rough descendants such as Ephraim. We know it is a messy, embarrassing tale a lot of the time.

We also know something else. We know this is *our* story. We have sin in our past. We have stubborn rebellion in our genes. We have all ignored God's word, and some of us have mistreated God's messengers. These stories make us cringe, for we see ourselves there and do not like what we see.

That is why it is so important to cling to the part of the family history told in 12:3–6. In his sin and desperation, Jacob clung to God and begged for his life. God forgave and protected him. God brought him safely home to the faith and safely home to his land.

Those of us who cling to God in Christ have a family history of grace, service, and glory no matter what else has happened. As Paul reminds us, "If you are Christ's, then you are Abraham's offspring, heirs according to promise" (Galatians 3:29), just like Jacob. "Honey, that is something you *do* want to know!" Do you know it? If so, you know the family history ends in forgiveness, not in judgment.

# 12

# Ransom from Death

HOSEA 13

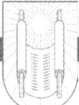

HUMAN HISTORY SHOWS THAT people hold onto their national pride even after they lose self-governance. They long for a return to at least some measure of former glory. Deep in their hearts, they hope for their nation's resurrection. Such was the case with Israel. Only two centuries after breaking with Judah, Israel fell to Assyria in 732 B.C. For the next ten years the people schemed to rid themselves of the Assyrians. Eventually Assyria tired of their rebellion and destroyed Israel's capital city, Samaria, in 722 B.C. For many more years Israelites clung to dreams of freedom from Assyria. They dreamed of resurrection. Yet no resurrection occurred. By 670 B.C. Assyria concluded that the Israelites would never learn. They deported hundreds of Israelites and replaced them with refugees from other lands.[1]

Hosea 13 indicates that Israel looked for resurrection in all the wrong places. They sought life from all the sources that brought death in the first place. The people kept turning to idols that could not save. They treated their covenant with God as either an emergency plan or as some quaint tradition they had outgrown.[2] New gods and new political plans seemed to them to be the best the way forward. Forgetting that there was no Savior but God (13:4–11), they bowed to idols skillfully made by artisans (vv. 1–3). Thus they chose to bear their guilt—the most awful penalty any person or nation can face (vv. 12–16). By rejecting the One who gave them life in the first place (vv. 4, 5), they fought against the only One who could give them new life (v. 9).

We are nearing the end of Hosea's book. It is time for us to take stock of our own situation. Perhaps some of us resent Hosea for his straight talk. We may have dug in and rebelled more than when we started these chapters. That is certainly what most Israelites did when they heard Hosea's message. If we follow their example, then we are rejecting the only God, the One who loves us and tells us the truth. We are pursuing a long and impatient death. But perhaps others of us have been awakened as if from a long sleep. We have come to realize that we have been fighting God and breaking our covenant vows for a long time. But now we want to come home. We want to serve the One who has ransomed us from death for as much time as we have left. If so, we are hearing Hosea, and we are hearing God. I pray that all of us will hear and give our hearts to the only Savior, who gives life.

### Idols Skillfully Made (13:1–3)

As he does in chapter 12, Hosea refers to Israel's history in this section. He begins by noting Ephraim's status when the nation began: "When Ephraim spoke, there was trembling; he was exalted in Israel" (13:1a).[3] As 1 Kings 12:1–24 recounts, because of Solomon's idolatry God gave ten of Israel's tribes to Jeroboam I, who ruled 930–909 B.C. As is often the case in Hosea, the name Ephraim stands both for the kingdom as a whole and for the strongest clan in the kingdom. Ephraim led the people of the north. So when he spoke, the others bowed to his wishes. More often than not, Judah also followed Ephraim's lead.

By now we know what Ephraim did with this God-ordained power and privilege. Instead of always serving the Lord, "he incurred guilt through Baal and died" (Hosea 13:1b). His spiritual death preceded his physical death by many decades. Nonetheless, he was dead in sin, as Paul describes all those who rebel against God in Ephesians 2:1–3.

Hosea says that like all who are dead in sin, Ephraim's life produced more and more sin (Hosea 13:2a). He turned repeatedly to "idols skillfully made of their silver, all of them the work of craftsmen" (v. 2b). Ephraim loved money, sex, and power. This is why he worshiped Baal, the god of fertility. He freely gave offerings of silver, and some of this silver was artfully made into idols by skilled artisans. They bowed before images crafted from money, the thing they loved the most.

In times of unusual trouble, people often become more religious. They pour out their hearts in prayer to their god or gods. They offer more extreme forms of piety. It seems this may have occurred in Israel. Simply bowing before idols did not give them liberty from Assyria. So they took more extreme measures.[4] In what seems to be a phrase spoken in those days, Hosea notes, "Those who offer human sacrifice kiss calves." A summary of that idea might go like this: "The people who offer human sacrifices are the ones who truly[5] worship what the images represent." Apparently they came to believe that for the god of fertility to help them, they had to sacrifice the most precious result of fertility: their children (see Jeremiah 32:35). They gave the full measure of their devotion.

Of course, devotion is not what makes things happen. The deity makes things happen. Since Baal is not real, the devoted get no help with their troubles. Sincere worship of a false god is sad, for people who worship them give their hearts and souls for nothing. In Israel's case, these worshipers will soon pass away. To make this point in Hosea 13:3, he uses metaphors drawn from the people's daily life. They will melt away like morning mist in the air or dew on the ground. They will blow away like chaff beaten from grain on a threshing floor or like smoke from a fire kindled for cooking or comfort. Their desperate devotion to Baal amounts to fog, dew, chaff, and smoke when it comes to solving life's true problems of sin, service, and survival. Israel will leave the land as surely as these light things quickly leave their respective places.

Throughout history people have thought that religion is a human choice verified by sincere devotion. They have believed that any religion is fine if it is honestly held and practiced. Hosea reminds us that these sentiments are not true. The God of the Bible is the only God. He alone saves, and he alone reveals true spiritual religion (see John 4:19–26). Israel strayed from God and gave their hearts to Baal and other unreal deities. Serious service of a nonexistent god did the people no good at all. We Christians can become prideful because we serve the only God, or we can, like Hosea, have compassion enough to share God's loving warnings with a world that earnestly worships gods that cannot save.

## No Savior but God (13:4–11)

Hosea is well-versed in Israel's history. To him, history is not useless information from bygone days. Hosea thinks the past is never dead. In fact, it is not even past.[6] The past keeps getting lived out in the present. There is no present or future without the past. The past informs the future if we have eyes to see. For Hosea, the fact that God is the only savior was the key to Israel's history and Israel's future. The same is true of all of us who are part of Abraham's family through faith in Christ. It is also true of all humanity, for God made us all.

Hosea 13:4–6 surveys Israel's history from the exodus to the prophet's day, a period of about seven centuries. God's work on Israel's behalf was extremely personal. In verse 4 he speaks emphatically, using his covenant name: "I, Yahweh, am your God" (AT).[7] He speaks historically and relationally, stating that "from the land of Egypt; you [have known][8] no God but me." Since God delivered Israel from slavery, they have known no other deity who has saved and loved them. We discovered in Hosea 1—4 that in the Old Testament, knowing someone involves one's heart, soul, mind, and body. It is quite personal. Yahweh became known by what he did and said as well as by whom he sent. In this sense, Israel has known no other such God. Baal has not saved them and cannot save them. Hosea adds that they have known no other such God because "besides me there is no savior" (13:4). This phrase does not just mean there is no God for Israel except Yahweh. It means there are no other gods *at all*.

Not only did God deliver Israel, he sustained them "in the wilderness, in the land of drought," according to verse 5. God fed them manna in the desert (Exodus 16). He found water for them in a dry land (Exodus 17:1–7). God provided for them in a place so inhospitable to life that the people had no reason thereafter to doubt his power and love. He did this because he quite emphatically knew them: "It was I who knew you in the wilderness" (Hosea 13:5). His personal commitment *to* them was evident by what he did *for* them.

So what happened? When and how did they turn away from God? Verse 6 continues the story. God brought them into Canaan, a land lush by comparison with the desert. After grazing in such good pasture, Israel got full and satisfied. When they got full, "their heart was lifted up" (v. 6b). That is, they became proud. They forgot who they were, where they came from, and how they got where they were. This was because, God says, "they forgot me." Unfounded pride led them to cast off their past, which marred their present. They forgot their God and lost themselves. Pride always wreaks this sort of havoc. When we give ourselves credit for what God has done, we lose God in the process. Success can lead to self-satisfaction, then to dangerous forgetting.

By this point in the book of Hosea, you know what this pride-induced forgetting means for Israel. It means God will discipline them through judgment. Indeed judgment lurks just around the corner, like a lion or leopard ready to pounce, according to 13:7. He will tear them like "a bear robbed of her cubs" or like a wild animal eating a carcass, according to 13:8. God has given Israel into Assyria's hands, and he will do still more. God's judgment has taken place in the past and continues in the present. If no change occurs, then it will also happen in the future.

The reason for this continuous incremental punishment is clear. Verse 9 says that Israel has forgotten God, who tells them, "You are against me, against your helper." God's help had extended over seven centuries at this point and had "made possible everything good in Israel's life (cf. Pss 33:20;

70:5; 115:9–10; 121:1–2; 124:8)."[9] God's help took concrete form. It was not theoretical, never abstract.

The people could not see God, but they could see a king. In Samuel's time the people cried out for a king. They wanted to be like other nations, and they were not content to have God rule over them. Then and throughout Israel's history, God gave kings and took them away, as Hosea 13:10, 11 states. The people often looked to the kings that God gave them instead of to God himself. As James L. Mays has observed, "Israel had looked to the military competence of the royal court for deliverance. In all the palace revolutions, assassinations, and anointings which punctuated every phase of the Assyrian crisis, Israel had been looking for salvation. The ruthless vehemence of Israel's royal politics was a testimony to their desperate belief that a proper king would save them."[10]

Hosea 13:1–3 has reminded us of the fact that devotion to a nonexistent god cannot save. Hosea 13:9–11 reminds us that a king God has not sent cannot save, however tough and ruthless he may be. No nation and no king are too tough to die. We must look to God, not to our devotion or the institutions God has ordained. Where does this leave us? It leaves us looking to what is unseen. It leaves us with faith in God and his word. Odd as it may seem, it leaves us with the source of all reality. It leaves us with the only God, and thus the only God who can save.

One more time we need to see ourselves in Israel's past, for this is our past. God has saved us from sin through Christ's death as surely as he delivered Israel from slavery in Egypt. He has given us brothers and sisters in Christ and all that we need to survive and serve him (see Matthew 6:19–34; 19:16–30; Mark 8:17–21), just as he gave us a homeland and kings. Will we grow fat, satisfied, proud, and forgetful of God as most Israelites did in Hosea's time? Or will we serve God no matter what others do? God continues to provide his word and all the lesser bread we need (see Deuteronomy 8:1–10), just as he did in the desert. God is our help. There is no ultimate savior but God. Whatever your circumstances, believe and cling to these promises. Let us take care lest we forget Yahweh, our God (see Deuteronomy 8:11–20).

## Ransom from Death (13:12–16)

For those of us blessed to live in the United States, it is easy in our age of amazing medical achievement to forget about death. Or at least it is easy to put off thinking about it. There always seems to be one more thing the doctors can do for us. Death gets postponed over and over in many of our lives and in the lives of those we love. An elderly friend once remarked, "It seems we've ensured that we will only die of the most hideous illnesses." Yet as we well know, doctors cannot ransom us from death.

Israel seemed to think there was always one more political rabbit they could pull out of their hats. They could always choose another king; they could always try a new foreign policy; some new technology for war was always on the horizon. But the nation was slowly but surely dying. Life comes from God alone, and most of the people had shut him out of their lives. Death stalked them because they forgot God.

Ephraim thought himself a powerful, wise, and wily survivor. God disagrees. Hosea 13:12 states that Ephraim has been bound by his iniquity. He has stored up sin and thus stored up wrath. This means "he is an unwise son" (v. 13). Though he fancies himself a great strategist, he is in fact like a baby who does not know when to be born. Ephraim is helpless and hapless. Ephraim's great plans are stillborn.

Now God asks a series of questions about Ephraim's plight in 13:14. God clearly knows what is at stake. Israel heads toward death and the grave. Will God let his child go? As in 11:1–11, he will not. He declares, "I will ransom them from Sheol [the grave]; I will redeem them from death"(13:14).[11] In 11:8, 9 God states that he will not make Ephraim like Admah and Zeboiim, the small places wiped out when God judged Sodom and Gomorrah. He will judge Israel, but he will not wipe him out. He will "ransom" (13:14). That is, he will pay the price necessary to avert death. He will "redeem." He will be like Ruth's Boaz, a kinsman who will take action to buy back what is lost if death prevails. God will save the child bent on death.

Since he will ransom and redeem, God now asks, "O Death, where are your plagues? O Sheol, where is your sting?"[12] Death and the grave thought they could snare Israel. All indications were that they were correct. But God had other plans. These questions are rhetorical. They assume their answer is that death and the grave have no power over God. He has chosen to keep life and hope and his people alive.

Just in case death and the grave wonder, God's decision is final: "Relenting is hidden from my eyes (v. 14)."[13] In other words, "Relenting from my chosen course of action is out of the question." Israel will live on in some form or fashion. God will not change his mind on this particular subject.

But this decision does not mean that the wicked people in Israel are off the hook. This promise of Israel's long-term survival does not mean there will be no current judgment of Israel's sin. God has made everlasting promises to Noah, Abraham, Israel, and David. These include the ongoing descendants of Abraham. All these promises must be accessed by faith, not by genetic code (see Genesis 15:6). God can keep his promises as long as one faithful Israelite exists, and Hosea is a faithful Israelite. Yet he is surrounded by hardened sinners headed for disaster.

Hosea 13:15, 16 details this horrific disaster. Verse 15 shows that judgment may well come swiftly at a time when Israel feels safe. Israel "may flourish among his brothers," but "the east wind"—the hot wind from the desert, which will be "the wind of the LORD"—will blow on them. They will never see what is coming. The result will be that "his fountain shall dry up; his spring shall be parched." Verse 15 ends with an image that reveals the desolating wind is an army: "It shall strip his treasury of every precious thing." Verse 16 confirms this. Because Samaria has sinned against God so consistently and for so long, "they shall fall by the sword." As was the case when Assyria conquered cities, the women and children will be abused and killed. By rejecting the only savior (v. 4) and their best helper (v. 9), they leave themselves open to a cruel oppressor. They have placed their families in a desperate situation. Their sins have led to their loved ones' deaths. They may blame God or their kings, but they should blame themselves.

Severe judgment looms. God will preserve some descendants of Abraham. He will not let the coming devastation wipe out Israel completely. Grace will prevail, though it will be a costly grace for God and for Israel. God will redeem and ransom through the suffering and death of prophets like Hosea and ultimately through the suffering and saving death of Jesus, his Son. Before and after Christ's death, faithful people like Hosea have suffered alongside the wicked to whom they minister.

## Conclusion

The Apostle Paul provides a better conclusion to this message than any I could conceive. Paul cites Hosea 13:14 in 1 Corinthians 15:50–58, the end to his great treatise on the resurrection as the culmination of the gospel (1 Corinthians 15). Like Hosea, Paul has been writing to an unruly, rebellious group of people. While claiming faith in Christ, they have sinned in a variety of shocking ways. They have followed false teachers and perpetrated false doctrine. Still, a few faithful ones have clung to true faith and obedience. With such results at one of his most promising church plants, how can Paul keep going?

He keeps going because God has sent Jesus his Son. Jesus has died on the cross, and God has raised him from the dead. Because believers love Christ, God will raise them from the dead. Jesus was the first of many persons whom God will raise. Like Hosea, Paul stands on the promise that God ransoms and redeems, so death and the grave cannot prevail. There may be sin everywhere.

Judgment may loom on the near horizon. Regardless, God's ransom and redemption from the grave stand between the believer and the death that the wicked die. Nothing can change God's decision. Therefore, together with Paul and Hosea, we serve in hope, even in harsh conditions. God in Christ triumphs, so we triumph.

Is this your faith? Have you turned from sin and turned to Jesus? Have you rejected idols skillfully made and given your life to the only Savior, the One who ransoms and redeems from death? Have you taken hope in Christ, knowing that your nation may fall but your spiritual family never will? Hosea and Paul offer you this faith and this confidence. They show you the way to be ransomed from death. As we near the end of Hosea, it is surely time for you to choose life.

# 13

# Repentance, Healing, Fruitfulness, and Wisdom

## HOSEA 14

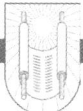

HOSEA 13 ENDS with some very sobering words:

> Samaria shall bear her guilt,
>   because she has rebelled against her God;
> they shall fall by the sword;
>   their little ones shall be dashed in pieces,
> and their pregnant women ripped open. (13:16)

For many years God protected Israel from Assyria, the fiercest and most cruel army the ancient world knew. Assyria was famous for atrocities, and Israel was on Assyria's conquest list. God warned Israel through his prophets and waited for repentance, to no avail. Finally, he gave Israel over to the consequences of their decisions. Assyria's armies came, and they destroyed Samaria, Israel's capital, in 722 B.C. God's severe promises were fulfilled.

Yet we also recall that 13:14 promised to ransom Israel from the grave. We remember that Hosea 1—3 stressed God's unquenchable love for Israel, his bride. We take heart that Hosea 11:1–11 emphasized God's undying love for his son, Ephraim. Assyria's invasion and conquest of Samaria is not the book's conclusion.

God's healing grace is the last word in Hosea. In chapter 14, the prophet offers a profound summary of God's unquenchable love for his people. He offers a beaten, battered, and shattered Israel instruction in repentance (vv. 1–3), healing from the effects of sin (v. 4), and future fruitful life (vv. 5–8). The book concludes by noting that wise people will accept God's offer of grace (v. 9). God's love continues to capture the hearts of those who trust him. This was Hosea's message before Samaria fell and after it fell. It remains God's word for us today. Have we heard it? If we are wise, then we will make sure that we have. We will find our lives fitting Hosea's grand conclusion.

## Repentance (14:1–3)

Why should Israel repent? Again Hosea is quite clear. He tells Israel, "You have stumbled because of your iniquity" (v. 1b). The Hebrew word translated here as "iniquity" basically means "twisted." The twisting of God's word and the twisting of our behavior amounts to iniquity, a particular type of disobedience. Hosea indicates that the people's twisted deeds take them on a twisted path. Therefore, he writes, "You have stumbled," a phrase that "denotes the lack of strength which incapacitates and topples previously fit and active men."[1] They have not stumbled just once. They have staggered time and again. As they disobey God, their path gets harder to walk on.

Why should we repent today? Repenting is the right thing to do primarily because we owe God our lives and our souls. He merits our faithful service. Sin precludes that service. Repenting is also the best thing to do because sin beats us down until we are too bruised to rise. Sin is foolish and self-defeating.

Next, Hosea states in 14:2, 3 how Israel may repent. Like the wonderful teacher he is, the prophet gives them clear steps to follow. First, they must think about how to confess sin ("Take with you words") and "return to the LORD" (v. 2a). Second, they must ask God to "take away all iniquity" that they have committed that led to their stumbling (v. 2b). Confession of sin includes the understanding that only God can bear with and remove sin. Third, they must ask God to "accept what is good" and say to him, "We will pay[2] the fruit[3] of our lips" (v. 2b). This fruit includes prayer, worship, and the keeping of vows.[4] Only a kind and giving God could accept the promise of one who has lied so often. Fourth, Israel must turn from their faith in political alliances and from bowing before idols (v. 3a). They must admit that no great nation, not even Assyria, can save them. They must not allow political scheming[5] to be their source of hope. They must stop loving money and the fertility gods that represent this love. They must "say no more, 'Our God,' to the work of our hands" (v. 3b).

Anything less than these steps falls short of turning from iniquity and trusting in God alone. It is false repentance, such as 7:14–16 described:

> They do not cry to me from the heart,
>     but they wail upon their beds;
> for grain and wine they gash themselves;
>     they rebel against me.
> Although I trained and strengthened their arms,
>     yet they devise evil against me.
> They return, but not upward;
>     they are like a treacherous bow;
> their princes shall fall by the sword
>     because of the insolence of their tongue.
> This shall be their derision in the land of Egypt.

True repentance comes from a humble heart through honest lips. True repentance stands ready to praise God through word and deed. True repentance leads to serving God.

Finally, 14:3c states why Israel can hope God will forgive them: "In you the orphan finds mercy." Israel discovered God's mercy for the poor and weak when God delivered them from Egypt. The word translated as "mercy" is the mercy a good mother has for her child (see 1 Kings 3:26, 27). God has parental compassion for the orphan, so surely he will have compassion on Israel, his son (see Hosea 11:1–11). God's mercy is Israel's hope.

Like Psalm 51 and 1 John 1:9, 10, Hosea 14:1–3 shows us the path of true repentance. We cannot justify our own sins, so we should not even try. Rather, we must own up to them. Only God can forgive and restore; no one else could even forgive all that we have done. God alone has limitless mercy. Take responsibility for what you have done, pray to the One you have offended, prepare for service, and wait on him. These are the first steps we must take. All other paths lead to destruction.

## Healing (14:4)

Americans today are obsessed with healing. We want the best doctors, we want cutting-edge medicines, and we want them to cost as little as possible. We often want extreme measures taken to extend life just a bit longer. We rightly rejoice when people get better, and I suspect health issues take up more space on our prayer lists than any other subject.

Oddly enough, we are not yet as interested in prevention techniques as one might guess, given our passion to live longer. We tend to want our cake and not have it eat us. Frankly, we have grown spoiled, having become accustomed to living as we wish and having doctors find some way to fix us. Too many of us desire healing without any accompanying personal responsibility.

Israel had wishes of this sort long before Americans did. They wanted to use their bodies, minds, politics, economics, military, and souls however they wished and suffer no consequences. They wanted to adore sex, money, power, prestige, and ease without the consequences of their idolatry. As time passed, however, they found themselves in a desolate land governed by a foreign power. They found themselves poor and needy. They awoke to the fact that their souls were even thinner than their bodies. Physicians and political advisers could have honestly and correctly told them, "There is nothing more we can do for you. I am afraid your choices have caught up with you."

Thus it is good news for them that God can heal what no one else can. His medicine is strange, and Hosea 14:1–3 has already described it. This sin-sick people must take an elixir of repentance. In verse 4, God declares that when they take it, "I will heal their apostasy; I will love them freely, for my anger has turned from them." He will do what they do not deserve. His grace will make them well.

God's healing deals with the cause of their illness, not just with its symptoms. The word the ESV translates as "apostasy" is a play on words in Hebrew. It is from the same root word as "return" in 14:1, 2. Therefore, Hosea basically says that when Israel turns to God, he will heal their turning away from him ("their apostasy"). By his grace and through his word he told them how to repent in 14:1–3. By his grace and through his word he now promises to provide the cure for their sin.

God will safeguard this healing through a marvelous therapy. He will "love them freely," without any trace of anger (v. 4). Love ultimately stands behind all that God does, for "God is love," according to 1 John 4:7, 8. Love motivated God's promises to Abraham, his deliverance of Israel from Egypt, and the giving of his standards to Israel through Moses (see Deuteronomy 7:6–11). In the Bible, love is not a sentimental emotion. It basically means choosing to commit to someone. Sentiment may accompany an appropriate choice, but one's commitment matters most.

God is committed to Israel. Because he loves Israel, he shows extreme anger at their extreme sin. But when true repentance comes, all that will be in the past. Anger's work is then done. God "has turned" his anger away when his people return to him (Hosea 14:4).

We have seen this love at work throughout the book but especially in Hosea 2:14–23 and 3:1–5. There God speaks of drawing Israel back to him, and he tells Hosea to go love Gomer again. God's love is always working. It may be patient or severe, but it is never dormant. Its goal is reconciliation, the healing of relationship with him. This reconciliation was always available to Israel. They only had to return to the Lord. It remains available to us through Jesus Christ.

## Fruitfulness (14:5–8)

Most of us want healing so we can get back to living. We do not consider good health simply a state of being; we have things we hope to accomplish. These things are the fruit of our healing. Similarly, God has fruit he wants to produce through a healed relationship with Israel. In these verses, Hosea uses several metaphors drawn from nature to show how Israel's restoration will lead to their good.

In 13:15, Hosea compared God's judgment to a searing "east wind . . . rising from the wilderness." This heat promised to dry up all supplies of water. But after Israel's repentance and God's reconciling love take effect, the opposite will occur. In 14:5, God pledges that he "will be like the dew to Israel." As Andrew Dearman explains, "Dew is associated with the morning clouds and early mist of the summer in ancient Israel, a season that is otherwise dry. A Mediterranean climate typically offers very little rain from April through October. Without the dew, the agricultural season is cut short, and ripening fruits will be stunted in development or not survive."[6] Israel's relationship with God is like a new crop recently planted. Without the help God provides, it will die. God will make certain that this new love will have what it needs to thrive.

In fact, God will make certain that there is a bumper crop of various kinds. God will make the people "blossom like the lily" (v. 5b), a plant that came up quickly and filled the desert with temporary beauty. Macintosh observes that this image means God "can bring life and vigour to his people (cf. Isa 26:19, where dew is used in connection with the notion of resurrection), so that Israel shall flower with all the glory of 'the lilies of the field' . . . the flowers . . . which flourish so strikingly in the wadis of the desert and among the thornbushes."[7] Furthermore, God will see to it that his people "take root like the trees of Lebanon" (Hosea 14:5c). Garrett notes, "Deep roots . . . signify endurance and hardiness, and call to mind the picture of the righteous person of Ps. 1:3."[8]

But this is not all, for Hosea 14:6 states that new growth[9] will follow. Israel's "shoots shall spread out." The ground will be covered with Israel's flourishing growth. What is more, this spreading growth will be lovely, like an olive tree in bloom and like the fragrant cedars of Lebanon. Finally, 14:7 declares that Israel will bear much fruit, like a full head of grain or a vine bearing many grapes. Grain and wine were staples of Israel's diet. They were also surplus products that Israel sold to other lands. Thus, this verse indicates that God will meet all the people's basic needs.

One can get excited about all this marvelous production and forget the source of these blessings. If so, 14:7 reminds us that all of this occurs because Israel comes under God's "shadow." That is, Israel has come under God's "protection and sphere of rule (Pss. 17:8; 36:7; etc.)."[10] Without this protection Israel lies exposed to heat and death. Likewise, Hosea 14:8 compares God to "an evergreen cypress," a tree that never dies.[11] From this continually living tree comes Israel's fruit. Whatever Israel needs for continuing spiritual, physical, and mental life comes from God. Therefore, they have no need of idols.[12] God alone loves them and cares for them. They have sought help from Baal in the past, but now Israel will see that only God is real, and only he can help. If Israel forgets the true source of their salvation and provision, all is lost. If they remember, though, the future will be incredibly bright.

God always redeems and blesses to make his people fruitful. He provides for us so that we may love him (Deuteronomy 6:4–9), love neighbors (Leviticus 19:18), and love strangers (Leviticus 19:34). He saves his people so that we can be a kingdom of priests declaring his glory to the ends of the earth (Exodus 19:5, 6; 1 Peter 2:9, 10). He teaches and empowers us so that we can be fruitful in character and conduct (Galatians 5:22–26). In short, by his grace God saves us from sin to do the works he prepared for us to do before he made the world (Ephesians 2:1–10). We bear the fruit he produces in us (Galatians 2:20). Our lives, homes, work, and communities are all changed as a result. As we trust him, we have all that we need to do his work, for the God who clothes the lilies of the field makes his people fruitful in his kingdom's work (Matthew 6:25–33). We need never worry whether such is the case (Matthew 6:34).

### Wisdom (14:9)

We now come to the last verse of Hosea. Here we find soul-searching words. Hosea has exposed great sin and offered rich grace. Now he writes, "Whoever is wise, let him understand these things; whoever is discerning, let him know them" (Hosea 14:9). This all seems mysterious at first. What is the standard for being "wise" and "discerning"?

The second half of verse 9 clarifies things. Those who are "wise" and "discerning" read this book and trust that "the ways of the Lord are right." We do not fully grasp the reasons and means of God's judgment. We cannot fathom the depths of his unquenchable love. We may disagree with his wrath or his kindness. Or we may become wise and know that the God who loves, disciplines, and reconciles knows what he is doing. If we love him as he has loved us, then we will trust his character.

Also, those who trust God's ways "walk in them." They walk the path of repentance, faith, obedience, and fruitfulness because he enables them to do so. They are the ones God considers "righteous."[13] Like Abraham they believe God, and God counts their faith as righteousness (Genesis 15:6). But those who "transgress" or "rebel" are doomed to "stumble" in God's ways. Thus Hosea returns to the metaphor he began this chapter with in 14:1. Stumbling and falling result from failing to trust God and failing to walk in his ways.

## Conclusion

One last time Hosea presents us with the choice between the path of life and the path of death. He has shown us that God is willing to be reconciled with sinners. He has alleviated our fears that our sin cannot be forgiven. Hosea has also put us on notice that we cannot love money, sex, and power and have salvation too. When we choose God, we choose whatever fruitfulness he gives us.

God is loving and just. He loved the world so much he sent his Son so that we might not be condemned. Yet those who do not believe are condemned already (John 3:16–21). If you have never done so, come out of condemnation into love. Repent of your sin and give your life to the Lord Jesus. If you have done this before and have been living on the wrong path, it is time to return to God. The One who loved you then still loves you now. He can make you flourish in his work again. Hosea promises this love, and Jesus embodied it. We need only turn to God in Christ for God to turn toward us, to receive us back as if we had never been gone.

# JOEL

*By Paul R. House*

# 14

# A Plague for the Ages

## JOEL 1

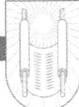

I THINK I WILL ALWAYS REMEMBER 2011 as a year of disasters.[1] Early in the year we saw videos of the earthquake and floods in Japan. It was sobering to see raging waters sweeping away homes, automobiles, and human beings. People entered eternity swiftly, in a matter of seconds. In April we had a night of tornadoes in Alabama, where I live. Several towns were struck. More than 200 people died across our state. The size of the tornado that landed 100 miles west of my home was staggering. The very next month, a tornado of similar size hit Joplin, Missouri, where my sister lives. The path of destruction was wide, and many people died. These places all learned that nature is not always kind. It can be a source of death as well as a source of life.

How should we think about such events? Should we simply consider them a bit of bad luck? Should we think they punish bad people? Should we think God is not in control of such events? Should we just put such terrible events out of our minds? How can we think Biblically about what seem to be freakish acts of nature?

I do not have all the answers to these questions. I do not fully understand God's ways. But I believe that studying Joel 1 will help us begin to find answers.

Here Joel describes a terrible locust plague. In fact, he states that it is a plague for the ages. It is one to tell your children and grandchildren about. It is one that people who experience it will never forget. More than that, Joel writes, it is an opportunity to seek God and return to him. This chapter invites us to see natural disasters as times when our faith in God can grow.

Joel uses a plague for the ages to build faith for the ages. Joel 1 is a tightly connected message. We cannot separate its contents the way we can some other Biblical passages. However, a few clear themes emerge. This passage stresses the day of disaster, the day of the Lord, and the day of prayer.

## The Day of Disaster (1:1–12)

The book begins by noting its origins. It is "the word of the LORD," the Creator and Ruler of the universe (1:1a). God has not made us and forgotten us. He speaks to us in words we can understand. He shapes our lives through his instruction. The Bible does not originate in the minds of human writers. It begins with God, who loves us enough to speak words of comfort and correction to us.

The Bible is written in human words through human ambassadors. God has given his word *through* "Joel, the son of Pethuel" (1:1b). Joel was a real man with a real father, not a mythical or legendary figure. However, the book does not reveal exactly when Joel ministered.[2] I believe that he wrote well before Babylon conquered Jerusalem in 597 B.C. and destroyed the city in 587 B.C. But a specific date eludes us. Like the other prophets, Joel was God's servant. He wrote God's words in a way that reveals his personality. Each prophet had a distinct writing style. God used each one's unique mind and situation to speak about real historical situations. God also led each prophet so fully and so well that each one wrote truthfully and without error (see 2 Peter 1:16–21).

Since this is God's word, Joel commands that all the people "hear" what he has to say. In Joel 1:2a he declares that every elder and inhabitant of the land must listen. Joel is about to announce an unprecedented event (v. 2b). People will be talking about it for generations, according to verse 3. Clearly this is an urgent message that affects the whole land. It is like the tornado sirens that warn Americans when a storm is approaching.

Verse 4 reveals the great danger. A locust plague would soon descend on the land. Joel lists four types of locusts that will eat away the nation's food supply. Whatever one type of locust leaves, another type will devour. Verse 6 compares these locusts to an unstoppable mighty army. Such plagues have been known to occur. James M. Boice described one that devastated Israel in 1915.[3] I have seen a video of one that occurred in Australia in 1935, when massive swarms of locusts flew through the land, darkening the sunlight and consuming everything in their path.

It may be hard for citizens of great cities to grasp what the text envisions. Imagine that you are in a rural place. Imagine all the crops and trees destroyed. Imagine livelihoods wiped out. Imagine economic disaster and panic, starvation, and desperation. Perhaps older people who have experienced war recall similar terrible images. Israel was an agricultural nation. It depended on its crops to survive. Joel's message means that everything the people knew and loved was at risk.

This disaster will affect everyone. Joel 1:5 tells the drunkard to mourn, for there will be no grapes for his wine. Verse 8 tells the whole land to mourn like a bride whose husband has died. Verse 9 tells the priests to mourn, for there will be no wheat and animals for sacrifices. Thus there will be nothing for them to eat. Verse 11 tells the farmers to be ashamed, for they have failed to produce crops. Sorrow always accompanies tragedy, and Joel envisions a tragedy of massive proportions. Verses 18 and 20 state that animals will suffer because they will have nothing to eat. All creation will suffer because of this terrible locust plague.

Joel 1:1–12 demonstrates creation's total dependence on God. Everything we have—every good gift—comes from God (James 1:17). We must make plans. We must plant crops and conduct business. It is right to use our knowledge and gifts to provide for our families. Yet we must realize how fragile life really is. We may act like we are independent and self-reliant. We may live in great nations and have fine allies. But God rules the universe. We must bow to his authority. We must recognize that we are but small children, helpless without our Father's help. We must bow before him, and he will lift us up.

## The Day of the Lord (1:15)

We will return to Joel 1:13, 14 in a moment. I ask you to look next at verse 15 because it explains why the plague has come. It has not come by accident. God has sent it. Joel reveals that this plague is "the day of the Lord." This is a familiar Biblical term we must study if we want to understand the prophetic books.

The day of the Lord is a concept that describes the different ways that God judges. The concept's historical roots go back to Sumeria, Abraham's home country.[4] As early as 2000 B.C., well before Israel was a nation, Sumerian poets wrote about times when their gods punished their cities. They wrote that the gods sent foreign armies to defeat them. They wrote of huge changes in weather associated with these invasions. They spoke of these times as "days" of the gods. Thus the concept of a divine judgment that occurs on particular days in particular ways predates Joel by more than a thousand years.

The Biblical roots of the concept go back to Moses. In Deuteronomy 27—28, Moses tells Israel the benefits of keeping their covenant commitments to God. He also explains the consequences of breaking their covenant promises.

He informs the people that God will discipline them when they sin. God promises to bring hardships on them to lead them to repent. If they refuse to repent, God promises worse problems, including crop failure and plague. If they still do not repent, Moses warns, God will drive them from the promised land. He will send them into exile. Clearly Moses taught that God loved his people enough to lead them to repentance (compare Deuteronomy 7:6–11). He also taught that God would not let sin go on forever. Thus, he taught that God is righteous and will therefore judge sin.

But judgment is not Moses's final word. Moses states in Deuteronomy 30:1–10 that God will cause the people to repent. Though he has punished them, he will restore them. They will repent and serve him with all their hearts. The prophets knew that judgment could come at any time, but they also knew that repentance and forgiveness were possible. They knew that God would always find and restore his people.

By the time Joel wrote his book, the concept of the day of the Lord was probably well known (see Amos 5:18–20). The Biblical writers believed in only one God. They believed that this one God made the world. They believed that he rules the world and judges the wicked. They taught at least three kinds of the day of the Lord. Context determines which type a text describes.

First, they taught that hard times could be a day of the Lord. God uses historical events to punish sin and lead people to repentance. The plague in Joel 1:1–12 is an example of this. Second, they taught that wars could be a day of the Lord—God can use armies to punish wicked persons and societies. God sending Babylon to destroy Jerusalem in 587 B.C. is an example of this type of day of the Lord. Third, the Biblical writers taught there would be a final day of the Lord. On that day, God will judge all nations and all people. Then there will be new heavens and a new earth. Isaiah 65—66 describe this type of day of the Lord. When this final day of Yahweh comes, there will be no more sin, sickness, sorrow, or death (Isaiah 65:17–25; cf. Revelation 21:1–7). All things will be made new.

Joel 1:15 indicates that the people in his day faced the first type of day of the Lord. God is sending them a message: they need to turn to him. Amos 4:6–13 is like Joel 1:15. Amos notes that God sent circumstances that led to a lack of food, and yet Israel did not repent (4:6). He writes that God withheld rain, and yet the people did not return to him (vv. 7, 8). He says that God sent plague and defeat in war, yet they did not return to him (vv. 9–11). Therefore, they must prepare to meet their God, the Maker of heaven and earth (vv. 12, 13). They ignored every sign that they needed to return to the Lord. They left themselves open to a worse kind of day of the Lord.

How should we think about and respond to times like Joel 1 describes? First, Hebrews 12:3–11 states that God disciplines those he loves. The Bible indicates that we should consider times of discipline opportunities to draw closer to God. Some of us walk with God daily. Yet we are still not sinless. We should search our hearts for ways God wants us to grow. Second, we should also pray for others. God can use such hard times to bring unbelievers to Christ or to bring straying Christians back to God. Third, some of us may know we have walked away from our covenant commitments. If so, then we need to see hard times as God's way of bringing us back to him. We must not rebel further. We must do as God says. He loves us enough to discipline us. Let us respond obediently to his love. Fourth, pastors must preach these things. In the United States, many pastors never speak of God's discipline or God's judgment. God expects pastors to care for people's souls. We must do so in a Biblical way. Sin is rebellion against the King of the universe. It is disrespect for his person. Despite such disrespect, God still loves people. He does forgive them when they ask. Pastors must teach these truths.

## The Day of Prayer (1:13, 14, 16–20)

Joel concludes chapter 1 by telling the people what steps they must take in their situation. The people have heard that the locust plague is a day of the Lord. Now they hear that they must call for a day of prayer. Just as the "day" of plague will last longer than twenty-four hours, so the prayers may need to last for a while.

Verses 13, 14 explain who should pray and how they should pray. The priests must take leadership. They must "consecrate" or "make holy" a time for prayer. This time of prayer will include putting on rough garments ("sackcloth") (v. 13) usually worn during times of mourning. In fact, they are to wear these garments all night. This time of prayer will include fasting. Wearing sackcloth and fasting indicate the priests' seriousness. The combination shows that God has their attention. But they are not to pray alone. The priests are to gather "the elders," which most likely refers to the community leaders (v. 14). They are also to call "all the inhabitants of the land" to prayer. The plague involves everyone, so everyone should pray. All should come to God's house and cry out in their time of need. Once again, Joel teaches us our dependence on God.

We must be careful to see what verses 13, 14 teach and do not teach. They teach us that prayer is the proper response to the troubles that God sends to awaken us. Of course, prayer is also the right response to life in general. Paul tells us to "pray without ceasing" (1 Thessalonians 5:17). This means, I think, that we must pray at all times, in all circumstances. Yet times of trouble especially call for serious prayer. Thus these verses also teach us that organized prayer and worship matter. It is good for God's people to come together in normal and unusual times. These verses teach that prayer should be serious and that it may be costly and time-consuming.

We also need to see what these verses do not teach. There is nothing magical about prayer. God does not give us specific blessings if we pray a certain number of hours. God does not hear us when we fast and not hear us when we do not. God does not answer only when we wear sackcloth. God looks at the heart. He desires a humble and submissive spirit (Micah 6:6–8). God hears serious prayer, however long it lasts.

What is serious prayer?

Joel 1:15, 16 indicate that serious prayer recognizes God's hand in daily life. Verses 17, 18 show that serious prayer addresses specific needs. They also show that serious prayer includes having pity for all God's creatures. Most importantly, verses 19, 20 show that serious prayer focuses on God. Serious prayer cries out, "To you, O Lord, I call" (v. 19). It cries out, "Even the beasts of the field pant for you" (v. 20). Prayer is ultimately about God, not about us. Prayer is not primarily about us getting what we want. Prayer is about God's kingdom coming and his will being done on earth as it is in Heaven (Matthew 6:10). It is about God's glory filling the earth (Isaiah 6:3). If God is glorified, then all will be well. Plagues will end, and the earth will be healed.

## Conclusion

Joel 1 is but a beginning. We stop here with the people called to prayer. The plague has not stopped, and worse times may come. Great promises that we will study together remain over the horizon. But we have learned some key points from this beginning.

First, things do not just happen. Disasters in nature are not accidents. They are opportunities to see God's hand in daily life. We can learn to repent, pray, and help others when disasters happen. God uses historical events to shape his people. For some people these events judge their sins. For others these events test their faith. For still others they provide opportunities to confess their faith alongside fellow sufferers. God is always working with every human being in many ways. Things do not just happen. We must avoid giving overly simple answers to hard questions, but we must not act as if there are no answers at all.

Second, God judges sin. First Timothy 5:24 states that some people's sins are judged in this life and some people's sins are judged afterwards. I think the

Bible also teaches that some people's sins are judged now and later. Regardless, God judges sin.

As I read Joel 1, I am concerned that people in the United States learn that God judges sin. Americans have many fine qualities. But Americans also covet money, power, sex, violence, and ease. We export our values around the globe. Sadly, American Christians sometimes share bad American values. We covet wealth, big churches, nice homes, new cars, the best university degrees, the best academic jobs, and the top place in our businesses. I have known Christians who want their children to be doctors and lawyers because they will earn big salaries. They cannot imagine their children being missionaries. We even have preachers who tell their people that God wants them to be rich and powerful. When will we learn that God judges his people's sin?

Third, we must recognize our dependence on God. We must come to him, for he alone can save us, provide for us, and teach us. Our prayers should reflect our trust in him. An awakened people will be a prayerful people.

Joel 1 shows us that it is not too late to seek the Lord. We may be in the middle of a personal plague. We may have nearly ruined our lives. Nonetheless, God sends his word to us through Joel. The Lord calls us to come back, just as he called the Israelites. May God help us see today as his day and thus see it as the day to pray.

# 15

# Even Now, Seek the Lord

JOEL 2:1–17

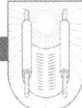

WHEN TALKING ABOUT TRAGIC national events, Americans often say where they were when the events occurred. For instance, my father recalls that he was working with his father on December 7, 1941, when a neighbor told them that Japan had bombed Pearl Harbor. I was with my mother and grandmother in November 1963 when we heard that President Kennedy had been assassinated. I was on my way to work at Wheaton College when I heard about the attacks on September 11, 2001. These national events touched all Americans. I suspect every nation has its own sad memories.

We also have tragic personal and family memories. People go through divorce. They lose loved ones. Their businesses fail. Their children disappoint them. In these awful moments we may feel all is lost. We may think things will never be normal again. We may feel that it is too late for us to recover. Worse still, some of us walk away from God. We used to serve him but not now. We may think it is too late to change. Or we may know and love someone who is old and still without Christ. It may seem hopeless to think they could come to faith now.

As we saw in the previous study, Joel 1 envisions a terrible plague that would afflict the whole land. I said then that terrible events should remind us of our dependence on God. They should also remind us that God judges sin both now and later. Finally, they should remind us it is time to repent. We must seize the chance to turn back to God. We must look beyond the circumstances to the One who rules all circumstances.

Joel 2:1–17 continues to warn that God judges. This time the prophet describes a military invasion. Scholars have long debated whether both chapters deal with the same event.¹ Some think so and argue that Joel compares locusts to an army.² Others argue the opposite.³ Still others think that Judah faced a plague and then an army.⁴ Judah certainly faced one or both at various points in their history. I think the last option is the best one, but one cannot be certain. All scholars think that chapter 2 describes more intense suffering than chapter 1 does. Thus, all think that in chapter 2, Joel tries even harder to get his readers' attention. All scholars also observe that God's final day of judgment will make all previous days of judgment look small in comparison.

In 2:1–17, Joel again leads us to prayer, repentance, intercession, ministry, and hope. He declares that it is not too late to turn to God. He bases his hope on God's character. He believes that God will forgive those who come to him. Joel tells us that "even now" we can come to the Lord (v. 12). Even though terrible things may have happened, it is not too late to repent. Joel declares that even though we have sinned, God will pardon if we repent. God still offers forgiveness, renewal, and wholeness. The world may crumble around us. Wars come and nations fall, but God is still there. God will receive us.

Joel presents this hope for the future in three parts. He states that God has a day (vv. 1, 2a), God has an army (vv. 2b–11), and God has mercy (vv. 12–17). Joel therefore teaches us that God is just, God is powerful, and God has perfect character.

## God Has a Day: God Is Just (2:1, 2a)

Joel 1:13, 14 tells the priests to gather the people for special prayer. They must do so because the locust plague they face is a day of the Lord. Now in 2:1, God himself tells the people to "blow a trumpet in Zion." He wants "all the inhabitants of the land" to "tremble." The day of Yahweh is not just coming, it is "near"! He continues in 2:2a, noting that the day is very dark, like a massive storm. We have alarms that warn us of fire. We have alarms that warn us of storms and military invasion. In the United States, we periodically test our national warning systems on television. In this verse, God sounds *his* alarm. The people are in mortal danger.

The Bible teaches that God is just. He punishes sin, but he warns before he punishes. The Scriptures and those who teach them are God's warning system. The concept of the day of the Lord highlights this truth. God reminds his people that the threats and promises found in Deuteronomy 28:15–68 remain true. They cannot sin and expect him to do nothing. The day of reckoning approaches. Storm clouds are gathering. His people need to respond appropriately.

This is not just an Old Testament doctrine. As I said previously, Hebrews 12:3–11 teaches that God disciplines his people. Also, Revelation 2—3 warns churches that God will not allow them to sin forever. Of course, God's work will go on. We can be sure of this, for Jesus said the gates of Hell will not prevail against him and his Church (Matthew 16:16–18). Our sin cannot stop God's work. The question is whether we will be part of his work and participate in his victory.

### God Has an Army: God Is Powerful (2:2b–11)

What is the danger? What storm is forming? Joel 2:2b–11 reveals that it is an army. In the second part of verse 2 God states that it is a mighty army of "a great and powerful people." There has never been a military force like this one. This army is so vast that it blackens the mountains. Joel may mean the enemy soldiers are so numerous that they cover the mountains. Or he may mean they are so numerous that their mere shadow covers the mountains.

Such massive invasions have occurred in history. I first visited Asia in 1991. I spent six weeks teaching in Singapore. An older Malaysian man told me about the fall of Singapore in 1942. He had very vivid memories of what he had seen. He said the invaders entered the city in waves, riding on bicycles—they were that unstoppable. I thought he exaggerated until a few years ago, when I saw films of exactly what he remembered.

The invasion that Joel envisions is similar to what my old friend saw. The invading army is powerful and large. Nothing can halt its advance. Joel 2:3 states that this army scorches the earth. The land in front of them is like the garden of Eden, but the land behind them is charred and desolate. I suppose that the land Joel describes looks like Hiroshima and Nagasaki after the atomic bombs or Vietnam after napalm bombs. I suppose it looks like the battlefields of France during World War I. The picture is bleak.

Verses 4, 5 state that this army has plenty of infantry, cavalry, and chariots. They have all the weapons of war they need. Verses 7–9 describe their discipline. They do not break ranks (v. 7). They do not run when the enemy fights them (v. 8). They take over cities quickly, according to plan (v. 9). Verse 10 declares that they fill the horizon. They block out the sun and make the ground tremble. The people being invaded see only the enemy army. This scene is terrifying, like a nightmare.

Verse 11 discloses something the first ten verses do not. Now Joel reveals that this army is God's army, and God is all-powerful. No enemy can defeat him. The army is so effective because he leads it. It is so large because they are his soldiers. It is so strong because his power stands behind it. Because this is

God's army, Joel wonders, "Who can endure it?" This is a rhetorical question. The clear answer is that no one can endure it. That is, no one can endure it unless God gives them the power to do so.

Joel 2:1–11 reminds us of two types of the day of the Lord.[5] It begins by appearing to describe a historical invasion of Israel. The descriptions of the armies could remind readers of the Assyrian and Babylonian armies. This should frighten people enough to bring them to repentance. But verse 11 takes us beyond normal historical invasions. It reminds us of the final day of the Lord when God will judge all sin. Only those on God's side can stand on that day. All others will be swept away.

Judgment in time and beyond time deserves our attention. Judgment is part of the gospel. What does the gospel include? God is the Creator. He is the Ruler of all nations. We are his subjects. He has revealed his standards to us. We have sinned against those standards. In love he has offered us forgiveness through his Son. He has told us how to walk with him as his people, his Church, his body. He has gifted us to minister to others in our homes, churches, and communities. He has also told us he will judge sin now and forever. Finally, he has told us he will send his Son again. This time his Son will have an army, according to Revelation 19:11–16. He will defeat all his opponents. He will do so because he is the judge of the living and the dead (Acts 10:42, 43). God has appointed us to preach this comprehensive message.

Do we preach the whole gospel? Without judgment there is no gospel. People may not wish to hear about judgment, but that is nothing new. Our job is to be faithful to God's word. We have an all-powerful and holy God to declare.

### God Has Mercy: He Has a Gracious Character (2:12–17)

Joel 2:11 leaves readers in a desperate situation. If the book ended here, there would be no hope. But God speaks words of grace in 2:12–14. He then reminds readers there is time to repent in 2:15–17 (compare 1:13, 14). In this passage—indeed in the whole Bible—human hope rests in God and his character. We need no other source of help. Believers desire no other source of help.

Verse 12 reflects the crisis that 2:1–11 describes. A plague has come. An army is about to attack. God himself is about to send his army to remove sin. The people have ignored every chance to repent. They are on the brink of complete disaster. At this point, God utters the words "yet even now." Like the thief on the cross, the people still have time to repent (Luke 23:41–43). Like the workers hired at the last hour in Jesus's parable, there is still time to work

(Matthew 20:1–16). Like Saul on the road to Damascus (Acts 9:1–19), there is still time to see the truth. Time has grown short, but there is still time.

But there is only time for one thing. There is no time to sin some more or to see if politics or economics can solve their problems. God tells his people there is only time to "return to me with all your heart" (Joel 2:12). This phrase makes plain what has been implied all along. The people have sinned and have not repented. This phrase also defines repentance. The Hebrew word usually translated as "repent" literally means "turn around." The context shows when it means "return" or "repent."

Joel does not list specific sins. Perhaps the people have turned to other gods. They may have turned to improper lifestyles. Regardless, they must turn around now and walk with God again. Repentance may begin with sorrow or regret. It may include a desire to do better. But repentance means an actual turning, an actual change. We should repent of sin every day, for we sin daily (1 John 1). We turn back to God often in our lives as Christians. But unless we turn back to God, we have not repented.

Joel 2:12, 13 describes what this turning requires. Turning back to God begins in the "heart." It starts as an internal change (compare Jeremiah 4:1–4) that the Holy Spirit causes. It can lead to fasting, weeping, and mourning, as Joel 2:12 states. All these can show how serious repentance can be. Unless we tear our hearts and not just our garments, we have not repented, according to verse 13. Without a true change of heart, fasting is a diet. Without a true change of heart, wearing sackcloth is a fashion statement. Without a true change of heart, weeping is an act. External conformity is not enough. Internal obedience is necessary. We must desire to return to fellowship with God. We must want to do his will again. We cannot remain lord of our own lives. We cannot play religious games. Our will must become one with God's.

When we return, we are not returning to an institution. We are returning to a person. Like 1:19, 20, Joel 2:13 reminds us that we have a relationship with the living God. We seek *him*. We do not simply seek freedom from judgment. We do not just seek help with our problems. We seek to love God with heart, soul, mind, and body (see Deuteronomy 6:4–9; Mark 12:28–32).

Joel now quotes one of the Bible's most important passages. He does so to show why it is possible to come to God "even now" (Joel 2:12). He cites Exodus 34:6, 7 and applies his people's situation to these verses. Because Exodus 34:6, 7 is crucial for understanding Biblical theology, I want us to spend some time on it.[6] We will then discuss how Joel uses it.

Exodus 34 comes after several important events. God delivers Israel from slavery in Egypt in Exodus 1—15. He provides food and water for Israel in the desert in Exodus 16—18. He brings Israel to Mount Sinai and calls them to be a kingdom of priests for his glory in Exodus 19:5, 6. This means Israel is God's instrument of salvation to the nations. God gives the Ten Commandments and other laws in Exodus 20—24. He and the people enter a covenant relationship. Sadly, Israel breaks this covenant by worshiping the golden calf in Exodus 32. So Moses prays for the people, and God agrees to give them a fresh start in Exodus 33:17. Moses then asks God to reveal his character. God does so in Exodus 34:6, 7.

The Lord defines his character through several key phrases. He says he is "merciful and gracious" (34:6). These terms appear together eleven times in the Old Testament. They can describe the kindness a parent has for a small child (see 1 Kings 3:26, 27). They can also describe the sort of kindness one shows to the poor. In each case they describe compassion for a weaker person. God also says he is "slow to anger, and abounding in steadfast love and faithfulness" (Exodus 34:6). He does not judge his people quickly. He is patient with them, like a good father with a child. His covenant love, often translated in English as "steadfast love," is a loyal love. He does not give up on his people. His faithfulness is reliable and truthful. He cannot lie. God says he keeps his covenant love with thousands (v. 7). Deuteronomy 7:9, 10 indicates that this phrase means "a thousand generations."

That is not all. In Exodus 34:7b, Yahweh relates why he displays this type of character. It is because he is "forgiving." He bears with covenant-breakers. He treats them as if they were always faithful. God uses three words to describe what he forgives. These three words help us develop a doctrine of sin.[7] They appear together thirteen times in the Old Testament. Thus, placing them together is a common way of expressing sin's totality. First, God forgives "iniquity" (*awon*).[8] This word basically expresses the conscious twisting of a personality, idea, or thing.[9] Second, he forgives "transgression" (*pesa*). This word describes rebelling against God.[10] Third, God forgives "sin." This word means "missing a goal" (*ht'*).[11] God's graciousness and compassion are amazing. By his grace and mercy he forgives people who twist his words. He forgives people who rebel against him and ignore the standards he has set. God displays complete covenant faithfulness. Exodus 34:5–9 reveals that he has clearly been faithful to his covenant with Abraham, Isaac, and Jacob, even long after they have died (see Exodus 2:23–25). He has also kept his promises to the current generation of Israelites (see Exodus 3:13–17).

In contrast, most of Israel has been unfaithful. They have worshiped idols. They have not kept the covenant as they promised to do. They do not reflect a right relationship with God. They have twisted, broken faith with, and missed the goals set by God in Exodus 20—24. To act in this twisted, treacherous, and wayward manner is what we call sin. The people made the golden calf. They declared this idol to be the god that brought them from Egypt. They had a wild festival. They treated God as if he was an option, not the living God (32:1–7). Yahweh had been unfailingly loyal, but the people had not.

God's forgiving nature does not mean he is unjust. Not at all. Exodus 34:7 states that he "will by no means clear the guilty, visiting the iniquity of the fathers on the children and the children's children, to the third and fourth generation." Based on Exodus 20:4, 5, the successive generations mentioned here are people who "hate" Yahweh. Therefore, this verse does not mean God punishes persons who have not sinned (see Ezekiel 18:17). Rather, it describes him punishing sin however long it occurs in a clan or nation.

To summarize, Exodus 34:6, 7 teaches that God's character has many traits. He is first and foremost gracious and compassionate. This means he is patient with sinners. His first instinct is to forgive. He stands ready to forgive every type of sin people devise. But he is not weak. He is just. He punishes sin wherever and however long it exists. He desires people to repent, to turn from their sins and return to him. He is willing to forgive even terrible sins, like worshiping the golden calf. But if no repentance occurs, then he is willing to judge the wicked.

Now let us return to Joel 2:12–14. Joel applies his people's situation to Exodus 34. His people are on the brink of disaster, like Israel was in Exodus 34. His people have apparently sinned greatly, like Israel had in Exodus 32. He wants his readers to feel that they are in the same position as Israel was earlier. He wants them to know the situation would be hopeless were it not for one important detail.

This detail is God's character. Joel uses part of Exodus 34 to motivate his people to return to the Lord. How is it even possible to return to him after all they have done? It is possible because God is "gracious and merciful," according to Joel 2:13. This means he is "slow to anger." God is amazingly patient. Not only that, God also has incredible covenant loyalty. He is no fair-weather friend. He sticks with the covenants he makes and the people with whom he makes them.

Since all these things are true, Joel knows that God "relents over disaster." The word translated as "relent" is often translated as "repent" in English versions. This is a different word than the one for "repent" that we have already studied. The word refers to stopping a course of action because conditions have been met. In this case, God does not send the threatened punishment because the people meet the conditions of repentance. Joel is telling the people that God will not punish even though he has the right to do so.

If the people return, then God will forgive. In verse 14, Joel exhorts the people to place themselves in God's hands. He reasons that if they turn to God, then God may turn to them. If they repent of their sins, God may relent of his punishment. In fact, he counts on this being true. They have not been destroyed. Hope remains. God's character is the only foundation for such hope.

With this irreplaceable foundation laid, Joel once again calls the people to prayer in 2:15–17. They must blow a trumpet to announce a fast (v. 15). They must gather all the people, from oldest to youngest (v. 16a). Even people just married should assemble (v. 16b). This assembly takes precedence over everything. Once together, the priests will lead the people in prayers of repentance (v. 17). But these prayers must focus on God. They are God's people, not independent individuals. Their desire must be that God's reputation be honored.

Here we see the essentials of true repentance. True repentance turns from our desires to God's will. It turns from what we want to what God wants. It turns from considering our reputation to protecting God's. It therefore turns from sin to renewed relationship with the Lord. Ultimately we sin because we do not currently want what God wants. We place our will above his. We need reformed hearts, wills, and affections. Our actions will follow.

## Conclusion

I find Joel 2:1–17 one of the most encouraging and challenging texts in the Bible. It is encouraging because it promises that "even now" (v. 12), even late in the day of sin, we can return to the Lord. We may think we deserve judgment, and this is true. But because God is gracious, merciful, and patient, we can come to him "even now." His character is the source of our hope. It is not too late to turn to him. The situation is not so terrible that he cannot save.

This passage is challenging because it requires ministers to sound the alarm. We must call people to see their condition and cry out to God. We must lead people to seek God and not just solutions to their immediate problems. This message may be rejected. It may not be popular. That is not up to us. Our job is to be faithful and to preach God's Word. Doing so never gets easier.

As I grow older, I find more and more comfort in God. He is kind. He is patient. He is just. We can count on his character daily. We can make declaring his glory the goal of our ministries. We can know that he is stable and helpful. Let all of us come to him for salvation, guidance, comfort, and hope.

# 16

# When God Answers Prayer

JOEL 2:18–27

SO FAR IN THE BOOK OF JOEL, the prophet has envisioned an unforgettable locust plague (1:2–20). He has also seen a powerful army that Judah cannot defeat. The invaders are God's army. He was its leader (2:1–11). God sent these visions of terrible trouble to effect repentance, not just to punish. Though the people have sinned for a long time, Joel has claimed it is not too late to be forgiven. In 2:12, he encouraged Judah "even now" to return to God. In 2:12–14, he reminded them that God is gracious and compassionate. He told them that God is patient and relents from sending disaster (v. 13). God will receive those who repent, those who turn *from* their sins and come *back* to him.

The people obey between 2:17 and 2:18, for in 2:18–27 God promises pity and renewal. He answers the prayers that Joel urged the people to pray. This passage is the first of three hopeful sections that end the book. Next in 2:28–32, God promises to pour out his Spirit. Finally, in chapter 3, he promises to judge the nations for sins they have committed against him and his people. Together these passages describe God's great acts that will occur after Joel's lifetime. They give Joel faith in the present by providing hope for the future.

These passages can also build our faith. We can grow in faith today by recalling that God has kept promises he made in the past.[1] From where we stand in history, God has already renewed Judah's land. In Christ, he was in their midst (see Joel 2:27; cf. John 1:14). He has already poured out the Holy Spirit. That occurred on the Day of Pentecost, according to Acts 2:1–21. He has not yet judged the world and ended sin. But his past faithfulness helps us believe the promises that he has made about the future. So we can believe that

God will bring complete justice and peace to the world at the end of time. Like the rest of the book, then, Joel 2:18–27 teaches us to trust God's promises.

Joel 2:18–27 also teaches us about answered prayer. The most important thing it teaches us is that answered prayer depends on God's character. Thus the passage teaches us to base our prayers on God's character and God's will. Furthermore, this passage gives us courage to pray, for it demonstrates God's great mercy toward us. He is kind, so he does even more than we ask or imagine (see Ephesians 3:20). Prayer is not magic. It does not force God to do what we want him to do. Rather prayer is conversing with our Father so he can shape our desires to his. As these verses unfold, in 2:18, Joel tells us that God's character is *why* God answers prayer. Then, in 2:19–26, Joel tells us *how* God answers prayer through his promises and power. Finally, in 2:27, the prophet tells us *where* God answers prayer, which is among his people.

### God's Zeal and Pity: Why God Answers Prayer (2:18)

By now readers of Joel may have given up on Judah. Joel has warned of plague and invasion, seemingly to no avail. One could easily expect to read next of the nation's complete downfall. But this is not what happens. In 2:15–17, Joel urges the people to call out to God. In 2:18, Joel portrays God acting for his people. They have turned back to him, and he has forgiven them. Why has he done this?

Joel 2:18 states that God turned back to his people because of who he is. He has not turned back to them because their prayers were fervent. He has not decided to help them because he does not care about sin. He has not pardoned them because of their good deeds. Rather, Joel explains that God acts according to his character, a subject that 2:12–14 introduced. Now Joel states that God hears, pities, acts, and heals. God's character is why he answers prayer.

Like many Hebrew sentences,[2] verse 18 begins with a conjunction. These are often translated in English as "and." Many Hebrew experts argue that such conjunctions reveal a causal connection between the sentences. Therefore, these conjunctions could be translated as "and that being so" or "then." Verse 18 indicates that, based on 2:15–17, the Lord has proceeded to do something. Because of what has happened, he "became jealous for his land"[3] (v. 18). Repentance has begun. God now promises to deliver the people based on their obedience to what he commanded. We should not think their repentance was ultimately what delivered them. God's word came first, not their repentance. God sent Joel to warn them. They would not know to repent had God not sent his word. They would have remained in their sins.

After the conjunction, the verse states that God "became jealous for his land" (v. 18). This verse troubles many Americans because the word "jealous" is mostly negative in today's American English. It is normally used to describe someone who merely imagines a spouse or lover has been unfaithful. It also often describes a suspicious, insecure, and immature person. Therefore, it can shock people to read that God is "jealous."

We must be clear that God's jealousy is not like this. His jealousy is zeal for what is right. So he is jealous to protect his people from idols, for idols are not gods. He is jealous that they learn righteousness, for he is holy. He is jealous to protect them from their enemies (Zechariah 1:14) so they can be secure. In short, he is jealous to keep his covenant promises. One of these promises is to forgive his people and deliver them from their enemies when they repent (see Leviticus 26:40–46; Deuteronomy 30:1–10). Now that they have repented, he is "jealous for his land" (Joel 2:18). This means he will drive out his people's opponents. He will keep his people safe. His kind and proper covenant jealousy will make these things happen. God's faithful care for his people is the key to their future.

Joel also states that God has "pity" for his covenant people (2:18). He has seen what the locusts have done to their land. He knows that foreign armies have killed and captured some of his people. God understands their pain and cares for them. Things did not need to get so bad. The people did not need to rebel against God. He did not fail them in any way. Still, he feels pity for them, as he did in Hosea 11:1–9. Though they have sinned, or even perhaps *because* they have sinned, he has pity for them. He knows they are but dust (Psalm 90:3). When they return to him, he helps them.

This short verse explains why God answers prayer. We may pray sincerely. We may pray often and fervently. We may pray with a pure heart and clean motives. It is good to pray in these ways. But none of these are ultimately why God answers prayer. He answers prayer because of his character, which includes proper jealousy and proper pity. As Joel 2:12–14 has already told us, God is gracious, compassionate, patient, and just. God's goodness is the key to answered prayer. He is always kinder to us than we deserve. We can always count on his zeal and pity. We must not be too proud to accept his pity. All answered prayers are in his hands. For flawed people like me, this is very good news indeed. Let us pray with faith in the Lord's goodness, not in our piety.

## God's Promises and Power: How God Answers Prayer (2:19–26)

How God answers prayer interests most of us. By that I mean that we seek the results of answered prayer. We scan circumstances and look for progress. We note when God uses others to answer our prayers. We try to determine when God has answered prayer and when we have merely engaged in wishful thinking. At our best we desire to praise God for answering us. At our worst we simply want to get what we want. All these things are part of learning about prayer. Yet none of these are ultimately most important. Once again we must get back to God himself. Only then will we know how he answers prayer. Only then will we understand prayer correctly. Joel 2:19–26 shows that God answers prayer through his promises backed by his almighty power.

Verses 19, 20 begin this section by declaring that God now answers his people. Several promises about the present and future follow in verses 21–26. First, God offers two summary promises in 19, 20. He pledges to heal the land and remove Israel's enemies from it. The healed land will yield "grain, wine, and oil" (v. 19; cf. Hosea 2:21–23). These staples of life will satisfy Israel's hunger and rebuild their economy. Removing their foes will take away their "reproach among the nations." This "reproach" is the shame that defeated and oppressed nations feel. Joel 2:20 notes that God's people have been harmed by a northern nation. Joel could refer to Assyria, Babylon, or Syria. Regardless of its identity, this foe "has done great things." It has wreaked great havoc in Israel. Thus, the foe's defeat will be spectacular. One end of its army will be in "the eastern sea." The other will be in "the western sea." This mighty military force will be scattered and beaten. It is not possible to identify this army. But at various times in history God rescued his people from Assyria, Babylon, Persia, and other foes. His promises were backed by his power.

Second, in verses 21, 22, God gives some specific promises that result from these two general ones, declaring the end of fear and the beginning of rejoicing. The people have been living in fear caused by worsening conditions. Their hopes have understandably fallen. Death by starvation and war has stalked them. Now the days of fear are over, for God will do "great things." These "great things" will exceed the great things done by his people's enemies. He will restore pastures and trees. The dried fields described in 1:12 will be refreshed. Crop losses will be replaced by a "full yield," according to Joel 2:22. His promises are backed by his power. He is the Creator. He rules land and nature. He has the strength and authority to do all that he says he will do.

Third, verses 23–26 give specific promises related to the future. In verse 23 God addresses those who trust him. These are the "children of Zion," those who will live with God forever (see Isaiah 4:2–6; 11—12; 56:1–8; 65—66). These people are now asked to "rejoice" in the Lord their God. They must recognize that he is the source of their changed situation. They must focus on him and enjoy his presence among them. He is the source of life-giving rain, according to Joel 2:23. He is the One who gives abundant harvest, according to verse 24. The people must focus on him and what he has already done. They can then trust his promises about the future. He pledges to "restore . . . the years" the locust plague took from them (2:25). Renewal will not be temporary. It will last. God's power backs these promises.

Fourth, verse 26 shows what the people will enjoy because of what God has done. They will "eat in plenty and be satisfied." This promise is the natural result of the restored people and land. They will also "praise the name of the LORD" their God. His name and his character are the same thing in the Old Testament. They will praise God's grace, compassion, patience, justice, pity, and covenant jealousy. They will recognize that he "has dealt wondrously" with them. Things have not simply *happened* to get better. God has made them better. He deserves the credit. The people have received good things from their good God. Their relationship with him has been repaired. They will "never again be put to shame." God's power backs these promises.

These verses may help us refocus our prayers. We may currently look solely for results. If so, we need to look again. We need to look at God. We need to read his promises in his Word. We need to believe that his power backs these promises. God does not answer prayers that conflict with his promises in his Word. He answers prayers that are anchored in his character for his glory. Once again we need to view prayer as the way to know God and to conform to his will. Prayer is not simply about getting what we want. It is about knowing God.[4] He answers prayers by his promises and his power.

### Where God Answers Prayer: God among His People (2:27)

By now this passage has taught us *why* God answers prayer. He does so because of his covenant jealousy and his proper pity. He does so because of his character. The passage has also taught us *how* God answers prayer. He does so by his promises and his power. This last verse is closely connected to 2:19–26. It is difficult to separate it from what precedes it.

Verse 27 teaches us *where* God answers prayer. He answers prayer "in the midst of" his people. He does this so that we may share his goodness with the world. He does this to show his sovereignty and his covenant love. He does this to show that he is God and there is no other. The goal of answered prayer is that the world will see God's glory and believe. God's presence with and in his people is the world's best hope. Answered prayer reveals reality to all who have eyes to see. It is a witness to the world, not just an encouragement and help to believers.

The verse begins with God promising his people, "You shall know that I am in the midst of Israel" (v. 27). The mention of Israel, not just Judah, indicates that he has reunited the people, as Hosea 3 also promises. The people will see the renewed land and the absence of enemies. They will enjoy praising the Lord. They will recognize that he is with them.

Of course, he has been with them since the beginning. And he has always been with them so they would witness to others. He chose Abraham to bless all nations (Genesis 12:1–8). He chose Israel, Abraham's descendants, to do the same. They were called to be a kingdom of priests to declare God's glory to the nations. Both Exodus 19:5, 6 and 1 Peter 2:9, 10 make this point. God delivered Israel from Egypt to display his power to Pharaoh and to the world. Israel's worship was intended to draw Gentiles to God (see 1 Kings 8:41–43). Israel's obedience to God's word had the same goal. God was in their midst to save them in the exodus, the desert, the conquest, and throughout their history. He was also in their midst to save others.

As the Bible proceeds, God comes in the flesh. Jesus Christ lives among his people. He teaches them, dies for their sins, is raised from the dead by his Father, and ascends to Heaven. God the Father and God the Son send the Holy Spirit to live with us. Joel 2:28–32 will deal with this latter subject. Jesus coming to us is in perfect continuity with God's previous deeds. God has always dwelled amidst his people. He has always done so to deliver from sin those who believe in him.

Answered prayer shows that God is in our midst. It reminds us that God loves us. It also serves as an invitation to others as we tell what God has done for us. It draws them to God and thus to his Church. Answered prayer is one way God expands our spiritual family. We should therefore find ways to tell others when God answers prayer.

This verse also states that God will not only show his people he is with them but will also prove he is God and "there is none else" (v. 27). The Old Testament is an unusual ancient Near-Eastern religious text. It is virtually the only one that claims there is only one God. Moses taught Israel they must confess there is no other god (see Deuteronomy 4:35–39; 5:8–10; 6:4–9 on this point). Moses taught them that God alone created and that he alone can save. All other gods are the work of human minds and hands. Isaiah and other prophets agree (see Isaiah 44:9–20). Christians respect persons who embrace other religions. We must not mistreat them. But we must also continue to teach kindly and consistently that there is one God. Joel 2:27 indicates that answered prayer helps demonstrate God's sovereignty and uniqueness. It demonstrates God's love for his people. They learn that there is no other God to whom they can turn. More importantly, they learn to want no other.

The verse ends with a final marvelous promise. The same promise appears at the end of 2:26. God tells his people that they "shall never again be put to shame." This promise has an ongoing nature to it. The Hebrew word translated as "never again" indicates a time as far as one can imagine. It is often translated as "forever." God promises that his dwelling in their midst and his proof that he alone is God will have permanent value. It will eliminate their shame. It will ensure that they do not fall into sin and idolatry again. The ultimate answered prayer is that God will keep us with him forever. Our deepest need is to know him. Because we know him, shame, sorrow, suffering, and death will not always be part of our future. He removes these from the place where we will dwell forever.

Knowing that God answers prayer "in the midst of" (v. 27) his people may help us in three ways. First, it may help fill us with gratitude and praise for his love for us. Second, it may help us witness to others. God dwells among us so that others may become part of his people. Answered prayer is part of that witness. Third, it may help us take comfort in the future. Every answered prayer now is a down payment of sorts. Each one encourages us to recall that our most pressing prayers will be answered in eternity. They will be answered when we are with him forever.

## Conclusion

This chapter has not been a typical one about prayer. I know that Christians often mention seasons of prayer and great experiences with God during such times. I am not speaking against such seasons or such experiences. I am asking us to remember that God is the focus of prayer. I am reminding us that his character and his will are paramount. I am urging each of us to turn to him, find him, and accept his answers to our prayers. His answers are best, and they are above all we can imagine or engineer.

Have you turned to God in prayer? Have you based your prayers on his character? Have you accepted his answers as what you need? Have you embraced why, how, and where God answers prayer? If so, then I expect that you have great testimonies of how God deals with his people. Joel knew this type of joy, and I believe all of us can as well. We have no greater help for our souls. We also have no greater hope for our families, communities, churches, and nations. Healing comes from God. It begins with repentance and dependence on God. It includes answers to prayer, answers that will last forever.

# 17

# God's Spirit for God's People

JOEL 2:28–32

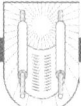

JOEL HAS BEEN TAKING US on a journey from judgment to renewal, a journey back to God. Let me summarize what he has told us so far. In chapter 1, he describes a terrible plague and declares that it is part of a "day of the LORD" (v. 15), a time of judgment, of correction. Therefore, if the people want relief, they must cry out to God for forgiveness and help. In 2:1–17, Joel describes a military invasion. There is no way Israel can defeat this invader, for it is God's army. God is about to use a foreign army to sweep sinners out of the land. But there is hope. Joel says that "even now" the people can turn back to God (v. 12). The Lord is gracious and compassionate and will forgive (v. 13). The prophet again asks the people to call out to God (vv. 15–17). In 2:18–27, Joel relays very good news: The people have repented, God will forgive them, and he will heal their land. God will send their enemies away. He will again dwell with them. The problems announced in 1:2—2:11 have thus been solved.

The book could have ended with 2:27. If it did, it would read like many other prophetic books, for several of them end with renewal.[1] But Joel is not finished. He looks farther into the future. In 2:28–32, he envisions God pouring out his Spirit on the people after the time of renewal. Then in chapter 3, he describes the Lord's final day of judgment. Thus, in 2:18—3:21, Joel promises that God will restore the people in the land (2:18–27), send the Spirit (2:28–32), and defeat the wicked (3:1–21).

By New Testament times God had blessed the people in the land, as 2:18–27 promised. The land was full of thriving communities. The Gospels teach that God sent Jesus, the Messiah, to the people. Jesus lived a sinless life. He died as a sacrifice for sins. God raised him from the dead and gave all authority to him. Many Jewish people believed in him. All his apostles were Jews.

The book of Acts teaches that God then poured out the Holy Spirit on the Messiah's followers in Jerusalem at the Pentecost festival (Acts 2). The Apostle Peter claimed that what happened was what Joel promised in Joel 2:28–32. As time passes in the book of Acts, the Messiah's Jewish followers tell other peoples that God's judgment is coming. Therefore, all people, not just Jews, should repent, bow to the Lord Jesus, and serve him while they await his coming (cf. Acts 10; 15:1–35; 16:6–40; 17:16–34). The writings of James, Peter, John, Jude, and Paul in the New Testament explain how believers throughout the ancient world accepted and lived these and other truths.

Therefore, Joel 2:28–32 is an important text for understanding what the Bible teaches about the Holy Spirit and the spread of the Christian message. Many American Christians do not think the Holy Spirit was active in the Old Testament, or they believe he was barely active. I hope to show that the Holy Spirit plays an important role in the Old Testament. I also hope to show that Joel and Acts present a unified message. Both texts emphasize God pouring out his Spirit on his people. Both texts stress God's people prophesying. Both texts announce God's coming day of judgment and his rescuing grace. Seeing the unity of Joel and Acts will help us trust God's promises and do God's work in our world.

### God's Grace and God's Spirit before Pentecost

Christians believe that there is only one God and that he exists as Father, Son, and Holy Spirit. The concept of one God in three persons is what we mean when we speak of the Trinity. Matthew 28:16–20 and 2 Corinthians 13:14 are particularly helpful on this subject. Christians also believe that God has always existed as the Trinity. God did not evolve into his current nature. John 1:1–18 and Colossians 1:15–20 help us understand this truth. Among other things, this means that the Holy Spirit was alive and well long before New Testament times.

Christians also believe that God started extending his saving grace to people who believed in him from the time human beings first sinned. Genesis 3—4 and Hebrews 11 make this point. Christians also believe that since God created the world, there have been people who have inexcusably refused to believe in him. Romans 1:18–32 teaches this point.

As time has passed, the accumulated total of God's grace has grown greater and greater. How so? The Bible reveals that God sent prophets who were wonderful preachers and writers. Many people believed their messages, though most did not. But people had enough grace to come to God. Then God did even more. He sent his Son, who was even greater than the wonderful prophets. Hebrews 1:1, 2 makes this point. We have been given additional times of grace, as Hebrews 2:1–4 indicates.

Besides the ministry of the prophets and other faithful persons, God led Moses, the prophets, and others to write the Old Testament Scriptures. See 2 Timothy 3:14–17 and 2 Peter 1:16–21 for confirmation of this point. Jesus warned that if people do not believe Moses and the prophets, they will not believe if someone rises from the dead (Luke 16:31). Having done all this, God did more. He inspired the New Testament writers to complete the revelation that the Old Testament began.

Those of us who live now have much more information about God and his grace than people in Jesus's time did. In other words, now people have received even more grace than in past times. As will be seen a moment, God's Spirit aided believers in the Old Testament. They had wonderful help from him. But Joel promises that God will do even more: He will give even more grace. He will pour out the Spirit on his people.

God's increasing grace is wonderful and frightening at the same time. It is wonderful because we have more knowledge of God and his ways than past generations did. Peter wrote that the prophets longed to know what we know (1 Peter 1:10–12). God has been kind to make plain his way of salvation and holiness. But with increased grace comes increased responsibility. Paul warns in Romans 3:19 that every mouth will be closed on the day of judgment. No one will have an excuse. No one can blame God then. As Hebrews 2:3 asks, "How shall we escape if we neglect such a great salvation?" Given these warnings, let us learn with awe how God the Holy Spirit has increased grace from Old Testament days until now.

Prior to the book of Joel, God's Spirit did several things. The Bible uses several interesting verbs to describe this work. Genesis 1:2 states that God's Spirit was involved in creation. That verse portrays God's Spirit "hovering over the face of the waters" like a protective mother bird. Exodus 31:1–3 states that God's Spirit "filled" the workman Bezalel to make the tabernacle. Numbers 11:24, 25 states that God's Spirit "rested on" Israel's elders. Moses said he longed for all the Lord's people to have God's Spirit rest on them (Numbers 11:29). He wished all the Lord's people would prophesy as he did. Judges 6:34 states that God's Spirit "clothed" Gideon to deliver Israel from the Midianites. Judges 14:19 states that God's Spirit "rushed upon" Samson to work for God. Isaiah 63:7–14 states that God's Holy Spirit caused Moses and the Israelites to triumph over Egypt. Micah 3:8 states that God's Spirit "filled" Micah with wisdom to preach and write.

The list could be extended, but the point is clear. In Old Testament times the Spirit hovered, filled, rested, clothed, rushed upon, gave victory, and carried. He was with the people, as Joel 2:27 indicates. He was actively involved in history. God's grace was at work.

In the New Testament, Luke 1:15, 41, 67 state that faithful believers were "filled with the Holy Spirit" before Jesus was born. Matthew 3:13–17 portrays how the Spirit descended on Jesus when John baptized him. Matthew 4:1 states that the Spirit "led" Jesus. Late in his life Jesus taught his disciples that the Holy Spirit had been with them, but now he would be in them (John 14:17). Their master offered the startling news that they would do greater things than he had done because of the Spirit (John 14:12–31). Jesus taught that they were about to have something greater. He was not teaching they would have something better than something bad. They were about to receive even more grace. They must use this incredible gift to take the gospel to the ends of the earth.

God's character has not changed. He has not altered his plans. He has not evolved. He has given more grace. Joel 2:28–32 delivers the promise of this grace and this power.

## God's Spirit Poured Out on God's People (2:28)

In Joel 2:27 God promises to be "in the midst of Israel." His presence is the key to their renewal. In Joel 2:28, 29 God promises still more. He says,

> I will pour out my Spirit on all flesh;
> your sons and your daughters shall prophesy,
>   your old men shall dream dreams,
>   and your young men shall see visions.
> Even on the male and female servants
>   in those days I will pour out my Spirit.

Moses's wish that all the people will prophesy (Numbers 11:24–29) will come true. This promise is universal and exclusive at the same time. It also has a definite purpose.

It is exclusive because it only comes upon God's people. The word translated as "your" refers to the people of God (Joel 2:27). The Spirit will not be poured out on unbelievers. Acts 1:15 reveals that there were 120 believing men and women waiting on God on the Day of Pentecost. God's Spirit fell on them. They then declared God's gospel. God's Spirit comes to all who believe

(Romans 8:9). This is God's seal, his proof of their salvation, according to Ephesians 1:13–14. But the Spirit does not come to those who do not believe. The Spirit is a special gift for God's servants.

This is universal; he will pour his Spirit on all kinds of "flesh" or persons as defined in these verses. God's Spirit will be poured out on young and old. He will be poured out on men and women. He will be poured out on leaders and servants. As Acts 10 shows, he will be poured out on Gentiles as well. Jewish persons take the gospel to the world. The gospel comes to the Jews first and then to the Gentiles (Romans 1:16). As the New Testament proceeds, "all flesh" means all who believe, regardless of race, gender, or social status. The Holy Spirit thus binds Christians together as a family. Asians and Africans bear a family resemblance. Caucasians and Indians do as well. We have the same family gifts. We have the same family heritage. We have the same family inheritance. The Spirit lives in all believers.

What Joel envisioned came true on the Day of Pentecost in Acts. God kept his promise to give more grace. God poured out his Spirit. This event is not repeatable, nor does it need to be. When God poured out his Spirit on them, he also poured it out on us. Therefore, when we trust Christ, we receive God's Spirit (Romans 8:9; Ephesians 1:13, 14). Those who believe have God's Spirit living in them.

### God's People Prophesying (2:29)

This pouring out is remarkable. It is very exciting. The Bible describes many other examples of wonderful experiences that the Holy Spirit gives. I hope that all of us can recall special times when the Spirit filled us with joy and awe. It is tempting to spend all our time replicating these experiences. Many Christians do this in America. But the Spirit is poured out for a specific purpose. He gifts us for gospel work. He gifts people to serve God for the sake of others. Passages like 1 Corinthians 12 show that all believers have spiritual gifts provided by the Holy Spirit. We have different gifts, but we all have gifts. We have different tasks, but we all have tasks. We are not to worry about being superior or inferior to other Christians. We are to embrace the Spirit's plans for our lives.

Joel and Peter note that the people will "prophesy" (Joel 2:28; Acts 2:17). The phrases "dream dreams" and "see visions" are synonymous with "prophesy." There are not three separate tasks described here. Joel uses the term "prophesy" broadly in 2:28. It means declaring God's gospel. It seems that in Acts 2, all 120 believers shared about Jesus. The same is true in the rest of the book of Acts. Men and women shared from God's Word about the Messiah and how to live for him. There are specific offices in the New Testament's churches. People prophesy in different ways and with different levels of authority. But all prophesy in the sense that they share God's word with others.

Of course, this is also what the Old Testament prophets did. We tend to focus on their predictions and visions. We enjoy the spectacular things they did. We appreciate the Scriptures they wrote. If you read closely, however, you will see they mostly did normal (some would say boring) ministry. They prayed. They taught the Bible. They encouraged the faithful, and they corrected the rebellious. They were also persecuted and ignored.

The Holy Spirit gifts us to do what the prophets did. If we find gospel work boring, then we may need to check our hearts. We all get discouraged and tired at times, but let us all realize that we have been called to the routine life of lay and ordained ministry. This is great work, for it is God's work. The Holy Spirit will enable us to persevere in faithful Bible teaching, preaching, and service. God's Spirit is not just in us for our benefit. He is in us so we can help others. Our ministries are about God, not about us.

### God's Coming Day of Judgment (2:30, 31)

Once again Joel returns to the theme of the day of the Lord. So far the book has emphasized the concept in relationship to God's people. Now Joel begins to shift from God's people to the whole world. This day of the Lord is not just a local event. It affects everyone. These two verses link the Day of Pentecost and the day of the Lord.

Verses 30, 31 describe wonders that will occur before final judgment comes. They contain metaphors that alert readers to future extraordinary events. Joel claims that unusual things will happen before the day of the Lord. These verses warn readers that God's coming day is more severe than they can imagine. The heavens and earth will be affected. Isaiah 2:6–22 also describes the day of the Lord. It warns that the day will be so terrible that the people will long for death. Zephaniah 1 also describes the day of the Lord. It declares that no amount of money will purchase safety then. People must see what God is doing and repent.

Peter teaches that these wonders have begun (Acts 2:14–36). What are these wonders? Jesus has come. He lived, died, and has been brought back to life. He has ascended to Heaven. God has poured out his Holy Spirit.

We have clearly been given enough signs to turn from sin. God is gracious. He may well send more wonders before his great day comes. But we do not deserve more. Why do we need more signs than those Jesus has done? Why do we need more signs than the ones done in the book of Acts? Why do we need more fulfilled prophecies? Why do we stand around staring into

Heaven looking for signs (see Acts 1:6–11)? Never lose the wonder of what God has already done in Christ through the Holy Spirit!

## God's Rescuing Grace (2:32)

When any day of the Lord comes, there is only one safe place to go, and that is to the Lord. People must flee to God's rescuing grace. Joel 2:32 states that "everyone who calls on the name of the LORD shall be saved." The word translated as "saved" is not the word normally translated this way. It is a word that expresses one fleeing to safety. The phrase "calls on the name of the LORD" usually refers to those who worship God alone. They call on him through prayer and through sacrifice. They seek his word through his prophets. The people who worship God alone will escape on the day of the Lord. Throughout Joel, the prophet declares God's grace. God seeks people in Joel. The fact that they even know to respond is due to his kindness.

Furthermore, Joel locates Jerusalem as the place of safety. The prophets and psalmists often use Jerusalem as a symbol for God's eternal city. This is the place where God's people are safe with him forever. This is where God's people worship him forever. Jerusalem was where the temple was. It was where the people gathered to hear God's word on the Day of Pentecost. It is hardly surprising that this city became a rich symbol for God's people.

For his part, Peter urged his hearers to flee from the coming wrath of God (Acts 2:40). He told them that God had sent signs and wonders (Acts 2:22–32). He told them God had sent his Son and that they had crucified him (Acts 2:36). He told them God had poured out his Spirit as promised (Acts 2:33). They understood that they deserved God's judgment, so they asked what they had to do. Peter told them to "repent and be baptized" in Jesus's name; God would fill them with the Holy Spirit (Acts 2:38). In other words, the apostle told the people to call on the name of the Lord Jesus. He told them to flee to the Savior.

Three thousand hearers obeyed! These Jews from around the world fled to Jesus. They were in Jerusalem, the Lord's city. They found safety and escape from judgment where Joel said they would find it. The apostles incorporated new believers into the Church (Acts 2:42–47). The survivors began to minister to the world.

## Conclusion

God kept all the promises he made through Joel. We may trust his message and the message that Peter gave based on it. Trusting this message could mean several things. I will mention just two possibilities.

First, the Bible clearly teaches that judgment is coming. The day of the Lord is near. It is near because God can judge whenever he wishes. It is also near because we could die at any moment. Do we believe these things? Do we preach these things? Do we act as if we are accountable to God?

Second, if you have not called on Jesus, I urge you to do so. Calling on him means accepting what the Bible teaches about him. It means believing he is Lord and Savior. It means living your whole life under his authority. He has died for your sins. He is worthy of worship and praise. He is the reason we can pray to the Father. Only faith in Jesus can save. Call on him now. Escape the coming judgment.

# 18

# When God Roars from Zion

JOEL 3

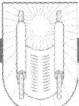

SO FAR IN JOEL, we have seen that Judah faced an unprecedented locust plague (1:1–12). This plague was a day of the Lord (v. 15). Joel urged the people to pray to (vv. 13, 14) and return to the Lord (vv. 17–20). It seems they did not do so right away. So Joel warned that an invasion was coming (2:1–11). This was to be the worst foe the people had ever faced. In fact, the opponent was the Lord's army. Thus, the people must ask the Lord to pardon them.

Joel reminded them that God is merciful, kind, and willing to relent (vv. 12–17). Thankfully, they prayed, and God took mercy on them. He promised to send rain and heal the land (vv. 18–26). More importantly, he promised to be in their midst (v. 27). After this renewal, God promised greater renewal. He pledged to pour out his Spirit on his people (vv. 28–32). He promised them shelter in his city on the day of the Lord.

These marvelous promises still leave final judgment on the horizon. Joel 3 settles this matter. The chapter reveals what God will do with the wicked nations that oppose his people. In 3:16 Joel portrays God as a roaring lion about to overcome his prey. This means that God will gather the nations and defeat them. Joel declares that all sin will be removed. The world will be made right. Joel 3 delivers this message in three parts. Verses 1–8 promise that God will judge those who harm his people. Verses 9–15 declare that God will decide the fate of rebellious nations. Verses 16–21 claim that God will be a refuge for his people.

## God Will Judge Those Who Harm His People (3:1–8)

The Bible teaches that God's people suffer for several reasons. They suffer due to their own sins and mistakes. They suffer because they are part of a fallen world where sinners do terrible things. They also suffer because of persecution. They are hated and mistreated by God's enemies because they love God. Indeed, Jesus told his disciples not to be surprised when persecution occurred: "In the world you will have tribulation. But take heart; I have overcome the world" (John 16:33). Joel 3:1–8 describes persecution. But it also describes God's final judgment of those who persecute his faithful people.

Joel 3:1 connects this chapter to 2:18–27 and 2:28–32. The prophet writes that "in those days and at that time" God will change Jerusalem's circumstances (3:1).[1] He treats renewal, the outpouring of the Spirit, and final judgment as three linked events. Any time between the second and third events must be seen as a period for warning.

Verse 2 begins God's indictment of the nations. God pledges to bring all nations into one place, "the Valley of Jehoshaphat." Obviously this name is symbolic, for there is no valley large enough to hold all of Judah's enemies. The name Jehoshaphat means "Yahweh judges." Therefore, Joel warns that God will bring the nations to the place where he judges. God clearly claims to be the supreme God over all gods. All these nations must answer to him. No other deity has the right to judge.

The Lord has a particular reason for gathering Judah's enemies for judgment. He says he will judge "on behalf of my people and my heritage Israel."

Verses 2, 3 provide the charges that God brings against the nations. They have done three things. First, they have "scattered [God's people] among the nations" (v. 2b). Second, they have divided up the land (v. 2c). Third, they have treated God's people as things, not people (v. 3). Scattering the people included selling them into slavery.

Verses 4–8 indicate that Tyre, Sidon, and Philistia sold some of the people to the Greeks. The Greeks then took them by sea to distant lands. They also sold them to the Sabeans. These desert traders took them by land to places far from Judah. Amos 1:6–12 condemns Tyre, Sidon, and Philistia for the same crimes. Human trafficking is not new. God has been condemning it for centuries.

Dividing the land occurred several times. Every time Israel lost major battles, their enemies took captives. Assyria also took parts of the land in 732, 722, and 701 B.C. Babylon took the whole land in 597 and 587 B.C. Persia did the same in 539 B.C. The Greeks and Romans came later and did the same thing. Exile and occupation became a way of life. It is hard to know what event or events Joel has in mind.

These nations have treated God's people in a shameless fashion. They place a low value on human life. Joel 3:3 says they trade a boy for time with a prostitute. It also says they trade a girl for wine to drink at a party. To these people, human beings are nothing but a means to an end. It is important to note that God denounces Israel and Judah for similar deeds in Amos 2:4–16. Amos accuses Israel of trampling the poor (Amos 2:7). He also says they sell the righteous for silver and the needy for the price of a pair of shoes (v. 6). There is no double standard. God rejects these sins regardless of who does them.

We should take note of how God wants us to treat other people. God calls us to deal justly with one another. He calls us to love our neighbor (see Leviticus 19:18). Love for neighbor stems from loving God (see Deuteronomy 6:4–9; Mark 12:28–32). We show our love for him partly by how we love others. People are not just a means for making money or having pleasure; they are the image of God in the world. How we treat them shows our true commitment to Jesus, as Matthew 25:31–46 indicates.

God's people are not safe if they have enemies. They certainly had enemies in Joel's day, in Jeremiah's day, and in the Apostle Paul's day. We still live in times of danger. Satan and his followers remain active. We lose brothers and sisters to persecution every day. I am grateful we can say of these Christians, "They have conquered him [Satan] by the blood of the Lamb and by the word of their testimony, for they loved not their lives even unto death" (Revelation 12:11). I have a very easy life compared to many Christians in the world today. I pray I will have their courage if I need it.

Joel teaches that God will hold those who persecute his people accountable. New Testament writers agree. They claim that God's people are all who believe in Jesus. These believers come from many nations (see Romans 9—11; Revelation 5:9, 10; 7:9, 10). Peter asserts that God will judge all who oppose God and his people (2 Peter 2:1–3). Paul reminds the Thessalonians that their sufferings help their faith grow (2 Thessalonians 1:3, 4). He also claims the day is coming when God will judge the wicked and deliver his people (2 Thessalonians 1:5–12). Revelation 19:11–16 shows Jesus leading an army that will defeat all nations that oppose his kingdom. Christians can take comfort in these words. God has saved us from sin. He will save us from all who hate us because they rebel against him.

### God Will Decide the Future of Rebellious Nations (3:9–15)

Several Bible passages describe the nations rebelling against God. One of the best known is Psalm 2. In that text the nations and their leaders are rebelling against God and his chosen king, the Messiah. They plot against God and his king (Psalm 2:1, 2). Their plotting does not worry God. He laughs at their big plans. He warns them to serve his chosen one or face judgment.

Joel 3:9–15 is much like Psalm 2. Here God shows his absolute control over the nations. He invites them to prepare for battle in Joel 3:9–12 and then describes their destruction in 3:13–15.

Speaking like a mighty king, God sends a proclamation to the nations in 3:9. He tells them to "consecrate" themselves "for war." This means they should set apart their best warriors, their "mighty men." They should choose their elite forces, their very best soldiers. In verse 10, God tells them to get their best weapons. They should melt down all their metal and make weapons so effective that even weak men will feel strong using them. Verses 11, 12 then challenge them to come fight God in the Valley of Jehoshaphat, the valley of judgment (see v. 2). They have been oppressing boys and girls (see 3:3). It is time to see how they will do against God.

The nations should bow down in fear at this challenge, but they do not. Rebellion against God is a strong emotion in human beings.

The outcome is not in doubt. In verse 13, God tells his army to "put in the sickle," as if the enemy soldiers are grapes to be cut from a vine. Once cut, the grapes can then be trodden to harvest their juice. The juice overflows, just as their evil has done. Evil will be pressed out as their blood ebbs from their bodies.

Verse 14 marvels at the sight of "multitudes" in the valley. There are two possible ways to understand the valley's name in this verse. The word translated in most English versions as "decision" ("the valley of decision") can mean "an absolutely settled decision." But the Hebrew word can also mean "cutting."[2] Either way, the nations have not been gathered to make a decision. They have either gathered to be cut down or gathered to receive God's firm decision. They cannot defeat God. Joel 2:1–11 has already made this point clear.

Believers should take comfort from these verses. God will secure our future. Persecution will not always exist. Injustice and evil will not ultimately prevail. God will defeat the wicked. We do not need to worry about taking revenge against our opponents. We can let God do his work, in his way, in his time.

Believers should also seek to win enemies of Christ to Christ. We all begin as God's enemies. We hated God and his ways before he brought us to faith in him. He commands us to love our enemies (Matthew 5:43–48). God calls us to take his good news to the ends of the earth. He asks us to reach out to the lost until Christ comes. God has loved us so much, and we must spread his love.

## God Will Be a Refuge for His People (3:16–21)

Joel concludes his book by describing a glorious future for God's people. Judah has suffered in the recent past. They have endured a terrible locust plague. People from foreign lands have oppressed them and taken over parts of their land. God has been disciplining them. But after the time of renewal and the outpouring of the Spirit, final judgment will come. God's people will be safe, for God himself will be their refuge and their avenger.

Joel 3:16–18 describes God as Judah's refuge. To the nations he is a roaring lion ready to tear its prey apart, according to verse 16. When he "roars," the heavens and earth shake. The ground moves beneath the enemy's feet. Few natural disasters are as frightening as earthquakes. The nations will have plenty to fear when God roars.

In contrast, God is "a refuge to his people." He is like a fortress, a walled city, or a safe tower. He provides complete security for them. Verse 17 states that "strangers"—in this case, dangerous people—will not enter this city. Egyptians, Assyrians, and Babylonians defeated or occupied Jerusalem in Old Testament days. No such enemies will disturb God's people in Zion.

Verse 18 promises that this place will also have all the provisions that the people will need. Joel uses metaphorical language here. He says the "mountains shall drip sweet wine, and the hills shall flow with milk, and all the streambeds of Judah shall flow with water." This will be the most fertile place imaginable. Water, milk, and wine will flow in abundance. This verse reminds us of passages like Isaiah 11:1–9, which says the wolf and lamb will lie together in God's kingdom. It reminds us of Ezekiel 47:1–12, which tells us that water from God's altar will heal the land. Safety and abundance await God's people in God's city.

Joel 3:19–21 presents God as Judah's avenger. Egypt and Edom have mistreated refugees in their lands. "They have shed innocent blood," according to verse 19. Verses 19, 20 state that God will make these nations desolate, but he will make certain that Judah is "inhabited." The book's final verse says that God will at last "avenge" his people's blood on the day he judges and reigns in Zion. These images may seem harsh to us. We must remember that God is just. He is very patient, but he will not clear the guilty (Exodus 34:6, 7). His people can trust in both his justice and his mercy.

## Conclusion

Joel ends with a flourish. God has completed his renewing work begun in chapter 1. In his mercy he has brought his people to himself. The plague he sent and the warnings he gave through Joel have succeeded. The people have prayed. They have received the outpouring of the Holy Spirit. They have been brought safely to Zion, God's eternal city. This is God's gospel. This is his news for us. We may begin in sin, but we do not have to stay in sin. We may come to the brink of destruction, but even then he will receive those who repent. We may pass through this life as pilgrims, but we have a home prepared for us. God's work for the sake of his people continues today.

We have a great God to share with the world. He is powerful, gracious, and just. He keeps his promises, and his word never fails. His word can shape lives now, just as Joel's words helped shape Peter's life on the Day of Pentecost. Joel's short book can transform lives as we share it afresh with our families, friends, and enemies. May God give us the courage to share and believe God's perfect word.

# AMOS

*By Paul R. House*

# 19

# The Shepherd, the King, and the Lion

AMOS 1:1, 2; 7:10–17

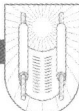

THE BOOK OF JOEL CLOSES with a section devoted to God's promise to protect his people and judge the wicked (see Joel 3). Near the end of the passage, Joel 3:16 proclaims,

> The Lord roars from Zion,
>   and utters his voice from Jerusalem,
>   and the heavens and earth quake.
> But the Lord is a refuge to his people,
>   a stronghold to the people of Israel.

Lions usually roar when they are warning or attacking. So Joel's words are ominous for those who oppose God and his faithful ones. But they are comforting to God's people.

Amos 1:2 echoes Joel 3:16. It declares, "The Lord roars from Zion and utters his voice from Jerusalem; the pastures of the shepherds mourn, and the top of Carmel withers" (Amos 1:2). Amos takes up Joel's urgent message. Both passages present God as fierce, powerful, and in a mood to attack. Both prophets declare necessary and terrifying words. These twin passages help link the two books and carry us on to stark truths presented by one of the Bible's most straightforward prophets.

Amos has received more attention from scholars and pastors than Joel. There are many reasons for this interest. First, Amos denounces sin specifically and extensively. He condemns individual and corporate sin in no uncertain terms. He spares no one. His words lash the lowly and the great alike. Second, Amos announces the day of the Lord in graphic, sometimes nightmarish, detail. Third, Amos demands justice for the weak and oppressed. Fourth, Amos declares that David's household will rule Judah, Israel, and the nations. Fifth, Amos's era is well attested in the Bible and has been illuminated by archaeological discoveries. The book has a lot to offer to a wide range of readers.

All these interesting historical and theological matters could tempt us to avert our eyes and close our ears from Amos's clear and pointed message that God roars like a lion against sin, so it is time to return to him. This message should strike fear in the heart of the wicked and inspire hope in the faithful. It is a timeless and weighty message. It is one we must hear today so we can repent and receive forgiveness from God. It is one we must hear if we wish to have meaningful Christian work, homes, churches, and communities, and if we wish to bear a spiritually healthy witness in society. These ancient words still carry God's grace and power for all who are willing to obey them.

Amos 1:1, 2 and 7:10–17 introduce the book's main themes by presenting ancient images foreign to most of us. We rarely encounter a shepherd, a king, or a lion, but we find them here. All three were common in ancient times. These images basically relate three major prophetic themes. First, God calls prophets to shepherd his people. They must feed, protect, and guide them. Second, God is the great King. He rules all earthly rulers. They are accountable to him. Third, like a lion God roars against sin wherever it occurs. He aims to devour it. These themes lead to the main intent of prophetic books, which is to turn people to God, their ruler and redeemer.

### The Shepherd: God Calls and Sends Amos (1:1; 7:14, 15)

Every prophet in the Bible has specific preparation and gifts for ministry. No two are exactly alike. Their hometowns, professions, families, writing and speaking abilities, level of insight, and grasp of God's ways contribute to how they communicated then and communicate now. The Bible does not tell us much about several of these special men and women. For instance, we have more information about Hosea, Amos, Jeremiah, and Huldah than we do about Joel, Obadiah, and Habakkuk. Happily, Amos 1:1, 2 and 7:14, 15 allow us a good glimpse into Amos's life before he began his prophetic work. Thus, we have some added insight into how he viewed himself and his ministry.

Amos opens the book by stating that what follows are "the words of Amos" (1:1). The Hebrew word translated as "words" can also mean "things" in the sense of the things that a person does. The book of Amos includes both words Amos spoke and things Amos did. Both his words and deeds were bold.

Amos's words are among the most pointed and powerful in the prophetic writings. His statements bear the stamp of a strong personality. They are clearly his. Yet the Bible claims these words did not originate with Amos. Rather these are words "he saw" (1:1), words that came from outside him. These are words from God that God sent Amos to proclaim. The book repeatedly prefaces Amos's statements with "Thus says the LORD" (1:3). Amos is God's agent, his mouthpiece, his ambassador.[1] Second Peter 1:19–21 declares that God "carried along" the Old Testament writers as they wrote and spoke. God led his prophets to write down his words as a message for future readers, for us, as 1 Corinthians 10:1–6 states. We must hear these words for what they are, God's word for us now. We should also remember to thank God for our older brother Amos, whose distinctive personal style resonates centuries after he died.

According to 1:1 and 7:14, 15, Amos had not been a prophet before God sent him from Judah to speak to Israel. Rather, he had been "among the shepherds of Tekoa" (1:1). He was not even raised in a priestly family, like Jeremiah was (see Jeremiah 1:1). He did not live near the temple, as Isaiah likely did. Tekoa was a village in Judah located about six miles southwest of Bethlehem, so about twelve miles south of Jerusalem. Due to Tekoa's high elevation, from that small town one could see Bethlehem, Jerusalem, the Dead Sea, and a long way east.[2]

The Bible seldom mentions Tekoa. According to 2 Chronicles 11:5–12, King Rehoboam of Judah (c. 930–913 B.C.), Solomon's son, made Tekoa a fortified city. It was probably still a military outpost in 760–750 B.C. when Amos began his ministry. It was a great place to observe the world.

Shepherding of all sorts was a normal trade in the ancient world. The wool and meat trades depended on shepherds in the fields, shepherds managing trade between countries, and shepherds managing high volumes of diverse types of sheep. Kings called themselves shepherds. Shepherding was a highly valued way of life.[3] Those of us used to Christmas sermons that assert all shepherds were considered thieving and dirty scoundrels will likely be surprised by the respect shepherds had in ancient times. In his case, Amos may have raised a special kind of sheep. The word translated as "shepherds" in the ESV only appears here and in 2 Kings 3:4. Both times, the word refers to owners of a small breed of sheep that was "valued for its abundant fine wool."[4]

In 7:14, Amos states he was not a prophet or a prophet's son before taking up his ministry. Rather, he says he "was a herdsman and a dresser of sycamore figs." This mention of being a herdsman parallels the comment in 1:1 that he was a shepherd. The phrase "dresser of sycamore figs" refers "to one caring for and pruning a tree that produced a fig usually consumed by poor people."[5] These trees may not have grown at an altitude as high as Tekoa's, so it is possible that Amos owned land elsewhere.[6] This means Amos may have been prosperous, but the text does not tell us this for sure. People often find it more remarkable when a person leaves a lucrative position to follow God than when a poor person leaves his job to do the same. The Bible does not encourage this sort of distinction. It emphasizes God's call, God's gifts, and the person's character and faithfulness.

In 7:15 Amos adds, "The LORD took me from following the flock, and the LORD said to me, 'Go, prophesy to my people Israel.'" In other words, God did not allow him to stay in his hometown and his job. God required him to leave Judah to go preach in Israel, which was a foreign country to Amos. It would be something like asking an American to go minister in Canada. This call, therefore, required a dramatic change in Amos's life and location. Ministry often requires such sacrificial change. It also requires divine direction. God did not leave him on his own to figure out where to serve.

God also did not leave him on his own to decide what to preach. Amos 1:1 notes that Amos "saw" what God wanted him to say. God gave him the necessary inner sight to know what, how, when, and where to speak. Of course, God also used what Amos knew already. As the book proceeds, it becomes clear that Amos had an excellent grasp of the history of Israel and of Moses's teaching. It is also clear that he had learned the sage advice once given to my friend Phillip Jensen by an older minister: "Never forget, sheep bite."

God continues to call people today to leave their homes and jobs to serve as shepherds of his people. Ministers come in all shapes and sizes. They have different gifts and backgrounds. Yet they all share some common traits. They must know God in Christ Jesus through the Holy Spirit. They must be willing to stay where they are or to leave anything and anyone God asks, to do God's work. They must be willing to prepare for the work as God directs. They must share God's words, not their own opinions. They must care about God's people or else they simply cannot sustain the work. As shepherds they must have the tenderness and toughness displayed by Jesus, the great shepherd.

Amos was this type of shepherd. As such, he remains a strong example of one willing to do whatever God requires. Are we willing to be like him? Are we willing to ask God to call such people into ministry? Are we willing to ask God even to call our own loved ones into such service?

### The King: God Rules History (1:1; 7:10–13, 16, 17)

God sent Amos to a straying flock and an unfruitful field. He did so in an era marked by notable kings, which demonstrates his kingship over all rulers. How do we know Israel was an unruly flock and a barren field? Amos 1:1 reveals that Amos served during the overlapping reigns of Jeroboam II (c. 782–753 B.C.) in Israel and Uzziah (c. 783–742 B.C.) in Judah. Both kings were outwardly fine monarchs. Both expanded their nations' borders. Both presided over economic prosperity. Uzziah followed God imperfectly but solely. He did not worship other gods or encourage his people to do so.

Jeroboam II was another story. He followed the religion of his namesake, Jeroboam I (930–909 B.C.) (1 Kings 11:26—12:33).[7] This cult began when Israel split from Judah after Solomon died in 930 B.C. God made Jeroboam king of Israel, but Jeroboam did not trust God to keep him on the throne. He feared that if his people went to Jerusalem, his rival's capital, they would turn away from him and depose him. Instead, he opened rival worship sites in Bethel and Dan (see Amos 4:4; 5:5), which were on his southern and northern borders, respectively. Jeroboam II supported these places nearly two centuries later. Worse yet, he allowed Baal worship to flourish. We learn from the book of Hosea that Baal was a fertility god. People believed he made women, land, and animals fertile. Baal worship encouraged sexual acts and other sensual behavior at official sanctuaries.

Bad theology always eventually leads to bad morals. As the people worshiped money, sex, and power, they abused the poor to make money (Amos 2:6, 7), and they did make money. Some could afford several houses (3:15) with expensive furnishings (6:4). They could also purchase expensive food and other luxuries (3:12; 4:1; 6:6). Alec Motyer summarized the situation as follows: "Money making and personal covetousness ruled all: the men lived for their offices (8:5), the women lived for excitement (4:1), the rulers lived for frivolity (6:1–6)."[8] In this society, the needy were sold into slavery for very small debts. The wealthy trampled the poor into the dust (2:6, 7). This era in Israelite history illustrates Jesus's blunt pronouncement that "you cannot serve God and money" (Matthew 6:24).

Amos dares to speak against these money-driven practices. In passage after passage he attacks greed, oppression, and immorality. He even dares to declare that God's judgment will fall on Israel if the people do not seek justice and righteousness (5:18–24). He warns that God is about to send a nation to punish Israel for all their sinful deeds (6:8–14).

Such preaching did not go unnoticed. Israel's religious and governmental leaders did not appreciate it. They did not like this man from Judah coming north to tell them how to live. According to 7:10–13, "Amaziah the priest of Bethel" warned Amos to stop speaking against the king and his religion. Amaziah assumed Amos was like other prophets of the day. He assumed Amos was in it for the money, so he told Amos to go back home and preach (v. 12). He must not dare to prophesy at the royal sanctuary at Bethel, "for it is the king's sanctuary, and it is a temple of the kingdom" (v. 13).

Amos gives a classic response. He works for a greater king than Jeroboam (v. 15). Amos declares that he must preach and that Amaziah and Jeroboam are heading for a fall (v. 17). Jeroboam is merely the king of Israel. Amaziah is merely the priest of Bethel. God rules all rulers. Amos is the ambassador of the great King. Amos outranks Amaziah.

Amos's words to Israel and Jeroboam resonate today. When Amos spoke to money-loving, covetous Israel, he spoke to all such peoples. Thus he still speaks to the United States, a nation I love, yet a nation morally crippled by lust for money, consumption of goods, and wastefulness. I cannot read Amos's words without hearing warnings for our homeland and for most of the Western hemisphere. This book is especially apt for believers caught in the web of a materialistic worldview. We must not be deceived; God is not pleased with those who say they love God but in truth love money and abuse people to get it.

Rulers often believe that they determine world history. They boast about their policies, their authority, and their legacy. They tempt their people to look to them as if they were God, as if they were the source of food, shelter, clothing, and peace. But they are not God, and they must not play God. Every one of them dies, but God lives on forever. None comes to power unless God allows it. All of them are accountable to God, no matter how differently things may look on the ground. God sees how rulers treat people and knows what or who they worship. God allowed Jeroboam II to rule over Israel, but God was not pleased with what he saw. Amos served the one true King, and he calls us today to bow before that all-powerful monarch.

### The Lion: God Judges and Saves (1:2)

It is hard for us to conceive of it now, but the Middle East was once a place where lions roamed. These fierce beasts were feared and respected then as they are now. Robert Stallman writes that Egypt had cults that utilized lions in their artwork and that rulers in Egypt and Mesopotamia compared their power to that of lions.[9] In the Bible, Israel's heroes and enemies are both portrayed as lions, and Solomon decorated his throne with twelve lions.[10] It is not surprising, then, for Amos to portray God as a lion who "roars from Zion," the place from which he rules (1:2).

God's rule has a vast scope and tremendous power. Though he roars from Zion, Jerusalem, his realm is not limited to Judah. It reaches to Mount Carmel in Israel. It stretches from the height of that great mountain to the lower pastures where shepherds graze their flocks. God rules everywhere, a point made even clearer in Amos 1:3—2:16. When he roars, all nature responds. His very breath scorches the earth, making the shepherds mourn and the top of Carmel wither. There is no avoiding the results of his declarations.

God, the great King, dispenses justice according to his character. Thus, in Joel 3:16, he is a lion that protects Judah. But in Amos 1:2 he is a lion that is about to punish Israel. Before he punishes, however, he roars a warning through Amos, an image picked up again in 3:8. Israel must decide if they wish this Ruler of the whole earth to be their unbeatable helper or their unsparing foe.

As the book proceeds, the lion's roar gets louder. It roars out the certainty of judgment on all sinful nations in 1:3—2:16. It roars out indignation against Israel's covenant-breaking, injustice, and unwillingness to repent in Amos 3—4. It roars out demands for justice to roll down lest there be woe in Samaria and Jerusalem in Amos 5—6. It roars out the coming of the day of the Lord in Amos 7:1—9:10. God speaks time and time again through his good prophet Amos, just as he has spoken through Hosea and Joel. As the book unfolds, it becomes apparent that the roar does not disturb the people. They get used to it and do not ponder what it means. Therefore, the Assyrians come, and the land mourns.

But the lion roars one last time in Amos 9:11–15. There God promises that these fallen, rebellious covenant people will one day return to God. He will give them a king from David's line again. Their enemies will fall away, and God will make nations bow before him. He will restore the people and plant them in the land. Acts 15:1–21 indicates that God keeps these promises as Israelites take the gospel of Jesus Christ to the nations. The lion of the tribe of Judah, Jesus Christ, is God's last word. He is the final roaring from God the King. God judges so that he might save.

## Conclusion

Thus, we begin to hear the word of the Lord that Amos "saw" through the power of the Holy Spirit. These words challenged people more than twenty-seven centuries ago, they challenged the early church, and they challenge us. Amos still tries to shepherd God's people, so we will recall that Jesus is the great shepherd. Amos still urges us to understand the difference between earthly kings who die and God the great King who lives and reigns forever through his chosen one, Jesus Christ. Amos warns us to hear God when he roars, for God protects those who trust in him and judges those who rebel against him. Amos warns those who know God and those who do not. Those who are wise will hear the words of the man who never planned to be a prophet, making his hard journey to the mission fields of Israel worthwhile.

# 20

# God's Authority and the Nations' Sins

AMOS 1:3—2:3

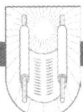

IN ONE OF THE BIBLE'S most famous texts, Romans 3:23, Paul declares, "All have sinned and fall short of the glory of God." He makes this statement after citing a series of Old Testament passages that begin with a paraphrase of Psalm 14:1: "None is righteous, no, not one" (Romans 3:10). Paul's comments indicate some very important points of Biblical theology. First, every person has disregarded God's person and character and has broken the laws he has set. They do so even though his character is glorious and his law is just and beautiful. Second, God assesses every person's deeds. He does not let sin go unpunished. Third, if every person is under God's authority, then every nation is likewise under his authority. In short, the God who created and rules the world is the One who defines sin and judges it wherever it occurs.

Amos's words agree with Paul's summary. He also offers evidence that such is the case. To be more specific, Amos 1:3—2:3 offers concrete proof that the nations surrounding Judah and Israel sinned in many ways. Amos 2:4–16 then demonstrates that sin infected Israel and Judah as well. Sin is as common as nations and people. Amos has already stated that God is roaring like a lion ready to pounce (1:2). Now he helps us understand why.

In Amos 1:3—2:3, the prophet slowly informs his Israelite audience of God's plans to defeat their enemies. He lists the peoples and lands around Israel, covering every geographical direction. He mentions Damascus first, which was (and is) northeast of Israel (1:3–5). Next, he denounces Gaza, which was (and is) southwest of Israel (vv. 6–8). Then he condemns Tyre, northwest of Israel (vv. 9, 10). Finally, he blasts Edom (vv. 11, 12), Ammon (vv. 13–15), and Moab (2:1–3), which were south and southeast of Israel. Whether first read or heard, one can imagine Amos's hearers cheering at each opponent's demise. They may have thought this was great preaching.[1] However, Amos will eventually include Judah and Israel in his declarations of judgment, and the people will be less happy. Amos slowly slips a verbal noose around their spiritual necks through this geographically informed sermon.

We must not think that the noose only fits ancient Israel. After all, we live in a culture that loves to condemn opponents, all the while rebuking others for judging us. In such a setting it is usually easier to see sins in others than in ourselves. Amos prods us to shed such hypocrisy. The world is filled with sins of many types, and none escapes God's gaze. He is the Creator and Ruler of the universe. Now and at the end of time, God holds all people accountable for what they do (Romans 14:11, 12; 2 Corinthians 5:10). We must face this fact if we are to know God, have our sins forgiven, and live ethically for him in a sinful world.

Amos denounces six places in swift succession. To do so, he uses a numerical formula best known in the Bible from the book of Proverbs (see Proverbs 30:15–33). He announces that "for three transgressions . . . and for four," the Lord will judge each place (Amos 1:3). The idea is that the sins just keep adding up. He could name more, but he must stop somewhere. After stating each place's sins, he concludes with a declaration of future fiery, devouring, and destructive judgment. Their punishment is as certain as their transgressions.

These sins have far-reaching consequences. They appear in many forms in our world. It would be nice if the sins Amos describes fell into two or three neat categories. However, the passage proceeds like water flowing down a river. Therefore, I will take the places and their sins in the order Amos presents them. I think you will see current sins in these ancient words.

### Damascus: Threshing People Like They Were Grain (1:3–5)

Amos begins with Damascus (1:3), the capital city of the Aramean kingdom. Bible translations often refer to the Arameans as "Syrians" and the kingdom of Aram as "Syria." The Damascus mentioned here was located near the city of the same name today. In fact, Damascus is one of the world's oldest cities. The Arameans were an old enemy of Israel and Judah. They were powerful during the time of Elijah and Elisha, a century before Amos, and they remained a threat in Amos's and Isaiah's days (see Isaiah 7:1, 2).

These verses refer to the fact that at some earlier point in time, the Arameans captured Gilead, a place located in disputed territory between Aram and Israel. This may have occurred when Hazael was king of Aram (see 2 Kings 10:32, 33),[2] but it is impossible to know. After all, the two nations fought over this land for decades. Bitter feelings resulted.

God denounces the Arameans for a war atrocity. He condemns them "because they have threshed Gilead with threshing sledges of iron" (Amos 1:3b). A threshing sledge was a device used to separate grain from chaff. It was normally made from planks that had stones attached to the bottom of them. Farmers pulled this device over grain until the chaff was gone. Aram used a sharper instrument than normal. Its sledge was made of iron, not stones. Aram threshed Gilead as if its people were the grain under the sledge.

Andersen and Freedman have explained that the threshing of a place "is a metaphor for the savage conquest of a territory. The war machine is like a gigantic threshing board, which slashes and pulverizes the whole land."[3] Similar imagery occurs in 2 Kings 13:7 when Israel defeats Aram. It also appears in Isaiah 41:15 where God promises Israel victory over their enemies. It is possible that the Arameans pulled threshing sledges over the bodies of victims. Or this may be an apt metaphor. Regardless, they treated people as if they were husks of corn, bits of straw, and chaff to blow away in the wind.

This threshing occurred in war. But God does not excuse the brutal behavior just because it happened in battle. As J. A. Motyer asserted, "War or no war . . . [Aram] had no liberty to treat people as if they were things. It is the first absolute moral principle for which Amos campaigns: people are not things."[4] As Jesus stated in Matthew 5:43–48, people deserve compassion even if they are one's enemies.

As the book unfolds, it becomes likely that this early passage in Amos, like some others, attacks war atrocities done to women, children, and other defenseless persons. Defeating a nation may be one thing; brutalizing and terrorizing them as part of that victory is quite another.

God will address the Arameans' sins. The punishment will not turn back. It will come. No timetable appears. Nonetheless, within a few decades the Assyrians invaded and defeated Aram. In 732 B.C. they took many Arameans captive and deported them to other lands, just as Amos 1:5 warns. In the Assyrians the Arameans faced a foe even more brutal than they were. What they did to Israel was done to them. Their sins came back to haunt them. God's roaring from Zion had its effect.

We must ask ourselves how innocent our country is of war atrocities. To our credit, the United States has often punished war crimes committed by our own soldiers in the past. We continue to debate the use of torture of enemy combatants and other tactics we do not think should be applied to American citizens. We retain some conscience in this matter. However, we also have a history of total war, of bombing cities filled with noncombatants. We have spoken of enemy peoples in terms usually reserved for animals. We have taken satisfaction in making people pay double for what they have done to us.

All nations must be very careful. God does not accept our anger and sense of vengeance as the standard. He calls for justice, compassion, and forgiveness, even when these are very hard to offer. Everything is not fair in love and war. We cannot treat people as if they were things.

## Gaza: Selling People into Slavery (1:6–8)

One of the most troubling aspects of early American history is the nation's support of buying and selling human beings against their will. The practice of this type of slavery lasted longer in the southern United States[5] than in the rest of the country, but the Northern states also had it for over a century. Famous Christians owned slaves. For example, it often surprises people to learn that Jonathan Edwards owned slaves. But such was the case.[6] I was once visiting a fellow church member and saw a bill of sale for slaves framed and hung on a wall devoted to Southern history. It was a sober reminder to me that slavery was real and that it still affects relationships between the races today.

America and Britain hardly invented chattel slavery. It was occurring centuries before Israel came on the scene. The Bible never condones the practice. In fact, it forbids all types of kidnapping, and it forbids the selling of people into slavery for the rest of their lives. The Bible allows types of indentured service, but it never approves of what most of us mean when we use the term *slavery*. Bondservants were indentured servants—they agreed to a period of service for certain considerations. The persons in this text had no such choice.

In 1:6–8 Amos denounces the people of Gaza because they "carried into exile a whole people to deliver them up to Edom" (v. 6). Like Damascus, Gaza was an ancient city that exists in basically the same place today. In Amos's day it was part of Philistia, which had a well-earned reputation for conducting effective warfare. The Gaza that Amos knew was a port city located southwest of Israel. It is possible that Gaza received persons taken captive in battles Philistia fought. It is also possible that these unfortunate people were taken captive by other nations, and Gaza simply transported them to Edom, which was famous for slave trading. From Edom the people could be taken across the desert to Babylon, Assyria, and other places. Gaza may have been captors and traders or simply middlemen in the slave trade.

Amos does not distinguish between those who take slaves and those who transport them. He holds all parties guilty. In fact, he holds all four major Philistine cities accountable. Gaza, Ekron, Ashdod, and Ashkelon all face God's judgment. All four will feel the power of God's hand against them. All have been involved, and all four will be held accountable. As was true of Aram, the Philistines fell to the Assyrians within thirty years of Amos's ministry. Many Philistines went into the sort of slavery they had inflicted on others.

Slavery remains a significant matter today. Human trafficking, particularly for prostitution, occurs worldwide. Women and children are particularly vulnerable. The stain of slavery still mars relationships between black and white Americans. One wonders how long this sin will harm humanity and our homeland. One may wonder if nations that practice the sins of Gaza will face God's judgment. Amos makes it clear that they will. This certain judgment will not turn back. It will happen.

### Tyre: Breaking the Covenant of Brotherhood (1:9, 10)

God's standards are not always hard to understand. In their simplest form they can be boiled down to one phrase: "Treat others the way you wish to be treated" (see Matthew 7:12; Luke 6:31). Jesus taught this idea, but he is hardly alone. Virtually every world religion has some version of this principle. It is ingrained in human consciousness. Even children can understand it; even children can break it. Amos 1:9, 10 states that Tyre broke this golden rule.

Like Gaza, Tyre was a port city. Located northwest of Israel, Tyre had been a key trading center for centuries by Amos's time. It was particularly strategic for the shipping trade west to Cyprus and beyond. Ships from Tyre had reached the ports of Spain by the time Amos ministered to Israel. Thus Tyre was known for its wealth, technology, and trading savvy.

Amos criticized Tyre for selling an entire community to Edom for slavery. This means that no one from the area in question was spared. No one was left. All were sold. No mercy whatsoever was shown. Young and old, male and female, rich and poor became slaves. Tyre considered people to be just another commodity. They were happy to be middlemen in the selling of human beings into a life of constant bondage.

Their actions proved that their lust for money exceeded their humanity. They were happy to treat others in a way they did not wish to be treated. Worse still, the phrase "covenant of brotherhood" (1:9) may also refer to an actual agreement. If so, Tyre not only sold the people into slavery, but they did so after assuring them they would not. They gained their victims' trust before selling them out.

God does not need a middleman to punish Tyre. He will take care of the task himself. He will send fire on Tyre's walls, which means that the city will suffer defeat and loss. Eventually the double-dealing and greedy people of Tyre will lose their precious money. God will hit them where it will hurt them most—in their wallets. In fact, God sent fire on Tyre's walls without the city falling to a foreign foe. By 709 B.C. the Assyrians ruled Cyprus and the land surrounding Tyre. Thus Tyre's trade and income were greatly curtailed. The city was shut off and made to suffer. The people of Tyre learned what it was like to face life without freedom.

Tyre's sin is basic. All of us have committed it. As individuals we can forget that we should not treat others in a way we do not wish to be treated. Children bully their brothers and sisters, though they hate the same treatment. Adults cheat others but are outraged if they get shortchanged. As a nation we often place burdens on others we do not want. We treat newcomers as fodder for labor that citizens will not do. Or we argue that it is fine for us to have weapons aimed at other countries but get upset when the reverse occurs. We have been known to twist the truth of treaties when it suits us. From the least to the greatest, we have the capacity to break "the covenant of brotherhood." When we do, we can expect God to act in the areas of our greatest devotion. Like Tyre, America can expect to lose money since that is what we seem to adore above all other things.

### Edom: Casting Off All Pity (1:11, 12)

We have already seen that Edom was the region's chief slave trader. There seemed to be no deal they considered too repulsive to make. They were willing to take portions of a people group into slavery, or take the whole lot. It really did not matter much to the Edomites.

As noted earlier, from Edom newly captured slaves could be sent across the desert to ancient lands such as Babylon and Assyria. But Edom also used forced labor locally. Edom was known for its mining operations. Scholars debate whether Edom or another nation controlled these mines, but the mining work proceeded at a heavy pace for a long time. Slaves did the most backbreaking and soul-killing labor. The wheels of the economy kept turning.

How does a nation manage to sell group after group into slavery? How does a nation keep its heart cold enough to look on while men, women, boys, and girls go off to the mines or off into the desert? How does money remain more important than anything else?

Amos supplies an answer. He describes Edom as indiscriminately vicious, perpetually angry, and ceaselessly cruel. Edom "pursued his brother with the sword and cast off all pity" (v. 11a). The word the ESV translates as "brother" can mean an actual brother, or it can mean a friend or close companion. Regardless, Edom treats a friend as an enemy. Edom does not play favorites; Edom mistreats everyone.

To do so, the Edomites must be in the habit of casting off any compassion that may creep its way into their hearts. Edom must fight off feelings of mercy by letting anger tear perpetually at their minds. No slight can be forgotten. No opportunity for vengeance can be missed. No good deed can go unpunished. One must feed a hard heart a steady diet of malice, hatred, and betrayal. Otherwise one might hesitate before selling the next girl into sexual bondage or the next man into the fiery furnace of a stifling mine.

This passage helps us understand the darkness of human hearts. How can we understand a man like Joseph Stalin who murdered millions more than Hitler? How can we explain Mao Zedong and his cultural revolution, which included the murder and starvation of millions? How can we reconcile in our minds a human being opening fire on helpless children in a school? Some of us point to mental insanity, and sometimes this is the answer. But Stalin and Mao were not insane. Their hearts were as hard as stone. They cast off any pity that might stop their deeds. They let anger tear at their souls until they could ignore God and human beings. As hard as it is to hear, my grandfather was right when he told me, after we heard about some atrocity and I wondered if the perpetrator was insane, "Boy, you need to learn that some people are just no good." Edom earned this description. It comes as no surprise for Amos to inform us that judgment fire will come upon Edom.

## Ammon: Ripping Open Pregnant Women (1:13–15)

Amos has already alerted us to the harsh realities of war. Damascus threshed people as if they were grain. Gaza took slaves as spoils of war. Edom stayed ready to fight at a moment's notice. Now Amos gets very specific about some of the most grotesque acts of terror that soldiers use against their foes. He also gets very specific about the petty reasons they do such massively cruel things.

Amos accuses Ammon of ripping open "pregnant women in Gilead" (1:13). Thus Gilead suffered at the hands of both Damascus (see v. 3) and Ammon. The soldiers slashed these women and killed them and their babies solely to intimidate, wreak vengeance, and warn against further opposition. After all, pregnant women and unborn children are hardly threats to full-grown men.[7] They have no strategic significance. The men kill them simply because they can. They do so even though they certainly do not want the same done to their wives and children. Similar atrocities have occurred in recent warfare.[8]

Why did the Ammonites do this? What did they gain from it? Amos states that they did it simply to "enlarge their border" (1:13). They did it to gain a bit more land, a bit more money, and a bit more fear for their nation. They did it simply to get a little more of the small things they valued. They did all this in vain, for today one must be interested in ancient studies or Biblical studies to have any interest in the Ammonites. Their quest for fame yielded short-term results, to say the least. It left them remembered for cruelty and for little else. It also left them open to God's certain judgment.

I was born in Kansas, but I grew up in Missouri. Citizens of both states recount tales of the days when Missouri and Kansas came into the United States. Missouri was a slave state and Kansas a free state. Each had people cross the border to pillage the other. To this day, when their sports teams play one another, they call it "the border war." As brutal as the Missouri-Kansas border wars were before and during the Civil War, they pale in comparison to the border wars fought in Europe, Africa, and the Middle East in the previous century and in our current one. Nations large and small fight for the chance to make a bit more money (or even lots of it) by expanding their borders. If women and children get in the way, they must be removed. Ammon's sin remains way too common.

### Moab: Pursuing Enemies beyond Death (2:1–3)

By now you may wonder what sin is left for Moab to commit. War crimes, slave trading, and a general lack of humanity have passed before our eyes. But Moab is up to the challenge of doing something that takes sin to new depths. Moab does not let even the death of their enemy satisfy them. They pursue their foes beyond death.

Amos notes that Moab and Edom, which shared a north-south border, fought against one another. This is hardly surprising in the war-torn setting he describes. What is unusual is that Moab did not stop with killing Edom's king or at least finding his grave. Moab "burned to lime the bones of the king of Edom" (2:1). It is not clear to us exactly why Moab did this. Perhaps they wanted to desecrate the grave to show their power and disrespect. Perhaps they wanted to eliminate any trace of the dead king's life. Even bitter enemies usually grant a truce to bury the dead from both sides. Such respect is customary. Moab is too angry to grant this basic courtesy. They do not just wish their opponent gone. They want him never to have existed.

Nations often have long memories where slights are concerned. When I traveled in the Middle East for the first time in 1987, I was amazed by some of the people's approach to time. They spoke of events that occurred centuries before as if they had happened that week. Those bent toward revenge were ready to use ancient atrocities as an excuse for current ones. On the one hand, it is great to recall good things that took place centuries ago and be glad. On the other hand, it is quite dangerous to nurse old grudges, especially in international politics. Forbearance and forgiveness are much better paths to follow. As Amos 2:2, 3 warns, seeking ceaseless vengeance leaves people and nations open to divine judgment carried out by the very people one afflicted unmercifully.

## Conclusion: Grace for Sinners

After such a catalog of sins, we may wonder if there is any hope for such sinners. The Bible is very clear on this matter. God judges and punishes sin, but he offers grace to those who repent. Moses and David killed people or had them killed, yet God forgave them and restored them. The Apostle Paul was a vicious man who loved hurting Christians, but God redeemed and cleansed him. Samson threw away great potential in wicked living, yet God forgave him. Peter denied Jesus, who forgave him. King Nebuchadnezzar of Babylon exalted himself over God and was struck with a disease. When he turned to God, the Lord forgave him and restored him to his throne (Daniel 4:28–37). Repentance brings renewal, for God forgives.

The Bible never lists sins just to condemn them. It always exposes sin to bring people to repentance, to turning to God in Christ. Just as Naaman from Syria (2 Kings 5:1–14) and Ruth from Moab (Ruth 1:6–18) came to the Lord, so can sinners of all sorts. The same God who saved the slave trader John Newton, author of "Amazing Grace," could save slave traders from ancient Gaza, Tyre, and Edom. The question is not whether God can forgive. He is ready to do so. The question is whether we are ready to repent. Are you?

# 21

# Israel and Judah Have Sinned

AMOS 2:4-16

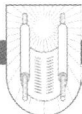

"ALL HAVE SINNED and fall short of the glory of God." This is the Apostle Paul's summary of humanity's spiritual condition without Christ in Romans 3:23. I recalled this verse in the previous chapter. I have heard both Reinhold Niebuhr and G. K. Chesterton credited with observing that this statement is empirically verifiable. Both men were great thinkers and writers. But they did not have to conduct exhaustive research to see that every person sins. Sinning is part of who we are. None of us should consider sinning acceptable, and surely none of us doubts that it exists.

As you know already, Amos certainly does not approve of sin. In 1:3—2:3, he exposes sin in the nations surrounding Judah and Israel. Amos 2:4–16 shows that Amos was not a nationalistic prophet. He did not see sin in other lands and fail to see it in Israel and Judah. He exposed sins in Judah and Israel as honestly as he did in the bordering countries. In fact, as the book proceeds, he uncovers the sins of those who claim to know and serve God in much greater and more graphic detail. The neighboring lands get off lightly in comparison.

This is as it should be. Israel had been given many advantages and thus bore more responsibility. God had delivered Israel from slavery in Egypt hundreds of years earlier. He had called the Israelites to be a kingdom of priests that ministered to other nations (see Exodus 19:5, 6; 1 Peter 2:9). Thus, they were supposed to set an example for their neighbors, not imitate these neighbors who did not know God. Furthermore, God gave them a homeland as a staging ground for worldwide ministry. He also sent Moses, David, and the prophets to guide them.

The Israelites clearly had a responsibility to God and to other people (see Deuteronomy 6:4–9; Leviticus 19:18). At times they fulfilled God's purposes. At times they failed slightly; at other times they failed miserably. Amos's times were of the latter type. To compare it to New Testament times, the Israelites of Amos's day were more like the Corinthians than the Philippians. They were more like the Laodiceans than the Ephesians (cf. Revelation 2:1–7; 3:14–22). Most of the people abandoned God and his covenant. They refused to fulfill their ministry to others. When God's people sin like the rest of the world, the world becomes a very dark place.

Amos is clear about what God thinks of this behavior. He considers it a breach of faith. He considers it the worst sort of personal betrayal, the rankest type of ingratitude. Amos calls Israel from their sins to return to their place as God's ministers to God's world. He exposes their lies, immorality, and injustice so that they may repent and be spared when God comes to judge.

We know now that most did not heed Amos's message. God speaks today through this passage so that we will not repeat their mistakes. He warns those of us who claim to know God in Christ through the Holy Spirit to turn from these sins and serve him again.

### Preferring Lies to God's Word: Judah's Sins (2:4, 5)

Israel might have taken some satisfaction in hearing Amos denounce Judah. After all, Israel split from Judah in 930 B.C. when Solomon died. Israel was the larger and richer of the two nations. Israel had their own version of religion, as I noted in the chapter on Amos 1:1, 2. Israel may have resented Judah's claims that they followed God more closely than their backsliding northern neighbors. Perhaps they even hoped Amos's statements about Judah meant that this prophet from the south was coming over to their way of thinking. Regardless, Amos denounced Judah in no uncertain terms. He focused on Judah's straying from the truth and embracing lies.

Amos uses the same formula to criticize Judah as he used to condemn Damascus, Gaza, and the others in 1:3—2:3. In 2:4 he warns that "for three transgressions of Judah, and for four" God "will not revoke the punishment" reserved for Israel's southern neighbor. When he finishes his description of their sins, he closes with the news that God "will send a fire upon Judah, and it shall devour the strongholds of Jerusalem" (2:5). The prophet warns that judgment will follow if nothing changes. This warning unfolds in three parts.

First, Amos claims that the people of Judah "have rejected the law of the LORD, and have not kept his statutes" (v. 4). The heirs of Abraham, the pupils of Moses, and the followers of the Davidic kingship have rejected God's word. When they reject God's "law," which can also be translated as his "instruction," they reject the governing document of their relationship with him. It is somewhat like an employer refusing to abide by a contract with an employee or a union refusing to stand by a labor agreement or a spouse refusing to abide by marriage vows. In each of these examples, the relationship is undercut. One of the parties involved has left the relationship or wants the benefits of the relationship without its responsibilities. Judah has walked away from the God who delivered them from Egypt, gave them their king and land, and kept them safe for centuries. They want to go their own way despite all God has done for them.

Second, Amos states why they have rejected God's instruction. They have done so because "their lies have led them astray" (2:4). By "lies" Amos most likely means "other gods."[1] Following these gods leads Judah to go astray, to wander about like a lost animal. They have probably wandered after false gods because they have followed false prophets who filled them with incorrect teaching.[2] As Israelite history unfolds, the majority of Judah rejects the words of Isaiah, Jeremiah, Micah, Habakkuk, and Zephaniah. They prefer the words of prophets who tell them what they want to hear, especially if those prophets promise peace, prosperity, and ease (see, for example, Jeremiah 23:9–40; 28:1–17). They want gods who fill their wallets and stomachs. They want preachers to tell them that all will be well, no matter what.

Third, Amos reveals the example that Judah follows. They follow lies "after which their fathers walked" (2:4). This phrase most likely refers to idolatry. Beginning with the golden calf incident in Exodus 32, idolatry was a recurring part of Israelite history. When the Israelites worshiped other gods, they simply acted like the nations around them, where believing in many gods was normal. But when they worshiped other gods, they cut themselves off from the only living God. They cut themselves off from the One who loved them the most and provided all they ever needed. Instead of following the example of people like Moses, David, and Deborah, who had flaws but never committed idolatry, they followed the examples of their worst ancestors.

Amos 2:5 states that judgment follows covenant infidelity. So Amos agrees with Moses, who warned Israel in Leviticus 26:14–39 and Deuteronomy 28:15–68 that God would discipline his people when they sinned. Moses also warned in these passages that if the people did not repent when God disciplined them, he would eventually drive them from the promised land. Thus,

Amos was simply agreeing with Moses when he made this pronouncement. He knew God's word, and he knew it was always true.

This warning has particular value for people who have enjoyed spiritual privileges. Many have grown up in Christian homes, yet walked away from God. Some went to faithful Christian colleges and seminaries yet no longer serve the Lord. We live in a land that has Bibles, commentaries, devotional literature, and sermons available in many types of media. We have lots of churches where I live. There are five or six within a mile of my home! We have so many churches that we treat them like commodities. People can shop for churches like they shop for groceries or like they shop for entertainment. We have so much spiritual help available in the United States that it is almost embarrassing.

This abundance makes us abundantly accountable to God. Few people in the United States can honestly say they know nothing of Christianity and its claims. We are accountable to God for what we have heard, seen, and read. If this is so, how culpable are those who walk away from God to serve such small gods as money, sex, and power—the unholy trinity of American culture? How responsible are we when we walk away from the Christian teaching that we have inherited to chase after lies? Jesus warned in Luke 12:48, "Everyone to whom much was given, of him much will be required, and from him to whom they entrusted much, they will demand the more." These words summarize Judah's guilt in Amos 2:4, 5. They also summarize the guilt of all who know God and yet reject his teaching in order to follow the gods of this or any other age.

### Greed, Sexual Immorality, and Irreverence: Israel's Sins (2:6–12)

Amos finally addresses his primary audience, Israel, and he hits them hard. He begins with the same formula as before: "For three transgressions . . . and for four" (v. 6). But he describes Israel's sins and judgment in more detail. He discusses their lack of character in more embarrassing terms. He leaves them with no excuse for their behavior. In later chapters he will add to the list of their moral failures. For now he is satisfied to reveal their greed, sexual immorality, and disregard of God and his ministers.

Greed is a plague on any life, any community, and any nation. It leads to other sins. It leads to stealing, adultery, false teaching, murder, and Sabbath-breaking. It is the twisted twin of coveting, the sin that summarizes all the others in the Ten Commandments. In these verses, greed fuels oppression and sordid sexuality, and it resists God's overtures of grace. It leads the people to live in a way that contradicts the salvation that God offers in the Bible.[3] It leads to the very opposite of the character that the people of God should exhibit before our watching world.

Amos describes what these greedy people are doing. In verse 6, he claims that they "sell the righteous for silver, and the needy for a pair of sandals." This accusation probably means they sold innocent, faithful, God-honoring poor people into slavery to pay very small debts.[4] This level of greed requires a very hard heart.[5] Moses taught that Israel should treat every person with respect and kindness (Exodus 22:25–27; Leviticus 25:35–38).[6] Instead they have acted like the nations around them. Like Damascus, Gaza, and the others, they treated people like objects.[7] They failed to be the holy people of God. They let greed lead them far from the path of justice and righteousness.

Amos 2:7a claims that this greed-induced cruelty resulted in the righteous poor being ground into the dust. The poor man can never get his head up. He can never get to his feet. He can never get anywhere in life. Sadly, the verse continues: if poor persons could get to court, they would find that the judges "turn aside the way of the afflicted," the mistreated (2:7a). The poor have no money to bribe judges, so they are treated as if they have no case. They are, in effect, treated as if they do not exist, as if they were invisible, as if they were not persons at all.

The Apostle Paul warned his fellow worker Timothy to shun the love of money. Paul knew some false teachers who thought that "godliness is a means of gain" (1 Timothy 6:5). They used people to get money. Thus Paul cautioned that "the love of money is a root of all kinds of evils. It is through this craving that some have wandered away from the faith and pierced themselves with many pangs" (6:10). This wicked love is certainly what had happened in Israel in Amos's time. The people valued money above all else, and to get it they pursued unjust practices that harmed their brothers and sisters. Their nation's death pangs soon followed.

God's people are not immune from temptations to love money and mistreat others. We must guard our hearts. Most American Christians hear and see dozens of advertisements per day. It is hard to avoid them if we listen to radio, watch television, browse websites, open our paper mail or our electronic mail, or glance at billboards as we drive home from work. These ads typically urge us to want something so we will buy something. They appeal to greed. They lure us into thinking that we are consumers first and people second, or third. They imply or assert that we deserve to have expensive things. If we are not discerning, we can easily fall into the trap of loving *things*, which is the start of loving money. What we do to get the money to buy the things we desire can be the opposite of how Christ tells us how to live.

In the second half of Amos 2:7, the prophet accuses Israel of sexual immorality committed during Baal worship. Amos claims that "a man and his father go in to the same girl, so that my holy name is profaned" (v. 7b). The words translated as "go in," "same," and "girl" in the ESV need clarification. The words "go in" could be more literally translated as "walk to" or "take a journey to" the woman in question. The word "same" is supplied by interpretation, not by a specific Hebrew word. The word translated as "girl" is literally "the young woman," which probably refers to a particular *category* of woman. In this case it is likely that "the young woman" refers to a cult prostitute. Therefore, Amos is probably indicating that a man and his father both take a journey to see a cult prostitute committed to Baal worship. However, they may or may not go to the same woman.

These men are supposed to lead their sons and daughters to worship the one living God, but instead they lead them to worship Baal. As part of worshiping Baal, the men engaged in sexual acts with women committed to serving Baal by giving their bodies for his glory. Moreover, as Hosea 4:14 has stated, these men's daughters become prostitutes for Baal. Thus, these Baal worshipers profane God's name, the body of the woman, and the family ties they represent.[8] They undermine everything sacred in life.

In Amos 2:8, the prophet connects their greed and their immorality. He notes that "they lay themselves down beside every altar." There are Baal altars throughout the country, and they are well attended. Furthermore, when the worshipers lie down with cult prostitutes, they do so "on garments taken in pledge." The garments in question were taken from poor men who would give the garment to secure a loan. Exodus 22:26, 27 and Deuteronomy 24:12, 13 required such garments to be returned to the debtor at night so he could keep warm.[9] The heartless men in Amos 2:8 failed to comply. They kept the garments, and they paid the cult prostitutes by giving them the garments. These men are faithless, cruel, callous, and lustful.

To become this greedy and immoral, Israel disregarded the fact that God freed their ancestors from slavery and gave them their homeland, according to 2:9, 10. Furthermore, Amos 2:11, 12 claims that the people have ignored God's word sent through God's messengers. God called prophets and sent them to warn the people to turn from their rebellious ways (v. 11a). Men such as Elijah and Elisha preached to them. Now Hosea and Amos have come on the scene. God also sent Nazirites, men who took vows to serve God in special ways. Numbers 6:1–21 describes these persons. A Nazirite gave up wine and other fine things to devote himself to God. Such persons contrast sharply with the Baal worshipers that Amos describes in 2:7, 8. The Israelites wanted no part of such reminders of God and his word. They told the prophets to stop preaching, and they forced Nazirites to drink wine (v. 12). Respect for God simply had no place in their society. It did not fit their values. It cramped their style.

It is important for us to note how Israel got into this condition so we can learn from their mistakes. Israel did not go from following God closely to worshiping Baal in one day. Their falling away happened over time. It began with forgetting what God had done for them (vv. 9, 10). They became ungrateful and inattentive. This led to rejecting God's word and then refusing to hear it at all (vv. 11, 12). Hearts grew harder and harder. Soon enough, the people turned to the gods of the land, to false deities that reflected their greed and lust (vv. 6–8).

Hosea and Amos spoke to people who were supposed to be God's people. We do not know people's hearts. God alone does. Yet we do know what people claim. Many people claim to have been saved by the blood of Jesus Christ. They hold membership in some church, even in our church. Yet they live for money. They live for sex. They reject God's words and God's messengers. Still, there is hope. Jesus still forgives. It is not too late, but the clock is ticking.

## "I Will Press You Down": God's Judgment on Israel (2:13–16)

As we come to Amos 2:13–16, we sense that we have been here before. After all, we have heard God denounce several cities and peoples by now. Yet this is different somehow, for God warns in more detail. There is nothing perfunctory about this passage. It reveals that God's judgment will be as thorough as Israel's rebellion. These verses are very systematic and very picturesque.

God will put great pressure on Israel. He states in verse 13, "Behold, I will press you down in your place, as a cart full of sheaves presses down." God will make Israel heavy, like a loaded cart; in fact, like a cart so burdened that its wheels cannot move. It is as if their sins are a bumper crop that farmers cannot get to market.

God will strip Israel of all defenses. Her best warriors will fail "in that day" (v. 16), the day he comes to punish. Verses 14, 15 describe their plight. Their swift warriors will have no speed. Their powerful men will grow weak. Their valiant men will lose courage. Their skilled bowmen will lose their nerve. Neither swift runner nor trained horseman will escape. The stoutest hearts and the strongest arms will "flee away naked in that day" (v. 16). They will drop everything and run for their lives. Men trained to face any foe and any threat cannot face God's judgment.

We only think we are ready to face God. I recall once hearing a speaker say that when he sees God, he will shake his fist in God's face and demand answers for what has happened on earth. We can only pity people who think this way. Remember how brave Job was in facing life's great problems and how he longed to call God into account? Yet when he saw God, he realized how little he knew and how great God is (Job 40:3–5; 42:1–6). Isaiah 2:6–22 states that when God comes to judge, the proud people of the earth will run and beg the rocks to fall on them. Babylon's King Nebuchadnezzar ruled the world, but when God pressed him down for his pride, the poor arrogant king lost his mind and ate grass like an animal (Daniel 4:28–33). Only when he praised God did he return to his senses (4:34–37). If the mighty warrior will flee on that day, then what chance do we normal people have?

## Conclusion

I must ask you, my friends, is God's hand pressing down on you? Do you feel the weight of your sins? Do you recognize yourself as one who loves sex, power, money, and pride instead of the living God? Do you realize that you will have nowhere to run and nowhere to hide on the day when God will judge? Are you one who claims to know God and yet hates his word and blocks out his memory?

If so, the good news is that there is hope for you. Your conscience has been stirred. You are coming to your senses. Some of you are realizing that you need to give your sins to Jesus. You need to be changed and made into a new person who follows him. You know you cannot save yourself. So why not admit your sins, ask Jesus to take them away, and bow to him as your Lord and only Savior? He can make you new.

Others of you may be awakening as if from a long sleep. You have been redeemed by Jesus, but you have profaned his holy name and his holy ways. You hardly recognize what you have become amidst all the Baal worshipers of our day. But you can come home. You do not need to linger beside the altars of a false god. You can stop loving money and stop harming the poor. You can start loving God and neighbor again. God can pick you up from "the garments taken in pledge" (Amos 2:8) and use you in his work again. He alone can do all this, and he will do it as you turn from irreverence, greed, and lust to the God of grace and holiness.

## 22

# Privilege, Responsibility, and Consequences

AMOS 3

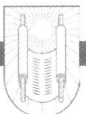

FROM A VERY EARLY AGE we are told that privileges come with responsibilities. And we are warned that when we do not take our responsibilities seriously, there will be consequences. I recall my father giving my brother Joel a thorough lecture on this subject when Dad let him purchase his first .22-caliber rifle. Dad gave me an equally stimulating version of the speech when I began driving. Our father warned Joel and me that recklessness could lead to a loss of privileges. Having been a father myself for a long time, I suspect that he was also concerned that recklessness with a rifle or an automobile could lead to the loss of our lives. Dad knew that we would make mistakes, but ignoring or rebelling against his instructions would not be allowed. He cared about us too much to be indifferent.

The principle of appreciating privileges by showing responsibility is a very Biblical one, and it is central to the message of Amos 3. The Bible proclaims that in love God chose and redeemed Israel and gave them a homeland (see Deuteronomy 7:6–26). This was partly so that Israel would, through word and deed, declare the news of God's love to other nations (cf. Exodus 19:5, 6; 1 Peter 2:9, 10). Their redemption was not for their sake alone. Therefore, God held Israel's people and leaders responsible for what they did with their privileges.

In 1:3—2:16 Amos stated that all have sinned, even persons in Judah (2:4, 5) and Israel (vv. 6–16). Amos has also stated that God has been merciful. He redeemed the Israelites, gave them a home, and sent prophets and Nazirites to teach them his ways (vv. 9–11). Yet they have ignored God and corrupted his servants (v. 12), so a terrifying time of judgment will come (vv. 13–16).

Amos continues his attempts to awaken the Israelites in chapter 3, this time by indicting them before other nations (vv. 9, 10). He declares that the Israelites have been a privileged people (vv. 1, 2), that faithful prophets have declared God's word to them (vv. 3–8), and that they are now subject to the penalties for ignoring God and his prophets (vv. 9–15).

Lest we think this is some superseded Old Testament pattern, similar texts appear in the New Testament. For instance, Jesus calls his followers to a careful and joyous walk with him (Matthew 5:13–20; 11:25–30). He reminds them to be doers of his words and not just hearers (5:21–26). He tells them that he expects much from them because they have received much (Luke 12:48). He warns his followers of the need to care for others, for when they care for others they care for him (Matthew 25:31–46). Paul directs stern words at professing believers in Galatians and 1 and 2 Corinthians, but no sterner ones than the author of Hebrews aims at his readers. First John 1:9, 10 reminds us that Christians sin, but also that God forgives confessed sins. Repentance and trust restore our relationship with him. We have every reason to thank God that he is merciful and to thank him for working in and through us (Galatians 2:20). Those who believe God heed God's warnings. Let us now hear and heed God's warnings given through his servant Amos.

### God's Privileged People (3:1, 2)

As God's people, we ought to remember all that God has done for us. For example, God called me to preach his Word decades ago. Every year on the anniversary of my call, I take some time to consider what this has meant to me. Though much time has passed, I have not forgotten the deep and humbling sense of gratitude to God that I had at that time for giving me the honor of serving him in ministry. I could scarcely believe that God would choose to use me in his work.

Now that I am older and more seasoned, I am still amazed. I think this is especially true for me because there was a time that it looked like I would not be allowed to continue in ministry. I have been privileged to be given an education, a family, a host of friends, and a generally rich life through the call to ministry. At this stage of my life I often ask myself what I am doing with all God has given me. This is a proper question for one deeply flawed and deeply blessed.

Israel was not reflecting on God's past and present goodness in Amos's day. The people were not wondering how to give back to God even a tiny measure of the good he had poured out on them. They felt no weight of grace, no sense of sustaining mercy. They felt free to live as they pleased. Throughout their history the Israelites had heard God's words spoken to them and for them, but now they hear God's word spoken "against" them (Amos 3:1a). This word concerns "the whole family" that God "brought up out of the land of Egypt" (v. 1b). In other words, both Israel and Judah are condemned, as in 2:4–16. God delivered Abraham's descendants from spiritual and physical slavery in Moses's day (see v. 10), but past actions seemingly have no relevance for Amos's generation.

But the past matters to God. He has not forgotten. In Amos 3:2 he reminds the people that "of all the families of the earth," he has only "known" them in the sense of delivering them from slavery for service to him. God chose Israel to be his people to bless "the families of the earth," not just to have freedom and possess and use a land (Genesis 12:3, 7). He called them to be "a kingdom of priests" to minister to others and to set an example for others (Exodus 19:5, 6; cf. Ezekiel 36:20). He gifted them for ministry, not for self-serving ease. Their unwillingness to serve in the ways that God requires twists their true purpose, which is the basic definition of "iniquities" (Amos 3:2b). He will punish their rebellion, just as he warned through Moses in Leviticus 26:14–39 and Deuteronomy 28:15–68. Their privileged position will not shield them from God's disciplinary measures.

I have already mentioned Revelation 2—3 as a parallel passage. There the Lord Jesus speaks to seven of his churches. We would do well to examine his words to all of them, but perhaps focusing on just one will help us make the connection.

Ephesus is the first church Jesus addresses (Revelation 2:1–7). It is hard to imagine a more privileged church. The Ephesians had been marvelously saved from idolatry. They received teaching from the Apostle Paul, the Apostle John, and the gifted evangelist Apollos (Acts 18:24—19:40; 20:17–38). The Ephesian church held a prominent place in Paul's mission strategy. The Ephesians were doctrinally sound (Revelation 2:1–7). Yet Christ reveals that over time they had abandoned the type of love they had at the first (2:4), a phrase that indicates they had gone away from what matters most. So Jesus warns them that if they do not repent, he will come and remove that church (2:5). They must live for Christ in light of all he had given them. This was not some sort of payoff they would give God to stay in his good graces. Rather, it was the most natural response they could give to God's grace.

One time, while speaking to members of my church, I asked everyone to pause and consider the privileges God had given our congregation. Those blessings included the following: He has sent his Son, his Word, his Spirit, our brothers and sisters in Christ, and his servants, our ministers. He has provided Biblical teaching. He has forgiven all our sins, healed all our diseases, and satisfied us with good things (Psalm 103:1–5). He has given us spiritual gifts for his service in his world (see 1 Corinthians 12). Concluding, I asked, "How else should we respond to such privileges but with thanksgiving, joy, and careful service?"

God's Faithful Prophets (3:3–8)

God's grace to Israel did not stop with deliverance from Egypt. It did not stop with giving the Israelites a homeland (see Amos 2:10). It did not even stop when Israel became unfaithful. In his love, God sent his prophets to instruct his people in his ways.

Amos does not come to Israel to preach on his own authority (see 7:10–17). God sent him. Like other good Old Testament prophets, Amos speaks logically and kindly about God's sovereignty, holiness, and love. As James Boice wrote, God's "love is not incompatible with justice."[1] God has given his Word and his messengers to build us up into the sort of people the world needs. Do we listen and respond Biblically, or are we carried along by the words and emphases of our day?

In 1:3—2:16, Amos declares the sins and punishments of eight nations. The last nation, Israel, is the focal point of the list. Everything that precedes 2:6–16 leads to those verses. Similarly, Amos asks eight questions in 3:3–8, with the final one providing the list's main point.[2] Each question is rhetorical, with the expected answer being "No." Each question highlights cause and effect. Each question hints at Israel's relationship with God. For example, people walk together when they have agreed to do so (v. 3), and God and Israel long ago agreed to walk together in covenant relationship (Exodus 20:1–17). The mention of roaring lions in Amos 3:4 reminds hearers of Joel 3:16 and Amos 1:2. Amos 3:6 reminds hearers of God's sovereign rule over all lands, a point made very plainly in 1:3—2:16.

But the final question focuses hearers' attention on the role of God's prophets. They have received God's "secret" (3:7), a word that in context refers to God's plans revealed to an intimate circle of close confidants.[3] But the prophets do not receive such a privilege for their own personal satisfaction or gain. They are God's "servants" (v. 7), tasked with speaking what God has spoken, according to 3:7, 8. What follows is not Amos's opinion. It is God's word. He might prefer not to declare such hard truths, but he has no choice in the matter. He hopes the people will respond to God as he has.

Those who share God's Word with others need Amos's example. At least three points come to mind. First, we explain and apply the Bible's ideas, not our own. Amos shared what had long been revealed, and he also received direct revelation from God that became Scripture. We are not the conduits of new scripture. But like Amos, we share truth long revealed. We help our family, friends, and neighbors see, believe, and obey what God has said. Second, we need God-given, Amos-like courage when we must share hard truths. We must remember that compassion and truthfulness are friends, not enemies. Third, we need Amos-like willingness to go where God sends us and to speak to those God gives us. This may mean going to places far or near. The choice is up to God.

### God's Verdict on Israel's Sin (3:9–15)

The faithful prophet declares what will happen to the privileged people. To do so, he includes a wider audience. In Amos 3:9, 10 God calls Ashdod and Egypt to hear his case against his people. Having heard the evidence against Israel, they learn how God will punish Israel's sins in 3:11–15.

In verse 9 God summons two expert witnesses, Ashdod and Egypt, to see what goes on in Samaria, the capital of Israel. According to 1:6–8, Ashdod captured and sold people. Of course, Egypt oppressed Israel before the exodus (see 3:1). Together the two represent small and large places that mistreat others. They will know oppression when they see it. God seats them on the hills surrounding Samaria, from which they can get a good view of what happens in Samaria. They view tumult and panic caused by oppression.

In verse 10 God declares his verdict. The oppressors in Samaria have lost all moral bearings. The people in these "strongholds" are storing up the results of "violence and robbery" in their most prominent city. As they have done so, they have lost the ability to tell right from wrong. This has occurred even though God's prophets have warned them to return to the right paths (see vv. 7, 8). Their willful ignorance scorns God's gracious warnings.

In verse 11 God delivers his verdict. The first half of the verse is hard to translate into readable English. The best option is that God declares that "an adversary" will put pressure on the whole land.[4] The second half of the verse is quite clear: Samaria, the great storehouse of oppression, will be plundered. God does not state that the city will fall to a foreign army, though Samaria suffered that fate in 722 B.C. For now he simply warns that the oppressors will receive the same sort of treatment they have inflicted on others. God's justice will prevail.

The punishment will be devastating. According to Amos 3:12, the people will be ravaged like a lion's unlucky prey. They will be as damaged as furniture swept up in a flood or ruined in a fire. Only small pieces of things will be rescued (i.e., salvaged). The word "rescue" or "deliver" seems ironic in English. The mention of "a couch" and "a bed" may refer to the luxuries the oppressors have enjoyed. They have mistreated the poor and needy to acquire the money to get the things they desired (2:6, 7; 3:9, 10). Their possessions will perish with them.

Verses 14, 15 show that Samaria will not be alone when God judges. Bethel, the place 7:10–13 discloses as a major center of false worship, will likewise experience God's disciplining hand. Wherever they exist in the land, large and ornate houses bought with tainted money will be no more (3:15). False religion, along with the oppression it causes, will end.

It is important to recall that Amos speaks before judgment falls. Israel does not yet have to go through what he describes. There remains time to awaken. Though the worst oppressors have forgotten how to do what is right, perhaps some whose consciences have not been seared will hear and change.

When first spoken, these words offered grace. Those of us hearing them now should seize them as a great gift. We can do now what Amos hoped people would do then.

## Conclusion

So what will we do with our privileges? Twenty-seven centuries after Amos lived—centuries that saw the completion of the Old Testament, the life of Jesus Christ, the writing of the New Testament, and the spread of Christianity—what will we do with our privileges? What will we do with the privilege of so many good pastors, so many helpful books, so many Bible translations, so many fellow believers, so many opportunities? What will we do with our wealth? What will we do with our freedoms? What will we do to show that we love and obey the God who redeemed us? These are just a few of the questions that this passage raises for me.

One thing is certain: our privileges are not guaranteed. If we squander them in favor of money and things gained at others' expense, we can be sure that God will not let us have them forever. They can be gone in a flash.

Worse yet, if we choose to ignore what God has given us, then we lose fellowship with God, and that is the greatest loss of all. Knowing him is the greatest privilege in the world. If we learn anything from Amos, let us learn that.

# 23

# You Did Not Return to Me

AMOS 4

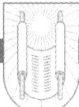

GOOD DISCIPLINARIANS are very purposeful people. They have healthy, useful goals. Good parents discipline children in appropriate ways intended to build proper character. Conscientious teachers want their students to learn material that will make them solid citizens, workers, and family members. They also instill work habits that will hopefully last a lifetime. Bosses who love their workers hold them to high standards so they can reach their potential and the company can flourish. Good disciplinarians have the other person's interests at heart, not just their own. Their methods seek higher aims than temporary order, money, or family pride.

God is an excellent disciplinarian. He holds people accountable—always for redemptive purposes. He convicts us of our sin to save us. He corrects us to change our destructive behavior. He knows that sin crushes souls. He knows that sin kills. Because God is loving and just (see Exodus 34:6, 7), he deals with sin.

Amos has already stated God's commitment to justice in chapters 1—3. He has also emphasized the need for God's covenant people to obey him for their own sake and for the sake of others. Thus, Amos has agreed with Moses (see Leviticus 26:1–45; Deuteronomy 28:1–68; 30:1–10) and with earlier prophets like Elijah (see 1 Kings 18:18).

Amos 4 presents God's efforts to discipline Israel. Their need for correction is clear. Rich and greedy men and women oppress others, all the while bringing tithes and sacrifices to worship centers (vv. 1–5). In response, God has sent several sorts of trouble meant to turn Israel back to him (vv. 6–11). But the result was not good. Five times God offers the refrain, "yet you did not return to me" (vv. 6, 8–11). So he commands the people to prepare to meet him, their God, who is also the Creator of the heavens and earth (vv. 12, 13). He will straighten them out then! Their sin will end. The question is whether they want things to get to that stage.

God's character does not change; he still disciplines today. Romans 5:1–11, Hebrews 12:3–11, James 1:2–4, and Revelation 2—3 make this point abundantly clear. He disciplines us whether we sin or not since we need endurance to give needed witness to a hurting world (James 1:2–4). When we sin, God disciplines us to conform our actions to the image of Christ (Romans 12:1, 2). Whatever the reason for the discipline, we should learn to embrace it. We should not object to it, pout about it, resent it, or ignore it. We should reflect, give thanks, and grow. Amos 4 shows the perfectly incorrect response to God's gracious discipline. It provides a cautionary tale for all who wish to avoid the lifestyle, stubbornness, and future of Israel's decadent rich.

### The Lifestyle of the Rich and Greedy (4:1–5)

Some years ago there was a television show called *Lifestyles of the Rich and Famous*. Its host, Robin Leach, had a lilting English accent. Each week he took viewers to opulent, luxurious homes owned by celebrities. In many ways it was the mother of many of today's so-called reality shows. Sometimes it was hard to tell which was bigger, the homes or their owners' egos. I guess I should add that it was hard to tell which was bigger, their homes or my envy!

Amos takes us on a short tour of Israel's rich and famous in 4:1–5. He begins in 4:1 by describing some women, saving the men for 6:1–7. As in 3:1, he demands a hearing for God's words (4:1). This time he addresses women "on the mountain of Samaria." Amos describes them as "cows of Bashan," which today would be an insult. In those days, however, it was a compliment. Ancient writers "regularly employed pastoral imagery to refer to beautiful women."[1] Bashan was a lush and lovely area (see Deuteronomy 32:14; Isaiah 2:13; Psalm 22:12),[2] so these are very attractive women.

Unfortunately, they have ugly hearts and unattractive habits. They "oppress the poor" and "crush the needy" (Amos 4:1), and they urge their husbands to do whatever is necessary to maintain their lavish lifestyles. They are addicted to drink. Apparently they contribute nothing productive to their communities.[3] They are consummate consumers. Of course, their husbands are no better, for they bow to their wives' wishes. As is true of the nations in Amos 1—2, they treat other people as disposable objects that exist to make them comfortable. They have become rich and famous at others' expense.

Their wealth will not last. God sees everything they have done. These women have sent their husbands to get them whatever they want. According to 4:2, God will send a foreign army to give them something they do not want. The Lord swears by his own holiness—the very essence of his character—that their days of excess are numbered (4:2a). An enemy will take them away using "fishhooks" (v. 2b).[4] As noted in the section on Hosea, Assyria often placed hooks through the upper lips of their captives, fitted a line through the hooks, closed the hook, made a line to other people, and marched groups into exile single file.

This process may be reflected in 4:3, which says the women will go out through breaches in battered city walls, "each one straight ahead."[5] They will pass by "Harmon," a reference to Mount Hermon, on their way to exile. It is hard to conceive of a more complete reversal of fortunes. The sleek city women will be herded away like animals on a leash. They were heartless, and this is a sad ending for these selfish women.

Verse 4 shows that these rich and greedy people were not irreligious. They participated in worship services at ancient sites. "Bethel" had been an important place for centuries. Jacob had his dream of angels on a ladder and received covenant promises at Bethel (Genesis 28:10–22). Samuel judged Israel there (1 Samuel 7:15, 16). "Gilgal" (Amos 4:4) was where Israel crowned Saul as their king (1 Samuel 11:14, 15) and where Joshua renewed the covenant (Joshua 5:1–9). Yet Amos cries out for the people to come to these places and sin! He is clearly being sarcastic. What does he have against the people going to these places?

Remember that when Solomon died, his kingdom was divided into two unequal parts. Judah and Benjamin banded together and continued to worship at the temple in Jerusalem. The other ten tribes united around Jeroboam I, who instituted a new religion that looked like worship in Jerusalem but was opposed to it. God commanded the Levites to lead worship. Jeroboam let people from many tribes be priests. God commanded that no images be used in worship. Jeroboam set up metal bulls to represent God. Moreover, God commanded centralized worship in Jerusalem. Jeroboam set up rival sites, including ones at Bethel and Gilgal. God commanded untainted worship. Jeroboam mixed in some fertility rituals from other religions. Bethel was the royal sanctuary of the king by Amos's day (see 7:13). Whoever went there honored the king and opposed the Davidic king in Jerusalem.

At Bethel and Gilgal, the people did what worshipers of that era did: they brought "sacrifices" and "tithes," according to Amos 4:4. But verse 5 highlights their bad motives, their "leavened" motives. Amos tells them to "proclaim freewill offerings, publish them; for so you love to do, O people of Israel!" Amos does not condemn sacrifices and offerings, though he does not approve of the places Jeroboam set up to receive them. Rather he condemns the worshipers' motives and attitudes. As James Limburg explained, "When the motivation for worship is recognition by others and satisfaction for self, then that religion is rebellion, says the prophet."[6] These people love to let other people know what big gifts they bring. The lifestyle of the rich and greedy includes giving gifts to be seen by others. Even religion has become a venue for self-serving, lavish hypocrisy. There is no love of God or neighbor (see Deuteronomy 6:4, 5; Leviticus 19:17, 18, 34–37), and there is no intention to repent (see Isaiah 1:10–20). Therefore, there is no worship. There is only rebellion and self-glorification.

Amos 4:1–5 strikes at the heart of ill-gotten wealth and human-centered worship. We must take pains to ensure that our wealth does not come through the mistreatment of others, especially the poor, weak, and needy. I say "take pains" because in today's global economy oppression abounds. Believers need to be free of oppression's foul taint, especially given the Church's cooperation with many kinds of oppression in the past. We must also take pains to honor God in our services, buildings, and practices. The Church has always faced the temptation of favoring the rich (see James 2:1–7), for it takes money to do ministry. But we must beware of wanting our names on buildings and our imprint on everything the Church does. We must beware of adopting the attitudes of the rich and greedy.

I worked at Beeson Divinity School of Samford University from 2004 to 2023. In 1988, Ralph Waldo Beeson gave more than sixty million dollars to start this seminary. He tried to give the money anonymously, but he could not due to the local media's understandable curiosity over who made such a large gift. He agreed to name the school after his father, John Wesley Beeson. It was only after his death in 1990 that the trustees overrode his wishes and decided to add Ralph Waldo Beeson's name to his father's. Mr. Beeson wanted no credit for this large gift. Thus he was the perfect antithesis to the people Amos describes.

Jesus warned that we must beware of giving gifts and doing religious deeds simply to be seen by other people. Otherwise being seen will be our only reward (Matthew 6:1–4).

### The Stubbornness of a Sinning People (4:6–11)

God did not leave Israel alone when they sinned. He loved them too much to do that. His gracious character did not allow him to let his covenant people descend into the abyss of sin without disciplining them. He took actions calculated to turn them back to him, back to the safety of holiness and faithfulness. As Amos 4:6–11 unfolds, however, it becomes clear that his efforts were largely unnoticed, ignored, or rejected. Every disciplinary situation God devised met with the same result: his people did not return to him.

First, God created a "lack of bread" in the land, according to verse 6. Food supplies ran short. In Leviticus 26:20, Moses warned Israel that if they sinned against God and failed to repent, "your land shall not yield its increase, and the trees of the land shall not yield their fruit." The Bible does not teach that every food shortage occurs because of human sin, but it does teach that such disasters can be a result of sin. Regardless of the cause, a lack of food demonstrates our absolute dependence on God and should thus lead to prayer. But Israel took no steps back to God. They simply kept refusing to repent and return to God.

Second, Amos 4:7, 8 notes that odd rainfall caused water shortages and desperate migration patterns. Three months before harvest—the time when one expects autumn rains to soften ground hardened by summer heat—no rain came (v. 7).[7] Therefore, the growing season was over before it began. Water supplies also ran dry, so people wandered from city to city to get water but did not even have enough liquid to slake their thirst (v. 8). Parched, weary from travel, and burned by the sun, the people still did not repent.

Third, verse 9 adds that God sent locusts and diseases that harmed crops. The people were helpless to stop the loss of their livelihoods. Figs and olive oil were large export items. Incomes dropped. Perhaps the people took all this in stride. Maybe they chalked it all up to the cost of doing business. What they did not do was return to the Lord. It seems they never considered that option.

Fourth, verse 10 says that God sent the plague of war. Leviticus 26:25 mentions war as one of the tools God will use to bring straying Israel back to covenant faithfulness. Israel was constantly at war during this era; first with Syria, then with Judah, and then with Assyria. Constant war blights any land. It stirs up people's baser instincts when it becomes routine. War's terrible effects should make any nation—much less one that claims to know God—turn to their Creator. Though war became so unpleasant it is compared to a "stench" in their nostrils (Amos 4:10), Israel did not return to God.

Fifth, verse 11 reveals that God gave much of Israel into the hands of foreign armies.[8] These places were overthrown suddenly and completely due to God's decision, just as Sodom and Gomorrah were. Leviticus 26:27 claims that God's discipline includes military defeat. When his people ignore loss after loss, they are on the brink of total and final destruction. Amos writes that what remained of Israel at this point was like "a brand plucked out of the burning" (4:11). Though spared from the fire, their escape did not lead them to return to their God.

Five levels of judgment have come and have been met by five levels of stubbornness. Israel refused to recognize and respond to God's evident restorative work. Natural disasters did not move them. Economic loss did not change them. Military disasters did not awaken them. Their stubborn march to oblivion continued. They were like lemmings going to the sea.

Unbelief has a terrible gripping effect—it binds us to spiritual rebellion and physical pain. Some of us may have trouble believing that God still uses historical events and natural disasters to discipline his people. J. A. Motyer wrote that Bible readers eventually have to decide if they will think as the Bible thinks or not.[9] He observed that we harm our own souls and those of others when we fail to recognize God's sovereignty and goodness in all realms of life.[10] God loves us, and he uses all the means at his disposal to discipline us for repentance and restored relationship. We need to take the opportunities that he gives us to come back to him. If troubles of any kind cause repentance, then we must be grateful that God loves us enough to take great pains to restore us.

### The End of God's Patience (4:12, 13)

The Bible portrays God as an extremely patient person. As Exodus 34:6, 7 puts it, he is "slow to anger, and abounding in steadfast love and faithfulness ... forgiving iniquity and transgression and sin." He was patient with Israel after the exodus, in the era of the judges, and throughout Biblical history. Amos 4:6–11 gives examples of that patience. Yet Exodus 34:7 also warns that God does not "clear the guilty." He takes purifying action. He puts an end to destructive behavior. In Amos 4:12, 13 God's prophet announces the end of God's patience. The people who have refused to return to their God must now prepare to meet him. They have no choice. Time is up.

Given their stubborn refusal to do what God wants, the people must now do something God had tried to avoid. He had sent disciplinary events to stave off the need for worse punishment. Rebuffed, he summons them for a face-to-face meeting in 4:12. He will encounter them in history, in person.[11]

When they meet him, it will not be as their gracious and patient covenant partner, because they have broken the covenant. Verse 13 says they will meet him as "he who forms the mountains and creates the wind"; in short, as the One who rules nature. They will meet him as the One who declares to people what they are thinking.[12] Nothing is hidden from him. He knows everything, so he can judge correctly. They will meet him as "the God of hosts," which means "the God of armies." The armies they face in the future are God's troops. God does not need weather forecasts to go to battle, for he controls the wind. He does not need flat ground to fight on, for he made the mountains. He does not need spies, for he knows the thoughts his opponents think. He does not need to raise an army or worry about reinforcements, for he has legions of soldiers at his command. This is the God his people must meet because they refused to return to him when he disciplined them.

The rich and greedy will soon meet God. They will learn what they refused to let discipline teach them. They will learn that God cannot tolerate sin and be loving and just. His patience cannot last forever, for sinners do not rule the world.

## Conclusion

Are you prepared to meet God? We have no option but to prepare to do so on his terms or face him as Creator and Judge rather than as Creator and Savior. Martyn Lloyd-Jones was a marvelous preacher, pastor, and spiritual adviser in twentieth-century Britain. A former doctor, he had no problem whatsoever reminding people they were going to die. In fact, he considered it foolish to avoid the question, "What will happen when you die?" The only issue, he reminded hearers, was whether we will die *in Christ* or *in our sins* (John 8:21).[13]

The people in Amos 4:1–5 foolishly acted as if they determined their own affairs. They gave no thought to death. Amos reminded them (and us) that we must all meet God. The Bible is clear that only those who trust in Jesus Christ and the reconciliation with God that he offers are truly prepared to meet their Maker. Have you prepared to meet God by meeting his Son, Jesus? If not, today can be your day of salvation.

Are you prepared to meet God? We Christians will one day stand before God to give an account of what we have done (see Romans 14:12; 2 Corinthians 5:10). God disciplines his people to make us sharper tools in his work (Hebrews 12:3–11). Do we see this discipline as love, as good in our lives (Romans 8:28)? Do we respond positively to his gracious use of time, nature, and history? I pray that we do, and I know that many of you do. Your lives testify to your growth in grace. May it always be so, for someday soon we will meet our God face-to-face.

# 24

# Seek the Lord and Live

AMOS 5:1–17

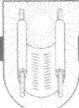

WE HAVE REACHED THE MIDPOINT of Amos's book, and Israel is at a national crossroads. Time has passed. Sin has piled upon sin. Most of the people show no sign of repenting. Therefore, God's punishing hand is raised. Enemies loom on the horizon. Israel has little time left before they suffer the consequences of their actions. With each passing day they are choosing to die rather than live.

Sensing the urgency in the situation, Amos 5:1–17 stresses the minor prophets' central theme. In 5:4 God tells Israel, "Seek me and live," and in 5:6 Amos says, "Seek the LORD and live."[1] This call to seek God is thus both a warning and a promise. It is a warning in that the people have a death sentence hanging over them. It is a promise in that seeking the Lord will protect them. With this great theme in mind, Amos directs the people to hear God's word in 5:1–3, to seek the Lord in 5:4–13, and to seek the good deeds that reflect their relationship with him in 5:14–17. Amos believes that those who truly hear God will seek him, and those who seek God will find him and the life he gives, and those who find the life he gives will pursue what he approves.

## Hear the Word of the Lord (5:1–3)

Public safety warnings have become a staple of American life. Flood warnings, tornado sirens, and fire alarms are lifesaving tools in a caring society. We question why people fail to respond when they hear them. God's prophets sounded the repentance and judgment alarm for his people. God sent prophets before disaster fell. He did so to save Israel from danger. When the people ignored the alarm, they chose danger over safety. Amos warns that as things stand now, Israel is as good as dead.

Amos begins by commanding Israel to "hear" what he has to say. He does not give them the kinds of messages we have read before. This time he sings a *qinah*, a funeral song, over them (v. 1).[2] The words of the song appear in verse 2: "Fallen, no more to rise, is the virgin Israel; forsaken on her land, with none to raise her up." This very sad song depicts Israel knocked to the ground, unable to rise, with no one around to give aid.

This funeral song indicates that God has left the Israelites to suffer the consequences of their actions. Israel would have no homeland unless God had given it to them. Israel would not have survived in the land had God not provided for them. Enemies would have routed Israel without God's protection. Therefore, if Israel lies beaten and forsaken, it is because they no longer enjoy God's covenant-based protection (cf. 2 Kings 14:23–27). Israel has begun to experience the consequences for disobedience outlined in Leviticus 26:14–39 and Deuteronomy 28:15–68. No wonder Amos sings a funeral song.

Amos 5:3 explains how death will occur. Places throughout Israel will be decimated. A city of 1,000 people will be reduced to 100. A squad of 100 soldiers will lose 90 percent of its men. War will do what it always does. It will devastate land and people.

All this sounds so final until we realize that Amos calls on Israel to hear this song and this report *before* the events described actually occur. He warns. He proclaims God's word so that the people will turn to the Lord while they still have time.

This passage is a bit like Charles Dickens's *A Christmas Carol*, when the third spirit, the Ghost of Christmas Yet to Come, shows Ebenezer Scrooge his grave. Moved, Scrooge wants to know if these are things that may be or things that must be. He is grateful that what he has seen are not things that must be. He is grateful for time to change, and he seizes the opportunity. By sending his dirge-singing prophet, God shows his warning grace to a straying people.

### Seek the Lord and Live (5:4–13)

Amos has given the people a glimpse of their own funeral in 5:1–3. Now he gives them glimpses of the pathway to life. Seeking God is the only way they can live, according to verse 4. The word "seek" denotes a persistent, regular, earnest, and demanding inquiring of God's will. People often sought God's will from a prophet or a priest at a shrine.[3] Yet in this passage God seems to be saying they do not need to go anywhere or seek the help of any prophet.

They need to turn to God himself. As Amos will soon state clearly, finding God's will is not like solving a mystery. Moses wrote what the people needed to know centuries before Amos prophesied.

Verse 5 reveals where they have been looking for God: they have been going to Bethel, Gilgal, and Beersheba. These were famous places. Jacob famously dreamed of angels ascending and descending at Bethel (Genesis 28:10–17). Gilgal was where Israel encamped before entering Canaan (Joshua 4:19). Abraham and Isaac encountered God at Beersheba (Genesis 21:33; 26:23–25). These historic places had become official sanctuaries where questionable practices occurred.[4] Amos 4:4 mentions Bethel and Gilgal as sites of self-serving religious practices. The Bible does not say much about the worship at Beersheba,[5] but it is safe to conclude that it was no better than what happened at Bethel and Gilgal. At those places the priests and people mixed the Biblical faith that God revealed through Moses with innovations that Jeroboam I (930–909 B.C.) introduced.[6] Bethel, Gilgal, and Beersheba were not places to find God. They were places for destruction.

Gilgal will "go into exile," (5:5), which God announces through a play on words in Hebrew. In a second play on words, he claims that Bethel, which means "house of God," will become a "house of nothing." Those who practice their religion there face exile. Those who seek God there find nothing. In fact, Israel did not need to go anywhere to seek God. They could seek him where they were through prayer and repentance.

In 5:6, Amos warns that fire will break out on Bethel, the king's own royal sanctuary (cf. 7:10–13). If the king's worship center is on fire, then it is safe to assume that an internal or external enemy controls the land. The reason that fire will consume Bethel is because it is part of the king's unjust and unrighteous policies. The king pays the priests and maintains the site. Thus, as 7:10–13 shows, Bethel's priests allow no criticism of the king. Therefore, the priests have no moral authority. They belong to the king, not to God.

But the king and the priests are not the only problem, according to 5:7. The people themselves turn the sweetness of "justice" into a bitter drink ("wormwood"). They turn the high goal of righteous living before God among one another into something to be cast to the ground. They do not value or practice justice and righteousness. They turn something good into something bad.

In contrast, God turns bad things into good things. Verse 8 says that God is the One

> who made the Pleiades and Orion,
> and turns deep darkness into the morning

and darkens the day into night,
who calls for the waters of the sea
and pours them out on the surface of the earth.

In short, God is their good Creator. He is also their judge, according to verse 9, for he "makes destruction flash forth against the strong, so that destruction comes upon the fortress." The people have every reason to believe, then, that if they seek the Lord, he can meet all their needs. They also have every reason to believe that he will judge them if they reject him. The One who made them and assesses their actions urges them to seek him, the all-powerful and all-seeing God. Amos offers them healing that only their Creator can give.

Unfortunately, verses 10–13 indicate that Israel does not want God's help, nor do they want to hear from God's prophet. Amos observes in 5:10, "They hate him who reproves in the gate, and they abhor him who speaks the truth." The Israelites he addresses have no use for true preachers of the word. Historically, when God's people reject God's messengers and refuse to seek the Lord, terrible results always occur. People who ignore God's commands to love their neighbor (see Leviticus 19:18, 34–37) and to respect their neighbor's life, property, and home (see Exodus 20:12–17) feel free to mistreat others. In 5:11 Amos notes that when the rich cast off God's expectations, they "trample on the poor" by levying unjust taxes. The rich use these extorted funds to build bigger homes for themselves. Furthermore, he adds in verses 12, 13 that they defeat and defraud the innocent ("the righteous") in court by bribing judges (v. 12), which silences wise and helpful people (v. 13).

These oppressors think they will get away with what they have done. But God spoke on this subject long before Amos's day. Six centuries earlier, Moses taught Israel God's ethical standards for his holy people (Leviticus 11:44), his kingdom of priests (Exodus 19:5, 6). He warned that when Israel broke his covenant, there would be consequences. He explained that those who pervert justice and take bribes merit God's judgment (Deuteronomy 28:19, 25). Such people may build houses and plant vineyards, but they will not keep them (v. 30). Therefore, Amos has God's word on his side when he writes in 5:11, "You have built houses of hewn stone, but you shall not dwell in them; you have planted pleasant vineyards, but you shall not drink their wine." God will ensure that the people's wickedness does not go unpunished. As Exodus 34:7 declares, God does not "clear the guilty." He knows who seeks his ways and who does not.

Failure to seek God is not a neutral act. It leads to self-centered behavior. It views human agendas as life's highest good. While human beings rarely act as badly as they can, pursuing our own plans can lead us down some very dark blind alleys. The book of Judges illustrates this point, as does Romans 1:18–32. Amos reveals that in pursuing personal wealth, many Israelites abandoned and used their neighbors. Not seeking God led to not seeking basic human decency. When we seek any god other than God, or a way of life other than the one chosen by the Giver of life, we are at the mercy of culture, circumstances, and current events.

Seeking God today requires us to first seek God in Jesus Christ, for no one comes to the Father except through him (John 14:6). Seeking Christ means trusting in him alone as our Savior, in his death for our sins as our only way to receive God's forgiveness, in his resurrection as our only means of eternal life, and in his will as our only way of life. Seeking Christ therefore requires recognizing and admitting our sins against God. It requires humbling ourselves before him and choosing his standards as our own. It requires keeping his commandments.

Once we trust Christ, seeking to do God's will becomes a way of life because he lives in us (Galatians 2:20). We pray, read the Bible, learn from good Biblical teachers, have friendship with other Christians, do the work God gives us to do, and learn from those who do not know Christ but live the way he teaches people to live. Abiding in God's ways brings joy, contentment, and proper challenge. As God reorients us, we become people committed to Jesus and his teachings, which we find in the Sermon on the Mount and elsewhere in the Gospels. We are not sinless, but we know where we are going. As Paul puts it in Philippians 3:13, 14, "One thing I do: forgetting what lies behind and straining forward to what lies ahead, I press on toward the goal for the prize of the upward call of God in Christ Jesus." Those who seek God as believers press on in uneven but certain triumph in Christ.

### Seek Good That You May Live (5:14–17)

Those who press on in seeking God gradually become like God. Romans 8:28, 29 encourages believers by stating that God works all things for our good so that we may be transformed into Christ's likeness. Similarly, Ephesians 2:8–10 states that God saves believers from sin so that we may do good works that God prepared for us to do before he created the world. Those who seek God and live therefore seek good while they live. They seek God because God first called them to hear his word (see Amos 5:1). They seek God because he warned them to do so (5:4–6). Thus the good they do praises God, who stands behind the work they do.

Amos 5:14 demonstrates that God's presence is the chief benefit of seeking good. Those who seek good by seeking God are assured that "the LORD, the God of hosts, will be with you." He is the Giver of life, so those who seek him will live. Of course, the bare fact that life can continue given the threat of judgment is good. Yet God's presence is the greatest gift a people committed to him desire. When Jesus sent his disciples to the ends of the earth in Matthew 28:16–20, the greatest promise he could give was his presence: "I am with you always, to the end of the age" (v. 20). The Apostle Paul states that God's Holy Spirit—his presence—gifts believers for service (1 Corinthians 12:1–11) and for ever-deepening godly character (Galatians 5:16–26).

Amos describes some of this character in 5:15a. Stated generally, those who through God's presence seek good "hate evil, and love good." In the Old Testament, the pairing of "hate" and "love" signals a choice for a particular purpose. The words do not convey loathing and emotional passion. Those who love God choose him, and he chooses them. For example, Malachi 1:2–5 says God loved Jacob and hated Esau. In the Biblical context, God was kind to both Jacob and Esau. Both received many blessings from God. Nonetheless, God chose Jacob to bear the promises made to Isaac and Jacob. God did not loathe Esau; he simply had other purposes for him. Those who love good choose it over evil. In this sense they hate evil. The verse in Amos encourages us to choose what is right.

More specifically, in Amos's day, those choosing good needed to reestablish "justice in the gate" (Amos 5:15a). They needed to avoid offering or receiving bribes (see v. 12). They needed to stop threatening God's prophets (v. 10) and mistreating honest folk (v. 12). They needed to treat their neighbors like people, not like dirt (v. 11). They needed to show that they loved good and hated evil. Only then would God demonstrate his gracious mercy (v. 15b). Only then would God stay his order of Israel's execution.

If no such repentance comes, if Israel continues to love evil and not good, then Amos 5:16, 17 reveals what Israel can expect.[7] The lament that 5:1 introduced will fill the land. From city square to rural Israel, the land will be filled with mourners (v. 16). Farmers and professional mourners will raise their voices as one. No part of and no person in Israel will escape (v. 17).

What is the source of this mourning? Oddly enough the answer is that God's presence will cause it. In 5:15 God promises his merciful presence to those who seek him and the good he wills in the world. In 5:17 he promises his punishing presence to those who refuse to obey. Egypt experienced this punishing presence in the exodus era when God passed through their midst while passing over the Israelites.[8] Now Israel must brace for their own experiencing of God's displeasure. But the blow has not fallen yet, so God's warning remains God's grace. Egypt's past does not have to become Israel's present.

## Conclusion

Some of the hardest funerals I have attended or conducted are those for a young person. These are particularly sad when a bad decision has led to death. The worst of them all is when a young person takes his or her own life. It is tragic when someone with seemingly years of life ahead chooses death. Such situations haunt us, leaving us with questions of what might have been had our loved one chosen life.

Amos implores Israel to seek the Lord and live. He laments the tragic, unnecessary choice the people are making and the consequences that choice will bring. As Hosea 8:7 says, the people are sowing the wind, but they will reap the whirlwind. They are planting greed, oppression, and injustice—in short, evil. They will harvest invasion, devastation, and death. So Amos sings a funeral dirge over them. But they are so busy sinning that they do not hear his song.

Do we hear the lament God sings for those choosing death? If we can discern even a faint echo of his warning, we should seek him and live. We should choose good over evil and walk in God's ways. God's own presence will direct us if we will but earnestly seek him. We do not have to endure his punishing presence. There is still time to cancel the funeral.

# 25

# Let Justice Roll Down

AMOS 5:18-27

THE CURRENT PASSAGE INCLUDES what is arguably Amos's best-known verse: "Let justice roll down like waters, and righteousness like an ever-flowing stream" (5:24). Like so many Bible verses, this one is often taken out of context by well-meaning people. It gets quoted by folks who rightly desire the end of injustice and corrupt human behavior. Yet one needs the whole context to understand how these principles turn into outcomes. Amos has stated clearly his and God's opposition to oppression of the poor, to bribery in the courts, and to lip service in religion. He has also made it clear that without a real relationship with God, one cannot understand or sustain just and right behavior. Without knowing the living God of the Bible, people revert to cultural pressures and personal preferences.

But with God, justice and righteousness are not only possible, they are necessary. Indeed, as we have learned already, God's justice is inevitable. This passage reminds us that our task is to know God, reflect his character, and fulfill his purposes in his world. Seeking God means seeking his justice and righteousness, or we are not seeking him at all. Seeking justice and righteousness without first seeking God is equally futile. Happily, Amos tells us that both God and justice can be found.

These verses begin a two-part emphasis on the woes associated with pursuing false religion (5:18–27) and self-serving luxury (6:1–14) without regard for justice and righteousness (5:24; 6:12). In the passages that follow these, Amos stresses the certainty of future judgment (see 7:1—9:10). Though the time of reckoning draws ever nearer, Israel still has time to turn from their sinful, destructive ways.

In this passage, Amos claims that Israel still has time to turn from their delusional desires and prepare for the day of judgment to come (5:18–20). There is still time to stop useless worship and start showing the fruits of a walk with God (5:21–24). There is still time to return to their spiritual roots before they are uprooted and thrown into a foreign land (5:25–27). There is still time, but Israel seems hardened in their ways, hardened against Amos's warnings. I fear that many of us have grown equally hardened. As God speaks to us through Amos, we must clear our ears, soften our hearts, and prepare to serve the living God—Father, Son, and Holy Spirit.

## Delusional Desires for Judgment Day (5:18–20)

Israel faced many problems. Their economy was fraying due to vast divisions between the poor and helpless and the rich and powerful. Neighboring countries sought to take chunks of Israel's territory and population (see Amos 1:3—2:3). People began to realize their dreadful situation. They desperately desired a solution. Where some of them turned may be a surprise.

They turned to theology. In particular, they turned to eschatology, the study of last things. Verse 18 says they longed for "the day of the LORD," the Biblical term for the day God judges his enemies and delivers his people.[1] They reasoned that God would crush their local and international foes and reward them for their belief in him. Times were hard for the moment, they thought, but God would soon put things right. Clearly they believed they were on the Lord's side and therefore had a very bright future. They convinced themselves they were the righteous ones.

Amos attacks their vain hope. He asks, "Why would you have the day of the LORD?" For them it will be "darkness, and not light." In fact, it will be a nightmare. In verse 19 he claims it will be like a man fleeing a lion only to meet a bear, then escaping into a house only to be bitten by a poisonous snake. He adds in verse 20 that for them, the day has only "gloom." There is no brightness in it for them. In short, they are the ones God will pursue when he judges. They will have nowhere to go, no place to hide, and no one to deliver them from God.[2] The day of the Lord will not be at all what they expect. It will bring them no comfort, no salvation.

Escapist theology did not die with Amos's audience. It endures today, taking on some specific forms. First, some fine Christians do not want to face a particularly hard situation. A loved one may be dying. A grown child may be acting badly. Their marriage may be troubled. Whatever the particulars of their circumstances, they will not deal with it realistically, which is another way of saying Biblically. Instead, they wish Jesus would come so they could avoid the issue. They escape to the future in an unhealthy way.

Second, some Christians take a dim view of all the sin in the world. They believe events prove that the world is getting worse by the day. In fact, forgetting large chunks of terrible human history (some of which happened in their lifetimes), they conclude the world has never been worse. These friends often take solace in believing only judgment day will sort it all out. So they quite often stop praying, ministering, and evangelizing. They also escape to the future in an unhealthy way.

Third, like the Israelites in Amos's day, some people believe themselves right with God when they are not. They trust in their place of birth, religious affiliation, or relative goodness compared to others, rather than in Jesus Christ. Other people are sinners, but they are not. Other people may need Jesus's atoning blood, but they do not. Like the Israelites, they think judgment day will punish the bad people and reward them. Their theological escapism is the most delusional of all, for they do not know God at all.

People who understand the day of the Lord tremble at the thought of it. They know that God's grace through Christ alone stands between them and well-deserved punishment. Given this awareness, they warn others to flee the wrath to come by accepting God's grace. Like Amos, they stay focused on God's redemptive work and do not take premature shelter in God's future judgment of the wicked. At the same time, they face the future with confidence, certain that God will end injustice of all kinds. Their theology has nothing to do with self-delusion.

### Let Justice Roll Down: The Fruits of Walking with God (5:21–24)

Israel did not just delude themselves with misguided end-times theology. Week by week and year by year they participated in religious observances that they thought must please God. Amos 4:4, 5 has already noted some of these practices. Israel thought the acts performed in worship were all that God asked of them. Thus if they came to the sanctuary at particular times with particular offerings, then surely God would be pleased. External religion was enough for them, so surely it was enough for God.

Amos 5:21 declares the opposite. God says, "I hate, I despise your feasts, and I take no delight in your solemn assemblies." Of course, these feasts were not the ones God revealed through Moses, and these assemblies did not occur in Jerusalem, the place God had chosen. As we learned before, Israel had followed an eclectic religion since the nation began in 930 B.C.[3] Yet as bad as meeting at the wrong times and wrong places was, this was not Israel's chief problem.

Similarly verses 22, 23 state that God does not approve of their sacrifices and singing. They bring lovely animals and sing lovely songs, but God will not look favorably upon their sacrifices or listen to their songs. Again the people had decided on their own what animals to bring, when to bring them, and what to sing when they did so. They preferred their own version of worship to what God gave them through Moses. Nonetheless, offering the wrong animals or strumming incorrect hymns, as bad as these were, was not their chief problem.

Their chief problem was that their lives did not reflect God's character. They did not know God. There was no fruit of their walk with God. Sacrifices, songs, festivals, and assemblies were supposed to reflect and fuel godly living. They were not supposed to provide cover for wicked behavior. Worship ought to be an outward reflection of an inner reality. For Israel during this era, worship services were simply meetings where attendees killed animals. This so-called worship was done in God's name by people who did not do God's will.

Amos 5:24 expresses what God wants faith and true worship to produce. God demands, "Let justice roll down like waters, and righteousness like an ever-flowing stream." The word translated as "justice" appears in many Old Testament contexts, always conveying the sense of proper decisions made. It stresses the need for correct charges, procedures, and verdicts. The word translated as "righteousness" conveys correct behavior in all circumstances. Taken together, the two words highlight the need for doing and deciding what is right in every realm of life, whether personal or societal.[4] As Thomas McComiskey explains, "Only when the personal concern of the law is incorporated into their social structure and 'rightness' characterizes their dealings with others will their worship be acceptable. A token practice of justice and righteousness will not do."[5] Believers in God practice justice and righteousness because God does. They produce the fruit of God's character because they walk with him. Their life and worship converge.

During the past few years there has been increased discussion in American society about justice. Harder financial times highlight disparities between the rich and the poor in areas such as wealth, educational opportunities, political clout, and health care. Everyone wants a fair shot at getting a satisfying piece of the nation's financial pie. By world standards the United States has a substantial pie. Such discussions tend to bring up other long-standing, understandable grievances over fairness in law courts, the treatment of the poor, immigration policy, fiscal responsibility, and a galaxy of related matters. Christians are part of the discussion, for they still constitute a healthy share of the general population. Evangelical believers join the conversation more often than in the past, which is appropriate for Bible-believing persons to do. Yet as Bible believers, they have an obligation to follow God's ways, not just represent Christians who argue no differently than secular people do. In fact, they know there is no lasting justice without following God's ways.

How does Amos help us answer God's demand that righteousness and justice flow like a mighty river? Though one chapter in a commentary cannot begin to answer this question in all its complexity, perhaps it can help us get started.

First, Amos 5:21–24 refuses to separate worship and righteousness. One cannot bring offerings to God while living off the backs of others and expect God to be pleased. Sacrifices and songs that are not backed up by behavior faithful to God's character and God's spoken word sicken him. Like Amos, Jesus makes it very clear that we cannot worship God *and* money (see Matthew 6:24). Paul and the author of Hebrews agree (see 1 Timothy 6:10; 2 Timothy 3:2–4; Hebrews 13:5). People who believe that money is the most important thing in life will use others to get money. This is the essence of unrighteousness, of ungodliness. Such folk can use part of that money to give gifts to the Church, but God is not impressed. Unlike many persons and institutions, he does not want dirty money.

The love of money has always been a danger. America did not invent lust for cash, but we are doing our best to perfect it. Currently our government, general culture, advertising, and economic systems teach us that human beings are first and foremost consumers. We are told that we exist to buy things. We are taught that it is our duty to make, borrow, and spend money. Thrift, saving, and conservation are valued mainly, if not solely, for how they allow one to consume later. Therefore, people, their labor, and their production are all treated as sheer commodities. They are all esteemed according to what they cost, consume, and control. No wonder, then, that people get used and thrown away in American culture.[6]

Christians cannot agree with or give in to this way of thinking. There is no way to baptize it or adapt it, for it is corrupt at its core. Like the writer of Genesis 1:26, 27, Amos believed people were made by God (4:13; 5:8, 9) in his image. Thus they shared in a "covenant of brotherhood," according to Amos 1:9. More than that, believers have made a covenant with God that directs their faith and its expression, according to 2:4—4:13. Because they know God, believers are required to love God with all their hearts (Deuteronomy 6:4–6) and their neighbors as themselves (Leviticus 19:17, 18, 34–37). They cannot treat people as consumers and commodities. They cannot put money above people and claim to know God, who created people in his image and sent his followers to declare his love to all persons. All the singing, offerings, and numerical growth in the world cannot make up for loving money more than God and people. Those who do so know nothing about God's righteousness, or they have forgotten what they once knew.

Second, Amos 5:21–24 refuses to separate worship and justice. The courts were corrupted by bribes, according to 5:12. Clearly when paying judges is necessary for one to get a favorable verdict, the poor are out of luck. Corrupt laws allowed people to be sold into slavery for small debts, according to 2:6, 7. Obviously a lender would prefer to have a person's labor rather than receive a small payment. This system violated the laws of lending and debt forgiveness outlined in Leviticus 25:35–55 and elsewhere. People were victims of unjust laws and crooked practices. When they tried to get justice in court, a bribed judge denied their claims (Amos 5:12). Under such conditions, the poor stay poor. Ironically the rich eventually run out of human capital to exploit and their profits recede. Injustice proves self-defeating in an incredibly short period of time.

Believers cannot accept such things as normal or inevitable. Christian businesspeople, judges, lawyers, and legislators must speak and act for justice. Christians can decide to learn about where goods come from and how they are produced. They can decide not to support the oppression of others by what they buy, how they vote, how they educate the next generation, and what they preach. But Christians will never act correctly in these matters unless and until they desire God's justice and righteousness more than they love money. Until we stand for justice, our so-called worship pleases no one but ourselves.

Sometimes we despair of making any real changes. But we can take heart. I live and work in Birmingham, Alabama. Sixty years ago and longer, brave men, women, and children stood against the injustice of Jim Crow segregation laws. Many paid for their convictions with their lives. But things changed. In Alabama the changes were led by ministers such as Martin Luther King Jr. and Fred Shuttlesworth, and by unheralded rank-and-file Christians of many types. Nonbelievers likewise played a huge role.

In his famous "Letter from a Birmingham Jail," King reminded clergy, "Injustice anywhere is a threat to justice everywhere." He further warned, "Far from being disturbed by the presence of the church, the power structure of the average community is consoled by the church's silent—and often even vocal—sanction of things as they are. But the judgment of God is upon the church as never before. If today's church does not recapture the sacrificial spirit of the early church, it will lose its authenticity, forfeit the loyalty of millions, and be dismissed as an irrelevant social club."[7] King's warning is as true today as it was sixty years ago. Yet his warning also reminds us that people who stand for justice can make a difference. Even if not, God still demands obedience.

Let me conclude by noting that Amos does not give us a big program for restoring justice. He insists that we do right where we are. God leads some of his people to individual action and some to corporate action. Those who take God's view of people, money, and worship find his ways. They follow his voice, as Amos did when he left home and made his way north to confront Israel. Are we ready to listen and act? Are we ready to produce the fruit of truly knowing God?

### Returning to Spiritual Roots (5:25–27)

In Amos 5, God does not ask the people to accept some brand-new religious outlook. He calls them back to their most basic spiritual roots. In Amos 5:25 he asks them, "Did you bring to me sacrifices and offerings during the forty years in the wilderness, O house of Israel?" This question takes them back to the exodus era. It does not imply that sacrifices were not part of God's plan for them; since God clearly ordered Moses to teach them about acceptable sacrifices.[8] Rather, it reminds the people that God's deliverance and their faith in him came first. Without their relationship with God, the sacrifices mean nothing.

Yet Israel has forgotten this basic truth. They seem unaware that sacrifices did not save them then and cannot save them now.[9] God saved them. By faith they left Egypt under his protection. Israel needs to nurture their relationship with God, not raise more animals for slaughter. Having bribed men, they think they can bribe God. They need to have the sort of faith in him that they had at the dawn of their history.

Instead of returning to foundational faith, however, they revert to the worst practices of their early years. The reason they had to spend "forty years in the wilderness" was because they did not believe God capable of giving them the land (see Numbers 14:11, 12). As a result, they turned against Moses and toward idols (see, e.g., Numbers 25:1–9). According to Amos 5:26, the Israelites of Amos's day worshiped Sikkuth and Kiyyun. These were probably Egyptian or Syrian astral deities.[10] The Israelites chose those gods over the Lord who delivered them from Egypt. They copied their ancestors' worst habits.

Since this is the case, Israel can expect another time of punishment. Israel's first generation spent forty years in the desert because of their unbelief. Verse 27 says that this generation will go "into exile beyond Damascus."

Unbelief and idolatry result in exile. No amount of animal sacrifice can change this scenario.

The Bible often asks straying believers to think back to their beginnings. Hosea started over with Gomer to represent how God renews relationship with his people (Hosea 3). The Apostle Paul urged the Galatians to recall that they were saved by "hearing with faith," not "by works of the law" (Galatians 3:2). The Lord told the Ephesians to "repent," return to their first love, and do the works they "did at first" (Revelation 2:4, 5). When we become discouraged, confused, or rebellious, sometimes it is best to get back to basics. It is best to recall that God saved us, gave us the gift of faith, and gives us good work to do, as Ephesians 2:1–10 teaches. It is good to remember that we worship God because of who he is and what he has done to make us new creations in Christ (2 Corinthians 5:17–21). Our worship delights God when we take this approach. Any thought that we can manipulate God through our religious activities is simply foolish. When we think this way, we must return to our spiritual roots.

## Conclusion

Amos has once again reminded us of some fundamental truths and has tried to get us to see reason. This time he has declared that only a delusional people could long for judgment day while sinning against God. He has told us that "purely ceremonial religion can never safeguard the truth or hold . . . people to the truth."[11] Rather "faith apart from works is dead," as James 2:26 states. Justice and righteousness are the fruits of true faith, not sacrifice and song. Amos has counseled us to get back to basics.

As we know, Amos was a veteran farmer. By now he may have felt as if he had labored hard in the fields of Israel. He had sown the seed of God's word. It seemed that these seeds fell on stony ground. Though probably tired, he did not quit. He kept on working, hoping to turn Israel to God. Through his book, he keeps preaching twenty-seven centuries later. His warnings echo down the years to us. He keeps farming souls.

Do not harden your heart to his words. There is still time to turn to Christ. There is still time to turn away from pretending to worship God while engaging in injustice, all the while saturated with greed. There is still time to do God's work and to "let justice roll down" (Amos 5:24). But we should not wait any longer. Those who wait too long find themselves in the desert, or beyond Damascus in exile, or in a place where the fire never stops and the worm of death never dies (see Isaiah 66:24). If justice does not roll down, judgment will roll through our lives and through our land, for God's justice will prevail.

# 26

# Undisturbed by Injustice

AMOS 6

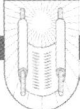

IN 5:18–27 AMOS GAVE US a view of worshipers who longed for the day of the Lord despite their unjust ways. Now he takes us to where Samaria's wealthy leading citizens hold their parties.[1] The people he portrays in this passage are unconcerned about the day of judgment, if indeed they believe in it. Self-indulgent pleasure is their god, and they worship their idol shamelessly, relentlessly, and successfully. Injustice fuels their lifestyle, so it does not disturb them at all. In fact, injustice is shattering their country, but they are blind to that reality. Instead, they are puffed up with nationalistic pride, materialism, and militarism. Therefore, Amos informs these social and cultural leaders that they will lead the way as Israel goes into exile.

In a sermon preached March 4, 1560, John Calvin described such persons and why they act as they do.

> Why is it that the great of this world, when they trust in their renown, in their might, in their munitions, in all the means they have to defend themselves with, act like they despise God, as the psalm says (cf. *Psa.* 10) and say that no storm can touch them and that they are exempted from the rank and file of common men? What is the reason for that except they are like blind men, deprived of common sense and ignorant of their weakness? They do not realize that everything here below is only wind and smoke.[2]

Calvin would not disagree with my adding that even if they think that life is wind and smoke, they do not turn to God, the Creator (see Amos 4:13; 5:8, 9). Amos says that they turn to themselves—their prominence (6:1–3), their money (vv. 4–7), their military (v. 8), and their manner of living (vv. 11–13).

Amos reminds us that those who live this way face coming trouble (v. 1). Judgment will overtake them (vv. 7, 14). He warns that these people, these ones undisturbed by injustice and unmoved by their nation's shattering (vv. 6,14), face a devastating future.

### Their Prominence (6:1–3)

Amos announces a "woe" on people who are "at ease in Zion" and who "feel secure on the mountain of Samaria" in 6:1. Thus, he includes both Judah and Israel, as he did in 2:4–15 and 3:1. Mentioning Judah keeps his audience from claiming that he overlooks the sins committed in his home country while denouncing Israel's sins.

The people he describes are seemingly carefree. They think their future is set. Amos addresses "notable men"—gentlemen marked by their importance, who live in what they consider the finest ("first") of all nations, Israel (6:1b). As Duane Garrett has explained, Amos "speaks to the conceit of the aristocracy of Samaria, who think of themselves as the best people of the best country in the world."[3] No one except an Israelite would have considered Israel the greatest nation of its time. Perhaps these men think Israel is a great place because "the house of Israel," the people of the land, must come to them for money and legal decisions (v. 1c). They are what a friend of mine used to call "big fish in a small pond."

But the big fish do not admit that they live in a small pond. Verse 2 quotes,[4] or at least reflects, their boastful speech. They think their cities are greater than Syria's Calneh and Hamath, not to mention Philistia's Gath (v. 2). Amos chooses these once-important places either because Israel or Judah rules them or because they have been conquered by foreign armies recently.[5] Either way, Samaria and Jerusalem are not bigger or less vulnerable to regional or distant foes. Saying otherwise is sheer bravado.

Amos 6:3 tells how things really are. Their big talk is just a way of putting "the day of disaster" far from their minds. The phrase probably refers to the day of the Lord, the very "day" they seem to disregard. Putting that day far from their minds has brought "near the seat of violence." Amos may mean that they bring violence near in the form of a coming destruction (see vv. 9, 10, 14). Or he may mean that the more they refuse to think of divine judgment, the more they act violently against others in their daily lives (see Amos 2:6, 7). Amos probably intends to convey both meanings, for both are true.

Their big talk stems from misguided, self-centered, and godless devotion to their country and culture. They probably considered themselves patriotic. They seem to have an "Israel first" mentality. As 6:4–7 will show, however, they are really "me first" Israelites. They equated their personal interest with the public's interests, without consulting the public.

We must beware of repeating their sins. Such personal selfishness feeds nationalism, the tendency to claim that our people are special and that our nation is the greatest in the world. On the one hand, it is good to love, cherish, and protect your people and your land. We should love our neighbors as ourselves (Leviticus 19:17, 18, 34–37) and care for the land that sustains us (Genesis 1:26–31). On the other hand, God requires believers to be humble in all realms of life and grateful to him for all good things (see James 1:16, 17; 1 Peter 5:6, 7). If so, how can Christians proclaim their land and their people as exceptional, the greatest, or always right? If so, how can Christians put their government's decrees above God's? In American history, conservative, moderate, and liberal Christians alike have fallen prey to so-called Christian nationalism—the belief that making America great is the best way to make Christianity great, or the belief that making Christianity great is a tool for making America great. This sort of thinking is exactly how German people lost their way in the 1920s and 1930s.

My wife once said the following profound sentence: "The word 'Christian' makes a bad adjective." She was and is right. Thus combinations like "Christian nationalism," "Christian Republican," "Christian Democrat," "Christian capitalist," and "Christian Socialist" are wrongheaded. Following Christ defines all that we are. Let other words specify what kind of Christian we are. Remind yourself that you are not primarily a party member or a certain kind of economic advocate. Remind yourself that you are a believer in Jesus Christ, and let the adjectives grow from Biblical truth anchored in our Lord's teachings. Anything else "bring[s] near the seat of violence" (Amos 6:3), whether we intend to do so or not.

## Their Money (6:4–7)

Amos pronounces a second woe on the prominent people in 6:4. He goes on to describe their opulent lifestyle in 6:4–6a, its effect on them in 6:6b, and what God will do about it in 6:7. Their love of luxury reveals their materialism, their love of money and objects above all else. It also reveals their callous and indifferent hearts.

The wealthy people in Samaria have the best of ancient luxuries.[6] According to verse 4, their beds are decorated with ivory carvings (v. 4a). They eat tender beef and mutton on a regular basis in an era in which most Israelites might have expected to eat meat only on a few special occasions each year (v. 4b). Verse 5a notes that they own expensive instruments that they use while writing new songs.[7] They take the sort of care to write their feasting songs that David used in writing songs about God (v. 5b). Verse 6a says they drink wine from specially crafted bowls normally used in religious ceremonies.[8] They choose only "the finest oils" to anoint their skin (v. 6b). They have what their hearts desire.

Sadly, having what their hearts desire hardens them against what God's heart desires. They "are not grieved over the ruin of Joseph" (v. 6c). Here "Joseph" stands for the whole land of Israel, the very people that he suffered to protect (Genesis 50:19, 20). His descendants have become rich like Joseph did, but their wealth makes them indifferent to their brothers and sisters. The country they consider so great (Amos 6:1) is decaying around them, but they do not care. Perhaps they are so hardened that they are incapable of caring. Their materialism has led to impenetrable callousness. They are undisturbed by injustice, the sin that 5:18–27 identified as crucial in their situation.

By now you know what comes next. With no hint of repentance in the air, God will judge them guilty and enforce the penalty for their actions. Amos 6:7 announces that these "first" citizens (6:1) will be "the first of those who go to exile" (v. 7). They are leaders, but they have been leading others into horrible losses that they can hardly fathom. They will lose everything they hold dear, including their beloved luxuries. Over the next several decades Israel experienced these losses, chiefly under the hand of the Assyrian Empire.

More than seven centuries later, Jesus spoke the following words: "Woe to you who are rich, for you have received your consolation. Woe to you who are full now, for you shall be hungry. Woe to you who laugh now, for you shall mourn and weep. Woe to you, when all people speak well of you, for so their fathers did to the false prophets" (Luke 6:24–26). Jesus had in mind the sort of people that Amos warned. The people who heard Amos had about twenty years before their many exiles began. The people who heard Jesus had less than forty years before Rome would blast through Judea, devastating Jerusalem in the process.

With more than twenty-seven centuries of warning about nationalism, materialism, and hardened hearts in our hands, we are truly without excuse. While some preachers may focus on how the behavior of non-Christians leads to disaster, I focus on myself and other regular churchgoers. The American church has gone deep into nationalism and materialism. Many of us gladly support politicians with low moral standards if they run under our party's banner. Many of us think that God's will and America's will are indistinguishable. Many of us love money and comfort. Many of our fellow professing believers put pleasure-seeking and money-making above our Christian community. As we do, so we bring near disasters of all sorts, as Amos 7:12–17 will reveal. It is time to soften our hearts and hear God's word.

### Their Military (6:8–10)

Amos has so far pronounced coming woe on Israel's chief citizens because they trust in their prominence and their money. Now he adds their trust in their military might. He hinted at this misplaced trust in 6:4, and he will deal with it explicitly again in 6:13. Here he emphasizes their pride in their fortified cities (v. 8) and declares that these towns will be emptied (vv. 9, 10).

It is hard to imagine a more emphatic statement than verse 8. God swears that what he announces will occur. Indeed, he swears by his own name since there is no higher power (cf. 4:2; 8:7). He uses two very strong words, "abhor" and "hate" (6:8) to state how much he dislikes their pride in their "strongholds," their cities that contain military installations. Put in today's terms, Amos might say that God hates our nuclear silos and our many military bases around the world. However strong Israel's defenses may be, God will deliver the place and its people to the enemy.

The losses will be catastrophic. Ten men was the smallest military unit in Israel. Verses 9, 10 portray one small unit left in one house. Presumably the rest of the soldiers have fought, fled, or died. None will survive. An aged relative will come and clear the bodies. This relative will be so scared of what God might do next that he will stop those seeking survivors from using God's name. Regardless, God is not with them to deliver them from danger. The army will be decimated.

Israel's military is no more able to stave off judgment than Israel's prominence or wealth. No army can stop God when he decides that a place will fall. Joel made that point clear in his first chapter. In Biblical times Egypt, Assyria, Babylon, Persia, and Greece were massively powerful empires. Each one fell. Again we must take note. Christians who trust in the power of American military might rather than in God are on the wrong side of history, not just on the wrong side of theology. The histories of the Roman Empire, the Japanese Empire, the British Empire, and the Soviet Empire can tell us that. The histories of the American Empire and the Chinese Empire will one day say the same thing. These are temporary powers in an old and enduring world. Christians know that the only enduring power rests in the Creator, the ever-living God. His kingdom is forever, and he has entrusted it to Jesus Christ and those who love him. Pride in one's military is as foolish as pride in one's prominence and one's possessions.

## Their Planning (6:11–14)

Throughout this passage, the wealthy people that Amos addresses have been making and executing plans that are the very opposite of God's plans. They live for themselves. They seek high positions and luxury. God's plan is for people to love him and to love others above themselves (Leviticus 19:17, 18, 34–37; Deuteronomy 6:4–6). His plan is for people to "seek good, and not evil" (Amos 5:14a). They seek security in their military. He offers security through his presence (v. 14b). Now Amos declares that God plans to devastate their big homes (6:11). He plans to unseat their plans to make injustice a societal norm (v. 12). He plans to reverse their military gains by sending an opponent that Israel cannot defeat (vv. 13, 14). Amos warns that their plans should follow God's plans. Any other plan is a bad plan.

Verse 11 is a bridge verse. It links 6:8–10 and 6:12–14. Bringing forward the image of an empty house in 6:9, 10 Amos states that God will bring down the big houses that the wealthy have built on the bent backs of the poor. He will pound the building stones into pebbles. His phrasing reminds me of Jesus's telling his disciples that not one stone of Jerusalem's impressive buildings would be left upon another (Matthew 24:1, 2).

In Amos 6:12, he exposes their terrible planning. Horses do not run on rocks and a farmer does not have his oxen plow on rocks. Doing so would just be stupid. Yet they have done something equally stupid. They have "turned justice into poison and the fruit of righteousness into wormwood." They have reversed God's plan that righteousness would lead to justice in the land, as 2:6–16; 4:1–3; and 5:18–27 have made abundantly clear. The word "righteousness" refers to the right actions of people in right relationship with God. Psalm 1 probably offers the Bible's clearest definition of a righteous person. A righteous person is one who knows God and therefore lives by God's instructions in his world. Justice is one fruit, one result of such relational living. As Amos has indicated (5:7), the Israelites in his day throw down justice as if it were garbage. Indeed, they throw down people as if they were garbage.

Amos 6:13 offers an example of their bad thinking and their bad planning. They think it was by their own strength that they captured Lo-debar and Karnaim. As Doug Stuart explains, the first place was a border town in Galilee, and the second was a place between Samaria and Damascus. Jeroboam II captured both because God took mercy on Israel (see 2 Kings 14:25–28).[9] God gave them relief from oppression, but they thought they had won a mighty victory through their strategy and military prowess.

Finally, Amos 6:14 reveals that because of their sins, God will defeat them from north to south. This is the very territory that 2 Kings 14:25 states that God gave Israel in Jeroboam II's time. Everything he achieved will be reversed. Israel thought they had defeated an oppressor, so now they could oppress their own people, not just those they conquered. They had the exact opposite belief from what God intended.

My cousin Cary is a successful man. When asked how to operate in business, in an extended family, or in any other realm of life, he always says one thing: "Proper planning prevents poor performance." Many of us who know him have attempted to state the opposite, something like "Pitiful planning produces poor performance." He does not even want to contemplate the opposite.

Israel had contemplated the opposite of God's good plans. They had performed their pitiable substitutes for God's blessings. Now the time drew near when they would pay for their poor planning, and the payment was destitution and death.

## Conclusion

It must have been very hard for Amos to see the Israelites continue down the path of destruction. In the first six chapters, he has tried to lead them away from deadly national and personal pride, materialism, militarism, and misguided planning and turn them to God. He has spared no one in his quest. Unfortunately, as Kyle Yates observed, "With increasing clarity and intensity, he has reached the sad and somber conclusion that only destruction and captivity lie ahead."[10]

Ultimately, the people had bad hearts. They were satisfied with injustice. They were satisfied with unrighteousness. They liked the temporary results of oppression more than they liked the favor of God. They did not grieve over their ruin. The lion was roaring (Amos 1:2), but they refused to hear and fear. Their days were numbered, whether they believed that or not. Assyria's invasions of Israel did not occur for a decade or two, depending on how you date the book of Amos. Before then, however, lots of the people Amos addressed died and met their own personal day of judgment. The fall of many souls always precedes the fall of nations.

Amos offered the people the good news that they could seek the Lord and live (5:4). They did not have to stay in their oppressive, unjust ways. Jesus told people the same thing while he was on earth. Now the Church takes up this message of hope. Times may be hard, and days may be dark, but those who seek the Lord Jesus find him, and they find his peace and his forgiveness. Whatever a person's circumstances, there is still time to seek him and live. There is time to stop being satisfied with injustice.

# 27

# No More Delaying of Judgment

AMOS 7

I LIVED IN A STATE that still executes some persons convicted of capital murder. There were few enough executions that our local television news often did a story when they occurred. The reporters typically stated when the murder was committed, how long the prisoner had been on death row, and how many appeals and stays of execution there had been. Often there had been decades of reprieves. Eventually time would run out.

Amos has been warning Israel that a time of severe judgment approaches. He has declared that the people have time to repent and avoid punishment, but they need to act—and act quickly. He has warned Judah, Israel, and other nations of their sins' consequences in chapters 1—2. In chapters 3—6 he has tried to get Israel to repent of various forms of injustice. The book has reported no positive responses like those we read about in Jonah, Haggai, and Zechariah. So far Israel's execution has been delayed, but it has not been canceled.

In chapters 7—9 we learn that the season of warning has concluded. Now Amos states how things will end for Israel. In chapter 7 he begins this final section of the book by reporting three visions and an encounter he had with the high priest of Bethel. The chapter unfolds in three parts: no more pardons (7:1–9), no more preaching (7:10–13), and no more divine protection (7:14–17).

## No More Pardons (7:1–9)

Amos loved the Israelites. He did not want to see them crushed under the weight of their own sins, even a destruction of their own making. In fact, in this passage he asks God not to judge the people as they deserve. Jeremiah followed in Amos's footsteps a century later. Early in his ministry he often asked God to overlook Judah's sins. God eventually ordered him to stop praying for this (Jeremiah 11:14; 14:11). Both Amos and Jeremiah accepted God's decision in their respective times. Never forget that they were loving people. Their messages were urgent, not mean-spirited. They did not enjoy chastising people.

Amos reports three visions in 7:1–9. In the first vision (vv. 1–3), God "showed" or caused Amos to see a phenomenon of nature. Locusts were "forming" in April, as the "latter" growth sprouted (v. 1a). The king had already taken his portion of the crop, so what remained belonged to the farmers (v. 1b). Amos apparently saw a massive number of locusts, something like what Joel 1:2–20 describes. The locust swarms "[eat][1] the grass of the land" (Amos 7:2a). The timing of this devastation would have left nothing for the people of the land to cultivate, harvest, and sell. The dry season had begun. No rain would fall for six long months. Amos sees a major disaster unfolding.

He does not accept what he sees as simply what the people deserve. In verse 2 he asks God to "forgive." This is the standard word that Old Testament texts use to describe forgiveness of sins (see Leviticus 4:26, 31, 35). He gives two reasons for his request. First, "Jacob"—a personal name for the nation called Israel at this time—could not "stand" in the face of what he would endure (Amos 7:2). A literal reading of the Hebrew would be "he cannot rise." Such a cataclysmic event would bring the people to their knees. Second, Amos claims that Jacob is "so small" (v. 2b). Their leaders may think the nation is mighty (compare 6:1–7), but Amos knows the truth.

So does God. Therefore, verse 3a states that he "relented" from carrying out the devastation he showed Amos. Depending on the context, the word translated as "relented" can refer to one having sorrow or regret, changing one's mind, sighing, taking or giving comfort, or turning aside from a course of action.[2] Since the context here is like Hosea 11:1–9,[3] either "relented" or "had compassion" is the best rendering. God was set on a particular, viable course of action, but he did not complete that course of action. He relented, which comforted Amos (7:3). Why did God do so? Because he is gracious, compassionate, and patient, as Exodus 34:6, 7 proclaims.

In the second vision (Amos 7:4–6), Amos sees God declaring or "calling for" a trial[4] ("judgment by [means of] fire" in verse 4.[5] The results of this fire were even worse than the locust plague. The fire "devoured"[6] the waters underground and "was eating up" vegetation above ground (v. 4b). The image may be of a subterranean fire or of a severe drought. Regardless, water will be in short supply above or below ground. As with the locust swarm, the lack of water would create a terrible agricultural and economic crisis. Many would die.

Amos intercedes for the people again. In verse 5 he asks God to "cease," to stop the horrible event. He repeats his claim that Israel will not be able to rise from such a blow, for Israel is too small. As before, God does not do what the vision portrayed (v. 6). Israel has more time. God's patience endures.

But it is not endless. A third vision follows. Amos sees God "positioned over a wall of tin" in verse 7.[7] In other words, God looms over a wall made of tin. Why tin? In ancient Palestine, tin was an expensive metal imported and "used almost exclusively as an alloy of bronze from which weapons were made."[8] Amos 6 highlights Israel's trust in their weapons. This vision shows that God has authority over their protective walls of weaponry. Thus he has been the One protecting them. The metal that makes their weapons is in his hand. He can use that metal to protect them or to attack them.

God clarifies the vision's meaning and prevents Amos from praying further in 7:8b, 9. He will put the military-grade tin "in the midst" of his people Israel, and he will "never again pass by them." The translation "never again" is too exclusive in current English usage. He has been passing by them, not judging them, but now he will judge them. The worship places for idols that have fixed buildings ("the sanctuaries"), the worship places for idols in the open air ("high places"), and the royal lineage of Jeroboam II will all meet their end (v. 9). All this will occur due to "the sword," the symbol of war. Presumably the sword will contain tin as an alloy.

The prophet's intercession and God's patience have reached their limits. Exodus 34:6, 7 states that God is patient and forgiving, yet it also warns that God does not clear the guilty. His patience is never indifference. It is never license. People forget this at their own peril. God has decided it is time for Israel's sins to be judged. Amos does not ask God to relent again. He accepts God's timing, just as he has accepted God's call in his life. There will be no more pardons, no more reprieves.

At least two applications deserve our attention. First, intercessory prayers for God's mercy must accompany Christian ministry. Since God is merciful, we must also be merciful. Asking God to delay judgment is not trying to get a harsh God to back off from a mean course of action. It amounts to praying in concert with how God's character operates through the long corridors of time. Second, it is necessary to accept God's decisions about the timing of judging wickedness. We will always hope that those we love will have time to change.

We can count on God's goodness. But we must accept God's timing for punishment, just as we welcome God's timing for blessing.

### No More Preaching! (Amos 7:10–13)

In case there has been any wondering about how people took to Amos's message, the next segment gives an idea. His preaching at Bethel must have caused a stir, for "Amaziah the priest of Bethel" felt compelled to send a report to the king. Amaziah also felt compelled to confront Amos and to offer him some "friendly advice." The upshot is that Amaziah felt that Israel's king, religion, and political environment would all be better if there was no more of Amos's preaching.[9]

Amaziah's reaction shows that he was completely devoted to and dependent on the king. His report to Jeroboam in 7:10, 11 about the effects of Amos's message mentions nothing about God or righteousness. Rather, he tells the king that Amos is a threat to peace and royal authority (v. 10). He claims Amos has said that either Jeroboam himself or Jeroboam's lineage will die by the sword, perhaps a reference to 7:9, and that Amos has declared Israel will go into exile (v. 11). His whole concern seems to be geopolitical.

But when Amaziah addresses Amos, we learn Amaziah's true concerns. Verse 12 shows that he assumes that Amos is preaching to "eat bread" (v. 12a); in other words, for the financial support he gets from it. So he tells Amos to go home to Judah where it is safer for him and preach there for money and food (v. 12). In verse 13 Amaziah tells Amos not to preach again in Bethel, "for it is the king's sanctuary," which means that the monarchy supports it financially (v. 13a). Indeed, it is "a temple of the kingdom" (v. 13b), which probably means it is a national shrine.[10] Amaziah's argument seems to be that when Amos preaches against Bethel, he preaches against the whole kingdom, and doing so is dangerous. It appears that Amaziah thinks Amos has the same motives for "ministry" that he has. Amaziah has gained money, position, and power from his religious activities. He cannot imagine giving these up, and he expects Amos to operate out of the same sort of expedient self-preservation.

One might argue that Amaziah operates out of misguided patriotism. He speaks what he feels is best for his king, people, and country. He may feel responsible for stopping crazy prophets from harming himself or others (compare Jeremiah 29:26). Let me repeat that he says nothing whatsoever about God. His response puts his nation in the place of the God he claims to serve.

Amaziah's solution to Israel's ills is for Amos to stop preaching the truth. This important priest wants to keep a lid on social unrest and keep his secure position in the process. He finds religion a useful tool for a good living. He finds currying favor with the king a prudent and effective way to be a priest. Through the centuries his number is legion. Self-promoting and politically well-placed religious leaders who have cautioned people like Amos have always been around, and they always will be. In our own time we have seen many ministers cozy up to presidents and governors and senators and congressmen and mayors and commissioners, supposedly to influence them for good when the real purpose has been to get themselves close to power, to enhance their ministry brand, and to make themselves feel important. Beware of the Amaziah near you!

Also, beware of closing your ears to the truth. Biblical preaching, rightly defined and presented with love, is not our enemy. In fact, it is the warning we need most.

### No More Divine Protection (Amos 7:14–17)

Amos has heard what Amaziah has said. Now he replies. Interestingly, he does not respond in anger. He does not say that he will preach where, when, and how he likes. Rather, he explains how it was that he came to preach in Israel (Amos 7:14, 15). Only then does he give Amaziah a terrible concluding prediction (vv. 16, 17). This prediction stresses that Israel's ending has begun. The God who forgave and protected in 7:1–6 will no longer protect Israel from the consequences of their actions.

Amos addresses Amaziah's misconceptions in 7:14, 15. Basically he tells Amaziah that his prophetic work has been a recent development. He had not been a prophet or had any training to be a prophet. The phrase "a prophet's son" refers to those who were pupils of prophets like Elisha (see 2 Kings 2:3–5; 4:1; 6:1; 9:1) or a member of a group of established prophets (see 1 Kings 20:35).[11] Amos reports that he was a farmer instead, one who tended trees that produced figs and who took care of sheep (7:14).[12] God sent him to prophesy to Israel; otherwise, he would still be pursuing his previous work (v. 15). He has been preaching God's words, not a politically or financially motivated message.

Though Amaziah has misunderstood Amos's mission, Amos understands perfectly what Amaziah has said to him. According to verse 16, Amaziah wants him to stop preaching negatively about Israel. Amaziah does not know that Amos's preaching has been God's lifeline to Israel. God has graciously sent an unusual messenger with urgent news. Amaziah's response is to demand that there be no more preaching.

Amaziah does not know that no more preaching means no more pardons. Left to their own devices, the people will no longer enjoy God's protection from harm. In 7:17, Amos gives Amaziah the sober news that Israel's rejection of God's call to repent will unleash war. War creates the situation that the chapter's final verse describes. During times of war young people "fall by the sword," people "go into exile," and women are abused. Choosing war is not the glorious thing that the people in Amos 6 think it will be. Choosing war means choosing nightmare scenarios.

Amos 7:14–17 reminds us of the necessity of hearing God's gracious warnings from God's good servants. Amos was unselfish. Israel's troubles were not his troubles. He was not even from that nation. Prophesying was not his job until recently. Yet he accepted God's call to be a bridge between God and the people. He was willing to take on an unfamiliar task in an unfamiliar land to help strangers avoid a devastating situation.

Jesus Christ is the greatest example of someone who took on problems he did not cause or approve of for the sake of others. In much smaller ways, God calls Jesus's followers to do the same. Those who imitate Christ do not simply ask who is to blame for a situation. They ask what they can do to take responsibility for bringing love and reconciliation to bear on hard situations.

The passage also reminds us that only God's protection holds back events that would punish human sins. When sin against the weak and lowly meets an unseen threshold, then God acts. As Leviticus 26:14–39 and Deuteronomy 28:15–68 indicate, war is the worst restorative measure that can unfold. War lets loose death, atrocities, hunger, displacement, widowhood, orphaning, and many other tragic circumstances. When Israel chose their own means of protection, they chose war—in this case, a war they would lose. When we choose money and military and national pride over God's ways, we may well be choosing war and all its horrors. As soon as possible, we ought rather to apply Jesus's promise that "blessed are the peacemakers" (Matthew 5:9).

## Conclusion

When Amos and Amaziah part, we have a strong sense of finality. The two men have not connected. Amaziah must have felt relieved when Amos departed for home. The national shrine was intact. The king was on his throne. The dissonant voice was no longer heard. He got his wish for Amos to stop preaching. Still one wonders if the farmer-prophet's words stayed in the recesses of his mind. At the very least, they may have come to Amaziah's mind again if he lived long enough for the horrors of war to overtake him, his family, his people, and his beloved shrine.

For Amos, there must have been at least the satisfaction of having done the job that God sent him to do. He had warned while he could. He had sought to turn Israel away from disastrous paths. Still, he surely also felt the sting of holy regret that God's warnings went unheeded. He had traveled, preached, prayed, and borne witness. If he lived long enough, he would have heard that Assyria had conquered Israel. He would have heard that Samaria, Bethel, and Dan were overrun. As he marveled at God's truthfulness and power, he might also have shaken his head over what might have been had the people not chosen no more pardons and no more protection.

Amos shows us the right way to approach doing God's work in hard times. He followed God's call to serve in the way God desired. Amos was at God's disposal. Furthermore, he prayed for mercy while preaching coming judgment. Finally, he accepted God's decisions about the timing of judgment. As we do God's work among the many varieties of people in this world, may we follow his example. As we hear God's Word, may we repent as needed before the time of protection ceases.

# 28

# The Ending Has Begun

## AMOS 8

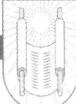

IN AMOS 7:1–3, the prophet received the first of five visions. The initial one occurred in April, the time for mowing. In 8:1–3, Amos reports that the fourth vision came in August, when the summer fruit had been harvested. Harvest was usually a time for gratitude to God for timely rain and good growing conditions. It was a time of satisfaction in work well done, a time for rejoicing and feasting with family and friends (see Deuteronomy 16:13–15). It was also a time for bringing offerings for the priests and the poor (see 16:16, 17; 26:1–15) and a time for learning how to serve God by listening to prophets and priests teach God's word. People traveled far and near to places of worship, feasting, and teaching. Seeing "a basket of summer fruit" (Amos 8:1) should mean seeing a symbol of joy.

When God shows Amos that basket of fruit, however, it is not to provide joy. Rather, it is to tell him again that life as Israel has known it has begun to end. Time for change that could have saved Israel's government, people, and land from destruction has expired. Great reversals will occur. As the chapter unfolds, Amos sees life replaced with death (vv. 1–3), the light of joy replaced by the darkness of mourning (vv. 4–10), and the usual feasting on God's word replaced by a famine of hearing God's word (vv. 11–14). The hope that remains for individuals resides where it always has in Amos, in seeking and serving God (see 5:4).

### Death Comes to Israel (8:1–3)

This fourth vision begins in the same unassuming way as the previous three. Amos opens the scene by stating, "This is what the Lord GOD showed me"

(8:1a). What he sees comes at God's initiative, not his own. He does not divulge any other information, such as how he felt or where he was. God showed Amos "a basket of summer fruit" (v. 1b), which again would normally have been a pleasant, welcome sight. When asked what he has seen, Amos replies naturally enough in verse 2: "A basket of summer fruit [*kayeetz*]." Things now take a sudden turn. God responds with a play on words: "The end [*kaytz*] has come upon my people Israel" (v. 2a). He then adds the explanatory phrase first found in 7:8: "I will not pass by them again" (8:2b, AT).[1] Like the third vision in 7:7–9, then, this vision stresses that the time for pardons has passed. The end has begun. The last harvest has arrived.

Amos 8:3 emphasizes great changes in the atmosphere at worship centers. As noted earlier, late summer to early autumn was the time of harvesting and bringing offerings to worship centers. It was also the time of the Feast of Booths, one of the three times that the people gathered from around the land (see Deuteronomy 16:13–15). Though the people in Israel's kingdom did not go to Jerusalem for the Feast of Booths anymore, they had set up alternative meetings in Bethel and probably elsewhere (see 1 Kings 12:25–33). Motyer explained that when this feast was observed properly, "token offerings of all the prosperity which the Lord had given to His people were brought in thankfulness and joy to Him." He added, "The sense of prosperity, with its attendant buoyancy towards the future, joy and the reminder of belonging to the unique people of the Lord would have filled the mind of the worshipers as they came bearing their harvest hampers to the shrines of Israel."[2] Or at least that is what *should* have been on their minds if their hearts were right with God. These happy occasions would have also provided opportunities for reunions and for meeting new people. Joyful singing would have been part of the festivities.

When the end comes upon Israel, joy will turn to sorrow. Temple singers will be wailing instead of rejoicing (Amos 8:3). The word translated as "temple"[3] does not necessarily refer to the temple in Jerusalem, which was in Judah, not Israel. The word can refer to any major building or to a specific house of worship, such as the one at Bethel (see 7:10–13). The singers will wail because there will be so many deaths. Instead of the roads being filled with worshipers coming to the feasts, the roads will be littered with dead bodies. The corpses will be scattered on the ground, not buried. Most of us have seen battlefield photography that depicts such conditions. Some of us have seen such places firsthand. Israel experienced these types of losses when Assyria conquered and occupied the country beginning in 732 B.C. Exiles occurred that year, as well as in 722, 701, and 670 B.C.

## Darkness Falls on Israel (8:4–10)

With the end of the story already told in the first three verses, Amos explains in Amos 8:4–10 why God has announced Israel's end. He declares the people's sins in 8:4–6, announces his verdict on them in 8:7, 8, and proclaims the effects of the sentence that the people will bear in 8:9, 10. As in 8:1–3, reversals are the order of the day.

Verse 4 begins with the now-familiar summons to hear what God has to say (see 3:1, 13; 4:1; 5:1).[4] The people commanded to hear are the ones "trampling the needy" (8:4, AT).[5] Amos first addressed such persons using these terms in 2:7. Now he adds that these persons "bring the poor of the land to an end" (8:4). The verb translated as "bring . . . to an end" is a form of a well-known word, *sabbath*. Festivals included sabbaths. The Sabbath was a day to stop working for a while. It was a day for rest and kindness. But these people saw it as a day to plot against the weak. They saw it as a day to put an end to the poor.

Indeed, those who trample the poor do not like holy days at all, for those days stop normal business transactions and give workers time off. Holy days cramp their style and delay their plans. Amos 8:5 depicts them longing for the weekly Sabbath and the monthly new moon gatherings to be over so they can get on with charging high prices for low-value grain.

Israel lived on a lunar calendar, with the new moon starting each month. Thus the month began dark and got lighter. Jacob Milgrom wrote the following about the new moon observances: "In early Israel, it was an important festival (Isa. 1:12–13; Hos. 2:13) celebrated by families and clans in a state of ritual purity at the local sanctuary (1 Sam. 20:5-6, 26). It was a rest day (Amos 8:5) on which one visited a man of God (2 Kings 4:23)."[6]

It is possible that new moon meetings occurred monthly or once a year. I lean toward the former possibility. If so, the people would rest one day each month on top of the weekly Sabbath rest. Those trampling the poor did not want any days of rest. They wanted continuous buying and selling. They wanted their employees to work every day. Their workers got ground down, trampled into the dust, worn to a frazzle.

Not to worry. There were lots of poor people to abuse. Amos 8:6 implies they could be bought or hired cheaply, for a bit of silver, for the price of "a pair of sandals." Cheap labor, high prices, and poor products were the essence of their business model. God's standards for rest and worship simply got in their way.

Several years ago Beeson Divinity School and Samford University, where I worked at the time, invited Truett Cathy and his family to give their testimony and talk about Christians in the workplace. Mr. Cathy founded the Chick-fil-A restaurant chain. His first restaurant was not open on Sundays. Cathy said that back when they started the business, no one would have come had they been open on Sunday. Now, he said, it was a way of giving people rest, letting them go to church if they wished, and containing costs. He also considered it part of their family's Christian witness.

Those who believe in the living God, the Creator and Provider, can rest from making money. We can also strive to pay people what they deserve. Work and money do not own us or other people. For years I have heard Christians say they do not have to keep a day of rest because they are not legalists. While legalism is lamentable, it is not legalism to rest as God directs. We need to beware, lest in our attempts to avoid legalism we enslave ourselves to unceasing activity and to money.

By now we have read enough of Amos to guess what follows. Verse 7 says God has seen, and he will not forget. Verse 8 says he will make the land tremble and will make it rise and fall, perhaps by means of an earthquake (compare 1:1). Amos 8:9 says the people who hate the quiet darkness of the new moon Sabbath will have darkness when they expect the noonday sun.[7] In other words, their moral darkness will lead to the darkness that judgment brings. According to verse 10, their feasting and their constant working will turn into funeral rituals—mourning, singing of laments, wearing rough garments, cutting their hair, and generally regretting their circumstances (v. 10a). It will be one "bitter day" after another when God judges what they have become and what they have done (v. 10b).

We must count the cost of conducting business that denies God's kind standards for bosses, laborers, customers, and their families. All of God's standards have people's good in mind. People are not raw materials to be consumed for profit. When Israel or any other nation acts otherwise, it is only a matter of time before God takes corrective action. As always in Amos, turning to God from such living is the right thing to do (see 5:4). Darkness did not have to fall over Israel. The eventual defeats by Assyria and others did not have to occur. We do well to remember that those who want money more than God, especially to the exclusion of God, bring darkness wherever they set up shop.

### Famine Spreads in Israel (8:11–14)

In Amos 7:10–17, we met Amaziah the priest, who wanted Amos to stop preaching. Amos 8:11–14 shows us what it will be like when he gets his wish. Amaziah thought the removal of the preaching of God's word, at least the words that Amos was preaching, would bring stability and peace to the land.

Instead, it eventually brought devastation (see 7:16, 17). Devastated places often suffer from famine, the loss of food. This passage portrays people who have food for their bodies but no food for their souls.

Harvest festivals were almost certainly times when young people saw one another and enjoyed one another's company. Many romances would have begun then. One of the striking sights of festival time would have been young people, the future of Israel, walking the roads to the worship sites. They would have needed guidance for the many decisions they faced.

Amos 8:11 announces a famine. This is not a famine of food but "of hearing the words of the Lord." This famine reminds us of Moses's words to the Israelites in Deuteronomy 8:3: "He [God] humbled you and let you hunger and fed you with manna, which you did not know . . . that he might make you know that man does not live by bread alone, but man lives by every word that comes from the mouth of the Lord." Jesus quoted Deuteronomy 8:3 when Satan tempted him (Matthew 4:1–4). Moses, Amos, and Jesus knew that God's word gave physical life (see Genesis 1—2). They also knew that God's word gave accompanying spiritual and moral strength as they heard and obeyed God's gracious guidance. When judgment comes on Israel, God's life-giving word will not be available.

Amos 8:12 describes an increasingly desperate situation. The people go about the land like sheep seeking pasture. Their search is extensive, "from sea to sea, and from north to east" (v. 12a). Then their search takes on more urgency, for they "run," pursuing[8] a word from God (v. 12b). Their pursuit seems to indicate growing intensity, perhaps driven by desperation. As the society they have known crumbles around them in the manner 8:7–10 describes, they seek to know what to do. Why can't they get an answer? Why can't they find a word from God?

Verse 13 indicates that young men and women will faint from thirsting for an authentic word from the Lord. This verse presents the reverse of the famous Isaiah passage, 40:27–31, where those who wait on the Lord run without weariness and walk without fainting. If the young people are falling, then the old and infirm have no chance. If they are seeking a word from God, why do they fail to get it?

Amos 8:14 gives us the answer. They are seeking the Lord where he cannot be found. They are seeking his word in places where people worship false gods. These seeking people have wandered far and wide. Samaria is in the middle of the land, Dan is in the north, and Beersheba is in the south. This verse shows that people were worshiping other gods in all these places, or perhaps worshiping perverted versions of God there. Either way, these poor seekers will never find God's word in such venues. Rather they shall faint and fall "and never rise again" (v. 14b).

Personally, I find verse 14 to be one of the saddest in the Bible. Having turned to false ideas about God, the people do not even know where to find the truth. Once the truth has been driven out of the land, there is no place to hear it. When I learn of places where Christian witness has been virtually eradicated, I mourn and pray.

I did some of the preparation for the sermon from which this chapter originated in our church library. I was surrounded by good books about God's good words for us. Most of the time I prepare sermons at home, where I keep a library provided for me by God's good gifts. I have lived my whole life in areas where God's people are doing God's work, though I have visited and studied in places where God's work has virtually vanished.

Most of us have many opportunities to hear God's Word. Thus, I have heard this passage preached as a warning. I have heard pastors tell hearers that the day could come when the United States is so secular that the Word of God will not be heard anymore. While I know that this scenario is possible, it is not what we face now—at least not where I live. The greater danger is that we stop listening to God ourselves. The immediate danger is that we prefer phony gods to the real God, phony ideas about God to true ones. If we are not careful, we can become so used to lies that we will not recognize or enjoy the truth. As a friend of mine once described a schoolmate, "That kid ate so much junk food that good food made him sick." We want to beware of fainting from spiritual famine even as other healthy people live on around us. We need to feed on God's Word.

## Conclusion

Famine, darkness, and death are sobering images. It is hard to believe that time to repent can run out, but it can. On a bright spring day, it is hard to imagine that darkness and death can engulf us, but it can, as any veteran of yearly tornado warnings can attest. When we are spiritually young and strong, it is hard to believe that we can get so spiritually out of shape that we faint when we most need to stand. But we have seen enough of life to know that this too can happen.

Amos helps us know that things do not need to go this way. Those who do not know Jesus can seek him and live. Those who know Jesus can always seek him, no matter what the time or trouble or triumph may be. We do not need to faint from spiritual malnourishment. We have ways to find his word if we seek it in the Scriptures and with God's people. As we exit this scene of darkness and fainting, let us never forget that this does not have to be our future. Amos shows us a better way.

# 29

# The Household of Jacob, the Booth of David, and the Remnant of Edom

AMOS 9

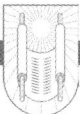

AS WE HAVE SEEN TOGETHER, the book of Amos has three major sections. In chapters 1—2, the prophet stresses God's rule over all lands and people groups. God sees and reacts against injustice of all sorts in every place, including Israel and Judah. In chapters 3—6, Amos urges erring Israel to seek God and live (see 5:4–6). With the vast majority of Israelites unmoved, God speaks to Amos through a series of five visions in chapters 7—9. God states that he will no longer "pass by" Israel (see 7:8; 8:2). Rather, he will discipline Jacob's sinning descendants. Death, mourning, displacement, and a famine of God's guiding words will occur (8).

In the closing chapter, Amos finishes his statements about judgment. Then, as all the prophets eventually do, he emphasizes the renewal that God's punishment produces. While doing so, he describes the future of three important Biblical groups—the household of Jacob (9:1–10), "the booth of David" (v. 11), and "the remnant of Edom" (v. 12). Ultimately, these prospects are incredibly positive (vv. 13–15). God's promises to each group provide instruction for all of us who, like Amos, seek God and live.

## The Household of Jacob (9:1–10, 13–15)

God sent Amos from his home in Tekoa in Judah to preach to Israel (1:1; 7:14). As you will recall, Israel and Judah divided from one another shortly

229

after Solomon died in 930 B.C. Thereafter they constituted two kingdoms with separate monarchs and governments until Assyria ended Israel's monarchy in 722 B.C. Judah's monarchy held on until 587 B.C. when Babylon put a stop to it. Israel had kings from various lineages, but Judah's kings all came from David's family. Technically speaking, both Israel and Judah were the household of Jacob, for both descended from Jacob, who was also called Israel (Genesis 35:9–15). Jacob was Isaac's son and Abraham's grandson. By Amos's time, the descendants who had separated from Judah were known as the "people of Israel" (Amos 9:7), "the house of Jacob" (v. 8), "the house of Israel" (v. 9), and "my people Israel" (v. 14).

Amos knows that this household is in grave danger. Judgment is about to commence. In verse 1, Amos sees God either above or beside the altar, presumably at a temple in Bethel, Samaria, or Dan (see 8:14). God commands that the top of the supporting columns be struck so hard that the whole structure will come down on worshipers' heads (9:1a). The image may remind veteran Bible readers of Samson pushing down the pillars of a Baal temple, killing himself and many Philistines (Judges 16:23–30). Anyone managing to survive will be cut down by a sword (Amos 9:1b). No one will escape.

They will try to flee, as people do. But verses 2, 3 indicate there will be no place to hide. Low or high, they will be found. Verse 4 adds that even if their foes capture them and take them away, God will find them in the foreign land and punish them. After all, verses 5, 6 remind us, God is the Creator and Ruler of the whole earth. He sees every person everywhere. The house of Israel is in deep trouble.

Verse 7 removes any notion that Israel will escape punishment because they are God's special ones. True, God brought Israel out of Egypt. But he likewise brought the Syrians and Philistines from distant places to where they resided in Amos's time.[1] Israel is not more special than the Cushites, people from the lands we know now as Sudan. Stated more positively, the Cushites are as special to God as the Israelites. It is worth recalling that Moses had a Cushite wife (Numbers 12:1). Later in the eighth century B.C., Isaiah proclaimed great promises to Cush (Isaiah 18:1–7). God cares for all these people.

Amos 9:8 reminds us once again (1:3—2:16) that God also holds all peoples everywhere accountable for their actions. God sees all that happens on earth. He sees any and every "sinful kingdom" (9:8), including Israel. God gives all peoples the benefits of his creation. He also holds all peoples accountable for what they do in his kingdom. Thus he will "destroy" the sinful kingdoms "from the surface of the ground," from where they have been used to enjoying God's good earth. This phrase may include harsh conditions or exile from one's homeland. The main point is that God is the One behind the destruction.

At the end of the verse, Amos offers a very significant qualification. Though God may destroy Israel's "sinful kingdom," he most certainly will not[2] eradicate Jacob's "house," his descendants.[3] The descendants of Abraham, Isaac, and Jacob will survive, just as God promised (see Genesis 12:1–9; 15:1–6; 26:1–5; 28:10–17; Exodus 2:23–25). Here God includes the tribes separated from Judah in the promises to the patriarchs and matriarchs. Exiled or oppressed in their homeland, the Israelites will survive, however reduced their numbers may be.

Amos 9:9, 10 indicates that the numbers will fall because of the vast number of wicked persons who will be removed. God will command others to shake Israel "as with a sieve" (v. 9).[4] This sieve is apparently death "by the sword" (v. 10), a metaphor for the ravages of war. All who believe that disaster will not overtake them, presumably because of their privileged relationship with God, will discover otherwise. The sieve of the sword will remove the wicked. God has decreed it. Nonetheless, this reduction of the people will not obliterate Israel. Jacob's household will survive to fulfill God's promises and purposes.

There are at least three applications we should draw from this rich and disturbing passage. First, God is both blessed Creator and thorough Judge (9:1–6). As 7:1–6 showed us, God does not punish quickly or lightly. In fact, he desires repentance, that people would return to him, seek him, and live, as 5:4–6 has made very plain. But when the Creator judges, he can find sinners wherever they are. None of us should think we can fool or elude God. The oppressed are counting on his justice, and he will not disappoint them.

Second, God's people serve God's purposes alongside other peoples (9:7–10). They are not special in the sense that they can get away with things that others cannot. They are accountable to God. They must treat others as God demands. Jacob's physical descendants, people we know as Jews, cannot do as they please. Jeremiah 7:1—8:3 makes this point clearly, as does Jesus's teaching. Thus it is simplistic and ungodly for Christians to consider justifiable anything and everything the current state of Israel does. Anti-Semitism is a stain on human history. It is inexcusable. That said—all people, Jacob's literal physical descendants included—answer to God. They are not free to do as they please.

Third, God kept his promise to preserve some Israelites from the judgment that began in Amos's time. After Assyria conquered Israel and took captives in 732 B.C., that great empire put down rebellions and took more Israelite captives in 722, 709, 701, and 670 B.C. Israel suffered alongside Judah when Babylon conquered Jerusalem in 597 B.C. and destroyed the city in 587 B.C. Some people always remained in the home places, but vast numbers went away, some with the victors and others into refugee communities. When Persia allowed Jews to go to the land of their ancestors in 538 B.C., the long, slow process of repopulation and rebuilding began. When Jesus was born fifty-three decades later, the land was filled again with Jacob's descendants. God did not destroy the people. His purposes continue through the ages, however bleak things may appear at any given time.

### David's Booth (9:11)

With his hard work of presenting judgment behind him, Amos moves to the hope that future days will bring. He reports God's promise to "raise up the booth of David that is fallen" (Amos 9:11a). He will "repair" where "breaches" in its walls have made it collapse (v. 11b). It will stand once again.

A "booth" was a good, temporary shelter where a person or persons could stay. Booths were portable. The Israelites lived in booths as they journeyed after the exodus. Moses instituted the annual Feast of Booths to memorialize God's guidance and sheltering in those days (Leviticus 23:33–44; Deuteronomy 16:13–17). Today we might think of camping tents, a pop-up camper, or an Airstream trailer if we want to get the concept. These are all good in their own way. They are not houses, churches, office buildings, courthouses, or other buildings meant to stand in one place for long periods of time.

This image of David's "booth" is an interesting variation on the concept of David's kingdom. David was ruler over all twelve tribes of Israel when he died (around 970 B.C.). Indeed, God had promised David an everlasting kingdom that would help all people, according to 2 Samuel 7:11–16, 19. Many psalms and prophetic texts reflect this promise. From these texts we learn of God's plan to send a permanent holder of David's throne, a messiah, Jesus from Nazareth. All these passages lead us to think about permanence, so why a booth?

This image reminds us that David's realm shrank from twelve tribes to two tribes after Solomon died in 930 B.C. God gave ten tribes to Jeroboam I, the first king of Israel (c. 930–909 B.C.), and to his successors. David's "booth"—his ruling household and its realm—had holes. Judah and Israel were separated, and both deteriorated. Now Israel was falling and was being scattered. Judah would follow in a few decades. David's booth was indeed falling apart.

This image also reminds us that Israelite refugees could find shelter in Judah, where David's descendants lived. Hosea may have done so.[5] Others certainly did. These people could find good, temporary shelter as they fled from life's harsh realities.

Finally, this image reminds us of Hosea 3:5. There Hosea envisions the reunion of Judah and Israel under the rule of David's family. When Israel's kingdom ends, the people must swallow their pride and reinstate David's lineage as their rulers. Hosea the Israelite and Amos the missionary from Judah agree on this point. The reuniting of Israel does not depend on Jacob's descendants returning to the land or having just any person, say a Caesar or a prime minister, ruling them. The ruler must be from David's family.

The New Testament clearly identifies that ruler as Jesus Christ. Matthew 1:1–17; Luke 3:23–38; and Romans 1:1–6 are just three passages that make this point. Zechariah 9:9—10:12, a passage written years after the Jews first came back to their ancestral homeland in 538 B.C., looks for a king to unite Judah and Israel. Though the people slowly filled the land, Israel and Judah remained at odds with one another. When Jesus called twelve apostles, he united the people. David's booth once again sheltered Israel and Judah. The Jewish people who believed in Jesus constituted a renewed and reunited household of Jacob. God's promises came to fruition.

We would do well to stop and marvel at God's resilient promises and people. Hebrews 11 offers a long, unbroken line of Israelite witnesses. Too often we can read the Old Testament story as one of consistent failure. While failure is part of the story, it is not the most important part. The most important part is that God keeps his promises, and he does so through his people. If not for these children of Jacob, Christianity would not exist. We owe God and our forebearers our thanks for what he has done through them.

### The Remnant of Edom (9:12)

God's purposes for rebuilding David's fallen booth extend beyond his plans for Judah and Israel. Amos 9:12 says that God will raise up David's booth in order "that they may possess the remnant of Edom, indeed, all the peoples called by my name" (AT).[6] This statement leads us to ask at least three questions. What does the term "possess" mean? What does the concept "the remnant of Edom" mean? What does it mean for a group of people to be called by God's name?

Let's begin with the last question and work our way back. After all, having a relationship with God is the chief benefit that the Bible offers to people. To begin with, the phrase places God above all else that Amos describes. God's "name" is his character shown by his actions. Amos has described God as Creator (4:13; 5:8–9; 9:5, 6), provider (4:6–12), redeemer (2:9, 10; 3:1; 9:7), and judge of all people (1:3—2:16; 9:8–10). Peoples called by his name recognize his rule over them wherever they are and wherever they may go. They must live somewhere, so the concept has geographical implications. But peoples may have to be on the move. Their name and the name of the king travel with them. Most importantly, the name of their God goes with them.

As God's people, Israel represented God to the world. Any blessings they enjoyed, any land upon which they lived, and any activities they did reflected well or poorly on God. This is what it meant for them to be a kingdom of priests, a holy nation (Exodus 19:5, 6). According to the Apostle Peter, this is also what it means to be a Christian church (1 Peter 2:9, 10). Any people group from all the nations that takes on God's name bears these responsibilities.

As for the second question, "the remnant of Edom" (Amos 9:12) may refer either to the Edomite people, the land they have left after war or natural disaster, or both. Edomite people were scattered from their homeland for the same reason that any people group gets scattered. Amos seems to have the same concern for Edom that Isaiah has for Moab in Isaiah 15—16, which is to treat them according to what befits a people who claim God's name, ways, and character. Such good treatment contrasts sharply with how some Edomites had treated others, according to Amos 1:6, 9. It also contrasts sharply with David's military conquests of Edom (see 2 Samuel 8:11–14). Like Israel, this minority of Edomites will be called by God's name wherever they live geographically.

As for the first question, "possess" means to lay claim on something or someone (Amos 9:12).[7] In this context it means to lay claim on Edom and other peoples for the sake of placing them under God's name in the sense that we just considered. It is true that David conquered Edom. Here the concept of the booth indicates shelter and protection, not conquest or exploitation. Even if one conceives of "possess" in the sense of "to own,"[8] the Old Testament teaches that God owns the land (Leviticus 25:23) and governs human life on it. Common American views of ownership clash with the Bible's views on the subject. *Possessing* means using something as God directs and helping someone live as God wills.

As we did with Jacob's household and David's fallen booth, let's trace Edom's remnant. Like Israel and Judah, Edom suffered at the hands of the Assyrians, Babylonians, and Persians. By the time Malachi prophesied in the mid-400s B.C. (see Malachi 1:2–5), the Edomites had been scattered. Those who remained were joined by refugees who had fled northward. Edom had truly become a place populated with a remnant of its original people and several other newcomers. Some Edomites moved northward into southern Judah, and that region became known as Idumea. Herod the Great (reigned 37–4 B.C.), who ruled Jerusalem and Bethlehem when Jesus was born, was from Idumea.

Thus, through the years, Edom and Jacob's household had not united. Neither side considered the other shelter.

Acts 15:16, 17 cites Amos 9:12, thus helping us connect the story. Jesus's earliest followers believed that Jesus was the promised descendant of David who united Israel and Judah (see Acts 2:25–36; 4:25–27; 5:42; 13:22–36). They preached in Jesus's name, just as the Old Testament prophets preached in God's name (see, for example, 5:41, 42; 8:12; 9:28). God led Peter (10:42, 43) and others (Acts 11:19–26) to preach the same message to non-Jews, the Gentiles. When a dispute arose over how Gentiles were to be included in the Messiah's people, Peter, Paul, and Barnabas gave evidence of God's full inclusion of Gentiles (15:1–12).

But it fell to James, Jesus's brother and the leader of the Jerusalem church, to give the conclusive word on the matter. He cited and interpreted Amos 9:12 (Acts 15:16, 17), not unlike how preachers do today. He could assume that all those present believed that Jesus was the One who raised up David's fallen booth. They confessed Jesus as Messiah and Lord of creation (15:11). They confessed him as the King in whose kingdom they lived (8:12). Before he ascended to Heaven, Jesus directed them to share the news about him with all people without reference to political power (1:8). Therefore, they knew Gentiles would believe. The question was how to receive them.

James interpreted Amos's comment on those called by God's name (Amos 9:12; Acts 15:17) as referring to anyone who decided to "seek the Lord," the concept that Amos 5:4–6 used to define a proper relationship with God. James included Amos's mention of "Edom" and "all the nations" (Amos 9:12) under the inclusive term "mankind" (Acts 15:17). Having raised up David's fallen booth and united followers from Judah and Israel under his rule, the Lord had now sent those followers to include Edom and all peoples in his kingdom. James concluded by requiring Gentiles to obey standards that Amos affirmed (vv. 19–21; cf. Amos 2:7, 8; 3:13–15; 6:1–7). Thus, James saw the work that Peter, Paul, Barnabas, and the church at Antioch had done as being in direct continuity with God's purposes that Amos 9:12 describes. God's reunification plans begin with Israel and Judah, but they do not end there, nor is there some two-stage, Jew-versus-Gentile plan. The reconciling God brings peoples together in the shelter of David's booth, which is the kingdom of Jesus Christ the Lord. This kingdom includes people from any land, race, or culture.

Let me bring this section to a close by offering some applications. First, as believers in Jesus Christ, Jews and Gentiles alike have a King we must obey. This is part of what it means to be called by his name and to call upon his name. His commands take precedence over those of any other lesser ruler. Second, this King is building a kingdom of peoples, not a kingdom of geopolitical entities. American government, Israeli government, or any other geopolitical entity cannot be equated with God's people or God's land, nor can oppressed persons be automatically equated with God's people. Third, God's people are like Amos and Jesus. They put God and neighbor first. They seek to reconcile people to God and people to one another. Amos represented God, not Judah. Fourth, reconcilers can get pinched between warring parties. Amos took a lot of heat for proclaiming his message, as we saw in 7:10–17. We know what happened to Jesus. Church tradition says that James died at the hands of Jews who did not like this fellow Jew's message. Yet this is the job, and it can be a very complicated and discouraging one. Fifth, reconcilers must think. They must serve. It is easier to pick a side and countenance oppression, revenge, and political maneuvering than it is to seek to be called by God's name. But as the old gospel song I sang as a boy puts it, "The way of the cross leads home."[9]

## Conclusion (9:13–15)

Amos concludes with his conviction that when the world's peoples take shelter in David's household, the world is transformed. When people follow the King, it is like constant harvest, as Amos 9:13 describes. When God replanted Israel in their land to rebuild and repopulate it, this was a beautiful development, as Amos 9:14 promises. This kingdom cannot be uprooted, as Amos 9:15 asserts. Now more than two millennia old, Christ's kingdom flourishes in God's world as the world's peoples embrace Jesus. It will flourish even more when God judges all wickedness for good.

There remains much to do. We must struggle better to unite our confession of Jesus as Lord and our care for the Creator's world. Amos the farmer would surely applaud such progress. We have miles to go before we fully embrace our role as reconcilers and shed nationalistic and racial prejudices, welcoming Edomites. Amos the preacher would surely applaud such progress. But we know the King to follow and the shelter he provides. This is the place to start and the path to walk.

As we leave Amos for Obadiah, let us give thanks for the man from Tekoa and the God who roars from Zion. Speaking for myself, I will never match Amos's visionary commitment to God and others. But I have been brought closer to God by Amos's words, which are also God's words.

# OBADIAH

*By Paul R. House*

# 30

# Brothers, Bystanders, and Betrayers

OBADIAH 1-11

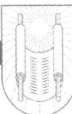

EDOM FIGURES PROMINENTLY at the beginning and end of the book of Amos. You will recall the prophet's stark descriptions of Edom's slave trading and implacable anger in Amos 1:6, 11, 12.[1] But also recall Amos's hopeful statements about Edom in 9:12 (cf. Acts 15:1–21, especially vv. 12–19). To these we might add God's plea to Edom found in Jeremiah 49:11: "Leave your fatherless children; I will keep them alive; and let your widows trust in me." Whatever we conclude from what we will hear about Edom from Obadiah, it must be anchored in God's loving concern for all peoples and his coinciding insistence that they are accountable to him for their actions.

Obadiah is the shortest book by word count in the Old Testament. Thus, it is also the shortest prophetic book. But it is about the same length as several surviving prophetic texts from other lands.[2] It is unlikely, then, that Obadiah would have been viewed as peculiar. Despite its brevity, the book exhibits prophetic literature's main themes: sin, punishment, and renewal. The prophet stresses God's sovereignty over all nations, humanity's responsibility for one another, God's just judgments, and God's ultimate victory over evil. Along the way he emphasizes the dangers of human pride and greed. Obadiah packs a lot into a very few words.

I wish I could tell you more about the man Obadiah, but his book is about all we know of him. His name is beautiful. It means "servant of the Lord." As God's servant, he shares God's words, stating four times that he speaks the words God has given him (see vv. 1, 4, 8, 18). Obadiah does nothing to draw attention to himself. Rather, he points readers to the fact that "the kingdom shall be the LORD's" (v. 21).

All that we can derive about the time in which Obadiah lived also comes from the book, particularly through what it says about Edom. We can then compare what we find here to what else we know about Edom from the Bible and other ancient writings.

Jacob, also known as Israel, was the father of Israel's twelve tribes. His twin brother, Esau, was the father of Edom's people (see Genesis 25—36). Therefore, it is no wonder that Obadiah calls Edom the brother of Israel and Judah (Obadiah 12). God gave Edom a homeland, just as he gave one to Israel (Deuteronomy 2:1–8). That homeland was a strip of territory about 110 miles long and forty miles wide, beginning at the southeastern tip of the Dead Sea. Eilat on the north edge of the Red Sea was its only port. However, Edom controlled seventy miles of key overland north-south trade routes. It also was a gateway to eastern trade routes across the desert. Edom had many ways to gather wealth. Sadly, one of the ways was human trafficking, as Amos 1:6 indicates.

Over the centuries Edom had an uneasy relationship with Israel and Judah. David and Solomon subjugated Edom c. 1000–930 B.C. Edom got free c. 850 B.C. By 734 B.C. Edom joined with Israel and Syria in campaigns against Judah, according to 2 Chronicles 28:1–21. This campaign included threats against Jerusalem that made King Ahaz and the people shake like a tree's leaves on a windy day (Isaiah 7:1, 2). Though Edom was part of an anti-Babylon coalition with Judah in 597 B.C. (Jeremiah 27:1–15), they had joined Babylon against Judah by 587 B.C. (Lamentations 4:21, 22; Ezekiel 35). I stop here because most scholars think that Obadiah was not written after this time. Ezekiel 35:10 states that Edom wanted Israel's and Judah's territory, probably because Edom was getting pushed out of their own land in the early sixth century B.C. Edom's losses became their motivation to mistreat Judah and Israel.

Obadiah speaks words of warning into this complicated scene. He calls Edom into account for being an unbrotherly brother and a bystander who turned into a betrayer (v. 10). He speaks about Jerusalem surviving when other places fall, so I place the book in the eighth century B.C. when Syria, Israel, Edom, and others threatened Jerusalem ( 735–733 B.C.) or when Assyria did so in c. 701 B.C. Most scholars date the book after 587 B.C., when Babylon conquered Jerusalem.[3] I think that Amos, Obadiah, Isaiah, and Micah all served during the last half of the 700s B.C.

Obadiah 1–11 provides a clear introduction for which verses 12–21 give us a fitting conclusion. The prophet announces God's decree against Edom in verses 1–4. This is a decree of destruction. Obadiah then portrays the decimation of Edom's resources in verses 5–9. In verses 10, 11 he explains why God has made this decision: Edom has stood aloof from his brother when his brother needed help. Indeed, Edom went from being a bystander to being a betrayer (v. 11). Edom did so because of pride (v. 3) and greed (v. 6). Obadiah goes on to warn Edom not to gloat over Jerusalem's troubles, for God's justice will prevail in all nations (vv. 12–16). Zion will endure, and those who serve God will have a home (vv. 17–20). Why? So that all peoples may know that God's kingdom never ends (v. 21).

But let's not get ahead of ourselves. We must first hear God's warnings to Edom so we can hear God's warnings to us. We ought to examine ourselves to see if we have been proper brothers and sisters, guilty bystanders, or betrayers. It is not too late to be God's family for one another.

### God's Decree of Destruction (vv. 1–4)

Obadiah reports that these twenty-one verses are a "vision" he has received from God (v. 1). Isaiah and Nahum use the same term for their books (Isaiah 1:1; Nahum 1:1). Obadiah writes about what he has seen. He testifies to what God has said. It was not his idea to write what follows. He is simply God's servant.

The first thing he saw was God sending out a decree (Obadiah 1). Kings great and small have issued decrees to their subjects from ancient times. In Obadiah's times, Assyria had the most powerful kings. They sent instructions to or about the various lands they ruled through ambassadors and other emissaries. Egypt's pharaohs had done so before Assyria rose, and Babylon did so after Assyria's fall. The Bible presents God as the actual ruler of the whole earth and all its peoples. Obadiah sees God sending out a message to all nations, and the message is that God commands his armies to battle Edom (v. 1b). The King of the universe has called for a war against this small desert country. We should note that no rebellion, no attack against an ally, was too small for Assyria to ignore. The ruler of all places, God himself, is no less vigilant.

In verses 2–4 the decree addresses Edom directly. Translated literally, verse 2a says that God will give Edom "smallness," that is, smallness of esteem, "among the nations." Indeed other lands will despise, ridicule, and hold Edom in contempt (v. 2b). Edom will become an object lesson for other rebels.

What has Edom done to merit this decree? We don't know yet.[4] Verse 3 focuses on why Edom has done whatever it is they have done. Their heart became filled with "pride." This small, wealthy, cliff-dwelling land thought itself invulnerable. The people believed that no one would dare to invade their well-protected little kingdom. They thought they could do as they pleased.

Verse 4 shows that God does not worry about Edom's difficult terrain. Even if Edom were as high as an eagle's nest, God could bring them down. The Assyrian kings often reveled in conquering distant or simply difficult-to-reach places. They bragged about victories in all kinds of landscapes.[5] If they could do such things, surely God the Creator could do so as well. In fact, he could use the Assyrians or others to do so.

Ancient rulers used similar decrees to get balky subjects back in line. They also sent messengers to rebels. Isaiah 36:1–21 recounts an Assyrian envoy's mission to Judah in 701 B.C. He fails to persuade King Hezekiah at that time. Isaiah 37:8–13 reports that the king of Assyria sent a threatening letter to Hezekiah. Though Hezekiah does not comply, he pays a heavy price, as 2 Kings 18:13–17 demonstrates. Obadiah presents God as a great king ordering one of his subjects to behave or pay the consequences.

Obadiah 5–9 reveals more about Edom's pride. The Edomites are proud of their nation, proud of their military, proud of their wisdom and learning, and proud of their allies. They are proud of their success. They are full of themselves—so full, in fact, that they have no room for anyone else. Their proud hearts are the source of their coming destruction.

The Scriptures uniformly oppose pride and affirm humility. Consider the warning in Proverbs 16:18: "Pride goes before destruction." Or James 4:6: "God opposes the proud but gives grace to the humble." Note that "the desires of the eyes and pride of life" are soul-killing dangers, according to 1 John 2:16. Humility and gratitude are the character traits God values.

Therefore, let us beware of boasting that we live in the greatest country, the greatest city, or the greatest state. Let us be careful not to boast that we attend the largest church, live in the most tasteful home, drive the most desirable car, or parent the most beautiful and intelligent children. Pride leads to all sorts of terrible results. Let us learn the most fundamental point of Obadiah's little book before we go any further. Self-exaltation dishonors God and demeans other people. Let us turn *now* from this flaw.

### God's Decimation of Edom's Resources (vv. 5–9)

Obadiah's vision continues. Now he sees words meant to drive home the threat that verses 1–4 announce. God wants Edom to imagine the future, one in which everything they lean on slowly will slip away. These verses declare the decimation of Edom's cherished resources.

Verses 5, 6 indicate that Edom's losses will be total. God compares what will occur to a robbery. Thieves and plunderers would only take what they could carry or could use (v. 5). Edom's invaders have no such limits. They go on a wild spree. The imagery seems to warn that the losses will not be small, such as Edom might experience in a raid. They will suffer great loss. The enemy will have time to find their closely guarded treasures (v. 6). These were often kept in palaces and temples. Therefore, the enemy will control Edom's cities and institutions.

How could such a thing happen? As history played out, it happened slowly, a bit at a time. It was not until the fourth century B.C. that the Nabateans forced Edom out of their territory into what had been southern Judah.[6] The displaced Edomites became known as the Idumeans. The Jewish leader Judas Maccabeus defeated the Idumeans in 164 B.C. His successor John Hyrcanus forced the Idumeans to accept Jewish religion in 120 B.C.[7] Herod the Great, who ruled the Jews and Idumeans and sought to kill Jesus, was Idumean. The Jews and Idumeans fought together in the catastrophic, futile war against the Romans in 70 A.D.[8] It took a long time for what Obadiah describes to unfold.

This means that Edom had lots of time and many opportunities to consider and change their ways. This may also help us understand why Isaiah, Jeremiah, Ezekiel, Amos, and Malachi said similar things about Edom over a period of three centuries or more (see Isaiah 34; Jeremiah 25:15–38; 27:1–11; 49:7–22; Ezekiel 25:12–14; Amos 1:6, 11, 12; 9:12; Malachi 1:2–5). God was dealing with Esau's descendants for a long time, just as he was with Jacob's. According to Acts 15:1–35, God was bringing some of Esau's descendants to faith in Christ within two decades of Jesus's death.[9] God did not give up on Edom.

With this in mind, let's go to Obadiah 7. Edom's slow decimation begins with a loss of allies. In fact, former allies turn against the Edomites. Obadiah uses three terms to describe these allies: men in covenant with them, men at peace with them, and men who go to battle with them.[10] The list is comprehensive. So is the list of what these allies do to Edom: they press them to the border, deceive them, and set a trap against them. They do their work so craftily that Edom has "no understanding" of what the villainous allies are up to.

With these external resources covered in verse 7, God proceeds to discuss Edom's internal resources in verses 8, 9. Their statesmen and counselors, their "wise men," will not possess the needed discernment (v. 8). Their "mighty men," their soldiers, will be "dismayed," taken by surprise, as a result (v. 9). As history develops, this twin failure occurs in Edom from the Assyrian era to the Roman era. But the Assyrian-era defeats are on the near horizon in

Obadiah. Amid these losses, the Edomites rekindled their national pride over the years. They too seldom asked who truly ruled their lives.

As I read these verses, it strikes me how much Edom acts as nations have acted before and since. National pride fills people. They trust in allies, armies, strategy, diplomacy, trade, and economic might. These cultural props erode slowly. Edom's decimation did not occur overnight. God was merciful and patient.

These verses lead me to think about Christians' role in a nation, even in the United States. In my opinion, many Christians have followed two wrong paths. First, we have sought to help build up American pride, might, financial success, and international importance and then asked people to receive Jesus in gratitude. This puts Jesus in second or third or fourth place in our message. Second, we have asked people to accept Jesus so that America might receive God's blessings. This makes Jesus a tool for getting wealth. Both approaches affirm nationalistic pride, whether intentionally or not.

The Bible leaves no room for personal or nationalistic pride. It does not offer God as a tool for success. Rather, it calls people to repentance, humility, and service. It indicates that God uses historical circumstances to lead people to repentance, humility, and service. Beyond a repeated ignoring of God's kindness lies inevitable decimation of the false gods we trust. Decimation may take years, decades, or centuries, but it will occur. Something like this is the message we carry to others, even as Obadiah carried it to Judah and Edom in his day.

### Brother, Bystander, Betrayer (vv. 10, 11)

We now finally learn why God decrees decimation and disaster for Edom. At least we get the beginning of the explanation. More reasons appear in verses 12–21. For now it is enough to learn that Edom has taken a very unbrotherly attitude toward his brother Jacob (v. 10). Rather than standing with Jacob, Edom has stood by while others have harmed Jacob (v. 11). Worse yet, Edom has often joined those harming Judah. Edom had the responsibility of a brother, a close relative, yet chose to be an unhelpful bystander and eventually joined those who destroyed.

Obadiah 10 summarizes the reason for and the result of God's anger at Edom. It is because of the killing, because of the violence[11] that Judah has endured and will endure. The reference to Judah's status as Edom's brother is telling. God declared Edom and Israel brothers, kinsmen, in Deuteronomy 23:7. Kinship required positive and helpful relationships. These relationships entailed solidarity in times of need, including times of attack.[12] Kinship meant that one could expect support in times of killing and general violence.

We must note that Edom, Israel, and Judah often failed to treat one another as family. David's treatment of Edom did not build up good relationships, for example. Neither did subsequent economically motivated wars against Edom.[13] Both could claim that the other party started the conflict. Seldom did either side try to make a lasting, relational peace. Many parents, supervisors, attorneys, and pastors will understand the problem. Therefore, God the Peacemaker had to act as God the Judge to create the space for renewed kinship.

Having ignored, rejected, or resented the family connection, Edom chose not to help. Obadiah 11 states that instead, "on the day" Judah needed assistance, Edom "stood aloof." This concept appears in 2 Samuel 18:13 when a soldier describes how Joab would have acted had that soldier killed Absalom and been forced to face David's wrath. It also appears in Psalm 38:11 in a lament that includes close relatives. These passages portray abandonment that amounts to hostility.[14] Edom was a bystander who could have done something to help. The Edomites were not powerless. They were not mere victims themselves.[15]

Edom did not help when "strangers" and "foreigners"—who in this case were enemies—"entered his [Jacob's] gates" (Obadiah 11). The phrase refers to Jacob's territory where they seized "wealth," which included goods and people.[16] Having entered Jacob's territory, they "cast lots" to see who would get Jerusalem. They had not yet invaded or captured Jerusalem. By standing aloof, Edom signaled their willingness to be "like one of them," which probably meant to move against Judah without formally joining a coalition.

When did Edom act this way? As I have said, they did so more than once. However, I think Obadiah's description best fits c. 734 B.C., when Israel and Syria invaded Judah and took many captives (2 Chronicles 28:1–15). They plotted to capture Jerusalem but did not do so (2 Kings 16:7; Isaiah 7:1, 2). Edom took captives and recaptured Elath from Judah at this time (2 Kings 16:6; 2 Chronicles 28:17). Jerusalem survived, but with no thanks to Edom, who acted like Israel and Syria even if they did not officially join their coalition. By not acting like a brother, Edom became a betrayer.

Those who accept the role of a family member cannot remain bystanders, innocent or otherwise. In Luke 10:25–37, Jesus tells the Parable of the Good Samaritan. The passage reaffirms the Old Testament's contention that love of God and love of neighbor are the essence of Biblical faith and eternal life. When asked to define the term "neighbor," Jesus tells the well-known story.

The person who showed "compassion" and "mercy" was a neighbor to the wounded man (Luke 10:33, 36, 37). In Matthew 25:31–46, Jesus commends visiting imprisoned brothers and sisters as well as feeding and clothing brothers and sisters in need. While Matthew 25:31–46 probably refers to *Christian* brothers and sisters, the parable of the Good Samaritan portrays all human beings as neighbors. When we simply walk away from people who need our mercy, we do not act like a brother or sister or neighbor. We will face many questions once we decide to be neighbors. But we will never gain proper answers if we think being a bystander is an option.

But what about real, live, active enemies? After all, Edom, Judah, and Israel often fought one another. A seldom-noticed account from c. 734 B.C. gives us answers. Second Chronicles 28:5–15 recounts Israel's and Syria's invasion of Judah. Oded the prophet and some of Israel's leaders kept the people from killing and enslaving men, women, and children that the Israelites had captured from Judah. Oded declared, "Have you not sins of your own against the LORD your God? Now hear me, and send back the captives from your relatives whom you have taken, for the fierce wrath of the LORD is upon you" (vv. 10b, 11). Vengeance is not an option. Second Kings 6:20–23 tells a similar episode when Israel had Syria trapped. Mercy is always an option, whether the opponent is a relative or not.

As I have already mentioned, the New Testament extends the mercy principle further. Jesus commands his followers to love, help, and pray for enemies. Moreover, Christianity is a worldwide family. Can we really justify killing Christian brothers and sisters in wars, even if they are political enemies? Can we really support wars between other nations as easily as we do? Can we really justify letting our allies act badly if we only send money or equipment, not soldiers?

Maybe I should ask simpler questions. How do I treat my wife and family members? How do I treat fellow workers? How do I respond to personal attacks? I don't know about you, but Obadiah 10, 11 gives me a lot to think about.

## Conclusion

Proud Edom failed to admit that Israel and Judah were their brothers and sisters. They saw these relatives and neighbors as opponents whose losses were their gain. They saw suffering Israel and Judah as getting what they deserved. Soon enough they went from bystanders to betrayers. God noticed, and he warned against such behavior.

Now is a good time for us to recall Jesus's grace toward sinners. It is a good time to recall his teaching about love for enemies. It is a good time to recall the Good Samaritan. It is a good time to humble ourselves, love God, love others, and mean it when we pray, "Forgive us our debts, as we also have forgiven our debtors" (Matthew 6:12). It is a good time to trust Jesus to guide us to be brothers and sisters, lest we become betrayers.

# 31

# The Kingdom Shall Be the Lord's

OBADIAH 12-21

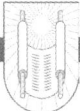

AT THE END OF THE PREVIOUS CHAPTER, we left Edom among those casting lots for Jerusalem (Obadiah 10, 11). At that point, Edom was bursting with pride (vv. 3, 4) and standing aloof from Judah (v. 11). Edom was at a turning point, an hour of decision. God had warned that he had prepared a decree of destruction for Edom (vv. 2, 5–9) if they joined other nations in pillaging Judah and plotting against Jerusalem. They have not done right by Judah so far, but they have not done their worst. There remains time for them to pull back. Indeed, there remains time for them to humble themselves and embrace the truth, which is that God is the ultimate King to whom all peoples answer. The kingdoms of Judah, Israel, Syria, Edom, and all other nations belong to God. Therefore, all kingdoms shall be the Lord's, for all kingdoms are already the Lord's. Like Edom, we need to accept this great fact and live accordingly. All other paths lead to destruction.

Obadiah 12–21 develops the key theme of God's kingdom in three stages. Verses 12–14 warn Edom against joining the day of injustice. Then verses 15–20 warn Edom about the day of the Lord's justice that is unfolding and will unfold. Finally, verse 21 concludes the book with the declaration of God's permanent, just rule. While Obadiah offers comfort to Judah in verses 15–21, he retains his focus on warning Edom. While I think the original setting is c. 734 B.C., Edom needed this message many times in succeeding centuries. As I will try to explain, we need such warnings too, for the message that God rules resounds in the New Testament with increased

249

urgency. We need this word to Edom now and always until God establishes his permanent, righteous kingdom.

### Edom's Day of Decision (vv. 12–14)

As you will remember, Edom stood aloof when his brother Judah needed help (vv. 10, 11). Edom chose to remain a bystander, which made him the betrayer of family obligations.[1] Now Obadiah reports eight negative commands (vv. 12–14). God warns Edom not to consider Judah's weakness, exult in it, or act upon it. On Edom's day of decision, God tells Edom not to join in the day of injustice that other nations perpetrate against Judah.

These eight prohibitions treat Edom as still able to step back from further wrongdoing. Since Edom joined in the destruction of Jerusalem in 587 B.C., many commentators consider these to be past actions placed here for effect.[2] But the text indicates no later setting. The eight prohibitions fall into two sets of four, with the same verb appearing in the first and fifth prohibitions.

This coordinating verb is a form of the word usually translated as "see" or "look." The type or intensity of the seeing usually depends on the context. The translation of "gloat" in Obadiah 12, 13 (see ESV) therefore interprets the word as looking on Judah's plight with derision or enjoyment.[3] There are also words that convey speech in the verses, and the series of eight prohibitions increases in specificity and severity. Thus, the first and fifth commands warn Edom against looking in the sense of sizing up possibilities.

Thus, verse 12 begins by telling Edom that they are not to "look" for the purpose of considering what they might do given Judah's new vulnerability. Translated literally, this new vulnerability is Judah's "foreignness." The word means that Judah's opponents treated them as people not in covenant or in alliance with the invaders. This fact led Edom to consider Judah the same way, though Judah was Edom's "brother" (cf. v. 10). The invaders treating Judah as a non-ally was a "misfortune," but the word conveys a specific type of misfortune.

Much like Eve, whose looking upon forbidden fruit contributed to her sin (Genesis 3:6), Edom's looking can only yield negative results. God names these results in the prohibitions that follow. Considering Judah's weakness will lead to rejoicing—an outburst of, in this case, unrighteous happiness (Obadiah 12). God warns against this expression of an illegitimate emotion when Edom views "the day" of Judah's destruction.[4] Moreover, once having rejoiced, Edom must not open their mouths (see ESV note for "boast") to speak on "the day of distress" (Obadiah 12). The word translated as "distress" refers to a variety of military situations, from exerting pressure to laying siege. Here opening the mouth may be boasting, as the ESV renders it, but in context it likely means talking about how to leverage Judah's difficulties to Edom's advantage. After all, prohibition number four in verse 13a states, "Do not enter the gate of my people in the day of their calamity."[5] The type of speaking that God forbids leads to entering Judah's "gate," a metaphor for Judah's territory and towns (see v. 11).

In verse 13b, Obadiah begins the second set of four prohibitions. The combination of using the same verb that opens verse 12 and the repetition of "calamity" from the preceding line links to the whole list. Edom must not[6] look on Judah's calamity, lest this looking lead to looting of the towns (v. 13). Two things come into view here. With Judah in trouble, Edomites could both steal their possessions and settle in their houses.

Verse 14 prohibits even worse activity. God prohibits Edom from standing "at the crossroads to cut off his fugitives." At first, doing so might simply be an attempt to block their flight. Regardless, doing so would be a sin against desperate folk. Furthermore, Edom must not gather up survivors to hand them over to the invaders, or perhaps to sell them into slavery. Amos 1:6 identified Edom as slave traders. Again, if Judah's people were removed, then Edom had a chance to take their land and property. They could also sell some of the fugitives and earn some cash on the side. Murder, rape, and human trafficking went hand-in-hand with war then, just as they do now. God warns Edom against walking down such sordid paths.

The Edomites had a decision to make. Would they see that Judah was weakened by enemies and take advantage of the situation? Or would they shelter refugees, refrain from looting, and leave deserted towns alone so people who had fled could come back home? Will Edom see people as brothers and sisters rather than property to be bought and sold? Will Edom set aside old wrongs that Judah has done to them so that a better relationship might develop? Will they treat their neighbors as they wish to be treated? God's warnings could not be clearer or more specific.

They remain valid today. Think how world history would be different if these basic prohibitions had been honored. Think of how different current domestic and foreign policies would be if these commands were obeyed. Think about how different our Christian witness would be if believers refused to be part of breaking these commands. Edom eventually chose the wrong path, as we know. We ought to beware of following their example. Their day of decision became a day of disobedience. We can choose a different way.

## God's Day of Justice (vv. 15–20)

Given what is ahead, God's warning of Edom is especially kind. The day of the Lord, a time of judgment, is on the horizon. In this case it is a day of reckoning for all the nations, not just for Judah or for Edom. Obadiah 15–18 primarily explains what this means for Edom, while verses 19, 20 focus on what this means for Judah and Israel. God's days of judgment restore justice. All nations need to be on God's side when he judges. Edom still has the chance to do what is right.

In his mercy God reveals what is to come. Edom has been involved in regional political, military, and economic battles. While doing so, they have become linked to the wider activities of nations like Assyria and Egypt. God states that they are part of something much bigger than these international political-military intrigues. Obadiah discloses that Edom's day of decision precedes "the day of the LORD," which "is near" for "all the nations" (v. 15a).

As we learned from Joel and Amos, the day of the Lord is a time in history or at the end of history when God restores justice (see Joel 1:15; 2:1, 11, 31; 3:14; Amos 5:18–20). The phrase "all the nations" (Obadiah 15) here refers at least to all the nations involved in attacking or defending Judah in Obadiah's time. As we know from other Bible passages, God will judge all people at the end of time (see Revelation 20). The very fact of God's judgment should foster obedience in Edom.

So should the basis upon which God will assess Edom and all peoples: "As you have done, it shall be done to you; your deeds shall return on your own head" (Obadiah 15b).

This decision is completely fair and just. After all, the Edomites get to set their own standard, their own punishment, and their own reward. This is the same standard God set for the Israelites in Exodus 21:24: "eye for eye" (cf. Leviticus 24:17–21). It is sad that our culture tends to cite this standard as a threat or as the right to take revenge rather than as a call to mirror God's righteousness. If Edom obeys the prohibitions in Obadiah 12–14, then God's continued kindness will prevail. If Edom disobeys, then what they have done will come back to haunt them. Showing mercy and kindness now is the way through the day of the Lord, which is a day of perfect justice.

Verse 16 continues the warning. There is no difference in the grammar or setting in the verse's clauses.[7] The way Edom acts toward Mount Zion is how Edom will be treated. The same is true for the other peoples. In the Old Testament Prophets, the imagery of drinking in a foreign city usually refers to attacking and consuming that city (see, for example, Isaiah 51:17–23; Jeremiah 51:7; Ezekiel 23:32, 33; Habakkuk 2:16). The nations attacking Judah want to drink up Judah until nothing remains. Given the standard set in Obadiah 15, these peoples "shall be as though they had never been" (v. 16b). What they intended for Judah will be what they receive.

It is important to note a historical difference here. In the eighth century B.C., the day of the Lord brought the discipline of Judah without resulting in Jerusalem's capture or destruction (see Isaiah 2:12; 10:5–34; Hosea 1:7). In the sixth century B.C., the day of the Lord entailed both (see Jeremiah 39—52; Lamentations 1—4). What the next four verses describe fits the last half of the eighth century, not the last half of the sixth century.

The invaders may do as they will. "But in Mount Zion there shall be those who escape," according to Obadiah 17.[8] This declaration reminds us of Joel 2:32, which likewise establishes Jerusalem as a place where fleeing people may find refuge. As Johan Renkema explains, "When the nations are confronted with YHWH's [God's] judgment, the refugees in their midst are also in danger. Zion, however, is the place to avoid danger."[9] Isaiah 37 uses similar terminology for Jerusalem when Assyria invaded Judah in 701 B.C.[10] Because it is a place of refuge, Jerusalem "shall be holy," set apart for this purpose (Obadiah 17b). Furthermore, "the house of Jacob"— which refers to Judah and Israel combined—"shall possess their own possessions" (v. 17c). They will stay where they are. Edom will not get their lands and towns now. It is not yet time for the day of the Lord to include the loss of Jerusalem and the rest of the land.

Verse 18 promises worse things for Edom if they attack. They will find either Judah and Israel ("the house of Jacob") or Israel alone ("the house of Joseph") to be a fire that consumes. Jerusalem will not be a place where invading Edomites will survive, at least not now. In 587 B.C. Edom helped Babylon conquer Jerusalem (see Lamentations 4:22).

Obadiah 19 states more specifically what Israel and Judah will possess.[11] The prophet describes a multidirectional retaking of land. People of Judah in the south ("the Negeb") will move eastward into Edomite territory ("Mount Esau"). People of Judah in the west ("the Shephelah") will take back land from Philistia west and south, and then move north to "the land of Samaria." Benjamin will go northeast to Gilead. As a result, Obadiah 19 describes movements that reestablish the boundaries of David's kingdom.[12] However, Obadiah says nothing about reuniting Israel and Judah under David's household, as Hosea 3:4, 5 does. The point here is that Edom will not have Judah's or Israel's territories now. In fact, people driven from their homes will return to them.

Obadiah 20 reinforces this point. People exiled from the outer defensive cities of Israel[13] will live as far north as Zarephath, a town between Tyre and Sidon (see 1 Kings 17:9). People exiled from the area of Jerusalem to the Mediterranean[14] will come live in the south ("the Negeb," Obadiah 20). Homes lost will be recovered. Obadiah does not say who will rule the returning people from Israel and Judah, but he emphasizes the fact that Edom will not rule them. The taking of captives was normal when opponents invaded. Returning was also common. God will put Judahites and Israelites back in their homes.

God's day of justice sets things right. It always has, and it always will. In Obadiah's time, Edom discovered that greed, violence, and oppression would not get them what they wanted. God forbids it. As Malachi 1:2–5 and Lamentations 4:21, 22 show, the Israelites endured despite Edom's actions. God saw to it.

At the end of time God will assess all persons and all peoples. God's people will endure forever, safe with him (Revelation 21:1–7). Those who suffered at oppressors' hands will experience justice. So will the oppressor. Their deeds will boomerang, to paraphrase Obadiah 15. Until then, God continues to preserve his people for his purposes. Let us take heart, as Obadiah must have done. Let our decision be the right one, for God's justice will be served.

### The Kingdom Shall Be the Lord's (v. 21)

The closing verse provides both warning and hope. It warns those who oppose God that they will not succeed. It comforts those who suffer that God's justice will prevail. The day of the Lord demonstrates God's rule over all peoples and places. This was true in Obadiah's time, and it is true in ours.

Obadiah circles back to Edom from the lands he mentions in verses 19, 20. "Saviors" or "deliverers" on Mount Zion will "rule," which means "exercise justice," on Mount Esau. It is interesting that the word "saviors" is plural. Most Christians are used to thinking of only one Savior, the Lord Jesus. We need to remember that the term is much broader in the Bible. Nehemiah 9:27 calls Israel's judges "saviors," for example. Two other terms deserve mention in this regard. Micah 5:5, 6 mentions seven "shepherds" and eight "princes" who will help Judah's king defeat Assyria. Isaiah 32:1 states that "princes" will help the king defeat Assyria. Isaiah 34:8–12 includes the land of Edom in that victory. God will provide the necessary leadership to rule Mount Zion and Mount Edom justly.

These officials must rule justly, for "the kingdom shall be the LORD's" (Obadiah 21). God's rulers reign through righteous deeds and correct decisions (see Isaiah 32:1). This is because God loves righteousness and justice (see Psalm 33:5). God's kingdom reflects his character, which is good, righteous, gracious, merciful, and patient (145:7–13). God and his helpers provide "supportive justice for the poor and wretched and punitive justice for those who do evil."[15] I make this point in case anyone thinks vengeance is the point. God's justice rules out revenge.

Edom must accept God's rule and God's King. In Obadiah's time, that meant Edom needed to set aside other gods and come under the leadership of David's descendants. Hosea 3:4, 5 says the same thing about Israel, who had rejected David's dynasty two centuries earlier. Of course, Edom and Israel were not always treated well by David or his descendants, and Edom and Israel responded in kind. Thus God asks Edom to submit to him and his servants, trusting that God will keep his promises, trusting that his kingdom is where they need to be.

Jesus took up the theme of God's kingdom early and often in his work (see Matthew 12:28; Mark 1:15; Luke 4:43; 22:18; John 18:36). His followers are members of his kingdom (Luke 6:20), and they obey his teaching (vv. 46–49). When we sin, we confess our sins, and he forgives us (1 John 1:9, 10). While we will experience his kingdom fully only at the end of time (see Revelation 21:1–8), his rule over all things has begun. Jesus expects us to do his work in his way in his kingdom until we die or he comes back. Like Edom, we must give up greed and other gods. We must trust God and serve David's descendant, Jesus. God will rule, whether we bow or not.

Let us not forget what we learned from Amos 9:12 and from James's interpretation of it in Acts 15:15–19. The early church's ministry led some Edomites to believe and to build up David's fallen tent—his fallen kingdom. Faith in Christ united Israelites and Edomites in the early church, which revealed that all kingdoms are the Lord's.

## Conclusion

Perhaps you stand at your own crossroads today. You can go your own way or pursue God's way. You can take advantage of other people, including God's people, or you can show trusting, unwarranted compassion. You can enter God's kingdom and follow his King, or you can serve yourself or some false god.

Know the truth. God is kind enough to warn and righteous enough to judge. A day will come when your choices will be assessed. What you have done will be revealed, as Obadiah 15 declares. You can either enter God's kingdom, which means trusting and obeying him, and rebuild David's fallen tent, or you can drink the cup of God's judgment. The merciful God who warned Edom warns us now. May we thank him and embrace his rule.

# JONAH

*By Stephen M. Coleman*

# 32

# Running from God

JONAH 1:1-6

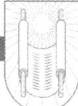

A LITTLE OVER A HUNDRED YEARS AGO, G. A. Smith wrote of the tragedy of the book of Jonah: "This is the tragedy of the Book of Jonah, that a Book which is made the means of one of the most sublime revelations of truth in the Old Testament should be known to most only for its connections with a whale."[1] The whale (literally, "great fish") for which the book is so famous appears in only three verses (1:17; 2:1, 10). Needless to say, *Jonah* is not primarily about a whale.[2] And despite its name, *Jonah* is not primarily about Jonah, either. God speaks both the first word and the last word of the book, a literary device that indicates his central role within the narrative. *Jonah* is primarily about God: specifically, it is about God's unwavering purpose to redeem a desperately wicked people for himself, a people comprised of both Jews and Gentiles. A central theme, if not *the* central theme of the book, is God's compassionate mercy—a mercy that at times offends and hardens hearts and yet at other times humbles and transforms lives.

Though recounting historical events, this remarkable little book was written not simply out of historical interest (i.e., to inform about the past).[3] *Jonah*, after all, is among the books of the prophets, and thus, unsurprisingly, it has an irreducibly prophetic message as it announces Israel's failure and God's faithfulness. This is to say, the story itself serves as a rebuke and a warning to Israel. It declares, in effect, that even though Israel, through her self-righteous disobedience and stubborn faithlessness, refused to fulfill her calling to be a kingdom of priests to the nations, God's promise to bless and to redeem the nations is not thwarted. In fact, through his sovereign and mysterious providence, God uses even Israel's sin and stubborn rebellion to accomplish this gracious purpose of extending mercy to Jewish sinners and Gentile sinners alike. We see this surprising work displayed in the life of Jonah as God uses his disobedient prophet to bring about the repentance of an entire city. However, God's surprising work through Jonah anticipates the even more surprising and ultimate work that God would accomplish through the greater Jonah, Jesus Christ (Matthew 12:38–41).[4]

Much more than an account of a peculiar encounter with a whale, *Jonah* is a story about sin and grace, repentance and forgiveness, death and life, and all of these grand themes are introduced in the opening verses. In fact, the opening scene might be thought of as a play within a play. In this little boat, as one author puts it, we have "in exquisite miniature, the situation of the world . . . a pagan world of many nations (represented by the mariners) threatened by the judgments of God, with Israel, (represented by Jonah) present in the midst."[5]

### God's (Un)surprising Commission (1:1–2)

Like a melody that opens and closes a piece of jazz music, so the divine words that bookend this narrative set the tone for the entire story. Both God's first word and God's last word reveal something of his deep and unwavering compassion for Gentile nations. In Jonah 1:2 God commands his prophet, "Arise, go to Nineveh, that great city, and call out against it, for their evil has come up before me." To be sure, God's initial command sounds much more like an intent to judge Nineveh than to pardon her. However, the prophet (as well as the informed reader) understands that such an announcement of imminent divine judgment is often an implicit offer of forgiveness and pardon to those who would turn from their wickedness and humble themselves before God in repentance. We suspect the prophet knows as much in chapter 1, and our suspicions are confirmed in chapter 4:2.[6]

At the close of the book, God puts the question to his indignant prophet: "Should not I pity Nineveh, that great city, in which there are more than 120,000 persons who do not know their right hand from their left, and also much cattle?" (4:11). God's pity and God's compassion reach from the greatest to the least, including even the beasts of the field in the scope of his grace. Like the other prophetic books, *Jonah* affirms the reality that God will judge the Gentile nations for their evil, wickedness, and oppressions. But alongside this message, and perhaps even overshadowing it, is the message that God's mercy and compassion extend beyond the walls of his covenant people Israel and are at times set upon the most unlikely and unexpected peoples of this world. This is in fact the catalyst for the dramatic action in the book of Jonah. The prophet is given the awesome responsibility of delivering this message of God's grace for sinners, and he responds by running in the opposite direction.

Now it is important to note that Jonah does not object to God's mercy in principle. In fact, outside of the book that bears his name, the only other appearance of Jonah in the Bible is in 2 Kings 14:24–26, an account that clearly demonstrates Jonah's willingness to announce God's grace toward Israel:

> [Jeroboam II] did what was evil in the sight of the Lord. He did not depart from all the sins of Jeroboam the son of Nebat, which he made Israel to sin. He restored the border of Israel from Lebo-hamath as far as the Sea of the Arabah, according to the word of the Lord, the God of Israel, which he spoke by his servant Jonah the son of Amittai, the prophet, who was from Gath-hepher. For the Lord saw that the affliction of Israel was very bitter, for there was none left, bond or free, and there was none to help Israel.

Three things are important to notice in this account. First, Jeroboam II (c. 793–753 B.C.)—and the people of Israel following in his footsteps—persisted in the "sins of Jeroboam the son of Nebat." Second, despite their sin, God restored territory that had been lost to them, a remarkable demonstration of his grace for a wicked and undeserving people.[7] And third, the announcement of God's grace toward undeserving Israel came through the ministry of Jonah, the son of Amittai, the prophet.[8] When it comes to Israel, Jonah, it appears, is a willing (or at least unobjecting) emissary announcing glad tidings of divine mercy and gracious provision for his own people.[9]

But when God says to this same prophet, "Arise, go to Nineveh" (1:2), Jonah objects, refusing and protesting in the clearest possible way by making a beeline toward Tarshish (Jonah 1:2, 3). Jonah understands that an announcement of judgment against Nineveh entails the possibility of mercy as well, and the prospect that God would extend mercy to the Ninevites causes Jonah to run from God in chapter 1 and plunge into a suicidal despair in chapter 4.[10]

From one perspective, the prophet's response is unsurprising. Assyria was, after all, an empire whose might was exceeded only by their cruelty. In the history of empires, the Assyrians were arguably the most brutal, violent, and cruel of any empire that arose either before or after.[11] Known for flaying their captives alive and displaying their corpses on pikes, the Assyrian Empire was established and expanded in large measure through acts of intimidation and terror. Furthermore, at this particular moment in history, the Assyrians were increasingly becoming a threat to God's people.[12] "Is now the time," Jonah would have wondered, "to warn Assyria of God's judgment?" Regarding the city of Nineveh in particular, in Jonah's day Nineveh's star was rising as a major city in the empire, and her rise would continue until she eventually became the capital city of the entire empire (c. 700 B.C.), making her the most powerful city in the known world.[13] Certainly the great need of the day was God's judgment on Nineveh and not his mercy. Or so Jonah thought.

However, from another perspective, God's instructions are not surprising at all, and the prophet would have understood at least something of God's good plans and purposes in his commission to go to Nineveh. At this period in redemptive history, God's blessing of Israel's enemies was a sign of his displeasure with his own people.[14] In the Song of Moses, God said of his people Israel, "They have made me jealous with what is no god; they have provoked me to anger with their idols. So I will make them jealous with those who are no people; I will provoke them to anger with a foolish nation" (Deuteronomy 32:21). In Jonah's day, God is doing precisely what he had promised to do: responding to his people's sin by blessing their enemies, strengthening those who would oppose Israel as a sign of his displeasure. In this way, Jonah's mission to Nineveh served as a warning to his own people to turn from their sin and to walk faithfully before the Lord their God. The prophet's flight may rightly be interpreted as the prophet running from the Lord's difficult word of discipline and judgment against Israel. In Jonah's mission to Nineveh, God is saying, in effect, "If Israel won't listen to my prophets, I'll see if Nineveh does any better."

The covenantal context of Jonah's commission, however, goes far deeper than the curses of the Mosaic covenant.[15] God's extension of mercy and forgiveness to wicked Nineveh recalls another, older covenant: God's covenant with Abraham in which he promised to bless the entire world through Abraham's offspring. In Genesis 12:3 God said to Abram, "I will bless those who bless you, and him who dishonors you I will curse, and in you *all the families of the earth shall be blessed.*" God's purpose in his sovereign election of Israel has always been to work through them to bring the light of his salvation to the very ends of the earth, to those nations and countries and peoples who are not Israel, making them one people, chosen by God (Ephesians 2:11–22). The redemption of the nations was never plan B for God. Though Israel's wickedness had so dimmed her witness that little could be seen of the glory and majesty of her God, God's promises and purposes were nevertheless certain. God would bring the light of his mercy and grace to the foreign nations either through his people's obedience or, as we see in the case of Jonah, through his people's disobedience.

Thus from its opening words to its closing, the book of Jonah teaches us that God's mercy is indiscriminate. It will often be given to those whom the world (and even the Church) would think to be the least likely to receive it. This serves as an important reminder for Christians in every age, that God's ways are not to seek and save the best and the brightest, the most moral and upstanding, the most promising and respectable this world has to offer. Neither is it to redeem those who seem like they'd fit in well with the Church, as if the Church were a sort of country club for generally good people. Rather, out of his abundant love and compassion, out of the unfathomable depth of his mercy, God seeks and saves the most unexpected and the most desperately wicked and sinful that this world has to offer. He seeks out those who, to the world's mind (and sometimes, sadly, even to the Church's mind), are the last people with whom a holy God would get involved, and it is these people whom God pursues with his grace and mercy.

At the end of the day, Jonah found God's grace to be offensive (Jonah 4:1–3). God's grace was perfectly fine when it was extended to those who Jonah thought deserved it, especially, as we see in chapter 2, when it is extended to him. But when Jonah discovered that God's mercy extended to the Assyrians, he wanted nothing to do with it.

It was for this same reason that so many of Jesus's own people objected to him in his day. They thought, *If God is going to save some people and condemn others, he will certainly save the good people and condemn the bad. He will save the preachers and teachers and condemn the prostitutes and tax collectors.* But when the religious authorities objected to Jesus eating with tax collectors and disreputable sinners, Jesus responded, "Those who are well have no need of a physician, but those who are sick. I came not to call the righteous, but sinners" (Mark 2:17). Jesus told the chief priests and the elders, "Truly, I say to you, the tax collectors and the prostitutes go into the kingdom of God before you" (Matthew 21:31). Like Nineveh, the tax collectors and the prostitutes responded to God's offer of mercy and forgiveness, while the religious leaders (for the most part) rested comfortably on their own merit, and in pride and self-righteousness would not respond to Jesus's call to repentance and faith.

J. I. Packer once wonderfully summarized the gospel in just three words: "God saves sinners."[16] God does not wait until sinners clean themselves up a bit, get their lives together, and kick some of those particularly ugly sins and habits. God saves sinners—Jews and Gentiles, rich and poor, educated and uneducated, deeply broken and even more deeply broken. God delights in saving those whom this world would least expect because in so doing he testifies both to his sovereignty in salvation and the greatness of his mercy.

## A Prophet's Surprising Response (1:3–5)

In a book in which we find the surprising seemingly at every turn, we may be tempted to miss just how unsurprising the opening verses of *Jonah* really are: "Now the word of the LORD came to Jonah the son of Amittai, saying, 'Arise, go to Nineveh, that great city, and call out against it, for their evil has come up before me'" (1:1, 2). Here we have a fairly typical prophetic commission. We find similar commissions, for example, to Elijah (1 Kings 17:2–4), Jeremiah (Jeremiah 13:3), and Ezekiel (Ezekiel 3:22). However, with Elijah, Jeremiah, and Ezekiel, this prophetic commission is immediately followed by a record of the prophet's obedience in declaring the word of God (cf. 1 Kings 17:5; Jeremiah 13:5; Ezekiel 3:23). Knowing this makes Jonah 1:3 all the more startling because we read, "But Jonah rose to flee to Tarshish from the presence of the LORD."

The unexpectedness of Jonah's response would be humorous if it were not so tragic. We have a prophet (and there is nothing suggesting Jonah was a false prophet) who has stood in the presence of the thrice-holy God and who has been commissioned as the official emissary of the Almighty, who receives his mission from his great King and responds by running in the opposite direction. Clearly something has gone terribly wrong.

Nineveh was approximately 500 miles northeast of Israel. Jonah rose and fled to Joppa, southwest of Israel, with the intent of traveling to Tarshish, most likely (though not certainly) on the coast of modern-day Spain.[17] To the ancient mind, Tarshish may have been considered the very end of the world. There is nothing in the text that suggests that God's instructions were unclear, and there is nothing in the text to suggest Jonah was directionally challenged. Jonah's actions provide a clear and straightforward response to the word of God, in which God's ambassador in effect says to the sovereign King of the universe, "No!"

We are given a little window into the character of Jonah's rebellion in the episode in the boat in 1:4, 5. Here we find the pagan sailors in crisis, frantically and passionately calling out to their false gods for deliverance; and we find Jonah, who knows the one true God and whose job it is to intercede with God, sound asleep.[18] Interestingly, the captain's words to Jonah echo God's instructions in verse 2 when he says, "Arise, call out to your God!" (v. 6). Like the original audience, we too understand that this is in fact Jonah's job as a prophet—to call out to his God and to intercede for those in need of divine mercy. Jonah in all likelihood heard his divine commission from verse 2 reverberating in the captain's words in verse 6.[19] However, God's prophet tragically responds with a deafening silence. In his hard-heartedness and stubborn rebellion, Jonah is an unmitigated failure as a prophet.

But what is driving the prophet's rebellion? It is striking that the author does not disclose all that Jonah found objectionable about the Assyrians, nor his disgust at his mission to the Ninevites, nor even his concern about what such a mission would have meant for Israel as a nation. While these were no doubt contributing factors to the prophet's flight, they do not get to the very heart of the matter. Twice in only six verses we read that Jonah fled "away from the presence of the LORD" (v. 3). With this the author is signaling to us that at the end of the day, it was not the Assyrians to which Jonah objected most strenuously but God. Jonah's flight was not a flight from the Assyrians; it was a flight from God himself.

The author captures something of the character of Jonah's flight from God by depicting it throughout the narrative as a descent. In verse 3 Jonah goes "down to Joppa." Next, in a more literal translation of the Hebrew, we read that Jonah went "down onto the ship." In verse 5 we're told that Jonah went "down into the inner part of the ship." Jonah's descent will come to a climax when the prophet *goes down* into the depths of the sea, to the very "belly of Sheol" (2:2).[20] This physical journey downward is meant to reflect the prophet's spiritual journey away from God. It is a journey away from the land, the temple, the altar, the priesthood, the very means by which God extends his grace and blessing to his people. God's presence is the place of life and blessedness. As the psalmist says, "You make known to me the path of life; in your presence there is fullness of joy; at your right hand are pleasures forevermore" (Psalm 16:11). As we witness Jonah's physical descent away from the presence of the Lord, we are meant to see a spiritual movement from life to death. God is the author and sustainer of life, and as Jonah flees from his presence, he is moving closer and closer to the realm of the dead.

Death is, in fact, the end of all rebellion against God, and sin is, in essence, a flight toward death itself. Though sin often promises joy, freedom, life, and blessedness, it is in reality nothing more than what one author called "a banquet in the grave."[21] At times God allows his children to run a great distance from him for a long time before he, in his mercy, is pleased to draw them back to himself. Often, like Jonah's, the journey back is incredibly painful. It is a journey marked by sadness and regret and hurt both to ourselves and to others. But it is nevertheless a good path because it is a path back to God, the true fount of life and joy and blessedness.

Ultimately the only thing more difficult than taking the path back to God, as hard as it can be, is not taking it. Not taking it means being left to our own devices, in our own sin and misery, careening toward an eternal death, apart from the blessedness and the joy of God's presence. In these opening verses, we witness Jonah, God's prophet, humorously yet tragically running from the

God of life, the fount of joy. Wonderfully, however, we also witness God's relentless pursuit of his rebellious prophet.

### God's Gracious Pursuit (1:6)

There is something deeply ironic in the captain's words to the prophet when he says, "Perhaps the god will give a thought to us, that we may not perish" (Jonah 1:6). As readers we know that, far from forgetting Jonah and the sailors, Jonah's God is very much "giving a thought" to this little crew and to his rebellious prophet. In fact, it is God's thought about this boat that is precisely why it is, at that moment, threatening to break apart. And yet, contrary to the pagan sailors' expectations, the terror and the chaos they are experiencing is not the result of divine anger but of divine compassion. As Jonah flees from the presence of God, God pursues Jonah, being willing to go with him even to the very gates of Sheol so that he might rescue him from death.

In this we see an expression of God's long-suffering patience and his infinite love. After Jonah's high-handed and petulant rejection of God's word, God would have been perfectly just to abandon Jonah to the fate he both desires and deserves. But here at the very beginning of the narrative, in this tempest on the sea, we are given the wonderful message that God is not only pursuing the hearts of the Ninevites, but he is pursuing the hearts of Israel as well. Jonah is running headlong toward death, and God in his grace is, in a sense, running after him. Such is the depth of God's love and compassion.

Every Israelite reading or hearing this story would have understood that while it is not less than a story about God's rebellious prophet, it is much more than a story about God's rebellious prophet. Israel would have understood that her own sinfulness is simply Jonah's rebellion writ large, and that Jonah's rebellion is in a sense a microcosm of Israel's.[22] What the prophet does physically is what the nation was doing spiritually—refusing to obey God and fulfill their calling as a kingdom of priests and a light to the nations.[23] The story, in this sense, is a prophetic indictment. It serves as a warning and a question. In effect, God is asking Israel, "Are you going to persist in your rebellion? In your sin and self-righteousness will you refuse to obey my command to fulfill your calling of being my witness to the nations?"

Tragically Israel's response to God was a resounding "Yes, we will!" Thus in 722 B.C., God raised up Assyria as the rod of his judgment to scatter Israel, an event depicted vividly by Jonah's contemporary, the prophet Hosea, when he declared, "Israel is swallowed up; already they are among the nations as a useless vessel" (Hosea 8:8). However, God would not ultimately accomplish his work of extending grace to Jew and Gentile through the work of an unfaithful prophet but through the work of a faithful prophet. It would not be through a disobedient prophet like Jonah but through the obedient prophet Jesus Christ. In contrast to Jonah, the anti-missionary, Jesus would in the fullness of time come as the embodiment of the missionary heart of God (Galatians 4:4). Jonah ran *from* his enemies, but Jesus ran *toward* them. Jonah withheld grace from his enemies, but Jesus prayed for them on the cross, saying, "Father, forgive them, for they know not what they do" (Luke 23:34). Jonah hated those who would kill him, but Jesus set his face toward Jerusalem and wept for the city (Isaiah 50:6, 7; Luke 9:51; 19:41–44). Where Jonah would rather die than see his enemies saved (Jonah 4:3), Jesus did die and experience the full weight of God's judgment so that he would see his enemies saved (Romans 5:8).

God sent Jonah to show Israel who they were—a stubborn and rebellious people. God sent his Son to be for Israel who they were meant to be—the obedient son and the faithful servant. In Jesus, God was victorious. God accomplished his mission of redeeming Jewish and Gentile sinners alike. The good news is that at every point where Israel failed, Jesus succeeded. At every point we have failed in our sin, in our self-righteousness, in our pride, Jesus obeyed God perfectly for us. Jesus declared himself the One greater than Jonah who would die and after three days rise again (Matthew 12:39–41). Jesus died and rose again once so that by the grace of God we might die to sin and rise to new life in Christ daily, and so that we might be humbled by the greatness of our sin and the greatness of God's mercy to sinners like Jonah, like Nineveh, and like us.

# 33

# Divine Pursuit

JONAH 1:7-16

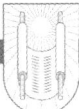

IT WAS IN THE EARLY-MORNING HOURS of September 28, 1994, that Europe experienced one of the worst maritime disasters in its history. As the luxury cruise liner the *MS Estonia* crossed the Baltic Sea, she encountered a ferocious storm, with waves over twenty feet high, creating a force that tore the bow from the ship. Within fifteen minutes the ship had rolled ninety degrees, and in less than an hour she had sunk below the waves, taking the lives of 852 of its 989 passengers.

In an article written for *The Atlantic*, William Langewiesche described the chaos that ensued in those last moments before the *Estonia* disappeared beneath the sea. In addition to rehearsing the tragic events themselves, Langewiesche captured the sense of hopelessness and helplessness that gripped the passengers in their race toward the upper deck in a final attempt to survive. He wrote, "There was no God to turn to for mercy. There was no government to provide order. Civilization was ancient history, Europe a faint and faraway place. Inside the ship, as the heel increased, even the most primitive social organization, the human chain, crumbled apart. Love only slowed people down. A pitiless clock was running. The ocean was completely in control."[1]

Much of Langewiesche's vivid description of the *MS Estonia*'s fateful night could apply equally well to the terrifying scene aboard the Tarshish-bound ship battered by a divinely appointed storm on account of a runaway prophet in the book of Jonah. In fact, the storm was so ferocious that we are told the well-seasoned sailors onboard—sailors who no doubt would have seen their fair share of storms in their lifetimes—"were afraid" (Jonah 1:5).

The crisis for these sailors is becoming more acute by the minute. As the severity of the storm increases, the ship's structure is becoming more and more precarious, a reality described vividly in verse 4, where we read that "the ship threatened [literally, thought] to break up." The reader can almost hear the ship's boards creaking on the verge of giving way to the relentless onslaught of the wind and waves.[2] Each sailor, having called out to his own deity (v. 5), must have concluded by this point that there was no help and no mercy to be had from any of their gods. In the words of Langewiesche, "A pitiless clock was running. The ocean was completely in control."[3]

It is in the disorienting chaos and danger of this storm at sea that these sailors receive a surprising revelation. From a reluctant prophet, these pagan sailors hear about the one true God who is sovereign over all of creation, who does as he pleases, and with whom there is mercy.

In his book *A Gracious and Compassionate God*, Daniel Timmer captures the dramatic tension of the scene. He writes,

> Their own gods (to whom they attributed the ability to control primarily just one sphere anyway) had failed to respond, or were unable to aid them, so that not just Jonah's words, but the sailors' present experience, remove all deities except Yahweh from the scene. The sailors and Jonah thus find themselves face to face with a deity who has unlimited power and has apparently begun to punish some sin among them.[4]

In this divinely appointed tempest we behold a remarkable display of God's sovereignty, power, and grace. However, in the Israelite prophet and the pagan sailors we meet two vastly different responses to God's sovereignty, power, and grace.

### The Sovereign Power of a Gracious God (1:7)

At first glance, God does not seem to be a major player in this scene, especially when we compare his clear presence and powerful actions in other parts of the story. In the opening scene, for example, we hear the Lord addressing Jonah directly: "Arise, go to Nineveh, that great city" (v. 2). We read in verse 4 that "the LORD hurled a great wind upon the sea." Immediately following this scene we read, "The LORD appointed a great fish to swallow up Jonah" (v. 17). At times God is speaking, hurling storms upon the sea, or appointing a great fish to do his bidding. But in this episode on the boat, God doesn't appear to be involved or even present. Consequently, we might be tempted to regard God as somewhat peripheral to the action onboard the vessel. However, to do so would cause us to miss perhaps the central message of this passage, because the author relates the events that take place in such a way as to highlight God's sovereign power and his complete control over every event, both large and small, that transpires on this little ship.

We read that the sailors cast lots, and "the lot fell on Jonah" (v. 7). Lot-casting was a common practice among pagans used to understand the mind or the will of the gods. It was believed to reveal things that the gods knew and that humans did not, and so would be used for determining, for example, guilt or innocence. Israel herself would at times cast lots for similar reasons.[5] In Joshua 7 Achan's guilt was revealed through the casting of lots (vv. 14, 15). In 1 Samuel 14:42 Jonathan was revealed as the guilty party through the use of lots. Though the sailors no doubt were appealing to any number of deities in their use of lots, the original audience of *Jonah* (and the contemporary audience) was meant to understand that the result of the lot-casting was nevertheless from the Lord. As Proverbs 16:33 says, "The lot is cast into the lap, but its every decision is from the LORD." It was not by chance, therefore, that the lot fell to Jonah. Yahweh was as sovereign over the lots that were cast in the laps of the sailors as he was sovereign over the winds of the sea that battered the ship.

The purpose of this episode, however, is not to offer a model for believers to discern the mind of God through the casting of lots. The point, rather, is to show how God condescended in such a way as to use this practice—common for pagans and familiar (if not common) to Israel—for his special redemptive purpose of exposing his prophet's guilt, an event that would set off a series of reactions that would lead to a wonderful revelation of God's grace and faithfulness. We see in this gracious condescension something of the missionary heart of God working all things together—including sinful pagan practices—to draw sinners to himself and, as we will see, to create worshipers of the true and living God.

We see God's sovereignty not only over the lots but also over the storm at sea. In Jonah 1:13, we read that as the sailors rowed hard to get back to dry land, "the sea grew more and more tempestuous against them." Who was it, we might ask, that caused the storm to "grow more and more tempestuous against them" and thus prevented the sailors and Jonah from reaching the shore? Clearly it was the same God who is sovereign over the great fish, the *qiqqayon* plant, and the east wind. In this tempest at sea, the Lord has a lesson both for Jonah and for the sailors, and the lesson could not be learned (at least not in the same way) with Jonah and the sailors reaching the safety of dry land. The astute reader, therefore, is meant to see the Lord's sovereignty over the terrifying and chaotic power of the storm and the sea. Everything is working together to expose Jonah's guilt and draw him back to God.

Strikingly, we see that the Lord is sovereign over not only the raging chaos of the sea but also over the otherworldly calm of the sea. Even more amazing than his ability to send the storm is God's ability to still the storm, thus bringing order out of chaos. When the sailors hurl Jonah into the sea, we're told that immediately "the sea ceased from its raging" (1:15). So sudden and so drastic was the change in the weather that it served as a final and undeniable confirmation of Yahweh's identity. Yahweh is, indeed, the Lord of the sea and the dry land.

As any parent of a two-year-old knows, it is much easier to cause chaos than order. Interestingly, in the Babylonian flood narratives, the gods were able to destroy the land with a flood, but they were not able to stop the chaos once it was unleashed.[6] We see a similar dynamic in the exodus event when Pharaoh's magicians were able to replicate the first two plagues, thus adding to the chaos and destruction of Egypt, but they were impotent when it came to ending the chaos and establishing order (Exodus 8:7, 8).[7] Yahweh, however, time and again brings order out of chaos. God not only sends the storm, he also stills the storm. He is equally sovereign over chaos and order, and he employs both to accomplish his sovereign will.[8]

Far from being uninvolved or remote from the events on this small vessel, God is in control of every lot that is cast; he is sovereign over every wave that strikes and threatens to destroy the little ship carrying Jonah and the sailors. Here we meet a God who is in absolute control over the smallest events of what many call chance, and he's sovereign over the greatest forces known to humankind. The winds and the waves obey his voice. So it is no wonder that the sailors respond the way they do. In Jonah 1:5, we are told that the storm was so severe, the sailors were afraid; but at the end, when they encounter the power of the God of the storm, we read, "The men feared the LORD" (v. 16). No longer the storm but God becomes the object of the sailors' fear.[9]

Who is it that could calm such a storm by the will of his power? In Mark 4 we read of Jesus's disciples caught in a storm on the Sea of Galilee (vv. 35–41). Gripped by fear, they wake their Master, who rebukes his disciples for their weak faith and then rebukes the sea, which immediately stands still. How do the disciples respond to the power and sovereignty of this man who calms the storm with a word? Mark tells us, "They were filled with great fear and said to one another, 'Who then is this, that even the wind and the sea obey him?'" (4:41).

However, in addition to offering a portrait of the sovereign power of God, this passage in Jonah 1 also offers a portrait of the sovereign grace of God. This becomes clear when we consider God's purposes in sending this awesome and awful storm, in the lot-casting revealing the culpability of his prophet, and in Jonah being tossed into the sea. What is God's purpose in all of this? In all of this, God is employing his sovereignty and power to stop his rebellious prophet in his tracks. Like a parent shouting at or grabbing a child careening into oncoming traffic, the storm has not been sent to punish Jonah. It has not been sent to terrorize Jonah for his disobedience. It has not been sent as poetic justice against the fleeing servant of the Lord. The storm has been sent to stop Jonah because Jonah was fleeing from the presence of the Lord of life.

The presence of the Lord is the place of life and blessedness. It is the place of wholeness and peace. To flee from the presence of the Lord is to flee toward death, a reality the prophet himself will acknowledge in his song from the depths: "I went down to the land whose bars closed upon me forever; yet you brought up my life from the pit" (Jonah 2:6).[10]

Along with this revelation of the unbridled power of God, we see also a revelation of the unfathomable love of God in which he marshals the created order to stop Jonah in his tracks so that he might draw him back to faith and submission to a loving God.

In this we find a precious gospel truth that is critical for Christians in every age. Whatever storms we might be facing—whether they be storms at work or in a relationship or in a marriage, struggle with a sin, suffering the consequences of a sin, illness, depression, anxiety, or anything else—we can know with certainty that the storms are not in control of our lives, and our lives are not out of control. God holds even our storms in the palm of his hand, and he is able, in his way and in his time, to use these storms for our good and to calm them for his glory. Though God may seem absent or his presence may be difficult to discern, Jonah 1 tells us that God is in fact present in every trouble, and he is in complete control. Not a wave struck Jonah's vessel, not a board groaned under the force of the sea, apart from God's sovereign good pleasure. God is sovereign—he's sovereign over the big things and over the little things. As Jesus reminded his disciples, not a sparrow falls to the ground apart from our Father's care (Matthew 10:29). More than that, we can see that our perfectly sovereign God is also perfectly good.

This storm no doubt felt to Jonah like God's judgment, like God was punishing him for his disobedience, his stubbornness, and his hard-hearted rebellion. Jonah probably felt hunted by God, threatened by God. The storm certainly didn't feel like God's loving-kindness toward him in that moment.

But God's hand of discipline, I suspect, rarely does. The reality is that God was pursuing Jonah every bit as much as he was pursuing the sailors and the Ninevites with his gracious, forgiving, redeeming love. Jonah was running straight toward the gates of Hell, and God moved Heaven and earth to stop him.

Jonah would have thought this was God's punishment; however, as readers, we know it was nothing of the sort. So it is with our trials as well. In fact, the Bible teaches throughout that God disciplines the one he loves (Psalms 94:12; Proverbs 3:12; Hebrews 12:6). For those who are in Christ Jesus by faith, not one of the storms we face in this life is punitive. We may be certain of this because Jesus, the Son of God, bore in his body the full extent of God's punishment for every one of our sins, past, present, and future. On the cross God poured out on his own Son his wrath and his curse for sins Jesus did not commit so that sinners might know God's loving hand of discipline. Though they may feel like the hand of God's judgment, even those disastrous consequences we experience on account of our foolish sin are in reality the disciplining hand of a loving Father who knows that if left to ourselves we, like Jonah, would run headlong into the very pit of Sheol (Jonah 2:2). In his mercy, in his lovingkindness, in his grace, God stops us in our tracks so that he might draw us back to himself in repentance and faith.

We do not call storms themselves good, but by faith we know and confess that the God of the storms is without question very good.

## A Prophet's Persistent Rebellion (1:8–15)

The centerpiece of this passage is undoubtedly Jonah's great confession. As the lot reveals Jonah to be the cause of the sailors' crisis, the sailors respond with a barrage of questions—all in an attempt to discern the reason for this great catastrophe, what the text refers to literally as an "evil" that has "come upon us" (1:8). "Tell us," they say, "on whose account this evil has come upon us. What is your occupation? And where do you come from? What is your country? And what people are you?" Jonah no doubt would have carried an aura of mystery about him.[11] Most on the ship would have been merchants, yet Jonah showed up with no merchandise. The sailors were crying to their gods for help, yet Jonah prayed not a word. In fact, some have suggested that the fare Jonah paid for the ship (v. 3) effectively chartered the entire vessel for his personal voyage.[12]

Who is this mysterious figure? The prophet responds to their queries with what is essentially a creed or confession of faith: "I am a Hebrew, and I fear the LORD, the God of heaven, who made the sea and the dry land" (v. 9).[13]

What are we as readers to make of this confession? On the one hand, we see in the prophet's confession a decidedly orthodox theology. Jonah identifies his God, Yahweh, translated as "the LORD," with the God who created all things. God is the God of Heaven, and he made the sea and dry land. Here the prophet uses a *merism*, where he cites two extremes to indicate everything in between—as, for example, to pray night and day is to pray all the time. Saying that the Lord is God of the sea and dry land is to say he is the God of the entire cosmos.[14]

In this remarkably brief confession there is a wealth of orthodox theology. Jonah's confession is a good confession. It is a true confession in the sense that what is expressed about God is true. However, we quickly learn that this good and true confession is uttered by the prophet in bad faith. In other words, there is a profound, even tragic, incongruity between what the prophet says with his mouth and what the prophet does with his life.[15]

The disconnect between Jonah's words and Jonah's actions is not lost on the sailors. After his confession Jonah presumably fills the sailors in on the backstory, making them aware of what has transpired between Yahweh and himself. The sailors, we're told, are exceedingly afraid, and they say to Jonah, "What is this that you have done!" (v. 10). Timmer has written that the sailor's response, "What have you done?" is a "cry of terror springing from knowledge."[16] The sailors have finally come to understand the truth of what is happening. They wonder, in utter astonishment, "How do you expect to flee from the presence of the God of Heaven, who is sovereign over land and sea? Where do you think you're going to go? How do you think you would succeed?"

It is a remarkable scene. In their astonishment we hear, as it were, the Gentile nations of the earth standing in judgment on Israel. The Gentile nations of the earth, represented by the sailors, surround Israel, represented by Jonah, and say, in effect, "What is this you have done?" In Jeremiah 2:10, 11 God speaks to his people with a similar note of astonishment:

> Cross to the coasts of Cyprus and see,
>   or send to Kedar and examine with care;
>   see if there has been such a thing.
> Has a nation changed its gods,
>   even though they are no gods?
> But my people have changed their glory
>   for that which does not profit.

It is a dark day when the pagan nations arise in righteous judgment on God's people. Jesus appealed to Jonah to make this very point: "The men of Nineveh will rise up at the judgment with this generation and condemn it, for they repented at the preaching of Jonah, and behold, something greater than Jonah is here" (Matthew 12:41).

The book of Jonah is a prophecy to and for Israel. The people of Israel were meant to see in the character of Jonah a portrait of themselves. Israel saw themselves in Jonah's disobedience as he refused to bring God's word to the nations, but Israel also was meant to see themselves in Jonah's confession. Like the prophet, Israel had correct theology, they had the covenants and the promises, they had God's word and God's revelation of Torah, and they could give the right answers. But when it came to their hearts, as God said through his prophet Isaiah, "this people draw near with their mouth and honor me with their lips, while their hearts are far from me" (Isaiah 29:13).

What Jonah says about God is true, but the tragedy is that he doesn't really understand it or believe it. Jonah says, "I fear the LORD" (Jonah 1:9), but the fundamental characteristic of someone who fears the Lord is someone who obeys the Lord. Though a God-fearer doesn't obey perfectly, one who fears the Lord is one who, when confronted, is willing to acknowledge his or her sin, repent of sin, and seek by God's grace to turn from his or her sin. The one thing that is conspicuously absent in this scene is any notion that Jonah grieves over his sin or repents of his rebellion. Unlike the sailors, Jonah doesn't pray. The one option that seems to go unmentioned is the option of repentance and renewed obedience.

Of course, we need to be careful about speculating about Jonah's heart. The author does not provide details of the spiritual state of the prophet. However, one thing we can say with certainty is that Jonah would rather die than obey the Lord. He would rather die than bring the word of God to the Ninevites.[17]

Jonah's response is surprising. It's surprising because Jonah should have known better. He had all the right theology, he knew all the right words, he had all the right credentials, and yet Jonah was entrenched in his rebellion and unrepentance and would rather die than submit to the will and word of God. Isn't this always the character of sin? It is a race toward death, and yet as we run headlong to our destruction, we convince ourselves that the way is good, right, beautiful, pleasant, and true.

Jonah's confession offers God's people a sobering warning. It's a warning against hypocrisy, against saying the right things and knowing the right things, but at the end of the day not seeing ourselves in need of the forgiving, transforming grace of God. It's a warning against giving voice to our faith in God and love of Christ and yet, in reality, refusing with an entrenched stubbornness to acknowledge God's rightful lordship over every area of our lives.

Yet the good news is that God pursues Jonah and that God's grace is sufficient for hypocrites and Pharisees as well. One of the surprising messages of the Gospels is that Jesus came for the most unlikely of people in his day: the pimps and the prostitutes, the traitors, thieves, and tax collectors. And in hearing this, we learn of the depths of God's love—that it can reach even these.

Time and again Jesus defended himself against charges from the Pharisees for sharing table fellowship with such disreputable sinners. It's tempting to think Jesus chose these and rejected the self-righteous, hypocritical Pharisees. But then we read passages like Luke 7, where we see Jesus eating with Simon the Pharisee (vv. 36–50). Here we see Jesus telling Simon the parable of the moneylender precisely because Jesus is pursuing the heart of Simon the Pharisee just as much as he's pursuing the tax collectors and prostitutes.

The fact is, we all run from God; we all can at times live hypocritical lives. But the good news is that the Son of God also laid down his life and bore the curse of sin for such as these. God continues to pursue hard-hearted, stubborn hypocrites with the very same gospel that can change even the most self-righteous hearts.

### The Gentiles' Humble Worship (1:16)

There is certainly something humorous in the flight of the prophet. As Jonah is running from his divine calling to preach to the Gentiles, we see the prophet inadvertently transforming an entire ship of Gentiles into worshipers of Yahweh.[18] These sailors were not, as Bryan Estelle has so helpfully noted, "innocent bystanders . . . caught up in the counteraction of a deity in hot pursuit of his aberrant prophet. Their own idolatries qualify them as the object of God's wrath (Rom. 3:10–18)."[19] Yet when the sea ceases its raging, we read, "Then the men feared the LORD exceedingly" (Jonah 1:16). Unintentionally, and unbeknownst to Jonah, who was at this point sinking into the heart of the sea, these pagan sailors had, at the very least, recognized Yahweh, the God whom Jonah preached to them. They recognized Yahweh as the God of the sea and dry land. Furthermore, they adopted the appropriate posture of a creature before its Creator. To "fear the Lord" refers to that posture of reverential awe before the majesty of the holy God who is the Creator and sustainer of all things.

The pagan sailors feared the Lord, and then we're told, "They offered a sacrifice to the LORD and made vows" (1:16). This is the language of worship. Offering sacrifices and making vows to the Lord were the basic elements of Israelite worship. Psalm 50:14, 15, for example, says, "Offer to God a sacrifice of thanksgiving, and perform your vows to the Most High, and call upon me in the day of trouble; I will deliver you, and you shall glorify me." Importantly, we're told that the sailors offered sacrifices and made vows "*to the Lord*" (Jonah 1:16). It was to Yahweh, the God of Israel, of whom they possibly had just heard only moments prior, that these sailors directed their worship.

We could not have more strikingly dissimilar portraits than that of Jonah and the sailors. One commentator put it like this:

> The reactions of the gentile sailors and the prophet of the Lord to the looming peril of death by drowning are poles apart and quite the opposite of what one might have expected. In contrast to the sailors' clear vision and perfect compliance with the voice of the Lord, as it rises from the waves of the storm-tossed sea, Jonah shuts his eyes against the truth and, when compelled to open them, persists in his stubborn refusal to obey.[20]

Jonah identifies himself as one who fears the Lord, and yet nothing in his behavior evidences the fear of the Lord.[21] By contrast we find the sailors, who know precious little about Yahweh, doing the very thing Jonah (and Israel) should be doing. Perhaps more surprising than Jonah's unresponsiveness to the grace and mercy of God are the sailors, who are depicted as engaging in the worship of the very God from whom Jonah is fleeing.

To be sure, I do not think the Biblical author here is claiming that every pagan sailor onboard became a faithful Yahwist from this day forward, submitted to circumcision, worshiped in Jerusalem, followed Torah, etc.[22] The point is, rather, that through their encounter with even a rebellious prophet and their experience of God's great power and mercy, they were transformed. They had an encounter with the sovereign God that would make an indelible impact on their hearts and minds, and they responded appropriately.

Ultimately, the sailors are transformed by submitting to the sovereignty of God. Their efforts to row to land having failed (v. 13), the sailors are left with one option: to hurl the prophet of God overboard, presumably to his death. Understandably concerned that God would hold them liable for the death of his prophet, they lay their petition before the Lord: "O Lord, let us not perish on account of this man's life, and lay not on us innocent blood, for you, O Lord, have done as it pleased you" (v. 14). They confess God's sovereignty in the events that have transpired on the sea: "O Lord, [you] have done as it pleased you." The sailors would have been deeply impressed with the reality of God as a God of justice as they witnessed the divine pursuit of a disobedient prophet. But what about God's mercy? Like Nineveh will do later, the sailors can only hope against hope that, perhaps, this sovereign God might possibly be inclined to show mercy to those who repent and call out for help in the midst of the storm of his judgment. So they cry out just before they lift Jonah and hurl him over the edge of the ship.

That Jonah had a death wish is clear. Why he insisted that the sailors hurl him overboard instead of, for example, jumping overboard himself is unclear (v. 12). It is suggestive that the word translated as "picked up" (v. 15) is only rarely used for individuals and is more commonly used for the removal of sin and guilt from the community.[23] Perhaps the prophet was deeply impressed with the reality of his guilt and yet, unwilling to repent of his sin, believed his only option was to submit to divine judgment. From one perspective, however, Jonah's psychology is immaterial. What the sailors experienced was that their lives were spared because of the self-sacrifice of a prophet of God. Dim as it was, the sailors beheld in this a faint shadow of another, future sacrifice, a sacrifice not of a disobedient prophet but of an obedient prophet, Jesus, the incarnate Son of God.[24] And this, we see, was enough for the sailors to fall on their faces in worship.

What a contrast to Israel! Here we see pagan, Gentile sailors worshiping the Lord. Look at how much they do with so little! They know nothing of the Torah or covenant; they know nothing of Abraham and the patriarchs; and they know nothing of the covenant of grace and the Messiah. And yet the last we hear of them, they are worshiping the God who made the heavens and the earth. But Israel, who has all of these blessings and privileges, is so slow to repent, so slow to turn, so slow to obey, and so half-hearted in worship. God's prophet reveals how unresponsive God's people have become to God's word. Of course, in the pagan sailors-turned-worshipers of the Lord, we're given a foretaste of what God will do in Nineveh. In Nineveh we will see an entire city of pagan Gentiles turning from their wickedness and repenting before the sovereign Judge of the universe (3:6–8).

In both of these events we are reminded of God's faithfulness to his covenant promises. He offers us a picture of the fulfillment of God's covenant of grace that promises that the blessings of Abraham will one day extend to the whole world. Genesis 12:3 says, "In you [Abraham] all the families of the earth shall be blessed." Israel had become unfaithful to their covenantal responsibilities and had forgotten their calling. However, just because Israel had become unfaithful and had forgotten did not mean that God had become unfaithful and had forgotten.

We see here that God is going to accomplish his purposes, not through Israel's obedience but despite Israel's disobedience. It will be through the obedience of the seed of Abraham—Jesus Christ—that the Abrahamic blessings to the nations will be fulfilled.

Even in Jesus's own lifetime we see hints and glimmers of what would come to pass at Pentecost as Jesus speaks to the Samaritan woman at the well (John 4:1–30) or as we hear about the faith of the Syro-Phoenician woman (Mark 7:24–29). But by and large Jesus's pre-resurrection ministry was a ministry to his own, yet as the Apostle John tells us, "His own people did not receive him" (John 1:11). In Jonah's day, God would use the wickedness and sin of his prophet to accomplish his purposes to preach the gospel to the nations.[25] However, in an even greater way in Jesus's day, God would use the sin of his people Israel to accomplish the redemption of the nations, Jews and Gentiles alike, when they nailed the Son of God to a cross (Acts 2:23, 39).

God sovereignly advances his purposes of redemption, renewal, and forgiveness in a world that strains under the curse of sin and that, like Jonah's boat, is threatening to break apart. God, by his common grace, is preserving this world, and God, in his saving grace, is pursuing sinners. Here too we discover another gospel truth: that the hope of the world, does not rest on our faithfulness to God but on God's faithfulness to us. We see God pursuing lost and broken people, Jews and Gentiles alike, with the hope of the gospel so that all who would believe and submit to his sovereignty and goodness will receive his mercy and forgiveness in abundance.

## 34

# Prayer from the Depths

JONAH 1:17—2:10

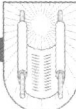

FOR OUR TWO- AND FOUR-YEAR-OLD CHILDREN (at the time) the highlight of living in a high-rise apartment overlooking Washington, D.C., was not the view we had of the National Cathedral, the Washington Monument, or the Capitol building. It was the view we had of the Discovery building that once a year decorated their office building with an enormous inflatable shark known affectionately to the locals as Chompy. Imagine a gigantic inflatable shark head on the front of a building, two enormous fins on the sides, a tail on the back, and a dorsal fin adorning the top, and you can easily understand why our children could spend hours at our window keeping an eye on (and sometimes talking to) Chompy. Chompy heralded the annual arrival of "Shark Week," which in those days was one of the longest-running and most successful cable television programs in history. The immense popularity of this program—which is basically the same year after year—attests to the insatiable fascination we have with these monstrous and dangerous creatures of the deep.

This fascination, however, is not only a modern phenomenon. The ancients also regarded the great creatures of the sea with a similar mixture of awe and terror. The sea itself was a symbol of chaos—a picture of the disordered world and a threat to human life.¹ The great sea creatures that inhabited it were common symbols of both evil and death.² Knowing this makes *Jonah*'s portrait of God all the more majestic because in *Jonah* we meet a God who exercises sovereignty and control over what were considered the most powerful, terrifying, and dangerous forces in the known world. At the beginning of chapter 1, God demonstrates his power over the winds and the seas, sending a storm to stop his rebellious prophet in his tracks. At the end of chapter 1, God appoints a great fish to swallow Jonah (v. 17). After Jonah's prayer from the depths we read, "The LORD spoke to the fish, and it vomited Jonah out upon the dry land" (2:10). In contrast to many pagan myths in which the gods do battle with the sea or a sea monster, what opposes God in the book of Jonah is not the sea or the sea creatures, but human beings.[3] And not just any human being but God's own prophet takes his stand in opposition to the Almighty.

Jonah opposes God, but God does not come after his rebellious prophet in a thundercloud of judgment. God does not assault Jonah to destroy him. Like he does with Jacob by the Jabbok river (Genesis 32:22–32), God assaults Jonah to save Jonah. The instrument of God's salvation is a great fish (all we're told about the fish is that it was "great") that he uses to reveal to Jonah, to Israel who first read this book, and to us today that he is not only a God who is sovereign, but he's also a God who is merciful. Jonah, for his part, comes to understand this in new and profound ways: the great fish is not an expression of God's judgment but God's mercy, and he responds by issuing a prayer of thanksgiving (Jonah 2:2–9).[4]

This prayer from the belly of the fish is an expression of the prophet's deep gratitude that God delivered him from certain and well-deserved death. In fact, the message of the prayer and probably the whole book of Jonah may be summarized in the last line: "Salvation belongs to the LORD!" (v. 9). What is not clear, however, is whether the prophet fully understands what "salvation belongs to the LORD" means. He certainly apprehends its truth in part, and he confesses it in a prayer of thanksgiving: God is a God of salvation. Though Jonah had been brought low on account of his sin and rebellion, God in his boundless grace has raised him up. The hymn or prayer itself follows this movement from death to life, from descent to the grave to ascent to newness of life.

## Jonah's Descent into Death (2:2–6)

As we witness the prophet's descent into the depths of the sea, we must remember that this descent is simply the last leg of a journey that began much earlier. When God commanded Jonah to go to Nineveh and preach repentance to the Ninevites, the prophet fled in the opposite direction, "from the presence of the LORD" (1:3). Throughout the narrative, the author speaks of Jonah's flight from the presence of God as a descent. In 1:3 we read that Jonah "went *down* to Joppa." There he bought a ticket on a ship headed for Tarshish, and we're told that Jonah "went *down*" into the ship. When God sends a storm on the sea that threatens to destroy Jonah's boat, we're told that Jonah had "gone *down* into the inner part of the ship" to sleep (v. 5).[5]

In Jonah's prayer he recalls that he was "cast into the deep, into the heart of the seas" (2:3). In 2:5, 6 he says,

> The waters closed in over me to take my life;
>     the deep surrounded me;
> weeds were wrapped around my head
>     at the roots of the mountains.
> I *went down* to the land
>     whose bars closed upon me forever.

Jonah's descent is not just his sinking into the sea, but he describes it quite appropriately as his descent into the realm of death itself.[6] In 2:2 Jonah says, "Out of the belly of Sheol I cried, and you heard my voice." The prophet had arrived at the belly of Sheol, and it was from Sheol that he issued his cry for help.[7] Sheol, for ancient Israel, was the place of the dead, a place of divine abandonment, if not punishment. It is the final destiny of the wicked, a sad, shadowy existence apart from God's gracious presence, and it is the very place to which Jonah had been fleeing.[8]

In this poem, the prophet paints a vivid picture. We can imagine this lone figure sinking slowly into the sea, struggling for breath, and experiencing the first pangs of that horrible and final reality we call death. The seaweed that entangles him foreshadows the chains that will bind him in his watery grave forever.[9] Jonah enters a state of panic, distress, despair, and grief. He is utterly hopeless and helpless.

The Biblical author records this terrifying experience not to celebrate Jonah's experience as a survivor or as a sort of celebration of his greatness or good fortune. The author records this experience in such vivid detail to show us precisely what God saved him from: God delivered Jonah from death. The imagery here suggests not just physical death but an eternal death. Hans Walter Wolff captures the scene well when he writes: "The 'bars' indicate the world of the dead conceived as a fortified city. . . . If these bars are closed 'behind' (*b'd*) a human being, they remain 'finally' shut. . . . Thus for the psalmist, Jonah's fate at the end of the voyage seemed to be an inescapable descent to death."[10] In his prayer Jonah is saying, in effect, that his experience of pain and terror, of agony and grief, of distress and helplessness and hopelessness at having run from God in rebellion and disobedience, can be best described and understood as entering Hell itself.

In this way, the author is showing us that Jonah's rebellious flight from God is nothing less than a flight from life since God is life in himself and he is the source of life for his people. It is in fellowship with God and in obedience to his commands that his people come to experience life in its fullest. Conversely, as the prophet bears witness, sinful rebellion against God and a refusal to submit to his word and will inevitably result in death and an absence from God's goodness and gracious presence. While it promises to be the road to freedom and self-realization, sin results in a life void of hope and joy and beauty.

Jonah's description of his entrance into Sheol is, of course, a metaphor. Jonah hadn't in reality entered the belly of Sheol. He hadn't literally entered that permanent state of divine abandonment. The bars of Sheol hadn't shut behind him forever. But there is one who would enter that state of God-forsakenness beyond anything experienced by Jonah—namely, Jesus Christ. Jonah's cry of dereliction is just a faint echo of Jesus's cry from the cross: "My God, my God, why have you forsaken me?" (Matthew 27:46). Whatever unimaginable distress, grief, and pain Jonah experienced in his descent into the abyss, it was nothing compared to what Jesus experienced on the cross at Calvary. John Calvin and others have rightly seen in Jesus's cry of dereliction what one commentator has called "the very finest commentary on the ancient creed, 'He descended into Hell.' "[11] Jesus experienced on the cross the ultimate and absolute abandonment by his Father. Yet the hell into which Jesus ran was not for his own sin but for ours. The hell from which Jonah was delivered, Jesus experienced in its fullness.

Jonah's descent to the gates of Hell serves as a helpful reminder of the seriousness and consequence of sin. This is something we need to be reminded of daily, as we are prone to forget and to treat our sin as a light, inconsequential matter. Far from inconsequential, our sin required nothing less than the Son of God to suffer an unimaginable death on a Roman cross, the immense horrors of which we will never fully comprehend. God would snatch Jonah from the jaws of death that Jesus would enter in Jonah's place. Such is God's love and mercy, even to those who flee his presence.

## Jonah's Judgment (2:3, 5)

Jonah's sin brought him down to the realm of death, but God's grace will raise him up. However, what of Jonah's (and, by implication, Israel's and our own) sin? What about God's judgment of his obstinate and disobedient servant? The answer to this is perhaps most clearly seen in another allusion in the prophet's prayer of thanksgiving.

Scholars have pointed out that Jonah's description of his death by drowning (Jonah 2:3, 5) draws on language derived from the ancient Near Eastern legal practice known as a trial by ordeal.[12] The trial by ordeal was a legal practice in which the accused would be subjected to a physical test, and his response to this test would reveal his guilt or innocence. It was believed that the response of the accused to the ordeal was the god issuing a divine verdict. Perhaps the most common trial by ordeal in the ancient Near East was the river ordeal in which the accused would dive into the river and swim a predetermined course. If he passed through in safety, he was pronounced innocent; if he succumbed to the river, he was pronounced guilty.[13]

While Israel did not practice the river ordeal as far as we know, they did practice other ordeals—specifically the drinking ordeal, as attested in Numbers 5:11–31. Just as the numerous references to "the cup of God's wrath" utilize the image of the drinking ordeal, so too do numerous passages (like Jonah's prayer) utilize imagery of the river ordeal.[14] Israel's poets used this dramatic judicial practice to describe their experiences both personally and as a nation. In his psalm, Jonah casts God as his accuser and judge when he says, "For *you* cast me into the deep." As he is beset on every side with the onrush of waters, he says, "All *your* waves and your billows passed over me." As he describes his descent to "the roots of the mountains" (2:6), Jonah is describing the place of judgment, and Jonah understands that his death was God's righteous judgment for his rebellion.

The prophet describes his ordeal with language from Israel's national anthem, the Song of the Sea recorded in Exodus 15:1–18. This song celebrates Israel's victory over Egypt with images of trial by ordeal as the Egyptian army is thrown into the depths of the sea and drowns while Israel passes through in safety and vindication. The prophet speaks of "the deep" (Jonah 2:3; Exodus 15:5), "the abyss" (Jonah 2:5; Exodus 15:5, AT),[15] "the heart of the seas" (Jonah 2:3; Exodus 15:8), and "the weeds [seaweed]" (Jonah 2:5; Exodus 15:4). It is striking, however, that the prophet identifies more with Egypt than with Israel. As he sinks down into the depths of the sea Jonah believes, "*Like Egypt before me, I am now drowning under the righteous judgment of the God I opposed.*" And yet Jonah, like Israel before him, does not ultimately sink into the abyss of God's judgment; rather, he experiences a remarkable act of God's saving power and grace.

Clearly Jonah's deliverance is not on account of his own righteousness. We know Jonah was, is, and would continue to be a sinner in need of God's grace. Jonah is delivered because of God's covenant faithfulness, mercy, and compassion for his people. Because God would judge his own Son—who was perfect and innocent, never rebelled, was never wayward, never opposed God—he would not judge Jonah. This is why, on more than one occasion, Jesus spoke of his death as a trial by ordeal. When, for example, James and

John asked Jesus if they could have positions of authority in his kingdom Jesus responded, "Are you able to drink the cup that I drink, or to be baptized with the baptism with which I am baptized?" (Mark 10:38). This is why, in the garden, Jesus prayed, "Father, if you are willing, remove this cup from me" (Luke 22:42).

The reason Israel could pass through the judgment waters at the Red Sea (Exodus 14), the reason Jonah could pass through the waters of judgment in the belly of a fish, and the reason we can pass through the waters of judgment symbolically represented in Christian baptism, is because Jesus drowned in the judgment waters on the cross. Therefore, God's words spoken through his prophet Isaiah,

> When you pass through the waters,
>   I will be with you;
> and when you pass through the rivers,
>   they will not sweep over you;
> when you walk through the fire,
>   you will not be burned (43:2, NIV)

remind us that whatever the reason for the trials and crises in our lives, the one thing we can know for sure is that they are not God's judgment upon us. God may be disciplining us, teaching us, growing us in faith and dependence on him, but if we are in Christ by faith, the hardships of this life are not divine judgment. Furthermore, God promises to be with us, even in and through the greatest trials and hardships we face.

### Jonah's Ascent to New Life (2:6–10)

The turning point in Jonah's prayer comes in Jonah 2:6 when the prophet says, "I went down to the land whose bars closed upon me forever; yet you brought up my life from the pit, O LORD my God." Jonah went down, but God brought him up. God delivered him from the pit, "the pit" being another common designation of the place of the dead.[16] Jonah then goes on to describe in more detail exactly what transpired at the gate of Sheol. He says in verse 7, "When my life was fainting away . . ." Here he uses an uncommon Hebrew expression that means something like "When I was on the verge of unconsciousness, when I was completely out of breath and slipping into oblivion and death, I remembered the LORD." The Lord God was Jonah's last thought. Of the Lord from whom he was fleeing, the Lord with whom he wanted nothing to do, Jonah says, "I remembered the LORD, and my prayer came to you, into your holy temple" (2:7).

There in the heart of the sea, at the gates of Hell, God heard Jonah's cry of faith. Notice that God does not say to his rebellious servant, "Well, save yourself and make your way back to Jerusalem on your knees; then we'll talk about salvation." God hears, responds, and delivers even on the basis of the faintest cry for help and mercy—a cry from a prophet who, as we will see, still has much to learn about divine compassion.

Jonah concludes his prayer with an expression of his confidence that he will again enter into God's worship, that God will accept him into his presence through the blood of sacrifices, commitments of loyalty, and a confession of faith. He says, "I with a voice of thanksgiving will sacrifice to you; what I have vowed I will pay" (v. 9).

Notice the prophet's confidence. I suspect that if I were in the belly of a fish, I would be tempted to wait to see how things played out before issuing my songs of joy. But Jonah is remembering his God and remembering his character, that God is a God who saves sinners. Jonah's God is a God who is quick to forgive, quick to extend grace to all who turn to him in faith (even the smallest faith). In remembering his God and experiencing God's gracious provision in this fish, Jonah expresses his confidence that he will again worship in God's presence. The presence from which he was fleeing is now, he says, his chief desire and delight.

Jonah's prayer from the depths is a magnificent song that vividly and powerfully celebrates the gospel of free grace for sinners. However, for the astute reader, this song in the mouth of Jonah rings a bit hollow. The prophet's contrast of himself with those who worship "vain idols" (v. 8) makes one wonder if he's in any position to declare his moral superiority to, for example, the sailors who we last saw worshiping God (1:16) or the Ninevites who will repent on the basis of so little by way of gospel promise (3:5).[17] It is a song that in itself is a pristine example of a psalm of thanksgiving, and as such is an appropriate expression of gratitude for God's salvation.[18] But it is sung by a prophet for whom its message has yet to capture his heart. It is sung by a prophet who, as the story unfolds, reveals that he really does not truly believe the significance of his final declaration: "Salvation belongs to the LORD" (2:9). After all, the story will conclude with the prophet sitting outside of Nineveh bitter, angry, and wishing to die because God has extended mercy to the Ninevites (4:2, 3).[19]

Jonah is not, as some suggest, offering readers a portrait of half-hearted repentance, a reality with which every believer struggles. Rather, Jonah offers readers a portrait of hypocritical repentance, the persistent stubbornness of a person who has correct theology but has not had those truths transform his heart. In this way, the prophet's experience serves as a mirror for Israel. Israel was meant to see in the prophet a reflection of their own behavior as they too, time and again, would experience God's grace and forgiveness. They would experience remarkable deliverances from threat and danger, only to fall quickly back into hard-hearted rebellion and disobedience. Consider, for example, the recurring pattern of sin–oppression–deliverance, only for Israel to fall back into sin once more, in the book of Judges (e.g., 3:7–12). So too with the wilderness generation. It seems that no sooner had Israel passed through the Red Sea and sung that remarkable victory song (Exodus 15:1–18) than they began grumbling, doubting, complaining, and questioning the very character of the God who delivered them (e.g., 17:1–7).

When read in the context of the larger narrative, Jonah's song from the depths offers a warning to Israel and to us. Throughout the narrative, Jonah reveals that he is an orthodox theologian. We see this in Jonah 1, 2, and 4—Jonah making good confessions.[20] Yet Jonah's heart seems far from God. God indicted Israel through the prophet Isaiah, saying, "This people draw near with their mouth and honor me with their lips, while their hearts are far from me" (Isaiah 29:13).

We are given a clue about how God regards Jonah's prayer from the depths in 2:10: "The LORD spoke to the fish, and it vomited Jonah out upon the dry land." A somewhat ignoble arrival back on land would put it mildly.[21] Throughout *Jonah*, God displays absolute sovereignty over his creation. He's sovereign over the storm at sea; he's sovereign over the great fish that swallows Jonah; he's sovereign over the plant that grows up overnight (4:6) and the east wind that scorches Jonah's head (v. 8). How does the sovereign God respond to his prophet's prayer? Immediately following the final note of Jonah's hymn of thanksgiving, we hear of this sovereign God ordering the great fish to vomit Jonah out.

Vomiting is almost never a positive thing, and unsurprisingly in Scripture, it is almost always associated with God's judgment. For example, in Leviticus 20:22 God says, "You shall therefore keep all my statutes and all my rules and do them, that the land where I am bringing you to live may not vomit you out." Here again the creation is said to vomit out God's people as a consequence of their persistent disobedience and failure to repent.

In this way Jonah's prayer from the depths warns against religion that is merely external. It is a warning against a religion that sings the right songs, prays the right prayers, even offers external obedience to the letter of the Law (as Jonah will do in chapter 3), and yet is a religion that does not issue from a heart that has been humbled before the sovereign majesty of God or transformed by the forgiving grace of God.

Jonah's prayer from the depths and his arrival on dry land offer not only a sober warning but also a wonderful promise. Regardless of Jonah's heart, what Jonah experienced was real and what he sings is true: God has made a way to deliver sinners like Jonah, sinners like the Ninevites, and sinners like us from the jaws of death itself. Acting through the great fish, God may be said to swallow up death itself. God, we learn, has power even over death—a reality demonstrated fully and finally in the resurrection of the Son of God. For this reason, the Apostle Paul declares through Christ's resurrection,

> "Death is swallowed up in victory."
> "O death, where is your victory?
>   O death, where is your sting?"
>
> The sting of death is sin, and the power of sin is the law. But thanks be to God, who gives us the victory through our Lord Jesus Christ. (1 Corinthians 15:54–56)

Jonah ascends from the realm of the dead by the power, grace, and provision of God, and he expresses his gratitude as one who has in a sense passed from death to life. The gospel message of Jonah's prayer is not "Be like Jonah, only better"; rather, it is, "Trust in the One whom Jonah prefigured, the One who declared, 'For just as Jonah was three days and three nights in the belly of the great fish, so will the Son of Man be three days and three nights in the heart of the earth'" (Matthew 12:40). To everyone who has faith in him, who hears his words and believes the One who has sent him, Jesus says, "He does not come into judgment, but has passed from death to life" (John 5:24).

# 35

# Portraits of Repentance

JONAH 3:1—4:1

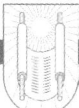

"SALVATION BELONGS TO THE LORD!" (Jonah 2:9). It is with these triumphant words that Jonah concludes his prayer of thanksgiving from the belly of the great fish. This is a fitting conclusion and one that in many respects captures the theme of the entire book. "Salvation belongs to the LORD!" The implication of this declaration is as clear as it is critical. Salvation doesn't belong to Jonah. It doesn't belong to Israel. It doesn't belong to the Church. It belongs to God, and God is free to bestow his saving grace on whomever he wills whenever he wills; he is accountable to no one.

The prophet himself had experienced a remarkable display of this reality. When on account of his rebellious flight from God, Jonah sunk into the depths of the sea, hopeless, helpless, and in great distress, down to the very gates of Hell, God rescued him and granted him new and undeserved life. This was not because of any merit on Jonah's part, but because he is a God of compassion who hears the prayers even of a rebellious prophet and who answers with a powerful display of his sovereignty and goodness. God caused a great fish to swallow Jonah and in so doing, snatched him out of the jaws of death. God had mercy on Jonah. Immediately following God's deliverance of Jonah, we see the prophet called to go and extend that same mercy to Nineveh.

Though not yet the capital, Nineveh was a major city of Assyria, the greatest empire in the known world. Mighty, vast, and brutal, Assyria was a merciless empire, known and feared for their violence and cruelty in warfare. More importantly, at this time in Israel's history, Assyria was the greatest threat in the international arena to God's people. Jonah is tasked with the mission of preaching to this great city, which the narrator describes, somewhat enigmatically, as a "great city to/for God/the gods" (3:3, AT). Though sometimes translated as a superlative ("an exceedingly great city"), it is more likely the case that the Biblical writer is signaling either Nineveh's role as Assyria's religious center (i.e., it was full of idols) or Nineveh's role in God's redemptive purposes.[1] Either way, surprisingly, amazingly, and wonderfully, Nineveh repents (vv. 5–9). As Nineveh turns from her evil ways, God for his part, surprisingly, amazingly, and wonderfully, turns from the evil (or the disaster) he had declared he would bring against this wicked city (v. 10). In this we see that God's mercy extends beyond the borders of Israel and is granted to even the most unexpected peoples.

This is the central message of Jonah 3: God extends great mercy to great sinners.

Now the obvious place we see God's mercy is in his forgiveness of the Ninevites. However, we must remember that the book of Jonah was not written for the Ninevites but for Israel; therefore, it contains a unique message for God's people. In this remarkable scene in Jonah 3, the three main characters of the drama finally come together—Jonah, Nineveh, and God. Each character in his or its own way exhibits a form of turning or repentance, and each character's repentance contains an important message for us about God and his mercy for sinners.

### Jonah's Repentance: A Warning to Israel (3:1–4)

The main (human) character of the book of Jonah makes a rather brief appearance in this climactic scene. In response to God's recommissioning of his disobedient prophet with words reminiscent of his original command (1:2), we read that "Jonah arose and went to Nineveh, according to the word of the LORD" (3:3) and that he went "a day's journey" and called out, "Yet forty days, and Nineveh shall be overthrown!" (3:4).[2]

That's all we hear from God's prophet. What do we make of our reluctant prophet here? Many have seen in the prophet's obedience an outward expression of inward remorse. On this reading, the prophet is genuinely sorry for his earlier flight from his divine commission, and here he appears chastened, humble, obedient, and submissive to the divine will.[3] Whereas his earlier response to God's call to arise and go to Nineveh was to flee to Tarshish (1:3), here we see Jonah rising and going to Nineveh "according to the word of the LORD" (3:3). It does indeed, at least on the surface, seem to be a definite improvement.

However, in the larger context of the narrative, Jonah's obedience here takes on a different hue altogether.[4] When it turns out that Jonah's somewhat half-hearted sermon receives the greatest response of any prophet in Israel's history, the prophet responds with suicidal depression (4:3). One author has described Jonah as "the most rebellious and the most successful of the prophets."[5] Yet in 4:1 we read the response of "the most successful of the prophets": "It displeased Jonah exceedingly, and he was angry." The prophet then proceeds to contend with Almighty God, arguing that God has made a terrible mistake and has violated his very nature as the God of justice. This hardly seems like a portrait of repentance.

It is certainly true that obedience is better than disobedience, and the narrative is written in such a way as to highlight that, this time, Jonah did obey God's command.[6] But God is not after Jonah's obedience. He is after Jonah's heart. If the goal of the story was simply to get Jonah to obey, then the narrative could have ended at chapter 3. However, God wants something much more than his prophet's obedience; God wants his loving submission.

In this we discover the significance of Jonah's recommissioning. Why does God recommission Jonah, of all people, to deliver his word to Nineveh? It is certainly not the case that Jonah is the only man for the job. God does not need Jonah. God could have easily sent the great fish to go and preach to Nineveh. God sends Jonah because he has an important lesson that Jonah, and Israel through Jonah, needs to learn.

In this period of Israel's history, when God sends his prophets to bless Israel's enemies, he does so as a word of judgment and curse against his own people. In Deuteronomy 32, the Song of Moses, God anticipated Israel's hardhearted rebellion, saying, "They have made me jealous with what is no god; they have provoked me to anger with their idols. So I will make them jealous with those who are no people; I will provoke them to anger with a foolish nation" (v. 21).

This is precisely what God is doing. Throughout Israel's history, when God's people fall into disobedience and faithlessness, God blesses Israel's neighbors so that they might become a thorn in Israel's side and a tangible sign of God's displeasure. We may recall, for example, Elijah's care for the widow of Zaraphath during a famine (1 Kings 17:8–24); Elisha healing the leprous Naaman, the Syrian officer (2 Kings 5:1–14; cf. Luke 4:27); and Elisha anointing Hazael, king of Damascus, thus giving Syria an even stronger king than Ben-hadad I, and one who would prove an even greater threat to Israel (2 Kings 8:9–15). While these are, on the one hand, genuine blessings for these individuals and these nations, they are at the same time signs of God's displeasure and judgment on his own people.[7] At the end of the day, God's forgiveness of Nineveh and his relenting of his judgment against them would have very real, very difficult, and very painful consequences for Israel.

We need to see both realities at play in the book of Jonah. On the one hand, *Jonah* carries with it a wonderful picture of the inclusion of the Gentiles into the great community of the redeemed. In this we're reminded that, from the beginning, God's purposes have been to work through one family and one nation to bring the blessing of salvation to the ends of the earth. Thus, *Jonah* offers a glimpse of the generous and compassionate missionary heart of God. God delights in showing mercy to even the most unworthy recipients. But Jonah's mission to Nineveh also contains another message, a warning that serves as a word of judgment for God's rebellious people. God's blessing of the Ninevites is an expression of his judgment against Israel. God's mercy to Nineveh adumbrates his eventual appointment of the Assyrians as the rod of his righteous anger (Isaiah 10:5) that will one day come against his covenant people.

How do we understand Jonah's obedience in chapter 3? As we see in his confession earlier, "I am a Hebrew, and I fear the Lord, the God of heaven, who made the sea and the dry land" (1:9), Jonah can say the right things. So too in chapter 3 we see that Jonah may even do the right things. But the tragic reality is that Jonah's heart remains far from God. In this way he represents Israel in his day. Israel may pray the right prayers, they may even externally obey God's word, but in Jonah's day, their hearts are not transformed by the gospel.

Is Jonah repentant? I think the message of the book is "Not yet."[8] Yet this is precisely what God is seeking in his dramatic engagement with Nineveh.

In Jonah's recommissioning we see the Hound of Heaven pursuing his prophet, and God's work in Nineveh is designed to preach a critical, life-giving word to his covenant people. As great as God's mercy to Nineveh is, there is an even greater mercy still: God's relentless pursuit of his own people, Israel, represented in the reluctant and hard-hearted prophet. Just as God's threat of judgment against Nineveh is at heart an expression of his mercy—an invitation to faith and repentance—so too is God's threat of judgment against Israel. It is a call for Israel to repent and find mercy in the only place it may be found. It is a reminder that Israel's God is a God of second chances. There is still time for Israel to repent and return to the Lord and to show forth the fruit of their repentance in living out their calling as a kingdom of priests and a holy nation (Exodus 19:6).

Here we find a warning for Christians as well. It is a warning to be wary of shallow repentance. Like Jonah, we are tempted to confuse good confessions, orthodox hymns, and proper behavior for genuine faith and true repentance. However, God doesn't simply desire our external obedience; he desires an obedience that is the fruit of a heartfelt trust and faith in him. The truth is that even our obedience can become a stumbling block to fellowship with God when it becomes the basis for our confidence in his love. So we should regularly, even daily, ask ourselves, *Does my obedience stem from my love for God and an apprehension of his grace to me in Christ? Or is it simply a means by which I convince others (and perhaps even myself) that I am deserving of God's grace?* Or, to put it another way, *Is the object of my faith my obedience or the Christ who promises me forgiveness through faith in him?*

This is not an encouragement for Christians to doubt their salvation. Rather, it is a call for Christians to find their assurance in the right place. It is a call for us to reorient the eyes of our heart, which are so constantly directed inward, to look outward to the Son of God as our only hope in this life and the next. In doing so, we discover that God's grace is free—free for us and free for others. In this discovery, our obedience to God changes from slavish duty to joyful privilege, privilege for the opportunity we have to showcase the transforming power of God's grace to sinners.

### Nineveh's Repentance: An Indictment of Israel (3:5–9)

After so much build-up surrounding Jonah's mission, so much effort, as it were, to get Jonah to Nineveh, it's a bit surprising that when it comes to the execution of his mission, we are only given one verse: "Jonah began to go into the city, going a day's journey. And he called out, 'Yet forty days and Nineveh shall be overthrown!' " (3:4).[9] In fact, the bulk of the chapter describes in considerable detail the thoroughness, the intensity, and the sincerity of Nineveh's response to Jonah's message.[10] We're told in verse 5 that Nineveh's repentance was "from the greatest of them to the least of them." Sorrow over evil wasn't the conviction of one small segment of the city; rather, it was the uniform conviction of every citizen from all strata of Ninevite society. The king himself not only decreed a time of national repentance and mourning over their evil ways, but he also participated in it, removing his royal robes and donning the dress of a poor and humble mourner as he sat in sackcloth and ashes (v. 6). Even the livestock participated in this expression of sorrow and lamentation over the evil of Nineveh (v. 8).

Though some have found a hyperbolic touch of humor in this mention of the animals participating in the mourning rituals of Nineveh, Douglas Stuart is closer to the mark when he notes that this "is the language of severity; it demonstrates the urgency of the situation in Nineveh rather than any awkward choices on the part of the king and his nobles."[11] In other words, Nineveh's repentance was serious business.

However, it is worth asking the question: For a book of only forty-eight verses, why spend so many of them on Nineveh's repentance?

The purpose of this lengthy description was to give Israel a vivid picture of what true, heartfelt, and thorough repentance looks like. The Ninevites expressed great sorrow for their great wickedness. In this way, Nineveh was meant to serve as a mirror in which the people of Israel could see themselves as they truly were and compare themselves to this notoriously wicked city that repented so deeply.

In contrast to Israel, Nineveh had very little information with which to work. No reason is given for God's judgment; no explanation or clarification is provided about which deity may be coming in judgment;[12] and no promise of grace is offered should they repent. The people of Nineveh received a word of judgment and were left to speculate and hope with little foundation about the possibility of mercy. Nineveh was left to surmise that this unknown God just might relent from judgment in response to their repentance. We hear this poignantly expressed in the king's question: "Who knows? God may turn and relent and turn from his fierce anger, so that we may not perish" (Jonah 3:9).[13]

Who knows indeed? As readers, we know that Jonah knows. But Jonah, from what we can tell, says nothing about the character of God, the reality of grace, and the possibility of forgiveness.[14] And yet with no other knowledge than that some God somewhere will punish their sins, the Ninevites respond with an unprecedented moral reform.[15] We're told in verse 5, "[They] believed God."[16] God spoke through his prophet, and his word in its dimmest form came with the most tremendous power. From the greatest to the least, the city was transformed. The message for Israel in their day and for us in ours is that wicked, pitiable, ignorant Nineveh did so much with so little.

The contrast with Israel could not be more striking. Israel had the Law and the prophets, the oracles of God and his covenant promises, the priesthood and the temple—all to teach them clearly and powerfully about God's judgment and mercy—and yet never in its history did Israel repent like Nineveh.[17] Thus Nineveh's repentance is an indictment of God's covenant people. God is saying, in effect, "Nineveh repented with so little, and you've been given so much. Will you not repent? Will you not turn? Will you persist in your evil and wickedness, disregarding my threats of judgment and ignoring my promises of forgiveness?" This is why Jesus would say to the Pharisees that he would give them no other sign than the sign of Jonah (Matthew 12:39; that is, his resurrection from the dead), and yet he knew that even then they would not believe. Therefore, the men of Nineveh would rise up in judgment against them (v. 41).

Nineveh did so much with so little, and yet the Pharisees would behold the dying and rising of the Messiah and refuse to believe.[18]

The Ninevites just hoped that something like a gospel existed. They hoped that maybe God's judgment isn't all there is and that there might be mercy. What Jonah didn't tell the Ninevites is something we've been told—God is merciful. God is gracious. God does forgive those who repent of their sins and turn to him in faith. In this way, Christians are like the people of Israel, who had the Law of God and the promises of God spoken in his word and displayed on his altar. Yet we have something far greater. We have the fulfillment of God's promises in Jesus Christ. We have the revelation that, through the death of Jesus Christ, God atoned for the sins of his people. In the cross we have the greatest display of God's mercy and grace. Therefore, we have the privilege of knowing an even greater revelation of God's purposes to redeem and forgive than Israel had. We know Christ, the fullness of God's revelation.

It is easy for us to look down on ancient Israel, whose failures at times are set so clearly on display in the pages of sacred Scripture, and not realize that we too can—more often than we care to admit—exhibit the same tendencies for spiritual lethargy and disobedience. We too need to be reminded of our great need for mercy and the greatness of God's provision for us in his Son. The question put to Israel is just as appropriately put to us: How often do we repent like Nineveh? How often do we in absolute contrition throw ourselves down like the prodigal son in Luke 15 and say, "Father, you owe me nothing," only to receive everything? If the cross doesn't drive us to our knees in humility and dependence, the Bible says God has nothing left to offer. The cross is God's final word to the world. It is his message of judgment—that this is what sin deserves. But also it is his message of grace—that for all who in faith and repentance turn to Christ, their judgment has fallen on Jesus.

### God's Repentance: A Promise to Israel (3:5–9)

Jonah 3:10 has been the cause of a fair amount of controversy in the history of the Christian Church. The reason for this controversy can be clearly seen in the more literal translation of the Hebrew in, for example, the King James Version when it says: "God saw their works, that they turned from their evil way; and God repented of the evil, that he had said that he would do unto them; and he did it not." What does it mean, "God repented"? Did God do something wrong for which he is morally culpable? Did God make a mistake and change his mind?

On the basis of this and similar verses, some have concluded this very thing: that God regretted the judgment he had purposed and declared to bring against wicked Nineveh. But the problem with this view is not only that it cuts against the grain of the Biblical witness in general (we're told in Numbers 23:19, "God is not man, that he should lie, or a son of man, that he should change his mind"; cf. 1 Samuel 15:29; Malachi 3:6), but it also cuts against the grain of the portrait of God within the Jonah narrative itself.

Thus far we've been given a portrait of God whose sovereignty is absolute, extending over the winds and the waves, over the monsters of the sea, and, in a way, even over death itself. Are we meant to think that the repentance of Nineveh, along with its powerful message to Israel, was an open question in God's plan? Certainly not. The expression translated as "God relented" is in fact the same expression that was used when Moses interceded for Israel and Yahweh "relented" from the judgment he had announced against them (Exodus 32:14). In Exodus as in *Jonah*, God announced his judgment against Israel to effect the very repentance he had foreordained. God knew all along—indeed, had foreordained—that Nineveh would repent, and God had purposed all along that he would relent from his threatened judgment.

It is important to remember that here again, as in every description of God, the Bible speaks analogically. As Calvin put it, God uses "a mode of speaking that ought to be sufficiently known to us."[19]

How do we think about and speak about a God who is infinite, who is beyond all measure and human understanding, who exists outside of time and knows the end from the beginning? The answer is that we speak God's words after him. God speaks to us in his revelation, and our speech about God repeats or rehearses what God has said about himself. When God speaks, he does so with words finite human beings can understand. Calvin put it like this:

> Strictly speaking, no repentance can belong to God: and it ought not to be ascribed to his secret and hidden counsel. God then is in himself ever the same, and consistent with himself; but he is said to repent, when a regard is had to the comprehension of men: for as we conceive God to be angry, whenever he summons us to his tribunal, and shows to us our sins; so also we conceive him to be placable, when he offers the hope of pardon. But it is according to our perceptions that there is any change, when God forgets his wrath, as though he had put on a new character.[20]

Theologians therefore speak of divine condescension. In his self-revelation, God condescends to the finite capacities of his creatures so that they can apprehend (though never comprehend) the majesty and the ways of the triune God. When we're told that God "relented of the disaster [or evil] that he had said he would do to them" (Jonah 3:10), we are not meant to think that

God regretted a moral evil, but that he responded to the change in Nineveh just as he had promised and purposed. As Nineveh turned from their wickedness, so God turned from his wrath. As the city turned, they experienced the unchanging and unchangeable God as having turned from his promised wrath to divine grace.[21] In this, God's people of every age are reminded that there is forgiveness to be found in the very God whose promises and purposes are as unchanging as he is (cf. Malachi 3:6).

This point is driven home when we consider not only what God accomplished (the transformation of Nineveh) but also how he accomplished it. Nineveh repented in response to the word of God delivered by his prophet: "Yet forty days, and Nineveh shall be overthrown!" (Jonah 3:4). Regardless of how inadequately or poorly the message was delivered, at the end of the day, Jonah preached the word of God, and when God blesses his word with the power of his Spirit, it achieves his purposes—it turns sinners from their sin and toward God in repentance, seeking mercy and forgiveness. This is the picture we are given: God, through the simple declaration of his word of judgment, transforms an entire city.

In a particularly arresting passage, Amy Erickson has described the power of God's work in Jonah 3:

> The instant that Jonah's five-word prophecy leaves his mouth, "the people of Nineveh believe in God" (v. 5), and the "turning" begins, spreading like a wildfire from the outskirts of the city until it reaches the king at the heart of the city. Jonah does not even need to go all the way into the city. He simply touches the first domino he encounters on his journey, and a chain reaction starts with the people and continues all the way to the king. The journey of the word is not hindered by the size of the city, rather, the spreading of the word and its immediate effects on every living creature in its path defies the expectation of a "three-day walk" (v. 3) and "forty days more" (v. 4).[22]

God's word is powerful. God's word can make sinners who by nature hate their neighbors love their neighbors. God's word can make dead people live (Ezekiel 37:1–14). As the Lord said through the prophet Isaiah, "So shall my word be that goes out from my mouth; it shall not return to me empty, but it shall accomplish that which I purpose, and shall succeed in the thing for which I sent it" (Isaiah 55:11). God's prophetic word of judgment is sometimes accompanied, as here, implicitly, with a prophetic word of mercy. Israel, the original audience, is here summoned back to this word. It is a word that overthrows sinners, but it is also a word that promises mercy to all who will turn in faith and repentance.[23]

The good news is that God is still working through his word. But today it is the Word of Christ. It is in the weakness and seeming inadequacy of God's word that God testifies to the fact that it is not by man's might or man's strength or man's message that salvation comes but by God's (1 Corinthians 1:20–31). It is not through human wisdom but through divine wisdom.

What was it that brought the mighty Ninevites to their knees? It was not a mighty army from without or a disaster from within. It was the word of God.

This is a constant application for Christians, both as individuals and as a church. Will we be faithful to preach God's word, to teach God's word, to trust God's word, to look to God to bless the word he's appointed to accomplish his ends? Or will we, like so many throughout history, seek to supplement God's word, "help" God's word, or change the ends for which it was appointed?

Jonah delivered what is arguably the weakest sermon in the history of sermons. However, consider its power and effect. As weak as it was, it nevertheless declared the truth, and God blessed it. It seemed foolish, inadequate, and weak. In this way, God says, "I'll receive the glory." God is at work glorifying himself as sinners respond to his word with faith and repentance. In this way, Jonah will come to know, Israel would come to know, and, by God's grace, we will come to know more and more the richness, beauty, and power of the precious truth that "salvation belongs to the LORD" (Jonah 2:9).

God's threat of judgment was not insincere. God wasn't playing the role of the indulgent parent, saying things he didn't mean. God here and throughout Scripture turned from a threatened judgment and extended mercy because he would reserve that judgment for his Son, who would bear it in full at Calvary. God's turning from the evil he had threatened was a turning of his holy anger from deserving sinners and a turning toward his undeserving and beloved Son. God's engagement with Nineveh was a revelation of his mercy. How much they understood about Yahweh is difficult to say, but they did have a profound experience of his mercy.

This entire episode was designed to reveal to Israel the greatness of God's mercy and compassion for undeserving sinners. Like Assyria, Israel was undeserving. And yet God's mercy and compassion extended to Israel and beyond Israel, even to the borders of Assyria.

Israel was meant to see that if God can extend so great a mercy so quickly and so lavishly upon a people who are not his people, how much more might he extend mercy to those who are his covenant people? This is the greatness of God's grace. The message of Jonah 3 is that God's mercy is for great sinners and hard-hearted Pharisees alike. God is at work through his word, summoning all manner of sinners to himself. Do you see yourself more in one than in the other? The invitation is the same. God's mercy is for all those who in repentance and faith turn to him.

# 36

# Lessons in Compassion

## JONAH 4

THERE IS AN OBVIOUS REASON why *Jonah* is the go-to book for speakers at Christian mission conferences. *Jonah* is one of the relatively few places in the Old Testament where we see God extending mercy to the Gentile nations. More often in the Old Testament, and in the prophetic literature in particular, God's posture toward the nations is one of judgment.[1] Time and again we hear Israel's prophets announcing God's judgment against the nations for their wickedness and cruelty, and especially for their oppression of his people.

In this way, the book of Jonah is somewhat unique among the prophetic literature because in this short story, the emphasis is not on God's wrath against the nations but on his great mercy and compassion for these nations as represented by Assyria. In Jonah we are reminded of God's desire to see the blessings of his covenant with Abraham extend to the nations around Israel and, by implication, to the farthest reaches of the earth. Yet Jonah 4 reminds us that as wonderful and as important as that message is, the book is not primarily about God's heart for the foreign nations.

If *Jonah* were solely or even primarily about God's mercy for the nations, then the story could have ended at chapter 3.[2] From the greatest to the least, the great Assyrian city of Nineveh—a city once characterized by injustice, oppression, and violence—experienced an unprecedented moral reform such that God "relented of the disaster that he had said he would do to them, and he did not do it" (3:10). We would expect the author at this point to conclude with the Hebrew equivalent of "They all lived happily ever after." However, we see in Jonah 4 that the story continues. God's attention turns from the evil of the Ninevites toward the evil of Jonah.

In his book *The Prodigal God*, Timothy Keller helpfully reminds us that Jesus's parable of the prodigal son (Luke 15:11–32) is not primarily about a father's love for his wayward and wicked prodigal son but rather is primarily about a father's love for the hard-hearted, self-righteous, angry older brother.[3] So too with *Jonah*. Jonah is not primarily about God's love for wayward and wicked Nineveh but about God's love for the hard-hearted, self-righteous, and angry prophet. While God's purposes for Nineveh had in a sense been accomplished, God's purposes for Jonah, and for Israel, had yet to be accomplished.[4] God's compassion for wicked Nineveh would serve this greater purpose of exposing the evil of Jonah's heart and reorienting the prophet to the reality of who God is as the Lord of salvation.

### Anger and Its Disastrous Consequences (4:1–4)

I still have vivid memories of our youngest child as a two-year-old being able to throw a temper tantrum like the world has never seen. At times my wife and I would hear her older siblings exclaiming something like, "Oh no, here she goes again! Grab her! Watch her head!" This was because Margaret, our two-year-old, had the capacity to become so consumed with rage that it appeared to take over her whole body so that she would collapse onto the floor in an uncontrollable fit of anger and bang her head on the ground. It is difficult to put into words the sight of a little two-year-old so completely consumed with anger, lashing out against any and all who got in her way, including even herself.

The author of Jonah goes to great lengths to express the all-consuming nature of Jonah's anger. When we're told in 4:1, "It displeased Jonah exceedingly, and he was angry," we have a somewhat understated rendering of the Hebrew that literally says, "It was evil, a great evil for Jonah, and he was furious."[5] Moreover, we see Jonah's anger in his response to God's question in verse 4: "Do you do well to be angry?" Jonah responds with silence. The prophet, in effect, says nothing and walks away.[6] This is almost never a good sign in a relationship. However, we see Jonah's anger perhaps most clearly in his death wish. Twice he announces that he would rather die than live, in verses 3 and 8. This is a portrait of a man so filled with anger that he does not know how he can continue living and so would prefer not to.[7]

Readers are not left to speculate as to what brought Jonah to this state of suicidal anger. The prophet himself discloses the source. In a furious outburst, the prophet pulls back the curtain on his inner emotional and mental state, saying, "O LORD, is not this what I said when I was yet in my country? That is why I made haste to flee to Tarshish; for I knew that you are a gracious God and merciful, slow to anger and abounding in steadfast love, and relenting from disaster" (v. 2).

The horrifying reality is that Jonah's anger is not a result of any confusion about God—his character, purposes, word, will, etc. It is not a result of a misunderstanding about who God is and what God is like. The tragic and heartbreaking reality is that Jonah is outraged precisely because he does know God.[8] He knows his character, his purposes, his word, and his will. And it is because he knows God that he ran from God's call to go to Nineveh at the beginning. Jonah is saying, in effect, "I knew this was going to happen! I know just what kind of God you are!" Jonah knows that Yahweh, the God of Israel, is a God of grace, and what the Assyrians need, Jonah believes, is justice. In this regard, Jonah is a prophet of strict and unrelenting justice.[9]

There is, of course, a tragic irony in Jonah's prayer. In verse 2 the prophet employs the same words God used to reveal himself to Moses at Mount Sinai. After Israel's astonishing act of high-handed disobedience in crafting and worshiping a golden calf, the Lord declared his intention to destroy Israel (Exodus 32:10). With Israel under a sentence of death, Moses took his stand as Israel's covenant mediator and interceded for the people. Wonderfully, the Lord heard him and relented from the disaster he was going to bring upon Israel. Shortly after, God revealed himself to Moses, declaring his name: "The Lord, the Lord, a God merciful and gracious, slow to anger, and abounding in steadfast love and faithfulness, keeping steadfast love for thousands, forgiving iniquity and transgression and sin" (Exodus 34:6, 7a).

This self-disclosure of the character and purposes of God is picked up throughout Scripture as a catalyst for praise. Psalm 103:8–10, for example, says,

> The Lord is merciful and gracious,
>     slow to anger and abounding in steadfast love.
> He will not always chide,
>     nor will he keep his anger forever.
> He does not deal with us according to our sins,
>     nor repay us according to our iniquities."[10]

Ironically, however, this confession of faith and basis for praise is, in the mouth of Jonah, not used to praise God but to condemn God.[11] The prophet, in effect, sits in judgment over God and delivers his sentence, seeing God as unjust. Phyllis Trible captures the ugly reality well when she writes, "Jonah accuses and condemns Yahweh for being Yahweh. He castigates divine mercy to justify himself. His anger attacks God's compassion. Thus he is far more 'wrathful' than the reader suspected. His reason for fleeing the command has to do, then, not with Nineveh itself, not with his views about foreigners, but with the very character of God."[12]

In his anger, Jonah has placed himself above God.[13] This is perhaps the most tragic revelation at the conclusion of the book. Jonah's anger is not ultimately directed toward the Ninevites, nor ultimately toward the Ninevites' repentance. Ultimately Jonah's anger is directed toward God. God, he believes, has acted unjustly by extending mercy and compassion to the Ninevites, and Jonah wants nothing more to do with him.

Jonah was delighted to be on the receiving end of God's mercy and grace and forgiveness, so delighted, in fact, that he burst forth in a song of praise and thanksgiving (2:2–9). But when he was called to extend that same mercy, grace, and forgiveness toward others, he could not stomach it.[14] Jonah loved the grace of God, but it was grace according to Jonah. Grace according to Jonah was for pretty good people who just need a little help getting over the finish line. Certainly Israel had her problems, and that's what grace was for. However, Assyria was infamously wicked—what one commentator called "international outlaws"—and, moreover, a threat (or potential threat) to Israel, and that, for Jonah, was who justice was for.[15]

Jesus faced a similar reality in his day. It is not the case that the scribes and the Pharisee and the other religious leaders who opposed Jesus were strict legalists, principally opposed to God's grace for sinners. Every single one of them would have affirmed their own need for God's grace. Yet when they saw Jesus in the company of tax collectors, prostitutes, and other known sinners, they grumbled among themselves and complained to Jesus's disciples. Yet what was Jesus's response? In Matthew 21:31, 32 Jesus said to the chief priests and elders of the people, "Truly, I say to you, the tax collectors and the prostitutes go into the kingdom of God before you. For John came to you in the way of righteousness, and you did not believe him, but the tax collectors and the prostitutes believed him." Similarly in Mark 2:17, Jesus said, "Those who are well have no need of a physician, but those who are sick. I came not to call the righteous, but sinners." God took on flesh to save sinners. He didn't come to lend a hand to those who were pretty good or to offer a supplement to the otherwise fairly healthy. Jesus came to raise dead people to life.

Jonah had forgotten the character of God's grace—that it is not just for little sins committed by basically good people. God's grace is sufficient for great sins committed by great sinners. Jonah had ceased to be amazed at God's grace that superabounded toward him and toward his people. As a result, Jonah was unable to live in a world in which God's mercy was extended to the likes of the Ninevites.[16]

It is too easy for readers to adopt a posture of superiority toward the irredeemably embittered prophet. We need to remember that we too are prone to place others outside the pale of God's forgiving, redeeming grace. We too can desire God's grace to extend to the whole world in principle while in practice thinking that what this group or that group, what this person or that person really needs is divine judgment. And we always have our reasons that naturally seem good.

However, Jonah had his reasons too—good reasons that made sense to Jonah and likely to most of Israel. It's a mistake to see Jonah's desire for God's unbridled judgment to come against the Ninevites as some sort of racism or ethnocentrism.[17] Though perhaps not at that particular moment, the Assyrians were nevertheless Israel's greatest threat in the eighth century. The Assyrians had attacked Israel's neighbors with a merciless cruelty that would baffle the imagination. It is quite possible that Jonah's friends or relatives suffered or died at the hands of the Assyrians. So it is not at all surprising that Jonah would desire justice and judgment to be meted out against such a wicked and cruel people.

Furthermore, we might consider what a suspended sentence for Nineveh would do to Jonah's reputation back home. What would this mean for Israel as well in the future? Jonah quite understandably could not see how God's relenting could possibly be good for his own people. Not only did God's sparing Nineveh contravene strict justice, it created innumerable difficulties for Israel as well. Jonah is not nursing a personal vendetta. Jonah is accurately representing Israel's objection: "This just won't do, God!" This, of course, is a feeling not unfamiliar to believers in every age—the feeling that God got it wrong, that this hardship or difficulty isn't the best thing for God's people. It is the feeling that if we do it God's way, we won't survive.

Jonah was convinced he had a good reason to be angry. So do we. We consistently think that our anger is righteous anger. Of course, there is such a thing as righteous anger (Ephesians 4:26). However, *Jonah* stands as a warning that we're prone to identify God's anger with ours, and in so doing, set ourselves up as the sovereign judges of the world. The author Anne Lamott once wrote, "You can safely assume that you've created God in your own image when it turns out that God hates all the same people you do."[18] Jonah was sure that his thoughts were God's thoughts, his ways were God's ways, and his enemies were God's enemies. In Jonah's anger we have an important reminder that God's ways are not our ways and God's thoughts are not our thoughts (Isaiah 55:8, 9).

God does not act according to our plans or our desires or our expectations. At the conclusion of his prayer in the belly of the great fish, Jonah declared those majestic words, "Salvation belongs to the LORD!" (Jonah 2:9). But did Jonah really believe this? God's mercy to the Ninevites tested Jonah's understanding of what this means. If salvation really belongs to the Lord, then that means God is free to extend mercy to whomever he chooses. He was not accountable to Jonah, nor is he accountable to us. The Apostle Paul writes, "What shall we say then? Is there injustice on God's part? By no means! For he says to Moses, 'I will have mercy on whom I have mercy, and I will have compassion on whom I have compassion.' So then it depends not on human will or exertion, but on God, who has mercy" (Romans 9:14–16).

The conclusion of *Jonah* highlights the horrible yet inevitable end of such deep anger. Twice Jonah expresses his desire to die. In this we see that nothing has changed for Jonah. The story begins with Jonah's desire to die rather than go to Nineveh as he tells the sailors to throw him into the sea (Jonah 1:12). Jonah experiences God's great mercy in the form of a fish and sings praise to God for his goodness and steadfast love (2:2–9). At the conclusion of the book, we see that Jonah's heart is just as hard and just as bitter and just as angry as ever, if not more so (4:1–3).[19] Jonah's flight in chapter 1 is described throughout as Jonah fleeing "from the presence of the LORD" (v. 2). The presence of the Lord in the Bible is the place of blessedness, of wholeness, of goodness, and of everlasting joy. It is this presence that Jonah flees, going down to the very gates of Sheol (2:2). In chapter 4 we can see in his death wish the same desire, the desire to have nothing more to do with this God who is "gracious . . . and merciful, slow to anger and abounding in steadfast love" (v. 2).

The end of such anger toward God—an anger that places itself over God and judges God—is death. Mercifully, however, Jonah doesn't get the last word. God responds to his embittered and intractably angry prophet with words full of both grace and a much-needed challenge.

## Compassion and Its Life-Giving Power (4:5–10)

In Matthew Jesus tells the parable of a king who takes pity on his servant and forgives him a debt so large he could never have repaid it in three lifetimes (Matthew 18:21–35). This servant finds a fellow servant who owes him the equivalent of a day's wage and mercilessly has him thrown in prison until he pays his debt. When the king hears of the servant's cruelty, he summons him and says, "'You wicked servant! I forgave you all that debt because you pleaded with me. And should not you have had mercy on your fellow servant, as I had mercy on you?' And in anger his master delivered him to the jailers, until he should pay all his debt" (18:34). The king's response to the servant's ingratitude resonates with us. This is fair treatment for such a wicked servant.

The parallels with Jonah are obvious. The disobedient prophet had been forgiven much. Yet when called to extend mercy to others, Jonah clams up and summons God to execute justice and judgment. There are striking similarities, but there are also striking differences. When God addresses Jonah, we don't see him adopting the posture of the king in the parable. God doesn't castigate Jonah. He doesn't condemn Jonah with the well-deserved rebuke, "You ungrateful servant." Rather, he questions Jonah: "Do you do well to be angry?" (Jonah 4:4). Again, in 4:9, "God says to Jonah, 'Do you do well to be angry for the plant?'"

Throughout the Bible God often poses questions in order to reorient sinners to the reality of who he is as the sovereign, redeeming God and who they are as sinners in need of saving. He is the Creator whose mind is unknowable, whose ways are unsearchable, while we are creatures, limited in both knowledge and understanding. This is seen most powerfully in Job, who finally gets what he asked for: an encounter with God. Notice how God responds to Job's questions with questions of his own: "Where were you when I laid the foundation of the earth? Tell me if you have understanding. Who determined its measurements—surely you know! Or who stretched the line upon it?" (Job 38:4, 5).

These questions, in Jonah as for Job, are expressions of God's mercy. They are means by which God stoops in love to meet his wayward, disoriented image-bearers where they are in their lives, in all their chaos and anger and frustration. God meets them and, like a father, tender but firm, questions them in such a way that they would remember before whom they stand—a God whose greatness and majesty and wisdom are unfathomable to the human mind; the God before whom the only proper response is to bow in humble awe, fear, worship, and adoration. God's questioning of Jonah in chapter 4 is an expression of divine compassion, as we see God here pursuing Jonah's heart and seeking to restore him to the proper posture of humility and reverence.

God's pursuit of his wayward prophet is seen perhaps most clearly in the episode of the plant (*qiqayon*) (Jonah 4:6). What were God's purposes with the plant? The obvious answer was to bring physical relief and comfort to the prophet. But if this were so, then why would God kill off the plant in an evening? Furthermore, why would God send a scorching east wind and a blistering sun to afflict his prophet (v. 8)? We're told in Jonah 4:6 that "God appointed a plant and made it come up over Jonah, that it might be a shade over his head, to save him from his discomfort." The Hebrew word translated as "discomfort" here is the same word in 4:1 that is translated as "displeased." It's a word that means literally "evil," as when we were told that Nineveh's repentance was "exceedingly evil to Jonah" (AT).[20]

What was the evil from which God desired to save Jonah? God's purpose for the plant was to save Jonah not chiefly from the physical evil he was experiencing from the blistering sun and scorching wind, but from the spiritual evil that had taken root in his heart. The divine compassion directed toward Nineveh in chapter 3 was directed toward his prophet in chapter 4. We're accustomed to seeing God's amazing grace in *Jonah* in the grace he extended to the Ninevites. While this was certainly amazing, as all divine grace is, the more amazing act of mercy and grace and compassion was God's pursuit of hard-hearted, bitter, ungrateful Jonah. This is the compassion of the father in Luke 15, who turns his fatherly love and concern from the prodigal son to the self-righteous older brother (vv. 25–32).

For God to effect this perhaps-greater repentance, he needed to bring trouble and discomfort into Jonah's life. The scorching wind and the blistering sun were not designed to punish Jonah but to humble and instruct him (Jonah 4:8). Their purpose was to remind Jonah that God is both sovereign and good. They were to instruct Jonah about God's freedom in election and salvation. In short, Jonah needed to remember that God is God and that his ways, though mysterious and at times difficult, are nevertheless good.

The death of the plant carries with it an important lesson for the prophet. What does Jonah have that God has not given him? What or who is the ultimate source of Jonah's gladness? Is not all of Jonah's gladness a result of God's unmerited love and favor? God has had such great compassion on Jonah, how could he not in small measure share in God's compassion for the Ninevites who, in contrast to Israel, are so ignorant in so many ways?[21]

This is what it means to have compassion. The word *compassion* came into English through the Old French from the Latin, with the basic meaning of "to suffer with." In compassion, we, in a sense, enter into the sufferings and sorrow of others and suffer with them. Their burdens become our burdens, their sorrows become our sorrows, their hardships become our hardships.

God is inviting Jonah to share in his compassion for the Ninevites, to sympathize with the Ninevites, a people who don't know their right from their left—that is, who are in large measure in the dark about the truth of God and the requirements of his moral law. God has compassion for hopelessly lost Ninevites and hopelessly hard-hearted Israelites.

This divine compassion expressed so powerfully in *Jonah* is expressed preeminently in God sending his own Son to take on human flesh. Throughout his life Jesus would extend the compassion of God by suffering with his people. Jesus at his baptism identified himself with sinful Israel (Mark 1:4–11). Throughout his life we see Jesus enduring trials and temptation. We see Jesus weeping at the tomb of Lazarus, touching the leprous and diseased, and undergoing all of the sorrows and temptations of this life. We do not worship a God who is unfamiliar with our sufferings, as the author of Hebrews tells us: "We do not have a high priest who is unable to sympathize with our weaknesses, but one who in every respect has been tempted as we are, yet without sin" (Hebrews 4:15).

But the greatest expression of divine compassion is seen not in Jesus's life but in his death. When Jesus, the Son of God, hung dying on a Roman cross, God was not just suffering with his friends but for his enemies, the righteous for the unrighteous. Paul says, "While we were enemies we were reconciled to God by the death of his Son" (Romans 5:10). Though Jonah is a prophet of unrelenting justice, he is, at the end of the day, inconsistent in his commitment. He desires unrelenting justice for Nineveh but not for Israel. God, however, is a God of unrelenting justice and is never inconsistent. The judgment that Nineveh deserved for their countless atrocities and unspeakable cruelty, the judgment that Jonah deserved for his arrogance, and the judgment that we deserve for our sins and rebellion, the Bible tells us, was laid on Christ. Jesus bore God's wrath in full measure. Jonah was called to declare God's mercy as one who had received God's mercy, but Jesus declared God's mercy as one who would receive God's judgment. God did not mitigate his judgment or turn aside from his justice to show us mercy. He bore it himself, in the person of Christ.

In Jesus's day, people were astounded that he would come for the pimps and the prostitutes, for tax collectors and murderers. Those persons were, in their minds, unredeemable. Yet Jesus came for such sinners as these. However, for us looking back, we don't see these socially marginal, pitiable people as the great unredeemables; rather, we see the Pharisees, the scribes, and the religious leaders with all their arrogance, self-righteousness, and judgmentalism as all but outside the pale of God's redeeming work. However, the good news of the gospel is that Christ died for these as well. So from the cross Jesus prays for the very ones who put him there: "Father, forgive them, for they know not what they do" (Luke 23:34).

God's compassion can break through even the hardest, most angry, arrogant, and embittered hearts. In Acts 8 we read that Paul's hatred for the

Christian Church was so great that he "was ravaging the church, and entering house after house, he dragged off men and women and committed them to prison" (v. 3). Paul was a member of the Pharisee party, who not only approved of the execution of Jesus but also were zealous persecutors of the Church itself. Paul was perhaps the most zealous, and yet on the road to Damascus, he encountered the risen Christ and was transformed by his grace and boundless mercy (9:1–18). The one who once persecuted the Church became the one who would write to Timothy,

> I thank him who has given me strength, Christ Jesus our Lord, because he judged me faithful, appointing me to his service, though formerly I was a blasphemer, persecutor, and insolent opponent. But I received mercy because I had acted ignorantly in unbelief, and the grace of our Lord overflowed for me with the faith and love that are in Christ Jesus. The saying is trustworthy and deserving of full acceptance, that Christ Jesus came into the world to save sinners, of whom I am the foremost. (1 Timothy 1:12–15)

This is the depth of God's compassion. It is a mercy that staggers the imagination and that, when truly beheld in the face of Christ, can only move us to exclaim with Paul, "Oh, the depth of the riches and wisdom and knowledge of God! How unsearchable his judgments and how inscrutable his ways! . . . For from him and through him and to him are all things. To him be glory forever" (Romans 11:33, 36). It is a compassion that extends beyond Israel to include the Assyrians, reaching even to their livestock (Jonah 4:11), a notice that suggests the expansiveness of God's love and mercy.

Bryan Estelle captures the power and poignancy of this closing chapter well when he writes,

> What we see in the final chapter is God's pity not just on the weak and helpless but on the strong and the mighty. Those who have egregiously sinned are actually the objects of God's concern, care, and pity (both the Ninevites and Jonah). It is easy for us to pity the pitiable, but what about those who are not? This is what makes God's mercy so profound. Once we grasp this theological point, our own lives may be transformed so that we too are able to exercise pity. Most significant is the fact that a deep and profound understanding of God's amazing pity toward those who are obviously sinners may actually move us to pity.[22]

*Jonah* is one of two books in the Old Testament that concludes with a question.[23] The question put to God's recalcitrant prophet in 4:11—"And should not I pity Nineveh . . . ?"—is meant for us as well. It sets before each of us the invitation to consider more deeply God's pity and compassion toward us, expressed in countless small ways yet supremely in the gift of his Son, that we might daily be transformed and moved to extend such pity and compassion toward others.

# MICAH

*By Stephen M. Coleman*

# 37

# Judgment Is Coming

MICAH 1

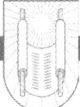

SHORTLY AFTER THE GERMAN invasion of Poland on September 1, 1939, W. H. Auden composed a poem in which he reflected on the tragedy and absurdity of war. The poem, which bears that infamous date as its title, contains some of the most haunting lines of any poetry in the English language. Perhaps chief among them are the following:

> Faces along the bar,
> Cling to their average day:
> The lights must never go out,
> The music must always play,
> All the conventions conspire,
> To make this fort assume,
> The furniture of home;
> Lest we should see where we are,
> Lost in a haunted wood,
> Children afraid of the night,
> Who have never been happy or good.[1]

With these lines Auden captured something of the human capacity to avoid, ignore, or even deny the dark realities of life. "The lights must never go out, / The music must always play." Why must the lights never go out? Why must the music always play? Because when the party comes to an end, Auden observed, we discover who we really are: "Lost in a haunted wood, / Children afraid of the night, who have never been happy or good." When the entertainments, amusements, and distractions come to an end, we realize that we are not nearly as safe, secure, content, or moral as we like to imagine.

We all have the intractable habit of surrounding ourselves with illusions that everything is going to be okay. Yet deep down we have that haunting suspicion, the nagging question, "What if it's not?" So, fearful of being exposed and condemned, we construct illusions that preach a continual message of safety and security.

Micah's opening oracle offers an uncomfortable antidote for those, both in his day and in ours, who prefer fiction to fact, illusion to reality. The prophet, in a sense, turns off the lights and shuts off the music so that the entire world can see and hear the unwelcome reality that judgment is coming. This is Micah's message in a nutshell: judgment is, in fact, coming.

We know very little about the prophet Micah himself. We are told that he came from Moresheth, a city whose location is currently unknown, although it was most likely located near the Philistine city of Gath.[2] We're told that Micah ministered during the reigns of the Judean kings Jotham, Ahaz, and Hezekiah (1:1), which places him in the latter half of the eighth century B.C. Micah, therefore, was a contemporary of the prophet Isaiah, and in fact his message bears many resemblances to that of the towering prophetic voice of the eighth century. But unlike Isaiah, who was at home in Jerusalem and familiar with the courts of kings, Micah was an unknown figure (at least to the Jerusalem elite) from a small and insignificant town on the outskirts of Jerusalem.[3] Yet it was from this small town that Micah was called to speak the word of God to the great seats of authority, power, and corruption in Israel and Judah. Stephen Dempster captures the challenge of Micah's ministry well when he writes, "Against Micah was arrayed all the organized structure of a corrupt economic, political, system. But Micah rose to the challenge and flatly contradicted false assurances of prosperity in the face of massive injustice."[4]

The opening chapter of Micah consists of two oracles, probably delivered decades apart from one another. The first oracle announces the imminent destruction of Samaria, the capital of the northern kingdom of Israel, a kingdom that Micah usually refers to as Jacob. The second oracle concerns Jerusalem, the capital city of Judah, and was likely delivered just prior to the invasion of Sennacherib in 701 B.C.[5] However, these two oracles are brought together in such a way that, as a unit, they provide an apt introduction to the book of Micah as a whole and together offer a single, coherent message for God's people.[6]

The message is as simple as it is terrifying: the God of all the world is coming in judgment. Micah's purpose, however, is not to leave his hearers hopeless and helpless in the face of an inexorable disaster. Ultimately the prophet's goal is to instill in God's covenant people a renewed faith and to effect heartfelt repentance that will bear the fruit of justice, mercy, and humility before so great and majestic a God (6:8).

## The Transcendent Judge and His Universal Judgment (1:2–5a)

The prophet opens his oracles with a summons, or, perhaps better, with a subpoena.[7] However, given what follows, the summons seems, at first glance, to be delivered to the wrong party and to the wrong address. Micah's opening oracles announce God's imminent judgment on his covenant people, the divided kingdoms of Israel and Judah. Yet the prophet says, "Hear, you peoples, all of you; pay attention, O earth, and all that is in it, and let the Lord GOD be a witness against you" (Micah 1:2). The addressees "you peoples, all of you" and "O earth" refer not to Israel and Judah, who are the objects of God's imminent judgment, but to the Gentile nations surrounding them.

However, the nations are invited to behold God's judgment on his own people, not as disinterested parties but as those who will receive the same judgment should they, like Israel, fail to repent, turn, and believe. The prophet addresses the nations, saying, "Let the Lord GOD be a witness against you, the Lord from his holy temple" (v. 2). God's judgment of Israel and Judah—about to be announced in details that are terrifying and horrific—contains a message, and it is a message not only for God's covenant people, Israel, but also for all the nations of the earth. One author helpfully describes the nations' interest in Israel's covenant relationship with her God as follows: "The whole historical covenant between Yahweh and Israel had from the beginning a universal dimension. The nations are real witnesses. Yahweh's saving actions, the punishments and the restoration that he imposed on Israel, were at the same time a preaching to the nations."[8] Israel and Judah are object lessons for the whole earth: God will judge the ungodly, Jews and Gentiles alike.

God's word to and for Israel therefore serves as a message for the world. It is the Lord bearing testimony or witness not only against his own people but against the entire world. [9] It is a message that should elicit from the Gentile nations the observation: "If the Lord is willing to utterly destroy his own people for their wickedness and idolatry, what is he willing to do to us for ours? If God will judge Israel, he will certainly judge us."

Here at the very beginning of Micah we have an important reminder that God's dealing with his particular covenant people, Israel, always had a universal purpose. The book carries a universal message of judgment and mercy. In fulfillment of God's promise to Abraham, in which he said, "I will bless those who bless you, and him who dishonors you I will curse, and in you all the families of the earth shall be blessed" (Genesis 12:3), the Gentile nations are summoned to observe, and in observing to learn, and in learning to seek refuge under the banner of the Lord and Judge of the world.

And what are the nations to observe? Micah's oracle opens with a portrait of God that is nothing short of breathtaking. The Lord is depicted as leaving his holy temple (Micah 1:3). Though many see this as a reference to the earthly temple, it is more likely that the heavenly temple, of which the earthly temple was a copy, is in view.[10] God leaves the heavenly throne room and descends to "tread upon the high places of the earth" (v. 3). From a human vantage point, if you wanted to tread upon the tops of the mountains there is only one way to get there: you must go up. As the psalmist said, "I lift up my eyes to the hills. From where does my help come?" (Psalm 121:1). From a human perspective, the tops of mountains are up (directionally) and difficult, if not dangerous (symbolically); yet for God, the heights of the mountains are far below him. His foot does not stumble, but he treads upon the heights, an image of sure-footedness and strength. God descending upon the highest places known to man and striding upon the most dangerous places known to man presents a vivid portrait of his transcendence, majesty, and power.

How great and how exalted must God be that he must descend in order to tread the heights of mountains!

> The LORD is high above all nations,
>     and his glory above the heavens!
> Who is like the LORD our God,
>     who is seated on high,
> who looks far down
>     on the heavens and the earth?" (Psalm 113:4-6)

In the book of Micah, the God who must look down to see the heavens comes down to tread on mountains. And yet, where God's transcendence is an impetus for praise in Psalm 113, his transcendence is an impetus for fear and lament in Micah 1. The One who looks far down on the heavens beholds the ways and the deeds of all flesh. His gaze penetrates even to the hearts and motivations of every man, woman, and child. And here in verse 3, God descends from Heaven to earth to express his dominion over and execute his judgment upon the earth that has taken its stand against his sovereignty.[11]

When he comes, the prophet declares, "the mountains will melt under him, and the valleys will split open, like wax before the fire, like waters poured down a steep place" (Micah 1:4). This is something of a conventional image in the prophetic literature. When Almighty God comes to this earth in judgment the world reels, the world order as we know it cracks and crumbles; it melts and is poured out. There are few things in our experience more permanent, more immovable, more inviolable than a mountain. And yet, before God's righteous judgment the very mountains melt "like wax before the fire." The valleys, similarly, split open to pour forth lava. The created order crumbles and melts, so great is God's power and so devastating his wrath.

Micah's portrait is both awesome and terrifying. The world is turned upside down. Everything that we thought was permanent, secure, and certain is revealed to be ephemeral, brittle, and frail before the power and judgment of the Holy One of Israel. Why? "All this is for the transgression of Jacob and for the sins of the house of Israel" (v. 5a). This is the God with whom Israel and Judah have to do. This is the God with whom the nations have to do; the God who, when he comes in judgment, causes the world to heave and to quake and to crumble.

The prophet's opening portrait is of a God who is more transcendent than we could ever imagine, whose greatness far surpasses the farthest reaches of the farthest universes, and yet who knows the heart of every man, woman, and child down to the most secret intentions and motivations. This God, Micah declares, is coming to judge even his own people, and when he does, the world will be turned upside down.

### The Fate of False Gods and the Failure of False Hopes (1:5b–7)

"What is the transgression of Jacob? Is it not Samaria? And what is the high place of Judah? Is it not Jerusalem?" (v. 5b). With these rhetorical questions Micah is locating Israel's wickedness at the very center of the nation.[12] The evil that was plaguing Israel and Judah was not a group of disenfranchised bandits living on the outskirts of society, wreaking havoc on the peripheries of an otherwise healthy nation. The evil was found, rather, in the very heart of society, in the leadership of the capital cities of Israel and Judah.[13] From there it spread to the cities and towns like a cancer. Samaria had become so corrupt that she is called "the transgression of Jacob"—the city essentially being identified with the nation's sin. And Jerusalem, similarly, is called "the high place of Judah." The high places were those sites where Israel, like her pagan neighbors, engaged in idol worship. The capital cities that should have been ruling God's people with equity, leading God's people in righteousness and serving God's people with mercy and compassion, were in actuality at the vanguard of Israel and Judah's idolatry, oppression, corruption, and violence.

Beginning with Samaria, God announces the fate of these wicked cities. Samaria was by any measure an impressive city. She was known in the ancient world for her immense wealth, which translated into great luxury for her citizens. Samaria was also well known for her security. It is believed that the city's walls were, in some places, thirty-two feet thick and constructed from incredibly expensive hewn stones combined with packed stones in places that made battering rams less effective.[14] Samaria instilled in its inhabitants, many of whom were the wealthy and elite of the northern kingdom, an unwavering sense of security and permanence. Their city seemed impenetrable. And yet God declares, "I will make Samaria a heap in the open country, a place for planting vineyards, and I will pour down her stones into the valley and uncover her foundations" (vv. 6, 7). This is quite a transformation.

The image here, however, is not so much what we might think when we think of a ruined castle, like those we might visit on a tour through Europe. The word translated as "heap" has the sense of a heap of stones.[15] Some have plausibly suggested that this is a reference to the stones that farmers would remove from their fields and discard in a pile at the far end of a field.[16] In other words, the once-glorious city has become an open country. No longer a thriving, vibrant center of commerce and culture, it is reduced to farmland. Her once-beautiful and expensive stones are now nothing more than an obstacle for farmers. What was once the source of her leaders' pride and the basis for their confidence will be reduced to a pile of bricks in a field, forgotten and abandoned.

When God says, "I will pour down her stones into the valley" (v. 6b), he is announcing a devastation that is as permanent as it is complete. The stones that made up Samaria's walls were so large that it was nearly impossible to bring them up from the valley below. But to add insult to injury, God says he will "uncover her foundations" (v. 6c). It is almost never a good sign when you can see the foundations of a building. Foundations are typically covered and hidden by the building itself. The foundations are exposed when the building is no more, and so it will be for Samaria. And when that occurs, it will be humiliating.

Scholars have noted the double entendre in the word "foundations," which is also used to refer to a person's backside (e.g., Habakkuk 3:13).[17] Cities in the ancient world are often depicted anthropomorphically as women, and we see this throughout Micah's prophecies.[18] Samaria's devastation will be humiliating. It will be a source of shame like that of a woman who is exposed with nowhere to hide and nothing with which to cover her nakedness as she is presumably led into exile.[19]

In Micah 1:7 the prophet announces that Samaria's idols will share the same fate as the city. Those objects of worship and adoration that served as the visible manifestation of the invisible deity or deities that Israel believed protected and blessed their great city will be revealed to be frauds, powerless to help and helpless themselves. So the prophet declares, "All her carved images shall be beaten to pieces, all her wages shall be burned with fire, and all her idols I will lay waste" (v. 7a). When God treads the high places (v. 3), he is in a sense accomplishing this very thing, crushing Israel's idols under his feet. When he comes in judgment, God will destroy the objects of Israel's misplaced devotion, revealing both their impotence and deception.

This provides the background to the somewhat difficult and obscure line: "for from the fee of a prostitute she gathered them, and to the fee of a prostitute they shall return" (v. 7b). Though some see this as a reference to temple prostitution, recent scholarship has revealed that there is little to no evidence that temple prostitution was ever practiced in ancient Israel.[20] Rather, the prophet seems to be employing an entrenched metaphor in which Israel's idolatry is cast figuratively as adultery.[21] Of course, as promises are broken and a relationship is destroyed, adultery provides a powerful and fitting analogy to describe the transgression of the covenant between God and man (cf. Hosea 1). In Micah 1:7, therefore, we see the principle of *lex talionis* at work: as Samaria gathered idols for the fee of a prostitute, effectively selling their souls to obtain them (likely though not exclusively through treaties with pagan nations), so these idols are going to be taken away for the fee of a prostitute. This is almost certainly a reference to the Assyrians carrying away the idols of her conquered peoples to display them in their own temples as trophies of their victories in honor of their false deities.

Micah's prophecy would be fulfilled in 722 B.C. or shortly thereafter. Samaria thought she was practically invincible; but the Assyrian king Shalmaneser V brought the city to its knees through a prolonged siege and eventually destroyed her. Either he or his successor, Sargon II, removed Samaria's inhabitants to resettlement communities across the Assyrian Empire, and Samaria and her environs were resettled by other displaced peoples. But the prophet wants Israel to know two things. First, God did this. This was not a result of Yahweh's weakness but Yahweh's strength. Samaria fell not because Ashur was stronger than Yahweh but because Yahweh is sovereign even over the greatest empires in the known world, and he bends even these nations to do his will.

Second, the prophet announces that God will judge sin. God is holy and his very character requires that he judge sin and wickedness. Though God's judgment is often delayed, his delay is intended to provide opportunity for repentance and reform. Too often God's slowness to judge sin is interpreted as disinterest, impotence, or both. Interestingly, there was a considerable time in which Micah's prophecy was not true before it became true. Commentators speculate that Micah suffered a good deal of public ridicule before he was acknowledged as a true prophet of God.[22] But in the year 722 B.C. the prophet was vindicated; Samaria was destroyed and her citizens scattered. In this the Lord revealed himself to be the Holy One of Israel who judges sin wherever it is found. Samaria's tremendous wealth, culture, education, fortification, and so-called gods could not deliver her from the wrath of God's judgment.

Micah's words are a sobering warning that serve as a wake-up call, if not to Israel and her capital Samaria, then to the surrounding nations that witness Samaria's downfall. The God of Israel does not suffer rebels, nor does he share his glory with another.

### An Invitation to Lament (1:8–16)

Micah 1:8, 9 serve as a transition, if not a hinge, between the two oracles. We can see this in verse 9 when the prophet says, "For her wound is incurable, and it has come to Judah." The incurable wound refers to the destruction of Samaria, and it is this wound that has now come to Judah.

It is never good to hear that a wound or illness is incurable, but what we hope comes next is something along the lines of "We can contain it, we can manage it," or perhaps even "We can cut it out." But what Micah says is that the wound is incurable and it has, essentially, reached the heart. The wound of which the prophet is speaking is the mighty Assyrian army that had devastated the countryside and villages, towns and cities of Judah, and has now reached the very doorstep of Jerusalem.[23] In this the prophet sees that the same sickness that was the cause of Samaria's ruin and destruction in 722 B.C. has now spread and "has reached to the gate of my people, to Jerusalem" (v. 9b).

Micah responds to this devastating news in the only way he can, with a cry of lamentation that erupts from the very depths of his soul. He responds with public expressions of mourning and grief and self-abasement, saying, "For this I will lament and wail; I will go stripped and naked; I will make lamentation like the jackals, and mourning like the ostriches" (v. 8). As he goes about stripped and naked, the prophet adorns the garb not so much of a mourner but of an exile.[24] His cries are likened to desert animals, the jackal and the ostrich—creatures known to make sounds that resemble cries and lamentations. Their desert habitat also brings into view an environment that is inhospitable to human life and flourishing. It is a place of loneliness, want, and death. Such is the future of Jerusalem.

Beginning in verse 10 the prophet's oracle takes the form of an invitation. He delivers a series of invitations to various cities and towns located southwest of Jerusalem. However, the invitations are not to a party but to a funeral. These are not invitations to a wedding but to a wake. These are invitations for those cities and towns to share in the prophet's grief and sorrow for the imminent destruction of the holy city, Jerusalem.

In these invitations Micah reveals that he is not only a prophet but a consummate poet, as he invites the cities to join him in mourning by means of puns or other plays on the names of the cities themselves. For example, in verse 10 he says, "In Beth-le-aphrah roll yourselves in the dust." Rolling in the dust was an expression of mourning in the ancient world. But what is striking here is that it is Beth-le-aphrah who is invited to do so because Beth-le-aphrah means "House of Dust," perhaps an expression of the desert location of the town. "House of Dust," Micah declares, "roll yourself in the dust." In other words, he commands the city to mourn in a way befitting her name. Each city's name thereby serves as a portent of her people's fate.

Similarly in Micah 1:11a the prophet says, "Pass on your way, inhabitants of Shaphir." Shaphir means "beauty," and yet they are told to "pass on your way . . . in nakedness and shame" (v. 11a). The city whose name means beauty has become vulnerable, exposed, and humiliated—evocative in every way of its coming fate of exile. The name Zaanan means something like "Exit," and to the inhabitants of the town of Exit, Micah says, "Do not come out" (presumably to fight, v. 11b). In other words, "Whatever you do, do not exit!" And though far from certain, Beth ezel may mean something along the lines of "House of Withdrawal," which the prophet depicts as a place of mourning, having been deprived of its "standing place" or "support," variously interpreted as its destruction or perhaps its ability to give support to neighboring cities (due to its grief).[25]

The next city, "Maroth" (1:12), is likely a play on Maraath (cf. Joshua 15:59), which would mean literally "Bitter Town." In Micah 1:12 he says, "For the inhabitants of Bitter Town wait anxiously for good, because disaster has come down from the LORD to the gate of Jerusalem." Maroth's waiting for good, however, is in vain; Jerusalem will not come to her aid. Her fate will bring new meaning to the residents of Bitter Town.

After Jerusalem, Lachish was the most important city in Judah. It was located in the low country southwest of Jerusalem and was heavily fortified. Archaeologists have discovered in it numerous stables, no doubt used for horses, probably war horses employed for the king's chariots. So it is unsurprising that in Micah 1:13 the prophet commands the inhabitants of Lachish to "harness the steeds to the chariots," almost certainly containing more than a hint of irony. With a pun on the name Lachish, the prophet is saying, in effect,

"Harness the horses . . . as if it will matter." Micah cleverly avoids the conventional word for war horses, employing instead the Hebrew word for messenger or racehorses, suggesting that the best use for their famous chariots is to flee and not fight.[26] It's possible, however, that the residents of Lachish did neither. Archaeologist David Ussishkin has suggested that Assyrian palace reliefs depict the citizens of Lachish hurling flaming chariots at their attackers.[27] You do not have to know much about ancient warfare to know that chariots were not typically designed to be set alight and hurled at the enemy, and yet moments of crisis often cause people to resort to anything to survive.

Lachish's invitation is noticeably longer than the others as the prophet offers the comment, "It was the beginning of sin to the daughter of Zion, for in you were found the transgressions of Israel" (v. 13). This elaboration has struck many commentators as obscure. What does Micah mean by, "the beginning of sin"?

In the law of the king recorded in Deuteronomy 17, Moses said regarding the future kings of Israel, "Only he must not acquire many horses for himself or cause the people to return to Egypt in order to acquire many horses, since the LORD has said to you, 'You shall never return that way again'" (v. 16). But in 1 Kings we read, "Solomon gathered together chariots and horsemen. He had 1,400 chariots and 12,000 horsemen, whom he stationed in the chariot cities and with the king in Jerusalem. . . . And Solomon's import of horses was from Egypt and Kue, and the king's traders received them from Kue at a price" (10:26, 28). Though somewhat speculative, it seems likely that Lachish was one of Solomon's chariot cities and thus the symbolic epicenter of the monarchy's original sin. Solomon had required God's people to return to Egypt, which God had strictly prohibited. He resorted to *realpolitik* at the expense of faithfulness. Perhaps worst of all, Solomon began to trust in chariots and horses rather than the Lord his God (see Psalm 20:7).

Lachish is then depicted as giving a dowry to the prophet's hometown of Moresheth-gath (Micah 1:14). This, however, is not the typical dowry, nor is it a happy occasion. The dowry is identified as "the houses of Achzib" and likely refers to the responsibility of defending this city. Achzib is itself described as "deceitful" since it is unable to withstand whatever disastrous onslaught is in view. Though somewhat obscure, the imagery seems to be that of the cessation of security and peace that results from the coming destruction. Lachish is dying, no longer able to offer protection. The protection falls to Moresheth-gath, which is burdened with the responsibility of guarding these deceitful towns.

Bookending the prophet's invitation to lament are two allusions that recall important events in the history of Israel's early monarchy. In verse 10 Micah declares, "Tell it not in Gath; weep not at all." These words are a clear reference to David's famous lament over the news of the death of Saul and Jonathan: "Tell it not in Gath, publish it not in the streets of Ashkelon, lest the daughters of the Philistines rejoice, lest the daughters of the uncircumcised exult" (2 Samuel 1:20). The deaths of Saul and Jonathan were an occasion for national lament, a crushing humiliation for Israel as a nation and a people. David's lament poignantly expressed deep heartbreak and emotional turmoil. Micah echoes David's fear that his enemies will hear and have reason to boast over him and his people; that they will witness Israel's humiliation and have occasion to rejoice at their downfall.

Closing the oracle, God speaks in the first person: "I will again bring a conqueror to you, inhabitants of Mareshah; the glory of Israel shall come to Adullam" (Micah 1:15). The mention of Adullam is an allusion to David's flight from Saul, recorded in 1 Samuel 22:1, 2 when he hid in the caves of Adullam. Who is "the glory of Israel" who will go into hiding in the caves (Micah 1:15)? Rabbis have noted that "the glory of Israel" is either a reference to the Lord himself or to the king of Judah—namely, Hezekiah.[28] Almost certainly the latter is in view; however, the latter stands in special relationship to the former, as the King of Judah is the Lord's Messiah (see Psalm 2:7–12). Once again the glory of Israel will find himself hiding in caves like a hunted animal, a symbol of the shame and ruin that will befall Israel's king.

Though the prophet's oracle is bookended by allusions to moments of national humiliation, disaster, and mourning, at the center of the poem stands the most startling announcement of all. In Micah 1:12b the prophet gives the simple notice that "disaster has come down from the LORD to the gate of Jerusalem." There is perhaps nothing more incongruous than disaster coming against the city of peace; and the fact that the disaster comes "from the LORD" highlights just how dire things have become for God's chosen city. The cause of Israel's ruin is not ultimately to be found outside of her but inside of her. It will come not from the power of a foreign deity but from the power of Israel's own God.

There is something both clever and humorous in the prophet's words. Yet the humor is a dark humor. We have to laugh; if we didn't, we'd cry. Micah's dark humor reveals not only that he is a consummate poet but also that he is a consummate theologian. By playing with, twisting, or ironically contradicting the names of these towns, the prophet is making a statement about Judah's identity. Names of towns, like names of people, are inextricably connected to their identity and were believed to reveal something about their destinies. Therefore, by connecting each town's name to its fate, the prophet is announcing that its fate is sealed. It is certain. Micah is saying, in effect, "You can no sooner change your fate than you can change your name. As surely as you are Beth-le-aphrah, so surely will you roll yourself in the dust and mourn over the destruction that is coming."

Names throughout the Bible reveal identities. In this case, names reveal how a city thinks of itself and how its inhabitants would like others to regard them. So Shaphir thinks of herself as beautiful, Lachish thinks of herself as powerful, and Moresheth-gath perhaps generous. So the prophet's clever puns and biting, ironic humor serve a deeper theological purpose of exposing the misplaced confidences of these treacherous cities. Their own conceptions of themselves do not align with God's conception of them. Micah powerfully sets on display the false hopes of these cities with what one commentator has memorably designated a "topography of terror."[29] Micah offers the important reminder that what matters far more than what we think of ourselves or what we call ourselves (or, to use our modern jargon, how we identify) is what God calls us and how God regards us.

Judgment against Judah's cities is as certain as their names, and there is nothing they can do to change it. Try as they might, there is nothing they can do to remove, withstand, or avoid the coming judgment. It has come to the very gate of Jerusalem; and with this, Micah's oracle comes to an end.[30] It concludes with one final invitation, and that is to join the prophet in his sorrow: "Make yourselves bald and cut off your hair, for the children of your delight; make yourselves as bald as the eagle, for they shall go from you into exile" (v. 16). Jerusalem's end is the exile of her children, a powerful symbol of the demise of the once-holy city and the cutting off of its future as symbolized in the deportation of her little ones.

These opening oracles of Micah end on a somber note of hopelessness and despair. We might rightly ask, Is there any hope for Judah at all? The answer is that Judah's hope lies in the arrival of a greater prophet and the receiving of a new name. Micah's lament is a human lament; yet it is a lament that anticipates a greater lament spoken by a greater lamenter. The Biblical prophets were called not just to proclaim the word of God but also, at times, to show forth God's emotions. Aaron, for example, was instructed to do this when he was prohibited from mourning the death of his sons Nadab and Abihu (Leviticus 10:1–6). By refusing to mourn, the high priest aligned his emotions with God's righteousness over against his family's sorrow. Of all the prophets we're given the clearest window into the inner life of Jeremiah, the weeping prophet, whose frequent and powerful lamentations over Israel's sin and Jerusalem's demise express not only human emotion but anticipate the sorrows of the incarnate Son of God.[31]

Likely unbeknown to Micah, his response to the judgment coming against Jerusalem anticipates this greater prophet. As Jesus approached this same Jerusalem, the Gospel writer Luke records that

> He wept over it, saying, "Would that you, even you, had known on this day the things that make for peace! But now they are hidden from your eyes. For the days will come upon you, when your enemies will set up a barricade around you and surround you and hem you in on every side and tear you down to the ground, you and your children within you. And they will not leave one stone upon another in you, because you did not know the time of your visitation.'" (19:41–44).

Jesus would not only lament for Jerusalem, he would die for her, that he might make her new.

When Micah roams about Jerusalem and her environs "stripped and naked" (1:8), he is not only adopting the posture of mourning but is embodying the curse that Jerusalem will endure. This is how Israel would go into exile: naked, humiliated, and ashamed.[32] The only songs on the people's lips were songs of lamentation, and their only prayers were prayers of grief and mourning. In this way Micah anticipated the Christ who would not only display Israel's judgment *on* his body but would bear Israel's judgment *in* his body.

What Jerusalem receives in part, Jesus would receive in whole—a truly incurable wound when he bore the wrath of God, stripped and naked and hanging on a tree. Indeed, the earthly Jerusalem would fall due to Israel's sin, but Jesus is even today building a new Jerusalem, a heavenly city "whose designer and builder is God" (Hebrews 11:10). This heavenly city will never be destroyed as it is built upon the finished work of the Son, who is its chief cornerstone (1 Peter 2:6–8).

Just as Israel's hope lay in a new city that God himself would build in righteousness, so too did their hope lie in receiving a new name that expressed their new identity through faith in the Messiah. Throughout the Bible God names and renames because, in so doing, he expresses a person's fate or sets on display their new identity through faith in him. For example, God names Hagar's son Ishmael, which means "God hears," saying,

> the LORD has listened to your affliction.
> He shall be a wild donkey of a man,
>     his hand against everyone

> and everyone's hand against him,
> and he shall dwell over against all his kinsmen. (Genesis 16:11b, 12)

God renames Abram Abraham (17:5), Sarai Sarah (v. 15), and perhaps most famously renames Jacob Israel (32:28). Though Israel is unable to change her fate, God is able.

In the book of Revelation, Jesus says to the church in Pergamum, "To the one who conquers I will give some of the hidden manna, and I will give him a white stone, with a new name written on the stone that no one knows except the one who receives it" (2:17). There is a degree of mystery about this "new name" that believers receive in glory. But what can be said with certainty is this: In baptism the triune God places his name upon his children. God gives us a new name, the name of the Father and of the Son and of the Holy Spirit.[33] Through this sign and seal of the covenant of grace God adopts us into his family. What we are unable to do for ourselves, God does for us as an act of his free grace. Indeed, our native identities in Adam are an occasion to mourn, but our new identities in Christ are occasions to rejoice.

Five hundred years ago Martin Luther wrote, "It is certain, man must utterly despair of his own ability before he is able to receive the grace of God."[34] Micah's opening oracle is intended to bring Israel and us to this point of utter despair. We must despair of our own abilities to avoid the coming judgment or to change our fate through our own efforts because only then are we in a place to receive the free grace of God and the salvation he offers in his Son.

# 38

# One Word of Truth

MICAH 2

THE RUSSIAN DISSIDENT Aleksandr Solzhenitsyn once remarked, "The simple step of a courageous individual is not to partake in the lie. One word of truth outweighs the whole world."[1] It's a powerful sentiment made all the more powerful when considered in light of Solzhenitsyn's life. For eight years Solzhenitsyn endured unspeakable horrors in a Russian gulag for criticizing the corruption and oppression of the Soviet leadership. The horrors that he both witnessed and experienced were designed to enfold him into the lies that supported the regime, and if not to bring him into conformity, at least to silence him. But remarkably, Solzhenitsyn was able to see through the manipulation, the mass hysteria, and the lies that sustained the Soviet regime, and even more remarkably, he was willing to speak out against them. In his three-volume international best-seller *The Gulag Archipelago*, which the novelist Doris Lessing famously said "helped to bring down an empire," Solzhenitsyn spoke that "one word of truth [that] outweighs the whole world."[2] In it he boldly and courageously exposed the wickedness, corruption, and oppression of the Soviet ruling class for what it was: evil.[3]

In Micah 2 we are given a window into a similarly dark period of Israel's history. It was a day characterized by the oppression of the poor by the rich, a day in which those with means leveraged their means to increase their wealth at the expense of the weak and vulnerable.[4] The rich were getting richer, and the powerful were becoming more powerful—not through legitimate means that blessed the city but through what amounted to state- and Church-sanctioned theft. The poor and the vulnerable in society were dehumanized and degraded as they were defrauded of their God-given inheritance and forced into servitude by the corrupt ruling class. From a human perspective there was little hope for reform, and things seemed to be going from bad to worse.

It is into this world turned upside down that God sends his prophet. Micah speaks that one word of truth that "outweighs the world." He exposes and denounces the corruption of Israel's ruling classes along with those who defend and justify their oppressive practices. God's plan for Israel's future blessing cannot and will not come through leaders such as these. Micah, however, points Israel's faithful remnant to a greater King who will one day lead his people into an inheritance that can never be stolen, and into a rest that will never come to an end.

### Oppressors Condemned (2:1–5)

In a few lines of exquisite poetry, the prophet paints a portrait that is as evocative as it is horrifying. He pronounces a "woe" upon "those who devise wickedness and work evil on their beds!" (Micah 2:1). The prophet's "woe" in this case is an ironic lamentation as it anticipates the demise and destruction of these wicked rulers.[5] It's an unsettling description made all the more unsettling by the surprising use of the verbs "devise" and "work." Commentators have observed that people don't typically work when they're lying on their beds, and so it would be more natural to read something along the lines of "those who work wickedness and devise evil on their beds."[6] But Micah, in showing that these oppressors "devise wickedness and work evil on their beds," is subtly signaling that their calculations are so certain and their will so powerful that their devising is as good as their doing. There is a seamlessness to the planning, execution, and realization of their wicked desires.[7]

Furthermore the prophet reveals that the energy, the intentionality, the intelligence, and the planning of these devisers of wickedness are matched only by their industry. They are up at the crack of dawn, with joy and drive and ambition to make their plans a reality: "When the morning dawns, they perform it, because [literally] their hand is to God" (Micah 2:1b, AT). This last expression is a bit obscure; however, it likely refers to the raising of the hand in oath to God, an action that affords these ruthless men the illusion of a divine endorsement for their wickedness.[8] Clearly these are men whose power and influence is such that they can accomplish whatever they will, and tragically, what they will is evil through and through. Consequently, the society in which they thrive has become so corrupt that such wickedness no longer needs to operate in secret, under the cover of darkness. Rather, in "the morning" (v. 1), at a time typically associated with hope and rejoicing (see, e.g., Psalms 30:5; 46:5; 59:16; 130:6), with prayers and sacrifices (1 Samuel 1:19;

1 Chronicles 16:40; Psalms 5:3; 88:13; Amos 4:4), and with just judgments (Jeremiah 21:12; Zephaniah 3:5), these men delight in making their wicked dreams a reality.[9]

What is this "evil" that these oppressors work on their beds and rise at dawn to execute? The notion that these are wealthy land barons seems to fit the description that follows: "They covet fields and seize them, and houses, and take them away; they oppress a man and his house, a man and his inheritance" (Micah 2:2). The word translated as "covet" means simply "desire," and does not necessarily denote a negative, much less evil, reality in the Bible.[10] However, in certain contexts like this, the word clearly refers to a sinful desire, rightly translated as "to covet." The determining factor has to do with the object of desire. Is it licit? Is it available for possession? Is it good for the person to possess? When the answer is no to any of these questions, we have moved from desire to covetousness, a sin that is at the root of so much oppression and misery. This is the same word used in the Tenth Commandment, in which God commands Israel, "You shall not covet your neighbor's wife. And you shall not desire your neighbor's house, his field, or his male servant, or his female servant, his ox, or his donkey, or anything that is your neighbor's" (Deuteronomy 5:21).[11]

These oppressors covet, and their covetousness produces theft. They not only covet the fields in their hearts, but their sinful desires produce action. Their desires are expressed in violence: "They covet fields and seize them, and houses, and they take them away" (Micah 2:2a). The seizure in view is not the violent seizure of bandits but the legally sanctioned seizure of those who manipulate the law—for example, offering unjust loans that are unlikely to be repaid for the purpose of causing default and foreclosure.[12] This, of course, is a kind of violence, a more subtle, genteel, insidious violence, but Micah instructs that it is violence nevertheless. The twisted desires of these land barons give birth to violent actions that enrich them at the expense of the poor and vulnerable.

As if this was not reprehensible enough, the prophet suggests that their wickedness surpasses mere theft of property and encompasses the destruction of life itself. He says, "They oppress a man and his house, a man and his inheritance" (v. 2b). The "inheritance" in view refers not simply to those material possessions that a child inherits from his father when the father dies but to the divinely granted and divinely apportioned land that each tribe, clan, and family were freely given when Israel entered the promised land.[13] The land was given to clans and families by God as an eternal inheritance. So permanent was this land inheritance that when such land was forfeited for a time it would, by divine law, be returned to the original owner in the Year of Jubilee (Leviticus 25:23–28).

The family was (and is) the foundational building block of life and society. For a man and his household to thrive in ancient Israel, they typically required land to work. Therefore, the offense in view here in Micah is not simply the deprivation of material possessions but the deprivation of those things that sustain life as God intended it for his covenant people.[14] Or, to place these actions within the broader redemptive historical framework, these land barons were dehumanizing God's image-bearers, stripping them of their God-given inheritance, which was a symbol, token, or down payment of their heavenly home.

The picture here in Micah is of an unbroken train, or, to mix the metaphor, a freely flowing stream that flows from desire to idea to action to accomplishment. There is very little friction slowing, checking, or exposing the evil of these ruthless land barons. There is nothing in the way of these oppressors realizing their most base and venal desires. The portrait is of men who are animated through and through by the thought of enriching themselves, and so they will do so at any cost, including the cost of destroying the lives and livelihoods of others. They are willing to steal and devastate the unalienable rights and possessions—unalienable because they are given by God himself—of the most weak and vulnerable of their society. In sum, the portrait of oppression that Micah paints is of those who take the good things God has given his people out of his abundant grace and kindness (land, wealth, strength, energy, industry, time, sleep, to name a few) and use them to crush those who bear his image. What was given to bless and to build up—namely, industry, intelligence, creativity, and wealth—is used instead to curse and to destroy that which God loves.

Few Biblical figures illustrate such corruption more clearly than the wicked Israelite king Ahab, who was so consumed with covetousness for his neighbor Naboth's vineyard that he refused to eat out of dejection and anger (1 Kings 21:1–16). His pagan wife, Jezebel, orchestrated false accusations of blasphemy, a kangaroo trial, and the execution of faithful Naboth to secure the property for her husband, the already land-rich king of Israel. The depth of depravity is staggering. A hundred years later, Micah shows us that the spirit of Ahab had spread and animated the leaders of both the northern and southern kingdoms so thoroughly that little help and little hope was to be found in their ranks.

The Lord responds to such wickedness, saying, "Behold, against this family I am devising disaster, from which you cannot remove your necks, and you shall not walk haughtily, for it will be a time of disaster" (Micah 2:3). What is immediately striking about the Lord's response is that he employs many of the same keywords used to describe the wickedness of the land barons.[15] Just as these oppressors "devise wickedness" (v. 1), so the Lord is "devising disaster" (v. 3). Just as the oppressors "work evil" (v. 1), twice we're told that the Lord is bringing this same word, here translated as "disaster," against this people (v. 3).[16] The significance of these lexical connections is not at all to suggest that God is culpable of the evil perpetrated by these land barons but rather that God will return upon their heads the evil they have committed against others. There is a time coming when these proud oppressors will be humbled, exposed, and condemned. It will be for them "a time of disaster." Micah announces that this time lies in the future, but he is clear that it is most certainly coming.

It is not perfectly clear who the "they" are in verse 4. "They" may refer to Israel's Assyrian captors or to those who suffered at the hands of the wicked land barons now being vindicated. Either way, "they" take up a taunt that serves to expose and humiliate these oppressive land barons: "We are utterly ruined; he changes the portion of my people; how he removed it from me! To an apostate he allots our fields" (v. 4).[17] Some scholars have understood these words to reflect the words of those who were oppressed, the lament they would raise when they were defrauded of land and home. In an ironic reversal, when God comes in judgment, these same words are used as a taunt as "they" mimic and mock the cries of the doomed oppressors.[18] It is another instance of *lex talionis*, the law of retribution. God's justice takes on a poetic character where he devises disaster against those who devise disaster, and those who cause others to lament will one day be singing the same lamentation with the result that "therefore you will have none to cast the line by lot in the assembly of the LORD" (v. 5).

In this sobering conclusion is implied both a word of judgment and a promise of salvation.[19] The lines that delimited Israel's land and property were established by God through Israel's casting of lots (Joshua 14:2). What Micah announces, therefore, is that when Yahweh comes in judgment, he will establish a new world order in which such oppressors will receive no property, no inheritance, no portion in the kingdom of God. Those who have laid up for themselves treasures on earth will find themselves destitute in the kingdom of God. Ultimately such treasure is useless, as Jesus taught his disciples: "Do not lay up for yourselves treasures on earth, where moth and rust destroy and where thieves break in and steal, but lay up for yourselves treasures in heaven, where neither moth nor rust destroys and where thieves do not break in and steal. For where your treasure is, there your heart will be also" (Matthew 6:19–21).

Hearing about the rank corruption and oppression of Micah's days, it's tempting to think something along the lines of *Well, I don't have much by way of means, influence or affluence; so Micah's words of judgment and condemnation don't have any application to me.* Solzhenitsyn, who had such penetrating insight into the corruption of the Soviet regime, observed that this same corruption found in the highest forms of government, among the elite ruling classes, and protected, if not enshrined, in the systems of Soviet society may in fact be found in every human heart. Perhaps his most famous quote captures it well: "The line dividing good and evil cuts through the heart of every human being. And who is willing to destroy a piece of his own heart?"[20] Less famous, though equally convicting, is Solzhenitsyn's observation that

> there is nothing that so aids and assists the awakening of omniscience within us as insistent thoughts about one's own transgressions, errors, mistakes. After the difficult cycles of such ponderings over many years, whenever I mentioned the heartlessness of our highest-ranking bureaucrats, the cruelty of our executioners, I remember myself in my Captain's shoulder boards and the forward march of my battery through East Prussia, enshrouded in fire, and I say: "So were *we* any better?"[21]

Though the prophet Micah denounces a very specific expression of oppression, he also, in the process, exposes the heart of oppression that lies within each of us. The sin that resides in every human heart is prone to use God's good gifts, graciously given, to harm those who bear his image. The commentator Stephen Dempster puts it well when he writes, "As the one from whom all power is derived, [God] demands an accounting for how that power is used."[22]

In this respect there is an immediate application to every man, woman, and child. Everything we have is given to us for the purpose of blessing God and blessing his image-bearers. And yet the human heart is so twisted and distorted by sin that we often use God's good gifts for just the opposite. Even if we're not adding to our real-estate portfolio, we are drinking from the same fountain of oppression any time we advance ourselves at the expense of others.

This is perhaps the most terrifying: to consider the oppressive, dehumanizing practices at work in the powerful, ruling classes of our day and to know that if we were given such means, wealth, and influence we would, more often than we'd care to admit, do the very same things. Micah's oracle reminds us that simply because something is licit does not mean it is good.

Ability (much less might) does not make right. God sees oppression in all its forms and will one day act to set all things right.

### Lies Exposed (2:6–11)

In Micah 2:6 we encounter another set of voices. These voices declare, "Do not preach! . . . One should not preach of such things" (Micah 2:6). Though the exact identity of these voices is unspecified, most interpreters understand these to be false prophets. They are depicted as doing the same thing that Micah is doing—namely, "preach[ing]" (literally "dripping"); however, their message and their agenda stand in marked opposition to the message and agenda of God's prophet.[23] These false prophets strive to contradict, if not shut down and completely silence, the message that Micah has to declare. Where Micah announces that Israel's oppressors will one day be exposed, humiliated, and publicly disgraced for their wicked deeds, the false prophets declare, "One should not preach of such things; disgrace will not overtake us" (v. 6).[24] To use the words of a latter prophet addressing the same situation, these are those who preach "'Peace, peace,' when there is no peace" (Jeremiah 6:14).

If this understanding of this difficult text is correct, then the portrait of oppression has become even darker. Israel's oppressive land barons are supported by false prophets, and the false prophets claim to be supported by God. The accountability structures are such that there is no accountability. The final mechanism to check sin and hold the wicked accountable has failed. The evil that has become rampant in Israelite society is legitimized by self-proclaimed spokesmen of God. Those who call evil good claim they are speaking for the Lord himself as they oppose the true word that exposes sin and directs the way toward true life.

In this dialogue, Micah reminds us that those who justify oppression, who defend oppressors, and who propagate the lies that sustain oppressive behaviors are complicit in the oppression even if they don't commit the act itself. It is tempting in days like today, when there is a great deal of attention given to uncovering systems of abuse, to accuse Israel of systemic oppression. However, the problem in Micah's day was not so much with the systems of power, leadership, governance, and law as it was a problem with the people engaged in these systems. The systems, in other words, might be more or less functional; the problem resides in the hearts of those who are in places of power and position. Israel's leaders were abusing the system, twisting it to their own advantage, and crushing countless people in the process.

Not content to leave it in generalities, God sets forth his evidence with specific examples:

> But lately my people have risen up as an enemy;
> you strip the rich robe from those who pass by trustingly
>   with no thought of war.
> The women of my people you drive out
>   from their delightful houses;
> from their young children you take away
>   my splendor forever" (Micah 2:8, 9).

Those "who pass by trustingly with no thought of war" (v. 8) likely refers to Israelites returning from battle, not suspecting until it is too late that their real enemy is to be found among their own people. Like the men earlier who were deprived of their houses and inheritance (v. 2), here we witness women deprived of that which gave their lives meaning and value in their society—namely, their homes and their children (v. 9).

But notice who has risen up as "an enemy" of "my people." Who is it who has assaulted the unsuspecting and the vulnerable? Who has deprived the weakest members of society of those things that give them not only identity but their lives? God identifies these wicked individuals as "my people" (v. 8). This designation recalls God's deliverance of his people from oppression in Egypt (Exodus 6:7), God's leading them through the wilderness on outstretched wings. They are the people God protected and to whom he gave a land so that they might live lives marked by obedience and the blessings that flow from it. "My people," God says, "have assumed the posture of my enemy as they assault, defraud, and oppress my people." They commit, defend, and justify dehumanizing atrocities.[25]

Things have gotten so bad that one wonders if there is any hope. Is there anything to be done to rectify the chaos wrought by Israel's leaders?

In Micah 2:10 the prophet gives the answer: "Arise and go, for this is no place to rest, because of uncleanness that destroys with a grievous destruction." In other words, "Run! Flee! Escape!" Why? This is "no place to rest." This expression is pregnant with significance as it essentially announces the reversal of God's good purposes and covenant promises for his people. In Deuteronomy 12:8–11a God had commanded Israel:

> You shall not do according to all that we are doing here today, everyone doing whatever is right in his own eyes, for you have not as yet come to *the rest and to the inheritance* that the LORD your God is giving you. But when you go over the Jordan and live in the land that the LORD your God is giving you to inherit, and when he gives you rest from all your enemies around, so that you live in safety, then to the place that the LORD your God will choose, to make his name dwell there, there you shall bring all that I command you.

Similarly, in his prayer of dedication, Solomon praised God for his fulfillment of his gracious promises: "Blessed be the LORD who *has given rest to his people Israel, according to all that he promised.* Not one word has failed of all his good promise, which he spoke by Moses his servant" (1 Kings 8:56). God had given his people rest in the land, yet the leaders of his people had made Israel's rest into hard labor, their peace into sorrow, their plenty into want, and their life into death. And astoundingly, those who should have called such wickedness to account supported it, encouraged it, and profited from it.

A people, it can be said, is known by their preachers. We can hear Micah's exasperation in his indictment: "If a man should go about and utter wind and lies, saying, 'I will preach to you of wine and strong drink,' he would be the preacher for this people!" (2:11). The lies peddled by these false prophets underwrite the indulgence and debauchery endemic to Judahite society. Micah's one word of truth threatened to be drowned out by messages of "Eat and drink and be merry; God approves of all that you do." The connection of the false prophets' preaching with their message of "wine and strong drink" is suggestive of what one commentator has called an "intoxicating effect on the hearers, dulling their senses and judgment regarding the reality of the precarious position and the truth of God's word."[26]

In this, Micah offers a powerful reminder: if we believe a lie long enough, and if we live according to that lie long enough, it becomes so much a part of our operating framework that we are no longer able to comprehend the truth, much less respond to the truth when we are confronted by it. Like a fish unaware that it lives in water, we can become so acclimated to evil and the lies that support it that we don't recognize it for what it is. Ultimately the only reliable thing we have to reorient us to the truth is the Word of God, a light shining in the darkness.

Practically, questions we can ask ourselves are: *Do I regularly sit under the reading and the preaching of the Word? Am I open to having my loves, hates, ideas, habits, and priorities challenged at the most fundamental level by a word from outside of me? And do I have anyone in my life—friends, family members, pastors, elders (preferably all of the above)—who can speak hard truths to me that expose the lies by which I am living and the sin they produce?* It is only when we open ourselves to correction by an authority outside of ourselves—namely, the God who is himself truth and who has spoken in his Word—that we, by his grace, have a fighting chance to no longer live according to the illusions and lies of this world but according to the truth of God and the reality of his kingdom.

### Deliverance Promised (2:12-13)

Beginning in 2:12 we see, as it were, a ray of sun breaking through the dark clouds. Oracles that thus far have been comprised of judgment and woe here give way to the first words of hope and blessing as God says,

> I will surely assemble all of you, O Jacob;
>     I will gather the remnant of Israel;
> I will set them together
>     like sheep in a fold,
> like a flock in its pasture,
>     a noisy multitude of men." (2:12)

Notice who is speaking. With these words God himself promises to do what Israel's leaders failed to do—namely, to shepherd "my people." Just as God's word of judgment against the oppressors contains an implicit word of hope for the oppressed, so too do these words of deliverance contain an implicit word of judgment against the oppressors. When God says, "I will surely assemble all of you, O Jacob; I will gather the remnant of Israel," he is, in effect, redrawing the lines of who constitutes "my people." He construes a remnant of Israel as "all of you, O Jacob," thus anticipating the Apostle Paul who would write to the Romans, "Not all who are descended from Israel belong to Israel, and not all are children of Abraham because they are his offspring" (Romans 9:6). Those in Israel who rob, oppress, victimize, and harm God's people will discover that they are not, in fact, God's people after all.

About this newly constituted Israel God says, "I will set them together like sheep in a fold" (Micah 2:12). Throughout the Bible God's people are consistently depicted as sheep and for good reason. Sheep need a shepherd. Without a shepherd sheep are exposed, vulnerable, wayward, and in great danger. God announces that he will become, to a remnant of his people who have been oppressed, abused, neglected, and scattered, a good and faithful shepherd. He will assemble them and set them in a place of safety and provision, like sheep in a fold, like a flock in its pasture.

This pastoral image will be taken up, developed, and expanded by another prophet years later. God will declare through his prophet Ezekiel, ministering in exile:

> Behold, I, I myself will search for my sheep and will seek them out. As a shepherd seeks out his flock when he is among his sheep that have been scattered, so will I seek out my sheep, and I will rescue them from all places where they have been scattered on a day of clouds and thick darkness. And I will bring them out from the peoples and gather them from the coun-

tries, and will bring them into their own land. And I will feed them on the mountains of Israel, by the ravines, and in all the inhabited places of the country. I will feed them with good pasture, and on the mountain heights of Israel shall be their grazing land. There they shall lie down in good grazing land, and on rich pastures they shall feed on the mountains of Israel. I myself will be the shepherd of my sheep, and I myself will make them lie down, declares the Lord God. I will seek the lost, and I will bring back the strayed, and I will bind up the injured, and I will strengthen the weak. (Ezekiel 34:11–16)

What generation after generation of leadership failed to do for God's covenant people, God himself would come and accomplish. And he would do so at the greatest cost to himself. At the Feast of Booths, Jesus stood among the crowds and announced the fulfillment of God's promises through his prophets of old when he declared, "I am the good shepherd. The good shepherd lays down his life for the sheep." (John 10:11). Where Israel's rulers routinely sacrificed their people in war or through deprivation to preserve their own lives and secure their own kingdoms, Christ would sacrifice himself, relinquishing the glory he had by nature as the Son of God to give up his own life for the sake of his people.

Micah's oracle, however, doesn't end with this hopeful scene of pastoral deliverance, security, and peace. In Micah 2:13 the prophet's metaphor shifts from the pastoral to the martial as God describes how he is going to accomplish the regathering of this remnant of his people.[27] He says,

> He who opens the breach goes up before them;
> they break through and pass the gate,
> going out by it.
> Their king passes on before them,
> the Lord at their head.

What was implicit in verse 12 is here made explicit: it is God himself who will deliver the remnant of his people. "The Lord is at their head" (v. 13). He will lead his people to a new place, to a new life, to a new world order characterized by safety and security and peace. And he will do this *as* or *with* "their king" (literally "their head"). Though it is ambiguous (perhaps intentionally so) whether the Lord is identified as their king or accompanies their king, the emphasis is on the Lord accomplishing the deliverance of his people through the strength and work of his Shepherd-King.

Strikingly, however, the direction of movement appears to be from inside a city outward. This is surprising because typically one flees to a city, not away from a city to find safety; he breaks into a city and not out of a city. Though Micah's prophecy will find its (penultimate) fulfillment in God's deliverance of Israel from the bondage of the Babylonian exile, in the immediate context the greatest threat to God's people is not the Assyrians or the Babylonians but the leaders of Jerusalem itself. The corruption of Jerusalem has become so great and its wickedness so pronounced that the only hope for the remnant is to escape the once-holy city (Micah 2:10).[28] It is for this reason that "he who opens the breach goes up before them; they break through and pass the gate, going out by it" (v. 13). Jerusalem is no longer the city of peace but a city of violence, no longer a place of refuge but a prison. Judgment will come against the wicked city. But praise God, the prophet says, in effect, that when judgment comes against Jerusalem and her intractably corrupt leaders, the Lord will gather his sheep and will lead his people to safety.

How will the Lord accomplish this deliverance? The first half of verse 13 has been the cause of considerable debate among scholars and commentators. "He who opens the breach" clearly refers to the royal, messianic figure who is identified with or stands in close relationship to the Lord. But what is the meaning of the designation "who opens the breach"? The word translated as "breach" (from Hebrew *pereṣ*) often occurs in contexts where God strikes out in righteous judgment against wickedness and unbelief, thereby creating a way of deliverance for his people. In 2 Samuel 5:20, for instance, we're told, "David came to Baal-Perazim [from the root *prṣ*], and David defeated them there. And he said, 'The LORD has broken through [Hebrew *pāraṣ*] my enemies before me like a breaking flood.' Therefore the name of that place is called Baal-perazim." Similarly, when well-intentioned Uzzah foolishly transgressed the boundaries of holiness when he touched the ark of the covenant, he was struck dead, and the text reads, "That place is called Perez-uzzah to this day" (2 Samuel 6:8; cf. Psalm 60:3).

In these instances God's breaking out, his creating a breach, describes a violent stroke that at one and the same time both destroys and delivers. The Philistines were destroyed; Israel was delivered. Uzzah was destroyed; the convoy carrying the ark was delivered. The prophet envisions a concrete event in which God frees his people from distress once and for all.[29]

Ultimately this one "who opens the breach" (Micah 2:13) would be fulfilled in the incarnate Son of God who finally and permanently made a way of deliverance and led his people to safety from every threat and danger that would harm them and every lie and deception that would mislead them. Yet the breach that King Jesus would open to deliver his people was not ultimately a breach in a wall around Jerusalem, Babylon, or Rome but a breach in his own body as he was struck so that those who believe on him might be delivered. In the words of the prophet Isaiah, "He was pierced for our transgressions; he was crushed for our iniquities" (Isaiah 53:5).[30] Such is the love of our good shepherd. "All we like sheep have gone astray; we have turned—every one—to his own way; and the Lord has laid on him the iniquity of us all" (v. 6).

In his commentary on Micah, Dempster astutely notes the striking contrast between the oracle of judgment in 2:1–11 and the oracle of salvation in 2:12, 13.[31] In the former, the reason for God's judgment is given. Why is God's judgment coming? Because of the covetousness, theft, lies, and corruption of the ruling classes. But when God declares the coming salvation and deliverance, strangely and amazingly no reason is given because God's redemption is an act of free grace. God simply shows up as Lord and King, the God of grace and mercy, to deliver a people for himself. He does this not because of anything in them or done by them but for his own glory, or in the words of the Apostle Paul, for "the praise of his glorious grace" (Ephesians 1:6).

# 39

# God's Mountain Ruined and Raised

MICAH 3:1—4:7

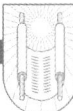

MOUNTAINS PLAY SOMETHING of a leading role in the Bible. The garden of Eden, where God dwelt in intimate communion with his image-bearers, was planted on a mountain (see Genesis 2:10–14; Ezekiel 28:14). Israel became a nation at Mount Sinai in the desert when the people entered into covenant with Yahweh. It was at Mount Sinai that Israel constructed the tabernacle—the architecture and symbolism of which was designed to be a representation of Mount Sinai, thus serving, in effect, as a portable mountain that could accompany Israel in her wilderness wanderings.[1] When Israel entered the promised land, she rehearsed the blessings and curses of the covenant on two mountains, Mount Ebal and Mount Gerizim (Deuteronomy 11:29). Later in Israel's history, the capital of the northern kingdom would be built on a high mountain in Samaria. And in the New Testament, Jesus not only delivered the law of the kingdom of God on a mountain (thus paralleling Moses's delivering of the Torah at Mount Sinai, Exodus 19:20ff.; Matthew 5:1ff.), but he also revealed himself in his glory to his disciples Peter, James, and John on what has become known as the Mount of Transfiguration (Matthew 17:1–8).[2]

Each of these mountains was important both in Israel's history and for Israel's theology. However, there is one mountain that indisputably overshadows them all in significance and indeed in glory—namely, Mount Zion. From the moment Israel departed Egypt, there arose on the horizon of history one mountain upon which their God would dwell and on which Israel would dwell with him in eternal fellowship and blessed communion. Israel sang of this great hope in the Old Testament version of the Apostle's Creed, Moses's Song of the Sea: "You will bring them in and plant them on your own mountain, the place, O LORD, which you have made for your abode, the sanctuary, O Lord, which your hands have established" (Exodus 15:17). The song concludes with one line celebrating the rule of Israel's God and King from this very mountain: "The LORD will reign for ever and ever" (v. 18).

Mount Zion was the mountain where God would choose to "make his name dwell" (Deuteronomy 12:11). There David brought the ark of the covenant (1 Chronicles 15:1–3); more importantly, there David's son Solomon constructed the temple for Yahweh, the God of Israel (1 Kings 6). From Zion, God's kingdom would be extended in righteousness, God's justice would be executed, and God's mercy would be apprehended by any and all who would submit to his kingship. God made Mount Zion his abode, and God planted his people on his holy mountain. Zion therefore stood as a symbol of God's glory and Israel's calling. On this mountain God's name would be glorified, and to this mountain the nations would stream. There are few places in the Bible where this is more evident than in the Psalms, so many of which sing of the supreme glory of Zion and the hope she is for the world. To give just one example, Psalm 87 opens with the following:

> On the holy mount stands the city he founded;
>    the LORD loves the gates of Zion
>    more than all the dwelling places of Jacob.
> Glorious things of you are spoken,
>    O city of God." (vv. 1–3)

In Micah 3, however, we see that something has gone terribly wrong. What was appointed as the place from which God would exercise his righteous kingship and expand his kingdom in justice and mercy has become the epicenter of corruption, violence, deception, and oppression. Once again God's prophet declares and denounces the deep wickedness of Jerusalem's ruling classes. Those whose station and calling it was to represent the justice of Yahweh have abused their positions of power for their own comfort and personal gain. As a result, God's mountain has become defiled. In Micah 3 the prophet condemns the corruption that has become endemic to Jerusalem's ruling elite and that has ruined God's holy mountain. God's judgment, however, is not his final word. In the wake of God's devastating judgment, Micah also announces the coming of a new day in which a new Zion will be raised and established forever. What has been corrupted, defiled, and destroyed on account of human sin, God promises to restore, renew, and glorify by his power and grace.

### Three Verdicts and the Ruin of God's Mountain (3:1–12)

*The Magistrates (3:1–4)*

What recourse did the average Israelite have to seek restitution from the oppressive, coercive, manipulating land barons addressed in Micah 2? The answer is obvious, and it is the same for us today: the legal system. It was the judges' and magistrates' duty, given to them by God, to render just judgments and to uphold righteousness. But as Bruce Waltke helpfully observes, "Whereas chapter 2 condemns the venal land barons, chapter 3 condemns the magistrates."[3] The scope of the corruption is clearly growing.

In 3:1, Micah addresses these leaders as "heads of Jacob and rulers of the house of Israel" and sets before them a scathing rhetorical question: "Is it not for you to know justice?"[4] The answer is, of course, an unqualified yes. The administration of justice was the primary responsibility of these leaders of Israel, given to them by none other than their God, the Lord of the covenant. The authority these magistrates held was to be exercised to the end that Israelite society would be ordered for the good of the people of God.[5] As faithful under-shepherds, Israel's leaders were to promote the thriving, peace, and blessedness of the people entrusted to their care. This was their world as God had designed it and had revealed its order to Israel.

And yet how have these "heads" and "rulers" discharged their duty? Micah answers this as he addresses them in horrifyingly grotesque terms:

> You who hate the good and love the evil,
> who tear the skin from off my people
>   and their flesh from off their bones,
> who eat the flesh of my people
>   and flay their skin from off them,
> and break their bones in pieces
>   and chop them up like meat in a pot,
>   like flesh in a cauldron. (3:2, 3)[6]

Far from rendering judgments according to truth and righteousness, judgments that preserve and promote life, these rulers were active participants and leaders in the destruction of the very people they were to be protecting. The prophet cleverly, if disturbingly, casts these magistrates' behavior in culinary terms, and the portrait is of men who are nothing short of monsters. The stripping of skin and separating of flesh from bones is what a butcher would do to a sheep or a goat. Cooks break bones and add them to a stew for flavor. And yet here it is not sheep, goats, or cattle that are being slaughtered, flayed, and cooked, but God says it is "my people" (an expression fraught with covenantal significance) who are being brutalized and mutilated to satisfy the appetites of these leaders.

These are God's covenant people, the apple of his eye, delivered from Egypt with a mighty hand and outstretched arm. Delivered from slavery and death by God's grace, it was the high calling of these men to protect God's people. But tragically we see them destroying God's people for their own gain. Some have taken this to be a literal description of the behavior of the magistrates, suggesting that they engaged in the same terrorizing measures as the Assyrians.[7] It is unlikely, however, that Micah's description is meant to be taken literally. The metaphorical connections with Assyria, however, are illuminating. Just as Assyria engaged in horrific brutalities to terrorize weaker nations into submission, so too do Israel's judges and magistrates align themselves with the spirit and practices of Israel's enemies. The metaphors serve, as one commentator puts it, to uncover "the vicious nature of the economic and legal processes by which the powerless are devoured."[8]

To be sure, these wicked leaders would not recognize themselves in this portrait. But the prophet exposes their actions for what they are—monstrous—and lays bare their hearts for all to see. Thus what we behold is a heart that is unwavering in its commitment to evil.

The point of the extended metaphor is to penetrate beneath the surface realities of lawsuits and courts, behind the threats, manipulations, lies, and deceit of politicians, behind the veneer of order and justice of the city's elders and leaders, to expose the horrific realities perpetrated against the weak and the vulnerable among God's people. When these appointed leaders decide in favor of those who line their pockets, perform favors for them, or advance their standing, they are in fact destroying life in the most base and grisly manner. Injustice goes under the guise of justice, lies wear the habit of truth, and oppression is set forth as righteousness. Here is a portrait of a world turned upside down.

Having rehearsed the charges against Israel's wicked magistrates, Micah then issues God's verdict: "Then they will cry to the Lord, but he will not answer them; he will hide his face from them at that time, because they have made their deeds evil" (v. 4). A day is coming, declares the prophet, in which these rulers of Israel will cry to the Lord in their distress, and like the cries of the poor and vulnerable that they met with indifference, and even scorn, so too will their cries be met with a deafening silence. Throughout the Bible deliverance from distress and certain death comes to those who cry to the Lord (e.g.,

Psalms 4:3; 22:5; 107:13). And in fact Israel's own cry of oppression in Egypt was to serve subsequent generations as a catalyst for pursuing justice in Israel.[9] The sentence Micah delivers, however, is that this way of escape from the coming crisis will be unavailable for the wicked and venal magistrates. Almost certainly the crisis in view is the Assyrian army, surrounding (or about to surround) Jerusalem. When these leaders cry for help and deliverance from this terrifying threat, Micah says, their cries will be answered with a silence that presages their ultimate destruction. These powerful leaders will one day cry out to God for justice and for mercy, but they will receive the same response they gave to the poor and the oppressed.[10] Silence.

*False Prophets (3:5–8)*

Micah's second indictment is leveled against false prophets, whom God speaks of as those who "lead my people astray, who cry 'Peace' when they have something to eat, but declare war against him who puts nothing into their mouths" (3:5). Like the magistrates, these false prophets pervert justice and twist the truth to satisfy their venal desires. The prophet's job was to serve God and to declare the truth of God to God's people. But these prophets serve neither God nor his people; rather, in the words of the Apostle Paul, "their god is their belly, and they glory in their shame, with minds set on earthly things" (Philippians 3:19).

Micah's expression in 3:5 is a little more vivid in the Hebrew than is often captured in translation, as he literally says, "Biting they cry out, 'Peace.'"[11] Against those who do not support their self-serving and corrupt message, these prophets literally "sanctify war."[12] They declare war and peace not according to God's truth but according to whatever promises to satisfy their greed and insatiable appetites. It is an appalling state of affairs. Religious leaders, purporting to speak for God, speak lies and deceptions and thereby manipulate God's people for their own gain. Sadly, the Church in our day too often witnesses the very same thing as pastors and leaders baptize indulgence, corruption, and wickedness in the name of Christ. Micah reminds us that this is not true religion but a shameful perversion that dishonors God and that will one day receive its due judgment.

Following the same pattern as before, the prophet Micah's indictment is followed by a verdict:

> Therefore it shall be night to you, without vision,
>    and darkness to you, without divination.
> The sun shall go down on the prophets,

> and the day shall be black over them;
> the seers shall be disgraced,
> and the diviners put to shame;
> they shall all cover their lips,
> for there is no answer from God." (vv. 6, 7)

Throughout the Bible, divine revelation, the basis of the prophetic vocation, is associated with light, sight, and honor (cf. e.g., Exodus 34:29–35; Numbers 12:6; 24:15, 16; Isaiah 29:9–14). Prophets were understood to be intermediaries between God and man. What they received from God, often in visions, they declared with their mouths. Here in Micah 3, God announces that the access to revelation for these (presumably) false prophets would be cut off in a public and humiliating way.[13]

Interestingly, Micah adopts and adapts traditional prophetic figures of judgment—the extinguishing of the heavenly lights and the encroaching darkness (3:6) (figures these prophets would likely have used to declare God's judgment on others)—to announce their dreadful sentence. What they lyingly claim to do (i.e., speak for God) they will be unable to do as their shame is set on full display for all to see and they "cover their lips" (v. 7), an act of grief and humiliation in Israel associated with the uncleanness and defilement of leprosy (cf. Leviticus 13:45).

These false prophets were no doubt incredibly powerful individuals in the Judean society of Micah's day. They would have commanded respect from the highest levels of society and would have wielded tremendous influence over king and court. It is against these pseudo-prophets that Micah takes his stand. This comes out clearly in 3:8, when the prophet uncharacteristically draws attention to himself and his own prophetic calling and ministry:

> But as for me, I am filled with power,
> with the Spirit of the LORD,
> and with justice and might,
> to declare to Jacob his transgression
> and to Israel his sin.

Micah embodies everything that the false prophets are not. He is one who is empowered by the Spirit of God who strengthens him for his calling. He is one who exhibits an unwavering commitment to justice, perhaps the quality most lacking in Israel's leaders. And he is one who declares the word of God faithfully, even and especially when his message is unpopular.

Micah, the true prophet, serves as a foil for the faithless and false prophets who enrich and engorge themselves by preaching lies to a weak and wounded people. But more than that, in his capacity as a faithful prophet of the Lord who in the strength of the Lord and by the power of the Spirit takes his stand for righteousness against the power brokers of Jerusalem, Micah anticipates a prophet greater than himself who would likewise come in the strength of the Lord and in the power of the Spirit to pronounce woe upon the religious leaders of his day for their corruption and hypocrisy (Matthew 23:13–36).

## *Magistrates, Prophets, and Priests (3:9–12)*

In Micah 3:9, the prophet broadens the scope of God's indictment. Along with the rulers and the prophets, Micah includes the priests, Israel's religious leaders. The corruption, it seems, is total. It has affected every aspect of Israelite society, from the judicial to the religious.

The accusation is likewise comprehensive in scope. The

> rulers of the house of Israel,
> . . . detest justice
> and make crooked all that is straight
> [and] . . . build Zion with blood
> and Jerusalem with iniquity. (vv. 9, 10)

Like the prophets who "practice divination for money," the priests "teach for a price" (v. 11), adjusting their instruction and adapting their legal opinions to the benefit of the highest bidder.[14] Perhaps worst of all is the fact that both groups (and perhaps all three) claim divine sanction and approbation for their wickedness: "Yet they lean on the LORD and say, 'Is not the LORD in the midst of us? No disaster shall come upon us'" (v. 11). The Old Testament scholar James Luther Mays summarized this tragic state of affairs well when he wrote, "The 'nouveau riche' in Jerusalem had drawn prophet and priest into their own environment where money talked louder than God."[15]

The comprehensive indictment is followed by an equally comprehensive verdict. Jerusalem is guilty and will receive the stroke of God's judgment. The prophet is explicit as to the cause of Israel's imminent demise: "Therefore because of you, Zion shall be plowed as a field; Jerusalem shall become a heap of ruins, and the mountain of the house a wooded height" (v. 12). The mighty mountain will be laid low. No longer glorious, Zion will become like Samaria before her—a field, plowed over presumably by an invading army.[16] Jerusalem will become "a heap of ruins," and the mountain of the house of the Lord will be abandoned and desolate and overgrown.[17] No longer will Jerusalem be a bustling, thriving metropolis, a city set on a hill as a beacon representing God's righteous rule to the world. Rather, Jerusalem will be humiliated, ruined, and abandoned—abandoned both by her citizens and, even worse, by her God.

The destruction of Jerusalem and the ruin of the temple were for many in Micah's day inconceivable. They held an aberrant view of God's protection of Jerusalem, and therefore to them the prophet's words bordered on blasphemy. Years later the prophet Jeremiah risked his life proclaiming this same message and was only spared the death penalty for blasphemy because Micah, by this time vindicated as a true prophet of Yahweh, had years earlier announced the same judgment (Jeremiah 26:16–18; Micah 3:12).

The judgments announced in Micah's three verdicts represent an escalation of divine absence. First, God will not hear (v. 4). Then God will not speak (v. 7). Finally, God will not abide in the midst of his people (v. 12). God becomes increasingly silent and eventually absent, the worst judgment imaginable. Divine abandonment leaves sinners to their own devices, devoid of divine grace and bereft of God's mercy.

Though leveled against those whose wickedness was egregious, we would be foolish to ignore the warnings these words of judgment contain for us even today. We too are prone to use others for our own advantage. We too twist the truth for our own gain. We too leverage whatever positions of power we may enjoy for our own benefit at the expense of others. Though in different ways, the depravity that so corrupted Mount Zion in Micah's day resides in our hearts as well.

In these sobering verdicts we catch only a glimpse of what each of our sins deserve and of the inevitable end of those who reject God and his kingdom. Those who live as if God were absent will eventually experience the true horror of that very reality: divine abandonment.

Yet Micah's verdicts against the faithless leaders, prophets, and teachers are significant not only for their vivid depiction of the humiliation and the sorrow and the misery that each of our sins deserve, but they are significant also in their vivid depiction of the humiliation and the sorrow and the misery of the One who would endure these judgments for sinners like us.

Like the rulers and magistrates who would cry out to God only to be met with silence, so Jesus, though perfectly innocent, would cry out from the cross, "My God, my God, why have you forsaken me?" (Mark 15:34). But unlike these magistrates, Jesus's abandonment by his heavenly Faither in his moment of distress would not be for crimes he committed but for the sins of others. The one who from all eternity knew nothing but the shining countenance of his Father's face would as the incarnate Son endure abandonment and utter rejection—the Father turning his face away from his Son so that those who believe in Jesus might hear the precious words of divine approbation: "The LORD bless you and keep you; the LORD make his face to shine upon and be gracious to you; the LORD lift up his countenance upon you and give you peace" (Numbers 6:24–26).

The covenant curses Micah announced against the faithless leaders of Israel would one day fall upon the perfectly good and perfectly faithful Prophet, Priest, and King. Jesus would willingly offer his life for vile sinners, bearing in his body the divine wrath so that those who are united to him by faith may escape so great and so awful a judgment. Micah's verdicts reveal not only the heinousness of our sin but also the greatness of God's love as Christ "redeemed us from the curse of the law by becoming a curse for us" (Galatians 3:13).

### God's Mountain Renewed and Glorified (4:1–7)

Micah 4 opens with a surprising reversal of events. Stephen Dempster is certainly correct when he writes, "In the context of the book, the razing of the temple to the ground (3:12) thus provides a deliberate foil to the raising of the temple to the sky. The heap of ruins will someday become the highest mountain!"[18] The prophet announces that the death and destruction wrought by sinful human hands is not the end of the story for God's mountain and for God's people. There will come a time that the prophet calls "the latter days" in which "the mountain of the house of the LORD shall be established as the highest of the mountains, and it shall be lifted up above the hills" (4:1).

Throughout the Bible the expression "latter days" is often used, as it is here, to denote the last days. It signals the end of time as we know it and the beginning of a new time or a new age, what theologians call the *eschaton*. It will be in this new age that God's mountain is established; that is, it cannot be moved, destroyed, or plowed into ruins ever again. It will be a permanent, immovable mountain, so permanent and immovable that we might even say it's an eternal mountain. Furthermore, it will be "the highest of the mountains." There is the basic cognitive association that bigger is better; the highest mountain is conceptually the most important mountain. There is the corollary notion that bigger is stronger. There is certainly the obvious implication that the highest mountain could be seen from miles around. Above all other mountains will tower immovable Zion.

In his description of this new and future mountain the prophet employs imagery that would have been familiar throughout the ancient Near East. Deities were often believed to dwell on the heights of mountains, and it is from these mountain dwellings that the gods would exercise their rule. This is a mountain the heights of which reach to Heaven, and we might see in this the sacred counterpart to the sacrilegious tower of Babel.[19] Babel was the mountain that man built in order to make a name for himself (Genesis 11:4). It served as a monument to human ingenuity exercised apart from God. But here in Micah, we're reminded that mankind's hope does not lie in a mountain that man will build; rather, the hope of the world resides in the mountain that God will build. This mountain will be exalted as the dwelling place of the one true God, and its greatness is global in proportion and prominence and power. Later in Israel's history, Daniel will interpret King Nebuchadnezzar's dream in which he saw a rock cut not by human hands grow into a mountain that fills the entire world, a picture of God's heavenly kingdom that will destroy and supplant all the kingdoms of this earth (Daniel 2:31–35, 44, 45).

The mountain is of cosmic significance not only geographically but also theologically. In contrast to the mountain that man made, the mountain from which the messianic king would deliver his people because of its corruption (Micah 3:12), God's new mountain will draw people from every tribe, tongue, and nation. Micah says that "peoples" and "many nations" will flow to it (4:1, 2). Some commentators have noted the other-worldly, supernatural image of a stream flowing not, as would be expected, down the mountain but rather flowing up the mountain (a seeming impossibility).[20] Like a flowing stream, people from every nation will come, saying to one another, "Come, let us go up to the mountain of the Lord, to the house of the God of Jacob, that he may teach us his ways and that we may walk in his paths" (v. 2).

Why this magnetism? What is the character of this mountain, this city, this God that draws peoples from across the globe to dwell on his mountain? From this mountain God will administer his rule with absolute justice and preside over a kingdom characterized by a grace the likes of which this world has never seen. The nations of the earth will thus be attracted to this new way and this new life of a kingdom that is not of this world.

The prophet then elaborates on this other-worldly kingdom rule by this other-worldly king, the Lord himself:

> For out of Zion shall go forth the law,
>   and the word of the Lord from Jerusalem.
> He shall judge between many peoples,
>   and shall decide disputes for strong nations far away;
> and they shall beat their swords into plowshares,
>   and their spears into pruning hooks;
> nation shall not lift up sword against nation,
>   neither shall they learn war anymore;
> but they shall sit every man under his vine and under his fig tree,

and no one shall make them afraid
for the mouth of the LORD of hosts has spoken. (Micah 4:2b–4)

It is striking that the Lord's mountain, the Lord's city, and the Lord's rule are depicted as the polar opposite of the mountain, city, and rule of Israel's judges, prophets, and priests.[21] Whereas Israel's leaders have taught, prophesied, or rendered judgments in order to line their own pockets regardless of the devastating effects on the poor and the vulnerable, the Lord, by contrast, will judge impartially between many peoples and shall decide disputes for strong nations far away.

We may also compare the mountains in terms of their results. Man's mountain results in a people with their skin flayed, their flesh torn off, their bones crushed and chopped up like meat in a pot (3:2, 3). The result of God's mountain, however, is swords beaten into plowshares and spears into pruning hooks because there is no more use for implements of war. In contrast to the outward flow of prisoners of war and plunder on account of Israel's sin is the inward flow of worshipers and wealth for Israel's king.[22] Finally, in its place the prophet says, "they shall sit every man under his vine and under his fig tree, and no one shall make them afraid" (4:4). Here Micah employs traditional prophetic imagery to express unqualified and never-ending peace, security, and prosperity for God's people. In place of warfare and oppression, in place of rampant violence and death, the Lord's kingdom is characterized by life and rest and peace. The Lord's mountain produces an abundance of food for a people free from fear and want.

Importantly, the citizens of God's mountain are identified not by race or ethnicity but by their faith in the one true God and King. Turning their back on their idols they declare, "All the peoples walk each in the name of its god, but we will walk in the name of the LORD our God forever and ever" (v. 5). "The peoples" in view are those who refuse to join the procession to the heavenly Mount Zion and to confess Israel's God as their own. These may expect the same fate as their idols and the earthly mountain, defiled by sin, which would be plowed like a field in God's judgment. "The peoples," however, are set in contrast to "we" who "walk in the name of the LORD our God." "We" refers to all—present and future—who confess their unwavering loyalty to God as their Lord and King. It refers to those who stream (back) to Mount Zion as citizens and worshipers of Israel's God (vv. 1, 2). God will never lack a people for himself. As God rejects and destroys those who are his people in name only, we see that he will gather even from the nations a people for himself, a people who will walk in his ways and internalize his law.

The "because of you" that identifies the cause of Zion's ruin in Micah 3:12 is in a sense answered in Micah 4:6, 7, where the prophet declares, in effect, "because of God." The Lord says,

> In that day . . .
>   I will assemble the lame
> and gather those who have been driven away
>   and those whom I have afflicted;
> and the lame I will make the remnant,
>   and those who were cast off, a strong nation;
> and the LORD will reign over them in Mount Zion
>   from this time forth and forevermore. (vv. 6, 7)

This language of assembling the lame and gathering those driven away is, of course, describing the work of a shepherd and recalls the prophet's earlier description of Yahweh as Israel's good shepherd (2:12).[23] A faithful shepherd gathers the sheep who are lost and binds up the wounds of those who are injured. Such a Shepherd-King was lacking in Micah's day, and yet God declares that he will come as the great shepherd of the sheep with power and mercy to restore, heal, and gather that which Israel's faithless shepherds had wounded and scattered.

This is precisely what Jesus did in his earthly ministry. Jesus came for the weak and the wounded, the hopeless and the helpless, the scattered and the lost, time and again calling them to himself and forming them into a new community of worshipers and disciples. In John 9, for instance, Jesus restored sight to a man who had been blind since birth. When the religious leaders saw the man healed and heard the man's testimony of the power of Jesus, they mocked him, ridiculed him, and eventually cast him out of the synagogue. In this we're given a particular example of what were no doubt thousands who had been similarly abused, mistreated, and harmed by Israel's faithless leaders. But we're told that when Jesus "heard that they had cast him out," he "found the man" (John 9:35) and revealed himself to him as the Son of Man; that is, the One to whom God would give "dominion and glory and a kingdom that all peoples, nations, and languages should serve him" (Daniel 7:14). What the faithless leaders have scattered, God in Christ gathers to himself.

It is perhaps unsurprising that immediately after this event Jesus declares himself to be "the good shepherd," saying, "All who came before me are thieves and robbers, but the sheep did not listen to them. I am the door. If anyone enters by me, he will be saved and will go in and out and find pasture. The thief comes only to steal and kill and destroy. I came that they may have life and have it abundantly" (John 10:8–11). Jesus organizes around himself a new people comprised not of the strong and the wise but the poor and the humble. Jesus came to and for the outcasts, both societal and religious, and brought them in, gathering them to himself as his disciples and, eventually, worshipers. In Christ, God made a way for those who are far off and under the sentence of death so they could draw near and have life in abundance.

This glorious mountain was, in fact, difficult to see in Micah's day. It took faith in God's word of promise to look beyond the wicked and corrupt Mount Zion as it stood seemingly immovable and to behold that heavenly mountain and that heavenly city "whose designer and builder is God" (Hebrews 11:10). Like the Israelites who walked by faith in the wilderness, believing that one day they would reach Mount Zion in the promised land, Christians too are called to live with the eyes of faith fixed firmly on the heavenly Mount Zion. For citizens of this heavenly city, Mount Zion still stands on the horizon, casting its long shadow into our present as we gather to worship our King and as we live in obedience and loyalty to our covenant God. This mountain is our true home, as the author of the letter to the Hebrews reminds us:

> But you have come to Mount Zion and to the city of the living God, the heavenly Jerusalem, and to innumerable angels in festal gathering, and to the assembly of the firstborn who are enrolled in heaven, and to God, the judge of all, and to the spirits of the righteous made perfect, and to Jesus, the mediator of a new covenant, and to the sprinkled blood that speaks a better word than the blood of Abel. (12:22–24)

# 40

# Road to Glory

MICAH 4:8—5:15

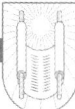

MY FIRST NIGHT AT COLLEGE I observed with some surprise and concern my new roommate setting an old-fashioned alarm clock. It was one of those analog clocks with two large steel bells on the top. He placed it next to his pillow and said to me, "I'm a heavy sleeper. If the clock doesn't work, use that," and he pointed to a small bucket of water sitting on his desk. Thankfully I never had to use the bucket. The alarm clock proved more than enough to wake my roommate, his roommate, and half of our freshman hall. Micah 4:8 and what follows hit us much like that blaring alarm, if not that bucket of water.

Just prior to these verses, we were given a portrait and a promise of a glorious day in which God would establish Mount Zion as the place of his righteous rule and his true worship. The prophet announced a future day in which the nations would flow to Jerusalem with joy and with love for God, seeking to worship Israel's God and to walk in his ways (4:1, 2). It would be a day in which the weak are strengthened and the wounded are healed (vv. 6, 7). It would be a day in which wars are a distant memory, so distant that instruments of war serve no conceivable function and are therefore beaten into instruments for farming (v. 3). Instruments of death will be transformed into instruments of life, and God's kingdom will be established forever and ever (v. 5).

This future glory is summarized in Micah 4:8, which functions as a hinge verse in which the prophet declares, "You, O tower of the flock, hill of the daughter of Zion, to you shall it come, the former dominion shall come, kingship for the daughter of Jerusalem."[1] "Tower of the flock" likely refers to Jerusalem, and thus the prophet here announces that the kingship will one day return to the capital city.[2] Kingship is coming again. Dominion is coming again. It will be like the dominion of old, a former dominion, which many scholars see as a reference to David or perhaps Solomon's kingship—dominions that had never been replicated for their glory at any point in Israel's subsequent history.[3] But the prophet announces that a day is coming in which Jerusalem's glory will yet again resemble that of her most glorious days of old.

Of course, there's an undesirable implication to this announcement. The implication of a kingship that is coming and a dominion that will return is that, at present, Israel's kingship was absent and her dominion nonexistent. This does not mean that Jerusalem had no king at the time but rather that the king who sat on the throne was deficient as a leader and shepherd of God's people.[4]

In what follows, we are, in effect, cast from Heaven to earth. Our attention shifts from the glorious future to the painful present, from our heavenly destination to the difficult road by which we get there. This present orientation is hammered home by the prophet's repeated use of the word "now." In contrast to the future glory so wonderfully set on display in Micah 4:1–7, in verse 9 we read, "Now . . ."; in verse 11, "Now . . ."; and in 5:1, "Now . . ." With these emphatic "nows," the prophet orients his audience to the painful, heartbreaking realities of their present existence and the difficult character of the road they will have to trod on their way to the glorious future God has promised. In this we too are offered the critical reminder that the way to glory is hard and fraught with, as the hymn puts it, "many dangers, toils, and snares."[5] And yet we're also reminded that this difficult and dangerous road is in fact the only way to true life and to joy unending. The path outlined by the prophet, though difficult, leads to an eternal life under the protection of a good shepherd who will one day very soon conquer all his and our foes.

### National Death (4:9, 10)

Each of Micah's oracles, in its own way, vividly depicts an imminent crisis, and each in its own way announces God's future deliverance. In his first oracle the prophet opens with a rhetorical question, probably uttered with a hint of sarcasm: "Now why do you cry aloud? Is there no king in you? Has your counselor perished, that pain seized you like a woman in labor?" (4:9). He is asking, Do you not have kings, O Judah? Do you not have counselors, O Jerusalem? Why the tears and cries of pain?

While some have taken "king" and "counselor" here to refer to God, Israel's true King and Counselor, the better reading in context is as a reference to Israel's failed leadership.[6] "Is there no king in you?" Well, yes and no! The implication is that Israel's leaders had failed at everything they were called to do, and the only thing they succeeded in was lining their own pockets through wickedness and injustice. The consequence of Israel's failed leadership was that the city was in agony, an agony that the prophet likens to the agony of childbirth. Israel had forsaken her true King and run to other kings, princes, and countries in hopes of finding the security that only Yahweh could provide. For Israel in the days of Micah, "Where is your king, O Israel?" is a searching question that exposed the false idols and misplaced hopes of the nation, and it may rightly serve us in just the same way today.

The result, however, of being effectively kingless and counselorless was that Jerusalem was exposed and vulnerable. Micah captures this by casting the city as a young woman in labor. She is called "daughter of Zion" and is commanded to "writhe and groan . . . like a woman in labor" (v. 10). The anguish of labor, which is commonly described as unparalleled and inexpressible, serves the prophet as the best analogy for the magnitude of the anguish that Israel will experience when they are taken into exile. Exile will be for Israel an agony that is unparalleled and inexpressible. Micah says, "Now you shall go out from the city, and dwell in the open country, you shall go to Babylon." This is the fate of the holy city and the people of God. They will be forcibly removed far from their home, that place of familiarity and comfort and security, and they will dwell in an open country, a place unprotected by walls and fortresses in which daily life is marked by vulnerability and insecurity.

Israel will live as aliens, strangers in a strange and unfamiliar land, a land that is characterized by enmity toward Israel and toward Israel's God. This is the significance of the reference to Babylon in verse 10. Babylon was a people and a place whose name evoked opposition to God and to his people.[7] But surprisingly we see that, unlike so many nations for whom exile meant complete annihilation, exile for Israel would be the occasion for them to experience healing. The place of death would become the place of new life as the prophet declares, "There [in Babylon] you shall be rescued; there the LORD will redeem you from the hand of your enemies" (v. 10b). It is only in exile, and only through exile, that Israel will come to know and experience God's redeeming grace.[8]

In this we see that Micah's metaphor, which likens Israel's trauma to that of a woman in labor, is a pregnant metaphor (pun intended) because the agony of labor is followed by the ecstasy of a mother holding a newborn baby in her arms. This is why some mothers, upon giving birth and holding that child in their arms, utter what sounds to their husbands like lunacy: "Let's do this again!" The inexpressible pain gives way to an even more inexpressible joy.

Though Israel will be handed over to her enemies because of her sin, she will be redeemed because of God's grace, power, and promise.

Exile was nothing short of a national death, and death is always a terrible and terrifying reality. But death does not receive the last word for God's people. Death and sorrow will give way to life and joy. Israel's redemption will come, and can only come, in the context of exile. This is why the prophet is so emphatic, declaring twice in verse 10 that it is "there" in Babylon that Israel "shall be rescued" and "there the Lord will redeem you." It will be "there," in Babylon—a city whose reputation for cosmic rebellion goes all the way back to the tower of Babel (Genesis 11:9)—that God will reveal his power and grace in unimaginable and certainly unexpected ways.

Israel must die in order to live. The cross must come before glory. So it is with the Christian as well, as Jesus told his disciples: "Unless a grain of wheat falls into the earth and dies, it remains alone; but if it dies, it bears much fruit. Whoever loves his life loses it, and whoever hates his life in this world will keep it for eternal life" (John 12:24, 25). In Babylon, Israel's death will give way to new life, and through Israel's great suffering will come Israel's even greater glory.

### Divine Provision (4:11–13)

In Micah 4:11 we're taken back to Jerusalem, and we hear the same song in a different key. The prophet declares, "Now many nations are assembled against you, saying, 'Let her be defiled, and let our eyes gaze upon Zion.'" Again God's people are threatened as the nations gather against Jerusalem with the intent of committing unspeakable atrocities, the result of which will be the defilement of Jerusalem, the daughter of Zion. The language here suggests the violence and degradation of rape, perhaps in this case the defiling of a pregnant woman. Jerusalem again appears helpless and hopeless. The nations are certain of victory, but the prophet declares a surprising reversal: "They do not know the thoughts of the Lord; they do not understand his plan, that he has gathered them as sheaves to the threshing floor" (v. 12).

God's plans are higher, deeper, and wider than man's, and they are certainly more profound and surprising than Israel (or we) could have ever dared to imagine. As God said through Micah's contemporary Isaiah,

> For my thoughts are not your thoughts,
>    neither are your ways my ways, declares the Lord.
> For as the heavens are higher than the earth,
>    so are my ways higher than your ways
>    and my thoughts than your thoughts. (Isaiah 55:8, 9)

The nations' thought is to thresh Jerusalem; God's thought is to thresh the nations who have arisen against him and set themselves against his people.

In contrast to the previous oracle that focused on the *location* of Israel's deliverance (Babylon), this oracle focuses on the *source* of Israel's deliverance—the Lord who strengthens his people. Jerusalem is in a hopeless situation. And yet into her hopeless situation comes the all-powerful word of God. In response to the violent, degrading, humiliating intentions of the wicked nations, God says

> Arise and thresh,
>   O daughter of Zion,
> for I will make your horn iron,
>   and I will make your hoofs bronze;
> you shall beat in pieces many peoples;
>   and shall devote their gain to the LORD,
>   their wealth to the LORD of the whole earth. (Micah 4:13)

Jerusalem is transformed from a vulnerable, exposed, helpless woman in the throes of labor to an unstoppable ox that "pulls a threshing sled and itself takes part in the trampling."[9]

This victory is from God. It comes from God's word that empowers as he summons his hopeless and helpless people to "arise and thresh" and as he transforms them for his marvelous purposes: "for I will make your horn iron, and I will make your hoofs bronze." As Israel is victorious over her enemies, she recognizes the source of her salvation and devotes the wealth of the conquered nations to the Lord. Israel freely and fully acknowledges that her victory comes not from her own strength but from her God. Israel's deliverance is, from start to finish, the work of her strong God who fights with and for his people.

God provides for his people. Even when the entire world seems set against them, Israel in Micah's day and Christians in our day have reason to hope, not in themselves but in their God who is sovereign. When faced with great trials, we can say with the psalmist,

> God is our refuge and strength,
>   a very present help in trouble.
> Therefore we will not fear though the earth gives way,
>   though the mountains be moved into the heart of the sea,
> though its waters roar and foam,
>   though the mountains tremble at its swelling. (Psalm 46:1–3)

The greatest powers of evil in this world, even death itself, cannot triumph over those who belong to God in Christ. When God says, "Arise" (Micah

4:13), nations are restored and even the dead themselves exit their graves. John Calvin was certainly correct to hear in God's command to besieged Jerusalem a dim echo of the words Christ will use to call his elect from their tombs, "Arise . . . O daughter of Zion."[10] In this divine word is a power not only for the last day but for every day in which we are laid low by the "slings and arrows" of this life such that "no strength, no vigour, remains in us."[11] As Calvin put it, Christians may arise daily "by the power of God, who by his voice alone can restore us to life, which seemed to be wholly extinct."[12]

## Faithful King (5:1–6)

In Micah 5 we see the same pattern recapitulated one last time. The opening verse is infamous for its difficulty, some taking the unusual Hebrew here as a call for Jerusalem to assemble for war ("Now muster your troops, O daughter of troops," ESV) or a summons to mourning ("Now you gash yourself in grief," JPS).[13] What is clear, however, is that the holy city is under siege again as the prophet declares, "Siege is laid against us; with a rod they strike the judge of Israel on the cheek" (5:1). Clearly this time something is different. The focus has shifted from the humiliation and degradation of the nation (4:9–13) to the humiliation and degradation of Israel's king. The judge of Israel—that is, her king—will be struck on the cheek with a rod, a painful and public symbol of his defeat and disgrace (cf. Job 16:10; Psalm 3:7; Isaiah 50:6).

But as before, God will deliver his people from their distress, and also as before, he will do so in the most unlikely and unexpected of ways so as to underscore for all who have eyes to see that salvation is from the Lord.

Bethlehem Ephrathah was a town so small and insignificant that it was not listed among the clans of Judah. Yet, speaking in the first person, God says, "From you shall come forth for me one who is to be ruler in Israel, whose coming forth is from of old, from ancient days" (Micah 5:2). This is surprising because Bethlehem was hardly a town that people would have expected to bring forth the ruler of Israel, much less the Ruler of the world. She was small, unremarkable, and by comparison to many of her neighboring towns, poor.

Yet Micah's announcement is at the same time unsurprising. It is unsurprising that Israel's deliverer would hail from Bethlehem precisely because Bethlehem's humility, in the words of one commentator, "befits the modesty Yhwh desires of His leaders."[14] Israel's greatest king, David, hailed from this small and insignificant town. Ever since it has been associated with royalty, if not the Davidic promise itself. The movement of the text from corrupt and conquered Jerusalem (v. 1) to the little town of Bethlehem (v. 2) suggests that "God is taking up his Messianic work from the beginning," breaking with the corruption of Jerusalem associated with the current Davidic line and starting again.[15] Bethlehem would once again bring forth Israel's Messiah, great David's greater Son. The focus on Bethlehem reminded Israel of the Davidic covenant, that though God would discipline David's royal descendants, he would never lack a descendant to sit on his throne (2 Samuel 7:12, 13). Though this future messianic king would come in the line of David, his origin was older than David and might in fact lie in eternity itself, a notion suggested by the enigmatic expression "whose coming forth is from of old, from ancient of days" (Micah 5:2).[16]

Though his origin is in eternity, the Messiah's rule will be established in history. His kingdom will be a kingdom in time and space. So the prophet offers an outline of history. It is a rough sketch to be sure, but it is sufficient for his purposes. Micah says, "Therefore he shall give them up until the time when she who is in labor has given birth" (v. 3). Just as parents can divide family history into life before kids and life after kids, Israel's history is divided into before the Messiah and after the Messiah—*before* one has "come forth" from Bethlehem and *after*. *Before* is a time in which God has given up his people to the trials and travails of exile, but *after* will be a new day that dawns with the advent of a new king who will "shepherd his people," not in his own strength and not for his own glory, but rather "in the strength of the LORD, in the majesty of the name of the LORD his God" (v. 4). At that time there will be a national reunion in which the ideal of Israel as one people and one nation is realized in a manner unprecedented in Israel's history: "then the rest of his brothers shall return to the people of Israel" (v. 3). A nation divided in Micah's day and a nation that will soon be scattered to the far corners of the earth will be gathered and united as one people under one King who will rule as God's faithful shepherd forever.

This future King and his future kingdom could not be more dissimilar to Israel's painful present reality. Their future shepherd can usefully be compared to Judah's King Ahaz, who shepherded God's people not in the strength of the Lord but in the strength of Assyria. When given the opportunity to place his faith in God and rely on his word declared by his prophet, Ahaz decided instead to trust in the strength of man, relying on the might of the ruthless and idolatrous nation of Assyria (Isaiah 7). This would prove to be a costly decision for the people he was appointed to shepherd, as Judah would from then on be subjected to the cruel and exploitive dominion of the brutal Assyrian Empire.

Sadly, the spirit of Ahaz persisted in Judah as, with few exceptions, her kings and rulers exemplified the same faithless self-reliance and the oppressive, exploitive rule over God's covenant people. When King Herod received news of the birth of the One who was King of the Jews, he inquired of his scribes where this child was to be born, to which they responded with the words of this prophecy from Micah: "You O Bethlehem, in the land of Judah, are by no means least among the rulers of Judah; for from you shall come a ruler who will shepherd my people Israel" (Matthew 2:6). But instead of bowing the knee to this infant king, Herod, like Pharaoh in the days of Moses, raged at the prospect of a rival king and a rival kingdom and ordered the murder of all the male children of Bethlehem two years old and younger (v. 16).

These kings and these kingdoms could not be more different.

In contrast to Ahaz's kingship and Ahaz's kingdom, and in contrast to Herod's kingship and Herod's kingdom stands the kingdom of the messianic Shepherd-King. His, Micah tells us, will be a universal dominion characterized by a universal peace: "They shall dwell secure, for now he shall be great to the ends of the earth" (5:4). Commentators are divided on the exact meaning of the next phrase, which reads literally, "This will be peace," or perhaps, "He will be the one of peace" (v. 5).[17] But whether it refers to the person ("This [one] will be peace") or the new government that he will establish, we nevertheless hear echoes of the prophet Isaiah, who declared,

> For to us a child is born,
>   to us a son is given;
> and the government shall be upon his shoulder,
>   and his name shall be called
> Wonderful Counselor, Mighty God,
>   Everlasting Father, Prince of Peace." (9:6)[18]

The reign of this shepherd will be a reign of unparalleled peace, for he will indeed be the Prince of Peace.

Consequently any threat or incursion by the enemy will be met by a more-than-sufficient resistance. Micah says, "When the Assyrian comes into our land and treads in our palaces, then we will raise against him seven shepherds and eight princes of men" (5:5).

The identity of these seven shepherds *plus one* has been the subject of much speculation, and there has not been anything close to a consensus. The most compelling suggestion has been proposed by Old Testament scholar Bruce Waltke, who notes that seven is the sacred number of completeness, and the plus one indicates that the resistance to any Assyrian threat would be more than complete.[19] These shepherds who would stand as God's answer to the faithless shepherds are, in a sense, whole or complete, with nothing lacking. And they have at their head one more, the eighth shepherd—perhaps the Messiah whom they would follow and with whom they would act in concert, defending God's flock.

The significance of the designation of these leaders as "shepherds" should not be lost on us as readers of Micah's prophecies. These future faithful shepherds stand in stark contrast to Israel's leaders in Micah's day, leaders who thus far have been exposed for their corruption and cruelty, and condemned by Yahweh's covenant prosecutor.

But notice that God's people are not only on the defensive.[20] These shepherds not only will shepherd Israel within their lands but will exercise authority over Assyria as well. The prophet declares that

> they shall shepherd the land of Assyria with the sword,
> and the land of Nimrod at its entrances;
> and he shall deliver us from the Assyrian
> when he comes into our land
> and treads within our border" (Micah 5:6)

This future day will be a day in which Israel is no longer ruled by Assyria, but Assyria is ruled by Israel. The messianic kingdom is no longer restricted to the land of Canaan and the people of Israel but extends to and indeed conquers the greatest empire in the known world.[21]

Great crisis gives way to even greater deliverance. Suffering, trials, and hardships are transformed by the power and sovereignty of God into victory and blessings. We may wonder why the prophet felt the need to rehearse this story three times in three ways and from three perspectives; those taken into exile are redeemed from the hands of their enemies (Micah 4:10); Jerusalem, besieged and hopeless, is delivered and is triumphant over their enemies (4:13); Israel's king is humiliated and yet his rule is established forever (5:2). Yet if we consider how we often respond to trial, difficulty, hardship, and suffering, we will soon discover the answer. The prophet's redundancy presses home God's plans and purposes for a people who are prone to fear and to doubt. Like Israel, we too need to be reminded often that God is sovereign over every trial we face, whether great or small. Suffering, even suffering for our sin, is not an accident, nor is it outside the control of a sovereign God. For those who do not know God and do not trust in his Messiah, loss, weakness, humiliation, and defeat in this life presage a divine forsakenness that will last for eternity. However, Christians also are tempted to internalize this message of divine displeasure and to interpret our crosses as indications that God has abandoned us to the fate our sins deserve.

In Jesus's day it was unthinkable that the crucifixion meant anything other than failure and defeat. Hopes were dashed and expectations of a national deliverance were revealed to be vain. At the cross when Jesus died it appeared that he had failed in everything he came to do. It seemed to his disciples that everything he had preached and promised was a fiction and that the miracles he had performed were ultimately meaningless. And yet the reality is that what appeared to be Jesus's greatest failure was in fact Jesus's greatest victory. Jesus's apparent defeat was his triumph. Paul tells us that at the cross, Jesus "disarmed the rulers and authorities and put them to open shame, by triumphing over them" (Colossians 2:15).

In Micah's three vignettes we witness Israel's trials—even those that came on account of their own sin and failure—being used of God to accomplish his greater, deeper, more profound purpose of saving helpless sinners for himself. Indeed Christ's kingship would not be established through strength but through weakness. So it is with Christ's Church. The Church in this present evil age is a Church militant. She is beset constantly by trials from without and temptations from within. She fails and falls often. And yet the Church of Christ is the flock of Christ, the people for whom he laid down his life and declared, "I should lose nothing of all he has given me, but raise it up on the last day" (John 6:39). While it is painfully obvious that the Church's pilgrimage is marked by great tribulation and unimaginable suffering, the Church nevertheless rests in the One who promised that "in the world you will have tribulation. But take heart; I have overcome the world" (16:33).

### New Conquest (5:7–9)

The stark contrast between a glorious future and a painful present applies not only to Israel but also to the nations. The nations that will one day stream to Mount Zion to walk in the ways of the Lord and to enjoy the benefits of his kingship and kingdom in Micah 4:1–7 are depicted in 4:8—5:6 as surrounding Jerusalem intent on brutalizing, humiliating, and destroying God's holy city. What distinguishes these two groups, the nations that stream into Jerusalem and the nations that destroy Jerusalem?

The answer comes in what follows: "Then the remnant of Jacob shall be in the midst of many peoples" (5:7). Not only are Israel's shepherds ruling throughout the nations (vv. 5, 6), represented by Assyria, but God's people are likewise scattered throughout the nations. This immediately raises a question: How will the remnant of Jacob be received by these nations? Typically in the Bible, being scattered among the nations is a sign of God's judgment on his people; yet here we see that the remnant of Jacob is not the object of God's judgment but the instrument of both his judgment and his mercy. How the nations and peoples respond to this remnant of Jacob will in fact determine their experience of divine blessing or divine cursing. It will determine whether these will be nations streaming into Jerusalem under the banner of salvation or nations threshed and pulverized under divine judgment.

Micah, always the poet, makes this point powerfully with the use of two similes. First, he compares the remnant of Jacob to "dew from the Lord, like showers on the grass, which delay not for a man nor wait for the children of man" (v. 7). With this simile, the remnant of Jacob is depicted as the source of life and blessing to the nations among whom they reside. What is largely ignored by us in industrialized societies was critical for life in an ancient Near Eastern context. Dew, for Israel, sustained life in the dry seasons. Rains produced the harvests and fruit that served as the basis for life and health and well-being in the rainy season (cf. Deuteronomy 11:14; Jeremiah 5:24). When the rains and the dew showered the earth, Israel experienced life, and, on her better days, she understood that these gifts of the dew and rain came from God, who is the Lord over all things. So the psalmist declares,

> Sing to the Lord with thanksgiving;
>   make melody to our God on the lyre!
> He covers the heavens with clouds;
>   he prepares rain for the earth;
>   he makes grass grow on the hills." (Psalm 147:7, 8)

However, in Micah 5:8 the prophet employs another contrasting simile:

> And the remnant of Jacob shall be among the nations,
>   in the midst of many peoples,
> like a lion among the beasts of the forest,
>   like a young lion among the flocks of sheep,
> which, when it goes through, treads down
>   and tears in pieces, and there is none to deliver."

The image could not be more different. Where the remnant of Jacob is the source of life and blessing among the nations in verse 7, in verse 8 the remnant of Jacob is the source of violence, death, and destruction. The remnant is likened to gentle showers on the grass and to a lion among the beasts of the forest. So which is it?

It is important to see that Micah is describing the same group ("the remnant of Jacob"), which has two drastically different effects on the nations among whom they live. For some, they are life-giving showers. For others, they are devouring and destroying lions. Which is it? The answer is, it depends upon the nations' response to this remnant of Jacob. More to the point, it depends upon the nations' response to the God of Jacob. The nations' experience of the remnant of Jacob will depend on the nations' posture toward Israel and her God. Will they bless Israel and honor her God, or will they oppress Israel and curse her God, as so many have done throughout her history?

Centuries earlier, God had made a promise to Abraham: "I will bless those who bless you, and him who dishonors you I will curse" (Genesis 12:3). Israel among the nations would be an instrument of God's blessing or cursing based on how the nations responded to her witness.[22] Waltke captures the prophet's meaning well when he writes, "The remnant of Jacob will be at the same time a source of benediction and a fomenter of misfortune; a channel of salvation and a cause of punishment; an instrument of hope and of tragedy. *In either case, though only a remnant, it is always triumphant with regard to the nations.*"[23]

This is where we see Israel's conquest. Israel will triumph over the nations by drawing them to their God and King and thus blessing them like showers upon the grass. But to those who take a stand against Israel and against her God, Israel will be a ferocious lion who, as in the days of Joshua's conquest, executes God's wrath and judgment. "Your hand shall be lifted up over your adversaries, and all your enemies shall be cut off" (Micah 5:9). God's people—harassed, oppressed, persecuted—will one day be victorious over all that threatens them. In this way God's people resemble their Savior, who would produce the very same paradoxical effects on the world, being at one and the same time both "a stone of stumbling" and a chief "cornerstone", "a rock of offense" and "an everlasting rock" (1 Peter 2:7, 8; Isaiah 26:4).[24] The Apostle Paul picks up on this connection between Christ and his Church in his second letter to the Corinthians: "Thanks be to God, who in Christ always leads us in triumphal procession, and through us spreads the fragrance of the knowledge of him everywhere. For we are the aroma of Christ to God among those who are being saved and among those who are perishing, to one a fragrance from death to death, to the other a fragrance from life to life" (2:14–16).

## Final Judgment, Final Deliverance (5:10–15)

The spotlight now shifts from the fate of nations surrounding Israel to the fate of Israel herself. God says to Israel, "In that day . . . I will cut off your horses from among you and will destroy your chariots; and I will cut off the cities of your land and throw down all your strongholds" (Micah 5:10, 11). The divine warrior will not only fight for his people—he will fight against his people as well. With this, Israel is reminded that they are not exempt from God's wrath and judgment against their own sin. They are not exempt from God's curses being rained down upon them like fire from Heaven for their own rebellion. They are not exempt from the call to holiness and righteousness. When God comes in judgment on the nations, this judgment includes Israel. And when God comes, what will he find?

The mention of horses and chariots (v. 10) and cities and strongholds (v. 11) does not simply refer to Israel's instruments of war and defensive fortifications, but in this context refers to those objects in which Israel was time and again tempted to place their trust. The psalmist wrote, "Some trust in chariots and some in horses, but we trust in the name of the LORD our God" (Psalm 20:7). However, throughout her history and certainly in Micah's day Israel time and again trusted in her chariots and horses, in military strategy and *realpolitik*, in place of the Lord, her covenant God. Like Ahaz who rejected the Lord's help and sign of assurance (Isaiah 7), preferring instead the help of the Assyrian military juggernaut, Israel preferred human strength and worldly wisdom to the word of God. These are the idols of strength and military might and human wisdom that tempted Israel, just as they tempt us, to place their trust in that which is no god and which cannot save.

That these are Israel's functional idols becomes clear as God proceeds to declare his judgment on Israel's illicit religious practices, specifically sorcery and fortune telling, carved images and pillars (features of pagan worship), and Asherah and cities (here possibly referring to cities that venerate the Asherah as a cultic object).[25] In the center of it all, God says, "You shall bow down no more to the work of your hands" (Micah 5:13b). Though far from exhaustive, this list is representative of the numerous ways Israel defiled themselves by worshiping the creature rather than the Creator. In all of these practices, we see variegated manifestations of the self-worship that stands at the heart of all human sin. And yet over and over God says, "I will cut off . . ." (vv. 10–13), an expression indicating complete and utter destruction. God will destroy every false hope and deceptive security along with those people who have entrusted their very lives and futures to these false gods.

As difficult as this climactic word of judgment would have been for Israel to hear, the concluding line would no doubt have been shocking as God includes his covenant people (about whom he has been speaking since verse 10) among the *gôyîm*, that is, the nations: "In anger and wrath I will execute vengeance *on the nations* that did not obey" (v. 15).[26] Israel is not exempt from God's judgment. God's judgment is universal; it includes Jews and Gentiles alike. Israel would be judged for her idolatry, just like the nations around her.

Though it is impossible to be certain, it seems likely that the prophet here delivers one more broadside against Israel's endemic Zion theology. It is not her genealogical descent that will save her, any more than her law or her temple. God alone is the source of Israel's hope and salvation.

This, of course, comes as a sober warning and a very real threat to all who persist in idolatry. "The wages of sin is death" (Romans 6:23). But the prophet's warning to Israel also entails a word of promise. For those who live by faith, the eschatological judgment announced in Micah's oracle is an announcement of the final destruction of all sin and temptation that besets God's people. The result of God's judgment will be a land and a people purified from idolatry and the innumerable sins that flow from it. When Israel failed to drive out the Canaanite nations from the promised land, the angel of the Lord came to Israel and said,

> I brought you up from Egypt and brought you into the land that I swore to give to your fathers. I said, "I will never break my covenant with you, and you shall make no covenant with the inhabitants of this land; you shall break down their altars." But you have not obeyed my voice. What is this you have done? So now I say, I will not drive them out before you, but they shall become thorns in your sides, and their gods shall be a snare to you. (Judges 2:1b–3)

Thus Israel had lived for centuries with thorns in their sides and snares in the form of false gods on high places throughout their country, beckoning for their devotion.

For the faithful in every age, life in a sin-cursed world is exhausting and constantly discouraging. But the good news of the Christian gospel is that this sin-cursed world will one day give way to a new creation. The prophet Micah's depiction of a land decimated by divine judgment reminds us that for those who are not united to Christ by faith, those who have not found refuge under the banner of God's Messiah who will shepherd God's people, the day of God's visitation will be a day of utter destruction. It will be a day in which every false source of hope and confidence and strength will be revealed to be illusions, unable to deliver from the One who declares, "In anger and wrath I will execute vengeance on the nations that did not obey" (Micah 5:15).

But for those who have heard the voice of Jesus, that great shepherd of the sheep, and have followed him in faith, the day of God's visitation will be a day in which sin and sorrow, temptation and struggle will be no more. Because the Son of God bore the sins of his people, Christians can long for this day of judgment in the sure knowledge that for them it will be a day of deliverance.

It will be a day in which God himself will wipe away every tear from our eyes (Revelation 21:4) and will restore to us all that has been lost and broken in this life. It will be a day in which the daily fight against sin and temptation will come to an end, and the reign of the Prince of Peace will dawn in fullness and finality. For this reason, believers have echoed John's closing prayer when they cry out, "Come, Lord Jesus!" (22:20).

# 41

# And to Walk Humbly with Thy God

MICAH 6:1-8

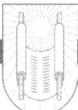

ON FEBRUARY 15, 1546, three days before his death, Martin Luther preached what would turn out to be his last sermon. He was not in Wittenberg at the time but was passing through Eisleben, the city of his birth, to mediate a dispute between dukes. He chose as his text Matthew 11:25–30 and focused especially on Jesus's words, "I thank you, Father, Lord of heaven and earth, that you have hidden these things from the wise and understanding and revealed them to little children" (v. 25). Typical of Luther, he contrasted a theology of glory—in this case, those who make great claims to wisdom (the pope, the emperor, kings, and lords) but are in reality those to whom the things of God are hidden—with a theology of the cross—those who are poor, meek, lowly, and faithful. It is to such as these that God chooses to reveal his Son and to give his kingdom.

But toward the end of his sermon, Luther began to rebuke the people of his home city for forgetting the gospel they had at one time so eagerly embraced. The people of Eisleben, like so many others who had once received the freedom that comes from the Reformation's recovery of the doctrines of grace, were once again making pilgrimages to relics and devoting themselves to the very superstitions that the Reformation rejected. They had, in some respects, forgotten the gospel. They had forgotten the means of grace, the recovery of which stood at the heart of the Protestant Reformation. These had begun to ring hollow in their ears and to have little effect on their hearts. So Luther did exactly what we would expect him to do, even in his frailty. He confronted the

Church's lukewarm affections and their wandering allegiances with the truth of God:

> Oh, people say, what is that? After all, there is preaching every day, often many times every day, so that we soon grow weary of it. What do we get out of it? All right, go ahead, dear brother, if you don't want God to speak to you every day at home in your house and in your parish church, then be wise and look for something else: in Trier is our Lord God's coat, in Aachen are Joseph's pants and our blessed Lady's undergarment; go there and squander your money, buy indulgence and the pope's secondhand junk; these are valuable things! You have to go far for these things and spend a lot of money; leave house and home standing idle![1]

Bored by the Word of God preached, tired of the Bible being read in their homes, they yearned for something more exciting. In Trier is Jesus's coat; in Aachen we can see Joseph's pants.

Many years earlier, another reformer, a prophet by the name of Micah, adopted a very similar posture and preached a very similar message to a very similar people. The prophet announced that Israel had forgotten God's love and rejected God's grace. Though they had time and again witnessed and experienced God's deliverance, they time and again had fallen away from trusting God and fallen away from the righteousness and justice that set them apart as a holy people and that stood at the very heart of God's covenant with them.

In Micah 6:1–8, we witness what is in a very real way a courtroom scene. Throughout these opening verses, there is an abundant use of legal terminology. The Hebrew words translated as "plead your case" (one word in Hebrew), "indictment," and "contend" are all words that are at home in the court of law.[2] These terms don't refer to a complaint based on an annoyance or a breach of convention or etiquette. These are words that refer to a breach of law, a violation of a covenant, constitution, or binding legal agreement. So the Lord is in a very real way bringing a lawsuit against his people, and through his prophet he is summoning them to appear in a court of law.[3]

On one common division, Micah 6:1 begins the third and final section of the prophet's book.[4] Verse 1 opens with an imperative: "Hear." It's an imperative we've heard before. The same word is used to open the book: "*Hear*, you peoples, all of you; pay attention, O earth, and all that is in it" (1:2). Similarly, in chapter 3 we read, "*Hear*, you heads of Jacob, and rulers of the house of Israel!" (v. 1). But whereas in chapter 1 the surrounding nations are summoned to hear, and in chapter 3 the leaders of Israel are summoned to hear, in chapter 6 it is all of Israel, as a nation, who are commanded to gather and to hear the Lord's complaint against his people.[5]

We hear God through his prophet essentially summoning his people to court, and we see God prosecuting them. For what? For their unresponsiveness to his word and their indifference to his love, a love expressed in more ways than they could ever count. They too have forgotten, and God's prophet calls them out and calls them back. Yet even in the Lord's prosecution of his people we hear an offer of forgiveness as God, through his prophet, shows his people the way back to full communion and unbroken fellowship with their gracious God.

## Divine Subpoena (6:1, 2)

The Lord speaks first to Israel commanding that they "hear" or attend to what he is about to say. The Lord then turns to his prophet/prosecutor Micah and declares, "Arise, plead your case before the mountains, and let the hills hear your voice" (6:1).[6] There are not two separate cases here, the prophet's case and the Lord's case. Rather, the prophet's case is the Lord's case. The Lord's case becomes the prophet's case, a reminder of the prophet's role as the mouthpiece of God. This prophet is told to plead the Lord's case, and to do so before the mountains and the hills. The mountains and hills are probably not the first things that come to mind when we think of the ideal jury or an ideal witness.[7] But this is essentially the role the mountains and the hills and the foundations of the earth are called upon to play in Israel's courtroom drama. They are called on to hear the charges and by implication, bear witness to their veracity.

Students of the ancient Near East have long noted that when treaties or covenants were ratified in the ancient world, it was customary to invoke deities as witnesses to the agreement.[8] Similar to many modern-day marriage licenses that require witnesses, the gods of the sun and the moon and the river might be listed at the bottom of a covenant document as witnesses to the agreement. These deities could be called upon to attest to the terms of the agreement or to enact the sanctions should the terms of the covenant be violated. But these scholars have also pointed out that when God established his covenant with Israel, he did not list deities to witness the agreement. The reason for this is obvious: there is only one God. To whom would God appeal? However, in the place of (false) gods, God appealed to the enduring elements of the created universe to serve as witnesses to the covenant.[9] So after Moses spoke the Law to Israel, and after he set out the blessings for obedience and the curses for disobedience, he declared, "Give ear, O heavens, and I will speak, and let the earth hear the words of my mouth" (Deuteronomy 32:1). Thus, throughout the prophetic literature, the created order is often called upon to bear witness, as, for example, in the oracle that opens the great prophecy of Isaiah: "Hear, O heavens, and give ear, O earth, for the LORD has spoken" (Isaiah 1:2).[10]

We have the expression "If walls could speak . . . ," the implication of which is that if what was done in secret were made known, then the truth that we all suspected but couldn't prove would be brought to light. In the mountains and the hills and the foundations of the earth we have witnesses whose age and endurance qualify them to speak and to render an accurate and impartial account of the facts, facts that would yield a clear verdict: *Guilty*.[11] They were there when Yahweh entered into covenant with Israel. They were there when Israel heard the terms of the covenant and swore in response, "All the words that the LORD has spoken we will do" (Exodus 24:3).

Now to be sure, God does not need a courtroom drama to adjudicate his case against Israel or his case against us. God does not need a jury or a judge to render a verdict. God is truth itself. He is the very definition or standard of truth. He can no more speak falsehood, twist the truth, or render an unjust verdict than he can stop being God. "So why," we might ask, "all the drama?" In this courtroom drama we witness God's condescension. God stoops to the level of his people, a level that a finite and sinful people can understand, and he enters into a legal dispute with them so as to make his point abundantly clear. God stoops so that his faithfulness and Israel's unfaithfulness, his perfect righteousness and Israel's wickedness, are made evident to all and especially to them. Like an intervention when everyone around the addict sees the problem except the addict himself, God marshals witnesses and evidence to set his case plainly before his people. Ultimately, God's purpose is salvific. He confronts Israel with her sin so that she might turn and live. Old Testament scholar Bruce Waltke puts it well when he says that the Lord "initiates the trial not to condemn Israel but to save them; so also he confronts mortals with the gospel of Jesus Christ not to condemn them but to save them."[12]

Before we even get to the substance of the divine indictment, the mere fact that God takes his people to court carries a message in itself. Israel's sin and guilt are indisputable, clearly evident to any and all who would consider the evidence impartially. God doesn't need a witness. But God's people do need a witness. God's people needed a witness just like we need a witness—because we are prone to forget just how apparent our sin and our guilt really are. We are so adept at self-justification that we begin to believe our own lies. But here in Micah 6, God is saying, in effect, "If even by the standards of creation your guilt is perfectly evident, how much more so before the divine court." We may think that our sins are small and therefore insignificant, or that they are atoned for merely by the passage of time. But here Micah reminds us that God both sees and knows; he reminds us that there is nothing hidden from God. Our secret thoughts and the deepest motivations of our hearts are laid bare before the Lord, and his judgments are perfectly just.

We have suspected all along who it is who is being summoned to court, but it is worth mentioning that in the flow of the prophetic lawsuit, the defendant is not named until the end of Micah 6:2. The prophet creates a degree of suspense. As the people of Israel first hear of God's complaint and then hear the jury being summoned, they are perhaps wondering who the accused might be. Who is the guilty party? Maybe Edom? Perhaps Ammon? Maybe Assyria? Instead they hear, "The LORD has an indictment against *his people*, and he will contend with Israel" (6:2). Though they shouldn't have been, Micah's original hearers were no doubt surprised to find their name listed on the indictment.

Israel was not the only nation harboring wickedness in the highest levels of society. She certainly wasn't the most oppressive and violent of the nations of the Near East in her day. But here again we see that God's covenant people are not exempt from God's righteous judgment. It is not enough to have witnessed God's mighty acts of salvation or to have outwardly benefited from them. As the author of the letter to the Hebrews reminds us, those who experienced God's deliverance from Egypt nevertheless perished in the wilderness on account of their lack of faith (Hebrews 3:16—4:2). If the substance of God's saving acts—namely, Christ himself—was not received by faith, if that gospel message, preached by each act of divine deliverance, was not believed with the heart, then it was of no value. The same is true for us today. It does us no good to hear the prophetic word and think it is only for the nonbeliever "out there." We need to hear it as the Church, knowing that we, like Israel, are prone to waywardness and wickedness and unbelief and therefore must find refuge in the only place it may be found.

### Divine Prosecution (6:3–5)

Beginning in Micah 6:3, God sets forth his case against his people: "O my people, what have I done to you? How have I wearied you? Answer me!" This is a charge that many have pointed out sounds more like a defense than an accusation.[13] God is asking his people, "What have I done to deserve your rejection and scorn?" In no uncertain terms, God demands an answer, an explanation, an accounting for Israel's behavior. What precisely has the Lord done to Israel to weary them?

Perhaps the prophet paused after this line to give Israel a moment to reflect and respond. But pause or no pause (time to answer would not have helped in any substantive way), God suggests possible answers, answers that simultaneously serve as evidence for the prosecution. He says in verses 4, 5,

> For I brought you up from the land of Egypt
>   and redeemed you from the house of slavery,
> and I sent before you Moses,
>   Aaron, and Miriam.
> O my people, remember what Balak king of Moab devised,
>   and what Balaam the son of Beor answered him,
> and what happened from Shittim to Gilgal,
>   that you may know the righteous acts of the LORD.

This last phrase, "the righteous acts of the LORD," unifies these events. Each of them is an instance of a "righteous act of the LORD," focusing on God's deliverance of Israel from slavery in Egypt and his guiding them through the wilderness to the point of their entry into the promised land.

All of this served the fundamental purpose expressed plainly in the accusation: *"that you may know* the righteous acts of the LORD" (v. 5). Needless to say, the Lord's goal in this courtroom drama was not to cultivate historical memory but to transform lives in light of his past goodness to his people and his faithfulness to his covenant promises.[14] God's purpose in all of these "righteous acts" was Israel's knowledge of him as their Savior and Deliverer, the One who redeemed them from slavery and who provided them with everything needful for their life and godliness.

With mighty signs and wonders, God revealed himself to be stronger than the greatest nation in the known world, the nation of Egypt. And with these same signs and wonders, he revealed himself as superior to the gods of the Egyptians. The Pharoah who had sought to destroy Israel in an ethnic genocide (Exodus 1:8–22) was himself humiliated and destroyed at the Red Sea (Exodus 14). When Israel was enslaved and without hope, God set them free from their bondage and oppression. When Israel was under a sentence of death, God raised them to new life. So God asks, in effect, "Was it this deliverance, a deliverance that astonishes the mind for its greatness, that you find so wearisome?"

Next, God brings forward as evidence his provision of Moses, Aaron, and Miriam who would lead God's people in their journey through the wilderness (Micah 6:4). These would serve Israel as guides, teaching them the Law and speaking to them God's word and will. Perhaps it was these leaders without whom Israel would never have made it to the promised land that burdened the people of God?

Third, God recalls the events on the plains of Moab when Balak, the king of Moab, summoned Balaam to come and curse Israel (v. 5). The significance of this event may not be immediately apparent to us, but it would be perfectly plain to Micah's original audience. Israel's superior military might had subdued the surrounding nations, and Balak knew that his army was no match against Israel on the battlefield. So he, at great cost, summoned a diviner of international repute in order to curse Israel. A diviner with Balaam's prestige would have been regarded as essentially a weapon of mass destruction.

To be sure, Micah is a bit vague on the details of the event when he says, "O my people, remember what Balak king of Moab devised, and what Balaam the son of Beor answered him" (6:5). The reason the prophet can be so vague is because, as commentator Stephen Dempster puts it, "Micah does not need to provide the answers, as even any Israelite child would know that the curse was turned into a blessing in Balaam's mouth because of the intervention of Yahweh (Numbers 22—24; Deuteronomy 23:5, 6)."[15] It was a marvelous and unforgettable episode in Israel's history in which God turned a curse into Israel's blessing. In it, Israel saw that God's purpose to bless his people was so settled and unwavering that the greatest diviner in the known world was unable to change it. Balak's curses were transformed into Balaam's blessings because God had promised to bless Israel and the world through them (Genesis 12:3).

The final piece of evidence that God brings forward sounds at first like little more than an itinerary. He refers to ". . . what happened from Shittim to Gilgal" (Micah 6:5). Shittim was the last place Israel camped before they crossed the River Jordan into the promised land (Numbers 25:1). Gilgal was the first place Israel camped when they entered the promised land. However, when we understand the significance of these places in Israel's history, we discover that this is perhaps the most compelling and devastating evidence of all because it was at Shittim that many Israelite men yoked themselves sexually (if not in marriage) to Moabite women. As it always did, this resulted in Israel yoking herself to Moabite deities, and we're told that the daughters of Moab "invited the people to the sacrifices of their gods, and the people ate and bowed down to their gods. So Israel yoked himself to Baal of Peor. And the anger of the Lord was kindled against Israel" (Numbers 25:2, 3).

What happened from Shittim to Gilgal? The answer, in short, is great sin and great grace. Shittim represented Israel's great sin, for which God's people should have been destroyed in a conflagration of his judgment, east of the Jordan, just outside the promised land. But Gilgal, inside the promised land, stood as an abiding witness to God's great grace that made a way for a sinful people, prone to idolatry, to arrive safe on Canaan's side.[16] God would again part the waters, this time the Jordan River (Joshua 3:7–17), and Israel would again pass through the waters of God's judgment and, by God's grace, arrive safely in the promised land.

In the midst of this remarkable rehearsal of God's goodness toward Israel—God's saving acts that were as astounding then as they are astounding to us today—we mustn't forget the context. Which of these or the countless other acts of grace and mercy has Israel found wearisome, so wearisome that they thought, *We can do better elsewhere*? We would think that a nation that had experienced so great and so many deliverances, with God proving his power and faithfulness in so many times and in so many ways, would have more readily and more devotedly entrusted themselves to their great God in acts of worship and obedience.

It is, in fact, easy for us to look at Israel from a position of superiority and to read these accounts of Israel's faithlessness and think, *Tsk, tsk, there she goes again, ungrateful, faithless, and perennially forgetful of God's saving grace*.

But the reality is that we too are prone to such forgetfulness, forgetfulness no less surprising and appalling. Before we look down our noses on Israel from a position of superiority, we must remember that we are in a superior position, and yet we do the very same thing more often than we would care to admit.

The fact of the matter is, God could put similar questions to each of us. "What is it that I have done to deserve your doubt? What have I done to deserve your waning affections and lukewarm loyalties? Was it when my eternal Son took on flesh and entered into the sorrows and suffering of your sin-cursed world? Was it when Jesus healed and restored and mended and raised to life those living under the shadow of death, thus announcing the arrival of my kingdom? Was it when the Creator of the world and the King of the Jews hung on a cross for your sins, thus paying the penalty you couldn't pay in a thousand lifetimes? What was it precisely that earned your ambivalence?" To which each of us, overwhelmed by our guilt and shame, could only wilt before the majesty and knowing gaze of our Creator.

If Israel was prone to treat God's great acts of salvation and deliverance as light matters—at times forgettable and at other times wearisome—we are prone to treat God's greatest act of salvation, the cross of Jesus Christ, the Son of God given for sinners, as of little consequence in our daily lives. And yet the remedy for forgetful and ungrateful sinners is to hear again the same gospel message we are prone to forget. Jesus Christ died for sinners like us. It is in this gospel alone that we find what the Apostle Paul calls "the power of God for salvation to everyone who believes" (Romans 1:16).

## The People's Plea and Response (6:6–8)

Much, much more could be brought forth by way of evidence against Israel, but Yahweh's case against his people is sufficient to demonstrate their guilt. In Micah 6:6, the people offer a revealing response to the Lord's indictment. What follows reveals that there is in fact no defense to be made. There are no justifications or explanations, no attenuating circumstances or different perspectives. It is fascinating and illuminating that the people's response turns to the possibility of atonement: "With what shall I come before the Lord, and bow myself before God on high? Shall I come to him with burnt offerings, with calves a year old?" (v. 6). In other words, Israel asks, "What can I possibly do to make my way back into the presence of my Creator and my God? What will he accept from me that will make me acceptable to him again?"[17]

Understandably, the first thing that comes to mind is the burnt offering. The burnt offering may be regarded as the most basic of Israel's offerings; its purpose was to provide atonement for a sinner who wished to enter into the presence of the holy God of Israel and find him to be a God of mercy.

Perhaps suspecting that a burnt offering is not enough and desiring assurance that something would actually accomplish this atonement, the questioner then suggests bringing a calf a year old. A calf was not a typical burnt offering and was considered somewhat more valuable and precious (perhaps because the meat was more tender and/or perhaps because the animal had so much life and usefulness ahead of it). Would a calf be sufficient to atone for sin? In this we can see the direction the questioner's mind is going. *If I can just find something valuable enough, then my sins will be forgiven and my iniquity atoned for.*

We can almost hear the mounting fear and desperation: fear that a year-old calf may not be sufficient and desperation to find something, anything to stand as a substitute.

The questioner then moves from quality to quantity. He asks, "Will the Lord be pleased with thousands of rams, with ten thousands of rivers of oil?" (v. 7). Few except kings would have the means to offer thousands of rams, and ten thousand rivers of oil would be impossible even for kings. Even if the standard is an impossibility, the human heart wants to know what it is. *What is sufficient to atone for my sins?* We do this perhaps because a standard, even an impossible, unattainable standard, offers the illusion that there is something we can do to atone for our sins.

In the second half of Micah 6:7, we hear a final offer, as horrifying as it is honest: "Shall I give my firstborn for my transgression, the fruit of my body for the sin of my soul?" In other words, will God accept the ultimate sacrifice—a life for a life?

Though it continues to be debated, child sacrifice seems to have been rare both in Israel and in her neighboring states. It was not, however, unknown. Jephthah in Judges 11 offered his daughter as a sacrifice in fulfillment of a foolish and ungodly vow (vv. 30–40). King Ahaz in 2 Kings 16:3 offered his son as a sacrifice, and most famously, King Manasseh of Judah burned his son as an offering (21:1, 6). I don't, however, think we're meant to hear in Micah's imagined dialogue a genuine offer to sacrifice one's child (6:7) but rather a cry of desperation that suspects there might not be anything at all that one can do to atone for one's sins. Micah's dialogue taps into a basic human fear, at times muted if not suppressed altogether, but always present and often haunting, that asks, "What is the cost of my life? What is the price of admission to divine blessedness? Do I have anything that will cause God to say of me, 'accepted' if not 'loved'?"

The questioner receives his answer. Speaking for God, the prophet utters what are perhaps the most famous lines in the entire book: "He has told you, O man, what is good; and what does the LORD require of you but to do justice, and to love kindness, and to walk humbly with your God?" (Micah 6:8).

The first thing that strikes us about this answer is the addressee. Micah doesn't say, "He has told you, *O Israel* . . ." but "He has told you, *O man* . . ." In this expression the prophet is expanding God's salvation beyond the walls of Israel, delimited by the Torah and the Mosaic covenant; it is not Israel alone but mankind as a whole to whom Micah says, "He has told you."[18] The command to "do justice, and to love kindness, and to walk humbly with your God" is not a command exclusive to Israel but summarizes the Law of God written on the heart of every man, woman, and child who bears his image.[19]

Also surprising is the opening phrase: "He *has told* you . . ." The answer that the questioner is scrambling to discover is not a secret guarded by the religious elite or a mystery discerned only by the spiritually sensitive. "*He has told you* . . ." clearly implies "You already have the answer." God's word is sufficiently clear, and always has been. "He *has* told you . . ." Israel's problem is at heart not an information problem but a will problem.

"What does the LORD require of you?" With this we come to the prophet's most striking claim: "to do justice, and to love kindness, and to walk humbly with your God" (v. 8). This is what the Lord requires. He requires "justice." Justice is what Israel refused to do, a refusal that Micah has been denouncing time and again. Justice was to uphold the cause of the poor, to protect the vulnerable, and to deal fairly in business. This is the sense of the Hebrew word translated as "justice"—actions that create an environment for human flourishing. Justice is not a disposition, a state of mind knowing what is right and wrong, what is fair and unfair. Justice refers to an action that establishes and promotes equity between man and man, woman and woman. It seeks order as God created it, and from that order emerges life and abundance and joy.

The Lord requires his people ". . . to do justice, and to love kindness." The word here for "kindness" is *hesed*, the meaning of which includes mercy but goes far beyond our notional concepts of mercy to include steadfast love or loyalty. God is a God of *hesed*. This is how he reveals himself to Moses: "The LORD, the LORD, a God merciful and gracious, slow to anger, and abounding in *hesed* and faithfulness" (Exodus 34:6). To love *hesed*, therefore, is to know and love the God who is himself the God of *hesed*. Unlike "doing justice," "loving kindness" (mercy) is an inward disposition that first loves the God of mercy and in turn seeks to extend that mercy to others as one who bears the image of the God who is *hesed* itself.

Finally, Micah concludes his summary of mankind's obligation; he is to "walk humbly with your God" (6:8). This is the posture of faith. "Walk[ing] . . . with God" expresses fellowship with and likeness to God. Just as we tend to take on the character and mannerisms of close friends, those who walk with God come to resemble him. As God loves justice, so too do those who walk closely with him. As God does righteousness, so also must those who belong to him. Walking with God is an orientation of one's entire life as one aligned with God, obedient to his Word, seeking his will, and, above all, trusting him in all things.

What is striking about the prophet's answer in 6:8 is that he responds to the questioner by saying, in effect, "Your calculus is all wrong." The Lord doesn't want something from you—he wants you.[20] He doesn't want your sacrifices; he wants your very heart and life. In other words, what the Lord desires from sinful people are lives transformed by his grace.[21] The prophet lays this before Israel not at all as a way for them to earn their salvation, as if works of justice and hearts that cherish mercy somehow merit God's favor and blessing. Rather, the prophet sets before the people a portrait of a life that has been transformed by the grace, mercy, and steadfast love of God. A life that has been transformed by God's grace, that has understood and believed the message preached by the countless "righteous acts of the LORD" (v. 5), is a life that will in turn act justly, love mercy, and seek to walk in humility and faithfulness with Almighty God.[22] The psalmist puts it like this: "You will not delight in sacrifice, or I would give it; you will not be pleased with a burnt offering. The sacrifices of God are a broken spirit; a broken and contrite heart, O God, you will not despise" (Psalm 51:16, 17). Similarly, the Apostle Paul writes to the Romans, "Present your bodies as a living sacrifice, holy and acceptable to God, which is your spiritual worship" (Romans 12:1).

Perhaps we could summarize the prophet's response like this: Bear fruit in keeping with repentance and repent in keeping with your faith in the God who has done great things for you.

Will God accept your firstborn for your transgression, the fruit of your loins for your soul? The answer is no, but he would accept his own. Only the incarnate Son's perfect life and substitutionary death could atone for the sins of the world and merit eternal life for those given to him by the Father. God would one day give his own Son for our sins so that we could, by his grace, day in and day out, do justice, love mercy, and walk humbly with our God. The most pressing question for us, therefore, is not whether we will God accept our firstborn to atone for our sins but whether we will accept his as he is freely offered in the gospel.

Is there an atonement we can make that will pay the price for our sins? No, there is not. But God who is rich in mercy did not spare his own Son but gave him up for us all, the righteous for the unrighteous, so that, as Paul tells us, "we might become the righteousness of God" (2 Corinthians 5:21). There is nothing more to be done. What was impossible for us is possible for God. God yet again, once and for all, has made a way where there was no way. We are saved; we are forgiven; we are accepted by grace alone, through faith alone, in Christ alone. This is all of God so that no one may boast.

# 42

# Lamenting in Hope

MICAH 6:9—7:7

IT IS COMMON IN A COURT of law that when the gavel goes down a cry goes up. The gavel, of course, punctuates the judge's announcement of a verdict either against the accused or against the accuser. The cry, then, goes up as a response, a sorrowful, pain-filled expression of hopes dashed and of futures irreparably changed, possibly forever. We may observe the same, or at least a similar, movement in Micah 6:9—7:7. In 6:9–16, we hear the divine verdict issued against Jerusalem announced and the sentence pronounced. The rod of judgment will fall against God's once-holy city on account of the rampant violence, deception, wickedness, and corruption that contaminated the city at every level of its society. God's verdict is unequivocal, and his sentence is as clear and certain as it is just. Jerusalem is guilty. Judgment is coming.

After the guilty verdict and a sentence of capital punishment, we hear in 7:1 another cry—this time of the prophet crying out in response to this dreadful pronouncement. In Micah's cry we hear the response neither of the guilty nor of the innocent. Rather, in Micah's lament we hear the cry of the faithful.[1] Micah cries out as a faithful Israelite in the midst of an unfaithful city doomed to destruction. He makes the only response possible in the face of such astonishing news—lamentation and unrelenting grief.[2] God's prophet laments and grieves as he beholds what has become of God's once-glorious city now defiled and corrupt to her very core.

How do we survive in a city, a world even, that is turned on its head? This question is as relevant today as it was in Micah's day. How do we live in a world that by all appearances is falling apart? The answer the prophet gives us—or enacts for us—is that we lament and grieve. But we see in the faithful prophet's lament that, just as Paul would later instruct the Thessalonian church, he does not lament and grieve as one without hope (1 Thessalonians 4:13). Despite the rampant wickedness and despite the certain judgment that is coming, the prophet finds that there is still reason to hope. His reason is not found in the city, which is beyond repair, but rather is found in God himself, specifically in who God is and what God has promised to do. In this we see a model for Christians even today. Yes, lament, and yes, grieve over the depravity and corruption, the lies and injustices that are all around us and in us. But we must do so as those who persist in hope—hoping in God, in his promises, and in his Christ, who came to seek and to save what is lost, to heal and to mend what is wounded, and to restore and renew what is broken. Or, to put it simply, we too must hope in "the God of my salvation" (Micah 7:7).

### Jerusalem's Verdict (6:9–16)

Micah opens his oracle with a formula that is unique among the prophets: "The voice of the LORD cries to the city . . ." (6:9a).[3] The Lord's judgment against Jerusalem is not a secret.[4] As it was earlier in the book of Micah, so it is again declared publicly and clearly for all to hear, so that when judgment comes, there will be (or should be) no surprises and no confusion about the cause of the disaster. Much like Lady Wisdom, who in Proverbs 1:20, 21 adopts the posture of a prophet and "cries aloud in the street, in the markets she raises her voice; at the head of the noisy streets she cries out; and at the entrance of the city gates she speaks," so the prophet Micah adopts the posture of Lady Wisdom and declares the wisdom of God to a foolish and broken city.[5] The meaning of the expression that follows, "it is sound wisdom to fear your name" (Micah 6:9), is infamously obscure.[6] However, the prophet seems to be setting up a contrast between a wise and a foolish response to the divine voice that is heard throughout the city.

Sound wisdom fears the name of God, and that fear of God brings forth repentance, and repentance produces obedience born of faith. Yet there are precious few who respond with sound wisdom to God's word delivered through his prophet. Proverbs 26:3 says, "A whip for the horse, a bridle for the donkey, and a rod for the back of fools," the prophet directs the attention of the foolish city to "the rod and . . . him who appointed it" (Micah 6:9). The prophet draws to our attention both the rod of judgment coming against Jerusalem (likely the Assyrian army) and the One who wields it—the Lord God himself.

After the prophet heralds the coming of the divine Judge and his judgment against unsuspecting Jerusalem, God speaks in the first person. He sets before the accused two rhetorical questions designed to expose Israel's sin and vindicate his judgment:

> Can I forget any longer the treasures of wickedness in the house of the wicked,
> and the scant measure that is accursed?
> Shall I acquit the man with wicked scales
> and with a bag of deceitful weights? (6:10, 11)

With these questions God asks, in effect, "How did you expect this to end? How did you think the Righteous One of Israel would respond to Jerusalem's lies and corruption?" Or, to use the words of Abraham, "Shall not the Judge of all the earth do what is just?" (Genesis 18:25).

When the Judge of all the earth considers Jerusalem, what he discovers is wickedness being stored up in the house of the wicked. This is a description of an unadulterated wickedness. It is wicked people acting according to their wicked nature and having an abundance of what it is they treasure in life—namely, wickedness. "Treasures of wickedness" is a metaphor that invites us to see such wicked practices as not only pervasive and tolerated but in some sense celebrated. As Jesus instructed his disciples, "Where your treasure is, there your heart will be also" (Matthew 6:21). Micah declares that Jerusalem's heart is set completely and utterly upon wickedness. Wickedness is their treasure, and it will pay its inevitable dividends. In circumstances such as these, there is little, if any, hope for reform.

God also sees in his holy city "the scant measure" (Micah 6:10); that is, a vessel that purports to measure a specific quantity but in reality measures less or more, whatever would favor the dishonest merchant. The same dishonesty is at work with "wicked scales" and "deceitful weights" (v. 11), both of which refer to corrupt business practices designed to steal and to deceive and to defraud—all for personal gain at the expense of those who are ignorant or powerless or both. "What precisely," God asks, "do you expect when the Judge of all the earth shows up?" It is not only the poor and ignorant who suffer. The wicked merchants themselves suffer as they debase themselves through stealing. The city itself likewise suffers as the character or ethos of the community increasingly becomes one of personal gain regardless of the cost or harm inflicted on others.[7]

Because Jerusalem has become corrupt and defiled to her very core, because it may be said of her that her treasures are nothing other than wickedness and lies, God issues the only verdict that a righteous judge could possibly issue: *Guilty*. Beginning in verse 13, God delivers Jerusalem's sentence in summary form: "Therefore I will make you sick, striking you, making you desolate because of your sins" (v. 13, AT).[8] The violent will themselves be struck, and the wealthy will become desolate.

This is, from a literary point of view, poetic justice. The sins and crimes of the people are visited upon the offenders; they suffer the same terrible fate that they inflicted upon so many others, and as a result, this once-beautiful city will become a desolation, just as God had promised so long ago.[9]

But what God declares against Jerusalem is not simply *poetic* justice, it is also *covenantal* justice.[10] God is going to mete out upon Jerusalem the sanctions of the covenant that he promised Israel in the days of Moses more than 500 years earlier. As God renewed the covenant with Israel on the far side of the Jordan River on the plains of Moab, he set before them blessings for obedience and curses for disobedience (Deuteronomy 28). Should Israel keep faith with Yahweh, walking in his statutes and keeping his commandments, Moses says, "The LORD will make you abound in prosperity, in the fruit of your womb and in the fruit of your livestock and in the fruit of your ground, within the land that the LORD swore to your fathers to give you. The LORD will open to you his good treasury, the heavens, to give the rain to your land in its season and to bless all the work of your hands" (vv. 11, 12). But if Israel breaks faith with her God, should she stray from the paths of righteousness and break the laws established by her God and king, Moses says, "You shall carry much seed into the field and shall gather in little, for the locust shall consume it. You shall plant vineyards and dress them, but you shall neither drink of the wine nor gather the grapes, for the worm shall eat them. You shall have olive trees throughout all your territory, but you shall not anoint yourself with the oil, for your olives shall drop off" (vv. 38–40).

What was the goal of Israel's wickedness and corruption, this violence and greed that characterized Jerusalem and especially her leaders in Micah's day? The answer, of course, was to grow rich, to achieve comfort, and to experience a deep and lasting joy. In short, these corrupt merchants, like the wicked magistrates, priests, and prophets addressed earlier, were seeking *shalom*. But God declares that all their labor and efforts to this end are ultimately in vain. These proud and affluent elites will experience nothing but the opposite of *shalom*—namely, futility, frustration, and eventually despair.[11]

We hear the covenant sanctions of Deuteronomy resonating behind the prophetic announcement when the prophet says, "You shall eat, but not be satisfied, and there shall be hunger within you; you shall put away, but not preserve, and what you preserve I will give to the sword. You shall sow, but not reap; you shall tread olives, but not anoint yourselves with oil; you shall tread grapes, but not drink wine" (Micah 6:14, 15). Jerusalem's leaders believed that by lying, deceiving, manipulating, and defrauding others through threat and violence, they would achieve the blessing and peace and life that is captured in the one Hebrew word *shalom*. But the reality is that faithlessness and disobedience always produce futility and frustration—the exact opposite of their intended goal. So it is with all sin. Our idols make promises of life and joy and satisfaction, none of which they have the power to supply in any true and lasting measure. The result is futility, frustration, and, if unremedied, eternal death.

In Micah 6:16, Yahweh delivers his verdict and Israel's sentence. It falls like a final, crushing blow upon the obstinately indulgent, wicked, and corrupt city: "You have kept the statutes of Omri, and all the works of the house of Ahab; and you have walked in their counsels." Though he receives only eight verses in the Biblical record, King Omri of the northern kingdom was immensely successful by the world's standards and immensely wicked by God's standards. We're told in the book of Kings that "Omri did what was evil in the sight of the Lord, and did more evil than all who were before him. For he walked in all the way of Jeroboam the son of Nebat, and in the sins that he made Israel to sin, provoking the Lord, the God of Israel, to anger by their idols" (1 Kings 16:25, 26).

The character of Omri is better known through his son Ahab, the acorn who didn't fall far from the proverbial tree. Ahab's reign was characterized by the very wickedness, oppression, greed, and self-indulgence that Micah denounces throughout his oracles. Ahab married the Phoenician princess Jezebel, who introduced and promoted Baal worship throughout the northern kingdom. Ahab (and Jezebel) not only repeatedly rejected the word of God as delivered by the prophet Elijah but on at least one occasion sought to kill the Lord's messenger (19:2). On another occasion, Ahab enriched himself through murder when his wife orchestrated the false accusation of blasphemy against faithful Naboth so that her husband could fulfill his voracious desire to enlarge his garden (21:1–24).

More than a hundred years later, Micah witnessed the sad reality that people follow their king(s), either for good or for ill. Where goes the heart of the king, so go the hearts of his people. Samaria had followed the wicked practices of her kings, and in the year 722 b.c. she paid the ultimate price. But Jerusalem, instead of learning from Israel's mistake, followed her example, imitating the wicked leaders of the northern kingdom. Judah adopted the spirit and practices of Omri and Ahab, and the Lord announced that they would experience the same fate as those wicked kings and their now-decimated city.

Even the language the prophet employs is crafted to expose the heart of Judah's offense and to convict the nation of the true character and tragic consequence of their sin. The expressions "keeping statutes," "doing commands," and "walking in counsels" are used throughout Israel's Law to describe her obligation to the Lord as her God and King.[12] But instead of its conventionally positive association of keeping the statues of Yahweh, instead of walking in the counsel of their God and King, Micah says Israel has "kept the statutes of Omri, and all the works of the house of Ahab, and you have walked in their counsels" (6:16). In the heartbreaking drama of 1 Samuel 8, the fateful day when Israel elected to be ruled by a king like the nations instead of being ruled by Yahweh, their covenant God, set the trajectory of the nation for centuries. The prophet Samuel exposed Israel's disloyalty to their great King, the Lord their God, and their faithlessness to the covenant to which they swore obedience. Israel has chosen for themselves another king like the kings of the nations around them—oppressive, brutal, and faithless—and he would lead them to utter destruction.

The consequence of Jerusalem's faithlessness to their great King is the city's destruction and its inhabitants' humiliation (Micah 6:16). How could it be any other way? In the ancient Near East when cities or nations rebelled against a greater king or emperor to whom they were subject, that city could expect that great king and his kingdom to come against them with a show of force that would boggle the mind for its brutality. What does Judah expect from her covenant Lord? It should be no surprise that the Lord declares, "I will make you a desolation, and your inhabitants a hissing; so that you shall bear the reproach of my people" (6:16, AT).

This is Jerusalem's just sentence: desolation, humiliation, and destruction. However, though God's sentence offers a critical reminder that though Jerusalem is corrupt to its very core, God's covenant community remains precisely that: a people whom God calls "my people," a term fraught with overtones of the covenant of grace (cf. Exodus 6:7).[13] In this expression we receive the faintest glimmer of hope. We hear that despite their clear failings to keep faith with and to live in obedience to God, and despite the fact that they will receive the stroke of God's judgment, there is nevertheless a bond between God and his people that cannot be broken because it has been forged by God himself through the covenant of grace. Though they will undergo the ultimate curse of God's judgment, a curse foretold by Moses when he declared, "You shall become a horror, a proverb, and a byword among all the peoples where the LORD will lead you away" (Deuteronomy 28:37), nevertheless they remain "my people," and by implication, God somehow amazingly remains "their God."[14]

## Hope in Hopeless Times (7:1–7)

But what about the faithful? Clearly there are not many. Micah, like his prophetic forebearer Elijah, feels completely alone in his faith and his trust in Yahweh. When the prophet says, "The godly has perished from the earth, and there is no one upright among mankind," (Micah 7:2) we hear echoes of Elijah, who cried out to God, "The people of Israel have forsaken your covenant, thrown down your altars, and killed your prophets with the sword, and I, even I only, am left, and they seek my life, to take it away" (1 Kings 19:14). "There is no one but me, Lord, and I myself am just barely alive" seems to be a common experience for these spokesmen of God. Yet we do have in Micah a remnant. And we have whoever it is that Micah is speaking to when he says, "Put no trust in a neighbor; have no confidence in a friend" (7:5). It seems that the prophet is offering wisdom for anyone who desires to survive such a dangerous and inhospitable city. Here again we have a glimmer of a remnant, those whom God has preserved in the faith, those whom he still calls "my people."

The prophet's lament, as we find it situated in the book that bears his name, comes as a response to the verdict God announced against Jerusalem for her crimes immediately prior. Micah cries out, "Woe is me! For I have become as when the summer fruit has been gathered, as when the grapes have been gleaned: there is no cluster to eat, no first-ripe fig that my soul desires" (v. 1). The prophet feels in his bones and in his being the desolation and destitution of the city. There is no longer any joy to be had because there are no longer good things to experience. As when the summer fruit has been gathered and the grapes gleaned, there is nothing left to desire, nothing to enjoy, and little to point to that offers hope for a brighter future. It's a vivid image of both hopelessness and helplessness.

Beginning in 7:2, the prophet pans back from his subjective experience of despondency to reveal its cause, saying, "The godly has perished from the earth, and there is no one upright among mankind; they all lie in wait for blood, and each hunts the other with a net." The character of the city is projected upon the world at large, and the world is cast as dangerous and unspeakably violent. Mankind hunts their neighbors like animals, stalking fellow human beings for blood. For what purpose we're not told. But the hunting imagery brings into view not only the satisfaction of carnal appetites, but also, in this case, the perverted pleasure that comes from tracking a prey and ending its life. Cruel exploitation has become the law of the land as one's neighbor is no longer viewed as the image of God to be honored and served but as a commodity to be used and abused for personal gain.

The prophet goes on to describe the practices of Israel's corrupt leaders, saying, "Their hands are on what is evil, to do it well" (v. 3a). These leaders strive to be experts in their fields and exceptional in their crafts. But what is their work and craft? They devote their minds and intellects and passions not to those things that would help and bless others; rather, what they seek to execute with excellence is evil. Those who are to be repositories of justice that allow communities and cities to thrive have become the epicenter of wickedness that both harms and corrupts the people they are appointed to serve. The great variety of evil intentions is woven together into a rich tapestry of pure evil: "The prince and the judge ask for a bribe, and the great man utters the evil desire of his soul; thus they weave it together" (v. 3b). Collaboration and teamwork are typically considered good things, but this city's judges and magistrates work together marvelously to accomplish unjust and wicked ends. John Goldingay captured the scene well when he writes, "The single thing they're good at is doing what is bad. One way they have both hands available for doing wrong is by having them open to receive a bribe in return for giving the decision someone wants."[15]

Those natural bonds that should bind a community together and be a source of solace and trust have disintegrated and no longer provide aid and support in desperate times. So the prophet advises, "Put no trust in a neighbor; have no confidence in a friend; guard the doors of your mouth from her who lies in your arms" (Micah 7:5). The natural order of natural relations has been turned on its head. Perhaps there is no more natural a relation than that between parents and children—fathers to sons, mothers to daughters. Yet as the prophet looks out, he sees that even this order has been twisted by the wickedness of sin, and the reigning chaos has made it so that "the son treats the father with contempt, the daughter rises up against her mother, the daughter-in-law against her mother-in-law" with the result that "a man's enemies are the men of his own house" (v. 6). The most basic human relations have become tainted with distrust and disloyalty such that even the faithful are given over to suspicion of those whom they most love and isolation from any who could offer succor in times of distress.

These are indeed hopeless times. There is no good thing within the city that the prophet can look to and say, "See, at least there is righteousness." Considering the dreadful state of affairs being described, Micah is remarkably measured in his response. He is not given over to hysteria, nor is he exaggerating. He is simply stating reality as he sees it and experiences it. The order that God has established for the thriving of human relations and the flourishing of society, the order designed to instill and promote life as God intended it, has degenerated into chaos, violence, brutality, and death. Those whom God has in his providence appointed guardians and overseers of order and justice are themselves the chief culprits, leading the way in human degradation, exploitation, and oppression. This is what is behind the prophet's description when he says, "The best of them is like a brier, the most upright of them a thorn hedge" (v. 4). Whoever these "best" and "most upright" are, they are not like a flower that blesses but rather like a shrub that harms. Don't get too close or you will get hurt! And these harmful, perhaps dangerous, individuals are not the worst that the city has to offer. They are the best.

The situation could not be more desperate. Corrupt to its core, Jerusalem has received God's word of judgment. The prophet looks in vain for reasons to hope. The order that God has established has been turned on its head; the *shalom* of the kingdom of God has been rejected, despised, and destroyed. In its place is man's order. Sin and corruption reign supreme. Deception and lies seem to be the law of the land. The prophet, like the city, has become devoid of life and joy. And yet, in Micah 7:7, like a light piercing the darkness, we hear an unexpected expression of hope ring out from our weary prophet: "As for me, I will look to the LORD; I will wait for the God of my salvation; my God will hear me."[16]

There is no hope to be found in Jerusalem, nor anywhere else in this world. Left to itself, this world is hopeless and helpless—"dead," as Paul puts it, "in . . . trespasses and sins" (Ephesians 2:1). The prophet's hope, however, is found not in this world but in the Lord his God, who stands apart from the created order and yet is near to those who call upon his name. "I will look to the LORD" (Micah 7:7) is the language of faith. Micah looks to Yahweh, the Lord, as the One who is able to bring order out of chaos, light out of darkness, life out of death. Such is the posture of faith; it looks to the Lord God alone for help in times of need. When rightly understood, all times in human life—every day and every hour, seasons of joy and seasons of affliction—are times of need.

Thus the prophet declares, "I will wait for the God of my salvation."

This sounds much like a later prophet who finds himself in a nearly identical situation and declares, "I will take my stand at my watchpost and station myself on the tower, and look out to see what he will say to me, and what I will answer concerning my complaint" (Habakkuk 2:1). Like a watchman on a tower, the prophet is reduced to silently waiting for the Lord to come, not just as the God of judgment but also as the God of salvation. There is in fact nothing else that the prophet can do but watch and wait. Happily, however, there is nothing else that needs to be done.

It is this confidence, this faith, that sustains Micah in his disorientation and despair; the confidence that though everyone around him is faithless, there yet remains One who is perfectly and unfailingly faithful—namely, "the God of my salvation" (Micah 7:7). We have the same reason for hope in our day. The God who is "the same yesterday and today and forever" (Hebrews 13:8) does not change, and his promises never fail (cf. Numbers 23:19; Malachi 3:6). In the midst of the chaos that we experience, the turmoils and afflictions that will undoubtedly come in this life, we have a sure anchor for our souls (Hebrews 6:19) in the God who commands his people, "Be still, and know that I am God" (Psalm 46:10).

This faith, expressed so powerfully for its succinctness by the prophet Micah, will later be expounded by his fellow prophet Habakkuk. As the Babylonians were marching against Jerusalem and the devastation that Micah prophesied was about to be realized in unspeakable acts of exploitive cruelty, Habakkuk could sing a song of faith perhaps unparalleled in Biblical literature for its beauty:

> Though the fig tree should not blossom,
>   nor the fruit be on the vines,
> the produce of the olive fail
>   and the fields yield no food,
> the flock be cut off from the fold
>   and there be no herd in the stalls,
> yet I will rejoice in the LORD;
>   I will take joy in the God of my salvation.
> GOD, the Lord, is my strength;
>   he makes my feet like the deer's;
>   he makes me tread on my high places. (Habakkuk 3:17–19)

In Micah's hope we are reminded that no matter how bad things get, God will preserve a remnant for himself, a people who are inwardly and truly God's people. God draws a line between those who belong to Israel in name only and those who are truly, internally, "my people." In this crushing indictment of his Church under the old covenant, we receive a sobering reminder of the distinction between the visible and the invisible Church. There are those who are members—citizens as it were—of the visible manifestation of the kingdom of God by the sign of the covenant, by the confession of faith, and in some measure by external obedience to the Biblical commands. The sad truth of the matter is that churches and their leaders can commit great and grievous sins, some of which reveal them to be outside the bounds of Christ's kingdom. But church leaders' failing or straying does not mean that Christ is unfaithful or that his kingdom has failed. The Christian's hope is not in Christ's Church but in Christ himself. Our hope is not in the people of God but in God himself. The Church can and does fail. She often will, this side of glory. But Christ can never fail. He never has, and he never will. The one who died for sinners and rose in power accomplished the salvation for which Micah waited and longed, and this Christ is faithful to save to the uttermost all those who place their hope in him.

As Micah witnessed the earthly Jerusalem cracking and crumbling, he looked to God, the perfectly faithful King, and longed for his kingdom of perfect justice and righteousness that can never be shaken. In this the prophet found a reason to hope in what were, by any measure, hopeless times. There is a better king, and there is a better kingdom. In this Micah models the life of faith for every believer. In even the deepest valleys of this life, when every new day seems to yield new disappointments, hardships, and sorrows, we, like the prophet before us, may look to God and find in him alone a firm anchor for our souls. Whatever our circumstances, no matter how bad things get, we too have a sure reason to hope because we know the God of our salvation as he has revealed himself ultimately in Jesus Christ, the Son of God, our Savior. John Newton, the famous slave trader turned priest, captures powerfully the Christian's other-worldly hope in the closing verse of perhaps his second most famous hymn, "Glorious Things of Thee Are Spoken":

> Savior, since of Zion's city
> I thro' grace a member am,
> Let the world deride or pity,
> I will glory in your name.
> Fading are the world's vain pleasures,
> All their boasted pomp and show;
> Solid joys and lasting treasures
> None but Zion's children know.[17]

# 43

# A Liturgy of Hope

MICAH 7:8-20

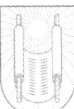

MICAH'S PROPHECY OPENS with a breathtaking depiction of God descending from his heavenly throne to execute a judgment on his people the scale of which and the horror of which borders on the inexpressible. This tone persists throughout the entire book. While it is certainly true that there have been glimmers of hope throughout Micah's oracles, it is also true that the center of gravity of the prophet's message is one of judgment. Israel's sin is too pervasive and the moral decay is too systemic to be remedied with education or minor adjustments to public policy. Micah's closing in this way echoes his opening: judgment is coming.

But here at the end of the book we hear another word, a final word alongside this unrelenting message of judgment. God's last and final word is not, in fact, one of sin and judgment, but of forgiveness and grace. In his conclusion, the prophet masterfully pulls together in a climactic summary the various themes and motifs that he has treated throughout his book: the sin of Israel and the impending judgment, the ingathering of the nations, the shepherding of the people, the victory of God over his enemies, and ultimately, the glory, majesty, and grace of God himself.[1]

Of the many difficulties presented by this exquisite book, perhaps the thorniest is the difficulty of identifying speakers. On more than one occasion we have discovered that we don't always know for certain who is speaking—God, his prophet Micah, the false prophets whom Micah is opposing, or someone (or perhaps something) else altogether (see, e.g., 2:5–8). With Micah's concluding oracle we come to the final instance of this difficulty. In 7:8 we read, "Rejoice not over me, O my enemy; when I fall, I shall rise;

when I sit in darkness, the LORD will be a light to me." These hopeful words immediately present us with a question: Who is speaking? Many take the "me" and the "I" in this verse as referring to the prophet himself. In this case, Micah is confessing his own personal sin and, on this view, is serving as a model for the remnant.[2]

Though this is certainly a possibility and a defensible line of interpretation, it strains a bit to explain the rationale for the abrupt transition from the sins of the people (and especially their leaders) that has been the focus throughout the book to focus here on the individual sins of the prophet. But perhaps even more suggestive that the speaker is someone or something other than the prophet is the fact that the pronoun in verse 10 is feminine. Though it does not come out in the English translation, when the enemy says, "Where is the LORD *your* God?," the "your" in Hebrew is feminine.[3]

This has caused many—this author included—to interpret Micah's concluding oracle not as the personal confession of the prophet but as a prayer of and for Jerusalem.[4] John Calvin puts it simply: "Here the Prophet assumes the character of the Church."[5] Micah assumes the character of the Church, that is, the city of God, the people of God. Therefore, what we have in Micah's concluding oracle is essentially a prayer or, perhaps more precisely, a liturgy.[6] This is a prayer not of Jerusalem the golden but for Jerusalem the conquered, defeated, and despoiled. Jerusalem, like her enemies and like her soon-to-be conquerors and captors, is most often depicted or cast as a woman. With this literary figure, the prophet is anticipating the judgment and ruin that will soon befall the city, but he is also giving the faithful a prayer to pray when it happens.[7] The prophet gives Israel a gospel word in which to hope when the darkness of God's judgment comes.

In his final oracle, Micah announces a great reversal of fortune for God's covenant people and his holy city. The prophet's central point is that this reversal will not come about, and indeed cannot come about, through human effort but only through divine gift and divine grace. It is not a salvation wrought by sinful man; it is a work wrought by the promise-making and promise-keeping God who has bound himself by covenant to save sinners for himself.

### God Will Raise His People from Death to Life (7:8–10)

The prophet, speaking as Jerusalem herself, addresses Jerusalem's enemies: "Rejoice not over me, O my enemy; when I fall, I shall rise; when I sit in darkness, the LORD will be a light to me" (Micah 7:8). Jerusalem's fall is certain. But her enemies are commanded not to rejoice over Jerusalem's certain destruction because just as certain as her falling is her rising. The image is one of moving from death and darkness to light and life. Thus even in the prophet's poignant lament we hear a note of hope and assurance. Jerusalem is at the same time both humble and confident. She is humble because when she contemplates the ruin and the shame that is about to befall her at the hands of her enemies, she knows that it is nothing less than she deserves. She says, "I will bear the indignation of the Lord because I have sinned against him" (v. 9). The indignity and humiliation that Jerusalem will endure does not come despite her God, as if Yahweh were somehow weak and defeated—it comes from her God. The Lord is the source of Jerusalem's ruin, but its cause is the people's intractable sin. For those sins and that wickedness that have been exposed and condemned in detail and at length throughout the book, Israel will endure God's judgment. The path that Jerusalem will have to trod on her way to glory is the path of repentance and faith.

Yet God's judgment is amazingly not his last word for his people. In verse 9 we learn not only of the cause of Israel's judgment but the basis for Israel's hope—namely, that the very same God who has spoken his word of judgment *against* them will one day speak *for* them. Jerusalem says, "I will bear the indignation of the Lord . . . *until* he pleads my cause and executes judgment *for me*."[8] In a surprising turn of events the prosecutor will speak for the defense; the One who has litigated the case against Israel will take up their cause and speak for them as their advocate. The result will be forgiveness, vindication, and new life: "He will bring me out to the light; I shall look upon his vindication" (v. 9). Israel does not vindicate herself. God's people don't justify themselves. But God has made a way through promise and covenant to redeem and deliver his elect from himself.

The guilty will rise to new life; those who had received the Lord's curse will one day receive his blessing. [9] Those who mocked her and who saw in her defeat the weakness of Israel's God or Yahweh's abandonment of his people, will be put to shame. "Then my enemy will see, and shame will cover her who said to me, 'Where is the Lord your God?'" (v. 10). Then it will be Israel's turn to "look" and "see," and what Israel will see is the humiliation of those who mocked her and celebrated the downfall of God's chosen people.[10]

In this way Israel in the Old Testament and Israel in the New Testament (what we call the Church) is given a critical reminder—namely, that God will vindicate his people. The basis of God's vindication is not that his people really weren't that bad or that their sins were not as bad as others' sins. Nor is it even that their sins were sufficiently atoned for with time served or punishments endured. God's vindication of his people is based on his sovereign electing love. God's love for and commitment to his people—the commitment

Israel's enemies imagined to be weak at best or nonexistent at worst when they mocked Israel saying, "Where is the LORD your God?"—will be revealed to be the strongest thing in the world, stronger than death itself. Those who mocked Israel for her ruin will themselves suffer devastation as they are "trampled down like the mire in the streets" (v. 10). The fates of these nations will be reversed. Those who had trampled Jerusalem into the mud and mire will themselves come to ruin, and ruined Jerusalem will rise in glory.

The source of Micah's poise and confidence is the promise-making and promise-keeping God. At no point does the prophet look to himself or to Israel as providing the catalyst for this great reversal of fortune. Just the opposite. Micah clearly and unequivocally confesses the sins and culpability of God's people, no doubt including himself as well. He acknowledges God's perfect justice in his judgments and curse: "I will bear the indignation of the LORD because I have sinned against him" (7:9). And yet he looks to God, whose judgment is severe, as Israel's only hope for forgiveness and for life.

### God Will Rebuild His City from Ruins to Glory (7:11–13)

Just as God's judgment is not the last word for his people, so too God's judgment is not the last word for his holy city. As Mark Gignilliat elegantly puts it, "The day of visitation yields to the day of restoration."[11] Yes, Jerusalem would be destroyed. Though not in Micah's day, her fate is certain because her citizens, like her kings, were prone to evil. Eventually this would result in the ultimate covenant curse being leveled against God's holy city. Jerusalem would undoubtedly fall. And yet just as God would raise a people from the dead, so too would God raise his city from the ashes and rubble. The darkness in which the city sits—the darkness of shame and guilt, of humiliation and indignation described so vividly in Micah 7:8–10—will one day pass, and a new day will dawn, a day the prophet describes as "a day for the building of your walls!" (v. 11).[12]

These "walls" (literally, "rule") will not be restricted to the old city of David, nor even just to the boundaries of Judah and Israel, the promised land. The boundaries of Jerusalem will extend to the farthest reaches of the known world, encompassing the very empires that have proven most hostile to God's people. Echoing (or anticipating) his contemporary Isaiah (Isaiah 54:1–3), Micah says, "In that day they will come to you, from Assyria and the cities of Egypt, and from Egypt to the River, from sea to sea and from mountain to mountain" (7:12). Assyria in the northeast; Egypt in the southwest; the River, that is, the Euphrates; and the cities of Egypt—all of these peoples will come

A Liturgy of Hope   403

streaming to Israel's rebuilt city, or perhaps the city will expand her walls to encompass even these distant and mighty kingdoms.

Some have suggested that this is a reference to the exiles of Israel and Judah, the Jews of the Dispersion returning home.[13] Though the prophet's words certainly include the Jews of the Dispersion, the prophet's vision and promise far exceed the Jews who have gone into exile. His words include the Gentile nations as part of those gathered into this new city whose boundaries extend to the "farthest corners of the world" and encompass even the mightiest and most hostile empires.[14] This is suggested by the prophet's use of the merisms "from sea to sea and from mountain to mountain" (v. 12), which serve to cast the scope of redemption on a global and universal scale reminiscent of the nations' streaming to Mount Zion in Micah 4:1–4. The image communicates a clear message: this new city will be inhabited by Jews and Gentiles alike. As God regathers those whom he has scattered, along with them will come those who were once far off.

Yet this universal scope of God's redemptive work is not a universalism. The prophet contrasts the rebuilt Jerusalem with the rest of the world: "The earth will be desolate because of its inhabitants, for the fruit of their deeds" (7:13). This future day is not a day of unqualified salvation. The salvation that Yahweh brings comes in the context of his judgment of the entire world. The desolation that Israel will experience at the exile "for the fruit of their deeds" is a microcosm of a final, global judgment that will be meted out against the world for "the fruit of their deeds." In the book of Revelation, John would relate his vision of this day of the Lord: "I saw the dead, great and small, standing before the throne, and books were opened. . . . And the dead were judged by what was written in the books, according to what they had done" (20:12). Both Israel and the nations will be judged according to the fruit of their deeds. Nevertheless, though the world lies desolate, and though many will be "trampled down like the mire of the streets" (Micah 7:10), the Lord will raise his city from dust to glory. The light of the Lord will shine, the city will be rebuilt, and a remnant will return to God and to his holy city.

### God Will Lead His People through Danger to Rest (7:14–17)

Beginning in 7:14, Micah returns one last time to the image of a shepherd.[15] Kings in the ancient world commonly employed this image to describe their rule and care for their citizens.[16] The prophets employed this same image to great effect as they time and again likened Israel's kings and leaders to venal and faithless shepherds who more often brutalized and exploited the sheep entrusted to their care (see, e.g., Isaiah 56:9–12; Jeremiah 23:1–4; Ezekiel 34:1–10; Zechariah 11; 13:7–9).

In this the prophets reveal Israel's (and our) greatest need: a good shepherd. So Micah declares, "Shepherd your people with your staff, the flock of your inheritance, who dwell alone in a forest in the midst of a garden land" (7:14). Israel, who would be scattered like sheep in the exile—wounded, helpless, and hopeless—will be sought out by God himself, the great shepherd of the sheep. God will guide them with his staff into fields of good food and abundant waters. This is the significance of the locations Bashan and Gilead (v. 14). Both were known as lush and desirable pastures, places in which sheep would thrive. Israel's hope is inextricably connected to their need for a Shepherd-King who would not use and abuse the sheep for his own benefit but who would protect and care for the sheep even at the cost of his own life.

In Micah 2:13 the prophet declared, "Their king passes on before them, the Lord at their head," a verse that is pregnant with ambiguity. It was unclear in this verse whether "king" and "the Lord" referred to the same or different persons. In 7:14, however, the ambiguity is resolved. It is the Lord who is identified as Israel's Shepherd-King and who is addressed in what many consider to be a liturgy in which the people cry out to God: "Shepherd your people with your staff," to which the Lord responds, "As in the days when you came out of the land of Egypt, I will show them marvelous things" (v. 15).

God declares that he is going to reenact the greatest act of deliverance Israel has ever known: the exodus from Egypt. In the exodus God revealed his sovereign power through signs and wonders. Through Micah, God promises to perform an event even greater than the greatest act of deliverance. There will be a second exodus, a new exodus. As in the first exodus, God will deliver his people and lead his people in such a way that the nations will stand back in astonishment.

> The nations shall see and be ashamed of all their might;
>   they shall lay their hands on their mouths;
> their ears shall be deaf;
>   they shall lick the dust like a serpent,
> like the crawling things of the earth;
>   they shall come trembling out of their strongholds;
> they shall turn in dread to the Lord our God,
>   and they shall be in fear of you. (7:16, 17)

The might and military prowess that was the source of the nations' confidence and boast becomes the source of their shame. They will be dumbfounded, speechless before the marvelous works of the Lord, and their might in which they trusted will be revealed to be worthless in the economy of the Most High. All that will be left for them to do is to acknowledge the greatness, worthiness, supremacy, and majesty of the one true God, and to submit to his rule: "They shall be in fear of you" (v. 17). This is not the fear of faithful worshipers but the fear of those confronted with the reality of the God they spurned, an event described by the Apostle Paul in Philippians when he says, "Every knee should bow, in heaven and on earth and under the earth, and every tongue confess that Jesus Christ is Lord, to the glory of God the Father" (2:10, 11).

In this we again hear the prophet alluding to Israel's celebration of the Lord's victory over Egypt (Micah 7:15). In Exodus Israel sings to Yahweh,

> You have led in your steadfast love the people whom you have redeemed;
> you have guided them by your strength to your holy abode.
> The peoples have heard; they tremble;
> pangs have seized the inhabitants of Philistia.
> Now are the chiefs of Edom dismayed;
> trembling seizes the leaders of Moab;
> all the inhabitants of Canaan have melted away.
> Terror and dread fall upon them;
> because of the greatness of your arm, they are still as a stone,
> till your people, O Lord, pass by,
> till the people pass by whom you have purchased. (15:13–16)

The exodus serves as a paradigm, a pattern, for an even greater and more glorious deliverance that God will accomplish in the future.[17] Israel shall again pass by the nations who look upon her deliverance as the work of a God whose greatness is beyond compare.

The prophet employs imagery of great abundance and deep rest, reminiscent of the imagery of Psalm 23, which is unparalleled in lyric poetry in any language: "The Lord is my shepherd; I shall not want. He makes me lie down in green pastures. He leads me beside still waters. He restores my soul. He leads me in paths of righteousness for his name's sake" (vv. 1–3). Yet unlike Psalm 23 in which God's flock is led through valleys of deep darkness, Micah sees no such trial or temptation, no such hardship or sorrow, in Israel's future. Israel's future will not be like her past as trial and temptation give way to triumph and peace.

### God Will Triumph over Sin Forever (7:18–20)

The final stanza opens with a rhetorical question: "Who is a God like you?" (Micah 7:18). It is a question that recalls and continues the sustained allusion to the Song of the Sea in which Moses asked, "Who is like you, O LORD, among the gods?" (Exodus 15:11).[18] More importantly, it is a question that resembles the name of the prophet himself. Micah's name means "Who is like Yahweh?"[19] The assumed answer is, of course, no one. There is no God like Yahweh. Israel's God (and our God) is incomparable. In any respect there is no god who compares to our God. "Who is a God like you?" (Micah 7:18). This rhetorical question is not meant to be answered but to become the catalyst for God's people to worship their incomparable God.

The prophet himself goes on to enumerate seven incomparable excellencies of Israel's God. The excellencies serve as the basis for Israel's hope for a brighter future. It is God's character that finds expression in his great acts of salvation in and throughout history and that serves as the sole basis for Israel's hope and our hope. God is a God who pardons iniquity and passes over transgression. He does not retain his anger forever because he delights in steadfast love. He is a God of compassion. For that reason the prophet and the Jerusalem he represents can have confidence that God will again have compassion on even the most sinful of people and the most wicked of cities. Micah declares, "You will show faithfulness to Jacob and steadfast love to Abraham, as you have sworn to our fathers from the days of old" (v. 20).

The prophet continues his earlier allusion to the exodus event when he declares that God "will tread our iniquities underfoot. You will cast all our sins into the depths of the sea" (v. 19). Just as God had hurled Pharaoh and his chariots into the heart of the sea, so he will again act to destroy Israel's sin.[20] As great an enemy and as dangerous a threat as Egypt was to Israel in the days of Moses, Egypt was not the greatest threat that Israel faced. While God delivered Israel from their Egyptian oppressors, he had yet to accomplish their greater deliverance from the curse of sin that indwells every human heart. As the wilderness generation can attest, an oppressor remained in Israel's lives long after Pharaoh and his chariots were drowned in the Red Sea. Bruce Waltke puts it like this: "God's memorial name initially became famous when he hurled the Egyptian army into the depths of the sea to keep covenant fidelity with the patriarchs. He will, however, add even greater luster to his name in the last days when he hurls Israel's iniquities into the depths of the sea to be true to his covenant with Abraham and Jacob (7:19–20)."[21] For the accomplishment of that greater deliverance, Israel would have to wait for the coming of her Messiah.

The prophet's soaring description of divine forgiveness suggests a question: Is this how we view our sin? Far greater than any threat *out there* is the threat and danger we face by the sin that resides in each of our hearts. God could triumph over Pharaoh and his army by the word of his power, but he could triumph over sin and its curse only by the death of his incarnate Son.[22] Jesus in his day would respond to the scribes who questioned his authority to forgive sins by asking, "Which is easier, to say to the paralytic, 'Your sins are forgiven,' or to say, 'Rise, take up your bed and walk'?" (Mark 2:9). It would be far easier for Jesus to heal than it would be for him to forgive sins. For the former he had to will and to speak; for the latter he had to suffer and die. Yet it was precisely to accomplish the latter that Jesus came.

The book that began with a revelation of God's judgment concludes with a revelation of God's mercy. It is striking that the prophet's concluding oracle opens and closes with rhetorical questions and that the concluding enumeration and celebration of the excellencies of God serve as an answer of sorts to the opening taunt. As Israel's enemies witness their woeful plight, they issue their mocking taunt: "Where is the Lord your God?" (Micah 7:10). Few things could be more self-evident to Israel's enemies than that Israel's God is impotent, he doesn't care, or both. "Where is the Lord your God?" These words ironically echoed in the mouths of the people of Israel themselves as they gazed at their Messiah hanging on the cross. The crowds that surrounded Jesus issued their own taunts, saying, "He trusts in God; let God deliver him now, if he desires him" (Matthew 27:43). In other words, "Where is the Lord your God?" (Micah 7:10).

Unlike Israel, who would bear the indignation of the Lord because they had sinned against him (Micah 7:9), Jesus would bear the indignation of the Lord "although he had done no violence," as Micah's contemporary Isaiah puts it, "and there was no deceit in his mouth" (Isaiah 53:9). Though he had done no wrong, Jesus was humiliated, defiled, defeated, and destroyed on a Roman cross so that Jerusalem in Micah's day and the Church in our day might see a light shining in the darkness and, by grace, rise again. Like Jerusalem of old, we too can know that the Lord will be a light to us because Jesus knew a darkness the horror of which we could never imagine. Christ bore our sins so that he could plead our cause as the risen Savior and Mediator of a better covenant. Between the guilty and God's judgment, the Son of God interposed his blood, and so, like Jerusalem of old, we may hope with confidence.

It is striking, however, that neither the prophet's rhetorical question, "Who is a God like you?" (Micah 7:18), nor what follows actually answers the taunting question "Where is the Lord your God?" (v. 10). The question "Where is the Lord your God?" is not really asking for the deity's location. It is essentially asking, "Where is God for you? Where is God acting for you, where is God caring for you, where is God defending you?" It's a question designed to taunt and to humiliate.[23] The implication is clear. By all appearances God can't be found. "God," the enemy implies, "has abandoned you; and you are as forsaken by God as you appear to be."[24] It's a question asked not only by others; sometimes it is a question that we in our darker moments ask ourselves.

What we need to remember, however, is that "Who is a God like you?" (v. 18) is at times the only and best answer to the question, "Where is the LORD your God?" (v. 10) because we can often have difficulty seeing how God is gracious to us in our daily lives, how God is working all things together for our good in moments of great trial.[25] Many if not most Christians have had seasons that move from disappointment to disappointment, which then gives way to loss and tragedy. Where is God in all of this? At moments like these, "Who is a God like you?" (v. 18) is not only the best response but the only response to the haunting question "Where is the LORD your God?" (v. 10). In this response, the prophet reframes the question from "Where . . . ?" to "Who . . . ," from "Where is God?" to "Who is God?"

At times it is difficult, if not impossible to point to this or that reality in our lives that demonstrates God is with us and for us. The tragedy can be so pronounced, the loss so great, the pain so intolerable, the sadness so deep. This certainly would have been the case for Israel as she bore the punishment for her sin in exile. Though we, like them, might not be able to see clearly how God is with us at the moment, how God is working our trials for our good, we can nevertheless know who God is and know him to be a light shining in our darkness (Micah 7:8). We can know his character, his purposes, and his promises as he has revealed them in his Son and in his Word. Though our circumstances change, the Son of God given for us will never change, and it's in him that we behold the fulfillment of Micah's liturgy of hope.

It is through Christ's atoning death and resurrection life that God pardons iniquity and passes over transgression for the remnant of his inheritance. In Christ God reveals himself to be a God who

> does not retain his anger forever,
>   because he delights in steadfast love.
> He will again have compassion on us;
>   he will tread our iniquities underfoot.
> You will cast all our sins
>   into the depths of the sea.
> You will show faithfulness to Jacob
>   and steadfast love to Abraham,
> as you have sworn to our fathers
>   from the days of old. (7:18–20)

This is who God is and who God has revealed himself to be fully and finally in Jesus Christ, who is the same yesterday, today, and forever.

The transition in verse 19 from third person "he" to second person "you" creates a sense of increasing intimacy: "He will tread our iniquities underfoot. You will cast all our sins into the depths of the sea." We can almost hear Jerusalem beginning to rise from the ash heap as she contemplates the character of her God and her confession transforms into worship. The good news is that even in our darkest moments, when we feel like we can't see God acting on our behalf, we can know who our God is, and this is sufficient to sustain us in our faith until the light shines in the darkness and faith becomes sight.

# NAHUM

*By Stephen M. Coleman*

# 44

# A Stronghold in the Day of Trouble

NAHUM 1:1–8

IN ADDITION TO HIS CREDENTIALS as a prophet of the living God, Nahum was also an accomplished taunter. In fact, the seventh-century prophet is perhaps the preeminent taunter in the Bible, offering more taunts per square inch of scroll than any other Biblical author. Scholars have identified four taunts in a book of just three chapters.[1] In chapter 2, for example, we have what is known as the lion's taunt in which the prophet employs the national symbol of Assyria, the mighty lion, to mock and to humiliate those enemies with a portrait of their downfall. "Where is the lions' den," the prophet asks, "the feeding place of the young lions, where the lion and the lioness went, where his cubs were, with none to disturb? The lion tore enough for his cubs and strangled prey for his lionesses; he filled his caves with prey and his dens with torn flesh. . . . I will cut off your prey from the earth, and the voice of your messengers shall no longer be heard" (2:11–13). The prophet depicts the Assyrian Empire as no longer a fierce and powerful lion but as a starved, frustrated, emaciated beast, unable to feed its starving lionesses or its hungry children. Later, in chapter 3 we have the harlot taunt (vv. 4–7), the historical taunt (vv. 8–13), and the locust taunt (vv. 14–17), each of which in its own way insults, derides, and humiliates what was in Nahum's day the greatest empire in the known world.

However, the prophet doesn't wait until chapter 2 to take up his taunt against Nineveh. The opening oracle itself, though formally a war oracle, is issued in the same spirit and with the same goal of mocking, ridiculing, and

413

humiliating the mighty Assyrian Empire. Students of the Psalms have observed that there are different types of divine warrior hymns. One type calls on God for help and provision in a time of crisis (e.g., Psalm 7).[2] A second type is probably meant to be sung (or envisioned as being sung) during battle and emphasizes the Lord's protection from harm (e.g., Psalm 91). The third type, however, was probably composed to be sung after a battle was won because it is a song of celebration and praise for the Lord's victory (e.g., Psalm 98).

It is striking that Nahum's opening hymn fits this third type.[3] When Assyria is at her strongest, when nothing in the world appears to rival or threaten her for dominance and glory, Nahum sings a victory song to the Lord.[4] We might wonder: Too soon? Nahum's hymn would be presumptuous and petulant if it were not prophetic. Nahum taunts Assyria, not because he has some insider knowledge about the empire's weaknesses but because he knows the Lord his God. Specifically, Nahum knows that the Lord is a divine warrior who fights against those who challenge his sovereignty or who threaten those who belong to him. One commentator summarized the matter well when he wrote, "What is said about Nineveh is based on what is known about YHWH."[5]

Like most of the so-called minor prophets, very little is known about the prophet Nahum. We know he was from a city called Elkosh (Nahum 1:1), though the exact location of the city is unknown. We know his name, Nahum, means "Comfort."[6] At first glance, the prophet's name seems ironic because Nahum offers very little in his prophecies that is explicitly comforting. Nahum is almost exclusively a prophet of pure and unrelenting judgment. The entire collection of oracles is in fact a sustained declaration of God's imminent judgment upon Nineveh, the capital city of the Assyrian Empire. But Nahum's name is not ironic because, when rightly understood, his message—for all of its words of judgment and woe—is, at the end of the day, a message of comfort for God's people.

Is there any comfort to be had in the here and now when you are languishing day in and day out under the oppressive yoke of foreign rule? Nahum's answer is a resounding yes! The prophet's war oracles, victory songs, and taunts all preach a message of deep and profound comfort to God's people in Nahum's day and to God's people in our day because that message announces with the utmost certainty that God will defeat and, in a very real way, has defeated all his and our enemies.

### A God of Vengeance (1:2–3a)

The prophet goes to great lengths to underscore the identity of the One before whom Assyria will fall. Three times in just one verse, the covenant name of

God is used, hitting readers (or hearers) almost like a drumbeat keeping time for an approaching army: "The LORD . . . the LORD . . . the LORD . . ." (Nahum 1:2). The cause of Assyria's demise will not be the weakness of her gods or the failure of her leaders; neither will it be through the strength of Israel or any other geopolitical force (though these will be used in the process). The prophet wants to make the point abundantly clear that the cause of Assyria's destruction will be none other than the might and will of Yahweh himself. It is with the Lord, the God of Israel, that Assyria will have to contend and by whom Assyria will be brought low.

This would have come as a surprise not only to the Assyrians but to many Israelites as well. A small and comparatively insignificant nation-state, Israel would probably be the last place the Assyrian emperor would expect to become a viable threat to his kingdom. And Israel, for the most part, would have thought the same thing. *Who is Israel and who is Israel's God that Assyria should be afraid?*

This question recalls a dramatic scene in the book of Exodus when Moses confronts Pharaoh with the divine command, "Thus says the LORD, the God of Israel, 'Let my people go'" (Exodus 5:1), to which Pharoah responds, "Who is the LORD, that I should obey his voice and let Israel go? I do not know the LORD, and moreover, I will not let Israel go" (v. 2).

"Who is the LORD?" Over the course of the next nine chapters in Exodus, the Lord answers this question in the most spectacular way. Pharoah soon discovers the identity of the Lord, the God of Israel, when plague after plague decimates his nation and humiliates Egypt's so-called gods.

Through the ten plagues that decimated Egypt, Yahweh revealed himself to Pharaoh more in his actions than in his words—and so he will again with Nineveh, when "he make[s] a complete end of his adversaries" (Nahum 1:8). Who is this Lord with whom Assyria will have to contend? Nahum answers this question in his opening hymn: "The LORD is a jealous and avenging God; the LORD is avenging and wrathful; the LORD takes vengeance on his adversaries and keeps wrath for his enemies" (v. 2). Three times the prophet declares that God is a God of vengeance (or "an avenger"). This is the principal characteristic of Yahweh that governs the entire book: the Lord is an avenger. Though some may regard vengeance as unbecoming of God, there is nothing inherently immoral in the action itself.[7] Vengeance has been defined by one scholar as "harsh punitive retribution in retaliation for wrongs committed against one."[8] When exacted by humans, vengeance may be twisted toward excessive or unjust ends, but when executed by God, "whose rule is the source of law," the punishment is perfectly fitting to the offense.[9]

In Nahum's hymn, God's vengeance is first connected with his jealousy, then with his wrath, and finally with his enemies. We might understand this as the cause, the effect, and the object of God's vengeance. Like vengeance, ascribing to God the attribute of jealousy likewise strikes many Christians as unseemly. This is no doubt due to the negative connotations that the word *jealousy* has for us. Jealousy, for us, carries the connotations of unfounded suspicions, pettiness, insecurity, and being illegitimately territorial. Experiences with jealous boyfriends or jealous coworkers come to mind. None of these, however, are rightly predicated of God, nor are they an aspect of divine jealousy. For this reason, many translations and commentaries will render the Hebrew word with the perfectly reasonable substitute "zealous."[10] However, many have pointed out that in certain circumstances, jealousy is far from a negative emotion; it is rather the most noble and fitting response to certain realities such as, for example, threats to loved ones or marital betrayal.[11] We might think of a wife's jealousy for her husband's faithfulness, a public figure jealous to preserve his honor, or parents' jealousy for their child's affection.

In the Bible, God's jealousy is first and foremost for his honor; secondarily, though connected, God's jealousy is for his people to whom he bound himself in covenant and for whom the incarnate Son would one day die. God's jealousy is not tainted by sin or suspicion. It is not excessive or in any way improper. God's jealousy, rather, is the fitting passion he has for his own honor and for the people on whom he has set his love. God's jealousy is perfectly pure and perfectly appropriate to who he is as Creator and Redeemer. When his honor is compromised or his people to whom he has bound himself in covenant are threatened, God manifests himself as justly and properly jealous.

If God's jealousy is the cause of God's vengeance, then God's wrath is its effect. Nahum declares, "The Lord takes vengeance on his adversaries and keeps wrath for his enemies" (v. 2). The wrath of God is his righteous anger that is realized in his executing judgment against those who have set themselves in opposition to him as their Creator. Wrath is the only proper response for a holy God to make against the wicked and the rebellious. God's wrath is an expression of his perfect and exacting justice, and the prophet tells us that this is stored up (1:2, 3); that is, it is awaiting the day when the floodgates will open and God will bring a complete end to his enemies, as the prophet says, "[pursuing them] into darkness" (v. 8).

God was not unaware of Assyria's cruelties or of Israel's afflictions at the hands of this cruel empire. God sees and God knows, and, though patient, he stores up his wrath until the right time. So, the prophet says, "The Lord is slow to anger and great in power, and the Lord will by no means clear the guilty" (v. 3).

With these words, Nahum is clearly alluding to one of the most famous and pivotal moments in redemptive history, the moment in which the Lord God revealed his name to Moses on Mount Sinai. Following on the heels of Israel's sin in worshiping God by means of a golden calf, God heard Moses's prayers for Israel and relented from the judgment he had announced against his covenant people. This is the context of God's great revelation to his servant Moses:

> The Lord descended in the cloud and stood with [Moses] there, and proclaimed the name of the Lord. The Lord passed before him and proclaimed, "The Lord, the Lord, a God merciful and gracious, slow to anger, and abounding in steadfast love and faithfulness, keeping steadfast love for thousands, forgiving iniquity and transgression and sin, but who will by no means clear the guilty, visiting the iniquity of the fathers on the children and the children's children, to the third and fourth generation." And Moses quickly bowed his head toward the earth and worshiped. (Exodus 34:5–8)

This unprecedented revelation of the name of God in Exodus emphasizes God's grace and the forgiveness of his people and his unwavering commitment to justice. Commenting on this scene, Thomas Renz writes, "Indeed, it may be the main contribution of this passage in the context of Exod 32–34 to affirm that God both forgives and certainly does not absolve. His relationship to Israel is restored by forgiveness, but the rebellion does not go unpunished."[12] God's mercy does not cancel out his wrath, but as his revelation to Moses implies, it is greater than his wrath, extending to thousands with the forgiveness of iniquity and transgression and sin.

Years later Nahum recalls and adapts this great revelation to Moses. However, Nahum replaces Moses's reference to God's abounding or great steadfast love with abounding or great power (Nahum 1:3). The God who is infinitely patient, Nahum reminds us, is also infinitely powerful. God's patience is not intended to underwrite sin but to provide occasion for repentance. One commentator put it well: "God's patience, not powerlessness, is responsible for the impression of divine inactivity in the face of evil."[13] Nahum sees a day in which God's patience will come to an end, and the Lord will come with infinite power against the guilty.

Nahum's confidence that Assyria would come to ruin was not simply the product of deduction: *God hates injustice, and Assyria is unjust. God also hates violence, and Assyria is violent.* All of this was true, but there were a lot of violent nations and a lot of unjust peoples in the ancient world, just as there are today. Why Assyria? Because Assyria was an increasing threat to God's people. Though God had appointed Assyria as "the rod of my anger" (Isaiah 10:5) to execute his judgment against his people for their own wickedness, Assyria executed her calling with an excessive and exploitive cruelty. Years later, God would characterize Assyria's cruelties, saying, "While I was angry but a little, they furthered the disaster" (Zechariah 1:15).

The whirlwind of divine judgment (Nahum 1:3) about to be unleashed on Assyria preaches not only the message that God hates injustice but also that God has bound himself to a people. God has so tightly and inextricably bound himself to his people that their enemies become his enemies and his enemies their enemies. As Assyria's grip gets tighter and tighter on Judah, the prophet understands that God's people and God's promises are under attack. God had promised that through the tribe of Judah he would raise up a descendant as a king who would rule his people (Genesis 49:10; 2 Samuel 7:4–17). It was when Pharaoh started drowning Israel's baby boys (Exodus 1:22) that Yahweh put on his armor and revealed himself as the divine warrior. So too in Nahum's day. When the Assyrian threat becomes great, God dons his armor. God mounts his storm-chariot. He paves a way before him in the midst of the sea. He takes a step; the mountains shake; the earth heaves before his majesty and anger (Nahum 1:3–5).

Many today think of a vengeful God as an antiquated, obsolete, or even primitive conception of God, a conception no longer relevant or appropriate for modern, enlightened men and women. Others think that God's vengeance is made obsolete through the revelation of God as love in the New Testament. Such views fail to reckon with the full witness of sacred Scripture. They reveal an embarrassingly blatant instance of mankind creating God in his own image instead of receiving God's revelation of himself in his Word and in his Son.

The God of the New Testament is no less a God of vengeance than the God of the Old. John the Baptist denounced the scribes and Pharisees seeking his baptism, saying, "You brood of vipers! Who warned you to flee from the wrath to come?" (Matthew 3:7). Jesus overturned the tables in the temple and drove out the money-changers with a whip (John 2:13–17) in fulfillment, John tells us, of Psalm 69:9: "Zeal for your house has consumed me." Jesus did not do this as a model for Christian ethics but as a manifestation of a divine wrath as pure as it is powerful. Paul wrote to the Roman churches, "Beloved, never avenge yourselves, but leave it to the wrath of God, for it is written, 'Vengeance is mine, I will repay, says the Lord'" (Romans 12:19).

The God of the New Testament is no less vengeful than the God of the Old. It is, in fact, the same God who reveals his unchanging and unchangeable character to his creation in word and deed. Both testaments, Old and New, univocally testify to a holy God who will one day come in judgment against his enemies. Though he is a God of mercy, "slow to anger," he is also a God who will "by no means clear the guilty" (Nahum 1:3). Elizabeth Achtemeier puts it well when she writes, "The God portrayed here is really God, different from all lesser imitations and different too from those impotent idols that we often project upon our universe."[14]

This is the God with whom Assyria, Israel, and we will have to do. In Nahum's opening poem we are confronted head-on with the true God, the living God who is both wrathful against his enemies and merciful to all those who find refuge in him.

## A God of War (1:3b–5, 8)

Though highly original in his expression, Nahum nevertheless employs conventional images of the arrival of the divine warrior. When God comes as the judge of Nineveh, the entire creation convulses. Nahum declares that Bashan and Carmel, two regions known for their rich pastures and verdant forests, will "wither" before him (v. 4).[15] Rivers will dry up, mountains once thought immovable will quake, and hills will melt before his awesome presence. "The earth heaves before him, the world and all who dwell in it" (v. 5). When its Creator appears, the creation trembles.

The prophet represents the breakdown of the created order in the form of a poem, writing the victory song of verses 1–8 as a broken acrostic.[16] Acrostics, which usually employ the letters of the Hebrew alphabet as the first letter of each line of poetry, are used throughout the Bible as a formal way of representing completeness or wholeness as, for example, in the book of Lamentations (1—4), Psalm 111, and perhaps most famously, Psalm 119. In Nahum, however, the prophet drops a letter and breaks off his acrostic at the Hebrew equivalent of the English letter *L*. Though some have doubted whether there is an acrostic in Nahum at all, many (myself included) see in the prophet's poem a creative and powerful representation of the created order, the world as we know it crumbling before our very eyes as order (represented by the Hebrew alphabet) gives way to disorder and chaos.[17]

However, the master poet not only employs vivid forms and imagery to depict the power of the Lord's advent, but Nahum also employs a number of allusions designed to convey God's purpose in his advent. When the prophet says, "His way is in whirlwind and storm, and the clouds are the dust of his feet" (Nahum 1:3), he is reminding Israel that Yahweh, not Baal or Adad, is the God of the storm.[18] It is likely that Nahum is recalling Elijah's contest with the 450 prophets of Baal, when the latter were unable to produce fire from Heaven and were subsequently destroyed in an act of holy war (1 Kings 18:20–40). When Nahum says, "He rebukes the sea and makes it dry; he dries up all the rivers" (1:4), he is of course recalling God's greatest act of redemption, the deliverance of his people from Egyptian slavery. Similarly, Nahum 1:8, "With an overflowing flood, he will make a complete end of the adversaries," clearly has in view God's triumph over Pharaoh at the Red Sea but may additionally signal a reversal of Isaiah's prophecy that foretold Assyria overwhelming Judah like a flood rising up to its neck (Isaiah 8:7, 8).[19]

What is the prophet doing with these allusions to Israel's past? The prophet's purpose is to connect Nineveh's imminent destruction to God's mighty acts of salvation in the past. In each of these events alluded to, God judged and saved; he destroyed and delivered. God judged the world in the flood but saved Noah. God judged the prophets of Baal but delivered Elijah and, through him, Israel. God judged Egypt but saved Israel. Nahum points his hearers to the past so that they might remember this pattern of deliverance and judgment, and so that they might grow in their confidence that God will so act on their behalf again. Nahum is confident that God will judge the enemies of his people in the future as he has in the past. The Lord God who time and again has donned his armor and defeated Israel's enemies in ages past will do so again, for he is the same today, yesterday, and forever (Hebrews 13:8).

When we read the Gospel accounts of Jesus against the background of the Old Testament, especially the Old Testament prophets, we see that Jesus came as this divine warrior. Jesus came as Lord and King to reclaim what the devil had stolen and to restore what sin and death had destroyed. In his earthly life Jesus entered into open combat with demons, overcame temptation, and battled sickness and disease. In the end Jesus conquered even death itself. Jesus came to pronounce judgment and curse on those who opposed God's kingdom, many of whom were the religious leaders of his day. But ultimately Jesus came not just to bring God's judgment but to undergo God's judgment. The Son of God became a curse so that those who have entrusted themselves to him by faith might pass through wrath to grace, from death to life.

While Christians can and should look back to these great acts of deliverance—Noah, Egypt, the Red Sea, the Philistines, Assyria, and numerous others—it is ultimately in the cross of Calvary that we find our surest comfort and unassailable hope. At the cross, God did battle for all who look to him in faith. Jesus was wounded that we might be healed. Jesus died that we might live. When we consider our world, when we consider our lives, it is often difficult for us to see God's victory over evil. The wicked seem to prosper. Christ's Church is persecuted around the world and is given over to division, infighting, and scandal. Our own lives show repeated failures in our attempts at holiness and obedience. And we wonder, understandably, *Where is God in all this?*

Nahum preached to a downtrodden, disoriented, despairing people that despite appearances, Assyria doesn't win. Yahweh wins. We in our day preach to a downtrodden, disoriented, despairing Church, "Rejoice, be of good cheer—your sin doesn't win, Satan doesn't win, even death itself doesn't win. Jesus wins." Jesus triumphed at the cross, decisively defeating sin, death, and the devil. And Jesus will one day come again to make all things new, just as he has promised.

### A God of Refuge (1:6, 7)

In Nahum 1:3, we read, "The LORD will by no means clear the guilty." Though Israel knew God to be patient and merciful, they also knew that their God is a God who judges sin. Israel's history and theology taught them that when God shows up in judgment, they themselves are by no means exempt. As the history of Judah would soon attest, God enters into judgment not only with Judah's enemies but with Judah as well. Just as he did with the northern kingdom of Israel in 722 B.C., as Judah's sin waxed stronger and stronger, God eventually would hand them over to their enemies, this time the Babylonians, who would devastate their land, city, and temple and then carry them off into exile.

God's people are not exempt from God's vengeance, wrath, and judgment. In less than fifty years after Nahum's prophecies, the prophet Jeremiah and the prophet Ezekiel would declare the destruction not of Assyria or Assyria's imperial successor, Babylon, but of Jerusalem. Why? Because Judah had become like Assyria. Her capital, Jerusalem, became a "bloody city, all full of lies and plunder—no end to the prey" (Nahum 3:1).

In 1:6, the prophet asks what is arguably the most important question anyone can ask: "Who can stand before his indignation? Who can endure the heat of his anger? His wrath is poured out like fire, and rocks are broken into pieces by him." Who can stand when the Lord comes in judgment? That question is asked throughout the Bible in a variety of ways. It is a question that has at its heart the longing of the human soul to experience the presence of God's blessedness, and yet, on the other hand, the deep and unshakable understanding that God cannot abide sin in his holy presence.

Like other Biblical authors who contemplate this question, Nahum provides a surprising response: "The LORD is good, a stronghold in the day of trouble; he knows those who take refuge in him" (v. 7). With these words the prophet sets before us the most counterintuitive idea. In the ancient polytheistic world, when a god was angry with you, you would typically seek the help and favor of another god. But for the people of Israel, who knew only one God—the true God—where could they run? Where could they go to escape the day of trouble? In verse 7 God says, in effect, "Run to me." Those who flee to the Lord in faith find him to be "a stronghold," safety and security from the water and fire of his judgment. In this we discover that God is not only a God of infinite wrath but is, at the same time, a God of infinite goodness and mercy. One commentator put it well when he wrote, "The goodness of YHWH ... is affirmed here not over against his wrath but because of it. YHWH's anger ensures that evil does not retain the upper hand, and thus he proves a reliable refuge for those who entrust themselves to him."[20]

The prophet provides a theological lens through which he wants his audience to view God's imminent judgment of Assyria. Nahum depicts the fall of Assyria with language that throughout the Bible is associated with God's judgment on the last day. Every Israelite knew there would come a day in which Yahweh would judge the nations; and when that day came, the entire cosmos would be turned upside down, the creation would be shaken to its core, and the natural order would cease to function as typically experienced (e.g., the sun is darkened). It is striking that Nahum describes God's destruction of Assyria in similar language when he says,

> He dries up all the rivers;
> Bashan and Carmel wither;
>   the bloom of Lebanon withers.
> The mountains quake before him;
>   the hills melt;
> the earth heaves before him,
>   the world and all who dwell in it. (vv. 4–5)

In the destruction of Nineveh, in the overthrow of Assyria and all their wickedness, God was giving Israel a foretaste, a picture, of a great day of judgment.[21] This will be a day in which God will sit in judgment on the nations, and he will judge every man, woman, and child according to what they have done. What hope did Israel have? What hope do we have?

It is important to note that this isn't the first time that a great day of judgment erupted into history.[22] The flood in the days of Noah was an inbreaking of judgment day. Israel's conquest of Canaan likewise was an inbreaking of judgment day. But it would not be the last. Babylon's destruction of Jerusalem would be presented in a similar fashion. Most importantly, however, when Jesus hung and died on the cross, we're told, "there was darkness over the land until the ninth hour. . . . And Jesus cried out again with a loud voice and yielded up his spirit. . . . And the earth shook, and the rocks were split. The tombs also were opened. And many bodies of the saints who had fallen asleep were raised" (Matthew 27:45, 50–52). Why was the sky darkened? Why did the earth shake? When Jesus died, God showed up as the divine warrior, as the Judge of all the earth pouring out his wrath on his Son for the sins of his people. Christians must never make the mistake of thinking that God does not judge his people, that believers are somehow exempt from divine judgment. The good news of the gospel is that when Jesus died on the cross, the righteous for the unrighteous, God judged the sin of his people once and for all. The God who must punish sin did so in a substitute whose death is of infinite value. On the cross Jesus cried out, "It is finished" (John 19:30). And so it was. The penalty was paid, the judgment was rendered, not against the offenders but against the offended. God himself in the person of his Son bore the penalty for the sins of his people. There is now, therefore, no word of judgment left for those who are united to Christ by faith, for to be so is to be united to Jesus in his death. The same God who is the Judge of the world is also the Refuge of the world to all who flee to him in faith.

## Nahum's Song: A Call to Courage (1:8)

If Nahum had to exhibit a staggering amount of courage to prophesy against Assyria, how much more courage would he need to taunt and mock her? His message at this time would certainly have been opposed by the ruling classes of Jerusalem who, generally speaking, wanted to curry favor with the Assyrians. If word got back to the Assyrians that there was an upstart prophet declaring their demise, the prophet may have suffered a fate none of us would care to imagine. Most cities and nations that submitted to Assyria's yoke did so because of the stories they heard, stories of men being flayed alive and impaled on stakes, still breathing. Yet Nahum spoke. Nahum *contra mundum*. Nahum spoke because the Spirit of God compelled him.

Nahum spoke with courage and conviction because he knew that the strength of the One who could break the yoke off Israel's neck was greater than the strength of the one who placed it there. He knew that standing above and behind the mighty Assyrian Empire was the even greater might of Yahweh, the God of Israel. Israel's God was able to return the terror, humiliation, and shame back upon the heads of the Assyrians, and this is precisely what the prophet heralded when he declared, "With an overflowing flood he will make a complete end of the adversaries, and will pursue his enemies into darkness" (Nahum 1:8).

When the nations looked at Assyria, it saw the greatest empire the world had ever known. Assyria descended upon her victims like a flood, completely overwhelming and utterly destroying any who dared to oppose her. She was a seemingly invincible empire whose might was matched only by her cruelty and before whom the only safe and rational response was homage, obeisance, and obedience. But when Nahum looked at Assyria, he saw yet another expression of the seed of the serpent, a wicked and arrogant people who defied the true and living God. So he moved forward with courage. Nahum's courage was not in himself but in his God, who he knew would fight and defeat all who stood opposed to him and who threatened his saving purposes. Christians today have the same reason for courage as we have inherited the same gracious promises and find refuge in the same God of vengeance and mercy.

### Nahum's Song: A Call to Hope

Commenting on Nahum's opening portrait, Klaas Spronk insightfully remarks, "The message of [God's] severe judgment is a comfort to those oppressed by evil powers and a source of hope for those who fear that these powers are invincible."[23] Embedded in Nahum's victory song, as well as in each of his taunts, was the conviction that these embodiments of wickedness and evil would soon fall to ruin. Nahum's victory song summoned Israel to hope, and it summons us to hope as well because it envisions a day in which God will remove every burden and affliction that we bear. Every threat, trial, and temptation will one day be destroyed, and God will say, "Though I have afflicted you, I will afflict you no more. And now I will break the yoke from off you and burst your bonds apart" (vv. 12, 13). Nahum's poem is a call to courage precisely because there's a reason to hope, and the hope is not in ourselves but in God, who has promised to make all things new.

When we think of the forces arrayed against Christ's Church—whether they be cultural, social, economic, or political—it's tempting to wonder with despair, *What chance does the Church have in the face of such power and hostility?* In Nahum's victory song, sung long before there was any evidence of coming victory, we have a powerful reminder that Christians have reason to hope in even the most troubled times. We have a reason for courage, poise, and even joy in the face of the greatest threats this world might supply. Our hope is not in the greatness of our plans or the genius of our strategies but in the greatness of our God and his power to save to the uttermost. Our hope is a sure hope because, in the resurrection of Christ, God has revealed his power and his purpose to triumph over all his enemies and to supply a refuge in the day of trouble for all those who flee to him for mercy.

# 45

# The Exalted Will Fall, and the Fallen Will Be Exalted

NAHUM 1:9—2:2

WHEN IT COMES TO ISRAEL'S PROPHETS, most of us no doubt sympathize with Martin Luther, who once remarked, "They have a queer way of talking, like people who, instead of proceeding in an orderly manner, ramble off from one thing to the next, so that you cannot make head or tail of them or see what they are getting at."[1] Israel's prophets abound with obscure references, abrupt transitions, and complicated figures of speech—all of which make this corpus of literature at times incredibly difficult to interpret.

Beginning in Nahum 1:9, we come to what some have argued is one of the most obscure and difficult passages in the entire prophetic corpus.[2] Questions abound. Why is Nineveh never named?[3] Who exactly is the "worthless counselor" (v. 11)? Where does the passage end? These are genuine difficulties. One commentator in fact has likened the reading of this passage to walking into the middle of a courtroom drama unfamiliar with the details of the case and ignorant of what has transpired so far. We hear the judge issuing verdicts and awarding damages, and we as readers are left to figure out what is going on with little guidance or explanation.

However, despite the numerous difficulties and lingering questions, the basic message of the text is sufficiently clear. The prophet announces that a day is coming in which God will humble the exalted and exalt the humble. When this day arrives, God will bring about a great reversal of fortunes. Those who in pride and arrogance have exalted themselves against God will be brought low, and those who have entrusted themselves to God and who, as the

Apostle Peter says, have humbled themselves "under the mighty hand of God" (1 Peter 5:6) will be exalted. This great reversal will happen, Nahum tells us, not because the universe has built into it a principle of karma but because the Lord himself has purposed and promised to do it.

The prophet Nahum, ministering in Judah in the mid- to late seventh century B.C., delivered this message to instill confidence and hope in difficult, uncertain, and perilous times. His goal was to remind God's people that their present afflictions will one day be turned to joy and that at the far side of this life, characterized as it is by a cross, lies an unimaginable glory for those whose hope is in God. At its heart Nahum's prophecy is a summons to faith in the character of God as a promise-making and promise-keeping God. It is a call to faith in the power of God: the One who has made such wonderful promises is able to accomplish all that he has promised to do. Though there is not a clear sense of progression in the prophet's oracles, they do nevertheless come in pairs; each oracle of judgment is followed by an oracle of salvation.[4] Happily, for preachers at least, there are three pairs in Nahum 1:9—2:2.

### Remove the Source of His People's Affliction (1:9–13)

The prophet opens with a question: "What do you plot against the LORD?" (Nahum 1:9).[5] Likely a rhetorical question, it is meant to emphasize the fact that whatever scheme Nineveh has hatched—to use Judah or to oppress Judah or to conquer Judah—will most certainly fail.[6] It will fail, the prophet says, because God has roused himself to fight with and for his people. God will bring an end to all that troubles his people. This rhetorical question, at the very least, exposes the vanity and futility of Assyria's plots against Judah. But the lack of naming perhaps broadens the referent, and thus we are on solid ground to expand the question "What do you plot against the LORD?" to include any and all who threaten God's people. They may expect only one fate: destruction.

But Nahum's question is designed to accomplish something else as well. The reality is that the Ninevites probably never really thought much about Yahweh, the God of Israel. In fact, Assurbanipal had likely never even heard of Yahweh. So we can imagine Nineveh replying to the prophet, "Plot against Yahweh? We've never heard of Yahweh!" But with this question the prophet is setting world history—all of the geopolitical maneuvering of kings and nations—in its proper theological context. When the Assyrian emperor looked at Judah, he saw another pawn on the chessboard, a minor city-state to be subjugated and exploited, intimidated and manipulated for his own purposes and his own pleasure. But Nahum reminds God's people that when the Assyrian emperor touches Judah he is in fact touching the apple of God's eye. In his oppression of God's covenant people, he has in fact set himself in rebellion against the King of the universe. Nineveh's plot against Israel is a plot against the Lord, and thus the prophet declares the futility and certain failure of all such schemes.

There is a hint of irony in all of this because Judah was a vassal state of the great Assyrian Empire, and arguably the greatest sin that any vassal could commit against her suzerain was the crime of treason. Any sort of rebellion against the great king would bring about crushing military action against the upstart vassal kingdom. In Assyria's estimation, they were the suzerain and Judah was the rebellious vassal. The prophet, however, uses a different calculus, and by it he reminds Israel of the reality of God. Assyria is subject to an even greater king, and her plots against God's people are plots against God himself. "What do you plot against *the Lord*?" (Nahum 1:9). The Lord will respond as any earthly suzerain would respond to a rebellious vassal king: "He will make a complete end; trouble will not rise up a second time" (v. 9).[7] The suzerain's retributive judgment will result in a comprehensive and decisive destruction of the mighty Assyrian Empire. How the tables have turned!

This trouble finds its epicenter not only in a nation (Assyria) or in its capital city (Nineveh) but also in an individual. Though in all likelihood a reference to the Assyrian king, possibly the great Assurbanipal, this unnamed individual is simply described as "a worthless counselor" (v. 11). The word "worthless" here may be derived from a proper name that originally referred to a demon, Belial. The word, however, has taken on connotation of that which is vile and rubbish. The plotting leader of Nineveh, with all his wealth and power and with all his idols and with whatever demonic forces lie behind them, has taken his stand against the Lord. Thus, despite all his external glory, he is in reality worthless and vile. But central to this *inclusio* identifying the plot (v. 9) and the plotters (v. 11) comes their fate (v. 10).

In Nahum 1:10a, the prophet likens Nineveh to an entangled thornbush and to a drunkard drinking—images of someone or something dangerous to approach, much less challenge and contradict. But then the significance of the simile changes. Nahum says, "They are consumed like stubble fully dried" (v. 10b). They are a danger not only to others but to themselves as well. Their plots will indeed bring destruction, but they will destroy themselves as they are consumed like a thornbush set ablaze. God regards Assyria's plotting against his people as an affront to himself, and he responds with a crushing and devastating judgment. It is a judgment that is comprehensive and efficient. Assyria will not live to fight another day.

But we see that the word of judgment against Nineveh is at the same time a word of salvation and deliverance for Judah. In the words of O. Palmer Robertson, "The judgment on Nineveh must be viewed from the perspective of God's intent to show mercy to his people. He responds to their cry for deliverance from oppression by sending judgment on their enemies."[8] This is evident in verse 12 as God shifts his address from Nineveh to Judah. Nineveh is now referred to as "they" and Israel, his covenant people, as "you":

> Though they are at full strength and many,
>   they will be cut down and pass away.
> Though I have afflicted you,
>   I will afflict you no more.
> And now I will break his yoke from off you
>   and will burst your bonds apart. (vv. 12, 13)

God announces to his people a gospel word. God reminds Israel that he is in control and in fact has been all along. By all appearances, according to Israel's day-to-day experience, Assyria was in perfect and complete control of the entire world as they knew it. Assyria was effectively sovereign not only over Israel but over most of the ancient Near Eastern world. But God reminds Israel that Assyria is the affliction that he has appointed for his people, and he, at the right time, will remove this affliction.

Assyria, by this period of history, had been an oppressive presence in the life of Judah for likely over a century. Many Israelites lived their entire lives under the shadow of Assyria's cruel suzerainty. The constant and ever-increasing tribute demanded by their Assyrian overlords, the military conscription requiring them to fight for their oppressors, and the threat of a devastating military attack should they not submit to every demand would have very much felt like a yoke on the neck of an ox or like shackles on the wrist and neck of a prisoner.[9] Yet God announces, "No more" (v. 12).

We don't know the exact dates of Nahum's prophetic ministry, but verse 12 suggests that it was when Assyria was at the height of her power: "Though they are at full strength and many . . ." This comment has led many scholars to place the prophecy during the reign of Assurbanipal (or perhaps immediately after), who ruled over Assyria when she was at the zenith of her power and influence.[10] The significance of this moment in history is that Nahum's prophecy of the utter, complete, humiliating destruction of Nineveh would have seemed like the rantings of a madman, deluded and declaring as certain that which was patently absurd. It is important to remember that when Nahum was announcing with certainty what was, from a human standpoint, an impossibility, he was not working with inside information about Assyria's political future. Rather, Nahum was simply trusting God's word over all appearances to the contrary.

Nahum's prophecy would have seemed like an impossibility. But in Nahum's day it was not only a promise of a brighter future but an invitation, even more, a summons, to faith in Israel's difficult present. What seemed like an impossibility at the time was fulfilled within fifty years at most, maybe less. In the year 612 B.C., God brought the armies of the Babylonians and the Medes against Nineveh, and she was utterly destroyed, never to rise again. Though in the eyes of the world the Assyrian Empire appeared invincible, in the eyes of God they were like grass to be mowed down (Nahum 1:12) and like a yoke to be broken apart (v. 13).

The prophet saw in Nineveh what David saw in Goliath: an affront to the majesty of Israel's God and a threat to God's people. Like David standing before Goliath, who was hurling taunts and threats (1 Samuel 17:45ff.), Nahum adopts the same posture of faith that produces courage and confidence (not to mention taunts and threats of its own). Nahum declares the ultimate and certain destruction of the seemingly invincible Assyria.

In this we hear the same summons to faith. We too read promises in Scripture that we have a hard time believing. By all appearances, this world and the things of this world are all there is, and yet Jesus tells us, "Lay up for yourselves treasures in heaven, where neither moth nor rust destroys and where thieves do not break in and steal" (Matthew 6:20). By all appearances, death is final. Yet Jesus tells us, "I am the resurrection and the life. Whoever believes in me, though he die, yet shall he live; and everyone who lives and believes in me shall never die" (John 11:25, 26). Our consciences condemn us, saying, "Your sins are too much and too bad to be forgiven," and yet God's Word tells us, "As far as is the east is from the west, so far does he remove our transgressions from us" (Psalm 103:12). Nahum's prophecy stands as a challenge to believers of every generation to trust God's word over and against all appearances to the contrary. This is the life of faith, trusting that God's word is true and living in light of his promises that will never fail.

### Establish His People in Eternal Worship (1:14, 15)

God's judgment now shifts from Assyria's rebellion to Assyria's pride. When God declares, "No more shall your name be perpetuated; from the house of your gods I will cut off the carved image and the metal image. I will make your grave, for you are vile" (Nahum 1:14), he is in a sense taking aim at those symbols of power, greatness, and permanence in which the Assyrians trusted.

Like the builders of Babel who sought through their building project to make a name for themselves (Genesis 11:4), the Assyrians—through their military conquests, through their massive building projects, and through their glorious temples and idols of their gods—have sought to make a name for themselves that would last forever. They have been seeking to achieve a type of immortality through their imperial greatness.

The cutting off of Assyria's name is likely a reference to the king's progeny who would perpetuate the king's name and, relatedly, the king's empire.[11] Assyria's kingship, Assyria's gods, Assyria's temple—these were the central institutions that gave Assyria her identity; without them, Assyria would cease to exist. This is precisely what God declares when he says, "I will make your grave, for you are vile." In other words, God says, "I will bury your defiled corpse." In the ancient world there were few things more dishonoring than being buried by your enemy in a place or in a manner that suggested defilement. This is not an honorable death. This is not a noble death.[12] Nineveh had become a symbol of utter wickedness, defilement, and impurity—all that is opposed to God, who is goodness, truth, purity, and life. Consequently, God will bury Assyria in an ignominious grave appropriate to her character, and the result will be absolute disgrace. With language and imagery reminiscent of the curses that Assyria would threaten against her vassals, Nahum announces that this once-great city will become the object of divine cursing and human derision.[13]

But this raises a question: What is Judah's role in all of this? Will Judah be the instrument of God's judgment on Nineveh? Will Judah be God's right-hand man in combat? The prophet declares: "Behold, upon the mountains, the feet of him who brings good news, who publishes peace!" (Nahum 1:15a). Here we see Judah's role. Judah is not the hero, the victor, the one who will triumph over wicked Assyria. Judah's role is passive and receptive. She will receive the good news of what God has done. The people of Judah have no role in this victory over evil; rather, they are the beneficiaries of its peace. If any role may be assigned, Judah is given the task of proclamation—the people are to declare the glad tidings of what God has done for them.[14]

How do God's people respond to the good news of what God has done for us? The answer Nahum gives is worship. What is worship but a rendering of all praise, all glory, all honor to God alone? It is lifting up our voices in thanksgiving because we have nothing with which we can repay God or in any way contribute to our salvation. This is the essence of what Judah is called to do: "Keep your feasts O Judah; fulfill your vows, for never again shall the worthless pass through you; he is utterly cut off" (1:15b). These vows were presumably vows promised should God deliver Judah from her oppressors, and these feasts were feasts of sacrifice and celebration for God's victory on Judah's behalf.

To be sure, the next-to-last line of chapter 1 ("never again shall the worthless pass through you") might, on first reading, raise some eyebrows for those who know that in less than fifty years the Babylonians marched through Judah, destroying her holy city and razing her temple to the ground. However, this categorical promise likely has in view the ultimate and permanent demise of "worthless" Assyria, who would not continue to harass and oppress Israel after her own defeat in 612 B.C. Nevertheless, in keeping with the symbolic world of the prophet (not to mention the Old Testament generally), we are on safe ground to see in Assyria's demise a symbol and foreshadowing of that ultimate destruction of all God's enemies and the permanent liberation of all God's people.[15] This, in our day as in Nahum's day, is cause for feasting and celebration with thanksgiving to the Lord.

This in fact is always the response of God's people when they behold his salvation. We may think of the numerous psalms of thanksgiving that preserve for us these great responses to God's provision for his people. In Psalm 18, for instance, Israel sings:

> The LORD lives, and blessed be my rock,
>     and exalted be the God of my salvation—
> the God who gave me vengeance
>     and subdued peoples under me,
> who rescued me from my enemies;
>     yes, you exalted me above those who rose against me;
>     you delivered me from the man of violence. (vv. 46–48)

When Israel witnessed God's victory over Pharaoh and his chariots at the Red Sea, the people took up a song of praise: "Sing to the LORD, for he has triumphed gloriously; the horse and his rider he has thrown into the sea" (Exodus 15:21).

Exuberant emotion is not an end in itself but the natural reflex of a heart overwhelmed by the grace and love and mercy of God. Every Christian at times has difficulty worshiping God. We come to church with distracted hearts or find that our affections for God are not what they once were. The solution, however, is to focus not on achieving an emotional experience but on the victory of God for us in Christ who died for us and rose triumphant over sin, death, and the devil. In other words, the solution is not to turn inward but to look outward. It is to hear declared what God has done for us once and for all.

To those who deserve nothing but a sentence of death, God sends a messenger who announces "Peace!"

In Romans 10, Paul reminds us that these heralds of good news are still to be found today in faithful preachers of the Word (vv. 14–17). Preachers every week stand and declare the good news that what is impossible for man is possible for God. God has reconciled sinners to himself through Jesus Christ. Christ is the substance of the Christian gospel and the heart of the good news, for as the Apostle Paul wrote to the Ephesians, "He himself is our peace" (Ephesians 2:14).

### Restore the Glory of His People (2:1, 2)

The final oracle of judgment in Nahum calls the Assyrian army and the city of Nineveh to prepare for battle:

> The scatterer has come up against you.
> Man the ramparts;
>     watch the road;
> dress for battle;
>     collect your strength. (Nahum 2:1)

It does not take a military expert to know that typically armies and generals don't tell the enemy when they are going to attack. The element of surprise has been the deciding factor in countless battles both ancient and modern. Why, then, is God telling the Ninevites that "the scatterer" is coming and to "man the ramparts" in preparation for an attack?[16] Consistent with the prophet's taunting throughout, summoning the enemy to battle is a rhetorical device intended to communicate the certainty of the Lord's victory. There is nothing Assyria can do to stop it. There are no defensive measures they can take to prevent it. There is no attack they could mount that would change it. The greatest army the world had ever seen is here summoned to prepare for the battle that will result in their utter destruction.

Here at the end of the oracle we're given, as it were, the big picture. What is God's purpose in the destruction of Nineveh? The prophet says, "The LORD is restoring the majesty of Jacob as the majesty of Israel, for plunderers have plundered them and ruined their branches" (v. 2). God has determined to restore the glory of Israel. Nineveh's doom is sure because God has covenanted himself to his people. By referring to Judah as "Jacob" and "Israel," Nahum is invoking God's covenant promises made first to the patriarchs Abraham, Isaac, and Jacob and reiterated to Israel in the days of Moses. Nahum announces that God will deliver Judah because he is faithful to his covenant.

When God looks at Israel, he sees a people who have been plundered and subjugated. Israel has been victimized, brutalized, harassed, and oppressed by Assyria. But we mustn't forget that Israel isn't simply a victim in all of this. God's people are complicit and bear responsibility for their own affliction. Israel's kings have been complicit. King Ahaz a century or so earlier had faithlessly formed an alliance with Assyria, and the prophet Isaiah prophesied that this nation that Ahaz was expecting to be Israel's savior would become Israel's oppressor: "Behold, the Lord is bringing up against them the waters of the River, mighty and many, the king of Assyria and all his glory. And it will rise over all its channels and go over its banks, and it will sweep on into Judah, it will overflow and pass on, reaching even to the neck, and its outspread wings will fill the breadth of your land, O Immanuel" (Isaiah 8:7). Israel, in other words, had covenanted themselves in a union that is best described as spiritual adultery.[17] Assyria enticed Israel with promises of provision and protection, of wealth and greatness under the banner of Assyria and, by implication, her deities.

Israel's oppression is attributable ultimately to her own sin, her own failures, and her own faithlessness. But God has set himself to a restoration project. Like Adam, who defiled the image of God in which he was created, yet God promised and purposed to restore, renew, and recreate sinful Adam in the likeness of the second Adam, so too Israel, who defiled herself through her own sin and faithless rebellion, will be restored to the former glory and majesty for which God created her.

While this prophecy is primarily about Nineveh and God's promise to destroy the Assyrian Empire, it's not only about Nineveh. This pattern of God allowing evil to wax strong for a time, God allowing his people to undergo affliction for a time, only to one day come in judgment against his enemies is a pattern that has played out again and again in redemptive history. We see it in the days of Noah when God allowed wickedness to wax strong until he sent the waters of his judgment. We see it in the days of Moses, when God allowed the Egyptians to enslave his people until he delivered them with his mighty signs and wonders. It is a pattern Judah will see again in the Babylonian exile. It is a pattern that was designed by God to point his people to the larger drama of redemptive history in which he will remove the afflictions of his people once and for all.[18]

The good news for Israel is not that God will destroy the Assyrian oppressors only to raise up Babylonian oppressors whom he will destroy only to subject his people to Persian overlords.[19] This would hardly be good news. When God says, "I will afflict you no more" (Nahum 1:12b), he is inviting Israel and he is inviting us to look beyond the afflictions of this world to a new world and a new time in which there will be no more pain and no more sorrow. Affliction will become a thing of the past, a distant memory, like a dream that can hardly be remembered. God is reminding his people that a time will come when "he will wipe away every tear from their eyes and death shall be no more, neither shall there be mourning, nor crying, nor pain anymore, for the former things have passed away" (Revelation 21:4). Such promises, almost too wonderful to comprehend, must be the substance of Christian hope and the object of daily meditation. Only in this way will our lives be transformed and governed by a reality that is as imperishable and unchangeable as the God who has made these promises. For those who are in Christ by faith, the affliction that we know as life in this sin-cursed world will indeed "not rise up a second time" (Nahum 1:9).

At the end of the day, it is critical to remember that the ultimate source of Judah's affliction wasn't Assyria. It was God himself. Notice that God says, "Though *I* have afflicted you, *I* will afflict you no more" (v. 12). The afflictions Judah was experiencing were God's judgment for their own sin and their own acts of rebellion against his suzerainty. Yet God could declare the ultimate removal of his judgment curse because his incarnate Son would one day bear God's affliction on their behalf. The price God would pay to be able to declare, "I will afflict you no more" is that his perfectly obedient Son would bear an affliction the order of magnitude of which is incomprehensible to the human mind. Jesus would become sin and bear the wrath of God for sinners on the cross. As the prophet Isaiah foretold,

> Surely he has borne our griefs
>     and carried our sorrows;
> yet we esteemed him stricken,
>     smitten by God, and afflicted.
> But he was pierced for our transgressions;
>     he was crushed for our iniquities;
> upon him was the chastisement that brought us peace,
>     and with his wounds we are healed.
> All we like sheep have gone astray;
>     we have turned—every one—to his own way;
> and the Lord has laid on him
>     the iniquity of us all. (Isaiah 53:4–6)

God would remove the affliction of the Assyrians by bringing the Babylonians and the Medes against Nineveh. But God could remove the affliction of sin and death only by bearing in the body of the incarnate Son the full wrath and judgment that Judah's (and our) sins deserve.

Jesus was abandoned, forsaken, oppressed, and afflicted with an unimaginable soul-crushing wrath to let guilty prisoners go free from the yoke of sin and death. It is on the cross at Calvary where these two words meet: God's word of *judgment* and God's word of *mercy*. We hear both words in the Christ who died for us, rose for us, and promised one day to return for us. Christians can know with certainty, therefore, that all their afflictions in this world are not the preface to God's eternal wrath, but the cruciform path we follow after our crucified Savior to an unfading glory, where we will worship God and feast with our Christ forevermore.

# 46

# God's Victory over the Pride of Man

NAHUM 2:3-13

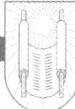

ALL THAT I KNOW ABOUT my grandfather's experience in World War II is that he was a jeep driver and that he drove transport during the Battle of the Bulge. I don't know anything of what he saw or experienced; I don't even know what he was transporting, though I have a pretty good guess. I don't know these things because, like so many others who experience combat, he wouldn't speak about it. And those who *do* speak about their experience of war often have difficulty capturing their experience with precision. This is perhaps not surprising. After all, what words can possibly express the disorienting horror of warfare? How does one describe the chaos, the carnage, the inhumane brutality, the blood, the smoke, the screams in such a way that civilians can understand something of what the experience of warfare is like? For most of us, the realities of war are simply too foreign to our everyday experience for us to truly comprehend.

In a BBC interview with veterans of World War I, Richard Tobin described the experience of going over the trenches like this: "As soon as you got over the top, fear has left you and it is terror. You don't look, you see. You don't hear, you listen. Your nose is filled with fumes and death. You taste the top of your mouth. . . . You're hunted back to the jungle. The veneer of civilisation has dropped away."[1] What's striking about Tobin's description is the way in which he highlighted the all-encompassing sensory experience of terror. All your senses are attuned to the danger that surrounds you—your eyes, ears, nose, even your taste; as Tobin said, "You taste the top of your mouth."

Similarly in Nahum 2:3–13, the prophet-poet strains to capture with words the disorienting horror of warfare, and he achieves this with some of the most sophisticated and powerful poetry in the Bible.[2] We're not told exactly what takes place. We're not given the specifics of all the military maneuvers, nor a blow-by-blow account of the assault on Nineveh. What we're given, rather, are brief glimpses or short vignettes of the terrifying power of God's assault on Nineveh and the painful, heartbreaking aftermath of the destruction of this once-great city.

The masterful poetry, however, serves a prophetic purpose. The prophet's goal is not simply to relate a gruesome account of another battle but to announce a gospel message to and for God's people. Nahum writes powerful poetry to capture the moment in which God triumphs over evil. For Israel, and all who suffered under the hands of the brutal Assyrian regime, it would be a glorious day—a day that for generations was unimaginable.

Even when Nahum declared it, it seemed impossible. But God's word is true. As God's prophet had declared it, so it came to pass that in 612 B.C. the mighty Assyrian Empire came to an end. But Assyria for Nahum was more than Assyria. The brutal empire represented all the forces of evil that had taken their stand against God and threatened his people.[3] The prophet's message, therefore, was good news not just for Israel in the seventh century B.C. but also for believers of every age. God has set himself against all that is evil in this world. The tyranny of evil, including the tyranny of evil in each of our hearts, is not how things will always be. There will come a day in which we will be able to look upon the ruins of evil itself and declare with the saints of every age, "Great is our God!"

### The Unimaginable Power of God's Wrath (3:3–6)

The scene opens with armies arrayed against Nineveh. We're not told who these armies are. We know from the fulfillment of this prophecy that these would be the combined forces of the Babylonians and the Medes who would raze Nineveh to the ground. But here they are simply identified as "his": "The shield of his mighty men is red; his soldiers are clothed in scarlet" (2:3). When the Babylonians and the Medes array themselves against Nineveh in 612 B.C., they do so as "his" army. Though unaware of it, they act according to God's sovereign will, executing his sovereign wrath against a wicked city.[4] They are, in this respect, God's army. Thus at the very outset, the prophet sets on display God's sovereign power. He is sovereign not only over his people but over all peoples, all kings, and all nations. As Nebuchadnezzar would later discover,

God's Victory over the Pride of Man    441

> his dominion is an everlasting dominion,
>    and his kingdom endures from generation to generation;
> all the inhabitants of the earth are accounted as nothing,
>    and he does according to his will among the host of heaven
>    and among the inhabitants of the earth;
> and none can stay his hand
>    or say to him, "What have you done?" (Daniel 4:34, 35)

God's army is described in full technicolor. Nahum speaks of the red shields and the scarlet uniforms; brilliant colors perhaps foreshadowing the blood this army is preparing to spill (2:3). They come adorned in red, their chariots gleaming in the sunlight, great cypress spears at the ready—all arrayed to perform the Lord's bidding. One commentator captures the awful and terrifying impression created by the Lord's army as follows: "Nineveh faces not a rag bag of soldiers but an organized and uniformly well-equipped army whose appearance is an aesthetic experience of color, brightness, order, and rhythm."[5]

In Nahum 2:4 the scene changes. Like a film director who cuts from one location to bring the audience to another, now we find ourselves inside the city, and we hear the chariots "race madly through the streets," rushing "to and fro through the squares."[6] These are probably the chariots of the Assyrians preparing for battle. The gleaming metal of the chariots reminds the observer of lightning that accompanies the thunder of their wheels as they tear through the narrow lanes. It's an ominous scene that anticipates the coming disaster. Throughout the Bible, the appearance of God as the divine warrior is accompanied by the sound of thunder and the flashing of lightning. These terrifying phenomena are foreshadowed by the gleaming chariots shaking the city of Nineveh as they prepare in vain for battle.[7]

Suddenly the battle commences. We're told, "He remembers his officers, they stumble as they go, they hasten to the wall; the siege tower is set up" (v. 5). What exactly is described here is uncertain. The stumbling possibly refers to the shoving and jostling of the attacking army as they swarm to enter the city. The word translated as "siege tower" is literally a mantelet, a kind of portable cover that gave soldiers approaching a wall some protection from rocks and arrows hurled from the ramparts.

Most interesting perhaps is the perspective the prophet offers the reader. What perspective are readers given of this terrifying scene? Where would you be standing to behold the color of the shields? From where would you hear the roar of the chariots tearing through the streets of Nineveh? Nahum places his readers/hearers inside the doomed city. He does this to help his hearers imagine the terror that the Ninevites will experience when the Lord God comes against them in his holy and righteous anger. The depiction of this attack is designed to capture the unbridled force of the onslaught and the disorienting horror of Nineveh's experience of being overwhelmed by this divine warrior and his terrifying army.

In this way the prophet is announcing to Israel that the horrors that Assyria had inflicted on countless others will one day in turn be visited upon them. The terror that countless nations experienced upon seeing the Assyrian army arrayed against their walls (probably dressed in scarlet with cypress spears brandished) will in turn be felt by the Assyrians. It's a vivid portrait of retributive and poetic justice. An eye for an eye, and a tooth for a tooth. A city for a city, death for death. The God of justice will exact complete and perfect retribution for the injustices of this wicked city.

But notice that no sooner does God's army attack than the battle is over: "The river gates are opened; the palace melts away" (v. 6). This is the moment: the great and mighty Nineveh has fallen. Based on Greek sources, some scholars have suggested that Nineveh was destroyed by the breaking open of the dams and the flooding of the city.[8] If this was the case, there is a bitter irony in the object of Nineveh's hope becoming the means of her undoing.[9] However, it is also possible that the prophet offers a metaphor for the onrush of an army since armies are often depicted as overwhelming rivers or floods in Scripture. What is important, however, is the fact that this expression of God's wrath against Nineveh is decisive. The prophet doesn't relate a struggle. He does not depict a battle whose outcome is uncertain. When the Lord pours out his wrath, the destruction comes with an overwhelming power and a decisive result.

In this we're offered a sobering reminder that God's wrath is a terrifying and terrible reality. Though today it is often made the punch line of jokes and the ironic lyric of songs, the reality is, as the author of Hebrews puts it, "It is a fearful thing to fall into the hands of the living God" (10:31). The Bible is perfectly clear: God's wrath against sin is real. God's judgment of sinners is real. The horrors of war as so vividly described by veterans like those who served in World War I and II will pale in comparison to the horror on the day when God judges the world in righteousness. Nahum's description of Nineveh's demise offers but a brief glimpse, a shadow (or foreshadow) of what will take place on that day.

Nineveh was a city that would have boggled the mind for greatness. It boasted a massive, eight-mile-long, seemingly impenetrable wall. Yet without a struggle, the God of Israel swept the city away by the word of his power.

Such a display of unopposable power in service of perfect justice should cause all who hear to sit up and take notice and to consider their true estate before such an awesome and terrifying God.

### The Unspeakable Sorrow of God's Judgment (3:7–10)

The scene then moves abruptly from the battle to its aftermath, and the prophet proceeds to take us on a tour of the ruined Nineveh. At the time Nahum prophesied, Nineveh was one of the great wonders of the world for its majesty and splendor. But now we're told, "Its mistress is stripped; she is carried off" (Nahum 2:7). A great deal of speculation attends the reference of the word translated here as "its mistress." The best suggestion is that it is a reference to the idol of Ishtar, the patron deity of Nineveh, who is carted off by the conquering forces to be set up in the temple of their own deity as an expression of their superiority and might.

Nineveh has become "like a pool whose waters run away" (2:8a). Like the city itself that has been washed away, so too her people disperse like water spilled on a flat surface, unable to be contained. No longer are they taking orders from their leaders and officials, no longer is the army answering to their commanders; the situation now is all men, women, and children for themselves.

As the people flee, we hear the vain shouts, "Halt! Halt!" (2:8b). There are always those who maintain hope of victory even after all has been lost. It is reported that in the final days of World War II, holed up in his bunker in Berlin, completely surrounded by Russian and American forces, hearing the constant bombardment of the city, Adolf Hitler vacillated between despair and delusions that there was still a path to victory. So too in Nineveh. "Halt! Halt!" they cry. Who is speaking? We're not told. It doesn't matter. No one turns back. It's a sad portrait of hopes dashed, lives and livelihoods ruined, and a few pitiful souls still harboring hopes that Assyria will rise again.

It's a tragic scene. It's a scene filled with irony and contrasts as the city is given over to plunder: "Plunder the silver, plunder the gold! There is no end of the treasure or the wealth of all precious things" (Nahum 2:9). Assyria's great wealth gained through terror and violence is now taken away by her conquerors through terror and violence. The plunderers have become the plundered. The vast wealth that preached greatness and security now becomes the possession of Assyria's conquerors. Through the prophet Nahum, Israel is made witness to this great reversal that their God will accomplish.

While the prophet depicts something of the objective desolation of the city, the focus is more on the subjective experience of the defeated Ninevites. We hear, for example, the "slave girls lamenting" and "beating their breasts" (v. 7). The beating of breasts is the posture of the deepest grief and mourning, as they are overwhelmed by the ultimate impotence of their deities that were the objects of their trust. Similarly, in verse 10 we're told simply, "Hearts melt and knees tremble, anguish is in all loins, all faces grow pale!" We're not given much by way of detail. But in the sparing way of a master poet, Nahum paints a portrait and creates the impression of utter hopelessness and sorrow. This is the end of rebellion against God, an unspeakable, indescribable, intractable sorrow. It is an anguish of the soul that only deepens when it realizes its hopelessness and helplessness.

Nineveh in her prime was the capital city of the largest and most powerful empire that the world had ever seen. Her army in Nahum's day was believed to be invincible. Her people believed themselves to be secure under the protectorate of their king, and the king believed himself to be appointed by the gods as their chief emissary and representative on earth. Nineveh was immensely rich; it was the center of culture and education, housing arguably the greatest library of the ancient world, the library of Assurbanipal. Everything about this city proclaimed power and permanence.[10] But God's prophet proclaimed it all to be an illusion. These too could and would come to an end, and so would all who entrusted their lives to them.

We are surrounded with many of the same illusions in our day—the false security offered by wealth, power, reputation, military might, education. This is what the author of Psalm 73 described when he looked at the wicked and observed, "Pride is their necklace; violence covers them as a garment. . . . Behold, these are the wicked; always at ease, they increase in riches" (vv. 6, 12). We can observe the same thing in politics, media, entertainment, and academic institutions in our day. Like the psalmist, we can be tempted to despair, thinking, "All in vain have I kept my heart clean and washed my hands in innocence" (v. 13). But it is in the temple that the psalmist is reoriented to the truth and confesses, "Truly you set them [the wicked] in slippery places; you make them fall to ruin. How they are destroyed in a moment, swept away utterly by terrors!" (73:18, 19).

We too need to be reminded of the reality that God's wrath lies in store for those who have set their hearts against Heaven. We have in God's destruction of Nineveh a portrait of such ruin. It is impossible to comprehend and fully express the horror of God's wrath against sin. Nahum 2:10 puts it simply and offers a summary of sorts. What has become of the once-almighty Nineveh? The prophet declares, "Desolate! Desolation, and ruin!" The reality of the horror and the bitter sorrow of God's judgment has settled into the hearts of the Ninevites, and they are undone.

The end of sin and rebellion against God is aptly summarized in the words "Desolate! Desolation and ruin!" Throughout all of Nahum's prophecies, however, God's word of judgment against Nineveh contains in it a word of gospel deliverance for God's people.

### The Unassailable Assurance of God's Deliverance (3:11–13)

Verse 11 exhibits a marked change of tone that may strike us as surprising because Nahum breaks into a particular form of speech called a taunt. Taunts in the ancient world were not all that dissimilar from taunts in the modern world. They were an aggressive way of expressing superiority: "I am better than you." They expressed assurance of victory: "You are going to fail, and you are going to fall. Get ready to be humiliated." Taunts were used to put people down, and they were a way of exalting oneself over another. Taunts were designed to condemn and denounce and humiliate the other.

This is precisely what Nahum does when he says, "Where is the lions' den, the feeding place of the young lions, where the lion and lioness went, where his cubs were, with none to disturb?" (v. 11). To understand the force of Nahum's taunt, it's helpful to know that the lion was an important symbol for the Assyrians.[11] Anyone who has been to the British Museum has probably seen the Colossal Lion of Assyria that once adorned the famous temple of Ninurta. The lion served as a national symbol for Assyria, and the Assyrian kings frequently compared themselves to this magnificent and terrifying creature.[12] What could be more appropriate? The lion is known, after all, as king of the jungle. Never mind that lions don't live in jungles. There certainly is a poise to lions, a power to lions, a (if you'll excuse the pun) pride to lions.

Lions move with a poise and a confidence that comes from their strength and their power. Mighty and ferocious, lions are able to defeat almost any threat that comes against them and to conquer any prey they so desire. It is no wonder, then, that the lion was conscripted to stand for the might of Assyria and her kings.[13] But the prophet invokes this symbol of Assyria's greatness to turn it against Assyria in a description of its ruin.

Where is the place, the prophet asks rhetorically, where the lions go to feed, that is, to rest, and feed in safety (2:11)? Nahum's implication is clear: the feeding place is gone! It used to be the case, as Nahum puts it, that "the lion tore enough for his cubs and strangled prey for his lionesses; he filled his caves with prey and his dens with torn flesh" (v. 12). It used to be the case that Assyria could eat her fill of the nations around her, plundering at will and enriching herself at the expense of her subject peoples. The king would feed himself and his family with delicacies, and he would fill his nobles and courtiers with the spoil and plunder of their victims. But now the once all-powerful lion has become impotent. On the day of God's wrath and judgment, the king will be unable to accomplish the most basic function of Near Eastern royalty—to defend his people, to protect his family, and even to provide food enough for himself. Where is the power? Where is the pride? Where is the might of Assyria? It is gone.

While we find taunts throughout the Bible and especially throughout the Prophets, Nahum, of all the Biblical authors, is the preeminent taunter. With this form of speech the prophet offers us not a lesson in cruelty but a lesson in faith. Specifically, Nahum teaches us about the posture of faith especially in the face of great danger and trials. Nahum is not speaking for himself but is expressing God's posture toward a city that has come to embody pure wickedness. Nahum taunts with and for God, who taunts Nineveh directly when he says, "I will burn your chariots in smoke, and the sword shall devour your young lions. I will cut off your prey from the earth, and the voice of your messengers shall no longer be heard" (2:13).

The prophet's confidence is not based on something he will accomplish in his own strength or something Israel will accomplish in theirs. Nahum's delight is not chiefly that his enemies or the enemies of his people will be cut off from the land of the living. Nahum's confidence and delight are in this: God's enemies will be vanquished and God's glory made manifest, and God's majesty and holiness will be vindicated among the nations.

Critical for understanding this gospel hope that Nahum expresses is verse 13: " 'Behold, I am against you,' declares the LORD of hosts." Who is the "you" referring to? Most scholars seem to agree that God is speaking to the city of Nineveh cast as an individual (perhaps as Christensen suggests) being summoned to a duel or individual combat.[14] But this raises a question: Why is the Lord against the Assyrian capital, and why is he summoning Nineveh to combat?

God's opposition to Nineveh is not simply because Nineveh is cruel and oppressive. Many ancient kingdoms and their capitals were cruel and oppressive. God is against Nineveh because Nineveh is against God's people. The king of Assyria had essentially exalted himself as a rival deity, offering himself to Israel as their lord and savior, their great provider and king. In countless ways such as art, literature, politics, military strategy, rhetoric, and religion, Assyria offered what one scholar calls a "propagandistic metanarrative"; that is, a message or worldview "designed to persuade lesser powers to come under its aegis and to convince those already under its control that it would meet all their needs and was worthy of their unreserved commitment and complete trust."[15]

## God's Victory over the Pride of Man 447

This is the corollary to Nahum 2:13: God is against Assyria because God is for his people. It is certainly true that God is against all kings and all governments and all peoples who are oppressive and cruel and unjust. God will judge such kings and governments, peoples and nations on the last day. But God broke into history in the seventh century B.C. not simply to reveal his antagonism toward cruel governments but to deliver his covenant people from oppression, from a false god-king who was nothing less than a shepherd of death. The gospel word that Nahum announced to Judah and the gospel word that Nahum continues to announce to us is that God is against everything that is against his people.

God is against that which is against us, not because we are somehow deserving of his favor and not because we are less rebellious than Nineveh or less cruel than the Assyrians. Inside every Israelite and inside every one of us lies a heart that has at times exhibited the same pride, lust, cruelty, injustice, and oppression that characterized wicked Nineveh. Yet the Bible says unequivocally that God is for us. God is for us because he loved us. There is no other explanation. Before the world began, God out of sheer love elected sinners to everlasting life. God could do this for his people because he would set himself against his own Son with a wrath and judgment far greater than what befell Nineveh, taking unto himself all the pain and sorrow, agony and fear that we deserve.

At a cross on Calvary, we come to understand that our greatest enemy is not an empire or a godless ideology but our very own hearts. God's wrath against Nineveh so vividly displayed by the prophet-poet is a dim picture of what each of us deserves on account of our sin. What the Bible declares in countless ways, the Apostle Paul puts simply: "The wages of sin is death" (Romans 6:23). Though many under her imperial rule would say that Nineveh got what she deserved, Jesus did not get what he deserved but rather what we deserve. Yet out of love for his own he died, the righteous for the unrighteous. The fear, isolation, doom, helplessness, and hopelessness that wicked Nineveh would endure at the hands of the Babylonians was but a type and shadow of the fear, forsakenness, and isolation that innocent Jesus would endure. He endured such forsakenness not only from his kindred but from his friends and family who abandoned him, and worst of all, from his Father in Heaven. And yet he would endure the sorrow, as the author of Hebrews tells us, "for the joy that was set before him" (12:2), that is, the joy of a people redeemed by his blood.

It is perhaps difficult to imagine taunting in a way that does not contain an element of sinful pleasure in the downfall of another. But apparently it's possible. Taunts are found throughout the Bible in the mouths of God's inspired prophets and, as we'll see, the apostles. Just as Paul instructed the Ephesians to "be angry and do not sin" (Ephesians 4:26), so too Nahum instructs us to taunt but not to sin. This is not a call to adopt a posture of scorn and derision toward those who disagree with us or oppose us for our faith. Rather, it's a call for believers to adopt the prophet's posture of confidence in our God and to share his confidence in God's sovereignty over all the evils that afflict us and threaten to undo us both in this life and in the next. It's a call to give voice to our faith in the promises of God in the face of the greatest trials and temptations of this world.

This is the faith that young David exhibited when he battled Goliath. While the Philistine and Israelite armies believed they were witnessing a confrontation between a humble shepherd and an enormous, battle-seasoned warrior, David saw the situation differently. As he strode to meet his opponent, David took up his taunt:

> You come to me with a sword and with a spear and with a javelin, but I come to you in the name of the LORD of hosts, the God of the armies of Israel, whom you have defied. This day the LORD will deliver you into my hand, and I will strike you down and cut off your head. And I will give the dead bodies of the host of the Philistines this day to the birds of the air and to the wild beasts of the earth, that all the earth may know that there is a God in Israel. (1 Samuel 17:45, 46)

David would not recognize a Bible story entitled, as it so often is, "David and Goliath." By faith he saw that this was a battle between God and Goliath. Though "God and Goliath" spoils the ending and is far less exciting, it is far more accurate to the reality of what took place.

Like David and Nahum (to name just two), we must learn to be those who give voice to our assurance that God is real and his promises are true. When we consider the sin in our own lives and the accusations of the devil that whisper to us, "If you were a real Christian, you wouldn't have done this or that," we must respond with the promises of God—a response that may at times take the form of a taunt.

Something I find endlessly amusing about Martin Luther is the conversations he would have with the devil, often yelling at him, rebuking him, throwing inkwells at him, and of course, taunting him. Luther would relate stories like the following:

> When the devil comes at night to worry me, this is what I say to him: "Devil, I have to sleep now. That is God's commandment, for us to work

by day and sleep at night." If he keeps on nagging me and trots out my sins, then I answer: "Sweet devil, I know the whole list. But I have done even more sin which is not on your list. . . . Write there also that I have crap in my breeches. Hang it around your neck and wipe your mouth on it." Then, if he won't cease to accuse me of sins, I say in contempt: "Holy Satan, pray for me."[16]

Though comical, Luther's taunts were serious expressions of a lively and abiding faith that was determined to believe and speak the truth in the face of great temptation and opposition. His taunts to the devil exhibit a confidence that should be the desire of every believer. Confidence in God's triumph over our enemies. Confidence in God's forgiveness of our sins. Confidence in the sufficiency of Christ's work. Confidence in our victory in him over all things.

To be sure, we do not know what God's deliverance will look like in any particular circumstance. God may grant us relief from suffering, triumph over our enemies, and victory over our sins, or he may grant us the grace to endure great suffering, perseverance in the face of horrendous persecution (a persecution that may end only in glory), and a daily struggle with temptation that drives us to greater repentance and faith in the sufficiency of the cross of Christ. Either way, through faith in Christ, we are nevertheless and always victors. For this reason the Apostle Paul could write to the Romans, "If God is for us, who can be against us? He who did not spare his own Son but gave him up for us all, how will he not also with him graciously give us all things?" (Romans 8:31, 32). Do you see what kind of confidence this gives the Christian? We are in Christ "more than conquerors through him who loved us" (v. 37).

It is difficult to imagine Judah's joy upon hearing God declare to Assyria, "I will burn your chariots in smoke, and the sword shall devour your young lions. I will cut off your prey from the earth, and the voice of your messengers shall no longer be heard" (Nahum 2:13). A day was coming when Assyria's mighty chariots would no longer terrify Judah into submission. No longer would Assyria eat up cities and nations like a lion pouncing on a gazelle, exacting crushing tribute so that the Assyrian king could live in luxury. No longer would Judah hear the voice of Assyria's emissaries demanding tribute and service on the pain of death. Yet Nineveh's demise is but a portrait of God's victory over our sins in Christ.

Christian, what stands against you? Your sin and the curse of sin? Satan and his temptations? Death and the painful reality of mortality? A day is coming in which we too will be able to say, "No longer!" This great day was anticipated by the Apostle Paul, who stared the greatest enemy we face square in the eye and uttered the most famous taunt in sacred Scripture: "'Death is swallowed up in victory.' 'O death, where is your victory? O death, where is your sting?'" (1 Corinthians 15:54, 55). He concluded, "The sting of death is sin, and the power of sin is the law. But thanks be to God, who gives us the victory through our Lord Jesus Christ" (vv. 56, 57).

# 47

# He Put Them to Open Shame

NAHUM 3:1-7

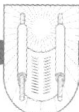

DURING MY YEARS in pastoral ministry, I officiated many funerals. All of them could be described as quiet, somber, and solemn affairs. All of them, that is, except one. I once had the privilege of participating in the funeral service for a member of my congregation who was from Cameroon, and the service was far from the quiet, somber, and solemn affair with which I was familiar. The family of the deceased expressed their grief with loud cries of sorrow. The widow, with wailing and tears, threw her body onto the casket. Throughout the entire service, a sound of loud lamentation would suddenly and slowly arise from the largely Cameroonian congregation as they grieved the loss of their beloved friend. As foreign as the whole experience was to me, I remember at the time being struck by the fact that what I was witnessing was no doubt much closer to the world of the Bible and much closer to the funeral practices of ancient Israel than the traditionally quiet, somber, organ-laden services to which I was accustomed.

The opening word of Nahum 3 ushers us into a funeral service with just such a cry. *Hôy, Hôy*, as it reads in the Hebrew, was a cry of lamentation. *Hôy* is a word that expresses deep and inconsolable sorrow, and it is a word associated most often with the mourning that takes place at funerals. Yet on the lips of the prophet this word—translated as "Woe" or "Alas"—takes on a distinctly sarcastic or ironic tone.[1] The prophet is not *lamenting* the demise of Nineveh. If anything, Nahum is celebrating, rejoicing over Nineveh's imminent destruction. So this woe oracle is uttered in the same spirit as the taunts that we have seen in chapters 1 and 2, where the prophet mocks the proud capital of the Assyrian Empire.[2] The function here, however, is more than ironic. It's also prophetic. One commentator summed up the matter well when he wrote, "The use of that form here indicates that Nineveh's demise is certain, as if the city were already dead and on its way to final burial."[3] A conduit of divine revelation, the prophet is certain of Assyria's demise—so certain that he is, in effect, donning his funeral attire, buying flowers for the casket, taking up his funeral lament, and making his way to the wake.

Now in all likelihood Nahum declared these words while the Assyrian Empire was at the height of its power. There was nothing that Nahum could point to and say, "Look here, this is how I know Nineveh is going to fall: this army is marching toward the capital," or "Their stock market is about to collapse." How is it that Nahum could be so certain of what would have seemed at the time so impossible? The answer is that Nahum knew the Lord his God, and he knew the promises of the Lord, and he trusted the word of the Lord.

The God that Nahum knew was the God who had revealed himself as one who judges the wicked, often returning upon their heads the very evil and sorrow they inflicted upon others.

This is precisely what we see in these opening verses of Nahum 3. Though in infinite patience the Lord might allow wickedness to continue for a time and might allow evil to increase and even flourish for a season, a day is coming, declares the prophet, in which God will utterly destroy the wicked from this earth. On that day God will expose their wicked deeds for all their corruption and depravity, and the world will behold them not as powerful, enviable, and glorious but as pitiable, despicable, and vile. As the prophet announces the certain destruction of Judah's oppressors, he invites God's people to share in his joyful anticipation of the Lord's triumph over all that opposes his kingship and afflicts his people.

As is customary of woe oracles, the prophet's message divides neatly into two parts: the enumeration of Nineveh's crimes (3:1–4) and the announcement of Nineveh's fate (vv. 5–7).

## Nineveh's Crimes and Their Woeful Consequences (3:1–4)

Nahum's lament quickly turns into a prosecution that begins with a summary of the charges: "Woe to the bloody city, all full of lies and plunder—no end to the prey!" (3:1). With these words the prophet captures the heart and character of the city of Nineveh. We know that cities can take on a sort of personality of their own. This personality is a product of the values and character of the city's leaders and residents. I was struck by this when I moved from Los Angeles to

Washington, D.C. Los Angeles was animated, as it were, by the entertainment industry, whereas Washington was animated by politics, and the feel of each city was markedly different as they had come to reflect the values and dynamics of their respective industries.

What animated ancient Nineveh in the seventh century B.C.? Nineveh, Nahum tells us, was a city animated by violence (a "bloody city"), deceit ("full of lies"), and theft, as she is described as full of the "plunder" of her victims. Furthermore, Nineveh is portrayed as indulgent as she gorges herself with an endless supply of "prey" (3:1). This was a city that was not only animated by but thrived on these realities—violence, deception, theft, and indulgence.[4]

Assyria had always been a brutal and cruel empire. But historians have noted that Assurbanipal, during whose reign Nahum was likely to have ministered, took cruelty to a new and unprecedented level. Reading his inscriptions glorying in violence is not for the faint of heart. To give just one illustration of his exploits, one reads, "I pierced his cheeks with the sharp-edged spear, my personal weapon, by laying the very hands on him which I had received to conquer opposition against me; I put the ring to his jaw, placed a dog collar around his neck and made him guard the bar of the east gate of Nineveh."[5] Assurbanipal secured his throne and extended his kingdom not only through violence but through acts of terror that would cause his victims to tremble at the very thought of his approaching army.

But no sooner does the prophet pronounce a woe upon Nineveh than he transports us, as it were, into the middle of a city under attack. Being a poet of extraordinary skill and imagination, Nahum even captures something of the horrific experience of being in the middle of battle.[6] First, you may hear from a distance "the crack of the whip, and the rumble of the wheel" (3:2a). When the army comes into view you would see the "galloping horse and bounding chariot!" (v. 2b) at a distance. Then the attack commences, and we are taken up into the chaos of "horsemen charging, flashing sword and glittering spear" (v. 3a). Finally we behold the grim aftermath—"hosts of slain, heaps of corpses, dead bodies without end" (v. 3b). There are so many dead bodies that it is impossible to move through the city without stumbling over piles of corpses (v. 3c). Many of us have seen Holocaust photographs of the bodies of murdered Jews piled high into mountains. The scene is mind-numbing. Observing these photos, we feel it is almost impossible to get our minds around the true extent of the horror. In Nahum, we are given a similarly terrifying scene of violence, bloodshed, and carnage, all of which expose the depths to which human violence and cruelty can go.

But this raises a question: Whose demise are we witnessing? Coming as it does on the heels of the charge that Nineveh is a bloody city, we're first meant to see this as a picture of the horrors that Assyria inflicted time and again on cities and nations throughout the Near East. Israel had no doubt heard stories about the terror and carnage that Assyria would inflict on her enemies. And yet as we read on, we discover somewhat surprisingly the reason for all of this death and destruction. The prophet says that this is "all for the countless whorings of the prostitute" (v. 4a). With this notice we realize that this is not a portrait of Assyria's cruelty in warfare at all, but it is in fact a description of the fate of Nineveh herself.[7] It's a picture of God's justice. Nineveh's cruel treatment of her neighbors, and especially Nineveh's cruel treatment of Israel, will come back upon her own head as she finds herself to be a city full of corpses.[8]

This judgment that Nineveh would experience would come as a consequence not only for her cruel violence toward her neighboring states but also on account of her deceptive political intrigues. Nineveh's unbridled violence that she unleashed against neighboring cities and states was often the end of a long progression of diplomatic deceit and manipulation. Nahum appropriately likens Nineveh's international policies to the work of a prostitute: "All for the countless whorings of the prostitute, graceful and of deadly charms, who betrays nations with her whorings, and peoples with her charms" (v. 4). Just as a prostitute lies and deceives, promises life and pleasure but delivers death and sorrow, so Nineveh in her dealings with other nations has made treaties and agreements only to betray her allies and destroy them.

Elizabeth Achtemeier has described these opening verses of Nahum 3 as "one of the finest poetic portrayals of a powerful nation to be found in literature." She writes, "Here we see political, military, and economic power in all its devious corruption."[9] We have first and foremost an announcement that God will destroy those governments and groups, those leaders and rulers who use their positions of authority to exploit those whom God in his providence has entrusted to their care. We can look at our world and see governments and regimes that are corrupt to their very core, that seem not only to get away with oppression but that thrive on account of it. It's often tempting to think they've gotten away with it and that justice will never be done. Nahum, however, reminds us that the wicked haven't gotten away with anything. Justice is coming, the scales will be balanced, and God will exact his vengeance upon the wicked of this earth.

But these verses are not only a denunciation of Nineveh and Nineveh-like governments wherever they are found. These verses may be understood equally well as a denunciation of those who are taken in by such governments and who allow themselves to be deceived by their false promises. Achtemeier again captures this powerfully when she says:

> We run to those with power, with wealth, with status. We even run to those whom we think have the solutions to our problems. The rich entice us with their ability to buy whatever is needful and desirable. The powerful lure us to their sides with their promises of security. The important shed on us their glory, and the wise seem to ease our perplexities. And so we take refuge in the petty powers of this world and "do not look to the Holy one of Israel" (Isa 31:1). We "carry out a plan" which is not God's plan and "make a league" that is not of his spirit (Isa 30:1). And that lures us to our doom as surely as a harlot lures her customers to theirs.[10]

We have a prime example of this very thing in the tragic character of Ahaz, king of Judah. When Judah was threatened by her northern neighbors Syria and Israel, fearful King Ahaz rejected the protection of the Lord in favor of an alliance with Assyria. The scene is dramatic. The prophet Isaiah calls Ahaz to trust Yahweh in the face of a very real threat with the famous words, "If you are not firm in faith, you will not be firm at all" (Isaiah 7:9). Furthermore, Isaiah offers Ahaz a sign "as deep as Sheol or high as heaven" to bolster his faith (v. 11). But how does Ahaz respond? Ahaz declares, "I will not put the Lord to the test" (v. 12). It sounds pious. But the truth is that Ahaz has already sent messengers to Assyria to make an alliance and secure Judah's safety through the provision and protection of Assyria and, by implication, Assyria's gods. Though Ahaz no doubt saw a net gain for himself and for his country in this alliance with Assyria, Isaiah would declare just the opposite to Judah's faithless king: "The Lord will bring upon you and upon your people and upon your father's house such days as have not come since the day that Ephraim departed from Judah—the king of Assyria!" (7:17). Judah's Assyrian alliance would not be a source of her blessing but a source of her cursing.

Like Isaiah's prophecy, Nahum's announcement of Nineveh's demise carries with it a warning. It is a warning to those in Judah who would be tempted to look to Nineveh as a source of hope and help and a way to gain power and security. A treaty with Nineveh and submission to the Assyrian king, which entailed a religious obligation to Assyria's deities, did indeed promise such security, privilege, and perhaps power.[11] But these promises were false, and the prophet warns Judah against putting confidence in kingdoms built on lies, bloodshed, and deceptive promises of life and peace. To make an alliance with Assyria would be to forsake God and to reject the blessings of the covenant he had made.

This of course stands as a warning to every believer as it poses the question, where do I place my hope? Is it in this world and the things of this world? Or is it in the "solid joys, and lasting treasures, none but Zion's children know"?[12]

### Nineveh's Tragic Fate: Her Glory Has Become Her Shame (3:5–7)

Divine sentencing and execution are not a private affair. God is not content with condemning Nineveh for her great wickedness and executing judgment against Nineveh for her great violence—he purposes to do so in the most public of manners because, in so doing, he reveals to the entire world the true character of this once immensely enviable city. God says through his prophet,

> Behold, I am against you,
>     declares the LORD of hosts,
>     and I will lift up your skirts over your face;
> and I will make nations look at your nakedness
>     and kingdoms at your shame.
> I will throw filth at you
>     and treat you with contempt
>     and make you a spectacle. (Nahum 3:5, 6)

This description of God's brutal and humiliating treatment of his vanquished enemies has made many modern readers uncomfortable. We recognize God's justice and goodness in the destruction of the wicked and recognize God's goodness and justice in overthrowing violent and oppressive forces, but what about the humiliation of the enemy? American soldiers who humiliate prisoners of war are court-martialed, and rightly so, because we recognize the dignity of human life, even the lives of those who would harm us.

It is critical to see, however, that God is not endorsing or adopting abusive policies when it comes to the treatment of prisoners. To understand the force of this vivid imagery here, we need to see that God is extending the metaphor introduced earlier in which Nineveh is likened to a prostitute: "All for the countless whorings of the prostitute" (3:4a). When God says, "I . . . will lift up your skirts over your face; and I will make nations look at your nakedness" (v. 5), he is saying that he is going to expose Nineveh for who she really is. God is going to uncover her nakedness, and what has been so alluring to the surrounding nations will be revealed to be sordid and vile, like a prostitute's body that, in the imagination of her customers, is perfect and delightful, yet is in reality covered with bruises and sores.

Once stripped and exposed, God says, "I will throw filth at you" (3:6a). This word is used most often for the detestable idols of the nations, and is used here to identify defeated, exposed, and humiliated Nineveh with her gods. God covers her with dirt, as one commentator puts it, "to better represent her true nature than her former outward appearance of beauty."[13]

What God is here announcing with this disturbing image is that in his destruction of wicked, brutal, and vile Nineveh, he will expose her wickedness to the world. Once she was the epitome of greatness. Her glory and her might and her wealth knew no rival, and everything about her declared invincibility and permanence. But now God declares that he will expose her corruption, and the whole earth will regard her as vile and disgusting.

There is a certain satisfaction we all experience at the thought of wickedness being exposed for what it really is and receiving the sentence that it justly deserves. This is what makes many novels and films so satisfying; in the end, the villain is finally revealed as the fraud, tyrant, abuser, liar, or thief he is and is defeated once and for all. Yet with this longing for evil to be exposed and judged, there is in each of us the haunting fear that we ourselves might also be exposed for what we are. We love it when other people's sins are brought to light and justice is brought to bear on offenses that are not our own, but deep down each of us is terrified that the searchlight might one day be cast on our own thoughts and actions, and that our own hearts, our true selves, might be revealed. As Paul wrote, "Therefore do not pronounce judgment before the time, before the Lord comes, who will bring to light the things now hidden in darkness and will disclose the purposes of the heart" (1 Corinthians 4:5).

The announcement that God is going to judge all that is evil in this world and will destroy all that is wicked is good news only if there is a way of escape and salvation. Judah's hope was not that they were morally superior to Nineveh. God doesn't promise to come in judgment only for the very wicked, as if the moderately wicked are perfectly safe. In fact, it would be said about King Manasseh of Judah that he erected altars to foreign gods in the temple, that he burned his own son as a sacrifice, and that he consulted fortune tellers and necromancers (2 Kings 21:1–6). "Manasseh shed very much innocent blood, till he had filled Jerusalem from one end to another" (v. 16). Israel herself was prone to the same level of corruption. Israel's hope could not rest in their ability to be a little better than Nineveh. Their hope would rest in their God who promised to cover over their sin and guilt with the blood of a perfect sacrifice.

In their state of innocence in the garden, Adam and Eve "were both naked and were not ashamed" (Genesis 2:25). But after their sin, "the eyes of both were opened, and they knew that they were naked. And they sewed fig leaves together and made themselves loincloths" (3:7). These crudely made coverings of fig leaves were our first parents' pitiable attempt to hide the shame of their sin and to hide from each other. This attempt was not only a symbol of the suspicion and recrimination that was introduced into their relationship but also a symbol of their desire to hide from God. So Adam said to God, "I heard the sound of you in the garden, and I was afraid, because I was naked, and I hid myself" (v. 10). Though God pronounced a curse on mankind, he at the same time uttered another word of grace and mercy. What Adam was no longer qualified and able to accomplish, God himself promised to accomplish through the seed of the woman. As a symbol and promise of the work that this messianic seed would complete, the Lord provided his own covering for our first parents: "The LORD God made for Adam and for his wife garments of skins and clothed them" (v. 21).

Many theologians have pointed to the fact that these garments of skins would have required the death of an animal,[14] a life for a life. Adam and Eve's hope in their day, Judah's hope in Nahum's day, and our hope in our day is that God would cover our sin and remove our shame, neither of which we could do on our own. This is precisely what Jesus came to do. The Son of God took on human flesh that he might bear in full the judgment for sins not his own and thereby cover—that is, atone—for the sins of his people.

Before he was nailed to the cross, Jesus was made a spectacle in his humiliation. He was beaten, he was spat upon, he was derided and despised, he was made a mockery with a crown of thorns and a purple robe. He was no doubt filthy, his skin covered with dirt and blood, and he was held in contempt by almost everyone who saw him. His closest friends having abandoned him in his hour of need, Jesus was without comforters. Nahum said of Nineveh, "All who look at you will shrink from you" (Nahum 3:7), and the prophet Isaiah said of the Suffering Servant, "His appearance was so marred, beyond human semblance, and his form beyond that of the children of mankind" (Isaiah 52:14). Jesus was "despised and rejected by men, a man of sorrows and acquainted with grief . . . one from whom men hide their faces" (53:3). The horrific judgment that Nahum pronounced against wicked Nineveh was but a dim reflection of the horror that Jesus would experience on the cross for the sins of his people.

The remedy for our sin and our shame is not to suppress it or to justify it or to minimize it. It is not to ignore it. The remedy is to look to Christ and by faith see him bearing our shame and our curse in full, and by faith finding in him God's perfect righteousness, covering us like a cloak and offered to us as a free gift. This great exchange is the heart of the Christian gospel. The horror of God's judgment on Nineveh, the humiliating exposure of Nineveh, offers a vivid portrait of what Christ has borne in our place and of what we've been spared through the grace and mercy of God.

It would not be through a massive army that God would overthrow the greatest forces of evil that we face. It would be through the death of his Son that God, as Paul puts it, "cancel[ed] the record of debt that stood against us with its legal demands" (Colossians 2:14). The apostle goes on to say, "This he set aside, nailing it to the cross. He disarmed the rulers and authorities and put them to open shame, by triumphing over them in him" (Colossians 2:14, 15). Christ has conquered a foe far more wicked and far more deceitful than a thousand Ninevehs. In Christ, God has triumphed over sin, death, and the grave. Christ has bound the forces of evil that, left unopposed, would irreversibly and permanently ruin those who bear the image of their Creator.

Nahum's woe oracle concludes with the announcement that Nineveh's wickedness will be exposed and recognized by the entire world as vile and disgraceful (3:7). On that day, no one will have sympathy for her. No one will desire her charms or privileges. No one will extend comfort to her. Rather, all will shrink back from the depravity of this wicked city, for the Lord of hosts has set himself against the wickedness of this world and will one day destroy it. He will expose it for what it is, and in so doing he will vindicate himself as holy, righteous, and just. God will unmask every pretender, and every false god will be revealed as powerless to save.

This is the fate of every idol and false god that we are tempted to serve. Wealth, power, sex, influence, beauty, strength—though seductive in countless ways—all prove in the end to be faithless friends and impotent saviors. Nahum's prophetic (and ironic) woe oracle serves as a reminder of the ultimate fate of idolatry and the insatiable pull it has on the human heart. Furthermore, Nahum's prophecy is a call for believers of every age to long for the day when Christ's victory over evil will come to its full consummation, when he will be revealed in all his glory and "every knee should bow, in heaven and on earth and under the earth, and every tongue confess that Jesus Christ is Lord, to the glory of God the Father" (Philippians 2:10, 11).

# 48

# A History Lesson

NAHUM 3:8-13

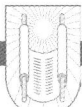

IN HIS FAMOUS POEM *Ozymandias*, Percy Shelley tells of a traveler who stumbles across the ruins of an enormous statue in the middle of the desert. He sees "two vast and trunkless legs of stone," and nearby he sees the shattered visage (face) lying "half sunk" in the sand. On the pedestal that once held this magnificent statue, the traveler finds these words:

> My name is Ozymandias, King of Kings;
> Look on my works, ye Mighty, and despair!

This is a remarkable expression of pride and power and invincibility. As if obeying the command of this great king, the speaker looks around and observes,

> Nothing beside remains.
> Round the decay of that colossal Wreck, boundless and bare
> The lone and level sands stretch far away.[1]

It's a sobering poem. All that is left of this once-mighty king, and all that is left of this once-mighty kingdom, is a broken and forgotten statue, half-buried in lone and level sands that stretch far away.

With this semifictitious King Ozymandias, Shelley captured the tragic reality of countless emperors, kings, and presidents and of countless empires, nations, and countries who throughout history have looked at their expansive kingdoms, their mighty armies, and their monumental building projects and thought to themselves, *I am perfectly secure. My kingdom will last forever*, only to one day find their nations destroyed, their buildings razed, their armies routed, and their legacy forgotten.

Not long ago China celebrated the seventieth anniversary of the founding of the People's Republic of China. Speaking from Tiananmen Square, President Xi Jinping declared, "There is no force that can shake the foundation of this great nation. . . . Today, a socialist China is standing in front of the world. . . . No force can stop the Chinese people and the Chinese nation forging ahead."[2]

We understand that presidents may at times be given to hyperbole and boasting. But the fact of the matter is that President Xi's remarks are really nothing new. They are simply one more example of the kind of pride, self-confidence, and self-reliance to which leaders and nations throughout history and across the world have been intractably prone.

In Nahum 3:8–13, we hear the prophet taunting Nineveh for this very thing—her pride, her self-confidence, and her false sense of security. To the strongest empire that history had ever seen, Assyria, the prophet says, in effect, "Your security is an illusion. Your doom is coming." In this taunt we are given the critical reminder that all those who place their hope in their own strength and who look to the things of this world for their security or their salvation will inevitably come to ruin. But in this the prophet offers God's people another equally, if not more important, reminder; specifically, that there is a king and there is a kingdom not of this world in which true refuge and true safety, eternal refuge and eternal safety, may be found—the kingdom of our Lord and of his Christ.

This taunt in Nahum 3 is sometimes called a history taunt because here the prophet offers important history lessons, the first and most prominent of which is the deceptiveness of idolatry.

### The Deceptiveness of Idolatry (3:8–10)

The prophet opens his taunt with a question: "Are you better than Thebes . . . ?" (3:8a). It is important to note that the Thebes in view here is not the familiar Greek city by that name but the Egyptian capital city that in its day was the crowning jewel of the vast, mighty, and immensely wealthy Egyptian Empire. Thebes was remarkable in part for her natural defenses due to her strategic location on the Nile River. The city was situated in upper Egypt at the major bend in the Nile, a bend so sharp that the river itself wrapped almost entirely around the city and thus served as a natural wall or moat protecting Thebes from attack. This is what the prophet is highlighting when he says she "sat by the Nile, with water around her, her rampart a sea, and water her wall" (v. 8).

Thebes was well protected not only with walls of water but also through her strategic alliances with neighboring kingdoms. When Nahum declares, "Cush was her strength; Egypt too, and that without limit; Put and the Libyans were her helpers" (3:9), he is referring to the diplomatic relationships that Thebes forged with neighboring kingdoms.[3] Through treaties and alliances, Thebes had secured the help and resources of Cush (modern-day Ethiopia) and Libya, for which Put is possibly another name.[4] Thebes, in other words, was surrounded by allies who would fight for her, just as she was surrounded by water and walls to defend her.

News outlets regularly put out lists of the best and the worst cities based on certain criteria—worst traffic, best place to raise kids, best gelato; you name it, there's likely a list on the internet. If there was a list of the safest, most secure cities in the ancient world, Thebes would almost certainly have been at the top of it. In her day Thebes was immensely wealthy and immensely powerful. Thebes was well connected and remarkably well protected. Yet in 663 B.C., Thebes fell to the Assyrians.

Thebes thought she was invincible. She could look at the water that surrounded her and her high walls and her massive army and her great wealth and feel inviolable. She could look to her powerful neighbors Cush, Put, and Libya, which provided a buffer between herself and hostile neighbors, and think there was nothing on this earth that could harm her. Yet despite her immense power, despite her high fortifications, despite her strategic alliances, Nahum declared,

> Yet she became an exile;
> she went into captivity;
> her infants were dashed in pieces
> at the head of every street;
> for her honored men lots were cast,
> and all her great men were bound in chains. (3:10)

How the mighty have indeed fallen! With this dreadful summary the prophet captures the horror, humiliation, and trauma that Thebes suffered in defeat.

It is somewhat surprising that Nahum would use Thebes as his example. Asking Assyria the question, "Are you better than Thebes?" (3:8) seems to lose something of its rhetorical power when it was Assyria who defeated Thebes. We can imagine the response: "We are better than Thebes, as evidenced by the fact that we razed Thebes to the ground." But I think this would be to miss the emphasis of Nahum's question. The emphasis of Nahum's question is, "Will you do better than Thebes? Will you fare better than Thebes? Are you so sure that the humiliations and the atrocities you committed against mighty Thebes will not one day return upon your own head?"[5] Of course, the implied answer to the prophet's taunting rhetorical question is an emphatic no!

The prophet engages in this history lesson to expose Nineveh's false sense of security. Like Thebes, Nineveh believed she was secure, unshakable, permanent because of her mighty army, her high walls, her great wealth, her magnificent temples, and her strategic alliances. All of these instilled in the Assyrians a sense of invincibility. Thebes had all this and more. Yet Thebes was not safe, her walls of water were not impenetrable, her alliances were not as strong as she thought, and her end was utter ruin.[6]

We see in Nineveh's false sense of security another portrait of the deceptiveness of idolatry. Just as Nineveh would look to her walls and her wealth and say, "For this reason I know I am safe," we, too, run to our idols in the hope that they will give us the help and the protection and the satisfaction that our hearts desire so deeply. Bank accounts, retirement accounts, job security, education, relationships (networks), spouses, children—all good things in themselves—are incapable of forgiving our sins or protecting us from our greatest threat, God's judgment of sin. The fact is, these idols and the safety they offer may be destroyed in an instant—through floods or famine, economic meltdowns or global pandemics, or the most inevitable catastrophe of all, death itself.

This is the nature of idols. They are full of lies. They promise life and deliver death. Like the false prophets of Jeremiah's day, our idols preach to our hearts, "Peace, peace, when there is no peace" (Jeremiah 6:14). Our idols constantly proclaim, "There is safety here, there is refuge here, there is satisfaction here, there is hope and happiness here," and yet God's Word exposes all these promises as lies. We should ask ourselves, *When the difficulties and uncertainties of life assail us, to whom or to what do we flee? Where do we find refuge?* The answer to this question will reveal our functional gods, the idols of our hearts.

### The Danger of Idolatry (3:11–13)

Beginning in Nahum 3:11, the prophet turns his attention from the tragic fate of Thebes and focuses on the certain future of Nineveh:

> You also will get drunk; you will pass out; you too will seek a refuge from the enemy. All your fortresses are fig trees with first-ripe figs—if shaken they fall into the mouth of the eater. Behold, your troops are women in your midst. The gates of your land are wide open to your enemies; fire consumes your bars. (Nahum 3:11–13, AT)[7]

With masterful poetry the prophet piles up and juxtaposes seemingly unrelated images. He likens, for example, Nineveh to a drunken man, a fig tree full of ripe figs, an army of women, and a city with its gates wide open. What do these things have in common? They all portray vulnerability. They depict a city that is on the verge of destruction.

Nineveh, he says, is like fat, ripe figs on a fig tree, weighing down the branches and just waiting for the slightest breeze to shake the branches and snap them off into the mouth of the eater, to be consumed. Nineveh is as naïve as a fig: comfortable, healthy, and yet ripe for falling. Nineveh's mighty soldiers, the prophet says, are like women. This is not a comment on women's strength, nor is it a comment on whether women should fight in combat. Nahum is simply utilizing the fact that women were not trained soldiers in ancient Assyria. To liken the powerful Assyrian army to an army of women is designed to expose it as weak, vulnerable, and ill prepared before the coming assault. Finally, Nineveh's massive gates, with thick iron bars designed to fortify the city from hostile intruders, are in reality wide open and destroyed, making the seemingly inviolable city utterly defenseless.

If the Ninevites had heard this description they would undoubtedly have laughed much like Goliath laughed mockingly at the little shepherd boy David when he strode onto the battlefield with a sling. When the Assyrians looked at themselves, they saw a fortress with an impenetrable wall. They saw an army the likes of which the ancient world had never seen. They saw eternal glory that knew of no rivals for power. But when Nahum looked at Nineveh, he saw a weak and vulnerable city, pathetic, degraded, and on the brink of destruction. How is that?

Nahum viewed Nineveh through the lens of his faith. Through the promises of God and by the word of God, Nahum saw the most powerful empire in the history of the world as a weak fig ready to fall to its destruction. Nahum chose to believe God's word over the very real, present, observable, and tangible experience of his and all Israel's everyday lives. It was a choice not too dissimilar from the choice Israel faced years earlier when they found themselves on the edge of the promised land, just to the south of Canaan, and preparing to enter the inheritance the Lord had promised their forefathers generations earlier. Moses had sent twelve spies to scout out the land, and the spies returned bringing with them the fruit of the land and reporting that the land was just as God promised, a land flowing with milk and honey. They also observed that "the people who dwell in the land are strong, and the cities are fortified and very large." They said, "We saw the descendants of the Anak there. The Amalekites dwell in the land of the Negeb. The Hittites, the Jebusites, and the

Amorites dwell in the hill country. And the Canaanites dwell by the sea, and along the Jordan" (Numbers 13:27–29).

Thus far the report was unanimous. All twelve of the spies agreed on the facts. But this was where the agreement ended, and the spies divided into a majority and minority report.

The majority of the spies said, "We are not able to go up against the people, for they are stronger than we are" (13:31). But two spies, Caleb and Joshua, objected and said, "If the LORD delights in us, he will bring us into this land and give it to us, a land that flows with milk and honey. Only do not rebel against the LORD. And do not fear the people of the land, for they are bread for us. Their protection is removed from them, and the LORD is with us; do not fear them" (14:8, 9).

Both the majority and the minority agreed on the facts: The land was good and desirable, and the land was filled with enemies from top to bottom. The difference was that the majority interpreted the facts from a posture of unbelief, and the minority viewed the facts through the lens of faith. Joshua and Caleb at that moment chose to position themselves firmly on God's promises that had come to their forefather Abraham generations earlier: "Know for certain that your offspring will be sojourners in a land that is not theirs. . . . And they shall come back here [i.e., to the land of promise] in the fourth generation" (Genesis 15:13, 16). By faith Joshua and Caleb called Israel to move forward in obedience to God and in reliance on his strength.

So too Nahum, years later, would issue the same call. The prophet called on Israel to view Nineveh from the same perspective of faith. It was tempting for Judah to view Nineveh as Nineveh viewed herself—invincible, powerful, secure. But Nahum summoned Judah (and summons us) to view this world and the powers of this world through the lens of faith, faith in God and faith in God's word. God's word creates reality and God's word is reality, and the reality that God has revealed in his word is that those who in their pride and rebellion stand opposed to him will eventually and most certainly fall to ruin. Those who have placed their hope in the things of this world, creatures rather than the Creator, will find that their idols are powerless to save in the day of trouble.

When Nahum looked at Nineveh, he saw a nation set in slippery places, about to fall to ruin, because it had set itself against the God of Heaven as it took to itself divine prerogatives of lordship and dominion. In their pride and arrogance, the Assyrians had touched the apple of God's eye as they oppressed those whom he called his own. Nahum knew by faith in God and trust in his word that Nineveh's fate would most certainly be one of destruction, and the destruction of Nineveh was good news for God's covenant people.

## Hope for Idolaters (3:11)

Admittedly on the surface, Nahum's taunt of Nineveh does not contain much that we might call good news. It is in its entirety a message of doom and of judgment against Nineveh. However, in seeking to understand the prophet's message, we must remember the primary audience to whom these oracles were delivered. Though Nahum's oracles are about Nineveh, they were not written primarily to and for Nineveh but to and for Judah. They were written for the people of God, and as such, they serve as a reminder that the evil Assyrian Empire would one day be destroyed. This is good news. Perhaps the major theme of the entire book is that this seemingly invincible empire whose might is surpassed only by her cruelty will one day experience the judgment and justice of God for all of her atrocities. The corollary of Nineveh's doom is that those who had been oppressed by the wicked city would be set free.[8]

As Israel heard of God's judgment on Nineveh, she would have been reminded of God's great provision of salvation for herself. Where it is said of Nineveh in verse Nahum 3:11, "You will seek a refuge from the enemy," Israel is reminded of Nahum 1:7, which says, "The LORD is good, a *refuge* in the day of trouble" (AT). What Nineveh seeks but is unable to find—refuge from the coming storm of God's judgment—Israel has found in the Lord her God. God shelters his people, protecting them ultimately from himself and the righteous judgment he will bring.

This of course raises the questions how? and why? The answer to these questions, the gospel according to Nahum, is seen perhaps most clearly earlier in the same verse. Nineveh's subjugation and defeat at the hands of the Babylonians is likened to the humiliation and degradation of a drunken man as the prophet declares, "You also will be drunken; you will go into hiding," meaning they will pass out (3:11). Here the prophet employs a conventional image in which God's wrath is depicted as a cup full of wine that his enemies will drink and, as a result, suffer the humiliation, degradation, and demise of a drunken man.[9] Psalm 75, for example, says,

> For in the hand of the LORD there is a cup
>   with foaming wine, well mixed,
> and he pours out from it,
>   and all the wicked of the earth
>   shall drain it down to the dregs. (v. 8)

For Israel, this image of a cup of God's wrath would have called to mind the legal practice of trial by ordeal, in which the accused was subjected to a physical test to determine guilt or innocence.[10] Of the variety of ordeals known and practiced in the ancient Near East, the only one known to be practiced in Israel was the drinking ordeal. In Numbers 5 we read that the woman suspected of adultery should submit to a drinking ordeal in which a solution is administered to her and the reaction of her body will reveal her guilt or her innocence (vv. 11–31).

It is this legal practice that is in view in the numerous references to the "cup of God's wrath" throughout the Bible. Thus what is in view in Nahum 3:11 is not just a humiliation and degradation (though that is certainly implied) but a judicial verdict. Nineveh's drunkenness will reveal their guilt and will manifest God's just sentence against them for their countless atrocities. Though they may run, their efforts to escape and their efforts to hide will be like the efforts of a drunk man trying to escape his pursuers. For Nineveh there is no refuge; there is no place to hide. They will drink the cup of God's wrath, their guilt will be exposed, and they will suffer the dreadful fate of those accursed by God.

But what about Israel? The question Nahum posed to Nineveh will soon be put to God's covenant people. Is Israel any better than Thebes? Is Israel any better than Nineveh? Nahum's taunt of Nineveh serves equally well as a reminder and warning to Israel. This terrifying portrait of God's judgment that will be unleashed against arrogant and wicked Nineveh should remind Israel that they are not exempt from the wrath of God and the judgment of God against their own sins. The cup of God's wrath is not only reserved for the Gentiles; the cup of God's wrath is also reserved for his own people. The psalmist said, "You have made your people see hard things; you have given us wine to drink that made us stagger" (Psalm 60:3).

Israel herself will drink of the cup of God's wrath, and she will experience God's judgment for her sins when God brings the Babylonians against Jerusalem. Yet unlike Nineveh, God has a plan and a future for his people. Isaiah wrote to these exiles,

> Wake yourself, wake yourself,
>     stand up, O Jerusalem,
> you have drunk from the hand of the LORD
>     the cup of his wrath,
> who have drunk to the dregs
>     the bowl, the cup of staggering. (Isaiah 51:17)

Why? "Thus says your Lord, the LORD your God who pleads the cause of his people: 'Behold, I have taken from your hand the cup of staggering; the bowl of my wrath you shall drink no more'" (Isaiah 51:22). Israel's future was not bright because she was better than Nineveh, but because out of the greatness of God's love that he had freely placed upon her, the Lord had taken the cup of his wrath from her hands.[11] And what Isaiah only alluded to, Jesus would announce—namely, that he had come to drink the cup of God's wrath to the bottom for sinners like us.

As Jesus was approaching Jerusalem, James and John came to him and asked if one of them could sit on his right hand and one on his left in his glory (Mark 10:37). James and John didn't have a clue what it would be like to be on Jesus's right and left hand when they got to Jerusalem (vv. 35, 37). Clearly they were imagining a coronation and a celebration, not a trial and an execution. They couldn't understand that on Jesus's right and left hand were the last places anyone would want to be. How did Jesus respond? "You do not know what you are asking. Are you able to drink the cup that I drink, or to be baptized with the baptism with which I am baptized?" (v. 38).

The cup that Jesus was to drink was the cup of God's wrath for the sins of his people. What Jesus experienced in his body was not only the penalty for sin but the declaration that he who knew no sin was regarded as guilty, vile, and wicked through and through. Jesus, the innocent Son of God, became like Nineveh and endured divine judgment, though it was a judgment far greater than Nineveh endured in 612 B.C.

It is difficult to imagine what must have been going through Jesus's mind in the upper room when he said to his disciples, who were ignorant of what was about to transpire, "This cup that is poured out for you is the new covenant in my blood" (Luke 22:20). As he handed them that cup and announced to them all the blessings that were theirs by grace—forgiveness of sins, freedom from bondage to sin, eternal life, hope, joy, peace with God—he knew that he would need to drink the cup of God's wrath down to the very dregs. Jesus would have to endure in his body and soul horrors that no human had ever experienced. It is no wonder that Jesus would pray, with sweat and tears, "Father, if you are willing, remove this cup from me. Nevertheless, not my will, but yours, be done" (v. 42). So terrible was the prospect, yet so great was the reward, that Jesus endured the cross, despising the shame for the joy set before him, the joy of communion with sinners redeemed by his blood.

How do we answer the question of whether Israel is any better than Thebes? Is the Church better than Nineveh? The answer is, "In ourselves, not at all." But for the grace and mercy of God, Nineveh's fate would be our fate. In ourselves we are no better than Nineveh, but in Christ we are so much better off. Jesus drank the cup of God's wrath down to the very dregs and thereby paid in full what we could never pay. He did this so that he could hand to us, as he does every week in the Lord's Supper, the cup of God's "blessing that we bless" (1 Corinthians 10:16).

# 49

# And Death Shall Be No More

NAHUM 3:14-19

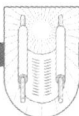

ON APRIL 20, 1945, in a bunker under Berlin's Old Reich Chancellery, Adolf Hitler celebrated what would be his last birthday. Berlin at this time was surrounded by Soviet forces that were rapidly closing in on the city. Nevertheless, Hitler's never-say-die inner circle would gather in the Chancellery to toast their Fuhrer's health to the distant sound of artillery fire and bombs. At some level, everyone standing with glasses in their hands knew that the Third Reich was doomed. Almost to a man, Hitler's closest friends—the leaders of the Third Reich—were each plotting escape from Berlin. Over the next several days, as the Soviet dragnet tightened on Berlin, these friends who had appeared so loyal would disappear.

When Nahum wrote his prophecy, there was nothing to suggest that the Assyrian Empire was on the brink of destruction.[1] There were no scandals rocking the palace. There were no economic collapses on the horizon. There were certainly no armies surrounding the city. When the Assyrians looked at their nation, they saw an empire that would last for a thousand years. Yet when the prophet Nahum looked at Assyria, he saw a scene much like that scene in April 1945: a nation surrounded by enemies, a city deserted by her leaders, and a king who would suffer an incurable wound from which he would never recover.

Nahum, the foremost taunter in the Bible, closes his prophecy with one final taunt, often referred to as the locust taunt. In this taunt Nahum offers a climactic announcement of the imminent destruction of mighty Nineveh.

Though Nahum's taunt is about God coming in judgment on Nineveh and his commitment to destroy this wicked city, the message of the prophecy pertains not just to an ancient capital of a failed empire but also speaks today about God's commitment to judge and destroy evil in every form, wherever it is found.

Nineveh was both a historical reality and a symbol. As a historical reality, it was the most recent iteration of oppressive tyranny and the most pressing cause of Israel's daily hardships and suffering. But as a symbol, Nineveh represented for Nahum and for God's people all that stood opposed to God and all that threatened to destroy God's people, whatever form it might take.

The prophet's climactic message may be helpfully summarized in a few memorable lines from Martin Luther's most famous hymn:

> The prince of darkness grim,
> we tremble not for him;
> his rage we can endure,
> for lo! His doom is sure;
> one little word shall fell him.[2]

Nahum speaks (and gives to all God's people) that little word: the devil and all his works will one day be crushed under the mighty hand of God's righteous judgment. The prophet's closing taunt orients us to that day, telling us not simply to look back to Nineveh but to also look forward with hope and with assurance that, in the words of the Apostle Paul, "The God of peace will soon crush Satan under your feet" (Romans 16:20).

### The Certainty of Nineveh's Destruction (3:14–15a)

Nahum's taunt begins with a call for Nineveh to prepare for battle. The two most critical resources for an ancient city hoping to survive a siege were strong defenses and plenty of water.[3] So the prophet commands the city's residents,

> Draw water for the siege:
>     strengthen your forts;
> go into the clay;
>     tread the mortar;
>     take hold of the brick mold! (Nahum 3:14)

Needless to say, these tasks were grueling work, typically reserved for slaves and the lowest classes of society. Yet the prophet instructs the entire city to take part in the work of storing up water and fashioning and setting mud bricks. He commands all the citizens of Nineveh—young and old, rich and poor—to throw all of their energies and resources into preparation for this great battle.

But no sooner does he tell them to get to work than he tells them that all their efforts are going to be utterly futile: "There will the fire devour you; the sword will cut you off. It will devour you like the locust" (v. 15). Nahum's message is clear. There is nothing Nineveh can do: No amount of preparation or defensive measures will prevent, mitigate, or enable them to escape the coming judgment. The best efforts of the greatest minds, the greatest army of the greatest nation, and the strongest wall of the strongest city are all useless before the fires of divine judgment. In this final taunt the prophet focuses on a final act of futility, that of preparing in vain to survive. This may serve them as it serves us: as a metaphor for all whose lives are not built on the foundation of God in Christ. All efforts at empire are useless as there is only one King whose reign is eternal and whose kingdom is forever.

Despite the Ninevites' most valiant efforts to defend their city and preserve their lives (if not their empire), the fires of God's judgment will break out in their midst; their city will be struck down by the sword. The prophet emphasizes the word "there" in order to signal that it will be in that very place, the place where the Ninevites have thought they were most safe, most powerful, most secure. "There" they will be consumed in a conflagration of God's wrath.[4] One Old Testament scholar vividly captures the dark irony of the scene when he says, "The walls of the city of Nineveh will become the borders of their tomb, not their defense."[5]

The prophet likens this devastation that Nineveh will experience to the devastation that is brought about by swarms of locusts (v. 15). As I understand it, at present in the United States we don't have a phenomenon comparable to the Middle Eastern locust swarm, so it is difficult for us to imagine the character and extent of the devastation wrought by locusts in the Near East. One commentator has remarked, "There are few natural events that can match the destructive power of a locust plague in the Middle East."[6]

The locust swarm was and remains infamous for its ability to devour everything in its path—so much so that when a locust swarm would move through a town, the crops would seem to vanish into thin air. One observer described his experience of a locust plague in 1915 like this:

> In passing the Jordan Valley these fliers of recent date came in clouds sufficiently dense to darken the sun and cleared this Jericho oasis of its vegetable gardens and the leaves from the fruit trees, rendering it for a while as

barren as the parched wilderness encircling it. The entire devastation was wrought by two visits lasting a day or so each, after which diligent search could not produce a single locust.[7]

For Nahum, the locust plague offers a picture of the scope of God's judgment. God's judgment will not be a minor inconvenience. It will not be a slap on the wrist. It will not be the unpleasantness of a siege that can be weathered with careful planning and hard work. When it comes, God's judgment will be complete, decisive, and final. Like a locust swarm that in a sense leaves nothing alive, so too God, when he judges sin, will judge sin completely and fully. There will not be those who get away. There will be no sin that goes unpunished.

With this the prophet offers a critical reminder of the reality and the gravity of God's wrath against sin. God will one day judge sin completely, and he has given us pictures of that future judgment in history. He gave us a picture when he came in judgment in the days of Noah, when he came in judgment against Sodom and Gomorrah, when he came in judgment against the Canaanites in the days of Joshua, and here when he came in judgment against the Ninevites. His judgment on these peoples and these places was in its own way comprehensive. These horrific events were meant to serve Israel, and they are meant to serve us as microcosms of a much grander, global reality—an ultimate, final day of judgment in which the devastation and destruction wrought against Nineveh in the seventh century will be extended to all who have taken their stand against God.[8] The Apostle Peter would write that just as the world that was formed through water was deluged and perished in the days of Noah, "by the same word the heavens and earth that now exist are stored up for fire, being kept until the day of judgment and destruction of the ungodly" (2 Peter 3:7).

Nahum's taunt teaches us that what we may experience as God's absence or God being unaware of the suffering of his people is in fact an expression of God's patience. The book of Nahum opens with a hymn that declares that God is "slow to anger," but goes on to say that God is also "great in power" and that he "will by no means clear the guilty" (1:3). Judgment will come. Christians mustn't mistake God's patience as a lack of concern or care, but rather should regard these days as expressions of divine forbearance. God's patience provides a daily opportunity to ask ourselves, *Have I found refuge in the only place refuge may be found? Have I found refuge not in the work of my hands or in pathetic attempts at self-defense and justifications for my sin, but rather in the God whom Nahum tells us is "good, a stronghold in the day of trouble" (v. 7)?*

Such questions are not designed to lead to doubt, much less despair, but rather to hope and an assurance that comes from the daily reminder that our lives have been bought with a price and are hid in Christ who is raised on high. The believer's hope is not in kingdoms of this world but "according to his promise we are waiting for new heavens and a new earth in which righteousness dwells" (2 Peter 3:13).

### The Failure of Nineveh's Hope (3:15b–17)

The locusts provide Nahum with a vivid picture not only of the comprehensive character of God's judgment but also of Nineveh's failed hope. Just as the prophet sarcastically calls Nineveh to prepare for battle though it will do no good, he sarcastically calls the Ninevites to multiply themselves. In a world before bombs, numbers meant a great deal in battle. Nineveh is commanded not only to multiply people but merchants in particular: "Multiply yourselves like the locust, multiply like the grasshopper! You increased your merchants more than the stars of the heavens" (Nahum 3:15b, 16a).

Nineveh's influence and affluence were in large measure due to her maintenance of an elite class of wealthy merchants. The accumulation of merchants made Nineveh in Nahum's day the economic center of the Near East. Nineveh was home to Assyria's Wall Street. These were the strong and the educated and the wealthy whose very presence in Nineveh was a constant reminder that they were in the right. They had the lion's share of economic capital, most of the intellectual capital, and almost all of the military capital—how could they be wrong?

But Nahum says, in effect, multiply them many times over, making them as many as "the stars of the heavens" (v. 16).[9] This is the only place in the Bible where someone other than Yahweh is said to multiply people like the stars of the heavens.[10] Here again, the prophet subtly yet powerfully exposes Assyria's pretensions to divine prerogatives.[11] The Assyrians seek to bring the entire world, including God's covenant people, under their authority and dominion. They do this through military strength, religious export, propaganda, and, as is suggested here, economic incentives and exploitations.

They may multiply their merchants many times over, but God says it will not make a difference. These sources of strength, wealth, and wisdom are themselves like locusts in that when they face danger they will fly away:

> Your princes are like grasshoppers,
>   your scribes like clouds of locusts
> settling on the fences

> in a day of cold—
> when the sun rises, they fly away;
> no one knows where they are. (3:17)

This is the merchants' and leaders' response to the coming crisis of God's locusts—they themselves will (ironically) become like locusts that disappear.

Many of the merchants who resided in Nineveh were not native Assyrians. Hailing from far reaches of the empire and beyond they brought great capital to the city, both intellectual and financial, yet they had no deep loyalty to Nineveh or its people. Unlike the common people, these merchants (along with the wealthy nobles and princes of the city) would have resources to flee before the danger arrived. What declared to the people of Nineveh a message of power and permanence—their wealthy and educated elite class—turned out to be fair-weather friends, fickle in the hour of need, willing to use others when it came to their benefit, but ultimately ephemeral and useless in the moment of crisis. Nineveh would learn the painful lesson that "the possessions and powers of this world do not avail against the Lord of Hosts."[12]

One of the difficulties of this text that has troubled scholars and commentators is the shift in the locust metaphor. In Nahum 3:14, 15a, it is the approaching army that is likened to locusts, and it is Nineveh who will be destroyed by the locust swarm. But in 3:15b–17, it is the Assyrian rulers and merchants who are compared to locusts who fly away at the sight of danger. However, this shift in the metaphor is part of the taunt itself.[13] Assyria was known for executing this type of complete destruction on cities and nations themselves. In fact, many believe that the destroying locusts of Joel's prophecy refer to the Assyrians, who would overwhelm their enemies so completely and decisively that they left nothing in their wake. But here Nahum is turning this metaphor against them. He says, in effect, "The cruel destruction that you wrought against countless cities and nations will come back upon your head as God brings the locust plague of the Babylonian army against you. You *are* like locusts, however, not in your powers of destruction but in your frailty and flight."[14]

These economic, military, and intellectual leaders were a source of Nineveh's confidence. These men, savvy, skilled, and wise, made the Ninevites boast, in effect, "If these are for us, if these are with us, who could possibly be against us?" Yet in the moment of crisis, the common men and the common women looked around to find they had been abandoned. The merchants had left, and the princes and marshals/scribes were nowhere to be found.

We too are tempted to tether our hopes to people and institutions. Perhaps it is professors or politicians, preachers or journalists, theoreticians or therapists, newspapers or news outlets. We too are prone to look to people and think, *If they believe it, then I must be on safe ground. If the group has a sleek website, they must be legit.* From my experience in the academy, I know that nothing sets off a flare of suspicion more quickly than the expression "Every scholar agrees . . ." This is not to suggest that there is no such thing as consensus or that scholarship should be disregarded but simply that the history of scholarship is littered with failed consensuses and the overthrowing of so-called assured results.

This message came to Israel as it comes to us, as a warning. Nahum warns us not to be fooled, not to be taken in by people or to place our eternal hope on mere men, movements, or institutions. It comes as a warning not to place our confidence in the things of this world that preach to us a message of power and permanence that is found in anything other than God himself and the revelation of God found in his Word. "The grass withers, the flower fades, but the word of our God will stand forever" (Isaiah 40:8). Those who place their eternal hope in pretenders to power will find themselves betrayed, hopeless, and helpless in the day of God's wrath.

Nahum 3:18 marks a significant shift in tone as Nahum shifts his speech from taunt to lament. The prophet offers a lament over the death of the king of Assyria. Of course, this lament is sung tongue-in-cheek and is just as sarcastic as the taunt that has preceded it. But the prophecy ends with a dirge sung over the tomb of a failed king and his failed kingdom.

### The Demise of Nineveh's Shepherd (3:18–19)

Throughout the book of Nahum, God's threats and judgments have been directed against an anonymous male figure. But it is not until the end of the book, in 3:18a, that our suspicions are confirmed. The identity of that mysterious and wicked figure is revealed to be none other than the king of Assyria himself: "Your shepherds are asleep, O king of Assyria; your nobles slumber." What the astute reader has suspected all along is now confirmed: the king and head of this cruel nation will, like the nation he has fashioned in wickedness, also come to ruin.

What is the root cause of Assyria's excessive cruelty and therefore the root cause of Assyria's terrible demise? From a human perspective it is that Assyria has at her head a wicked king and faithless shepherds. Assyria, like Israel, followed the predictable pattern of the people of a nation following their leaders and especially their king. When the king of Nineveh in the days of Jonah repented of his great evil, the city followed their king in repentance (Jonah 3:6–10). But now, a century later, the Ninevite king engages in excessive acts of cruelty, treachery, and violence, and the people follow. Therefore, God's judgment against this wicked city finds its ultimate focus on the wicked king himself: "Your shepherds are asleep, O king of Assyria; your nobles slumber. Your people are scattered on the mountains with none to gather them. There is no easing your hurt; your wound is grievous" (3:18b, 19a). Much like the city, the Assyrian king is depicted as abandoned by his nobles, and the mention of their sleeping suggests that they have died.[15] As for the people of the city, they are scattered on the mountains, perhaps because they have been slaughtered as they fled the doomed city.

Kings and rulers in the ancient world would commonly liken themselves to shepherds, even taking the designation as a title of sorts.[16] In his famous law code, Hammurabi of Babylon referred to himself as the "shepherd of the slaves and the oppressed."[17] The self-designation "shepherd" represented something of a sovereign's responsibility to care for and protect his or her people. Yet Nahum declares the king of Assyria to be a failed shepherd. He has not fulfilled the most basic duty of the king—namely, the protection of his people. His people are scattered, his nobles (likely) dead, and the king himself has suffered an incurable wound. He is envisioned as wounded and presumably dying. Every illusion of permanence and greatness that animated Assyria for generations has been exposed as false, and the wicked king slowly dies in the painful realization that his kingdom has fallen and his future has been cut off.

The author of Psalm 49 observed, "Man in his pomp will not remain; he is like the beasts that perish. . . . Like sheep they are appointed for Sheol; death shall be their shepherd" (vv. 12, 14). The king of Assyria was a shepherd of death. In his cruelty he led his people along paths of death that eventually ended in the place of death.

In Nahum's announcement that Assyria's wicked king and Assyria's faithless rulers would suffer the irreversible judgment of God, there is an implicit reminder to Judah and to us that where the king goes, the nation goes. Israel's only hope in escaping the same judgment as Assyria, and our only hope of escaping the same judgment as Assyria, is that God would raise up a good shepherd, a faithful king to rescue an intractably wayward people.

The fact is that Israel herself also suffered under a series of wicked kings and faithless shepherds. Not long after the days of Nahum, the prophet Ezekiel would declare to Israel's rulers:

> Thus says the Lord GOD: Ah, shepherds of Israel who have been feeding yourselves! Should not shepherds feed the sheep? You eat the fat, you clothe yourselves with the wool, you slaughter the fat ones, but you do not feed the sheep. The weak you have not strengthened, the sick you have not healed, the injured you have not bound up, the strayed you have not

brought back, the lost you have not sought, and with force and harshness you have ruled them. So they were scattered, because there was no shepherd, and they became food for all the wild beasts. My sheep were scattered; they wandered over all the mountains and on every high hill. My sheep were scattered over all the face of the earth, with none to search or seek for them. (Ezekiel 34:1–6)

God's response to the plight of his people at the hands of their worthless shepherds is: "For thus says the Lord God: Behold, I, I myself will search for my sheep and will seek them out. As a shepherd seeks out his flock when he is among his sheep that have been scattered, so will I seek out my sheep. . . . I will seek the lost, and I will bring back the strayed, and I will bind up the injured, and I will strengthen the weak" (vv. 11, 16a). God himself will come, and he will himself shepherd his people in righteousness and justice and compassion and mercy. He will be to them a shepherd the likes of which they have never seen. Even the greatest shepherd of Israel, King David himself, was susceptible to great sin. He too would use the sheep for his own gain, harming them to satisfy his own lusts and desires.

At the conclusion of Nahum, God comes in judgment as the mighty warrior king, as the shepherd of his people, to deliver them from the oppression of Assyria. With the destruction of wicked Assyria, God is not only judging evil—he is delivering a people. This is implied in the final verse: "All who hear the news about you clap their hands over you" (Nahum 3:19). Such clapping is an expression both of derision and celebration. All who have suffered the oppression of the cruel Assyrian emperor will experience the deliverance of the mighty God who sets the prisoner free. God is the good shepherd, the mighty king who fights for his people and delivers them from all their enemies. But God's destruction of Nineveh and the Assyrian Empire is only a picture of a much greater deliverance to come.

The Gospel writers often depict Jesus in just such a royal and pastoral role. In Mark 6, for example, we read, "When [Jesus] went ashore he saw a great crowd, and he had compassion on them, because they were like sheep without a shepherd. And he began to teach them many things" (v. 34). Jesus comes to gather the sheep that are scattered, to bind up the wounds of the injured, to feed those who are hungry, and to establish them in places of life. The selflessness of the good shepherd does not end with his hospitality but, as he declared in John 10, would extend even in his death on their behalf: "I am the good shepherd. The good shepherd lays down his life for the sheep" (v. 11).

Jesus came as the perfectly good shepherd. Unlike the Assyrian princes, scribes, and merchants, who saw danger and fled, Jesus, knowing the horror that awaited him there, set his face like a flint to go to Jerusalem (Isaiah 50:7; Luke 9:51). Unlike the Assyrian king who would send countless Assyrians to their death in a futile attempt to secure his own throne, Jesus gave up his throne and laid down his own life to secure the lives of his sheep. Christ suffered and died so that those who have gone astray like lost sheep might be brought back to God and given thrones in glory that they've neither earned nor deserved.

Nahum is one of two Bible books that conclude with a question. Interestingly, both books feature Nineveh as a central figure. God asks Jonah, "Should not I pity Nineveh, that great city, in which there are more than 120,000 persons who do not know their right hand from their left, and also much cattle?" (Jonah 4:11). The Lord's compassion and pity for lost and wayward Nineveh set on brilliant display in Jonah finds its corollary and balance in the Lord's final question to the king of the doomed city in Nahum: "There is no easing your hurt; your wound is grievous. All who hear the news about you clap their hands over you. For upon whom has not come your unceasing evil?" (3:19).

Nahum's climactic rhetorical question is uttered in the same taunting spirit as so many of his previous prophecies.[18] It is a question that reveals the cause of Nineveh's ruin—namely, their vast and unceasing evil perpetrated against countless victims and "emanating from the Assyrian king."[19] Even more importantly, Nahum's question is uttered in a spirit of vindication and triumph as well. So many who were victimized, brutalized, and cruelly oppressed at the hands of king and empire would behold the downfall of this once-proud and glorious kingdom. This symbol of wickedness and evil would come to ruin.

Of course, God's triumph over wicked Assyria and the downfall of the king of Assyria served Israel (and us) as both a type and a shadow of his greater triumph in Christ. At the cross, Jesus would overthrow one whom he called "the ruler of this world" (John 12:31), whose unceasing evil is not limited to the destruction of a human body but encompasses the ruin of body and soul together. As Paul reminded the Ephesian church, "We do not wrestle against flesh and blood, but against the rulers, against the authorities, against the cosmic powers over this present darkness, against the spiritual forces of evil in the heavenly places" (Ephesians 6:12).

The Christian life is a life of struggle. At times it certainly feels like (and sometimes looks like) we are on the losing side. Beset by sins over which we've gained little by way of victories, possessed of bodies that succumb to sickness and disease and eventually that last and greatest enemy we call death, the Christian life by all appearances is one of loss and defeat. Yet by faith in the risen Son of God, we are given a different song to sing—not a song of lamentation but of praise, not a dirge but a song of triumph. The prophet's closing question is in essence a gospel word. It's a public announcement of the ultimate demise of Satan and all his minions. It is an announcement of the overthrow of the death that he has sown in the world from the beginning. It is an announcement of the triumph of God's kingdom over all that has been touched by the evil of sin, death, and the devil.

The prophet envisions a day in which Assyria's victims will look in triumph on the ruins of this once-mighty empire. In a temporal and provisional way, that day came in 612 B.C., when the Medes and Babylonians overran the city of Nineveh and reduced its fortresses to rubble. But it would be at Calvary that Nahum's prophecy was fulfilled in full. When Jesus died for the sins of the world and rose to newness of life on the third day, it was then that God's people could look in triumph on the greatest enemies we face. The Apostle Paul could write to the Colossian churches about this very reality when he said,

> You, who were dead in your trespasses and the uncircumcision of your flesh, God made alive together with him, having forgiven us all our trespasses, by canceling the record of debt that stood against us with its legal demands. This he set aside, nailing it to the cross. He disarmed the rulers and authorities and put them to open shame, by triumphing over them in him. (Colossians 2:13, 14)

Though the unceasing evil of sin, death, and the devil has come upon us all, the good news of the gospel is that God has triumphed over them all in his risen Son, the Savior of sinners.

# HABAKKUK

*By Paul R. House*

# 50

# Seeking God in Troubling Times

HABAKKUK 1:1-11

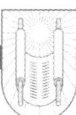

THIS SIDE OF THE NEW JERUSALEM (see Isaiah 65:17–25; Revelation 21:1–8), we will always live in troubling times. Right now[1] our national worries are the Iraq War, spiraling gas prices, a weak dollar, and a national election. Of course, we still have our perennial personal worries. We still have issues with our own spiritual growth, our children's walk with the Lord, our parents' health, and so forth. We also have matters of concern in our church. It is never easy to proclaim the gospel at home and abroad or to support those who represent us in Great Commission ministry.

History teaches us that things do not change all that much. In the past there were wars, elections, recessions, and depressions. In the future there will be more of the same until Jesus comes. We should not and must not be surprised at the existence of trouble in our world. Jesus told us there would be tribulation (John 16:33a). Yet he also told us to be of good cheer because he has overcome the world (v. 33b). Through him we also overcome the world. The good news that Jesus has overcome all obstacles to eternal life is the Bible's message. It should come as no surprise to us, then, that the book of Habakkuk helps us apply these great truths to our lives.

Habakkuk knew a lot about troubling times. He lived in the latter decades of the seventh century B.C. and perhaps in the early portion of the sixth century B.C. During his time Josiah, Judah's last righteous king, ruled from 640–609 B.C.[2] He turned to the Lord and sought to lead the nation to do the same. The nation had a lot that they needed to change. Jeremiah, Habakkuk,

Nahum, Zephaniah, and other faithful prophets in that era decried violence, oppression, dishonesty, immorality, idolatry, and other sins. Josiah tried to root out idolatry and other religious vices, but most of the people refused to repent.

When Josiah died in 609 B.C., a new era in Judah's history began. Judah lost political autonomy. First Egypt and then Babylon determined who would rule Judah and what its policies would be. Jeremiah and the other prophets had warned that worse things would occur if Judah did not wake up and turn to God. They failed to persuade most of the people. Thus in four devastating stages Babylon took some of Judah's best young leaders, then many of its most accomplished artisans and seasoned community leaders, then thousands of its people, and finally some remaining community leaders.[3] Daniel and his friends were part of the first deportation, and Ezekiel was part of the second. Jeremiah was part of the fourth. In short, Judah grew increasingly morally culpable until God sent the Babylonian army to destroy its cities and take many of its citizens to other lands. All these things took place in accord with the warnings Moses had given the people eight centuries earlier (see Leviticus 26:14–45; Deuteronomy 28:15–68).

Habakkuk saw the decline, and it appalled him. He discussed what he saw with the Lord. His book reports that conversation. To summarize the contents quickly, Habakkuk wonders (in 1:2–4) why evil persons in Judah escape punishment. He notes that the wicked are violent, unjust, destructive, and divisive, and yet God does not stop them (v. 3). Their actions paralyze the courts and pervert justice (v. 4). So he asks God "How long?" such things will continue (v. 2).

Yahweh responds in 1:5–11, telling Habakkuk that the Chaldeans, an old tribe in Babylon, will punish Judah's wicked people. Exile will cleanse the land of unjust and violent persons. Not yet satisfied, Habakkuk observes that the Chaldeans' defeat of Judah leaves the wicked still prospering. So in 1:12—2:1 he asks who will punish the Chaldeans, the evil conquerors of wicked Judah.

The Lord's answer comes in two parts. First, Yahweh tells Habakkuk in 2:4 that in the devastating days ahead, "The righteous [person] shall live by his faith." Only faith in the Lord will sustain the faithful in tough times. The Apostle Paul built his theology around this concept. Martin Luther, John Calvin, and John Wesley formed Christian movements on their beliefs about this verse. This verse remains essential to all persons who preach salvation by faith in Christ. Second, Yahweh assures Habakkuk in 2:6–20 that the Chaldeans will pay for their sins. Thus the wicked never escape. All nations that build empires by bloodshed (v. 12) and idolatry (v. 19) will perish. God remains in control of the whole earth (v. 20).

These answers satisfy Habakkuk. In a concluding hymn (3:1–15), he praises God's sovereignty and goodness. He pledges to live by faith (v. 16). According to 3:17–19, regardless of how difficult times become, Habakkuk knows that God will be his strength and will direct his steps. He has begun to live by faith in the new and threatening times he faces. God's promises sustain him.

Though Yahweh's day of judgment has not come yet when the book ends, Habakkuk knows punishment is inevitable. God's days of judgment will affect foreign sinners. Even powerful peoples are under God's control. God's days of judgment will also affect domestic sinners. Habakkuk includes Judah in the list of the wicked. If the covenant people can expect devastation, then what should the other nations expect? Under God's direction, Habakkuk predicts his nation's fall as a warning while there is still time to seek the Lord. Soon enough what he has threatened comes to pass.

The book's first eleven verses set the tone for the whole prophecy. Habakkuk presents his case for being God's prophet and for the problems he sees in Judah. He also receives his first response from God. Here he tells the truth about what always happens when people fall into long-term, degrading sin.

What he wrote then can warn and instruct us now and in possibly worse days if we let his book shape us into people who can trust God in troubling times. Let us turn to this man of God to find an anchor for our lives and a voice for our concerns. If we do, by faith we will see God at work. We will learn afresh that he is completely trustworthy and is always delivering his people.

### The Message Habakkuk Saw (1:1)

Like Hosea and Isaiah (see Hosea 1:1; Isaiah 1:1), Habakkuk begins his book by saying its contents are a "burden" (ESV, "oracle") that he "saw." These seemingly conflicting images could mean several things, but chief among them is that this burden came from outside the prophet. He saw something beyond himself. This something, this burden, came from God as Habakkuk experienced life in seventh-century B.C. Judah. When the burden materialized in real time as divine revelation and instruction, Habakkuk saw it. And he saw it as a prophet, as God's messenger, friend, ambassador, and herald. As O. Palmer Robertson writes, "He must be heard because he was the bearer of God's message, not because of what he was in himself."[4]

We need to grasp the significance of having God's written word before our eyes and in our hands. The prophets did not speak or write on their own initiative. According to the Apostle Peter, the prophetic word that we have with us today surpasses even Peter's eyewitness experience of Jesus's transfiguration in terms of revelational certainty. He writes in 2 Peter 1:19–21:

> And we have the prophetic word more fully confirmed, to which you will do well to pay attention as to a lamp shining in a dark place, until the day dawns and the morning star rises in your hearts, knowing this first of all, that no prophecy of Scripture comes from someone's own interpretation. For no prophecy was ever produced by the will of man, but men spoke from God as they were carried along by the Holy Spirit.

Whether orally or in writing, prophets spoke by the power, authority, purity, and truthfulness of the Holy Spirit who is God, who is trustworthy and wholly good. Isaiah, Jeremiah, Hosea, Habakkuk, and the other Biblical prophets spoke and wrote words that came from beyond themselves, words that came from God.

Thus the words we read from Habakkuk carry the authority of the God who gave them to him. We must let them shape us into their mold, for the mold was made by the Holy Spirit. When we are truly Bible-formed believers, we are Holy Spirit-formed believers. May God shape us into people who see and feel Habakkuk's vision and burden!

These words are useful and sufficient for our instruction because they are God's Word. Note how Psalm 19:7–9 combines the Scriptures' purity and usefulness:

> The law of the LORD is perfect,
>   reviving the soul;
> the testimony of the LORD is sure,
>   making wise the simple;
> the precepts of the LORD are right,
>   rejoicing the heart;
> the commandment of the LORD is pure,
>   enlightening the eyes;
> the fear of the LORD is clean,
>   enduring forever;
> the rules of the LORD are true,
>   and righteous altogether.

The Apostle Paul offered a similar twofold emphasis in 2 Timothy 3:16, 17: "All Scripture is breathed out by God and profitable for teaching, for reproof, for correction, and for training in righteousness, that the man of God may be complete, equipped for every good work." While "man of God" means a minister of God, the Bible clearly claims that the Scriptures shape all believers (see 1 Corinthians 10:1–13; Hebrews 4:1–13). The Bible offers us a life-shaping message that carries God's authority, usefulness, and accuracy. When Habakkuk shares with us how he came to trust God in troubling times, we do well to apply our lives in the same way in our times.

### The Prophet's Concerns about Judah's Wickedness (1:2–4)

Habakkuk gets right to the point in 1:2. He sees things in Judah that cause him great personal concern.[5] The three verses 1:2–4 are shaped by three very common human expressions: "How long?" "Why?" and "So . . ."

Like other Biblical writers, Habakkuk asks "how long" the Lord will fail to hear his prayer and act (see Psalms 13:1; 79:5; 89:46; Revelation 6:10). Like other writers of laments, he says that he cries for help yet gets no answer. He cries out about, or proclaims, the violence in his homeland, but God does not save them from distress. He may wonder why earlier prophecies of judgment, like Micah 6:12–16, have not come true.[6] He may wonder why God does not hear his cries for deliverance the way he heard Israel's pleas for help in Moses's day (Exodus 2:23–25).

God's silence when we call out to him can confuse and frustrate us. We know that God has the power to act, that he knows what is going on, and that he will stop all sin on judgment day. Yet the world slogs on, sin evident everywhere. As Elizabeth Achtemeier writes:

> Habakkuk's time is out of joint, as is every human era, because the world lives under slavery to sin rather than to the righteousness of God. And the prophet is weary—weary with the world as it is. "What is the world coming to?" is his question and the question of every faithful soul like him. Where will it all end? When will the wicked be defeated and God's order be established over all? Is God doing nothing about setting up his righteous rule on the earth? Has his purpose for humankind finally failed? Living in our age, in a society such as ours, those are our questions too.[7]

Though we can never fathom the mind of God with anything near full comprehension, it may be helpful to keep two basic Biblical teachings in mind. First, God is patient with sinners—all sinners, not just us. God explained his own character to Moses in Exodus 34:6, 7 in the following terms:

> The LORD, the LORD, a God merciful and gracious, slow to anger, and abounding in steadfast love and faithfulness, keeping steadfast love for thousands, forgiving iniquity and transgression and sin, but who will by no means clear the guilty.

In confusing times of seemingly unanswered prayer, we must remember the first part of God's self-definition. He is patient, merciful, and gracious. When we need his patience, we are happy to have it. Let us strive to be patient with his patience with others, assured that, as Peter writes, "The Lord is not slow to fulfill his promise as some count slowness, but is patient toward you, not wishing that any should perish, but that all should reach repentance" (2 Peter 3:9). This patience means sin will continue and sin will bring suffering in its wake. Sinners will sin. Hurters will hurt. But believers take on God's nature, and he is patient for the sake of salvation. May we be the same. May we be like the prodigal son's father—long-suffering, patient, alert to the returning sinner (Luke 15:20–24).

Second, in confusing times we should also recall God's concern for ultimate realities rather than temporary ones. We too often focus on today's setting, today's opportunities, today's effort, today's joys. God has a much broader, multifaceted, long-term goal in mind. He is saving sinners through his Son's death and resurrection. He is gathering a people who will be his means of declaring and showing his kingdom until he comes. He calls us to view history the way he does, with a long lens and a keen kingdom eye. Today may be marvelous or maddening, but God asks us to keep our eye on the final goal, which is a new heaven and earth, where God's people will live with him forever in the absence of sin and death (see Isaiah 65:17–25; Revelation 21:1–7).

Habakkuk continues his prayer in 1:3. Like us and like believers through the centuries,[8] he wonders "why" he must see and experience so many negative things. God makes him see[9] things such as "iniquity," which means "wickedness leading to sorrow," and "wrong," which means "distress leading to sorrow."[10] He sees sin and its consequences played out daily. He sees the pain and sorrow sin brings to sinners and their victims.

He also wonders why God seems to "idly look at wrong." How can a pure God let these things go on unaddressed? "Destruction and violence" to persons and injustice are apparent. Strife between individuals grows. Therefore, violence and "contention," perhaps better translated as "lawsuits," multiply. People fight and sue one another. Issues never get resolved. Abuses and chaos abound. No wonder Habakkuk laments.

Habakkuk concludes his opening prayer in verse 4 by describing the worst results of what has been happening in Judah ("So"). First, God's "law" (the *torah*) and the "justice" that results from adherence to it "never goes forth"; it is "paralyzed." A more literal translation is that justice is "stillborn." When God's word no longer governs their affairs, the people are left with human opinion and its ever-changing ways. Second, the wicked, those who transgress the standards for right relationship with God and others, are like a mob surrounding "the righteous," those who keep faith with God's standards for relationship with him and others. God's people live under threats. They are persecuted. In such times justice is perverted.

Without question, we can use Habakkuk's words to ask "Why?" and assert "So . . ." today. But I think we need to be careful to care about what Habakkuk cared about. He was concerned about God's reputation, God's word, God's justice, and God's people. His concerns were not money, luxury, recreation, ease, preferment, and self-promotion. Habakkuk united his concerns with God's and asked God to act according to his character. All complaints and laments are not created equal. Let us strive to coordinate our concerns with God's.

### The Lord's Solution to Judah's Wickedness (1:5–11)

The Lord answers. He says that he is not inactive. He has a plan to address all of Habakkuk's concerns. As he told Moses in Exodus 34:7, he will not clear the guilty. He will judge sin in Judah by sending another nation against Judah. Just as he sent Israel as a means of punishing the sins of the people of Canaan, and just as he sent Assyria to judge the sins of Israel, Judah, and other countries, so he will send the Chaldeans to remove all the wicked and their wickedness in Judah (see Genesis 15:12–16; Leviticus 18:1–5; Isaiah 10:5–34; Zephaniah 1). What will occur is God's astounding, forceful, and thorough work. As always, this judging work intends to encourage people to repent and see better days.

Habakkuk has asked why God seemingly sits idly by, doing nothing while wickedness expands (1:2). God tells Habakkuk in verse 5, "Look among the nations, and see; wonder and be astounded. For I am doing a work in your days." Using the same words for "see" and "idly look" that Habakkuk chose in 1:3, God commands the prophet to see and look at the fact that God rules these lands and to see that he is working among them. Francis Andersen observes, "The purposes of God for one person or one nation can be understood only in terms of the whole world. This means that God alone understands it all, while humans get glimpses. The purpose of God for one period of time . . . can be understood only in terms of eternity (v. 12) and eschatology."[11] World events can only be understood properly when one takes God's sovereignty into account.

God's work will surprise Habakkuk. The prophet would not believe it if he did not hear of it from God, according to verse 5. Verse 6 adds that God's shocking work is that he will send the Chaldeans to judge Judah's wicked people.

How is this shocking? If God made this statement prior to 626 B.C., it would have astounded Habakkuk that anyone besides Assyria would be God's instrument of punishment. Babylon did not defeat Assyria until c. 612–609 B.C. If God sent the word between 609 and 605 B.C. it would not have been surprising because one would expect Egypt, not Babylon, to rule Judah's affairs. The Egyptians killed Josiah in 609 B.C. and placed Jehoiakim on David's throne later that year (see 2 Kings 23:28–35). Regardless, the effect was the same. God had plans to judge sin. Habakkuk now knew these plans.

Wickedness never goes gently into the night. It must be rooted out. Sometimes wicked persons and nations are punished when people harsher than themselves defeat them. God had chosen to allow Babylon to be the harsh punisher of the wicked people Habakkuk saw.

Make no mistake about it. Babylon was not a righteous nation. Habakkuk 1:7a says that the Babylonians were "dreadful and fearsome," in part because they believed they were a law unto themselves. They felt no need to look beyond themselves to find "justice and dignity," according to verse 7b. As verse 11 summarizes their character, the Babylonians were "guilty men, whose own might is their god." Such was the nature of Judah's sin that God used wicked Babylon to judge them.

Babylon's armies were well-trained, well-equipped, and well-motivated from 626 B.C. onward. Their cavalry and charioteers moved swiftly and met foes with fierceness, as verse 8 indicates. Having lost to Assyria for decades, verse 6 notes that they were "bitter" for revenge and in a hurry to achieve glory. They were also brave and effective. Verse 9 states that they only moved "forward"; they did not retreat. They feared no king, and they met every challenge and met every objective, according to verse 10. The section closes by observing that they were hungry for further conquest (v. 11a). Judah had no chance against such a foe without God's help, and he was the One sending Babylon in the first place.

Babylon was a harsh, proud, and self-consumed nation. Most of all, however, Babylon loved violence and all it gave them. The violence in Judah would soon be quelled by greater violence. Soon Judah's wickedness would cower before a greater wickedness. Soon the violent ones roaming Judah's streets would be overrun.

God's judging work has at least two major goals. The first is to remove sin, as we have just seen. The second is to effect repentance. The prophets constantly call on people to repent. This word basically means "turn." People who repent decide to turn away from opposing God and his instruction and to turn to God and his service. Jonah, Haggai, and Malachi all saw people repent, as did John the Baptist, Jesus, Peter, and Paul. Repentance is wise and beautiful. It changes lives.

Habakkuk's prayer for judgment led to God's promise of judgment. In times of judgment one needs to repent and come to God through Jesus Christ by the power of the Holy Spirit. The prophet's concerns led to the Lord's work. Are you prepared for that work to come? Have you repented of your sins and made God's concerns your concerns?

## Conclusion

Judgment has never been a popular subject. It is just too depressing, too raw, and too real. We may avoid the subject because it makes too much sense to us. We can see that sin should not be left unpunished. Worse yet, we can see that we have sinned and that only God can save us. We have no way out but through repenting of our sin, asking God to forgive us because Jesus died and was raised for us. When we come to our senses and turn to him, we can trust him to forgive us.

Christians, the day may also come for us when we must suffer through the punishing of the wicked as Habakkuk did. Are we ready? Are we able? Are our concerns God's concerns? Are we willing to pray, wait, serve, and trust? If so, then we will be like Habakkuk—people who trust God in troubling times, people who reflect God's concerns and embrace his work.

# 51

# Praying in Troubling Times

HABAKKUK 1:12—2:5

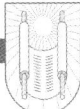

THE BIBLE GIVES US many examples of mothers seeking God on behalf of their children and husbands.[1] For instance, Hannah prayed for a son and promised to give him to God's service if God granted her request (1 Samuel 1:9–20). When God gave her Samuel, she kept her word (vv. 21–28), and she prayed a prayer of thanksgiving to God for his goodness to her (2:1–10). In Lamentations 2:20, Mother Jerusalem pleaded to God for her suffering children, and in Matthew 15:21–28, a Canaanite woman begged Jesus to heal her daughter. We can probably safely assume that Eunice prayed for her son Timothy many, many times (see 2 Timothy 1:5).

The prayers of mothers also adorn church history. Saint Augustine's mother, Monica, prayed for her son years before he took up the Bible and eventually confessed that Jesus is Lord.[2] John Wesley's mother prayed for her many children. Her sons John, Samuel, and Charles helped lead a revival movement that spread from England to many lands.[3] Her prayers were answered in abundance.

Christian mothers also often pour out agonized prayers. Perhaps their husband or children are not believers, or they are at best indifferent to things of the Lord. Maybe their parents are sick and need care, or they have died, and the pain of separation lingers. For others, their husbands have left the family or are leaving. Perhaps health is an issue or money is an issue or world events are an issue. Mothers keep praying through it all.

We join them. We share in the problems, the searching, the intercession, and the waiting. Like those mothers who are Bible-formed believers, we pray for salvation, healing, and understanding. We pray for God's will to "be done, on earth as it is in heaven" (Matthew 6:10).

In the text under consideration in this chapter, Habakkuk teaches us to pray, especially in troubling times, for he knew all about such times. He lived in Judah 600 years before Jesus, during the era in which his nation was disintegrating.[4] Corruption and injustice were common. Lack of covenant faith and political intrigue walked hand in hand. When Habakkuk prayed about these troubling matters in 1:2–4, the Lord promised in 1:5–11 to deal with Judah's sin by sending Babylon to punish the wicked people in Judah. God promised that he would indeed judge the wicked. Basically, he told Habakkuk not to worry; the wicked would ultimately not succeed in their schemes.

But Habakkuk does worry. Despite this first answer, Habakkuk plows on in prayer. He feels that God's promise that the wicked Babylonians will punish the wicked people in Judah does not address his concerns fully. He wants to know if God still rules and if he still rules justly. He wonders if God still distinguishes between the righteous and the wicked and if God has specific instructions for living in desperate times. As before, God answers Habakkuk's prayer. What God tells him echoes down to us, not just through Habakkuk but also through Paul, James, and the author of Hebrews, as we shall see. What God tells him and how Habakkuk prays gives us help for praying in troubling times and gives us a challenge to meet whether we are mothers, fathers, young people, or children—the challenge to live by faith.[5] As the text unfolds, it teaches us to pray with confidence in God's character (1:12), to pray committed to patience and service (1:13—2:1), and to pray expecting to live by faith (2:2–5).

### Pray with Confidence in God's Character (1:12)

As I have already indicated, Habakkuk did not find God's response to his initial prayer satisfying. He needed, or at least wanted, more. So he prayed again, seeking answers by asking hard questions. Yet he asked in faith, not in unbelief.[6]

What he did first was to stop and think about some fundamental principles. As the noted Welsh preacher Martyn Lloyd-Jones wrote about this text:

> We must first remind ourselves of those things of which we are absolutely certain, things which are entirely beyond doubt. Write them down and say to yourself: "In this terrible and perplexing situation in which I find myself, here at least is solid ground." When, walking on moorlands, or over a mountain range, you come to bogs, the only way to negotiate them is to find solid places on which you can place your feet. The way to get across the morasses and the places in which you are liable to sink is to search for footholds. So, in spiritual problems, you must return to eternal and absolute

principles. The psychology of this is obvious, for the moment you turn to basic principles, you immediately begin to lose your sense of panic. It is a great thing to reassure your soul with those things that are beyond dispute.[7]

The most basic premises we should affirm in our hearts consist of what we know to be true about our God, the Lord, the ruler of the universe, from the infallible word of God. What can we know? Where can we start?

Habakkuk starts with a rhetorical question in 1:12 that results in him confessing that God is "from everlasting."[8] Habakkuk's confession means that God is the permanent solution to what worries him. God is, as the writer of Psalm 90 prayed, "our dwelling place in all generations. Before the mountains were brought forth, or ever you had formed the earth and the world, from everlasting to everlasting you are God" (vv. 1, 2). He is the starting place and the answer to all our prayers.

Habakkuk thereby confesses that God does not change, for he is complete as he is. He does not grow weak. He does not lie, and he does not mislead. God is the rock upon which we can build our lives (see Deuteronomy 32:4; Matthew 7:24–27). Habakkuk reminds us that we have security in insecure times because God is "from everlasting." This conviction anchors our prayers in unchanging, permanent reality.

Habakkuk knows it is not enough for God to offer security unless he offers it personally—in other words, to *me* or *us*. Habakkuk clings to the fact that God has entered into a personal relationship with Israel and with Habakkuk through his covenants with Abraham (Genesis 12:1–9), Israel (Exodus 20—Deuteronomy 34), and David (2 Samuel 7:4–17). He affirms the truth that God acts on his faithful ones' behalf by saving them from sin and delivering them from enemies (Deuteronomy 28:1–14). He also knows that God forgives those who repent when they have failed (Deuteronomy 30:1–10).

How much more should we pray in the confidence of having a personal relationship with God?

We know about God because we now have the whole Bible. We know him through his Son, Jesus, the clearest and most wonderful self-revelation God has ever made. As Hebrews 1:1, 2 asserts, "Long ago, at many times and in many ways, God spoke to our fathers by the prophets, but in these last days he has spoken to us by his Son, whom he appointed the heir of all things, through whom also he created the world." We know God through the Holy Spirit who lives in us, comforting and teaching us (John 14:15–17). Because of this personal relationship, we can, through prayer, come boldly "to the throne of grace, that we may receive mercy and find grace to help in time of need" (Hebrews 4:16).

Habakkuk understood that God is not just everlasting and personal. He is also holy, set apart, different from human beings and the other so-called gods of the prophet's day. He is set apart from people because he does not decay, wear out, lie, or change his mind. He is set apart from the other gods because he is living, powerful, able to save, and willing and able to love the entire creation. Other gods have no power (Jeremiah 10:1–16). They are figments of human imaginations (Isaiah 44:9–20; Jeremiah 10). But God is real. He is holy. He does what is right. He delivers, restores, and heals.

He also teaches his people to be holy as he is holy (Leviticus 11:44). This means that we must love him and love our neighbors (Leviticus 19:18; Deuteronomy 6:5). It means that we must seek justice, love mercy, and walk humbly with God (Micah 6:8). It means that we are his servants (Isaiah 43:10) whose goal must be to act as a kingdom of priests to declare his glory to other nations (Exodus 19:5, 6; 1 Peter 2:9, 10). He has set us apart to share him with others who then become holy as they become his followers by faith.

After calling God the "Holy One," Habakkuk makes a statement that the ESV translates as "We shall not die" (1:12a). It is possible that the best translation is "You shall not die," for Hebrew scribes may have wished to preserve reverence for God at this point.[9] If so, then the assertion may affirm God's enduring nature (compare Psalm 90:2).

However, the ESV option is also viable. It is possible that Habakkuk again recalls Moses's teaching. He may have remembered that God warned Israel through Moses that if Israel broke faith with him by serving other gods and mistreating one another, he would discipline them. He would send prophets to call them to repentance. He would send trouble and enemies so they would look to him. Failing all else, he would take them out of the land (Deuteronomy 28:15–68). God would do all this to preserve Israel, not to kill them. God is faithful to raise up and renew. Judgment is not the end. Rather, grace is the goal. He promises to take Israel back when they turn to him (30:1–10). Both options honor God for his abiding faithfulness.

Habakkuk understands that God sends enemies "as a judgment" and that their coming is "for reproof" (1:12b). God will do what he says he will do. This truthfulness is not the kind we usually like from God. We prefer God's truthfulness to always be in our favor. But his words about judgment are as trustworthy as his promises of forgiveness. Though no doubt with regret at the circumstances, Habakkuk confesses that God has been a truthful and reliable covenant partner. Judah has not.

Habakkuk will soon move on to his concerns, but he has begun in the right place. He bases what follows on what is always true. We must likewise begin with what is true, with what is real. We must do so especially when our world has been shaken to its core, when airy dreams and wishful thinking simply will not do. From this strong, enduring, and certain base, we can praise, lament, request, and learn. But starting here gives us the perspective to carry on in the right direction.

### Pray Committed to Patience and Service (1:13—2:1)

Prayer almost always requires patience born of waiting on God. Some of us are not very patient in any realm of life. When I used to make one of my infrequent trips to the mall, I noted folks, usually males, sitting forlornly on benches or slouched in puffy chairs waiting . . . waiting . . . waiting. Some waited patiently, some not so much.

Clearly Habakkuk must wait, and for him this entails noting what makes the waiting hard and what makes the waiting worthwhile.

The next four verses (1:13–16) indicate that Habakkuk finds waiting for justice very hard. First, in 1:13 he asks God, "[So] why do you idly look at traitors and remain silent when the wicked swallows up the man more righteous than he?" In other words, "Since you are of holy character, why are you not doing something about the wicked?" The term "swallows up" often appears in passages that describe one nation devouring another, and that is the case here (see, for example, Isaiah 49:19; Jeremiah 51:34, 44; Lamentations 2:2, 5, 16; Hosea 8:8). Thus Habakkuk wonders why God would allow a wicked nation like Babylon to swallow up nation after nation. It makes no sense to him.

Second, he compares people to fish being caught by Babylon's hook and net in Habakkuk 1:14, 15. When Babylon snags these "fish," her people will gain wealth and will rejoice in their wealth. In love with luxury and riches, they sacrifice to their net—in other words, to their power and to the idols they associate with this power, according to verse 15. The living God is never in their minds. They think only of money, ease, prestige, plundering, pillaging, partying, power, and their other desires.

Third, with all this stated, Habakkuk asks in 1:17, "Is he then to keep on emptying his net and mercilessly killing nations forever?" In other words, "If suffering and idolatry abound, what good can possibly come of such things? Why does God not judge and get some quick glory? Why is he so patient? Why is he so patient with Babylon?"

The answer is that God will be patient with Babylon the way he has been patient with Judah. God once gave the Amorite people 400 years to change before Israel could have the promised land (Genesis 15:13–16). God endured Israel's behavior 850 years before judging them. God delays judgment so that sinful people like us can have time to turn around. He is not slow to judge the way *we* count slowness. Rather, he is unwilling that any should perish (2 Peter 3:1–13).

I need that sort of patience, and I need to stand with God as he shows patience with others (see Matthew 20:1–16). Some of your waiting may be terribly costly. I do not want to minimize that fact. If your waiting is costly, please know that your suffering is distinctly Christlike, for so he suffered for others. We can remain patient in such settings knowing that God does act in due time. He does not clear the guilty (Exodus 34:7).

Such waiting is worthwhile. The Bible teaches that we were placed on earth to do God's will, to trust in Jesus Christ and then do "good works, which God prepared beforehand, that we should walk in them" (Ephesians 2:10). He gifts and instructs those he saves (Romans 12:3–8; 1 Corinthians 12:1–11). He gives his people meaningful tasks to do, and he expects us to serve in his power and in his way.

Habakkuk was called and gifted as a prophet. Like his contemporary Ezekiel, he was a watchman for God in the world (Ezekiel 33:1–9).[10] As the watchman, Habakkuk warned the people of coming danger and future hope.[11] So when he says in Habakkuk 2:1 that he will station himself on the watchtower, he is not just saying that he will wait for an answer. He is saying he will keep doing what God has asked him to do. He will wait for God to address his complaint, but he will do so while remaining faithful to God and helpful to others. He has decided to be like the author of Psalm 37, who advised readers to wait for the Lord without fretting and to wait with trust and delight in God (vv. 1–4). Habakkuk will serve while he waits.

We can certainly expect God to answer as we commit our issue to him and look to him in faith. But the waiting will be more meaningful as we serve and grow. Our service will not force God's hand or show how serious we are about our prayers, for God is sovereign over time and circumstances. Our service is what we owe our Savior (Romans 12:1). Our service is a way we grow and take God's grace to others.[12]

I once had the privilege of studying the life of May Hayman, a young missionary nurse martyred in New Guinea in 1942.[13] I was amazed at her daily, normal, faithful service as she risked her life for her Papuan patients before Japanese soldiers murdered her. Her letters to her fiancé described her calm and normal service in the face of danger and death. Clearly she waited on the Lord, and he renewed her strength (Isaiah 40:31). Perhaps you are not facing death, but many of you face trials of many kinds. As you wait on God's answer to your prayers keep serving, keep redeeming the hours as you wait.

### Pray Expecting to Live by Faith (2:2–5)

God answers Habakkuk's second prayer in 2:2–20. He says that we have two choices short of Heaven: we can live by faith, or we can live by woe, by certain disaster. In the first part of this answer the Lord calls Habakkuk to faith in God and his word. This faith is necessary for a saving relationship with God, and it is also necessary for living faithfully in troubling times. God unpacks what this faith means and how Habakkuk may possess it and share it with others.

God begins in verse 2 by commanding Habakkuk to do his job as a prophet. He must "write the vision"; he must "make it plain" so that persons running by it or with it can read it.[14] There must be no mistake about what God intends. Thus Habakkuk must preach and write of sin, judgment, repentance, and hope, prophecy's great themes. Faith means doing the tasks God has given you to do to serve Jesus Christ in the world. Once again, waiting is not killing time. It is doing God's will.

Next, in verse 3 God promises that the vision "hastens to the end." That is, the vision of God's victory over sin through judgment will happen. It may seem slow, so Habakkuk must "wait for it," yet "it will surely come; it will not delay." By "delay" the text means "be held up one minute past when God has determined for it to be fulfilled." In this case it will not delay past 587 B.C., when Babylon conquered Jerusalem, or past 539 B.C., when Persia conquered Babylon. As F. F. Bruce concludes, "God has fixed the appointed time; the prophet must wait for it. But though it seems long in coming, it will not be later than the time of God's appointment."[15]

Finally, in 2:4, 5, God declares outright what has been implicit in his answer all along: Habakkuk must trust God that all these promises will come to fruition, for God is trustworthy. Otherwise, he is wasting his time to write the vision or wait for its fulfillment. God tells Habakkuk that the wicked are "puffed up" (v. 4), swollen with conceit, and filled with "greed . . . as wide as Sheol" (v. 5). They do what their appetites dictate. In stark contrast, God says, "The righteous shall live by his faith" (v. 4).

Scholars have debated what Habakkuk 2:4 means. The issue is that the word translated as "faith" can mean "faith" or "faithfulness." Of course, one leads to the other. Neither word exists without the other, though a faith relationship must precede faithfulness. Here the word indicates and includes both. Here lies the essence of how one *enters* the Christian life and how one *lives* the Christian life. We seek a relationship with God by faith that believes that God "exists and that he rewards those who seek him" (Hebrews 11:6). We enter that faith relationship with God through Jesus Christ. I cannot improve on what Paul writes in Ephesians 2:1–10:

> You were dead in the trespasses and sins in which you once walked, following the course of this world, following the prince of the power of the air, the spirit that is now at work in the sons of disobedience—among whom we all once lived in the passions of our flesh, carrying out the desires of the body and the mind, and were by nature children of wrath, like the rest of mankind. But God, being rich in mercy, because of the great love with which he loved us, even when we were dead in our trespasses, made us alive together with Christ—by grace you have been saved—and raised us up with him and seated us with him in the heavenly places in Christ Jesus, so that in the coming ages he might show the immeasurable riches of his grace in kindness toward us in Christ Jesus. For by grace you have been saved through faith. And this is not your own doing; it is the gift of God, not a result of works, so that no one may boast. For we are his workmanship, created in Christ Jesus for good works, which God prepared beforehand, that we should walk in them.

Did you hear the *entering* part? We are saved by grace through faith. Did you hear the *living* part? God has created us and saved us so that we might do good works that he has prepared in advance, indeed from before creation (see Ephesians 1:3, 4).

Hebrews 11, the great essay on faith, teaches the same thing. All those who know God do so "by faith," a phrase that appears fifteen times in 11:1–31. Those who did great deeds and persevered in terrible persecution did so by faith, according to 11:32–40. As God told Habakkuk, we enter a relationship with God and also live for him by faith (Habakkuk 2:4). This is the faith that Paul and James agreed is living faith as opposed to dead faith (Romans 6:15–23; Ephesians 2:1–10; James 2:14–26).

Will you enter this relationship with Christ by faith? Will you learn how to be a faithful person by first becoming a faithful servant of Jesus Christ? Will you who are Christians walk by faith and thus redeem the days in which you live? If so, then the troubling times will still be troubling, but the troubling times will end at last when the vision hastens to its fulfillment.

## Conclusion

When Habakkuk prayed in troubling times, God answered. He still answers today as we wait, serve, and trust. It may be that the answer will come soon, or it may not. It may be that we will live to see the answer, or perhaps not. Timing matters little in the end, for God's will matters most.

This is best for all concerned. Our prayers are part of our growth in Christ. As my friend Don West wisely has observed, even God's delayed or denied answers "are necessary ingredients in the struggle that each Christian assumes when he or she carries the shield of faith (1 Peter 1:6; 4:12–15)."[16] We will have some prayers answered in the "now" and some in the "not yet."[17] The answers belong to God, and we, like Habakkuk, can be sure that God's character is good, his service is good, and living by faith is good. Even if a particularly nasty set of Babylonians are at our gate, let us pray in faith, pray in hope, and pray in love. The Holy Spirit will come to us afresh in the way that we need him. May we all learn to pray in troubling times.

# 52

# God's Answer to Troubling People

HABAKKUK 2:6-20

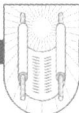

THIS PASSAGE INCLUDES the second part of God's answer to Habakkuk's second prayer. God has told Habakkuk to "write the vision" (2:2), to trust God's timing (v. 3), and to "live by . . . faith" (v. 4). Obedience to these commands separates the Lord's followers from arrogant unbelievers (v. 5). This obedience is all Habakkuk really needs to continue his ministry, yet God gives him more. He tells Habakkuk what will happen to the people who are troubling Judah. He reveals what will happen to the wicked.

What will happen is that "woe" will eventually come on the wicked Babylonians and on all who adopt their ways. While Habakkuk and the righteous live by faith that leads to faithfulness, Babylon will live by inflicting woe that will lead to woefulness for them. Babylon's oppressive ways will lead to their own oppression by others. Babylon's love for unjust gain will lead to their being plundered.

"Woe" is not a word we use much today, but it appears in many Bible translations to render the Hebrew word *hoy*. This word reflects "trouble," "disaster," "pain," "setback," and general loss of all that is good in life. It is a word reserved for those who resist God's will and reject God's ways and suffer the consequences for doing so. Thus where it appears, we should take it as a word of warning or, if necessary, as a word of correction.

Habakkuk can afford to wait for woe to come on the wicked, for he knows God's victory and ultimate rule are certain. These woes will come as surely as God's judgment has fallen on Israel and is in the process of falling on Judah.

Only those who trust in God (v. 4) can avoid the woe of being on the wrong side of the day of the Lord's removal of sin in all its forms. These woes are presented as actions done by people we may recognize. Their actions betray their lack of understanding that the Lord rules the world.

## Woe to the Wicked Banker (2:6–8)

God asserts that someday all the people that Babylon has harmed will sing a taunting song against their former overlord. The Lord never mentions Babylon directly, but as Francis Andersen observes, "Underneath this language, it is easy to make the metaphorical application to a nation as an oppressor."[1] God identified the Babylonians as the agent of Judah's punishment in Habakkuk 1:6.[2] Thus the descriptions that follow encourage readers to think of Babylon's behavior.

The first "woe to him" verse of the taunt song describes a corrupt banker. According to 2:6, this banker seizes what does not rightfully belong to him, and he piles up loan agreements ("pledges") from people who do not wish to be in debt. Today it would be something like a bank having the power to *force* people into a loan they could never pay. This banker is part bully and part loan shark. He is totally corrupt.

Of course, this imagery fits Babylon. They conquered nations and forced them to pay tribute money, a high tax extorted from beaten foes. None of the fallen countries wished Babylon to conquer them, and none of them wanted to take out such "loans."

Just as loan sharks and bullies often fall prey to their former victims, so Babylon will face the wrath of their debtors. Verse 7 says that the debtors will "suddenly arise" to make Babylon pay. Verse 8 adds that the plundered ones will someday plunder their oppressor. The blood that Babylon has spilled to gain tribute money and to grab territory will come back to haunt them. The unjust banker will pay the last penny. He will reap what he has sown.[3] He will become as poor as the weakest person he ever oppressed.

## Woe to the Wicked Builder (2:9–11)

Babylon hoped to construct a secure future on the backs of others' suffering. All the "evil gain" they gathered from their conquests was taken in hopes that they could have a "nest on high" to "be safe from the reach of harm" (v. 9). They wished their cities to be as safe from invasion as an eagle in a nest is from attack by a ground predator. They wished their economy to be safe from the shifting fortunes of trade and production. In many ways, Babylon succeeded in having such wealth and security in Habakkuk's day. Marvin Sweeney writes:

> During the Neo-Babylonian period, and especially during the reign of Nebuchadnezzar, the city of Babylon was rebuilt into a magnificent capital city with major palaces for the king, the hanging gardens of Babylon, a processional way through the city, and the ziggurat Entemenanki, which served as the focal point for the Akitu New Year celebration. It was at the temple located at the top of the Entemenanki that the Babylonian king received the tablets of destiny that authorized his kingship for another year.[4]

Clearly Babylon built quite a "nest."

Verse 10 states that Babylon did not know that the building-up of this kingdom would in time bring shame, not glory. Babylon sinned against its own future by what it did. Babylon's leaders no doubt thought their policies amounted to good politics. But as Waylon Bailey writes, "God saw the plan from a different perspective. Such a plan incurred guilt and thus promised sin's wages—death."[5] By taking lives, Babylon forfeited its own. The walls and rafters of this evil house—in other words, the nations upon which Babylon has built—cry out against the builder in verse 11. The house rebels against its maker. Death will come to those who build on death.

### Woe to the Wicked City Planner (2:12–14)

Now the prophet compares Babylon to an individual planning a whole city, not just a house. As Habakkuk 2:8 has already indicated, Babylon's empire was built by spilling the blood of its opponents. Habakkuk repeats this fact in verse 12a when describing the work of "him who builds a town with blood." Such actions lead to a city built "on iniquity" (v. 12b). This city cannot last.

Expending time, energy, and resources on killing for the purpose of national expansion is vain. Verse 13a reminds us that God did not create people so they could "labor merely for fire," so they could burn other people's homes and plunder other people's bank accounts. He did not create nations to "weary themselves for nothing" (v. 13b) by chasing after temporary pleasures and vicious goals. Human beings were made for so much more than this. They were made by God for relationship with him and for service of others (Genesis 1:26–28).

People who turn aside from trivial pursuits and instead choose to seek God learn what life is about. They embrace God's kingdom. They discover the joy of knowing that "the earth will be filled with the knowledge of the glory of the LORD as the waters cover the sea" (Habakkuk 2:14). They are glad that his kingdom will come and that his will shall be done on earth as in Heaven. They serve the King of kings, the Lord of lords, the present and permanent Ruler of the universe (see Revelation 19:16).

The Babylonians sought to usurp God's role and God's realm, but they failed. Knowledge of the living God will prevail, and all pretenders to his throne and their wearying ways will be destroyed. God will bring his people to Zion, his city, and he will live with them there in the absence of sin forever (see Isaiah 4:2–6; 65:17–25; Revelation 21:1–7).

## Woe to the Date Rapist (2:15–17)

As if the preceding characterizations were not loathsome enough, the prophet offers a still more troubling portrait of Babylon's activities. Habakkuk 2:15 states that Babylon makes other countries drink the cup of defeat so these nations will get drunk and expose their nakedness, weakness, and vulnerability, so Babylon can take advantage of them. In other words, he portrays Babylon as a date rapist. Babylon has gotten other lands drunk with despair at Babylon's victories. Then Babylon violated the victim. This portrait demonstrates the vile, self-serving, and lust-driven nature of Babylonian national foreign policy. Such behavior cannot be justified on any grounds.

As the previous "woes" have already warned, what Babylon has done to others will be done to Babylon. They will be uncovered and violated. This threat came to pass in 539 B.C. when Persia conquered Babylon. At that time Babylon experienced "shame instead of glory," as verse 16a threatens. At that time, Babylon, which once made other countries drink the bitter cup of defeat, drank from this same cup. Habakkuk reminds readers that this "cup" came from "The LORD's right hand" (v. 16b).[6] Babylon drank because God ordained it as a punishment. The blood of those they wronged cried out against them (v. 17) as surely as Abel's blood cried out after Cain's murder of Abel (Genesis 4:10). God heard Abel at the dawn of time, he heard Babylon's victims in Habakkuk's day, and he hears now.

History is filled with examples of the tables turning on oppressors. One has only to recall Berlin's and Tokyo's plight after World War II, Rome's plight when the barbarians came, or Jerusalem's desperation when Babylon conquered that city to see the principle in practice. Such occurrences are not accidents of history. They reveal God at work in real time. Every nation must take this truth to heart and amend any errant, unjust ways lest it find itself on the wrong side of God's cup of judgment.

### Woe to the Worshiper of Idols (2:18, 19)

In many ways this last woe is the source of all the others. Idolatry leads to self-service, leading to oppression, misuse of things, and mistreatment of people. It is the most foolish of sins (see Isaiah 44:9–20) and the most dangerous of errors. No wonder, then, that the First Commandment declares, "You shall have no other gods before me" (Exodus 20:3).

Habakkuk wonders aloud in verse 18 what one hopes to gain by worshiping an idol. After all, an idol's "maker has shaped it" (2:18a). Therefore, whoever trusts in an idol "trusts in his own creation" (v. 18b), nothing more.

Babylon had official idols, but they also made idols of power, sex, money, and fame. Elizabeth Achtemeier observes that all "the false gods of the tyrants and oppressors and military powers will be unable to save their people from the curse of the only true God."[7] Trusting in these idols amounts to trusting in human beings.

Those who trust in "speechless idols" (v. 18c) have no guidance in perilous times. Idols cannot awake. They cannot arise. They cannot teach their worshipers, as verse 19 warns. They are lifeless things. Babylon has shaped gods for themselves out of their own imaginations in the image of their lusts. Apparently they considered oppression and greed qualities commanded by their gods. If so, then their worship is a primary source of their destruction. Woe is the only result they should expect.

These verses highlight the danger and cruelty associated with idolatry. We must never forget the woe of idolatry as we pass our days in a pluralistic environment. Trusting in anything other than the one true and living God revealed in Scripture is dangerous. It is destructive. It is to base one's life on a lie. Such trust cannot save, for idols cannot remove sin. Neither can idols teach their worshipers how to live as our Creator directs people to live. Any religion, cult, or practice that takes one away from a relationship with God through Jesus Christ leads to spiritual death (see John 14:6; Acts 4:12). As John Calvin warned, "As then idols are dead things, it follows that they are most palpable impostures of Satan, by which he fascinates the minds of men, when they thus devote themselves to dead things."[8] Such truths are not comfortable or popular today, but they remain the plain and merciful teaching of God's written Word. Woe awaits those who worship non-gods.

### The Path Away from Woe (2:20)

Habakkuk makes it clear that the woes he describes are not permanent. Troubling people will come and go. The wicked banker, builder, city planner, date rapist, and idolater will continue to live among us. Babylon is not history's last terrible oppressing nation, and vicious societies and individuals are with us still. We must be realistic about how the world works.

Nonetheless, Habakkuk concludes this section with a strong statement about God's sovereignty that puts all these woes into perspective. Idolaters will continue to worship what their hands can make—money, power, sex, empires, images, technology, and knowledge. Fulfilling their desires will harm others. "But the LORD is in his holy temple; let all the earth keep silence before him" (2:20).

Habakkuk conceives of reality much like Isaiah did. Isaiah saw God "sitting upon a throne, high and lifted up" in a room patrolled by flying fiery beings calling out God's holiness (Isaiah 6:1–3). Isaiah envisioned God as sitting high above the earth ruling the world (40:21–23) and as receiving tribute from earth's kings (18:4, 7). Similarly, Habakkuk portrays God as governing the nations from his temple—the physical symbol of his spiritual presence in the physical world—for the sake of his people. This reality contrasts with idols, which are physical symbols of beings that do not exist. God is real. He rules creation. He is utterly different than the gods that wicked people worship.

The fact that God rules should comfort believers and chasten those headed for woe. It should comfort believers because it reminds them that their suffering and sorrow will not last forever. Thus we can be patient as we serve Christ, knowing we are secure in him. As David Garland observes, "The covenant people know a security that the idolaters can never experience. The God who watches over the righteous is the God of heaven, omnipresent and omnipotent."[9]

Believers can and will struggle to understand and deal with pain, suffering, injustice, persecution, and sickness. They will continue to ask the sorts of questions that Job asked. They will be called upon by God to learn to confess what the Apostle Paul does in Philippians 4:10–13:

> I rejoiced in the Lord greatly that now at length you have revived your concern for me. You were indeed concerned for me, but you had no opportunity. Not that I am speaking of being in need, for I have learned in whatever situation I am to be content. I know how to be brought low, and I know how to abound. In any and every circumstance, I have learned the secret of facing plenty and hunger, abundance and need. I can do all things through him who strengthens me.

We can make this confession because, as Paul adds, "My God will supply every need of yours according to his riches in glory in Christ Jesus. To our God and Father be glory forever and ever. Amen" (Philippians 4:19, 20).

Only the God who rules the earth can "supply every need." Comfort comes from trusting this God.

Yet it is important to remember that this comfort is reserved for those who trust God by putting their faith in Jesus Christ through the power of the Holy Spirit. This comfort only comes to those who receive the gift of faith and obedience that Habakkuk 2:2–4 describes. Those who receive Christ will eventually praise him before his throne in Heaven, but those who reject Jesus will face the fires of eternal woe (Revelation 20).

## Conclusion

Troubling persons and troubling nations are not a permanent problem for Christians. Our God who rules the world from "his holy temple" (Habakkuk 2:20) will call the wicked into account. He will not fail to judge them. We can endure trouble, then, for we know that the God who ruled Judah and Babylon then rules all the nations of the earth now. Those who trust in him need not fear troubling times and those who cause them.

# 53

# Rejoicing during Troubling Times

## HABAKKUK 3

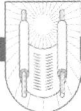

VERY FEW THINGS are as challenging and rewarding as rejoicing in troubling times. I have persevered in tough times. I have grown through tough times. But those few times I have rejoiced in hard times are among the dearest and precious and irreplaceable in my life. Many of you have no doubt had similar experiences.

Maybe your experience was like it was for the believers described in Acts 5:17–42. Having been jailed, released, and threatened, "they left the presence of the council, rejoicing that they were counted worthy to suffer dishonor for the name" (v. 41). These disciples of Jesus were experiencing his words from Matthew 5:11, 12: "Blessed are you when others revile you and persecute you and utter all kinds of evil against you falsely on my account. Rejoice and be glad, for your reward is great in heaven, for so they persecuted the prophets who were before you." They were learning to do what James 1:2–4 commands: "Count it all joy, my brothers, when you meet trials of various kinds, for you know that the testing of your faith produces steadfastness. And let steadfastness have its full effect, that you may be perfect and complete, lacking in nothing."

Such words are countercultural these days in Christian circles. We emphasize happiness, numerical growth, successful parenting, and so forth. We highlight our martyrs from time to time, but we are more interested in ease. We spend little time learning to rejoice in the situations that Jesus, James, and Habakkuk described.

This situation is odd to me, for there is much to trouble us. Wherever we live, people have troubles at work, in their families, and in their churches. They lose loved ones. They deal with broken relationships. So it seems quite practical to me to let Habakkuk shape us into people who know how to handle reality joyfully.

The prophet has faced reality squarely so far. He has already prayed about wickedness in Judah and was told that judgment would solve that problem (Habakkuk 1:1–11). He has prayed about God's character and Babylon's wickedness and has been reassured that faith and faithfulness are the way the righteous must live in such times (1:12—2:5). He has learned that woe awaits the wicked (2:6–20) but also that "the earth will be filled with the knowledge of the glory of the Lord as the waters cover the sea" (v. 14). Having embraced God's answers, he now prays a third time.

This time he incorporates Israel's past and present into prayers for the future. He uses Israel's history to gain perspective on the present. As Habakkuk prays, he asks God to renew his great past deeds (3:1, 2), he recounts God's past deeds for present comfort (vv. 3–15), and he commits to rejoicing in God regardless of future circumstances (3:17–19). I will spend less time on the first two points than on the third, but each part builds on what precedes it. Each part leads us forward on the path of rejoicing in tough times.

## Humbly Ask God to Renew His Past Great Deeds (3:1, 2)

I enjoy reading Christian biographies and histories of Christian events. I have learned much about godliness from books about J. C. Ryle, Marcus Loane, D. B. Knox, John Knox, Charles Simeon, May Hayman, and others. My hope is that wonderful past events can happen afresh in our day. After all, the same God still rules the universe.

Habakkuk prays in the same spirit in 3:1, 2. He notes that he has been told of what God has already accomplished in verse 2. Very importantly, these reports lead him to reverence for God. This reverence produces humility. Habakkuk recognizes that all is lost unless God revives his work. All is lost unless, amid his justifiable wrath, God shows mercy. The people are utterly dependent on God and his decision to revive, restore, and renew. His person and his grace are all they have or need. We must learn this humility. James Montgomery Boice asks:

> What are the elements of faithful prayer? The first and most essential is humility. We cannot succeed in prayer if we come into God's presence demanding things because of who we are. We cannot succeed if we think that somehow we deserve to be there and deserve to be heard.[1]

Part of this humility is recognizing that we are dependent on God doing now what he has done before. Will we ask him to heal again, save again, forgive again, drive out Satan again, or rebuke us again? If we will, then we can be on our way to rejoicing in troubled times. Let us hear and learn and pray.

### Faithfully Recount God's Past Deeds for Present Comfort (3:3–15)

Having prayed humbly *for* God to do what only God *can* do, Habakkuk comforts himself by recounting what God has done in the past. He knew that strength and hope for the present come from trusting in God's future provision based on God's past provision.[2] So he prays back to God what God has done. As he does so, he emphasizes God's relational love (vv. 3–5) and God's supreme power (vv. 6–15).

Habakkuk's prayer mentions God coming from Teman and from Mount Paran (3:3a). As he confessed in 1:12, 13, the prophet asserts again here that God is the Holy One, the pure one, the different one. It is possible that these places remind readers of "the steps by which God led Israel into the possession of the land."[3] Teman represents Edom, the area south of Judah, while Paran represents Sinai and Egypt.[4] God certainly brought Israel along this route.

But it is more likely, I think, that this mention of Teman and Paran refers to God coming to the region of Mount Sinai with the people to join them to him in loving covenant bonds. Deuteronomy 33:2–5 states:

> The LORD came from Sinai
>   and dawned from Seir upon us;
>   he shone forth from Mount Paran;
> he came from the ten thousands of holy ones,
>   with flaming fire at his right hand.
> Yes, he loved his people,
>   all his holy ones were in his hand;
> so they followed in your steps,
>   receiving direction from you,
> when Moses commanded us a law,
>   as a possession for the assembly of Jacob.
> Thus the LORD became king in Jeshurun,
>   when the heads of the people were gathered,
>   all the tribes of Israel together.

In other words, Habakkuk recalls when God delivered Israel from slavery in Egypt, sustained them in the desert, and brought them safely to Sinai. There God taught Israel how to be "a kingdom of priests and a holy nation" (Exodus

19:6; see also 1 Peter 2:9). There God committed himself to the people, and they committed themselves to him (Exodus 24:1–8). God proved himself to be Israel's loving father.[5] Love and instruction were the order of the day, as I hope it is in all our homes. Protection (in the form of "brightness") and "plagues" kept Israel's enemies at bay, as Habakkuk 3:4, 5 recalls. They were a safe, instructed, committed people.

Habakkuk recalls these days and takes heart. He treats them as facts, not as myths; not even as kernels of truth greatly expanded.[6] As Martyn Lloyd-Jones argues:

> If God did not actually do the things recorded in the Old Testament for Israel, then the whole Bible may be just a piece of psychology meant to keep me happy. The Bible, however, plainly shows that my comfort and consolation lies in facts—the fact that God has done certain things and they have literally happened.[7]

And they happen each day. God loved Israel, and Habakkuk desires that real, demonstrable love will envelop his people again.

Once Israel left Mount Sinai (Numbers 10:11, 12) they began their long journey in the desert. After they crossed the Jordan into Canaan, the Lord gave them victory after victory. He gave Israel the land promised to Abraham hundreds of years earlier (see Genesis 12:7; 15:12–16). Before giving them the land, Habakkuk 3:6 says, he measured it all out according to his "everlasting ways" (Habakkuk 3:6). Verse 7 says that Cushan and Midian, lands on Canaan's outskirts, trembled at what the Lord was about to do. Verses 8–10 proclaim that the earth did God's bidding, while verse 11 states that "the sun . . . stood still," which is likely a reference to Joshua 10:1–15. Habakkuk 3:12–15 portrays God marching, threshing, crushing, laying bare, piercing, and trampling the wicked for Israel's sake. In doing so he saved Israel, his "anointed" (v. 13).

This picturesque imagery highlights God's power. It is immeasurable. It is unstoppable. It works justice for those who love and serve him. Habakkuk recalls this power in prayer as a way of asking God to use it again.

Our prayers reveal our fears and our confidences. Our God loves us with devotion proven by the blood of his Son and sealed by the presence of the Holy Spirit (Ephesians 1:3–14). His power is great like his love. Great comfort can be gained by recalling such truth. What problem cannot be overcome by such strength? Love and strength are a potent combination, and God gives them to us in full measure. Take heart, then, and face reality. Learn to rejoice in troubled times.

## Commit to Rejoicing in God Regardless of the Circumstances (3:16–19)

We now reach the prayer's grand conclusion. Habakkuk's humble asking and God's faithfulness have led him to commit to rejoicing in God no matter what happens. He will wait for God's word to come true even though that word scares him (3:16). He will rejoice in God even though he may suffer economic deprivation (vv. 17, 18). He will trust in God's strength even though he must go to high, treacherous places (v. 19). These promises constitute a proper commitment to the all-loving and all-powerful God.

What God has told Habakkuk and what he has recalled makes the prophet's knees buckle. In verse 16, the Lord's servant says that he "trembles." He confesses that his "lips quiver" and he feels as if he will collapse. God's great past deeds are awe-inspiring. God's revelation of present and future judgment on his people hardly settles Habakkuk's nerves. The prophet speaks realistically about his own frailty and God's glory.

Regardless, he will "rest quietly for the day of trouble to come to the nations [that] will invade us" (3:16b, AT).[8]

Some scholars have wondered if this turnabout from fear is too abrupt and suggest that a textual error has occurred. Others rightly observe the prophet's growth in faith. J. J. M. Roberts writes:

> Nonetheless, even in his terror, the prophet recognizes the promise implicit in the vision, and the response of his will to the vision is precisely what God demanded in Hab. 2:3. In light of the vision, Habakkuk is willing to cease from his complaints and to wait quietly for the vision's fulfillment, for the day of judgment to come upon the Babylonian oppressor.[9]

F. F. Bruce agrees. He comments, "As he recovers and considers the vision, Habakkuk expresses his faith in the spirit of 2:4b. . . . Yahweh's righteous retribution may be slow in coming, but come it will [compare 2:3b]."[10]

Francis Anderson also agrees, and he adds that this verse represents "a lyrical synthesis of faith and love that is the height of adoration—Yahweh, terrible and compassionate."[11]

Faith operates even when fear is present. Faith trusts God and God's plans even when we feel afraid. God gave Jesus this courage as he prepared to bear God's judgment of sin on the cross.[12] God gave Jeremiah the strength to serve while knowing that terrible judgment was coming (Jeremiah 21—45). God gives this courage now. He never fails, and he is with us "always, to the end of the age" (Matthew 28:20). Thus we can wait restfully, quietly, faithfully, not simply in a spirit of resignation. It will seem odd to the world that we have this peace, but "take heart," Christ has "overcome the world" (John 16:33).

Habakkuk is no fool. The book to this point has certainly proven this. He knows that a Babylonian invasion and occupation followed by a defeat of Babylon will destabilize the region and its economy. Any further disaster, such as drought, could prove devastating. That said, Habakkuk 3:17 terrifies a former farmer like me, much less real farmers like my dad and my brother. If there are no figs, grapes, grain, sheep, or cattle, then the olive oil, wine, grain, and animal markets will fail. There will be no cash and no way to get any. This description is like Pittsburgh's economy when the steel industry died in the early 1980s. It is like what happened to the airline industry right after September 11, 2001. It is like what happened to the New Orleans economy after the levees broke in 2005.

Even if such a collapse comes—and he has good reason to think it will—Habakkuk will rejoice. In what? In Yahweh, the Savior. No one can take that relationship from him.

Few ministers of the Church of England endured more slander, verbal abuse, snubbing, and outright humiliation than Charles Simeon (1759–1836) did in the first two decades of his ministry in Cambridge. Marcus Loane recounts :

> At Holy Trinity [Simeon's church] there were wild scenes of riot and tumult, with filth and stones flung on all sides. One eyewitness relates how he saw Simeon on his way back to King's [his home], his face and clothes streaming with rotten eggs which had been hurled at him as he left the church.[13]

As years passed, Simeon gained fame and respect, but lessons learned in those early years were never forgotten. Later he commented on Habakkuk 3:17, 18:

> The Christian is not exempt from trials and troubles; yet is he far happier than any unregenerate man. . . . A carnal mind cannot form any estimate of the Christian's joys. To know what is meant by communion with Christ, by the witness of the Spirit, and by the love of God shed abroad in the heart we must experience them ourselves; and without such experience we are as incapable of judging of them as a blind man is of colors, or a deaf man of sounds. No words can fully express the joy with which the Christian is sometimes favored.[14]

Simeon knew that fame may or may not come, and respect might be long in being bestowed, but a relationship with Christ Jesus is eternal. It is deep and lasting. It cannot be taken away, and believers cherish it above all earthly pleasures.

I have seen Christians of all types agree with Habakkuk and Charles Simeon. I have seen parents lose children and yet trust in Christ. I have seen people lose homes and jobs and yet trust in Christ. I have seen people abandoned by spouse or friends and yet trust in Christ. I have seen people jilted by lovers and rejected by schools and yet trust in Christ. As Peter replied when Jesus asked if the disciples were leaving him, "'Lord, to whom shall we go? You have the words of eternal life, and we have believed, and have come to know, that you are the Holy One of God'" (John 6:68, 69). When you have the God of your salvation, all else can go, however hard those losses may be.

Habakkuk concludes his book by confessing that God is his "strength" in 3:19. Therefore, he can trust God to give him sure footing on high, treacherous terrain. F. F. Bruce comments, "As the sure-footed hind makes its way in rocky and precipitous places without slipping, so the prophet's faith empowers him to surmount his adversities and live on that higher plane where the soul is in direct touch with God."[15] O. Palmer Robertson adds, "Surefooted, untiring, bounding with energy, the Lord's people may expect to ascend the heights of victory despite their many setbacks."[16]

I am no mountain climber, but I have tramped up long inclines. In the summer of 2007, I spent time on the Isle of Skye in Scotland, and I enjoyed going up higher to get better views of the sea. Once I went way up when, breathless from the climb and from being careful where to put my feet, I reached a ledge, only to be eyed by suspicious sheep led by a wary ram. I was outnumbered and on their ground. I retreated.

Habakkuk would not be surprised by the climb of life or at finding enemies at the top. But he knew his strength came from God, his Savior, his strength, the Judge, the Holy One, the King, the revealer of truth, the One worthy of faith, the One who would welcome him into the eternal kingdom. Thus he knew he could rejoice and sing in the tough times he faced. He confessed, and his confession challenges me to the core of my soul.

## Conclusion

Habakkuk has been on quite a faith journey. He has prayed about his country and about Babylon. He has questioned God and been called to faith. He has trusted, and he has conquered. With God's great deeds reviving, God's love continuing, and God's power enriching, he has triumphed over his circumstances.

We may do the same. The locusts may eat what the Babylonians leave behind, but "the righteous shall live by his faith" (Habakkuk 2:4), for "the earth will be filled with the knowledge of the glory of the Lord as the waters cover the sea" (v. 14) and the Lord is our "strength" (3:19). Therefore, we may rejoice, for so the persecuted prophets before us rejoiced. The times will still be troubling, but we will rise to new heights where the permanent things dwell. We will serve Christ there until we live with our brothers and sisters of all ages with our Savior, where times are no longer troubling.

# ZEPHANIAH

*By Paul R. House*

# 54

# God Won't Be Used: Renewal and Its Limits

ZEPHANIAH 1:1 AND 2 CHRONICLES 34-35

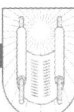

THE NEED TO "SEEK THE LORD AND LIVE"[1] continues to grow more urgent for Judah (Amos 5:6). Israel has lost its monarchy and thousands of exiles to Assyria since the days of Hosea and Amos (see 2 Kings 15:29; 17:1–6, 24). Assyria remains the dominant international power. More than seventy years have passed since the Assyrian invasion of Judah in 701 B.C. that Micah described. Judah has survived with David's lineage at the helm because David's lineage has played by Assyria's rules. Meanwhile, Nahum has noted the fall in 663 B.C. of the great Cushite dynasty that ruled Egypt. Nahum has promised that Assyria's own fall is coming, and Habakkuk has delivered the astonishing news that Babylon will rise. Habakkuk has no word of Judah rising. Rather, he envisions a minority of God's people living by faith (Habakkuk 2:4) amid great loss.

Enter Zephaniah, serving as God's spokesman in the days of Josiah (Zephaniah 1:1). He declares the need for renewal in virtually every part of Judah's life. For the first time since the days of Hezekiah (715-687 B.C.), Judah has a king who wants the renewal that the prophets advise. Reigning 640–609 B.C., Josiah uses his influence and power to effect significant changes. However, these acts of renewal, proper as they are, will not save Judah's economy, military, or corrupted culture. God is not a tool of national greatness. He will not be used.

In fact, Zephaniah has no interest in any greatness except God's. He fastens his attention, and hopefully ours, on a great God and a people humble and lowly enough to serve him in all circumstances (2:2, 3). It is these people who seek God and live. Though virtually unseen, these "humble of the land" are the only people with a bright future (v. 3). For them, having God is enough. He is their reward, their hope. Zephaniah was one of these people, and he urges us to be one of those humble, lowly, satisfied people.

### Zephaniah and Josiah (Zephaniah 1:1)

The book opens with an assertion, an unusual genealogy, and a notation about its setting. The assertion is that what follows is "the word of the LORD," consisting of words that "came" to Zephaniah (1:1). To underscore the words' divine origin, the book often provides indicators of quotations, such as "declares the LORD" (vv. 2, 3, 10). Zephaniah is quite a messenger. As the book progresses, Zephaniah's poetic skill, vivid imagination, theological intelligence, and keen observation of humanity become evident. God chooses an extremely capable partner.

Zephaniah's name likely comes from the verb usually translated as "hide," "hid," or "hidden." Exodus 2:2, 3 uses the verb to describe Moses's parents hiding him during the deadly days of Egypt's killing of newborn Israelite boys. We can only wonder if Zephaniah's parents felt that their son had been born in similarly dark days.[2] After all, he was likely born in the long, politically and morally dark days of King Manasseh's rule (c. 697–642 B.C.) (2 Kings 21:1–9). Regardless, their faith and their son's faith do not stay hidden. Zephaniah's ministry makes sure of that.

The genealogy is unusual because it includes four generations prior to Zephaniah (Zephaniah 1:1). Eight of the Biblical prophets have no stated genealogy, six name only the prophet's father, and only Zephaniah lists both a father and grandfather.[3] The Hezekiah mentioned in the verse may be King Hezekiah of Judah, who ruled c. 715–687 B.C. (2 Kings 18:1–8). If so, the prophet bridges the time gap between Hezekiah and Josiah, the nation's last two reforming kings. At the very least, the genealogy suggests that Zephaniah had deep roots in the Jerusalem community. He was no outsider. He knew the situation that he describes firsthand.

These words came to Zephaniah in Josiah's times, which were momentous times. They inform subsequent eras, including ours. Jeremiah, 2 Kings, and 2 Chronicles provide a great deal of information about and insight into these times. Since 2 Chronicles 34—35 gives key material not found elsewhere, I will now focus our attention on those chapters so we can see better what follows in Zephaniah. Both Zephaniah and 2 Chronicles stress renewal's aims and limits.

## Basic Steps of Renewal (2 Chronicles 34:1–7)

Second Chronicles 34:1–7 provides a great deal of important information about Josiah's reign. Verse 1 states that Josiah was just eight years old when he became king in 640 B.C. Amon, his father, had only ruled two years before "the people of the land" conspired to assassinate him, according to 2 Chronicles 33:21, 25. During his lifetime Amon refused "to humble himself before the LORD" (v. 23). Instead, he worshiped other gods and bowed down to the images that represented them (v. 22). It is unclear why the people wanted him gone. Frankly, times were good. Perhaps Amon wanted to rebel, which would have upset the thriving economy and brought Assyria's wrath. Assyria still ruled Judah and was quite harsh when challenged. The people may have expected the boy king's advisers to keep things settled down once he succeeded his father.

Eight years later, in c. 632 B.C., Josiah "began to seek the God of David his father," according to 2 Chronicles 34:3. Seeking the Lord is a major theme in both the Minor Prophets and in 1 and 2 Chronicles. Seeking God means pursuing God's will through prayer, reading Scripture, and asking advice from wise believers.[4] Those who seek God humble themselves, for they confess that they need his help. They are pre-committed to obedience once they know what God desires. They confess that "the God of David" (v. 3) is the only God they trust and serve. This was Josiah's confession by the time he was sixteen.

This confession led to action. In 628 B.C., when he was twenty, he began to use his authority to cleanse Jerusalem of three types of improper worship, according to 2 Chronicles 34:3, 4. First, he removed "the high places" (v. 3). This general term likely refers here to unauthorized places where people claimed or tried to worship Yahweh. People could have been led astray by bad prophets and priests. Possibly they had simply rebelled against God's decision that the temple was where approved worship was to occur (see 2 Chronicles 6:1–11).

Second, Josiah removed the Asherim (34:3), images that venerated Asherah, the "principal goddess of Tyre and Sidon."[5] Third, Josiah "chopped down the altars of the Baals" (v. 4). As we learned in the chapters on Hosea and Amos, Baal was a deity that people believed gave fertility to land, animals, and women.[6] Elijah had battled Baal worship as long ago as c. 869–850 B.C. Why was the Baal cult so popular for so long? Perhaps because worshiping Baal allowed people to venerate sex, money, and power and to be considered righteous while doing it. Josiah sought to eliminate these old rivals to the living God.

Having begun these acts of renewal in Jerusalem, Josiah then proceeded to do the same in the territory of the old Israelite kingdom, according to 2 Chronicles 34:6, 7. This activity might have had political implications. Assyria was declining before their last great king, Asshur-banipal III (who reigned c. 669-627 B.C.), died. Assyria had ruled Israel since 732 B.C. Josiah may have had Assyria's approval or he may simply have taken a risk fueled by zeal for the Lord. Either way, he sought to bring all Abraham's descendants back to God. Second Chronicles 30:1, 2 indicates that Hezekiah had a similar motive for asking Israel to celebrate Passover in Jerusalem decades earlier.

Josiah understood that renewal begins with exclusive commitment to God demonstrated by proper worship. Put simply, as a follower of the Lord, he obeyed the first two of the Ten Commandments (Exodus 20:3–6). He also agreed with Deuteronomy 6:4–9 that loving God is the basis for life and ethics. Old rivals to God, such as Baal and Asherah, must be laid aside. So must corrupt means of so-called worship that God denounces.

These steps of renewal are so basic that one should fear what else has gone wrong when we must start with them. Yet start with them we must. We do not truly "seek the LORD" (Amos 5:6) unless we do.

### Renewal's Rewards and Limits (2 Chronicles 34:8–28)

Six more years pass. It seems that it took this long to achieve the level of reform that 2 Chronicles 34:1–7 describes. Not even very basic renewal can happen quickly if bad practices have gone on long enough. These six years were probably the time when Zephaniah began his work since he mentions a remnant of Baal and much more to be done (see Zephaniah 1:4–6). Second Chronicles 34:8–28 reveals what happened between 628 and 622 B.C.

Josiah considered repairing the temple to be a next logical step of renewal. Thus 2 Chronicles 34:8–13 says that he commissioned officials to oversee various aspects of renovation. In such work many things typically are found, then saved or thrown away. During this process, "Hilkiah the priest found the Book of the Law of the LORD given through Moses," according to 34:14. The writer does not state whether the priest knew the book's contents or not; neither does the writer divulge how much of Moses's writings were in this scroll or how long the king listened. But 2 Chronicles 34:19 records Josiah's reaction: "he tore his clothes." That is, he performed an act that in his culture represented sorrow. The words affected him deeply.

Having grasped the text's meaning, the king sends messengers to "inquire of the LORD" in 34:21. He wonders what the future holds and what the people need to do. So far he has sought the Lord through personal relationship and service and by hearing and obeying God's word. Now he reaches out to someone able to advise further action. As Josiah sends messengers, he confesses that God's "wrath" has been on Judah due to their disobeying God (v. 21). At the very least, he can see that Judah has been under Assyrian control and oppression since 732 B.C. because of rebellion against their ultimate King. He longs to know what God will do and what God expects him to do. Josiah seeks the Lord.

Verse 22 states that he sent Hilkiah the priest and some others to Huldah, the wife of Shallum, a high official in the king's government. She is a prophetess, clearly one Josiah trusts. Like Zephaniah, she knows and speaks God's words (v. 23). She knows God's written word, for she declares that the consequences the book describes are coming into effect. Thus she very likely has passages like Leviticus 26:14–39 and Deuteronomy 28:15–68 in mind when she says in 2 Chronicles 34:25 that God's judgment on Judah "will not be quenched."

Huldah also can see into the future, a gift only her all-knowing God can bestow. She acknowledges Josiah's tender, humble, repenting, and seeking heart in 34:26, 27. She adds in 34:28 that because he has turned to the Lord, he will be allowed to die before Judah and Jerusalem suffer what is to come. He will not live through what people like Daniel, Ezekiel, and Jeremiah faced. This is a promise just for him.

This hard mercy brings out two important points. First, Josiah is right to humble himself, pray, and seek God's direction (compare 2 Chronicles 7:14). Our relationship with God must come without conditions. Second, Josiah's walk with God will not stave off Judah's demise. His death will come as a kindness to one who cares deeply about his God and his people. God is Josiah's reward. God determines the limits of what personal faith will do in the lives of others.

### Renewal in One's Own Time (2 Chronicles 34:29—35:27)

Huldah's words leave Josiah to serve God without any promise of national survival. True to his character, the king does the right thing. For the next thirteen years, he works to put God at the forefront of his life and his people's lives. Second Chronicles 34:29—35:27 demonstrates that he does what is available to him in his own time.

Josiah gathers the people and their leaders to hear "all the words of the Book of the Covenant that had been found in the house of the Lord" (34:30). He commits his own life to obeying these words (v. 31) and makes all those present agree (v. 32). He enforces the covenant effectively in his days (v. 33).

According to 35:1–19, he also oversees a Passover service that was better than any since Samuel's days more than four centuries earlier. These were faithful things to do. He did them because they were right, not because they guaranteed a happy future.

Sadly, 2 Chronicles 35:20–24 reports that Josiah died in 609 B.C. at the hands of Egypt's Pharaoh Neco. By this time Babylon had crippled Assyria, though the older empire fought to cling to what was left of its crumbling power. Egypt marched out to help Assyria fight Babylon. Josiah wanted to stop Neco's advance. Neco warned Josiah to stay away, a warning 2 Chronicles 35:22 says were "words . . . from the mouth of God." Josiah proceeded anyway, and he died, a greatly loved and much-mourned figure, as 35:25 reports.

As Huldah had promised, he died before Judah fell. When he died, all possibility of top-down, imposed renewal ended. What had looked like national repentance showed itself largely to be the majority going along with the power in place. Renewal comes from within, not from a leader's decree, even if that leader is Josiah.

Nonetheless, there were others who kept trusting and serving God, keeping the covenant as Josiah had done. Jeremiah and his friend and ministry partner Baruch certainly did. They called the people to turn back to God a mere four years after Josiah died (Jeremiah 36; 45:1–5). Even sooner, just months after Josiah's death, Jeremiah preached in the temple, warning the people that unless they repented the temple and Jerusalem would soon be finished (26:1–6). When the temple priests and prophets condemned Jeremiah (v. 11), "certain of the elders of the land" intervened, recalling words by Micah, a true prophet like Jeremiah (vv. 17–19). These people kept the old faith. So did eighty men "from Shechem and Shiloh and Samaria" who brought offerings to Jerusalem after Babylon destroyed the temple ( 41:5). God's work went on, and Josiah's humble faithfulness had a part in that work.

Conclusion

Zephaniah's words in the rest of his book are in concert with Huldah's and Jeremiah's. From beginning to end he pronounces judgment on Judah and the surrounding lands. Even mighty Assyria will fall (Zephaniah 2:13–15). Judah will experience God's disciplining punishment for turning to other gods and acting in ways that God always disapproves. As Huldah told Josiah, serving the Lord is correct and good. Josiah will have a deep relationship with God. So will many other individuals and some communities. But the government will fall.

In a time when many people fear the future, it is worth remembering that God will not be used to save our personal security. Turning to God in Christ in faith and service is the right thing to do every day. He loves and comforts those who seek him as Josiah did, as Jeremiah did, and as our Christian ancestors did. Just remember that God does not promise to prop up our portfolio or swell our college fund. He will not be used to meet our professional and retirement goals. God is enough. He promises to care for us, as Matthew 6:25–34 shows.

In a time when many Christians think the United States of America is in moral decline, it is worth remembering that God will not be used to save this or any other country. We should not be praying for spiritual renewal and an increase in followers of Jesus so that America will survive and flourish. God will not be used as an instrument of nationalism. History has shown that God is enough for believers who have been displaced, whose nations have been obliterated. Their brave faith is the faith of Josiah, Huldah, and Jeremiah.

Today let us all decide that faith in God alone is and will be our faith. God will not be used, but he will receive all who come to him, who seek him as Josiah, Zephaniah, and Huldah did.

# 55

# The Great Day of the Lord Is Near

ZEPHANIAH 1:2-18

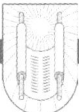

WHILE KING JOSIAH was learning to put God at the center of his life in 628 B.C., most of the people of Judah were keeping the Lord well on the margin of theirs.[1] They certainly knew how God had delivered their ancestors from Egypt. His temple, now more than three centuries old, was in a prominent location on Mount Zion. As Zephaniah 1:2–18 shows, common people spoke God's name and had opinions about him (v. 12). Religious and political leaders put him in the mix of national life (v. 5). Military personnel probably counted on his help when they needed it (v. 14). The people thought of God as a deity who was part of their nation's story.

At the same time many, if not most, of the people also sought the help of other gods (v. 4). Political leaders adopted the religion of Assyria's ruling elite (v. 8). Priests satisfied the public's demand for services devoted to other traditionally important gods, such as Baal (vv. 4, 5). Business owners put profits ahead of ethics, reasoning that God was not involved in commerce (v. 12). They apparently considered business a world of its own.

In short, God was not at the center of most people's lives. It appears that most of the people of Judah had forgotten the first of the Ten Commandments: "I am the LORD your God who brought you out of the land of Egypt, out of the house of slavery. You shall have no other gods before me" (Exodus 20:2, 3). Their forgetting was akin to Christians forgetting Jesus's words in John 14:6: "I am the way, and the truth, and the life. No one comes to the Father except through me." Or John 14:15: "If you love me, you will keep my commandments."

On a more positive note, there were people like Zephaniah, people who trusted and served the Lord. Zephaniah 2:3 calls them the "humble of the land," folks who kept God's word and did what was right. The problem was that they were a small minority of the whole population. Like God, they were on the margin of Judah's society.

Because God had been pushed to the margins, Zephaniah declares that "the day of the LORD" is coming (1:7). As we have seen many times in the Minor Prophets, this "day" is a time when God the Judge restores justice by punishing wrongdoing. These days occur in history, such as when Israel fell to the Assyrians. There will also be a final day of the Lord at the end of human history. After that day there will be no more sorrow, sin, suffering, or death (Revelation 21:1–7).

Zephaniah warns that judgment is coming soon. He warns that the day of the Lord will impact all types and classes of people. My late friend and outstanding Old Testament teacher Elmer Martens used to tell his students that the day of the Lord was a time when God "filled the whole horizon." When God judges, the fact that he is always at the center of reality becomes very apparent.

Zephaniah 1:2–18 warns Judah's people that God is about to fill the horizon of every nook and cranny of their lives. Those who know him or will now come to know him will find him to be the calm at the eye of the coming storm. Those who keep him on the margins of their lives will find him to be the storm itself.

As we will see, Zephaniah probably speaks these words to folks gathered for the great autumn Feast of Tabernacles. He tells them that God has gathered them for destruction (1:2–6), that he is searching for any remaining wicked people (vv. 7–13), and that he will make a complete end of all the wicked (v. 14–18). He will not remain on the margins.

## Gathered for Destruction (1:2–6)

Zephaniah's opening section announces God's decree concerning Judah and other peoples in the region. You will recall that Obadiah began with God's decree about Edom.[2] The image is of a great king declaring what will occur in his realm. Here in Zephaniah, God decrees destruction on earth (vv. 2, 3), with particular reference to Judah and Jerusalem (v. 4). These five verses also imply a setting for the book's first audience. Zephaniah uses verbs that convey gathering, cutting, and removing. These are all harvest words. God's people were supposed to gather in Jerusalem in the autumn after harvest to participate in the Feast of Booths, a celebration of the exodus from Egypt (see Exodus

23:14–19; Leviticus 23:33–43; Numbers 29:12–40; Deuteronomy 16:13–17). While we cannot be certain, it is reasonable to interpret the book as a declaration on such an occasion.[3]

Imagine a gathering of Judah's people in Jerusalem. The harvest has been completed. Folks are relieved and happy to see one another. They want to hear about God's delivering acts and enjoy days of feasting. They are ready to offer sacrifices as required. Among them are everything from faithful believers to worshipers of other gods. Zephaniah speaks to an array of folks with differing points of view.

The first two verses set the tone for the whole book. Zephaniah explodes any sense of easygoing so-called faith. In 1:2, the prophet announces God's intention to gather for removal[4] creatures and human beings alike from "the face of the earth."[5] He begins with two Hebrew words that only appear together elsewhere in Jeremiah 8:13 and Micah 2:12. Both passages refer to gathering. Of course, gathering is a removal from the plant or tree on which the grain or fruit grows. One then must decide the quality of the grain or fruit and what use to make of it. In Zephaniah 1:3, God speaks of himself as the One harvesting. He says that he will stretch out his hand and "cut off" animals and people as if he held a giant scythe (cf. Hosea 4:3). While animals were often killed and eaten—a sort of harvest— people were not harvested. Zephaniah implies that something strange and bad is afoot.

He brings the message home in Zephaniah 1:4–6. The people of Jerusalem are about to be harvested. God will cut them off. But why? Verse 4 says that Baal worshipers, "idolatrous priests," worshipers of "the host of the heavens" (v. 5), people who swear they worship God when they do not, and people who no longer serve God live there. God has a lot of bad fruit to cut off in Jerusalem. The problem is not somewhere far away. It is in "this place" (v. 4), right where the people are standing.

These four groups of people require some explanation. The mention of "Baal" and "idolatrous priests" in 1:4 indicates that Josiah has yet to remove these from Jerusalem, an action he took after 622 B.C. (2 Kings 23:4–20).

As we learned when we studied Hosea, Baal worshipers claimed that he was the god of fertility. Baal priests and prophets had been in the land for years. The "hosts of the heavens" that Zephaniah mentions in 1:5 were astral deities, probably imported to Jerusalem from Egypt, Mesopotamia, or Assyria.[6] In verse 5, those who swear that they serve God actually serve "Milcom," the chief god of Ammon. Zephaniah mentions Ammon in 2:8. Sadly, many people used to worship God but no longer do so. They do not "seek" out God (1:6) for worship, guidance, or ethical decision-making.[7] They do not "inquire of him," which means they do not pray to him. Taken together, these groups represent a very bad spiritual harvest.

Zephaniah's portrait of the people may sound familiar to us. When we gather for worship, we have stalwart people like Zephaniah, folks who serve God in Christ in good times and bad. They believe, share, and obey God's Word, and they want others to do the same. Yet there are often people who used to seek God's will and ways who have stopped doing so. Perhaps they became discouraged. Perhaps life has hit them hard. Or maybe they got greedy or chose to engage in selfish behavior. Worse still, we may have people who worship other gods while claiming to worship the true God. Americans often worship money and power, even while saying that they worship God. Jesus spoke plainly on this matter: "You cannot serve God and money" (Matthew 6:24). As we worship we may also think of loved ones who now no longer gather with us, for they have turned to other religions or to causes that they have put in Christ's place. Zephaniah speaks to us today.

He also speaks to us about judgment. In time and at the end of time God gathers the wicked for removal. He can use historical circumstances to punish sin. He can use death to remove wicked people and stop wicked deeds. He can and will judge anywhere on earth, including in Jerusalem or our hometown.

Zephaniah shared these words so that people would seek God and live. As we have learned, prophets did not utter words of inevitable doom. They spoke a loving God's words so that people could live. Let each one of us decide to stand with Zephaniah and all those who serve God. Let us choose life.

### Searching for the Wicked (1:7–13)

Good harvesters pay close attention to their work. They do not want to leave behind any portion of the grain or fruit that they seek. God is a careful harvester in this passage. He seeks out every wicked person. He will find them all.

When the Israelites met for the Feast of Booths, they brought sacrifices (see Leviticus 23:36; Numbers 29:12–40; Deuteronomy 16:13–17). Zephaniah says that the wicked people whom God finds and eliminates are themselves sacrifices (1:7). He describes who they are (vv. 8–11) and warns that God will search until he finds them (vv. 12, 13). All these things are part of "the day of the Lord" (v. 7), a concept we have heard of many times in our journey through the Minor Prophets.

God has been the speaker in 1:2–6. In verse 7, Zephaniah speaks. He warns the people to "be silent before the Lord God." They should make no defense, offer no protest. Instead, they should listen and do what God says.

There is no time for arguments or explanations, for "the day of the LORD is near." It is close at hand. It could unfold at any time.

In anticipation of this day, God has "prepared," or "confirmed," the sacrifice for the occasion. As the next few verses unfold, it becomes apparent that the wicked people are the sacrifice. They will die for their sins. Given the terrible nature of judgment, perhaps Zephaniah counsels silence because of the gravity of what will happen.

Verses 8–11 specify the various guests who are the sacrifice. First, Zephaniah mentions "the officials and the king's sons" in verse 8. These are the people who administer the king's rule over the kingdom. The phrase "the king's sons" probably refers to members of the royal family of various ages, not to children descended from Josiah. They and others in Judah "array themselves in foreign attire" (v. 8), which probably means that they adopt standards and behaviors that contradict God's. Rather than live by God's word, they live by the cultural and professional standards of Assyria, the ruling nation, or some other country.

Second, among these leaders exists a particularly bad group, according to verse 9. These persons are "[ones] who [leap] over the threshold, [ones] who fill their master's house with violence and fraud."[8] The first phrase is strange, but in context it likely refers to crossing a line that should not be crossed. After all, the second half of the verse describes actions that should not occur in a just kingdom. Some of Judah's officials abuse their power for personal gain.

Third, Zephaniah singles out Jerusalem's merchants in verses 10, 11. The buyers and sellers in the various portions of the city will be targets on the day of the Lord. Those who have lived for commerce and cash will cease to do business.

Fourth, Zephaniah mentions a subgroup of the moneymakers in 1:12, 13. These are not merchants who sell a few fish or a bit of grain per day, like the folks in 1:10, 11. They have bigger aims. They want to build houses, presumably larger ones, and they want to plant vineyards (v. 13). In short, they are entrepreneurs. They plan to expand their operations. This will require more workers and more capital. They are like the landowners Isaiah described in Isaiah 5:8–30. They think God will do nothing to stop their plans (Zephaniah 1:12). They do not consider God a factor at all.

They could not be more wrong. None of their plans will come to fruition. Verses 12, 13 depict God searching Jerusalem like a watchman with a lamp, like a harvester working late into the night. Nothing escapes his attention. Punishment awaits officials, merchants, and entrepreneurs alike—not because they are involved in government or business but because they break God's laws for government and business, because they do not think about God at all when they do their work. On the day of the Lord, God will judge their wickedness. God sees what they are doing. If they know what is good for them, they will turn to the God they have ignored.

When I was a child I learned a song at church that included the phrase "There's an all-seeing eye watching you." The application of this phrase depended on the adults teaching me. Some used it as a warning. God was watching, so I ought to do what was right. Or God was watching, so I should not be afraid.

The people Zephaniah addresses here in 1:12, 13 needed the first application. They needed to know that God saw their wicked deeds. On the other hand, people like Zephaniah could take comfort in knowing that God saw everything and would act appropriately. The wicked caused suffering, even as they prospered. However, such would not always be the case. The day of the Lord is coming, and wickedness cannot endure it. Now is the time to move from the group facing punishment to the side of those who follow the Lord.

### The End of the Wicked (1:14–18)

Zephaniah now brings his opening message to a grand conclusion. He has introduced the day of the Lord in 1:7–13. Now he describes its nature and effects in clear and telling detail. His message is urgent, for the day is near and terrible (vv. 14–16). His message is personal, for it relates to people deluded into thinking that their wealth shelters them from God's judgment (vv. 17, 18).

Verses 14–16 offer as clear a portrait of the day of the Lord as exists in the Old Testament. Several vivid images unfold in rapid succession in verse 14. The first image stresses time: in this case, the day's nearness (v. 14a). The day is not only "near" in proximity. It is also "hastening fast," moving quickly toward Judah. Time is of the essence. The second image emphasizes the sense of sound. The day sounds like a brave soldier wailing due to mortal wounds (v. 14b). Judah's death throes have begun.

Six more images flow in rapid succession. According to verse 15, the day of the Lord is "a day of wrath," which probably means it is like an army taking revenge on an enemy. The word translated as "wrath" literally means an overflowing—in this case, one of anger rather than water.[9] What will overflow? "Distress and anguish" will overflow. Fear, anxiety, and relentless mental distress will overflow. Also, "ruin and devastation" of cities and villages will overflow. To make matters worse still, "darkness and gloom" as well as "clouds and thick darkness" will overflow. One imagines that there will be so much smoke and confusion that the people being attacked will not be able to see. Or the sky itself will turn dark just when people most need to see. The people will be living a nightmare. Finally, according to Zephaniah 1:16, trumpet blasts and battle cries will overflow. The enemy armies will come upon the people. It will be too late to run. There will be nowhere to hide. Not even "the fortified cities" equipped with the best weapons will survive. An invading army will overflow the defenses Judah will put up.

This not only refers to Judah's defenses. According to verse 17, the day will present "distress on mankind." The book's first two verses have already introduced this topic, and chapter 2 will deal with it in some detail. People outside Judah will experience overflowing darkness. They will "walk like the blind" because they share Judah's spiritual blindness. The invading army will treat them like "dust" or "dung" (1:17). Any human being who opposes the invader will be seen as an obstacle, not as a human being.

When faced with such overwhelming odds, many people will try to negotiate. They think that surely there is some price that the aggressor will accept to call off the devastation. Verse 18 removes this possibility. Their silver and gold will have no effect on the day of overflowing, the day of God's wrath. God's zeal for removing sin, his "jealousy," will be like a raging fire. That fire will consume the surface of the earth and all the wicked ones there. Though the verse does not specify the wicked as the "inhabitants of the earth" that Zephaniah mentions, the context surely makes that identification certain. God does not want money. God wants the eradication of wickedness, and he will have what he desires.

When I was a boy growing up in Baptist churches, R. G. Lee was one of the most famous Baptist preachers in the country. He preached one sermon hundreds of times. Entitled "Payday Someday," it was a retelling of the story of King Ahab, Queen Jezebel, and the prophet Elijah in ninth-century B.C. Israel. His point was that God's judgment might be delayed but eventually will fall. The American country music singer Johnny Cash made a similar point in an iconic song that includes the lyrics "You can run on for a long time . . . sooner or later God'll cut you down."[10]

Virtually every culture has a version of these beliefs. Christian or not, people realize that judgment by a deity is on the horizon. Zephaniah, Isaiah, Jeremiah, Jesus, Paul, and John made the same point in their own ways. Wickedness may endure for a while but not forever.

## Conclusion

Christians believe that Jesus Christ is the ultimate judge of the world. Eventually every knee will bow to him (see Isaiah 45:22, 23; Philippians 2:9–11). He is the "King of kings and Lord of lords" (Revelation 19:16). Until he comes again, Christians tell the world that serving the great and good King puts us on the right side of the coming day of judgment. It also places us in the company of people like Zephaniah and the people who have loved God and served others through the centuries. Christians know that wickedness will meet its just end.

We also believe that there is still time to turn to God through Jesus Christ. The day of the Lord is coming. It is near in time or will come at the end of time. You do not have to be among those consumed by God's righteous removal of injustice, greed, hatred, and idolatry. There is hope. We invite you to join us forgiven and trembling Christians in embracing this hope. We invite everyone to find the hope behind Zephaniah's stern warning. We invite everyone to gather for joy rather than for destruction.

# 56

# Gather to Seek the Lord

## ZEPHANIAH 2

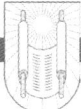

IN CHAPTER 1, Zephaniah warns religious festival-goers that God will gather the wicked for destruction. He says that the day of the Lord is on the horizon. Those who ignore this warning do so at their own peril. Now in chapter 2, the prophet tells them to gather for a more positive reason. Since judgment has not yet fallen there is still time to change. Thus Zephaniah urges the people to gather to seek the Lord, to do his will, and to be hidden when God's day of punishment comes (2:1–3).

Seeking the Lord is a key theme in the Minor Prophets, as we have seen before.[1] Seeking God requires wanting no other god and no other way of life. It includes finding God's will in Scripture, through prayer, and by ethical living. Zephaniah urges the "humble of the land" to seek God now (2:3) before woe falls on lands near (vv. 4–11) and far (v. 12–15).

The setting is the same as chapter 1. People from around the small nation of Judah have come to Jerusalem, probably for the fall harvest festival, the Feast of Tabernacles. The time is likely between King Josiah's early reforms in 628 B.C. and his more serious ones in 622 B.C. Looking ahead, Babylon will capture Jerusalem in 597 B.C. and will destroy the city in 587 B.C. Though they did not know it at the time, the people had a scant thirty or forty years to seek the Lord or face the consequences. Those who cared about their children and grandchildren needed to act.

Immediate action is always the best response to any legitimate announcement of the imminent day of the Lord. May we remember this truth as we examine this chapter together. May we seek the Lord and be his humble people in our own land, in our own times.

## Seek the Lord, All You Humble of the Land (2:1–3)

These verses introduce the people who turn to God and will survive the coming day of the Lord. They share Zephaniah's faith in God. They are humble enough to know God and do his will. They will possess the land after God removes the wicked, according to 2:7. These people want God, and he will come to them. Therefore, they will have what they want and need most.

Zephaniah returns to harvest imagery in 2:1. In 1:2, 3, he tells the people gathered for the harvest festival season that God will gather them for destruction. Now he tells them (in the Hebrew) to "gather yourselves" (2:1),[2] then adds, "and stiffen" (AT)[3] for what is to come. He addresses these commands to Judah, which he calls a "shameless nation." Zephaniah's descriptions in 1:7–13 certainly mark them as such.

Zephaniah 2:2 relates the good news that there is still time to feel justifiable shame and to turn to God. Death and destruction are not inevitable outcomes. The prophet's use of the vital word "before" makes this point.[4] He equates "the decree" with the day of God's "burning anger." God is not out of control. Quite the opposite, in fact. He has been exercising self-restraint, holding back the punishment the people have earned. Now his anger will burn away the wicked, much like farmers burned off any stubble left after all harvesting was completed. This burning will proceed swiftly, like "the chaff" blown away by wind. Therefore, while there is still time "before" these awful times come, action is essential.

Verse 3 specifies the necessary action for avoiding burning, which is appropriate seeking. Those who heed Zephaniah's advice are the "humble of the land." J. A. Motyer defines this group as "those at the bottom of life's heap, those who can be pushed around by the influential, by vested interests (Ps. 9:12–13)."[5] This group appears often in the Old Testament (e.g., Psalm 37:11; Isaiah 61:1). They are unlike the wealthy in Zephaniah 1:6, who refuse to seek the Lord, who prefer to make money from cooperation with foreign nations. Motyer adds that the humble ones "are ready to see themselves at the bottom of the heap in God's eyes, those who have no power to help themselves nor any influence to bring pressure on God (Pss. 25:9; 149:4). Characteristically, the humble cry out to the Lord (Ps. 10:17) and seek him (Ps. 69:32)."[6] They display no spiritual pride.

Their seeking is threefold. First, they seek only the Lord, not any other god (Zephaniah 2:3). They pursue no other alternative deity or way of life. Second, they seek "righteousness," which means doing God's "just commands."[7] Third, they show "humility," constant attention to putting God first in their lives. These appropriate actions mark them as those who love God and put their neighbors' interests above their own (see Leviticus 19:17, 18, 34–37; Deuteronomy 6:4–9). They may be put down by others. Rather than retaliate or seek their own piece of the wicked's pie, however, they turn to God and do what he has commanded.

Their reward is wonderful and ambiguous at the same time. They may well be "hidden" when the day comes. They will not get burned up like the wicked. But they will in fact experience hard days. The key point is that they will have a right relationship with God, one another, and their neighbors. Remember that Noah, Elijah, Jeremiah, Baruch, Ezra, Nehemiah, Naomi, Esther, and Deborah suffered as they served God and his people. They went through hard circumstances in Old Testament times.

Jesus mentioned the same group in the New Testament. He called them "the poor in spirit" (Matthew 5:3), "the meek" (v. 5), and simply "the poor" (Luke 4:18; 6:20). Jesus is their leader. He is the ultimate humble one, as Paul attests in Philippians 2:5–11. His followers included Lazarus, Mary, Martha, Peter, James, John, Paul, Timothy, Barnabas, Titus, and Phoebe, to name just a few. These people had no evident power, no visible influence. They had God in Christ through the Holy Spirit. They had one another. They had God's work to do. They were satisfied. Long departed from this earth, they remain satisfied (Hebrews 12:1).

We ought to take note of what Zephaniah 2:1–3 teaches. God intervenes in history to sweep away the wicked. If nothing else, God removes wicked people via death every minute of every day. But he also governs all human events. Whether we admit it or not, we are but "the humble" of the earth compared to him. It is time for all of us to bow before Christ the King and to do what he asks. It is also time, I think, for Christians to give up visions of influence, power, dominance, or prominence. It is time to be the "humble of the land" who do his just commands" (v. 3). There is still time, however late the hour may be.

### Woe to the Neighboring Lands (2:4–11)

Having warned Judah to seek the Lord, Zephaniah now declares God's decision about neighboring places. He deals with the coastal people west of Judah (2:4–7) before moving on to the lands southwest of Jerusalem (vv. 8–11). While doing so, the prophet keeps God's faithful seeking ones in mind (vv. 7, 9). They will carry on living in the land after their foes have vanished. They will do so because their God is the only living God, the great King to whom all lands and people will bow (v. 11).

Verse 4 states that God's judging fire will reach the four major cities of the old Philistine kingdom: Gaza, Ashkelon, Ashdod, and Ekron. Indeed they may be the first to feel the fire, for invading armies often came down the coast before heading east or further south. These places had ready access to sea trade and thus to the supply that armies in the field needed. Assyria had long considered these places strategically important in their financial empire. It would not have surprised people in Zephaniah's day that these places were constantly vulnerable. Amos had said as much a century earlier (see Amos 1:6–8). But it would have surprised the people that an invader would devastate the coastal cities as completely as Zephaniah 2:5 describes. God's decree, his word, specifies removal of inhabitants. Verses 6, 7 explain why. Shepherds and their flocks will replace seacoast traders and their businesses (v. 6). More specifically, shepherds from Judah will graze their flocks there (v. 7).

Even more specifically, these shepherds will be "the remnant of the house of Judah," those who survive the coming day of the Lord (v. 7), those who seek God, humility, and righteousness (see v. 3). Ultimately, this minority within Judah will emerge because "the LORD their God will be mindful of them and restore their fortunes" (v. 7). The word the ESV translates as "mindful" is a standard Hebrew term for when God visits someone for benefit or punishment. In 1:8, 9 God visits to "punish," but here he visits to "restore" (2:7) what the people have lost.[8] In this case, they had lost their homes to the Philistines due to Assyria taking that land from them.[9] The phrase "restore their fortunes" is a play on words in Hebrew that refers to restoring things to how they were in the past. It does not mean "get their money back." Things will change because of what a faithful God can achieve for faithful people.

In verses 8–11, Zephaniah shifts focus to the southeast. Moab and Ammon took advantage of Judah's weakness.[10] Perhaps with Assyria's approval or Egypt's help, these small neighboring countries took lands along their borders with Judah. This is likely what Zephaniah means when he mentions in verse 8 their "boasts against their [Judah's] territory." God has heard these boasts and will thwart them.

He will do so decisively. Moab and Ammon will become like Sodom and Gomorrah, according to verse 9. Such a comparison usually indicates one of two things: the swiftness or the thoroughness of the place's destruction. Verse 9 highlights the latter. Moab and Ammon, once devastated, will not soon recover, if ever.

According to verse 9, God's minority will live in these places. To be more specific, they will live again in the borderlands taken from them. In this case the phrase "plunder them" (v. 9b) means "resettle in lands that had been taken from them." God's remnant will "possess" (v. 9b) or, more literally, "have as an inheritance" these towns and areas. God will provide these as homes for them. There is no mention of the remnant regaining the territory through armed action.

Verses 10, 11 give two reasons for God's actions against Moab and Ammon. First, verse 10 charges that they "taunted" "the people of the LORD of hosts." Swollen with pride, they considered Judah and Judah's God too weak to respond. Second, they therefore considered their gods greater than the Lord, the living God. The word translated as "famish" in verse 11 indicates that as God acts, the idols that Moab and Ammon worship will slowly fade from view. When God's power becomes evident, "all the lands of the nations" will "bow down," will worship the Lord (v. 11). Chapter 3 will revisit this image of the nations' worshiping God. Ultimately, God's day of judgment will benefit many lands, not just Judah.

We considered some worldwide implications of God's day of judgment when we considered Zephaniah 1:2–18. We will see some more of them when we study chapter 3. Right now I want to discuss what it means for God's "humble of the land" (2:3) to possess the land (v. 7) as an inheritance (v. 9). I believe that both the Old and New Testaments testify to what it means for God to guide and protect his seemingly powerless minority during a time of judgment.

The Old Testament states the basic facts of what it means for people to possess land. First, God created all land (Genesis 1:1). Thus, God owns all land; people never do (Leviticus 25:23). Second, he gives people portions of his land as a gift to steward for a time, sometimes a lifetime (Genesis 1:26–31; Leviticus 25:23–34). Land is a good gift granted with the provision that people use it according to God's standards (Deuteronomy 8:11–20).[11] Third, God gives land to his people and to people who do not follow him (2:1–8). Fourth, love of God and love of "neighbor," a term that includes foreigners, mark God's people as his own (see Leviticus 19:17, 18, 34–37; Deuteronomy 6:2–9) as they live in the land. Seen this way, God's people live in God's land for their own good and for the good of their neighbors. Fifth, when people betray God, misuse land, and abuse neighbors, they violate the terms of their tenancy. God is patient with such sins but not endlessly so. Loss of land through exile or less dramatic circumstances may ensue. More positively, faithfulness to the land and to God in the land brings enormous good to people (Leviticus 26:1–13; Deuteronomy 28:1–14). God's promises to give the remnant homes in the land are among Zephaniah's most encouraging words.

The New Testament assumes these texts; it does not override them. But the New Testament applies them in new ways. I think the New Testament particularly shows how God's minority can live in lands dominated by people unsympathetic to their way of life. In this way the Thessalonian believers, for example, paralleled the humble, afflicted people in Zephaniah's time. They were being afflicted, and God would afflict their oppressors when Christ came again (2 Thessalonians 1:5–10). Until then, God would give them homes, work, and witness (1 Thessalonians 4:11, 12; 2 Thessalonians 3:6–12;). Writing to Timothy, who was then based in Ephesus, Paul urged prayer for all leaders so that believers could "lead a peaceful and quiet life" (1 Timothy 2:2). Paul knew that God gives his minority people places for home, work, worship, and witness. In short, God's people in New Testament times possessed the same sort of quiet portions of places that Zephaniah described.

We need to receive and cultivate the places God provides for us. He gives us places for our families to live quietly and helpfully. He gives us work to do and responsibilities to fulfill. He gives us comfort and beauty along with challenges and sorrows. This is what it means for the meek to inherit the earth, as Jesus promised in Matthew 5:5. The day will come when the wicked will no longer try to push God's people out. Until then, God still provides us with homes and a quiet life. Let us embrace this blessing even if the lands and people near us reject it, even if they oppose our efforts to extend God's blessings to more people.[12] Let us live in God's kingdom.

### Woe to the Great Distant Lands (2:12–15)

In Zephaniah's time, it was easy to see how places like Judah, Philistia, Moab, and Ammon could be swept away by the flood tides of history. They were small. They had tiny armies. They had little influence. They lived in the wake of the great nations, nations like Egypt and Assyria.

For decades, Judah and their neighbors had been pinched between Egypt and Assyria as the two superpowers battled for supremacy. For more than a century, Assyria had been the victor most of the time. Large, powerful nations often think themselves immune to the sorts of problems that dog insignificant nations. Zephaniah 2:12–15 warns them to think again. The prophet asserts that God rules and judges these places no less than he governs and punishes smaller ones.

Verse 12 simply adds the "Cushites" to the list of people who will be "slain by [God's] sword." The Cushites were an ancient people group that had formed into a monarchy called Cush. The Cushites ruled Egypt from c. 716–664 B.C. Isaiah wrote about these people decades before (see Isaiah 18:1–7).

This kingdom stretched as far south as today's Uganda and Ethiopia. We know from Nahum 3:8, 9 that when Assyria conquered portions of Egypt in 664 B.C., they removed the Cushites from power.

Zephaniah indicates that the Cushites will not regain power over Egypt. They will stay defeated. On a more positive note, Isaiah 18:7 says that the Cushites will worship God, a promise that Acts 8:26–40 recalls.

Zephaniah 2:13–15 address Assyria, the mightiest nation of Old Testament times. Assyria had defeated the Cushites and subdued Egypt in 664 B.C.[13] By 628–622 B.C., however, when Zephaniah ministered in Judah, Assyria was much weaker. Ashurbanipal, Assyria's last powerful king, died c. 627–626 B.C. The nation's power had already ebbed during his final years. Afterward, Babylon and its allies attacked Assyria. They succeeded in ending Assyria's run as the world's greatest power by 612–609 B.C.

According to Zephaniah 2:13, 14, the people who defeated the Cushites will not last much longer themselves. Time is running out on this oppressive superpower, as the book of Nahum has already stressed.

Why is time running out? Zephaniah 2:15 tells us. Nineveh, Assyria's major city, represents the attitude of the whole Assyrian Empire. Nineveh acts as if no one else matters, as Nahum has so eloquently stated. Thus, the Ninevites break the Bible's two most basic commands; they neither love God nor their neighbors. They are completely selfish.

As Biblical history rolled on, the Babylonians defeated the Assyrians, then fell to the Persians. The Persians fell to the Greeks. The Greeks fell to the Romans. Though the New Testament ends with Rome still being the world's dominant power, the book of Revelation gives every indication that this latest great oppressor of God's people will not last forever. From this pattern it is fair to conclude that no power, however rich and strong, can oppress and kill forever. God's justice will prevail, both in history and at the end of history.

Zephaniah's words about the Cushites and Assyria have at least two important applications for us today. First, we all need to remember that humbly seeking God, not endless war and expansion of territory, is the mark of both persons and nations that please God (see v. 3). God judged these two mighty powers for abusing others, not for good behavior. The history of many countries, including the United States of America, includes lust for war and conquest. Repentance for past sins and determination not to repeat past mistakes are always in order. As the book of Jonah has shown us, God forgives those who repent.

Second, we all need to remember that God judges the wicked to protect his people. Judah had suffered at the hands of Assyria and Cush for more than a century. They suffered from being Assyria's vassal, and they suffered from Egypt's broken promises (see 2 Kings 18—19; Isaiah 18, 28—29, 36—37). They suffered whenever Assyria and the Cushites fought one another in Judah. Now these old sources of pain will not be a factor. God's people will have breathing space. What all Judah's people will do with that breathing space remains to be seen. But the "humble of the land" will use the breathing space to seek the Lord and to do his will (Zephaniah 2:3, 7, 9). As God gives us blessed relief from sorrow, pain, and difficulties caused by others, let us determine to thank him and seek him.

## Conclusion

Zephaniah 2 has portrayed God's judgment as the gathering and burning of stubble (v. 1). Wicked people from lands near and far, great and small will be consumed along with all false gods (vv. 2, 4–15). On the day God judges, all gods and their people will bow to him (v. 11), regardless of their past or current fame or power (vv. 12–15).

But Zephaniah includes some very good news. Before any of this happens, it is possible to turn to God (2:2). How should we turn to God? The answer here is the same as it is throughout the Bible. We must turn to God humbly, recognizing his right to rule us (v. 3a). We must turn to God honestly, with the intention of keeping his commandments (v. 3b). In short, we must turn to God by faith in his word with obedience as our goal. We must respond positively to Jesus's admonition: "If you love me, you will keep my commandments" (John 14:15; cf. v. 21). There is still time.

There is more good news. God provides homes now and forever for his people. As nations great and small pass from history, God's humble ones remain in the land, in quiet places that God has given them (Zephaniah 2:3, 7, 9). If we want to be like Assyria and Cush, then we have no future in the land. If we are happy to be God's people in God's places for God's purposes, then we have a future, as Jesus promised in Matthew 6:25–34. If we are happy with whatever humble life God gives us now, then we will be prepared for the stupendous everlasting future that awaits us. I believe Jesus. "The meek . . . shall inherit the earth" (Matthew 5:5) now and always.

# 57

# A Singing God

## ZEPHANIAH 3

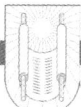

IT IS IMPORTANT TO HEAR the prophets' whole message. Yes, they stress sin and the need to change. Yes, they emphasize coming woe and divine judgment if repentance does not happen. But they also celebrate the renewal that follows repentance and even judgment. Because the prophets know and trust God, they know that the future is bright. Zephaniah closes on this great trajectory from sin to judgment and inevitably to restoration. He concludes with the amazing image of God singing for joy because of his people.

As we have seen, Zephaniah has been preaching in the days of Josiah (c. 640-609 B.C.), most likely between 628 and 622 B.C.[1] He probably spoke these messages at one of Judah's and Israel's annual festivals, perhaps the Feast of Tabernacles, which occurred after harvesting was finished. In 1:2–18, the prophet writes of gathering for sweeping away, for removal. In chapter 2, he writes of preparing to be cut down (v. 1). Yet in 2:3, 7, and 9, Zephaniah mentions the humble people in the land who seek God. They will inherit the land. They will survive and find life when arrogant people in lands great and small disperse and die. It is possible that 3:1–5 continues the message that begins in 2:1 since 2:5 and 3:1 both call out "woe" on wicked people. However, Zephaniah 3:1–5 announces woe on Jerusalem, not on a foreign city. Therefore, it is defensible to treat verses 1–5 as beginning the book's final segment.

In this final segment, the prophet declares that God has patiently waited and worked for Jerusalem to move from a situation of woe to one of renewal. Jerusalem has disappointed him. So in 3:6–13, God declares that he will act decisively to renew the people of Judah and cause people from many nations to worship him. In this wonderful gathering, this fantastic harvest, the humble ones who seek God will have company. Their numbers will grow. When this renewal occurs, God will sing with joy over what the people and their place have become, according to 3:14–20.

Zephaniah leaves us with the great news that our God is a singing King who takes delight in what we have become. We need this encouragement daily. Our God is not a gloomy, angry, finger-pointing God who cannot be pleased no matter what we do. He is the Lord of the universe, and he delights in those of us who seek him, who are the humble of the earth.

### God's Patience (3:1–5)

The opening section resumes Zephaniah's declarations against sin in Jerusalem. In three distinct segments he claims that Jerusalem is a wicked city (3:1, 2) that is afflicted with wicked leaders (vv. 3, 4), though God has been just and righteous (v. 5). Despite Zephaniah's previous messages, the people have not yet awakened. They remain prone to "woe," to trouble they will wish they had never experienced.

Verse 1 here sounds much like 2:13–15. Until we get to 3:2 we could easily think that Zephaniah is still denouncing Nineveh. I think that is the point. Zephaniah sees little difference between how Jerusalem and Nineveh act. Assyria was Judah's overlord for decades leading into Zephaniah's and Josiah's time.[2] It seems that Jerusalem had become like Nineveh—oppressive, "rebellious" against God, and "defiled" in the sense of doing exactly what God says not to do (3:1). In short, Jerusalem remains as Zephaniah described the place in 1:4–6. God has waited. He has sent his servants, the prophets. Thus far his patience has not been rewarded.

Having announced Jerusalem's basic flaws in 3:1, Zephaniah states in verse 2 how the city became so much like Nineveh. There are four things that most of the city's inhabitants have refused to do. First, they do not listen to God or anyone else who tells them to change. Second, they accept no correction from God, a point that Zephaniah will make in more detail in 3:6, 7. Third, they do not trust God. Instead, they trust alliances, wealth, and soldiers to meet their needs, as we learned in 1:4–13. Fourth, because they do not trust God, they do not "draw near" (3:2) to him through worship, prayer, and obedience. Taken together, this is a poisonous recipe for leaving God and staying away from him. Rebellion and oppression (v. 1) are the fruits of such behavior. There is no positive way forward unless these actions change. Zephaniah has devoted his life to helping people make these changes.

Jerusalem's inhabitants have had a lot of assistance in developing their rebellious and oppressive ways. In another four-fold statement the prophet claims in 3:3, 4 that officials, judges, prophets, and priests have ravaged the people. The officials and judges were supposed to ensure that justice and equity prevailed in courts and legal systems. Instead, they are like "lions" and "evening wolves" who devour the people, which likely means that they abuse their offices to line their pockets (v. 3).

For their part, the prophets were supposed to correct bad behavior among the people and encourage faithfulness to God and one another (see Leviticus 19:17, 18; Deuteronomy 6:4–9). Priests were supposed to teach folks about holiness, which here refers to living in the presence of their holy God (see Leviticus 11:44). The prophets are instead "fickle . . . men" (Zephaniah 3:4) whose message changes with the times and the payments for services rendered. The priests "do violence to the law," just as the prophets do violence to the people (Zephaniah 3:4). Again, the implication is that the civil and religious leaders are out for themselves. They have lost the correct definition of their vocations.

In stark contrast to the leaders within the city (see v. 1), verse 5 states that the Lord "within" their midst is "righteous." Indeed, he "does no injustice" whatsoever. Instead, each morning and evening he does the right thing for and among the people. Meanwhile, "the unjust" leaders are unashamed at what they do.[3] Thus they have no intention of changing. God will not change either. He will keep doing what is right. Unfortunately for the wicked leaders and those who follow them, his righteousness requires their punishment.

God has remained patient in the face of much rebellion against him and his ways. Manasseh, whom the Bible portrays as one of Judah's worst monarchs, ruled from 697–642 B.C. (2 Kings 21). After a brief reign of two years, the people deposed his son, Amon, replacing him with the boy-king Josiah in 640 B.C. (vv. 17–26). By now Josiah has done some reforming,[4] but Judah's days are numbered, for the world is changing. Babylon will soon rise. Assyria will cease to be a major power. All that Judah has known for decades will change. For tiny Judah to survive, they must turn to God, their true King, as Zephaniah 3:15 will make plain. God has waited long enough. The humble of the land will survive, just as God promised in 2:3, 7, and 9. Who, if anyone, will join them?

God's patience is one of his chief virtues. He is patient with the wicked, for he gives them time to repent even when giving them more time leads to problems for those who serve him (2 Peter 3:9). He is "slow to anger," patient with his people when they turn from him (Exodus 34:6). Through his servants he warns people repeatedly to turn from sin to grace (see 2 Kings 17:13). He waits, warns, and grieves. As we recognize his patience with us, may we reward his patience with faith and obedience. As his righteousness sets the world right, let us believe that he has not moved rashly or harshly.

### God's Renewal (3:6–13)

God never punishes simply to be punitive. He judges to renew. That was one of the chief things I learned when I wrote a book on Zephaniah more than three decades ago.[5] Indeed, renewal and reconciliation are God's aims in everything he does. After all, when the Apostle Paul summarizes his preaching, his understanding of God's gospel, he emphasizes reconciliation with God (2 Corinthians 5:16–21).

Zephaniah holds out the same possibility. Yet he does so only after stating that most of Judah's people have failed to learn from other nations' destruction and will face punishment themselves (Zephaniah 3:6–8). The prophet then proceeds to claim that God's judgment will lead to many nations' learning to worship him (vv. 9, 10). He concludes by describing the fall of Judah's wicked people and the rise of the humble ones who seek the Lord (vv. 11–13). Renewal will not be easy or quick, but it will be wonderful.

Verses 6, 7 demonstrate the dangers of failing to learn from other nations' destruction. Verse 6 offers a series of images that depict destruction. God has "cut off nations," laying waste their "battlements" (defenses), "streets," and "cities" in the process. The verse offers a general statement. It offers no details that might help us date the events God describes. Still, we know that God did this hard work through the armies of nations like Assyria, Babylon, Egypt, and others in Josiah's times. Zephaniah's point is that these were not just instances of bad policy or bad luck. God oversaw this destruction. In verse 7 God explains that he wanted Judah to see, fear, and "accept correction"[6] when they saw what he had done in other lands. He hoped that they would avoid what others had endured. Instead they were "all the more . . . eager to make all their deeds corrupt."

Given Judah's failure to learn, God utters a new command in verse 8: "Therefore wait for me . . . for the day when I rise up to seize the prey." The word translated as "wait" is not the usual word for "wait," but rather one that means "waiting with patient endurance."[7] If so, then God addresses people who are already waiting for him to act—in other words, the meek and humble believers in the land (compare 2:3, 7, and 9), folks like Zephaniah. Since their compatriots will not learn from God's work in the world, they must wait for him to act further.

This expectation reminds us of Habakkuk's need to trust God no matter what happened.[8] As in Habakkuk, times will get harder for all in Judah, including the faithful ones. Echoing wording from Zephaniah 1:2, God pledges "to gather nations, to assemble kingdoms" (3:8) for judgment. During this judgment, "the land" (v. 8, AT)[9] will be cleared by burning, which echoes 2:1. Just as farmers cleared land of old crops and weeds by burning, so God will clear the land of wicked people and wicked deeds (compare 2:3–11). God's people will need patient endurance while all this occurs.

Their patient endurance, and God's, will be rewarded. Zephaniah 3:9, 10 states that the faithful ones in Judah will eventually have company. God will change "the speech of the peoples" to "pure speech" (v. 9a), which the context defines as calling "upon the name of the LORD" and serving "him with one accord" (v. 9b). Here, as in Psalm 73:1, purity amounts to confessing and serving only the living God. As Marvin Sweeney writes, such speech recognizes God's sovereignty over creation.[10] It will not simply be a reversal of the Tower of Babel account.

When this occurs, worshipers from distant lands like Cush will come to worship God, presumably in Jerusalem (Zephaniah 3:10) given the context. Both "the peoples" (v. 9, Gentiles) and "my [God's] dispersed ones" (v. 10, Jews) will be part of "my worshipers" (v. 10). This combination echoes Isaiah 66:17–23, where we read that a multinational group worships God after burning clears the ground.

Zephaniah 3:11 builds on this imagery. On "that day," the day when God changes idolatrous speech to pure speech, the people will "not be put to shame" for all that the whole group ("you") has done while rebelling against God. It is important to note that the faithful ones shared in the rebellion. Though they are not as culpable as the worst rebels, they are responsible for their part in what has happened. This principle is evident in community laments in which all the people, not just the worst perpetrators, pray together for forgiveness. As verses 11, 12 continue, God distinguishes between the faithful and the wicked. The faithful are not too proud to admit their wrongdoing, while the wicked remain "proudly exultant."

Verse 12 states that the removal of the wicked will "leave in your midst a people humble and lowly," the very people that 2:3, 7, and 9 feature. These people choose God. They "seek refuge" (3:12) in him, a phrase that commonly describes faithful ones in the book of Psalms (see, for example, Psalms 2:12; 7:1; 71:1; 91:2). Zephaniah may have in mind all the deportations that Judah and Israel had suffered at Assyria's hands. Here a divine deportation leaves the faithful ones "in the midst" of the land (Zephaniah 3:12).

Zephaniah 3:13 links these people to the ones that 2:3 mentioned. This remnant, this minority—"those who are left in Israel" (3:13)—does not act unjustly. They do not speak deceitfully. They conduct themselves according to God's standards in their life and work. These humble and lowly people are shepherds, for they will graze their flocks "and none shall make them afraid" (cf. 2:7, 9). As in 2:1–11, God's meek ones inherit the land. They have all that they need. Their patient endurance has been rewarded. God has done his renewing work.

This passage reminds us of the massive importance of patient endurance. As I consider what Zephaniah writes about this, I am reminded of three couples. All three are in ministry. All three have lost daughters through early death. The husband in one couple and the wife in another teach the Old Testament. The husband in the third couple is a pastor. All six people have retained their Christian faith. All three couples wait patiently to see their children again. All three have faithfully raised their other children.

I could add more examples, but these witnesses suffice to make my point. I have seen patient endurance in action, and I have met the humble and afflicted ones in our midst. If you are one of them, I want you to know that God hears your faithful, pure speech. He sees your righteous and truthful witness, as do I and many others.

### God Sings (3:14–20)

I would guess that if you asked a thousand people to name something that God does, at best a tiny handful would say that God sings. Yet this is what Zephaniah 3:14–17 says. A few more people might say that God gathers, as in gathering people to himself or to Heaven. Verses 18–20 present him bringing his people together for their good. Taken together, these verses portray God like a bridegroom singing about his bride or a harvester singing while he works. Having read much about God's sorrows in Zephaniah and other books of the Minor Prophets, it is wonderful to close our study of this book on such a high note.

With God's faithful and humble ones safe in the land (3:13), God calls on Jerusalem to "rejoice" in verse 14. Then he gives four reasons for this rejoicing in verse 15. First, God has set aside "the judgments against" the people (compare v. 11). As in Hosea 5:1, the word translated as "judgments" refers to judicial verdicts that did not go in their favor. The people with pure speech and righteous lives have been pardoned (compare Zephaniah 3:11–13). Second, God has turned back Judah's enemies (v. 15). His people are safe (compare v. 13). Third, and most important, God is their "King" and lives among them (v. 15). Fourth, they do not have to fear "evil," that is, harm or trouble, anymore. Forgiveness, safety, divine rule, and permanent safety are all marvelous reasons to rejoice. Taken together, they explain the best parts of life now and the permanent life that believers will eventually enjoy with God forever (cf. Isaiah 65:17–25; Revelation 21:1–7).

Others join the rejoicing in Zephaniah 3:16, 17. An unidentified bystander will exhort Jerusalem not to fear "on that day" (v. 16), for all her sorrows are behind her. But God is the most significant jubilant person. In verse 17 Zephaniah repeats that God is in Jerusalem's midst. He dwells there. His presence shows that he is "a mighty one who will save." In the ancient world, a king's presence in the capital city meant that foes were subdued elsewhere and the kingdom was at peace.

The next phrase is difficult. God either "quiets" his beloved, Jerusalem, or he "plows" on behalf of his beloved.[11] The first option would mean that God quiets all the people's fears, in keeping with verse 15. The other option would indicate that having subdued all enemies and having taken up residence at home, the King now settles down to planting crops. Both resonate in context, but the second is in keeping with the royal imagery. It also provides less of a contrast with the next phrase. Finally, God sings loudly "over" or "on account of" his people. He is ecstatic about being at home with his beloved people. His love for his people delights him, so he sings.[12]

In Zephaniah 3:18–20, the Lord speaks. The book began with harvesting imagery, and now it ends with harvesting imagery. In each of these final verses, God says that he will "gather" his people. In verse 18, he promises to gather those "who mourn for the festival." Sweeney states that this phrase probably refers to people that God gathered for destruction in 1:2–18 and 2:1, 2.[13] If so, their days of mourning are over. In 3:19 God promises to gather "the lame" and "the outcast," folks who represent weakness and rejection. This promise reminds readers of passages like Isaiah 35 and of Jesus's ministry to the broken and hurting (Luke 4:17–21; 7:21, 22). In Zephaniah 3:20, God promises to make his people "renowned" after he changes their circumstances. This reversal of fortunes is glorious when it occurs now, and it will be even more glorious when it becomes a permanent condition. God's harvest is vast. It will amount to harvesting all good things for all of creation. It will amount to a complete renewal of all that was ruined.

In July 2023, my father died at age ninety. Dad had many talents, but singing was not among them. He could not begin or carry a tune. He liked hearing singing, but he could not sing. When I preached his funeral, I noted that the next time I saw Dad he would be able to sing. God makes all things new. It will be nice to hear Dad sing well for the first time. It will also be wonderful to hear God sing joyfully over his harvest work, over his beloved people.

## Conclusion

In June 1983, I was pastoring a small Baptist church in Medora, Indiana, and teaching world literature at a Catholic college in Louisville, Kentucky. I was set to begin doctoral studies in Old Testament in the fall semester at Southern Seminary. One morning my daily devotional Bible reading brought me to Zephaniah. By the time I finished reading those fifty-three verses and praying over them, I felt led to write my dissertation on the book. This sense of direction was a great blessing to me as I navigated my doctoral program over the next three years. Thirty days after my graduation, a good academic press accepted the manuscript for publication, which helped me get a position at Taylor University in July 1986. Thus studying Zephaniah launched me into what is now many happy years of studying, teaching, and preaching the unity of the Bible anchored in the unity of God's character. Spiritually, intellectually, and financially I owe a lot to Zephaniah.

As we conclude this section on Zephaniah, I hope that we all feel that we owe a lot to the prophet. He has been a herald and a watchman to us, a true prophet of God. He has announced God's decree of judgment on Judah, the surrounding lands, and distant countries. His announcement comes soon enough to give the people of Judah time to change before the day of the Lord comes. Before judgment falls, they have time to "seek the LORD" (2:3) and join the righteous "humble of the land" (vv. 3, 7, 9), the people who will survive when nations great and small get swept away (vv. 4–15).

Even after judgment falls (3:1–6), if they "wait" with patient endurance (v. 8), people of all nations can be his humble people in his place forever (vv. 9–13). He will be their King who sings over them with joy (vv. 14–20). God's harvest of renewal will grow out of his harvest of judgment. What the prophet said then applies to us now, as we have seen. I am sure that we all owe a lot to Zephaniah. Let the rejoicing and singing begin!

# HAGGAI

*By Stephen M. Coleman*

# 58

# Work, for the Lord Is with You

HAGGAI 1:1–15A

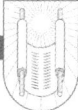

"SOLITARY, POOR, NASTY, BRUTISH, AND SHORT."[1] Though these words of the philosopher Thomas Hobbes are often used to describe life in medieval Europe, they may be applied equally well to describe life in postexilic Israel. The year was 520 B.C., and it had been eighteen years since Cyrus the Great issued his famous decree allowing the Jews to return to their homeland, to rebuild their temple, and to worship their God (Ezra 1:2–4; 6:2–5). Israelites living in exile in Babylon rightly understood Cyrus's decree to be the long-awaited fulfillment of God's promises to their fathers. Though God's sword of judgment fell upon his people for their sins, though Israel was cast off into exile, God had promised to have mercy on his people, to restore a remnant of his people to their land, and, more importantly, to restore a remnant to himself.

The initial return to the promised land had been an occasion for great celebration and thanksgiving, and the initial efforts to rebuild the temple were accompanied by great optimism and fervor. But Israel's energy quickly faded, enthusiasm waned, and the work ground to a halt. Life back in the promised land, it turned out, was much more difficult than the returnees had imagined. Their efforts to rebuild met with opposition, their labors produced barely enough to get by, and they lived under the sovereign rule not of a king in the line of David but of the pagan Persian emperor (Ezra 4:4—5:5).[2]

Before they knew it, eighteen years had passed, and God's temple still lay in ruins. The returnees who were expecting a glorious return to Israel's golden age were left struggling to simply sustain life in what had come to feel like a distant, backwoods, forgotten corner of the Persian Empire. It would be difficult to overstate the discouragement the postexilic community felt at this time. Without too much effort we can imagine the questions that haunted this community day in and day out: "Is this the glorious future God had promised? Has God abandoned us? Would life have been better for us had we stayed back in Babylon?"

It's in this context of bewilderment, discouragement, and spiritual lethargy that the word of the Lord bursts onto the scene with its transforming and life-giving power. Through his prophet Haggai, God declares a word of both judgment and mercy with the result that God's people are transformed, and through them God's city is transformed.[3] In this we witness something of the power of the word of God. God's word is powerful and effective, accomplishing the purpose for which he sends it forth (Isaiah 55:11).[4] Through his word announced by his prophet Haggai, God reorients his disoriented people, reminding them of who he is as their covenant Lord and who they are as his covenant people. Centrally, though, God reminds Israel how they are called to live and what they're called to be about as pilgrims in this life. Thus, in the midst of their despair, Israel is given a reason to trust, to hope, and to work to the glory of their God.

God does this for us as well. We too can find ourselves disoriented, bewildered, wondering if God has abandoned us, wondering if what we are experiencing is the best that Christianity has to offer. So Haggai's prophecy bears an important message for Christians today as it comes to us through its fulfillment in Christ, the One in whom God's justice and God's mercy meet.

### God's Sobering Complaint (1:1–11)

To say that God issues a complaint about his people is not at all intended to cast God as an impatient parent grumbling about his kids. When God issues a complaint, he is, in effect, filing a legal charge against them in a court of law. The prophets were administrators of the Mosaic covenant, and as such, their job was to remind God's people of the terms of the covenant—the laws and the statutes that were to govern Israel as a nation holy to God. Most importantly, however, Israel's prophets reminded them of the blessings God promised for obedience and the curses God promised for disobedience.[5]

The heart of the Lord's complaint is seen in Haggai 1:2: "These people say the time has not yet come to rebuild the house of the LORD." We're not told explicitly why the people are saying that "the time has not yet come." It's not difficult, however, to imagine quite a number of reasons why the postexilic community felt this way. Perhaps they were feeling the burden of paying particularly heavy tribute to the Persian Empire, as we know that Darius was preparing to invade Egypt. Or perhaps, as was common in the ancient world, the postexilic community was waiting for a sign from their God that now was the time to build.[6] In fact, it may have been the case that their inauspicious moment signaled that this was positively *not* the time to engage in such a building project.[7] Or perhaps it was the feeling that it was all they could do to get food on their tables. How could they possibly have time and resources to build a temple? As one commentator memorably puts it, "Why worry about the presence of God when reality is dictated by famine and fate and foreign power?"[8]

Whatever their reasons for the delay, God's word breaks into Israel's excuse-making, effectively silencing them as he issues an uncomfortably searching and revealing question: "Is it a time for you yourselves to dwell in your paneled houses, while this house lies in ruins?" (v. 4).[9] Apparently the postexilic community was not opposed to working on houses. They were simply opposed to working on God's house, preferring to spend their time, energy, and resources building their own houses instead. The people of Israel were building houses for themselves, and God's question highlights the incongruity of Israel's behavior. Israel's actions speak more loudly than their words, and their actions betray the reality of their chief loves and primary devotions. Israel had said they were devoted to God, that they desired to glorify God with all their heart, soul, strength, and mind, and yet their actions revealed that their chief desire was not for God's glory and God's house but for their own glory and the glory of their own houses. God's word through Haggai exposed the sinfulness of their hearts: their hypocrisy, their self-justification, and their faithlessness.

The fact of the matter is that postexilic Israel had put their own comfort, interests, and agenda over the glory of God. God pulls back the curtain and sets on display his people's true love and their functional gods. Regardless of their confession, this postexilic community is serving the gods of safety, ease, comfort, and material wealth. In this, we're reminded that we, like Israel, always have excuses for our idols. We justify to ourselves (if not to others) why we're right in our sin, saying things like "I'm of more service to the Lord when I'm comfortable" or "I can be a blessing to more people if I make more money." We too always need to hear God's word and be reoriented by his call to faith and obedience. Every day we need God's word to shine its light into the darkness of our hearts, as uncomfortable and disrupting as this is, to tell us the truth of what we're living for and to call us back to him.

God not only exposes the sinful realities of his people's hearts but also, in a sense, exposes the impoverished reality of their daily experience. He says,

"Consider your ways. You have sown much, and harvested little. You eat, but you never have enough; you drink, but you never have your fill. You clothe yourselves, but no one is warm. And he who earns wages does so to put them into a bag with holes" (Haggai 1:5, 6). Israel is experiencing futility in their work and a deep frustration in their livelihoods. It seems as if the more they work, the less they earn. Their sowing is not producing the expected harvest, their clothes are not keeping them warm, and their food and drink do not satisfy their hunger. Why? God answers, "You looked for much, and behold, it came to little. And when you brought it home, I blew it away. Why? declares the Lord of hosts. Because of my house that lies in ruins, while each of you busies himself with his own house" (v. 9).

Israel's experience of futility in their work, dissatisfaction in their labor, and want in their yield was directly related to their faithlessness in rebuilding the temple. This was not a coincidence but God's direct response to his people's faithlessness and disobedience.

Futility was at the heart of the covenant curses. In Deuteronomy 28, Moses had promised that if Israel was careful to obey the word of God, "the Lord will make you abound in prosperity, in the fruit of your womb and in the fruit of your livestock and in the fruit of your ground. . . . The Lord will open to you his good treasury, the heavens, to give the rain to your land in its season and to bless all the work of your hands" (v. 11). Yet here in Haggai, the Lord proclaims the exact opposite. God declares through his prophet, "Therefore the heavens above you have withheld the dew, and the earth has withheld its produce. And I have called for a drought on the land and the hills, on the grain, the new wine, the oil, on what the ground brings forth, on man and beast, and on all their labors" (1:10, 11).

These words echo the covenant curses that God had promised to bring upon Israel for their disobedience.[10] Deuteronomy 28:23 says, "The heavens over your head shall be bronze, and the earth under you shall be iron." Later in the same chapter we read, "You shall carry much seed into the field and shall gather in little, for the locust shall consume it. You shall plant vineyards and dress them, but you shall neither drink of the wine nor gather the grapes, for the worm shall eat them. You shall have olive trees throughout all your territory, but you shall not anoint yourself with the oil, for your olives shall drop off" (vv. 38–40).

Because Israel was so prone to live according to the illusion of self-sufficiency, according to the illusions promised by their idols, they needed to be reoriented to reality. This was the reality for Israel: their frustrations were not the result of not working hard enough or not being smart or savvy enough in their farming, but because of their disobedience. Israel had been experiencing God's hand of judgment and curse because of their own sin and faithlessness.

This dynamic was unique to ancient Israel as they lived under the Mosaic covenant. The temporal blessings for obedience and the curses for disobedience do not characterize the new covenant in which we find ourselves. This is important to remember. This means that it would be wrong to go to our Christian friend who has lost his job and is having difficulty providing food for his family and to say to him, on the basis of this passage or similar passages, "This is because you have been faithless and disobedient to God." That would be a gross misuse of this Scripture. The primary purpose of the covenant curses was to display for Israel something of the penalty that their sins deserved and something of the curse that the Son of God would bear on behalf of his people. The conditionality of the Mosaic covenant pointed Israel forward and points us backward to Jesus Christ, the second Adam, who would obey God's law perfectly and yet bear in his body the covenant curses as if he broke every law of God a thousand times over. He would do it out of his immeasurable love for us.

Though our experiences of difficulty in this life are not necessarily the direct result of our sin and faithlessness the way they were for Israel, though we're not under the Mosaic covenant with its conditionality of blessing for obedience and cursing for disobedience, we may nevertheless still learn the lesson Israel's covenant curses have to teach. They teach us, as they taught Israel, that idolatry will always end in frustration. Our idols can never deliver what they promise—comfort, lasting happiness and joy, significance and satisfaction for our deepest longings and desires. As we chase after material wealth, power, popularity, and comfort, we will always end up feeling empty, frustrated, and anxious.

Jesus taught his disciples, "Therefore do not be anxious, saying, 'What shall we eat?' or 'What shall we drink?' or 'What shall we wear?' For the Gentiles seek after all these things, and your heavenly Father knows that you need them all. But seek first the kingdom of God and his righteousness, and all these things will be added to you" (Matthew 6:31–33). This is always a critical reminder—to ask, "What do my actions reveal about my priorities?" Not "What do my words say is first in my life?" but "If I take a realistic view of how I use my time, how I use my money, how I use my gifts that God has given me, what do my actions reveal to be my first love?"

When understood in this light, we all stand condemned by God's penetrating question: "Is it a time for you yourselves to dwell in your paneled houses?"

(Haggai 1:4). Not one of us has put God's kingdom first even for a day, much less a lifetime. But God not only issued a sobering complaint; he also declared a gracious promise.

### God's Gracious Promise (1:7, 8)

Though the great bulk of the message delivered by Haggai contains a sobering complaint, at the center of the prophet's message is not a word of judgment *against* sinners but a promise of grace *for* sinners. In the middle of this crushing announcement of God's judgment the Lord declares, "Consider your ways. Go up to the hill and bring wood and build the house, that I may take pleasure in it and that I may be glorified" (vv. 7, 8).[11] Clearly there remains a way forward. There remains the possibility that God will once again delight in his people as they stand in his presence.

Though Israel was at that very moment experiencing God's judgment, verses 7, 8 remind us that the purpose of his judgment is often designed to get his people to wake up. This is what he meant when he said, "Consider your ways." God was calling his people to take a realistic and truthful assessment of themselves. He said, in effect, "Snap out of it! Look at what you've become!" Like the prodigal son in Luke 15, who we're told "came to himself" (v. 17), countless Christians have experienced God shaking them out of a spiritual stupor. When this happens we become aware of our sin in a new and profound way, and we come to once again regard our sin as God regards our sin—as something abhorrent from which to flee. God in Haggai's day shook his people, calling them to consider their ways and to set themselves about the task of rebuilding his temple.

It is important, however, to remember God's goal in all of this. God is not commanding his people to build him a temple because he needs a new house (cf. 2 Samuel 7:5–7). God is not cold from having to camp outside, nor is he jealous of his people's paneled houses, thinking, *I want one of those*. God wants his people to build a temple not for his own sake but for theirs. God knows that what his people need more than anything else—more than shelter and clothes, food, or even health—is to know him and worship him as their Lord and Redeemer.

What Israel needed most was to dwell in the presence of God and to know his blessing and favor, a relationship that could only be established through the ministry of the temple.

This was the significance of the temple for Israel. It was the place God had appointed and designed so that a sinful people might commune with a holy God. It was the place in which and through which the creatures might enjoy that relationship with their God for which they had been created. God purposed to repair and restore that relationship, which was ruined by human sin. In Israel's day, he would do this through the ministry of the temple. Through the temple, God said to Israel, in effect, "Because in your sin you cannot come to me, I will come to you, and I will make a way back into my blessed presence. I will dwell in your midst, and I will make a way for ruined sinners to once again stand in the presence of a holy God and experience not the hot wrath of my judgment but the sweet smile of my fatherly love."

The way back into the presence of God was through the ministry of the temple. It would be from this place that God would begin his great restoration project whereby he would reverse the woeful effects of the curse. It would be through the washing with water and the blood of the sacrifices and the ministry of the priests that Israel could hear the gracious words, "The LORD bless you and keep you; the LORD make his face to shine upon you and be gracious to you; the LORD lift up his countenance upon you and give you peace" (Numbers 6:24–26).

The focus of this passage is not the people's obedience, as if God were saying, "If you just work hard enough, and if you just get this temple built, then there will be grace for you," as if God's grace is for the hard-working temple builders of life. The promise of grace centers on the temple itself. God would take pleasure in the temple because this is where he would be glorified by his people. It represents the relationship between God and man restored, with his image-bearers once more orienting their hearts toward him as their Creator and worshiping him as their Redeemer and Lord.

God's people needed this temple as a constant reminder of their need for a greater temple, a final temple, a true temple who would come in the person of Jesus, about whom John wrote, "The Word became flesh and dwelt [or "tabernacled"] among us, and we have seen his glory, glory as of the only Son from the Father, full of grace and truth" (John 1:14). Put another way, God's people needed a temple to teach them their need for Christ and the ministry of Christ; that the way back into God's presence would come not from an earthly temple built by human hands, with its washings and sacrifices and priesthood, but through the ministry of the heavenly temple, through the blood of the Lamb of God and the ministry of Christ—the great high priest who never dies—and through the cleansing of our consciences by the Holy Spirit.

When Jesus declared in John 2:19, "Destroy this temple, and in three days I will raise it up," he was not speaking of a building but of his body. Christ's body that would be crushed and broken for human sin would three days later be rebuilt and restored as the inaugural resurrection life. God would take pleasure in Israel's temple because it was a type and shadow of Jesus, of whom the Father would say, "This is my beloved Son, with whom I am well pleased" (Matthew 3:17). The promise in Haggai's day of a rebuilt temple in which God would once more dwell with man for their blessing was ultimately a promise of the Christ who would come and tabernacle among his people, a light shining in the darkness. This temple was Israel's hope in the midst of judgment.

### A People's Surprising Response (1:12–15)

Haggai's is not the first complaint that God has issued against his covenant people through his prophets, nor will it be the last. However, what is somewhat surprising about this particular episode in Israel's history is the response God's word receives.

How did Israel typically respond to God's word spoken by his prophets? Israel's typical response to God's prophets was well summarized by Jesus, who cried, "O Jerusalem, Jerusalem, the city that kills the prophets and stones those who are sent to it!" (Luke 13:34).

But in Haggai 1:12 we read, "Then Zerubbabel the son of Shealtiel, and Joshua the son of Jehozadak, the high priest, with all the remnant of the people, obeyed the voice of the Lord their God, and the words of Haggai the prophet, as the Lord their God had sent him." Similarly, a few verses later we read, "They came and worked on the house of the Lord of hosts, their God, on the twenty-fourth day of the month, in the sixth month, in the second year of Darius" (vv. 14b, 15).

This is a picture of large-scale, city-wide obedience. From the greatest to the least—both Zerubbabel the governor and Joshua the high priest—are mentioned (v. 14). There is a complete turnaround and commitment to the task that God has given them. We're told that "all the remnant of the people" with them "obeyed the voice of the Lord" (v. 12).[12] The expression "all the remnant of the people" is pregnant with meaning, as Iain Duguid has helpfully noted: "Calling them 'the remnant of the people' focuses attention on the judgment for unfaithfulness that God's people have already experienced, but at the same time also on God's promises that his judgment upon their sin would not completely obliterate them."[13]

All the remnant of Israel are following all their godly leaders in obedience to the word of God delivered by his prophet. This is a portrait that stands in stark contrast to that of Israel's forefathers.

Lest we mistake the people's obedience as simply outward, as simply an act of self-preservation, an obedience of those who want the heavens to open yet want no relationship with the One who opens the heavens, we're told in verse 12, "The people feared the Lord." "The fear of the Lord" is the language of faith. The obedience we see here is not born of fear but of faith. The people's obedience is the fruit of heartfelt trust in Yahweh and a trust in Yahweh's word. The postexilic community believed the word of God spoken through his prophet, and their obedience in rebuilding the temple was the fruit of that faith.

In Israel's obedience we learn something of the character of faith—that faith believes God's word above all things, especially above feelings, experiences, and even reason. We notice that nothing about Israel's circumstances has changed. The postexilic community was still under the rule of the pagan Persian Empire. Israel still lacked a Davidic king on the throne. Israel was still struggling to put food on the table. Yet Israel obeyed God because they believed the word of God. Israel ceased acting according to what they thought, experienced, or felt at that moment and acted on the basis of God's word. This is the character of true faith: trusting God's word and acting on the basis of God's word in opposition to our own thoughts and feelings about what is good for us. As the Apostle Paul says, "Let God be true though every man were a liar" (Romans 3:4).

In Haggai's brief account of the people's obedience, we also learn something about the origin of faith. Though we're told in 1:12 that Zerubbabel, Joshua, and all of the people feared God and obeyed God, the author also tells us that even this is ultimately from God. We read in 1:14, "The Lord stirred up the spirit of Zerubbabel the son of Shealtiel, governor of Judah, and the spirit of Joshua the son of Jehozadak, the high priest, and the spirit of all the remnant of the people. And they came and worked on the house of the Lord of hosts, their God." Why did these people obey God? Why did they exercise faith? Was it because they were just a little better than their forefathers? Was it because they were a little more spiritual or moral or intelligent? Ultimately, we're told, the obedience of the postexilic community was the fruit of God's redeeming and transforming work in their hearts.

Certainly Zerubbabel made a deliberate decision to believe God, and certainly he made a deliberate decision to obey God. God didn't turn Zerubbabel into a robot in order to force him to obey. Zerubbabel was a free moral agent just as we are free moral agents, and yet the author here reminds us that the transformation that took place in Jerusalem was ultimately the work of God, whose Spirit captured the heart of Zerubbabel and Joshua and the people and made them willing servants of the living God.

There is, of course, a deep mystery to this. How is it that we freely choose what God has ordained us to choose before the foundation of the world? I, for one, am at a loss to explain the mechanics of it. But what I can say with confidence is that this is what the Scriptures teach from beginning to end. This is why Paul commanded the Philippians to "work out your own salvation with fear and trembling, for it is God who works in you, both to will and to work for his good pleasure" (Philippians 2:12b, 13). Obedience is doing something we're commanded to do, and the Bible throughout commands us to obey God. And yet just as faith is a gift from God, so too is the obedience that flows from faith. So in the end, the Christian has nothing to boast in except God's grace and mercy alone (1 Corinthians 1:31; Galatians 6:14; Ephesians 2:9).

Zerubbabel obeyed God, Joshua obeyed God, and the people obeyed God, and this was God's doing. Though we can't know everything we'd like to know about how God accomplishes this transforming work, this passage teaches at least that it is through the gospel. Central to this remarkable transformation of God's people from faithless to faithful, from disobedient to obedient, was this wonderful gospel promise we see in Haggai 1:13: "Then Haggai, the messenger of the LORD, spoke to the people with the LORD 's message, 'I am with you, declares the LORD.'" Ultimately it is not the threat of judgment that is going to move sinners to glorify God, but it is God's promise of mercy—a promise captured beautifully in the words "I am with you"—that can transform even the hardest hearts.

It is not uncommon for pastors and churches to think that the only way to get people to behave themselves is to proclaim the Law of God and the judgment of God against lawbreakers more loudly. But the power of God for salvation is not the thundering judgments of the Law but the sweet promises of the gospel that proclaim Christ and all his benefits that are freely given to those who trust him. It is helpful, therefore, to consider the question, where do I go for help and strength in my struggle against sin? "I am with you," declares the Lord (v. 13). God's presence is not only the glorious end of our pilgrim journeys, but it is the driving and sustaining force throughout them as well. God is with us, and God is for us.

This is the great comfort and hope of the Christian life, that God is with us now and that he will be with us always. This permanent presence of God for our blessings has been established once and for all through the finished work of his own Son. As the incarnate Son of God hung and died on a Roman cross, he cried out, "Eli, Eli, lama Sabachthani? My God, my God, why have you forsaken me?" (Matthew 27:46). In this we hear expressed the deepest pain and most agonizing sorrow a human being could ever feel: the abandonment of God. The worst was not the unimaginable pain of being nailed to a Roman cross but the pain of being forsaken by the Father with whom the Son had forever enjoyed a loving communion the depths of which we could never fully know or possibly understand. Jesus endured the forsakenness that we deserve so God could say to sinners like us, "I will never leave you nor forsake you" (Hebrews 13:5). Because Jesus was forsaken, those who trust in him will never be forsaken. Neither in life nor in death will God fail to be with us and for us. As God through the prophet Isaiah declared,

> Fear not, for I have redeemed you;
> I have called you by name, you are mine.
> When you pass through the waters, I will be with you;
> and through the rivers, they shall not overwhelm you;
> when you walk through fire you shall not be burned,
> and the flame shall not consume you.
> For I am the Lord your God,
> the Holy One of Israel, your Savior. (Isaiah 43:1–3)

This word announced to postexilic Israel more than 2,500 years ago is just as relevant for us today. Our experience as Christians living under the new covenant inaugurated by Christ is in many striking respects quite similar to that of the postexilic community. Just as they lived in the gap between promise and fulfillment, we find ourselves knowing and experiencing that great deliverance from the captivity of sin through the death and resurrection of Christ and yet awaiting an even greater fulfillment of God's promises in the consummation of the new heavens and the new earth. As we live between the first and second coming of Christ, we too must live by faith and hope and with faithfulness and obedience to God although we, like postexilic Israel, at times can't see how God is working all things together for the good of his people and for his own glory. We too are prone to bewilderment, discouragement, and spiritual lethargy and need to be reoriented by the Word of God, in which God assures us of his presence with us through even the greatest trials we face. The call for us today, therefore, is the same: "Work, for the Lord is with you."

# 59

# Future Glories

HAGGAI 1:15B—2:9

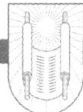

OUR MONTH OF JANUARY derives its name from the Roman god Janus. When Janus was depicted in visual art, he was commonly portrayed as having two faces pointing in opposite directions. Now for most of us, being depicted with two faces doesn't seem like a desirable thing, but for the Romans, this was a physical representation of the deity looking to the past and looking to the future. Janus was the god of transitions. As such, he was associated with beginnings and endings. January, therefore, is a fitting name for the first month of our calendar year, as it is a time in which we often look back to the year behind and forward to the year ahead.

Consequently, since January comes only once a year, many if not most of us are in the habit of taking the time to look back and look forward with thoughtfulness, care, and intentionality only once a year. However, the prophet Haggai's second oracle teaches that this posture of looking back and looking forward is a fitting one for believers at all times and in every age.

In Haggai, God calls Israel to adopt a sort of Janus-like posture, looking backward to the past and looking forward to the future. This is almost certainly the significance of the date appended to this oracle: ". . . in the second year of Darius the king. In the seventh month, on the twenty-first day of the month . . ." (1:15b—2:1a).[1] The twenty-first day of the seventh month places Haggai's oracle on the next-to-last day of the annual Feast of Booths (Leviticus 23:33–43; Numbers 29:12–39; Deuteronomy 16:13–17).

Also called the Feast of Ingathering, the Feast of Booths would have been a natural time to address the entire covenant community, as the whole community was gathered together along with their leaders. But this date is also significant because of what the Feast of Booths commemorated. The Feast of Booths was a commemoration and, in a sense, a reenactment of Israel's wanderings in the wilderness. For this feast, God commanded Israel to build booths as they had done in the years of their wilderness wanderings and to live in them for a week. For Israel this would be a time to look back and remember God's faithfulness to them in the past when he guided and sustained their forefathers and -mothers through their forty-year wanderings in the Judean desert.

The Feast of Booths was not only a time to look back in reflection and commemoration, but it was also a time to look forward with hopeful anticipation. God prescribed the Feast of Booths as a yearly reminder to Israel that was to be celebrated even after they were settled in the promised land, to say, in effect, that even though they were in the promised land, even though they had received their earthly inheritance, there was yet a greater land and yet a greater inheritance still to come. In a very real sense, Israel was still in the wilderness, dependent on God for his provision, looking forward to a greater and more glorious day.

This had been important for Israel to remember in her glory days of old, when she was wealthy and strong and independent, but it was also important for Israel to remember when she was poor, weak, oppressed, and discouraged.

This is the heart of Haggai's message to the postexilic community. The prophet calls Israel to look back and to look forward, and he declares to them that there is a far more glorious day yet to come, a day more glorious than their glory days of old. As they wait for that day, they are to wait trusting God, working for God, and hoping in God. The prophet does this by first calling the postexilic community's attention to what was almost certainly the elephant in the room (or city, as the case may be): the temple they were building was noticeably inferior to the temple that had been destroyed. Yet this inglorious temple would stand as an important symbol for Israel, a symbol that had important things to teach this postexilic community.

## Lessons from an Inglorious Temple (2:3–5)

One of the things my wife and I teach our children is that if they notice that something is wrong, deficient, inferior, or lacking, it is not incumbent upon them to mention it. If, for example, their little sister's drawing of her dad is missing a torso, they don't need to mention it. However, God instructs his prophet Haggai to announce publicly to the entire postexilic community the fact that their temple is conspicuously inferior to the temple of their forefathers: "Who is left among you who saw this house in its former glory? How do you see it now? Is it not as nothing in your eyes?" (Haggai 2:3).

God is here inviting witnesses to speak up and testify to the superiority of Israel's former temple. Some of the very old people in the postexilic community could remember seeing Solomon's temple and were therefore in a position to relate something of its glory and splendor.[2] Included among these were Levites, priests, and heads of families; in other words, leaders whose estimations had the potential to shape those of others.[3] The prophet's point, however, is that this former glory and splendor is now lacking in the new temple currently under construction and, by implication, missing for this postexilic community.

Why does God do this? He is not highlighting the inferiority of the second temple to make his people feel bad about their labors. Nor is he highlighting its inferiority to make them work harder, as if the temple's glory is ultimately a matter of human skill and effort. Rather, God is highlighting the inferiority of the second temple to teach this postexilic community something of the character of the age in which they are living.

Israel would have an inglorious temple because Israel was living in an inglorious age. This time in her history was not going to be a time marked by outward displays of Israel's power, wealth, and influence. In the former times, as evidence of God's favor, Israel could point to their king reigning from the throne of David and leading Israel in victory over any who opposed them or their God.[4] In ages past, Israel could point to the splendor of their city or their great wealth or their sovereignty over other nations, all of which displayed something of the glory of Israel and the glory of Israel's God.[5] But those days were gone, now a distant memory preserved in stories about the good old days.

Things had clearly changed, and from the perspective of the postexilic community, not for the better. Now the people found themselves without a king, without great wealth, without national autonomy, and wondering if their best days were behind them. We know from Haggai's contemporary Zechariah that many regarded their day as "the day of small things" (Zechariah 4:10), and many were discouraged. Many, no doubt, were tempted to give up on building the temple, thinking, *What's the point?* They were deeply and daily impressed with their identity as conquered people who were just one small cog in the machine of the great Persian Empire. Furthermore, it was tempting to question and to doubt whether God's purposes for them and his promises to them were still in effect.

Notice, however, what God does *not* do. God does not say, "You're really looking at it wrong—you really are a great nation." God isn't a relativist

("Every nation is a great nation!"). God doesn't deny that his people are living in an inglorious age. Rather, he responds by teaching them how to live well in an inglorious age. He calls them to faithfulness even in a day of small things. God says, "Be strong. . . . Work, for I am with you, declares the LORD of hosts" (Haggai 2:4). In this call to strength and courage, God is not calling his people to pull themselves up by their bootstraps. God is not saying, "Buck up and work harder." God is calling his people, rather, to persevere in faithfulness in the face of great obstacles. This call to "be strong" is a call to obedience to the tasks that the Lord has set before them.

But more than that, this call would have reminded Israel of previous calls to previous servants of God. Servants like Joshua, to whom God said, "Be strong and courageous, for you shall bring the people of Israel into the land that I swore to give them" (Deuteronomy 31:23). Then the Lord added, "I will be with you." So it was in Haggai's day. Zerubbabel, Joshua, and the entire postexilic community were called to "Be strong. . . . Work" (Haggai 2:4). As he did with Joshua centuries earlier, so God assured the postexilic community of his presence: "Work, for I am with you, declares the LORD of hosts" (Haggai 2:4).

As they worked, they would do so in the sure knowledge that God was present with them.

By all outward appearances, the Lord seems to be far from his people. The outward symbols that would have told the world that Israel belongs to the sovereign Lord of the universe are gone. But Israel is reminded that they have something far more precious and profound, something infinitely more valuable than symbols of their glorious status: they have God himself. "The LORD of hosts [literally, armies]" is their God, and as their assurance, they have his word of promise that can never be broken. God says, "Work, for I am with you, . . . according to the covenant that I made with you when you came out of Egypt" (vv. 4, 5). God's covenant promises are still in effect. Though Israel might break the covenant, though Israel has been and will be faithless toward the covenant, ultimately God's grace, as it is expressed clearly in his covenants, will never fail.

On the basis of these truths Israel can persevere and work. As they do, Israel's confidence is not in themselves but in their God who is with them and for them. He is still working all things together to bless his people and fulfill his good purposes for them. God is at work in the day of small things just as much as he is in the day of big things. Simply because Israel lacks glory doesn't mean Israel's God lacks glory. Though Persia's emperor certainly appears to be the king of kings and the commander of the greatest army the world has ever seen, Haggai reminds God's people that their God was and is and always will be the Lord of hosts, that is, the Lord of armies. Israel's God and our God is sovereign over all the affairs of men and is sovereign over his people, even when they don't feel it or can't see it. Even when the entire world seems to speak the contrary, God nevertheless is at work in and through his people.

This message to the postexilic community is just as relevant in our day as it was in theirs because we too can feel like we're living in a day of small things. This is certainly true for the Church. Christianity in America is on the decline. Not too long ago a Pew research poll indicated that Wiccans now outnumber Presbyterians in the United States.[6] Fewer and fewer people seem interested in the claims of Christianity, and the gospel of Christ is increasingly met with boredom if not open opposition.

While Christianity is on the decline in the secular West, around the world there is continued, if not increased, persecution of the Church in places like Nigeria, Pakistan, Libya, and China, to name a few. As Christians we're tempted to wonder, *Is God really in control of all of this? And if God is in control, why does he allow his people to be persecuted, imprisoned, harassed and at times slaughtered?* The solution is not to pretend as if the day of small things is a day of big things or by denying the harsh circumstances in which we live.

We can certainly feel this way about the Church, but we can also feel this way in our own lives when it seems as if we're making very little spiritual progress. When our Christian walk feels like a crawl at best, when the gospel that once thrilled our hearts can seem to ring hollow in our ears as we continue to struggle with the same besetting sins, we wonder, *Is this the victorious Christian life I was promised?* We too need to hear that God is still with us according to his unfailing and unchanging promise. God is with his people and is at work, even though we at times struggle to see it and fear that it's not true. In all of our struggles and trials, it is critical to remember that God remains the Lord of Hosts who is with his people—in the days of big things and in the days of small things. The Spirit of God himself dwells with and in his people. The God who is with us has promised to work in us and through us.

God's call for us is to work. We are called to labor in those tasks that he in his providence has laid before us. We're not called to understand all that God is up to, as there is much that God does that remains mysterious. Nor are we called to do great things for Jesus in the way the world would measure greatness. Like the postexilic community, we're called to trust God and to live in faithful obedience to him in the small and mundane tasks to which all of us are called as fathers, mothers, students, teachers, employees, and church members. So much of what we're called to be about lacks any outward display of glory, power, or triumph, but God's promise is for us today. God is with us.

Looking back teaches Israel something about the character of their present—it teaches them something about their calling in the present to work and to wait; and it also, perhaps more importantly, serves to instill in them a hope for a more glorious future.

### Promises of a More Glorious Future (2:6–9)

If you've been around Presbyterians any length of time, you know that we easily and often fall into the "good old days" mentality. This is a mentality in which the Church's past becomes a sort of golden age, and the Church's present is regarded as just short of a return to the dark ages. There is a nostalgic longing to return to the good old days when pastors were pastors, congregants were churchmen, and children knew their catechisms. However, God is not pointing Israel to the past to instill in them a longing to return to a mythical golden age (was Solomon's age really all that great after all?) but to instill in them a longing for the future. He's telling them to look back because in looking back Israel can learn something about what lies ahead.

God declares, "The latter glory of this house shall be greater than the former" (Haggai 2:9). The former glory of Israel's temple is meant to serve as a reference point for comparison. God is saying, in effect, "Remember the glory of Israel's former temple because I am going to build and I am going to adorn a temple so beautiful and so glorious that the former temple will seem like a run-down shack by comparison." God is saying that there is coming a day for his people that will be so glorious that the glory days of old will by comparison seem like days of poverty and suffering, and our days of poverty and suffering will seem like a distant dream.

Notice how this glorious day is going to come about. It is not going to come about through Israel's efforts at temple-building. Nor is it going to come about by Israel's obedience in law-keeping and evangelism. It's going to come about by God shaking the world in such a way that the created order as we know it will be turned upside down: "For thus says the LORD of hosts: Yet once more, in a little while, I will shake the heavens and the earth and the sea and the dry land" (v. 6). These couplets, "the heavens and the earth and the sea and the dry land," are in a sense polar opposites. This is a common literary form called a *merism* in which two extremes are mentioned in order to indicate everything in between. "The heavens and the earth and the sea and the dry land" is a way of saying, "Everything." Everything in the entire cosmos is going to be subject to this divine shaking.

The promise of a cosmic shaking is, from a human perspective, a terrifying prospect. Not many of us would look forward to or long for an earthquake of cosmic proportions. When we think of an earthquake, we think of a terrifying event that leaves our well-ordered world in chaotic disarray. We could think of images we have seen of the horrific aftermath of an earthquake where all that remains of a once-great city is rubble and smoke. But according to the Bible, what we think of as an ordered world is in fact a world that groans under the effects of the curse of sin, wickedness, and injustice. Paul tells us in Romans 8 that sin caused God's well-ordered creation to be "subjected to futility" and that the earth now under the curse of sin is in "bondage to corruption" (vv. 20, 21). It is a world, as Psalm 73 reminds us, in which the righteous are oppressed and the wicked prosper (vv. 3–9).

This was Israel's experience. The pagan Persian Empire seemed to go from victory to victory—the Persian king amassing immense wealth and exerting what in the ancient world would have been considered near-worldwide dominance. On the other hand, God's covenant people were poor, oppressed, and weak. Was this not a world that was out of joint?

In this, we're reminded that this world we inhabit is already upside down. But when God shakes the earth, the silver and the gold, the wealth and power and glory of the nations, will come flooding into his house, and his people will enjoy God's blessing and will display God's glory. This is a picture of the world set right. At the very time that the postexilic community is suffering from a meager crop harvest (Haggai 1:6), they hear that the Lord is going to bring about an ingathering of his own.[7]

This image of the silver and gold of the nations pouring into the temple of the Lord (2:8) is a metaphor. What we look forward to, what we long for, is not literal gold or silver; our greatest longing is for God himself. There is no greater joy that we can experience than the joy of communion with our Creator, and there is no greater fulfillment that we can experience than that which comes from knowing the smile of God's favor and love. The same psalmist who once desired the fleeting prosperity of the wicked would sing, "Whom have I in heaven but you? And there is nothing on earth that I desire besides you. My flesh and my heart may fail, but God is the strength of my heart and my portion forever" (Psalm 73:25, 26).

This is what God was promising when he said, "The latter glory of this house shall be greater than the former" (Haggai 2:9). Some have pointed out that in many respects this second temple was not all that different from the first temple. The second temple, in fact, had the same basic footprint. In terms of square footage, the general measurements were about the same.[8] A temple realtor would have sold them for about the same price. In what way, then, was the second temple so noticeably inferior to the first that God could say, "Is it not as nothing in your eyes?" (v. 3).

The answer is found in the word "glory" when the prophet speaks of the "latter glory" (v. 9). This word would almost certainly have reminded the postexilic community of "the glory of the LORD" that descended upon the temple 440 years earlier. When Solomon dedicated the first temple, also during the Feast of Tabernacles, we're told in 1 Kings 8:10, 11 that "when the priests came out of the Holy Place, a cloud filled the house of the LORD, so that the priests could not stand to minister because of the cloud, for the glory of the LORD filled the house of the LORD." This *Shekinah*-glory cloud was a visible manifestation of God's gracious presence with his people. It was this glory of God that departed from the temple and Jerusalem at the exile, memorably depicted in Ezekiel's vision of the departure of the glory of the Lord (Ezekiel 10).

Ultimately, this was the glory that was missing from the second temple, perhaps represented by the ark of the covenant.[9] God withheld this theophany to create in his people a longing and a watchfulness and a readiness for the Word who would become flesh and dwell among us. John said, "We have seen his glory, glory as of the only Son from the Father, full of grace and truth" (John 1:14). The glory of the Lord would return to the temple, but it would not come in the brilliant spectacle of a blindingly bright pillar of cloud and fire. It would come in the person of the incarnate Son, humble and riding on a donkey (cf. Zechariah 9:9).

In Mark 11 we read of Jesus's triumphal entry into Jerusalem in which he is hailed as the Davidic Messiah with loud shouts of "Hosanna! Blessed is he who comes in the name of the Lord! Blessed is the coming kingdom of our father David! Hosanna in the highest!" (vv. 9, 10). Then we read, surprisingly, "He entered Jerusalem and went into the temple. And when he had looked around at everything, as it was already late, he went out to Bethany with the twelve" (v. 11). What is striking about this scene is that here Israel beholds and, in a sense, receives what she had been waiting for so long. The glory of God finally returns to his temple. But tragically and ironically, no one is there to greet him. The crowds seem to have peeled away. Jesus enters his Father's house seemingly alone. The crowds were expecting a day of big things, a salvation that involved great spectacle and outward trappings of victory. Yet the truth is that Israel's redemption and our redemption could only come in the humiliation of the Son of God, the true King of kings dying on the cross for our sins.

It is not a coincidence that on that day the sun was darkened, and the earth shook. The great earth-shaking that Haggai promised began on Calvary when the Son of God, Israel's true King, died for the sins of his people. The earth shook, and God began building his house around the chief cornerstone, the Lord Jesus Christ.

At the end of the day, the God who owns the cattle on a thousand hills is not really interested in the precious metals that are possessed by the nations; rather, he is interested in fallen sinners redeemed, sanctified, and glorified by the precious blood of the Lamb. He is interested in ransoming those who are slaves to sin and setting them free in Christ. That is the great renovation project begun at Calvary as God calls men and women, boys and girls from every tribe, tongue, and nation to new life in his Son. God will beautify his house, but he will do so with people. As the Apostle Paul reminded the Corinthians, "Do you not know that you are God's temple and that the God's Spirit dwells in you?" (1 Corinthians 3:16). Similarly, Peter wrote, "You yourselves like living stones are being built up as a spiritual house, to be a holy priesthood, to offer spiritual sacrifices acceptable to God through Jesus Christ" (1 Peter 2:5).

The effect of this for those who are united to Christ by faith is that we are enabled by the Spirit to live lives without fear. Apart from Christ, the realities of this present evil age are terrifying. The same was true for the postexilic community in Haggai's day. But at the end of Haggai 2:5, God said through his prophet, "Fear not."

There is in this world so much to fear—so much uncertainty, so many dangers. But God says to his people, "Fear not," because their end is certain and their fate secure, and both are glorious beyond human comprehension. In the very place where the world seems most out of joint God says, "I will give peace" (v. 9). The promised peace and rest are found ultimately in the Son of God who tabernacled among his people as the true temple and who promises his disciples, "Peace I leave with you; my peace I give to you. Not as the world gives do I give to you. Let not your hearts be troubled, neither let them be afraid" (John 14:27).

Like Israel, we are called to look back and to look forward. However, we look back not to the glory of an old temple but rather to a wondrous cross "on which the Prince of Glory died."[10] When Jesus was nailed to that cursed tree, so too were the sins of his people. When Jesus was buried in that tomb, he took with him the sin and shame of those united to him by faith. Thus, we can look forward with the assurance that whatever trials, hardships, and griefs we endure, and whatever pains and sorrows we bear are—in the scope of eternity—but light, momentary afflictions compared to the weight of glory yet to be revealed when God one last time shakes the earth and makes all things new.

# 60

# Defiled People, Divine Blessing

HAGGAI 2:10-19

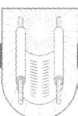

IF YOU'RE TRAVELING through Maine and ask for directions, it's quite possible that you'll hear, "Well, you can't get there from here." This expression strikes many non-Mainers as funny because, in theory, you can get anywhere from anywhere. With enough time, money, energy, and technology you can get to almost any point on this globe from any other point on this globe. So if we're talking about directions, the expression "You can't get there from here" seems patently and humorously untrue. However, what is patently untrue when it comes to travel is painfully true when it comes to our relationship with God. From the moment Adam was expelled from the garden paradise, the overriding question for the human race has been, how do we get back? How do we return to that estate of innocence and blessedness and joyful communion with our Creator? To put it another way, how can sinful man stand in the presence of the holy God?

Of course, a variety of answers have been offered, and even more have been attempted. Some, for example, look to their own morality, thinking, *If I'm just good enough (or at least better than most), then surely God will look favorably upon me.* Others look to religiosity and outward acts of piety designed to appease God or to endear God to them. Still others seek a mystical experience to try and achieve communion with the divine. But the answer the Bible gives throughout is, try as you might, you can't get there from here. The Bible says that the human predicament is so desperate and the estate of sin so dire that there is nothing man or woman, boy or girl could ever do to earn his or her way back into the presence of God.

That is the bad news. The good news, however, is that Jesus said to his disciples, "What is impossible with man is possible with God" (Luke 18:27). This is the message that Haggai brought to the postexilic community. What is impossible for mankind to accomplish on account of their innate uncleanness and impurity, God accomplishes through the work of his pure Son. While human effort ends in cursing, God's work results in blessing.

The prophet begins his message with what we might call an object lesson or a case study meant to illustrate a greater, more profound reality.

### The Power of Impurity (2:10–13)

God commands the people to "ask the priests about the law" (Haggai 2:11). There is, in fact, nothing unusual about this, as it was the priest's job not only to offer sacrifices and prayers on behalf of God's people but also to answer questions and make judgments about the Torah, that is, what the Law of God teaches on a matter.[1] This was especially important when a particular situation arose that was not explicitly addressed in the Bible. The priests would reason based on the principles of the Law in order to render an answer.

This is what is going on in Haggai's third oracle. The prophet is instructed to set this question before the priests: "If someone carries holy meat in the fold of his garment and touches with his fold bread or stew or wine or oil or any kind of food, does it become holy?" (v. 12). At its heart, the prophet's line of questioning has in view the communicability of holiness.[2] In what situations and under what conditions is purity or impurity transferred from one object to another?

In the days before pockets, much less Ziploc bags, people would carry meat in the fold of their garment. The situation envisioned here is one in which someone is carrying meat that has been consecrated by the priests. Meat consecrated by the priests was holy and its use limited. Though some offerings (e.g., the burnt or holocaust offering) were completely consumed on the altar, most of the other offerings preserved a portion of the victim to be consumed by the priests as their portion. In one instance, however, the sacrificial victim was eaten by the worshiper along with his or her family.[3] This was the fellowship or peace offering. The worshiper and his family could consume the meat of the sacrifice up to two days after it was offered.

In all likelihood, the situation envisioned here in Haggai 2 is that of a fellowship offering in which meat is being transported from one place to another, and it somehow comes in contact with stew, wine, or oil.[4]

Should this happen, thoughtful Israelites would wonder, "What is the status of the oil that comes into contact with a holy item belonging to a holy God? Is the oil holy? Is the wine holy?" The answer the priests give is an unequivocal no. Ordinarily a holy object does not transmit its holiness to a common object. This was the principle at work in the priests' verdict: holiness is not contagious or transferrable.[5] So they answer in the negative.

Then God asks a second question: " 'If someone who is unclean by contact with a dead body touches any of these, does it become unclean?' and the priests answered and said, 'It does become unclean' " (Haggai 2:13). Keeping everything the same, what about uncleanness? Is impurity contagious? According to Biblical law, the answer the priests give is perfectly correct: Contact with the unclean undoubtedly makes the wine or the stew or the oil ritually unclean. Consequently, that wine or stew or oil would make someone unclean who drinks it or eats it. The principle at work here is clear: in contrast to holiness, impurity is extremely contagious and transfers easily to anything with which it comes into contact.

The point of these prophetic case studies is to teach Israel something about the character of sin and the curse of sin: specifically, sin is both powerful and pervasive. The curse of sin is not something that is easily undone. When children run across a pristine new carpet with dirty shoes, they leave dirt everywhere. Running across the now-dirty carpet with clean shoes does not make the carpet clean. Rather, in all likelihood it makes the clean shoes dirty. The carpet is still as dirty as ever. This is the point that God is making: it is much easier to make the carpet dirty than clean. And once the carpet downstairs is dirty, it is much more likely that the carpets upstairs will get dirty as well. Once present, the dirt transfers and contaminates easily. The effects of sin, in other words, are not reversed easily.

Now it is important to remember that these categories of uncleanness and cleanness, pure and defiled, are not necessarily moral categories.[6] They may include moral issues; for example, if someone intentionally eats an unclean animal, this becomes a moral issue.[7] But in essence, these categories are ritual categories. They refer to one's status within the community and will determine whether or not he is permitted to enter into God's presence in temple worship. That those who are unclean are not welcome in the temple is a symbol of the fact that the impure and the defiled have no place in the presence of God. Though purity doesn't have in view particular sins, the entire system of clean and unclean brings into view the reality of the curse of sin and the dreadful consequences of sin. It is a way for Israel to highlight in their society the power and pervasiveness of sin and to remind themselves that those who are under the curse of sin have no place in the presence of our holy God. The curse of sin goes to the very core of who we are as fallen human creatures, and it touches every aspect of the created order and every aspect of our societies.

In Haggai, God is reminding his people of the power of sin and the pervasiveness of sin. He is reminding them of the power of the curse and the pervasiveness of the curse. The curse has affected every aspect of human existence; it has disrupted human flourishing in every respect.

This comes as a critical reminder for believers of every age. We too can be tempted to think of sin as a small thing, limited for the most part to outward actions. In so doing, we can fail to see how deep our sin really goes, how powerful and how pervasive sin really is in human life, and we can fail to see how many aspects of our lives sin has corrupted and defiled. Consequently, we tend to focus on the presenting issues and fail to consider and address the deep spiritual sicknesses and the deep underlying idols of our hearts. As we are accustomed to say in the Reformed tradition: we're not sinners because we sin—we sin because we're sinners. The impurity of sin, the stain of sin, goes to our very hearts and, as a consequence, affects our thoughts, our emotions, our motivations, our desires.

### The Problem of Impurity (2:14, 16, 17)

The purpose of this case study was not to indulge the legally minded with abstract, ultimately pointless theoretical speculation. God is not engaging in a parlor game. The purpose of this case study was to teach the postexilic community something critical about themselves. In Haggai 2:14, the prophet applied this principle of the power and pervasiveness of sin to Israel's present experience: "Then Haggai answered and said, 'So is it with this people, and with this nation before me, declares the LORD, and so with every work of their hands. And what they offer there is unclean.'"[8]

The postexilic community has been harvesting grain, raising animals, and pressing oil and bringing these as offerings to the Lord as expressions of their love and devotion. But how does God respond? God responds by declaring that Israel's offerings are defiled, corrupt, polluted, and therefore unacceptable. In fact, God uses startling language here when he refers to the postexilic community as "this people" instead of his common designation "my people." It's a bit subtle but telling. It's similar to my wife referring to one of our children as "your daughter" instead of "our daughter." This designation reveals a certain posture. "This people's" sacrifices are unacceptable not because the sacrifices are unclean but because *the people* are. As they bring what they think are acceptable sacrifices, God says, in effect, "These are unclean because you are unclean."

Like the story of King Midas who needs to eat, yet everything he touches turns to gold, these people need to offer sacrifices to atone for sin, and yet every time they touch one to bring it to the Lord, it becomes unclean. Their offerings are vain; their efforts are vain. They could offer sacrifices day and night, they could bring the absolute best to God, but it is all for nothing because they are themselves unclean, and thus even their best is stained with the contamination of sin.

When rightly understood, the postexilic community is in an impossible situation. They can't get there from here. The very thing Israel needs is the very thing they can't provide because of who they are—sinners, unclean and defiled. As a consequence, they are experiencing the frustration, futility, and misery of God's covenant curses. In 2:16, God rehearses the experience of the postexilic community: "When one came to a heap of twenty measures, there were but ten. When one came to the wine vat to draw fifty measures, there were but twenty." And then, lest the people mistakenly attribute their misfortunes to bad luck, God identifies himself as the cause of their troubles: " 'I struck you and all the products of your toil with blight and with mildew and with hail, for you had nothing directed towards me, declares the LORD" (2:17, AT).[9]

Blight and mildew were features of the futility curses promised in Deuteronomy 28:22. Hail was a common affliction God brought against those who opposed him, as, for example, at the time of the exodus (Exodus 9:13–35; cf. Psalm 78:47; Isaiah 28:17). God's people were experiencing God's covenant curse and his hard judgment, but to what end? Negatively, God's purpose was to reveal to Israel that the people's sin was more serious and their situation more impossible than they had ever imagined. Positively, God's purpose was to reveal to them their need for the temple.

This elaborate and demoralizing case study was designed to teach Israel and to teach us something about humanity's helpless and hopeless estate apart from God's grace so that they and we might find God's grace where it may be found. In Haggai's day, this was the earthly temple, and in our day, this is the true temple, Jesus Christ.

We learn from this that apart from the merit and mediation of Christ, even our best efforts to love, serve, please, honor, and obey God are in vain.

No worship is acceptable in God's sight apart from the mediation of the risen Son. No acts of obedience are pleasing to him apart from the merit of the covenant-keeping Christ. Speaking about our best works, the Westminster

Confession of Faith says that "as they are good, they proceed from His Spirit, and as they are wrought by us, they are defiled, and mixed with so much weakness and imperfection, that they cannot endure the severity of God's judgment" (16.5). Similarly, the Heidelberg Catechism asks, "But can those converted to God obey these commandments perfectly?" The answer opens with the words, "No. In this life even the holiest have only a small beginning of this obedience" (Q&A 114).

Even the holiest, the Heidelberg Catechism says, are unable to obey perfectly. Even the holiest find that their best and most selfless good deeds are nevertheless stained with the corruption of sin. And as such, in and of themselves, these good works are defiled and cannot endure the severity of God's judgment, much less provide the righteousness necessary to stand in his presence.

It is impossible for good deeds, defiled by human sin, to merit favor and find acceptance in the presence of a holy God. You can't get there from here, and yet what is impossible for man is possible for God.

### The Provision for the Impure (2:15, 18, 19)

Many of the dates given in the books of Haggai and Zechariah correspond to important dates in Israel's annual festival calendar. Understanding something about the origin, purpose, and character of those festivals sheds light on the prophetic oracle that comes on that particular day. But surprisingly, the date given in this text, "the twenty-fourth day of the ninth month, in the second year of Darius" (Haggai 2:10), does not correspond to any important feast or festival in Israel's life. It does not mark an important day in the annual calendar. However, it does mark one of the most important days in Israel's history. Time and again throughout this text, God emphasizes the importance of this particular day. In verse 15, for example, God says, "Now then, consider from this day onward . . ." And again in verse 18, "Consider from this day onward, from the twenty-fourth day of the ninth month." And then in verse 19, "From this day on I will bless you."

This day, "the twenty-fourth day of the ninth month," marks a major turning point in Israel's history. What is it that is so special about this day that it marks the turning point from cursing to blessing? We're told in verse 18, "Since the day that the foundation of the LORD's temple was laid . . ." It is the completion of the foundation of the temple that makes all the difference.[10]

To be sure, we don't know what happened on this day that signaled the completion of the foundation. Was there a ceremony, a celebration of some sort? Was there a ceremonial placement of a final stone? The text doesn't tell us.

But whatever it was that marked the completion of the temple foundation, it is clear that "this day" was the day the foundation was completed; therefore, from "this day," the postexilic community would experience God's blessing in place of his cursing.[11]

God says, "Is the seed yet in the barn? Indeed, the vine, the fig tree, the pomegranate, and the olive tree have yielded nothing. But from this day on I will bless you" (v. 19). Israel's future will be one of blessing, but not because they are going to be more obedient. God is not a life coach telling Israel, "You've got this!" Neither will they experience God's blessing because they're going to bring better sacrifices. Israel's future will be one of blessing because of the temple, because of all that the temple represents, and because of all that the temple accomplishes for God's people in making a way for sinners back into the presence of their holy God.

For the postexilic community, the ministry of the temple changes everything. The temple is the place where God revealed himself to his people not only as sovereign Lord of the universe, the great Lawgiver and Judge, but also as the God of grace and mercy to those who look to him in faith. It is through the temple that God revealed himself as the One who forgives broken and contrite sinners and who heals the weak and wounded. If you wanted to know God as Creator and Judge, you didn't need the temple. But if you wanted to meet God as a God of grace, the place you could do that was in the temple.

Through the washings with water, the blood of the sacrifices, and the mediation of the priests, God made for sinners a way back into his blessed presence. When Israel approached God apart from the temple, even their best efforts were defiled and abhorrent to a holy God. But when Israel approached through the ministry of the temple, their sacrifices were accepted, and they were accepted, and they knew and experienced the blessing of the Lord God.[12] Through the temple, Israel could be assured that they were accepted by God, that he delighted in them, and that he rejoiced over them as a father rejoices over a child whom he loves and adores.

What we have in the temple is the reminder that, though hopeless and helpless in themselves, though they were unable to enter God's presence through any effort or work of their own, God came to Israel and made a way. God said, in effect, "If you meet me here, if you enter through this temple, you will find that the judgment you deserve has been transformed into blessing."

God gave his people the temple to teach them and to teach us of their and our need for Christ, who said, "I am the way, and the truth, and the life. No one comes to the Father except through me" (John 14:6). Jesus, John tells us, is "the Word [who] became flesh and dwelt among us" (John 1:14); he is the true temple that would be torn down and rebuilt in three days (John 2:19–21). Jesus is the perfect priest who mediates between God and man. Jesus is the once-for-all sacrifice whose blood takes away the sins of the world. Jesus is the One out of whose heart flows living water, and he sends his Spirit into the world to cleanse the hearts of his people. Christ accomplishes what the temple promised: God's purification of an impure people.

We see this throughout Jesus's ministry. Think of how often Jesus came into contact with the impure and the unclean of his society. He interacted with the ritually impure—lepers, a woman with a hemorrhage, corpses. He interacted with what you might call the spiritually impure—demoniacs, for example. He interacted with the morally impure, eating with tax collectors, prostitutes, and known sinners. To what end? In all of Jesus's interactions, he bore witness to the fact that he came to bring purity, cleanness, and holiness to a desperately impure, unclean, and sinful world. In contrast to the holy meat that lacked the power to transfer purity, Jesus came to grant purity to all who would by faith entrust themselves to him.

We see this perhaps most strikingly in Jesus's healing of a leper in Mark 1. In this episode, Jesus is approached by a leper who kneels before him and says not what we might perhaps expect: "If you will, you can heal my leprosy." Rather, he says, "If you will, you can make me clean" (v. 40).

This leper understood that his greatest problem was not his leprosy but the obstacle it created for him to enter into the presence of God in worship. Then we read that Jesus stretched out his hand and touched him (v. 41).

Mark is presenting the scene in slow motion, providing what is, for him, an uncharacteristic amount of detail. Why? Of course, you need to stretch out your hand to touch someone. Why mention it?

We know from other accounts that Jesus didn't have to touch the leper to heal him. He healed people from a distance without touching them—for example, in Luke 17, where he healed ten lepers by the word of his power (vv. 11–19). But Jesus touched this man in Mark 1 intentionally (v. 41). In this action, Jesus is showing the price that he would pay to make this man clean and to make us clean.

Jesus was saying, in effect, "I am willing to become unclean so that you can become clean. I'm willing to become impure myself for a time so that you might experience the fullness of joy in the presence of my Father."

This great exchange is dramatically portrayed in the conclusion of the narrative. Mark writes that after Jesus heals the leper,

Jesus sternly charged him and sent him away at once, and said to him, "See that you say nothing to anyone, but go, show yourself to the priest and offer for your cleansing what Moses commanded, for a proof to them." But he [the man] went out and began to talk freely about it, and to spread the news, so that Jesus could no longer openly enter a town, but was out in desolate places, and people were coming to him from every quarter. (Mark 1:43–45)

The man who disobeys Jesus is restored to his community. He can go about sharing and conversing in fellowship with his kinsmen. But where is Jesus? Jesus, Mark tells us, is left outside the city, in the desert and the lonely places.

It was no small price that Jesus would pay to be able to say to the unclean man, "I will; be clean" (Mark 1:41). In this scene, Jesus quite literally switched places with this leprous man—the man reentered life in the city while Jesus was left on the outskirts of society, thus adumbrating what would transpire at Calvary. On the cross, in the place of cursing, outside of the city, Jesus took all our) uncleanness and gave us his purity before the Father so that we could not only enter into fellowship with one another but with God himself.

It would be on the cross that the perfectly pure, perfectly clean, perfectly holy Son of God became unclean, despised, and rejected, not just by his fellow Jews (as painful as that was) but by his Father, who laid on him the sins of us all.

Through his blood, Christ makes the impure pure and the unclean clean. Though apart from Christ our best works are so stained by sin and corruption that they could not possibly merit standing before a holy God, yet in Christ even our weakest endeavors, our most pitiful efforts are sanctified by the blood of Christ and are therefore pleasing to our Father in Heaven as the fruit of genuine faith in Christ. We are defiled, but the risen Christ says, "I paid for that in full." As this is the fruit of the working of God's Spirit, God receives all the honor. So at the end of the day all glory, laud, honor, blessing, and praise go to God and to God alone.

# 61

# Christ Victorious

HAGGAI 2:20-23

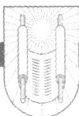

THERE IS AN EXPRESSION that supposedly originated in the U.S. Army: "Hurry up and wait." This is, of course, a somewhat humorous expression that I hear captures life in the military—the experience of needing to hurry and hustle to an assignment only to find oneself waiting for someone else to act or give an order. This expression also captures something of Israel's experience in the postexilic period because this was a moment in which Israel needed to hurry up: Israel was called to work diligently with renewed energy on rebuilding the temple of the Lord. Under the leadership of Zerubbabel, the governor and Joshua the high priest, the people of God were working faithfully and tirelessly to complete this temple project. Why? We're given the answer in Haggai's final oracle. Israel had to work tirelessly to complete the temple so they could wait!

This abrupt transition from diligent working to faithful waiting is evident in the transition from imperatives that dominated the first three oracles to indicatives that pervade the final oracle.[1] Commands to "go up . . . bring wood, and build" (Haggai 1:8), to "be strong" (2:4), and to "consider" (1:7; 2:15) give way to promises: "I am about to shake . . . and to overthrow . . . and to destroy" (vv. 21, 22); "I will take you, O Zerubbabel . . . and make you like a signet ring, for I have chosen you" (v. 23). The culmination of Israel's temple-building would not be the glorious future that God had promised them. The kingdom of God did not appear in glory when the last stone was set in place. Rather, when the temple was complete, Darius would still be the emperor of Persia, Israel would still be a small, insignificant vassal state in the vast

589

Persian Empire, and the people of God would still lack a Davidic king on the throne. Israel would have to wait.

But in their waiting, Israel was reminded that their glorious future would not come as a result of their temple-building; it would come, rather, as a result of God working and acting in the world.[2] So Israel would have to wait. However, Israel's waiting was not a pointless waiting. They were not waiting for Godot, the nonexistent character in Samuel Beckett's famous play, whose imminent arrival preoccupies the characters on stage but who never actually arrives.[3] Israel's waiting was an intentional waiting for a God and for a Messiah who would and who did one day come in the flesh. Israel's was therefore a purposeful, meaningful waiting. We could even say it was a sanctifying waiting, as God had much to teach Israel as they waited on the Lord for deliverance.

In Haggai's final prophecy, we hear God instructing his people on precisely how they are to wait, how they can be faithful as they await the fulfillment of God's great promises of a brighter future. Israel is to wait hoping for God's future deliverance. They are to wait remembering God's faithfulness in the past. They are to wait serving God faithfully in the present. Though today we live in a markedly different covenantal context, Haggai's message speaks to us as well, as we too are called to live faithfully in our present circumstances. The call for us is to do so like Israel—hoping, remembering, and serving.

### Hope for God's Deliverance in the Future (2:20–21)

As with the previous oracles, the prophet's final oracle is introduced with a date formula that provides the exact date Haggai delivered his message: "The word of the LORD came a second time to Haggai on the twenty-fourth day of the month" (2:20). When compared with 2:10, we see that this is the second message that the prophet received and announced on the twenty-fourth day of the ninth month. Like the other oracles whose dates are significant in that they connect the message to Israel's feasts, so the final two oracles in Haggai come on an important occasion—this time not connected with Israel's sacred feasts but with the official laying of the second temple's foundation. The immediately preceding oracle makes it clear that as Zerubbabel, the governor of Judah, was overseeing the ceremonial laying of the foundation of the temple, the word of God's blessing came to God's people. Once again, God would abide with his people, and once again God's people would have access into his gracious presence through the priesthood and through the sacrifices. Israel had a path back to God through the ministry of the temple.

Unsurprisingly, the hearts and minds of God's people turned to the question of the kingship and kingdom, much like Jesus's disciples, who, after witnessing the resurrection, asked, "Lord, will you at this time restore the kingdom to Israel?" (Acts 1:6). Perhaps they had in mind the Davidic covenant, wherein God connected the building of his own house (the temple) to the building of David's house, that is, his eternal dynasty (2 Samuel 7:4–17). The people were no doubt wondering, "Is now the time? Is Zerubbabel the king who will establish God's kingdom?"

God's answer is, in effect, a reiteration of Psalm 2: God will establish his kingdom, and he will do so through his Messiah. In answer to the question, "When?" God answers, in effect, "Soon." When God says in Haggai 2:21, "I am about to . . . ," he uses an expression that communicates the immanence of his kingdom.[4] It is an expression designed to keep God's people looking forward with hope, longing, and expectation.

To help his people persevere in hope, God describes something of this future advent of his kingdom.[5] When God's kingdom arrives, it will come with unimaginable power and glory. God says to Zerubbabel, "I am about to shake the heavens and the earth, and to overthrow the throne of kingdoms. I am about to destroy the strength of the kingdoms of the nations, and overthrow the chariots and their riders" (v. 21). This is an announcement of a comprehensive cosmic judgment. It is an announcement that those kings and kingdoms, those rulers and principalities that oppose God and his rule will one day soon be decisively overthrown. God is saying, in effect, "I am about to turn the world as you know it upside down." When Israel's God arrives as King and Judge of the world, those things that seem to us to be the most stable and most certain—things like the earth below and the heavens above—will be shaken to their very core and will collapse before his matchless power.

As we saw in Haggai's second oracle (1:15b—2:9), this announcement of universal, cataclysmic undoing of the natural order sounds terrifying. This is the stuff of nightmares and tragedy. Yet the cosmic shaking that God promises is not a shaking that will turn the order of this world into chaos, destruction, and death. This is a shaking of a chaotic world, a world that is already broken. This is the shaking of a world characterized by violence and injustice, a world in which lies are regarded as truth, and the truth is regarded as a lie.

God's covenant people in Haggai's day were acutely aware that things were not how they should be. It was not a world in which Yahweh and his anointed king ruled to the very ends of the earth, but a world in which the Persian king ruled what seemed to be the very ends of the earth. It was Darius to whom the world bowed as lord. This was the world that God promised to shake, a shaking that would result not in disorder but in order, not in chaos but in the kingdom of God.

This message should come to us as an encouragement. If we listen to the news media, it seems like our world is falling apart through pandemics, economic collapse, wars, and famines. The ominous lines of the poet come often to mind:

> Things fall apart; the centre cannot hold,
> mere anarchy is loosed upon the world,
> the blood-dimmed tide is loosed,
> and everywhere the ceremony of innocence is drowned;
> the best lack all conviction,
> while the worst are full of passionate intensity.[6]

As we look at our world, we see it unraveling and falling apart. The message of Haggai for us is a message of hope.[7] It is a call to look to the future and to know for certain that how things are today is not how things always will be. God's kingdom is coming soon, and when it does, this broken world will be set right.

God's promise through Haggai comes also as a challenge. As we hear about an imminent shaking of this world, we are prompted to ask ourselves, *Have I become comfortable and complacent in a sin-cursed world?* The truth is that, more often than we care to admit, our hearts secretly resonate with the lyrics of the country song: "Everybody wants to go to heaven, but nobody wants to go now."[8] Do this world and the things of this world have their hooks in our hearts such that we don't long for the kingdom of God to come? For many of us, our lives can become so comfortable that we cease to look forward, longing for that better city "whose designer and builder is God" (Hebrews 11:10).

Haggai's language of cosmic cataclysm is the language of theophany. This is what happens when God appears, particularly when God appears as the divine warrior who will fight with and for his people against all that opposes and oppresses them. These are familiar images used throughout the prophets. In Habakkuk 3, for example, the prophet vividly describes the appearance of the divine warrior:

> You stripped the sheath from your bow,
>    calling for many arrows.
> You split the earth with rivers.
> The mountains saw you and writhed;
>    the raging waters swept on;

> the deep gave forth its voice;
>   it lifted its hands on high.
> The sun and moon stood still in their place
>   at the light of your arrows as they sped,
>   at the flash of your glittering spear.
> You marched through the earth in fury;
>   you threshed the nations in anger.
> You went out for the salvation of your people,
>   for the salvation of your anointed. (Habakkuk 3:9–13a)

By echoing the promises declared by the preexilic prophets, God was saying, "My purpose for my people, my purpose to bless and not to curse, has not changed on account of Israel's sin." God's promises had not changed on account of the exile. They had not changed on account of the loss of political autonomy and the Davidic kingship. They had not changed because God's purposes are at heart gracious, dependent upon the God who promises and the God who acts in history with power and sovereignty.

In this we see that human sin and failure cannot disrupt or derail God's settled purpose to redeem his people, to care for them, to lead them, and to usher them into a new creation absent of sorrow, sickness, death, disease, loss, and heartbreak, and full of the abundance and life for which we were created. This day of the Lord and the great transformation it entails is yet to come. The Scriptures are clear: the day of the Lord will be a day of judgment for all who stand opposed to Christ and his kingship. Yet it will also be a day of deliverance for those who through faith in Christ have been reconciled to God and numbered among the citizens of Heaven.

Haggai calls God's people to be (or become) uncomfortable with the status quo and thus to look forward with hope and expectation, with longing and desire, for a day in which the will of God will be done perfectly on earth as it is in Heaven.

### Remember God's Faithfulness in the Past (2:21–22)

Many scholars have noted that God's word to Zerubbabel through Haggai is replete with traditional images and conventional phraseology. For example, God says in 2:21, 22, "I am about . . . to overthrow the throne of kingdoms," and many have pointed out that this is the same word God used to describe his judgment against Sodom and Gomorrah in Genesis 19:25 ("[God] overthrew those cities, and all the valley, and all the inhabitants of the cities, and what grew on the ground" (cf. Amos 4:11). Similarly, when God says, "I am about to *destroy* the strength of kingdoms" (Haggai 2:22), the word *destroy* would have reminded Israel of God rooting out the Canaanites from the promised land. Moses said in Deuteronomy 7:23, "The Lord your God will give them over to you and throw them into great confusion, until they are *destroyed*."

The mention in Haggai 2:22 that "their riders shall go down, every one by the sword of his brother" is a reference to God's promise to fight Israel's battles for them. One of the signs that Israel's victories belonged to the Lord is that their enemies were thrown into panic, chaos, and confusion.[9] Their fighting was futile and only resulted in destroying themselves as, for example, in Gideon's victory against the Midianites: "When they blew the 300 trumpets, the Lord set every man's sword against his comrade and against all the army" (Judges 7:22).[10] But perhaps the clearest and most familiar allusion is the image of "chariots and their riders. And the horses and their riders shall go down" (Haggai 2:22). Here Haggai is drawing on what would have been for Israel an old-covenant version of the Apostles' Creed, a confession that has become known as the Song of the Sea (Exodus 15). The Song of the Sea was sung by Israel on the far side of the Red Sea after witnessing the Lord's triumph over the greatest war machine in the known world, the Egyptian army. In Exodus 15, Israel sang, "I will sing to the Lord, for he has triumphed gloriously; the horse and his rider he has thrown into the sea. . . . Pharaoh's chariots and his host he cast into the sea, and his chosen officers were sunk in the Red Sea" (vv. 1, 4).

As Haggai reuses these evocative words and expressions, there's not much here that we'd say is either creative or new. The prophet offers a sort of amalgamation or pastiche of a variety of familiar Old Testament depictions of God's victory over Israel's enemies. However, the rhetorical effect of Haggai depicting God's future salvation in terms reminiscent of his past deliverance of his people is that Haggai is in essence calling on Israel to remember. "Remember," he is saying, "God's great acts of judgment and salvation in ages past. Remember God's arrival to fight for his people and to deliver his people and to provide for his people in the past, and let those objective historical events encourage you in the present. Let them be an encouragement to believe that God's promises are sure and that he will indeed one day come and deliver his people again."

This is something that all Christians are to do, but especially those who are discouraged, weary, or given over to doubt and despair. To these, God says, "Remember." Israel could look back to countless ways in which Yahweh, their God, preserved and delivered his people from what would have been certain destruction. Christians today, however, have something far better. We look back not just to the Red Sea and the conquest but to God's ultimate judgment and deliverance: the dying and rising Messiah. We have Calvary and the cross, we have the empty tomb, and we have the promise that "this Jesus, who was taken up from you into heaven, will come in the same way as you saw him go into heaven" (Acts 1:11). The opening words of Psalm 124 may be sung with utter sincerity by believers of every age:

> If it had not been the LORD who was on our side—
> let Israel now say—
> if it had not been the LORD who was on our side
>    when people rose up against us,
> then they would have swallowed us alive. (vv. 1–3a)

The sad truth, however, is that Israel's history was a history of forgetting. Too often Israel forgot their God and his promises. They forgot their identity as a holy people and their calling as a kingdom of priests.

It is tempting for us to judge them for what seems an intractable forgetfulness. But how often do we too forget God's love? How often do we too forget God's care and provision for us? How often do we forget the great price God paid for our sins? Is not a little bit of forgetfulness mixed in with each of our sins as we forget the goodness of God's Law and the truth of his Word and the freedom that is ours in Christ? We too are prone to forget. Haggai calls us still today also to remember who God is and what he has done for us in Christ.

### Serve Faithfully in the Present (2:23)

As Haggai delivers this oracle to Zerubbabel in a public setting, the rest of the postexilic community is invited to listen in and to receive instruction from what God is saying to their governor. What God's people are meant to hear in God's commendation of Zerubbabel is that, to use the language of another postexilic prophet, we must not "[despise] the day of small things" (Zechariah 4:10).

Zerubbabel's day was, in the world's eyes, a day of small things. Though descended from a king, their governor was not a king but only a minor government official serving the interests of a pagan overlord. Zerubbabel's status was highlighted in God's command to his prophet to "speak to Zerubbabel, governor of Judah" (Haggai 2:21). Furthermore, Judah was no longer an autonomous state whose palace and king commanded honor or even respect among the nations. Judah, rather, was a backwater province of the great Persian Empire. Israel's temple would have been just one of countless temples commissioned by the empire, an attempt to endear and indebt a conquered people to Persia's lordship. We can imagine the Jews in Haggai's day, and we can perhaps imagine Zerubbabel along with them, wondering, "Does anything we're doing matter? Does anything we do here at this time and place matter in the grand scheme of things?" Especially as they looked back on the former glory of Israel, it is not surprising that the people and their governor would wonder, "Does a rebuilt temple to Yahweh matter?"

But Zerubbabel, uncharacteristically for Israel's leaders, listened to and obeyed the word of God spoken through his prophet. Zerubbabel led Israel in rebuilding the temple so that God's people could once again assemble in the presence of the Lord to render worship acceptable to him. This would have been a small matter in the world's eyes, but in God's eyes it was of immense consequence. God delighted in Zerubbabel's zeal for his house. Therefore, when God said to Zerubbabel, "On that day . . . I will take you, O Zerubbabel my servant, the son of Shealtiel, declares the LORD, and make you like a signet ring, for I have chosen you, declares the LORD of hosts" (v. 23), he was saying at the very least, "Well done, good and faithful servant. You have been faithful over a little; I will set you over much" (Matthew 25:23).

God is honored by our faithfulness and obedience in our callings, whether they are outwardly glorious or, as is often the case, mundane and ordinary. One commentator put it like this: God's "future intervention casts its shadow forward into the present."[11] The certainty that God will one day come in judgment and mercy imbues our current actions with significance as we set our hands to our God-given tasks and callings. That great day of God's appearance will also be a day in which our work, even that which seems insignificant or trivial in the world's eyes, will be vindicated as God-honoring and Christ-glorifying. Some labors, perhaps the most trivial in the world's eyes, will be revealed to be of utmost eternal value.

Undoubtedly, we see in Zerubbabel a model for personal obedience and thus a call to faithfulness. But we see more than that. We also see in him a prefigurement or type of Christ to come.[12] As Haggai draws his oracle to a close with this final word to Zerubbabel, he shifts his focus from Zerubbabel, governor of Judah (2:21), to Zerubbabel "the son of Shealtiel" (v. 23), a designation that brings into view his royal lineage.[13] Shealtiel was a son of King Jehoiachin, a connection that highlights Zerubbabel's descent from King David. Also in verse 23, Zerubbabel is called "my servant," a designation used notably for King David.[14] Perhaps most strikingly, in verse 23 God reverses the curse that he leveled against Zerubbabel's great-grandfather Jehoiachin through the prophet Jeremiah.

In Jeremiah 22, God declared, "As I live . . . though Coniah the son of Jehoiakim, king of Judah, were the signet ring on my right hand, yet I would tear you off and give you into the hand of those who seek your life, into the hand of those of whom you are afraid, even into the hand of Nebuchadnezzar king of Babylon" (vv. 24, 25). But now, almost a hundred years later, God was declaring to Zerubbabel, "On that day . . . I will . . . make you like a signet ring" (Haggai 2:23).[15]

In the ancient world, a signet ring was a precious item—it represented the king's authority and, as such, was jealously protected by its owner either by being worn on the hand or on a chain around the neck.[16] Contrary to some suggestions, God was not promising to make Zerubbabel a king to stand in opposition to the Persian emperor and to mount a revolt against the empire.[17] Rather, God was promising to reward Zerubbabel's obedience in temple-building by reversing the curse he had declared against Jehoiachin and renewing his unchangeable promise to establish his king on David's throne in Zion. Zerubbabel would not hold royal office, but he pointed to the One who would.[18]

In Haggai's day, God's people could look to Zerubbabel and see in him a glimmer of the One who was to come, one who would obey God and, through his obedience, establish the source of God's blessing for his people. It would not be Zerubbabel, the descendant of King David, who would accomplish this; it would be great David's greater Son, who would come as a descendant of Zerubbabel (cf. Matthew 1:12; Luke 3:27).

Jesus, like Zerubbabel, was not regarded as significant by any nation or empire of this world. Jesus would also come in humility and meekness, preferring to be faithful to his Father in Heaven rather than to receive the honors and recognition of this world. Zerubbabel rebuilt the temple awaiting the day when the true temple would appear in Christ. Zerubbabel exhibited a zeal for the Lord's house, prefiguring the day when the Son of God would come and fulfill the prophecy, "Zeal for [the Lord's] house will consume me" (John 2:17; cf. Psalm 69:9). Like Zerubbabel, Jesus would render to his Father obedience; specifically, obedience in building God's temple, which, as he told his disciples, referred ultimately to his own body rebuilt in resurrection life (John 2:21) and to the Body of Christ, the "living stones" who are his people (1 Peter 2:4, 5).

However, on the cross, Jesus more closely resembled Jehoiachin than Zerubbabel. The precious signet ring was cast aside, humiliated, rejected, and accursed as he paid the price for the sins of his people. The King of glory, power, and splendor was reduced to the ultimate humiliation of suffering and death. But it was in his suffering, death, and resurrection on the third day that God began his shaking of the heavens and the earth. God accomplished his victory over those thrones and kingdoms and powers that have set themselves in opposition and hostility to his rule. As Paul wrote to the Colossians, at the cross God "disarmed the rulers and authorities and put them to open shame, by triumphing over them in him" (Colossians 2:15).

God has begun his shaking, but he has not completed it. Like the Jews in Haggai's day, we look forward to the last and final shaking that will accompany Christ's return. The author of Hebrews reminds us that this great and awesome day is yet to come, and this future reality casts a shadow on our present lives:

> If they did not escape when they refused him who warned them on earth, much less will we escape if we reject him who warns from heaven. At that time his voice shook the earth, but now he has promised, "Yet once more I will shake not only the earth but also the heavens." This phrase, "Yet once more," indicates the removal of things that are shaken—that is, things that have been made—in order that the things that cannot be shaken may remain. Therefore let us be grateful for receiving a kingdom that cannot be shaken, and thus let us offer to God acceptable worship, with reverence and awe, for our God is a consuming fire. (Hebrews 12:25–29)

As Israel waited for that day, they had to live by faith—faith in the promises of God and in the tokens of those promises meant to sustain them in their faith. The same is true for us. Living as those who look to the past and look to the future, we too are called to faithfulness, not despising the day of small things but waiting in faithful obedience to the One who lived for us and died for us as we look forward to the great day when we will behold our Savior face to face. Iain Duguid captures this calling well when he writes:

> In the meantime, though, as we wait for the final shaking of the heavens and earth, our calling is to be faithful. Like Zerubbabel, we are to be faithful in the little things, the daily grind of chores and studies, of work and witnessing, of laboring for God and for our daily bread. Sometimes our task may seem to us like that given to Sisyphus in Greek mythology, who daily rolled a stone up the hill, only for it to be returned to the bottom every night. Christian ministry, in particular, often looks like the ministry of stone-rolling. But none of our labors will be wasted in the purposes of God. So we trudge on, hoping that we too may simply hear the words of our God: "Well done, good and faithful servant! You have been faithful over a little; I will set you over much."[19]

# ZECHARIAH

*By Stephen M. Coleman*

# 62

# Breaking with the Past

ZECHARIAH 1:1-6

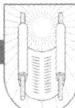

"WHAT'S IN A NAME? That which we call a rose by any other name would smell as sweet."[1] With these words, Shakespeare's Juliet famously pontificates about the arbitrariness and insignificance of names, especially when the name—in this case, Romeo's—disrupts her love life. However, the Biblical authors could not disagree more. Names in the Bible are far from arbitrary and are often of such significance that Biblical characters would not smell nearly as sweet (to use Shakespeare's phrase) should they be called by another name. Names can, for example, serve as a window into a person's character. Here we might think of Abigail's husband, Nabal, whose name in Hebrew means "foolish," a characteristic he exhibited in spades in his interactions with David (1 Samuel 25:25).[2] Or we could think of the patriarch Jacob, whose name means literally "heel grabber" and can suggest someone who is conniving or underhanded, characteristics that certainly describe Jacob's dealings with so many in his life (Genesis 25:26).[3]

At other times, however, a name may serve a prophetic role as it adumbrates a person's significance in redemptive history. Eve, we're told, was so named because she through faith would become the mother of the living (3:20), and Abram's name was changed to Abraham as he would become "the father of a multitude of nations" (17:5). Yet at other times, Biblical names function less as descriptions or prophecies and more as sermons. The name Joshua, for example, means "Yahweh saves," and Josiah means "Yahweh supports" or "Yahweh heals"—both profoundly important messages for God's people in their days.[4] It is this last function that we see at work in the name of the eponymous prophet of the book of Zechariah. Zechariah's name means "the Lord remembers."[5]

This message "Yahweh remembers" could not have been more timely for Israel at this particular moment in history. Zechariah was ministering at a time in which God's people would very much have felt like they were forgotten. Gone were the glory days of kingdom and kingship. Gone were the glory days of palace and temple. Postexilic Israel existed as a small, poor, backwater province of the mighty pagan Persian Empire. We're told in the opening verse that Zechariah delivered his message "in the eighth month, in the second year of Darius" (1:1), which places this prophecy somewhere in October or November in the year 520 B.C. Instead of dating the year of the prophecy to one of Israel's kings, as was the custom throughout Israel's recording of their history, the author dates Zechariah's prophecy to the second year of Darius, the Persian king, a pagan emperor. This is, as one author puts it, "a painful moment in the book: every dating formula in Zechariah is a reminder of the fact that there is no king in Jerusalem."[6]

Israel had been back in the land almost eighteen years. The temple rebuilding project had ground to a halt, the community was plagued with opposition from without and compromise from within, and the vast majority of the people had been left struggling simply to survive. No doubt many were wondering, "What about all those wonderful promises and prophecies of Israel's glorious restoration?" Speaking of Israel's release from exile, the great prophet Isaiah had declared:

> You shall go out in joy
>   and be led forth in peace;
> the mountains and the hills before you
>   shall break forth into singing,
>   and all the trees of the field shall clap their hands.
> Instead of the thorn shall come up the cypress;
>   instead of the brier shall come up the myrtle;
> and it shall make a name for the Lord,
>   an everlasting sign that shall not be cut off. (Isaiah 55:12, 13)

Needless to say, postexilic Israel's experience was a far cry from rejoicing mountains and clapping trees.[7] There was in fact very little that the postexilic community could point to and say, "See, look at this! Here is proof that we are the treasured possession of the God of the universe!" By all appearances, the postexilic community was forgotten.

It is into this context of discouragement and spiritual despondency that God sends his servant Zechariah to remind his people that God has not forgotten them. Just the opposite: God remembers his people, and he remembers the promises he has made to them.[8] This, we might say, is the central purpose of Zechariah's prophecies: to renew God's people with the assurance that, contrary to appearances, God's plans and purposes are sure. The curse of exile has not derailed God's gracious purposes for his people nor disrupted his plan to bless the world through them (Genesis 12:3).

This message is, of course, just as relevant for Christians today as it was for the covenant community in Zechariah's day. Christians too can hear God's wonderful promises, such as when the Apostle Paul says, "If anyone is in Christ, he is a new creation" (2 Corinthians 5:17), and then look at our own lives and think, *Really? Is this the new creation that God promised?* Like postexilic Israel, Christians can often feel forgotten and can wonder if God is in fact at work in their lives. Such feelings of hopelessness and despair are not at all unfamiliar to Christians today. In this way, Zechariah's name preaches to us as well. Regardless of what our circumstances might suggest to us or to anyone else, the Lord could never forget those whom he has called to himself in his Son.

We are not told much about the prophet Zechariah—probably because Zechariah was a common name—though the prophet is further identified as "the son of Berechiah, son of Iddo" (1:1). It seems highly probable that the Iddo mentioned in Zechariah 1:1 is the same Iddo named in Nehemiah 12:16, who was one of the Levitical priests who returned from Babylon along with Zerubbabel.[9] If this is the case, Zechariah would have been a Levitical priest, an identity that explains many of the major themes and interests that recur throughout the prophecy. The temple, the priesthood, issues of defilement, the temple menorah, the relationship between high priest and king, and the propriety of certain fasts and feasts would have all been a preoccupation of the priesthood. While we shouldn't insist upon it (the way we must, for example, with Ezekiel), we're on safe ground to read the prophecies of Zechariah through the lens of the Levitical priesthood. Whether he was a priest or not, Zechariah was certainly a prophet, and the book opens with a familiar prophetic message. In Zechariah 1:1–6, we hear the prophet calling the postexilic community to break with the sins of their forefathers and to renew their commitment to their God through heartfelt repentance and faith.

## A (Surprising) Call (1:2–3)

When we think of the Biblical prophets, most of us probably think of them primarily in terms of their remarkable ability to see and declare future events, sometimes long before they would take place. However, the fact is that Israel's prophets were just as preoccupied with Israel's past as they were with Israel's future. Just as Israel was to live in light of glorious future realities yet to come, Israel was to live in light of their past, having learned from both the successes and (more often) the failures of their forefathers and foremothers.

This is where Zechariah begins—turning Israel's attention to their past: "The LORD was very angry with your fathers" (1:2). The expression "your fathers" could refer to any number of previous generations of Israel that had been unfaithful to God, though in all likelihood the principal generation in view is the generation that experienced God's ultimate covenant curse, which came in the form of the Babylonian exile in 587/86 B.C.[10]

Simply because God's anger had burned against their forefathers, however, does not mean that it must burn against them. This postexilic generation has the opportunity to break with the sinful ways of their forebearers and to live faithfully in covenant fellowship with their God. To this end, God instructs his prophet to declare his word: "Return to me, says the LORD of hosts, and I will return to you, says the LORD of hosts" (1:3).

Zechariah's call to repentance is, on the one hand, completely unsurprising. "Return to the LORD" is at the heart of the prophetic message (cf., e.g., Isaiah 44:22; Joel 2:12; Amos 4:6; Malachi 3:7). The verb "return" is used throughout the Prophets to call God's people to repentance. The act of repentance is being construed as a movement or a turning, an appropriate metaphor that casts repentance as a turning from sin and a turning toward God or a movement from sin and self into the gracious presence of God as offered in his gospel. Thus, in one respect, Zechariah's call to repentance is completely unsurprising, as this is the central burden of the prophetic ministry—to call God's people to repentance and faith.

On the other hand, when we consider his audience, Zechariah's call to repentance is in fact quite surprising because Zechariah is addressing those Israelites who have returned to the promised land. As such, they would regard themselves as those who have already repented, their willingness to return to the land of promise being the chief evidence that they have already returned to the Lord.

Like Naomi whose "return" (same word) to Bethlehem from the fields of Moab was a sign of her repentance (Ruth 1:6), the returnees would have been inclined to think their return to the land was sufficient evidence of their commitment to God and of God's commitment to them.[11] *It is those who stayed in Babylon*, they would have thought, *who need to repent and return to God by returning to his land.* And yet, God's prophet calls this postexilic community, those who had returned physically to God, to return spiritually as well. "Return to me, says the LORD of hosts, and I will return to you" (Zechariah 1:3).

Zechariah was ministering at the same time as the prophet Haggai and was presumably addressing the same sins that Haggai had in view (i.e., idolatry expressed in a disregard for the Lord's house, worship of comfort, and doubting the Lord's provision; cf. Haggai 1:4–6).

God promises, "Return to me says the LORD of hosts, and I will return to you" (Zechariah 1:3). The prophet not only delivers a call to repentance but also announces the motivation for repentance: "I will return to you, says the LORD of hosts." To be sure, the prophet is employing a pun to make his point.[12] The return that God is promising to his people is not the same returning that Israel is called to undertake.

What does God mean when he promises to return to his people? It would be a mistake to interpret God as in any sense repenting or changing in himself—that is, in terms of who he is as God. God's promise to return to his people is predicated precisely because God is an unchanging God, as he said through another postexilic prophet, Malachi: "I the LORD do not change; therefore you, O children of Jacob, are not consumed" (Malachi 3:6). However, as God's people change from unbelief to belief, from faithless to faithful, they find the unchanging God to be no longer a God of wrath and judgment but a God of grace and mercy. The unchanging God's actions or disposition toward them changes from curse to blessing, from wrath to grace.

The reality being described in this metaphor of turning is, of course, that of forgiveness. Here we're given a picture of covenant fellowship, communion between the Creator and his creatures. This promise has at its heart a promise of forgiveness. It is the prospect of forgiveness that draws sinners to God in repentance and faith. Consider the prodigal son of Luke 15, whose hope that his father might forgive him enough to treat him as a hired servant motivates him to rise and go to his father in contrition, only to find his father more gracious and more forgiving than he had ever hoped or imagined (vv. 11–24). So too for Israel. As they are called to wake from their spiritual slumber and turn again to God in repentance, the sure and certain promise is that they will find Yahweh not only willing but quick to return to his people in love, grace, and mercy.

The spiritual reality of God's return to his people had, in Zechariah's day, a concrete expression in the Lord's return to the temple he had earlier abandoned. This return is a major theme in the visions and prophecies of Zechariah. God will one day return to his temple in glory, a manifestation of his power and presence the likes of which had not been seen since the days of

Solomon, when the glory-cloud representing Yahweh's presence descended on the temple. As Israel longs for a glory that seems to be a thing of the past, God promises a greater, more glorious advent that will make Israel's most glorious day of old seem like a day of small things.

## A Call to Faith (1:4–5)

In 1:4, Zechariah issues a warning in the form of a history lesson: "Do not be like your fathers, to whom the former prophets cried out, 'Thus says the LORD of hosts, Return from your evil ways and from your evil deeds.' But they did not hear or pay attention to me, declares the LORD." Sadly, the prophet's description here could summarize just about any point in the history of Israel from Moses to the Babylonian exile. Time and again throughout their history God's people closed their eyes, stopped up their ears, and hardened their hearts to the prophetic word of warning.

To drive home the lesson that the postexilic community must learn from their history, the prophet issues three rhetorical questions: "Your fathers, where are they? And the prophets, do they live forever? But my words and my statutes, which I commanded my servants the prophets, did they not overtake your fathers?" (vv. 5, 6). With these questions God is contrasting the frail, fading, and ephemeral nature of human life with the eternal, unfading, unchanging word of God.[13] God's word is reliable, and his promises, both for good and for ill, are absolutely certain.

"Your fathers, where are they?" (v. 5). They are either dead, killed by the brutal and ruthless Babylonian army, or if they weren't killed, they were likely living out their last years in exile, away from their home and their land, away from the temple of God, and away from their inheritance. Of the prophets, God asks, "Do they live forever?" Some biblical scholars have suggested that these are the false prophets who have misled God's people into the illusion that all is well.[14] But it is more likely a reference to true prophets like Samuel, Elijah, Isaiah, and Jeremiah.[15] God is asking, "Where are they?" The point being made is that even the mediators of God's word—those who have access to the divine counsel and to whom God speaks his word and will—do not live forever.

Neither the best nor the worst in Israel can claim for themselves what God claims for his word: "My words and my statutes, which I commanded my servants the prophets, did they not overtake your fathers?" (v. 6). God's word is what is sure and endures forever. This language of God's word "overtak[ing] your fathers" has military or hunting overtones and is an allusion to the covenant curses promised in Deuteronomy 28:15–68. There Moses said, "If you will not obey the voice of the Lord your God or be careful to do all his commandments and his statutes that I command you today, then all these curses shall come upon you and overtake you" (v. 15).[16] Similarly, in verse 45: "All these curses shall come upon you and pursue you and overtake you till you are destroyed, because you did not obey the voice of the Lord your God, to keep his commandments and his statutes that he commanded you." Many in Israel had not believed the word of God delivered by Moses and announced by the prophets Jeremiah, Zephaniah, and Ezekiel. The result was wave upon wave of covenant curses culminating in the destruction of Jerusalem and the exile of God's people.

Zechariah directs the people of Israel to their history that they might remember the failures of their forefathers and might learn anew where their ultimate trust must lie. In the words of the prophet Isaiah, the postexilic community must learn that "the grass withers, the flower fades, but the word of our God will stand forever" (Isaiah 40:8). In this the prophet is calling this struggling community to trust God's word above all things.

In the midst of many trials and hardships, postexilic Israel was tempted to trust their own assessment of their lives and circumstances. They believed their best days were long gone and their present day was a day of small things in which God was impotent, if not absent. It seemed like their best hope for survival (if not flourishing) was through building their own houses, attending to the immediate needs of their families, and taking care of what they considered to be the necessities of life before they attended to the things of God. But Zechariah reminded Israel, and he reminds us, that what is more sure than even our experiences is God's word of promise. What is more important than attending to our own needs, as important as they are, is the worship of the true and living God.

The call to believe God's word over our own ideas and experiences is in essence a call to faith. God has promised to return in grace and mercy to his repentant people. He assures them that the blessedness they seek can only be found in his gracious presence.

The place where that grace and mercy could be apprehended in the postexilic period was in the temple; in our day, the place where God's grace and mercy may be apprehended is in the Christ who tabernacled among us and who in his earthly ministry declared, "Destroy this temple, and in three days I will raise it up" (John 2:19). Israel's return to the Lord found its chief and most tangible expression in their building of the temple, not because God needed a temple but because the chief expression of both Israel's faith and Israel's obedience was true worship of the living God.

### Portrait of Repentance (1:6)

Most of us are familiar with the expression that something doesn't "make one iota of a difference." This expression comes from the Arian controversy of the fourth century in which the Church's expression of the full divinity of Christ rested on the presence or absence of a single Greek letter, *iota*, distinguishing *homoiousias* from *homoousias*. Zechariah 1:6 presents the first of many exegetical difficulties in the book of Zechariah, and while it would go too far to say that the difficulty "doesn't make one iota of a difference," we can say with confidence that no essential Christian doctrine hangs on the correct answer to the problem we face in this verse.

Nevertheless, we are faced with an important interpretive question regarding the subject of repentance in verse 6. Who is said to repent? Is it Israel's forefathers, who in exile acknowledged God's righteousness in his judgment and pled for mercy (e.g., Daniel 9:1–23)?[17] Or is the passage describing the postexilic community's response to the prophetic word of warning and call to repentance? To put it another way, where should we close the quotation? The English Standard Version closes the quotation at the end of Zechariah 1:6b, which implies that it is Israel's forefathers in exile who acknowledged God's justice in his judgment. However, other translations and commentators end the quote after "fathers" (v. 6a), in which case it is the postexilic community that is being portrayed as repenting. On balance, given what has already been said about Israel's forefathers and the postexilic community's need to break from their ways, it seems more natural to see the repentance as the repentance of the postexilic community.[18] This is the same surprising response witnessed in Haggai's ministry just two months earlier (Haggai 1:12–15).[19]

On either reading, however, what we see in Zechariah 1:6 is a portrait of repentance. Verse 6 does not tell us everything we need to know about repentance. It's not a treatise on repentance. But it does offer us a picture of repentance as we're told, "So they repented and said, 'As the LORD of hosts purposed to deal with us for our ways and deeds, so has he dealt with us'" (v. 6b). The people's repentance is expressed by way of confession. When the postexilic community says this, they are acknowledging God's righteousness and justice in his judgments against them. They are acknowledging not only God's righteousness but their own unrighteousness. Implicit in the postexilic community's repentance is a confession that their experience of God's covenant curses of famine, drought, pests, and opposition is a righteous judgment against a sinful people.

This scene should give us great encouragement. What we see here is in a sense a recapitulation of the wilderness generation. Israel's wilderness years may be understood as a tale of two generations. The first generation was a generation characterized by faithlessness and disobedience. What sets the second generation apart? What is it that in a sense qualifies them for entrance into the land? That they have not been disobedient? That they have never sinned or doubted or grumbled? No. The main difference is that when confronted with their sin, they repented.

So too with King David. The central difference between David and Saul was not that Saul was very sinful and David was less so. A good argument could be made that David's sins were more grievous than Saul's. David through faith in God knew what Saul did not know: that God is not only the God of judgment but also the God of mercy. God promises to forgive any and all who return to him, that is, who look to him in repentance and faith. So too in this text a contrast is being made between the postexilic community and their forefathers. The difference is not sinful and sinless but unrepentant and repentant.

Unlike their forefathers, the postexilic community responded to God's word announced by his servant, the prophet Zechariah, by acknowledging the righteousness of God's judgments and, by implication, the greatness of their own sinfulness. It has been said that repentance involves taking God's side in his case against you. This is what we see Israel doing. They were not denying their sinfulness. They were not objecting to the fairness of the discipline. Rather, they were affirming God's holiness, justice, and righteousness in his punishments and yet fleeing to this holy, righteous, and just God to find in him mercy and forgiveness.

This was what Israel needed to hear again. Samuel Johnson once wrote, "Men more frequently need to be reminded than informed."[20] What the prophet announced was not new news. It was old news that God's people needed to hear again and again: God's word is sure, and his promises will never fail. God had promised Israel a glorious future, and though they couldn't imagine how he could bring this about in their present circumstances, their future glory was as certain as God's word of promise.

In this we are reminded of the power of God's word. As God said through the prophet Isaiah, "My word that goes out from my mouth, it shall not return to me empty, but it shall accomplish that which I purpose, and shall succeed in the thing for which I sent it" (Isaiah 55:11). Similarly, the author of Hebrew said, "The word of God is living and active, sharper than any two-edged sword, piercing to the division of soul and of spirit, of joints and of marrow, and discerning the thoughts and intentions of the heart" (Hebrews 4:12).

The central challenge facing the postexilic community was the rebuilding of the temple. This was going to require not only effort but tremendous faith. Israel would never be in the proper position to complete the temple until they had repented of their selfishness, self-reliance, and faithlessness. The temple, for the postexilic community as for the preexilic, would stand as the physical, tangible sign of God's presence with them. It mediated God's blessings to his people through the ministry of the priests and the offering of sacrifices. However, the temple was only the penultimate expression of God's greater, ultimate turning toward his people that would take place years later when he would take on human flesh and dwell among his people. "The Word became flesh and dwelt among us, and we have seen his glory, glory as of the only Son from the Father, full of grace and truth" (John 1:14). God's turning toward his people in love, grace, and mercy was not an easy or trivial act but one that would come only at a great cost to himself.

God's turning toward Israel in Zechariah's day and God's turning toward us in our day is only possible because, at the cross, God would turn his back on his Son, and Jesus would bear in himself the God-forsakenness that we deserve. Though he had never committed an evil deed in his entire life, never uttered a false or deceptive word, and never harbored an ungodly thought or intention, Jesus was "pierced for our transgressions; he was crushed for our iniquities" (Isaiah 53:5). God's countenance shines upon his people, not because they are perfect but because they are repentant and have been united to Christ by faith and justified by his blood.

The prophet called the covenant community to break with the past and to recommit themselves to God's calling to be a kingdom of priests and a holy nation. In this we find the heartbeat of the Christian gospel. When Martin Luther penned his ninety-five theses that sparked the Protestant Reformation, the very first thesis read as follows: "When our Lord and Master Jesus Christ said 'Repent' (Matthew 4:17), he willed the entire life of believers to be one of repentance."[21]

Turning from sin—that is, turning from self and turning to God in faith and toward our neighbor in love—is not a one-time event. It is the very character of the Christian life. Day after day after day, Christians must heed the call of our Lord and Master to repent in the sure knowledge that God has turned toward us in Christ, and therefore he will never and can never turn away.

# 63

# How Long, O Lord?

ZECHARIAH 1:7-17

THE PAINTINGS OF the surrealist Salvador Dali usher us into a world that is disorientingly bizarre, grotesque, and otherworldly. Dali's world is one in which clocks melt, elephants walk on bony stilts, and giant human faces hover above the earth like balloons. Bizarre, grotesque, and unsettling to say the least—and yet, at the same time, Dali's paintings pulse with that uncomfortable familiarity like that of a strange dream or a haunting nightmare. Dali himself once remarked, "Surrealism is destructive, but it destroys only what it considers to be shackles limiting our vision."[1]

There was a similar goal animating the apocalyptic or protoapocalyptic visions of the prophet Zechariah. To say that Israel's vision had become limited would be a gross understatement. Israel's vision had become profoundly myopic. Life in postexilic Israel was incredibly difficult and painfully mundane. Little of note was happening in and among God's covenant people, and the glorious future that had been prophesied of old had yet to be realized. Daily life was marked by seemingly endless toil that yielded barely enough to survive. Bereft of king and kingdom, the people in that impoverished backwater province of the great Persian Empire regarded themselves as utterly insignificant, irrelevant on the grand stage of history. Their God seemed absent or impotent or both.

It is in this context that the prophet Zechariah receives his famous night visions: fantastic, bizarre, and disorienting dreamlike experiences that, like Dali's paintings, destroy the shackles limiting Israel's vision in Zechariah's day and destroy the shackles limiting our vision of who God is and what he is up to in the world in our day as well. In Zechariah's visions, the familiar and mundane combine seamlessly with the fantastic and otherworldly. Horns appear out of nowhere, an enormous scroll flies overhead, and women with stork wings carry a woman in a basket to Babylon.

This is not reality as we experience it. But this highly symbolic world serves as a powerful reminder that there is more going on in Heaven and earth than we could ever possibly understand. Though unfamiliar, bizarre, fantastic, and symbolic, what the prophet sees is at the same time familiar, meaningful, and significant for the postexilic community. In these visions it is as if the veil separating the spiritual world from the physical has been pulled back so that the prophet (and we along with him) may behold the spiritual realities at work in this world—realities at work in the prophet's day, in our day, and in the days to come.

Some interpreters have made much out of the seeming disconnect between the prophetic formula that opens these visions ("the word of the Lord came to the prophet Zechariah . . . saying . . . ," 1:7) and the fact that the prophet does not hear a word but sees a vision: "I saw in the night, and behold, a man riding on a red horse!" (v. 8).[2] However, in this apparent disconnect between word and vision, we're given the important reminder that the prophet's visions not only contain the word of the Lord but the visions themselves may properly be regarded as a word from the Lord. These visions *are* a revelation of God, the word of God to his prophet, and the revelation is found in both the visions and the word spoken within them.[3]

The opening night vision sets the stage for the subsequent visions in that it serves as God's answer to his people's lingering question and deepest fear: Does God know about the struggles, burdens, and anxieties that we bear day in and day out? And if he knows, does he care? And if he cares, will he do something about it?

These questions plagued the postexilic community every day; however, they were not peculiar to the postexilic community. Christians of every age have at times been haunted, if not crippled, by these questions. The message of Zechariah's opening night vision is therefore just as important for us to hear today. Despite appearances to the contrary, despite our feelings and experiences, God knows his people, he cares for his people, and he will fulfill his gracious promises to his people.

### The Meaning of the Horsemen (1:8–10)

It is interesting that as the prophet relates his night visions, he does so in a way that brings us as his hearers or readers into the bewilderment, surprise, and disorientation that he experienced when he first received these extraordinary visions.⁴ As he, in a sense, awakes in a dream, the first thing that catches the prophet's attention is a "man riding on a red horse" (v. 8). This is not itself a particularly exceptional sight in Zechariah's day, especially when we know that the Hebrew word often translated as "red" does not refer to an unnatural barn red but can refer to a reddish-brown or chestnut color that is a common color for horses.

The prophet's attention then moves from the horseman to his location, and we are told that he is "standing among the myrtle trees in the glen" (v. 8). Though not certain, a good case can be made that the glen here is reminiscent of the garden palace of Parsagadae, the capital of the Persian Empire.⁵ Perhaps more certain, however, is the fact that these myrtle trees are evergreens and would thus have provided a cover of darkness and a note of secrecy and concealment for the horseman.

Then finally the camera pans back, as it were, and Zechariah observes that the man is not alone. Behind him are a number of other horses, chestnut and white and sorrel in color, and all presumably mounted by horsemen. Though for us these carry an air of mystery, the horsemen in the opening night vision would have been immediately recognizable to the prophet's original audience.

In its day, the Persian Empire was the largest empire the world had ever seen, and one of the chief means that the Persian king employed to exercise remarkable control over his vast empire was scouts or spies. These scouts included riders of the imperial postal service, couriers who relayed information to and from the king to the farthest reaches of Persia's expansive empire and no doubt beyond.⁶ The Greek historian Herodotus famously described the Persian courier service in these words:

> There is nothing mortal that is faster than the system the Persians have devised for sending messages. Apparently, they have horses and men posted at intervals along the route, the same number in total as the overall length in days of the journey, with a fresh horse and rider for every day of travel. Whatever the conditions—it may be snowing, raining, blazing hot, or dark—they never fail to complete their assigned journey in the fastest possible time.⁷

The postexilic community would have been familiar with Persia's horsemen. Located at a major artery in the empire, Judah would have seen these horsemen and thus would have been reminded routinely that the Persian emperor had eyes and ears everywhere.⁸

Though their identity is not immediately evident, it is clear to the prophet that these are not Darius's spies. He inquires of the interpreting angel

(Zechariah 1:9), and the angel responds, "I will show you what they are." The angel's "showing" comes in the form of dramatic action: "the man who was standing among the myrtle trees" declares, "These are they whom the LORD has sent to patrol the earth" (v. 10). Like the chariots of fire surrounding the Syrian army that were revealed to the prophet Elisha (2 Kings 6:17), these horsemen are the heavenly corollary to the Persian couriers, reminding Zechariah that Yahweh sees all things and knows all things.[9]

This, of course, would have been a comforting message for the postexilic community, as they would have daily wrestled with significant questions: Does Yahweh see? Does Yahweh know? Is our God aware of the suffering of his people? Does he know the hardships we endure? Here the prophet is reminded that the answer is a resounding and unequivocal yes. God sees, God knows, and most important of all, God cares. Furthermore, God does not accidentally come into this information about the state of this world; the Lord is the One who sent these horsemen to patrol the earth (Zechariah 1:10).

The scene seems to be one of a secretive gathering. The cover of darkness afforded by the myrtle trees suggests that God's awareness of his people's troubles is not always evident.[10] We don't always see that God sees; we're not always aware that God knows. Like Israel, our experience often suggests just the opposite.[11] But here we too are given the critical reminder that often despite appearances, our God does in fact know all things, he cares deeply about his creation, and he cares even more deeply about his people. Every tear that is shed in the dark, every pain that is suffered in quiet, every anxiety and doubt that we bottle up, God knows.

The God who is sovereign over the whole world knows the suffering of his people and, as will soon become clear, he is more zealous to do something about it than we could ever imagine. The horsemen are in a sense themselves a message for God's people, but they also come bearing a message.

### The Message of the Horsemen (1:11)

The horsemen deliver their report to the angel of the Lord, saying, "We have patrolled the earth, and behold, all the earth remains at rest" (v. 11). On the face of it, this report sounds like good news. The world is at rest! There is peace throughout the land!

Isn't this what we all long for? Countless songs, poems, novels, and political and philosophical treatises attest to the fact that an earth at rest or, more familiarly, a world at peace, is the great longing of the human soul, and here the horsemen announce its arrival. The date formula probably offers insight into the historical context of the horsemen's report. We're told that the word of the Lord came to the prophet "on the twenty-fourth day of the eleventh month, which is the month of Shebat, in the second year of Darius" (v. 7), placing these visions on or about February 15, 519 B.C.

Darius's succession to the Persian throne in 522 B.C. was far from smooth. After overthrowing the legitimate heir to the throne, Bardiya, and then mounting a campaign to discredit Bardiya (claiming that he only killed a magus pretending to be Bardiya), Darius was confronted with a series of major revolts throughout the empire. Many historians believe that his hold on the empire was tenuous for the first two years of his reign, and it wasn't until 520 B.C. that the rebellions were largely suppressed and the empire was firmly under the imperial rule of Darius the Great.[12] World peace, yes. But at what cost? And under whose kingship?

It was plain from the angel of the Lord's response, "How long?" (v. 12), that this announcement of world peace was far from good news for God's people. The reason a world at rest was far from good news for the postexilic community was because the world was at rest under the reign and rule of the Persian emperor, Darius. It was not the rest of the kingdom of God expanded to the farthest corners of the globe but the rest of the kingdom of Persia that, by all appearances, had conquered the entire known world. The nations of the earth were not streaming to Yahweh's temple in Zion to pay homage to Israel's God; they were streaming to Parsagadae to pay homage to Darius. This was not the glorious eschatological future that God had promised for his people; it was not the realization of Israel's longings and dreams.[13] For Israel, this report was much closer to a nightmare—what John Calvin called an "accursed happiness"—suggesting as it did that the current state of affairs was as good as it would get.[14]

The great tragedy of the earth at rest was that the earth was at rest in her wickedness. By all appearances, the nations had triumphed, and there was no sign of the messianic king or the messianic kingdom on the horizon. As far as the eye could see, the mighty, pagan Persian Empire ruled over all.[15]

The horsemen's message and the angel's response pose a question for us today. How do we envision world peace? What would a world at rest look like or feel like for us? Have we settled for a pseudo-peace achieved through the efforts of *realpolitik* rather than the realization of the eschatological kingdom of Christ, that future glory of the new heavens and the new earth? The angel's prayer is, on one level, an invitation to join him in longing and praying, *How long, O Lord?* Or, to put it in New Testament terms, "Your kingdom come, your will be done, on earth as it is in heaven" (Matthew 6:10).

## The Angel's Lament (1:12)

The angel of the Lord responds to the horsemen's report by calling to the Lord: "O LORD of hosts, how long will you have no mercy on Jerusalem and the cities of Judah, against which you have been angry these seventy years?" (Zechariah 1:12). This cry echoes the refrain found throughout the psalms of lament. The psalmist of Psalm 13, for example, asks,

> How long, O LORD? Will you forget me forever?
> How long will you hide your face from me?
> How long must I take counsel in my soul
>   and have sorrow in my heart all the day?
> How long shall my enemy be exalted over me? (vv. 1, 2)

"How long?" is the cry of the downcast and downtrodden, of those who, in their helplessness, grief, and pain, look to God for justice and vindication.

The angel's lament, however, becomes all the more powerful and poignant when we consider the identity of the one who prayed it. This figure called "the angel of the LORD" appears throughout the Old Testament, at times fulfilling the ordinary role of an angel as a heavenly messenger or emissary who speaks *for* God, and at other times appearing as one speaking and acting *as* God himself.[16]

It was this angel of the Lord who, for example, found Hagar by a spring of water in the wilderness and comforted her with promises that only God could make, saying, "I will surely multiply your offspring so that they cannot be numbered for multitude" (Genesis 16:10). Hagar's response to the angel's extraordinary promise (and subsequent revelation that she was pregnant) indicates that she realized that she had actually encountered God himself in the form of an angel: "So she called the name of the LORD who spoke to her, 'You are a God of seeing,' for she said, 'Truly here I have seen him who looks after me'" (v. 13).

Similarly, in Exodus 3, we're told that "the angel of the LORD appeared to [Moses] in a flame of fire out of the midst of the bush" (v. 2), and yet, when Moses turned aside to behold this wonder, "*God* called to him out of the bush, 'Moses, Moses'" (v. 4). It was almost certainly this angel of the Lord who appeared to Joshua outside Jericho and before whom Joshua fell on his face and worshiped, saying, "What does my lord say to his servant?" (Joshua 5:14). To which this commander of the Lord's army responded, "Take off your sandals from your feet, for the place where you are standing is holy" (v. 15).

Only God makes ground holy, not mere angels. The fact that this Biblical figure generally designated "the angel of the LORD" is both identified with

God (in his authority, his holiness, his works, etc.) and yet distinguished from God has led many theologians to conclude, I think rightly, that the angel of the Lord is a visible manifestation or revelation of the preincarnate Son of God.[17]

God the Son appears in human form as a heavenly messenger, an angel, in order to reveal something of the work he will one day accomplish on behalf of his people, though this time not through a visible manifestation of God (what theologians call a theophany) but through the bodily incarnation of the Son of God. In Zechariah's vision, the prophet is given a revelation of Christ's intercessory work for his people.[18] In Christ, the Son of God identifies himself with sinful humanity so that through the merit of his blood, he might serve as the only mediator between God and man.

Beginning with his baptism (Mark 1:9–11), we see throughout the Gospels Jesus identifying himself with sinful humanity so that he might represent them before his Father. On the night in which he is betrayed, we see Jesus still praying for his people. He says to his clueless and self-centered disciple Peter, "Satan demanded to have you, that he might sift you like wheat, but I have prayed for you that your faith may not fail" (Luke 22:31, 32).

Between Satan and his people, Jesus stands praying for those who know him. Even on the cross, Jesus was praying for those who put him there, saying, "Father, forgive them, for they know not what they do" (23:34). This is not a work that came to an end with his earthly life and ministry; the resurrected and ascended Christ continues this ministry in Heaven. The author of the letter to the Hebrews says that as a consequence of Jesus's eternal priesthood, "he is able to save to the uttermost those who draw near to God through him, since he always lives to make intercession for them" (7:25).

God not only knows about his people's sufferings, sorrows, and unfulfilled longings for the realization of his kingdom but, in the incarnation, he would enter into the sorrows and miseries of this world. He would identify himself with his sinful people not only in his baptism in the Jordan River (Mark 1:9) but also in his baptism of the cross (10:38). The Spirit of Christ that indwells believers, Paul tells us, "helps us in our weakness. For we do not know what to pray for as we ought, but the Spirit himself intercedes for us with groanings too deep for words" (Romans 8:26). This is a tremendous encouragement to believers. When we are keenly aware of the inadequacies of our prayers we can remember that God the Holy Spirit will take even the weakest of our prayers and make them perfect in God's presence. God hears the groanings of his people who are united to Christ by faith, and he cares more deeply about these groanings than we could ever imagine.

There is a lovely expression used in my denomination's baptismal liturgy in which parents promise prayer *with* and *for* their child.[19] This is precisely what the incarnate Christ does for his people perfectly and perpetually. Jesus prays *with* and *for* his people. Having taken upon himself all the sorrows and miseries of this life, and having borne in himself the penalty we justly deserve, Jesus then prays with us and for us for all eternity.

### The Lord's Gracious Response (1:13–17)

Technically we're not told exactly what the Lord said to the angel; we're only told the character of his words, specifically, that they were "gracious and comforting" (Zechariah 1:13). The implication seems to be that the substance of God's words is what the angel instructs the prophet to declare in verse 14 and following. But before moving quickly to the content of God's words, it is worthwhile to consider the significance of the gracious and comforting character of God's response, because in this we see the Father's response to his Son's intercession for those for whom he will one day die.

What is God's posture toward his people? How does God respond to the prayers of his saints? He responds with "gracious and comforting words." This is in fact a powerful portrait of the Christian gospel: God speaks a gracious and comforting word toward undeserving sinners on account of the mediation of the Son. Apart from the Son we have no standing in God's presence and should expect to receive no hearing. The only word we deserve to hear is the word spoken to the serpent in the garden: "cursed are you . . ." (Genesis 3:14). But wonderfully, through the Son, God has spoken an unexpected and undeserved word, a gospel word, a word of grace for sinners and comfort for those afflicted in this present evil age.

Having overheard the gracious and comforting words the Father speaks to the Son in response to the Son's lament and plea, the prophet is then given his mission. He is instructed to "cry out, Thus says the LORD of hosts: I am exceedingly jealous for Jerusalem and for Zion. And I am exceedingly angry with the nations that are at ease; for while I was angry but a little, they furthered the disaster'" (Zechariah 1:14, 15).

The historian Paul Johnson wrote, "There is no logic or justice in history—only chronology."[20] This is indeed how life often feels, and apart from God's supernatural revelation, this would certainly be true. However, God has disclosed both the logic and the justice of history in his Word. He has not done so exhaustively, nor in such a way as to answer and satisfy our idle curiosities. But really and truly, we find in Scripture a compass that orients us in a disorienting world and reveals God's plans and purposes in what appear to be the chance vicissitudes of history.

In these verses God discloses to his prophet something of what he is doing on the stage of history. Like Israel, whom God had raised up as his sword of judgment against the Canaanites in the days of Joshua, so God raised up nations, particularly (though not exclusively) Assyria and Babylon, as his sword of judgment against Israel. God calls Assyria "the rod of my anger" (Isaiah 10:5) and Nebuchadnezzar "the king of Babylon, my servant" (Jeremiah 27:6), whom he was raising up against Israel for her idolatry (Isaiah 10:11). This is how Israel was to understand their humiliation and their exile—as God's righteous anger against his people for their sin and rebellion.

Unaware of their role in God's drama of redemptive history, unaware of their accountability to a higher, holier, and more just Judge, these nations far exceeded God's intended judgment on his people.[21] God said, "While I was angry but a little, they furthered the disaster" (Zechariah 1:15). In their pride Assyria and Babylon committed unspeakable atrocities against Israel, atrocities for which they were accountable. Though God appointed these nations as his instruments of justice against his people, this did not excuse the cruelty and brutality of their treatment of Israel. In his Pentecost sermon, the Apostle Peter spoke similarly of the crucifixion of Jesus when he said, "This Jesus, delivered up according to the definite plan and foreknowledge of God, you crucified and killed by the hands of lawless men" (Acts 2:23). Though God had foreordained the death of his Son, those who committed the greatest injustice in the history of the world were nevertheless held accountable for their lawless actions.

The divine logic and justice revealed through Zechariah is that the triumph of wicked nations over God's chosen people is not the final act of the drama. The injustices that Israel experiences at the hands of lawless men will not be left unresolved or unaccounted for. There is a visitation yet to come, and when that day of visitation comes, all will be made right. The prophet declares, "Therefore, thus says the LORD, I have returned to Jerusalem with mercy; my house shall be built in it, declares the LORD of hosts, and the measuring line shall be stretched out over Jerusalem" (Zechariah 1:16).

What God has torn down in judgment, he will rebuild in mercy. What God has broken, he will heal. What he has abandoned in judgment, he will again visit with his grace. Grace will indeed have the last word in Israel's story. God will do this not because Israel deserves to be rebuilt and glorified but because of his unwavering love set upon this undeserving people from before the foundation of the world.

Zechariah declares that Israel's glory is not just a thing of the past, a dim memory never to be seen or experienced again. Rather, God promises that his house will be rebuilt, and the holy city will be rebuilt, and this city that at the moment was impoverished and in ruins will "again overflow with prosperity" (v. 17). God through his prophet cries out to his people the good news that the future glory of Jerusalem will indeed be greater than her past.

This is a promise that would be quite literally unbelievable if it weren't spoken by the Lord of Heaven and earth. It is a promise of a new Jerusalem in which the Lord himself will again reside.

This unbelievable prophecy would be fulfilled in part when the temple was rebuilt in Zechariah's day, in 516 B.C., and when Jerusalem was rebuilt in the days of Nehemiah in the mid-fifth century.[22] Yet God's return to his temple would come much later. The New Testament authors teach that this was fulfilled in the Son of God, who came to and for his people. In Christ, God would again dwell in the midst of his people. Though many did not recognize him, those who had eyes to see beheld his advent with awe and wonder. The Gospel writer Luke records that when Mary and Joseph brought the baby Jesus into the temple to be consecrated to the Lord, they met a man named Simeon who was "waiting for the consolation of Israel" (Luke 2:25). When Simeon beheld the Christ child,

> he took him up in his arms and blessed God and said,
>
> > "Lord, now you are letting your servant depart in peace,
> > according to your word;
> > for my eyes have seen your salvation
> > that you have prepared in the presence of all peoples,
> > a light for revelation to the Gentiles,
> > and for glory to your people Israel." (vv. 28–32)

The glory of God had returned to his temple in the person of the infant Jesus.

However, Zechariah's prophecy is fulfilled not only in Christ's earthly ministry but also in his heavenly ministry. The risen and ascended Christ is at work even today, by his word and Spirit, building a spiritual city and living temple of which he is the chief cornerstone. The Apostle Peter writes, "As you come to him, a living stone rejected by men but in the sight of God chosen and precious, you yourselves like living stones are being built up as a spiritual house, to be a holy priesthood, to offer spiritual sacrifices acceptable to God through Jesus Christ" (1 Peter 2:4). Zechariah's prophecy is being fulfilled in the gift of the Holy Spirit whom Christ has sent to indwell his people (1 Corinthians 6:19). It is fulfilled in the ingathering of the nations, a multitude of people from every tongue and tribe and nation that cannot be numbered (Revelation 7:9–12). It is fulfilled in the prosperity of Christ's people as through him they share in "every spiritual blessing in the heavenly places" (Ephesians 1:3).

Though God's promises have been fulfilled in part at the advent of his Son and in his Church that is united to him by faith, the final fulfillment of this prophecy has yet to be realized in its full and consummate glory. In Revelation 21, John received a vision of a new creation, new heavens, and a new earth in which the former things had passed away and all things had been made new (v. 1). John says, "I saw the holy city, new Jerusalem, coming down out of heaven from God . . . having the glory of God, its radiance like a most rare jewel, like a jasper, clear as crystal" (vv. 2, 11). John saw that there is a glory yet to be revealed: a beauty, blessedness, and prosperity for God's people that will be absolute, permanent, and perfect, beyond our ability to even describe in ordinary language. The best we can do is resort to analogies and symbols.

Just as the prophet's words were designed to keep Israel looking forward in hopeful, confident anticipation of this glory yet to come, so they have the same design for us today. Though we've beheld the glory of Christ, the true temple, we are nevertheless, like Abraham before us, "looking forward to the city that has foundations, whose designer and builder is God" (Hebrews 11:10). Elizabeth Achtemeier captures well the Christian's hope when she writes, "The time is coming for the covenant people when all the earth will be quiet; but that tranquility will be the fruit not of the conqueror's oppressive hand but of 'the peace of God which passes all understanding'" (Phil. 4:7).[23]

# 64

# Glorious Things of Thee Are Spoken

ZECHARIAH 1:18—2:13

> Glorious things of thee are spoken,
> Zion city of our God.
> He whose word cannot be broken
> formed thee for his own abode.
> On the Rock of Ages founded,
> what can shake your sure repose?
> With salvation's walls surrounded,
> thou may'st smile at all thy foes.[1]

The opening stanza of John Newton's famous hymn captures well Israel's view of Mount Zion throughout much of Old Testament history. The hymn is a soaring portrait of Mount Zion that Newton painted using various lines and images derived largely from Israel's psalms, the most obvious of which is Psalm 87, which opens with these words:

> On the holy mount stands the city he founded;
>   the LORD loves the gates of Zion
>   more than all the dwelling places of Jacob.
> Glorious things of you are spoken,
>   O city of God. (vv. 1–3)

This celebration of Mount Zion and this delight in God's holy city, Jerusalem, persists throughout much of the Hebrew psalter. Psalm 46, for example, says, "There is a river whose streams make glad the city of God, the holy habitation of the Most High. God is in the midst of her; she shall not be moved; God will help her when morning dawns" (vv. 4, 5). Psalm 125 says,

> Those who trust in the LORD are like Mount Zion,
> which cannot be moved, but abides forever.
> As the mountains surround Jerusalem,
>   so the LORD surrounds his people,
>   from this time forth and forevermore. (vv. 1, 2)

The list could go on.

Mount Zion was the place of God's holy city, Jerusalem, and Jerusalem was the place of God's holy temple. God established these as the place of his habitation, the means by which he would dwell in the midst of a people called by his name. Mount Zion, Jerusalem, and the temple were founded in a sense on God's promises and therefore, like God himself, were unshakable. They were Israel's glory, a symbol of the greatness of her God and the security that he provides for his people. The walls of Jerusalem were like the arms of God, protecting his people, keeping them safe and secure from all their foes.

There were times, however, in which the glorious portrait of God's glorious city was far from evident to anyone, especially to Israel herself. There were times when these psalms sounded much more like the wishful thinking of an idealist or sentimentalist (at best) or the rantings of a madman (at worst) rather than the praises of the faithful. In 586 B.C., Jerusalem was sacked, the temple razed to the ground, and her treasures carted away to Babylon as spoil, some never to be seen again. In Zechariah's day, the once beautiful city lay in ruins. The glories of Mount Zion and the security of God's holy city seemed like a thing of the past, never to be repeated.

But what did this state of affairs imply about Israel's God? Had his promises, so richly and wonderfully symbolized by Mount Zion—the promises of security and provision and abundance, the promises of peace and life everlasting—come to an end as the result of Israel's faithlessness and the curse of the exile? These questions weighed heavily on the hearts of the postexilic community who had returned to the ruins of Jerusalem, and it was these questions that received their answer in Zechariah's second and third night visions. The somewhat bizarre and disorienting drama of these visions revealed a glorious future for God's city and a glorious future for those whose citizenship was in it. The primary purpose of these visions, however, was not simply to relay information about the future but rather to encourage God's people in the present to press on in faith, hope, and obedience in the tasks that lay before them in the sure knowledge that God had not and would never abandon his people or forsake his promises. All that Zion represented for God's people would most certainly come to pass, and Zion's future glory would far surpass that of even her most glorious days of old.

## Jerusalem's Glorious Future (1:18–2:5)

### Enemies Overthrown (1:18–21)

Zechariah's second night vision begins somewhat abruptly with the prophet beholding four horns (1:18). Like most things in the night visions, these four horns have been the subject of a great deal of speculation, discussion, and disagreement. What are these four horns that the prophet sees? Suggestions range from the horns of animals, the four corners of a (pagan) altar, and animal horns decorating a warrior's helmet.[2] Whatever they were, whatever they were made of (bone, metal, wood, stone), and whatever they were attached to (if they were attached to anything at all), they were clearly and immediately recognizable as horns so that when the prophet inquires of the interpreting angel, "What are these?" (v. 19), the angel does not disclose their identity (the prophet already knows that they are horns) but rather discloses their symbolism and their significance. "These are the horns," he answers, "that have scattered Judah, Israel, and Jerusalem" (v. 19).

Often in the Bible a raised horn is used as a symbol of power, strength, and victory (especially military victory). In her song of thanksgiving, for example, Hannah sang, "The LORD will judge the ends of the earth; he will give strength to his king and exalt the horn of his anointed" (1 Samuel 2:10). So too the psalmist praised God, saying, "You are the glory of their strength; by your favor our horn is exalted" (Psalm 89:17). When used of the wicked and the oppressive, however, a raised horn is associated with arrogance and tyranny. In Psalm 75, for example, we read, "I say to the boastful, 'Do not boast,' and to the wicked, 'Do not lift up your horn; do not lift up your horn on high, or speak with haughty neck'" (vv. 4, 5; cf. Daniel 7:7, 8). The horns in Zechariah's vision were clearly used in this second sense. These horns represented those menacing nations who scattered Judah, Israel, and Jerusalem.

As was seen in the first vision, these nations were used by God as his sword of divine judgment, but they acted with arrogance, pride, and excessive cruelty. Thus God had declared, "While I was angry but a little, they furthered the disaster" (Zechariah 1:15). "These are the horns that scattered Judah" in a decisive and humiliating victory, as the angel says, "so that no one raised his head" (v. 21). Archaeologists have discovered numerous reliefs from the ancient world depicting a victorious king with his foot on the neck of his conquered foe. It was a posture designed to glorify the victor and to humiliate and dehumanize the conquered. Literally or metaphorically, this was the posture of the nations toward Israel, nations with their foot on the neck of God's people.

Interestingly, Israel is named alongside Judah and Jerusalem in 1:19, thus bringing into view all of God's covenant people. Historically we know that Assyria and Babylon were the nations that destroyed Israel and Judah. The former scattered Israel in 722 B.C., and the latter scattered Judah and razed Jerusalem in 586 B.C. But the fact that neither Assyria nor Babylon are mentioned by name, along with the fact that there are four horns, utilizing the number symbolic of completeness, suggests that something greater, more expansive, might be in view.[3] These historical entities are imbued with cosmic significance and have come to represent in divine revelation and the prophetic imagination all that opposes God and oppresses his people.

But no sooner does the prophet receive this awesome and terrifying vision of extraordinary power and blasphemous arrogance than he receives another equally surprising and equally terrifying vision of four craftsmen (1:20). Again the prophet inquires into the significance of these figures, and the interpreting angel responds, "These are the horns that scattered Judah, so that no one raised his head. And these have come to terrify them, to cast down the horns of the nations who lifted up their horns against the land of Judah to scatter it" (v. 21).

Somehow these four craftsmen are God's response to the four horns. This is made clear by the way the angel sets these two groups against each other, perhaps gesturing toward each as he does so: "These are the horns that scattered Judah. . . . And these have come to terrify them." The craftsmen are on a mission to do to the nations what the nations did to Judah and to Israel. They will terrify them and cast them down.[4] It is a vision of justice executed according to the principle of *lex talionis*, "an eye for an eye, a tooth for a tooth" (Leviticus 24:19, 20).[5]

The nations who have set themselves against God and against his people will one day be brought low. Like the nations in Psalm 2, who rage against the Lord and against his anointed, the One who sits in Heaven laughs (vv. 1–3). In Psalm 2 God responds to the nations' arrogance with the announcement of the coronation of his messianic King: "As for me, I have set my king on Zion, my holy hill" (v. 6). Where God responds to the arrogant kings and nations with his messianic King in Psalm 2, he responds with craftsmen in Zechariah's second vision.

Perhaps more mystifying than the four horns are these four craftsmen sent to destroy them. For most of us, craftsmen would probably not be our first choice for a champion to send out against the greatest forces of evil and tyranny. A great king, a mighty warrior, a cunning politician perhaps, but not a craftsman. Some scholars, in an attempt to make more sense of the vision, have interpreted "craftsmen" more narrowly as blacksmiths, which evokes the idea of strength and force suitable for destroying the power of empires and nations.[6] However, the word is rarely used for blacksmiths, and this view assumes that the horns are metal, an assumption that is far from certain.

The word, rather, is typically used for masons, artisans, and other craftsmen, those who work with wood, stone, jewels, and precious metals.[7] Important for this text, however, is the fact that this is the word used for those who constructed the tabernacle in the wilderness (e.g., Exodus 35:35; 38:23) and for those who worked on the temple in Jerusalem. For example, in 2 Kings the same word is used for "the carpenters . . . who worked on the house of the LORD" (12:11; cf. 22:6). The significance of the craftsmen is not their strength or their effectiveness on the battlefield but rather their skill and their calling to work on the temple.[8]

The craftsmen are a threat to the hostile nations opposing Israel, and, when rightly understood, a threat to every evil that exists in this world, not because of who they are but because of what they are coming to do—namely, to rebuild the temple of God. The temple is the throne room of God. It is the focal point of his redemptive work in the world. It is the place from which he will expand his kingdom, the kingdom of God, a kingdom characterized by justice, righteousness, and peace. It is the place where his people may gather and find a refuge in God as their fortress and their strong tower. But perhaps most important, it is the place where God's people can find refuge and protection from God himself, as it is the place of forgiveness, restoration, reconciliation, and communion.

The temple, with all it stood for, was God's answer to the hostilities and dangers Israel faced because it pointed them, as it points us, to the true temple, Jesus Christ. Jesus would fulfill all that Israel's temple represented. Zechariah announced that it would be through the work of these craftsmen building God's temple that the nations who lifted up their horns against the land of Judah to scatter it would be terrified and cast down (1:21). Paul announces its fulfillment at the cross, where Jesus "disarmed the rulers and authorities and put them to open shame, by triumphing over them in him" (Colossians 2:15). The forces of evil arrayed against God's people are much stronger, much crueler, much more terrifying than the worst rulers and worst armies of Assyria and Babylon (Ephesians 6:12). But the good news is that at the cross, Jesus conquered them all. Ultimately it would not be through the building of the temple that God would defeat his foes but through tearing it down (John 2:18–22). Jesus triumphed when his body was torn apart on a Roman cross, and he was declared victorious when that same body was raised on the third day to resurrection life.

When we consider the many forces arrayed against the Church of Christ, it is tempting to respond with the means and mechanisms of the world, things like political lobbying, military force, or social media campaigns, to name a few. In fact, there were likely voices encouraging Zerubbabel to usher in Israel's future glory by leading them in military revolt against their Persian overlords. But these craftsmen reminded Israel in Zechariah's day, as they remind us in ours, that the future glory of God's people would not be a result of their own efforts—militaristic or otherwise—but in entrusting themselves to the God who fulfills all his promises in his way and in his time.

*Population Multiplied (2:1–4)*

If the second vision presents the catastrophic future of Israel's enemies, the third vision presents the glorious future of Israel herself. The prophet sees a man holding a measuring line in his hand (Zechariah 2:1). This young man is apparently on the move as the prophet asks him, "Where are you going?" He replies, "To measure Jerusalem, to see what is its width and what is its length" (v. 2). The city, like the temple in Zechariah's day, lay in ruins; rebuilding anything even approximating Jerusalem's former glory seemed nothing short of impossible. But the energy and eagerness of this young man to measure the city suggests that the holy city might be rebuilt.[9] This future city might resemble, at least in some small measure, the glories of the Jerusalem of old.

But no sooner does this thought lodge in the prophet's mind than it is interrupted with an announcement of a future far more glorious than Zechariah or the postexilic community could ever have imagined.

Zechariah's angel is confronted by another angel commanding him to run after the young man with the measuring line and tell him, in effect, "Don't bother" (vv. 3, 4). Why? "Jerusalem shall be inhabited as villages without walls, because of the multitude of people and livestock in it" (v. 4).

The implication of this whirlwind drama is that the inhabitants of God's new Jerusalem will be so numerous that it is not humanly possible to build a city large enough to house them. There is no line long enough to measure the city that God is building. As the first man and the first woman were called to "be fruitful and multiply and fill the earth" (Genesis 1:28), so God himself will fulfill that mandate as he fills his holy city with a people too numerous to count. The mention of livestock also suggests the wealth and abundance that will characterize this city of God. Measuring Jerusalem with a view toward building houses and walls enough for its future inhabitants is a fool's errand because the young man's vision and the prophet's vision of God's future kingdom is not nearly expansive enough to capture its glory and its greatness.

This vision contained a critical message for postexilic Israel. The size and stature of the postexilic community would have presented an enormous challenge to their faith. The people of Israel looked and felt like an utterly insignificant people, a drop of water in the ocean of the Persian Empire. How could anything good, much less great, come out of so insignificant a place? Israel had little by way of influence or strength within the larger geopolitical landscape, and no prospect of change was visible on the horizon of history.

But in this vision, God announces a future glory for Israel that is nothing short of staggering. It is a glory that far transcends the most glorious days of Israel's past and fulfills the most glorious promises in which Israel had dared to trust. Glorious things of Zion, the city of God, will once again be spoken.

The Church today needs to hear and heed this same message. Christians in the West, as in many parts of the world, are becoming increasingly marginalized and ostracized. Consequently, it is tempting to lose hope that the Church will ever be anything other than a small group of little significance, eking out an existence at the fringes of society. We are tempted to adopt the world's standards of significance and to measure ourselves by what the world regards as greatness, which can only result in compromise. But Zechariah reminds us that God has a different measure and a different plan. The current state of the Church—beset as she is with infighting, weakness, sin, and error—is not indicative of her future. In fact, her future is just the opposite. Paul wrote to the Corinthians,

> So we do not lose heart. Though our outer self is wasting away, our inner self is being renewed day by day. For this light momentary affliction is preparing for us an eternal weight of glory beyond all comparison, as we look not to the things that are seen but to the things that are unseen. For the things that are seen are transient, but the things that are unseen are eternal. (2 Corinthians 4:16–18)

Often contrary to appearances, God is at work building a city that can never be shaken, whose inhabitants will be beyond numbering and whose glory will be nothing short of the glory of God himself. What appears weak and insignificant in this present evil age will one day be revealed to be more important and more consequential than we could ever imagine, so much so that we will wonder how we could have ever thought otherwise. It will all be so obvious.

### *Safety Secured (2:5)*

The promise of a city without walls because her inhabitants are so many was a heartening and heartwarming prospect, and at the same time a discouraging and fear-inducing prospect. Walls, after all, served an important function in the ancient world; they kept a city's enemies out, and they kept the citizens and inhabitants of a city safe and secure within. A city's walls were its glory because they spoke of wealth, power, security, and permanence. Typically, the greater the city, the higher and thicker the walls. A village was, almost by definition, a wall-less city, and the daily experience of those who lived in villages was one of vulnerability and insecurity.[10] This constant feeling of vulnerability and insecurity was postexilic Israel's daily experience. The Jerusalem of Zechariah's day was a wall-less city. It wouldn't be until years later, under the leadership and ministry of Nehemiah, that the postexilic community would set their hands to rebuilding the walls of Jerusalem.

But there was at least one city in the ancient world that was a city without walls, not because it lacked greatness, but because it was the capital of an empire that was so great, powerful, and secure that the emperor thought there was no need for walls. That city was Parsagadae, the capital of the Persian Empire.[11] It is likely that this notion of a city without walls as a sign of greatness and as a sign of the permanence of the empire was behind Zechariah's third night vision. But the Persian Empire of which Parsagadae was a symbol would one day fall. The permanence of the empire would be revealed to be an illusion.

Zechariah, however, beholds a city that will truly need no walls made of stone or brick because it will have God himself. God will be Jerusalem's protection as a wall of fire around it, a wall that is as impenetrable as it is permanent (Zechariah 2:5). That image evokes not only the altars of fire surrounding Parsagadae, but closer to home it is an image that evokes Israel's past, when in the days of Moses Yahweh stood as a pillar of fire between Israel and the Egyptians who could destroy them. Biblically, God often appears in smoke and fire, a powerful and terrifying revelation of his presence. Here we see that God's presence will answer the longing of every human heart for safety, security, and rest.

But even greater than the wall of fire around Israel will be the fire in Israel's midst. This is perhaps a summary of the entire Bible: the presence of God will one day be restored to his people. This is the glory that descended upon the tabernacle in Moses's day, glory that was so powerful Moses had to flee from before it. It is the glory that descended on the temple in Solomon's day as a visible manifestation of the presence of God with his people. It is the glory Ezekiel saw departing Jerusalem in the days of the exile—God abandoning his city. But here Zechariah announces its return. The God who is the wall of fire about his people will also be the glory in their midst. He will again take up residence in and among his own and thereby fulfill his promise of old: "I will be your God, and you shall be my people" (Jeremiah 7:23).

## Living in Light of Israel's Glorious Future (2:6–13)

The acronym FYI flies around emails and offices to mark a point of information that is important to know but does not necessarily require action, decision, or a change of behavior. It is simply "for your information," something for recipients simply to be aware of. Zechariah's visions of Jerusalem's glorious future were anything but an FYI for postexilic Israel, and they are anything but an FYI for us today. Though the wonderful promises Zechariah received in these visions announced what God would do for his people in the future, by these visions God was summoning his people to respond to these promises in how they thought, felt, and lived in the present, with all its trials, temptations, and hardships.[12]

As good preachers are trained to apply the message of their sermons to different groups in their congregations—believers, unbelievers, young, old, married, single, etc.—so the prophet applies his message to three groups of people—namely, the residents of Babylon, the citizens of Jerusalem, and the entire world.

### *Residents of Babylon (2:6–9)*

Though some Jews chose to return to the land of promise, others (likely the majority of Jews) chose to stay in Babylon. The reasons for this were no doubt varied. Some had put down roots and didn't want to leave the homes and communities they had known their entire lives. Others would have established successful livelihoods and meaningful relationships that they didn't want to abandon to start afresh in Jerusalem. Still others had achieved positions of influence within the foreign court and were thus disinclined to abandon an opportunity for advancement. Life, in other words, had become comfortable.

Babylon was a thriving cultural, economic, and religious center of the ancient world. Leaving Babylon for Jerusalem would be like leaving New York City for a Midwest ghost town. In fact, life in exile was now much improved since a remnant of Israel had returned to rebuild the temple. The return of their kinfolk allowed the Jews who remained in Babylon to worship from afar and to know that God was being served back home while they thrived outside the land.

And yet Babylon was not the home of God's people. Designated "the land of the north" (Zechariah 2:6), Babylon represented all that stood against God:

wickedness, oppression, violence, and idolatry.[13] Those who returned to the land did so not because it was to their advantage economically, socially, or politically but because they understood that the God who had sent them into exile on account of their sin had called them to return to the land on account of his grace. Israel's return to the land represented their return to God and God's return to them. Their return was at heart an act of faith. Of course, there was still much to do to reestablish the covenant relationship, yet the land of promise and Jerusalem, the holy city, remained the theater of God's redemptive work among his people.

Simply put, the message of Zechariah's second and third night visions for those who remained in Babylon was, "Run! Flee! Escape!" "Up! Up!" the prophet declares in verse 6. "Flee from the land of the north, declares the LORD. For I have spread you abroad as the four winds of the heavens, declares the LORD. Up! Escape to Zion, you who dwell with the daughter of Babylon" (vv. 6, 7). The absolute dichotomy between the kingdom of God and the kingdoms of this world is here highlighted—those who dwell with the daughter of Babylon and those who have fled to Mount Zion. Spiritually speaking, there is no city in between.[14]

Those who dwell with the daughter of Babylon have in a sense built their houses on a train track. It might be some time before the train comes, and the household might grow and thrive, and yet its fate is certain. God says in verse 9, "Behold, I will shake my hand over them, and they shall become plunder for those who served them." The plunderers will become the plundered. Those who have grown wealthy through oppression and violence will themselves be oppressed and destroyed. Though by all appearances and by any human measure Babylon was a city marked by power and wealth, influence and affluence, culture and civilization at its highest, God says its fate is destruction and spoiling. One day God will shake his hand over them, and judgment will come against Babylon and all that this wicked city represents. So the prophetic call goes out: "Up! Flee!" (v. 6). "Flee," the prophet says, in effect, "to the only place where safety may be found, Mount Zion."

Mount Zion is the only place of safety from the wrath and judgment of God, not because it is a magical mountain but because it is the place where God said, in effect, "There you will find me as the God of grace." In Zechariah's day, if you wanted to know God as the God of grace, he could be found in Jerusalem on Mount Zion; he could be found in his holy temple by those who approached him in faith.

For us, Zechariah's words are no longer a summons to flee to the Jerusalem temple but a summons to flee to the One who, speaking of his body said,

"Destroy this temple, and in three days I will raise it up" (John 2:19). In Jesus, the Gospel writer tells us, God "tabernacled among us, and we have seen his glory, glory as of the only Son from the Father, full of grace and truth" (John 1:14, AT). It is in Christ alone that God may be found as the God of all grace and mercy, and it is ultimately to this Christ we must flee for salvation.

*Citizens of Jerusalem (2:10–12)*

But what of those who have returned? What about those living in and around Jerusalem who have by faith in God's promises returned to the promised land but who have yet to see God's promises realized and whose lives are marked by daily struggle and hardship? To these God says, "Sing and rejoice, O daughter of Zion, for behold, I come and I will dwell in your midst, declares the LORD" (Zechariah 2:10).

This is a somewhat surprising thing to say to a group of people whose daily life is characterized by tremendous struggle and hardship. But in calling the returnees to shout and rejoice, God is reminding his people that of all the peoples of the earth, this small band of faithful Israelites has reason to be glad, because of all the peoples of the earth, God is dwelling in their midst for their blessing.

It is this singular truth—that God is with us and for us—that enabled the postexilic community and has enabled believers in every age to rejoice in the face of daily struggle, great danger, and fierce persecution. Though despairing at the prosperity of the wicked and the oppression of the righteous, the psalmist was nevertheless able to sing, "Whom have I in heaven but you? And there is nothing on earth that I desire besides you. My flesh and my heart may fail, but God is the strength of my heart and my portion forever" (Psalm 73:25, 26). Paul and Silas were stripped, beaten, and placed in stocks in a Philippian jail, yet they could bear witness to their unshakable hope as they prayed and sang hymns to God (Acts 16:25).

Here in Zechariah, God tells his people to rejoice not only because he is with them in their present afflictions but also because there is a more glorious day yet to come. When God speaks of "that day," he is directing Israel's attention to the future: "Many nations shall join themselves to the LORD in that day, and shall be my people. And I will dwell in your midst" (Zechariah 2:11). With these words, God is repeating his promises of old that he declared, for example, through Isaiah:

> It shall come to pass in the latter days
>   that the mountain of the house of the LORD

> shall be established as the highest of the mountains,
>   and shall be lifted up above the hills;
> and all the nations shall flow to it,
>   and many peoples shall come and say,
> "Come, let us go up to the mountain of the LORD,
>   to the house of the God of Jacob,
> that he may teach us his ways
>   and that we may walk in his paths." (Isaiah 2:2, 3)

God's promises have not failed, and God's purposes for his people have not been derailed on account of their sin. God has promised to restore lost and broken Israel to a land and a home that will burst forth with beauty and bounty. This does not refer to Israel alone; with Israel will come the lost and broken nations that join themselves to Israel and to her God in worship and obedience. God's promise to Abraham, "I will bless those who bless you, and him who dishonors you I will curse, and in you all the families of the earth shall be blessed" (Genesis 12:3), has not been abrogated because of Israel's great sin. God's covenant of grace is precisely that: gracious.

## The Whole Earth (2:13)

Yet the final command goes not to the daughters of Babylon or the daughter of Zion but to all flesh—that is, the entire world, Jews and Gentiles alike. The prophet concludes these fantastic visions not with a call to lamentation at destruction or shouts of joy at deliverance but with a call to silence: "Be silent, all flesh, before the LORD, for he has roused himself from his holy dwelling" (Zechariah 2:13). When we behold the majesty of God and the mystery of his ways in the world, neither of which we can ever fully comprehend, the most appropriate response is silence induced by awe and wonder.

This was the silence of Job when he encountered Yahweh in the whirlwind (Job 40:5). Similarly, the veil separating the visible from the invisible was lifted for a moment, and the prophet Zechariah beheld a small part of what God was up to in the world, and he called on the nations to respond with the only response possible: namely, fear and awe before the power, sovereignty, holiness, and wisdom of God.

The nations were summoned to silence. The prophet said to them, in effect, "Behold the God of Israel." This was not a summons to become disinterested spectators.[15] This was a summons to take a stand with Israel or against them. It was a summons to identify either with the daughter of Zion in their joy and glory or with the daughter of Babylon in their sorrow and destruction.

When the earth beholds what God is up to in and through his people—God's ways of judgment and God's ways of mercy—and when they behold the invitation that goes to them as well (Gentiles invited into this great drama of redemption), they will be struck speechless in wonder and awe at the glory of Israel's God dwelling in the midst of his blood-bought people. The question for them and for us is, How will we respond?

# 65

# Clothed in Righteousness

ZECHARIAH 3

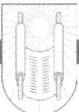

WEARING THE RIGHT CLOTHES is important. What is appropriate for a baseball game might not be appropriate for a wedding, and what one wears to the beach would almost certainly need to be changed before a funeral. Appropriateness in attire takes into account not only the event to which one is going but also the person who is dressing for the occasion. The mother of the bride is typically discouraged from wearing a white dress to her daughter's wedding, and donning a police uniform when you are not a police officer might very well land you in jail (unless it's Halloween).

However much this is true in radically individualistic and dispositionally countercultural America, it was that much more true in the communally oriented and comparatively conservative ancient world in which Zechariah ministered. Generally speaking, people dressed according to their station in life, and office holders especially would dress in a manner fitting for and appropriate to their office.[1] This was true of kings and courtiers, generals and soldiers and it was particularly true of Israel's priests, whose uniform was not only a matter of societal convention but also of divine prescription. The Law of Moses laid out in exquisite detail the proper clothing for the priests and the high priest who served in the tabernacle and later in the temple (cf. Exodus 28; Leviticus 8:1–13). The priests' clothing was highly symbolic and of vital importance for the covenant community because the priests' faithfulness relative to their own bodies qualified them for the critical work as mediators between God and Israel.[2]

Violation of not only social custom but divine law stands at the center of Zechariah's fourth night vision.

637

Together with the fifth night vision, this fourth vision serves as the centerpiece of the entire cycle of night visions. These two central visions feature the two central leaders of the postexilic community—Joshua, the high priest, and Zerubbabel, the governor.³ These two men have been called to lead Israel in the task of rebuilding the temple and thus reconstituting Israel as the people among whom the God of the universe dwells. It is a task of immense importance not only for Israel but for the entire world. As the whole world will be blessed through Israel's God, so Israel's obedience in building the place where God will extend his blessings to the world, where he will receive sinners into his presence, is of no little consequence.

However, there's a problem here. The prophet sees the high priest Joshua standing before the Lord in filthy garments (Zechariah 3:3), a state of affairs that would have had profound implications for the covenant community, as it would disqualify him from his ministry on their behalf.⁴ The filth, of course, is more than filth—it represents sin, probably both his own as well as the sins of the people of Israel. In one of the most dramatic displays of the gospel in the Old Testament, the prophet Zechariah witnesses God's removal of the high priest's sin as one removes a filthy garment, and he witnesses as well God's provision of the righteousness that makes him fit to stand in the presence of the holy God.

Zechariah's fourth night vision dramatically displays God's provision for Israel's high priest, and through Israel's high priest, God's provision for his people. In this the prophet announces to God's people in every age that God will ransom them from the crucible of divine judgment and affliction through the ministry of a faithful great High Priest.

### God's Provision for the High Priest (3:1–5)

As the curtain rises on the fourth vision we feel, much like the prophet himself, as if we're walking into the middle of a courtroom drama. We're not given any of the backstory of the case. We know nothing about the who, what, when, where, and why of it all. But as the drama unfolds we very quickly realize that the stakes could not be any higher—and not just for the accused but for all of Israel as well. The placement of the characters themselves is somewhat revealing. Joshua the high priest, we're told, is "standing before the angel of the LORD," with "Satan standing at his right hand to accuse him" (Zechariah 3:1). The high priest clearly stands as the accused and is on trial. The angel of the Lord is presiding as either judge over the hearing or perhaps as Joshua's advocate. To Joshua's right is Satan (literally, "the Satan"), who clearly stands as the prosecutor and whose name means "the Accuser."

However, it seems that no sooner does the trial begin than the case is thrown out. The angel of the Lord declares, "The LORD who has chosen Jerusalem rebuke you! Is not this a brand plucked from the fire?" (v. 2). The Accuser never speaks; he is never given the opportunity to present his case. This is somewhat surprising because the Accuser in fact has a clear and indisputable case against Joshua.

We learn a few verses later that the high priest is clothed in filthy garments (v. 3). In other words, the high priest is standing before the bar of God's perfect justice exposed, defiled, ashamed. He says nothing, perhaps because there is nothing he can say. There are no excuses, justifications, or attenuating circumstances. The priest is himself a sinner and is therefore defiled, and as such he is unfit to stand before or minister in the presence of the Holy One of Israel, the One of whom the prophet Habakkuk declared, "You who are of purer eyes than to see evil and cannot look at wrong . . ." (Habakkuk 1:13).

If ever there was an open-and-shut case, this is it. The Accuser's evidence is literally caked on the accused at this very moment. It is like the accused showing up in court with the blood of his victim on his hands and clothes. The high priest is robed in filthy garments (Zechariah 3:3)—the evidence of his disqualification to minister in the temple of the Lord is evident for all to see. He stands exposed, humiliated, and ashamed. The offense is indisputable. But in a remarkable turn of events, the Lord dismisses the charges, rules any evidence to be inadmissible, and, perhaps most startling of all, issues a rebuke to the prosecutor himself.[5]

How can this be? Clearly the basis for the Lord's acquittal is not the innocence of the high priest. The Lord does not deny the defilement of the high priest, adopting, as my kids often do, a sliding or relative scale of cleanliness. The basis of God's dismissal of the charges, and thus the rebuke of the Accuser, is God's electing love and redeeming grace: "The LORD who has chosen Jerusalem rebuke you! Is not this a brand plucked from the fire?" (Zechariah 3:2). It is God's sovereign election of Jerusalem that stands against the accusations of the devil. The Lord has rescued Joshua as one might snatch from the fire a stick that has just begun to burn.

The language here is a clear allusion to Amos 4:11, in which God says to Israel, "I overthrew some of you, as when God overthrew Sodom and Gomorrah, and you were as a brand plucked out of the burning; yet you did not return to me." In contrast to the remnant in Amos's day, the remnant in Zechariah's day did return to the Lord. They returned to the land in faith, leaving the Babylon of their birth to rebuild the temple and the city of God. Not only did they return to the Lord by physically returning to the land, but they returned to the

Lord spiritually as they responded to the prophetic word with repentance and faith. The book of Zechariah opens with a notice of this very thing: "So they repented and said, 'As the LORD of hosts purposed to deal with us for our ways and deeds, so has he dealt with us'" (1:6; cf. Haggai 1:12–15).

However, it is not enough that the charges against Joshua are dismissed. The manifest problem of the high priest's defiled garments is yet unresolved. Therefore, the angel of the Lord commands those who are "standing before him," presumably other angels or heavenly beings in attendance in the heavenly courtroom: "Remove the filthy garments from him" (Zechariah 3:4a).[6] This action is attended by the interpretive word in which the angel of the Lord declares, "Behold, I have taken your iniquity away from you, and I will clothe you with pure vestments" (v. 4b). Then, somewhat surprisingly, the prophet himself speaks: "Let them put a clean turban on his head" (v. 5a) As the Lord spoke in the beginning and it was so, again the Lord's word is no sooner uttered than obeyed, and we're told, "So they put a clean turban on his head and clothed him with garments. And the angel of the LORD was standing by" (v. 5b).

For all its many points of ambiguity and uncertainty, the message of the drama is perfectly clear: the righteousness God requires to stand in his holy presence, God provides for his elect. There is in fact no other way for a sinner to stand in the presence of God. Sin is defiling, and no amount of good works can atone for sin and make one fit for the presence of God. No amount of sacrifice or prayer qualifies sinners for God's presence. What makes the gospel good news is not that God grades on a curve but that God provides the righteousness he requires in his perfectly righteous Son given for sinners. For this reason the Apostle Paul would despise not only his sin but also his righteousness:

> If anyone else thinks he has reason for confidence in the flesh, I have more: circumcised on the eighth day, of the people of Israel, of the tribe of Benjamin, a Hebrew of Hebrews; as to the law, a Pharisee; as to zeal, a persecutor of the church; as to righteousness under the law, blameless. But whatever gain I had, I counted as loss for the sake of Christ. Indeed, I count everything as loss because of the surpassing worth of knowing Christ Jesus my Lord. For his sake I have suffered the loss of all things and count them as rubbish, in order that I may gain Christ and be found in him, not having a righteousness of my own that comes from the law, but that which comes through faith in Christ, the righteousness from God that depends on faith. (Philippians 3:4b–9)

At the heart of the Protestant Reformation was a recovery of the Biblical understanding that in Christ, God freely gives the righteousness that he requires—what Martin Luther called "an alien righteousness."[7] What makes sinners acceptable to a holy God is not what God does in them but what God does for them in the life, death, and resurrection of Jesus. Critics of this doctrine have suggested that alien righteousness is in fact alien to the Old Testament and is therefore, at best, a Pauline invention or perhaps a modern misunderstanding of Paul. It is far from the truth, however, to say that the Old Testament is ignorant of the need for the imputation of an external righteousness. Perhaps the best example of this is Zechariah's fourth night vision, which not only teaches this critical gospel truth but vividly displays it in the unfolding of a courtroom drama.[8]

Joshua the high priest and the Israel whom he represented were unfit for the presence of God. Their sin was as apparent to the world and, more importantly, as apparent to God as an excrement-covered wedding dress on a bride walking down the aisle. God's word, God's initiative, and indeed God's amazing grace remove sin along with all its guilt and shame. More than simply removing sin (as marvelous as that is), God also provides a perfect righteousness symbolized in the pure vestments with which he clothed Joshua, thus making him fit for the divine presence and for his priestly work as a mediator between God and man.

### God's Provision of a Priest (3:6–10)

After this dramatic scene, Zechariah's vision takes something of a strange turn. This remarkable display of God's gracious removal of sin and its defiling guilt—God's free gift of righteousness represented in the pure vestments—gives way to a series of conditions: "The angel of the LORD solemnly assured Joshua, 'Thus says the LORD of hosts: *If* you will walk in my ways and keep my charge, then you shall rule my house and have charge of my courts, and I will give you the right of access among those who are standing here'" (Zechariah 3:6, 7). The expressions "walk in my ways" and "keep my charge" refer to the priests' role in temple upkeep and service as well as their duties in teaching and modeling Torah observance.[9] The reward for Joshua's obedience is authority over God's temple and, even more wonderful, access to the very presence of God with all the glory and blessedness that entails.

How are we to understand these conditions that are placed before Joshua? On one level, God's command to Joshua is simply the call to faithfulness to the terms of the covenant.[10] Joshua's forgiveness and the provision of an alien righteousness are not license for moral laziness or carelessness in his duties. In this respect, we may rightly see here the call to godly living that attends all who have experienced the grace of God in the forgiveness of sins. And yet with Joshua, this call to godliness and covenant fidelity operates at another level as well. God's calling of the high priest to faithfulness and obedience in his duties reminds Israel of their need for a perfectly faithful priest, a priest whose right of access into the heavenly throne room and whose rule over God's house will be achieved by his own faithfulness to God and his own obedience to God's word. This is the heart of God's promise to Joshua—that through his obedience, he and those he represents will enjoy access to the presence of God and the blessings of the covenant. In this respect, Joshua is a type, a picture or foreshadowing, of the work of Christ.

This isn't the first time in the Old Testament that a single individual has had this dual function of both needing and typifying the Christ who would come. Noah clearly functioned as a type of Christ, one whose righteousness qualified him to provide shelter and safety from the floodwaters of God's judgment not only for himself but for his family who entered the ark. However, as events following the flood made abundantly clear, Noah was not perfectly righteous, and he himself needed God's grace and the imputation of the righteousness of the very one of whom he was a type.

So too with Abraham. Though God promised that he would graciously and unconditionally bless Abraham with a land and offspring, the angel of the Lord appeared in order to make God's unconditional and gracious promises conditioned on Abraham's one act of obedience:

> By myself I have sworn, declares the LORD, *because* you have done this and have not withheld your son, your only son, I will surely bless you, and I will surely multiply your offspring as the stars of heaven and as the sand that is on the seashore. And your offspring shall possess the gate of his enemies, and in your offspring shall all the nations of the earth be blessed, because you have obeyed my voice. (Genesis 22:16–18)

Though the only way Abraham would receive God's eternal covenant blessings would be on account of God's unmerited grace received by faith alone, nevertheless his one act of obedience in offering up his son Isaac served as the basis for Israel receiving God's earthly blessings, thus foreshadowing the obedience of the Son whose one act of obedience merited eternal blessing for those who share the faith of Abraham. Despite his remarkable act of faith and obedience, Abraham still needed the perfect obedience of the Christ who the patriarch's true but imperfect obedience typified.[11]

This list could go on to discuss Moses, David, and others whose sins required forgiveness and whose failures required the imputation of an alien righteousness but whose obedience, though imperfect, was used by God to foreshadow the work of his perfectly obedient Son. It is along these lines that we can make sense of the conditions set before Joshua the high priest.[12] The forgiveness of sins so dramatically displayed in the reclothing of Joshua would be accomplished through the obedience of a high priest of whom Joshua is a type. In his faithfulness and obedience, Joshua would foreshadow the work of this future High Priest whose perfect faithfulness would merit his right of access to the Father's presence, not for himself but for those who are united to him by faith.[13]

But it is not only Joshua who serves as a sign pointing to a greater Priest to come. The angel of the Lord expands the scope of his address to include Joshua's "friends who sit before you" (Zechariah 3:8). These "friends" were probably the priests who served alongside Joshua and whose very presence was called a sign or a portent. That is, they served as a constant reminder to Israel of something greater to come. What was that greater thing yet to come? God told them: "Behold, I will bring my servant the Branch."

In all likelihood, "the Branch" does not strike most of us as a particularly impressive epithet, especially for one who will accomplish so great a mission. But in this promise God is recalling the promise he had made years earlier through the prophet Jeremiah: "Behold the days are coming . . . when I will raise up for David a righteous Branch, and he shall reign as king and deal wisely and shall execute justice and righteousness in the land" (Jeremiah 23:5). God has not forgotten his people, and his purposes in redemption haven't faltered. He will one day raise up that Branch of David to shepherd his people Israel.

Though much about the connection between the priests and the Branch remains obscure, the vision does seem to adumbrate the connection between the kingship and the priesthood that will be developed in greater detail in Zechariah 6. Joshua and his fellow priests are a sign that this Messiah is yet to come, but when he does come, he will fulfill these two central offices in the life of Israel, the kingship and the priesthood.

It is not only the priests who serve as portents of better days yet to come. God says, "Behold, on the stone that I have set before Joshua, on a single stone with seven eyes, I will engrave its inscription, declares the LORD of hosts, and I will remove the iniquity of this land in a single day" (Zechariah 3:9). With this stone and this promise we move from the obscure to the opaque. The nature of this seven-eyed or seven-faceted stone is far from clear, and theories abound. Some have connected the stone to a feature of the temple, which is clearly central in Zechariah's night visions. However, the suggestion that this stone refers to a precious gem (or gems) that was part of the high priest's uniform makes better sense in the immediate context.[14]

Whatever its exact nature, what was clear about the stone was the promise contained in its inscription. Like the priests who reminded postexilic Israel of the coming messianic King, this stone reminded Israel of the work this Priest-King would accomplish, as it was inscribed with the words "I will remove the iniquity of this land in a single day" (Zechariah 3:9). The removal of iniquity was the prerogative of the priests, especially the high priest on the Day of Atonement. However, the Day of Atonement only came around once a year, a reality that reminded Israel of the insufficiency of the atonement that was accomplished. However, the removal of iniquity testified to by this stone was of a different sort. There was a finality to it, a once-for-all character of an accomplished atonement. The daily repetition of Israel's sacrifices and the yearly celebration of the Day of Atonement would give way to a sacrifice whose perfection and value made it the final, once-and-for-all accomplishment of all that these sacrifices represented. As Barry Webb puts it, "What Zechariah has just seen done symbolically for Joshua the high priest will one day be done actually for the whole *land* (the entire community)—in a single day, once and for all, when the Messiah comes."[15]

Zechariah's vision does not tell us exactly how God would accomplish this, but perhaps we're given a hint. We're never told what happened to Joshua's excrement-covered clothes in the drama that unfolded before the prophet, but we are told what happened to Joshua's clothes in the drama of redemptive history. When Jesus of Nazareth was stripped naked, beaten, humiliated, and nailed to a Roman cross, he in effect took up Joshua's excrement-covered clothes and our excrement-covered clothes and put them on. The sin and the guilt and the shame that Joshua's clothes represented were adorned by the sinless Son of God out of love for those who would nail him to the cross.

Though the how would be revealed in the fullness of time, Zechariah is made privy to the result as the Lord declares, "In that day ... every one of you will invite his neighbor to come under his vine and under his fig tree" (3:10). This image of rest and refreshment, friendship and peace between man and man is a conventional image of the blessings that attend obedience to the covenant. It is a picture and promise of community and unbroken fellowship among God's people. It is a promise of safety when the land is free from plague, pestilence, and the devastations of war and disaster. It is a promise of life in the fullest sense of that term—abundance, deep delight, and perfect rest. It is, in short, a promise of a new creation, new heavens and a new earth where God's people will receive the blessings of the covenant not because of their efforts but because of the finished work of their Messiah who would remove iniquity and its curse from the land in a single day.

This remains the hope for God's people even today. Though Christians have seen the fulfillment of Zechariah's remarkable vision in the death and resurrection of Christ, our perfect High Priest, we nevertheless wait for a greater, ultimate fulfillment of that life, that rest, that abundance, and that peace promised so wonderfully in this image: "Every one of you will invite his neighbor to come under his vine and under his fig tree."

# 66

# A Day of Small Things

ZECHARIAH 4

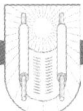

IN ALMOST EVERY PROFESSION, sport, art, and industry there is a single accomplishment that represents ultimate success. In the film industry it's the Oscar. In television it's the Emmy. In music it's the Grammy. For journalists it's the Pulitzer. For Olympic athletes it's the gold medal. The list could go on. For a king in the ancient world, even more than a great victory on the battlefield, the single accomplishment that represented ultimate success, the climax of the king's reign, was the construction of a temple.¹ The construction and especially the completion of a temple for the king's and the nation's deity marked the high point of the reign of a Near Eastern king.² In fact, archaeologists have unearthed numerous inscriptions that were buried in the foundations of such temples commemorating the building or rebuilding of these houses for gods. For example, the famous Sippar Cylinder of Nabonidus commemorates the restoration of no less than three temples by the Neo-Babylonian king. In it he boasts:

> I cleared its foundations and laid its brickwork. I mixed its mortar with beer, wine, oil and honey and anointed its excavation ramps with it. More than the kings my fathers [had done], I strengthened its building and perfected its work. That temple from its foundations to its parapet I built anew and completed its work. Beams of lofty cedar trees, a product of Lebanon, I set up above it. Doors of cedar wood, whose scent is pleasing, I affixed at its gates. With gold and silver [glaze] I coated its walls and made it shine like the sun.³

Though less boastful on their better days, Israel's kings shared similar values and exhibited the same priorities. It was when King David enjoyed "rest from all his surrounding enemies" that his heart turned to the last great feat he could hope to accomplish—namely, the building of a house for God (2 Samuel 7:1, 2). The construction of God's temple would perfectly express his devotion to his God and King, and it would secure his legacy for years and generations to come. So obvious was temple-building as the next and greatest step in David's royal career that when he announced his plans to Nathan the prophet, the prophet didn't bother consulting God but simply responded, "Go, do all that is in your heart, for the Lord is with you" (v. 3). It was that obvious and that fitting that King David should build a temple. Later, however, the prophet would have to reverse course as God revealed that David would not build a house for God; rather, God would build a house for David.

God did not have in view a physical house for David but, in the most famous pun in the Bible, a household or dynasty that would last forever. The honor of building a physical house—that is, a temple—for God would be the prerogative of David's son Solomon. King Solomon built a temple with such grandeur and beauty that the thought of replicating it seemed impossible for later generations. Temples expressed the glory of the gods they housed and were the pride of the people who gathered to them for worship.

However, much had changed since the days of Solomon and since the destruction of Solomon's temple. Zerubbabel was not a king; he was a governor. He was not an autonomous ruler but served at the behest and under the authority of the great Persian emperor. Israel, or Yehud as it was called at this time, was not an independent state but rather a remote province of the vast Persian Empire. As for Jerusalem, the holy city was a dim picture of the glorious city of old. In Zerubbabel's day Jerusalem lay in ruins, without walls and without a temple. What exactly would a rebuilt temple represent? What purpose would it serve? The glory of the first temple, the glory of Israel, and the glory of Israel's God seemed to be a thing of the distant past, a magnificence never to be repeated.

The fifth night vision opens somewhat abruptly, not only for us as readers but for the prophet Zechariah as well: "The angel who talked with me came again and woke me, like a man who is awakened out of his sleep" (Zechariah 4:1). The prophet is startled awake, only to find himself in another dream sequence in which he is immediately confronted with the question, "What do you see?" (v. 2). The prophet responds, "I see, and behold, a lampstand all of gold" (v. 3).

No sooner would the original audience have heard the words "a lampstand all of gold" than they would have made the immediate connection to perhaps the central feature of the temple.[4] The ordinary lampstands with which the common people were familiar were rarely if ever made all of gold.[5] However, every Israelite would have known of the golden lampstand that adorned the house of the Lord in the days of Moses and the ten golden lampstands that Solomon set in his temple (Exodus 25:31–40; 1 Kings 7:49; 2 Chronicles 4:7). The lampstands that stood in the temple represented God's presence with his people and, even more specifically, the light of his countenance ever shining upon his people with his grace and favor.[6] They served as a visible and powerful reminder of the Aaronic blessings: "The Lord make his face to shine upon you and be gracious to you; the Lord lift up his countenance upon you and give you peace" (Numbers 6:25, 26).

However, as is typical in Zechariah's night visions, the familiar and sacred are again transformed into the otherworldly and the bizarre. The prophet describes this golden lampstand as configured with "a bowl on top of it, and seven lamps on it, with seven lips on each of the lamps that are on the top of it. And there are two olive trees by it, one on the right of the bowl and the other on its left" (Zechariah 4:2, 3). The prophet, in other words, beholds what one commentator has called a "super menorah."[7] Like a dream in which the familiar is represented in profoundly unfamiliar (and perhaps symbolic) ways, the prophet recognizes that this both is and is not the lampstand in the temple. It is clearly the temple lampstand, and yet it is configured differently. But it is precisely in these differences that the super-menorah relates a critical message both for Zerubbabel and for the postexilic community. What is the meaning of this bizarre vision? The prophet is as curious as we are, and he inquires of the angel, "What are these, my lord?" (v. 4). The angel responds, "Do you not know what these are?" (v. 5).

Perhaps we're meant to hear a gentle rebuke as Zechariah, the representative of Israel, should have known something of the message of the lampstand. Or perhaps the angel simply desires the prophet to acknowledge that there is much about God and his ways in the world that Zechariah does not know or understand.[8] Either way, Zechariah's fifth night vision contains a powerful message that is far from evident to Israel in her daily experience. It declares a message of divine presence and divine provision. God is with his people for their good. Furthermore, Zechariah's vision announces that God will accomplish the work he has promised, and he will do so in the most unexpected, unassuming, and ordinary means—through the faithfulness of a provincial governor and through the humble temple of a humble people.

Why does God work in this way? The answer is simple: so that he alone will receive all the glory. When Zerubbabel accomplishes the impossible it will be evident to everyone who has eyes to see and ears to hear that the Lord, the God of Israel, has done this. Yet as incredible as it would be to all who see it, Zerubbabel's temple-building anticipates the greater work of the greater Zerubbabel, King Jesus, who on the third day would rebuild the temple of his body and who himself would construct a temple far more glorious than even King Solomon could have imagined, for it would be a temple built of living stones purchased at the cost of his own blood.

### God Will Build His House (4:6, 7)

When faced with the task of rebuilding the temple in Jerusalem, Zerubbabel was confronted with countless and seemingly insurmountable obstacles. There were the obvious physical obstacles of having to clear enormous blocks of ruined stone and then reset enormous freshly cut stones in their place. There were the economic obstacles of having to secure materials at great cost and perhaps from great distances. There were the social obstacles of leading a discouraged and despondent people in a task that appeared all but impossible. Perhaps most challenging were the spiritual obstacles of having to reorient to the Lord a disoriented people who had until recently been more concerned with building their own houses than with rebuilding the Lord's.

All of these obstacles (and no doubt many more) proclaimed to Zerubbabel, "Impossible!"

But in response to the obstacles that declare, in effect, "No!" Zerubbabel has the word of God that says, "Yes!" What appears to the world to be impossible is announced to be God's settled purpose. Where there appears to be no way, God promises to make a way. The angel declares what may be the most famous lines in the entire book: "This is the word of the LORD to Zerubbabel: Not by might, nor by power, but by my Spirit, says the LORD of hosts" (Zechariah 4:6). It will not be through Zerubbabel's strength, skill, ingenuity, or wisdom that God's house will be rebuilt and the blessings of the covenant will again be enjoyed by God's people. Zerubbabel's strength is inadequate for the task that lies before him. But as Jesus reminded his disciples, "With man it is impossible, but not with God. For all things are possible with God" (Mark 10:27). God declares to Zerubbabel that he will do it.

Furthermore, the language of "might" and "power" carry connotations of military might, and thus the angel may have in view a show of political or military strength in which the governor would lead a rebellion against Persia and establish himself as king in the line of David.[9] To any who are thinking along these lines, the angel says, in effect, "No!" Again, to use Jesus's words, "My kingdom is not of this world" (John 18:36). God will accomplish his purposes, and he will do so in his way, in his time, and in accordance with his purpose to redeem a people for himself.

God reveals not only *what* he will do through Zerubbabel but also *how* he will do it—namely, through his Spirit (Zechariah 4:6). God the Holy Spirit will superintend the rebuilding of this temple so that what the world has thought, what Israel has thought, and what Zerubbabel has thought impossible will be accomplished through the strength of the Lord.

The mention of the Spirit reminded Israel of God's power both in creation and redemption. It was the Spirit of God who hovered over the face of the deep in the very beginning. It was the Spirit who parted the waters of the Red Sea, making a way where there was no way for Israel to pass through to safety. It was the Spirit who in the days of the judges empowered Gideon and Samson to deliver Israel from her foreign oppressors. This same Spirit would be with Zerubbabel in his work of temple-building and would guarantee its completion. God would do it, and he would do it through the power and working of his Holy Spirit.

So certain are God's promises and so mighty is God's power that his angel (or God himself) issues a taunt: "Who are you, O great mountain? Before Zerubbabel you shall become a plain. And he shall bring forward the top stone amid shouts of 'Grace, grace to it!'" (Zechariah 4:7).[10] It is not perfectly clear what particular mountain, if any, is being addressed.[11] The mountain might be a figurative way of referring to all of the obstacles Zerubbabel faces in the temple rebuilding project. But whether literal or figurative, the angel's taunt is designed to instill in Zerubbabel a confidence in the work that lies before him. Zerubbabel is to lead Israel not from a posture of doubt and fear but of assurance and courage. His confidence and courage are not in himself but in the power and promises of God. Zerubbabel, in other words, is here being called to faith as he is summoned to view reality in light of or through the lens of God's promises. He is being called to live by faith and not by sight. Sight says, "Rebuilding the temple is impossible." Faith says, "God has promised to build his house, and I will act accordingly."

God's certain promise does not mean that Zerubbabel does not need to work, nor does it mean that the people don't need to break a sweat. What God's word means is that Zerubbabel may have assurance that he will be successful in this task of temple-building because God is with him to strengthen and to guide. The wisdom Zerubbabel needs, God will supply. It is Zerubbabel's job to be faithful in leading God's people in obedience in rebuilding the temple, an obedience symbolized in the governor's bringing forward "the top stone" (v. 7), or better translated as "the premier stone." This stone was likely an important stone from the earlier temple that would serve as part of the foundation for the second temple and thus symbolically unite the two structures. Some have suggested that it was this setting of the premier stone that effectively began the rebuilding project. Zerubbabel's leadership would be recognized by the people, who respond with praise and acclaim saying, "Grace, grace to it!" (v. 7).

When it comes to misunderstanding and misapplying this passage for Christians today, the road is wide and the way is easy. It is tempting for us to hear in God's promise to Zerubbabel a promise to remove every obstacle we face in our lives. We all have challenges and face a variety of obstacles, and we all long for a day in which we will enjoy success in our labors and victory over the obstacles we face. However, such a direct application to the lives of believers misses the redemptive historical context of God's promise.

Zerubbabel was in the line of King David. Though Israel did not have a Davidic king on the throne, they had a Davidic heir as their governor, and this was sufficient for them to recall God's promise to King David when he said, "Your house and your kingdom shall be made sure forever before me. Your throne shall be established forever" (2 Samuel 7:16).

This figure was sufficient for Israel to hope for a greater King David yet to come. Zerubbabel was a type of Christ, a foreshadowing of the One who would rebuild God's temple in his body and, through his resurrection life, rebuild God's temple with living stones united to him by faith.

The good news that the prophet's words to Zerubbabel has for us today is not that God will flatten all our mountains or raise all our valleys, nor is it that God will grant us victory over all our hardships and challenges. The promise is that Christ will build his Church, and "the gates of hell itself shall not prevail against it" (Matthew 16:18).

Like Zerubbabel and Israel rebuilding the temple, we too labor for Christ in loving and serving our neighbors, in speaking the truth in love, and in bearing faithful witness to what we believe. But as we labor, we do so knowing that ultimately our success depends not on ourselves but on the Lord and that thankfully our Lord has promised to be with us always, even to the end of the age (Matthew 28:20). We don't change hearts, God does. He does so through the powerful and mysterious work of his Holy Spirit, who brings life out of death.

Even today God is building his Church, often in contexts where it seems almost impossible for the Church to grow, much less thrive. In many parts of the world those who confess Christ are threatened with imprisonment and violence, and in many other parts of the world Christians suffer marginalization for their commitment to follow Christ and live according to his teachings. The thought that Christ's Church would grow, and not only grow but thrive in these contexts, seems nothing short of an impossibility. And yet, in many of the places where Christians are most persecuted, Christ's Church is growing the most. Zerubbabel would learn what Paul articulated so well when he wrote to the Corinthians, "I planted, Apollos watered, but God gave the growth. So neither he who plants nor he who waters is anything, but only God who gives the growth" (1 Corinthians 3:6, 7).

### God Will Vindicate His Servants (4:8–10a)

Beginning in Zechariah 4:8, the prophet draws attention to the painful realities of Israel's present moment. The postexilic community in Zechariah's day is living in a time between promise and fulfillment, a time between small beginnings and great accomplishments. The prophet says, "Then the word of the Lord came to me saying, 'The hands of Zerubbabel have laid the foundation of this house; his hands shall also complete it. Then you will know that the Lord of hosts sent me to you'" (vv. 8, 9).

The message of this oracle is that Zerubbabel will accomplish the reconstruction project that he started. Though Zerubbabel had overseen the laying of the foundation of the temple, progress had ground to a halt, and the erection of the temple had become an impossibility in the minds of the people. It seems likely that the people believed that God would rebuild his temple someday, but surely today is not the day. "Someday, perhaps far in the future, long after we're gone, God may accomplish this great work, but our day is 'the day of small things.'" They wrongly assumed that God did not and perhaps could not do great things in a day of small things. But God responded that the very person who began this work would see its completion. This is a remarkable promise. Zerubbabel, not a king but a mere governor of Judah, would accomplish what even the great King David was not permitted to accomplish.

There seems to have been a sizable group in Zerubbabel's day who doubted, ridiculed, and perhaps even opposed the governor (and no doubt opposed any who encouraged him, like Zechariah) in his endeavor to rebuild the temple. While this would have been profoundly discouraging for both governor and prophet, it should not have been surprising. God's work in the world always confounds the so-called wisdom of the wise. As Paul wrote to the Corinthian church, "God chose what is foolish in the world to shame the wise; God chose what is weak in the world to shame the strong; God chose what is low and despised in the world, even things that are not, to bring to nothing things that are, so that no human being might boast in the presence of God" (1 Corinthians 1:27–29).

The day is coming when those who mocked and laughed at Zerubbabel and the prophets who supported him, despising "the day of small things," will "see the tin stone in the hand of Zerubbabel" (Zechariah 4:10, AT).[12] This tin stone might mark the refoundation or possibly the completion of the temple, but either way it will vindicate Zerubbabel as God's chosen servant, who was faithful in building the house of God. Zerubbabel does not have to worry about vindicating himself, defending himself, or securing his own honor and reputation. In his own good time, God will publicly vindicate his servant.

God will vindicate not just Zerubbabel but Zechariah as well. When Zerubbabel stands with the plumb line in his hand, the prophet who has declared God's word of promise will be revealed to have been faithful and true. This is the test that Israel was to use to discern the true and the false prophet.

When God established the office of prophet for Israel, he instructed them, "When a prophet speaks in the name of the LORD, if the word does not come to pass or come true, that is a word that the LORD has not spoken; the prophet has spoken it presumptuously. You need not be afraid of him" (Deuteronomy 18:22). People in Zechariah's day may very well have questioned his legitimacy. Was Zechariah perhaps a false prophet? Along with the governor, the veracity and integrity of the prophet Zechariah would likewise be vindicated when, in 515 B.C., the temple was rebuilt against all odds and expectations, and worship resumed.

God again would make a way, albeit temporary and provisional, to dwell in the midst of his people for their blessing. Then again Israel would know and see that God was in it all along. In this we're reminded that those who in obedience to God's word labor for God's kingdom will not be put to shame. No matter what the cost personally, professionally, financially, whatever is lost will be returned a hundredfold from the One who is able, as the hymn puts it, "to supply from his own fullness all he takes away."[13]

God's answer to those who have little regard for the small and seemingly insignificant things of the faith is not to supplement these things with what our world would regard as great things, nor are we to pretend that small things are big things. Rather, the answer is to trust God to vindicate himself, his ways, and his people in his perfect time. Zechariah's oracle carries with it a sobering reminder of the danger of despising the day of small things. There is nothing wrong or shameful in living in a time or a place where God appears to be doing very little. The sin and shame come when we despise such a time or place because we have difficulty seeing God's plans or purposes being fulfilled. Zechariah reminds us that God is working even when we can't see it. "As the heavens are higher than the earth, so are my ways higher than your ways and my thoughts than your thoughts" (Isaiah 55:9).

In Zechariah's day, no one would have thought anything of significance was happening in Judah, and any claim to the contrary was downright laughable. And yet it was there in Jerusalem that the sovereign Creator of the universe was making a way to welcome sinners back into his presence. Similarly, 500 years later, very few thought anything of significance was happening in Bethlehem, but in reality the Creator of the world took on flesh and "tabernacled among us" (John 1:14, literal translation) so that he might reveal to us the grace and truth of God. When few thought anything significant could come out of Galilee, the Son of God came to inaugurate a new creation reality. And at the cross, at the very moment Jesus was most despised and rejected by men, God was in fact ransoming sinners and triumphing over forces of evil greater than we could ever comprehend.

How could those whose lives were purchased by an execution on a Roman cross despise small things? God may work equally through small churches and large churches. He may be working as much through outwardly unsuccessful missions as he is through evidently successful missions. He may be doing great things through Christians who seem to be a mess as much as he is through Christians who seem to have it all together. We are not to determine how, when, why, and through whom God accomplishes his purposes. Rather we are to pursue obedience in taking up the means of grace and in loving our neighbors as ourselves, all the while trusting God to bless and to grow our weak endeavors for his glory.

### God Will Sustain His People (4:10b–14)

The prophet's oracles to Zerubbabel and through him to all of Israel are nothing short of glorious. But what do these two oracles announcing God's purpose to build his house and God's work in vindicating his servants have to do with the super-menorah that opens and closes Zechariah's vision? The connection is not immediately clear. As is the case with the other visions, the prophet himself is at a loss as to its significance. In fact, the connection between the vision and the oracles has proven so elusive that some commentators have concluded that the oracles come from a later editor who awkwardly interrupted the visionary material.[14] This, however, misses the significance of how the vision of the menorah and the olive trees works in tandem with the oracles to communicate a critical message to Zerubbabel, Zechariah, and the entire postexilic community.[15]

The vision closes with the angel revealing the significance of the seven lamps, each with seven lips, affixed to the bowl of the golden lampstand: "These seven are the eyes of the LORD, which range through the whole earth" (Zechariah 4:10). The seven lamps, presumably, or perhaps the seven lips of the seven lamps represent the eyes of the Lord.[16] Seven times seven—seven times the number of perfection—represents the scope and completeness of God's sight and therefore his knowledge. The horsemen of the first vision have been transposed into lamps that would have set the room ablaze with light.

In this spectacular and overwhelming vision, the postexilic community would have been reminded that their God does indeed see, does indeed know, and does indeed care about his people. The forty-nine lights (seven times seven) would have brought to mind the Jubilee year, the fiftieth year in which all that had been lost would be restored and all who were bound would be set free. A symbol for the temple in which it stood, the super-menorah was quite literally a brilliant reminder of God's presence with his people.[17] Though the pillar of cloud and fire was gone, the fire of God was alive and well and burning in the midst of his people.

But even after the angel's explanation, there are still questions left unanswered. The prophet inquires again, "What are these two olive trees on the right and the left of the lampstand?" (4:11). Not receiving an answer, he asks again, somewhat more specifically, "What are these two branches of the olive trees, which are beside the two golden pipes from which the golden oil is poured out?" (v. 12). The angel responds, "Do you not know what these are?" The angel asked the same question in verse 5. With this question the prophet is reminded that he is a mere instrument of divine revelation and that there are great mysteries he cannot understand apart from God's revelation to him. If Zechariah has difficulty understanding what he sees, Israel should proceed with caution and humility as they seek to understand God's ways in the world, as should we.

It is only when the prophet acknowledges his lack of knowledge that he is given insight. The angel says, "These are the two anointed ones who stand by the Lord of the whole earth" (v. 14). Theories abound about the identity of these two individuals. The mention of oil associated as it is with the act of anointing has suggested to some that the offices of king and priest are in view. In context, both Zerubbabel and Joshua would make good candidates.[18] The problem with this view, however, is that the Hebrew word translated as "oil" is not the word typically used for oil in anointing. Rather, the Hebrew word refers to new, unmanufactured oil and is found throughout the Old Testament in contexts of agricultural produce. Perhaps more importantly, however, the sons of oil in this passage are not anointed but anointers.[19] That is to say, they are the ones through whom the blessing of God's life-giving and sustaining grace comes. For this reason, prophets (perhaps Haggai and Zechariah) might be more likely candidates, as they would have access to the divine counsel and at times were those who anointed Israel's kings and priests.[20] However, since the context is not one of anointing but rather of supplying the menorah with fuel for "the eyes of the LORD" (v. 12) that range through the earth, these two might refer to heavenly beings like the horsemen in the first vision who patrol the earth as the eyes and ears of the great King.[21] Needless to say, like much in Zechariah's night visions, it's difficult to be certain.

Whoever they are, what we do know for sure is what these anointers are doing: they serve the Lord of the whole earth. More specifically, we know that through their work—or, better, their ministry—they supply the means for the fire of God's gracious presence to burn among his people and never go out. There will be a constant supply of oil that will never run out because it is supplied directly from olive trees.

When the oil for the menorah was dependent upon Israel's obedience in bringing the tithe, that fire was in constant danger of going out. And when through her disobedience Israel's temple was destroyed and its furniture (including the menorah) was carried into exile, the fire of God's presence was extinguished seemingly forever. But God through his prophet reveals that a day is coming in which God's presence with his people will be permanent. God is going to make a way; God will supply the means to cause the fire of his presence to burn brightly and gloriously among his people for their blessing. This is precisely what Christ accomplished in his death when the veil of the temple was torn in two, from top to bottom. The curtain was torn because God, not man, made a way for fallen sinners to be welcomed back into the very presence for which they were created (Mark 15:38; Hebrews 10:19–22).

In Zechariah's vision, we're given a reminder that God has made a way for sinners like us to dwell with him in holy, sweet communion, a bond of fellowship and inexpressible joy, for all eternity. This revelation of God's plans for his people was and is meant to transform how they lived then and how we live in the present. Whatever trials we are enduring today, whatever obstacles, fears, doubts, and anxieties we are facing, though the days may seem like days of small things or our circumstances seem dark, our heavenly Father wants us to know that he is with us. He will never leave us or forsake us; he will be with us always, even to the end of the age.

# 67

# Thy Kingdom Come

ZECHARIAH 5:1—6:8

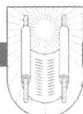

"THE MORE THINGS CHANGE, the more they stay the same." This familiar English proverb comes to us from the French and has become so common in both languages that it is often shortened to simply, "The more things change . . ." or *"Plus ça change . . ."* The rest can be supplied by those familiar not only with the proverb but also with the shared experience the proverb captures.

As with most proverbs, "The more things change, the more things stay the same" has gained currency in numerous cultures and languages because of how well and how memorably it captures a common and somewhat unpleasant experience. Things do change. People change, cultures change, institutions change, circumstances change, governments change. And yet despite the constant and ever-quickening pace of change (dare one say *progress*?) people still display the same old foibles, frailties, and failings. Institutions make the same old mistakes. New governments, having promised brighter days, engage in the same old political posturing, intrigue, and malfeasance as their predecessors. The more things change, the more they in a very real way stay the same.

This proverb would have resonated with God's people in Zechariah's day. Much had indeed changed for postexilic Israel. They had experienced the glorious release from captivity and the even more glorious experience of returning to the land of promise. Israel was no longer under the oppressive tyranny of Babylon, and they had been given a fresh start back in the land of promise with the commission to rebuild the temple of their God. Furthermore, Israel had broken with the disobedience of their forefathers in deep and profound ways as they listened to and obeyed the voice of the Lord delivered through his prophets Haggai and Zechariah. This was certainly a welcome change.

However, though much had changed, much remained the same. Israel still lived in the gap between promise and fulfillment. Though living in the land of promise, postexilic Israel was still a pilgrim people, waiting for the fullness of God's promises to be realized in their midst. They had to live by faith, trusting the promises of God even and especially when they couldn't see or understand how these gracious promises could possibly come to pass. Furthermore, the particular sameness that is in view in this passage is the sameness of God's judgment against sinners. Postexilic Israel was still under the same Mosaic covenant as their forefathers, at the heart of which stood blessings for obedience and curses for disobedience (Leviticus 26; Deuteronomy 28). It was especially the latter, the curses for disobedience, that would have reminded Israel that they were not home yet.

The last three of Zechariah's night visions vividly depict God's response to his people's sin. God will judge sin; he cannot do otherwise. But in his final visions, Zechariah sees that one day God will remove and destroy sin forever. When he does, God's kingdom will be finally and fully established on earth for all eternity.

### Apostates Judged (5:1–4)

Much in keeping with the previous visions, the prophet is immediately confronted with a bizarre, otherworldly, and bewildering sight: "Again I lifted my eyes and saw, and behold, a flying scroll!" (Zechariah 5:1). This scroll that the prophet beholds is unusual in almost every respect. Most obviously, this scroll is flying. Not only is the scroll unusual in its movement, it is unusual in its dimensions. In his response to the angel's query, the prophet observes the scroll's dimensions: "I see a flying scroll. Its length is twenty cubits, and its width ten cubits" (v. 2). In other words, the scroll, presumably unrolled to some extent, is enormous, approximately thirty feet by fifteen feet.[1] Finally, as the angel describes the purpose of the scroll, another surprising feature emerges: the scroll features writing on both sides (v. 3).[2] Since ancient scrolls typically contained writing on only one side, it has been suggested that the writing on both sides of the scroll was perhaps reminiscent of the tablets of testimony delivered to Moses on Mount Sinai.[3]

As described, this is a truly bizarre vision. One can only imagine the bewilderment, if not terror, that the prophet experienced when he saw it. In addition to the uneasiness created by the bizarre and fantastical quality of the scroll, there would no doubt be a profound sense of dread created by the ominous hovering and perhaps the dark shadow cast over the land by the threat of judgment and destruction. But what is the meaning of the gigantic flying scroll with writing on both sides? These bizarre and fantastical features are clearly not the stuff of daily life and experience, so as with most things in Zechariah's night visions, they need to be interpreted symbolically.

Thankfully, the interpreting angel provides the prophet (and us) with insight into its significance when he identifies the scroll as "the curse that goes out over the face of the whole land" (Zechariah 5:3a). This is the divine curse that God has pronounced against sinners wherever they may be found throughout the entirety of the land of Israel. The expression "goes out over the face of the whole land" lends insight to the significance of the scroll's flight and the scroll's size. A flying scroll would have an uninhibited line of sight—a symbol, perhaps, of God's omniscience. There is no sin that goes unnoticed, and no sinner is able to escape God's perfectly righteous judgment. The curses written on this scroll will find their intended target and will clean out "everyone who steals . . . according to what is on one side, and everyone who swears falsely shall be cleaned out according to what is on the other side" (v. 3b).

Commentators have noted that the two particular offenders mentioned—thieves and those who swear falsely—likely represent violators of the two tables of the Law.[4] The Ten Commandments have traditionally been divided in two, with commandments one to four emphasizing duties toward God and commandments five through ten emphasizing duties toward neighbors. The thief in this case represents those who violate their duty toward their neighbors, and the one who swears falsely brings into view those who violate duty toward God whose name was, and often still is, invoked in oath-swearing and vow-taking.

Theft and swearing falsely were often found together and, left unchecked, became a societal cancer. Without a witness, an accusation of theft in ancient Israel could be adjudicated by the accused swearing before God. Such an oath was considered sufficient evidence of innocence. The situation in view is likely that of a thief who is not only willing to steal (which is bad enough) but who is also willing to compound the offense with blasphemy; that is, swearing by the name of Yahweh, Israel's covenant God, that his or her lie is the truth.[5] Though such an offender might escape human judgment, that person, Zechariah is assured, will in no way escape divine judgment.[6] Seeking to build their own houses with wealth and influence, liars and thieves will find their homes utterly consumed, both timber and stone together.

The message of the scroll is fairly straightforward: God is going to purify the land. Even after the Babylonian exile, the promised land to which Israel has returned remained defiled, not because of any stain native to the soil but because its inhabitants are intractably sinful.[7] The message that Zechariah receives in the sixth night vision is that defilement is not the end of the story for the land or for the people. God will judge sin, and one day he will destroy it forever. He will root it out from the land so that its presence will no longer be felt, and its contamination will no longer stain a purified community living in a purified land. The daily injustices and deceptions that have come to plague the postexilic community are not the way things will always be. God sees, and God will act.

In this we are reminded that the covenant curses promised years earlier in the Mosaic covenant are still in effect. Israel may expect covenant blessings for obedience and covenant curses for disobedience. The conditions of the covenant must be kept.

In this sense, the exile had changed nothing in Israel's relationship with God. Their covenantal situation created a longing for a new and better covenant to be inaugurated by a new and better covenant mediator.

### Idolaters Deported (5:5–10)

The transition from the sixth to the seventh night vision is more seamless than the others as the prophet's attention is essentially redirected from the flying scroll to a basket. True to form, however, the prophet is confused about the significance of the vision and inquires as to its meaning, to which the interpreting angel responds, "This is the basket that is going out. . . . This is their iniquity in all the land" (Zechariah 5:6).

On the surface, the message seems clear enough and somewhat in line thematically with the previous vision. However, the seventh vision moves from the bizarre to the macabre as the basket's leaden lid is lifted and the prophet beholds a woman sitting in the basket (Zechariah 5:7). The angel identifies the woman, saying, "This is Wickedness" (v. 8). And then we're told that he "thrust her back into the basket, and thrust down the leaden weight on its opening." The macabre then gives way to the fantastic when the prophet witnesses two women with wings "like the wings of a stork" lifting the basket between earth and Heaven and flying the basket out of sight (v. 9).

It's a somewhat violent scene. It's certainly a disturbing scene. But what does it mean?

Much is enigmatic in this vision, and much promises to preoccupy scholars and students of the Bible for years to come. What, for example, did the prophet see in the basket? Was it an actual woman or, as some have suggested, was it an image or idol of a woman?[8] What is the significance of the basket (literally, an ephah, a unit of measure) and the lead cover? And why do the women transporting the basket have the wings of a stork as opposed to some other bird or even no wings at all?

Fascinating and thought-provoking explanations of the symbolism of the various aspects of this vision abound. Perhaps the woman in the basket (animate or inanimate) is an allusion to Israel's idolatry, which is often cast throughout the Old Testament in terms of marital infidelity. Perhaps the basket and lead cover are a veiled reference to corruption in the marketplace where such units of measure (ephahs and leaden weights) were commonplace. Perhaps the identification of the women with storks connects them to the realm of the unclean, thus making them fit transports for Israel's wickedness. This list of "perhapses" could go on and on.

What can be said with certainty, however, is that this otherworldly vision unmistakably declares a message of hope. While sin is clearly an enormous threat to Israel, we see in this vision its containment and its ultimate removal from the midst of God's people. Israel's iniquity, dangerous as it is, is nevertheless contained in the basket. It is secured by a leaden cover. The angel exercises remarkable power and control over this dangerous reality as he thrusts it into the basket and thrusts the leaden weight over its opening.[9]

This, after all, was the constant struggle for God's people: their intractably sinful hearts and the curse that their sinful hearts deserved. But here in Zechariah 5, God announces that one day sin will be no more. Temptation to sin will be no more. The defilement and corruption of sin will be no more. Sin, rather, will be relegated to a place appropriate to its character. It is understandable, therefore, that the most pressing question for the prophet is, "Where are they taking the basket?" (v. 10), to which the angel responds, "To the land of Shinar, to build a house for it. And when this is prepared, they will set the basket down there on its base" (v. 11).

Shinar was another name for Babylon, and Babylon represented for Israel the archetypal enemy of God and his people.[10] In Babylon would be built a house or temple fitting to house Israel's sin and wickedness, essentially a blasphemous corollary to God's holy temple on Mount Zion. In fact, the various elements of this vision evoke a parody of Israel's true religion, what one commentator summarizes as "an 'anti-ark' carried by 'anti-cherubs' to an 'anti-temple' in an 'anti-Jerusalem.'"[11] In this response the angel declares an ultimate and final separation of the righteous and the wicked, the holy and the unholy, the clean and the unclean.[12]

God will one day separate the righteous—those who belong to him, whom he has called by name and united to his Son by faith and filled with his Spirit—

from the wicked. But God will not only separate his people from the wicked, he will remove the wickedness of his own people once and for all. It's not the people who are going to Babylon; their sin is in a sense being cast into Hell.

When taken together, visions six and seven offer a portrait of the ultimate covenant curse: exile. As Zechariah's generation was no doubt painfully aware, exile consisted of the destruction of home and property and the deportation of people from the land. Israel's exile offered a portrait of cosmic, eschatological judgment.

The last and final judgment that will be rendered with perfect knowledge and unbending righteousness is prefigured in Israel's Babylonian exile, and here in Zechariah it is promised again. The message for Zechariah and postexilic Israel was as clear as it was simple: God will judge sin. The exile has changed nothing in this respect. The covenant that God made with Israel through Moses at Sinai is still in effect, and Zechariah's sixth vision invokes this image of God's covenant curses pursuing and overtaking an unfaithful people. In Deuteronomy 28 God expounds on the blessings that Israel will receive if she obeys the terms of the covenant and the curses that Israel will receive if she violates the terms of the covenant: "If you will not obey the voice of the LORD your God or be careful to do all his commandments and his statutes that I command you today, then all these curses shall come upon you and overtake you" (v. 15).

What could possibly change for the postexilic community such that their history would no longer be a constant cadence of disobedience that leads to a covenant curse? The answer is a new covenant in which the covenant mediator bears the curses so that only blessings are left for God's people.

On the night when he was betrayed, Jesus announced to his disciples this new and better covenant that he would ratify through his own blood: "This cup that is poured out for you is the new covenant in my blood" (Luke 22:20). The blessings and curses of the Mosaic covenant come to their fulfillment in Christ who, though he deserved God's blessings for his perfect obedience, suffered God's curse in place of his people. The lion of Judah became the Lamb of God who once and for all bore away the sins of his people. In the words of the Apostle Paul, "For our sake [God] made him to be sin who knew no sin, so that in [Christ] we might become the righteousness of God" (2 Corinthians 5:21).

Jesus was no thief. Yet he would be crucified as a common criminal, in the company of two thieves, bearing in his body the covenant curse for even such as them. Though truth incarnate, he was condemned as both a blasphemer and a liar by those who swore falsely. Yet these too could find forgiveness in the blood they themselves caused to be shed. To use the theological symbolism of

Zechariah's night vision, on the cross the perfectly innocent Jesus was carried to the house of Shinar, and though he had always worshiped God alone, he suffered the fate of the wicked so that even the most wicked who look to God in faith and seek his forgiveness through Christ might be pursued not by the curses they deserve but by a love they could never imagine.

Because Christ bore our curse, we may sing with the psalmist, "Surely goodness and mercy will follow me all the days of my life, and I shall dwell in the house of the LORD forever" (Psalm 23:6).

### God's Kingdom Come (6:1–8)

Zechariah's penultimate vision of the stork-women and the basket of wickedness creates a tension as it raises the specter of an eternal struggle between two temples, two mountains, two lands, and two peoples—the temple of Yahweh and the people of Yahweh on the one hand, and the temple of wickedness and the people who serve her on the other. Will there ever be ultimate victory?

Zechariah's eighth and final night vision resolves this tension. It is perhaps with this question in his mind that the prophet once again lifts his eyes: "Four chariots came out from between two mountains" (Zechariah 6:1). These are not ordinary mountains. "They are mountains of bronze" (v. 1), apparently serving as a "gateway of heaven."[13]

The night visions opened with the prophet's vision of horses, and here at the conclusion we meet horses again as the four chariots are pulled by horses of different colors—red, black, white, and dappled (Zechariah 6:2, 3).[14] The scenes, however, are strikingly different. Whereas the first vision was characterized by a note of secrecy, with the horsemen gathering in a glen under the cover of darkness provided by the myrtle trees (1:8), the horses and their horsemen in the eighth vision show no such concern for concealment. The horses ride in plain view, no doubt producing a sound like thunder as they ride forth from between two mountains of bronze (6:1). These mountains would be recognized as bronze only in daylight, and daylight striking two bronze mountains would bathe the scene in a nearly blinding riot of sunlight. Furthermore, the mounted horsemen of the first vision were clearly spies (1:10, 11); here in the final vision, the horsemen are charioteers, likely warriors, no longer riding forth in secrecy to gather information but riding forth to declare the establishment of God's kingdom.[15] As before, they are identified as divine messengers, literally "the four winds of heaven who are going forth from standing before the Lord of the whole earth" (6:5, AT).[16] Like the previous horsemen, these wind-chariots are on a mission that is cosmic in scale, encompassing the entire world in its scope.

These heavenly emissaries are depicted as faithful and eager to do God's will. Zechariah observes, "When the strong horses came out, they were impatient to go and patrol the earth" (v. 7). In this we see the fulfillment of the longing of every angel in Heaven and every saint who has ever lived and prayed, "Thy kingdom come, Thy will be done, in earth, as it is in heaven" (Matthew 6:10, KJV). These emissaries are eager to see God's kingdom established not only in Israel but throughout the entire world.

Sometime after the mighty horses and chariots have set out on their patrol, the angel cries out in a loud voice, "Behold, those who go toward the north country have set my Spirit at rest in the north country" (Zechariah 6:8). Though it is not obvious at first, this angelic cry is an announcement of the Lord's absolute, universal dominion over all the earth. These messengers of the Lord of all the earth establish his victory and declare his peace to its farthest corners (v. 5), and most especially in the north country. Not wanting to traverse the inhospitable desert to the east of Israel, Israel's enemies from the east (e.g., Babylon) would typically come against them from the north. "The north country" refers, therefore, to the most hostile and dangerous forces that would set themselves against Israel and against her God.[17]

Thus Zechariah's final vision is an announcement that all the wickedness, idolatry, and rebellion symbolized so powerfully in the temple of wickedness in Babylon will one day be subdued, overwhelmed, and destroyed by Yahweh's kingdom. As the Lord's chariots go forward to the four winds of Heaven, they go in the power of the Spirit, and as the angel announces to the prophet, "They have set my Spirit at rest in the north country" (v. 8). The subjugation of the north country represents the ultimate triumph over the greatest enemy that Israel faced.

The night visions of Zechariah opened with the horsemen's announcement that "all the earth remains at rest" (1:11), an announcement that elicited from the angel of the Lord the lament, "How long?" (v. 12). It was a world at rest not under the righteous and just dominion of Israel's God and his Messiah but under the dominion of Persia, the latest iteration of a world empire established through the force of violence, manipulation, and oppression. True, Persia was better than Babylon. But as the postexilic community quickly learned, the kingdom of Cyrus, Cambyses, and Darius was a far cry from the kingdom of God. The exile, however, did not annul or change God's promises found, for example, in Psalm 2, which says,

> He who sits in the heavens laughs;
> the Lord holds them in derision.

> Then he will speak to them in his wrath,
> and terrify them in his fury, saying,
> "As for me, I have set my King
> on Zion, my holy hill." (vv. 4–6)

Zechariah's climactic night vision has dramatically announced the coming of God's kingdom. When the kingdom comes, it will come in power, like four horse-drawn chariots thundering out from the presence of their Lord, intent on doing his will perfectly and completely. The power and the glory, the triumph and the dominion of God that Zechariah foresaw, summarized in the expression "set my Spirit at rest" (6:8), would arrive years later in the person and work of King Jesus.[18] With the coming of the King, the kingdom of God drew near and triumphed over the power of sin, death, and all the works of the devil.

Though the kingdom of God was revealed clearly in the earthly ministry of Jesus for those who have eyes to see and ears to hear, it was nevertheless partial, provisionary, and, in a word, veiled. The kingdom of God revealed in Christ's earthly ministry lacked the scope and the finality promised in Zechariah's night vision. Jesus himself would teach his disciples to look forward to another, greater, final advent of the Son, at which time this world order will fall apart and give way to the inbreaking of a new creation and a new kingdom in its consummate glory:

> Immediately after the tribulation of those days the sun will be darkened, and the moon will not give its light, and the stars will fall from heaven, and the powers of the heavens will be shaken. Then will appear in heaven the sign of the Son of Man, and then all the tribes of the earth will mourn, and they will see the Son of Man coming on the clouds of heaven with power and great glory. And he will send out his angels with a loud trumpet call, and they will gather his elect from the four winds, from one end of heaven to the other. (Matthew 24:29–31)

So too in the book of Revelation, John was given a vision of Christ's second coming that is so glorious in splendor and otherworldly in character that he, like Zechariah before him, had to resort to highly figurative and symbolic language:

> Then I saw heaven opened, and behold, a white horse! The one sitting on it is called Faithful and True, and in righteousness he judges and makes war. His eyes are like a flame of fire, and on his head are many diadems, and he has a name written that no one knows but himself. He is clothed in a robe dipped in blood, and the name by which he is called is The Word of God. And the armies of heaven, arrayed in fine linen, white and pure, were

following him on white horses. From his mouth comes a sharp sword with which to strike down the nations, and he will rule them with a rod of iron. He will tread the winepress of the fury of the wrath of God the Almighty. On his robe and on his thigh he has a name written, King of kings and Lord of lords. (Revelation 19:11–16)

The longing so powerfully expressed by the angel of the Lord in Zechariah's first night vision is here in the final vision fulfilled in the last day. The rest for which God's people long will one day be realized in the kingdom of God on earth. It is not a rest realized by any human king or geopolitical kingdom. It will be a kingdom established by the Spirit of God coming to rest even in "the north country" (Zechariah 6:8), that is, overcoming the greatest foes we face in this life.

Christians live by faith. The kingdom of God as it exists in this world (as the Church of Christ) remains imperfect and incomplete. Sin still plagues each of us as we struggle with the lusts of the flesh and the love of this world. Nevertheless, the gospel continues to go forth, and sinners continue to be added to the number of the redeemed, just as Jesus promised: "I will build my church, and the gates of hell shall not prevail against it" (Matthew 16:18). It is with this assurance that we continue to pray, "Thy kingdom come, Thy will be done, on earth as it is in heaven" (Matthew 6:10), until the day when faith becomes sight and Heaven and earth are united under their one King.

# 68

# Behold, Your Priest-King!

ZECHARIAH 6:9–15

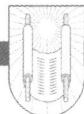

"POWER TENDS TO CORRUPT and absolute power corrupts absolutely."[1] History has proven the truth of Lord Acton's insight more times than we could possibly count and more times than most of us would wish to remember. Absolute power in the hands of sinful humanity results inevitably and always in abuse, oppression, injustice, or violence of one sort or another.

It was in part a concern over such tyrannical abuses of power that motivated the framers of the United States Constitution to distribute power between three branches of the federal government in an attempt to limit the abuse that attends the concentration of power in one individual or institution.[2] This was also in part the reason for God's laws for ancient Israel that strictly separated royal authority from priestly authority. Israel's kings must come from the line and the tribe of Judah, and Israel's priests from the line and tribe of Levi. Judahites and Levites, kings and priests—never the twain shall meet in the days of the old covenant. Israel's kings could not hold the office of priest, and Israel's priests could not hold the office of king.

This reality serves as the background for the astonishing announcement that Zechariah declares literally in the most dramatic of ways. In Zechariah 6:9, the Lord instructs his prophet to perform a prophetic sign-act, that is, a drama the actions and elements of which are highly symbolic and serve as a prophecy to and for Israel.[3] Like Hosea whose marriage to a prostitute vividly depicted Israel's intractably wayward hearts, or Ezekiel whose bizarre diet and sleeping arrangements foretold the destruction of Jerusalem, so it is with Zechariah's crowning of the high priest Joshua.[4] God instructs his prophet to perform what is essentially a drama in which he announces the future union of the two offices—the kingship and the priesthood—in one person: namely, the messianic Branch. It would be through the once-for-all work of this single individual that God's purposes of redeeming his people and ruling over his people—priestly and kingly actions, respectively—would be accomplished.

The prophet's message is so astonishing, if not scandalous, that the opening notice is critical: "The word of the LORD came to me" (6:9). Zechariah emphasizes that the drama he performs is not his own script or the product of his own imagination but is from God. The drama is God's script, God's idea, and therefore it announces God's message to his people. This Messiah who would come (and we know has come) in the person of Jesus of Nazareth would come as *both* priest and king. As Israel's Priest-King, he would fulfill both royal and priestly functions so that God's people would not need to approach him through any other priest, and God's people would be ruled by no other king.

## A Crown (6:9, 10)

Central to the dramatic action is a newly fashioned crown. The prophet is commanded to "take from the exiles Heldai, Tobijah, and Jedaiah, who have arrived from Babylon, and go the same day to the house of Josiah, the son of Zephaniah. Take from them silver and gold, and make a crown, and set it on the head of Joshua, the son of Jehozadak, the high priest" (Zechariah 6:10, 11).

Though we don't know much about the individuals Heldai, Tobijah, and Jedaiah, we do know that they are from Babylon, that they've come to Jerusalem, and that they've come bearing gifts or tribute for the temple. It seems unlikely that the gold and silver were their personal tribute; more likely they were a gift and tribute from and on behalf of the Jews who remained in Babylon to support the temple rebuilding project.[5] These three—Heldai, Tobijah, and Jedaiah—therefore function in the drama as representatives of the covenant community who remain in exile.

Having received their tribute of gold and silver, the prophet is commanded to go to the house of Josiah, son of Zephaniah, who is to fashion a crown. Again, uncertainty abounds. Presumably Josiah, son of Zephaniah was a metalworker of sorts such that his house would be the appropriate place to fashion a crown of gold and silver. As is the case with most prophetic sign-acts, the meaning or significance of the drama is far from self-evident. Thus Biblical sign-acts were typically accompanied by an interpretive word that expounded the significance of the dramatic action. However, before we pass too quickly to the interpreting word, it is important to consider the significance of the embassy bearing tribute.

It has been noted that a composite crown of silver and gold was unusual in the ancient world, and its significance probably had less to do with the symbolism of its wearer's glory and more to do with its fulfillment of God's promises.[6] Not long prior to this event, the Lord had declared to Zerubbabel through the prophet Haggai, "I will shake all nations, so that the treasures of all nations shall come in, and I will fill this house with glory, says the Lord of hosts. The silver is mine, and the gold is mine, declares the Lord of hosts. The latter glory of this house shall be greater than the former, says the Lord of hosts. And in this place I will give peace, declares the Lord of hosts" (Haggai 2:7–9). All the treasures of the earth belong to the Lord, and one day these treasures will flow into God's house, a public display of God's kingship and glory.

With the tribute in Zechariah, we see small beginnings of the fulfillment of God's promise through Haggai.[7] The silver and the gold of the nations have begun to make their way to Jerusalem as tribute to Israel's God and King. What begins as a trickle will one day become a torrent when the wealth of this world flows into the house of God and his kingship/kingdom is revealed in its glory.

Those who had eyes to see in Zechariah's day beheld a token or foretaste of this glorious work. God would beautify his temple, and the world would acknowledge Israel's God as the Lord to whom belongs all things. Thus this crown belongs to God and represents God's kingship.

Notice, however, the means by which this gold and the glory it represents come to the house of God. It is through exiles who return bearing tribute to their king.

The epicenter of God's redemptive work in this world would not be in the great halls of power found in Babylon and Susa, Alexandria and Persepolis. Rather, it would be from the city of God's choosing, and it would be through those who by faith returned to rebuild the temple.[8] Few would have thought that Jerusalem was the right place for such a crown and such a promise. But again, God had chosen the weak things of this world to shame the wise, as he would "again choose Jerusalem" (Zechariah 1:17) to be the place of his dwelling. Jerusalem would again be the place where God could be found to be gracious and merciful.

Though God is everywhere at all times (what theologians call his omnipresence), he is found to be gracious and merciful only in the time, place, and means he appoints. In Zechariah's day, it would be through the ministry of God's temple, foreshadowing the ministry of his Son, that God's grace would be apprehended by faith. Though from a human perspective Jerusalem was of little significance on the stage of human affairs, from God's perspective

Jerusalem was the place that he had appointed to establish his kingdom. From this unlikely city God's kingdom would expand throughout the entire world. In this composite crown we catch a glimpse of the coming King and his glorious kingship.

## A Coronation (6:11–13)

Though the drama begins with the receiving of tribute from the exiles and continues with the crafting of a composite crown by Josiah, clearly the climax of the drama comes with the coronation of Joshua, the high priest. As the prophet Zechariah places this crown, newly fashioned of silver and gold, on the head of Joshua, he is told to announce to Joshua and all present (presumably to Heldai, Tobijah, and Jedaiah, and most likely others), "Behold, the man whose name is the Branch" (6:11, 12).[9] This identification of Joshua with the Branch connects this prophecy to the fourth night vision of chapter 3:1–10. There the priests themselves were designated a sign or a portent of this messianic Branch who was to come.

This theme is picked up again here in Zechariah 6. But strikingly and surprisingly, it is Joshua alone who is crowned as the Branch, thus connecting the future messianic figure not only to the priesthood but also to the kingship, since both the crown and the task assigned to the Branch—namely, temple building—were distinctly royal prerogatives: "He shall branch out from his place, and he shall build the temple of the LORD. It is he who shall build the temple of the LORD and shall bear royal honor, and shall sit and rule on his throne. And there shall be a priest on his throne, and the counsel of peace shall be between them both" (6:12, 13).[10]

Though it contains an extraordinary message of hope and comfort for the postexilic community, there is nevertheless something quite scandalous about this drama. Priests could not be kings, and kings could not be priests. A man could be from the tribe of Judah or he could be from the tribe of Levi, but he could not be from both. Thus the Law of Moses did not have legislation for such a dual office and could not anticipate such a figure from within its structures. The reason for this is not specified; however, it does not seem to be at all a stretch to imagine that, at least in part, the division of authority in Israel was designed to prevent the abuse and oppression endemic to kings who would wield absolute authority.

The fact that the office of a priest-king was prohibited by the Mosaic law did not stop Israel's kings from assuming priestly prerogatives and authorities for themselves that often, if not always, resulted in disastrous consequences. Saul, the newly minted king, bristled at waiting for the prophet Samuel to offer sacrifices during war and sinfully offered the sacrifices himself (1 Samuel 13:8–14). No sooner had Jeroboam assumed kingship over the northern kingdom than he set up rival temples and a rival cult to prevent his people from traveling to Jerusalem to worship. He himself assumed priestly prerogatives, offering sacrifices at the altars that he had made (1 Kings 12:32–34). Even the good King Uzziah was led astray by the temptation to such comprehensive authority. In 2 Chronicles we read about Uzziah that "when he was strong, he grew proud, to his destruction. For he was unfaithful to the Lord his God and entered the temple of the Lord to burn incense on the altar of incense" (26:16). Tragically, Uzziah was struck down with leprosy, disqualifying him from public worship for the rest of his life (vv. 19, 22).

For Israel's kings, the great attraction of priestly authority was the desire for total and complete authority over every sphere of Israel's life. As it stood, the king's authority came to an end at the temple courtyard. The king needed the priests to approach God in worship and to experience the blessing of God's presence. Kings needed priests, and priests needed kings. All of Israel needed both, priests and kings. They needed kings to rule them in righteousness and justice as faithful undershepherds of their divine King and heavenly shepherd. And Israel needed priests to represent them before God in their prayers and to offer sacrifices to God on their behalf. Total, complete authority in the hands of a single sinful individual could end only in disaster. Distributed power could bless and sustain Israel until, in the fullness of time, the One qualified to hold both offices and perform both functions perfectly and completely would come to his people.

In Zechariah's prophetic sign-act, God declared that when Messiah comes, he will unite these two offices of priest and king, and will execute both with faithfulness and righteousness (6:13).[11] There will be a Priest-King sitting on the throne and serving in the temple. This was not a possibility according to the Mosaic covenant, and yet this was a necessity for the consummation of God's kingdom. The salient point, therefore, is that the work of the messianic Priest-King required the abrogation of the old covenant and the inauguration of a new one.

In this we see the temporary character of the Mosaic covenant. That covenant was never meant to last forever; it was never intended to be God's final word to his people. The Mosaic covenant had woven into it its own annulment when its conditions would be fulfilled. Its types and shadows would give way to the substance and fulfillment in the Messiah.

Joshua was not the priest-king any more than Zerubbabel, conspicuously absent from this drama, was the priest-king. However, Joshua, the crowned high priest, symbolized this coming figure, this royal Branch who would "branch out from his place" and "build the temple of the LORD" (Zechariah 6:12).

When the priest takes his seat on the royal throne, "a counsel of peace shall be between them both" (v. 13). Though some have suggested that "them both" refers to the priest and the king, two figures who would rule jointly as co-messiahs, the absence of Zerubbabel from the scene strongly suggests that the union of the two offices in one person is in view.[12] The result of this enthronement of the messianic Priest-King will be the establishment of a counsel of peace, that is, a rule characterized by things that cultivate human flourishing.

King David was prevented from building God's temple on account of his reign being characterized by bloodshed.[13] That privilege would fall to his offspring, whose reign would be characterized by peace: first Solomon and then the One of whom Solomon was a type (1 Chronicles 22:8, 9). The reign of the messianic Priest-King would be characterized by the peace requisite for a final, consummate temple-building.

### A Memorial (6:14)

Though the prophetic sign-act reaches its climax in the symbolic coronation of Joshua as a priest-king, the drama is not yet finished. After the prophet performs the coronation and announces his message, the Lord instructs him to place the crown in the temple of the Lord "as a reminder to Helem, Tobijah, Jedaiah, and Hen the son of Zephaniah" (Zechariah 6:14). There is a great deal of uncertainty as to why the names of these individuals only partially match the names of those mentioned earlier. Perhaps we're dealing with nicknames or, in the case of Hen, titles.[14] What is certain, however, is that the crown is to have an ongoing function in the life of God's covenant people. The prophet's message and its attending sign-act have been designed to minister to God's people for generations to come.[15]

This, I suspect, would have signaled to Heldai, Tobijah, and Jedaiah that the fulfillment of God's promise to raise up the Branch and, through him, to build the Lord's house might lie a long way off. Therefore, they (and perhaps their children and grandchildren) would benefit from a memorial to remind them that the Messiah, the Deliverer of Israel, would indeed come.

The sad fact of the matter is that memories fade, doubts creep into the human heart, and people would begin to wonder, *Are God's promises true?* Knowing the frailty and weakness of the human heart, God in his kindness often accompanies his gracious promises with signs meant to remind his people of the truthfulness and the certainty of his word.

When God promised that he would make Abraham the father of many nations, would give his offspring the land of Canaan as an everlasting possession, and would be their God (Genesis 17:4–8), he accompanied his promise with the institution of circumcision, which, among other things, served as a reminder that God's gracious covenant was for Abraham and for his children after him, throughout their generations (v. 10). When God promised to spare Israel's firstborn from the angel of death who would pass through Egypt, he gave them a sign in the form of the Passover feast, which would become a yearly memorial in which Israel remembered God's deliverance from Egypt and looked forward to an even greater deliverance to come (Exodus 12:43—13:10). When Israel crossed the Jordan to enter the promised land, God commanded Joshua to erect memorials of twelve stones, according to the number of the tribes, on the bank of the river and in the midst of the river to serve as reminders of God's faithfulness to bring them into the promised land (Joshua 4:1–10).

Even now, these physical, tangible signs represent something of God's redemptive purposes in this world. They are expressions of God's infinite compassion and fatherly condescension. As the One who "knows our frame . . . [and] remembers that we are dust" (Psalm 103:14), God knows that the trials and difficulties of this present evil age can drown out the realities of his promises. So God graciously accompanies his promises with memorials designed to reorient his often-disoriented people to the truth of his word.

Like Israel before us, we too can be given to doubt and unbelief as we wonder if the gospel is true. And like Israel before us, God stoops down to offer signs and seals to his covenant of grace.

Thus in the waters of baptism, God vividly depicts the cleansing by Christ's blood shed for sinners. In the bread and wine of the Lord's Supper, Jesus offers his body and blood to be received by faith. More than memorials, God provides these sacraments as means by which he proclaims the grace of the gospel to sinners and assures their hearts of the realities represented. The Heidelberg Catechism speaks of this assurance powerfully with the little expression "*as certainly as* . . ." in the answers to questions 69 and 75:

**Question 69:** How it signified and sealed unto you in holy baptism that you have part in the one sacrifice of Christ on the cross?

**Answer:** Thus, that Christ has appointed this outward washing with water, and has joined therewith this promise, that I am washed with his blood and Spirit from the pollution of my soul, that is, from all my sins, *as certainly as* I am washed outwardly with water whereby commonly the filthiness of the body is taken away (emphasis mine).

**Question 75:** How is it signified and sealed unto you in the Holy Supper that you partake of the one sacrifice of Christ on the cross and all his benefits?

**Answer:** Thus, that Christ has commanded me and all believers to eat of this broken bread, and to drink of this cup, and has joined therewith these promises: First, that his body was offered and broken on the cross for me, and his blood shed for me, *as certainly as* I see with my eyes the bread of the Lord broken for me, and the cup communicated to me; and, further, that with his crucified body and shed blood he himself feeds and nourishes my soul to everlasting life, *as certainly as* I receive from the hand of the minister, and taste with my mouth, the bread and cup of the Lord, which are given me as certain tokens of the body and blood of Christ (emphases mine).

An assured people is not indicative of presumption or arrogance but is a testimony to God's love and goodness. In the same way that a child's assurance of his or her parents' love is a testimony to the parents' goodness and faithfulness to that child, so it is with believers. God delights in an assured people because he loves us and because our assurance of his love for us testifies to his fatherly care.

The memorial crown in Zechariah's day served its purpose of pointing Israel to the Priest-King who was to come. The waters of baptism and the bread and wine of the Lord's Supper continue to serve this purpose of pointing us to the Savior who has come, and to the same Savior who is coming again, just as he promised (Acts 1:11).

### A Response (6:15)

In Zechariah 6, we see that this sign and this word and this work of temple-building is not only for the benefit of the Branch and the Jews who have returned to the land. The prophet expands the scope of the work: "Those who are far off shall come and help to build the temple of the Lord" (v. 15). Who does the prophet have in view with the designation "those who are far off"? While some have suggested this refers to Diaspora Jews—those who did not return to the land after the exile—the expression and its near synonyms that appear in other places in the prophetic literature typically refer to the Gentile nations.[16]

There will be magnetism to Israel's obedience in building the temple. Those who are not Israelites by birth or members of the covenant community by birth nevertheless will be drawn to the work because of the greatness of Israel's God and the righteousness of his rule. Israel's act of temple-building is going to include those who are far off. The peoples and nations who are not part of the postexilic community will in some way contribute to the construction of God's habitation on earth.

The nations joining Israel in building the temple and in the worship of God, which is the great goal of it all, will vindicate God as that work fulfills his promises made generations earlier, and it will vindicate Zechariah as a true prophet who faithfully declared the at times unbelievable word of the Lord. So Zechariah says, "You shall know that the LORD of hosts has sent me to you" (6:15). Then, invoking the same typological works principle that he did in his vision of the high priest, he says, "This shall come to pass, if you will diligently obey the voice of the LORD your God".[17] Joshua is a type of the Priest-King to come, and his obedience in temple-building will serve as a pointer to the greater temple builder to come.

One commentator put it well when he wrote, "In view of what the symbolic act itself signified, this promise must refer to something far greater than anything that happened during the building of Zerubbabel's temple."[18]

There is no indication that Joshua, Zerubbabel, or anyone else exercised both priestly and kingly authority in Zechariah's day. And it is hardly the case that the nations came streaming to assist in the temple rebuilding efforts in Zechariah's day or anyone else's day thereafter. To what, then, does Zechariah's prophecy refer? Though Zechariah's prophecy and promise find their penultimate fulfillment in the construction of the second temple, their ultimate fulfillment is found in the advent of Jesus, the true temple, and his Church that is built of "living stones" (1 Peter 2:5) and is united to him by faith.

The temple that Jesus would build is not a temple of wood and stone but the temple of his body, torn down on the cross and rebuilt by the power of the Spirit in his resurrection. The fulfillment of Zechariah's prophecy therefore may be seen in the incorporation of Gentiles into the kingdom of God, an influx that began at Pentecost and continues to this day.[19] No one was qualified to don the crown that sat in the temple until Jesus came as Israel's king from the tribe of Judah and a priest according to the order of Melchizedek. As the perfectly righteous, perfectly faithful Priest-King, the resurrected and ascended Jesus reigns over his people at his Father's right hand and intercedes for them with his blood that, as the author of Hebrews reminds us, purifies "our conscience from dead works to serve the living God" (9:14).

# 69

# Mourning into Dancing, Fasting into Feasting

ZECHARIAH 7—8

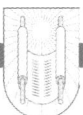

GOOD TEACHERS KNOW that sometimes questions need answers, and other times questions need questions. Throughout his earthly ministry Jesus often responded to questions with questions of his own. The rich young ruler, for example, asked Jesus, "Good teacher, what must I do to inherit eternal life?" (Mark 10:17). Jesus replied, "Why do you call me good? No one is good except God alone" (v. 18). When Nicodemus inquired about the new birth, asking, "How can these things be?" (John 3:9). Jesus responded, "Are you the teacher of Israel and yet you do not understand these things?" (v. 10). When James and John asked to sit on Jesus's right and left hand in glory, Jesus replied with a question of his own: "Are you able to drink the cup that I drink, or to be baptized with the baptism with which I am baptized?" (Mark 10:38). Why not just answer the question? Ever the consummate teacher, Jesus's questions were designed to penetrate to the heart of the matters that burdened, confused, or spiritually blinded his conversation partners, thereby revealing the real issues at stake and the things that mattered most.

Centuries earlier, God imbued his prophet Zechariah with the same spiritual discernment and penetrating insight. In Zechariah 7, the prophet responds to a question from a Jewish embassy with questions of his own. Sharezer, Regem-Melech, and their men had been sent from Bethel to Jerusalem to ask the prophets and priests of the city, "Should I weep and abstain in the fifth month, as I have done for so many years?" (v. 3).[1] As was customary with questions of Israelite law and ritual observance that were not directly addressed by the

Torah, the priests' judgment was sought out. The question here concerns ritual mourning. The weeping and abstaining (from food) were expressions of sorrow and contrition. As is often the case, there is a question behind the question. For the embassy from Bethel, the question behind the question was, "Is our exile almost over?"[2]

The embassy's question clearly has in view Israel's future. It is, in a sense, a question quite similar to that of Jesus's disciples when they asked the resurrected Christ, "Lord, will you at this time restore the kingdom to Israel?" (Acts 1:6). The answer that comes in Zechariah 7, however, directs Israel's attention to her past. Why does the prophet answer this way? Israel must first learn the lessons from her past before she can be in a position to embrace the grace of God in the present and to enjoy the salvation in store for her in the future.

### The Demands of the Law (7)

From the outset, we observe not only the embassy's question but also their purpose in asking it. "Now the people of Bethel had sent Sharezer and Regemmelech and their men *to entreat the favor of the Lord*" (Zechariah 7:2). The postexilic community living in and around Jerusalem was keenly and painfully aware that though they were recipients of God's grace and favor, though they had returned to the land of promise in fulfillment of God's faithfulness and mercy, nevertheless there was a greater grace and greater favor yet to come. To put it another way, though they had returned home, they were not home yet. Though they had returned from exile, there was a greater return yet to be realized, and it was for this final, consummate realization of God's kingdom that they longed.[3]

The sorrow that attended Israel's exile and longing for God's forgiveness and restoration both during their exile and afterward had produced the custom of ritual mourning and fasting to commemorate the great events that led to their punishment in exile. As the date formula of Zechariah 7:1 indicates, the seventy years that Jeremiah had prophesied for Israel's exile is coming to an end and the embassy wants to know, "Is it close? Is the kingdom almost here?"

Through his prophet, God responds to his people's question, "Should I weep and abstain in the fifth month?" (Zechariah 7:3), with a question of his own: "When you fasted and mourned in the fifth month and in the seventh, for these seventy years, was it for me that you fasted? And when you eat and when you drink, do you not eat for yourselves and drink for yourselves?" (vv. 5, 6). In this response, God reconfigures the breadth and depth of the question. It's not just weeping and abstaining; it's fasting and mourning as well. And it's not just in the fifth month but the fifth and the seventh months. God goes on to say, in effect, "Let's not just talk about abstaining and fasting—let's also talk about eating and drinking. Why do you do any of it?" God's response addresses not just ritual fasting in one month but the entirety of Israel's outward expression of mourning and contrition, of sorrow and penitence.[4] God's question cuts through outward ritual to the posture and disposition of the heart.

Israel's law always addressed not only outward behavior but inward heart motivation as well. It was not enough to be circumcised in the flesh of the foreskin. Moses had commanded Israel to "circumcise therefore the foreskin of your heart" (Deuteronomy 10:16). What was the postexilic community's motivation for their fasting and mourning? God asked, "Was it for me?" The fact of the matter was that God had never commanded Israel to weep and abstain or fast or mourn over the exile in the fifth month, the seventh month, or any other month for that matter. These were human traditions, not inherently wrong but potentially distracting from the weightier matters of the Law.

Instead of focusing on what God had not commanded, he instead directs Israel's attention to what he had commanded: "Thus says the LORD of hosts, Render true judgments, show kindness and mercy to one another, do not oppress the widow, the fatherless, the sojourner, or the poor, and let none of you devise evil against another in your heart" (Zechariah 7:9, 10). These words are hardly original to Zechariah. On the contrary, the prophet here plants himself firmly within the stream of the Israelite prophetic tradition, echoing the message of his prophetic forebears.

Centuries earlier, the prophet Samuel had announced the Lord's rejection of King Saul, saying, "Has the LORD as great delight in burnt offerings and sacrifices, as in obeying the voice of the LORD? Behold, to obey is better than sacrifice, and to listen than the fat of rams" (1 Samuel 15:22). The prophet Micah had asked,

> With what shall I come before the LORD,
>     and bow myself before God on high?
> Shall I come before him with burnt offerings,
>     with calves a year old?
> Will the LORD be pleased with thousands of rams,
>     with ten thousands of rivers of oil?
> Shall I give my firstborn for my transgression,
>     the fruit of my body for the sin of my soul? (Micah 6:6, 7)

To these questions the prophet uttered the famous words, "He has told you, O man, what is good; and what does the LORD require of you, but to do justice, and to love kindness, and to walk humbly with your God?" (v. 8).

Zechariah's response to the envoy from Bethel rehearses the law of God that was known to every Israelite and indeed every human being created in God's image. What God cares about is not outward, formal, ritual action but sincere and heartfelt obedience to his word as the fruit of genuine faith. Israel was to care for the weak and vulnerable in their midst, represented here by the widow, the fatherless, the sojourner, and the poor (Zechariah 7:10). This is an elaboration of that comprehensive summary, "You shall love your neighbor as yourself" (Leviticus 19:18).

But the prophet doesn't stop at correcting Israel's misplaced priorities and revealing the true demands of God's Law. He also points Israel to the dreadful consequences of faithlessness and disobedience by pointing to her painful history. Zechariah reminds the postexilic community of their forefathers, the preexilic community who refused to heed God's word and obey God's Law. The prophet describes their disobedience with vivid metaphors: they "turned a stubborn shoulder and stopped their ears that they might not hear. They made their hearts diamond-hard lest they should hear the law and the words that the LORD of hosts had sent by his Spirit through the former prophets" (Zechariah 7:11, 12). These images of stubborn shoulders, stopped ears, and diamond-hard hearts all highlight the willfulness and intentionality of Israel's sin and rebellion.

While often attending to the outward and visible expressions of obedience, Israel's forefathers neglected the deeper and weightier matters of love of God and love of neighbor. The destruction and devastation of the Babylonian conquest was not the result of misunderstanding or miscommunication, much less coincidence or misfortune. The Babylonian conquest of Israel was an expression of God's anger against his people's willful disobedience and culpable ignorance. "Therefore great anger came from the LORD of hosts" (Zechariah 7:12).[5] In an expression of divine justice, Israel experienced the fitting sentence of divine silence: "As I called and they would not hear, so they called, and I would not hear" (v. 13). The result was literally devastating. God's chosen people were scattered among foreign nations, and their home and land were left desolate and destroyed.

What was the postexilic community to learn from this history lesson? God was not rebuking his people for ritual mourning and fasting but was pressing them to consider its purpose and to warn them about allowing outward, man-made rituals to displace true religion and the necessary acts of loving service toward God and neighbor. Outward action apart from inward faith is worthless in the eyes of the One who observes the thoughts and intentions of hearts.[6] Expressions of sorrow over sin apart from renewed obedience profit nothing.

The same applies to us, as James reminds us: "Religion that is pure and undefiled before God the Father is this: to visit orphans and widows in their affliction, and to keep oneself unstained from the world" (1:27). The postexilic community was warned against believing the illusion that they had peace with God through outward formalities and rituals. Peace with God, true peace, comes only through faith and the obedience that inevitably flows from it.

Israel's question revealed not only a misunderstanding about what God really cares about (obedience rather than sacrifice) but also a misunderstanding of the relationship between their working and their future glory. At the end of the day, the postexilic community would no more usher in the kingdom of God by their ritual mourning than by their temple-building.[7] Nor would their obedience and good works be the catalyst for the arrival of God's kingdom on earth. Israel's calling was not to know the day or the hour of Messiah's coming but to live by faith and to bear the fruit of obedience in keeping with that faith, obedience that expresses itself in loving and sacrificial service to others.

### The Grace of the Gospel (8)

The sudden transition from stern warning in Zechariah 7 to unconditional gospel promises in chapter 8 reminds us that God's kingdom will come not as a result of Israel's (or our) obedience but as a result of God's gracious promise. Notice that at no point are conditions given. God does not say, "*If you obey my voice*, I will return to Zion." Rather, God simply announces the good news of the gospel, that apart from Israel's works of the Law, God has purposed to restore and renew his covenant people in accord with his gracious promises. It is not Israel's unfaithfulness in the past that determines their future but God's faithfulness to his promises.[8]

God's ultimate purpose for Israel is not fasting but feasting. In a series of prophetic oracles, God reveals something of the glory and grandeur of the kingdom that he is about to establish. This kingdom will stand in stark contrast to Israel's present hardships, as God is going to transform those hardships into unimaginable blessings.

### *New City (8:1–8)*

When God speaks of being "jealous for Zion with great jealousy" and being "jealous for her with great wrath" (Zechariah 8:2), he is speaking about his holy zeal for his own honor and for his own people to whom he has bound himself in covenant and upon whom he has placed his name. Like a husband's passion for his wife's honor and well-being, so God declares once again his unwavering, passionate commitment to Zion, his holy city, and to her citizens who find protection within her walls. Though God's jealousy is expressed in his protection of and provision for his people, that same jealousy is expressed in his great wrath against all who stand opposed to him or who threaten those who belong to him.[9]

Because of Israel's sin, God had abandoned Zion in the days of their forefathers. But here again God declares his presence with his people who had returned to Jerusalem, and he declares his intention to once again dwell in their midst (v. 3). God's presence will utterly transform the holy city that in Zechariah's day lay in ruins—a visible, tangible, painful reminder of Israel's failure to keep faith with her God.

Jerusalem had been destroyed because of Israel's sin. But God declares that Jerusalem will be rebuilt into a metropolis the likes of which this world has never seen because of his gracious presence. Jerusalem will be so transformed from ruin to glory that she will become known by a new name: "faithful." The city that was once called a faithless city will be called "the faithful city." This "mountain of the LORD of hosts" will be called, rightly and properly, "the holy mountain" (v. 3).

God accompanied these promises, which would have seemed completely impossible when they were uttered, with a depiction of a city so full of life and joy that it would have utterly astonished the prophet's original hearers. The author of the poems of Lamentations (maybe the prophet Jeremiah) opens that book of sorrow with these words:

> How lonely sits the city
> that was full of people!
> How like a widow has she become,
> she who was great among the nations!
> She who was a princess among the provinces
> has become a slave. (Lamentations 1:1)

Between the days of Jeremiah, when these poems were written, and the days of Zechariah, not much had changed. The city was still a sight to behold for its ruins, a heartbreaking testimony to her bygone glory and the unfaithfulness that brought this devastation upon her.

Into this scene of sin and woe, ruin and sorrow, God speaks his word of promise: "Old men and old women shall again sit in the streets of Jerusalem, each with staff in hand because of great age. And the streets of the city shall be full of boys and girls playing in its streets" (Zechariah 8:4, 5). No longer will lives be cut short by wars and illness, plagues and famines. Men and women will grow old, using staffs to move about because of their great age. The streets will be full of boys and girls, no doubt laughing, playing, and running. Children running and playing, shouting and laughing, serve as a symbol of joy and a future for the city. Old men and old women serve as a symbol of the safety and provision of this transformed city. What about the middle-aged adults? Perhaps their presence is implied through merism; the mention of the young and the old implies everything in between. Or perhaps their absence suggests that neither the young nor the old are in need of the protection or provision typically associated with middle-aged adults in this new Jerusalem.[10]

This portrait of a city transformed, renewed, and, in a sense, brought from death to life seemed like an impossibility to those living amidst its rubble and ruins.[11] To those prone to doubt, the Lord said, "If it is marvelous in the sight of the remnant of this people in those days, should it also be marvelous in my sight, declares the LORD of hosts?" (v. 6). God was saying, in effect, "Don't limit your vision of what I can do with what you think is possible." As Jesus would put it years later, "What is impossible with man is possible with God" (Luke 18:27). The One who is both strong and faithful would certainly accomplish all he had promised to do.

This is precisely how Zechariah's oracle concludes, with a reminder that God will fulfill his covenant promises summarized simply and powerfully throughout the Old Testament with the words: "They shall be my people, and I will be their God" (Jeremiah 32:38). Regarding those who had been scattered to Egypt in the east and Assyria/Babylon in the west, the Lord says, "Behold, I will save my people from the east country and from the west country, and I will bring them to dwell in the midst of Jerusalem. And they shall be my people, and I will be their God, in faithfulness and in righteousness" (Zechariah 8:7, 8). Those who had been scattered in judgment would be gathered in mercy to a new Jerusalem that, in contrast to its state of ruins, would brim with life and joy and peace.

### *New Blessing (8:9–13)*

Beginning in verse 9, Zechariah returns to a theme that he, along with his prophetic colleague Haggai, touches on time and again: the centrality of the temple in God's economy of redemption. Both Haggai and Zechariah labored to instill in the postexilic community—and especially the community's leaders, Joshua and Zerubbabel—a zeal for rebuilding the temple of the Lord. Through his prophets, God has declared in no uncertain terms the function that this temple will have in the life of the community. It will be through the ministry of Israel's temple that God will transform Israel's curses into blessings.

Haggai proclaimed this same message in what was likely his first public prophecy, recorded in Haggai 1:2–11. Zechariah refers back to Haggai and perhaps others when he declares, "Let your hands be strong, you who in these days have been hearing these words from the mouth of the prophets who were present on the day that the foundation of the house of the Lord of hosts was laid, that the temple might be built" (Zechariah 8:9).[12] This command to be strong was a call to faithfulness and courage issued to God's covenant servants such as Joshua and Zerubbabel. But here it is issued to all "who were present on the day that the foundation of the house of the Lord of hosts was laid" (v. 9).

Though the temple was not even close to complete, the laying of the foundation served, as it were, as the switch that was flipped, as the moment when God replaced his covenant curses with his covenant blessings, and the difference for Israel could not be more evident. Prior to the temple foundation, or as Zechariah puts it, "before those days" (Zechariah 8:10), Israel experienced the curses of the covenant in countless ways, both large and small, and the general experience of all their labors was that of futility. God describes it like this: "There was no wage for man or any wage for beast, neither was there any safety from the foe for him who went out or came in, for I set every man against his neighbor" (v. 10). However, those days are now a thing of the past as God says, "*Now* I will not deal with the remnant of this people as in the former days, declares the Lord of hosts. For there shall be a sowing of peace. The vine shall give its fruit, and the ground shall give its produce, and the heavens shall give their dew. And I will cause the remnant of this people to possess all these things" (vv. 11, 12).

Even before it is complete, the temple serves as the basis for Israel's new relationship with their God, a relationship characterized no longer by divine curses but by divine blessings. Their experience of futility will be transformed into prosperity as now their labors will produce the very thing we all desire from our work: peace: "For there shall be a sowing of peace" (v. 12).

Covenant curses have been replaced by covenant blessings. Why? It would be a mistake to regard Israel's temple-building as God being coerced into blessing Israel. Neither was it meritorious, as if it had an innate value that God must reward or repay. Rather, the temple serves as the catalyst of Israel's blessings because of its ministry. It is the place that God has appointed to dwell with his people as their God. Through the sacrificial offerings, the ritual washings, and the mediation of the priests, God extends his grace and mercy to undeserving sinners.

By means of the temple, God transforms the fate of his people. In place of the cursed fate that they deserve on account of their sin, God grants life and peace and blessings. Those who have been the object of ridicule by the nations will not only be blessed themselves, but in fulfillment of the Abrahamic promise they will turn and bless the very ones who cursed them: "As you have been a byword of cursing among the nations, O house of Judah and house of Israel, so will I save you, and you shall be a blessing" (Zechariah 8:13).

Interestingly, the oracle closes in the same way it opened, with a summons to strength and courage: "Fear not, but let your hands be strong" (v. 13). The grace of God is not license for laziness or passivity. Israel clearly still has work to do. The temple is far from complete. Yet as the people work, they are to do so not to earn God's grace and favor but with gratitude for God's grace and favor already received through the ministry of the temple.[13]

This is in fact the only way we can truly serve God: as those who have apprehended the gospel of the Son and who, in gratitude for a gift we could never earn and can never repay, obey freely out of love for the One who has loved us and given his life for us.

## *New Life (8:14–17)*

The next verses can easily be misunderstood. On the surface, it may sound as if God keeps changing his mind and doesn't quite know what he is doing when he declares, "As I purposed to bring disaster to you when your fathers provoked me to wrath, and I did not relent, says the LORD of hosts, so again have I purposed in these days to bring good to Jerusalem and to the house of Judah; fear not" (Zechariah 8:14, 15).

What are God's purposes for Jerusalem? The key to understanding God's words here is to begin at the end: "Fear not." God's goal for his people is to drive out the fear and anxiety that had perhaps understandably taken root in the hearts and minds of this remnant. This command concluded the previous oracle and is central to the message of this oracle—namely, that Israel might be assured that God's purposes for them are for their good. The Lord's desire for his people to know and to be assured of his love for and commitment to them is at the heart of the comparison between past and present.

God draws his people's attention to their history when, after literally centuries of pleading, imploring, threatening, forgiving, waiting, and entreating, he declared that his judgment was coming.

This is the point of the comparison and the grounds of Israel's assurance: God declares that as surely as he brought disaster upon Israel for their sins, *so surely* will he bring good to Jerusalem. So "fear not."

Both were God's purpose. God purposed to punish Israel for their disobedience to his word, for flouting his covenant. And just as certainly as God's declared curse came upon his people, so his blessing and goodness would come upon them as well.

But there is a critical difference. The cause of God's curse is stated plainly; the cause of God's blessing is not. The cause of God's curse was their forefathers' sin: "Your fathers provoked me to wrath, and I did not relent" (Zechariah 8:14). What is the cause of God's blessing? We know from the previous oracle that the rebuilding of the temple will serve as the occasion for God to shower his people with blessings, but the temple is not the cause. Even the temple is a gift of God's grace. God's grace toward the postexilic community, like his grace toward us, is not caused by anything in them or done by them. It is not caused by something we build or a project we complete. God's favor flows solely from God alone, who has purposed in the mysterious counsel of his will to pour out blessings on sinners who deserve nothing but his curse. The gospel changes everything.

Beginning in Zechariah 8:16, God once again summarizes the demands of the Law: "These are the things that you shall do: Speak the truth to one another; render in your gates judgments that are true and make for peace; do not devise evil in your hearts against one another, and love no false oath, for all these things I hate, declares the LORD" (vv. 16, 17).[14] These commands are the same in substance and nearly identical in wording as the summary in chapter 7: "Render true judgments, show kindness and mercy to one another, do not oppress the widow, the fatherless, the sojourner, or the poor, and let none of you devise evil against another in your heart" (vv. 9, 10). But while in Zechariah 7 these were used to highlight Israel's failure to keep the Law, in Zechariah 8 they are set forth as Israel's grateful response to God's mercy and grace.[15] Those who have had fear expelled from their hearts by the love of God evidence that new life by loving what God loves and hating what God hates. As God is truth itself, those who love him speak truth to one another in love. As God maintains justice, so those who love him strive to uphold justice in their communities and societies. This is the new life of the believer—freedom from fear because we have been freed from the curse of the Law, and freedom to obey because God has redeemed us for the purpose of loving and blessing those who bear his image.[16]

## *New Season (8:18, 19)*

Confronted as they were with a future so glorious that it bordered on the unimaginable and seemed impossible, it's easy to forget that all these promises served as God's answer to a simple question: "Should I weep and abstain in the fifth month, as I have done for so many years?" (Zechariah 7:3). Though the embassy who posed this question to the priests was no doubt looking for a simple yes or no answer, what they received was an avalanche of oracles relaying the demands of God's Law and the comfort of God's gospel.[17]

For almost seventy years, many in Israel had been marking moments of crisis, loss, and sorrow through ritual fasting. The fast of the fourth month remembered the day the walls of Jerusalem were breached (2 Kings 25:3, 4; Jeremiah 39:2; 52:6, 7); the fast of the fifth month marked the day the city fell (Jeremiah 52:12–15); the seventh month commemorated the day Gedaliah was assassinated (2 Kings 25:25; Jeremiah 41:1–3); and the fast of the tenth month marked the beginning of the siege of Jerusalem (2 Kings 25:1; Ezekiel 24:1, 2).[18] Israel's life was characterized by constant mourning over the suffering and loss they experienced on account of their sin. Eventually the mourning produced the repentance requisite for a return to the land. But even in the land, Israel kept these fasts and marked these occasions because they understood there was a greater deliverance yet to come. The question behind the embassy's question was simple: "Are we almost done? Is the exile almost over for good? Is the kingdom of God close? When will our sorrow and suffering be over?" (see Zechariah 7:3).

In the prophet Zechariah's penultimate oracle in this central section of his prophetic book, he finally comes around to answering the original question. As we might expect, the answer is far deeper and wider than what was conceived in the question, but it answers the question nevertheless: "Thus says the Lord of hosts: The fast of the fourth month and the fast of the fifth and the fast of the seventh and the fast of the tenth shall be to the house of Judah seasons of joy and gladness and cheerful feasts" (8:19). Though the embassy only inquired about the fast of the fifth month, Zechariah brings into view the fasts of the fourth, the seventh, and the tenth as well. By expanding the scope of the answer, the prophet is straining to communicate something of the comprehensive and exhaustive transformation that God is going to effect. This is his way of saying that every fast and every reason to fast will give way to and be replaced by feasts and every reason to feast.

It is notable that God does not add feasts to the yearly holiday calendar, trying, as it were, to balance or drown out Israel's grief and sorrow with occasions for joy and gladness. Rather, God promises to replace the fasts with feasts. The fasts "shall be to the house of Judah seasons of joy and gladness and cheerful feasts" (v. 19). The implication is that there will be no more fasting because there will no longer be any reason to do so. The glory of this future day will be so weighty, the joy so overwhelming, that the griefs and sorrows of former days will be considered of little consequence.

Here we're given the critical reminder that one day God will take even the most tragic events in our lives, including our sin and its dreadful consequences, and will transform them into occasions for celebrating his goodness and grace, his power and mercy. This is not a portrait of rejoicing over our sin and failures. Rather, it is a picture of God's people rejoicing over the greatness of a God who can bring good out of something as awful as sin and death.

The practice of fasting, inasmuch as it flowed from a spirit of repentance, was certainly appropriate for Israel's day and time. Life in this world, for postexilic Israel and for us, is characterized by the cross. Jesus promised as much when he told his disciples, "If anyone would come after me, let him deny himself and take up his cross and follow me. For whoever would save his life will lose it, but whoever loses his life for my sake will find it" (Matthew 16:24, 25). There is no way around it. God's people must pass through the crosses of this life to enter their glory. In so doing, they follow the pattern of their Savior, for whom it was necessary that he suffer before he entered his glory (Luke 24:26).

That God can restore what sin and the curse have ruined is difficult if not impossible for us to imagine this side of glory. As any who experience significant suffering, sorrow, or loss can relate, there are some griefs that can't be healed in this life. There are some holes that cannot be filled. This indeed is the character of life in a sin-cursed world. Sin and its curse, however, are not the end of the story for those who trust in God's promises and look in faith to God's Son. Glory will not be a distraction from our sorrows but a revelation of how God used even the greatest tragedies we experienced on earth for our good and for his glory. As the Puritan John Flavel wrote in his classic treatise, "It will doubtless be a part of our entertainment in *heaven*, to view with transporting delight how the designs and methods were laid to bring us hither."[19]

*New People (8:20–23)*

Finally, we see that that God's gospel promises don't only go deep in transforming Israel from the inside out, or wide in gathering the remnant of God's people from their exile in the far reaches of the earth (Zechariah 8:7), but they go even deeper and wider as they transform and draw Gentile nations to God, making of them both—Jews and Gentiles—one people of God. Such was the goal of God's covenant of grace from the very beginning. The blessings of the covenant were never meant to stop at the borders of Abraham and his offspring. Rather, God promised Abraham, "In you all the families of the earth shall be blessed" (Genesis 12:3). Zechariah proclaims the fulfillment of this promise when he declares, "Peoples shall yet come, even the inhabitants of many cities" (8:20).

The prophet doesn't leave it at that but gives us, as it were, a front-row seat to the excitement and spread of the good news: "The inhabitants of one city shall go to another, saying, 'Let us go at once to entreat the favor of the Lord and to seek the Lord of hosts; I myself am going'" (Zechariah 8:21). Those peoples and cities who once used God's people and God's city as "a byword of cursing" (v. 13) will now find them to be unimaginably desirable and delightful.

What could effect such a change? The gospel of God that has been so vividly set on display in Zechariah's sermons is, as Paul tells us, "the power of God for salvation to everyone who believes, to the Jew first and also to the Greek" (Romans 1:16).

This is not a coalition of the weak, seeking strength in numbers. Rather, these nations who are drawn to the lordship of God will be as "strong" as they are diverse (Zechariah 8:22).[20] They will in fact be so numerous that they will outnumber Jews by a factor of ten to one: "In those days ten men from the nations of every tongue shall take hold of the robe of a Jew, saying, 'Let us go with you, for we have heard that God is with you'" (v. 23).

Of course, Zechariah's prophecy is not meant to provide exact ratios of Jews and Gentiles in the kingdom of God. Rather, the prophet highlights the global scope of God's purposes in salvation. The transformation will be so great that those who make up the majority of God's kingdom in Zechariah's day will become a minority as the good news that "God is with you" extends to the ends of the earth. Even the strong nations of this earth will find in the kingdom of God something far stronger and far more desirable and far more glorious than any kingdom of this world. As a result, they will urgently seek to unite themselves to the fellowship of God's chosen people and come under the Lordship of Israel's one true God in true humility and submission.[21]

# 70

# The Return of the King

ZECHARIAH 9

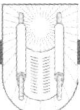

WHEN THE KING COMES, everything will be okay. This basic plotline drives countless stories that continue to capture our imaginations. We might think of young Arthur who draws the sword from the stone to be proclaimed king over Britain, the king whose rule brings order to a land ravished by lawlessness and chaos.[1] Similarly Robin Hood fights for the poor and oppressed in the knowledge that when good King Richard returns, his lawlessness will be vindicated and justice will again reign throughout the land.[2] Perhaps the best-known example is J.R.R. Tolkien's aptly named *The Return of the King*, in which Aragorn, the rightful king, leads the armies of men in defeating the forces of Mordor and whose kingship over Arnor and Gondor inaugurates a new era of peace throughout Middle Earth.[3] When the king comes, everything will be okay.

These stories are, of course, fiction. And yet even as fiction (or better, myth), they trade on something that is both undeniably real and true—what C. S. Lewis called the myth that became fact in Christianity.[4]

In Zechariah 9, the prophet declares the true story behind the stories, the story of the gospel of Jesus Christ. Israel's true King is coming home, and his return will mark an unparalleled change in the course of human history. With Israel's King will come righteousness, deliverance, and peace in both Israel and throughout the entire world. When the King comes, everything will be okay.

Zechariah 9 marks a significant shift in the tone and message of the book, so much so that many scholars believe chapters 9—14 come from another hand altogether, an anonymous author writing some time much later

693

than the prophet and whose work has been mistakenly ascribed to Zechariah. However, such a hypothesis is unnecessary. A better explanation is that in chapters 9—14 we observe that Israel's days of faithfulness and obedience under the leadership of Joshua and Zerubbabel are a thing of the past, and the postexilic community has returned to the spiritual waywardness and apostasy that characterized their forebears.[5] God's people again need deliverance from oppression, temptation, and, most of all, sin and idolatry. The good news, however, is that God promises to send just such a deliverer for his people. In response to Israel's plight, God renews his promises of old to inaugurate his kingdom, the kingdom of his Messiah, for Israel and for the world.

Zechariah 1—8 focused on the postexilic community's task of rebuilding the temple, the house of the Lord, under the leadership of Joshua, the high priest, and Zerubbabel, the governor in the kingly line of David. Throughout these visions and oracles, God reiterated his promise that he would one day return to his house in power and glory (e.g. 1:16; 2:5, 11; 8:8, 22). Beginning in chapter 9, Zechariah describes this very thing: the return of the Lord to his city, his house, his people.

This return of Israel's God will not be a secret or a quiet affair; rather, it will be the catalyst for establishing a new world order, a new life for God's people. It will be a world that is turned upside down, or better, right side up. The oppressors will become the oppressed. The prisoners will become victors in battle. Those who have been the most pitied will become the envy of the nations as they are revealed to be God's chosen people. All of this will take place when God, the King, returns.

### God Returns to His Temple (9:1-8)

Zechariah's oracle opens with a series of judgments pronounced against Israel's neighbors and traditional enemies. This judgment begins with Israel's neighbors to the north, "the land of Hadrach and Damascus" (9:1). Hadrach, Damascus, and Hamath (vv. 1, 2) were the major urban centers of Syria, a nation that was a particularly painful thorn in the side of Israel throughout the ninth and into the eighth centuries B.C.

From Syria to the north, God's march of judgment moves west to the Phoenician cities of Tyre and Sidon, two coastal towns northwest of Israel. Tyre in particular is singled out, as she was known for her impregnable fortress and incredible wealth, both of which contributed to her sense of security and pride.[6] "Tyre has built herself a rampart and heaped up silver like dust, and fine gold like the mud of the streets" (Zechariah 9:3).

Tyre enjoyed an almost unimaginable security largely attributable to its strategic location on the coast. Combined with the enormous stronghold surrounding the city, this cultivated a sense of invincibility. Added to this was the enormous wealth created from its location and function as a port city. The consequence of all of this was arrogance, pride, and the conviction that no harm could befall this great city.

Yet in response to Tyre's pride and hubris, the Lord declared a judgment fitting the offense: "Behold, the Lord will strip her of her possessions and strike down her power on the sea, and she shall be devoured by fire" (Zechariah 9:4). The very things that were the source of Tyre's security and the basis for her pride proved to be false hopes as the Lord stripped Tyre of her great possessions and her security was revealed to be an illusion.

From the Phoenician cities of Tyre and Sidon, God's trail of judgment and destruction moves south along the coast to the Philistine cities of Ashkelon, Gaza, Ekron, and Ashdod. Historically the Philistines were Israel's inveterate enemies. But as these cities witnessed the awesome power and utter destruction that Yahweh meted out to his enemies, they would melt in fear and be consumed with the terror that was coming upon them: "Ashkelon shall see it, and be afraid; Gaza too, and shall writhe in anguish; Ekron also, because its hopes are confounded" (v. 5).

The opening of Zechariah 9:7 continues the portrait of God's judgment on Philistia as it brings into view the Philistines' idolatrous practices, especially the practice of consuming sacrificial victims with the blood still in the meat.[7] This of course was a practice prohibited for Israel, for it represented not only the monstrosity of idolatry but the temptation of Israel to do the same (Genesis 9:4; Leviticus 17:10–14). In response to Philistia's pride and idolatry, God declares, "I will take away its blood from its mouth, and its abominations from between its teeth" (Zechariah 9:7a), a response well deserved on both counts.

However, no sooner does God announce his violent and just judgment on the Philistines than the oracle takes a surprising turn, and God's judgment is transformed into a remarkable blessing: "It too shall be a remnant for our God; it shall be like a clan in Judah, and Ekron shall be like the Jebusites" (v. 7b). The removal of the idolatry from the mouths (literally) of the Philistines will become, for some, an expression of the transforming power of God's grace. Some among the Philistines will not be the objects of God's judgment and curse but recipients of his grace and mercy as he removes from them their idolatrous practices and, even more, as he engrafts them into his covenant community. Just as the postexilic community is a remnant snatched from the conflagration of the exilic judgment, so too will these Philistines be a remnant of the Gentiles delivered from God's righteous judgment and incorporated into the one people of God.

Importantly, this Philistine remnant will not be second-class citizens in the kingdom of God. Rather, God says they will be "like a clan in Judah" (v. 7b). Ekron, one of the five major cities of Philistia, will be "like the Jebusites" whom David drove out of Jerusalem, many of whom were assimilated into the life and worship of the people of God.

Though traditionally thorns in Israel's side, these countries and city-states were not threats to the postexilic community in Zechariah's day. In fact, it is a bit surprising that these (as opposed to the major world powers of Persia and Egypt, or the earlier powers, Assyria and Babylon) were singled out as objects of God's judgment. However, this is not a case of God picking a fight with easy targets. Instead, the significance of God announcing his purposes of judgment and mercy toward these particular city-states is their location. If you were to plot these city-states on a map of ancient Palestine, you would quickly observe that the order and organization are far from random. Beginning with Syria north of Israel and moving southwest to the Phoenician city-states of Tyre and Sidon, after which God's judgment moves south along the coast to the Philistine cities of Ashkelon, Gaza, Ekron, and Ashdod, we observe Yahweh following an essentially north-to-south route, the significance of which is that it follows the path God will take when he returns to his home in Jerusalem.[8] In other words, as we witness God's judgment on the move, we see him returning to his home, again taking up residence amidst his covenant people.

Thus after his work of judgment and salvation in Philistia, the Lord says, "Then I will encamp at my house as a guard, so that none shall march to and fro; no oppressor shall again march over them, for now I see with my own eyes" (Zechariah 9:8). Years earlier the prophet Ezekiel had witnessed Yahweh's dramatic and tragic departure from his house and from his city. However, in a wonderful reversal of Ezekiel's vision, Zechariah witnesses the Lord returning to his house and leaving in his wake unimaginable judgment and destruction on Israel's enemies. Yet God's homecoming is not only judgment and destruction on the Gentile nations surrounding his covenant people, it is also the occasion for mercy and redemption of the least likely citizens of the kingdom of God. The King is indeed coming home, and the world is beginning to be set right as the Lord conquers and subdues Israel's traditional enemies and establishes the boundaries of the promised land.[9]

The Lord's destruction of his enemies will be so decisive that they will no longer pose any threat, either in the present or the future, to God's covenant people. God's residence will be that of a guard, his temple and his city no longer vulnerable to armies marching to and fro throughout the land. The eyes of the Lord that served as a theme in chapters 1—8 appear here again as a reminder of God's constant care for and watchfulness over his people. No evil can thwart his purposes, no opposing power surprise him, no oppressor ever again afflict his people.

Zechariah's opening oracle in chapter 9 offers a grand vision of the divine warrior on the march, triumphing over those who have taken their stand against his kingship and his kingdom. These nations, representing Israel's traditional enemies, appear to be thriving and secure. Their pride and godlessness seem to be rewarded by success, while Israel, for their part, struggles to maintain even a meager existence. Yet the prophet announces that this state of affairs will not always be the case. Israel's God, the divine warrior, will one day return to his temple and to his people. His advent will inaugurate a new era of peace, security, and freedom for all who are citizens of his kingdom.

Zechariah's vision of the world set right through divine judgment and mercy would be reiterated years later by John the seer, who would hear the seventh angel blow his trumpet and loud voices in Heaven announcing, "The kingdom of the world has become the kingdom of our Lord and of his Christ, and he shall reign forever and ever" (Revelation 11:15).

### Messiah Comes for His People (9:9–13)

Beginning in Zechariah 9:9, the perspective shifts and our attention is focused no longer on the judgment and redemption of the nations surrounding Israel but on Jerusalem, for whom the coming of the King means deliverance from warfare and oppression. The oracle opens with a call:

> Rejoice greatly, O daughter of Zion!
>   Shout aloud, O daughter of Jerusalem!
> Behold, your king is coming to you;
>   righteous and having salvation is he,
> humble and mounted on a donkey,
>   on a colt, the foal of a donkey. (v. 9)

These verses may be so familiar to Christians, who know of their fulfillment in Jesus's triumphal entry into Jerusalem, that we might overlook the significance of the commands to "Rejoice" and "Shout!" for the postexilic community. Even the saints of Zechariah's day, the citizens of Jerusalem, the daughters of Zion, had reason to shout and rejoice, not because their King had come or because he could be seen on the immediate horizon but because of the promise that their King would one day come. As it turned out, the arrival of Jerusalem's

King was almost a half a millennium away. Nevertheless the knowledge that he was coming, that Israel's sin had not disrupted God's good purposes or canceled his gracious promises, was enough for the postexilic community to rejoice and shout in their day. Even in the midst of their daily hardships and trials, they had the assurance that God had not forgotten his people, that he would return in power and glory, that the promised Messiah would most certainly come, and would instill hope, confidence, and even joy in their present evil age.

## The Character of the King (9:9)

Israel is told not only that her King is coming; she is also told something about the character of this coming King. Zion's King is "righteous" and has "salvation"; also, he will come "mounted on a donkey, on a colt, the foal of a donkey" (Zechariah 9:9). Zechariah's portrait highlights the humility and faithfulness of this coming King. He will be a righteous King.

This was, in fact, the inveterate problem with Israel's kings. Even the greatest of them, the most righteous among them, was a sinner with feet of clay. Israel's greatest king, David, committed adultery and murder, and his parental negligence plunged the people of God into civil war with devastating and lasting consequences. If we learn anything from the book of Judges, it's that Israel needed a king, and if we learn anything from Samuel and Kings, it's that Israel needed a righteous king. The King who was coming, Israel's Messiah, would be that righteous King who would judge with equity and rule with compassion.

The expression sometimes translated as "having salvation" is probably better rendered in the passive sense, as one who is "saved" or "delivered" (Zechariah 9:9).[10] Depicting this king as "saved" presents this figure as the ideal king, one who entrusted himself to the Lord for his victory in battle. While far too many of Israel's kings trusted in the strength of their fortress, the size of their army, and the number of their chariots (as King Ahaz, for example, trusted in Assyria's military might rather than the Lord his God), this King who is coming will above all else trust in the Lord and entrust himself to the Lord.[11]

Furthermore, this King will come in a posture that was largely unthinkable for ancient Near-Eastern monarchs—humility. "Behold, your king is coming . . . humble and mounted on a donkey, on a colt, the foal of a donkey" (9:9). The humility of Israel's king signals his association with the poor and lowly. As Isaiah foretold of the Servant of the Lord, he would not "cry aloud or lift up his voice, or make it heard in the street; a bruised reed he will not break, and a faintly burning wick he will not quench" (Isaiah 42:2, 3).[12] Even more, the King's humility reflects his submission to God, his willingness to rule in complete obedience and submission to Yahweh's word.

Yet this King's humility mustn't be mistaken for weakness.

It is true, as many commentators have pointed out, that there is nothing particularly unkingly about riding a donkey.[13] The donkey on which he will ride into Jerusalem, however, stands in contrast to the warhorses and chariots that kings, especially despots and tyrants, would ride into battle.[14] This donkey symbolically reveals that the King comes as one who, through the strength of his God, has triumphed over his enemies and is inaugurating a new era for the citizens of Jerusalem.[15] That Israel's king would come riding a colt is likely an allusion to an ancient messianic prophecy spoken by the patriarch Jacob. In Jacob's deathbed prophecy he declared that the royal scepter would not depart from the tribe of Judah and that "binding his foal to the vine and his donkey's colt to the choice vine, he has washed his garments in wine and his vesture in the blood of grapes" (Genesis 49:11). While clearly alluding to this messianic Ruler from the warlike tribe of Judah, Zechariah downplays the violence and warfare suggested by garments "washed in wine . . . and the blood of grapes"(Genesis 49:11).[16] This coming King will not establish his kingdom through warfare but through humility and dependence on his God, who will fight for him and triumph over all his foes.[17]

The Gospel writers rightly saw the fulfillment of Zechariah's prophecy in Jesus's triumphal entry into Jerusalem. Jesus himself was cognizant of his identity as the King of Israel and his calling to a mission of humility that would culminate in humiliation and degradation beyond human imagination. Knowing what awaited him, Jesus instructed his disciples to secure a donkey and a colt for him to ride into Jerusalem as Israel's true king (Matthew 21:1–9; Mark 11:1–10; Luke 19:29–38). Saying more than they fully understood, the crowds hailed their king: "Hosanna to the Son of David! Blessed is he who comes in the name of the Lord! Hosanna in the highest!" (Matthew 21:9). Here indeed was the long-awaited King, righteous and humble, who in complete submission to his Father's word and will remained faithful to the very end.

### *The Mission of the King (9:10–13)*

This Messiah's advent is coincident with God's destruction of the implements of war that plagued Israel and his establishment of peace to the farthest reaches of the earth. God declares,

> I will cut off the chariot from Ephraim
> and the war horse from Jerusalem;

> and the battle bow shall be cut off,
> and he shall speak peace to the nations;
> his rule shall be from sea to sea,
> and from the River to the ends of the earth. (Zechariah 9:10)

Daily life for Israel will no longer be characterized by vulnerability and danger, violence and warfare. The struggle that marked Israel's existence since her founding will give way to unprecedented rest and peace.[18]

The Lord's deliverance is not only a deliverance from warfare and oppression, but also a deliverance from bondage, specifically the bondage of Israel's own sin. God declares, "As for you also, because of the blood of my covenant with you, I will set your prisoners free from the waterless pit" (Zechariah 9:11). Though the postexilic community had returned to the land and had completed the project of rebuilding the temple, their experience was still that of a conquered and subject people. As seen time and again throughout Zechariah's prophecies, postexilic Israel longed for a greater deliverance yet to come. Though it is this bondage to foreign nations that is principally in view, it is critical to understand this bondage to be the result of Israel's sin, and therefore to understand freedom from "the waterless pit" to be a powerful image of that deliverance from all oppression, both from without and within. God promises to work such a decisive and permanent deliverance because of "the blood of my covenant with you."

When covenants were made in the ancient world, they were ratified with blood. When God made a covenant with Israel at Mount Sinai, both parties swore to keep the terms of the covenant, and subsequently the blood of a sacrifice was sprinkled on both parties (Exodus 24:8).

However, even this covenant relationship was based on an older, more foundational covenant—namely, that made with Abraham in Genesis 15. In contrast to the later Mosaic covenant, at the ratification ceremony for the covenant with Abraham, God alone walked down the aisle of blood, thus swearing to suffer the consequences should he fail to fulfill his gracious promises and keep the terms of his covenant of grace (Genesis 15:12–21).[19]

Abraham's hope, Israel's hope, and our hope is fundamentally based on God's gracious promises that God sealed not in the blood of bulls and goats but in the blood of his own Son, who, on the night when he was betrayed, declared, "This cup that is poured out for you is the new covenant in my blood" (Luke 22:20). No longer captives of sin, much less prisoners of Babylon, Persia, Greece, or anyone else, the people of Israel were now "prisoners of hope" (Zechariah 9:12). Their hope, like ours, was not in themselves or their improved obedience to the covenant but in the One to whom the blood of the covenant points, Jesus Christ, the Lamb who was slain. On the cross Jesus, the true Israel, bore the penalty for Israel's and our faithlessness to the covenant. Unlike Israel, Jesus was not delivered from the waterless pit, nor did he find a stronghold in his Father. On the contrary, hopeless and helpless, Jesus suffered the full weight of God's wrath so that those who belong to him might receive back double what sin and the curse had stolen from them.

Strikingly, however, the overthrow of the implements of war and Israel's deliverance from sin and bondage would not happen without conflict. The peace that God would establish would not be based on strategic negotiations, political compromise, or agreements to maintain borders. God's kingdom would be a kingdom that triumphs over any and all who would ever stand opposed to his rightful sovereignty.

Just as God employed Assyria and Babylon as instruments of his judgment against Israel, he depicts his judgment against his enemies in the same fashion: his covenant people will be deployed as his weapons of war against all who threaten to oppress and destroy them. Judah will become God's bow, bent and ready to shoot. Ephraim will be the Lord's arrow and, taking aim at Javan (often translated as "Greece," though likely referring to "unknown peoples on the edge of civilization"), the final battle will commence (Zechariah 9:13).[20]

### Final Victory (9:14–17)

The picture that Zechariah paints in verse 14 has been painted many times before, not only in his own prophecies, but in the prophecies of so many of his prophetic forebears.[21] It is the portrait of God as the divine warrior fighting his enemies and the enemies of his people. Zechariah 9:13 has already set the stage: God depicts Judah as "my bow" and Ephraim as "its arrow" and Zion as "a warrior's sword." God is assembling his people in preparation for war. The arrows are loaded, and bows are bent. The sons of Zion are prepared and ready to be wielded as a sword in the hand of the divine warrior.

In Zechariah 9:14, however, the battle commences: "Then the LORD will appear over them, and his arrow will go forth like lightning; the Lord GOD will sound the trumpet and will march forth in the whirlwinds of the south." The Lord's appearance over his people provides shade or a covering that affords protection even as they engage in combat. God's arrows are released, the trumpet is sounded, and the Lord's people march forth in battle. When the Lord delivers his people from their exilic prison and restores them to himself and to his city, then he will lead them into battle once again as the divine warrior fighting with and for his people. It is unclear whether verse 15 continues the description of this final battle or presents a victory celebration.[22] In either case, the outcome is the complete and unqualified triumph of God's people over their enemies. The cause of their triumph is clear: "the LORD of hosts will protect them" (v. 15).

The result of this final, cataclysmic battle between good and evil is certain: victory for God and for his people. It will be the fulfillment of all of God's good promises. The prophet declares, "On that day the LORD their God will save them, as the flock of his people; for like the jewels of a crown they shall shine on his land" (v. 16). The divine warrior is the good shepherd, a theme that appears throughout the book of Zechariah.

Like David whose work in protecting his father's flock from lions and bears prepared him to protect Israel from Goliath and the oppressive suzerainty of the Philistines, so God would lead his flock against a greater foe and through a more dangerous battle. David was just a faint shadow of this far greater King and far better shepherd who would lay down his life for his flock to not only deliver them from their sin but also glorify them for all eternity. As the jewels of a crown beautify that crown—the outward glory of a king—so Christ's Church would beautify God's holy land as a people redeemed, justified, sanctified, and glorified by their great Shepherd-King.

Contemplating so great a salvation, Zechariah breaks out into expressions of praise and wonder and invites us to do the same: "For how great is his goodness, and how great his beauty!" (v. 17). What other response can God's children have when they behold the good news of the gospel? God has bound himself to bestow the blessings of the covenant freely and graciously to undeserving sinners. The "grain [that] shall make the young men flourish, and new wine the young women" (v. 17) are the covenant blessings promised to covenant keepers in Deuteronomy 33:28. Yet even Israel's former exiles, despite their clear improvements, were a far cry from being covenant keepers. The grain that causes young men to flourish and the new wine that enlivens the hearts of young women God will give as a free gift to undeserving sinners, purchased by the blood of the covenant, shed by the precious Lamb of God to take away the sins of the world.

Like Israel in Zechariah's day, the coming of our King changes how we live in the present. We too have reason to rejoice greatly and to shout aloud because our King is coming, and with him, salvation and peace. Even amidst the greatest trials we could possibly face in this life, we nevertheless remain prisoners of hope, with lives oriented toward the future because, as the angels reminded Jesus's disciples, "This Jesus, who was taken up from you into heaven, will come in the same way as you saw him go into heaven" (Acts 1:11). However, when Messiah does come again, he will not come in humility, riding a donkey, but in majesty, riding on a great warhorse appropriate to the judgment he will bring (Revelation 19:11). But those who have been sprinkled with the waters of baptism and washed in his blood by faith may be assured of this: when King Jesus does come in power and glory, he will establish his kingdom "from sea to sea" (Zechariah 9:10), and then finally and forever, everything will be okay.

# 71

# The Work of the Good Shepherd

ZECHARIAH 10

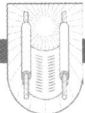

WAYWARD AND DISSOLUTE throughout many of his teenage years, Robert Robinson was converted to Christ at age nineteen through a sermon by the revivalist preacher George Whitefield.[1] In 1757, when he was just twenty-two years old, he penned these memorable words:

> Prone to wander, Lord, I feel it,
> prone to leave the God I love.
> Here's my heart. O, take and seal it,
> seal it for thy courts above.[2]

Understandably Robinson's lyrics have become well-known and oft-quoted as they so powerfully and poignantly capture the common, perhaps daily, Christian experience of wandering at times far from the very God we love. Those who know their own hearts well know they are susceptible to all manner of temptations to waywardness, sin, and rebellion. Yet the longing of every true believer is to be rescued from such wandering; to be delivered from the corruption that still resides within even the most sanctified human heart; and to be established, made new, or, as Robinson put it, sealed for the courts of Heaven itself, the very presence of the triune God.

This dynamic that is evident in the heart and life of every believer is a microcosm of the dynamic that was at work in the larger covenant community. It is this dynamic that we see in the prophet's oracle to the postexilic community in Zechariah 10. Israel's past was characterized by wandering from their God.

705

As a result, many Israelites remained scattered throughout the nations and empires of the world. Yet it was not only those outside the land who were prone to wander. Those who had returned home still found themselves beset with trials and temptations. Furthermore, Israel's shepherds had failed them in the past, and by all appearances the leaders in Zechariah's day had begun to follow their dreadful legacy of injustice, oppression, violence, and abuse. In short, Israel was once again acutely and painfully aware of their need for a good shepherd.

Though Israel's shepherds had failed them once again, the prophet announced that Israel's great shepherd, God himself, was still faithful. Israel's God himself would assume the role of the good shepherd, that leader who would be faithful to care for his sheep, gathering those who were lost, strengthening those who were weak, and healing those who were wounded. But not only would God provide help and healing for his sheep, he also would set himself against all that would threaten them. Like King David before him, this faithful shepherd, we discover, is also a mighty warrior, One who will fight with and for his people.

### Providing for His Flock (10:1, 2)

The opening of Zechariah 10 makes it clear that we are some distance from the spiritual revival that took place under the leadership of Zerubbabel and Joshua.[3] How long after, we cannot say with certainty, but it is evident that Israel has fallen back into their old ways of sin and spiritual rebellion. The idolatry of her forefathers has taken root in the hearts of many in the postexilic community, and God's people are again looking for their sustenance and provision, their hope and their help, in the false gods of the surrounding nations.

Zechariah's oracle opens with an invitation, or perhaps more accurately a command:

> Ask rain from the LORD
> in the season of the spring rain,
> from the LORD who makes the storm clouds,
>   and he will give them showers of rain,
>   to everyone the vegetation in the field. (10:1)

The expression "from the LORD" is used twice, indicating that the emphasis here is not so much on *what* Israel should ask for (i.e., rain) but *who* they should ask (i.e., the Lord). Rain from the heavens and the vegetation that it produces from the earth are what make human life and flourishing possible. As one Old Testament scholar put it, "No rain, no life. It was just that simple in OT times in the Promised Land."[4] Reading between the lines, we can surmise that Israel has returned to Baal worship or the worship of a similar deity associated with storms and rain. This is why the prophet emphasizes that it is Israel's God, Yahweh, who "makes the storm clouds" and who provides "showers of rain" whereby his people might enjoy the fruit of the land and prosper.

That the Lord's invitation is also a reprimand is made clear in Zechariah 10:2 as Israel is again tempted to craft and serve "household gods." They are inclined to listen to the counsel of pagan diviners who "tell false dreams and give empty consolation" (v. 2). These household gods and false prophets make promises of provision, life, and blessing, but Zechariah exposes these promises as deceptive lies that lead God's people away from the truth and the life that God promises to those who worship and serve him alone.[5]

The result of serving these false gods and listening to the false prophets who serve them is as terrible as it is inevitable: "Therefore the people wander like sheep; they are afflicted for lack of a shepherd" (Zechariah 10:2). The postexilic community is cast as lost and wandering sheep, exposed, vulnerable, and malnourished.

This is not the first time Israel has been in this position. Prior to her exile, Israel's leaders notoriously used and abused the people of God, and God's prophets exposed their wickedness for what it was: self-serving abuse of those entrusted to their care. Perhaps the most sustained example of this came from the prophet Ezekiel, who castigated Israel's leaders:

> Ah, shepherds of Israel who have been feeding yourselves! Should not shepherds feed the sheep? You eat the fat, you clothe yourselves with the wool, you slaughter the fat ones, but you do not feed the sheep. The weak you have not strengthened, the sick you have not healed, the injured you have not bound up, the strayed you have not brought back, the lost you have not sought, and with force and harshness you have ruled them. So they were scattered, because there was no shepherd, and they became food for all the wild beasts. (Ezekiel 34:2–5)

Tragically, history was repeating itself and Israel was again "wander[ing] like sheep; they are afflicted for lack of a shepherd" (Zechariah 10:2). Such is always the effect of idolatry.[6] God's people had lost their way as they heeded and followed faithless leaders.[7] While, as we will see, this was in part due to faithless shepherds, it is not sufficient to simply blame the leaders for Israel's predicament. The people willingly, perhaps even eagerly, followed those who pointed them to "household gods" for help and led them in consulting diviners.

The people were not only victims in the waywardness Zechariah described so vividly but also complicit in wandering from the truths of God's word and the faith once for all delivered to the saints.

These opening words come as a summons. God speaks as a king summoning his people to himself. Also, to change the metaphor, God speaks as a shepherd calling his sheep to look to him for protection and provision. Every Sunday churches around the globe sing and so confess God's provision with the familiar words, "Praise God from whom all blessings flow." With these words believers call one another to acknowledge that God has made us who we are and is able to provide all that is needful to us. This God is the true God from whom all blessings flow, and it is the duty of everyone who bears his image to acknowledge this God and his blessings with thanksgiving and worship.

Zechariah's summons is just as important for us today as it was for the postexilic community in his own day. We too are prone to attribute our well-being and blessings to our idols. Though success, education, wealth, influence, or sex may have replaced the rains from Baal as our functional gods, the net effect is the same. We are tempted to regard the good things we know and enjoy in this world as gifts from the creation, products of our own strength and ingenuity rather than blessings from our Creator and Redeemer. As a consequence we end up worshiping and serving these false gods with our affections, devotion, time, or money in place of the One from whom comes "every good gift and every perfect gift" (James 1:17).

The prophet's summons is a summons to recognize our idols for what they are: false gods who make false promises and offer a counterfeit salvation. There is no true and lasting rest to be found in the wealth we make; rather, one finds only a relentless, merciless taskmaster with whom there is no forgiveness for failure but only "empty consolation" (Zechariah 10:2). The call for sheep prone to wander is to hear the summons of our God and his Christ, the great shepherd of the sheep. God calls us to find in him and from him all that is genuinely needful for us in this life, for he has promised, and he alone is able, to provide blessings without measure to those who look to him in faith.

## Protect His Flock (10:1–5)

Saying that God's people "are afflicted for lack of a shepherd" (v. 2) is like saying a child is socially maladjusted for lack of a father. Of course, the child had a father (every child does), but the child's bad behavior may be the result of an absentee, negligent, or abusive father. Similarly, Israel had shepherds.

They had governors, elders, self-proclaimed prophets, priests, and (probably) wise men. The problem was not that they didn't have governors, officials, and leaders, but that those holding these offices executed them to the detriment of the sheep under their care.[8]

In Zechariah 10:3, therefore, the Lord responds to the abuse of his sheep, declaring his word of judgment against these wicked shepherds: "My anger is hot against the shepherds, and I will punish the leaders." The Hebrew word translated as "leaders" is literally "he goats" or "billy goats." These goats may refer to a second tier of leadership that is coming under God's judgment as they, like the shepherds, have dealt harshly and selfishly with the sheep under their care.[9]

Though at times popular and well loved, those who abuse, deceive, or mistreat God's people will come under God's wrath and will be held accountable for their negligence, selfishness, and deception. But Israel's hope was not only that God would judge those who oppressed them and who led them away from their God with false promises and empty consolations—Israel's hope was that God would himself assume the role of the faithful shepherd, as Zechariah goes on to say, "for the LORD of hosts cares for his flock, the house of Judah" (v. 3).[10] It is precisely because the Lord cares for his flock and is aware of all their struggles, hardships, and afflictions that he will oppose and destroy the false shepherds of Israel.

In this image of Yahweh as Israel's shepherd, Zechariah is again utilizing imagery that has a long and established history in Israel's sacred literature. Of course, the most famous example is Psalm 23 in which King David, the shepherd of Israel, says,

> The LORD is my shepherd; I shall not want.
>    He makes me lie down in green pastures.
> He leads me beside still waters.
>    He restores my soul. . . .
>
> Even though I walk through the valley of the shadow of death,
>    I will fear no evil,
> for you are with me;
>    your rod and your staff,
>    they comfort me. (Psalm 23:1–3a, 4; cf. Genesis 48:15; Numbers 27:17; Psalm 80:1)

The Lord's care for his weary and wounded sheep is a recurring theme throughout the prophetic literature as well. In Micah, for instance, God says, "I will surely assemble all of you, O Jacob; I will gather the remnant of Israel;

I will set them together like sheep in a fold, like a flock in its pasture, a noisy multitude of men" (2:12). After pronouncing a woe upon the faithless shepherds of Israel, God says through Jeremiah, "Then I will gather the remnant of my flock out of all the countries where I have driven them, and I will bring them back to their fold, and they shall be fruitful and multiply. I will set shepherds over them who will care for them, and they shall fear no more, nor be dismayed, neither shall any be missing, declares the LORD" (23:3, 4). Unsurprisingly Ezekiel offers the most detailed portrait of the Lord's work as the shepherd of Israel:

> For thus says the Lord GOD: Behold, I, I myself will search for my sheep and will seek them out. As a shepherd seeks out his flock when he is among his sheep that have been scattered, so will I seek out my sheep, and I will rescue them from all places where they have been scattered on a day of clouds and thick darkness. And I will bring them out from the peoples and gather them from the countries, and will bring them into their own land. And I will feed them on the mountains of Israel, by the ravines, and in all the inhabited places of the country. I will feed them with good pasture, and on the mountain heights of Israel shall be their grazing land. There they shall lie down in good grazing land, and on rich pasture they shall feed on the mountains of Israel. I myself will be the shepherd of my sheep, and I myself will make them lie down, declares the Lord GOD. I will seek the lost, and I will bring back the strayed, and I will bind up the injured, and I will strengthen the weak, and the fat and the strong I will destroy. I will feed them in justice. (Ezekiel 34:11–16)

Where Israel's leaders have failed the people and led them astray, God himself has promised to intercede and assume the mantle of the shepherd, leading his wayward people to the safety and security of lush pastures and flowing waters.

Though Zechariah takes up this well-worn theme, he does so in a new and somewhat surprising way as he announces, "The LORD of hosts cares for his flock, the house of Judah, and will make them like his majestic steed in battle" (10:3). No longer is the Lord's care envisioned as rescuing the lost, healing the wounded, and feeding the hungry. Nor is it even protection in the midst of danger, as when David sang, "You prepare a table for me in the presence of my enemies" (Psalm 23:5). Now the Lord's shepherding turns decidedly martial as he promises to transform his flock to be like a majestic warhorse ready for battle.[11] Sheep, of course, are known for their weakness and vulnerability. But with this extraordinary image, the prophet is declaring that God will transform his weak and vulnerable sheep into a strong and majestic creature known for inflicting rather than receiving harm.[12] God does not promise that his people will be free from danger, difficulty, hardship, and trial. Rather, God promises that he will be with them, and he will arm and strengthen them for the trials and dangers they will face.

Though obscure, these provisions of "the cornerstone," "the tent peg," and "the battle bow" (Zechariah 10:4) have royal, even Davidic, overtones, and "rulers" likely describes the renovation of the lower-level leaders (represented by the he goats)—all of which equip and lead Israel in battle.[13] God will protect his people by strengthening them, by providing leaders for them, but perhaps most of all by supplying his own gracious presence. The reason God's people can go forth with confidence is not ultimately because of their strength or because of their equipment, but because God is with them: "they shall fight because the LORD is with them, and they shall put to shame the riders on horses" (v. 5).

Postexilic Israel would have been acutely and painfully aware of their sheeplike qualities—their weakness, their helplessness, and their vulnerability. Though aspects of the prophet's oracle are puzzling (some scholars think intentionally so), the overall message is perfectly clear: The Lord will strengthen his people against those who oppress them, and their victory is assured because their Lord is with them. This is not a hymn to Israel's victory but to the Lord's. Israel's only hope is the Lord, and Zechariah reminds Israel (and he reminds us) that there is no greater or more certain hope.

The point of the martial imagery is not to call the Church in Zechariah's day nor the Church in our day to militarize themselves against those who would oppose them. The Church's warfare, as Paul reminds us, is not "according to the flesh," but rather through the power of God to "destroy arguments and every lofty opinion raised against the knowledge of God, and to take every thought captive to obey Christ" (2 Corinthians 10:3, 5). Nor is it a call to take pleasure in the downfall of the Church's enemies. The point of the prophet's vivid imagery is to depict a radical change in the estate of God's people. From a weak, wounded, lost, and afflicted people, God will create an army of faithful believers able to storm the very gates of Hell itself.

With the resurrection of Christ, this eschatological reality has begun even today. God equips his Church, providing for her leaders—pastors, teachers, elders, deacons, and evangelists—to care for his flock as undershepherds, representatives of the great shepherd of the sheep who are accountable to him and his word. Nevertheless, like postexilic Israel, the Church still waits in faith, hope, and love for God's kingdom to be revealed in its fullness and glory. At that time the Church will be transformed from weak, wounded, frail, and often wayward sinners into strong, healed, holy saints of the Lord.

## Restore His Flock (10:6–10)

Zechariah 10:6 functions like a hinge; it looks backward and it looks forward as God says, "I will strengthen the house of Judah, and I will save the house of Joseph" (v. 6a).[14] Here God reiterates and summarizes the work he will do in strengthening Judah, described in verses 3–6, and then introduces the work he is going to do in gathering Joseph in verses 6–12. In fact, it will be by means of the former (the strengthening of the house of Judah) that God will accomplish the latter (the gathering of the house of Joseph).[15]

Judah and Joseph refer to two of the largest tribes of Israel. These tribes became identified with the two nations of the divided kingdom, Joseph in the north and Judah in the south. Though kinsmen, these two nations had very different experiences. The southern kingdom of Judah was exiled in 586 B.C. and kept more or less intact as a people in Babylon. The northern kingdom of Israel (here called "Joseph"), however, was exiled almost 150 years earlier, not by the Babylonians but by the Assyrians, who had a very different philosophy of empire-building and control. The northern kingdom of Israel was not resettled together in exile; the people were scattered to various regions of the empire and, as a result, from a human perspective, had disappeared from human history. We have no record of what happened to the tribes that made up the northern kingdom after their Assyrian exile. Their territory was resettled by other displaced people groups, and it would seem that this part of God's covenant people was lost forever.

But Zechariah reminds us that God knows his people and will restore not only Judah but Joseph as well. He says, "I will bring them back because I have compassion on them, and they shall be as though I had not rejected them, for I am the LORD their God and I will answer them" (v. 6b). Similarly in a stunning reversal of his announcement through Isaiah where God whistled for Egypt and Assyria to come in judgment against his people (Isaiah 7:18), God now says, "I will whistle for them and gather them in, *for I have redeemed them, and they shall be as many as they were before*" (Zechariah 10:8). Like a shepherd whose whistle can be heard at great distances, so the Lord God will whistle and gather his people from even the farthest reaches of the world to which they have been scattered in judgment. As Jesus would say, "I am the good shepherd. I know my own and my own know me, just as the Father knows me and I know the Father; and I lay down my life for the sheep" (John 10:14, 15).

This image is, of course, a picture of God's reversal of the covenant curses. The scattering of the northern kingdom was not a result of God's lack of attentiveness to his people, much less a result of his being overpowered by another god. Israel's demise was the result of their sin of idolatry and the monstrous practices that flowed from it. In Zechariah 10:9, God says, "Though I scattered them among the nations, yet in far countries they shall remember me, and with their children they shall live and return." Remembering the Lord was the prerequisite for forgiveness. It refers to a remembrance of God's promises to forgive those who turn to him in faith and the repentance that is its first and chief fruit.

The mention of Egypt and Assyria (v. 10) is not meant to limit God's redemptive reach, but to represent the farthest limits of the known world and the powers arrayed against his people, as these were the two superpowers that consistently harassed and oppressed God's people throughout her history. The Lord is saying, in effect, "However far from me your sin has taken you, however hopeless you are in sin's strong hold, I will find you and I will bring you home and establish you in pastures of peace and places of rest." This is the significance of the regions of Gilead and Lebanon. These places were known for their rich and abundant agricultures, the very places where sheep would thrive and enjoy peace and rest. Yet even these wide and abundant places will not be large enough to contain the flock of God's redeemed, so great will be their multitude—a testimony to the greatness of God's grace, mercy, and power. Though Israel's sin, like our sin, has driven them far from their God, he, the Good shepherd, has promised and will be faithful to bring them home.

## Guide His Flock (10:11, 12)

How would God accomplish so great a deliverance? In Zechariah's climactic image, the shepherd's whistle is transformed into a warrior's stride. Zechariah declares, "He shall pass through the sea of troubles and strike down the waves of the sea, and all the depths of the Nile shall be dried up. The pride of Assyria shall be laid low, and the scepter of Egypt shall depart" (Zechariah 10:11).

The divine warrior is on the march again. The prophet draws on numerous images to depict this future ingathering and deliverance of God's people as a second, greater exodus. The Lord again adopts the posture of a warrior who will do battle with oppressive nations that threaten to destroy his people and the waters of chaos that threaten to overwhelm them.[16]

The mightiest powers imaginable, Egypt and Assyria, had in Zechariah's day become mythic as symbols of evil and oppression. Yet the pride of Assyria would be laid low and the scepter of Egypt would depart. As in the days of the exodus, God would again triumph over anything and everything that threatened his people or obstructed his leading them into a wide, good, and plentiful land.

God's work in Judah is described as strengthening (v. 12), but God's work in Joseph is depicted as gathering (v. 10). God knows what his people need. Though Judah was back in the land, they were incredibly weak, like wounded sheep, unable to help themselves. God declares that he will strengthen the weak and the wounded. Jesus said, "Come to me, all who labor and are heavy laden, and I will give you rest. Take my yoke upon you, and learn from me, for I am gentle and lowly in heart, and you will find rest for your souls" (Matthew 11:28, 29). Joseph was not so much weak as lost. God declares that he will gather from the farthest corners of the world everyone who belongs to him.

Zechariah's great burden in his oracle is to announce that God will do everything necessary to restore his weak, wounded, and wayward people to himself. Though from Israel's standpoint this seems impossible, God can and will do what is in fact impossible for man to do. Judah could not strengthen himself. Apart from God's grace and provision, Judah would have disappeared from the pages of history. Joseph could not gather himself. So lost were these people that restoration and return were impossible. But God announces his purposes and reiterates his promises of old for a weak and weary, lost and wayward people: " 'I will make them strong in the Lord, and they shall walk in his name,' declares the Lord" (Zechariah 10:12). Israel's strength here, like our strength, comes from the Lord, is in the Lord, and, by his grace, is directed to the Lord's glory.

Our great shepherd's commitment to rescuing his wayward sheep does not end at providing, protecting, gathering, and guiding them but includes laying down his life for them (John 10:11), as Jesus would declare. This is in fact the chief quality of a faithful shepherd—his willingness to lay down his life to protect the flock entrusted to his care. This is precisely what Jesus did at Calvary. Before he could pass through the sea of troubles, Jesus would drown in them as he hung dying on a Roman cross. Before he could strike down the waves of the sea, symbolic of chaos and evil, he himself would be struck down by them as he was stricken and afflicted for transgressions not his own. Before he could make his people strong in the name of the Lord, the Lord himself had to become weak, wounded, humiliated, and rejected by men. Yet it was in his defeat that our Savior triumphed.

Wonderfully, however, the One who in weakness laid down his life for his sheep, in strength took it up again in resurrection power (John 10:17). As the risen and ascended Lord, Jesus continues to provide for, protect, gather, and guide his Church even today as he calls church leaders, elders, and deacons to serve under his watchful oversight. Such leaders are God's gifts to his Church and the means by which he continues to nurture and care for his people by the power of his Holy Spirit.[17] Nevertheless, there are times when elders, deacons, church leaders, and church courts will let us down. They will make wrong decisions, sin against us, and fail us. Like the sheep, the undershepherds are also prone to wander and must daily look to God for help and strength lest they fall. But the good news is that Christ, the good shepherd, will never fail us. He will never be faithless to his flock that he rescued at the cost of his own blood.

If Zechariah's oracle teaches us anything, it offers a powerful reminder that the Christian's ultimate confidence and only hope is not in the Church or in her leaders, who have feet of clay, but in Christ who lived for us and died for us and has promised to be with us always, even to the end of the age. Our ultimate allegiance, therefore, and the object of our faith must only be God and his Christ, whom the author of Hebrews called "the great shepherd of the sheep," for he alone is able to fulfill his promise to "equip you with everything good that you may do his will, working in us that which is pleasing in his sight, through Jesus Christ, to whom be glory forever and ever. Amen" (13:20, 21).

# 72

# Death Shall Be Their Shepherd

ZECHARIAH 11

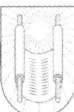

TODAY IN WHAT WAS ONCE a Nazi concentration camp in Dachau, Germany, stands a memorial on which are emblazoned in five languages the words "Never Again." These words have become the slogan for the United States National Holocaust Museum and serve in part to answer the question, "Why erect a museum in the center of Washington, D.C., completely devoted to one of the most horrific events in human history, an event that most people understandably would prefer to forget?" To put it another way, why dwell on the past, especially one so horrific and so shameful? This museum is designed to stand as a monument to the victims of the Holocaust. As such, it is intended to help the world remember the atrocities that led to the systematic murder of Jews, gypsies, homosexuals, and others in Nazi Germany in order to prevent such evil from ever happening again. *Never again.*

History, we know, has a habit of repeating itself. The hope is that the evil that led to the Holocaust will never again plague our world. We remember and rehearse the past in order to learn from mistakes, sometimes very costly mistakes, with a view toward never repeating them.

Zechariah 11 is widely considered one of the most challenging texts in the Old Testament.[1] Much of the dramatic action described in this passage is obscure and the characters difficult to identify. Perhaps the central difficulty has to do with the symbolic referent of the drama that the prophet is instructed to perform. Does it refer to realities in Israel's past, present, or future?[2] This question, however, may be a bit misleading. As we will see, all three temporal horizons are likely involved in some way and perhaps intentionally blurred together in the dramatic sign-act that Zechariah is commanded to perform.[3]

The drama is oriented to the past as God commands his prophet to reenact events that led up to the ultimate covenant curse of the Babylonian exile in 586 B.C.[4] But this is not a reenactment of Israel's past for the sake of history enthusiasts. This is a reenactment of the past for a present prophetic purpose. That is, Zechariah's performance of this drama declares a prophetic word to the postexilic community in their present moment, a moment that had begun to show an increasing resemblance to Israel's sinful and sordid past.[5] All of this speaks a word about Israel's future. Should they return to the idolatry and wickedness that characterized earlier generations, postexilic Israel should expect the same judgment to come against them that came against their forefathers at the time of the exile.[6] Rehearsing God's judgment on the preexilic community therefore serves as a powerful, sobering reminder that God's justice and judgment are real and that the most dreadful experience for a human being is that of being delivered over to the devices and desires of their own sinful hearts.

The enigmatic narrative that comprises the bulk of Zechariah 11 is bookended by two short poems. These poems introduce and conclude the central theme of the narrative—the failure and fate of Israel's faithless shepherds. The opening poem depicts Israel's leaders as the mighty trees of Lebanon and Bashan—regions that were well known in Israel's day for their magnificent and majestic trees, especially cedars, cypresses, and oaks. These trees are somewhat conventional Biblical figures for arrogant leaders or nations. The heights of their tops and the depths of their roots give them the appearance of permanence and invincibility; they stand tall and, we might say, proud. But these mighty trees are nevertheless vulnerable to destruction by fire and by ax. "Open your doors, O Lebanon, that the fire may devour your cedars! Wail, O cypress, for the cedar has fallen, for the glorious trees are ruined! Wail, oaks of Bashan, for the thick forest has been felled!" (vv. 1, 2). Though the opening of this poem suggests that this is simply another oracle against the foreign nations (continuing the theme of chapter 10), the conclusion presents a startling and dreadful revelation: "The sound of the roar of the lions, for the thicket of the Jordan is ruined!" (v. 3b).[7] The divine judgment that God declared against the nations around them has made its way to Israel as well.[8] Israel is given the important reminder that they are not exempt from divine judgment. These shepherds who will be destroyed are not the rulers of foreign nations but the arrogant and ruthless leaders of the postexilic community.

This, of course, is not the first time we've encountered this theme. In Zechariah 10:3, God declared, "My anger is hot against the shepherds, and I will punish the leaders, for the LORD of hosts cares for his flock." The rest of chapter 10 focused on developing the latter portion of the prophet's oracle—namely, the Lord of hosts caring for his weak and wayward flock. But whatever became of those faithless shepherds?

Zechariah 11 circles back to address this very issue.[9] How does God's hot anger against his shepherds manifest itself in the life of the postexilic community? It is this anger and the punishment that follows that are vividly depicted in Zechariah's prophetic sign-act, what one commentator calls "a chilling account of a God who shows no pity to his people, breaks his covenant with them, and commands his prophet to play the role of leaders who will neglect and abuse them."[10] What we discover in this outline of the script the prophet is to perform is that something has gone horribly wrong in the postexilic community. Zechariah's haunting sign-act is designed to serve as a warning to his generation that those who reject the Lord as their good shepherd will in turn be rejected by him just as their forefathers had experienced. Though almost exclusively negative in its outlook and message, the prophet does not leave us without hope, for the drama concludes with a poem announcing the ultimate destruction of those faithless shepherds who would harm God's people and separate them from their faithful Shepherd-King.

## Outlines of a Tragedy (11:1–6)

We have already seen at least one prophetic sign-act in the book of Zechariah. In chapter 6, the prophet was instructed to place a crown on the head of Joshua the high priest, a sign and symbol of the coming messianic Priest-King. However, if the coronation of the high priest in chapter 6 was the dramatic equivalent of a one-act play, the sign-act recorded in chapter 11 is more like a Wagnerian opera (one of which took four nights to perform!). That is to say, the sign-act in Zechariah 11 is exceedingly involved and highly elaborate both in its performance as well as in its symbolism.[11] Though much about this sign-act is obscure, the general message of the play is sufficiently clear and outlined for us in its broad contours at the beginning as Zechariah recounts God's instructions to him in verses 1–6.

When God commands his prophet to "become shepherd of the flock doomed to slaughter" (Zechariah 11:4), he immediately calls to mind the now familiar metaphor of Yahweh as the shepherd of Israel. In the first of the two dramas, the prophet is directed to play the role of the good and faithful shepherd, a direction that connects him to God himself. God, after all, is the perfectly good shepherd, the One of whom David said, "The LORD is my shepherd; I shall not want" (Psalm 23:1). Zechariah, representing the Lord, is called to shepherd a flock whose destiny is certain: they are a flock "doomed to destruction" (11:4, AT). Moses himself had understood that under the stipulations of the covenant God made with Israel at Mount Sinai, Israel's fate was sealed. Therefore, he could say in Deuteronomy 30:1, "*When* all these things come upon you, the blessing and the curse, which I have set before you, and you call them to mind among all the nations where the LORD your God has driven you . . ." Israel's failure was not the result of a deficient covenant but of a deficient people who would one day stray from their God so far and so irreparably that divine judgment was certain even to Moses.

After commanding his prophet to play the role of a shepherd, God then describes the circumstances of this doomed flock: "Those who buy them slaughter them and go unpunished, and those who sell them say, 'Blessed be the LORD, I have become rich,' and their own shepherds have no pity on them" (Zechariah 11:5). This is a portrait of the commodification of God's people; they are bought and sold like sheep in a market. Those who buy them do so not to shepherd them in safety, that is, to care for them, but rather to slaughter them for their own benefit. This is a depiction of the oppressive violence and abuse of Israel's leaders prior to the exile, abuse denounced so vividly, for example, by Micah, who said to the leaders of Israel,

> Is it not for you to know justice?—
>   you who hate the good and love the evil,
> who tear the skin from off my people
>   and their flesh from off their bones,
> who eat the flesh of my people,
>   and flay their skin from off them,
> and break their bones in pieces
>   and chop them up like meat in a pot,
>   like flesh in a cauldron. (Micah 3:1-3)

Those in positions of authority used their power to commodify the people of God for their own gain and benefit, to the detriment and destruction of God's people.

Even worse, they did so with immunity: they "go unpunished" by the magistrates, judges, priests, and other officials whose God-given calling was to protect the innocent and to render just judgments. Perhaps worst of all, however, these faithless shepherds cloaked their wickedness in piety. They interpreted their success as the Lord's approbation as they declared, "Blessed be the LORD, I have become rich" (Zechariah 11:5). This was indeed a world turned on its head. Evil was regarded as good and good as evil. Gains achieved through oppression and violence, through manipulation and abuse of the system, were regarded as tokens of divine favor that in turn sanctioned further and greater abuse. Under such leaders the people were indeed doomed to death and destruction.

On account of these ruthless and wicked leaders, God says he will "no longer have pity on the inhabitants of this land" (Zechariah 11:6a). The result? When God removes his grace and compassion, the result is self-destruction. God says, "I will cause each of them to fall into the hand of his neighbor, and each into the hand of his king, and they shall crush the land, and I will deliver none from their hand" (v. 6b).

When God removes his grace and mercy, the result is nothing short of horrific self-destruction. Neighbor destroys neighbor, the strong destroy the weak, and they themselves will be destroyed by those stronger still. The result? God concludes, "They shall crush the land." No longer providing sustenance and protection for God's people, the land that the Lord appointed to be heaven on earth will become ruined, pulverized by human recklessness, wickedness, and sin.

Prior to the exile, God's people had begun to presume upon God's grace. They had forgotten that God's pity and patience toward them had a purpose—namely, that they might turn from their sin and turn toward him in repentance and faith. God's patience was interpreted as license for further sin and greater oppression. The implication is clear enough: the postexilic community had begun to walk down this same, well-trod path of oppression and presumption. Her leaders had again begun to abuse those entrusted to their care, commodifying and exploiting the flock of God.

The prophet Zechariah was instructed to enact Israel's history as a stern warning to the postexilic community. God would not be presumed upon, and wickedness will always end in destruction for those who do not repent. The Apostle Peter writes, "The Lord is not slow to fulfill his promise as some count slowness, but is patient toward you, not wishing that any should perish, but that all should reach repentance" (2 Peter 3:9).

In Zechariah's prophetic sign-act we are reminded that God's patience will one day come to an end, God's pity is not to be taken for granted, and his mercy is not to be presumed upon. God's long-suffering toward sin should not lead to presumption and complacency, much less greater sin and wickedness. Rather, God's patience is meant to lead to repentance and a celebration of God's kindness in withholding his judgment to provide an opportunity to turn toward him in faith, repentance, and renewed obedience. This was a lesson Israel's forefathers failed to heed. Would the postexilic community follow in their footsteps?

### The Rejection of the Good Shepherd (11:7–14)

Having received the script of the drama he must perform, Zechariah executed his mission beginning in verse 7. Whatever the exact nature of the prophetic sign-act, it is clear that the prophet performed his assigned role creatively and effectively.[12] He became a shepherd and took up two staffs with which to shepherd the sheep. While there is nothing unusual about a shepherd employing two staffs in his occupation (cf. Psalm 23:4), a shepherd naming his staffs certainly seems unique. However, consistent with the highly symbolic nature of the drama, Zechariah related that he named his staffs "Favor" and "Union" (11:7), representing God's covenant with Israel and the unity that covenant created among the tribes of Jacob.[13]

Zechariah's work as a faithful shepherd showed some early signs of success. He said, "In one month I destroyed the three shepherds" (11:8a). I'm not completely sure what a good time frame is for destroying shepherds, but the implication seems to be that Zechariah set his hands to his work with diligence, eagerness, and effectiveness.

The identity of these three shepherds is another aspect of the drama that has yielded much by way of speculation and little by way of consensus, with one commentator noting at least forty different proposals![14] Plausible but uncertain suggestions have ranged from three individuals (e.g., Saul, David, and Solomon, or Cyrus, Cambyses, and Darius) to three offices or groups (prophet, priest, and king, or priests, Levites, and scribes).[15] Since we are dealing with a prophetic sign-act, these numbers might not be meant to be taken literally. Three often symbolizes completion, and "one month" here is probably significant as a reference to a short period of time.[16] Whoever these shepherds were, we can say with confidence that they were the leaders guilty of or at least complicit in the abuse, harm, and destruction ("slaughter") of the sheep. Zechariah's destruction of these ruthless shepherds therefore represents God's sovereign care for his people and his provision of protection from those who would harm them.

If the Shepherd-King's success in destroying his enemies is somewhat unsurprising, the sheep's response to their deliverance from certain death is nothing short of astonishing. Zechariah relates, "I became impatient with them, and they also detested me" (11:8b). The sheep have come to despise the very one who is protecting, nurturing, and caring for them, with the result that the Lord, represented by his prophet, has become weary or "impatient." To be sure, the Lord's impatience is not identical to our impatience. Our impatience is, more often than not, an expression of our self-centeredness, whereas God's impatience is an expression of his sovereign freedom and perfect wisdom in withdrawing his mercy from those who treat it as inconsequential and use it as license for wickedness.

The word translated as "impatient" is used elsewhere to refer to "an inability to endure a situation."[17] The Lord became impatient with his people's disregard of his law and their unresponsiveness to his grace. The sheep, remarkably, did not respond to God's redemption and rule with the joy, gratitude, and loving devotion that we would expect; rather, they detested the God who had saved them and despised the very one who cared for them.

God responds to his people's rejection of his kingship by rejecting them as his people: "So I said, 'I will not be your shepherd'" (Zechariah 11:9a). This is the terrifying reversal of the covenant promise, "I will be your God, and you shall be my people" (Jeremiah 7:23), or, to use the symbolism of the prophetic sign-act, "I will be your shepherd, and you will be my sheep." God renounces his role as the shepherd of his people with the dreadful sentence, "What is to die, let it die. What is to be destroyed, let it be destroyed. And let those who are left devour the flesh of one another" (v. 9b).

Punctuating the Lord's death sentence, the prophet breaks his staff named Favor, "annulling the covenant that I had made with all the peoples" (Zechariah 11:10).

"Covenant . . . with all the peoples" likely refers to the covenant God made with Israel at Mount Sinai.[18] It was this covenant that established Israel as a nation under the rule of God as their Lord and King. It was to the terms of this covenant that Israel swore, "All that the LORD has spoken we will do, and we will be obedient" (Exodus 24:7). Yet time and again they broke faith with Yahweh, violating their promises and their covenant with God. Though much about the prophet's drama is obscure for us as readers and hearers 2,500 years removed from the event, his point was not lost in the least on his original audience: "So it was annulled on that day, and the sheep traders, who were watching me, knew that it was the word of the LORD" (Zechariah 11:11). Those leaders who witnessed the destruction of Jerusalem finally realized that the words of warning issued time and again through the prophets were in fact the words of God. But it was too late. The covenant was annulled, and Israel was destroyed.

How much did Israel's leaders, these faithless shepherds and wicked sheep traders, value God's kindness and compassion? Tragically, the leaders whose corruption and wickedness were exposed responded with resentment and derision. I once heard of a waitress receiving her tip in the form of a nickel pressed into a pat of butter. That clearly (albeit uncharitably) revealed what the customers thought of her service. Similarly, the leaders revealed what little regard they had for God's shepherding by paying him thirty pieces of silver (Zechariah 11:12). Though thirty pieces of silver was not an insignificant amount of money, the amount itself, as many commentators have noted, revealed hearts that desired to control God as they dismissed his messianic representative with the sum designated in their law as the price of a slave's life (cf. Exodus 21:32). Elizabeth Achtemeier summarizes the issue well when she says, "The irony consists in the fact that the leaders are actually paying their Messiah!—as if he were their servant and they were not his subjects! They want a Messiah who can be bought, whom they can hire or dismiss at will. In short, they want to run their own community."[19] God in turn commanded Zechariah to throw "the lordly price at which I was priced by them" to the temple potter (Zechariah 11:13), a clear denunciation of the state of the temple complex and priesthood that maintained it.

In response to the leaders' rejection, the prophet breaks his second staff, Union, thereby "annulling the brotherhood between Judah and Israel" (v. 14).[20] The rejection of God's kingship resulted in the traumatic and, from a human perspective, irreparable division of the kingdom into two nations in the days of Rehoboam. Rehearsing this traumatic event served as a warning to Israel's leaders in Zechariah's day who, it appears, had cooled to the prophet's ministry and were showing distressingly similar tendencies toward the Lord's word. Most tragic, however, would be Israel's rejection not of Zechariah but of God's Messiah, adumbrated in the prophet's drama.

How much would Israel value the good shepherd, the Son of God incarnate? The Gospel writer tells us that Judas Iscariot betrayed the Lord of glory for the same sum of "thirty pieces of silver" (Matthew 26:15). Convicted of the enormity of his offense but unable to return it, Judas repeated Zechariah's sign-act by leaving the payment for a slave in the temple, a not-so-veiled condemnation of the religious authorities in his day as well (27:5). The only one whose life was of infinite worth was betrayed, condemned, and crucified for the price of a slave.

The realities that Zechariah's sign-act represented in his day and the realities that were fulfilled in Christ's day set on display the depth of the depravity of the human heart. In the words of Jeremiah, "The heart is deceitful above all things, and desperately sick; who can understand it?" (Jeremiah 17:9). Apart from the transforming, vivifying grace of God, we prefer darkness rather than light, and when confronted with the grace and truth of God himself, clothed in human flesh, we would nail him to a cross rather than bow the knee in humility and repentance.

However, Zechariah's prophecy speaks a sobering word even to those who have embraced Christ by faith. Christians too can often treat Christ and the price he paid on the cross as something of little consequence and of slight import for our daily lives. Every time we view our sin as a light and inconsequential matter we display the same spirit of unbelief as those who dismissed God's Messiah with the price of a slave's life.

Zechariah's grim drama reveals the sad fact that God's covenant people chose death over life. God's patience, mercy, pity, and long-suffering came to an end, and he turned his people over to their wicked desires and the consequences that inevitably flowed from them. Thankfully, however, there is one final act to this sad drama, an act that offers a glimmer of hope for hopelessly wayward sinners.

### And Death Shall Be Their Shepherd (11:15–17)

In Zechariah 11:15, the prophet relates his reception of a second script: "Then the LORD said to me, 'Take once more the equipment of a foolish shepherd.'" This time Zechariah will play another role. He is no longer cast as God, the good shepherd who searches for, protects, feeds, and heals the sheep; rather, he will play the role of the foolish and faithless shepherds who commodify and victimize God's people: "For behold, I am raising up in the land a shepherd who does not care for those being destroyed, or seek the young or heal the maimed or nourish the healthy, but devours the flesh of the fat ones, tearing off even their hoofs" (v. 16).

Such was the brutality of Israel's shepherds of the past. If the postexilic community continued to reject God's rule and spurn his grace, God would again turn his people over to kings after their own hearts. As in the days of Samuel when Israel demanded a king "to judge us like all the nations" (1 Samuel 8:5), for which they received the monomaniacal King Saul, so God would again raise up kings and rulers who would rule Israel with an iron fist, exploiting, maiming, violating, and oppressing them on account of their rejection of the Lord's sovereign kingship.

The fundamental message of Zechariah's sign-act is "Beware of your desires." Apart from the regenerating, justifying, and sanctifying grace of God, the human heart desires that which will ultimately lead to death and destruction. The worst thing God can do to us is to leave us alone, because in so doing he is handing us over to ourselves, and we will become victims of our own desires.

In Zechariah's second sign-act, God offers a picture of this very thing: a foolish shepherd for foolish sheep. Though many suggestions have been proposed, it is likely that this foolish shepherd refers not to a single individual but rather not to a series of rulers and leaders who would continue the long and well-established tradition of cruelty, oppression, violence, and self-indulgence that has characterized Israel's kings and rulers.

The fulfillment of Zechariah's sign-act may be seen in the train of rulers who, it seems, governed postexilic Israel with ever-increasing violence and brutality that was at times nothing short of breathtaking for its cruelty. Perhaps the parade example is King Herod the Great. Though a brilliant general and an effective politician, Herod was deeply insecure, power-hungry, paranoid, oppressive, and excessively cruel in his rule over Judea. In the words of the Jewish historian Josephus, "Herod had immersed his people in poverty and utter lawlessness, and overall the miseries which Herod had inflicted on the Jews in a brief span of years were more than everything suffered by their forefathers in the entire time since they left their exile in Babylon and returned home in the reign of Xerxes."[21] Bouts of suspicions, jealousy, and cruelty led Herod to murder his wife, his uncle, his wife's grandfather, his mother-in-law, three of his sons, and countless citizens he suspected of disloyalty.[22]

Josephus recounted Herod's order that numerous prominent Jewish citizens were to be slaughtered in the Hippodrome upon his death. Why? So that Herod, aware of his unpopularity with the people, could be sure there would be sufficient lamentation upon his death.[23] Though this account may be apocryphal, we do know for sure that Herod's pride and paranoia led him to massacre the baby boys of the entire town of Bethlehem, an episode reminiscent of Pharaoh's attempted genocide in the days of Moses (Matthew 2:16–18). Following closely in his father's footsteps, Herod's son (also named Herod) imprisoned John the Baptist for speaking a word of truth about his illicit marriage (Mark 6:17–20). This same Herod ordered the execution of John the Baptist in order to save face in front of his nobles and make good on a foolish promise (vv. 21–29). These Herods, father and son, were just two embodiments of the ruthlessness, cruelty, indifference, and violence prophesied by Zechariah. But there were many who came before them, and not a few who came after, who shared their same spirit.

Those who reject God's kingship and God's shepherding will be handed over to the shepherd of their desires: a king after man's own heart, one who will, like Saul, enslave, oppress, and eventually destroy those who desire his kingship. Thankfully, God concludes this dark tragedy that exposes the depths of depravity of the human heart with the reminder that he will not forsake his people to a shepherd of death. The prophet's drama concludes with a poem that contains a message of judgment or, more specifically, a woe against these shepherds of death:

> Woe to my worthless shepherd,
>     who deserts the flock!
> May the sword strike his arm
>     and his right eye!
> Let his arm be wholly withered,
>     his right eye utterly blinded! (Zechariah 11:17)

The maiming described here would render these shepherd leaders impotent and worthless in battle. No longer strong and powerful, these wicked shepherds will be unable to execute their wicked desires and brutalize the sheep they have led astray.

In this we see the triumph of God's grace over his judgment. The good shepherd will not ultimately abandon his sheep, forsaking them to those who would destroy them.

Christ, the good shepherd, has come to and for his sheep, wayward and intransigent as they are, to seek and to save those who are lost. Though many in his day would despise and reject him, Jesus knows who are his. He declared, "My sheep hear my voice, and I know them, and they follow me. I give them eternal life, and they will never perish, and no one will snatch them out of my hand" (John 10:27, 28).

Ultimately, the good shepherd triumphs over the wicked and faithless shepherds, whom Christ identified as thieves and robbers (v. 1). In fact, God would use the betrayal, rejection, and murder of the good shepherd to accomplish his purpose of redeeming the very ones who would crucify Christ. On the cross, Jesus suffered the fate of a faithless shepherd, bearing in his body the woe and the wounds deserved by Israel's worthless leaders and those who followed them. He did this to redeem his flock, doomed to destruction by the most terrifying shepherds of all: sin and death. In Christ, therefore, we see that God's final word is not the pitiless judgment that his sheep deserve, leaving them to the fate of their own sinful devices and desires. Rather, God's final word is the destruction of the false and faithless shepherds who would deceive and destroy the flock of his people.[24]

It is striking that immediately following Herod's beheading of John the Baptist—a terrible injustice, violence, and innocent bloodshed resulting in (literally) a head on a platter—we find Jesus, the true shepherd, exhausted, seeking rest and solitude, being chased down by a crowd of people. Mark 6:34

records, "When he went ashore he saw a great crowd, and he had compassion on them, because they were like sheep without a shepherd. And he began to teach them many things." When it grew late, Jesus tended to his flock by feeding them with loaves and fish miraculously multiplied (vv. 41–44). Lest we miss the significance of Jesus's actions, Mark introduces the episode as follows: "Then he commanded them all to sit down in groups on the green grass. So they sat down in groups, by hundreds and by fifties" (vv. 39, 40).

In this wonderfully pastoral scene we see Jesus taking up the mantle of the good shepherd and causing his weary and needy sheep to sit in the green grass. He looked out at a people and saw a flock that was scattered, starved, and oppressed by faithless leaders, and we're told he had compassion on them and he fed them. However, the most important feeding that took place there in the wilderness was not the miracle of the multiplying loaves and fish but the teaching of many things. In Jesus's teaching, the flock who deserved death received words of life.

Few scenes in the Gospels are more poignant. The good shepherd came not to the halls of power but to the wilderness. There in the wilderness God had compassion on his people who were like sheep without a shepherd, and he cared for them both physically and spiritually. Christ's compassion for his people hasn't changed. God's heart for his people is full of compassionate love that would go to the ends of the earth, even hell on a cross, to rescue even one wayward and lost sheep. For good reason Psalm 23 is the most well-known and best-loved psalm: "The LORD is my shepherd; I shall not want [lack]" anything either in this life or in the life to come (v. 1). "Surely goodness and mercy shall follow me all the days of my life, and I shall dwell in the house of the LORD forever" (v. 6).

# 73

# By Thy Transforming Power

ZECHARIAH 12—13

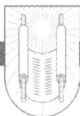

TODAY, PERHAPS MORE THAN any other time in the history of the world, we possess a remarkable ability to transform ourselves. Through diet, surgery, therapy, technology, fitness, and education we are able to effect a deep, profound, and sometimes lasting transformation of our minds and bodies. While much (though not all) of this ability is to be celebrated, the net effect of these wonders of self-transformation is the common illusion that because we are able to transform *some* things, therefore we are able to transform *all* things. Such a view, however, is patently false. There are some things in life—race, gender, biological family, to name a few—that we are simply unable to change about ourselves, no matter how hard we try and no matter how much human ingenuity and technology are applied to the enterprise.

The sobering message of the Bible is that when it comes to the most basic and most important aspects of who we are, our very hearts, we are utterly incapable of effecting even the smallest transformation for our improvement. Left to ourselves, apart from the grace of God, we are, in the words of the Apostle Paul, "dead in trespasses and sins" (Ephesians 2:1). But the good news of the gospel is that what is impossible for man is possible for God. God has promised to effect a transformation of his people so comprehensive and so profound that the best way to describe it is, again in the words of Paul, "a new creation" (2 Corinthians 5:17). Indeed, "the old has passed away; behold, the new has come."

Zechariah 12—13 depict this promised transformation, a transformation in this case not of an individual but of an entire nation. Israel's future is so different from her present that it is difficult even to capture it with words. So the prophet employs wildly fantastic and at times bewildering images to communicate something of this radical new creation that God is going to bring about in the life of the nation.

God through his prophet announces a transformation so glorious in its character and so comprehensive in its scope that the mind reels and the heart is tempted to disbelieve that such a thing could ever be possible. But as if to preclude such objections and doubts, the prophet opens with a reminder of who it is who is promising: "The oracle of the word of the LORD concerning Israel: Thus declares the LORD, who stretched out the heavens and founded the earth and formed the spirit of man within him" (Zechariah 12:1). It would be a mistake to pass too quickly over this familiar messenger formula because the prophet expands the traditional identification ("Thus declares the LORD") to include the description of God as the One "who stretched out the heavens and founded the earth and formed the spirit of man within him."

With this expanded formula, the prophet emphasizes the identity of the One who will accomplish the extraordinary transformation of Israel about to be described in spectacular detail. It is Yahweh, the God of Israel, who established the earth below and who stretched out the heavens above by the very word of his power. It is Yahweh who created mankind as the centerpiece of his creation, forming, as the prophet says, "the spirit of man within him." By emphasizing God's sovereign power in creation at the beginning, the prophet is reminding his hearers of the Lord's credentials.[1] Israel's God is no local deity, limited in his power to people or place. Rather, these opening words remind them and us that the fate of Judah and Jerusalem will in fact have cosmic significance as God brings about a redemption that is global in scope. But perhaps even more importantly, Zechariah highlights the fact that the One who created the world in the beginning can and will do it again as he brings about a new creation and a new world order.[2]

## A Strong People (12:1-9)

What do the following have in common: a cup of staggering, a heavy stone, a blazing pot, and a flaming torch? What connects these seemingly unrelated realities is their potential to inflict devastating harm. A flaming torch will utterly consume surrounding sheaves, and it does so without suffering harm itself. Likewise, a blazing pot will set alight the pile of wood over which it is placed, again without itself suffering harm. Though not a threat to anyone in and of itself, a heavy stone may inflict considerable damage when someone attempts to lift it.

Beginning in Zechariah 12:2, God describes his great transformation of his people with these metaphors and similes. He says, "I am about to make

Jerusalem a cup of staggering to all the surrounding peoples." Similarly in verse 3, he says, "On that day I will make Jerusalem a heavy stone for all the peoples. All who lift it will surely hurt themselves." And in verse 6, God says, "On that day I will make the clans of Judah like a blazing pot in the midst of wood," then, changing the simile ever so slightly, "like a flaming torch among sheaves. And they shall devour to the right and to the left all the surrounding peoples."

With these vivid figures, the prophet offers different perspectives on and different portraits of the same event, a final cataclysmic battle between God's enemies and God's people. It is an event in which Jerusalem will face a tremendous crisis as its inhabitants find themselves surrounded by hostile nations on all sides. That this conflict transcends ordinary warfare is suggested by the fact that "all the nations of the earth will gather against [Judah and Jerusalem]" (Zechariah 12:3).[3] This is not a battle between two or three nations. This is a global, cosmic conflict.[4] Yet amazingly, as Israel's enemies surround Jerusalem, certain of victory, God will transform his city into "a cup of staggering" (v. 2), "a heavy stone" (v. 3), and "a blazing pot" (v. 6).

This event will stand in stark contrast to Jerusalem's recent past. Unlike the destruction at the hands of the Babylonians, who moved Jerusalem (to put it mildly) and set Jerusalem ablaze, this time those who would move Jerusalem will find the city to be inviolable and themselves to be moved to their own destruction. Those who wish to burn Jerusalem to the ground will themselves be set ablaze and consumed. Those who set themselves against God will drink not the cup of victory but the cup of staggering.

This image of "a cup of staggering" creatively adapts the common Biblical image of the cup of God's wrath that will render its drinkers incapacitated (cf., e.g., Psalm 75:8; Isaiah 51:17, 22; Jeremiah 25:15–29; Ezekiel 23:31–34; Habakkuk 2:16). Scholars have long noted that the cup of wrath is derived from the ancient Near Eastern legal practice known as the trial by ordeal.[5] In this judicial procedure, the accused would undergo a physical test (in this case, drinking a potion). It was believed that the potion would reveal the accused's guilt or innocence by creating a physiological reaction in his body, and that this reaction was a revelation of the god or gods.[6] Though perhaps not technically an ordeal, God employed something similar as part of Israel's Law as a way to discern the guilt or innocence of a wife suspected of adultery (Numbers 5:11–28), and it was likely the ordeal procedure that stood behind the events at Marah in Exodus 15:23–26.[7] So compelling was this practice, probably for the terror it invoked, that Israel's prophets routinely employed this image of the cup of God's wrath—or, as Zechariah takes up the image, the "cup of reeling"

(12:2, AT)—to describe the revelation of guilt, the exposure, and the judgment that will be meted out against those who rebel against God.[8] Those who seek Israel's harm and Jerusalem's destruction will find God's chosen people to be a cup of wrath that reveals their guilt in an expression of divine judgment as they stagger, reel, and fall to their peril.

With each of these images, God offers a vivid portrait of the transforming work he will accomplish in his people. Taken together, they reveal that God is going to provide for and protect his people in a way that demonstrates both his sovereignty and his power. There is no notion that Israel is going to transform themselves. Israel's transformation, and therefore their hope, is all of God.

Though they face unspeakable danger, God will strengthen and equip his people for the challenges and hardships, the threats and dangers they will face. In fact, God's purposes in strengthening his people are clearly declared twice by his prophet: "Then the clans of Judah shall say to themselves, 'The inhabitants of Jerusalem have strength through the LORD of hosts, their God'" (Zechariah 12:5). A few verses later, he says, "On that day the LORD will protect the inhabitants of Jerusalem, so that the feeblest among them on that day shall be like David, and the house of David shall be like God, like the angel of the LORD, going before them. And on that day I will seek to destroy all the nations that come against Jerusalem" (vv. 8, 9). The feeblest inhabitant of Jerusalem will be like the greatest king and ablest general Israel has ever known, David. The house of David will become so great that the only thing to compare it to is God himself (v. 8). Specifically, the prophet likens the house of David to the angel of the Lord who went before Israel in the wilderness, an angel who led Israel through the trials and dangers of the desert to the safety and provision of the promised land.

In the face of danger and hardship, temptation and failure, the Christian's hope is not that we will strengthen ourselves or that we will transform ourselves. Our only hope is that God will provide for his people as he has promised and that he will deliver us according to his purposes. Like postexilic Israel, the Church often appears (and often is) remarkably weak. But here we are reminded that weakness serves a purpose in God's economy. It reminds us that we are constantly dependent on God. It reminds us that we lack the resources needed to face the countless threats and dangers that we encounter in this life. Left to ourselves we would most certainly perish on the way. We would be destroyed, if not from hostile nations without, then from the corruption of sin within. In an apocalyptic idiom appropriate for the needs of his day, the prophet Zechariah expresses what Abraham learned on Mount Moriah: "God will provide" (Genesis 22:8, 14). Though our trials may be beyond severe, the Lord is able and is faithful to provide, in the words of the great hymn, "strength for today and bright hope for tomorrow."[9]

Weakness is not the end of the story for God's people. It is not a preface to defeat and ultimate destruction. Nor is it the final state of affairs—the way things will always be. Weakness, rather, serves the Christian as a reminder that our hope and our strength are in God, who has promised and is able to deliver those he calls his own. For this reason, Paul was able to boast even and especially in his weakness: "For the sake of Christ, then, I am content with weaknesses, insults, hardships, persecutions, and calamities. For when I am weak, then I am strong" (2 Corinthians 12:10).

## A Repentant People (12:10–14)

The transformation that God promises affects Israel not only regarding their foes from without but also their enemies from within—namely, the enemy of their own hearts. God says, "I will pour out on the house of David and the inhabitants of Jerusalem a Spirit of grace and pleas for mercy" (Zechariah 12:10, AT). Again, God is the One who will work this remarkable change in the hearts of his people, and he will do so by his Spirit.[10] Just as God will transform Israel physically from weak to strong, he also will transform them spiritually as he pours out upon them "a Spirit of grace and pleas for mercy." By the power of his Spirit, God will work faith and repentance in the hearts of his people. The effect of God's transforming work is that his people are so overwhelmed and undone by their sin and the offense of their holy God that they are moved to a state of utter humility and heartfelt repentance that looks to God alone for mercy.

God, however, often works through means. What means will God the Holy Spirit use to convict people of their sin and to drive them to God for grace and mercy? It is here that we approach, in the words of Barry Webb, "the most mysterious and profound part of Zechariah's message, and it has to do with the necessary place of suffering and weeping in the coming of the kingdom of God."[11] The catalyst for such a radical transformation is the apprehension of the true horror and offense of their sin depicted in this vivid expression: "When they look on me, on him whom they have pierced, they shall mourn for him, as one mourns for an only child, and weep bitterly over him, as one weeps over a firstborn" (v. 10). Though Israel will be victorious in battle, their victory will not be without casualties. In fact, Israel will suffer perhaps the greatest loss: their messianic King sustains a mortal wound.[12] Just as the victory of the seed of the woman over the seed of the serpent would not come without suffering—"he shall bruise your head, and you shall bruise his heel" (Genesis 3:15)—Israel's champion will be wounded in their victory.

And yet it is not only the death of their King that will cause Israel inconsolable sorrow, but the fact that it is by a spear thrust that comes from God's own people: "When they look on me, on him whom they have pierced..." (Zechariah 12:10). Clearly the responsibility for the Messiah's wound lies with Israel. It is this realization that cuts God's people to the heart. When God's people realize the true cost of their deliverance, the price God pays to redeem a people for himself, their hearts melt in sorrow, their tears flow in contrition, and their lips tremble for a mercy without which they are utterly lost.

The prophet likens the depths of Israel's sorrow to the mourning that took place at or for Hadad-rimmon in the plain of Megiddo (Zechariah 12:11). His reference to Hadad-rimmon is somewhat cryptic. Some have suggested that the mourning in view here is the ritual mourning for the Canaanite deity Baal when worshipers grieved the deity's death and descent to the underworld. More likely, however, this may refer to the place where King Josiah was killed in battle on the plain of Megiddo, a national calamity for which the chronicler tells us "all Judah and Jerusalem mourned" (2 Chronicles 35:24). In either view the prophet is clearly conveying the scope of the sorrow that will grip the land. The entire land, the entire nation, the entire kingdom will see and will know the great shame of their sin and the great cost of their deliverance.

However, the national, corporate nature of Israel's sorrow does not minimize its individual character. The prophet goes to great lengths to stress the personal contrition of individuals and families.[13] "The land shall mourn," he says, "each family by itself" (Zechariah 12:12). This, in other words, will not be a day of blame-shifting and excuse-making. There will not be appeals to ignorance or mitigating circumstances. Rather, every individual will acknowledge his or her own guilt, sin, and complicity in the wound that pierced their God and King. Importantly, Israel's leaders are not exempt from the blame. Just the opposite. As Israel's kings and priests so often have led Israel in disobedience in the past, in a wonderful reversal Israel's leaders will lead the nation in repentance. The leading families represented here as the houses of David, Nathan, Levi, and the Shimeites will rend not only their garments but their hearts, acknowledging their sins before God.

The depth of Israel's grief, however, is perhaps captured most powerfully in the central image when the prophet says that Israel's mourning would be "as one mourns for an only child" and weeps "as one weeps for a firstborn" (v. 10). Nothing in this world compares to the grief of losing a child. That this child should be a firstborn and an only child evokes a circumstance so painful that words fail to fully capture the depth of such grief. Of course, this image evokes not only a common understanding but Israel's history as well, bringing to mind Israel's infant boys whom Pharaoh sentenced to death in the days of the exodus. It also brings to mind Abraham's son Isaac, whom he was willing to offer to God in an act of faith. Such events pointed Israel and they point us to the loving heart of God, who gave up his own Son to death for us all.

What God declared through Zechariah's figures of speech was in fact fulfilled and accomplished in time and space. The Roman soldiers who wanted to hasten the death of those being crucified set out to break their legs. However, John tells us that when they got to Jesus, they saw that he was already dead (John 19:33). So perhaps to make sure, one soldier thrust his spear into Jesus's side, and "at once there came out blood and water" (v. 34). This happened, the Gospel writer tells us, to fulfill Scripture, which says, "They will look on . . . him whom they have pierced" (Zechariah 12:10; cf. Revelation 1:7).

Those who benefit from the death of the Son are those who, in looking at the crucified Jesus, understand that it was their own sins that put him there. Though most believers did not crucify Jesus personally, the expression "When they look on me, on him whom they have pierced . . ." (Zechariah 12:10) reminds every believer that Christ suffered the Father's wrath on a Roman cross for our sins. As the prophet Isaiah said, "He was pierced for our transgressions; he was crushed for our iniquities; upon him was the chastisement that brought us peace, and with his wounds we are healed" (Isaiah 53:5). As one recent hymn puts it,

> It was my sin that held Him there
> Until it was accomplished.[14]

## A Cleansed People (13:1–6)

Perhaps contrary to expectations, confession of guilt results not in the stroke of God's judgment but the gift of God's mercy. Juxtaposed to this scene of mourning, isolation, and heart-rending grief over sin in Zechariah 12 is a contrasting scene of life, cleansing, and purity in Zechariah 13. In response to the people's sorrow and grief over their sin, God causes a fountain of life to erupt: "On that day there shall be a fountain opened for the house of David and the inhabitants of Jerusalem, to cleanse them from sin and uncleanness" (Zechariah 13:1). The "sin and uncleanness" that disqualifies us from the presence of God is addressed by this cleansing fountain that will "cleanse them [Israel] from sin and uncleanness."

The cleansing that God will accomplish is not only the cleansing of his repentant people but of the land itself. God says he will remove the idols from the land; he will "cut off [their] names, . . . so that they shall be remembered no more" (Zechariah 13:2). By removing the idols from the land, God removes Israel's perennial temptation to trust and serve false gods. These idols and the temptation that they present will no longer be remembered, and Israel will be free from the struggles, failures, and sins with which they have so long been burdened.

God will cleanse the land not only of the false gods and (presumably) those who serve them but also of those who serve the true God falsely. God will cleanse the land from those who speak lies in his name: "Also I will remove from the land the prophets and the spirit of uncleanness. And if anyone again prophesies, his father and mother who bore him will say to him, 'You shall not live, for you speak lies in the name of the LORD.' And his father and mother who bore him shall pierce him through when he prophecies" (Zechariah 13:2b, 3). Admittedly, this vignette of filicide sounds strange to modern sensibilities. However, the prophet's goal in this little dialogue is to depict a people whose loves and loyalties are so attuned to God's righteousness that they are willing to forsake even the strongest natural bonds for the sake of his kingdom. The purity of the kingdom of God is cast in terms of the people's devotion to the Mosaic covenant, which required that false prophecy, even that uttered by one's children, be punished by death as an affront to the majesty, holiness, and truthfulness of the Lord God (cf. Deuteronomy 13:1–5; 21:18–21).

Furthermore, the visions of these false prophets will become a source of shame, and the "hairy cloak" that was donned—likely as a symbol of the prophet's status as a mouthpiece of God—will be cast aside, no longer a source of honor (Zechariah 13:4). However, the false prophet remains true to form as he continues to deceive in an attempt to cover his sin and save his life by claiming, "I am no prophet, I am a worker of the soil, for a man sold me in my youth" (v. 5). When questioned about wounds on his back, probably self-inflicted in an attempt to manipulate God, as was often done in pagan religions, he will again lie, saying, "The wounds I received in the house of my friends" (v. 6). There is much that is obscure about this prophecy. But what shines through clearly is this: what was once a lucrative and reputable career in divination and idolatry will become a source of shame and mortal danger for those who practiced it. When God's kingdom comes, false prophets will be exposed as liars, deceivers, and frauds who are willing to profit by harming others. In this way, the prophet Zechariah offers a vivid picture of a corrupt people purified and a defiled land cleansed. A land that once celebrated godlessness and corruption will become a land marked by purity and holiness.

God is holy and has purposed to create a holy people with whom he will dwell in a holy land. Zechariah announces the fulfillment of that reality as God cleanses the penitent and destroys the wicked from his land. Here believers of every age are given the critical reminder that the trials of this life and the shame of sin will not last forever. Those who hate their sin will one day be free from it; those who long for holiness will one day be cleansed so thoroughly that it will be impossible to remember the temptations that haunt people daily in this present evil age. After Jesus declared his blessing upon those who "hunger and thirst for righteousness," he promised, "They shall be satisfied" (Matthew 5:6).

### A Scattered People, a Gathered People (13:7–9)

How is it that the Lord will accomplish so great a transformation? Zechariah 13:7 marks a major transition in the oracle, so major that many commentators and preachers treat the verses that follow as a separate unit, somewhat unrelated to what comes before and potentially misplaced.[15] However, the poem in verses 7–9 forms an apt conclusion to the previous oracles, as it brings resolution to issues of leadership, testing, punishment, and deliverance.[16]

In 13:7, God once again, and for the last time in the book, invokes the image of a shepherd. We met the shepherds earlier in Zechariah's prophecies. In chapter 10, Israel's shepherds are the object of divine wrath: "My anger is hot against the shepherds, and I will punish the leaders; for the LORD of hosts cares for his flock, the house of Judah" (v. 3). Again in chapter 11, the prophet announces, "The sound of the wail of the shepherds, for their glory is ruined!" (v. 3). The shepherd motif is taken up as the controlling metaphor for the prophetic sign-act in chapter 11 (vv. 4–17), where the prophet enacts Israel's tragic rejection of God, their good shepherd. In Zechariah 13, we meet a shepherd again, this time the good shepherd. The shepherd is described as one closely associated with the Lord himself, as God calls him "my shepherd" and one "who stands next to me" (v. 7).[17] Yet surprisingly and inexplicably, God calls for this shepherd to be struck down: "'Awake, O sword, against my shepherd, against the man who stands next to me,' declares the LORD of hosts" (v. 7).

No reason, cause, or explanation is given; only the result. The result of a stricken shepherd is scattered sheep. This, in fact, is God's purpose; he will turn his "hand against the little ones" (v. 7). This scattering is an act of judgment and testing. Just as Israel's wilderness wanderings had been an expression of

God's judgment upon the first generation but a time of testing and refinement for the second generation who would enter the land, and just as Israel's exile had been a period of judgment for national Israel for their rebellion against God but a period of refinement for those who would look to the Lord in repentance and faith, so too will the stricken shepherd serve as the occasion for both God's judgment and God's mercy. From those who are scattered, God preserves a remnant who will be tested, refined, and purified by his grace.[18] God says, "In the whole land, declares the LORD, two thirds shall be cut off and perish, and one third shall be left alive. And I will put this third into the fire, and refine them as one refines silver, and test them as gold is tested" (vv. 8, 9).

Jesus himself invoked this verse as he foretold his disciples' rejection and denials. "When they had sung a hymn, they went out to the Mount of Olives. Then Jesus said to them, 'You will all fall away because of me this night. For it is written, "I will strike the shepherd, and the sheep of the flock will be scattered"'" (Matthew 26:30, 31). And so they did—even Peter, who insisted and swore that though everyone else should fall away, he would remain with Jesus (v. 33). Peter would deny Jesus not once or twice but three times (vv. 69–75). Indeed, Jesus's closest friends were scattered. Out of embarrassment, cowardice, misunderstanding, and fear, they left their shepherd utterly alone, a preface to his abandonment by his Father in Heaven. And yet God would use precisely this stricken shepherd to accomplish his purposes to forgive sins, defeat the power of the devil, and bring healing to the nations. Jesus not only foretold his death and his disciples' rejection but also his resurrection and his disciples' restoration: "After I am raised up, I will go before you to Galilee" (v. 32). The crucified and risen Lord would gather a people to himself.

This poem in the book of Zechariah is about the way of salvation and the cost of discipleship. At the center of God's new creation stands a stricken shepherd. The blow this shepherd receives is the catalyst for God's judgment and God's mercy. Yes, God's stricken shepherd will cause many to be scattered. They will find in the cross a stumbling block of offense. For others, however, the stricken shepherd will become the cause of their redemption and the ingathering of God's elect. Those who take their stand with the stricken shepherd, the crucified Messiah, are the true recipients of God's covenant promises summarized so wonderfully in the prophet's concluding lines: "They will call upon my name, and I will answer them" (Zechariah 13:9b). Like a child calling out to her father or longing for the voice of her mother, those who by faith take up the reproach of Christ will cry out to God, and God promises, "I will answer them." What is God's response to his tried and tested people?

The oracle concludes with Israel's restored relationship with her God, captured in a liturgical variation of God's gracious promise, the summary of the covenant of grace: God says, "I will say, 'They are my people'; and they will say, 'The LORD is my God'" (v. 9c).

# 74

# On That Day . . .

ZECHARIAH 14

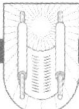

"THIS IS THE WAY THE WORLD ENDS, This is the way the world ends, This is the way the world ends, Not with a bang but a whimper." These final lines of T. S. Eliot's poem "The Hollow Men" are, at least according to one source, "probably the most quoted lines of any 20th century poet writing in English."[1] This is unsurprising, as Eliot so memorably captured the disillusion, despair, and sense of futility that had gripped the modern consciousness in the early part of the twentieth century. In a world without purpose, what should we expect except an end without meaning, a conclusion that is no conclusion at all? For Eliot and so many others at the time, there was no longer any room for a climactic culmination of history that would make sense of all the suffering, tragedy, and absurdity of the modern world as they conceived it.

Zechariah's climactic prophecy stands in stark contrast to the hopelessness and lifelessness of Eliot's haunting poem. To modify Eliot, we might say that Zechariah declares, "This is the way the world ends, This is the way the world ends, This is the way the world ends, Not with a whimper but with a bang." In Zechariah 14 the prophet announces that the world as we know it will one day come to an end. It will end not in the way many modern-day prophets predict—through rising oceans, a new ice age, or the explosion of the sun—but through the inbreaking of the kingdom of God, an inbreaking of such cosmic proportions that it will be impossible to miss. This is what Zechariah declares in this highly symbolic final vision: God's otherworldly reign and rule upending this present evil age with such finality that the world order as we know it will be fundamentally and permanently transformed.

Concluding both his final oracle, which began in chapter 12, and his book as a whole, Zechariah's prophecy of the end of the world is not meant to be read as a precise timeline or literal description of what will happen or when it will happen.[2] Like most things in Zechariah's prophecies, the prophet employs rich and allusive symbolism drawn from Israel's Scriptures as well as from Israelite culture to express what is in many respects inexpressible. The prophet utilizes the familiar to convey the unfamiliar by way of analogy. The great and awesome day of the Lord is described in different ways and from various angles, moving forward and backward in time with a fair degree of fluidity. In this we see that the prophet's purpose is not to provide Israel (or us) the details of what to expect with historical or scientific accuracy.[3] Rather, his purpose is, on the one hand, to overwhelm us with the power and terror of God's final judgment on this rebellious world and, on the other hand, to encourage and instill hope by reminding his hearers that God has promised to provide a way of escape and to one day make all things new, imperishable, and incorruptible. The Lord will make a new world of unimaginable glory and unending blessing where those who worship him in this life will worship him for all eternity.

Zechariah 14 reminds us that the way things are now is not how things always will be. A new day, a better day, is coming. Though disorienting in its arrangement of events, the vision does relay a narrative of sorts, a narrative that moves through great trial to great triumph.[4] "Through many dangers, toils, and snares" God will preserve his people and bring them safely to their heavenly home.[5]

### Day of Great Trial (14:1–2)

In his concluding oracle, Zechariah returns to a message he's labored hard to impress upon the hearts of God's covenant people—namely, that the road to glory is not an easy road filled with sunshine and rainbows. Rather, the road to glory is filled with tremendous struggle as God's people encounter trials and temptations, loss and hardships of every kind.

The prophet's vision of the day of the Lord opens with an announcement that is nothing short of terrifying: "Behold, a day is coming for the Lord, when your spoil will be divided in your midst" (Zechariah 14:1, AT). A day is coming in which Israel will again witness their enemies distributing their wealth "in your midst," that is, in the midst of the city of Jerusalem itself.[6] Israel is presented as helpless and even hopeless. Her walls have been breached, and she has clearly suffered great loss and humiliation. By all appearances her defeat is certain. The prophet then offers a flashback of sorts that rehearses how Israel got to this point of defeat and desperation. God speaks in the first person: "For

I will gather all the nations against Jerusalem to battle, and the city shall be taken and the houses plundered and the women raped" (v. 2).

The scene is clearly one of war, with God's people besieged within the walls of the holy city. The fortifications of Jerusalem are not strong enough to withstand the attack. The walls are breached, the houses plundered, the women raped. These are the horrors of war. The heartbreaking loss of home and property, symbolizing the livelihoods built up over years and generations, happens in a day. However, this pales in comparison to the loss of life and the defilement of human dignity that is depicted in the rape of Jerusalem's women. This future disaster that Zechariah describes so vividly is intentionally reminiscent of the past destruction of Jerusalem in 586 B.C., when the Babylonians razed the city to the ground under the leadership of Nebuchadnezzar.[7] Zechariah sees in this past event a type or a prefiguring of a future, eschatological event in which God will again come in judgment. His people will again suffer unimaginable violence and destruction at the hands of those who despise them and their God.

For many in Israel, this day is a day of God's judgment. Zechariah says, "Half of the city shall go out into exile, but the rest of the people shall not be cut off from the city" (14:2). In the Bible, the language of "going into exile" and "not being cut off" is the language of death and life, respectively. Simply being an outward, visible member of the covenant community is not enough to spare an Israelite from divine judgment. Half of the city will suffer the stroke of divine judgment and, like the nations themselves, will come under divine wrath for their faithlessness and sins. Once again there will be a separation within the covenant community between those whose circumcision is merely external and those whose circumcision is both external and internal, that is, of the heart (13:7–9; cf. Deuteronomy 30:6; Romans 2:28, 29). Paul says, "Not all who are descended from Israel belong to Israel, and not all are children of Abraham because they are his offspring" (Romans 9:6, 7). For those who did not learn the lesson of the first exile, Zechariah says, there awaits another terrible and final exile.

In Zechariah's day, like our day, the covenant community consisted of both believers and unbelievers. But this state of affairs would not last forever. One day there would be an ultimate separation, not between Jews and Gentiles but between those in Christ and those in Adam—those who have trusted in God for their salvation and those who have taken their stand against God and against his Messiah (Psalm 2:1, 2). In a parable, Jesus taught that the master will allow the wheat and weeds to grow together for a time, but the day of harvest will come when the master will tell the reapers, "Gather the weeds first and bind them in bundles to be burned, but gather the wheat into my barn" (Matthew 13:30).

Perhaps the most startling aspect of this brutal scene in Zechariah is not the warfare itself but God's involvement. God says, "For I will gather all the nations against Jerusalem to battle" (Zechariah 14:2). Why would God, whose eyes are too holy to look upon evil, involve himself in such a horrific event? There are a few things to keep in mind when encountering this and similar texts. First, God is not putting an evil desire into the heart of these nations that is not present already. The sinful impulses and desires inclining these nations toward such brutality find their origin in the human heart (see James 1:13–15) and not in God. Rather, the Lord is allowing sinful human beings to act on the evil intentions present in their hearts and minds to accomplish his appointed ends. Second, the prophet emphasizes God's gathering of the nations against Jerusalem to highlight God's sovereignty over Jerusalem's final trial. God is not reacting; he is in control from start to finish. In fact, third, God's control reveals his ultimate purposes. While the nations gather no doubt to destroy and plunder Jerusalem, God gathers the nations to destroy and plunder them. God will employ the nations as his rod of judgment against unbelief, and yet the ultimate fate of those who wickedly oppose God and his people is as certain as it is dreadful. Once and for all God will overthrow his enemies and, as we will see, deliver his people.

The expression "War is hell" is attributed to William T. Sherman, who served as a Union general in the American Civil War. War, of course, is not hell in the literal sense. But it is perhaps the closest analogy we have in this life to the horror, sadness, loss, grief, panic, and despair that is the reality of Hell. Hell is an existence (the word *life* might be misleading) completely void of God's goodness, God's mercy, and even God's common grace. The warfare depicted so vividly by the prophet Zechariah presents a small glimpse of the eternal fate that awaits those outside of Christ and the salvation he came to bring to the world, to Jews and Gentiles alike. In this way, Zechariah 14 serves as a warning to those outside the Church that this world and this life are not all there is; a day of reckoning and of judgment is coming. But it is a warning to those in the Church as well, reminding us that our external association with the Church, while vitally important, is not sufficient. The visible covenant community itself will be divided between those who live by faith in God's promises and those who, like the unbelieving nations, live by sight.

The Church must not be surprised when trials and temptations come. Jesus promised that they would come, and that the only road to glory is a road that runs through trial—sometimes even great trials as symbolically depicted in Zechariah's prophecy. But here we receive the critical message that God is sovereign over the trials of his Church, and he will use even the greatest trial the Church will ever face, a trial that by all appearances adumbrates the annihilation of the Church herself, to accomplish his purposes of judgment and mercy.

## A Day of Great Deliverance (14:3–5)

Into Israel's day of great trial erupts an even greater deliverance. Zechariah declares that at the very moment when all hope seems to be lost, "The LORD will go out and fight against those nations as when he fights on a day of battle" (Zechariah 14:3). God does not wait until the last moment because he has a flair for the dramatic. He waits until, from a human perspective, all hope is lost because in so doing he demonstrates to the entire world that salvation is from the Lord (cf. Jonah 2:7–9). Only God could deliver Jerusalem, and Zechariah reminds us that only God *will* deliver Jerusalem.

When God appears, he does so as the divine warrior. The expression "as when he fights on a day of battle" (Zechariah 14:3) would have reminded Israel of the countless times God had gone before them into battle, defeating their enemies often in extraordinary displays of his power and sovereignty. The most obvious example, of course, had been the Lord's defeat of the Egyptian army in the time of the exodus. But the Lord fought for his people countless times throughout their history—in the days of the judges, in the days of David, and in the days of Hezekiah, to name a few.

Here, one last time, God is again taking his stand with and for his people.

His stand this time is quite dramatic, as the earth not only shakes but splits under his appearing. Zechariah says, "On that day his feet shall stand on the Mount of Olives that lies before Jerusalem on the east, and the Mount of Olives shall be split in two from east to west by a very wide valley, so that one half of the Mount shall move northward, and the other half southward" (v. 4). It is a vivid scene, the drama of which is meant to highlight the seemingly impossible nature of God's deliverance. Jerusalem is besieged all around; there is no hope or help in sight. It is into this impossible scenario that the Lord, the divine warrior, plants his feet on the Mount of Olives east of Jerusalem, a hill associated in Israel's history with idolatry, and as in the days of the exodus, God makes a way where there is no way.[8]

The mountain splits apart, a path of escape is made, and God's people are delivered. Zechariah says, "You shall flee to the valley of my mountains, for the valley of the mountains shall reach to Azal. And you shall flee as you fled from the earthquake in the days of Uzziah king of Judah. Then the LORD my God will come, and all the holy ones with him" (v. 5). The only analogy that Israel has for the destruction and devastation of that day is an earthquake that took place centuries earlier, the destruction of which was so great that it served as a touchstone for catastrophe for years to come. When the Lord takes his stand, the earth will shake, the mountain will split in two, and God's people will flee to a place of safety, far from the battle that the Lord will fight.[9]

The believer's hope in every age is in the Lord who has promised to fight for his people. God will take a stand against all the forces of evil arrayed against his elect. When from a human perspective there is no hope of deliverance, God promises to make a way. The battle is clearly not a joint endeavor. It is not a salvation ushered in by the prayers or piety of God's people. It is not the result of Israel's (or our) obedience to God's Law. It is God's salvation from first to last. God, perhaps leading the forces of Heaven itself, will come to deliver his people from certain death.[10]

In this depiction of a final battle, the prophet emphasizes God's sovereignty over even our greatest trials and victory over our greatest foes. In those trials, where we feel as if we've entered the gates of Hell itself, God assures us that he is with us and that he is in control over every evil that threatens us. The message for God's people in Zechariah's day and the message for God's people in our day is that faith in God in this life does not exempt us from grave trials and great difficulties. This is as true for the Church corporately (which is the focus of Zechariah's prophecy) as it is for individuals. The road to glory is a road of great difficulty, hardship, sorrow, and temptation. Yet here we're reminded that God wins in the end. There are no powers or principalities in this world that will ultimately triumph over Christ's Church. God will deliver those who belong to him. We will at times feel hopeless and helpless. We will look around and not see a way of escape. Our imaginations cannot fathom how God can bring good, much less salvation out of the crises we encounter in this world. Yet Zechariah declares in no uncertain terms that God is able to make a way where there is no way. He has done it countless times before ("as when he fights . . . ," 14:3), and he will do it again.

Israel's hope, like our hope, is not to be found in this world or in the powers of this world. It is not to be found in their wisdom or in their ability to manage the situations in which they find themselves struggling, if not drowning. The prophet promises that God himself will come to deliver his people and, as we will see, he will triumph over all that threatens them either in this life or in the life to come.

## A Day of New Creation (14:6–11)

The aftermath of war is chaos. War never creates order. It destroys and decimates what has been built up sometimes over generations. Not so with the war that the Lord will wage for his people. The result of God's battle against his enemies is not chaos, ruin, and mass destruction but order. It is not exposure and vulnerability for the weak and wounded but safety and security for those who have found refuge behind the banner of the Lord. In short, it is not death but life.[11]

Beginning in 14:6, Zechariah describes a new world order so profound that it is nearly impossible for our minds and our imaginations to comprehend it. It will be like this creation with which we are familiar, yet it will not be like this creation in fundamental ways. However, since the only reference point we have for understanding a new creation is this present creation that we know and experience every day, Zechariah describes this new creation reality in terms of the old. He says, "On that day there shall be no light, cold, or frost. And there shall be a unique day, which is known to the LORD, neither day nor night, but at evening time there shall be light" (14:6, 7). There is perhaps nothing more certain in this life than the fact that the sun will come up tomorrow. Every day we have lived on this earth we have known morning and evening, day and night, light and darkness. This is part of the creation as God designed it at the very beginning: "God said, 'Let there be light,' and there was light. And God saw that the light was good. And God separated the light from the darkness. God called the light Day, and the darkness he called Night. And there was evening and there was morning, the first day" (Genesis 1:3–5).

From the dawn of creation, light and darkness, connected as they are to the sun and the moon (vv. 14–19), are part of the warp and woof of the created order. But when God comes in glory, Zechariah says, he will bring about a new creation in which "light . . . cold . . . frost" (Zechariah 14:6)—possibly references to those original astral bodies and their effects on the world—will be no more.[12] It will be a world and an existence that is marked by perpetual light, a wonderful image that is picked up in the book of Revelation in which John sees a vision of the new heavens and the new earth and a new Jerusalem. He writes, "The city has no need of sun or moon to shine on it, for the glory of God gives it light, and its lamp is the Lamb. By its light will the nations walk, and the kings of the earth will bring their glory into it, and its gates will never be shut by day—and there will be no night there" (21:23–25). Just as God was the sole witness to his works of creation at the beginning, so again this day will be a day "known [only] to the LORD" (Zechariah 14:7). He alone is the architect of this new creation reality, a city, as the author of Hebrews tells us, "that has foundations, whose designer and builder is God" (11:10).

Corresponding to the transformation of the heavens above comes a transformation of the waters below. "On that day living waters shall flow out from

Jerusalem, half of them to the eastern sea and half of them to the western sea. It shall continue in summer as in winter" (Zechariah 14:8). Intersecting the north-south axis of the Jordan River comes a new river flowing east to west, from the Mediterranean to (presumably) the Dead Sea. These waters being designated as "living" refers to the never-ending supply of the life-giving and life-sustaining waters that will flow from Jerusalem. Such cosmic waters were somewhat conventional features of ancient Near-Eastern sanctuaries; here they are a clear allusion to the waters that flowed from and around Eden at the beginning (Genesis 2:10–14). Quite unlike most of the rivers and wadis with which Israel was familiar, these new, living waters would flow in season and out of season, in summer and in winter, making provision from farming and agriculture reliable and Israel's daily bread secure.

From the heavens in Zechariah 14:6, 7 to the waters in verse 8, the prophet lastly comes to the transformation of the land itself. In verse 10, the prophet declares, "The whole land shall be turned into a plain from Geba to Rimmon south of Jerusalem. But Jerusalem shall remain aloft on its site from the Gate of Benjamin to the place of the former gate, to the Corner Gate, and from the Tower of Hananel to the king's winepresses." The highlands of Judah are characterized by often steep and craggy cliffs. From the perspective of Israel's agricultural life, the leveling of the land represents ease of farming and the abundance such farming would produce. However, the agricultural interests are secondary to the theological interests of Judah's refashioned topography.[13] The leveling of Judah effectively exalts Jerusalem, which itself is greatly expanded in size.[14] The goal of the leveling of the Judean highlands and the expansion of Jerusalem is to exalt the city of God. Jerusalem will "remain aloft" in glory and splendor.

The point, of course, is both the exaltation and security of Jerusalem. From this height Jerusalem would be an impregnable fortress. Never again would she be susceptible to attack, much less destruction.[15] Even more, the exalted Jerusalem will reflect its status as the highest city, the city of God, the place from which he rules as Lord of all.[16] The geographical security corresponds to the Lord's purpose for his holy city summarized succinctly in Zechariah 14:11: "It shall be inhabited, for there shall never again be a decree of utter destruction. Jerusalem shall dwell in security."

The rich imagery used for this new creation is designed to impress upon the hearts of the faithful the profound difference between their present and their future. The present of the postexilic community in Jerusalem is marked by insecurity, uncertainty, deprivation, and humility. Jerusalem's future, by contrast, will be breathtaking in its glory, marked as it is by unimaginable security, provision, abundance, and life in the fullest sense of the term. Not only will the new Jerusalem enjoy a new day, but it will be impossible for her ever to return to the days of old. God says, "There shall never again be a decree of utter destruction." Implied in this new creation is a new relationship, a new covenant unlike the covenant that set before Israel blessings for obedience and curses for disobedience (Leviticus 26; Deuteronomy 28).[17] No longer will disobedience and God's just judgment be a specter for a sinful people, a lingering possibility should they return to their old ways; God's justice will be satisfied and his people sanctified by the Son, whose perfect obedience and shed blood brings to an end the old covenant and inaugurates the new.

This new creation will be nothing less than the kingdom of God. Central to this marvelous description of a new creation is what many scholars believe was a confession of faith perhaps used in Israel's temple worship: "The LORD will be king over all the earth. On that day the LORD will be one and his name one" (Zechariah 14:9). Of course, God is King even now over all the earth. But God's kingship will one day be made manifest perfectly, plainly, and fully for all to see at the consummation of this world and the advent of the next. On that day every tongue will acknowledge the truth of Israel's creed, "Hear O Israel: the LORD our God, the LORD is one" (Deuteronomy 6:4). As Paul puts it in his letter to the Philippian church, "Therefore God has highly exalted him and bestowed on him the name that is above every name, so that at the name of Jesus every knee should bow, in heaven and on earth and under the earth, and every tongue confess that Jesus Christ is Lord, to the glory of God the Father" (Philippians 2:9–11).

This day of a new creation has dawned in the resurrection of the Son of God. However, what has begun in Christ's body has yet to be fully realized. For that we await this future day. John, the author of Revelation, describes this new creation with imagery that recalls Zechariah's prophecy: "Then I saw a new heaven and a new earth, for the first heaven and the first earth had passed away, and the sea was no more. And I saw the holy city, new Jerusalem, coming down out of heaven from God, prepared as a bride adorned for her husband" (21:1, 2). Later, John will tell us, "The city has no need of sun or moon to shine on it, for the glory of God gives it light, and its lamp is the Lamb. By its light will the nations walk, and the kings of the earth will bring their glory into it, and its gates will never be shut by day—and there will be no night there" (vv. 23–25). God's deliverance of his people will usher them into a new day and a new creation where mourning, tears, pain, and even death will be no more (v. 4). This creation, which now groans under the curse of sin and death, will one day be liberated and transformed into a new creation, the firstfruits of which have already appeared in the resurrected body of our Lord Jesus Christ (1 Corinthians 15:20).

## A Day of Reckoning (14:12–19)

Moving back and forth in time, the prophet then describes this coming day of the Lord as a day of reckoning. Two diametrically opposed fates will befall two diametrically opposed peoples. The first fate is the gruesome judgment that will befall those who have taken their stand against God, his city, and his people. Zechariah says in 14:12 that the Lord will strike them with a plague: "Their flesh will rot while they are standing on their feet, their eyes will rot in their sockets, and their tongues will rot in their mouths." The prophet is not trying to score cheap points by resorting to grotesque scare tactics. The point rather is that those who have assembled themselves in opposition to God will be subject to his devastating curse. The mention that this will take place "while they are still standing on their feet" suggests its immediacy; through a supernatural intervention, this rebellious assault will be stopped in its tracks.[18] Those who have mounted the assault will receive the stroke of divine justice, causing their flesh, their eyes, and their tongues to rot.

The nature of the curse is important. It entails a corruption and destruction of the organs that facilitate human life in the fullest sense of the term. Rotting, of course, is associated with death. However, these corpses rot "while standing on their feet." To be alive and rotting at the same time is a vivid portrait of the horrible fate awaiting those who posture themselves against their Creator.

Furthermore, the plague is accompanied by panic: "On that day a great panic from the Lord shall fall on them, so that each will seize the hand of another, and the hand of the one will be raised against the hand of the other. And Judah too will fight with Jerusalem" (Zechariah 14:13, 14a, AT). Panic is a common feature of holy war when God routes his enemies (maybe in this case including even unbelieving Israelites) by turning them against each other.[19] The turning of soldiers against fellow soldiers is an indication that the Lord has intervened in such a way that his people have to do little to nothing except watch as their enemies destroy themselves. To give just one example, when Gideon and his men blasted 300 trumpets, "the Lord set every man's sword against his comrade and against all the army" (Judges 7:22; cf. also 1 Samuel 14:20).

The plague and the panic are indiscriminate. When God placed the Canaanites under the ban in Joshua's day, the Israelites were not to leave anything alive. Men, women, children, beasts, livestock—everything with the breath of life must die because God was in this way anticipating and foreshadowing the reality of eschatological judgment. Zechariah receives a vision of this judgment day when the devastation of God's holy wrath consumes all that breathes in the camp of the ungodly. So the prophet sees the plague fall on all living creatures: the "horses, the mules, the camels, the donkeys, and whatever beasts may be in those camps" (Zechariah 14:15).

There is one final aspect of this judgment-day curse that Zechariah sets forth in technicolor. He says, "If any of the families of the earth do not go up to Jerusalem to worship the King, the LORD of hosts, there will be no rain on them" (v. 17). Of course, the lack of rain produces drought and famine and results in starvation. For reasons that continue to elude commentators and scholars, Egypt is especially singled out (vv. 18, 19). It's been suggested that Egypt is the parade example of a nation (here designated as a "family") that has opposed God as in the time of the exodus, or perhaps Egypt's regular supply of water from the Nile deludes them into thinking they are immune from the curse of plague, panic, and famine.

With these, Zechariah vividly and creatively paints a picture of divine curse. All who have taken their stand against God and opposed his people will receive the dreadful stroke of divine judgment. The prophet draws on the familiar—Israel's history and experience with war, famine, drought, plague, and death—to describe a reality whose horror is beyond human comprehension. Such, he says, will be the fate of those who have taken their stand against their Creator and their God.

Yet this dreadful curse is set in contrast to the fate of God's people, here represented by Judah and Jerusalem. For Judah and Jerusalem, this day of the Lord will be a day of victory, vindication, and blessing. Zechariah sets forth a reversal of fortunes in which the nations who were gathered against Jerusalem to divide her spoil in her midst (v. 1) will themselves be despoiled as Jerusalem divides their spoil in her midst: "The wealth of all the surrounding nations shall be collected, gold, silver, and garments in great abundance" (v. 14).[20]

But greater than the wealth of the nations streaming into Jerusalem is the Lord God, the glory of Israel, dwelling in her midst. Just as verse 2 depicted a division in Israel between believers and unbelievers, so too verse 16 depicts a division within the Gentile nations. There will be some survivors from the nations, and these survivors who once gathered for war will now gather for worship.[21] They will join Israel's worship as they "shall go up year after year to worship the King, the LORD of hosts, and to keep the Feast of Booths" (v. 16). A central feature of Zechariah's vision of the new creation is the worship of Israel's God by Jews and Gentiles alike.[22]

Two peoples, two fates. It is striking, however, that the division does not align with popular notions of who will be saved and who will not. We see that it is not the moral versus the immoral, the spiritual versus the unspiritual, or the religious versus the irreligious. The division is decidedly between those who worship the Lord and those who do not. For Zechariah, the remnant is by definition those who go up year after year to Zion to worship Yahweh at the Feast of Booths, the yearly festival most closely associated with the Lord's kingship.[23] Those who refuse to bow the knee to God in worship and fidelity will suffer a curse far more devastating than is depicted in the prophet's apocalyptic vision. However, those who do submit to the Lord's reign and rule, who are numbered as citizens of his kingdom, will receive in the next life a joy far more glorious than the prophet's vision and imagination is able to relate. In glory, believers will receive the Lord himself—Father, Son, and Holy Spirit—in the fellowship and communion bond for which we were created, and it will stagger the human mind for its blessedness and joy.

### A Day of Holiness to the Lord (14:20, 21)

The expression "Holy to the LORD" is used in the Bible to refer to realities set apart or sanctified for the Lord. It is used of the altar of incense (Exodus 30:10), the Sabbath day (31:15), the peace offering (Leviticus 19:8), the tithe of land or flock (27:30, 32), and the people of Israel themselves (Deuteronomy 7:6). In Exodus 28 God describes in detail the priestly uniform that Aaron and his sons were to wear as they ministered in the tabernacle of the Lord. In verse 36 God commands Moses, "You shall make a plate of pure gold and engrave on it, like the engraving of a signet, 'Holy to the LORD.'" The literal crowning jewel adorning Aaron's exquisitely and beautifully fashioned uniform marked Aaron and the priests who would come after him as sacred and set apart for the Lord in a special way. They were made fit for service in the house of God. Their status was separate and distinct from the common and the profane realities of everyday life. This distinction between the sacred and the profane, the holy and the common, was fundamental to Israel's life and faith. Transgression of that boundary always resulted in disaster, as the stories of Uzzah and Uzziah, to name just two, attest.

But Zechariah beholds a new day in which the division between sacred and secular, holy and common, will be utterly erased. He says, "On that day there shall be inscribed on the bells of the horses, 'Holy to the LORD.' And the pots in the house of the LORD shall be as the bowls before the altar. And every pot in Jerusalem and Judah shall be holy to the LORD of hosts, so that all who sacrifice may come and take from them and boil the meat of the sacrifice in them" (Zechariah 14:20, 21a).

Neither horses nor the daily cookware in the houses of Jerusalem were considered sacred in Zechariah's day. Not only were horses unclean, they were associated with warfare and a source of Israel's misplaced hope.[24] But no longer! What Zechariah was describing with these concrete examples was the complete removal of the distinction between sacred and common. The world of God and the world of man would no longer operate in separate spaces; the world of man would one day become the world of God. And everything that remains in it would be transformed and made fit for God's sacred and holy realm. The sacrifices that had become sanctified and reserved only for those who were sanctified—namely, the priests—would become freely available for any to take. The world would be remade. Every square inch of it would be holy and sacred to God.

The prophet concludes somewhat enigmatically, saying, "There shall no longer be a trader in the house of the LORD of hosts on that day" (Zechariah 14:21b). The word translated as "trader" is literally "Canaanite," and many, I think rightly, see here a symbol of Israel's perennial enemy who not only harassed Israel militarily but tempted Israel's to sin spiritually.[25] It was the presence of the Canaanites in the promised land (and here possibly a reference to their business dealings in the temple) that proved a constant source of trouble, sorrow, and temptation for God's covenant people. Thus, the designation became a pejorative term for all foreigners unfit for the Lord's presence.[26]

The prophet's goal in this depiction of a new people worshiping in a new Jerusalem in a new creation is to instill in God's people a hope and a longing for the advent of this future glory. Those realities that have held Israel in bondage—the realities of sin and the separation it creates between God and man—will one day be removed permanently. The longing for intimate communion with our Creator that resides in the heart of every human will one day be realized. The fellowship with God that was available occasionally and only for the priests under the old covenant will be freely available to all as the separation between the holy God and unholy creatures is removed through the work of our Mediator, our Priest-King, Jesus Christ.

Israel's longing is also our longing as we struggle in this world. We struggle with sin and the effects of the curse that continue to ravage God's good creation in us and around us. The Church exists today as an admixture of believers and unbelievers, and she finds herself in many parts of the globe harassed and marginalized, if not outright persecuted for her confession of faith. Zechariah's oracle speaks to us as it reminds us that our hope and our help is not to be found in this world but in the God who has prepared another world of unimaginable glory for those who have placed their faith in his Son, King Jesus. Jesus will come again just as he has promised, and then finally "on that day the Lord will be one and his name one" (v. 9).

# MALACHI

*By Stephen M. Coleman*

# 75

# Questioning God's Love

MALACHI 1:1–5

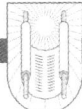

MALACHI IS A DIFFICULT BOOK. It is not difficult in the sense that it is difficult to understand (though some passages, as we will see, prove challenging). *Malachi* is difficult in the sense that it contains a difficult message—or better, a series of difficult messages—made all the more difficult because these are messages for an already beleaguered and discouraged people. The book consists of six disputations or accusations, each of which unfolds in a similar pattern: God levels a charge against his people, his people respond with an objection, and then God proves his case with a penetrating and painful demonstration of Israel's sin.[1]

As Israel quickly discovers, God's accusations do not merely address their outward behavior, as concerning as this is, nor even just their inner thoughts, though these too are exposed and condemned. God's accusations cut to the deepest heart attitudes and motivations of his covenant people, revealing the staggering depth and breadth of their spiritual bankruptcy. In this way, there is a relentless quality in the book of Malachi. As complaint follows complaint and accusation follows accusation, Israel's spiritual sickness is revealed to be more systemic, debilitating, and fatal than they ever could have imagined.

It is precisely this penetrating and relentless quality of God's accusations that makes the opening oracle even more striking. As the Lord prepares to unfold the sins of his people, how does he begin? The first word that God speaks to his people is a declaration of his unwavering, unqualified, unconditional love for his people. "'I have loved you,' says the Lord" (1:2). God has loved Israel in their sinful past, God continues to love them in their sinful present, and God will love Israel in their sinful future. This does not excuse or minimize the seriousness of Israel's sin. But it does provide a critical lens through which Israel (and we ourselves) must understand the hard and difficult words that follow.[2] God confronts his people with their sin because he loves them. God is calling his people to repentance because of his unwavering commitment to redeem them and to give them a future characterized not by curse and death but by blessing and life.

In Malachi's opening disputation we discover what is, in a sense, at the very heart of Israel's sin and rebellion, what we might call the sin beneath the sins. At the heart of all the various sins and shortcomings soon to be exposed and condemned lies a fundamental doubt and disbelief. Israel doubts God's love for them. Israel doubts that God cares about their sorrows and afflictions. Israel doubts that God is for them and that he will deliver on his promises to usher his people into a glorious future. God responds to Israel's doubting and distrustful hearts with a declaration and demonstration of his sovereign, electing love.

Though what follows Malachi's opening oracle will be hard and difficult words, we learn at the very beginning that God's ultimate goal is not to crush his people but to heal them. God desires to engender in his people of every age a deep faith, heartfelt repentance, and unwavering hope in him, in his Son, and in the world to come. But just as the revelation of God's love that would come in the person of Jesus would meet rejection from his own people, so God's love declared by his prophet Malachi is met with resistance and opposition. This is the first thing we see in our text—namely, God's love being questioned by God's covenant people.

### God's Love Questioned (1:2)

Something I think every teacher knows is that there are different kinds of questions. Some questions are asked out of genuine curiosity and concern, and some questions are asked to challenge and oppose. Immediately following God's unqualified and unequivocal declaration of his love for his people, his people respond with a question of this latter sort: "But you say, 'How have you loved us?'" (1:2). In this question, Israel is not expressing genuine curiosity or confusion. Israel's question is an opposing question. It is intended to contradict and to challenge.[3] "How have you loved us?" is saying, in effect, "No, you haven't."

Such a response likely strikes us as somewhat surprising. How could God's covenant people imply that their God hasn't acted lovingly and faithfully toward them? Given all that God has done for Israel, how could they possibly question God's love for them? I recall an incident as a young boy returning home from an entire day with my family at an amusement park and hearing a phone message from my friend inviting me to a sleepover. Taking into consideration how exhausted I was, my parents said I couldn't go to the sleepover. I remember looking them straight in the eyes and, without a hint of irony, saying, "You *never* let me have any fun!" This is how many hear Israel's question: like that of a child whose swimsuit is still wet from the waterslides accusing his parents of withholding fun.

But this would be to miss the point. Israel isn't ignorant of the fact that God has loved them in ages past. From their youth, every Israelite would have heard the remarkable account of God's acts of deliverance in the days of Moses, when God brought his people out of Egypt with great signs and wonders. They would have been familiar also with God's faithfulness in raising up King David, the man after God's own heart, to lead and rule his people. They would have heard of God's faithfulness in blessing King Solomon with great wealth, wisdom, and renown; and they certainly would have been familiar with the glories of the temple that Solomon built. Even closer to their own day, the postexilic community would have perhaps remembered, perhaps even firsthand, God's faithfulness in delivering them from the curse of exile and restoring them to the promised land. Israel's response, "How have you loved us?" doesn't deny these great demonstrations of God's love and faithfulness, but it implies that they are of little present value.[4] The people are asking, in effect, "How have you loved us lately? What good is your love in ages past for us today, in our present sufferings, struggles, and afflictions?"[5]

Though we can't pinpoint the date of Malachi's ministry with the exactness we would like, we can be fairly confident that he ministered in the postexilic period.[6] Life in postexilic Israel was incredibly hard. Many saw their day, to use the words of Zechariah, as a "day of small things" (Zechariah 4:10). Gone were the glory days of Israel's king and kingship. Gone were the glories of Solomon's temple. Gone were Israel's national independence and influence on the world stage. What about those promises of the great prophets of old? Centuries earlier, Isaiah had declared to those who would return from Babylon, "Arise, shine, for your light has come, and the glory of the Lord has risen upon you. . . . And nations shall come to your light, and kings to the brightness of your rising" (Isaiah 60:1–3). What about the great promises of Ezekiel, who spoke of Israel's future, saying, "They shall dwell securely, and none shall make them afraid. . . . They shall . . . no longer suffer the reproach of the nations" (Ezekiel 34:28, 29)? What about the more recent prophecies of Zechariah? God declared through him,

> There shall be a sowing of peace. The vine shall give its fruit, and the ground shall give its produce, and the heavens shall give their dew. And I will cause the remnant of this people to possess all these things. And as you have been a byword of cursing among the nations, O house of Judah and house of Israel, so will I save you, and you shall be a blessing. Fear not, but let your hands be strong. (Zechariah 8:12, 13)

What had become of these glorious promises? They all had yet to be realized. None had come to pass, and many in Malachi's day doubted they ever would.[7]

Israel was asking, in effect, "How is your faithfulness in the past of use for us today?" When seen in this light, we can understand how Israel's struggles were not all that different from our own. We too are prone to doubt and question God. For many Christians, the struggle is not in believing that Jesus lived, that he died for our sins, or that he rose on the third day. We might believe this to be true and yet fail to see its significance in the here and now. As a consequence, the gospel message can begin to ring hollow in our ears.

We too can struggle with being so preoccupied by the difficulties and worries, fears and sorrows of our daily lives that we fail to see the present value of the beauty and blessing of God, who is with us and for us.

We too are prone to question God's love for us and his commitment to us. Before we stand in judgment on Israel, thinking, *You had the exodus, you had the covenants, you had the kingdom, you had the prophets, you had the restoration from exile. How could you possibly question God's love for you?* we must remember that we have Christ, the fullness of God incarnate, and the fulfillment of all of God's promises. We have a cross on Calvary and an announcement of an empty tomb. We have the message of a resurrected Christ who died for us and rose in triumph over a foe far greater than Edom. Yet we can find ourselves questioning God's love, wondering what significance a dying and rising Savior has for us in our daily work, marriages, relationships, churches. We can find ourselves wondering if God knows and if he cares. If Israel was culpable in Malachi's day (and they were), how much more so are we? How does God respond to the challenging, questioning, doubting hearts of his culpable people?

## God's Love Demonstrated (1:2b–3a)

God does not respond to his people's doubting hearts and opposing tongues with the answer we might expect. We would probably expect God to respond with a somewhat exasperated version of Elizabeth Barrett Browning's famous Sonnet 43, which begins: "How do I love thee? Let me count the ways."[8] Then we'd expect God to enumerate the manifold ways in which he daily showers his people with mercy and kindness. But God doesn't respond like this at all. Rather, he responds to Israel's doubting and disputatious hearts with a history lesson: "'Is not Esau Jacob's brother?' declares the LORD. 'Yet I have loved Jacob but Esau I have hated'" (Malachi 1:2b, 3a).

God is referring to Israel's origins as the descendants of the great patriarch Jacob. During her pregnancy, Jacob and Esau's mother, Rebekah, received an oracle from the Lord adumbrating the future of her children: "Two nations are in your womb, and two peoples from within you shall be divided; the one shall be stronger than the other, the older shall serve the younger" (Genesis 25:23). Then we're told, "When her days to give birth were completed, behold, there were twins in her womb. The first came out red, all his body like a hairy cloak, so they called his name Esau. Afterward his brother came out with his hand holding Esau's heel, so his name was called Jacob" (vv. 24–26).

I don't typically think of twins as being older and younger. Their entrance into this world seems to have happened at roughly the same time. But I do know twins who speak this way, having recently heard one remind his sister that he's older, so she has to listen to him. But in the ancient Near East at the dawn of the second millennium B.C., birth order was of immense significance.[9] For many cultures, the oldest son (even if oldest by only a few seconds) received the lion's share of the family inheritance, and he would exercise a degree of power and authority within the family and community.

But God is reminding Israel that he did not choose Esau—the oldest, the strongest, the father's favorite, and the one culturally acceptable for privilege—to be the child of the promise. He chose Jacob—the younger, the weaker, and certainly culturally unacceptable—to be the one through whom he would raise up a people for himself and through whom would come the Savior of the world.[10] This is the significance of the language of "loved" and "hated" in Malachi 1:2, 3.[11] This is covenantal language, language that does not primarily have to do with emotions. God is not referring to his emotional life; rather, when the Lord says, "I have loved Jacob," he is referring to his commitment to a relationship and his faithfulness to that relationship that he has established with Jacob and his descendants.[12]

The significance of that commitment coming, in a sense, when Jacob was still in the womb is that it taught Isaac and Rebekah and it taught Israel and it teaches us something of God's sovereignty in election. God didn't choose Jacob because he was morally superior to Esau. In fact, a good case could be made that in many ways throughout his life, Jacob was morally inferior to his elder brother. God didn't choose Jacob because he was more spiritually sensitive. God didn't choose Jacob because he was stronger or more gifted or intelligent. Nor did he choose any of us today for these reasons. Furthermore, God did not choose Jacob because he foresaw that Jacob would have faith in him or because he saw that Jacob would reform his life in obedience to God's word. Rather, Jacob exercised faith in God and reformed his life (albeit modestly) in obedience to God's word precisely because God elected him. God's election came first.

It was while Jacob and Esau were still in the womb, Paul reasons, that "though they were not yet born and had done nothing either good or bad—in order that God's purpose of election might continue, not because of works but because of him who calls—she [Rebekah] was told, 'The older will serve the younger.' As it is written, 'Jacob I loved, but Esau I hated'" (Romans 9:11–13). Jacob's standing before God, Israel's standing before God, and our standing before God as righteous and beloved is all due to God's grace. It's all due to God's superabounding mercy for undeserving sinners. God elected Jacob out of his mere good pleasure; according to the inscrutable counsel of his will, he set his electing love upon him. From before the foundation of the world, God set his love upon Jacob and claimed this sinner as one for whom the incarnate Son would lay down his life.

God's response to Israel's doubt is not only surprising but also challenging. It challenged them and it challenges us to consider how the reality of God's election is a comfort and encouragement for us in our daily lives, especially in times of discouragement. This is the real function of the doctrine of election in the Bible. The doctrine of election is not revealed for the sake of philosophers to engage in metaphysical speculation or so that students in Christian colleges would have something to debate over lunch. Rather, throughout Scripture there is a clear pastoral purpose to the doctrine of election. It's used to minister to God's people. It is revealed to instill humility in those tempted to have pride, as Paul reasons in Ephesians 2 when he says that our salvation is a gift of God's grace "so that no one may boast" (v. 9). All who are proud and tempted to boast are brought back to this doctrine of election. Not because of anything in us or done by us but purely on the basis of God's grace alone in Christ may we stand in his presence.

The doctrine of election is set forth throughout Scripture to minister to God's people, especially in times of hardship and struggle, because it reminds us that the One who began a good work in us will most certainly see it to "completion at the day of Jesus Christ" (Philippians 1:6). It reminds us that our hope is not ultimately in our love for God but in God's love for us and that the God who loves us will hold us fast even and especially at times when our faith is weak (2 Timothy 2:13; 1 John 4:10).

In Malachi's day, as Israel struggled to see God's love for them in their present moment, God set forth his election of Jacob as his response to his people's doubting hearts. In response, Malachi grounded Israel's hope in God's election of Jacob. In times of doubt and in times of struggle, Israel needed to look to God and to God's word and remember that God would never leave them or forsake them.

The Old Testament scholar and theologian Geerhardus Vos famously wrote, "The best proof that [God] will never cease to love us lies in that He never began."[13] Less famous, though no less powerful is what Vos wrote next:

> What we are for Him and what He is for us belongs to the realm of eternal values. Without this we are nothing, in it we have all. Ours is the paean of Paul, "For we know that to them that love God all things work together for good . . . for those whom he foreknew [that is, eternally loved] he also predestinated to be made like unto the image of his Son . . . for I am persuaded, that neither death nor life, nor angels, nor principalities, nor things present nor things to come, nor powers, nor height nor depth, nor any other creation, shall be able to separate us from the love of God which is in Christ Jesus our Lord." (Rom. 8:28, 38, 39)[14]

In this gospel truth that God has loved us in Christ from before the foundation of the world, we have, as Vos reminded us, all we could ever need.

However, in Malachi, God not only points Israel to the past to demonstrate how his lovingkindness has protected and preserved his people throughout their generations, he also points Israel to the future in which his commitment to his people and the scope of his salvation will be displayed clearly before the entire world.

### God's Love Vindicated (1:3b–5)

It is not the case that Israel and Edom (Esau) in Malachi's day had no evidence of God's electing love in their lives. True, they struggled to see it. But the fact is that God's electing love was manifest, in part, in the history of these two great nations. Israel comprised the descendants of Jacob, and Edom the descendants of Esau. The Edomites were a constant scourge on Israel; when not a threat militarily, they were a thorn encouraging and supporting Israel's destruction in any way they could. The prophet Obadiah portrayed the delight and the rejoicing of the Edomites over the downfall of Israel (cf. Obadiah 11). For this reason God, through his prophets, announced his coming judgment on Edom, as for example, in Ezekiel: "As you rejoiced over the inheritance of the house of Israel, because it was desolate, so I will deal with you; you shall be desolate, Mount Seir, and all Edom, all of it. Then they will know that I am the LORD" (35:15).

There was something particularly appalling about the Edomite hostility toward Israel. This may be traced to an intuitive understanding we have of family bonds and the obligations to love and care for one another that they naturally produce.[15] How should brothers treat each other? They share a common ancestry, and this should be a sufficient motivation to weep at the downfall of one's kindred. There is an obligation to, at the very least, adopt a hands-off policy toward nations that move militarily against one's brothers. Yet Edom joined in the pillaging of Jerusalem and rejoiced over the destruction of their kindred.

The fruit of God's election of Israel for blessing and his election of Edom for cursing can be seen in some small measure in Malachi's day. God says, "I have loved Jacob but Esau I have hated. I have laid waste his hill country and left his heritage to jackals of the desert" (1:2b, 3).[16] Edom at that moment lay in ruins, a haunt of jackals—a conventional image of God's judgment and curse. Now Israel, being in an objectionable mood, might think, *Well, sure, Edom is desolate at the moment. But the fortunes of Edom, like our fortunes and the fortunes of so many states in the ancient world, rise and fall. Kingdoms are built up, they are destroyed, and often they are built up again.*

Edom had been destroyed before, only to rebuild and again harass and oppress Israel. Who was to say this wouldn't happen again? Was this how it would always be—a constant struggle with Israel rebuilding and Edom falling, and Edom rebuilding and Israel falling? To this God said in sum, "No!"

In Malachi 1:4a, we hear two visions for Edom's future. The first is Edom's vision for her future: "If Edom says, 'We are shattered but we will rebuild the ruins . . .'"[17] Here Edom acknowledges their defeat but makes plans to rebuild their ruined city with a demonstration of their power and might, a reassertion of their autonomy, arrogance, and rebellion. Edom's rebuilding no doubt implies a renewal of their threat to God's people.

But then we discover that Edom's plans are not God's plans.

In response to Edom's arrogant assertion of their future power and glory, the Lord of hosts (armies) declares his plans for Edom: "The Lord of hosts says, 'They may build, but I will tear down, and they will be called 'the wicked country,' and 'the people with whom the Lord is angry forever'" (v. 4b). The Lord declares that Edom's greatest efforts and most ingenious plans to establish themselves as a mighty kingdom will come to nothing. They may employ the greatest technology, building their walls twice as thick and making their defenses twice as strong. They may surround themselves with the greatest allies and purchase the most sophisticated weaponry—all of which preach power and security and wealth and wisdom—and yet God says, "They may build, but I will tear down." This is the ultimate fate of Edom: not eternal life but eternal destruction. In their arrogance Edom says, "We will rebuild," to which God in his righteous anger says, "I will tear down." The Edomites will seek to make a name for themselves. Just as those who built the tower of Babel sought to make a name for themselves, so Edom will seek to establish themselves in permanence and power. But God declares that their ultimate fate will be judgment and destruction.

Edom's fate will be summarized in their new name: "They will be called 'the wicked country,' and 'the people with whom the Lord is angry forever'" (Malachi 1:4b). These undesirable epithets disclose the identity and the fate of this country. Edom is a country characterized by wickedness and evil, and as such, it is a country that has received a word of divine curse and stands under divine judgment forever. This is how they will be known for all eternity.

In this we have the critical reminder that it is not Edom's word about themselves that determines their future; it is God's word about Edom that determines their future. The same is true for the Israel of God. Israel's word about themselves is less important than God's word.

Israel thought their circumstances would never change. They thought they would always be a subject people, struggling to survive in a backwater province of a vast pagan empire. Postexilic Israel hardly felt like a people chosen, beloved, and treasured by the Lord of the universe.

We can feel similarly. Most of us had the feeling during the global pandemic that it would never end and things would never change. At times we feel this way about our lives, jobs, marriages, relationships with friends or children, church, or health. Yet God announced the ultimate demise of all that stands opposed to his people. In so doing, God was reminding Israel that their present struggles would not last forever. Their present struggle, affliction, and humiliation were not the last word on the matter. God would one day publicly and permanently vindicate himself and his people.

So he declared, "Your own eyes shall see this, and you shall say, 'Great is the Lord beyond the border of Israel!'" (Malachi 1:5).

God's power was barely evident within the borders of Israel, and it was imperceptible beyond her borders.[18] But on this last day, God's people would see and understand that their God is not only sovereign now but has been sovereign all along. They would see that their God's power is not limited to his people or their land but encompasses the entire globe, and that indeed he has been working all things together for good for "those who love God" and have been "called according to his purpose" (Romans 8:28).

At the moment, Yahweh's greatness beyond the borders of Israel is an article of faith. But God announces a day in which their faith will become sight, and God's people will see the ultimate and final destruction of all that stands opposed to God and all that stands opposed to his people. Israel will in that day stand in awe, worship, and praise as they behold not their triumph but God's triumph over evil.

This is a picture, of course, of the last day when "every knee [will] bow, in heaven and on earth and under the earth, and every tongue confess that Jesus Christ is Lord, to the glory of God the Father" (Philippians 2:10, 11). But it is a picture that isn't reserved for the last day. This is a victory that began at the cross. At the cross Jesus triumphed over enemies far greater than Edom—the enemy of sin and the curse of sin, which is death. There God has defeated Satan and thrown down the rulers and principalities of this world.[19]

The truth is that in and of themselves, Israel deserved the exact same fate as Edom. But when God elected Israel and when he elected us, he elected them and us in Christ, as those for whom the Son would suffer and die. Israel's future would be different from Edom's, not because Israel was morally superior but because Jesus, the true Israel, would be torn apart on a Roman cross for sins not his own. Jesus suffered the full weight of God's wrath and judgment and received a name he didn't deserve: wicked and accursed. The only one who knew no sin became sin "so that in him we might become the righteousness of God" (2 Corinthians 5:21). On the cross Jesus received the fate of Edom so that sinners like us might know the unchanging and unfading love of our Father in Heaven. In the empty tomb and the risen Son we see God's victory over all that threatens to undo and destroy us, and we stand in awe, worship, and praise in the confession, "Great is the LORD beyond the borders of Israel!" (Malachi 1:5).

For those who are in Christ by faith, God speaks the opposite of what he declared to Edom. God said to Edom, "They may build, but I will tear down" (v. 4). But God says to us, "You may tear down, but I will rebuild." We tear down every day. We tear down with our sin and our doubts. We tear down with our words and our actions. We tear down every time we fall and live in ways unbecoming of followers of Christ. Every day we tear others down, and we tear down ourselves. But Malachi announces that, tear down as we might, God is faithful to raise us up. We have been united to the risen Son by Spirit-wrought faith, and God has promised that our ultimate fate is not destruction but resurrection life. Why? The answer is simple: because he loves us.

Israel's hope was not that they could build better or plan better. Israel's hope was not that they were wiser or richer or better connected than Edom.

Israel's only hope was God's unmerited, unwavering, unconditional love that had been set upon them before they were born, or as Paul puts it, "before the foundation of the world" (Ephesians 1:4). In and of themselves they were no better than Edom, and apart from God's saving grace they would justly receive the same dreadful fate. But Israel was reminded that God would vindicate himself as the God of justice and righteousness, and at the same time, he would vindicate his people as those whom he has loved and redeemed to the praise of his glorious grace.

This promise serves as a call for Christians today as well. It is a call to hope and perseverance in the face of hardship, trials, and temptations. We persevere precisely because we have reason to hope. We hope in the sure knowledge that one day God's promises that we have believed in our hearts will be seen with our eyes when Christ returns to claim us as his own, and we join with all of God's people past, present, and future in the glorious chorus, "Great is the Lord beyond the border of Israel!" (Malachi 1:5).

# 76

# Our Great High Priest

MALACHI 1:6—2:9

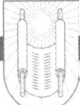

THE GREAT PREACHER and evangelist Billy Graham once remarked, "Give me five minutes with a person's checkbook and I will tell you where his heart is." However, it's not only a checkbook that reveals a person's character. Similar claims have been made about calendars, friends, and use of leisure time—all of which provide penetrating and accurate insight into a person's values and character, his or her loves and commitments. Why? Because all these realities reveal patterns of behavior; they are windows into one's activities and priorities. This is why the familiar English proverb "Actions speak louder than words" is mirrored in countless cultures and languages around the world. It is universally recognized that talk is cheap and that we all have the intractable habit of presenting something of an idealized portrait of ourselves to the world and to ourselves. If we really want to know what someone loves, if we really want to know what someone values, if we really want insight into a person's character, it is not enough to listen to his or her words. We must observe the person's actions. Our actions, at least in part, reveal our true selves. They reveal who we are; they have a sort of voice of their own, for better or for worse.

Malachi's second oracle to postexilic Israel contains a lawsuit directed primarily if not exclusively at Israel's priests (Malachi 1:6), whose profession of faith stood in stark contrast to their actions. There is no indication that the priests' theology was fundamentally flawed. They almost certainly would have given correct responses to at least the basic questions of Israelite theology and praxis. However, their actions revealed that their hearts were in fact far from God, that Yahweh, the God of Israel, was neither their first love

769

nor their greatest joy. Worship for the priests had become a burden, and as a consequence, these priests were leading God's people in a worship that was, at its heart, defiled and thus abhorrent to Israel's holy God.

However, though this oracle was directed toward the priests, it would be a mistake to understand Malachi's second oracle as relevant only to the priests of ancient Israel, and by extension, the clergy and church officers today.[1] Malachi's message to the priests is fundamentally a message about worship, and therefore it is relevant for every worshiper of God.[2]

Like all of Malachi's prophecies, this is an uncomfortable message. Here the prophet exposes not only the corruption and defilement that stain every human heart but also the lengths to which we go to convince ourselves that this is not true. Furthermore, it is a message that vividly sets on display the devastating judgment that every act of idolatry and false worship deserves. But ultimately Malachi's message is a message of hope because, in the midst of the uncomfortable exposure of sin and the announcement of God's curse, the prophet heralds the coming of another priest—a perfect worshiper who will walk before the Lord in perfect integrity, speak the word of God faithfully, and lead God's people into the presence of the all-holy God through repentance and faith. It is in and through this perfect worshiper, Jesus Christ, that even the greatest idolater may find cleansing for sin and hope for the future.

### Defiled Worship Exposed (1:6–13)

When Jesus declared, "If you then, who are evil, know how to give good gifts to your children, *how much more* will your Father who is in heaven give good things to those who ask him!" (Matthew 7:11), he was employing a traditional form of rabbinic reasoning known as *qal wahomer*, which may be translated as "from the light to the heavy." This is roughly equivalent to what we know conventionally as an argument from the lesser to the greater, from a minor to a major premise, in which a principle that is commonly agreed to apply to a lesser reality must logically and with perhaps even more certainty apply to the greater reality.[3] This conventional mode of rabbinic reasoning predated Jesus by centuries at least, and we see it here in Malachi's disputation with the priests of the postexilic community.[4] But unlike Jesus's words, in which he encouraged his people with the assurance of their heavenly Father's care for them, God through his prophet uses this mode of reasoning to expose his people's sin, to demonstrate that they've violated not only the principles of God's holy law but also the principles of humankind's custom and convention.

God's lesser argument is found in Malachi 1:6a: "A son honors his father, and a servant his master." Here God draws Israel's attention to proper relations that stand at the bedrock of any well-ordered society.[5] Children are to honor their parents, and servants are to obey their masters. To do otherwise would be to turn the proper order of the world on its head.

Having established a point of general agreement, God then presents his charge: "If then I am a father, where is my honor? And if I am a master, where is my fear? says the LORD of hosts to you, O priests, who despise my name" (Malachi 1:6b). It was the priest's chief calling to sanctify the name of the Lord in worship and in turn to place his holy name upon his people in the Aaronic blessing. However, God charges the priests here with doing the exact opposite. The priests have failed to perform their most basic duty—to sanctify the name of God. God says, in effect, "You have not feared me, O priests; you have despised my name" (v. 6b).

The priests' response, however, reveals that the problem is in fact far deeper and far worse than we have perhaps imagined. When confronted with the depth of their sin and failure, the priests respond with a claim of ignorance: "How have we despised your name?" This response says, in effect, "Prove it!" To which the Lord replies, "By offering polluted food upon my altar" (Malachi 1:7a). When the prophet Nathan confronted King David with his sin, David responded with utter contrition, clearly acknowledging his sin and God's righteousness in his judgment (cf. 2 Samuel 12:13; Psalm 51). The scene Malachi rehearses is the exact opposite. Far from contrition in dust and ashes, the priests double down with a second objection: "How have we polluted you?" (Malachi 1:7), to which the Lord responds, "By saying that the LORD's table may be despised. When you offer blind animals in sacrifice, is that not evil? And when you offer those that are lame or sick, is that not evil?" (vv. 7, 8a).

The priests claim ignorance, but the Lord who knows the heart of man down to the very bottom demonstrates that the priests are not ignorant by calling to mind their actions: "Present that to your governor; will he accept you or show you favor?" (Malachi 1:8b). Similarly, verse 9 is likely meant sarcastically when the prophet says, "Now entreat the favor of God, that he may be gracious to us. With such a gift from your hand, will he show favor to any of you?"[6]

Here we see the *qal wahomer* again. The Lord demonstrates that the priests are, in fact, far from ignorant of what is proper tribute for their king. They know what gifts are appropriate to give to a governor. The reality is that the priests would spare no effort or expense in offering to their governor a pristine gift so as to gain a hearing in his presence. And yet, at the end of the day, the governor is just that, a governor: a fallible, sinful, petty official set over an earthly territory for a limited period of time. But God? What they wouldn't present to a governor of a remote province of the Persian Empire they unabashedly present to the Creator and King of the universe.

In this we see the heart of the priests' problem. Theirs was not an information problem. They were not confused about the finer points of Mosaic law. They knew what God required of them, a requirement echoed in the cultures and conventions even of Israel's pagan neighbors: you honor your superiors by presenting them with your best.[7] The priests' problem rather was a heart problem. They had lost their first love, their loyalties to Yahweh had drifted, and their responsibility to lead God's people in right worship no longer gripped their hearts.

In this we discover the connection between this second oracle and the first. In Malachi's opening oracle God declared his love for his people, to which they responded, "How have you loved us?" (1:2). Like so many in Israel, the priests also had come to doubt God's love. They were no longer captivated by the unmerited, unconditional, unqualified, electing, and redeeming love of the God of the universe for sinners like themselves. Doubting God's love will inevitably lead to worship that wanders from God as the proper object of our love and loyalty, and instead leads toward loving things of this world.[8] God had become small, remote, abstract. And as the priests' hearts grew indifferent to the things of God and thus drifted, so did their worship. The constant refrain throughout Scripture is that how we worship reflects who we worship.[9] Just as the gifts we give reflect what we think of the recipient, so too the worship we bring reflects what we think about the One whom we worship. Clearly, these priests had come to think little of their God.

The only thing worse than not worshiping God at all is thinking that we're worshiping God when we are not but are instead offending him with our hypocrisy. At least those who never go to church know they are not worshipers, but those who go through the motions, trusting in token acts of piety and devotion, are in a far more dangerous place. They regard themselves as worshipers when in fact they are not. This is why, in Malachi 1:10, God longs for someone to lock the doors of the sanctuary: "Oh that there were one among you who would shut the doors, that you might not kindle a fire on my altar in vain!" (v. 10). It's better to shut the doors, lock the windows, and turn off the lights so that at least Israel wouldn't be living under the delusion of thinking that they were right with God.

The prophet paints a deeply unsettling portrait that reveals the human capacity to convince ourselves that we're worshiping God when in fact we are offending him and defiling his holy name. The truth is, we all struggle with—and often give in to—the temptation to offer something less, often something far less, than our best to the Lord. We are prone to cut corners, thinking that God doesn't really care. Our lips might say with the psalmist, "My soul longs, yes, faints for the courts of the LORD; my heart and flesh sing for joy to the living God" (Psalm 84:2), but our actions (not the least of which are our offerings) often reveal that we are far more devoted to comfort, respectability, affluence, influence, career, education, sports, money, or entertainment than we are devoted to the One who created us out of his goodness and redeemed us by his grace.

The truth is that God requires something far, far greater from us than a perfect animal. He requires lives lived in faith and devotion and obedience to him as our Creator. When Jesus responded to the Pharisees, "Render to Caesar the things that are Caesar's, and to God the things that are God's" (Matthew 22:21), he laid claim to our entire lives. As Caesar's image was on the Roman denarius, so God's image is indelibly stamped on every man, woman, and child. Our lives therefore are in every respect to be, in the words of the Apostle Paul, living sacrifices, "holy and acceptable to God, which is your spiritual worship" (Romans 12:1).

Many of us give more to our work or our leisure than we give to the Lord. And when we do open our Bibles or sit in the pews, our minds drift, our prayers are unfocused, and our hearts are, like Israel's in Malachi's day, far from our God. Some days, perhaps many or even most days, God is a second thought or an afterthought. Yet God's Word is clear: God is jealous for his worship, and he refuses to play second fiddle to anyone or anything in our heart's loyalty and affection.

In the face of such a requirement who can stand? Though addressed to the priests, the prophet's message is crushing for the entire postexilic community, and it's crushing for us as well, as we can see too much of our own hearts in the half-hearted worship of Israel's priests. What is the consequence? God not only exposes the defiled and corrupt worship of Israel's priests, but he also announces his word of judgment upon half-hearted worshipers.

## Defiled Worship Condemned (1:14—2:3, 8, 9)

Malachi declares, "Cursed be the cheat who has a male in his flock, and vows it, and yet sacrifices to the Lord what is blemished" (1:14a). This is someone who wishes to put on a good show of religion by publicly announcing his tribute to the Lord, yet when it comes time to hand over the offering he offers a second-rate substitute. God responds with the only verdict that he can as a holy and righteous judge: guilty and "cursed." Yet there are more curses to come should these priests not respond to God's word with faith and repentance:

"Now, O priests, this command is for you. If you will not listen, if you will not take it to heart to give honor to my name, says the LORD of hosts, then I will send the curse upon you and I will curse your blessings" (2:1, 2).

It is not perfectly clear what blessings are in view when God says, "I will curse your blessings" (v. 2). One suggestion is that the blessings refer to the blessings of the land and the blessings of the people's tithes that the priests received from the people as a result of a land that was blessed by God and therefore fruitful.[10] In other words, those things in life that God has ordained for the priests to know and enjoy as a token of God's good pleasure will be taken from them and will be replaced with bitter and difficult realities as a sign of God's curse upon them.[11]

We are given a glimpse of this reality later in the book of Malachi when God rebukes Israel for withholding their tithes from his worship, saying, "You are cursed with a curse, for you are robbing me, the whole nation of you" (3:9), and a couple of verses later says, "I will rebuke the devourer for you, so that it will not destroy the fruits of your soil, and your vine in the field shall not fail to bear, says the LORD of hosts" (v. 11). Israel had been experiencing crop failure due to a locust plague. What was to be a source of blessing for Israel for their obedience to the covenant became a source of misery and frustration, indeed a curse, on account of Israel's disobedience.

However, another proposal is that the blessings in view here are not the blessings the priests were to receive and enjoy but the blessings that the priests were to bestow upon the people of God.[12] The most famous blessing is the Aaronic blessing in which God commanded the high priest, "Thus you shall bless the people of Israel: you shall say to them, The LORD bless you and keep you; the LORD make his face to shine upon you and be gracious to you; the LORD lift up his countenance upon you and give you peace" (Numbers 6:23–26). God then said, "So shall they put my name upon the people of Israel, and I will bless them" (v. 27). In this view, the priest's blessings that are God's appointed means of blessing his people would not bless them but curse them instead.

A third (and in this author's view, preferable) option is that both meanings are in view.[13] All of the priests' blessings—both those that they receive and those that they give—will be transformed into cursing, and as a result, life will become nothing but sadness, frustration, and endless sorrow. This is God's judgment for false and idolatrous worship. As evidence that this is not an empty threat, the Lord declares that the priests have already begun to experience God's judgment in some measure: "Indeed, I have already cursed them, because you do not lay it to heart" (Malachi 2:2). These troubles and sorrows that have already begun are a foretaste of Hell itself if these priests do not turn to God in faith and repentance. This is how seriously God regards his worship. As Nadab and Abihu could attest, God is deadly serious (cf. Leviticus 10). The penalty for defiled worship is the forfeiture of divine blessings.

However, it is critical to see that the priests' blessings being turned into cursings was not only a problem for Israel's priests. This was a problem for the entire covenant community. Without a functional priesthood, Israel in their entirety would be left without access to God as the source of their hope and blessing. Like the rest of the world lost in sin, they would have free and unmediated access to God's cursing (a person didn't need a priest to know God as a Creator and Judge of sinners). But if they wanted to know God as the God of mercy and grace, as the Savior and Redeemer of sinners, they needed a priest. Israel needed a priest to stand as the mediator between themselves and their holy God. They needed a priest to offer sacrifices and prayers on their behalf. They needed priests to offer instruction and guidance from God's word. Without the priests and without a functional priesthood in Israel's day, God's blessing would have been inaccessible.

This threat that the priests would be disqualified and ineffective in their ministry is seen most clearly and vividly when God says, "Behold, I will rebuke your offspring, and spread dung on your faces, the dung of your offerings, and you shall be taken away with it" (Malachi 2:3).[14] The priesthood was handed down from father to son within the Levitical line. So when God says, "I will rebuke your offspring," he's declaring that their reproach will fall also on their children and will last for generations, thus precluding any hope that perhaps the next generation will be better.

As for this generation, God says that he will "spread dung on your faces, the dung of your offerings, and you shall be taken away with it." There are few things we can think of that are more defiling than excrement, and here the threat of wiping excrement on priests and their offerings is a startling way of declaring that all that they are and all that they do is unacceptable to the Lord. God will, in effect, give them what they've asked for. They wish to offer defiled sacrifices, so they will reap the woeful consequences of defiled sacrifices: they will be carried away with them.

The laws regulating Israel's sacrifices stipulated that the excrement of the animals did not go on the altar because it was not for the Lord (cf. Leviticus 4:11, 12). The excrement and the organs that held it were to be disposed of outside the camp. So God says to the priests, "You shall be taken away with it" (Malachi 2:3). The threat, therefore, is the threat of cutting off the priesthood altogether. Their position would no longer be a place of honor but a place of humiliation, as one commentator put it, "from the sanctuary to the dung heap!"[15] It's a grim picture that serves as a powerful reminder that the God of the Bible is not an indulgent grandparent; he is a consuming fire whose holiness can in no way countenance sin and whose righteousness demands obedience in every aspect of his people's, and most especially their worship.

In this we find one more *qal wahomer*: if Israel couldn't even manage to offer an unblemished animal, what chance did they have of offering unblemished lives? Not a hope in the world. Neither do we. Yet in the middle of this woeful portrait and promise of a divine curse, there breaks forth an announcement of divine grace for just such lost and hopeless sinners.

### Defiled Worship Remedied (2:4–6)

Beginning in Malachi 2:4, the prophet announces another priest and another priesthood, a priest and a priesthood that in almost every respect stands in contrast to the corrupt priesthood of his own day. God says, "So shall you know that I have sent this command to you, that my covenant with Levi may stand." Since this is the only time in the Bible that the expression "covenant with Levi" is used, there is much discussion about exactly which covenant is in view.[16] Most agree that the incident of the golden calf stands as the background (if not the foreground) to this expression. When Moses witnessed Israel's great sin of crafting a golden calf by which they might worship their God like the pagan nations around them worshiped theirs, he called out to the community, "Who is on the LORD's side? Come to me" (Exodus 32:26). Then we read, "All the sons of Levi gathered around him. And he said to them, 'Thus says the LORD God of Israel, "Put your sword on your side each of you, and go to and fro from gate to gate throughout the camp, and each of you kill his brother and his companion and his neighbor."' And the sons of Levi did according to the word of Moses" (vv. 26–28). Out of their zeal for God's holiness the Levites carried out God's judgment against their fellow Israelites. As a result, Moses declared, "Today you have been ordained for the service of the LORD, each one at the cost of his son and of his brother, so that he might bestow a blessing upon you this day" (v. 29). The Levites' unwavering zeal for God's holiness earned them the privilege of serving in the temple as priests of the one true God.

However, given the description of God's "covenant with Levi" as a covenant "of life and peace" (Malachi 2:5), it seems that a later, related covenant is primarily in view—the covenant that God made with Phineas in Numbers 25.[17] The context is unquestionably one of the darker days in Israel's history. Though poised on the edge of the land of promise, a land with abundance and provision bespeaking of the eternal blessedness of Heaven itself, Israel tragically falls into sexual sin with Moabite women (v. 1). The attraction of the Moabite women quickly led to a corresponding attraction to their deities, and Israel fell into idolatry, yoking themselves no longer to Yahweh, the God who had led them through the wilderness to the land of promise, but rather to "Baal of Peor" (vv. 2, 3).

Once again the Levites stood in the gap between God's judgment and God's people: "When Phinehas the son of Eleazar, son of Aaron the priest, saw it, he rose and left the congregation and took a spear in his hand and went after the man of Israel into the chamber and pierced both of them, the man of Israel and the woman through her belly. Thus the plague on the people of Israel was stopped" (Numbers 25:7, 8). The zeal for God's holiness that animated the Levites at Sinai animated another son of Levi, Phinehas, such that he sought to cleanse the camp from the corruption of idolatry and infidelity. In response to Phinehas's zeal, the Lord says to Moses, "Phinehas the son of Eleazar, son of Aaron the priest, has turned back my wrath from the people of Israel, in that he was jealous with my jealousy among them, so that I did not consume the people of Israel in my jealousy. Therefore say, 'Behold, I give to him my *covenant of peace*, and it shall be to him and to his descendants after him the covenant of a perpetual priesthood, because he was jealous for his God and made atonement for the people of Israel'" (vv. 11–13).

This "covenant of peace" that God made with Phinehas and his descendants centuries prior is the same as (or perhaps a continuation of) this "covenant of Levi" that stands as God's answer to the unfaithful priests of Malachi's day (2:4). In contrast to these unfaithful priests, Phinehas and his priestly ministry are depicted in idealized language: "My covenant with him was one of life and peace, and I gave them to him. It was a covenant of fear, and he feared me. He stood in awe of my name. True instruction was in his mouth, and no wrong was found on his lips. He walked with me in peace and uprightness, and he turned many from iniquity" (vv. 5, 6).

One might wonder if this is a perfectly accurate description of Phinehas or any other Levitical priest for that matter. Did Phinehas fear Yahweh perfectly? Did he always stand in awe of God's name? Was no wrong ever found on his lips? The answer, of course, is no. Phinehas was not perfect.

And yet God presents him in these terms because Phinehas's actions in the days of Israel's rebellion were a type of the One who is perfect. Phinehas prefigured or foreshadowed the greater Phinehas to come, so much so that the psalmist could sing of him:

Then Phinehas stood up and intervened,
and the plague was stayed.

> And that was counted to him as righteousness
> from generation to generation forever. (Psalm 106:30, 31)

While God's description of Phinehas is certainly true, its idealized character caused Israel (and it should cause us) to look for another, greater Phinehas of whom it can be said, "He stood in awe of my name. True instruction was in his mouth, and no wrong was found on his lips. He walked with me in peace and uprightness, and he turned many from iniquity" (Malachi 2:5, 6). These realities, seen truly yet imperfectly in Phinehas, are found perfectly and ultimately in Jesus Christ.

In his zeal for God's holiness and his mediation for God's people, Phinehas served as a type of a priest who was to come.[18] His one act of righteousness counted for the many and saved God's people from judgment. However, the blessings of the covenant are not reserved for Phinehas alone; they extend to his descendants as well (Numbers 25:13). This gospel word would have caused Israel in Phinehas's day, and would have caused Israel in Malachi's day, not only to look backward but to look forward for another priest who would embody the same spirit and exhibit the same zeal for God's holiness. This priest arrived in the person of Jesus of Nazareth, who perfectly fulfilled every duty and calling of Israel's priests. Jesus, as one consumed with a zeal for God's holiness, rid the temple of those who would corrupt it (John 2:17; cf. Psalm 69:9). Whereas the priests of Malachi's day offered defiled and corrupt sacrifices, Jesus would offer the perfect sacrifice of his own body. The priests in Malachi's day "caused many to stumble by [their] instruction" (Malachi 2:8), but of this Jesus it can be said without any qualification that true instruction was always in his mouth; no wrong was ever found on his lips. He walked with God his Father every moment of every day in peace, wisdom, and uprightness, and he "turned many from iniquity."[19] The commentator Gordon Wenham, however, observes an important difference: "Whereas it was Phinehas' spear that pierced the sinners that made atonement for Israel, it was the nails and the spear that pierced Jesus that made atonement for the sins of the whole world."[20]

In Christ we have a priest greater than Phinehas, greater even than Moses. As the author of Hebrews puts it, "When Christ appeared as a high priest of the good things that have come, then through the greater and more perfect tent (not made with hands, that is, not of this creation) he entered once for all into the holy places, not by means of the blood of goats and calves but by means of his own blood, thus securing an eternal redemption" (9:11, 12).

And yet though innocent and without blemish, though he himself was the perfect worshiper of God, Jesus nevertheless would die the death of an idolater so that idolaters like the priests in Malachi's day and we in our day could be forgiven. Those covenant curses so vividly threatened by the prophet Malachi would fall on the Son of God on the cross when the innocent Jesus would be rejected by God and man, hanging defiled and accursed on a tree, bearing in his body divine wrath for the sins of others so that idolaters like those in Malachi's day and idolaters like us could be forgiven and set free. Jesus, the perfect worshiper of his Father, would die the death of an idolater so that we who by nature hate God might be transformed into true worshipers of the true God.

Though our worship remains imperfect, our efforts too often half-hearted, our hearts and minds too prone to distraction and wandering, nevertheless our worship is acceptable to God and, more than that, is even pleasing to God. God delights in the worship of his people not because it's perfect (it's not) but because it is offered by faith in the One who worshiped God perfectly and who died for those who don't. As the author of the letter to the Hebrews writes:

> Every priest stands daily at his service, offering repeatedly the same sacrifices, which can never take away sins. But when Christ had offered for all time a single sacrifice for sins, he sat down at the right hand of God, waiting from that time until his enemies should be made a footstool for his feet. For by a single offering he has perfected for all time those who are being sanctified. (10:11–14)

Though the priests in Malachi's day appeared to derail God's redemptive purposes for his world, the good news is that God would accomplish his gracious and redemptive purposes despite our sin. With no thanks to those priests in Malachi's day, and contrary to the practices of faithless worshipers in the postexilic community, God declared, "For from the rising of the sun to its setting my name will be great among the nations, and in every place incense will be offered to my name, and a pure offering. For my name will be great among the nations, says the Lord of hosts" (Malachi 1:11).[21] God determined to have worshipers in every place, beginning in Old Testament times among faithful Jews of the Dispersion and proselytes to the Jewish faith, and continuing into the New Testament as the gospel goes out among the Gentiles.[22]

In this we see the universal scope of God's redemptive purposes. God's gracious covenant promises made to Abraham (Genesis 12:3) will come to pass because God has sworn it. And so it is even today. God's promise made through Malachi centuries ago is being fulfilled as the gospel of Christ is proclaimed to the farthest corners of the globe and worshipers of every tribe, tongue, and nation are gathering to confess the greatness of the triune God through Jesus Christ, the perfect and consummate great High Priest.

# 77

# Created for Faithfulness

MALACHI 2:10-16

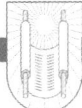

THE NEWS THAT DIVORCE is on the decline sounds at first like a welcome piece of good news. That is, until we learn that the reason divorce is on the decline is because marriage is also on the decline. In America, as in many Western societies, the reason couples are getting divorced less is because couples are getting married less. Rather than getting married, many are settling for the pseudo-marriage of cohabitation, the breakup of which is unaccounted for in divorce statistics.[1]

Yes, divorce is on the decline, but at what cost? In this we can see how far we have fallen from the glory God intended for marriage. Just when we think things couldn't get much worse than half of marriages ending in divorce, we learn that this number has gone down not because of a renewed commitment to marital fidelity or because of a renewed understanding of God's intentions for and purposes in marriage, but because we've in greater measure and in more profound ways exchanged the real for a counterfeit, the truth for a lie.

Perhaps this should not come as a surprise. The first consequence of the first sin, we're told in Genesis 3, is a breakdown in the marriage relationship: "Then the eyes of both [the man and his wife] were opened, and they knew that they were naked. And they sewed fig leaves together and made themselves loincloths" (v. 7). Broken communion with God is attended by the breakdown of communion in marriage. The alienation of the first man and the first woman from God produced an alienation from one another. The breakdown of this marital bond was furthered when the man blamed both God and his wife for his sin: "The woman whom you gave to be with me, she gave me the fruit of the tree, and I ate" (v. 12). The marital bond is arguably the greatest gift given to God's greatest creation; the man and the woman who bear his image become "one flesh" in this union (1:26; 2:24). The communion and intimacy enjoyed in marriage is perhaps the greatest earthly analogy to the love God has for his Church (Ephesians 5:25). Thus it is not at all surprising that throughout the Bible, the chief reflex of spiritual infidelity is marital infidelity, and the chief reflex of marital infidelity is spiritual infidelity. The two seem to go hand in hand, so much so that when we encounter one, we almost always find the other.[2]

While Malachi's previous oracle focused primarily on the failures of Israel's priests, his third oracle brings into view the failures of the people.[3] The sickness of the heads of the community had traveled throughout the body.[4] The particular failure that is in view is Israel's faithlessness in marriage. The books of Ezra and Nehemiah attest to the fact that during the postexilic period, especially in the mid-fifth century, intermarriage between Israelites and non-Israelites was prevalent in the postexilic community (Ezra 9, 10; Nehemiah 13:23–31). In this period, Israel's heart, like Solomon's before them, was led astray. Marriage to foreign women and the worship of foreign deities that almost inevitably followed revealed that Israel's hearts were indeed far from God. As a consequence, the covenant community experienced broken fellowship with God and disunity within the body.

In his third oracle, Malachi denounces the rampant intermarriage between Israelites and non-Israelites and exposes the far-reaching consequences of their faithlessness in the areas of worship and family life. But though the dark clouds of God's judgment hang ominously over this postexilic community on account of their infidelity, they are not left without hope. The prophet issues a call for renewed faithfulness first to their God and second to their spouses.

God had a purpose for marriage that indeed exceeded the common grace blessings that attend this gift. It would be through the holy seed of the woman that he would bring forgiveness and salvation to the world (Genesis 3:15).

### Created for Fidelity (2:10)

In an oracle focused on Israel's faithlessness in marriage, it is surprising that the prophet does not begin his lawsuit with marital union in view but with covenantal union, the union that God's people enjoy as the family of God. The prophet opens his third oracle with a series of questions: "Have we not all one Father? Has not one God created us? Why then are we faithless to one another, profaning the covenant of our fathers?" (Malachi 2:10). The first two questions are rhetorical. *Of course*, Israel would have thought, *we have one Father. Of course, the one God created us.* As in his previous oracles,

Malachi begins with a generally accepted truth that serves as the basis for his prosecution.

It is important to note that the relation in view in the prophet's questions is not the relation of Creator to creature but of Redeemer to redeemed. When Malachi speaks of "one Father" and "one God" creating us, he is referring to that special and particular work of God in redeeming Israel and setting her apart as a peculiar people for himself.[5] The Fatherhood of God is the special relationship that God established with Israel, whom he calls "my son" (Exodus 4:22, 23). The creation in view here is God's creation of Israel as a nation (Deuteronomy 32:9–11). It is in and through Israel that God's new-creation purposes for the world will be realized and the glory of the one true God will be set on display in the unity of his people.

If this is true (and the rhetorical questions suggest this was generally accepted), "Why then," the prophet asks, "are we faithless to one another, profaning the covenant of our fathers?" (Malachi 2:10). The prophet postpones the specifics of Israel's offenses to focus on the deeper spiritual issues and implications. As in his earlier oracles, Malachi is interested in the sin beneath the sins, the root of the matter.

The faithlessness in Israel's marital unions is not a private matter between two individuals. The nature, state, and health of the marriages of the people of Israel are of great concern for the entire community.[6] How the covenant community regards marriage, how it treats marriage, what it values in marriage all have far-reaching consequences that extend beyond the homes of the individuals involved. As sin in marriage is not only tolerated but perhaps even encouraged and promoted within the covenant community, there results a breakdown in the fellowship of the community. Children are affected. Extended families are affected. The clans and tribes are affected. Underlying it all is a breakdown in the fellowship of the covenant community with their God. Heightening the intensity and the urgency by including himself in the offense, the prophet asks, "Why have we profaned the covenant of our fathers?"[7] Though it is not certain which covenant is in view, the most likely candidate is the Mosaic covenant, which clearly set forth laws regulating marriage and divorce (see Deuteronomy 7:3, 4; 24:1–4).[8] This covenant that constituted Israel as a nation and enshrined her most treasured possession, the Law of God, has been defiled and profaned by the very people it was designed to bless.

Malachi's third oracle reveals that it is not only the priests who have defiled the sanctuary by offering second-rate offerings on the Lord's altar (Malachi 1:12); the people also have defiled the sanctuary by their faithlessness in marriage.[9] Malachi declares that Judah has "profaned the sanctuary of the

LORD, which he loves, and has married the daughter of a foreign god" (2:11b). How exactly does Israel's intermarriage profane the sanctuary of the Lord? God has redeemed Israel so that they might set on display the glory of his faithfulness, reconciliation, and love as they themselves manifest faithfulness, reconciliation, and love within the covenant community. The fruit of Israel's faithfulness to God is their faithfulness to and love for one another, the chief relationship, of course, being that of marriage. Israel's faithlessness defiles the covenant they swore to obey (Exodus 24:3) and profanes the name of their God who has redeemed them in love and bound himself to them in faithfulness.

The prophet's point is both simple and clear: Israel has been redeemed for fidelity to God and one another.

The good news of the gospel is not only what we are saved *from* but also what we are saved *for*. Both are equally glorious realities. We are saved from the eternal consequences of our sin and rebellion. We are saved from an eternal death. We are saved from the bondage of sin. But for what purpose? The purpose for which we are saved is principally to love God and to love our neighbors. Malachi here reminds us that we are saved for fidelity—fidelity to God and fidelity in our relationships, the most important of which is our relationship with our spouse (if we are married).

God is perfectly faithful in all his ways and has redeemed a people to show forth his faithfulness to the world as they are faithful to one another. It is this rehearsal and reminder of who God is for his people, a God who is loving and faithful, that sets in bold relief the enormity of Israel's sin.

### Faithlessness in Marital Union (2:11, 12)

The presenting symptom of Israel's faithlessness is their marriage to women outside the covenant community (Malachi 2:11). On the plains of Moab, Moses had warned Israel of the dangers of intermarriage with the peoples of the land of Canaan: "You shall not intermarry with them, giving your daughters to their sons or taking their daughters for your sons, for they would turn away your sons from following me, to serve other gods. Then the anger of the LORD would be kindled against you, and he would destroy you quickly" (Deuteronomy 7:3, 4).

It is critical to note that the reason given for this prohibition is not that the race, ethnicity, or nationality of these men and women disqualified them as marriage partners.[10] Rather, the reason God's people were forbidden to unite with foreigners in marriage was fundamentally religious. As pagans, these men and women worshiped false gods, and their piety was characterized by superstition and divination. The complete devotion to one's spouse that is the foundation and goal of marriage is irreparably disrupted when a believer binds himself or herself to a spouse who hates his or her first love. It is both difficult and dangerous to love a spouse who hates the God we love. Either our love for God will drive a wedge into our love for our spouse, or our devotion to our spouse will distance us from our God.

The examples of Moses and his Cushite wife and Boaz and Ruth clearly demonstrate that Israel was indeed permitted to marry non-Israelites should those non-Israelites join themselves to the covenant community through faith in Israel's God and obedience to Israel's law. Further evidence may be found in those non-Israelites who joined the postexilic community for Passover in Ezra 6: "It was eaten by the people of Israel who had returned from exile, and also by every one who had joined them and separated himself from the uncleanness of the peoples of the land to worship the LORD, the God of Israel" (v. 21). The fact that Malachi designates these women as "daughter[s] of a foreign god" (2:11) underscores the issue at stake—the loyalties and devotion of these women lie with a god who is not Yahweh, and as a consequence they will almost certainly lead the hearts of Israel away from Israel's God.[11] For this reason, one author has recently labeled these unions as "apostasy marriages."[12] Apostasy marriages are motivated by hearts that have rejected God's will, and they in turn inevitably push those hearts further and further from faith in God.

This is precisely what happened with one of Israel's greatest kings, King Solomon. Though he was great in both wisdom and wealth, though as the future king he had received every privilege and opportunity imaginable, his heart nevertheless went astray because of his marriages to many foreign women.

> Now King Solomon loved many foreign women, along with the daughter of Pharaoh: Moabite, Ammonite, Edomite, Sidonian, and Hittite women, from the nations concerning which the LORD had said to the people of Israel, "You shall not enter into marriage with them, neither shall they with you, for surely they will turn away your heart after their gods." Solomon clung to these in love. He had 700 wives, who were princesses, and 300 concubines. And his wives turned away his heart. For when Solomon was old his wives turned away his heart after other gods, and his heart was not wholly true to the LORD his God, as was the heart of David his father. For Solomon went after Ashtoreth the goddess of the Sidonians, and after Milcom the abomination of the Ammonites. . . . Then Solomon built a high place for Chemosh the abomination of Moab, and for Molech the abomination of the Ammonites, on the mountain east of Jerusalem. And so he did for all his foreign wives, who made offerings and sacrificed to their gods. (1 Kings 11:1–5, 7, 8)

It was not their race, ethnicity, or nationality that disqualified these foreign women from being King Solomon's wife (not to mention "wives" plural, but that's another matter). It was their religion. Solomon's love for his foreign wives translated into his serving their foreign gods, and the consequences both for Solomon and for his country were disastrous.

Though we're not told explicitly, many scholars believe that the men of the postexilic community were drawn to these "daughter[s] of foreign gods" for much the same reason that Solomon was drawn to his foreign wives.[13] Just as Solomon's marriage to 700 princesses was not driven by romance and love but by the political advantage such unions provided, so too the men of the postexilic community desired foreign women because these unions promised to improve their social, economic, or political standing within the community. Perhaps we might think of them as small-scale royal marriages. As kings would often enter into marriages to secure relations with other kings and empires, so these Israelite men found a way to improve their lives, to secure and promote their position in society, through strategic marriages with the daughters of the people of the land, yet without regard for the consequences of these unions to their own souls and to the well-being of the community.

The seriousness of this sin is seen clearly in Malachi 2:12, where the prophet issues an imprecation: "May the Lord cut off from the tents of Jacob any descendant of the man who does this, who brings an offering to the Lord of hosts." The language of being "cut off from the tents of Jacob" invokes the curses of the covenant and refers to exclusion from the covenant community and the blessings that God has promised to give to his people.

The ESV's translation "any descendant" is an attempt to make sense of an expression that is used nowhere else in the Bible and that says literally, "the one who wakes and answers." The proposals trying to make sense of this obscure expression are legion and inconclusive. However, one recent commentator has observed that what unites most if not all of the various proposals is the idea that the prophet is using a literary device to indicate totality.[14] In other words, it's a way of saying, "everybody" or "all" who marry foreign women and who then bring offerings to Yahweh shall be cut off from the blessings of the covenant and the community that is called by the Lord's name. To be "cut off" was, in effect, excommunication and was regarded with the utmost seriousness as it announced to offenders that they no longer had access to the grace, mercy, and forgiveness of God.

Such intermarriage was no small matter either for the individuals married or for the community at large. It has been said that every generation of Christians is one generation away from heterodoxy. If one generation is not faithful to pass on not only the practices of the faith but the content of the faith, the next generation will not understand why they do what they do, and the generation after them will not only not understand but will not do it.

Though our priorities may be different today, the temptation is nevertheless the same. For most, at least in the West, social standing and economic security have been replaced by romantic attraction and self-fulfillment as the driving criteria for choosing a spouse. While these are important, even critical, things to consider in marriage, when they surpass God in our loyalty and devotion, they compromise our fellowship with him and our ability to serve him. In other words, they become idols.

While much is different between our context and that of postexilic Israel, Paul nevertheless reiterates the command that believers must not be yoked with unbelievers (2 Corinthians 6:14) but must marry "in the Lord" (1 Corinthians 7:39). This is not because Paul wishes to narrow the Christian's dating pool but because he understands that God's design for marriage is not our self-actualization but the glory of God. In his instructions to the churches in Ephesus, Paul wrote that in marriage believers have the unique privilege of setting on display Christ's love for his Church through submission and sacrificial love, a calling that is nearly impossible to fulfill when one spouse doesn't love or serve the Lord of the other (Ephesians 5:25–33).

Few things about the Christian ethic are more bewildering to our culture than the Christian ethic of sex and marriage. Yet in Malachi 2 we're reminded again of what it means to live by faith. It is to live according to God's will as he has revealed it in his Word even and especially when it contradicts our culture's values or even our own desires and vision for what will make us happy.

## Faithlessness in Marital Life (2:13–14)

Beginning in Malachi 2:13, the prophet addresses a second sin (likely related to the first): divorce without cause.[15] Like the sin of faithlessness in marital unions, groundless divorce disrupts the communion between God and his people. Malachi says, "You cover the LORD's altar with tears, with weeping and groaning because he no longer regards the offering or accepts it with favor from your hand" (v. 13). Clearly these worshipers regard God's rejection of their worship as inexplicable and arbitrary. Not able to conceive of a single reason their offerings would be rejected, they cry out in objection, "Why does he not?" (v. 14a), a question that reveals hearts that are oblivious to the great violence they are committing against their wives and children, whom they have abandoned.

To this objection Malachi replies, "Because the LORD was witness between you and the wife of your youth, to whom you have been faithless, though she is your companion and your wife by covenant" (2:14b). The prophet says, in effect, "Because God was there when you promised to love and to cherish your wife as long as you both shall live." While we don't know the exact promises made in Jewish marriages in the fifth century B.C., the prophet designates the wife as literally "the wife of your covenant" (2:14).[16] Just as marriage vows today require witnesses, so God was and is a witness to every promise and vow that his people make, including and especially our marriage vows. In ancient Israel, God's name was no doubt invoked in the promises of the marriage covenant, the breach of which could not be committed with impunity or overlooked by the divine witness.

We're not given the specific reasons for these divorces. In all likelihood, however, many if not most of them took place because husbands wished to marry "daughter[s] of a foreign god" (Malachi 2:11) in the hopes of achieving greater wealth, influence, or social status and the like.[17] God, however, doesn't address the surface explanations and self-justifications that inevitably attend divorce; rather, he cuts right to the heart of the matter. Verse 16 reads literally, "The one who hates and sends [divorces] . . . covers his garment with violence, says the LORD of hosts" (v. 16, AT). At root, the motivation for these unjust and oppressive divorces is not a spouse's infidelity, abandonment, or abuse but hatred. These husbands have grown to hate their wives—the exact opposite of the ever-growing love and intimacy that God intended for marriage. This rending of the marital union has been done, apparently, without any thought to the harm it would cause the family and the community. Even worse, it has been done without any thought to the obstacle it would create between the individual and Almighty God.

In this we observe that divorce is the last stage of a journey that almost certainly began much earlier. Hatred doesn't bloom overnight. It is the product of many small, sinful choices. Choices to put one's own interests and desires ahead of the other's. Choices to harbor resentment rather than seek forgiveness. Choices to pursue happiness and fulfillment down avenues God has prohibited. This is the opposite of God's design for marriage. Marriage in the Bible is a covenant, a commitment animated by selfless and sacrificial love (cf. Genesis 2:24, 25; Ephesians 5:25–33). Love in marriage is manifest in the willingness, even delight, in giving oneself for the benefit and glory of the other. While the decision to divorce might happen over the course of a day or a week, the hatred that leads to it does not.

It is striking, however, that these divorces in the book of Malachi accomplish the exact opposite of their intended purpose. The goal for these faithless husbands was no doubt to achieve greater happiness, fulfillment, flourishing, or in a word, blessedness. The sad reality, however, is that the man who divorces his wife in this fashion "covers his garment with violence" (Malachi 2:16). This is an image trading on the Biblical notion that one's outward garments reflect or even reveal an inward reality. Regardless of appearances (their garments might be white as snow), the reality is that they are stained with the violence these husbands have committed against their wives by covenant and the children that the marriages produced. But even worse than the offense against and alienation from the spouse is the offense against and alienation from God. Faithlessness in marriage places a barrier between the worshiper and God. How can a husband approach God in worship when he hates his wife? The contradiction is so apparent that the Apostle Peter could write, "Husbands, live with your wives in an understanding way, showing honor to the woman as the weaker vessel, since they are heirs with you of the grace of life, *so that your prayers may not be hindered*" (1 Peter 3:7).

Thankfully, not every marriage that harbors bitterness and hatred, that fails to express selfless love and sacrifice, ends in divorce. The truth is that every marriage in some way fails to live up to the standard of perfect love and fidelity that God sets forth in his Word. Every husband and every wife has exhibited the resentment, bitterness, compromise, and selfishness that is the seedbed of hatred. Thus the prophet's words to Israel expose our sins and failures as well. Wonderfully, however, the prophet doesn't only expose sin but also sets forth a renewed vision for marriages, even those tainted with great sin and shortcomings.

## Hope for the Faithless (2:15, 16)

What hope is there for faithlessness in marriage? The answer that Malachi gives is a renewed apprehension of the grace of God and a renewed appreciation for his purposes in the marriages of believers. Twice the prophet calls on the postexilic community to "guard" or "keep watch" over their spirits (2:15, 16). Fidelity in marriage is a constant fight and calls for constant watchfulness. Sin in our own hearts and lies from our culture pull our loyalties and affections away from our God and from our spouses. The remedy set forth by the prophet is watchfulness and mindfulness that is animated by God's vision and purposes for Christian marriage.

When Biblical commentators get to this passage in Malachi, it is customary for them to highlight the numerous impenetrable difficulties it presents.[18]

Most will say something along these lines: "Now we've come to what is perhaps the most difficult and obscure text in the entirety of the Old Testament."[19] Furthermore, most seem to agree that of the seven verses in this most difficult and obscure text in the Old Testament, verse 15 is probably the most difficult and the most obscure. These sentiments are for the most part true. However, despite its many grammatical and exegetical difficulties, it is also true that of all the verses in this difficult text, verse 15 most clearly sets on display the hope of the gospel for sinners. Without denying the numerous exegetical difficulties that this verse presents (some of which I'll touch on in passing), the focus will remain on what is clear and what may serve as a source of hope and confidence for all who know themselves to be faithless more often than they'd like to admit.

The crux of the difficulty is found in the referent of the adjective "one" when the prophet literally declares, "What was the one seeking?" Who is "the one" who is seeking? Some interpret "the one" as referring back to the Israelite who united himself in marriage to the daughter of the foreign god. Earlier in 2:15, this union is referred to as being made one, so it is argued that later in this verse, it is this ungodly union that is in view. By this interpretation, the prophet is probably being sarcastic, saying, in effect, "What blessing did you think would come from this faithless union? Godly offspring? Covenant children?" The implication is that covenant blessings such as godly children should not be expected from covenant infidelity.

Other interpreters, however (including the ESV), supply the word "God," which is not present in the original Hebrew but is a perfectly defensible referent: "What was the one God seeking?"[20] According to this view, the prophet is underscoring God's purposes for marriage, especially the marriages of his covenant people. What was the one God seeking when he gave them a portion of his spirit in their union? The prophet answers, "Godly offspring." By this interpretation, God's intention for marriage is not just to produce children in general but also and especially for his covenant community to produce godly offspring. It is this design for marriage that is jeopardized by apostasy marriages. What god will the children of such unions be taught to worship? Mom's or Dad's? To whom will these children pray? Where will they go to worship? What law will they follow? Which god will they serve?

On either interpretation, the prophet brings into view the idea of godly offspring.[21] Godly offspring are either God's intention for marriage within the covenant community or the misplaced desire of a faithless Israelite. The mere fact, however, that in a world that stands under the curse of sin there is the possibility of a *zera' 'elohim*—literally "a seed of God"—is a staggering announcement of God's grace. These words would have recalled for Israel (and should recall for us) the first announcement of hope for sinners, the *protevangelium* of Genesis 3:15 in which God says to the serpent, "I will put enmity between you and the woman, and between your offspring and her offspring; he shall bruise your head, and you shall bruise his heel."[22] With this promise of a seed of the woman, God begins to heal and restore what the man and the woman had broken and destroyed, both in their relationship to each other and in their relationship to God himself. The broken marriage between husband and wife and between God and mankind will be healed by a godly offspring.

The expression "seed of God" (or "godly seed") therefore must be understood in the context of redemptive history.[23] The possibility of covenant children is rooted in the promise of the covenant child, the seed of the woman who will one day crush the head of the serpent. Certainly the penultimate longing for every Israelite was for faithful covenant children who would prosper in the land and carry on their family's name after they died. This reality preached to Israel about resurrection life, though in a veiled way. Nevertheless, any hope of resurrection life rested on the work of the one godly seed, the offspring promised to Abraham who would triumph over the seed of the serpent and reverse the woeful effects of the curse.

This is what God is seeking—a godly offspring who will in faithfulness to his Father and in faithfulness to his blood-bought bride produce godly offspring who will worship him in spirit and in truth.

Where do we find hope for broken marriages? The answer is, in the grace of God. It is the grace of God that announced a word of life to Adam and Eve when they deserved nothing but a word of curse and death. It is the grace of God that clothed naked, ashamed, and undeserving Adam and Eve with the skin of animals and that also clothed them and us with the righteousness of his obedient Son. Though perfectly innocent, Jesus would wear garments covered quite literally by the violence of sinners—a blood-stained robe and a crown of thorns—setting on full display not his own violence but that of his people. Though his offering was perfect, on the cross Jesus was "cut off from the tents of Jacob" (Malachi 2:12), crucified outside the city as one abandoned and forsaken by God. The good news for those who fail in their marriages is that God has made a way of reconciliation with our spouses and with himself. The gospel of Jesus Christ announces hope for those whose pasts seem irredeemable and help for those whose present seems unsustainable.

Any pastor who has been in his position more than a week knows that marital issues are always complicated. Guilt is not easily assigned. Hurts are not healed overnight. Divorce, when it happens, is almost never an easy decision. Malachi's denunciation of divorce is not a blanket condemnation of all divorce. The Bible makes clear allowances for divorce in certain circumstances such as adultery, abandonment, and abuse (Matthew 5:31, 32; 19:8, 9; 1 Corinthians 7:15). But even when such a divorce takes place, the prophet demands that we see it for what it is: a rending in two of what was designed to be one, a breaking apart of what was designed to be whole (Genesis 2:24, 25; Mark 10:9). It is an effect of the fall and the result of the sin of at least one, if not both, parties. Its consequences are far-reaching, and the scars never go away.

Any interpretation of Malachi's prophecy that minimizes the seriousness and sadness of divorce is a gross misinterpretation of the text. However, any interpretation that misses the grace of God available for great sinners is an equally gross misinterpretation. The entire narrative arc of sacred Scripture may be summarized in a wedding between a perfect groom, Jesus Christ, and his imperfect bride, the Church. The theme of the romance is well summarized by the Apostle Paul, who writes, "If we are faithless, he remains faithful" (2 Timothy 2:13). Though human marriage bonds are at times severed beyond repair, the marriage bond between Christ and his Church can never fail. Jesus is the perfectly faithful husband whose selfless and sacrificial love for his bride did not just require him to lay down his wants and desires but his very life.

There are no perfect husbands. There are no perfect wives. In marriage we witness the union of two sinners, both in daily need of God's grace. Yet in marriage we believers have an invaluable opportunity to set on display the selfless, sacrificial love of God as we love our spouses, forgive offenses, and pursue reconciliation. Though we will never do so perfectly, we may nevertheless truly set on display Christ's love for his bride, the Church.

After offering instructions to husbands and wives to love one another selflessly and sacrificially, caring for the other as one would their own body, Paul says, "This mystery is profound, and I am saying that it refers to Christ and the church" (Ephesians 5:32). Christ loved his Church to the point of dying for her on a cross, so that his blood-bought bride might in every way—not the least of which is in her marriages—show forth his grace as husbands and wives love and care for one another in humility, gentleness, faithfulness, and love.

# 78

# A Consuming and Purifying Fire

MALACHI 2:17—3:5

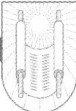

H. L. MENCKEN ONCE DEFINED a cynic as "a man who, when he smells flowers, looks around for a coffin."[1] For most people flowers are associated with life and love and beauty; for the cynic, always questioning motives and always assuming the worst, flowers speak of death and decay and loss. We may find a somewhat more accurate if less colorful description of a cynical person in *Merriam-Webster*, which offers the definition "contemptuously distrustful of human nature and motives." The inclusion of the word "contemptuously" in this definition is key. Cynicism isn't simply distrust; it is distrust attended with an air of superiority and arrogance that looks on others with contempt. This is precisely what is addressed in Malachi's fourth oracle: a deep-seated, acerbic cynicism that has taken root in the heart of the covenant community. However, Israel's cynicism isn't so much a contemptuous distrust of human nature (which is unbecoming, though perhaps understandable) as much as it is the far worse contemptuous distrust of the divine nature. It is a cynicism that casts aspersions on God's very character and calls into question the truth and the reliability of his promises and his purposes.

There can be little doubt that we live in a highly cynical culture where almost every claim to truth, goodness, and beauty is fair game for ruthless parody, mockery, and skepticism. Christians, likewise, are constantly tempted to assume this cynical posture toward life, toward others, and even toward God. In Israel's cynicism we see our own hearts set on display as we too are prone to doubt, prone to question, and prone even to rebuke God in anger and frustration. More importantly, in Malachi's oracle we hear God's response to the toxic, hopeless cynicism of his people. It is a response that confronts and condemns Israel's cynicism with an announcement that judgment is indeed coming in which the scales of divine justice will be perfectly leveled and all that is defiled and defiling will be consumed from this earth.

It is a response that warns Israel about the dangers of cynicism and its poisonous fruit—namely, presumption and complacency. Yet it is at heart a response meant to encourage the faithful as God again promises that one day soon even impure Israel, tempted as they are with cynicism and prone to despair, will be purified. Once purified by the work of a pure priesthood, Israel will enjoy a perfect and unbroken fellowship with their Creator and Redeemer.

### The Cynic's Complaint: "Where Is the God of Justice?" (2:17)

Malachi's fourth disputation opens somewhat more abruptly than his first three. Without introduction the prophet launches immediately into the divine accusation: "You have wearied the LORD with your words" (2:17). God accuses Israel of trying the Lord's patience, of burdening him unnecessarily with their words. True to form, recalcitrant Israel responds with a question meant to object to and challenge God's allegation. "How have we wearied him?" they ask. The postexilic community can't imagine any words that they have uttered, either out loud or in their hearts, that would displease their covenant Lord, so they demand specifics. Malachi responds to Israel's doubting, objecting, challenging hearts with the crushing revelation of the truth: "By saying 'Everyone who does evil is good in the sight of the LORD, and he delights in them.' Or by asking, 'Where is the God of justice?' " (v. 17). Whether they said these things aloud or nursed these suspicions in their hearts, we're not told. But the prophet here exposes the deep-seated cynicism that had become endemic in the postexilic community.

To be sure, "Where is the God of justice?" is not necessarily an impious or cynical question. Numerous laments throughout the psalter feature such cries for God to rise and act on behalf of his people, bringing about justice and righteousness in a world that has been torn apart and broken by sin. In Psalm 74, for instance, the psalmist cries out: "How long, O God, is the foe to scoff? Is the enemy to revile your name forever? Why do you hold back your hand, your right hand? Take it from the fold of your garment and destroy them!" (vv. 10, 11). Feelings of bewilderment and despair at the wickedness and injustices of this world rightly elicit from the faithful cries of frustration and longing for God to act decisively to establish justice upon the earth.

But these are not the cries of Malachi's disputants. The immediately preceding statement clearly reveals that Israel's question arises not from faith but from doubt; that is, from hearts that have begun to question God's very integrity.[2] The people accused God of approving what is evil, and not just approving but delighting in it as well. "Where is the God of justice?" on the lips of this postexilic community was rhetorical, even cynical, as it implied that God was nowhere to be found.[3] Israel had come to believe that God was not concerned about the injustices of this world and, more than this, that he actually took joy and pleasure in the violence, oppression, lies, and greed that increasingly characterized the postexilic community and the world in which they lived.[4]

Perhaps the most powerful portrait of this cynical spirit that had taken root in postexilic Israel is found in Psalm 73, where the psalmist confesses that he had become "envious of the arrogant when I saw the prosperity of the wicked" (v. 3). The psalmist observes that the wicked "have no pangs until death; their bodies are fat and sleek. They are not in trouble as others are; they are not stricken like the rest of mankind" (vv. 4, 5). The psalmist sees those who have taken a stand against God both in their words and in their deeds enjoying lives that may best be described as nothing less than charmed. In contrast, the psalmist voices frustration and perhaps even regret at having served God: "All in vain have I kept my heart clean and washed my hands in innocence. For all day long I have been stricken and rebuked every morning" (vv. 13, 14). In other words, "Where is the God of justice?" Obedience and faithfulness appeared to be in vain. Injustice, violence, and chaos appeared to yield the fruit of blessing.

So it was with the postexilic community in Malachi's day. When Israel looked at their world they saw the Persian Empire thriving, going from victory to victory as they amassed more and more territory and unimaginable wealth. Closer to home and of more immediate concern, Israel looked within their own territory and city and beheld rampant corruption, oppression, idolatry, and infidelity. *If God is the God of justice*, they thought, *surely he would have acted by now. Surely he would have punished the evildoers and rewarded the faithful.* But instead of crying out in faith, "How long, O Lord?" (Psalm 35:17) they began to doubt God's character as a God of justice and compassion. They began to reflect the wilderness generation of old as they grumbled and complained against God.

While we are meant to assume a critical posture toward those in Malachi's day who had become cynical toward God, we mustn't assume a superior posture. The fact of the matter is that we are susceptible to the same cynical spirit taking root in our hearts. We too are prone to make our experiences and our understanding the arbiter of truth, including the truth of who God is and what he is up to in the world. We too can look at the horrors taking place around the globe, the injustices in our own societies, and the corruption that is present even in our own churches, and conclude that God doesn't see, or if he does, he doesn't care.

Evil often appears to prosper and thrive while the faithful are weighed down with burdens and sorrows that seem at odds with their status as God's chosen and beloved. It is not at all improper to observe and lament these realities; in fact, just the opposite, believers have an obligation to acknowledge the reality of sin and injustice wherever it is found. But we must interpret such injustices by faith that responds not with cynicism, doubt, and recrimination but with heartfelt prayers for justice ("How long, O Lord, will you look on?" [Psalm 35:17]) and longing for God's kingdom to come in glory ("Your kingdom come, your will be done, on earth as it is in heaven" [Matthew 6:10]).

### The God of Justice Is Coming (3:1)

What is God's answer to the doubting, disoriented, and cynical hearts of his people? Simply put, God's answer is that the King is coming. In the ancient Near Eastern world, the arrival of a king would be preceded by the arrival of the king's messenger or herald.[5] It was the messenger's job to announce the imminence of the king's arrival and to summon the people to make all the preparations necessary for the king to receive a welcome befitting his office.[6]

When the Lord says, "Behold, I send my messenger, and he will prepare the way before me" (Malachi 3:1), he is declaring that the King of all the earth is coming. God is not unaware of the injustices. He is not unconcerned and aloof from the sufferings of his people. He is, Malachi says, coming to his temple, that is, God's earthly palace (v. 1). Later in the same verse, another messenger is mentioned, "the messenger of the covenant," a mysterious figure who has received a great deal of scholarly attention. Is this referring to the same messenger preparing the way for the King or to the King himself?[7] Though the same word for "messenger" is used for both, it seems from the context that the phrase "the messenger of the covenant" stands in apposition to "the Lord whom you seek" and therefore should be understood as referring to God himself.[8] God "will come to his temple," and he will come as "the messenger of the covenant."

God's response—in effect, "the King is coming"—implies several things. It implies that God is not unaware of the sufferings of his people or the injustices of this world. God does not deny the reality of sin and suffering, saying, "No, you're just looking at it incorrectly; there's really no problem here." Nor is God unaware. He doesn't say, "Wait! What's going on? I had no idea." He says in essence, "The Lord your God is coming." This is not an advent recently, quickly, or haphazardly planned; it is an arrival that has been eternally decreed.

"The King is coming" also implies that he is coming on his timetable and not Israel's (or ours). This is the significance of the notice that "the messenger of the covenant" will come suddenly to the temple. Though God had announced it beforehand, though he will send a messenger to prepare the way before him, nevertheless there is an unexpected quality to the Lord's arrival because it will be according to God's plan and not man's. God is in perfect control, and he will arrive at just the right time.[9] In the fullness of time, God will arrive in his holy temple.

In this response, God is saying, in effect, "I do see, and I do care." Though it did not look like it at their present moment, and though it did not feel like it in their experience, Israel was called to remember that the Lord remembers his people, and one day soon the Lord would act decisively to address every evil and to right every wrong. What Israel misunderstood and mischaracterized as disregard for evil, disinterest in justice, and a lack of concern for the suffering of his people was in reality an expression of God's patience to give time for his people to prepare. This time of preparation would come to a climax with the arrival of the messenger who would herald the advent of the King.

God's response to his people's cynical and accusatory complaints reminded them and reminds us that he is sovereign and that he is working all things together according to his perfectly good and perfectly wise purposes. The reality of the imminent coming of the Lord to his temple was meant to transform God's people in Malachi's day. It was not a call to deny or minimize the genuine suffering and hardships that God's people observed all around them. It was, however, a call to not despair. It was a call to not give up trusting that God would act as he had promised. It was a call to remember that God acts in his way and in his time, a way and a time that more often than not confounds the expectations and wisdom of mankind.

God graciously responded to Israel's accusations, but he didn't leave it there. God now had questions of his own. The most pressing question for Israel was not, "Where is the God of justice?" Israel should have known that the God of justice was alive and well. Rather, the most pressing question for Israel was, "What will we do when the God of justice arrives?"

## Who Can Stand? (3:2a)

At this point, God turns the tables. No longer is God on the defensive, answering the faithless complaints and accusations of his people. Instead, he adopted the posture of the prosecutor. His spokesman, Malachi, put a question of his own to Israel: "Who can endure the day of his coming, and who can stand when he appears?" (3:2a). With straightforward questions the prophet said, in effect, "Be careful what you wish for."[10]

When the King of Glory does arrive, what will he find? The experience of the exile had taught Israel that they were not exempt from God's judgment. Just as Israel was God's instrument of judgment against the Canaanites on account of their great wickedness, so Babylon was God's instrument of judgment against Israel on account of their great wickedness. God's judgment is indiscriminate, and the prophet calls Israel to look to themselves and consider what God will find in them when he comes. Will he find a people whose justice, righteousness, holiness, and purity will be able to stand in the face of a judgment that discerns the very thoughts and deepest intentions of the heart? Or will he find in Israel the very disregard for justice and the condoning of evil of which they were accusing God?[11]

When God sits in judgment, he will do so as one whose knowledge is complete, whose integrity is perfect, and whose standards are exacting. The result, Malachi tells us, will be twofold: God will do a refining work in Israel, and God will do a consuming work in Israel.

## Refining Fire (3:2b–4)

The prophet employs two images to describe God's work of purification, that of a refining fire and that of a fuller's soap. Both were used in the ancient world to purify completely what had become corrupt and defiled, whether from dirt or from contamination by other metals.

God is himself pure. He is the very standard and definition of purity: "He is like a refiner's fire and like fullers' soap" (Malachi 3:2b). Therefore, when he arrives, he will judge his people according to the standard of purity or holiness that he himself is. God's very presence will reveal the corruption and defilement of his people as they, as it were, pass through the fires that test metal and reveal even the slightest hint of impurity.

Though the images of refining with fire and cleansing with lye carry with them overtones of judgment—as the wickedness that characterized the current priesthood would be burned away, perhaps including the priests themselves—God's work of burning and bleaching was not ultimately designed to destroy but to heal Israel. It would redress the corruptions and defilements that had crippled the community and disrupted her worship seemingly beyond repair as the priests themselves engaged in corrupt practices that defiled the altar and misled the people. With this image of the refining and purifying of the Levitical priesthood, God announced the reversal of Israel's present circumstances.

When the priesthood ceased to operate, the worship for which Israel was created ceased as well. An impure priesthood had disastrous consequences for the entire covenant community. But Malachi declares that God "will sit as a refiner and purifier or silver, and he will purify the sons of Levi and refine them like gold and silver, and they will bring offerings in righteousness to the LORD" (v. 3). The purity that was impossible for Israel to achieve on their own was not only possible with God but was promised by God.[12] God was the agent of Israel's purification and therefore the cause of their purified worship. God would purify Israel's priesthood, thereby equipping them to lead his people in acceptable worship of the living God.[13] "Then," Malachi declares, "the offering of Judah and Jerusalem will be pleasing to the LORD as in the days of old and as in former years" (v. 4).

Israel's prophets often spoke in the idiom of the old covenant to describe the nearly indescribable glories of the new. The fulfillment of Malachi's promise was not found ultimately in a purified priesthood of the tribe of Levi but in the perfectly pure Priest after the order of Melchizedek, to whom Levi himself paid tithes while he was still in the loins of his father, Abraham (Hebrews 7:9, 10). In Christ, God provided precisely what Israel needed but could not provide for themselves, the pure priest who would "bring offerings in righteousness to the LORD" (Malachi 3:3). The offering Jesus would provide would not be the unblemished bulls or goats that Israel was required (but refused) to bring. Jesus would offer himself as the Lamb of God, the once-for-all sacrifice who would take away the sins of the world. This pure priest would make possible pure worship for the covenant community. This is what God promised when he said, "Then the offering of Judah and Jerusalem will be pleasing to the LORD" (v. 4). The pure priesthood led by the pure Priest would make even the imperfect worship offered in faith pure and acceptable in the presence of God. Even more than acceptable, it would be pleasing to him. The King of the universe delights in the worship of his people.

How is Christian worship ever to be pure and pleasing to God? The reality is that in this life our worship is never perfectly pure. Even when it may get close, it does so only for a moment before our minds are again distracted, our hearts again given over to doubt, or our offerings again tainted with hints of resentment. But when offered through faith in Jesus Christ and in the power of his Spirit, even half-hearted worship, prone to distraction and doubt, is in fact honoring and pleasing to God. To interpret this as license for laziness or inattentiveness in worship would be to miss the point. Malachi offers a powerful reminder that in Christ, God has provided a mediator whose perfection makes possible true communion and perfect fellowship with God, the very fellowship and communion for which we were created and in which we experience true blessedness.

### Consuming Fire (3:5)

Unlike the United States, in which the executive branch of government is separate and distinct from the judiciary, ancient Near Eastern kings functioned as supreme rulers as well as supreme judges. Adjudicating disputes and issuing verdicts was one of the chief functions of the king. By doing so, kings would demonstrate their commitment to uphold the order of society. We could think of King Solomon adjudicating the dispute between the prostitutes who each claimed that a child was her own (1 Kings 3:16–28). Likewise, the great King, when he came to his temple to establish his kingship, would sit in judgment: "Then I will draw near to you for judgment. I will be a swift witness against the sorcerers, against the adulterers, against those who swear falsely, against those who oppress the hired worker in his wages, the widow and the fatherless, against those who thrust aside the sojourner, and do not fear me, says the LORD of hosts" (Malachi 3:5). In this we see that the divine justice that purified some—namely, the sons of Levi, and through them God's covenant people—would at the same time consume and destroy others. As Charles Spurgeon once said, "The same sun which melts wax hardens clay."[14] The same fire of God's judgment refines and destroys.

God's enumeration of offenders and offenses in verse 5 is by no means exhaustive but is rather meant to highlight particular sins to which the postexilic community was prone and that, according to Israel's law, deserve the most serious censures, including capital punishment. These include sins against God, as in the case of consulting sorcerers. The majority, however, have in view sins against neighbors, such as adultery, swearing falsely, oppression of the weak and vulnerable, and neglect of the sojourner. Israel, like us, was prone to care more about offenses to themselves than to God, and so these are likely the evils that Israel had in mind when they said, "Everyone who does evil is good in the sight of the LORD" (2:17). But here in Malachi 3, God responds with an unequivocal affirmation of his commitment to justice and a promise to realize his justice in his judgments against the wicked and ungodly.

God declares that when he comes as King and Judge of all the earth, he will indeed bear witness against the wickedness and oppression that plagues the postexilic community and that appears to go unnoticed and unresolved. God once again assumes the prerogative of both witness and judge (cf. Malachi 2:12, 14), an ominous message for any who hoped to escape on a technicality. There will be no legal loopholes on that day. God will take his stand as the perfectly reliable witness, and he will issue his judgment as the perfectly just judge against every manner of evil conceived in the heart of mankind. In identifying his role as not only that of judge ("I will draw near to you for judgment") but also as a "swift witness" (3:5), God is declaring that his work in rendering judgment against sin will not be forestalled by a prolonged court case or an indecisive jury.[15] It will be as quick as it is clear and decisive. Here we find the sobering reminder that a reckoning is coming, and no sin and no sinner will go unpunished. As the author of the letter to the Hebrews says, "It is appointed for man to die once, and after that comes judgment" (9:27).

With this we return to the central question, a question that is as important for us today as it was for Israel in Malachi's day: "Who can endure the day of his coming, and who can stand when he appears?" (Malachi 3:2). When we long for justice for the oppressed and long for judgment upon the wicked and the evil of this world, we almost always envision ourselves on the side of the just and the righteous. Malachi's question is just as important and searching for us today as it was for Israel in that day. When the King and Judge of the earth arrives, who will be able to endure that day? Who will be able to stand in his holy presence when he appears? When the God who knows the deepest secrets of our hearts appears to render a judgment on this world, what will he say about us? One commentator put it well when she wrote, "All our feeble claims to righteousness and faith, much less excuses for indifference and unbelief, will be unavailing before that fire. Unless God himself saves his people, they cannot endure his coming."[16]

The Psalms again capture this reality powerfully when the psalmist asks, "O Lord, who shall sojourn in your tent? Who shall dwell on your holy hill?" (15:1). The answer is given:

> He who walks blamelessly and does what is right
>   and speaks truth in his heart;
> who does not slander with his tongue
>   and does no evil to his neighbor,
>   nor takes up a reproach against his friend;
> in whose eyes a vile person is despised,
>   but who honors those who fear the Lord. (vv. 2–4)

The psalmist concludes, "He who does these things shall never be moved" (v. 5).

When the Lord arrives to render judgment on the wicked and the unjust, what judgment will Israel receive? The prophet has already revealed something of how deeply Israel's own depravity runs. Who among them could claim to walk blamelessly, do what is right, and do no evil to his neighbor? Clearly the implication of the prophet's question is, "No one." No one in Israel could withstand the fire of God's judgment on his or her own merit, which points to only one hope—the merit of another.

How is it, though, that the God of perfect justice can be a consuming fire to some and a purifying fire to others? The answer is that when Jesus hung on the cross, he bore in his body the consuming fire of God's judgment for the sins of his people so that sinners who look to him in faith would experience the purifying fires of God's grace. At the cross God bore witness against his Son. Though innocent, Jesus was counted as a sorcerer, an adulterer, a liar, and an oppressor of widows, children, and sojourners, for such were the sins of the people for whom he died. Convicted of sins he never committed, Jesus set free from sin's bondage and curse those who belong to him. This is the answer to perhaps the most important question any of us will ever face: "Who can stand when he appears?" (Malachi 3:2). The answer is Jesus, the Son of God, and all who by faith stand in him.

Jesus is the ultimate answer to our cynical hearts. Where is the God of justice? He's stripped, beaten, mocked, pierced, and hanging on a Roman cross suffering the greatest injustice this world has ever witnessed. Very often our cries for justice come not so much from a desire for justice for others but from a desire for justice for ourselves. Jesus suffered the greatest injustice in human history so that when the God and King of the universe sits to balance the books, there might be a people—the Bible tells us more people than could possibly be counted—who are accounted righteous, pure, blameless, and holy because the sinless Son of God bears witness, saying, "I died for him; I died for her. They've been bought with a price, and they are mine."

God doesn't give us all the answers for why he allows such great suffering and injustice to occur in our world. We see this all around us every day, and it seems to be inexplicable. Even though we cannot explain it or see any greater purpose for the suffering and injustice of our world, the cross of Christ teaches us that God can and does. This truth should cause our cynical hearts to melt into hearts of childlike faith and deep trust in God. We can know with absolute certainty that he is working "all things . . . together for good, for those who are called according to his purpose" (Romans 8:28; cf. Psalm 131).

Our response to evil and injustice is faith in the living God that produces gratitude, and true gratitude to God inevitably leads to doxology. As the author of Hebrews writes, "Therefore let us be grateful for receiving a kingdom that cannot be shaken, and thus let us offer to God acceptable worship, with reverence and awe, for our God is a consuming fire" (12:28, 29). In his mercy, God bore in himself the consuming fire, so that we will ever more be refined by his grace and live to his glory.

# 79

# Putting the Lord to the Test

MALACHI 3:6–12[1]

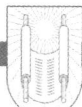

PUTTING GOD TO THE TEST is a phenomenally bad idea. God explicitly forbids it (Deuteronomy 6:16). Countless events in Scripture bear out the disastrous consequences that follow it. Perhaps the most famous (or better, infamous) is the event that took place in the wilderness when the people of Israel encamped at Rephidim and "quarreled" with Moses, saying, "Why did you bring us up out of Egypt, to kill us and our children and our livestock with thirst?" (Exodus 17:3). The word "quarreled" understates the matter considerably, as Moses cried out to God in response, "What shall I do with this people? They are almost ready to stone me" (v. 4). Though the Lord would respond with a remarkable demonstration of his power and grace, causing water to burst forth from a rock, thus providing life for a people who deserved death, the event nevertheless goes down in the history of Israel as the touchstone for faithlessness and rebellion against Almighty God and against his servant Moses.

The location itself, Rephidim, was renamed Massah and Meribah, which mean respectively "testing" and "quarreling," thus memorializing Israel's sin and God's grace (v. 7). Some forty years later, Moses would invoke this event when he commanded Israel on the plains of Moab, "You shall not put the LORD your God to the test, as you tested him at Massah" (Deuteronomy 6:16). Even more memorably, this event is cited as a warning for all generations in Psalm 95, which concludes by saying,

> Today, if you hear his voice,
>   do not harden your hearts, as at Meribah,
>   as on the day at Massah in the wilderness,

> when you fathers put me to the test
> and put me to the proof, though they had seen my work.
> For forty years I loathed that generation
> and said, "They are a people who go astray in their heart,
> and they have not known my ways."
> Therefore I swore in my wrath,
> "They shall not enter my rest." (vv. 7b–11)

Putting God to the test is, at its heart, an expression of faithlessness. It says, in effect, "God, your saving acts in the past and your word of promise in the present are not enough for me to believe you. You must do more for me so that I may believe that your word is true and that you are worthy of my trust."

What is striking is that the "more" that is required of God is never enough. As Abraham said to the rich man in Jesus's parable, "If they do not hear Moses and the Prophets, neither will they be convinced if someone should rise from the dead" (Luke 16:31). Unsurprisingly, it is this temptation to put God to the test that the devil employed against Jesus in the wilderness. Matthew tells us that Satan brought Jesus to the pinnacle of the temple and said to him, "If you are the Son of God, throw yourself down, for it is written, 'He will command his angels concerning you,'" to which Jesus responded, "Again it is written, 'You shall not put the Lord your God to the test'" (Matthew 4:6, 7; cf. Deuteronomy 6:16).

These illustrations would appear to settle the matter clearly, definitively, and without qualification. But there *is* an important qualification. We are not to put the Lord our God to the test *unless God himself invites us to do so*.[2]

We must make this qualification because there have been certain occasions when God invited and even encouraged his people to test him in such a way that to refuse would in fact have been an expression of unbelief.[3] Perhaps the parade example was God inviting King Ahaz through his prophet Isaiah to "ask a sign of the Lord your God; let it be deep as Sheol or high as heaven" (Isaiah 7:11).[4] In other words, Isaiah said to Ahaz, "Put God to the test."

In this invitation, we see God stooping down to a weak, doubting, sinful, and often world-weary people and saying, "Though my word should be sufficient, let this sign also help bolster your faith in the midst of doubt." The reason for such an invitation was God's kindness and condescension to mankind's inherent, sin-born weakness that produces doubt. God at times invites his people to put him to the test so that their weak faith might be strengthened.

While God's word should be more than enough for us to stand with confidence, the reality is that we are all plagued with sin and doubts that at times shake us to the core. But God in his mercy and tender compassion stoops down to offer signs and tokens of his fatherly affection to assure our doubting minds and comfort our weary hearts. So it is in the present passage. In Malachi's penultimate oracle, we witness God inviting the postexilic community to put him to the test. He says, "Bring the full tithe into the storehouse, that there may be food in my house. *And thereby put me to the test*, says the LORD of hosts, if I will not open the windows of heaven for you and pour down for you a blessing until there is no more need" (Malachi 3:10).

The root of Israel's reluctance is in fact their unbelief, their doubt that God will make good on his promises to bless an obedient people. However, God in his patience, goodness, and infinite mercy extends a remarkable invitation to his weak and sinful people. "Try me. Try obedience to my commands," God says, "See if I'm true to my word."

For Israel to withhold God's tithes is the fruit of their lack of faith. The call to return to the Lord is a call to faith, repentance (which is the inevitable fruit of faith), and obedience (which is the fruit of both).

### God's Unchanging Character (3:6)

God through his prophet opens this oracle with a declaration that is, on the one hand, perfectly clear, straightforward, and in a way, simple. Yet on the other hand, it is so profound and mysterious that philosophers and theologians can spend their lives studying it and never fully understand it. God says, "Truly I the LORD do not change" (Malachi 3:6a, AT).[5] This immediately sets Yahweh, the God of Israel, in stark contrast to the gods of Israel's neighbors. The gods of the nations were constantly changing. They changed their minds and their moods, their loves and their loyalties, their preferences and purposes, but unlike these gods, Yahweh never changes. He is in himself infinitely perfect, complete in all of his attributes and in all of his ways.[6]

Theologians have observed that for God to change would mean that he is either improving (and therefore wasn't perfect in the first place) or is weakening or diminishing in some respect, and though he may have been perfect at one point, he is no longer.[7] Neither of these portraits accurately describes the God of the Bible, who is repeatedly revealed to be perfect in every respect. As the book of James teaches, "Every good gift and every perfect gift is from above, coming down from the Father of lights; with whom there is no variation or shadow due to change" (1:17).

This is an incredibly difficult doctrine to fully comprehend. It is difficult in large measure because change is all that we as creatures know and experience. We change all the time, every day, every moment. Our circumstances change. The world in which we live changes. Times change. Seasons change. Change seems to be all that there is. This led the Greek philosopher Heraclitus to maintain that change (or flux) is at the center of reality, a view captured in his famous expression that it is impossible to step into the same river twice.

Though we can never understand fully what it means for God to be unchangeable, our understanding of change offers a little help. We know what it means to change, and the Bible says that God doesn't do it nor is he subject to it.[8]

Theologians have often appealed to Malachi 3:6 (among other verses) to demonstrate this central claim of Christianity—what is called, in theological terms, the *immutability of God*—and rightly so.[9] That God is unchangeable in himself is the clear and undeniable (though certainly mysterious) teaching of this and many other texts. However, it is also clear that the prophet Malachi is not offering a discourse on the metaphysics of deity.[10] He is instead prosecuting another covenant lawsuit against God's covenant people. That is to say, God's unchangeable character is of immense practical importance for God's people in their (and in our) particular moment in redemptive history. This is clear from what follows: "For I the LORD do not change; therefore you, O children of Jacob, are not consumed" (v. 6).[11]

It seems that the postexilic community had begun to wonder if in fact their God had changed toward them.[12] But the prophet reminds them that Israel's continued existence and her daily experience of God's grace and lovingkindness was exclusively the result of God's unchanging character and his commitment to his covenant promises. The implication is obvious. If God did change, if his affections waxed and waned, if he could change his decrees and purposes (like so many other deities in the ancient Near East), then Israel most certainly would have been consumed by his righteous judgment ages ago.

God's unchanging promises are rooted in his unchanging character. The importance of this doctrine was wonderfully expressed by Martin Luther, who once asked, "If God were not immutable, who can believe his promises?"[13] Just as God can no sooner stop being holy, wise, or just than he can stop being God, so too he can no sooner go back on his promises than he can cease being the self-existent God. God is who he is, and he will never— he *can* never—be anything other. He is the promise-making, promise-keeping God, and since he doesn't change, neither do his promises to and purposes for his people.

To be sure, God appears to change at times in the Bible as he interacts with his changing creation. God is said to regret, to repent, to be pleased one moment and angry the next; all of this seems to suggest some sort of change in God. In fact, even in the very next verse (Malachi 3:7), God declares, "Return to me, and I will return to you," a promise that certainly suggests God changing toward his people. These are *anthropomorphisms* or *anthropopathisms*. That is to say, these are figures of speech, ways of speaking about the unchangeable God genuinely and truly engaging with his changeable creation. As he condescends to interact with his creation, God is certainly perceived and experienced by his creation as changing, and yet we are told that it is the perfectly unchangeable, immutable God who is so acting within the created order to accomplish his unchangeable purposes.[14]

Divine immutability is certainly a profound mystery. However, we learn from Malachi 3:6 that God's unchangeable character is not an esoteric, abstract doctrine for the philosophically and theologically inclined. The fact that God is immutable is the foundation of the Christian's faith and hope. The God who gave his Son to die for sinners will not withdraw him. The God who promises to never leave us or forsake us today will not leave us and forsake us tomorrow. The grace that he has extended to us today will not be removed and unavailable for us tomorrow. Believers can sing those precious words of John Newton's famous hymn, "'Tis grace has led me safe thus far, and grace will lead me home,"[15] because the grace that we received in the past and in which we stand today will be available for us tomorrow precisely because our God doesn't change. One commentator summarized it well when he wrote, "In v 6 the people are confronted with the gospel."[16]

This is especially important to hear because we *do* change, very much and very often. Our obedience changes, and we go through seasons of waywardness and hard-heartedness. Our emotions change. At times we feel God's presence and provision acutely, and at other times we feel distant from God or even altogether abandoned. Our bodies change, at times for the better and at other times for the worse. As finite creatures, we can never fully comprehend what it means for God to be unchanging, but we can apprehend its truth sufficiently to understand that our God is "the same yesterday and today and forever" (Hebrews 13:8). He will never change because he can never change, and this means that his love for and faithfulness toward his people will never change. This mystery should not frustrate us as we seek to understand how this may be. Rather, it should drive us to greater thankfulness and deeper worship of this God who, though in himself beyond our comprehension, has nevertheless revealed himself in ways we can understand—unchanging in who he is in himself and in who he is to us and for us as our Rock and our Redeemer.

## God's Unchanging People (3:7–9)

Though God's unchanging character was the foundation of Israel's hope, there was nevertheless a problem. God, it turns out, was not the only party in this relationship who did not change. God's people were also described as unchanging. God said, "From the days of your fathers you have turned aside from my statutes and have not kept them" (Malachi 3:7). Like their forefathers, Israel was unchanging in their faithlessness and rebellion against God.

To be clear, God was not saying there has never been an Israelite who lived by faith and walked in righteousness and obedience to his laws. Neither was he saying that there had never been a generation that could accurately be described as faithful. In fact, in the preceding oracle, God spoke about acceptable offerings of Judah and Jerusalem "in the days of old and as in former years" (v. 4). Clearly there had been numerous individuals, even generations who received divine approbation. God was saying, however, that this postexilic community had failed to break with the faithlessness, idolatry, doubt, and distrust that characterized Israel throughout her generations.

Though some individual Israelites kept faith with Yahweh and though some generations had been more faithful than others, the overall portrait that Malachi paints of Israel throughout her history is that of a faithless people who have not honored God in their obedience, a people who have served other gods and have sought provision from the idols of the nations rather than from their Creator and their Redeemer. Those individuals and even those generations who had been faithful were the exceptions that proved the rule. Israel, when considered as a nation and when considered throughout their long history as God's chosen people, has lived more like the pagan nations around them who did not know God and did not have his laws and his covenant promises.[17] This fact is underscored by the prophet, who addresses Israel with a term typically reserved for the foreign nations: "the whole nation [*gôy*] of you" (v. 9).[18]

Whereas God is unchanging by virtue of who he is as God—that is, according to his divine nature—Israel is unchanging by virtue of their will—that is, according to their sinful affections and desires. God is unchanging in his loving-kindness, his forgiveness, and his covenant love for his people, but Israel, for their part, is unchanging in their stubborn rebellion, their faithlessness, and their disobedience. This fact is hinted at in the Lord's address of them as "children of Jacob" instead of "children of Israel" (Malachi 3:6), a designation that connected them with the patriarch whose name was associated with striving for God's covenant blessings through one's own sinful efforts (cf. Genesis 32:22–32). Perhaps the chief indication of the deep entrenchment of Israel's sin is that they cannot even see it when it is brought to their attention. God calls them to repentance saying, "Return to me, and I will return to you," to which the people respond, "How shall we return?" (Malachi 3:7). This is not an inquiry into the correct practice of repentance; rather, it is an expression of the people's confusion. They are essentially saying, "Why would we need to repent?" because they see nothing wrong.

Though there were no doubt many things to which God could have appealed to prove his case, he keeps his accusation simple and practical. He says, "Will man rob God? Yet you are robbing me" (Malachi 3:8a). Unconscious of any wrongdoing, perhaps as a result of their lack of instruction, the people respond, "How have we robbed you?"[19] (v. 8b), to which the Lord replies, "In your tithes and contributions. You are cursed with a curse, for you are robbing me, the whole nation of you. Bring the full tithe into the storehouse, that there may be food in my house" (vv. 8c, 9a). "Tithe" refers to the tenth of all Israel's produce that God had commanded to be set apart as "holy to the LORD" (Leviticus 27:30) and used in the maintenance of the sanctuary personnel, the Levites (Numbers 18:28). Though Israel was not the only culture that practiced the tithe, it served a special purpose as a reminder that everything they had and everything they were—their very lives—were gifts of God's grace.

Martin Luther once famously said, "God doesn't need your good works, your neighbor does." Similarly, God did not need Israel's tithes, but Israel needed to tithe because of what it said about God and their relationship to him. Israel did not need to cling to every ear of wheat or grain of barley. They did not need to keep every sheep that was born to their flock or every calf that was born to their herd. They could give back to God with freedom and joy because God is a good Father who owns the cattle on a thousand hills and is able to provide for his people in abundance. Indeed, he had promised to do precisely this for the postexilic community.

We are not told why the postexilic community refused to obey God in their tithes. It doesn't take much of an imagination, however, to identify a number of plausible motivations. For some it was likely fear that they wouldn't have enough for themselves.[20] For others it was a lack of faith that obedience in this area would in fact lead to genuine blessing. Still for others it is probable that their reluctance to tithe stemmed from laziness, putting off obedience until a more convenient time. There were likely other motivations as well. Almost all of these were exacerbated by the fact that the more Israel withheld, the more God withheld his covenant blessings, which further hardened an already hard-hearted people in their refusal to obey. As a result, the postexilic community experienced a vicious cycle of want that led to hardened hearts that led to withholding tithes. This resulted in more want that led to more hardening that led to more withholding, and so it went on from there. As a consequence, the postexilic community drifted farther and farther from God, which resulted in a profound insensitivity to God's warnings and rebukes that came through his prophet Malachi. So in their disorientation they ask, "How have we robbed you?"

The root of all of this, of course, is the sin of self-reliance. It is a sin to which Israel was constantly prone, and it is a sin to which we are constantly prone as well. It is a sin that says, in effect, "If I am going to be blessed, it will be through my own wisdom, effort, and work." Yet God had demonstrated to Israel in countless ways, in word and deed, that their happiness and blessing could only and ultimately be found in him. Blessing is found in the grace that God alone offers those who look to him in faith.

The presenting of tithes to Yahweh was at the heart of Israel's life and worship. It was the means by which the work of the temple was supported and sustained, the work of prayer and sacrifices and teaching. Importantly, however, the tithe was designed to represent something about Israel's heart, specifically that they recognized that everything they had been given was a gift of God's free and unmerited grace. The bringing of the tithe was an act of worship, a way of presenting to God a symbolic portion of one's labors and thus returning to the Lord a portion of those good things that he had given to his people.

Yet it is easy to see how giving to God a portion of one's wealth and resources seems counterintuitive. It seems contrary to our understanding of how the world works: if you want to accumulate wealth and if you want to enjoy the blessings of abundance, you must save and preserve and store up. To put it another way, you gain by keeping. Yet God says again and again in his Word that true gain, true joy, and true blessings are not found in amassing wealth but in spreading wealth. The God who owns the cattle on a thousand hills did not need Israel's tithes. Israel, rather, needed to be a people who freely, willingly, and joyfully gave to God as an expression of their faith in him and their confidence that he could and would provide all that was needful and good for his people.

To be sure, neither the tithes in the Old Testament nor the offerings in the New Testament are ways for us to live our best lives now. These are not ways of manipulating God or coercing him into giving us what we think will make us happy. Rather, giving to God is an expression of trust that God will provide all that is needful for us. It is a way of acknowledging that all we have belongs to God, and therefore we are happy to return a portion to him in thanksgiving, knowing that the One who has provided for us thus far will continue to do so in a way that is best for us.

This is at times difficult to believe, both for Israel in Malachi's day and for us in our own day. Though the tithe as it was legislated under the old covenant does not govern Christians under the new covenant, the New Testament is perfectly clear that Christians can and should give generously to the Church and to charity.[21] Christians are to give so generously, in fact, that their generosity confounds the wisdom and values of the world. Yet how often do we balk and withhold just as Israel did? How often do we give grudgingly, giving only and exactly what we believe is required of us? How often do we give doubting or wondering if God will provide for us?

What do our bank statements and credit card bills reveal about our priorities and our values? We too can doubt God's clear promises that the way to true blessing is through giving not just of our resources (financial or otherwise) but giving ourselves in love and in sacrificial service to others. As God revealed through his prophet, this is the life of faith.

## God's Unchanging Purpose (3:10–12)

God responds to his people's faithlessness, doubt, and disobedience with an invitation to put him to the test. He says, "Bring the full tithe into the storehouse, that there may be food in my house. And thereby put me to the test, says the Lord of hosts, if I will not open the windows of heaven for you and pour down for you a blessing until there is no more need" (3:10). In other words, God says, "Try doing things my way, and let's see how it goes."

Israel was seeking happiness, joy, contentment, and satisfaction—in a word, peace—by doing things their own way. Through clinging to the little they had, through withholding what they should have freely given, through keeping for themselves what they should have offered to God in obedience and worship, Israel believed that they would know what little joy and blessedness they could hope for in the difficult times in which they found themselves. But the result was a far cry from joy and blessedness. The result was covenant curses that yielded profound lack and abiding misery.

It is clear that Israel had been suffering for some time with crop failure and harvests decimated by locusts, what the prophet calls "the devourer" (v. 11). These, God reminds Israel, were from his hand, the rebuke of their covenant King. Yet God invites his people back to the ways of faith and obedience with the promise that should they repent (i.e., "return"), they will experience blessings that will astound the mind. Such blessings are not new promises but old. These are variations on the covenant blessings God had promised

Israel through Moses generations earlier (cf. Leviticus 26:1–13; Deuteronomy 28:1–14). In these blessings God is proving his word to be true and himself to be faithful to all he has promised.

It would be a mistake to interpret God's invitation to "put me to the test" as an invitation to moralism, thinking that God wanted Israel's tithes regardless of their heart attitudes, as if he needed Israel's offerings to satisfy his hunger or to provide for his priests. Rather, the invitation here is for Israel to display the fruit of faith by presenting to God the offering that his law requires. This will indeed require much faith. It will require faith that God is able to provide enough for their families to survive when they give a portion of their harvest to the Lord. God, however, promises that he will not only provide enough for Israel to survive but will provide for them with a harvest so abundant that it would boggle their minds, and not theirs alone: the nations would sit up and take notice of the abundant provision of Israel's God: "Then all nations will call you blessed, for you will be a land of delight, says the LORD of hosts" (Malachi 3:12).

As his people looked to him in faith and bore the fruit of repentance in their humble obedience and trust, they would find God to be lavish in his provision and care. God promised to roll back the causes of Israel's hardships and suffering, saying, "I will rebuke the devourer for you, so that it will not destroy the fruits of your soil, and your vine in the field shall not fail to bear, says the LORD of hosts" (v. 11). Instead, God would decree a fullness of life and health symbolized by the vine that never fails to give her fruit, thereby providing constant delight and refreshment to the soul.

Israel was being reminded that their God is a God who is rich in mercy and who is able to drive away the painful and sorrowful effects of the curse. Throughout this oracle we see the theme of reversal as God promised to transform Israel's curses into blessings. The rebuke that he issued against Israel would be turned against "the devourer"; "the windows of heaven" (3:10), an expression that recalled God's means of judgment in the days of Noah, would "pour down for [them] a blessing until there is no more need" (v. 10).[22] In this we see God's gracious purposes. God delights in showering the blessings of Heaven itself upon a people called by his name. No sooner did the first man plunge the human race into death than God issued a word of gospel promise and blessing revealing his purpose to bring life out of the death of mankind's making (Genesis 3:15). No sooner would the postexilic community return to the Lord than he would return to them with blessings unimaginable, such that even the nations around them would sit up and take notice of Israel and her God.[23]

Yet even in this, Israel is reminded of the condition: covenant blessings come through covenant obedience. The curse that Israel had been experiencing was a curse of their own making. Israel had been robbing God and, as a consequence, was suffering the penalty for their sin. Sadly, this behavior revealed that the postexilic community was not all that different than the preexilic community. That is to say, though they might obey for a time, keeping faith for a generation or two at best, the inevitable trajectory of the human heart is toward sin. When divine blessings are predicated upon human obedience, the blessings will be occasional and short-lived.

Could Israel hope for anything better? Though Israel might obey for a time and though they might experience God's blessings for a time, there is a temporary and conditional quality that is palpable throughout the prophecy. This was a function of the blessings and curses of the Mosaic covenant—it would teach Israel, and it teaches us, that ultimately eternal blessings and joys that never fade, and don't wax and wane with our obedience must be earned through a perfectly and perpetually obedient Israel.

Sadly, we see that postexilic Israel was no more an obedient son than was preexilic Israel; "one higher, purer, and 'better' was needed."[24] This higher, purer, and better one who was needed is the One who, in the fullness of time, God would provide in the person of his incarnate Son. This Son, Paul tells us, "did not count equality with God a thing to be grasped, but emptied himself, by taking the form of a servant . . . becoming obedient to the point of death, even death on a cross" (Philippians 2:6–8).

Jesus was obedient in everything and in every way all the time. He didn't merely pay the temple tax in obedience to God's Law; he offered what the temple tax represented—namely, his entire life lived perfectly in singular devotion to his Father, never turning from the paths of righteousness either to the right or to the left (see Romans 12:1). Jesus walked the path of obedience even when it led to a Roman cross and to a tomb. The Son did not have to take on human flesh and die for the sins of the world, but he did this freely, out of love for lost sinners and a broken world. As Paul told the Corinthian church, "You know the grace of our Lord Jesus Christ, that though he was rich, yet for your sake he became poor, so that you by his poverty might become rich" (2 Corinthians 8:9).

Though perfect, the Law of God does not have the power to change hearts. This power is found only in the gospel of Jesus Christ given for us, "the power of God for salvation to everyone who believes" (Romans 1:16). The temporal blessings of food in abundance, freedom from pestilence, and a land that is recognized the world over as delightful are but dim pictures of the blessings that God has purposed for his people through the obedience of his Son. They are a foretaste of a new Heaven and a new earth in which there will be no more hunger or famine or war. It will be a land in which pain, sorrow, sickness, sadness, and loss are things of the past, and the present is marked by "fullness of joy" and "pleasures forevermore" (Psalm 16:11).

The blessings that the postexilic community would experience for their obedience point us not only to the obedient Son, whose obedience merited God's blessings for all who are united to him by faith; they also point us beyond Christ to a principle that is as true for us today as it was for Israel in Malachi's day. Simply put, God blesses his people's obedience. To be clear, God's blessings do not always come in a tangible, physical form like they did for Israel in Malachi's day—food in the storehouses, freedom from the hardships of pestilence and war—though sometimes they do. But this does not negate the fact that Christians should expect God to bless their efforts to honor and obey him, even their weak and at times misguided efforts. Though the Christian life will be characterized by the cross, as Jesus promised, it will also be characterized by the Lord blessing the obedience of his people who by faith walk paths of righteousness as they follow their righteous Savior.

While the Old Testament tithe is no longer required for Christians under the new covenant, the support, including financial support, of the work of the Church certainly is (1 Corinthians 16:2; 2 Corinthians 8:1, 2).[25] We support the Church and give generously to those in need, not out of slavish duty nor out of a mercenary expectation that God therefore owes us something even better than whatever we sacrificed.[26] We give out of sheer gratitude and love for God, who has made us who we are and who has given us all that we have. God has given us himself in the person of his incarnate Son. What more could we possibly need?

Those things that are needful for us in this life, we may have confidence that the God who owns the cattle on a thousand hills can and will provide in abundance. As Paul says, "He who did not spare his own Son but gave him up for us all, how will he not also with him graciously give us all things?" (Romans 8:32). Only the gospel of God's love for us in Christ can possibly change seemingly unchangeable hearts because the gospel tells us to give not in order to get but to give because we have been given everything in Christ, and through him have received "every spiritual blessing in the heavenly places" (Ephesians 1:3). Thus through faith in Jesus Christ, fear—fear of want, of loss, of missing out, or whatever else—gives way to love, and love gives generously and with confidence that God loves and will most certainly bless "a cheerful giver" (2 Corinthians 9:7).

# 80

# When Faith Shall Be Sight

MALACHI 3:13—4:6

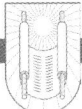

THOUGH WE KNOW precious little about the inner life of the prophet Malachi, I don't think we'd be at all surprised to learn that he suffered the same bouts of spiritual depression, anxiety, and loneliness as his prophetic forebearer Elijah. In a particularly dark moment of his career, the prophet Elijah cried out to God, "The people of Israel have forsaken your covenant . . . and I, even I only, am left" (1 Kings 19:10). Elijah's assessment serves as an equally appropriate summary of the state of affairs in Malachi's day. In fact, each of the six covenant lawsuits that make up the book of Malachi reinforces this basic point: the people of Israel had forsaken their covenant with God. After five prophetic disputations we've heard of no exceptions, no variation, no qualification . . . until now. In Malachi's final oracle we're given the wonderful reminder that God preserves a remnant for himself. We see that no matter how dark the day, no matter how desperate and hostile the circumstances of God's people, God is faithful to preserve a people who bear witness to the truth of God and the reality of the gospel.[1]

Just as Elijah discovered that there were in fact 7,000 in Israel who had not bowed the knee to Baal (1 Kings 19:18), so we too discover that there was a group in Israel—how large we don't know—who in the face of widespread doubt and cynicism persisted in living by faith, hope, and obedience to Yahweh. This remnant persisted in faith even and especially when their circumstances, their experiences, and even their fellow Jews had told them that it was vain and foolish to do so. In this final courtroom drama, God casts a spotlight on this remnant, and in a number of ways sets them in contrast to the faithless and cynical postexilic community to whom Malachi was called to minister.

Of course, Malachi's purpose in offering these contrasts was not to simply provide a taxonomy of different types of people who had different beliefs, values, and lifestyles. The prophet, unsurprisingly, had a prophetic purpose for his oracle. These contrasts served as an invitation—more than an invitation, a divine summons—to Israel in Malachi's day, and they serve as a divine summons to us in our day to walk by faith in the midst of a bewildering, difficult, and often hostile world in the sure knowledge that one day our faith will become sight, and God will vindicate both himself and his people. The prophet sets before his readers and hearers two lives and two fates, both of which continue even today to have profound implications for how we live in the present and how we hope in the future.

## Two Lives (3:13–17)

God's final lawsuit opens much like all the others. God levels a charge against his people: "'Your words have been hard against me, says the Lord" (3:13a). The expression "have been hard against me" (or "have been strong against me") is not a common one, and scholars debate its precise meaning.[2] It is of interest, however, that though this expression is uncommon, the word translated as "to be strong" is common and is used throughout the Old Testament in contexts of God calling his people to faith and courage in the face of great obstacles. As he was preparing to enter the promised land, God commanded Joshua, "*Be strong* and courageous" (Joshua 1:6). The word was especially common in this postexilic period; for instance, God declared through the prophet Haggai, "Yet now *be strong* O Zerubbabel, declares the Lord. *Be strong*, O Joshua, son of Jehozadak, the high priest. *Be strong*, all you people of the land, declares the Lord" (2:4). In light of this, Malachi's usage likely takes on an ironic tone as God denounced his covenant people, saying, in effect, "The only strength you're exhibiting is strength in opposing me and in violating my law."[3]

True to form, the people responded by going on the defensive, claiming complete ignorance of ever having spoken hard words against God. "How have we spoken against you?" they objected (Malachi 3:13b). Yet again, for the last time, God brings forth his evidence: "You have said, 'It is vain to serve God. What is the profit of keeping his charge or of walking as in mourning before the Lord of hosts?'" (v. 14).

This cynicism was addressed in Malachi's fourth oracle, and here it comes into focus again.[4] God's covenant people have come to doubt either God's goodness or his power or perhaps both. They have come to question God's care for his people, asking, in effect, "What good is it to know and to be known by the sovereign God of the universe? What advantage is it to be the

Lord God's treasured possession" or, in the words of Zechariah, "the apple of his eye" (2:8)?

To whatever extent nepotism exists in American politics and the entertainment industry, it is nothing compared to the nepotism and favoritism practiced in the ancient world. The ancients would not have known about equal opportunity employment. Israel would certainly have reasoned, "Surely we should enjoy some benefit, some advantage, on account of our obedience (i.e., "keeping his charge," (Malachi 3:14) and some privilege on account of our acts of devotion (i.e., "mourning," v. 14)."[5] However, as months turned into years and years turned into decades and the decades went on, the postexilic community found themselves still a far cry from the glorious promises made by the prophets of old, promises of Zion being exalted as the highest mountain to which the nations would flow, into which the treasures of the nations would come. These promises had come to seem like daydreams of fools rather than promises yet to be realized.

For many in Malachi's day, the answer to the question, "What good is it to know and to be known by the almighty, sovereign God of the universe?" was, "Very little." Many in Israel had reached the sad conclusion that the wicked were better off than the righteous. It seemed as if the arrogant and the evildoers were the real winners in this world. So they declared, "Now we call the arrogant blessed. Evildoers not only prosper but they put God to the test and they escape" (Malachi 3:15). But unlike the previous lawsuits, God didn't simply set forth his evidence; this time he brought forth witnesses.[6] In verse 16 we glimpse a ray of light shining in this dark place. The prophetic oracle breaks off, and we're given a single verse of Hebrew narrative: "Then those who feared the Lord spoke with one another. The Lord paid attention and heard them, and a book of remembrance was written before him of those who feared the Lord and esteemed his name" (v. 16).

There was, to use Presbyterian parlance, a minority report. There was a community within the community, and though we know very little about them, we do know the most important thing about them: their identity as "those who feared the Lord" (v. 16). This is what set them apart from the unbelief and cynicism that beset the larger community (even if some were perhaps tempted or participated for a time).[7] This group was identifiable by the fact that they feared the Lord. The expression "the fear of the Lord" is used throughout the Old Testament as the language of faith. In the midst of the cynicism and the acerbic doubt that had come to pervade the postexilic community, this group persisted in trusting Yahweh and in ordering their lives according to the reality of God and the truthfulness of his word.

We have no reason to think that the experience of this faithful remnant was any different than the experience of the unbelieving majority. They would have experienced the same trials and travails of life in postexilic Israel. They would have struggled with the same doubts and discouragements. But these, we're told, responded not with cynicism and grumbling but with faith. We don't know what this group said to one another in Malachi 3:16. Clearly the content is not as important as the fact of their speaking. Their speaking to one another sets them in contrast to the grumbling of the cynics in verse 13.

In this we're reminded of the importance of Christian fellowship and Christian community. Christian fellowship is one of the primary means by which we build one another up in faith and in courage to press on in the face of seemingly insurmountable difficulties and daily challenges. We do this even in those moments when our faith is plagued with doubts and we cannot discern God's ways in the world or even in our own lives. Especially in those moments when the last place we want to be is in church, we're reminded that one of God's many purposes for his Church is to be a community of faith that speaks to one another words of truth and hope in the face of lies and skepticism. The Church both in Malachi's day and in ours is the countercultural community of people who organize themselves around the word of God and are themselves organized by the Word of God, and who by faith take their stand on God's promises regardless of their appearances or experiences.

The prophet's brief narrative reveals the heart of the difference between these two groups, the cynics on the one hand and the God-fearers on the other. It is not a difference in education. It is not a difference in social or economic status. It is not a difference in personality. It is at heart a difference of faith. It is the difference between living by faith and living by sight.

For those who live by sight and not by faith, experience is king. As the majority in Israel looked at their world and examined their lives, their experience said, "Blessed are the arrogant, the wicked, the greedy, the haughty, the liars, the cheats." Those who feared God planted themselves firmly on God's promises, trusting that God's word was more true than their experiences.[8] Those who lived by faith embodied those values enumerated so beautifully in the opening of Psalm 1:

> Blessed is the man
> who walks not in the counsel of the wicked,
> nor stands in the way of sinners,
>   nor sits in the seat of scoffers;
> but his delight is in the law of the LORD,
>   and on that law he meditates day and night. (vv. 1, 2)

We're not told whether the larger community of cynics was aware of or took notice of this faithful remnant. It's quite possible that they were not aware and did not notice. But we are told that the Lord was aware and that the Lord took notice. We must not miss the magnificence as well as the irony of the notice that "the Lord paid attention and heard them" (Malachi 3:16b).

The first accusation leveled against the Lord by unbelieving Israel was that he was disinterested in the affairs of his people, or even worse, that he was actually approving of evil and wickedness; that obedience was going unrewarded and disobedience resulted in blessedness and prosperity. The prophet, however, pulled back the curtain of Heaven and revealed that the Lord does in fact see and does indeed remember. The prophet beheld what he called "a book of remembrance . . . written before him," and in it were the names of those who feared and esteemed the Lord (Malachi 3:16b).

Kings and emperors in the ancient world kept records of those who performed acts of loyalty to the king.[9] Perhaps the most famous account of this practice is the episode in the book of Esther when King Ahasuerus, suffering from insomnia, called for the book of memorial deeds to be read before him (6:1). In this book, he heard the record of Mordecai's faithfulness in exposing the plot against the king's life (v. 2). The king then remembered, and he rewarded accordingly (vv. 3, 10).

Unlike the Persian king, the Lord had not and could never forget his people. The point of the prophet's vision is to remind God's people that their Lord remembers them, that they are not forgotten. This is important for God's people of every age, but it is especially important to hear in moments when our experiences and our circumstances declare to us that we've been abandoned. When we feel as if God has forgotten us, that he has perhaps forsaken us, God assures us that he always remembers the plight of his people.[10]

God knows those who fear his name. He knows their needs, and he cares about them with a love and a loyalty so great that it is impossible for the finite mind to comprehend it. When God declares, "They shall be mine . . . in the day when I make up my treasured possession" (Malachi 3:17), he uses a term that refers to a possession of great value and personal significance.[11] Then, as if reaching yet further for an analogy that communicates the depth of his affection, God resorts again to filial language: "I will spare them as a man spares his son who serves him" (v. 17).

God loves his people. So jealous is he for his people that the Son of God would be forsaken by his Father, crying out," My God, My God, why have you forsaken me?" (Matthew 27:46) so that his people could be assured that their God remembers them and that he will never leave them or forsake them (Deuteronomy 31:6).

In response to the charge that God had forgotten, that he didn't see, and that he didn't care stands this book of remembrance (Malachi 3:16), in which are written the names of every man, woman, and child who belongs to God. Then, as if to answer the second charge that God will not act, we're given another contrast: the life of faith and the life of sight will receive two different fates.

## Two Fates (3:18—4:3)

These two diametrically opposed ways of life result in two diametrically opposed fates. In Malachi's day, as in our day, there was no obvious, external distinction between believers and unbelievers. Both met with successes and failures. Both enjoyed health or suffered illness. As Jesus taught in the Sermon on the Mount, God "makes his sun rise on the evil and on the good, and sends rain on the just and on the unjust" (Matthew 5:45). But the prophet does remind us that this will not always be the case. When God comes in judgment, there will be a distinction and a separation made "between the righteous and the wicked, between one who serves God and one who does not serve him" (Malachi 3:18). The difficulty in Malachi's day (as in our own) was not that there was no distinction between the righteous and the wicked, those who live by faith and those who live by sight; the difficulty was that they could not see the distinction.

A day is coming, the prophet declares, when God will make what is invisible visible. The Lord will separate the righteous from the wicked—as Jesus said, he will divide the wheat from the tares, "the sheep from the goats" (Matthew 13:30; 25:32). This day that is coming is described vividly. Malachi says the day will be "burning like an oven," and then, to extend the metaphor, he says that "all the arrogant and all evildoers" are likened to "stubble" (Malachi 4:1). The result is obvious. It's as inevitable as it is natural. When stubble meets a burning oven, it is utterly consumed and so destroyed that the only evidence that the stubble ever existed, possibly, is the ash that it may leave on the ground or toss into the air. It will be a day that the prophet says "shall set them ablaze . . . so that it will leave them neither root nor branch" (v. 1).

The picture here is that of complete and total destruction. There is nowhere to go to escape. The day itself is a burning oven. If a region of the world was a burning oven, one might avoid it. If an army were a burning oven, it might be outrun or outmaneuvered. But there is no way to escape a day.

There's a certain inevitability about the coming of tomorrow and the next day and the next. Something pastors quickly discover upon entering the ministry is that Sunday has the habit of coming around every week. The picture Malachi paints is of a coming day in which there will be total, inescapable, comprehensive judgment that leaves nothing behind.[12]

The great irony is that this destruction is coming against the same group mentioned in Malachi 3:15, "the arrogant" and "evildoers." When Israel says, "Now we call the arrogant blessed. Evildoers not only prosper but they put God to the test and they escape," God responds here by saying, in effect, "Not at all." For these arrogant evildoers who are regarded as blessed and enviable for their ability to flaunt God's word and get away with it, a day of reckoning is most certainly coming. The wicked will be exposed in their wickedness, the arrogant in their pride, the cruel in their cruelty, and all will be judged accordingly.

However, this day could not be any different for those who "feared the LORD" (Malachi 3:16). The day that will be a burning oven for the arrogant and evildoers will be a day in which "the sun of righteousness shall rise with healing in its wings" (4:2a). Many scholars have seen a common ancient Near Eastern image behind the prophet's reference of a sun disk featuring rays that come out of its sides like wings.[13] The disk typically represented a deity, and the wings the deity's protection of and care for his or her people.[14] Those who have been the victims of violence, oppression, and injustice at the hands of Israel's leaders and recipients of scorn by their neighbors will receive on that day healing, restoration, and wholeness, as that day will be marked by a sun whose rays shine forth pure righteousness.[15]

The next picture is one of new life breaking forth, like a calf shooting out of the barn on the first warm day of spring: "You shall go out leaping like calves from the stall" (v. 2b).[16] There is no threat and thus no fear. The wicked have already become ashes, such that they are perhaps unwittingly stomped on under the soles of feet.

It is hard to imagine two more diametrically opposed fates: the utter destruction of stubble passing through the fierce heat of an oven on the one hand, and the young calf bursting out of the barn into the warm sun of a spring day on the other. For the former, it will be a day of utter destruction. For the latter, it will be a day of joy and health the likes of which have never been experienced in this life.[17]

To the charge that God does not care and will not act against the proud and the wicked, God says, in effect, "What I am going to do about it will so utterly astound and terrify you that there will be no words to describe its power and glory." Psalm 107 puts it like this: "The upright see it and are glad, and all wickedness shuts its mouth" (v. 42).

God is shutting the mouths of the foolish. But even more than this, the Lord is instilling greater hope, assurance, and strength to the faithful. He declares that the injustices, sorrows, and hardships that we will suffer and are even now enduring will not last forever. There is a world beyond this world, a creation beyond this creation, a life beyond this life that is so real and so glorious that it will cause the afflictions of this present evil age to seem like a distant dream. As Paul writes to the Corinthian church, "No eye has seen, nor ear heard, nor the heart of man imagined, what God has prepared for those who love him" (1 Corinthians 2:9).

Having announced such unimaginable glories that lie in store for those who fear the Lord, the prophet Malachi takes us, as it were, from Heaven to earth. The sun of righteousness has not yet dawned for God's people. The healing and wholeness and abundant life described so vividly have yet to be realized. That victory over enemies and vindication of God's people as the treasured possession of the Most High God has yet to come to pass. So the prophet concludes with a sober reminder and kind encouragement in which he answers the unspoken question, "How do we live now? What does the life of faith look like in a world so fraught with hardship, discouragement, and disappointment? What does life look like for the wheat among the tares?"

## How Shall We Then Live? (4:4–6)

How are God's people to live by faith in a world that is not their home? The answer God gives through his prophet is twofold. First, God says, "Remember the law of my servant Moses, the statutes and rules that I commanded him at Horeb for all Israel" (Malachi 4:4).[18] How were God's people to comport themselves in a hostile world? They were to keep covenant with God by knowing God's word, believing God's word, and conforming their lives to God's word that he had delivered through his servant Moses.

This is what it means to remember—to always be mindful of and animated by the word about which Moses said, "It is no empty word for you, but your very life" (Deuteronomy 32:47).

The need to remember the Law of Moses seems to us to be so obvious that it hardly deserves repeating. But the fact is that Israel was prone to forget. Much like us, they were prone to become distracted and to wander from God and his word. They, like us, were prone to temptations—the temptation to take matters into their own hands through, for example, retreatism (that is, withdrawal from Israel, like the community at Qumran) or the temptation to revolution in which they might try to hasten the vindication of God and themselves by force. But God here reminded Israel, and he reminds us, that the life of faith is the way of the cross and is characterized by a humble obedience to God's word.

Especially in America, we greatly desire a new plan and a new method to meet the new challenges presented by these so-called unprecedented times, as if our lives and our situations are so fundamentally different from those of Israel or the New Testament Church. Malachi reminds us that the way of the cross is not the way of a shiny new method but the old, well-worn ways of God's people who embrace God's word. In response to Israel's desire to atone for sin through their own efforts and merit, God replied through an earlier prophet, "He has told you, O man, what is good; and what does the LORD require of you but to do justice, and to love kindness, and to walk humbly with your God?" (Micah 6:8). So it was for God's people in Malachi's day, and so it is for us today. How do we live in these difficult times? God says, in effect, "I have told you. Remember my word."

Life in this present evil age is to be characterized by obedience to God's Word but also by hope for the future. This is how God closes the prophetic word of the old covenant: with a call to watchful preparation and a confident hope. The Lord says through Malachi, "Behold, I will send you Elijah the prophet before the great and awesome day of the LORD comes. And he will turn the hearts of fathers to their children and the hearts of children to their fathers, lest I come and strike the land with a decree of utter destruction" (Malachi 4:5, 6). Israel was not only to be looking back to Moses, remembering the Torah given in ages past, but they were to do so keeping their eyes fixed as well on the future. God was going to send Elijah the prophet, and his appearance would herald the inauguration of that great day of judgment and mercy.

This Elijah figure would come on a mission that is described as turning the hearts of children to fathers and the hearts of fathers to their children. This is a picture of reconciliation. Is there a greater illustration of the brokenness of this sin-cursed world than the alienation that can exist between a parent and a child? This natural bond of love and selfless care can be severed such that the son is set against the father and the father against the son, a heartbreaking portrait of the disintegration of the covenant community.[19] But God promises to send Elijah to accomplish the work of reconciling and restoring what Israel had broken and severed. It will be a reconciliation within families and, by implication, a reconciliation between generations represented by fathers and children and children and fathers.

But this beautiful portrait of familial reconciliation is designed to serve as an earthly analogy to the even greater reconciliation that this Elijah will bring—namely, the reconciliation between God and mankind.[20] In Malachi 1:6 God employed this human relation of a son to his father as an analogy for Israel's relationship with himself: "A son honors his father, and a servant his master. If then I am a father, where is my honor? And if I am a master, where is my fear?"

Israel's transgressions against God are likened to the dishonor of a spiteful and rebellious son. The alienation and brokenness that exists between man and man is only a picture of the even greater alienation that exists between God and man. The prophet does not say, "Israel will raise up," but rather, "[God] will send" (Malachi 4:5), suggesting the divine initiative in this work of reconciliation. Reconciliation will be God's work, God's doing, God's sending. He will send this prophetic figure whose word will bring about a reconciliation before the arrival of that day. The only way for that day to be one of healing and not destruction is for Israel to heed the word of this Elijah whom God will send.

We, of course, know the fulfillment of this promise. We know about John the Baptist as the last prophet of the old covenant who appeared dressed like Elijah, "baptizing in the wilderness and proclaiming a baptism of repentance for the forgiveness of sins" (Mark 1:4). Jesus himself identified John as this prophet who came in the spirit of Elijah in fulfillment of God's promise through Malachi (see Matthew 11:9, 10). The appearance of this prophet who came to announce the fulfillment of all the prophets and their prophecies that had come before him presaged this great day of judgment that would arrive in the incarnate Son. This was John's mission, to point Israel to Christ. Arguably the greatest prophet Israel ever had would say about Jesus, "He must increase, but I must decrease" (John 3:30).

But what about this great and awesome day of judgment? John came. Jesus came. But what about that day? John came and declared a word of reconciliation to God and man in Christ. Jesus came and, in his miracles and in his teaching, announced the kingdom of God that comes with righteousness and with healing in its wings. But what about the day burning like an oven? This day did in fact arrive for one man. This day came for Jesus as he hung beaten, naked, condemned, and dying on a Roman cross. At Calvary, the Son of God who committed no sin was made stubble and set ablaze in the furnace of God's wrath for the sins of his people. Jesus was never arrogant. Jesus never committed evil. Yet he bore in his body the punishment of the wicked so that even the greatest of sinners might be forgiven for all their sins.

Apart from Christ, the land stood under the ban; that is, a sentence of "utter destruction" (Malachi 4:6). The only escape from God's covenant curse would be found in the One whom God provided to bear this covenant curse not for his own sins but for the sins of all who would entrust themselves to and hope in him alone.

The prophet could declare that God "will spare them as a man spares his son" (3:17) precisely because God "did not spare his own Son but gave him up for us all" (Romans 8:32).

The day of judgment came for Jesus, and on that day it came for all who are united to him by faith. The reason this coming day that the prophets announced time and again will be a day of healing, life, and joy for God's people is because God's Son bore their judgment curse, the blazing furnace that consumed him body and soul.

Though God's final judgment erupted into history at Calvary, this great day of judgment is still yet to come when Jesus returns just as he has promised. Jesus promised that he will come again not as the suffering Servant but as the risen King, riding on a white horse and bringing destruction in his train for all those who have spurned his kingship and rejected his mercy. Like the saints in the old covenant who were called to live as "prisoners of hope" (Zechariah 9:12), we too are called to live lives of eager anticipation, not for Elijah who arrived in the person of John the Baptist but for the One to whom John bore witness. So we pray, "Your kingdom come" (Matthew 6:10) because hopelessness is not an option for those who are by faith united to the risen and ascended Christ.

So this last word of the last Old Testament prophet is just as important for us in our day as it was for Israel in Malachi's day. We too need to heed this call to persist in serving the Lord, come what may, in the sure hope that the trials and travails of this present evil age will one day give way to a future more glorious and more shot through with life and joy and blessing than we could ever dare to imagine. To the world's eyes, the Church often appears insignificant, her faith of little consequence, and her obedience to God a waste of time (at best). But in God's eyes, the Church is so precious, so important, and so loved that the best earthly analogy that gets close to capturing this reality is the love that a father has for a son, a parent for a child.

The faith, obedience, and hope of God's people are not in vain. The Church will one day be vindicated before the entire world as the people of God are revealed to be his treasured possession, purchased at the cost of the lifeblood of the incarnate Son.

And Lord, haste the day
When the faith shall be sight,

The clouds be rolled back as a scroll;
The trump shall resound,
And the Lord shall descend,
Even so, it is well with my soul.[21]

*Soli Deo gloria!*

# Acknowledgments

SEVERAL PEOPLE HAVE EARNED my thanks during the twenty years it took me to complete my part of this volume.

I am grateful to my friend and former pastor Kent Hughes for the opportunity to contribute to this series.

My wife, Heather, encouraged the preparation, delivery, and writing of these sermons. Her advice always improved my preaching's clarity.

Her parents, David and Dawn Oldfield, showed me what daily courage looks like, as did my sister Suzanne Kingsley.

My daughter, Molly, and grandchildren Caleb, Eleanor, and Veronica gave me perspective on the value of the minor prophets for coming generations.

My sister Sunday and her husband, Jeff, came alongside me at a crucial time.

My friends are precious gifts from God. Several of them gave steady encouragement: Scott and Debara Hafemann, Ben and Nancy Mitchell, Richard and Leanne Bailey, Josh and Jennifer Turner, Wendell and Tanya Berry, Hunter and Liz Twitty, Jason and Jenna Varnadore, and Lane and Ebeth Dennis.

Beeson Divinity School of Samford University provided financial support that Timothy George, David Hogg, Grant Taylor, Doug Sweeney, and Tom Fuller administered.

As the writing progressed, Roy House, Sarah House, Jim Dixon, Mike Tucker, Lee Bullock, Richard Condrey, Tom and Sydie Allen, Harry Reeder, and others showed me how to die in the Lord, trusting that the future is incredibly bright.

The members of the Homestead and Deeper Life Classes at Briarwood Presbyterian Church listened to most of these sermons, always with kindness and grace. I dedicate my portion of this volume to them and their lasting testimony of seeking God.

For these and other kindnesses I am very grateful.

—Paul R. House

I wish to thank those congregations who often received these sermons with a generosity of spirit that far exceeded what the messages deserved. Special mention must be made of Wallace Memorial Presbyterian Church (College Park, Maryland), Christ Presbyterian Church ARP (Glenside, Pennsylvania), and Calvary Orthodox Presbyterian Church (Glenside, Pennsylvania). I am especially grateful for the many questions and comments that pushed me to clarify or sharpen my exegesis of a text, which I hope is reflected in this published version.

I wish also to thank those individuals without whose help and encouragement this work would never have come to fruition. A thousand thanks are due to Kent Hughes not only for his invitation to contribute to this series but also for his many encouragements along the way. It is a tremendous honor for me to coauthor this volume with Paul House, a scholar from whose work I have benefited in more ways than I can adequately articulate. Thank you, Paul, for the privilege of partnering with you in this endeavor. May God indeed use this work to draw his people closer to himself.

Special thanks go to Peter Lillback, Dave Garner, and the board of Westminster Theological Seminary, who supported me in this endeavor and translated their support into two sabbaticals that provided me invaluable time and space to write.

As always, my deepest and heartfelt gratitude goes to my darling wife, Carrie, who sat through some of these messages more than once and whose feedback always serves to strengthen (and shorten) my sermons.

—Stephen M. Coleman

# Notes

Chapter One: God's Enduring Love for Israel

1. For a survey of options, see Norman Snaith, *Mercy and Sacrifice* (London: SCM Press, 1953), 27–35; Douglas Stuart, *Hosea–Jonah*, Word Biblical Commentary 31 (Waco, TX: Word, 1987), 11–12; Duane Garrett, *Hosea, Joel*, New American Commentary 19A (Nashville: Broadman & Holman, 1997), 50–54; and A. A. Macintosh, *Hosea*, International Critical Commentary (Edinburgh: T. and T. Clark, 1997), 9–10.

2. James L. Mays, *Hosea*, Old Testament Library (Philadelphia: Westminster Press, 1969), 27.

Chapter Two: God's Disciplining Love

1. The ESV has "plead" in this verse.

2. Duane A. Garrett, *Hosea, Joel*, New American Commentary 19A (Nashville: Broadman & Holman, 1997), 75.

3. Thomas McComiskey, "Hosea," in ed. Thomas McComiskey, *The Minor Prophets* (Grand Rapids, MI: Baker, 1992), 1:36.

4. A. A. Macintosh, *Hosea*, International Critical Commentary (Edinburgh: T. and T. Clark, 1997), 60.

5. Macintosh, *Hosea*, 69.

Chapter Three: Go Love Again: God's Determined Love for Israel

1. Jon Hassler, *Simon's Night* (New York: Ballantine Books, 1979).

2. See the chapter on Hosea 1:1—2:1 in this volume. The scholars who hold that Gomer could not have been an actual prostitute generally treat 1:2 and 3:1 as symbolic, though symbolic of vital truth.

3. Douglas Stuart, *Hosea–Jonah*, Word Biblical Commentary 31 (Waco, TX: Word, 1987), 64. Note this rationale on 63–65.

4. See Francis I. Andersen and David Noel Freedman, *Hosea*, Anchor Bible 24 (New York: Doubleday, 1980), 115–17, 294; and Thomas McComiskey, "Hosea," in ed. Thomas McComiskey, *The Minor Prophets* (Grand Rapids, MI: Baker, 1992), 1:50.

5. Andersen and Freedman, *Hosea*, 298; Stuart, *Hosea–Jonah*, 65–66.

6. Stuart, *Hosea–Jonah*, 59.

7. For the opposite viewpoint, see McComiskey, "Hosea," 1:51; and James Montgomery Boice, *The Minor Prophets: An Expositional Commentary* (Grand Rapids, MI: Zondervan, 1983), 1:30–31.

8. For discussions of this phrase, consult J. Andrew Dearman, *The Book of Hosea*, New International Commentary on the Old Testament (Grand Rapids, MI: Eerdmans, 2010), 142–45; Duane A. Garrett, *Hosea, Joel*, New American Commentary

19A (Nashville: Broadman & Holman, 1997), 104; James L. Mays, *Hosea*, Old Testament Library (Philadelphia: Westminster Press, 1969), 60; Hans W. Wolff, *Hosea*, trans. Gary Stansell, Hermeneia (Philadelphia: Fortress Press, 1974), 63. They all consider the phrase a later addition to the text, though no ancient version lacks it.

9. Derek Kidner, *Love to the Loveless: The Message of Hosea*, The Bible Speaks Today (Downers Grove, IL: InterVarsity Press, 1981), 44.
10. Kidner, *Love to the Loveless*, 44
11. Dearman, *The Book of Hosea*, 141–42.

Chapter Four: Like People, Like Priest: God's Lawsuit against Israel

1. Derek Kidner, *Love to the Loveless: The Message of Hosea*, The Bible Speaks Today (Downers Grove, IL: InterVarsity Press, 1981), 46.
2. Duane A. Garrett, *Hosea, Joel*, New American Commentary 19A (Nashville: Broadman & Holman, 1997), 110.
3. James L. Mays, *Hosea*, Old Testament Library (Philadelphia: Westminster Press, 1969), 63.
4. J. Andrew Dearman, *The Book of Hosea*, New International Commentary on the Old Testament (Grand Rapids, MI: Eerdmans, 2010), 148.
5. Garrett, *Hosea, Joel*, 111. It should be noted that only the last three sins in the list of five are identical in Hebrew to their counterparts in Exodus 20:1–17. Nonetheless, the other two words relate concepts that are the same as the commandments noted.
6. Hans W. Wolff, *Hosea*, trans. Gary Stansell, Hermeneia (Philadelphia: Fortress Press, 1974), 68.
7. Francis I. Andersen and David Noel Freedman, *Hosea*, Anchor Bible 24 (New York: Doubleday, 1980), 338.
8. Note how Eli's sons did the opposite (1 Samuel 2:12–25).
9. See the chapter on Hosea 1:1—2:1 in this volume.
10. Garrett, *Hosea, Joel*, 118–19.
11. Mays, *Hosea*, 70.
12. Dearman, *The Book of Hosea*, 162.
13. Consult A. A. Macintosh, *Hosea*, International Critical Commentary (Edinburgh: T. and T. Clark, 1997), 151–52; and Garrett, *Hosea, Joel*, 122–23 for options.
14. Garrett, *Hosea*, 136.
15. Garrett, 136.

Chapter Five: Earnest Seeking of God

1. See Francis Brown, et al., *The Brown-Driver-Briggs Hebrew and English Lexicon* (1906; repr. Peabody, MA: Hendrickson, 1996), 1007.
2. Regarding seeking the Lord, see the chapters on Hosea 3; Hosea 10; Amos 5:1–17; and Zephaniah 1:2–18 in this volume.
3. This definition of the word and its ancient context is based on N. H. Snaith, *The Book of Amos, Part Two: Translation and Notes* (New York: Abingdon Press, 1946), 84.
4. Some scholars think the phrase the ESV translates as "the judgment is for you" indicates that Hosea is presenting charges against the leaders. See James L. Mays, *Hosea*, Old Testament Library (Philadelphia: Westminster Press, 1969), 79–81; and Thomas McComiskey, "Hosea," in ed. Thomas McComiskey, *The Mi-*

*nor Prophets* (Grand Rapids, MI: Baker, 1992), 1:75. Others claim the leaders were charged with the responsibility of dispensing justice and failed to fulfill this responsibility. See A. A. Macintosh, *Hosea*, International Critical Commentary (Edinburgh: T. and T. Clark, 1997), 176; and Hans W. Wolff, *Hosea*, trans. Gary Stansell, Hermeneia (Philadelphia: Fortress Press, 1974), 98. The context includes sins besides failing to dispense justice, so I think the first option is probably correct.

5. Duane A. Garrett, *Hosea, Joel*, New Amercian Commentary 19A (Nashville: Broadman & Holman, 1997), 143.

6. See J. Andrew Dearman, *The Book of Hosea*, New International Commentary on the Old Testament (Grand Rapids, MI: Eerdmans, 2010), 172.

7. Macintosh, *Hosea*, 181.

8. This is the situation that Pharaoh faced in Exodus 5—14. Also see Isaiah 6:9, 10.

9. Dearman, *The Book of Hosea*, 174.

10. Martyn Lloyd-Jones, *Why Does God Allow War?* (1939; repr. Wheaton, IL: Crossway Books, 2003), 63.

11. Lloyd-Jones, *Why Does God*, 68–74.

12. Lloyd-Jones, 92.

13. Lloyd-Jones, 93–94.

14. Lloyd-Jones, 105–26.

15. For a good short summary of events, see David A. Hubbard, *Hosea: An Introduction and Commentary*, Tyndale Old Testament Commentary (Downers Grove, IL: IVP Academic, 2009), 127–30.

16. Mays, *Hosea*, 88.

17. McComiskey, "Hosea," 81 suggests the mention of these cities may indicate that an invader would pass through Benjamin on the way to Judah. Macintosh, *Hosea*, 197 thinks the verse may threaten an invasion of Benjamin by Judah. See the ESV textual note on "we follow you" (5:8).

18. Mays, *Hosea*, 93.

19. Dearman, *The Book of Hosea*, 188.

Chapter Six: Real Repentance and Foolish Rebellion

1. For example, God appeared to Moses and Israel on Mount Sinai on the third day (Exodus 19:10–16).

2. Thomas McComiskey, "Hosea," in ed. Thomas McComiskey, *The Minor Prophets* (Grand Rapids, MI: Baker, 1992), 1:88.

3. The ESV reads "love," but the same word appears here as in 6:6, which the ESV renders "steadfast love." The phrase "steadfast love" translates *hesed*, the typical word for covenant loyalty in passages depicting God's covenant with Israel.

4. The word translated as "overflowed" (ESV, "transgressed") indicates wrongdoing.

5. See Duane A. Garrett, *Hosea, Joel*, New American Commentary 19A (Nashville: Broadman & Holman, 1997), 164–65; A. A. Macintosh, *Hosea*, International Critical Commentary (Edinburgh: T. and T. Clark, 1997), 247; J. Andrew Dearman, *The Book of Hosea*, New International Commentary on the Old Testament (Grand Rapids, MI: Eerdmans, 2010), 199; James L. Mays, *Hosea*, Old Testament Library (Philadelphia: Westminster Press, 1969), 102; and McComiskey,

"Hosea," 94, 97–98. Mays and Macintosh suggest that a later editor has added this mention of Judah, but Hosea 6:4 has already included Judah with Israel in this denunciation of sins. Following the verse divisions in the Masoretic Text, the ESV translates 6:11 as a promise to Judah, but this is probably incorrect. Both 6:11b and 7:1 begin with a temporal clause ("when"), so 6:11b and 7:1 should both be read as what God did for the people that had no effect on them.

6. Mays wrote, "By 733 there had been a rash of revolutions; within the previous twelve years four kings had been victims of assassinations." *Hosea*, 104.

7. Mays, 110.

8. McComiskey, "Hosea," 112.

9. See Macintosh, *Hosea*, 284. The ESV reads "upward," which amounts to the same thing.

### Chapter Seven: The Vulture, the Whirlwind, and the Fire

1. Charles Simeon, *Expository Outlines of the Whole Bible: Volume Ten (Hosea–Micah)*, 8th ed. (1847; repr. Grand Rapids, MI: Zondervan, 1956), 93.

2. Simeon, *Expository Outlines*, 93, 94.

3. Simeon, 95.

4. Simeon, 95.

5. The bird may be a vulture or an eagle. Regardless, it is searching for prey on the ground.

6. Francis I. Andersen and David Noel Freedman, *Hosea*, Anchor Bible 24 (New York: Doubleday, 1980), 484.

7. Douglas Stuart, *Hosea–Jonah*, Word Biblical Commentary 31 (Waco, TX: Word, 1987), 131.

8. A. A. Macintosh, *Hosea*, International Critical Commentary (Edinburgh: T. and T. Clark, 1997), 303. For an extended discussion of the calf's symbolism, see J. Andrew Dearman, *The Book of Hosea*, New International Commentary on the Old Testament (Grand Rapids, MI: Eerdmans, 2010), 224–26.

9. Dearman, *The Book of Hosea*, 223.

10. The ESV reads "and." The conjunction here may be translated either way. The second half of the verse is clearly in contrast with the first.

11. James L. Mays, *Hosea*, Old Testament Library (Philadelphia: Westminster Press, 1969), 120.

12. Dearman, *The Book of Hosea*, 230.

13. Dearman, 230.

14. Macintosh, *Hosea*, 324.

15. Dearman, *The Book of Hosea*, 230.

16. Macintosh, *Hosea*, 324.

17. As opposed to the basis of the beginning of a relationship with God, which is faith in God (Ephesians 2:1–10).

18. Stuart, *Hosea–Jonah*, 137.

### Chapter Eight: Leaving Harvest Joy Behind

1. Douglas Stuart, *Hosea–Jonah*, Word Biblical Commentary 31 (Waco, TX: Word, 1987), 142. For more information on prophetic sermons set at the time of the Feast of Booths, see the chapters on Zephaniah in this volume.

2. James L. Mays, *Hosea*, Old Testament Library (Philadelphia: Westminster Press, 1969), 127.

3. There is no Hebrew pronoun corresponding to "it" here. The force of the verse may be best conveyed by a colon after "shall know." See A. A. Macintosh, *Hosea*, International Critical Commentary (Edinburgh: T. and T. Clark, 1997), 351–52.

4. Thomas McComiskey, "Hosea," in ed. Thomas McComiskey, *The Minor Prophets* (Grand Rapids, MI: Baker, 1992), 1:146.

5. See Mays, *Hosea*, 136.

6. McComiskey, "Hosea," 154.

7. Macintosh, *Hosea*, 377.

Chapter Nine: Time to Seek God, Time to Sow Righteousness

1. On the theme of seeking God, see the chapters on Hosea 3; Hosea 5; Amos 5:1–17; and Zephaniah 2 (esp. vv. 1–5) in this volume.

2. See Philip J. King, *Amos, Hosea, Micah—An Archaeological Commentary* (Philadelphia: Westminster Press, 1988), 137–61.

3. James L. Mays, *Hosea*, Old Testament Library (Philadelphia: Westminster Press, 1969),139.

4. See Francis Brown, et al., *The Brown-Driver-Briggs Hebrew and English Lexicon* (1906; repr. Peabody, MA: Hendrickson, 1996), 323.

5. For a discussion, see J. Andrew Dearman, *The Book of Hosea*, New International Commentary on the Old Testament (Grand Rapids, MI: Eerdmans, 2010), 261n40.

6. Thomas McComiskey, "Hosea," in ed. Thomas McComiskey, *The Minor Prophets* (Grand Rapids, MI: Baker, 1992), 1:160.

7. The ESV reads "empty oaths." The word is the same as the one translated as "vain" in Exodus 20:7: "You shall not take the name of the Lord your God in vain."

8. For a discussion of the significance of bulls in ancient rituals, see Duane A. Garrett, *Hosea, Joel*, New American Commentary 19A (Nashville: Broadman & Holman, 1997), 210–11; and King, *Amos, Hosea, Micah*, 95–97.

9. For similar imagery see Isaiah 2:17–22; Luke 23:30; Revelation 6:16.

10. See previous comments on 10:9.

11. See Isaiah 10:5–12 on this point.

12. Derek Kidner, *Love to the Loveless: The Message of Hosea*, The Bible Speaks Today (Downers Grove, IL: InterVarsity Press, 1981), 97–98.

13. The ESV reads "wickedness," but the ESV usually translates *awon* as "iniquity." The word here is *rasha*. See Brown, et al., *Brown-Driver-Briggs*, 957.

14. Francis I. Andersen and David Noel Freedman, *Hosea*, Anchor Bible 24 (New York: Doubleday, 1980), 570–71.

Chapter Ten: "How Can I Give You Up, O Ephraim?"

1. For a succinct analysis, see Duane A. Garrett, *Hosea, Joel*, New American Commentary 19A (Nashville: Broadman & Holman, 1997), 220–22.

2. This practice is the likely background of Amos 4:1, 2.

3. Assyrian artwork and records of battles depict these acts.

4. Thomas McComiskey, "Hosea," in ed. Thomas McComiskey, *The Minor Prophets* (Grand Rapids, MI: Baker, 1992), 1:191. See Genesis 14:20.

5. James L. Mays, *Hosea*, Old Testament Library (Philadelphia: Westminster Press, 1969), 157.
6. The ESV reads "recoils."
7. For a discussion of this phrase, see J. Andrew Dearman, *The Book of Hosea*, New International Commentary on the Old Testament (Grand Rapids, MI: Eerdmans, 2010), 291–92.
8. Mays, *Hosea*, 158. See Jeremiah 25:30; Amos 1:2, 3:8; Joel 3:16
9. See B. D. Napier, "Prophet," in ed., G. A. Buttrick, *Interpreter's Dictionary of the Bible* (Nashville: Abingdon, 1962), 4:910–19.

## Chapter Eleven: Idols, Money, and Prophets: A Family Story

1. In the Hebrew text, verse 12 begins chapter 12.
2. The name here stands for Israel, the ten northern tribes.
3. The ESV has "prevailed," which sounds as if Jacob won the wrestling match. The word translated as "prevailed" in the ESV denotes endurance in Isaiah 1:13 and elsewhere. See Douglas Stuart, *Hosea–Jonah*, Word Biblical Commentary 31 (Waco, TX: Word, 1987), 185–86.
4. A. A. Macintosh, *Hosea*, International Critical Commentary (Edinburgh: T. and T. Clark, 1997), 485.
5. This is the most natural way to read the Hebrew, though most translations have "found him" because they miss the transition to the whole nation that occurs at this point.
6. The ESV has "by the help of your God, return," but there are no Hebrew words corresponding to "by the help of" in the verse.
7. The Hebrew word here is *hesed*, which typically refers to covenant loyal love in similar contexts.
8. Hans W. Wolff, *Hosea*, trans. Gary Stansell, Hermeneia (Philadelphia: Fortress Press, 1974), 215.
9. J. Andrew Dearman, *The Book of Hosea*, New International Commentary on the Old Testament (Grand Rapids, MI: Eerdmans, 2010), 312.

## Chapter Twelve: Ransom from Death

1. Compare 2 Kings 17:24–41 and Ezra 4:1, 2, which mentions Esarhaddon, king of Assyria c. 669–627 B.C.
2. Douglas Stuart, *Hosea–Jonah*, Word Biblical Commentary 31 (Waco, TX: Word, 1987), 202.
3. This verse is yet another difficult one to translate. The word translated as "trembling" in the ESV appears only here in the Old Testament. Nonetheless, the context seems to indicate Ephraim's decline and coming punishment. For a discussion of the verse's syntax, consult Duane A. Garrett, *Hosea, Joel*, New American Commentary 19A (Nashville: Broadman & Holman, 1997), 248n208; and A. A. Macintosh, *Hosea*, International Critical Commentary (Edinburgh: T. and T. Clark, 1997), 518–22.
4. Macintosh, *Hosea*, 524, notes that 13:2b indicates an increase in devotion over time. For a summary of the main epochs in Israel's Baal worship, consult David A. Hubbard, *Hosea: An Introduction and Commentary*, Tyndale Old Testament Commentary (Downers Grove, IL: IVP Academic, 2009), 226–27.
5. On this interpretation of their worshiping, see Macintosh, *Hosea*, 522.

6. I have heard this phrase attributed to William Faulkner, but I have been unable to trace the source.

7. The ESV reads, "But I am the LORD your God."

8. The ESV has "know," but the verb and context imply a past action that continues to the present.

9. Hubbard, *Hosea*, 230.

10. James L. Mays, *Hosea*, Old Testament Library (Philadelphia: Westminster Press, 1969), 177, 178.

11. This translation follows the Septuagint, Vulgate, NASB, NIV (1984), and ESV (2016). There is no question in this Hebrew phrase. Though implied rhetorical questions are not unheard of in the Hebrew Bible (see Genesis 27:24), there is no sufficient contextual reason in my opinion to supply the rhetorical question here. The context here is like that of Hosea 11—12: judgment includes promise, and promise does not exclude future or present judgment. However, promise does exclude annihilation, which is the issue here. For discussions of this issue, consult Macintosh, *Hosea*, 546–50; Mays, *Hosea*, 181–83; and Hubbard, *Hosea*, 233–34.

12. See 1 Corinthians 15:55. These questions are marked by a Hebrew word in the text. See Stuart, *Hosea–Jonah*, 200.

13. The ESV reads, "Compassion is hidden from my eyes." The Hebrew word *naham* may mean "comfort, compassion, sorrow, relief, or relent," depending on the context and which Hebrew verb stem an author uses. The ESV often translates this word "relent," and I think that rendering is correct here, given my reading of the context.

## Chapter Thirteen: Repentance, Healing, Fruitfulness, and Wisdom

1. A. A. Macintosh, *Hosea*, International Critical Commentary (Edinburgh: T. and T. Clark, 1997), 560.

2. Macintosh, *Hosea*, 562, notes that this verb "in the *Piel* [Hebrew stem] denotes the payment of a debt or obligation; in relation to God 'vows' are frequently found as an object but also 'praises' or 'thank-offerings.'" Compare Psalms 51:17–19 and 56:13.

3. The words for "fruit" and "bulls" (ESV) are very similar. Given the imagery in Hosea 14:4–7 and the use of "fruit" in 14:8, the context leads to translating the word "fruit." See the ESV note and David A. Hubbard, *Hosea: An Introduction and Commentary*, Tyndale Old Testament Commentary (Downers Grove, IL: IVP Academic, 2009), 239.

4. Hubbard, *Hosea*, 239.

5. The phrase "we will not ride on horses" in context likely means "we will not send our representatives to other countries to get help." See Macintosh, *Hosea*, 566.

6. J. Andrew Dearman, *The Book of Hosea*, New International Commentary on the Old Testament (Grand Rapids, MI: Eerdmans, 2010), 341.

7. Macintosh, *Hosea*, 571.

8. Duane A. Garrett, *Hosea, Joel*, New American Commentary 19A (Nashville: Broadman & Holman, 1997), 274.

9. Garrett, *Hosea, Joel*, 274.

10. James L. Mays, *Hosea*, Old Testament Library (Philadelphia: Westminster Press, 1969), 189.

11. Scholars disagree over exactly what tree this verse mentions. Nonetheless, they agree that the verse depicts a tree that never ceases to be fruitful or alive. For a discussion of ideas, see Macintosh, *Hosea*, 576–79.

12. The Hebrew and Septuagint differ over whether God asks what he has to do with idols or God asks what Ephraim has to do with idols in 14:8. Either way, this is a rhetorical question, and its answer is, "Nothing."

13. The ESV reads "the upright," but the plural noun is the standard Hebrew word for "the righteous." See Psalm 1:1–6 for similar Hebrew phrasing.

Chapter Fourteen: A Plague for the Ages

1. These chapters were adapted from sermons first preached in Seoul, Korea in 2012. I am grateful to my friend Sehoon Jang for inviting and hosting me. Readers may notice that the sentences in these chapters are shorter than the ones in Hosea, Amos, Obadiah, Habakkuk, and Zephaniah. This was intended to aid translation.

2. Scholars have suggested dates ranging from the ninth century B.C. to the fourth century B.C. Today most experts probably prefer a postexilic (post-587 B.C.) date. For a summary of opinions, see Duane A. Garrett, *Hosea, Joel*, New American Commentary 19A (Nashville: Broadman & Holman, 1997), 286–94; and John Barton, *Joel and Obadiah*, Old Testament Library (Louisville: Westminster John Knox Press, 2001), 14–18.

3. James M. Boice, *The Minor Prophets: Two Volumes Complete in One Edition* (Grand Rapids, MI: Kregel, 1996), 101.

4. The comments in the rest of this paragraph are based on Paul R. House, "The Day of Yahweh as a Unifying Concept in Isaiah 1–12," *Trinity Journal for Theology and Ministry*, vol. III, No. 1 (Spring 2009): 90–96.

Chapter Fifteen: Even Now, Seek The Lord

1. For a succinct survey, see Irvin A. Busenitz, *Joel and Obadiah*, Mentor Commentary (Fearn, Scotland: Christian Focus, 2003), 113–17.

2. See John Barton, *Joel and Obadiah*, Old Testament Library (Louisville: Westminster John Knox Press, 2001), 70.

3. See Raymond Dillard, "Joel," in ed. Thomas E. McComiskey, *The Minor Prophets: An Exegetical and Expository Commentary* (Grand Rapids, MI: Baker, 1992), 1:277.

4. See John Calvin, *A Commentary on the Prophet Joel*, trans. John Owen (London: Banner of Truth, 1958), 36–37.

5. For further discussion of the various types of the day of the Lord, see the chapter on Joel 1 in this volume.

6. Much of what follows on Exodus 34 is based on Paul R. House, "God's Character and the Wholeness of Scripture," *Scottish Bulletin of Evangelical Theology* 23/1 (Spring 2005): 4–17.

7. For a discussion of these three terms as foundational to the problem of sin in the Old Testament, see T. V. Farris, *Mighty to Save: A Study in Old Testament Soteriology* (Nashville: Broadman & Holman, 1993), 120–39; and Ludwig Kohler, *Old Testament Theology*, trans. A. S. Todd (Philadelphia: Westminster Press, 1957), 169–71.

8. Alex Luc, *"awon,"* New International Dictionary of Old Testament Theology and Exegesis, ed. Willem VanGemeren (Grand Rapids, MI: Zondervan, 1997), 3:351.

9. Rolf Knierim, *"awon,"* *Theological Lexicon of the Old Testament*, trans. Mark E. Biddle, eds. Ernst Jenni and Claus Westermann (Peabody, MA: Hendrickson, 1997), 2:863–64.

10. Knierim, *"pesa,"* *Theological Lexicon*, 2:1036.

11. Knierim, *"ht'"* 1:406–11.

Chapter Sixteen: When God Answers Prayer

1. My good friend Scott Hafemann has often stressed in writing, lectures and conversations the fact that current faith comes from recalling what God has done in the past and thereby believing what God will do in the future. See for example Scott J. Hafemann, *The God of Promise and the Life of Faith* (Wheaton, IL: Crossway, 2001).

2. This is especially true of Hebrew narrative sentences.

3. It is also possible to translate the verb in the future tense ("will"), as the NIV does. However, the past tense is the more normal way to translate the wording here. Regardless, the chain of events in 2:18–27 and 2:28–32 have occurred, and they are in the past from where we stand in time today.

4. On this important subject, see J. I. Packer, *Knowing God* (Downers Grove, IL: InterVarsity Press, 1973).

Chapter Seventeen: God's Spirit for God's People

1. For instance, note Hosea 14:1–9, Amos 9:11–15, Micah 7:18–20; Zephaniah 3:9–20.

Chapter Eighteen: When God Roars from Zion

1. I prefer "change Jerusalem's circumstances" to "restore the fortunes of Judah and Jerusalem" (ESV) because the latter phrase in current English sounds to many people like "give Jerusalem's wealth back."

2. Irvin A. Busenitz, *Joel and Obadiah*, Mentor Commentary Series (Fearn, Scotland: Christian Focus, 2003), 213; compare Douglas Stuart, *Hosea–Jonah*, Word Biblical Commentary 31 (Waco, TX: Word, 1987), 269.

Chapter Nineteen: The Shepherd, the King, and the Lion

1. See the chapters on Hosea 1:1—2:1 and Joel 1 in this volume.

2. For this description of Tekoa, I'm indebted to John D. W. Watts, *Vision and Prophecy in Amos* (Grand Rapids, MI: Eerdmans, 1958), 5.

3. These assertions about shepherds and shepherding are greatly informed by Timothy Laniak, *Shepherds after My Own Heart: Pastoral Traditions and Leadership in the Bible*, New Studies in Biblical Theology 20 (Downers Grove, IL: InterVarsity Press, 2006), 42–74.

4. N.H. Snaith, *The Book of Amos, Part Two: Translation and Notes* (New York: Abingdon Press, 1946), 6.

5. Snaith, *Book of Amos*, 127. See also Duane A. Garrett, *Amos: A Handbook on the Hebrew Text* (Waco, TX: Baylor University Press, 2008), 223.

6. Watts, *Vision and Prophecy*, 8.

7. The descriptions of Jeroboam's rise, reign, and religion that follow are based on 1 Kings 11:26—12:23. See also the chapter on Hosea 1:1—2:1 in this volume.

I find that short reminders of such facts when introducing prophetic books help audiences learn vital basic material.

8. J.A. Motyer, *The Day of the Lion: The Message of Amos*, The Bible Speaks Today (Downers Grove, IL: InterVarsity Press, 1974), 15.

9. Robert C. Stallman, "Lion," *New International Dictionary of Old Testament Theology and Exegesis*, ed. Willem A. VanGemeren (Grand Rapids, MI: Eerdmans, 1997), 1:514.

10. Stallman, *New International Dictionary*, 1:514–16.

Chapter Twenty: God's Authority and the Nations' Sins

1. See John D. W. Watts, *Studying the Book of Amos* (Nashville: Broadman & Holman, 1966), 36, 37.

2. Duane A. Garrett, *Amos: A Handbook on the Hebrew Text*, Baylor Handbook on the Hebrew Bible (Waco, TX: Baylor University Press, 2008), 25. For a survey of the history between Aram and Israel, consult G. V. Smith, *Amos*, Mentor Commentary Series (Fearn, Scotland: Christian Focus, 1998), 72–74.

3. Francis I. Andersen and David Noel Freedman, *Amos*, Anchor Bible 24a (New York: Doubleday, 1989), 229.

4. J. A. Motyer, *The Day of the Lion: The Message of Amos*, The Bible Speaks Today (Downers Grove, IL: InterVarsity Press, 1974), 39–40.

5. I lived in Birmingham, Alabama, when I first preached these chapters as sermons.

6. For a discussion of Edwards's slave-owning and slavery in colonial America, see Richard A. Bailey, *Race and Redemption in Puritan New England*, Religion in America Series (New York: Oxford University Press, 2011); and eds. Richard. A. Bailey and Gregory A. Wills, *The Salvation of Souls: Nine Previously Unpublished Sermons on the Call of Ministry and the Gospel by Jonathan Edwards* (Wheaton, IL: Crossway, 2002).

7. Smith, *Amos*, 60.

8. There were reports of this very act from the war in Kosovo in the late twentieth century.

Chapter Twenty-One: Israel and Judah Have Sinned

1. Jeffrey Niehaus, "Amos," in T. E. McComiskey, ed., *The Minor Prophets* (Grand Rapids, MI: Baker, 1993), 1:361.

2. Francis I. Andersen and David Noel Freedman, *Amos*, Anchor Bible 24A (New York: Doubleday, 1989), 299.

3. See J. A. Motyer, *The Day of the Lion: The Message of Amos*, The Bible Speaks Today (Downers Grove, IL: InterVarsity Press, 1974), 56.

4. G. V. Smith, *Amos*, Mentor Commentary Series (Fearn, Scotland: Christian Focus, 1998), 119.

5. Erling Hammershaimb, *The Book of Amos: A Commentary*, trans. John Sturdy (Oxford: Basil Blackwell, 1970), 47.

6. Smith, *Amos*, 119.

7. Motyer, *Day of the Lion*, 57.

8. Hammershaimb, *Book of Amos*, 49.

9. Smith, *Amos*, 123–24.

Chapter Twenty-Two: Privilege, Responsibility, and Consequences

1. James M. Boice, *The Minor Prophets: Two Volumes in One Edition* (1983, 1986; repr., Grand Rapids, MI: Kregel, 1996), 9.

2. James Limburg, *Hosea–Micah*, Interpretation (Atlanta: John Knox Press, 1988), 96.

3. Francis I. Andersen and David Noel Freedman, *Amos*, Anchor Bible 24A (New York: Doubleday, 1989), 399.

4. For a discussion of possibilities, see Andersen and Freedman, *Amos*, 407–8.

Chapter Twenty-Three: You Did Not Return to Me

1. Duane A. Garrett, *Amos: A Handbook on the Hebrew Text*, Baylor Handbook on the Hebrew Bible (Waco, TX: Baylor University Press, 2008), 107.

2. Erling Hammerschaimb, *The Book of Amos: A Commentary*, trans. John Sturdy (Oxford: Basil Blackwell, 1970), 65.

3. See Marvin A. Sweeney, *The Twelve Prophets: Volume One*, Berit Olam (Collegeville, MN: Liturgical Press, 2000), 225.

4. For other options, see Garrett, *Amos*, 111–13.

5. Sweeney, *Twelve Prophets*, 226.

6. James Limburg, *Hosea–Micah*, Interpretation (Atlanta: John Knox Press, 1988), 103.

7. N. H. Snaith, *The Book of Amos, Part Two: Translation and Notes* (Nashville: Abingdon, 1946), 74.

8. Some experts think the cities were "overthrown" by an earthquake (e.g., Hammerschaimb, *Book of Amos*, 73) and/or some other natural disaster (e.g., Sweeney, *Twelve Prophets*, 230), but the context indicates an unexpected and sudden military loss (see Amos 4:10).

9. J.A. Motyer, *The Day of the Lion: The Message of Amos*, The Bible Speaks Today (Downers Grove, IL: InterVarsity Press, 1974), 96.

10. Motyer, *Day of the Lion*, 97.

11. James L. Mays, *Amos: A Commentary*, Old Testament Library (Philadelphia: Westminster Press, 1969), 82.

12. The "his" in the phrase "declares to man what is his thought" refers to man, not God. See Hammerschaimb, *Book of Amos*, 75.

13. Hear his sermon on John 8:21, 22, available through the Martyn Lloyd-Jones Trust.

Chapter Twenty-Four: Seek the Lord and Live

1. Compare Hosea 3:5; 5:15; 10:12; Zephaniah 1:6; 2:3; 3:12; Zechariah 8:21, 22; Malachi 2:7; 3:1.

2. In *qinah* meter, three Hebrew words are followed by two Hebrew words in successive half lines. The meter descends from three to two words as the whole line unfolds. Thus the verse's rhythm matches the verse's theme, which is Israel's fall, her defeat by a foreign army. Compare 2 Samuel 1:17–27; Jeremiah 9:1–22; Lamentations 1.

3. This definition of the word and its ancient context comes from N. H. Snaith, *The Book of Amos, Part Two: Translation and Notes* (New York: Abingdon, 1946), 84.

4. See the chapters on Amos 1:1, 2; 7:10–17; and Amos 4 in this volume.

5. See Gary V. Smith, *Amos*, Mentor Commentary Series (Fearn, Scotland: Christian Focus, 1998), 221 and the chapter on Amos 8 in this volume.

6. Note the description of this religion in the chapters on Amos 1:1, 2; 7:10–17; and Amos 4 in this volume.

7. Amos 5:16, 17 may be treated as the conclusion to 5:1–15 or as the introduction to 5:18–27. It is clearly a bridge text between the lament announced in 5:1 and the woe oracle that begins in 5:18.

8. See Exodus 11:4, 5; 12:2; and Smith, *Amos*, 234.

### Chapter Twenty-Five: Let Justice Roll Down

1. For a discussion of the historical roots and theological importance of the day of the Lord, consult Paul R. House, "The Day of the Lord," in eds. Scott J. Hafemann and Paul R. House, *Central Themes in Biblical Theology: Mapping Unity in Diversity* (Nottingham: Inter-Varsity Press, 2007), 179–224.

2. For similar imagery see Isaiah 2:6–22.

3. See the chapters on Amos 1:1, 2; 7:10–17; and Amos 4 in this volume.

4. See James L. Mays, *Amos: A Commentary*, Old Testament Library (Philadelphia: Westminster Press, 1969), 91–93.

5. Thomas E. McComiskey, "Amos," in ed. Frank E. Gaebelein, *Expositor's Bible Commentary* (Grand Rapids, MI: Zondervan, 1985), 1:316.

6. Most of the ideas in this paragraph have been influenced by the writings of Wendell Berry. See his *The Unsettling of America: Culture and Agriculture*, 3rd ed. (San Francisco: Sierra Club Books, 1996).

7. Martin Luther King Jr., "Letter from a Birmingham Jail," https://www.khanacademy.org/humanities/us-history/x71a94f19:primary-documents/x71a94f19:primary-documents-lesson/a/letter-from-birmingham-jail. Accessed August 22, 2024.

8. Some scholars argue that the laws concerning sacrifice were added to the Pentateuch long after Moses's time. On this subject see Erling Hammershaimb, *The Book of Amos: A Commentary*, trans. John Sturdy (Oxford: Basil Blackwell, 1970), 91–92.

9. Mays, *Amos*, 110–11.

10. Gary V. Smith, *Amos*, Mentor Commentary Series (Fearn, Scotland: Christian Focus, 1998), 254.

11. J. A. Motyer, *The Day of the Lion: The Message of Amos*, The Bible Speaks Today (Downers Grove, IL: InterVarsity Press, 1974), 236.

### Chapter Twenty-Six: Undisturbed by Injustice

1. On this transition, see George Adam Smith, *The Books of Amos, Hosea, Micah*, rev. ed. (New York: Harper & Brothers, 1928), 178.

2. John Calvin, *Sermons on Genesis: Chapters 11–20*, trans. Rob Roy McGregor (Carlisle, PA: Banner of Truth, 2012), 295. The quotation comes from a sermon on Genesis 15:1–4.

3. Duane A. Garrett, *Amos: A Handbook on the Hebrew Text*, Baylor Handbook on the Hebrew Bible (Waco, TX: Baylor University Press, 2008), 179.

4. For the idea that Amos quotes the men, see James L. Mays, *Amos: A Commentary*, Old Testament Library (Philadelphia: Westminster Press, 1969), 115; and James Limburg, *Hosea–Micah*, Interpretation (Atlanta: John Knox Press, 1988).

5. Erling Hammerschaimb, *The Book of Amos: A Commentary*, trans. John Sturdy (Oxford: Basil Blackwell, 1970), 97.

6. For detailed descriptions of the luxuries in these verses in their ancient context, consult Philip J. King, *Amos, Hosea, Micah: An Archaeological Commentary* (Philadelphia: Westminster Press, 1988), 137–61.

7. I prefer this interpretation of the difficult Hebrew phrasing to the ESV's reading as meaning that the people invented new instruments. See Francis I. Andersen and David Noel Freedman, *Amos: A New Translation with Introduction and Commentary*, Anchor Bible 24A (New York: Doubleday, 1989), 544, 563.

8. Jörg Jeremias, *The Book of Amos: A Commentary*, trans. Douglas W. Stott, Old Testament Library (Louisville: Westminster John Knox Press, 1998), 113.

9. Douglas Stuart, *Hosea–Jonah*, Word Biblical Commentary 31 (Waco, TX: Word, 1987), 365.

10. Kyle M. Yates Jr., *Studies in Amos* (Nashville: Convention Press, 1966), 97.

Chapter Twenty-Seven: No More Delaying of Judgment

1. As the passage proceeds, Amos will use various forms of this word to make his points. Technically speaking, he will utilize wordplay, but the term seems too light for what this passage conveys.

2. See Ludwig Koehler, Walter Baumgartner and J. J. Stamm, *The Hebrew and Aramaic Lexicon of the Old Testament*, trans. and ed. M. E. J. Richardson, 4 vols. (Leiden: Brill, 1994–1999), 1:688–89.

3. See the chapter on that passage in this volume.

4. The word here is a form of *riv*, which usually means "court case" or "trial." It may mean "judicial decision" here, but the phrase may also parallel the English phrase "trial by fire."

5. For other options for translating this rare phrase, consult Duane A. Garrett, *Amos: A Handbook of the Hebrew Text*, Baylor Handbook on the Hebrew Bible (Waco, TX: Baylor University Press, 2008), 209–10.

6. The Hebrew words in this verse translated as "devoured" and "was eating up" are forms of the same verb as "eat" in 7:2a.

7. Verses 7, 8 are hard to translate due to the fourfold use of a word for a particular metal. These four uses are the only places that the word appears in the Old Testament. The word has been interpreted as "plumb line," the idea being that the metal might have been a tool. The ESV has the traditional reading of "standing beside a wall built with a plumb line." There are no words corresponding to "built with" in the Hebrew text. Also the word translated as "beside" is the standard word for "on," "upon," "concerning," or "over."

8. Jörg Jeremias, *The Book of Amos: A Commentary*, trans. Douglas W. Stott, Old Testament Library (Louisville: Westminster John Knox Press, 1998), 131.

9. Note that the first chapter on Amos in this volume included some exposition of 7:10–17.

10. Richard S. Cripps, *A Critical and Exegetical Commentary on the Book of Amos* (London: SPCK, 1929), 232.

11. Jeremias, *Book of Amos*, 140.

12. For more on the kind of farm work that Amos did, see Philip J. King, *Amos, Hosea, Micah: An Archaeological Commentary* (Philadelphia: Westminster Press, 1988), 116–17.

Chapter Twenty-Eight: The Ending Has Begun
1. See the comments on Amos 7:8 for a rationale for this translation. The ESV reads, "I will never again pass by them."
2. J. A. Motyer, *The Day of the Lion: The Message of Amos*, The Bible Speaks Today (Downers Grove, IL: InterVarsity Press, 1974), 177.
3. I take the ESV textual note as the best reading of the Hebrew text. The Hebrew word translated as "the temple" in the ESV text is not definite in Hebrew.
4. Gary V. Smith, *Amos*, Mentor Commentary Series (Fearn, Scotland: Christian Focus, 1998), 340.
5. The verb is a participle, indicating that this is their normal and ongoing course of action. The ESV reads "who trample."
6. Jacob Milgrom, *Numbers*, JPS Torah Commentary (New York: Jewish Publication Society, 1990), 242. Milgrom comments on Numbers 28:11–15, which specifies sacrifices for new moon observances.
7. The image is likely that of a solar eclipse, like those that took place in 784 and 763 B.C. See Robert Khua Hnin Thang, *The Theology of Land in Amos 7–9*, Langham Monographs (Carlisle, Cumbria, UK: Langham, 2014), 141.
8. The word translated as "seek" in the ESV is not the same as the one in 5:4. This word denotes pursuit.

Chapter Twenty-Nine: The Household of Jacob, the Booth of David, and the Remnant of Edom
1. Scholars disagree over the location of Caphtor and Kir. Most experts agree that the exact location of Kir cannot be determined. Some conclude that "Caphtor" refers to Crete, while others think it was a place in Asia Minor. See Gary V. Smith, *Amos*, Mentor Commentary Series (Fearn, Scotland: Christian Focus, 1998), 364–65.
2. The Hebrew here is emphatic.
3. The Hebrew word *beth* may be translated as "house" or "household," depending on the context.
4. For a discussion of what this image conveys, consult Duane A. Garrett, *Amos: A Handbook on the Hebrew Text*, Baylor Handbook on the Hebrew Bible (Waco, TX: Baylor University Press, 2008), 277–79.
5. See the chapter covering Hosea 1 in this volume.
6. My translation. The verse begins with a word that clearly conveys purpose. Furthermore, I take the conjunction translated in the ESV as "and" in "and all the nations" to be explanatory. Finally, I believe that the Hebrew word translated in most English Bibles as "nations" should be translated as "peoples" unless the surrounding context includes statements about a king or government.
7. Erling Hammerschaimb, *The Book of Amos: A Commentary*, trans. John Sturdy (Oxford: Blackwell, 1970), 141.
8. See, for example, James L. Mays, *Amos: A Commentary*, Old Testament Library (Philadelphia: Westminster Press, 1969), 164–65.
9. Jessie Brown Pounds, "The Way of the Cross Leads Home" (1906).

Chapter Thirty: Brothers, Bystanders, and Betrayers
1. See the chapter on Amos 9 in this volume. See also Joel 3:19.

2. Compare the Assyrian texts in James B. Pritchard, *Ancient Near Eastern Texts Relating to the Old Testament*, 3rd ed. (Princeton, NJ: Princeton University Press, 1969), 449–52.

3. I find that many writers only consider this option. They do not consider all the other times that opponents threatened Jerusalem. Also some commentators omit 2 Chronicles 28:1–21 in their analysis of Obadiah's setting.

4. The indictment comes in verses 10, 11. See Johan Renkema, *Obadiah*, trans. Brian Doyle, Historical Commentary on the Old Testament (Leuven, Belgium: Peeters, 2003), 127.

5. King Sennacherib (c. 705—681 B.C.) captured many cities in mountainous countries. See Josette Elayi, *Sennacherib, King of Assyria* (Atlanta: SBL Press, 2018), 48–50, 94–96.

6. Irvin A. Busenitz, *Commentary on Joel and Obadiah*, Mentor Commentary Series (Fearn, Scotland: Christian Focus, 2003), 237.

7. Busenitz, *Commentary on Joel and Obadiah*, 237.

8. Busenitz, 238.

9. See the chapter on Amos 9:1–15 in this volume.

10. See the ESV note on the phrase "eat your bread" (Obadiah 7). The Hebrew words for "bread" and "make war" are very similar. It is possible that the phrase indicates "those who share bread in a military camp."

11. The ESV translation of verses 9, 10 obscures the presence of two consecutive explanatory words at the end of verse 9 and the beginning of verse 10. It reads the first term as "by slaughter" rather than as an explanatory phrase that begins a new thought. The verses perhaps should read one of two ways. I slightly prefer the first option.

Option 1: "And your mighty men shall be dismayed, O Teman, / because every man shall be cut off from Mount Esau, / on account of the killing. / On account of the violence against your brother Jacob, / you will be covered with shame, / and you will be cut off endlessly." (AT)

Option 2: "And your mighty men shall be dismayed, O Teman, / because every man shall be cut off from Mount Esau. / On account of the killing, on account of the violence / against your brother Jacob, / you will be covered with shame, / and you will be cut off endlessly." (AT)

For a discussion of the Hebrew words involved, see Renkema, *Obadiah*, 156–58.

12. On the dynamics and responsibilities of kinship, see Renkema, *Obadiah*, 160–61.

13. For other examples of how the two mistreated one another, see the summary in Busenitz, *Commentary on Joel and Obadiah*, 237.

14. Renkema, *Obadiah*, 164.

15. For nuances in the definition of "bystander," see Victoria J. Barnett, *Bystanders: Conscience and Complicity During the Holocaust* (Westport, CT: Greenwood Press, 2000), 10.

16. Renkema, *Obadiah*, 164–65.

## Chapter Thirty-One: The Kingdom Shall Be the Lord's

1. See the preceding chapter in this volume.

2. See the discussion in Johan Renkema, *Obadiah*, trans. Brian Doyle, Historical Commentary on the Old Testament (Leuven, Belgium: Peeters, 2003), 171–72.

3. See James D. Nogalski, *The Book of the Twelve*, Smyth and Helwys Bible Commentary (Macon, GA: Smyth and Helwys, 2011), 1:387.

4. While "ruin" (Obadiah 12 ESV) is a possible translation, the Hebrew word here is the common general term for various types or levels of destruction. The word is also the first in a series of words in verses 12–14 that sound like "Edom."

5. The word translated as "calamity" sounds like "Edom."

6. The command is emphatic here.

7. The ESV has a past tense verb ("have drunk") followed by three future tense verbs ("shall drink" [2x] and "shall be").

8. There is no Hebrew form corresponding to the ESV's "those who." Verse 17 establishes Mount Zion as a place of refuge.

9. Renkema, *Obadiah*, 198.

10. Renkema, 198.

11. Hans Walter Wolff, *Obadiah and Jonah*, trans. Margaret Kohl (Minneapolis: Augsburg, 1986), 67.

12. Nogalski, *Book of the Twelve*, 391.

13. The ESV reads "host" or "army." The Hebrew word refers to human or material defenses beyond a city wall. See Francis Brown, et al., *The Brown-Driver-Briggs Hebrew and English Lexicon* (1906; repr. Peabody, MA: Hendrickson, 1996), 298.

14. Compare Joel 3:4–8. The location of Sepharad (Obadiah 20) is unknown. For options consult Irvin A. Busenitz, *Joel and Obadiah*, Mentor Commentary Series (Fearn, Scotland: Christian Focus, 2003), 280 and Nogalski, *Book of the Twelve*, 392.

15. Renkema, *Obadiah*, 218.

Chapter Thirty-Two: Running from God

1. George A. Smith, *The Book of the Twelve Prophets*, vol. 2 (New York: A. C. Armstrong and Son, 1898), 492.

2. Throughout these chapters I will distinguish references to the character of Jonah from the book that bears his name by placing the latter in italics or by using the designation "the book of Jonah." Of course, the titles ascribed to Biblical books are not original to the composition.

3. Many scholars reject the historicity of the book of Jonah, preferring to see it as a fable, legend, or allegory of sorts. Reasons for this, of course, are varied. Certainly one of the chief reasons for denying the historicity of the account is the episode with the great fish, which, on a secular view of the world, is regarded as an impossibility. However, the book's clear identification of the prophet with the historical figure Jonah ben Amittai, who prophesied in the mid-eighth century B.C. (2 Kings 14:25), as well as Jesus's use of Jonah's experience as a type of his death and resurrection (Matthew 12:40), suggests the narrative was written to relate historical events. Daniel C. Timmer has made the important observation that the expression "the word of the LORD came" (Jonah 1:1) occurs eighty-five times in the Old Testament and "always introduces recipients of the divine word, whom the biblical authors present as historical individuals (e.g., 1 Sam. 15:10; 2 Sam 7:4; 1 Kgs. 6:11; Jer. 1:4; Ezek. 3:16; Hab. 1:3; Zech. 4:8)." *A Gracious and Compassionate God: Mission, Salvation, and Spirituality in the Book of Jonah*, New Studies in Biblical Theology 26 (Downers Grove, IL: InterVarsity Press, 2011), 60. Cf. T. D. Alexander, "Jonah and Genre," *Tyndale Bulletin* 36 (1985): 35–59. According to John Stek, "[Jonah] is

offered as history; that is, as an account of events that have happened in history. But it is not merely a report of those events, such as a modern technical historian might attempt to offer, leaving it to the philosopher or theologian of history to make of it what he can. It is *interpreted* history, the prophetic writer himself providing the interpretation, and so disclosing its inner meaning." "The Message of the Book of Jonah," *Calvin Theological Journal* 4 (1969): 23–50 (quote on 34, emphasis original).

4. For a clear, concise, and careful discussion of a Christocentric interpretation of *Jonah*, see Bryan Estelle, *Salvation Through Judgment and Mercy* (Phillipsburg, NJ: P&R: 2005), 1–7; 27–30.

5. Stek, "Message of the Book of Jonah," 39.

6. Uriel Simon, *Jonah* (Philadelphia: Jewish Publication Society, 1999), 35.

7. Citing 2 Kings 14:26ff., Stek writes, "The prosperity currently enjoyed was not the reward of God upon a repentant and now faithful people, but was rather Yahweh's gracious relief of a nation which He had recently chastised with great severity because of its waywardness." "Message of the Book of Jonah," 24, 25. Cf. Douglas Stuart, *Hosea-Jonah*, Word Biblical Commentary 31 (Nashville: Thomas Nelson, 1987), 447.

8. "The author has taken pains to connect our Jonah with the Jonah alluded to in 2 Kings 14 by the way he opens his story in the Hebrew language. Additionally, the way in which the Septuagint—an ancient Greek translation (third century B.C.) of the Hebrew text—rendered 1:9 is further evidence that those in the ancient world took pains to connect the Jonah alluded to in 2 Kings. Similarly, early rabbinic interpretation unanimously connects the prophet of the book of Jonah to the prophet of 2 Kings 14. Although one should recognize that this connection between Jonah 1 and 2 Kings 14 is one of the most difficult issues in interpreting the book, the connection should not be quickly dismissed." Estelle, *Salvation through Judgment and Mercy*, 18. Cf. Thomas Bolin, *Freedom Beyond Forgiveness: The Book of Jonah Re-examined*, Journal for the Study of the Old Testament Supplement Series 236 (Sheffield, UK: Sheffield Academic Press, 1997), 151.

9. Timmer, *Gracious and Compassionate God*, 63.

10. "But Jonah would also recognize—as would the hearers/readers of this story in ancient Israel—that to give advance warning of the imposition of covenant sanctions was to open the door to the possibility of repentance." Stuart, *Hosea-Jonah*, 449–50, cf. 452.

11. The rise of the Neo-Assyrian Empire is typically dated to the reign of Ashur-dan II (934–912 B.C.). For the next 300 years the empire would expand its borders to include territories from the Arab-Persian Gulf to the Commagene in Western Turkey and even, for a time, Egypt. Their tools of expansion were infamous. Assyrian palace reliefs document the methods of torture and psychological warfare that were employed to terrify cities and nations into servitude, including flaying and impaling victims, amputation, castration, blinding people, or burning people alive (including children). For a popular-level treatment of Assyria's use of terror and torture, see Erika Bleibtreu, "Grisly Assyria Record of Torture and Death," *Biblical Archaeology Review* 17.1 (1991): 52–61.

12. The Black Obelisk of Shalmaneser III (858–824 B.C.) depicts the Assyrian king exacting tribute from Jehu, king of the northern kingdom of Israel (842–815 B.C.). James B. Pritchard, *Ancient Near Eastern Texts Relating to the Old Testament*, 3rd ed. (Princeton, NJ: Princeton University Press, 1969), 281, 283–84.

13. Regarding the sense of *hā'îr haggədôlâh* ("the great city"), Stuart has rightly urged caution against importing modern notions of "capital cities" onto ancient societies like Assyria. Though Nineveh was not technically the capital city of the Assyrian Empire in Jonah's day, it was certainly an important religious center that housed a royal residence. *Hosea—Jonah*, 441–49.

14. Stek, "Message of the Book of Jonah," 25–26; Estelle, *Salvation Through Judgment and Mercy*, 24–26.

15. Estelle, *Salvation Through Judgment and Mercy*, 16, 27.

16. J. I. Packer, Introduction to John Owen, *The Death of Death in the Death of Christ* (Carlisle, PA: Banner of Truth, 1967), 10.

17. For a brief discussion of the various proposals for the location of Tarshish as well as a defense for modern-day Spain as the most likely option, see JoAnna M. Hoyt, *Amos, Jonah, & Micah*, Evangelical Exegetical Commentary (Bellingham, WA: Lexham, 2019), 349, 350.

18. The significance of the deep, trance-like sleep designated by the Hebrew verb *rādam* has been variously interpreted as the sleep of individuals, especially prophets, prepared to receive revelation from God (Daniel 8:18; 10:9; and with the nominal form *tardēmâ*, Genesis 2:21; 15:12; 1 Samuel 26:12; Job 4:13; Isaiah 29:10). See Jack Sasson, *Jonah*, Anchor Bible 24B (New York: Doubleday, 1990), 102; and Bolin, *Freedom Beyond Forgiveness*, 80. Others, however, connect it to the sleep associated with death (Judges 4:21; Psalm 76:6) and as perhaps another expression of the prophet's death wish. See Amy Erickson, *Jonah: Introduction and Commentary* (Grand Rapids, MI: Eerdmans, 2021), 251; and Jonathan Magonet, *Form and Meaning: Studies in Literary Techniques in the Book of Jonah* (Sheffield, UK: Almond Press, 1983), 67–69.

19. Stuart, *Hosea–Jonah*, 458.

20. The Hebrew *yārad* ("to go down") occurs four times in the book of Jonah (1:3 [2x]; 1:5; 2:6). Though Hans Walter Wolff, erroneously in my opinion, understood the psalm in chapter 2 to be a later addition, his discussion of Jonah 1:5 is nevertheless insightful: "This is the third time we are told about Jonah's 'descent'. He is going down further and further. The person who inserted the psalm may have already discerned the direction leading to death (2:6f.), to which the disobedient man or woman, like the fool, 'descends.' Cf. Prov 5:5 and the frequent association of *yārad* with death, the grave, and the underworld (1 Sam 26:10; Ps 22:29; Job 33:24). The sequel also suggests that there is a metaphorical echo here: Jonah goes down into 'the lowest part of the ship.' In Isa 14:15 *yrkty bôr* means the lowest depths of the grave, and is parallel to the underworld (*šᵊ'ôl*) as the end of the 'descent.'" *Obadiah and Jonah: A Commentary*, trans. Margaret Kohl (Minneapolis: Augsburg, 1986), 112.

21. Edward Welch, *Addictions: A Banquet in the Grave* (Phillipsburg, NJ: P&R, 2001).

22. On Jonah as a representative of Israel, comparable to Hosea (1—3) and Ezekiel (4; 5; 12:1–20; 24:15ff.), see Stek, "Message of the Book of Jonah," 37–38. Cf. Estelle, *Salvation Through Judgment and Mercy*, 33–34; Edmund Clowney, *Preaching and Biblical Theology* (Phillipsburg, NJ: P&R, 1961), 98; and Timmer, *Gracious and Compassionate God*, 62.

23. Timmer, *Gracious and Compassionate God*, 62.

Chapter Thirty-Three: Divine Pursuit

1. William Langewiesche, "A Sea Story," *The Atlantic*, May 2004, https://www.theatlantic.com/magazine/archive/2004/05/a-sea-story/302940/.

2. Phyllis Trible captured the author's literary sophistication and subtlety in her analysis of this expression: "Three rhetorical devices sustain the attention given the ship: prosopopoeia, onomatopoeia, and assonance. Prosopopoeia attributes a human category to an inanimate object: 'the ship thought.' Onomatopoeia uses words that sound like their meaning, namely boards cracking from the force of the water: *ḥiššebâ lehiššābēr* (thought to-break-up). Assonance identifies similar or identical sounds between the internal vowels of proximate words: the vowels i, e, a, and i, a, e, in *ḥiššebâ lehiššābēr*. Focused on the ship, these devices underscore the terror of the storm hurled by Yhwh. They paint an unusual picture. Hence, a modest sentence acquires immodest proportions." *Rhetorical Criticism: Context, Method, and the Book of Jonah*, (Minneapolis: Fortress, 1994), 132. Cf. Jack Sasson, *Jonah*, Anchor Bible 24B (New York: Doubleday, 1990), 96.

3. Langewiesche, "Sea Story."

4. Daniel C. Timmer, *A Gracious and Compassionate God: Mission, Salvation, and Spirituality in the Book of Jonah*, New Studies in Biblical Theology 26 (Downers Grove, IL: InterVarsity Press, 2011), 70.

5. Sasson, *Jonah*, 108–10.

6. See, for example, *The Epic of Gilgamesh*, trans. Andrew George (New York: Penguin, 1999), 92; *Atrahasis*, in *Before the Muses: An Anthology of Akkadian Literature*, 3rd ed., trans. Benjamin R. Foster (Bethesda, MD: CDL Press, 2005), 249–52.

7. I am thankful to my colleague Iain Duguid for this observation.

8. "It is interesting to note that the grammar of the book of Jonah simultaneously seems to emphasize the futility of human efforts and the successful acts of God. More specifically, Jonathan Magonet has demonstrated that when an infinitive is used in the book of Jonah . . . to describe an action undertaken by humans (e.g., 1:3; 1:5; 1:13; 4:2), then those actions fail. In contrast to this, when an infinitive is used of an action undertaken by God (e.g., 1:17; 4:6 twice), whatever is endeavored by the Almighty succeeds." Bryan Estelle, *Salvation Through Judgment and Mercy* (Phillipsburg, NJ: P&R: 2005), 52. Cf. Jonathan Magonet, *Form and Meaning: Studies in Literary Techniques in the Book of Jonah* (Sheffield, UK: Almond Press, 1983), 31.

9. Estelle observes that "a theme of fear is carefully woven throughout this first chapter." *Salvation Through Judgment and Mercy*, 41.

10. "So then, life in the Old Testament means more than a beating heart; life is better described as fullness of life (a robust life), something compromised by the shadow of death. Life and death are in constant tension." Estelle, 78.

11. About Jonah's confession, Trible writes, "The taciturn, recalcitrant, enigmatic character begins to reveal himself. Or does he?" *Rhetorical Criticism*, 140.

12. Amy Erickson, *Jonah: Introduction and Commentary* (Grand Rapids, MI: Eerdmans, 2021), 270.

13. Stuart sees a possible allusion to Psalm 95:5. Cf. Exodus 10:13–19; 14; 15; Numbers 11:31; Job 26:12; Psalm 135:7; Isaiah 50:2; Jeremiah 49:32–36; Amos 4:13. Douglas Stuart, *Hosea-Jonah*, Word Biblical Commentary 31 (Nashville: Thomas Nelson, 1987), 461.

14. Trible, *Rhetorical Criticism*, 141.

15. Trible, 141 has noted that the irony is even embedded into the syntax of the prophet's confession: "The structure of his own sentence traps him. In splitting the theological formula 'Yhwh God-of the-heavens . . . who made the-sea and-the-dry-land,' Jonah surrounds himself with the God he is fearing. The splitting illustrates the rhetorical device *hyperbaton* (literally, 'transposed'), the separation of words that usually belong together. The arrangement recalls the narrator's surrounding of Jonah's flight from Yhwh with the presence of Yhwh (1:3). But how much stronger is the irony now because Jonah's own words undercut him." Trible.

16. Timmer, *Gracious and Compassionate God*, 70, n. 33.

17. Uriel Simon, *Jonah* (Philadelphia: Jewish Publication Society, 1999), 13; Erickson, *Jonah*, 257.

18. Hans Walter Wolff, *Obadiah and Jonah: A Commentary*, trans. Margaret Kohl (Minneapolis: Augsburg, 1986), 109.

19. Estelle, *Salvation Through Judgment and Mercy*, 42.

20. Simon, *Jonah*, 7.

21. Trible, *Rhetorical Criticism*, 141; John Goldingay, *Hosea-Micah* (Grand Rapids, MI: Baker, 2021), 384.

22. Estelle has written, "Now I do not think that the text warrants squeezing conversion stories out of the chapter at this point. Calvin says essentially the same when he explains the limitations of the concept of the fear of the Lord that our text says these sailors experienced." *Salvation Through Judgment and Mercy*, 55. Cf. John Calvin, *Commentaries on the Twelve Minor Prophets*, vol. 3, trans. John Owen (Grand Rapids, MI: Baker, 2003), 61–62; similarly, Stuart, *Hosea-Jonah*, 464. For a counterview, see Timmer's detailed treatment of conversion in the Old Testament with a special focus on the book of Jonah, *Gracious and Compassionate God*, esp. 72–74.

23. Cf. Leviticus 5:17; 16:22; Numbers 14:18. See Sasson, *Jonah*, 124; and Erickson, *Jonah*, 276.

24. "What Jonah could not do, but his attitude announces, is done by Jesus Christ. He it is who accepts total condemnation. . . . It is solely because of the sacrifice of Jesus Christ that the sacrifice of Jonah avails and saves. It is solely because Jesus Christ has accepted malediction that Jonah's acceptance has something to say both to the sailors and to us." Jacques Ellul, quoted in Estelle, *Salvation Through Judgment and Mercy*, 60.

25. "His prophetic function adheres to Jonah wherever he goes; he magnified the name of the Lord among the gentiles even when he ran away from him." Simon, *Jonah*, 8.

Chapter Thirty-Four: Prayer from the Depths

1. "The cosmic sea, however, also symbolizes the continued threat the forces of chaos pose against God and creation. The sea pushes against the boundaries established for it (Job 38:8-11; Jeremiah 5:22). The Bible adapts its neighbors' creation myths of a primeval battle between a creator god and a sea monster of chaos called Leviathan, Rahab, or the dragon or serpent (Job 41). Unlike the myths of neighboring nations, God creates the chaos monster and places it in the sea (Genesis 1:20-21; Psalm 104:24-26). The monster stirs the cosmic sea but is wounded and subdued by God (Job 26:12; Psalm 74:12-14; 89:9-10; Isaiah 51:9) and will ultimately be

vanquished in the end times (Isaiah 27:1). As the home of the chaos monster who can be roused, the sea symbolizes the threat of the reemergence of chaos (Job 3:8)." *Dictionary of Biblical Imagery*, eds. Leland Ryken, James Wilhoit, and Tremper Longman III (Downers Grove, IL: InterVarsity Press, 1998), 765. Cf. Hans Walter Wolff, *Obadiah and Jonah: A Commentary*, trans. Margaret Kohl (Minneapolis: Augsburg, 1986), 136.

2. Robert S. Fyall, *Now My Eyes Have Seen You: Images of Creation and Evil in the Book of Job* (Downers Grove, IL, InterVarsity Press, 2002) 83–100, 157–174.

3. See, for example, Baal's combat with Yam ("Sea") in the Ugaritic Baal cycle. An accessible translation may be found in *Ugaritic Narrative Poetry*, SBL Writings from the Ancient World Series, ed. Simon B. Parker (Atlanta: Scholars, 1997) and Marduk's combat with Tiamat in *Enuma Elish* (i.e., *The Epic of Creation*), Benjamin R. Foster, *Before the Muses: An Anthology of Akkadian Literature*, 3rd ed. (Bethesda, MD: CDL Press, 2005), 459ff. Cf. John Day, *God's Conflict with the Dragon and the Sea: Echoes of a Canaanite Myth in the Old Testament* (Cambridge: Cambridge University Press, 1985).

4. On the appropriateness of Jonah's psalm of thanksgiving (as opposed to a lament), see Douglas Stuart, *Hosea-Jonah*, Word Biblical Commentary 31 (Nashville: Thomas Nelson, 1987), 439.

5. Wolff, *Obadiah and Jonah*, 112; Amy Erickson, *Jonah: Introduction and Commentary* (Grand Rapids, MI: Eerdmans, 2021), 246.

6. "In the phraseology of the psalms, 'the flood' (*nhr*) which encompasses the petitioner is more reminiscent of the mythical underground rivers of chaos and death which belong to the underworld (Isa. 44:27; Ps. 24:2; 93:3) rather than the Mediterranean, especially since the whole passage (vv. 3–6) repeatedly echoes the mood and language of Ps. 18:4f." Wolff, *Obadiah and Jonah*, 134.

7. Many interpreters will identify "the belly of Sheol" (2:2) with "the belly of the fish" (2:1). On this view, the fish is not envisioned as the instrument of God's salvation but the Sheol-grave in which Jonah is unsure of his fate and from which he appeals to the Lord for salvation. Often those who take this view regard Jonah's prayer as composed separately from the prose tale, either much earlier or much later than his sojourn in the belly of the fish, and only placed into the mouth of the entombed prophet for literary and theological reasons (e.g., Gerhard von Rad, *God at Work in Israel*, trans. John H. Marks [Nashville: Abingdon, 1980], 68; Wolff, *Obadiah and Jonah*, 131–32, 140–42; Jack Sasson, *Jonah*, Anchor Bible 24B [New York: Doubleday, 1990], 172, 205–8, 102). As Stuart has rightly observed, "The trouble with this view is, of course, that the fish is precisely a vehicle of rescue in the story. Once Jonah is inside the belly of the fish he has been delivered from drowning." *Hosea-Jonah*, 439. Furthermore, the fact that two different words for "belly" are used (*mē'eh* in 2:1; *beten* in 2:2) makes the identification of the fish's belly with Sheol somewhat tenuous. Also, this view fails to account for the prophet's mention of an earlier prayer, presumably a lament (2:2, "I called out to the LORD out of my distress"), referenced in his prayer of thanksgiving.

8. Philip S. Johnston, *Shades of Sheol: Death and Afterlife in the Old Testament* (Downers Grove, IL: InterVarsity Press, 2002), esp. 69–124.

9. "Reed or seaweed suggests the growth on the ocean floor in which one could get fatally entangled; it also suggests a parallel image to the ropes with which She'ol

catches and holds its victims." John Goldingay, *Hosea-Micah* (Grand Rapids, MI: Baker, 2021), 389. Cf. Wolff, *Obadiah and Jonah*, 134, 136.

10. Wolff, *Obadiah and Jonah*, 136 notes, "On *l 'wlm* is a legal term for what is unalterable.'" See also Hans Walter Wolff, *Hosea*, Hermeneia (Minneapolis: Fortress, 1974), 52.

11. Bryan Estelle, *Salvation Through Judgment and Mercy* (Phillipsburg, NJ: P&R: 2005), 86.

12. P. Kyle McCarter, "The River Ordeal in Israelite Literature." *Harvard Theological Review* 66 (1973): 403–12; Estelle, *Salvation Through Judgment and Mercy*, 92–95.

13. See, for example, the second law of the *Code of Hammurabi*. An accessible version may be found in *The Context of Scripture*, vol. 2, eds. William Hallo and K. Lawson Younger Jr. (Leiden: Brill, 2003), 337.

14. For images of the drinking ordeal, see Psalms 60:3; 75:8; Isaiah 51:17, 22; Jeremiah 25:15; Obadiah 16; Revelation 14:10.

15. The ESV translates Hebrew *tᵉhôm* variously as "deeps" in Jonah 2:5 and "floods" in Exodus 15:5.

16. "For Yahweh to 'lead out' the helpless is his very own, most characteristic act of salvation, ever since the Israelites were led out of Egypt. . . . Psalms 30:3 and 71:20 also use [*'lh*] for a rescue from death." Wolff, *Obadiah and Jonah*, 137.

17. JoAnna M. Hoyt, *Amos, Jonah, & Micah*, Evangelical Exegetical Commentary (Bellingham, WA: Lexham, 2019), 470.

18. Goldingay, *Hosea-Micah*, 386; Erickson, *Jonah*, 293.

19. Stephen Coleman, "Reading Jonah Backwards: Reconsidering a Prophet's Repentance." *Unio Cum Christo* 5 (2019): 155–71.

20. "The credal statement in 1:9 and the credal statement given in 4:2 are literary cruxes. That is, they are extremely important to the story and must not be passed over lightly." Estelle, *Salvation Through Judgment and Mercy*, 50. To these I would add Jonah's prayer from the depths in chapter 2 as serving the same literary, theological, and prophetic functions.

21. "The reader will detect a bitter humor and a mocking note in these undignified dealings with Jonah. The word *qy'* is only used in the Old Testament in images that rouse disgust (Isa. 19:14; 28:8; Jer. 48:26; Job 20:15; Lev. 18:28); it is a coarse word which we might translate as 'to throw up.'" Wolff, *Obadiah and Jonah*, 139.

## Chapter Thirty-Five: Portraits of Repentance

1. JoAnna M. Hoyt, *Amos, Jonah, & Micah*, Evangelical Exegetical Commentary (Bellingham, WA: Lexham, 2019), 358, 477. For a discussion of the difficulty of taking *lē'lōhîm* as a superlative, see Jack Sasson, *Jonah*, Anchor Bible 24B (New York: Doubleday, 1990), 228.

2. Many commentators have seen the shift from *'al-nînəwēh* in Jonah 1:2 to *'el-nînəwēh* in 3:2 as suggesting a change in the nature of the mission from "call out against . . ." to the more neutral "call out to . . ." See, e.g., Amy Erickson, *Jonah: Introduction and Commentary* (Grand Rapids, MI: Eerdmans, 2021), 356. While this is possible, it is far from a necessary understanding of these roughly equivalent expressions. Cf. Bruce K. Waltke and Michael Patrick O'Connor, *An Introduction to*

*Biblical Hebrew Syntax* (Winona Lake, IN: Eisenbrauns, 1990) §11.2.2; §11.2.13b. For a balanced treatment of the issue, see Hoyt, *Amos, Jonah, & Micah*, 420–23.

3. See, for example, John Calvin, *Commentaries on the Twelve Minor Prophets*, vol. 3, trans. John Owen (Grand Rapids, MI: Baker, 2003), 94; Cassiodorus, quoted in *The Twelve Prophets*, vol. 14, Ancient Christian Commentary on Scripture, ed. Alberto Ferreiro (Downers Grove, IL: IVP Academic, 2003), 137. For a thorough treatment of the history of interpretation of the book of Jonah, see Yvonne Sherwood, *A Biblical Text and Its Afterlives: The Survival of Jonah in Western Culture* (Cambridge: Cambridge University Press, 2000); and Thomas Bolin, *Freedom Beyond Forgiveness: The Book of Jonah Re-examined*, Journal for the Study of the Old Testament Supplement Series 236 (Sheffield, UK: Sheffield Academic, 1997).

4. Stephen Coleman, "Reading Jonah Backwards: Reconsidering a Prophet's Repentance." *Unio Cum Christo* 5 (2019): 155–71.

5. Ben Zvi, *Signs of Jonah: Reading and Rereading in Ancient Yehud*, Journal for the Study of the Old Testament Supplement Series 367 (Sheffield, UK: Sheffield Academic, 2003): 87.

6. "Here Jonah's hyperbolic resistance (1:3) is replaced with exaggerated efficiency. Jonah does exactly what he is told. . . . The wording in v. 3 used to describe Jonah's subsequent actions mirrors the wording of the divine command: Jonah got up (*qûm*) and went (*hlk*) to Nineveh (*'el-nînəwēh*). The narrator even adds, for good measure, 'in compliance with the word of YHWH' (*kidbar YHWH*). The Jonah of ch. 3 is the reverse of the Jonah of ch. 1." Erickson, *Jonah*, 356.

7. I am indebted to John Stek for this argument in "The Message of the Book of Jonah," *Calvin Theological Journal* 4 (1969): 25, 26.

8. "Stubborn and unrepentant himself to the end, [Jonah] could not abide seeing God show compassion and grace to the enemies of his people." Douglas Stuart, *Hosea-Jonah*, Word Biblical Commentary 31 (Nashville: Thomas Nelson, 1987), 509. Cf. Hoyt, *Amos, Jonah, & Micah*, 474.

9. Some have interpreted Jonah's going a day's journey into a city that is described as "three days' journey in breadth" as suggestive of the prophet's reluctance. (e.g., Hoyt, *Amos, Jonah, & Micah*, 477–78). While this is quite possible, the exact meaning of descriptions "a day's journey" (*maḥᵃlak yôm 'eḥāḏ*) and "three days' journey" (*maḥᵃlak šᵉlōšeṯ yāmîm*) continues to elude interpreters. One common view is to take these as descriptions of the time it would take to travel through the city (and perhaps also its environs) or to travel all the streets within the city. So, e.g., André Parrot, *Nineveh and the Old Testament* (New York: Philosophical Library, 1955) 85–86; and C. F. Keil and Franz Delitzsch, *The Twelve Minor Prophets*, vol. 1, trans. James Martin (Edinburgh: T&T Clark, 1874), 405. This view is not without its problems (e.g., see Sasson, *Jonah*, 230, 233, for a critique of these and other proposals). David Marcus has made the compelling suggestion that the expressions may be used figuratively for short and long distances, respectively. In this case, the author may be emphasizing Jonah's connection to his prophetic forebears who could, at times, cover great distances in a short time through supernatural empowerment (such as in 1 Kings 18:46). "Nineveh's 'Three Days' Walk (Jonah 3:3): Another Interpretation," in *On the Way to Nineveh: Studies in Honor of George M. Landes*, eds. Stephen L. Cook and S. C. Winter (Atlanta: Scholars, 1999), 42–53. Needless to say, Jonah's reluctance may be deduced from the larger context of the narrative.

10. Hoyt, *Amos, Jonah, & Micah*, 474, 483.
11. Stuart, *Hosea–Jonah*, 485.
12. Erickson, *Jonah*, 358.
13. Erickson, *Jonah*, 360–61 has keenly observed that the king's words make a twofold allusion to David's mourning over his sick son (2 Samuel 12:22) and to Moses's intercession for Israel after the episode of the golden calf (Exodus 32:12).
14. The question of whether Jonah's five-word sermon (in Hebrew) recorded in verse 4 represents his entire message or a summary of his message is moot. If the latter, it must be recognized as a faithful summary of the prophet's entire message and not assumed to have been supplemented with substantive further explanations of who, what, why, etc. See Hoyt, *Amos, Jonah, & Micah*, 478.
15. As with the sailors earlier, it is not necessary to interpret Nineveh's repentance as conversion to Yahwism. While this may have been the case for some, what the text describes is the external moral reform of the city. For a good discussion of the nature of Nineveh's repentance, see Hoyt, *Amos, Jonah, & Micah*, 483–86; and Daniel C. Timmer, *A Gracious and Compassionate God: Mission, Salvation, and Spirituality in the Book of Jonah*, New Studies in Biblical Theology 26 (Downers Grove, IL: InterVarsity Press, 2011), 111–13.
16. The Hebrew *wayya'ᵃmînû 'anšê nînᵉwēh bē'lōhîm* does not necessarily describe Nineveh's conversion to Yahwism. Timmer, *Gracious and Compassionate God*, 101n32 notes that it is often used to describe a response to God's word (e.g., 2 Chronicles 20:20).
17. Though Stuart mentions the possible exception of the postexilic community in the days of Ezra (Ezra 10:1–17) and Nehemiah (Nehemiah 9:1–3). See Stuart, *Hosea-Jonah*, 496.
18. Hoyt, *Amos, Jonah, & Micah*, 495.
19. Calvin, *Commentaries on the Twelve Minor Prophets*, 115.
20. Calvin, 115.
21. Herman Bavinck beautifully captured the Bible's teaching on the interaction between the immutable God and the mutable creation: "The immutability . . . should not be confused with monotonous sameness or rigid immobility. Scripture itself leads us in describing God in the most manifold relations to all his creatures. While immutable in himself, he nevertheless, as it were, lives the life of his creatures and participates in all their changing states. Scripture necessarily speaks of God in anthropomorphic language. Yet, however anthropomorphic its language, it at the same time prohibits us from positing any change in God himself. There is change around, about, and outside of him, and there is change in people's relations to him, but there is no change in God himself. . . . Without losing himself, God can give himself, and, while absolutely maintaining his immutability, he can enter into an infinite number of relations to his creatures." *Reformed Dogmatics, Vol. 2: God and Creation*, trans. John Vriend (Grand Rapids, MI: Baker, 2004), 158, 159. Vriend is not included in chap. 79, note 9 citation for this title
22. Erickson, *Jonah*, 359.
23. To the question of Jonah's "failed" prophecy, it should be noted that prophetic announcements of divine judgment often (though not always) contained an implicit contingency should the threatened party repent and amend their ways (Jeremiah 18:7–10). Many scholars, however, have pointed out the ambiguity of Jonah's

prophecy—"Yet forty days, and Nineveh will be overthrown!" (*nehpāḵeṯ*)—and suggested that the prophecy would be fulfilled either through Nineveh being overturned in destruction (cf. Genesis 19:21) or through Nineveh being overturned (i.e., transformed, cf. Exodus 14:5) in moral reformation. In this latter sense, Nineveh was certainly overturned. See the discussion in Erickson, 372.

### Chapter Thirty-Six: Lessons in Compassion

1. Each of the so-called major prophets (and many of the minor) contain extended sections devoted to oracles (largely) of judgment against the nations. These include Isaiah 13—24 (or 27); Jeremiah 46—51; and Ezekiel 25—32.

2. Ben Zvi, *Signs of Jonah: Reading and Rereading in Ancient Yehud*, Journal for the Study of the Old Testament Supplement Series 367 (Sheffield, UK: Sheffield Academic, 2003), 15; Douglas Stuart, *Hosea-Jonah*, Word Biblical Commentary 31 (Nashville: Thomas Nelson, 1987), 435.

3. Timothy Keller, *The Prodigal God* (New York: Penguin, 2008).

4. Regarding this prophetic purpose of *Jonah*, John Stek writes, "We must ask whether the purpose of God with this mission terminated solely on the Ninevites. Was He perhaps also pressing His claims on His own wayward people by means of this prophetic mission to the notorious and greatly feared Assyrian capital, doing so after the pattern of his blessings upon Gentiles in the days of Elijah and Elisha? It would appear that the prophetic writer of the book of Jonah has answered this question in the affirmative. His narrative concerning this mission, let it be remembered, is addressed to *Israel*." "The Message of the Book of Jonah," *Calvin Theological Journal* 4 (1969): 32 (emphasis original).

5. Stuart, *Hosea-Jonah*, 502. Uriel Simon has noted that the internal accusative "reinforces the contrast between Jonah's negative reaction to the deliverance of the city and the sailors' positive reaction to the deliverance of the ship, it too expressed by an internal accusative (1:16)." *Jonah* (Philadelphia: Jewish Publication Society, 1999), 36. Cf. Hans Walter Wolff, *Obadiah and Jonah: A Commentary*, trans. Margaret Kohl (Minneapolis: Augsburg, 1986), 165. It should be noted that the most likely antecedent of the unexpressed subject ("It was evil") is the notice that God relented from the disaster he had threatened against Nineveh (Jonah 3:10).

6. On the significance of Jonah's silence, see Daniel C. Timmer, *A Gracious and Compassionate God: Mission, Salvation, and Spirituality in the Book of Jonah*, New Studies in Biblical Theology 26 (Downers Grove, IL: InterVarsity Press, 2011), 126.

7. "Psychologically, [Jonah] is motivated by the death wish that assails him whenever the course of his life reaches the end of a blind alley: first, when the storm impeded his flight, and now, when the pardon granted to the wicked city undermines his confidence in the validity of God's judgment." Simon, *Jonah*, 34. Cf. Timmer, *Gracious and Compassionate* God, 124; Landes, "The Kerygma of the Book of Jonah," *Interpretation* 21 (1967): 3–31(4)4; and Stuart, *Hosea-Jonah*, 503.

8. "By including in the story Jonah's admission of the fact that he had fled from God because he knew God was compassionate, the narrator effectively silences all speculation about Jonah's motives. Regardless of any other religious or political notions Jonah may have had, it is evident that he hated the fact that Yahweh was truly consistent in being merciful and patient—that is, consistent *among* the nations as

well as *within* Israel. 'What is God really like?' is thus a more important question in this book than the question 'What was Jonah really like?' About the latter question one may speculate; about the former question the book leaves no doubt: he is a God of grace of whom it is hopeless—indeed hypocritical—to expect a display of grace only to his own people. It was God's grace that Jonah resented so violently; except of course, when he was the recipient." Stuart, *Hosea-Jonah*, 443 (emphasis original), 503.

9. Simon, *Jonah*, 35.

10. See also Numbers 14:18; Nehemiah 9:17; Psalms 86:15; 145:8; Joel 2:13.

11. Simon, *Jonah*, 34–35.

12. Phyllis Trible, *Rhetorical Criticism: Context, Method, and the Book of Jonah* (Minneapolis: Fortress, 1994), 204.

13. Timmer has made the insightful comment, "Since only God has been angry to this point in the book (against Nineveh's sin, 3:9), we might ask ourselves if Jonah is somehow taking to himself divine prerogatives, especially given the enormously different reasons for his and God's anger." *Gracious and Compassionate God*, 119.

14. Commenting on the literary and thematic use of Hebrew *r'h* in 4:1, Wolff observes, "Now—since both Nineveh and God have turned away from their intention—this will to do harm overcomes Jonah. He is especially obsessed with the thought of Nineveh's wickedness, now that God has withdrawn his threat of disaster. Thus the repeated catchword does not merely accentuate Jonah's opposition to God's judgment; it also stresses that Jonah and Nineveh have actually exchanged roles. That it should be God's very mercy that brings 'great wickedness on Jonah' is both dramatic and satiric." *Obadiah and Jonah*, 165.

15. Stuart, *Hosea–Jonah*, 502.

16. Stuart, 503.

17. R. E. Clements, "The Purpose of the Book of Jonah," in *Congress Volume Edinburgh 1974*, Supplements to Vetus Testamentum 28 (Leiden: E. J. Brill, 1975), 16–28. Cf. Zvi, *Signs of Jonah*, 9n24, 103.

18. Anne Lamott, *Bird by Bird* (New York: Anchor, 1994), 22.

19. Stephen Coleman, "Reading Jonah Backwards: Reconsidering a Prophet's Repentance." *Unio Cum Christo* 5 (2019): 158–62.

20. For a helpful discussion of "evil" (Hebrew *r'h*) as a leitmotif in *Jonah*, see Jonathan Magonet, *Form and Meaning: Studies in Literary Techniques in the Book of Jonah* (Sheffield, UK: Almond Press, 1983), 22–25.

21. The expression "who do not know their right hand from their left" (4:11) almost certainly has in view the Ninevites' moral ignorance, perhaps even of a childlike nature. Amy Erickson, *Jonah: Introduction and Commentary* (Grand Rapids, MI: Eerdmans, 2021), 426–27.

22. Bryan Estelle, *Salvation Through Judgment and Mercy* (Phillipsburg, NJ: P&R: 2005), 143.

23. There are an increasing number of scholars who prefer to read Jonah 4:11 as a declarative, "I will not have pity . . ." (e.g., JoAnna M. Hoyt, *Amos, Jonah, & Micah*, Evangelical Exegetical Commentary [Bellingham, WA: Lexham, 2019], 516–22; and Philippe Guillaume, "Rhetorical Reading Redundant: A Response to Ehud Ben Zvi," *JHebS* 9 [2009]: 1–9) rather than a rhetorical question. While either a declarative or interrogative is grammatically possible, the traditional reading of

a rhetorical question is to be preferred based on, among other things, the logic of the divine argument that, in verses 10 and 11, moves from the minor premise to the major premise—what later became known in rabbinic discussions as *qal wahomer*. See Jack Sasson, *Jonah*, Anchor Bible 24B (New York: Doubleday, 1990), 307–9.

### Chapter Thirty-Seven: Judgment Is Coming

1. W. H. Auden, "September 1, 1939," in *Selected Poems* (New York: Vintage, 2007), 95–99. For a discussion of the significance and immense influence of Auden's poem, see Ian Sansom, *September 1, 1939: A Biography of a Poem* (New York: Harper, 2019).

2. "Although Micah veils his autobiographical information, his messages of judgment rest on the lofty ethical standards given to Israel on Sinai (Mic 6:1–8), his messages of hope on God's unchanging faithfulness to Abraham. Rebuffed by his audience (2:6; 6:6–11), this flashing preacher lifted his almost solitary voice from the highest peaks of ethical standards above the clamorous masses." Bruce Waltke, *A Commentary on Micah* (Grand Rapids, MI: Eerdmans, 2007), 2.

3. Many understand Micah's lack of patronymic in 1:1 as an indication that he was largely unknown to the cities to whom he ministered (cf. Isaiah 1:1; Jeremiah 1:1). See, e.g., Stephen G. Dempster, *Micah*, The Two Horizons Old Testament Commentary (Grand Rapids, MI: Eerdmans, 2017), 59.

4. Dempster, *Micah*, 7.

5. Though 701 B.C. is the most likely date for Micah's second oracle in 1:10–16, other possible options are discussed in Dempster, 74n54.

6. Dempster, 75.

7. On the function of the courtroom trial as a sustained metaphor in Micah 1:3–5, see Juan Cruz, *"Who Is Like Yahweh?" A Study of Divine Metaphors in the Book of Micah* (Göttingen: Vandenhoeck & Ruprecht, 2016), 86–89.

8. Walter Vogels, *God's Universal Covenant: A Biblical Study* (Ottawa: University of Ottawa Press, 1986), 67–68. Similarly, Thomas McComiskey and Tremper Longman III, "Micah," in *The Expositor's Bible Commentary*, vol. 8, rev. ed. (Grand Rapids, MI: Zondervan, 2008), 403: "If God does not fail to judge his own, he will certainly judge those who do not belong to them."

9. "Such a summons to the nations is quite appropriate in an oracle which announces impending doom on Israel, because the prophets considered Yahweh's punishment of Israel a model or pattern for Yahweh's future punishment of the nations. The nations are to see Yahweh's *witness against* (accusation of) them (vv. 2–4) in His punishment of His own people (vv. 5–7)." John T. Willis, "Some Suggestions on the Interpretation of Micah I 2," *Vetus Testamentum* (1968): 372–79 (quote on 378, emphasis original). Cf. Waltke, *Commentary on Micah*, 57; contra Cruz, "Who Is Like Yahweh?," 83.

10. See, for example, Hans Walter Wolff, *Micah: A Commentary*, trans. Gary Stansell (Minneapolis: Fortress, 1990), 55; and Francis Andersen and David Noel Freedman, Anchor Bible 24 Doubleday: New York, 2000), 157. However, while admitting the possibility of this reading, John Calvin noted, "There is nothing inconsistent in saying that God descended from his temple." *Commentaries on the Twelve Minor Prophets*, vol. 3, trans. John Owen (Grand Rapids, MI: Baker, 2003), 157–58. Similarly, see Marvin A. Sweeney, *The Twelve Prophets: Micah, Nahum, Habakkuk,*

*Zephaniah, Haggai, Zechariah, and Malachi*, vol. 2. (Collegeville, MN: Liturgical Press), 350.

11. Though the emphasis of the expression *wᵉdārak ʿal-bāmôtê ʾāreṣ* in Micah 1:3 is clearly on divine judgment, Dempster makes the important observation that the expression "to tread upon the high places" is often used "to indicate ownership over the territory of someone: God is the owner of the earth because he treads upon its high places. No one else can do so." *Micah*, 70. Cf. Job 9:8; Amos 4:13.

12. "The rhetorical question 'What is Jacob's rebellion?' might be an echo of Jacob's reply to Laban in Genesis 31:36 *mâ-pišʿî mâ ḥaṭṭāṯî* 'What is my rebellion? What is my sin?' People in Micah's audience might repeat that question pretending that they had no idea of for what the prophet was reproaching them." Johannes C. De Moor, *Micah*, Historical Commentary on the Old Testament (Leuven, Belgium: Peeters, 2020), 66. Cf. Calvin, *Commentaries on the Twelve Minor Prophets*, 163.

13. Micah's use of the interrogative *mî* ("who?") instead of the expected *mâ* ("what?") in 1:5b is a feature of his poetic imagination in which he personifies the capital cities. This metonymically brings into view the city's leadership. See Andersen and Freedman, *Micah*, 173; and Waltke, *Commentary on Micah*, 50.

14. Kathleen Kenyon, *Archaeology in the Holy Land* (London: Ernest Benn, 1960), 265.

15. Ludwig Koehler, Walter Baumgartner and J. J. Stamm, *The Hebrew and Aramaic Lexicon of the Old Testament*, trans. and ed. M. E. J. Richardson, 4 vols. (Leiden: Brill, 1994–1999), 816.

16. See, e.g., De Moor, *Micah*, 68.

17. See, e.g., De Moor, 71.

18. See, e.g., Micah 4:11; 5:1 (Hebrew 4:14); 7:10.

19. The depiction of Samaria as a disgraced woman, stripped and humiliated, is not, as is sometimes suggested, a reference to the unproven notion that such was the punishment for a woman caught in adultery. Rather, as Daniel Smith-Christopher has cogently argued, the stripping naked is a depiction of the common Assyrian and (probably) Babylonian practice of stripping their prisoners to be sent into exile (cf. Isaiah 20:3, 4). *Micah*, The Old Testament Library (Louisville: Westminster John Knox Press, 2015), 57–59. Contra, e.g., Andersen and Freedman, *Micah*, 178.

20. Those who see a reference to temple prostitution include Dempster, *Micah*, 71; Delbert R. Hillers, *Micah* (Philadelphia: Fortress, 1984), 20–21; and Waltke, *Commentary on Micah*, 54. For a popular-level treatment of this common misconception, see Edward Lipiński, "Cult Prostitution in Ancient Israel," *Biblical Archaeological Review* 40:1 (2014): 48–56, 70. For a thorough scholarly treatment of the issue, see Stephanie Lynn Budin, *The Myth of Sacred Prostitution in Antiquity* (Cambridge: Cambridge University Press, 2008).

21. De Moor, *Micah*, 76. However, John Goldingay makes the compelling suggestion that the image of prostitution could refer to "whorish activity by making treaties with people such as the Aramaeans and the Assyrians (which involved recognizing their gods) and profiting in some way from the relationship. So the impressive aids to worship in the sanctuary were the fruit of whoredom." *Hosea-Micah* (Grand Rapids, MI: Baker, 2021), 423. Cf. James Luther Mays, *Micah: A Commentary*, The Old Testament Library (Philadelphia: The Westminster Press, 1976), 47–48.

22. See, e.g., De Moor, *Micah*, 71.

23. This assumes that this prophecy dates to the siege of Sennacherib in 701 B.C. or immediately prior. It is possible, however, that Micah is prophesying long prior to the siege, in which case the devastation of the Judean cities had not yet taken place, but are related as present realities according to prophetic idiom.

24. Contra De Moor, *Micah*, 77. According to Wolff, *Micah*, 58: "Elsewhere the OT states only once that someone goes about 'barefoot and naked'; indeed, it is said of Isaiah (20:2–4)." Cf. Waltke, *Commentary on Micah*, 65; Smith-Christopher, *Micah*, 64.

25. It is widely agreed that the prophet's comment about Beth-Ezel is the most difficult of this section. See, e.g., Hillers, *Micah*, 26; and Mark S. Gignilliat, *Micah: An International Theological Commentary* (London: T&T Clark, 2019), 97. Space does not permit a rehearsal of the nearly countless proposals of interpretation. Needless to say, one should not be dogmatic on the meaning of this half-verse. For the suggestions represented here, see De Moor, *Micah*, 100; JoAnna M. Hoyt, *Amos, Jonah, & Micah*, Evangelical Exegetical Commentary (Bellingham, WA: Lexham, 2019), 613–14; and Gignilliat (above).

26. Hebrew *rekeš* instead of *sûs* (cf. Esther 8:10, 14; Isaiah 2:7; Micah 5:10). See Waltke, *Commentary on Micah*, 79.

27. David Ussishkin, "The Assyrian Attack on Lachish: The Archaeological Evidence from the Southwest Corner of the Site," *TA* 17 (1990): 53–86 (75, 81). It should be noted that Ussishkin's thesis is highly controverted.

28. De Moor, *Micah*, 110.

29. Dempster, *Micah*, 64.

30. The fact that, due to Hezekiah's faith and repentance (Isaiah 37), Jerusalem would not fall until years after Micah prophesied is immaterial to the point at hand.

31. Christopher Wright's description of the prophetic quality of the emotional life of Jeremiah applies equally well to Micah: "Naturally, when we read texts that speak in the first person of weeping, mourning, and crying out, we imagine the prophet himself giving vent to his grief in those ways. And we can be sure that he did. But as we shall see, in many of those texts the words of the prophet and the words of God blend together so closely that it is difficult to be sure who the weeping speaker is. It is not merely that Jeremiah speaks God's words; he also feels God's feelings. The prophet embodies the message to such an extent that his whole person and being—thoughts, feelings, words, actions—vibrate with the whole range of its emotional pitch and tone." *The Message of Jeremiah* (Downers Grove, IL: InterVarsity Press, 2014), 28. Cf. Gignilliat, *Micah*, 93.

32. "Micah, in addition to being the first to see the impending catastrophe and so the first to suffer, is not merely performing a lament ritual, but supplements and completes it by symbolizing Judah as going into exile." Waltke, *Commentary on Micah*, 65.

33. "In the ancient world and the OT, to know someone's name, especially that of God, often meant to enter into an intimate relationship with that person and to share in that person's character or power. To be given a new name was an indication of a new status. And when God's name was applied to a place in the OT (e.g., the temple), it often indicated that his presence was there. When someone gave a name to another person or thing it meant that they possessed that person or thing." G. K. Beale, *The Book of the Revelation: A Commentary on the Greek Text*, New International Greek Testament Commentary (Grand Rapids, MI: Eerdmans, 1999), 254.

34. Martin Luther, *Heidelberg Disputation* (1518), in *Martin Luther's Basic Theological Writings*, ed. Timothy F. Lull (Minneapolis: Fortress, 1989), 42.

Chapter Thirty-Eight: One Word of Truth

1. Though often quoted in this manner, this is a composite quote taken from Solzhenitsyn's Nobel Lecture delivered in 1970. The speech is easily accessible online and may also be found in *The Solzhenitsyn Reader: New and Essential Writings*, ed. Edward E. Ericson Jr. and Daniel J. Mahoney (Wilmington: Intercollegiate Studies Institute, 2006), 512ff.

2. "[*The Gulag Archipelago*] helped to bring down an empire. Its importance can hardly be exaggerated." Doris Lessing, *Sunday Telegraph*, August 31, 1980.

3. Aleksandr I. Solzhenitsyn, *The Gulag Archipelago 1918–1956 An Experiment in Literary Investigation*, 3 vols., trans. Thomas P. Whitney (New York: Harper & Row, 1974, 1975, 1978).

4. Waltke makes the important observation that Micah "has often been called 'the prophet of the poor,' but in fact he is a prophet of the middle class, which he saw being reduced to intractable poverty by the rich (2:1-5, 6-11)." Bruce Waltke, *A Commentary on Micah* (Grand Rapids, MI: Eerdmans, 2007), 3.

5. For a brief and helpful discussion of the connection between lamentation and prophetic woe oracles, see the summary in JoAnna M. Hoyt, *Amos, Jonah, & Micah*, Evangelical Exegetical Commentary (Bellingham, WA: Lexham, 2019), 628–29.

6. Cf. Psalm 21:11; Isaiah 59:6; Ezekiel 11:2. Francis I. Andersen and David Noel Freedman, *Micah: A New Translation with Introduction and Commentary*, Anchor Bible 24E (New York: Doubleday, 2000), 263–64; Mark S. Gignilliat, *Micah: An International Theological Commentary* (London: T&T Clark, 2019), 102.

7. Stephen G. Dempster points to the "phonological cohesion" of verses 1, 2, which suggests "that the criminal activity is working like a smoothly oiled machine: everything is occurring according to plan." *Micah*, The Two Horizons Old Testament Commentary (Grand Rapids, MI: Eerdmans, 2017), 83.

8. Johannes C. De Moor, *Micah*, Historical Commentary on the Old Testament (Leuven, Belgium: Peeters, 2020), 130–31.

9. Daniel Smith-Christopher, *Micah*, The Old Testament Library (Louisville: Westminster John Knox Press, 2015), 82.

10. Gignilliat, *Micah*, 104–5.

11. In contrast to the commandment given in Exodus 20:17, Deuteronomy 5 explicitly mentions "fields" (*śāḏēhû*, cf. Micah 2:2) as an object of illicit desire, another point supporting John Calvin's suggestion that whereas Micah 1 focuses on Israel's violation of the first table of the Law (e.g., 1:7), Micah 2 emphasizes Israel's breach of the second. *Commentaries on the Twelve Minor Prophets*, vol. 3, trans. John Owen (Grand Rapids, MI: Baker, 2003), 184. Cf. Gignilliat, *Micah*, 103.

12. Ehud Ben Zvi, "Wrongdoers, Wrongdoing, and Righting Wrongs in Micah 2," *Biblical Interpretation* 7 (1999): 87–99 (see esp. 88); Delbert R. Hillers, *Micah* (Philadelphia: Fortress, 1984), 33; M. Hoyt, *Amos, Jonah, & Micah*, 632.

13. "*Fields, house,* and *households* are the inheritance of God's people given by God alone who is the sole landowner in Israel (Lev. 25:23; cf. Isa. 5:8; Deut. 5:21)." Gignilliat, *Micah*, 105. Cf. Smith-Christopher, *Micah*, 83.

14. "The economic and social ideal of ancient Israel was of a nation of free landholders—not debt-slaves, share-croppers, or hired workers—secure in possession, as a grant from Yahweh, of enough land to keep their families." Hillers, *Micah*, 33.

15. Hans Walter Wolff, *Micah: A Commentary*, trans. Gary Stansell (Minneapolis: Augsburg, 1990), 73, 79.

16. Contra Ben Zvi, "Wrongdoers," 90, the incongruity between the wicked land barons of verses 1, 2 and the "family" or "clan" (Heb. *hammišpāḥâ*) as the object of God's judgment in Micah 2:3–5 is more apparent than real. As Daniel C. Timmer has noted, those in view in verses 3–5 are further identified as "the proud" or "haughty" (*rômâ*), consistent with the portrait of the land barons in verses 1, 2. *Obadiah, Jonah, and Micah: An Introduction and Commentary*, Tyndale Old Testament Commentaries (Downers Grove, IL: InterVarsity Press, 2021), 132. Furthermore, throughout his prophecies Micah redraws the traditional lines of God's covenant people to represent the realities of the new covenant community (e.g., 4:2). In 2:3, 4 the prophet is simply construing the aforementioned wicked land barons as a "clan" or "family" who will suffer talionic justice and be without representation in the redistribution of the land in the new creation (2:5). Smith-Christopher, *Micah*, 86 argues similarly: "Thus Micah calls this group of greedy elite a 'tribe,' setting themselves over against the legitimate tribes and clans and their rightful expectation of land distribution."

17. The alliteration of the Hebrew of 2:4 is suggestive of the groaning or crying of the oppressors turned oppressed: *wᵉnahâ nᵉhî nihyâ* ("We are utterly ruined").

18. See, e.g., Dempster, *Micah*, 84. It is possible that this taunt originates from their Assyrian captors. So Gignilliat, *Micah*, 111.

19. Gignilliat, *Micah*, 111–12.

20. Solzhenitsyn, *Gulag Archipelago*, vol. 1, 168.

21. Solzhenitsyn, *Gulag Archipelago*, 616.

22. Dempster, *Micah*, 65.

23. Identifying the speakers in Micah 2:6, 7 is an infamous *crux interpretum*. This author follows the configuration of voices suggested by Wolff and others who assigned 2:6, 7a (with the exception of *yaṭṭîpûn*, "they preach" in 2:6a) to the false prophets. Micah then responds to the false prophets in 2:7b: "Is it not so that my words mean well for him who lives uprightly?" Wolff, *Micah*, 68, 73.

24. For the grammatical disagreement between the subject *kᵉlimmôt* and the verb *yissag*, see *Gesenius' Hebrew Grammar*, ed. E. Kautzsch, trans. A. E. Cowley, 2nd ed. (Oxford: Oxford University Press, 1910) §145. Cf. Deuteronomy 32:35; 1 Kings 11:3; Isaiah 8:8; and esp. Jeremiah 23:40. Waltke, *Commentary on Micah*, 113.

25. Gignilliat, *Micah*, 118.

26. Gignilliat, 120.

27. Though verses 12, 13 both describe, from Micah's perspective, events in the future, the verbal forms in 2:13 (two *qatal* verbs followed by three *wayyiqtol*) suggest that the idyllic gathering of the remnant in verse 12 is subsequent to, and in this case the result of, the events in verse 13. Hoyt, *Amos, Jonah, & Micah*, 663.

28. "The sequential situation, *wayyēṣᵉ'û* (*and they will go out through it*), clarifies that the previous action was not by the enemy breaking into the city through its

gate but by I AM and his army breaking out of the enclosed city." Waltke, *Commentary on Micah*, 138. Though his late dating of verses 12, 13 may be safely ignored, see James Luther Mays, *Micah: A Commentary*, The Old Testament Library (Philadelphia: The Westminster Press, 1976), 75–76.

29. Waltke, *Commentary on Micah*, 142.

30. Throughout the Bible, buildings are often connected to bodies. The high priest's vestments, for example, reflect the materials of the tabernacle (cf. Exodus 26; 28), and Jesus identified his body with the temple (John 2:21). The Body of Christ, the Church, is envisioned as a new Jerusalem (Revelation 21:2). Within the larger symbolic and typological world of the Old Testament, the breach in the wall of God's holy city that leads to deliverance may legitimately be connected to and anticipate the body of Christ pierced for our transgressions.

31. Dempster, *Micah*, 99.

### Chapter Thirty-Nine: God's Mountain Ruined and Raised

1. For a discussion of the tabernacle as a "portable Sinai," see Nahum Sarna, *Exodus* (Philadelphia: Jewish Publication Society, 1991), 237; and L. Michael Morales, *Who Shall Ascend the Mountain of the Lord? A Biblical Theology of the Book of Leviticus* (Downers Grove, IL: InterVarsity Press, 2015), 93–100.

2. There is disagreement over whether this was Mount Tabor, Mount Hermon, or possibly another mountain.

3. Bruce Waltke, *A Commentary on Micah* (Grand Rapids, MI: Eerdmans, 2007), 153.

4. If, as some have argued, "house of Israel" and "justice" in Micah 3:1 is an allusion to Hosea 5:1, then this is another example of the prophet connecting the sins of Jerusalem in his day to those of Samaria before her. So, e.g., Mark S. Gignilliat, *Micah: An International Theological Commentary* (London: T&T Clark, 2019), 130.

5. "Micah views these leaders in light of traditions like those recorded in Ex. 18.13–27 and in Deut. 1.9–18, which define their obligation to be righteous judges, free from partiality and impervious to bribery. The right decision was the concern of God himself (Deut. 1.17), *so the righteousness of a judge was an obligation to YHWH*." James L. Mays, *Micah: A Commentary*, The Old Testament Library (Philadelphia: The Westminster Press, 1976), 79 (emphasis mine).

6. The ESV is almost certainly correct in following the LXX in reading $kīšə\,’ēr$ ("like meat," from Greek $hōs\ sarkas$) for $ka\,’^{a}šer$.

7. While open to the metaphorical interpretation adopted here, Andersen and Freedman suggest that 3:2, 3 may be a literal description of violence and perhaps cannibalism attending human sacrifice. See Francis I. Andersen and David Noel Freedman, *Micah: A New Translation with Introduction and Commentary*, Anchor Bible 24E (New York: Doubleday, 2000), 353–54.

8. Mays, *Micah*, 79. Cf. Gignilliat, *Micah*, 132.

9. Gignilliat, *Micah*, 132.

10. Mays, *Micah*, 80.

11. This expression may have in view the biting of a snake, thus elaborating the harm these false prophets cause to the community: "Like malevolent serpents they kill their victims to feed themselves." Waltke, *Commentary on Micah*, 159.

12. For a discussion of the significance of wᵉqiddᵉšû ʿālāyw milḥāmah, ("they sanctify war against him") see Waltke, 161.

13. First Kings 22:23 offers a helpful parallel for understanding the nature of the false prophets in Micah 3:5–7. Yahweh allowed a spiritual being from his heavenly council to be "a lying spirit in the mouth of [Ahab's] prophets," thus misleading Ahab in his plans for war. Though they were no doubt successful in their prophesying for a time, these prophets were eventually exposed as false and Micaiah vindicated when Ahab fell in battle. For other options for understanding the character of the prophets and the nature of their judgment in Micah 3:5–7, see JoAnna M. Hoyt, *Amos, Jonah, & Micah*, Evangelical Exegetical Commentary (Bellingham, WA: Lexham, 2019), 682.

14. Micah certainly has in view money received illicitly, above and beyond the regular tithes.

15. Mays, *Micah*, 83.

16. Micah 3:12 uses the same word ʿiyyîn ("ruins") for Jerusalem as was used for Samaria in 1:6.

17. Dempster has noted the intensifying expansion of desolation from Zion (the name of the Canaanite fort) to Jerusalem (the name of the city) to the mountain (the hill where the city was located). Strikingly, the expression "the mountain of the house" leaves out the expected specification "house *of Yahweh*," which Dempster, following Wolff, has astutely observed suggests the divine abandonment so conspicuous in this section. Stephen G. Dempster, *Micah*, The Two Horizons Old Testament Commentary (Grand Rapids, MI: Eerdmans, 2017), 113. Cf. Hans Walter Wolff, *Micah: A Commentary*, trans. by Gary Stansell (Minneapolis: Augsburg, 1990), 120.

18. Dempster, *Micah*, 129.

19. Dempster, 122.

20. Johannes C. De Moor, *Micah*, Historical Commentary on the Old Testament (Leuven, Belgium: Peeters, 2020), 202.

21. "The place where false leadership, false prophecy, and false teaching were institutionalized will one day become the place where true leadership, true prophecy, and true teaching will be installed since Yahweh in person will teach his ways." Dempster, *Micah*, 122. Cf. De Moor, *Micah*, 205.

22. Daniel Smith-Christopher, *Micah*, The Old Testament Library (Louisville: Westminster John Knox Press, 2015), 131.

23. De Moor, *Micah*, 211.

Chapter Forty: Road to Glory

1. Bruce Waltke, *A Commentary on Micah* (Grand Rapids, MI: Eerdmans, 2007), 234.

2. Some interpret *migdal ʿēder* as a reference to Bethlehem largely on the basis of Genesis 35:21 (e.g., Francis Brown, et al., *The Brown-Driver-Briggs Hebrew and English Lexicon* [1906; repr. Peabody, MA: Hendrickson, 1996], 154; and Marvin A. Sweeney, *The Twelve Prophets: Micah, Nahum, Habakkuk, Zephaniah, Haggai, Zechariah, and Malachi*, vol. 2. [Collegeville, MN: Liturgical Press], 383–84). The identification of *migdal ʿēder* with Bethlehem or a town in its vicinity is tenuous (see Johannes C. De Moor, *Micah*, Historical Commentary on the Old Testament [Leuven, Belgium: Peeters, 2020], 233); and as Francis I. Andersen and David Noel

Freedman observed, "The syntax of . . . *Ophel of Daugher-Zion* is in apposition to *Tower of the Flock*, as if both had the same referential meaning." *Micah: A New Translation with Introduction and Commentary* Anchor Bible 24E (New York: Doubleday, 2000), 439. Cf. Waltke, *Commentary on Micah*, 230–31. JoAnna M. Hoyt has noted its significance as a designation of Jerusalem: "The idea of a tower to watch over a flock is a great picture of what Jerusalem was intended to be. Jerusalem, as the center of the religious life and the government, was responsible for watching over the people and guiding them religiously, socially, and politically. Even though it had not done this job consistently well, its purpose had not been forgotten, and the mere use of this phrase for such a rebellious city provides hope beyond measure." *Amos, Jonah, & Micah*, Evangelical Exegetical Commentary (Bellingham, WA: Lexham, 2019), 709.

3. Mark S. Gignilliat, *Micah: An International Theological Commentary* (London: T&T Clark, 2019), 167; John Goldingay, *Hosea-Micah* (Grand Rapids, MI: Baker, 2021), 455; De Moor, *Micah*, 235–36; Waltke, *Commentary on Micah*, 234. However, Daniel C. Timmer has made the compelling suggestion that "the former dominion" (4:8) may refer to Yahweh's kingship that predated David's reign. *Obadiah, Jonah, and Micah: An Introduction and Commentary*, Tyndale Old Testament Commentaries (Downers Grove, IL: InterVarsity Press, 2021), 169.

4. Of the three kings who reigned during Micah's ministry (Micah 1:1), Ahaz (who ruled 735–715 B.C.) best fits the portrait of the faithless ruler implied in these opening verses (Charles S. Shaw, *The Speeches of Micah: A Rhetorical-Historical Analysis*, Journal for the Study of the Old Testament Supplement Series 145 [Sheffield, UK: JSOT Press, 1993], 156–60), though Hezekiah (who ruled 716–687 B.C.) can't be ruled out. So Delbert R. Hillers, *Micah* (Philadelphia: Fortress, 1984), 59.

5. John Newton, "Amazing Grace," in *Olney Hymns* (1779).

6. Stephen G. Dempster, *Micah*, The Two Horizons Old Testament Commentary (Grand Rapids, MI: Eerdmans, 2017), 135; Hillers, *Micah*, 59.

7. Though Assyria was the presenting threat to Judah at the time, Micah's reference to Babylon draws on the entrenched conception of Babylon as the "epitome of evil and death." As Waltke put it, "What Rome was to the Middle Ages, Babylon was to the ancient Near East. It was the 'Mecca' of the pagan religions, the very antithesis of Jerusalem. From its very commencement it was a type and symbol of pagan imperial power (cf. Gen. 10:10)." *Commentary on Micah*, 247, 248.

8. Waltke, 248.

9. Goldingay, *Hosea-Micah*, 462.

10. John Calvin, *Commentaries on the Twelve Minor Prophets*, vol. 3, trans. John Owen (Grand Rapids, MI: Baker, 2003), 288–89. Reflecting on Calvin's comments, Gignilliat notes that "Calvin requires little to no heavy hermeneutical lifting as he moves from God's speech to ancient Israel to God's current speech to the Church. These two entities share in the same divine economy and thus share in an overlap of substantial identities. When the Church suffers, even because of its own doing, the character of God on display in Mic 4:13 gives heart to the weary." *Micah*, 169.

11. Calvin, *Commentaries on the Twelve Minor Prophets*, 288–89.

12. Calvin, 288–89.

13. For an excellent summary of proposals for interpreting this difficult verse, see Hoyt, *Amos, Jonah, & Micah*, 721–22.

14. Gignilliat, *Micah*, 174.
15. Gignilliat, 174
16. Christian theologians have long interpreted Micah 5:2 [5:1 in Hebrew] as a reference to the eternal generation of the Son from the Father. See, e.g., Herman Bavinck, *Reformed Dogmatics*, vol. 2 (Grand Rapids, MI: Baker, 2004), 275. This interpretation has fallen out of favor in recent years for a number of reasons, some of them exegetical. Space does not permit a rehearsal of arguments for and against this view. As is clear from Bavinck's commentary, he believes that the expressions *miqqeḏem mîmê ʿôlom* ("from of old, from ancient days") in this case likely refer to the Messiah's origins lying in eternity. One contemporary proponent of this view has written, "Not only have Christians not abused this text when allowing it a substantive role in the doctrine of the eternal generation of the Son, but they in fact are reading the text well in light of the Trinitarian subject of Scripture. . . . His [the Son's] processions are from eternity, emerging from the eternal counsel of God's own inner-Trinitarian communication and a singular divine will given to the creation and redemption of the world." Gignilliat, *Micah*, 177, 178. Andersen and Freedman, *Micah*, 467 also come close to this view.
17. For the latter, see Bruce K. Waltke and Michael Patrick O'Connor, *An Introduction to Biblical Hebrew Syntax* (Winona Lake, IN: Eisenbrauns, 1990) §19.5.
18. "Whether 'this' looks forward . . . or backwards to the promised king with 'this' translated as 'he' or 'this one,' the promised peace of 5:5 resists detachment from the promised king of 5:2–4. Jeremias cuts the Gordian knot of this ambiguous phrase by claiming that the coming king is either the mediator of this coming salvation or the personification of it: *he is peace*. Both are grammatically possible." Gignilliat, *Micah*, 182.
19. Waltke, *Commentary on Micah*, 290.
20. Waltke, 291.
21. On the figural reading of Assyria as all that threatens Christ's Church in both the old and new covenants, see Gignilliat, *Micah*, 185.
22. Gignilliat, 187, emphasizes the instrumental function of Israel's work as dew/lion among the nations by appealing to Hosea's use of the same imagery with reference to Yahweh's acts of vengeance and redemption (cf. Hosea 5:14; 14:5).
23. Waltke, *Commentary on Micah*, 317 (emphasis mine).
24. I am grateful to my friend Michael Seufert for this insight.
25. Hoyt, *Amos, Jonah, & Micah*, 747. Cf. Judges 6:28.
26. "Like the surprising list of nations in Amos 1–2, so too here in the final form of Micah's prophetic book, faithless Israel is identified and linked with the nations who did not hear." Gignilliat, *Micah*, 190.

### Chapter Forty-One: And to Walk Humbly with Thy God

1. Martin Luther, *Luther's Works*, vol. 51, ed. and trans. John W. Doberstein (Philadelphia: Muhlenberg Press, 1959), 390–91.
2. Hebrew *rîḇ* (verb 1x; noun 2x) and *yiṯwakkoḥ* (from *ykḥ*).
3. On the legal covenantal function of the prophetic office in Israel see Meredith Kline, *The Structure of Biblical Authority*, rev. ed. (Grand Rapids, MI: Eerdmans, 1975), 57–62.
4. See, e.g., Bruce Waltke, *A Commentary on Micah* (Grand Rapids, MI: Eerdmans, 2007), 14–15; and Daniel C. Timmer, *A Gracious and Compassionate God:*

*Mission, Salvation, and Spirituality in the Book of Jonah*, New Studies in Biblical Theology 26 (Downers Grove, IL: InterVarsity Press, 2011), 93–94.

5. Stephen G. Dempster, *Micah*, The Two Horizons Old Testament Commentary (Grand Rapids, MI: Eerdmans, 2017), 153.

6. That the Lord is speaking to Micah and not Israel is indicated by the singular forms of the imperatives *qûm* and *rîb*.

7. That the natural elements possess this dual function of witness and jury finds its parallel in suzerain vassal treaties that feature divine witnesses who also superintend obedience to the covenant and execute covenant curses upon its breach.

8. See, e.g., George E. Mendenhall, *Law and Covenant in Israel and the Ancient Near East* (Pittsburgh: The Biblical Colloquium, 1955), 34; and Herbert B. Huffmon, "The Covenant Lawsuit in the Prophets." *Journal of Biblical Literature* 78 (1959): 285–95.

9. Huffmon, "Covenant Lawsuit," 292; Dempster, *Micah*, 154.

10. On Deuteronomy 32 as a model of the covenant lawsuit that served as the basis for later prophetic lawsuits, see Meredith Kline, *Treaty of the Great King: The Covenant Structure of Deuteronomy: Studies and Commentary* (Grand Rapids, MI: Eerdmans, 1963), 138–44.

11. Mark S. Gignilliat has astutely observed, "The extremity of mountains and their underworld foundation suggest a merism of the material creation in its entirety, from its highest heights to lowest depths (cf. Isa. 24:18)." *Micah: An International Theological Commentary* (London: T&T Clark, 2019), 194.

12. Waltke, *Commentary on Micah*, 377.

13. See, e.g., Gignilliat, *Micah*, 196; and Waltke, *Commentary on Micah*, 378.

14. "The form is a way of stating a theological axiom of the OT that YHWH is recognized in his historical deeds; they are the revelation of his identity and the occasion of confession actualized in trust and obedience. Such a response is the true answer YHWH seeks in his *rīb*." James L. Mays, *Micah: A Commentary*, The Old Testament Library (Philadelphia: The Westminster Press, 1976), 135.

15. Dempster, *Micah*, 158.

16. Rodney Hutton, "What Happened from Shittim to Gilgal? Law and Gospel in Micah 6:5," *Currents in Theology and Mission* 26 (1998), 94–103; Dempster, *Micah*, 158; Daniel Smith-Christopher, *Micah*, The Old Testament Library (Louisville: Westminster/John Knox, 2015), 192.

17. Mays, *Micah*, 136.

18. Smith-Christopher, *Micah*, 196. Contra Johannes C. de Moor, who argues that *'āḏom* refers to an individual (in this case, King Ahaz). *Micah*, Historical Commentary on the Old Testament (Leuven, Belgium: Peeters, 2020), 294.

19. Contra Mays, Micah, *141*. Cf. Dempster, *Micah*, 159.

20. Mays, *Micah*, 136.

21. In a particularly striking passage, Bruce Waltke summarized the situation as follows: "Outwardly the worshipper appears very religious as he bows before God with gift in hand, but in truth his insulting questions betray a desperately wicked heart. Blinded to God's gracious character and acts, he reasons within his own depraved frame of reference: he need not change, God must change." *Commentary on Micah*, 387.

22. "The pronouncement in v. 8 (from the court?) recalls and outlines the requirement which has always been the appropriate response to YHWH's saving deeds—not sacrifice, but a life submitted to the will of God." Mays, *Micah*, 138.

Chapter Forty-Two: Lamenting in Hope

1. Reading Micah's response as a model for or literary expression of the prayers of the faithful remnant rather than the cry of the nation/city as a whole answers Francis I. Andersen and David Noel Freedman's concern that the prophet's posture is "somewhat distanced from the people since there are descriptions of the evils rampant in society (third person) in vv 2–3 and 6." *Micah: A New Translation with Introduction and Commentary*, Anchor Bible 24E (New York: Doubleday, 2000), 563. On the issues surrounding the speaker in verses 1–7, see discussion under Micah 7:8–20 below.

2. "The use of a lament form ('Woe is me!') and the dropping of direct address ('you') put the reproach under the umbrella of the lament form. The mood is also that of lament. The lament, however, thinly veils that vv 1-4A are in fact an accusation giving the reason for the judgment in vv. 4B-6." Bruce Waltke, *A Commentary on Micah* (Grand Rapids, MI: Eerdmans, 2007), 423.

3. Waltke, 396 has noted the possibility that "A voice" (*qôl*) might be read as an exclamation rather than a construct ("A voice! The Lord cries out . . .").

4. Though some think the prophetic lawsuit in Micah 6:9–16 was originally pronounced against Samaria (e.g., JoAnna M. Hoyt, *Amos, Jonah, & Micah*, Evangelical Exegetical Commentary [Bellingham, WA: Lexham, 2019], 769), largely on the basis of the mention of Omri and Ahab in verse 16, the expression *lāʿîr* ("the city," with a definite article) in verse 9 along with the connection to the concluding liturgy that envisions Jerusalem restored suggest that the southern capital is in view. Cf., e.g., Jeremiah 6:6; 8:16; 17:24; Lamentations 1:19; 2:12; Ezekiel 4:3; 5:2; 7:15. Also James Luther Mays, *Micah: A Commentary*, The Old Testament Library (Philadelphia: The Westminster Press, 1976), 149; and Hans Walter Wolff, *Micah: A Commentary*, trans. by Gary Stansell (Minneapolis: Augsburg, 1990), 190.

5. John Goldingay, *Hosea-Micah* (Grand Rapids, MI: Baker, 2021), 476.

6. See the discussion of Andersen and Freedman, *Micah*, 544–46.

7. Mays, *Micah*, 147.

8. Following Hoyt's rendering of *heḥĕlêtî* as "to make sick," the general term for sickness brings into view the covenant curses that describe physical illness (e.g., Leviticus 26:16; Deuteronomy 28:22, 27, 59–61). *Amos, Jonah, & Micah*, 773–74.

9. Waltke, *Commentary on Micah*, 407; Hoyt, *Amos, Jonah, & Micah*, 769.

10. Cf. Deuteronomy 28:15–68. Hoyt, *Amos, Jonah, & Micah*, 773–76.

11. "The very fabric of the community whose ideal and shared goal was the rest and human flourishing of the promised land has broken down. They have been shown *the good* but exist in its very opposite: the house of wickedness." Mark S. Gignilliat, *Micah: An International Theological Commentary* (London: T&T Clark, 2019), 210.

12. Leviticus 18:4–5; 26:3; Deuteronomy 6:2; 8:6; 19:9; 30:10. Hoyt, *Amos, Jonah, & Micah*, 775.

13. Though some read wᵉ*ḥerpaṯ ʿammî tiśśāʾû* (literally, "and the scorn/reproach of my people you will bear," 6:16, AT) as a subjective genitive in which the "you" is

the object of "my people's scorn" (see, e.g., Johannes C. De Moor, *Micah*, Historical Commentary on the Old Testament [Leuven, Belgium: Peeters, 2020], 314–15; Delbert R. Hillers, *Micah* [Philadelphia: Fortress, 1984], 82; Mays amends *ammî* to *ammîm* following LXX, *Micah*, 148; Andersen and Freedman argue a mediating position, *Micah*, 550, 560), the more likely meaning is as an objective genitive in which the "you" is identical with "my people" and the sense is "the scorn that (you) my people (deserve)." See, e.g., John Calvin, *Commentaries on the Twelve Minor Prophets*, vol. 3, trans. John Owen (Grand Rapids, MI: Baker, 2003), 358–59; Hoyt, *Amos, Jonah, & Micah*, 775–76; and Waltke, *Commentary on Micah*, 406. This interpretation understands verse 16 as following the general progression of the covenant curses of Deuteronomy 28. Micah's use of *šammâ* ("desolation" or "horror") in 6:16 echoes Moses's use of the same word in Deuteronomy 28:37. Interestingly, both follow a list of futility curses (Deuteronomy 28:30–35; Micah 6:13–15).

14. "There is still a future beyond the punishment as long as eternal, omnicompetent *I AM* owns them as his people." Waltke, *Commentary on Micah*, 414 (emphasis original).

15. Goldingay, *Hosea-Micah*, 483.

16. Commentators are divided on whether verse 7 concludes the preceding unit (vv. 1–6) or opens the following unit (vv. 8–20). Following Hillers (among others), I take the *wa'ănî* of verse 7 as a strong disjunctive establishing a contrast between the speaker's hope and the hopelessness of the city described in the prior verses (cf. Habakkuk 3:18). Hillers's qualification, however, is helpful: "Of course, even if v. 7 belongs with the foregoing, it may still serve as a bridge to vv. 8-20." *Micah*, 85. Similarly, Waltke, *Commentary on Micah*, 429–31.

17. John Newton, "Glorious Things of Thee Are Spoken," in *Olney Hymns* (1779).

Chapter Forty-Three: A Liturgy of Hope

1. Delbert R. Hillers, *Micah* (Philadelphia: Fortress, 1984), 89.

2. See, e.g., Johannes C. De Moor, *Micah*, Historical Commentary on the Old Testament (Leuven, Belgium: Peeters, 2020), 351.

3. Though De Moor, *Micah*, 354 cites a number of medieval manuscripts that attest to the masculine singular pronominal suffix *'ĕlōhekā*, these are almost certainly instances of scribal correction. It is more likely that the feminine form (*'ĕlōhāyik*) would give rise to the correction to the masculine than the other way around.

4. Mark S. Gignilliat, *Micah: An International Theological Commentary* (London: T&T Clark, 2019), 224–25; John Goldingay, *Hosea-Micah* (Grand Rapids, MI: Baker, 2021), 485; Hillers, *Micah*, 90; Stephen G. Dempster, *Micah*, The Two Horizons Old Testament Commentary (Grand Rapids, MI: Eerdmans, 2017), 183; Hans Walter Wolff, *Micah: A Commentary*, trans. Gary Stansell (Minneapolis: Fortress, 1990), 215. Interestingly, the Targum adds, "Jerusalem says . . ." at the beginning of verse 9.

5. John Calvin, *Commentaries on the Twelve Minor Prophets*, vol. 3, trans. John Owen (Grand Rapids, MI: Baker, 2003), 373.

6. The identification of Micah 7:8–20 as a liturgy is not meant to underwrite Hermann Gunkel's famous thesis of the independence and cultic origin of the piece ("The Close of Micah: A Prophetical Liturgy," in *What Remains of the Old Testa-*

*ment and Other Essays*, trans. A. K. Dallas [New York: Macmillan, 1928], 115–49), but only to highlight the dialogical (e.g., vv. 14, 15) and doxological qualities of the text. As Gignilliat has observed, "The recognition of the liturgical or Psalm-like character of Micah's ending aids in understanding this final section as a fitting response to the hard passage leading to the book's end." *Micah*, 223–24.

7. Goldingay, *Hosea-Micah*, 485.

8. Cf. Lamentations 3:58: "You have taken up my lawsuit, O Lord; you have redeemed my life" (author's translation).

9. "As the 'light' of his community, Yahweh liberates it not only from its enemies (v. 8), but even more from its own guilt (v. 9a)." Wolff, *Micah*, 221.

10. Wolff, 223 notes that the collocation of the Hebrew *r'h* with the preposition *b-* emphasizes the "intensity of the experience of 'seeing.'" He says, "What is seen becomes a feast for the eyes; the view is pleasing."

11. Gignilliat, *Micah*, 225.

12. Dempster, *Micah*, 181–82. Speaking of 7:11–13, Goldingay notes, "Once again there is no formal connection between the subsections, but there is a substantial link in that the promises that follow [i.e., vv. 11–13] can be seen as a response to the confession of faith and confession of sin in vv. 8–10." *Hosea-Micah*, 487.

13. See, e.g., James Luther Mays, *Micah: A Commentary*, The Old Testament Library (Philadelphia: The Westminster Press, 1976), 162; Wolff, *Micah*, 224. This view is also suggested by the Targum.

14. Gignilliat, *Micah*, 226; Dempster, *Micah*, 184–85.

15. "The picture of God as shepherd recalls the same imagery in 2:12 and 5:4; thus this imagery occurs in each of the three 'hope' sections of the Micah book." James Limburg, *Hosea—Micah* (Atlanta: John Knox, 1988), 194.

16. See, e.g., "The Laws of Hammurabi," trans. Martha Roth, in *The Context of Scripture*, vol. 2 (Leiden: Brill, 2003), 336.

17. "The Exodus of Israel's past is in mimetic relation to [God's] future deliverance of his people. In those future moments, tethered as they are to the wonderous deeds of the past, Yhwh will go before them (2 Sam 5:24; Mic. 2:12-13)." Gignilliat, *Micah*, 228. For a thorough analysis of the exodus motif in the Bible, see Bryan Estelle, *Echoes of Exodus: Tracing a Biblical Motif* (Downers Grove, IL: InterVarsity Press, 2018). For allusions to the exodus in Micah 7:7–20, see Lesley DiFransico, "'He Will Cast Their Sins into the Depths of the Sea . . .' Exodus Allusions and the Personification of Sin in Micah 7:7-20," *VT* 67 (2017): 187–203. Cf. Waltke, *Commentary on Micah*, 450.

18. Gignilliat, *Micah*, 230. This is an important link to the exodus motif in the previous section (Micah 7:14–17) that is further developed in 7:19. Waltke has made the important observation: "When Israel's prophets imply the existence of other gods, such as Micah does in his question 'Who is a god like you?' they are using religious language, not catechetical teaching that recognizes their ontological reality." *Commentary on Micah*, 463.

19. It is widely agreed that Micah's name (Hebrew *mîkâ*) is a shortened version of *mîkāyâ*, meaning "Who is like Yah(weh)?" The long form is attested in the northern prophet Micaiah ben Imlah (1 Kings 22:8; 2 Chronicles 18:7).

20. DiFransico, "He Will Cast Their Sins," 197.

21. Waltke, *Commentary on Micah*, 1.

22. For a detailed discussion of Micah's conceptualization and personification of sin as an enemy to be overcome and destroyed, see DiFransico, "He Will Cast Their Sins," 200–201.
23. Dempster, *Micah*, 184; Wolff, *Micah*, 222–23. Cf. 1 Kings 18:27; Psalms 42:3; 115:2; Joel 2:17.
24. Goldingay, *Hosea-Micah*, 486.
25. For a discussion of this central theme of "seeing" in Micah 7:8–20, see Dempster, *Micah*, 182.

Chapter Forty-Four: A Stronghold in the Day of Trouble

1. See, e.g., Dan Timmer, *Nahum: The Divine Warrior as Avenger and Deliverer* (Grand Rapids, MI: Zondervan, 2020), 50–51; and Tremper Longman III, "Nahum," in *The Minor Prophets*, vol. 2, ed. Thomas McComiskey (Grand Rapids, MI: Baker, 2004), 778.
2. The following taxonomy is derived from Longman, "Nahum," 788.
3. Longman, 788.
4. Though it is generally agreed that Nahum's ministry must have fallen somewhere between the fall of Thebes (663 B.C.; cf. Nahum 3:8) and the fall of Nineveh (612 B.C., clearly still envisioned as a future event), 1:12 strongly suggests a date leading up to or during the reign of Assurbanipal (c. 668–c. 631?), during whose reign Assyria could be said to be "at full strength" and after whose reign Assyria was clearly on the decline as a military and political force. See, e.g., Thomas Renz, *The Books of Nahum, Habakkuk, and Zephaniah* (Grand Rapids, MI: Eerdmans, 2021), 41; and Longman, "Nahum," 798. Dates for Neo-Assyrian kings follow Amélie Kuhrt, *The Ancient Near East: c. 3000-300 B.C.* (New York: Routledge, 1995), 479.
5. Renz, *Books of Nahum, Habakkuk, and Zephaniah*, 42.
6. Francis Brown, et al., *The Brown-Driver-Briggs Hebrew and English Lexicon* (1906; repr. Peabody, MA: Hendrickson, 1996), 637.
7. "Just as jealousy can be regarded as an aspect of love, vengeance is related to justice." Klaas Spronk, *Nahum*, Historical Commentary on the Old Testament (Leuven, Belgium: Peeters, 1997), 34.
8. J. J. M. Roberts, *Nahum, Habakkuk, and Zephaniah: A Commentary*, The Old Testament Library (Louisville: Westminster John Knox Press, 1991), 49.
9. Roberts, *Nahum, Habakkuk, and Zephaniah*, 49.
10. E.g., Renz, *Books of Nahum, Habakkuk, and Zephaniah*, 63; Duane L. Christensen, *Nahum: A New Translation with Introduction and Commentary*, Anchor Bible 24F (New Haven: Yale, 2009), 176; Walter A. Maier, *The Book of Nahum: A Commentary* (St. Louis: Concordia, 1959), 149. The root *qn'* only occurs twice as the adjective *qannô* (cf. Joshua 24:19; the spelling *qannā'* is more common); however, based on the sense of the noun *qin'āh*, the Jewish Publication Society's translation "passionate" probably strains the semantic range of this adjective.
11. See, e.g., Longman, "Nahum," 788; O. Palmer Robertson, *Books of Nahum, Habakkuk, and Zephaniah*, New International Commentary on the Old Testament (Grand Rapids, MI: Eerdmans, 1990), 60; and Renz, *Books of Nahum, Habakkuk, and Zephaniah*, 67.
12. Renz, *Books of Nahum, Habakkuk, and Zephaniah*, 69.
13. Renz, 70.

14. Elizabeth Achtemeier, *Nahum—Malachi*, Interpretation (Louisville: Westminster John Knox Press, 1986), 8.

15. On the basis of Isaiah 2:12ff., Spronk suggests that Bashan was also associated with the pride often produced by amassing great wealth. *Nahum*, 41.

16. Though there is much debate about the presence of an acrostic in Nahum 1:2–8, that the appearance of Hebrew *'aleph* through *kaph* (minus *daleth*) at the beginning of the poetic lines is a coincidence seems to strain credulity (e.g., Alfred O. Haldar, *Studies in the Book of Nahum* [Upsala: Lundequist, 1947]). For a recent defense of the position that the prophet intentionally included a broken acrostic, see Thomas Renz, "A Perfectly Broken Acrostic in Nahum 1?" *JHebS* 9 (2009): 1–26. Cf. Timmer, *Nahum*, 72–73; Longman, "Nahum," 773, 775.

17. Longman, "Nahum," 775.

18. "The reference to *clouds* as *the dust of his feet* stresses the majesty and transcendence of YHWH because it situates YHWH well above the clouds. We could think of the clouds in the sky as the mere footstool of YHWH's throne." Renz, *Books of Nahum, Habakkuk, and Zephaniah*, 71.

19. Robertson, *Books of Nahum, Habakkuk, and Zephaniah*, 71.

20. Renz, *Books of Nahum, Habakkuk, and Zephaniah*, 78.

21. Though Nineveh is clearly at the center of the book, "the opening hymn reaches far beyond the borders of the Assyrian empire and gives the whole a universal scope." Timmer, *Nahum*, 67. It is notable that Nineveh is not mentioned by name in the opening hymn, a feature that implies that God's imminent judgment of the Assyrian capital has cosmic implications.

22. The following is based on the work and insights of, among others, Meredith G. Kline. See, e.g., "The Intrusion and the Decalogue," *Westminster Theological Journal* 16.1 (1953): 1–22.

23. Spronk, *Nahum*, 15.

## Chapter Forty-Five: The Exalted Will Fall, and the Fallen Will Be Exalted

1. Martin Luther, quoted in Gerhard von Rad, *Old Testament Theology*, vol. 2, trans. D. M. G. Stalker (New York: Harper & Row, 1965), 33.

2. Especially verse 10. See Duane L. Christensen, *Nahum: A New Translation with Introduction and Commentary*, Anchor Bible 24F (New Haven: Yale, 2009), 205ff.

3. Related is the thorny issue of numerous pronouns, the antecedents of which are unspecified and at times ambiguous. Tremper Longman III suggests a literary and rhetorical motivation for this, as the postponement of clear referents builds suspense with the effect that it "gives interest to the story and opens up the book to much broader application." "Nahum," in *The Minor Prophets*, vol. 2, ed. Thomas McComiskey (Grand Rapids, MI: Baker, 2004), 795.

4. Longman, "Nahum," 295.

5. The "you" here is masculine plural. It is also possible to take the Hebrew *mah* as an indefinite ("*whatever* you plot against the Lord"; so Christensen, *Nahum*, 201) rather than an interrogative. Cf. Bruce K. Waltke and Michael Patrick O'Connor, *An Introduction to Biblical Hebrew Syntax* (Winona Lake, IN: Eisenbrauns, 1990) § 18.3.e; GKC §137.c.

6. Commentators are divided over the referent of the pronoun "you." Some take it as referring to Judah and thus translate the verb *tᵉḥaššᵉḇûn* (from *ḥšb*) as "think" or "ponder about." Thus Thomas Renz translates the line, "What do you ponder concerning YHWH?" *The Books of Nahum, Habakkuk, and Zephaniah* (Grand Rapids, MI: Eerdmans, 2021), 84. Similarly, C. F. Keil and Franz Delitzsch, *The Twelve Minor Prophets*, vol. 10, trans James Martin (Edinburgh: T&T Clark, 1874; repr. Peabody, MA: Hendrickson, 2001), 360; J. J. M. Roberts, *Nahum, Habakkuk, and Zephaniah: A Commentary*, The Old Testament Library (Louisville: Westminster/ John Knox, 1991), 52–53; and O. Palmer Robertson, *The Books of Nahum, Habakkuk, and Zephaniah*, New International Commentary on the Old Testament (Grand Rapids, MI: Eerdmans, 1990), 72–73. While this reading is possible, it seems more likely (to this author at least) that the referent is to the Assyrians and, by extension, all enemies of Yahweh. Variant preposition (*'al* vs. *'el*; cf. Genesis 4:8; 22:12; Numbers 32:14) and direct object (cf. 2 Samuel 14:13) collocation notwithstanding, the same verb is used in Nahum 1:11 with the meaning "plot against." Furthermore, verse 11 serves to explicate the meaning of verse 9, according to Klaas Spronk, *Nahum*, Historical Commentary on the Old Testament (Leuven, Belgium: Peeters, 1997), 51. This was the understanding of the translators of the LXX, who rendered the expression *logizesthe epi* ("calculate against"). Spronk is almost certainly correct when he writes, "The question is directed at the opponents of YHWH," 51. Similarly, Christensen, *Nahum*, 201; and Longman, "Nahum," 795–96.

7. Though it is not perfectly clear what the first trouble (implied by the expression "trouble will not rise up a second time") would be, the common suggestion that it has in view the siege of Sennacherib in 701 B.C. is plausible. See e.g., Longman, "Nahum," 796. Spronk, however, prefers "a more general meaning . . . the enemies of YHWH do not get the opportunity to recover (cf. Ps. 18:39)." *Nahum*, 53.

8. Robertson, *Books of Nahum, Habakkuk, and Zephaniah*, 69.

9. On a cylinder commemorating campaigns against Egypt, Syria, and Palestine, Assurbanipal boasted of such oppressive measures: "[I] took the shortest road to Egypt and Nubia. During my march 22 kings from the seashore, the islands and the mainland . . . [including] Manasseh king of Judah . . . servants who belong to me, brought heavy gifts to me and kissed my feet. I made these kings accompany my army over the land—as well as over the sea-route with their armed forces and their ships." James B. Pritchard, *Ancient Near Eastern Texts Relating to the Old Testament*, 3rd ed. (Princeton, NJ: Princeton University Press, 1969), 294.

10. See note 7 above.

11. "It was a high priority of a king to ensure an heir to the throne and a peaceful succession. Also, there is evidence that in Mesopotamia, as in Canaan, it was the responsibility of the son to care for the corpse of his father." Longman, "Nahum," 799.

12. "The implication of Yahweh preparing the grave would appear to underscore the lack of anyone else to perform the task. There is no family left, and the dead ruler is too despised for anyone else to bother with his burial." Roberts, *Nahum, Habakkuk, and Zephaniah*, 54.

13. For a discussion of the numerous and illuminating parallels between Nahum and Neo-Assyrian treaty curses, see Kevin J. Cathcart, "Treaty-Curses and the Book of Nahum," *Catholic Bible Quarterly* 35 (1973): 179–87 (here, 180–81).

14. Cf. Romans 10:15. Robertson, *Nahum, Habakkuk, and Zephaniah*, 83.

15. Contra Longman who restricts the referent solely to Assyria itself. "Nahum," 800.

16. The historical referent of "the scatterer" (Hebrew *mēpîṣ*) is unclear. Spronk was certainly correct when he wrote, "The most important thing the poet wanted to make clear is that the one who is going to besiege Nineveh is sent by YHWH. The verb used here leaves open the possibility that it is YHWH who is coming himself." *Nahum*, 83. Similarly, Longman, "Nahum," 801; and Roberts, *Nahum, Habakkuk, and Zephaniah*, 64.

17. Gregory Cook argues that Israel's spiritually adulterous relationship with Nineveh serves as the context of Nahum's oracles against Assyria. "Covenant Sin in Nahum," *Journal for the Evangelical Study of the Old Testament* 6.1 (2020): 1–10.

18. For an excellent discussion of the symbolic and typological role of Assyria's destruction, see Robertson, *Books of Nahum, Habakkuk, and Zephaniah*, 83–84.

19. "Everyone is familiar . . . with those deliverances that last only a short time. But the prophet promises the end of this ceaseless round of troubles. But of course, there are the Babylonians. The Assyrians may be wiped from the face of the earth, but demons seven times worse emerge in the form of the Babylonian oppressors. This kind of problem in understanding prophetic promises necessitates an ultimate deliverance that shall break the bonds of the Old Testament teaching models. God's word is true, and all its fulness shall be realized. In the final analysis, this realization comes only on the occasion of the replacing of the old covenant forms with the new covenant realities." Robertson, 74.

## Chapter Forty-Six: God's Victory over the Pride of Man

1. Jasper Copping, "Unseen Interviews with WW1 Veterans Recount the Horror of the Trenches," The Telegraph Media Group, March 6, 2014; www.telegraph/history/world-war-one/10681656/Unseen-interviews-with-WW1–veterans-recount-the-horror-of-the-trenches.html.

2. There is admittedly little by way of consensus regarding the beginning of this pericope. I've followed Tremper Longman III, who delineates a new unit at 2:3 [Hebrew 2:4] on the basis of form and genre considerations. "Nahum," in *The Minor Prophets*, vol. 2, ed. Thomas McComiskey (Grand Rapids, MI: Baker, 2004), 769, 804. Note, for example, the shift from second-person to third-person pronominal suffixes.

3. Dan Timmer, *Nahum: The Divine Warrior as Avenger and Deliverer* (Grand Rapids, MI: Zondervan, 2020), 174–75.

4. "This shatterer is God, working his will through the conflicts of nations, restoring in his jealousy (cf. 1:2) his covenant people whom Assyria has plundered." Elizabeth Achtemeier, *Nahum—Malachi*, Interpretation (Louisville: Westminster/John Knox, 1986), 20. Cf. Timmer, *Nahum*, 122.

5. Thomas Renz, *The Books of Nahum, Habakkuk, and Zephaniah* (Grand Rapids, MI: Eerdmans, 2021), 123.

6. Renz, *Books of Nahum, Habakkuk, and Zephaniah*, 118 explains the sticky issue of verb-form variation throughout the passage (*yiqtol* and *qatal*) with reference to the rhetorical effect of drawing readers into the drama of the events as they unfold.

7. It is also possible that Nahum is depicting the enemy (i.e., Babylonian) chariots racing through the streets of Nineveh and that verse 4 is dischronologized

from verse 5, a phenomenon not uncommon in either Hebrew prose or poetry. So Klaas Spronk, *Nahum*, Historical Commentary on the Old Testament (Leuven, Belgium: Peeters, 1997), 91–92. Renz has made the compelling suggestion that the text is intentionally ambiguous about which army is racing through the streets, an ambiguity that captures something of the chaos of warfare. *Books of Nahum, Habakkuk, and* Zephaniah, 117–18. Regardless of the referent (i.e., Assyrians, Babylonians, or uncertain), the adumbration of the advent of the divine warrior still stands.

8. Achtemeier, *Nahum—Malachi*, 19–20.
9. Achtemeier, 21.
10. Timmer, *Nahum*, 178.
11. For a comprehensive treatment of leonine imagery in the Old Testament, see Brent Strawn's monumental work, *What Is Stronger Than a Lion? Leonine Image and Metaphor in the Hebrew Bible and the Ancient Near East*, Orbis biblicus et orientalis 212 (Göttingen: Vandenhoeck & Ruprecht, 2005). While it is true that many nations represented themselves and their rulers with leonine imagery and rhetoric, Assyria demonstrated a unique emphasis on this symbol among ancient Near East kingdoms and cultures. See G. Johannes Bötterweck, "ארי," in *Theological Dictionary of the Old Testament*, 1:374–87. For a discussion of the Neo-Assyrian sources and their connection to Nahum 2:11–13 in particular, see Gordon H. Johnston, "Nahum's Rhetorical Allusions to the Neo-Assyrian Lion Motif," *Bibliotheca Sacra* (2001): 287–307.
12. Cf. Isaiah 5:29–30. Also Strawn, *What Is Stronger*, 52; and J. J. M. Roberts, *Nahum, Habakkuk, and Zephaniah: A Commentary*, The Old Testament Library (Louisville: Westminster John Knox Press, 1991), 67.
13. To be sure, leonine imagery was employed as a symbol for other rapacious nations as well; for example, Babylon in Jeremiah 51:38, and even wicked Israel and Judah in Ezekiel 19:2–9.
14. Duane L. Christensen, *Nahum: A New Translation with Introduction and Commentary*, Anchor Bible 24F (New Haven, CT: Yale, 2009), 317; following Paul Humbert's thesis: "Die Herausforderungsformel 'hinnenî êlékâ,' " *Zeitschrift für die alttestamentliche Wissenschaft* (1933), 101–8.
15. Timmer, *Nahum*, 178.
16. Martin Luther quote adapted from Carolyn M. Schneider, *I Am a Christian: The Nun, the Devil, and Martin Luther* (Minneapolis: Fortress, 2010), 148. For source, see WA, Tr 2:131–32.

Chapter Forty-Seven: He Put Them to Open Shame

1. Klaas Spronk, *Nahum*, Historical Commentary on the Old Testament (Leuven, Belgium: Peeters, 1997), 117.
2. James D. Nogalski, *The Book of the Twelve: Micah-Malachi* (Macon, GA: Smyth & Helwys, 2011), 628.
3. Duane L. Christensen, *Nahum*, Anchor Bible 24F (New Haven, CT: Yale, 2009), 346.
4. "It is not merely that the city has slipped occasionally into these abuses. Instead, the poisonous vapors diffusing from every heart pollute the total atmosphere of the community." O. Palmer Robertson, *The Books of Nahum, Habakkuk, and*

*Zephaniah*, New International Commentary on the Old Testament (Grand Rapids, MI: Eerdmans, 1990), 100.

5. Cited in James H. Pritchard, ed., *Ancient Near Eastern Texts Relating to the Old Testament*, 3rd ed. with supplement (Princeton, NJ: Princeton University Press, 2016), 174.

6. Regarding verses 1–4, Jerome commented that no translation can do justice to the beauty of its language. Spronk, *Nahum*, 115.

7. Spronk, 119.

8. J. J. M. Roberts, *Nahum, Habakkuk, and Zephaniah: A Commentary*, The Old Testament Library (Louisville: Westminster/John Knox, 1991), 72–73.

9. Elizabeth Achtemeier, *Nahum—Malachi*, Interpretation (Louisville: Westminster John Knox Press, 1986), 23.

10. Achtemeier, *Nahum—Malachi*, 24.

11. For a discussion of the religious component of Assyria's imperialism, see Daniel C. Timmer, "Nahum's Representation of and Response to Neo-Assyria: Imperialism as a Multifaceted Point of Contact in Nahum," *Bulletin for Biblical Research* 24 (2014): 349. An excellent summary may be found in the same author's commentary, Dan Timmer, *Nahum: The Divine Warrior as Avenger and Deliverer*, Exegetical Commentary on the Old Testament (Grand Rapids, MI: Zondervan, 2020), 37.

12. John Newton, "Glorious Things of Thee Are Spoken," in *Olney Hymns* (1779).

13. Spronk, *Nahum*, 124.

14. See, e.g., Peter Martyr Vermigli, *In Primum Librum Mosis* (1569), 18r, translated in *Genesis 1-11*, Reformation Commentary on Scripture, OT 1 (Downers Grove, IL: InterVarsity Press, 2012), 176; Bruce Waltke with Cathi J. Fredricks, *Genesis: A Commentary* (Grand Rapids, MI: Zondervan, 2001), 95; and Meredith G. Kline, *Genesis: A New Commentary* (Peabody, MA: Hendrickson, 2016), 24.

Chapter Forty-Eight: A History Lesson

1. Percy Bysshe Shelly, "Ozymandias," public domain. Originally published in *The Examiner*, London, 1818.

2. See https://www.cnn.com/2019/09/30/asia/china-oct-1-national-day-intl-hnk/index.html.

3. Contra Thomas Renz, *The Books of Nahum, Habakkuk, and Zephaniah* (Grand Rapids, MI: Eerdmans, 2021), 170–71, the ESV is almost certainly correct in following the LXX reading *boēthoi autēs* ("her helpers," Hebrew $b^{e c}ezrā\underline{t}āh$) instead of $b^{e c}ezrā\underline{t}ēk$ ("your helpers"), which would imply Put and Libyans were on the side of the Assyrians. This reading is also found in the Targums, Peshitta, and some manuscripts of the Vulgate. Duane L. Christensen, *Nahum: A New Translation with Introduction and Commentary*, Anchor Bible 24F (New Haven, CT: Yale, 2009), 356; Klaas Spronk, *Nahum*, Historical Commentary on the Old Testament (Leuven, Belgium: Peeters, 1997), 130.

4. Spronk, *Nahum*, 130.

5. Cf. Genesis 12:3. Also Christensen, *Nahum*, 354; and Renz, *Books of Nahum, Habakkuk, and Zephaniah*, 167.

6. Some scholars suggest that Nahum's portrayal of Thebes is rhetorically designed to evoke Nineveh, especially its emphasis on its water fortifications. So Renz, *Books of Nahum, Habakkuk, and Zephaniah*, 168–69 citing the work of John R.

Huddlestun, "Nahum, Nineveh, and the Nile: The Description of Thebes in Nahum 3:8-9," *Journal of Near Eastern Studies* 62 (2003): 97–110.

7. Translation following Longman, esp. his rendering of *naʿălāmâ* as "to pass out." "Nahum," 822.

8. Dan Timmer, *Nahum: The Divine Warrior as Avenger and Deliverer*, Exegetical Commentary on the Old Testament (Grand Rapids, MI: Zondervan, 2020), 180.

9. Elizabeth Achtemeier, *Nahum—Malachi*, Interpretation (Louisville: Westminster/John Knox, 1986), 26–27; Christensen, *Nahum*, 361, 369–71.

10. For a comprehensive (though dated) treatment of this important ancient Near East legal phenomenon, see Tikva Simone Frymer-Kensky, "The Judicial Ordeal in the Ancient Near East" (unpublished PhD dissertation, Yale University, 1977).

11. Achtemeier, *Nahum-Malachi*, 27; Christensen, *Nahum*, 370.

## Chapter Forty-Nine: And Death Shall Be No More

1. Though the exact date of Nahum's prophecies is unknown, the internal evidence of Assyria being "at full strength and many" (1:12) strongly suggests a mid-seventh-century date, most likely during the reign of Assurbanipal (669–631 B.C., with 663 being the *terminus post quem* and 612 being the *terminus ante quem*, see chap. 44, note 4 above). The reign of Assurbanipal is considered by many scholars to be the zenith of Assyria's might and prosperity.

2. Martin Luther, "A Mighty Fortress Is Our God" (1529).

3. Thomas Renz, *The Books of Nahum, Habakkuk, and Zephaniah* (Grand Rapids, MI: Eerdmans, 2021), 181.

4. Hebrew *šām* is placed at the beginning of the clause for emphasis.

5. Tremper Longman III, "Nahum," in *The Minor Prophets*, vol. 2, ed. Thomas McComiskey (Grand Rapids, MI: Baker, 2004), 823.

6. Duane L. Christensen, *Nahum: A New Translation with Introduction and Commentary*, Anchor Bible 24F (New Haven, CT: Yale, 2009), 394.

7. John D. Whiting, quoted in John D. Whiting, quoted in Christensen, *Nahum*, 394.

8. Dan Timmer has noted, "The fall of Assyria is a faint shadow of the judgment that looms over all who are unreconciled to God (John 3:18)." *Nahum: The Divine Warrior as Avenger and Deliverer*, Exegetical Commentary on the Old Testament (Grand Rapids, MI: Zondervan, 2020), 177.

9. O. Palmer Robertson astutely noted that the variation in the masculine and feminine forms *hitkabbēḏ* and *hitkabbeḏî* suggests "the greatest possible fulness, or the totality of the nation in all its respects." *The Books of Nahum, Habakkuk, and Zephaniah*, New International Commentary on the Old Testament (Grand Rapids, MI: Eerdmans, 1990), 125. Cf. GKC §110k. Contra Timmer, *Nahum*, 169n96.

10. Cat Quine, "Nineveh's Pretensions to Divine Power in Nahum 3:16," *VT* 69 (2019): 498–504 (500).

11. Quine, "Nineveh's Pretensions," 500–501.

12. Elizabeth Achtemeier, *Nahum—Malachi*, Interpretation (Louisville: Westminster/John Knox, 1986), 28.

13. "Once again the writer inverts the metaphor for purposes of sarcasm." Longman, "Nahum," 825.

14. Timmer makes the compelling suggestion that the "choice of the locust as opposed to other entities that are characteristically numerous (e.g., sand on the sea-

shore) may reveal Nahum's awareness of Neo-Assyrian military self-descriptions in terms of locusts." *Nahum*, 169.

15. Cf. Isaiah 14:18; Jeremiah 51:39. Longman, "Nahum," 828; J. J. M. Roberts, *Nahum, Habakkuk, and Zephaniah: A Commentary*, The Old Testament Library (Louisville: Westminster/John Knox, 1991), 77.

16. Klaas Spronk, *Nahum*, Historical Commentary on the Old Testament (Leuven, Belgium: Peeters, 1997), 142.

17. "The Laws of Hammurabi," trans. Martha Roth, in *The Context of Scripture*, vol. 2 (Leiden: Brill, 2003), 336.

18. Longman, "Nahum," 828 has insightfully noted that Nahum's unanswered questions employed throughout the book traffic in the same spirit as the formal taunts.

19. Renz, *Books of Nahum, Habakkuk, and Zephaniah*, 191.

Chapter Fifty: Seeking God in Troubling Times

1. This chapter is adapted from a sermon that was first preached for the Homestead Class of Briarwood Presbyterian Church, Birmingham, Alabama, in January 2008. About eighty adults attended this class.

2. See the chapter on Zephaniah 1:1 in this volume.

3. These stages occurred in 605, 597, 587, and 582 B.C., respectively.

4. O. Palmer Robertson, *The Books of Nahum, Habakkuk, and Zephaniah*, New International Commentary on the Old Testament (Grand Rapids, MI: Eerdmans, 1990), 136.

5. F. F. Bruce, "Habakkuk," in T. E. McComiskey, ed., *The Minor Prophets* (Grand Rapids, MI: Baker, 1993), 2:844.

6. Marvin A. Sweeney, *The Twelve Prophets*, Berit Olam (Collegeville, MN: Michael Glazier, 2000), 2:463.

7. Elizabeth Achtemeier, *Nahum—Malachi*, Interpretation (Atlanta: John Knox Press, 1986), 36.

8. John L. Mackay notes, "'Why' is the cry of bewilderment which also occurs in the psalms of lament (Pss. 10:1; 44:23–24; 74:1, 11; 80:12; 88:14)." *Jonah-Zephaniah*, Focus on the Bible (Fearn, Scotland: Christian Focus, 1998), 180.

9. The stem of the Hebrew verb here is causative (*hiphil*).

10. On the consequential nature of the nouns, see Robertson, *Books of Nahum, Habakkuk, and Zephaniah*, 140n2; and C. F. Keil, "Habakkuk," in C. F. Keil and Franz Delitzsch, *Commentary on the Old Testament*, trans. James Martin, (1868; repr. Grand Rapids, MI: Eerdmans, 1980), 10:56.

11. Francis I. Andersen, *Habakkuk*, Anchor Bible 25 (New York: Doubleday, 2001), 141.

Chapter Fifty-One: Praying in Troubling Times

1. This chapter was adapted from a sermon that was preached at College Church, Wheaton, Illinois, on Mother's Day, May 11, 2008.

2. See B. J. Grundlach, "Augustine of Hippo," in Walter A. Elwell, ed., *Evangelical Dictionary of Theology*, 2nd ed. (Grand Rapids, MI: Baker, 2001), 122.

3. See Ronald H. Stone, *John Wesley's Life and Ethics* (Nashville: Abingdon Press, 2001), 29–41.

4. For a description of the times, see the chapter on Habakkuk 1:1–11 in this volume and F. F. Bruce, "Habakkuk," in T. E. McComiskey, ed. *The Minor Prophets* (Grand Rapids, MI: Baker, 1993), 2:832–34.

5. John L. Mackay, *Jonah–Zephaniah*, Focus on the Bible (Fearn, Scotland: Christian Focus, 1998), 191.

6. O. Palmer Robertson, *The Books of Nahum, Habakkuk, and Zephaniah*, New International Commentary on the Old Testament (Grand Rapids, MI: Eerdmans, 1990), 156–57.

7. D. Martyn Lloyd-Jones, *From Fear to Faith: Studies in the Book of Habakkuk* (London: Inter-Varsity Fellowship, 1953), 25.

8. Marvin A. Sweeney, *The Twelve Prophets*, Berit Olam (Collegeville, MN: Michael Glazier, 2000), 2:467; Francis I. Andersen, *Habakkuk*, Anchor Bible 25 (New York: Doubleday, 2001), 175.

9. For a discussion of the text-critical issues related to this phrase, see J. J. M. Roberts, *Nahum, Habakkuk, and Zephaniah*, Old Testament Library (Louisville: Westminster John Knox Press, 1991), 101.

10. See also Isaiah 21:6–9 for a similar image.

11. Bruce, "Habakkuk," 857.

12. See Lloyd-Jones, *From Fear to Faith*, 34–39.

13. See Diana Dewar, *All for Christ: Some Twentieth Century Martyrs* (Oxford: Oxford University Press, 1980), 73–74; and Robert Wilson, "A Canberra Nurse Who Became a Martyr," *Anglican Historical Society Journal* 14 (October 1992): 37–40.

14. The phrase either means that the vision must be written so that a messenger can read it easily and take it to others, or so that a person passing by can easily read a stationary message composed on wooden or stone tablets. For discussions of the phrase, see Mackay, *Jonah–Zephaniah*, 198–99; Robertson, *Books of Nahum, Habakkuk, and Zephaniah*, 168–70; and Sweeney, *Twelve Prophets*, 2:470–71.

15. Bruce, "Habakkuk," 859.

16. Don West, "Petitionary Prayer in the 'Now' and 'Not Yet,' " in eds. Peter G. Bolt and Mark D. Thompson, *Donald Robinson Selected Works: Appreciation* (Sydney: Australian Church Record/Moore College, 2008), 239.

17. West, "Petitionary Prayer," 235–40.

Chapter Fifty-Two: God's Answer to Troubling People

1. Francis I. Andersen, *Habakkuk*, Anchor Bible 25 (New York: Doubleday, 2001), 233.

2. Elizabeth Achtemeier, *Nahum—Malachi*, Interpretation (Atlanta: John Knox Press, 1986), 49.

3. Ralph L. Smith, *Micah-Malachi*, Word Biblical Commentary 32 (Waco, TX: Word, 1984), 111.

4. Marvin A. Sweeney, *The Twelve Prophets*, Berit Olam (Collegeville, MN: Liturgical Press, 2000), 2:475.

5. Kenneth L. Barker and Waylon Bailey, *Micah, Nahum, Habakkuk, and Zephaniah*, New American Commentary 20 (Nashville: Broadman & Holman, 1999), 335.

6. For other texts with similar cup imagery, see Jeremiah 25:15–17; Lamentations 4:21; Revelation 16:19.

7. Achtemeier, *Nahum—Malachi*, 51.
8. John Calvin, *Commentaries on the Twelve Minor Prophets, Volume Four: Habakkuk, Zephaniah, Haggai (1559)*, trans. John Owen (1848; repr. Grand Rapids, MI: Baker, 1996), 129.
9. David Garland, "Habakkuk," in J. Clifton Allen, ed., *The Broadman Bible Commentary* (Nashville: Broadman & Holman, 1973), 7:263.

Chapter Fifty-Three: Rejoicing during Troubling Times

1. James Montgomery Boice, *The Minor Prophets: Two Volumes Complete in One Edition* (1983, 1986; repr. Grand Rapids, MI: Kregel, 1996), 2:99.
2. For an elaboration of this principle as a central concept in Biblical theology, see Scott J. Hafemann, *The God of Promise and the Life of Faith: Understanding the Heart of the Bible* (Wheaton: Crossway, 2001).
3. O. Palmer Robertson, *The Books of Nahum, Habakkuk, and Zephaniah*, New International Commentary on the Old Testament (Grand Rapids, MI: Eerdmans, 1990), 222.
4. Marvin A. Sweeney, *The Twelve Prophets*, Berit Olam (Collegeville, MN: Michael Glazier, 2000), 2:483.
5. For a discussion of this theme in the Old Testament, see Christopher J. H. Wright, *Knowing God the Father Through the Old Testament* (Downers Grove, IL: InterVarsity Press, 2007).
6. D. Martyn Lloyd-Jones, *From Fear to Faith: Studies in the Book of Habakkuk* (London: Inter-Varsity Fellowship, 1953), 70–71.
7. Lloyd-Jones, *From Fear to Faith*, 71.
8. The ESV's "quietly wait" captures the essence of the Hebrew word, but the word comes from *nuach*, the root that "Noah" comes from, and this root includes the sense of rest, not just waiting.
9. J. J. M. Roberts, *Nahum, Habakkuk, and Zephaniah*, Old Testament Library (Louisville: Westminster John Knox Press, 1991), 157.
10. F. F. Bruce, "Habakkuk," in ed. T. G. McComiskey, *The Minor Prophets* (Grand Rapids, MI: Baker, 1993), 2:893.
11. Francis I. Andersen, *Habakkuk*, Anchor Bible 25 (New York: Doubleday, 2001), 345.
12. Robertson, *Books of Nahum, Habakkuk, and Zephaniah*, 244.
13. Marcus Loane, *Cambridge and the Evangelical Succession* (1952; repr. Fearn, Scotland: Christian Focus, 2007), 146.
14. Charles Simeon, *Expository Outlines on the Whole Bible* (1847; repr. Grand Rapids, MI: Zondervan, 1956), 10:383, 384.
15. Bruce, "Habakkuk," 893–94.
16. Robertson, *Books of Nahum, Habakkuk, and Zephaniah*, 247.

Chapter Fifty-Four: God Won't Be Used: Renewal and Its Limits

1. See Amos 5:4–6 and the chapter on Zephaniah 1:2 in this volume.
2. I owe this suggestion to Kadie Haase Smith.
3. See O. Palmer Robertson, *The Books of Nahum, Habakkuk, and Zephaniah*, New International Commentary on the Old Testament (Grand Rapids, MI: Eerdmans, 1990), 252.

4. See 2 Chronicles 7:11–18. See also the chapters in this volume on Hosea 3; Amos 5:1–17; and Zephaniah 2.

5. Michael D. Coogan and Mark S. Smith, *Stories from Ancient Canaan*, 2nd ed. (Louisville: Westminster John Knox Press, 2012), 273.

6. See the chapters on Hosea 1:1—2:1 (see esp. 1:1–11); 2:2–23; and Amos 2:4–16 in this volume.

Chapter Fifty-Five: The Great Day of the Lord Is Near

1. See the preceding chapter on Zephaniah 1:1 in this volume.

2. See the chapter on Obadiah 1–11 in this volume.

3. See Arvid S. Kapelrud, *The Message of the Prophet Zephaniah: Morphology and Ideas* (Oslo: Universitetforlaget, 1975), 22; and Marvin A. Sweeney, *Zephaniah: A Commentary*, Hermeneia (Minneapolis: Augsburg Fortress Press, 2003), 52–53.

4. The RSV and ESV translate the first two Hebrew words in Zephaniah 1:2 as "I will utterly sweep away," which conveys the phrase's emphatic nature. The word "sweep" sounds like the two verbs used, but the verbs themselves do not mean "sweep" anywhere else in the Old Testament. Rather, they convey "gather" and "bring to an end," respectively. Virtually every commentator on Zephaniah notes the difficulty of rendering these two Hebrew verbs into understandable English. See Adele Berlin, *Zephaniah: A New Translation with Introduction and Commentary*, Anchor Bible 25A (New York: Doubleday, 1994), 72; and Thomas Renz, *The Books of Nahum, Habakkuk, and Zephaniah*, New International Commentary on the Old Testament (Grand Rapids, MI: Eerdmans, 2021), 466.

5. Or "ground," since the Hebrew word often refers to arable land, not the whole planet.

6. Note the discussions in Sweeney, *Zephaniah*, 69; and Johannes Vlaardingerbroek, *Zephaniah*, Historical Commentary on the Old Testament (Leuven, Belgium: Peeters, 1999), 68–69.

7. I believe that seeking God is the key theme in the Minor Prophets. See Amos 5:4–6.

8. The ESV implies there are two groups. There is no conjunction in the phrase, so the verse probably gives two actions done by the same group.

9. For similar usages of the word, see Hosea 5:10; Amos 1:11; and Habakkuk 3:8.

10. Johnny Cash, vocalist, "God's Gonna Cut You Down," by Orlandus Wilson, Clyde Riddick, Willie T. Johnson, and Henry L. Owens Jr., track 2 on *American V: A Hundred Highways*, released July 4, 2006, by American Recordings.

Chapter Fifty-Six: Gather to Seek the Lord

1. See Hosea 3:5; 5:15; 10:12; Amos 5:4–6, 14; and the preceding chapter on Zephaniah 1:2–18.

2. The verb is a reflexive command. The ESV's "Gather together" seeks to convey the command into readable English. The verb is rare. It is not the same verb that occurs in 1:2. See Ludwig Koehler, Walter Baumgartner, and J. J. Stamm, *The Hebrew and Aramaic Lexicon of the Old Testament*, trans. and ed. M. E. J. Richardson, 4 vols. (Leiden: Brill, 1994–1999), 2:1155.

3. The verb here is similar, but not identical, to the first verb in the verse. There is a conjunction connecting the second word to the first, but there is no word corresponding to the use of "yes" in the ESV. This second verb is best translated as "stiffen." See Koehler, Baumgartner, Stamm, *Hebrew and Aramaic Lexicon*, 2:1151–52. As in 1:2, the ESV translators have tried to render into readable English a difficult combination of two like-sounding words with different meanings and emphatic force.

4. The Hebrew text uses the word three times. The ESV adds a fourth instance for clarity's sake.

5. J. A. Motyer, "Zephaniah," in *The Minor Prophets, an Exegetical and Expository Commentary*, ed. T. E. McComiskey (Grand Rapids, MI: Baker, 2000), 3:927.

6. Motyer, "Zephaniah," 3:927.

7. As Motyer, 3:927 noted, God's "just commands" are "what he has decided is the right course of action for his people."

8. O. Palmer Robertson, *The Books of Nahum, Habakkuk, and Zephaniah*, New International Commentary on the Old Testament (Grand Rapids, MI: Eerdmans, 1990), 301.

9. Marvin A. Sweeney, *Zephaniah: A Commentary*, Hermeneia (Minneapolis: Fortress Press, 2003), 130.

10. Sweeney, *Zephaniah*, 135–38.

11. See Wendell Berry, *The Gift of Good Land: Further Essays Cultural and Agricultural* (Berkeley, CA: Counterpoint, 1981), 267–81.

12. The applications in this section are in no way intended to keep people from seeking further justice in society. Other Biblical texts make this point. Also, living as God's humble people is a form of resistance against evil.

13. For summaries of this historical setting, see Thomas Renz, *The Books of Nahum, Habakkuk, and Zephaniah*, New International Commentary on the Old Testament (Grand Rapids, MI: Eerdmans, 2021), 568–70; and Sweeney, *Zephaniah*, 145–48.

## Chapter Fifty-Seven: A Singing God

1. For details on Josiah's reign, see the chapter on Zephaniah 1:1 in this volume.

2. See the chapters on Hosea 5 and Zephaniah 1:1 in this volume.

3. The Hebrew words translated as "injustice" and "unjust" are virtually the same, thus highlighting the contrast.

4. See the chapter on Zephaniah 1:1 in this volume.

5. Paul R. House, *Zephaniah, A Prophetic Drama*, Journal for the Study of the Old Testament Supplement Series 69/Bible and Literature Series 16 (Sheffield, UK: Almond Press, 1988).

6. Compare Hosea 5:1, 2. The Hebrew word basically means "instruction intended to change behavior."

7. See the discussion of Hebrew words normally translated as "wait" in Thomas Renz, *The Books of Nahum, Habakkuk, and Zephaniah*, New International Commentary on the Old Testament (Grand Rapids, MI: Eerdmans, 2021), 598.

8. See the chapters on Habakkuk 1:12—2:5 and Habakkuk 3 in this volume.

9. The ESV's "earth" (Zephaniah 1:2) seems to me to lead readers to envision a much wider area than the context indicates.

10. Marvin A. Sweeney, *Zephaniah: A Commentary*, Hermeneia (Minneapolis: Fortress Press, 2003), 183.

11. Sweeney, *Zephaniah*, 202–3.
12. J. A. Motyer, "Zephaniah," in *The Minor Prophets, an Exegetical and Expository Commentary*, ed. Thomas Edward McComiskey (Grand Rapids, MI: Baker, 2000), 3:958.
13. Sweeney, *Zephaniah*, 204.

### Chapter Fifty-Eight: Work, for the Lord Is with You

1. Thomas Hobbes, *Leviathan*, i. xiii. 9.
2. As Carol L. Meyers and Eric M. Meyers have written, "The hegemony of Persia in all local affairs is presupposed by both prophets [i.e., Haggai and Zechariah]." *Haggai, Zechariah 1–8*, Anchor Bible 25B (Garden City, NY: Doubleday, 1987), xl.
3. Like Obadiah and Habakkuk, we have no information about Haggai's ancestry or biography other than his clear role of prophet in the postexilic community. His name is derived from the Hebrew word for "festival" (*ḥag*) with an adjectival ending, so "festal." Many speculate from this that Haggai was born on a feast day. See, e.g., Pieter A. Verhoef, *The Books of Haggai and Malachi*, New International Commentary on the Old Testament (Grand Rapids, MI: Eerdmans, 1987), 4.
4. Verhoef, *Books of Haggai and Malachi*, 43.
5. On the legal covenantal function of the prophetic office in Israel, see Meredith G. Kline, *The Structure of Biblical Authority*, rev. ed. (Grand Rapids, MI: Eerdmans, 1975), 57–62.
6. William T. Koopmans, *Haggai*, Historical Commentary on the Old Testament (Leuven, Belgium: Peeters, 2017), 85–86.
7. Frank Patrick, "Time and Tradition in the Book of Haggai," in *Tradition in Transition: Haggai and Zechariah 1-8 in the Trajectory of Hebrew Theology*, eds. Mark J. Boda and Michael H. Floyd (New York: T&T Clark, 2008), 40–55. Similarly, Koopmans, *Haggai*, 86.
8. Elizabeth Achtemeier, *Nahum—Malachi* (Louisville: Westminster/John Knox, 1986), 98.
9. "The emphasis brought to the foreground through the syntax of the present construction in 1:3 immediately silences the observation attributed to the people by overriding the popular opinion with a divine word. The word (*dābār*) of YHWH has performative power and signals that reality is about to change." Koopmans, *Haggai*, 89.
10. "The descriptions of crop failure and hardship in Hag 1:6 must be viewed in the broader context of covenant curses or futility curses." Koopmans, *Haggai*, 96. Cf. Delbert R. Hillers, *Treaty-Curses and the Old Testament Prophets*, Biblica et Orientalia 16 (Rome: Pontifical Biblical Institute, 1964), 29; Hans Walter Wolff, *Haggai: A Commentary*, trans. Margaret Kohl, Hermeneia (Minneapolis: Augsburg, 1988), 33, 43–44.
11. Achtemeier suggests that this verse contains not only the central message for this passage but for the book as a whole. *Nahum—Malachi*, 94.
12. That the expression "all the remnant of the people" (*kōl šeʾērît hāʿom*) refers to all the inhabitants of Judah at the time (as opposed to the suggestion that it refers to a smaller, faithful subgroup of the inhabitants), see John Kessler, *The Book of Haggai: Prophecy and Society in Early Persian Yehud*, Supplements to Vetus Testamentum 91 (Leiden: 2002), 254.

13. Iain M. Duguid, *Haggai, Zechariah, Malachi*, EP Study Commentary (Carlisle: Evangelical Press, 2010), 33.

Chapter Fifty-Nine: Future Glories

1. For a discussion of the beginning of Haggai's second oracle at 1:15b ("in the second year of Darius"), see Max Rogland, *Haggai and Zechariah 1-8: A Handbook on the Hebrew Text*, Baylor Handbook on the Hebrew Bible (Waco, TX: Baylor University Press, 2016), 27–29; John Kessler, *The Book of Haggai: Prophecy and Society in Early Persian Yehud*, Supplements to Vetus Testamentum 91 (Leiden: 2002), 41–51; and William T. Koopmans, *Haggai*, Historical Commentary on the Old Testament (Leuven, Belgium: Peeters, 2017), 134–41.

2. Mignon R. Jacobs, *The Books of Haggai and* Malachi, New International Commentary on the Old Testament (Grand Rapids, MI: Eerdmans, 2017), 71; Carol L. Meyers and Eric M. Meyers, *Haggai, Zechariah 1–8*, Anchor Bible 25B (Garden City, NY: Doubleday, 1987), 71. Contra Pieter A. Verhoef, *The Books of Haggai and Malachi* (Grand Rapids, MI: Eerdmans, 1987), 95, 96.

3. Jacobs, *Books of Haggai and Malachi*, 75.

4. On the political implications of the inferiority of the second temple, see Meyers and Meyers, *Haggai, Zechariah*, 72–74.

5. Meyers and Meyers, 73.

6. As one author points out, the comparison is between Wiccans and members of the mainline Presbyterian church (PCUSA). Mark D. Tooley, "Witches Outnumber Presbyterians?" *The Christian Post*, December 28, 2018, https://www.christianpost.com/voices/witches-outnumber-presbyterians.html.

7. Koopmans, *Haggai*, 148.

8. Meyers and Meyers point to the fact that the second temple was rebuilt using the ruins and footprint of the first temple. *Haggai, Zechariah,* 72.

9. This is not to deny other aspects that contributed to the inglorious status of the second temple, including the economic and political realities mentioned by Meyers and Meyers, *Haggai, Zechariah*, 72–76. Here, however, I'm highlighting the ultimate glory, the presence of God, manifested visibly as a theophany in the days of Solomon, that was held in abeyance after the exile until the fullness of time. It is the absence of this glory, perhaps symbolized by the ark, that caused some to weep when the foundation was complete (Ezra 3:12). The presence of God as a present yet future reality is a major theme in Zechariah as well (cf. Zechariah 1:16; 2:5).

10. Isaac Watts, "When I Survey the Wondrous Cross," in *Hymns and Spiritual Songs* (1707).

Chapter Sixty: Defiled People, Divine Blessing

1. See Deuteronomy 33:10; Jeremiah 18:8; Ezekiel 7:26; Micah 3:11. David L. Petersen, *Haggai and Zechariah 1–8*, Old Testament Library (Philadelphia: Westminster/John Knox, 1984), 73. Cf. Carol Meyers and Eric M. Meyers, *Haggai, Zechariah 1–8*, Anchor Bible 25B (Garden City, NY: Doubleday, 1987), 55; William T. Koopmans, *Haggai*, Historical Commentary on the Old Testament (Leuven, Belgium: Peeters, 2017), 220; Mignon R. Jacobs, *The Books of Haggai and Malachi*, New International Commentary on the Old Testament (Grand Rapids, MI: Eerdmans, 2017), 96.

2. Jacobs, *Books of Haggai and Malachi*, 97.
3. Meyers and Meyers, *Haggai, Zechariah*, 55.
4. That the situation is one of a fellowship offering being transferred by nonpriests to their places of residence is suggested by the garment hypothetically coming into contact with "stew" (Hebrew *nāzîd*), which is never mentioned as a feature of Israel's temple cult. Petersen, *Haggai and Zechariah*, 78; Koopmans, *Haggai*, 224–25. Jacobs sees significance in the individual being identified as an *'îš* ("a man") instead of a *kōhēn* ("a priest"). *Books of Haggai and Malachi*, 97.
5. Much ink has been spilled on the relation of the priests' ruling in 2:12 to the regulations given in Leviticus 6:20 (and to a lesser degree, the implications of Ezekiel 44:19), with some scholars concluding that the priests' response was incorrect. See, e.g., J. L. Koole, *Haggai* (Kampen, Netherlands: Kok, 1967), 77. While this is possible, the prophet's response does not seem to suggest any deficiency in the priests' answer but rather applies their (presumably correct) legal principle to the situation that obtains in the life of the postexilic community. Koopmans, *Haggai*, 225 has correctly observed that, though similar, the situations envisioned in both Leviticus 6:20 and Ezekiel 44:19 "involve circumstances that are not identical to the hypothetical question of Hag. 2:12."
6. "The issue addressed in this context is ritual fitness—defilement is not a matter of idolatry or of sin." Meyers and Meyers, *Haggai, Zechariah*, 55.
7. Meyers and Meyers, 58.
8. I adopt the view that "this people" and "this nation" stand in parallel and refer to the same group, namely the postexilic community in its entirety. See Meyers and Meyers, *Haggai, Zechariah*, 57. For an excellent discussion of the anti-Samaritan and general-population interpretations as well as a brief and able defense of the latter, see Koopmans, *Haggai*, 209–11.
9. Translation of the infamously difficult phrase *wᵉ'ên-'eṯkem 'ēlay* follows Max Rogland's proposal to read it as a possessive clause (as above), which harkens back to the situation addressed in the prophet's first oracle in which the people did not direct their material possessions toward the Lord. "Haggai 2,17—A New Analysis," *Biblica* 88 (2007): 553–57.
10. Koopmans, *Haggai*, 212.
11. "From this day" (*min-hayyôm hazzê*) is used three times in this passage (2:15, 18, 19) to focus the hearers'/readers' attention on the significance of this particular day for the life of the community. The completion of the temple foundation marks a shift in Yahweh's relation to his people. Meyers and Meyers, *Haggai, Zechariah*, 65.
12. "Haggai . . . regards the people as 'unclean' or 'defiled' because the temple is not yet completed and because the uncleanness that abounds cannot yet be restrained." Meyers and Meyers, 57.

## Chapter Sixty-One: Christ Victorious

1. "The pattern of anticipated human action is dramatically broken in the final oracle. . . . The use of a single imperative for Haggai to speak to Zerubbabel without subsequent human action demanded from the person addressed is indicative that the ultimate security and future of the people will depend upon YHWH as their divine

king." William T. Koopmans, *Haggai*, Historical Commentary on the Old Testament (Leuven, Belgium: Peeters, 2017), 278.

2. Koopmans, *Haggai*, 277 makes the important observation that though Zerubbabel is an important figure in Haggai's final oracle, the Lord is the central actor. God is the one who speaks (2:20), "shakes" (2:21), "overthrows "(2:22), and "takes" and "makes" Zerubbabel his signet ring (2:23). Cf. Pieter A. Verhoef, *The Books of Haggai and Malachi* (Grand Rapids, MI: Eerdmans, 1987), 145.

3. Samuel Beckett, *En attendant Godot*, 1953. Published in English by Samuel Beckett, *Waiting for Godot: A Tragicomedy in Two Acts* (London: Faber and Faber, 1955).

4. $^{\prime a}nî$ with Hiphil participle $mar^{\epsilon}îš$ may be used as a "*future instans* that reflects the imminent action of YHWH, consistent with the theme introduced in Hag. 2:6." Koopmans, *Haggai*, 278–79. Similarly, Verhoef, *Books of Haggai and Malachi*, 143; *Gesenius' Hebrew Grammar*, ed. E. Kautzsch, trans. A. E. Cowley, 2nd ed. (Oxford: Oxford University Press, 1910) §116p.

5. On the eschatological focus of this passage, see Carol L. Meyers and Eric M. Meyers, *Haggai, Zechariah 1–8*, Anchor Bible 25B (Garden City, NY: Doubleday, 1987), 66.

6. W. B. Yeats, "The Second Coming," in *The Collected Poems of W. B. Yeats* (New York: Scribner, 1996), 187.

7. Koopmans, *Haggai*, 208 has suggested, "The double oracular activity on the final day structurally gives added emphasis to the message of hope that is associated with the day of refoundation."

8. Kenney Chesney, "Everybody Wants to Go to Heaven," on *Lucky Old Sun* (RCA: Nashville, 2008).

9. Koopmans, *Haggai*, 282.

10. Mark J. Boda suggests a closer parallel in Ezekiel's depiction of the defeat of Gog (Ezekiel 38:21). He also makes the compelling suggestion that such confusion and self-destruction among God's enemies might have been recognized and anticipated in the chaotic circumstances surrounding Darius's rise to the throne. *Haggai, Zechariah*, New International Version Application Commentary (Grand Rapids, MI: Zondervan, 2004), 162–63.

11. Iain M. Duguid, *Haggai, Zechariah, Malachi*, EP Study Commentary (Carlisle: Evangelical Press, 2010), 63.

12. Though Verhoef cites A. S. Van der Woude's rejection of a typological interpretation of Zerubbabel approvingly, he seems to equivocate in his conclusion: "The splendor of the new temple and the glory of the throne of David will, amid the turmoil in nature and among the nations, be fulfilled in Christ, centrally at his first and finally at his second advent." *Books of Haggai and Zechariah*, 149–50.

13. Boda, *Haggai, Zechariah*, 164.

14. Cf. 2 Samuel 3:18, 7:5, 8; 1 Chronicles 17:4; Psalms 78:70; 89:3; 132:10. To be sure, the designation is used of others: e.g., Abraham (Genesis 26:24), Moses (Numbers 12:7, 8), and Nebuchadnezzar (Jeremiah 25:9; 27:6), as well as nations (Isaiah 41:8; 44:1) and prophets (Jeremiah 7:25; Ezekiel 38:17). Mignon R. Jacobs, *The Books of Haggai and Malachi*, New International Commentary on the Old Testament (Grand Rapids, MI: Eerdmans, 2017), 122. Nevertheless, the complex of allusions to David's royal lineage suggest that Israel's greatest king is principally in view.

15. Though Hebrew *ḥôṯom* may mean "seal" or "signet ring" (Francis Brown, et al., *The Brown-Driver-Briggs Hebrew and English Lexicon* [1906; repr. Peabody, MA: Hendrickson, 1996], 368), the clear allusion to Jeremiah 22:24 that mentions God's "right hand" (*yaḏ yᵉmînî*) suggests that the latter is the sense in Haggai 2:23.

16. Jacobs, *Books of Haggai and Malachi*, 123–24.

17. Verhoef, *Books of Haggai and Malachi*, 146; Elizabeth Achtemeier, *Nahum—Malachi* (Louisville: Westminster John Knox Press, 1986), 104.

18. "Haggai," in *Dictionary for Theological Interpretation of the Bible*, ed. Kevin J. Vanhoozer (Grand Rapids, MI: Baker/ London: SPCK, 2005), 274.

19. Duguid, *Haggai, Zechariah, and Malachi*, 64.

## Chapter Sixty-Two: Breaking with the Past

1. William Shakespeare, *Romeo and Juliet*, 2.1:837–38, Quarto 2 (1599).

2. Cf. Robert Alter, *The David Story: A Translation with Commentary of 1 and 2 Samuel* (New York: Norton, 1999), 152.

3. "The grabbing of the heel by the younger twin becomes a kind of emblem of their future relationship, and the birth, like the oracle, again invokes the struggle against primogeniture. The original meaning of the name Jacob was probably something like 'God protects' or 'God follows after.'" Alter, *David Story*, 128.

4. Francis Brown, et al., *The Brown-Driver-Briggs Hebrew and English Lexicon* (1906; repr. Peabody, MA: Hendrickson, 1996), 221, 278.

5. Ludwig Koehler, Walter Baumgartner and J. J. Stamm, *The Hebrew and Aramaic Lexicon of the Old Testament*, trans. and ed. M. E. J. Richardson, 4 vols. (Leiden: Brill, 1994–1999), 271.

6. Wolter H. Rose, "Zechariah and the Ambiguity of Kingship in Postexilic Israel," in *Let us Go up to Zion: Essays in Honour of H. G. M. Williamson on the Occasion of his Sixty-Fifth Birthday*, ed. Iain Provan and Mark J. Boda, Supplements to Vetus Testamentum 153 (Leiden: Brill, 2013), 219–31 (quote on 220).

7. "To a limited extent restoration from exile had taken place in Zechariah's day, but the political conditions were not fundamentally changed. Persia, the second beast power from the deep in Daniel 7 still ruled over the heritage of covenant promise." Meredith G. Kline, *Glory in Our Midst: A Biblical-Theological Reading of Zechariah's Night Visions* (Overland Park, KS: Two Age Press, 2001), 14.

8. "The name captures in a single sentence an important theme of Old Testament religion: the God of Israel has not forgotten his covenant promises. As a name given to a Jewish child born in exile, it testifies to his parents' faith that God had not utterly abandoned his covenant people." Al Wolters, *Zechariah*, Historical Commentary on the Old Testament (Leuven, Belgium: Peeters, 2014), 36.

9. Elizabeth Achtemeier, *Nahum—Malachi* (Louisville: Westminster/John Knox, 1986), 111; Mark J. Boda, *The Book of Zechariah*, New International Commentary on the Old Testament (Grand Rapids, MI: Eerdmans, 2016), 16–17.

10. Boda points to Zechariah 7:7–14 as evidence that the prophet has in view the final generation before the exile. *Book of Zechariah*, 70. Cf. Carol L. Meyers and Eric M. Meyers, *Haggai, Zechariah 1–8*, Anchor Bible 25B (Garden City, NY: Doubleday, 1987), 92; Wolters, *Zechariah*, 32.

11. Peter H. W. Lau, *The Book of Ruth* (Grand Rapids, MI: Eerdmans, 2023), 119–21.

12. Al Wolters, "Word Play in Zechariah," in *Puns and Pundits: Word Play in the Hebrew Bible and Ancient Near Eastern Literature*, ed. Scott B Noegel (Bethesda, MD: CDL Press, 2000), 223–30 (223).

13. Boda, *Book of Zechariah*, 82.

14. Michael R. Stead, *The Intertextuality of Zechariah 1-8*, Library of Hebrew Bible/Old Testament Studies 506 (London: T&T Clark, 2009), 83–84.

15. Barry Webb, *The Message of Zechariah* (Downers Grove, IL: InterVarsity Press, 2003), 58; Boda, *Book of Zechariah*, 82.

16. On the military and hunting imagery of *hiśśîgû*, see Iain M. Duguid, *Haggai, Zechariah, Malachi* (Carlisle: Evangelical Press, 2010), 72; Carol L. Meyers and Eric M. Meyers, *Haggai, Zechariah 1–8*, Anchor Bible 25B (Garden City, NY: Doubleday, 1987), 96; and David L. Petersen, *Haggai and Zechariah 1–8*, Old Testament Library (Philadelphia: Westminster/John Knox, 1984), 134. Contra Boda, who creates a false dichotomy between hunting imagery and covenantal sanctions as the conceptual background to the verb. *Book of Zechariah*, 83.

17. Webb, *Message of Zechariah*, 55; Wolters, *Zechariah*, 39.

18. Max Rogland has noted, "Some take this as continuing the reference to the actions of the forefathers in verses 4-6a, describing the repentance of a previous generation. In light of what has been said of the forefathers already (e.g., 1:2, 4-5), however, this seems most unlikely. Instead, this is to be taken as a narrative comment indicating the penitent response of Zechariah's audience." *Haggai and Zechariah 1-8: A Handbook on the Hebrew Text*, Baylor Handbook on the Hebrew Bible (Waco, TX: Baylor University Press, 2016), 66.

19. Meyers and Meyers, *Haggai, Zechariah*, 93; Boda, *Book of Zechariah*, 59–60; Byron G. Curtis, *Up the Steep and Stony Road: The Book of Zechariah in Social Location Trajectory*, Society of Biblical Literature Academia Biblica 25 (Atlanta: SBL Press, 2006), 129.

20. Samuel Johnson, *The Rambler*, No. 2, March 24, 1750.

21. Martin Luther, *Ninety-Five Theses or Disputation on the Power and Efficacy of Indulgences* (1517), in *Martin Luther's Basic Theological Writings*, ed. Timothy F. Lull (Minneapolis: Fortress, 1989), 21–29 (quoted on 21).

## Chapter Sixty-Three: How Long, O Lord?

1. Salvador Dali, quoted in Dominika Ruszkowska-Buchowska, "Cubist Aesthetics in Stevens' 'The Man with the Blue Guitar': Defence Against Surrealism," *Studia Anglica Posnaniensia* 40 (2004): 344.

2. Carol L. Meyers and Eric M. Meyers supply "[*and Zechariah said*]" in an attempt to smooth out what they regard as a problematic sequence of actions. *Haggai, Zechariah 1–8*, Anchor Bible 25B (Garden City, NY: Doubleday, 1987), 109.

3. Al Wolters, *Zechariah*, Historical Commentary on the Old Testament (Leuven, Belgium: Peeters, 2014), 48.

4. Mark J. Boda, *The Book of Zechariah*, New International Commentary on the Old Testament (Grand Rapids, MI: Eerdmans, 2016), 118.

5. Wolters, *Zechariah*, 47.

6. According to Wolters, 56, the connection with the imperial postal system has been observed since the nineteenth century. Cf. Meyers and Meyers, *Haggai,*

*Zechariah*, 111; Iain M. Duguid, *Haggai, Zechariah, Malachi*, EP Study Commentary (Carlisle: Evangelical Press, 2010), 79.

7. Herodotus, *The Histories*, trans. Robin Waterfield (Oxford: Oxford University Press, 1998), 520.

8. Wolters, *Zechariah*, 56.

9. Wolters, 45.

10. It is also possible that the Hebrew *bamm$^e$ṣulâ* ("in the glen") refers to a "shady area" (cf. Wolters, *Zechariah*, 52–53), which would further support the clandestine ambiance. Meredith G. Kline, however, made the interesting though speculative connection between the *bamm$^e$ṣulâ* and "the deep" as a symbol of anti-God chaos (cf. Daniel 7). *Glory in Our Midst: A Biblical-Theological Reading of Zechariah's Night Visions* (Overland Park, KS: Two Age Press, 2001), 6–15.

11. Elizabeth Achtemeier, *Nahum—Malachi* (Louisville: Westminster John Knox Press, 1986), 111.

12. Meyers and Meyers, *Haggai, Zechariah*, 115, 130. Wolters, *Zechariah*, 59 has objected, citing subsequent (post-520 B.C.) conflicts with the Elamites and the Scythians recorded as an addendum in the Behistun inscription. Joyce G. Baldwin's comment serves as a fitting response: "Whether or not every trace of fighting had ended is beside the point. It was sufficiently clear that the riots of 521 had not been the beginning of eschatological battles ushering in the Messianic age. Instead, Darius was firmly in control of his empire." *Haggai, Zechariah, Malachi: An Introduction and Commentary*, Tyndale Old Testament Commentary (Downers Grove, IL: InterVarsity Press, 1972), 96.

13. Boda, *Book of Zechariah*, 133 sees Zechariah 1:11, 12 as an allusion to Isaiah 14:7: "Whereas the peaceful dwelling of 'all the earth' in Isa 14:7 prompts 'shouts of joy,' the peaceful dwelling in Zech. 1:11 prompts 'lament' to Yahweh in 1:12."

14. John Calvin, quoted in Achtemeier, *Nahum—Malachi*, 113.

15. Kline, *Glory in Our Midst*, 32, 35.

16. Kline, 1–4.

17. Kline, 2–4; John Calvin, *Commentaries on the Twelve Minor Prophets*, vol. 5, trans. John Owen (Grand Rapids, MI: Baker, 2003), 38.

18. Some commentators have noted the intercessory character of the angel's prayer without identifying the angel as a Christophany. See, e.g., Achtemeier, *Nahum—Malachi*, 114; and Wolters, *Zechariah*, 45.

19. *Book of Church Order of the Presbyterian Church in America: Directory for Worship*, 56–5.

20. Paul Johnson, *A History of the American People* (New York: HarperPerennial, 1999), 744.

21. "The nations God employed to execute his threatened curse-sanction would misunderstand this event and exalt themselves, discounting the God of captive Israel." Kline, *Glory in Our Midst*, 47.

22. Kline, 53.

23. Achtemeier, *Nahum—Malachi*, 115.

Chapter Sixty-Four: Glorious Things of Thee Are Spoken

1. John Newton, "Glorious Things of Thee Are Spoken," published as "Zion, or the City of God," in *Olney Hymns* (1779).

2. For a brief survey of various proposals and their sources, see Al Wolters, *Zechariah*, Historical Commentary on the Old Testament (Leuven, Belgium: Peeters, 2014), 71. This author agrees with Wolters's conclusion regarding the nature of these horns: "The text does not tell us. In the absence of any clear textual indication to the contrary, it is probably safest to take the קרנות in their most common and everyday sense, that is, as the familiar horns of certain animals (bulls, rams, and wild oxen) which throughout the OT are a symbol of power."

3. "[Zechariah] sees four single horns, which are indicative not of four specific enemies but of all those nations that have attacked Israel, perhaps from the four corners of the earth." Elizabeth Achtemeier, *Nahum—Malachi* (Louisville: Westminster/John Knox, 1986), 115. Cf. Wolters, *Zechariah*, 70; Iain M. Duguid, *Haggai, Zechariah, Malachi*, EP Study Commentary (Carlisle: Evangelical Press, 2010), 86.

4. I read *lᵉhaḥᵃrîd 'ōtom* with ESV as "to terrify them [i.e., the arrogant nations]." Contra Wolters, *Zechariah*, 73, who sees an incoherence to "terrifying" inanimate objects like "horns" and implausibility to it referring to the nations they represent. See discussion in Carol L. Meyers and Eric M. Meyers, *Haggai, Zechariah 1–8*, Anchor Bible 25B (Garden City, NY: Doubleday, 1987), 141–42.

5. Duguid, *Haggai, Zechariah, Malachi*, 86–87.

6. See, e.g., Meyers and Meyers, *Haggai, Zechariah*, 139. Mark J. Boda's translation of *ḥārāšîm* as "farmers" requires a revocalization unattested in various versions and furthermore fails to make better sense of the fantastic imagery than the traditional rendering "craftsmen." *The Book of Zechariah*, New International Commentary on the Old Testament (Grand Rapids, MI: Eerdmans, 2016), 164.

7. Francis Brown, et al., *The Brown-Driver-Briggs Hebrew and English Lexicon* (1906; repr. Peabody, MA: Hendrickson, 1996), 360. Boda, *Book of Zechariah*, 164 cites the following: Exodus 28:11; 2 Samuel 5:11; 2 Kings 12:12; 22:6; 1 Chronicles 14:1; Isaiah 40:19; 44:13; Jeremiah 10:3.

8. Few commentators have explicitly made this connection between the promise of a rebuilt temple in vision one (Zechariah 1:16) and the craftsmen associated with temple-building in vision two (1:20). For a concise and compelling argument to this effect, see Barry Webb, *The Message of Zechariah* (Downers Grove, IL: InterVarsity Press, 2003), 76–77.

9. Achtemeier makes the helpful observation, "The man is not an angel but a visionary symbol for human expectations." *Nahum—Malachi*, 116.

10. Wolters, *Zechariah*, 76; Duguid, *Haggai, Zechariah, Malachi*, 89. Duguid, 248n17 cites Ezekiel 38:11 as representative of how unwalled villages were perceived.

11. "That Zechariah had Pasargadae in mind is also made likely by the fact that the imperial capital also forms the likely background of Vision 1." Wolters, *Zechariah*, 77.

12. Achtemeier, *Nahum—Malachi*, 118.

13. Achtemeier, 118, 119.

14. Peter R. Ackroyd's assessment of Zechariah 2:8 (Hebrews 2:12) that "this notoriously problematic passage cannot be satisfactorily explained" only slightly overstates the matter. *Exile and Restoration: A Study of Hebrew Thought of the Sixth Century B.C.* (Philadelphia: The Westminster Press, 1968), 180n31. For an

incomplete survey of proposals for the meaning of ʾaḥar kāḇôḏ šᵉlāḥanî, see Wolters, *Zechariah*, 80–82. Though it is likely that the text has suffered in transmission, Duguid (*Haggai, Zechariah, Malachi*, 91) offers a straightforward rendering of the text as it stands: "In pursuit of [his own] glory, [the LORD of hosts] send me [Zechariah, with a message] concerning the nations that plundered you." Cf. Max Rogland, *Haggai and Zechariah 1-8: A Handbook on the Hebrew Text*, Baylor Handbook on the Hebrew Bible (Waco, TX: Baylor University Press, 2016), 99-104.

15. "In some texts those before whom something happens are not merely spectators, but witnesses, who are supposed to take a position as well (Deut. 31:7; Jer. 28:1, 5, 11). It is often said that Yahweh has bestowed his benefits in favor of Israel in the eyes of the nations. In other words, the nations are witnesses, but at the same time they are invited to take a personal stand." Walter Vogels, *God's Universal Covenant: A Biblical Study* (Ottawa: University of Ottawa Press, 1986), 65–66.

Chapter Sixty-Five: Clothed in Righteousness

1. For a discussion of clothing and its significance in ancient Israel see Philip J. King and Lawrence E. Stager, *Life in Biblical Israel* (Louisville: Westminster John Knox Press, 2001), 259–75.

2. For a helpful discussion of the priestly vestments and their symbolism, see Jacob Milgrom, *Leviticus 1–16*, Anchor Bible 3 (New Haven, CT: Yale, 1991), 501–8.

3. Though the number and structure of the night visions in Zechariah is a matter of debate, I take the majority view that there are eight night visions with chapters 3 and 4 standing as the central two visions (numbers four and five). Al Wolters, *Zechariah*, Historical Commentary on the Old Testament (Leuven, Belgium: Peeters, 2014), 26. For alternate views and arrangements, see Meredith G. Kline, *Glory in Our Midst: A Biblical-Theological Reading of Zechariah's Night Visions* (Overland Park, KS: Two Age Press, 2001), 241–58; and Carol L. Meyers and Eric M. Meyers, *Haggai, Zechariah 1–8*, Anchor Bible 25B (Garden City, NY: Doubleday, 1987), liv.

4. Iain M. Duguid, *Haggai, Zechariah, Malachi*, EP Study Commentary (Carlisle: Evangelical Press, 2010), 98–99; Barry Webb, *The Message of Zechariah* (Downers Grove, IL: InterVarsity Press, 2003), 85–86.

5. Duguid, *Haggai, Zechariah, Malachi*, 97–98.

6. Meyers and Meyers, *Haggai and Zechariah*, 217.

7. See, e.g., Martin Luther's "A Sermon on Two Kinds of Righteousness" (1518) in *Luther's Works*, vol. 31 (Philadelphia: Fortress, 1957), 297–306.

8. "In a context where filthy garments represent iniquity, these 'festival clothes' can only represent an altogether new righteousness that accompanies Joshua's new status, which is imputed to him by grace." Duguid, *Haggai, Zechariah, Malachi*, 99.

9. Though it is grammatically possible to read wᵉgam-ʾattâ tāḏîn ʾet-bêṯî wᵉgam tišmōr ʾet-ḥᵃṣēroy ("then you shall rule my house and have charge of my courts") as part of the protasis (e.g., Jewish Publication Society; Wolters, *Zechariah*, 96; and Max Rogland, *Haggai and Zechariah 1-8: A Handbook on the Hebrew Text*, Baylor Handbook on the Hebrew Bible [Waco, TX: Baylor University Press, 2016], 120–21), it is preferable to see this as part of the apodosis (e.g., LXX, KJV, NIV, NRSV, ESV). As Meyers and Meyers have noted, "The shift from *ʾim* to *gam* seems sufficient cause to understand that the second set of clauses denotes the scope of Joshua's authority, so long as he obeys God's word." *Haggai, Zechariah,*

194. Mark J. Boda's comment, however, may be more decisive: "It appears then that a clause beginning with particle *wegam* ('and also') can occur in the protasis or the apodosis, *but never occurs in the initial position.*" *The Book of Zechariah*, New International Commentary on the Old Testament (Grand Rapids, MI: Eerdmans, 2016), 245 (emphasis mine).

10. Duguid, *Haggai, Zechariah, Malachi,* 100. Cf. Moshe Weinfeld, "The Covenant of Grant in the Old Testament and in the Ancient Near East," *Journal of the American Oriental Society* 90 (1970): 184–203, esp. 186.

11. For a discussion of Abraham's covenantal obedience functioning as a type of the Messiah's, see Meredith G. Kline, *Kingdom Prologue: Genesis Foundations for a Covenantal Worldview* (Overland Park, KS: Two Age Press, 2000), 320–26.

12. "The covenant of works proposal to Joshua lifts our thoughts above to the Father's covenantal proposal to send his Son to replace the Aaronic priesthood and to be a second Adam. This Son-Servant would be an obedient Adam, keeping his covenant of works, faithfully performing his priestly church, and thereby he would merit for himself and those the Father gave him the promised place of acceptance, audience, and access in heaven. And in God's typological arrangements under the old covenant, Joshua, high priest of Israel, was a sign of that coming Servant of the Lord." Meredith G. Kline, *Glory in Our Midst: A Biblical-Theological Reading of Zechariah's Night Visions* (Overland Park, KS: Two Age Press, 2001), 119.

13. "No one who comprehends the obedience required of Joshua, the atoning authority invested in him, and his privileged access to God should interpret this chapter without seeing its New Testament parallel in the high priesthood of Jesus as set forth in The Letter to the Hebrews." Elizabeth Achtemeier, *Nahum—Malachi* (Louisville: Westminster John Knox Press, 1986), 123.

14. Boda, *Book of Zechariah*, 259; Duguid, *Haggai, Zechariah, Malachi,* 101–2. Wolters, *Zechariah*, 102–4 takes the Hebrew *'eben* ("stone" or often "precious stone"; cf. Francis Brown, et al., *The Brown-Driver-Briggs Hebrew and English Lexicon* [1906; repr. Peabody, MA: Hendrickson, 1996], 6) as a collective referring to the fourteen precious stones or jewelry (cf. Exodus 28:17; 1 Kings 10:2) that adorned the high priest's uniform, though the collocation with the adjective "one" or "single" (Hebrew *'aḥat*) militates against this view. Meyers and Meyers have suggested that the referent is intentionally ambiguous, thus serving to unite the priestly and monarchic prerogatives in the person of Joshua. *Haggai, Zechariah,* 204–8, 226.

15. Webb, *Message of Zechariah,* 88.

### Chapter Sixty-Six: A Day of Small Things

1. "Pride of place among the defining marks of greatness in domestic achievements goes to royal construction projects. As in Assyria, so in Syria-Palestine: great kings create 'constructed space.'" Douglas J. Green, *I Undertook Great Works: The Ideology of Domestic Achievements in West Semitic Royal Inscriptions,* Forschungen zum Alten Testament 2. Reihe 41 (Tübingen: Mohr Siebeck, 2010), 307.

2. Carol L. Meyers and Eric M. Meyers, *Haggai, Zechariah 1–8,* Anchor Bible 25B (Garden City, NY: Doubleday, 1987), 269.

3. William W. Hallo, ed., *The Context of Scripture,* 3 vols. (Leiden: Brill, 1997), 2:313.

4. Al Wolters, *Zechariah*, Historical Commentary on the Old Testament (Leuven, Belgium: Peeters, 2014), 115; Meyers and Meyers, *Haggai and Zechariah*, 262.

5. Meyers and Meyers, *Haggai, Zechariah*, 263.

6. Observing the static quality of the menorah in contrast to the dynamic characters and objects in the other visions, Meyers and Meyers, 262 have noted: "The menorah . . . stands fixed and immobile in the center of the prophet's visionary field. It represents the presence of Yahweh himself . . . and as such its immobility suggests the permanence and eternity of God's existence, especially as manifest within his earthly dwelling."

7. Iain M. Duguid, *Haggai, Zechariah, Malachi*, EP Study Commentary (Carlisle: Evangelical Press, 2010), 106.

8. The significance of the unusually extensive dialogue in the fifth night vision is obscure. Meyers and Meyers, *Haggai, Zechariah*, 261 suggest a dramatic and rhetorical function of drawing the audience "as completely as possible into the prophetic task of comprehending the vision. Its message is one upon which all of Zechariah's prophecies hinge, and so such devices of discourse as the extended dialogue and the duplication of queries function to draw extra attention to the resplendent objects and their meaning." These suggestions are not, however, mutually exclusive.

9. Meyers and Meyers, 269.

10. "As construed by the Masoretes, these words constitute a mocking challenge to the 'great mountain,' not unlike the rhetorical questions addressed to Job in the Yahweh speeches of Job 38, 39. Compare also Paul's words in Romans 9:20, 'But who are you, O man, to talk back to God?' " Wolters, *Zechariah*, 122.

11. For a wonderfully brief and yet exhaustive survey of possibilities, see Wolters, 122.

12. On the translation of *hāeben habbᵉdîl* as "tin stone," see Meyers and Meyers, *Haggai, Zechariah*, 253, 272.

13. Kathrina von Schlegel, "Be Still, My Soul" (1752).

14. See, e.g., David L. Petersen, *Haggai and Zechariah 1–8*, Old Testament Library (Philadelphia: Westminster/John Knox, 1984), 238–44.

15. Wolters, *Zechariah*, 111.

16. That *'ênê yhwh* refers to "eyes" and not "springs of YHWH," see Mark J. Boda, *The Book of Zechariah*, New International Commentary on the Old Testament (Grand Rapids, MI: Eerdmans, 2016), 308. Contra Joyce G. Baldwin, *Haggai, Zechariah, Malachi: An Introduction and Commentary*, Tyndale Old Testament Commentary (Downers Grove, IL: InterVarsity Press, 1972), 123.

17. Contra Elizabeth Achtemeier, *Nahum—Malachi* (Louisville: Westminster/John Knox, 1986), 124–25 who interprets the menorah as a symbol for the covenant people, Wolters is on firmer ground in connecting the menorah to the temple, "the holy place where the Lord will again take up residence after the exile." *Zechariah*, 111. Cf. Boda, *Book of Zechariah*, 310. Of course only through the work of Christ (whose body is the Church) and the power of the Spirit can the menorah be applied to the covenant people. Meredith G. Kline, *Glory in Our Midst: A Biblical-Theological Reading of Zechariah's Night Visions* (Overland Park, KS: Two Age Press, 2001), 132–33.

18. See, e.g., Barry Webb, *The Message of Zechariah* (Downers Grove, IL: InterVarsity Press, 2003), 93. Achtemeier, *Nahum—Malachi*, 125 suggested that a future king and a future high priest are in view.

19. For thorough treatment of the relevant evidence, see Wolter H. Rose, *Zemah and Zerubbabel: Messianic Expectations in the Early Postexilic Period*, Journal for the Study of the Old Testament Supplement Series 304 (Sheffield, UK: Sheffield Academic Press, 2000), 193–95.

20. Boda, *Book of Zechariah*, 315–16. If this is correct, Rose summarizes the meaning as follows: "Just as the two olive trees provide oil for the lampstand to burn, so the two prophets, presumably by speaking the word of YHWH, provide the means of sustenance for the people of God." *Zemah and Zerubbabel*, 203.

21. Rose, *Zemah and Zerubbabel*, 202–6; Duguid, *Haggai, Zechariah, Malachi*, 111.

### Chapter Sixty-Seven: Thy Kingdom Come

1. Al Wolters has noted that this is roughly the size of the average billboard beside highways in the U.S. Though many have suggested a significance to these dimensions (e.g., a connection to Solomon's temple porch, the Holy of Holies, etc.), Wolters rightly cautions that "it is doubtful whether the vision of the scroll is meant to be referring to them." *Zechariah*, Historical Commentary on the Old Testament (Leuven, Belgium: Peeters, 2014), 157–58.

2. Cf. Exodus 32:15. This seems to be the best reading of the admittedly difficult Hebrew, *mizzê kāmôhā* (literally, "from this according to it," feminine singular). That *mizzê . . . mizzê* is a spatial idiom indicating alternate sides or ends, see Exodus 17:12; 25:19; 26:13; Numbers 22:24; 1 Samuel 14:4; 17:3; 23:26; Ezekiel 45;7; 47:7. Mark J. Boda, *The Book of Zechariah*, New International Commentary on the Old Testament (Grand Rapids, MI: Eerdmans, 2016), 332. Cf. Francis Brown, et al., *The Brown-Driver-Briggs Hebrew and English Lexicon* (1906; repr. Peabody, MA: Hendrickson, 1996), 262; Thomas Edward McComiskey, "Zechariah," in *The Minor Prophets*, vol. 3 (Grand Rapids, MI: Baker, 1998), 1095; Meredith G. Kline, *Glory in Our Midst: A Biblical-Theological Reading of Zechariah's Night Visions* (Overland Park, KS: Two Age Press, 2001), 178. For alternate views, see Wolters, *Zechariah*, 158–60; Max Rogland, *Haggai and Zechariah 1-8: A Handbook on the Hebrew Text,* Baylor Handbook on the Hebrew Bible (Waco, TX: Baylor University Press, 2016), 155–56; and Carol L. Meyers and Eric M. Meyers, *Haggai, Zechariah 1–8*, Anchor Bible 25B (Garden City, NY: Doubleday, 1987), 286. Though a different expression is used, it should be noted that a double-sided scroll is featured in Ezekiel's visionary experience with perhaps the same symbolic function (Ezekiel 2:10).

3. Iain M. Duguid, *Haggai, Zechariah, Malachi*, EP Study Commentary (Carlisle: Evangelical Press, 2010), 115.

4. Elizabeth Achtemeier, *Nahum—Malachi* (Louisville: Westminster/John Knox, 1986), 127; Duguid, *Haggai, Zechariah, Malachi*, 115–16.

5. Boda, *Book of Zechariah*, 336; Duguid, *Haggai, Zechariah, Malachi*, 116.

6. "The scroll is heavenly and possesses the omniscience of its divine source." Meyers and Meyers, *Haggai, Zechariah*, 292.

7. Duguid, *Haggai, Zechariah, Malachi*, 114.

8. Duguid, 117–18 understands the woman in the basket to be an idol, suggesting a possible connection to Israel's faithlessness in marrying foreign unbelieving wives, a significant problem for the postexilic community. He notes that these two

issues often go together. Nevertheless, Duguid acknowledges that something bigger, namely all iniquity, seems to be in view.

9. "This surprisingly violent action on the part of the messenger suggests that he was fearful of the prospect of the woman being on the loose." Wolters, *Zechariah*, 167.

10. Wolters, 169.

11. Wolters, 163, following Michael R. Stead's seminal work, *The Intertextuality of Zechariah 1-8*, Library of Hebrew Bible/Old Testament Studies 506 (New York: T&T Clark, 2009), 196–207.

12. Meyers and Meyers observe, "The carrying of Wickedness away to Babylon serves as the counterpart to the return of Yahweh to the land he had chosen and to his rightful temple in Jerusalem." *Haggai, Zechariah*, 314.

13. Wolters, *Zechariah*, 173.

14. Wolters, 172.

15. Duguid, *Haggai, Zechariah, Malachi*, 121–22.

16. Wolters, *Zechariah*, 174 has noted that the Hebrew *ruḥôt* "normally has the meaning 'winds,' and by extension '(cardinal) points of the compass' (north, south, east, west). Zechariah seems to be playing on both of these meanings." The identification of the horse-drawn chariots as *'arbaʿ ruḥôt haššāmayim* ("four winds of heaven") likely connects these chariots to the common image of God as the rider of the clouds (cf. Psalm 68:5).

17. Kline, *Glory in Our Midst*, 211–14.

18. Though some have understood the expression *hēnîḥû 'et-rûḥî* ("have set my Spirit at rest") to refer exclusively either to God's judgment (e.g., Wolters, *Zechariah*, 178; and Boda, *Book of Zechariah*, 379–80) or to God's mercy (e.g., Kline, *Glory in Our Midst*, 214–15), this author agrees with those who understand both divine judgment and mercy to be in view. See, e.g., C. F. Keil and Franz Delitzsch, *Minor Prophets*, Commentary on the Old Testament in Ten Volumes, trans. James Martin (Grand Rapids, MI: Eerdmans, 1989), 580–81. The coming of God's kingdom so vividly and symbolically depicted in this vision consists of elements throughout both Zechariah and the prophetic literature generally (see, e.g., 14:12–19).

## Chapter Sixty-Eight: Behold, Your Priest-King!

1. As they pertain to the matter under consideration, Lord Acton's remarks are worth quoting in full: "I cannot accept your canon that we are to judge Pope and King unlike other men, with a favourable presumption that they did no wrong. If there is any presumption it is the other way against holders of power, increasing as the power increases. Historic responsibility has to make up for the want of legal responsibility. Power tends to corrupt and absolute power corrupts absolutely. Great men are almost always bad men, even when they exercise influence and not authority: still more when you superadd the tendency or the certainty of corruption by authority. There is no worse heresy than that the office sanctifies the holder of it." Letter to Archbishop Mandell Creighton, April 5, 1887, in *Historical Essays and Studies*, ed. J. N. Figgis and R. V. Laurence (London: Macmillan, 1907), https://oll.libertyfund.org/title/acton-acton-creighton-correspondence.

2. See, e.g., Alexander Hamilton or James Madison, *The Federalist Papers: No. 51* (1788), https://guides.loc.gov/federalist-papers/text-51-60#s-lg-box-wrapper-25493427.

3. Elizabeth Achtemeier, *Nahum—Malachi* (Louisville: Westminster/John Knox, 1986), 130. For helpful discussions of prophetic sign-acts as ancient Near East and Israelite phenomena, see W. David Stacy, *Prophetic Drama in the Old Testament* (London: Epworth, 1990); and Kelvin G. Friebel, *Jeremiah's and Ezekiel's Sign-Acts: Rhetorical Non-verbal Communication*, Journal for the Study of the Old Testament Supplement Series 28 (Sheffield, UK: Sheffield Academic Press, 1999).

4. For exegetical treatments of the major prophetic sign-acts including Zechariah 6:9–15, see Åke Viberg, *Prophets in Action: An Analysis of Prophetic Symbolic Acts in the Old Testament*, Coniectanea biblica: Old Testament Series 55 (Stockholm: Almqvist & Wiksell International, 2007).

5. Al Wolters, *Zechariah*, Historical Commentary on the Old Testament (Leuven, Belgium: Peeters, 2014), 183.

6. Iain M. Duguid, *Haggai, Zechariah, Malachi*, EP Study Commentary (Carlisle: Evangelical Press, 2010), 125.

7. Duguid, *Haggai, Zechariah, Malachi*, 125.

8. Duguid, 125.

9. Citing Ezekiel 21:26, Wolters makes the compelling observation, "The curse on the last king of Judah before the exile is matched and reversed by the blessing on the first high priest of Judah after the exile." *Zechariah*, 185.

10. Barry Webb has noted that the turban was the customary headdress for the priest while kings wore crowns as here. *The Message of Zechariah* (Downers Grove, IL: InterVarsity Press, 2003), 107–8.

11. Webb, *The Message of Zechariah*, 109; Achtemeier, *Nahum—Malachi*, 132; Duguid, *Haggai, Zechariah, Malachi*, 128.

12. That *šᵉnêhem* refers to the union of two roles or offices instead of the cooperation of two individuals, see Wolters, *Zechariah*, 191–93.

13. Mark J. Boda, *The Book of Zechariah*, New International Commentary on the Old Testament (Grand Rapids, MI: Eerdmans, 2016), 403.

14. Duguid, *Haggai, Zechariah, Malachi*, 127.

15. Duguid, 127, has noted that "the primary function of a memorial (*zikkārôn*) is to keep the matter constantly before the Lord, rather than the people, which is why it is located in the temple." Nevertheless, he specifies that the crown serves *secondarily* "as a reminder to the community of God's plans for their future. . . . It serves as an assurance for the people of God's determination to bring these things to pass."

16. Cf. Isaiah 49:12; Jeremiah 25:26; Joel 3:8. Boda, *Book of Zechariah*, 412 acknowledges that *rᵉḥôqîm* typically refers to "foreigners" or "Gentiles," though he believes that here it refers to Jews who have remained in exile as these would be the ones invited to build the physical temple in Jerusalem. Cf., e.g., Isaiah 43:6; 49:12; 60:4.

17. See the discussion of Zechariah 3:6–10 above.

18. Webb, *Message of Zechariah*, 109.

19. "From fallen mankind, exiled from God's presence and paradise as the aftermath of Adam's transgression, from the diaspora of the Gentiles augmented by the diaspora of the Jews (cf. Rom 11:30–32), from far off they come to Christ, God's

temple (John 2:18–21; Eph 2:12, 13). They come and participate in the building of the extended temple, the church-body of which Christ is the head, the temple of which he is the chief cornerstone and his apostles and prophets the foundation." Meredith G. Kline, *Glory in Our Midst: A Biblical-Theological Reading of Zechariah's Night Visions* (Overland Park, KS: Two Age Press, 2001), 232.

Chapter Sixty-Nine: Mourning into Dancing, Fasting into Feasting

1. Many commentators take *bêṯ-'ēl śar-'eṣer* as a personal name (Bethel-Sharezer) of an official who, along with Regem-Melech, probably sent an embassy to Jerusalem from Babylon. See, e.g., Jewish Publication Society; Max Rogland, *Haggai and Zechariah 1-8: A Handbook on the Hebrew Text,* Baylor Handbook on the Hebrew Bible (Waco, TX: Baylor University Press, 2016), 187–88; David L. Petersen, *Haggai and Zechariah 1–8*, Old Testament Library (Philadelphia: Westminster/John Knox, 1984), 281; and Iain M. Duguid, *Haggai, Zechariah, Malachi*, EP Study Commentary (Carlisle: Evangelical Press, 2010), 131. In a similar vein Joyce G. Baldwin takes Bethel-Sharezer as the subject and Regem-Melech as the object. *Haggai, Zechariah, Malachi: An Introduction and Commentary*, Tyndale Old Testament Commentary (Downers Grove, IL: InterVarsity Press, 1972), 142–43. Similarly, Al Wolters, *Zechariah*, Historical Commentary on the Old Testament (Leuven, Belgium: Peeters, 2014), 211–12. While these interpretations are grammatically possible and do in fact have much in their favor from a historical and perhaps archaeological perspective, Mark J. Boda is on firmer ground in appealing to the Masoretic Text accentuation (*zâqēp parvum* on 'ēl) that seems to cast Bethel as an individuated entity, as well as appealing to the connection between Zechariah 7:2, 3 and the matching verses at the end of chapter 8 (vv. 19–23), which "reveals the 1cs voice of a representative of a city speaking to another (city), similar to the 1cs voice of Shar-ezer speaking on behalf of Bethel." *The Book of Zechariah*, New International Commentary on the Old Testament (Grand Rapids, MI: Eerdmans, 2016), 434–35. Cf. Andrew E. Hill, *Haggai, Zechariah, Malachi: An Introduction and Commentary*, Tyndale Old Testament Commentary (Downers Grove, IL: InterVarsity Press, 2012), 183; Carol L. Meyers and Eric M. Meyers, *Haggai, Zechariah 1–8*, Anchor Bible 25B (Garden City, NY: Doubleday, 1987), 383.

2. Duguid, *Haggai, Zechariah, Malachi*, 135.

3. Commenting on the expression *lᵉḥallôṯ 'eṯ-pᵉnê yhwh* ("to entreat the favor of the LORD"), Boda, *Book of Zechariah*, 435 writes, "When used in relation to God, it often appears in contexts where people are seeking relief from the anger of God and often attendant experience or threat of discipline (Exod. 32:11; 1 Kgs. 13:6; 2 Kgs. 13:4; 2 Chr. 33:12; Jer. 26:19. . . . ). This evidence suggests, then, that the question presented here by the Bethel contingent is not merely a request for liturgical direction, but rather a muted plea that God would bring an end to the period of discipline."

4. Duguid, *Haggai, Zechariah, Malachi*, 132–33.

5. Wolters, *Zechariah*, 225.

6. "God takes no notice of piety that does not issue out of a listening and obedient heart (vv. 8-12; cf. Jer. 5:3, 21; 7:26; 8:5; 11:10; 17:1, 23)." Elizabeth Achtemeier, *Nahum—Malachi* (Louisville: Westminster John Knox Press, 1986), 135.

7. "[Zechariah] appears to be confronting an attitude in the community of the early Persian period that the building of the physical structure of the temple was evidence of the restoration of the community and the return of God's blessings." Mark J. Boda, "From Fasts to Feasts: The Literary Function of Zechariah 7–8," *Catholic Bible Quarterly* 65 (2003): 390–407 (quote on 399).

8. Duguid, *Haggai, Zechariah, Malachi*, 144.

9. Contra Wolters, *Zechariah*, 231, 232 who understands both God's *qin'ô gᵉdôlâ* ("great jealousy") and *ḥēmâ gᵉdôlâ* ("great wrath") as directed toward Zion. Cf. Zechariah 1:15. See also Boda, *Book of Zechariah*, 478–79.

10. Yair Zakovitch, "A Garden of Eden in the Squares of Jerusalem: Zachariah [*sic*] 8:4-6," *Gregorianum* 87 (2006): 301–11 (303).

11. Zakovitch, "Garden of Eden," 308.

12. Wolters, *Zechariah*, 237–43 has noted several links that connect Zechariah 8 and Haggai.

13. Achtemeier, *Nahum—Malachi*, 140–41.

14. Zechariah's opening words of verse 16, *'ēllê haddᵉḇārîm* ("these are the things") echo the opening words of Deuteronomy, which suggests that the laws specified in Zechariah 8:16, 17 are representative of the whole Torah. Wolters, *Zechariah*, 245.

15. Achtemeier, *Nahum—Malachi*, 136; Duguid, *Haggai, Zechariah, Malachi*, 136.

16. "The blessing that would come from the work begun with the raising up of the temple should provide the motivation to lives of renewed obedience." Duguid, *Haggai, Zechariah, Malachi*, 142.

17. Wolters, *Zechariah*, 246.

18. *ESV Study Bible*, 1761. Wolters's verdict of an "unsubstantiated hypothesis" regarding the ancient Jewish exegetical tradition supplying these connections (e.g., Talmud, Jerome) is slightly overstated. *Zechariah*, 214–15.

19. John Flavel, "The Mystery of Providence," in *The Works of John Flavel*, vol. 4 (Edinburgh: Banner of Truth, 1968), 340 (emphasis mine).

20. Wolters's preference for translating the Hebrew *ᶜaṣûmîm* as "numerous" instead of "strong" is based on a false dichotomy. There was at least some correlation between population size and strength in the ancient world. Though his suggestion "strong in numbers" is better (*Zechariah*, 250), the meaning of the word typically has to do with strength or might, which may only be partially related to population size. Cf. Psalm 10:10; Proverbs 18:18; Daniel 8:24; Joel 2:11. See also Boda, *Book of Zechariah*, 512.

21. For an excellent survey of the expression *wᵉheḥᵉzîqû biḵnap* ("they will take hold of the robe") in the Old Testament and cognate literature and its significance, see Wolters, *Zechariah*, 251–52.

## Chapter Seventy: The Return of the King

1. The most famous version is probably by Sir Thomas Malory, *Le Morte D'Arthur*, ed. William Caxton, 1485.

2. There are many versions and iterations of Robin Hood; one of the earliest that serves as the foundation for modern adaptations is the early sixteenth-century Middle English ballad *A Gest of Robyn Hode*.

3. J. R. R. Tolkien, *The Return of the King* (London: George Allen & Unwin, 1955).

4. C. S. Lewis, "Myth Became Fact," in *God in the Dock: Essays on Theology and Ethics* (Grand Rapids, MI: Eerdmans, 1970), 63–67.

5. For an excellent treatment of Zechariah's social location and its effect on his prophetic message, see Byron G. Curtis, *Up the Steep and Stony Road: The Book of Zechariah in Social Location Trajectory*, Society of Biblical Literature Academia Biblica 25 (Atlanta: SBL Press, 2006).

6. Al Wolters, *Zechariah*, Historical Commentary on the Old Testament (Leuven, Belgium: Peeters, 2014), 265.

7. Wolters, *Zechariah*, 273.

8. Barry Webb, *The Message of Zechariah* (Downers Grove, IL: InterVarsity Press, 2003), 130.

9. "The borders of that area are not arbitrarily set, but outline what ancient Israel tradition held to be the ideal kingdom of the Jews." Paul D. Hanson, *The Dawn of Apocalyptic: The Historical and Sociological Roots of Jewish Apocalyptic Eschatology*, rev. ed. (Philadelphia: Fortress, 1979), 317.

10. The Hebrew *yš'* occurs in two other passages in the Old Testament, both clearly passive: Deuteronomy 33:29 and Psalm 33:16. See Rex Mason, "The Use of Earlier Biblical Material in Zechariah 9-14: A Study in Inner Biblical Exegesis," in *Bringing Out the Treasure: Inner Biblical Allusion in Zechariah 9-14*, ed. Mark J. Boda and Michael H. Floyd, Journal for the Study of the Old Testament Supplement Series 370 (New York: Sheffield Academic Press, 2003), 36; and Carol L. Meyers and Eric M. Meyers, *Zechariah 9–14*, Anchor Bible 25C (New York: Doubleday, 1993), 126–27. Agreeing on the meaning "saved," Anthony Robert Petterson's further comment deserves consideration: "Yet in the context of Yahweh's victory in Zech 9:1-8, it also seems appropriate to understand the king's salvation in the sense of a victory that he brings to share with others. The salvation of the king means the salvation of his people, and in this sense the king 'has salvation' or 'brings salvation' and so the difference between the passive and the reflexive is not that great when it comes to the final meaning." *Behold Your King: The Hope for the House of David in the Book of Zechariah*, Library of Hebrew Bible/Old Testament Studies 513 (New York: T&T Clark, 2009), 139. Petterson's "final meaning" might be better understood as an implication.

11. Mason, "Use of Earlier Biblical Material," 39.

12. For a full discussion of the relationship between the king in Zechariah 9:9ff. and the servant in Isaiah's Servant Songs, see Mason, 34–38.

13. Cf. Judges 12:14. See Iain M. Duguid, *Haggai, Zechariah, Malachi*, EP Study Commentary (Carlisle: Evangelical Press, 2010), 149.

14. Iain M. Duguid, "Messianic Themes in Zechariah 9—14," in *The Lord's Anointed: Interpretation of Old Testament Messianic Texts*, ed. Philip E. Satterthwaite, Richard S. Hess, and Gordon J. Wenham (Grand Rapids, MI: Baker, 1995), 265–80, esp. 268.

15. "What seems to be indicated here, therefore, is that the king who comes brings victory and deliverance with him for the people. But it is God's victory which he has experienced, and which he mediates to the community *by virtue of his right relationship to God.*" Mason, "Use of Earlier Biblical Material," 36 (emphasis mine).

16. Duguid, "Messianic Themes," 268.
17. Duguid, 268.
18. Many commentators have noted that Psalm 72 likely served as a source for the prophet's language and imagery. In addition to the numerous conceptual parallels (e.g., the king's rule characterized by the cessation of warfare; cf. 72:7), there is a nearly exact parallel between Psalm 72:8 and Zechariah 9:10c. See Meyers and Meyers, *Zechariah*, 136–37; and Mason, "Use of Earlier Biblical Material," 39.
19. "The blood of this covenant testified that, even though the people deserved death for transgressing the covenant made at Sinai, God himself would none the less bring to fruition his purpose to have a people for himself." Duguid, *Haggai, Zechariah, Malachi*, 150.
20. Elizabeth Achtemeier, *Nahum—Malachi* (Louisville: Westminster/John Knox, 1986), 147. Duguid has noted that "in Genesis 10 'the sons of Javan' is a more general term that encompasses many of the coastal Mediterranean peoples. These peoples included the Greeks, so that later it became natural to use this term to denote the Greeks, but here the more general meaning is in view." *Haggai, Zechariah, Malachi*, 151.
21. Duguid., 147.
22. See, e.g., Achtemeier, *Nahum—Malachi*, 147 who interpreted Zechariah 9:15 as a victory celebration; and David L. Petersen, *Zechariah 9–14 and Malachi* (Louisville: Westminster/John Knox, 1995), 65 who interprets this verse as (continuing) the depiction of an eschatological battle. Wolters has asserted: "This portion of the text is hopelessly obscure," and "It is unclear whether the protagonists are themselves joining in the fight or enjoying a festive banquet as the battle rages elsewhere." *Zechariah*, 295.

Chapter Seventy-One: The Work of the Good Shepherd
1. Leland Ryken, *40 Favorite Hymns on the Christian Life: A Closer Look at Their Spiritual and Poetic Meaning* (Phillipsburg, NJ: P&R, 2019), 58.
2. Robert Robinson, "Come, Thou Fount of Every Blessing," in *A Collection of Hymns used by the Church of Christ in Angel-Alley, Bishopsgate* (1759).
3. Elizabeth Achtemeier, *Nahum—Malachi* (Louisville: Westminster/John Knox, 1986), 155.
4. Mark Futato, quoted in Al Wolters, *Zechariah*, Historical Commentary on the Old Testament (Leuven, Belgium: Peeters, 2014), 309.
5. Barry Webb, *The Message of Zechariah* (Downers Grove, IL: InterVarsity Press, 2003), 138.
6. "Bad leadership is a perennial problem, and it always leads to scattering and lostness." Webb, *Message of Zechariah*, 139.
7. That "shepherds" refers to rulers and leaders in general (as opposed to kings or prophets), see Iain M. Duguid, "Messianic Themes in Zechariah 9—14," in *The Lord's Anointed: Interpretation of Old Testament Messianic Texts*, ed. Philip E. Satterthwaite, Richard S. Hess, and Gordon J. Wenham (Grand Rapids, MI: Baker, 1995), 270; and Mark J. Boda, *The Book of Zechariah*, New International Commentary on the Old Testament (Grand Rapids, MI: Eerdmans, 2016), 608–9.
8. Duguid, "Messianic Themes," 270.

9. Carol L. Meyers and Eric M. Meyers, *Zechariah 9–14*, Anchor Bible 25C (New York: Doubleday, 1993), 196.

10. Boda, *Book of Zechariah*, 611 has noted the wordplay in Zechariah 10:3 with a variation of the sense of the Hebrew *pāqad* in *'epqôḏ kî-pāqaḏ* ("I will punish . . . for the LORD of hosts *cares* for his flock").

11. The character of Yahweh's warhorse in Zechariah 10:3 may be elucidated by Job 39:19–25 (esp. v. 20).

12. Boda, *Book of Zechariah*, 612.

13. Iain M. Duguid has noted that "the cornerstone" (*pinna*) recalls Isaiah 28:16 and Psalm 118:22, and "the tent peg" (*yātēd*) recalls Isaiah 22:20–23. *Haggai, Zechariah, Malachi*, EP Study Commentary (Carlisle: Evangelical Press, 2010), 156. Similarly, Meyers and Meyers, *Zechariah*, 200–201.

14. Wolters, *Zechariah*, 238.

15. "It appears that Judah's restoration is the first step in a program that will then impact the tribes of the former northern kingdom (see 10:6a)." Boda, *Book of Zechariah*, 612, cf. 622.

16. Webb, *Message of Zechariah*, 142.

17. "[God] is the subject of the verbs in [Zechariah 10:] 6-12. As the context makes clear, however, the means by which he brings about this remarkable reversal in the condition of his people is his getting rid of bad leaders (3a), and providing good ones in their place (3b-5). In short, strong leaders raised up and empowered by God, are essential for the welfare of God's people." Webb, 141.

Chapter Seventy-Two: Death Shall Be Their Shepherd

1. S. R. Driver called it "the most enigmatic in the Old Testament." *The Minor Prophets: Nahum, Habakkuk, Zephaniah, Haggai, Zechariah, Malachi*, The Century Bible (Edinburgh: T. C. & E. C. Jack, 1906), 253. Cf. Al Wolters, *Zechariah*, Historical Commentary on the Old Testament (Leuven, Belgium: Peeters, 2014), 346.

2. Anthony Robert Petterson, *Behold Your King: The Hope for the House of David in the Book of Zechariah*, Library of Hebrew Bible 513 (New York: T&T Clark, 2009), 168; Wolters, *Zechariah*, 357.

3. Carol L. Meyers and Eric M. Meyers, *Zechariah 9–14*, Anchor Bible 25C (New York: Doubleday, 1993), 260.

4. This author agrees with those who see the primary referent of the sign-act as Israel's history prior to the exile. See, e.g., Meyers and Meyers, *Zechariah*, 248–304; and Barry Webb, *The Message of Zechariah* (Downers Grove, IL: InterVarsity Press, 2003), 287–301. The breaking of the two staffs "Favor" and "Union" (Zechariah 11:7) seems to refer to the preexilic events of God's annulment of the Mosaic covenant that led to exile and the division of the kingdom after the days of Solomon, respectively. The latter is likely an allusion to Ezekiel's sign-act in Ezekiel 37:15–28. Furthermore, the depiction of cannibalism in Zechariah 11:9 reflects the conditions of Jerusalem immediately prior to its fall in 586 B.C. (cf. Jeremiah 19:9). For a helpful survey and evaluation of the various proposals for understanding Zechariah 11:4–17, see Petterson, *Behold Your King*, 168–94.

5. Zechariah 10:2 makes it clear that the postexilic community was again tempted with the idolatry that plagued their preexilic forefathers.

6. Eugene H. Merrill summarizes the multiple horizons in view in the prophetic sign-act: "The shepherd imagery pertained to events of the past, that Zechariah in fact was reliving the history of his own people. That history indeed provided a prototype for future events occasionally (as in vv. 12–13) but essentially was antecedent to the prophet's own time (i.e. was preexilic)." *An Exegetical Commentary: Haggai, Zechariah, Malachi* (Chicago: Moody, 1994), 303.

7. For a similar rhetorical device, see Amos 1:2—2:8. "It is not, however . . . , a matter of using a literary form originally meant for the nation and now adapted to Israel, but rather of deliberately setting a rhetorical trap for the readers, initially lulling them into thinking that the judgment announced is over Israel's enemies, and then, with the very last word, turning the tables on them by making the judgment apply to their own land." Wolters, *Zechariah*, 348.

8. Webb, *Message of Zechariah*, 144–47. Based on its connection to Jeremiah 25, Mark J. Boda argues that the Jewish leaders in view have connections to foreign nations. *The Book of Zechariah*, New International Commentary on the Old Testament (Grand Rapids, MI: Eerdmans, 2016), 644. Contra, e.g., David L. Petersen and others who see the trees as representing foreign nations. *Zechariah 9–14 and Malachi*, Old Testament Library (Philadelphia: Westminster John Knox, 1995), 80–82.

9. Elizabeth Achtemeier, *Nahum—Malachi* (Louisville: Westminster/John Knox, 1986), 155–56.

10. Wolters, *Zechariah*, 357.

11. So much so that Wolters, 357–58 has suggested that the sign-act could only be performed in the context of a dream or vision or, perhaps more accurately, a nightmare. While this is possible, it is not necessarily the case, as the prophet might have enacted this complex sign-act publicly in a manner that eludes our ability to easily conceptualize.

12. It is difficult to conceptualize exactly how the prophet performed the sign-act described in 11:7–15. This has led some to suggest that Zechariah was offering an account of a vision or a dream. See, e.g., Wolters, *Zechariah*, 357–58. While this is possible, it seems more likely that the prophet performed a skit of sorts that incorporated the various characters and actions.

13. "Together the two staffs symbolize the blessedness of life in covenant relationship with God." Webb, *Message of Zechariah*, 149.

14. Joyce G. Baldwin, *Haggai, Zechariah, Malachi: An Introduction and Commentary*, Tyndale Old Testament Commentary (Downers Grove, IL: InterVarsity Press, 1972), 181–83.

15. For these suggestions and more, see Wolters, *Zechariah*, 373.

16. John Calvin, *Commentaries on the Twelve Minor Prophets*, vol. 5, trans. John Owen (Grand Rapids: Baker, 2003), 316; Meyers and Meyers, *Zechariah*, 265; Iain M. Duguid, *Haggai, Zechariah, Malachi*, EP Study Commentary (Carlisle: Evangelical Press, 2010), 164; Webb, *The Message of Zechariah*, 149n139. Wolters takes *bᵉyeraḥ ʾeḥoḏ* as "in the first month" with a similar meaning: "the prophet-shepherd set to work immediately." *Zechariah*, 373–74.

17. Cf. Numbers 21:4; Judges 10:16; 16:16; Job 24:1-4. See also Boda, *Haggai, Zechariah*, 464.

18. Though the covenant in view in the expression *ʾet̠-bᵉrîṯî ʾᵃšer kāratî ʾet̠-kol-hāʿammîm* is difficult to determine with certainty, the Mosaic covenant makes

the most sense in the context. Though rare, Israel is on occasion referred to with ʿammîm. See, e.g., Genesis 27:29; 48:4; 49:10; 1 Kings 22:28; Isaiah 3:13. See also Meyers and Meyers, *Zechariah*, 271; and Petterson, *Behold Your King*, 192. For alternative views, see Duguid, *Haggai, Zechariah, Malachi*, 164.

19. Achtemeier, *Nahum—Malachi*, 157.

20. Webb has made the important point that "the breaking of the second rod *Union* (14) depicts . . . the breaking up of the once united Israel. Historically it began after the death of Solomon, but continued in stages over the next several centuries. The final fracturing came with the fall of Jerusalem and the scattering of its people." *The Message of Zechariah*, 151.

21. Josephus, *The Jewish War*, trans. Martin Hammond (Oxford: Oxford University Press, 2017), ii.86.

22. Josephus, *Jewish War*, i; *Antiquities*, xiv–xv.

23. Josephus, *Antiquities*, xvii, 161, 173–79, 193–95. Thankfully, Herod's orders were disobeyed.

24. Iain M. Duguid, "Messianic Themes in Zechariah 9—14," in *The Lord's Anointed: Interpretation of Old Testament Messianic Texts*, ed. Philip E. Satterthwaite, Richard S. Hess, and Gordon J. Wenham (Grand Rapids, MI: Baker, 1995), 273–74.

## Chapter Seventy-Three: By Thy Transforming Power

1. Mark J. Boda, *The Book of Zechariah*, New International Commentary on the Old Testament (Grand Rapids, MI: Eerdmans, 2016), 693. Boda has noted that the same verbs (Hebrew *nāṭâ* and *yāsad*) are used together only in Isaiah 51:13, thus drawing his hearers' mind to an earlier instance of God delivering his people out of an impossible situation.

2. Carol L. Meyers and Eric M. Meyers, *Zechariah 9–14*, Anchor Bible 25C (New York: Doubleday, 1993), 311; Iain M. Duguid, *Haggai, Zechariah, Malachi*, EP Study Commentary (Carlisle: Evangelical Press, 2010), 169.

3. On the basis of Zechariah 12:2 (*wᵉgam ʿal-yᵉhûḏâ yihyê ḇammāṣôr ʿal-yᵉrûšālāim*), commentators have suggested that even Judah will join the nations in the siege of Jerusalem, possibly under compulsion. See, e.g., Al Wolters (appealing to the Targum), *Zechariah* (Leuven, Belgium: Peeters, 2014), 404–6; and Elizabeth Achtemeier, *Nahum—Malachi* (Louisville: Westminster/John Knox, 1986), 161. However, Meyers and Meyers have argued that this reading disagrees with the rest of the passage and that the text is reasonably clear in identifying Judah with Jerusalem as under siege. *Zechariah*, 307, 315–16. Similarly, Boda has argued that *ʿal-yᵉhûḏâ* should be understood as "regarding Judah," thus connecting Judah with Jerusalem. *Book of Zechariah*, 701.

4. Boda, *Book of Zechariah*, 701.

5. The classic treatment of this ordeal as an ancient Near East legal phenomenon is Tikva Simone Frymer-Kensky's, "The Judicial Ordeal in the Ancient Near East" (Ph.D. diss., Yale University, 1977). For a brief introduction to the ordeal in ancient Israel, see Karel van der Toorn, "Ordeal," D. N. Freedman, ed., *Anchor Bible Dictionary* (New York: Bantam Doubleday Dell, 1992), 5:42–44.

6. Van der Toorn, "Ordeal," 42.

7. Cf. Exodus 32:20. Though the *Sotah* has often been identified as a trial by ordeal (e.g., W. McKane, "Poison, Trial by Ordeal, and the Cup of Wrath" *Vetus Tes-*

*tamentum* 30 [1980], 474–92), Tikva Frymer-Kensky argues on the basis of formal features that it is closer to an imprecatory oath. "The Strange Case of the Suspected Sotah (Numbers V 11-31)," *Vetus Testamentum* 34 (1984): 11–26. Cf. van der Toorn, "Ordeal," 40. However, the two procedures are closely related.

8. Meyers and Meyers, *Zechariah*, 313–14.

9. Thomas O. Chisholm, "Great Is Thy Faithfulness," in *Songs of Salvation and Service*, ed. William Runyan (Chicago: Moody, 1923).

10. Achtemeier, *Nahum—Malachi*, 162.

11. Barry Webb, *The Message of Zechariah* (Downers Grove, IL: InterVarsity Press, 2003), 159.

12. I follow Iain M. Duguid in identifying the wounded figure as Israel's coming messianic King. He has written, "Accepting that *dqr* usually means a stab wound inflicted by a sword, is it not better to identify the pierced one of Zechariah 12:10 with the shepherd of Zechariah 13:7-9, against whom God's sword is coming? The death of that royal figure, which clearly has tragic consequences for the flock (Zc. 13:7), seems an appropriate cause for the intense mourning of the whole community, mourning as intense as that which followed the tragic death of Josiah at Megiddo." "Messianic Themes in Zechariah 9—14," in *The Lord's Anointed: Interpretation of Old Testament Messianic Texts*, ed. Philip E. Satterthwaite, Richard S. Hess, and Gordon J. Wenham (Grand Rapids, MI: Baker, 1995), 276. Cf. Thomas Edward McComiskey, "Zechariah," in *The Minor Prophets*, vol. 3 (Grand Rapids, MI: Baker, 1998), 1214–15, 1223.

13. Achtemeier, *Nahum—Malachi*, 162.

14. Stuart Townend, "How Deep the Father's Love for Us," *Thankyou Music* (1995).

15. See, e.g., Stanley Brice Frost, *Old Testament Apocalyptic: Its Origins and Growth* (London: Epworth, 1952), 135–36; and Paul D. Hanson, *The Dawn of Apocalyptic: The Historical and Sociological Roots of Jewish Apocalyptic Eschatology*, rev. ed. (Philadelphia: Fortress, 1979), 368–69.

16. Joyce G. Baldwin, *Haggai, Zechariah, Malachi: An Introduction and Commentary*, Tyndale Old Testament Commentary (Downers Grove, IL: InterVarsity Press, 1972), 197. David L. Petersen sees it as a "transitional piece"; the "imperative rhetoric with which this brief poem begins will initiate the events that will eventuate in the appearance of Yahweh's day." *Zechariah 9–14 and Malachi*, Old Testament Library (Philadelphia: Westminster/John Knox, 1995), 129

17. Meyers and Meyers, *Zechariah*, 387. Anthony Robert Petterson has made the connection to the covenant formula adapted at the conclusion: "I will say, 'They are my people' " and "They will say, 'The LORD is my God' " (Zechariah 13:9). *Behold Your King: The Hope for the House of David in the Book of Zechariah*, Library of Hebrew Bible 513 (New York: T&T Clark, 2009), 197.

18. Iain M. Duguid, "Messianic Themes in Zechariah 9—14," in *The Lord's Anointed: Interpretation of Old Testament Messianic Texts*, ed. Philip E. Satterthwaite, Richard S. Hess, and Gordon J. Wenham (Grand Rapids, MI: Baker, 1995), 274.

Chapter Seventy-Four: On That Day . . .

1. From T. S. Eliot's obituary, *New York Times*, January 5, 1965.

2. To be sure it has been read as such in the history of Christian interpretation. For a helpful survey of interpretations of this difficult text and views about its fulfillment (or non-fulfillment), see Al Wolters, *Zechariah*, Historical Commentary on the Old Testament (Leuven, Belgium: Peeters, 2014), 452–54.

3. Wolters, *Zechariah*, 251.

4. David L. Petersen, *Zechariah 9–14 and Malachi*, Old Testament Library (Philadelphia: Westminster/John Knox, 1995), 16. Though there is a fair degree of movement and disorder to the events related in Zechariah 14, we may observe two general patterns of the Divine Warrior conquering his foes, after which he takes his seat as King of the world: Divine Warrior, 14:1–5, 12–15; Divine King, 14:6–11, 16–21. As numerous ancient Near East myths attest, these two images, warrior and king, are closely related (e.g., *Enuma Elish*; *The Baal Cycle*).

5. John Newton, 'Amazing Grace,' in *Olney Hymns* (1779). See also Iain M. Duguid, *Haggai, Zechariah, Malachi*, EP Study Commentary (Carlisle: Evangelical Press, 2010), 179.

6. Though some take the ambiguous "your spoil" (*šəlālēk*) to refer to what Israel acquired from their enemies (e.g., Barry Webb, *The Message of Zechariah* [Downers Grove, IL: InterVarsity Press, 2003], 178), it more likely refers to spoil that had been taken from Israel—Jerusalem in particular—and that is being distributed before their eyes (e.g., Carol L. Meyers and Eric M. Meyers, *Zechariah 9–14*, Anchor Bible 25C [New York: Doubleday, 1993], 410–11). This is consistent with the sustained allusion to the first destruction of Jerusalem in 586 B.C. Mark J. Boda has made the important observation that *šālāl* ("plunder") "more often refers to that which is taken from someone (Deut. 20:14; Josh. 8:2; Ezek. 29:19; 2 Chr. 20:25; Esth. 3:13; 8:11) than by someone (Judg. 8:24; Isa. 10:2). Furthermore, in Amos 7:17 the subject of the Pual of *ḥālaq* ('be divided') is 'your land' (*'admāṯeḵā*), and the pronominal suffix refers to those who originally possessed the land which was plundered." *The Book of Zechariah*, New International Commentary on the Old Testament (Grand Rapids, MI: Eerdmans, 2016), 749.

7. Meyers and Meyers, *Zechariah*, 495–96.

8. Cf. 1 Kings 11:7; 2 Kings 23:13. See also Wolters, *Zechariah*, 456. Webb has noted that "standing" is "symbolic for 'taking possession.'" *The Message of Zechariah*, 178n238. Cf. Deuteronomy 11:24; Joshua 1:3; Job 19:25.

9. Though the exact location is unknown, scholars believe Azal may refer to an unknown city somewhere east of Jerusalem or perhaps may simply be a more general reference to the region east of Jerusalem and east of the Mount of Olives. See discussion by Mark J. Boda, *Book of Zechariah*, 758.

10. There is much uncertainty surrounding the expression *ûḇā' yhwh 'ĕlōhay kol-qəḏōšîm 'immāḵ* (literally "and YHWH my God will come [with?] all the holy ones with you"). Wolters, *Zechariah*, 459 is almost certainly correct that this reading has suffered textual corruption. The suggestion that *qəḏōšîm* ("holy ones") refers to the saints (alive or dead) fighting with YHWH (Webb, *Message of Zechariah*, 179; Boda, *Book of Zechariah*, 760) is far less likely than the suggestion that this is a reference to the angelic heavenly host following their King into battle. See Meyers and Meyers, *Zechariah*, 429–30. Cf. Job 5:1; 15:15; Psalm 89:6; Daniel 8:13. Wolters's repointing of the text, placing *qəḏōšîm* in apposition with *'ammô*, has much to commend it and deserves consideration. *Zechariah*, 459.

11. "Throughout this chapter, the theme of radical transformation is central. Dealing with the age-old problems of Israel's economic and political vulnerability, it sees the resolution of those problems in the radical changes that God will effect in the world. There will be a new creation." Meyers and Meyers, *Zechariah*, 493.

12. Following the Qere, *wᵉqippāʾôn* ("frost"). On the meaning of the more difficult Ketib *lōʾ-yihyê ʾôr yᵉqārôṯ yiqpᵉʾûn*, see Boda, *Book of Zechariah*, 762.

13. Duguid, *Haggai, Zechariah, Malachi*, 182.

14. Meyers and Meyers, *Zechariah*, 444–47; Wolters, *Zechariah*, 463.

15. Wolters, *Zechariah*, 463.

16. The prophet is clearly alluding to and developing the earlier prophecies of Isaiah (Isaiah 2:1–4) and Micah (Micah 4:1–4).

17. "There will be a new creation. Only then will God's creation of Israel become eternally assured. It will no longer be internally contingent; rather, it will be externally validated." Meyers and Meyers, *Zechariah*, 493.

18. Elizabeth Achtemeier, *Nahum—Malachi* (Louisville: Westminster John Knox Press, 1986), 167.

19. The notice *wᵉgam-yᵉhûḏâ tillāḥēm bîrûšālāim* is perplexing, and I have followed Wolters, *Zechariah*, 468–69 in preserving the ambiguity in the Hebrew as to whether Judah is fighting *with* or *against* Jerusalem.

20. Duguid, *Haggai, Zechariah, Malachi*, 182–83.

21. "Like chapters 9–14, as a whole, it moves from one kind of gathering (for war) to another kind (for worship), with verse 16 serving as a neat summary." Webb, *Message of Zechariah*, 177.

22. Meyers and Meyers, *Zechariah*, 506.

23. Duguid, *Haggai, Zechariah, Malachi*, 183.

24. Wolters, *Zechariah*, 472; Boda, *Book of Zechariah*, 779, 780.

25. See, e.g., Wolters, *Zechariah*, 473.

26. Achtemeier, *Nahum—Malachi*, 168; Meyers and Meyers, *Zechariah*, 506. Duguid sees a reference to "those Gentiles who had been there in the temple merely for business reasons, whose presence defiled the holiness of the Lord's house (see Ezek. 44:9)." *Haggai, Zechariah, Malachi*, 184. Cf. Joyce G. Baldwin, *Haggai, Zechariah, Malachi: An Introduction and Commentary*, Tyndale Old Testament Commentary (Downers Grove, IL: InterVarsity Press, 1972), 208; Webb, *Message of Zechariah*, 182.

### Chapter Seventy-Five: Questioning God's Love

1. For a useful (though dated) discussion of the structure of Malachi as well as a defense of the six-oracle division of the book followed in this commentary, see Andrew Hill, *Malachi: A New Translation with Introduction and Commentary*, Anchor Bible 25D (New York: Doubleday, 1998), 26–34.

2. "Yahweh's claim forms the foundation of the book and provides the context for understanding the relationship depicted throughout the book—a fractured relationship with the resulting dynamics and efforts at repair." Mignon R. Jacobs, *The Books of Haggai and Malachi*, New International Commentary on the Old Testament (Grand Rapids, MI: Eerdmans, 2017), 157.

3. Jacobs, *Books of Haggai and Malachi*, 160, 163.

4. S. D. (Fanie) Snyman, *Malachi*, Historical Commentary on the Old Testament (Leuven, Belgium: Peeters, 2015), 29.

5. Iain M. Duguid, *Haggai, Zechariah, Malachi*, EP Study Commentary (Carlisle: Evangelical Press, 2010), 191.

6. For a brief sketch of the various proposals as well as an up-to-date bibliography of the major discussions on the issue of dating Malachi's oracles, see Jacobs, *Books of Haggai and Malachi*, 130–37.

7. "For those jaundiced by apathy and despair as a result of 'failed' salvation oracles pronounced previously by Haggai and Zechariah, Malachi's message served as a much-needed corrective to wrong thinking about covenant relationship with Yahweh." Hill, *Malachi*, 162. Cf. Elizabeth Achtemeier, *Nahum—Malachi* (Louisville: Westminster/John Knox, 1986), 175.

8. Elizabeth Barrett Browning, *Sonnets from the Portuguese*, first published 1850. Public domain.

9. For a discussion of the practice of primogeniture in ancient Israel, see Philip J. King and Lawrence E. Stager, *Life in Biblical Israel* (Louisville: Westminster/John Knox, 2001), 37, 47–48.

10. Jonathan Gibson has noted that even the word order is suggestive of the surprising divine reversal of expectations: the rhetorical question $h^a l\hat{o}$'-'$oh$ $^c\bar{e}\acute{s}ow$ $l^eya^{ca}q\bar{o}\b{b}$ "follows the sequence of the twins' births in the Genesis narrative. Esau is named first because he was the firstborn; but, in the next clause, Jacob is named first because YHWH chose him to be heir of the covenant promises by setting his love upon him." *Covenant Continuity and Fidelity: A Study in Inner-Biblical Allusion and Exegesis in Malachi*, Library of Hebrew Studies/Old Testament Studies 65 (London: Bloomsbury T&T Clark, 2016), 50.

11. William Moran, "The Ancient Near Eastern Background of the Love of God in Deuteronomy," *Catholic Bible Quarterly* 25 (1963): 77–87.

12. "The declaration of Yahweh's love for his people may be an expression of emotion, but it is also, and perhaps foremost, an expression of a covenantal relationship. When Malachi uses this concept during the mid-5th century, it certainly echoes the language so well known in deuteronomistic theology. Yahweh and his people are bound into a relationship where love is the governing force on both sides. The verb love is also used in close connection with Israel's election (בחר) as the people of Yahweh. For Yahweh to choose or to love Israel are two sides of the same coin." Snyman, *Malachi*, 34. Similarly, David L. Petersen, *Zechariah 9–14 and Malachi*, Old Testament Library (Philadelphia: Westminster/John Knox, 1995), 168.

13. Geerhardus Vos, "Jeremiah's Plaint and Its Answer," in *Redemptive History and Biblical Interpretation: The Shorter Writings of Geerhardus Vos*, ed. Richard B. Gaffin Jr. (Phillipsburg, NJ: P&R, 1980), 298.

14. Vos, "Jeremiah's Plaint," 298.

15. Consider, for example, Moses's reasoning with Edom in Numbers 20:14–21.

16. Gibson has noted that the prophet's language reflects both ancient Near East treaty curses and prophetic judgments against the nations. *Covenant Continuity and Fidelity*, 53. Cf. Delbert Hillers, *Treaty Curses and the Old Testament Prophets*, *Biblica et Orientalia* 16 (Rome: Pontifical Biblical Institute, 1964), 53.

17. Reading the opening conjunction *kî* as marking a conditional clause. GKC §159.bb; Bruce K. Waltke and Michael Patrick O'Connor, *An Introduction to Biblical Hebrew Syntax* (Winona Lake, IN: Eisenbrauns, 1990) §§38.2a, c, d; 39.3.4e. Hill's contention that *kî* is marking an *irreal* conditional (*Malachi*, 156) is unlikely.

As Jacobs astutely notes, "The deterrent to Edom's behavior is not that the rebuilding is *irreal* or impossible; rather, the claim for the condition depicted *is* possible. At issue is how Yahweh will respond to Edom—a response that will be born out of Yahweh's choice regarding Israel." *Books of Haggai and Malachi*, 170. Ronald J. Williams cites Ruth 1:12 as the sole example of *kî* in an unreal conditional sentence. *Williams' Hebrew Syntax*, Third Edition, Revised and Expanded by John C. Beckman (Toronto: University of Toronto Press, 2007), §446.

18. Contra Pieter A. Verhoef, who wished to read the Hebrew *mēʿal* as "over," "above," or "upon" (i.e., "above the borders of Israel"), thus limiting God's greatness to its manifestation within Israel. *The Books of Haggai and Malachi* (Grand Rapids, MI: Eerdmans, 1987), 194, 206. The rendering "beyond" is to be preferred, as it encompasses both God's greatness within Israel as well as his greatness manifested beyond her borders as he will do in his destruction of Edom. See Douglas Stuart, "Malachi" in *The Minor Prophets*, vol. 3., ed. Thomas McComiskey (Grand Rapids, MI: Baker, 1998), 1292. Snyman, *Malachi*, 40 has suggested intentional ambiguity with both senses in view.

19. "[In] Israelite prophecy, Edom was understood as the type of all those who oppose God; and her downfall was seen as an indispensable part of the picture of the messianic age (cf. Isa. 34:5–6; 63:1–6; Jer. 49:13, 17, 18)." Achtemeier, *Nahum—Malachi*, 177.

Chapter Seventy-Six: Our Great High Priest

1. Pieter A. Verhoef observes that though the message is directed toward the priests, "the people were also guilty . . . because they provided the unworthy animals, and in doing so they were trying to deceive the Lord (v. 14)." *The Books of Haggai and Malachi* (Grand Rapids, MI: Eerdmans, 1987), 214.

2. Elizabeth Achtemeier, *Nahum—Malachi* (Louisville: Westminster John Knox Press, 1986), 178.

3. Verhoef, *Books of Haggai and Malachi*, 219.

4. For the use of the *qal wahomer* form in the Old Testament, see Louis Jacobs, "The *Qal Va-Ḥomer* Argument in the Old Testament," *Bulletin of the School of Oriental and African Studies* 35 (1972): 221–27.

5. "Nobody living in an ancient Near Eastern social environment during the 6th–5th century B.C.E. would dispute the truth of this statement." S. D. (Fanie) Snyman, *Malachi*, Historical Commentary on the Old Testament (Leuven, Belgium: Peeters, 2015), 44.

6. A genuine appeal to the priests to again take up their office (so Snyman, *Malachi*, 66) does not fit the flow of the disputation that continues with a divine plea to "shut the doors" of the temple (Malachi 1:10). Cf. John Calvin, *Commentaries on the Twelve Minor Prophets*, vol. 5, trans. John Owen (Grand Rapids, MI: Baker, 2003), 493; Verhoef, *Books of Haggai and Malachi*, 220; Andrew E. Hill, *Malachi: A New Translation with Introduction and Commentary*, Anchor Bible 25D (New York: Doubleday, 1998), 182; Jacobs, *Books of Haggai and Malachi*, 193.

7. The sacrificial victim was to be without defect and blemish. See, e.g., Exodus 12:5; 29:1; Leviticus 1:3; 22:20–25; Deuteronomy 15:21.

8. Iain M. Duguid, *Haggai, Zechariah, Malachi*, EP Study Commentary (Carlisle: Evangelical Press, 2010), 199.

9. This foundational Biblical and theological point has been developed at length by Michael Horton, *A Better Way: Rediscovering the Drama of Christ-Centered Worship* (Grand Rapids, MI: Baker, 2002); and D. G. Hart and John R. Muether, *With Reverence and Awe: Returning to the Basics of Reformed Worship* (Phillipsburg, NJ: P&R, 2002), and is the corollary principle to that developed by Gregory Beale, *We Become What We Worship: A Biblical Theology of Idolatry* (Downers Grove, IL: InterVarsity Press, 2008).

10. See, e.g., Snyman, *Malachi*, 49. Calvin's view was close to this: *Commentaries on the Twelve Minor Prophets*, 514–15.

11. David L. Petersen has suggested a direct connection between the second-rate sacrifices offered by the priests and the second-rate (cursed) portions the priests receive as a result. *Zechariah 9–14 and Malachi*, Old Testament Library (Philadelphia: Westminster/John Knox, 1995), 188–89.

12. See, e.g., C. F. Kiel, *The Twelve Minor Prophets*, vol, 10. trans James Martin (1874, repr. Peabody, MA: Hendrickson, 2001), 645. Though acknowledging both possibilities, this view is favored by Duguid, *Haggai, Zechariah, and Malachi*, 208; and John Goldingay and Pamela Scalise, *Minor Prophets II*, New International Biblical Commentary (Peabody, MA: Hendrickson, 2009), 336.

13. This was essentially the view of Verhoef, *Books of Haggai and Malachi*, 239. See also Hill, *Malachi*, 199. Jacobs, *Books of Haggai and Malachi*, 213 allows this as a possibility.

14. Masoretic Text *hazzeraʿ* ("offspring") is to be preferred over LXX τὸν ὦμον, Hebrew *hazzerōaʿ* ("shoulder"). See Jonathan Gibson, *Covenant Continuity and Fidelity: A Study in Inner-Biblical Allusion and Exegesis in Malachi*, Library of Hebrew Studies/Old Testament Studies 65 (London: Bloomsbury T&T Clark, 2016), 97–98. On the covenant sanctions being meted out on the offspring of the offender, see Deuteronomy 28:18, 32, 41, 53, 55, 57.

15. Verhoef, *Books of Haggai and Malachi*, 243.

16. Jeremiah 33:21 is the closest parallel. There God speaks of "my covenant with the Levitical priests my ministers."

17. Beth Glazier-McDonald, *Malachi: The Divine Messenger*, Society of Biblical Literature Dissertation Series 98 (Atlanta: Scholars, 1987), 79–80. It is possible that the "covenant with Levi" in Malachi 2:4 refers to an earlier, unspecified covenant made with the tribe identified here by their eponymous ancestor (possibilities include Exodus 32:26–29; Numbers 3:5–13; 18; Deuteronomy 33:8ff.). If this is the case, the covenant with Phinehas is clearly related to, of a piece with, and a continuation of, this earlier covenant. The covenant with Levi would on this reading find a further expression and advancement in God's covenant with Phinehas, perhaps analogous to the Davidic covenant advancing the Abrahamic.

18. Gordon Wenham, *Numbers* (Downers Grove, IL: InterVarsity Press, 1981), 189.

19. On the clear wisdom motifs in Malachi 2:6, 7, see Snyman, *Malachi*, 90, distilling the more extensive exegetical work of Karl William Weyde, *Prophecy and Teaching* (Berlin: Walter de Gruyter, 2000), 190–92, 195–97.

20. Wenham, *Numbers*, 189.

21. Verhoef notes that these offerings "were exactly opposite to the unworthy sacrifices of the local priests." *Books of Haggai and Malachi*, 225.

22. Contra Snyman, *Malachi*, 46 who interprets the worshipers "in every place" as referring exclusively to Jews of the Diaspora. See Verhoef, *Books of Haggai and Malachi*, 222–32 on the now-and-not-yet Old Testament and New Testament horizons of Malachi's prophecy of worship, '*baggôyim*' ("among the nations"), in Malachi 1:11. Verhoef, 225 made the important observation: "According to the law it would be impossible to bring pure offering in the heathen countries because those countries were deemed impure on account of idolatry. This text, then, presupposes a radical alteration in the circumstances, making those countries sacred places of worship. Principally this could only be obtained on the basis of the conversion of the heathen nations, the breaking through of the wall of partition."

Chapter Seventy-Seven: Created for Faithfulness

1. See, e.g., Belinda Luscombe, "The Divorce Rate Is Dropping. That May Not Actually Be Good News," *Time*, November 26, 2018, https://time.com/5434949/divorce-rate-children-marriage-benefits/, based on a study by Philip N. Cohen, "The Coming Divorce Decline." https://osf.io/preprints/socarxiv/h2sk6/.

2. "Intermarriage with foreign women would have gone hand in hand with the worship of foreign gods." M. E. Tate, "Questions for Priest and People in Malachi 1:2-2:16," *Review and Expositor* 84 (1987): 391–407 (quote on 402).

3. Pieter A. Verhoef, *The Books of Haggai and Malachi* (Grand Rapids, MI: Eerdmans, 1987), 263.

4. "Corruption of the priesthood leads to the corruption of the people." Elizabeth Achtemeier, *Nahum—Malachi* (Louisville: Westminster John Knox Press, 1986), 178.

5. Achtemeier, *Nahum—Malachi*, 181. Cf. Deuteronomy 32:6.

6. "Marriage is more than a mutual contract between a man and a woman; it also has religious and social consequences for the community at large." S. D. (Fanie) Snyman, *Malachi*, Historical Commentary on the Old Testament (Leuven, Belgium: Peeters, 2015), 97–98.

7. Andrew E. Hill, *Malachi: A New Translation with Introduction and Commentary*, Anchor Bible 25D (New York: Doubleday, 1998), 224.

8. Hill, *Malachi*, 227 points to "the echo of Deuteronomic language and the explicit social obligation of the Mosaic law" as evidence for the Sinaitic covenant. Cf. Beth Glazier-McDonald, *Malachi: The Divine Messenger*, Society of Biblical Literature Dissertation Series 98 (Atlanta: Scholars, 1987), 87–88; Verhoef, *Books of Haggai and Malachi*, 267; Jonathan Gibson, *Covenant Continuity and Fidelity: A Study in Inner-Biblical Allusion and Exegesis in Malachi*, Library of Hebrew Studies/Old Testament Studies 65 (London: Bloomsbury T&T Clark, 2016), 123.

9. Hill has made the intriguing observation, "The priests may have been guilty of sanctioning such marriage and divorce; in fact, Ogden and Deutsch are probably correct in linking the misteaching of the priests (2:1-9) with the practice of intermarriage and divorce in postexilic Yehud (2:10-16)." *Malachi*, 223.

10. Peter Adam, *The Message of Malachi*, Bible Speaks Today (Downers Grove, IL: InterVarsity Press, 2013), 84.

11. Though the phrase *baṯ- 'ēl nēḵor* ("daughter of a foreign god") has been described as "totally uncommon and ambiguous" by Markus Zehnder, "A Fresh Look at Malachi II 13-16," *Vetus Testamentum* 53 (2003): 224–59 (quote on 227),

the larger context clearly depicts a situation in which intermarriage leads to apostasy such that Lena-Sophia Tiemeyer could write about this passage: "It is the interrelations between intermarriage and apostasy that *give the text its complete meaning*: intermarriages lead to unorthodoxy." *Priestly Rites and Prophetic Rage: Postexilic Prophetic Critique of the Priesthood*, FAT 2. Reihe 19 (Tübingen: Mohr Siebeck, 2006), 195 (emphasis mine). Given its uniqueness the expression must find its meaning with reference to this context.

12. Gary Edward Schnittjer, *Old Testament Narrative Books: The Israel Story* (Brentwood, TN: B&H Academic, 2023), 17.

13. See e.g., Iain M. Duguid, *Haggai, Zechariah, Malachi*, EP Study Commentary (Carlisle: Evangelical Press, 2010), 215.

14. Snyman has captured the sense of the merism with his literal translation, "one who is awake and one who responds," which he renders colloquially as "each and everybody." *Malachi*, 108–9. Jonathan Gibson has made the intriguing suggestion that the Hebrew ʿēr wᵉʿōnê is a hendiadys that refers more specifically to the descendants of the individual who will be cut off, thus invoking the covenant curses of Deuteronomy 28:15-20. "Cutting off 'Kith and Kin,' 'Er and Onan?' Interpreting an Obscure Phrase in Malachi 2:12," *Journal of Biblical Literature* 133 (2014): 519–37.

15. Achtemeier, *Nahum—Malachi*, 181–82.

16. For a thorough treatment of marriage and divorce in ancient and postexilic Israel, see Gordon P. Hugenberger, *Marriage as Covenant: A Study of Biblical Law and Ethics Governing Marriage, Developed from the Perspective of Malachi*, Supplements to Vetus Testamentum 52 (Leiden: Brill, 1994).

17. D. N. Freedman, ed., *Anchor Bible Dictionary* (New York: Bantam Doubleday Dell, 1992), 4:564. Hill, *Malachi*, 242.

18. See, e.g., Snyman, *Malachi*, 99; and Hill, *Malachi*, 222.

19. See, e.g., Verhoef, *Books of Haggai and Malachi*, 263.

20. Hill, *Malachi*, 246.

21. Gibson, *Covenant Continuity and Fidelity*, 136.

22. Gibson, 139 has argued persuasively that Malachi 2:10–16 evidences clear allusions to Genesis 2, especially Genesis 2:23–24. He does, however, suggest that Malachi gestures toward the larger context, especially Genesis 1:26–27 and 3:15, the latter of which informs the argument here.

23. Hill *Malachi*, 248 comes very close to this view: "The superlative expression 'the seed of God' is better understood as 'what is free from all vice and blemish . . . for what is excellent is often called God in Hebrew' (Calvin: 558). . . . Yahweh seeks 'the seed of God,' descendants of Abraham, Isaac, and Jacob who love him, obey him, and hold fast to him (Deut 30:19-20) and those who love justice, hate wrongdoing, and act faithfully (Isa 61:8-9). If the idea of the superlative sense of the divine name 'God' (*ʾĕlōhîm*) is that which belongs to God, then Israel will be 'the seed of God' only when they imitate his holiness through covenant obedience." By connecting Israel's hope for *zeraʿ ʾelohim* to its fulfillment in Christ, the interpretation above takes Hill's remarks to their logical next step from the perspective of redemptive history. Jesus is the one *zeraʿ ʾelohim* (cf. Galatians 3:16) "free from all vice and blemish," the descendant of Abraham, Isaac, and Jacob who loves God, obeys him, and holds fast to him, etc.

Chapter Seventy-Eight: A Consuming and Purifying Fire

1. *Writers on Writing: A Book of Quotations*, ed. Alysoun Owen (London: Bloomsbury, 2021), 53.

2. "By charging God with injustice, the people actually endorsed a theology of doubt that impeached the divinity of the Godhead and challenged the very existence of God." Andrew Hill, *Malachi: A New Translation with Introduction and Commentary*, Anchor Bible 25D (New York: Doubleday, 1998), 285.

3. Elizabeth Achtemeier, *Nahum—Malachi* (Louisville: Westminster John Knox Press, 1986), 184.

4. "Although the temple was completed, the dawn of a new future did not materialize as Haggai and Zechariah foresaw it. It was a time of crop failure and pests (3:11); religious laxity (1:6-14); and moral decay (2:10-16), and they were still subjects of the Persian Empire, with little or no expectation of political independence.... On a more personal level, little is seen of justice and righteousness so characteristic of Yahweh and embodied by the Torah. This observation leads to an accusation in this regard, an accusation that wearies Yahweh." S. D. (Fanie) Snyman, *Malachi*, Historical Commentary on the Old Testament (Leuven, Belgium: Peeters, 2015), 121–22.

5. Pieter A. Verhoef, *The Books of Haggai and Malachi* (Grand Rapids, MI: Eerdmans, 1987), 287.

6. "It may even be that the Persian king is thought of here on a mission through the empire, moving from one part to the other, during the time of the change of the season." Snyman, *Malachi*, 132.

7. For a good summary of the various proposals, see Synman, 132–35.

8. For a clear presentation of the literary features that lead to the "inevitable conclusion that the *ha'adon* and *malak haberit* must be seen as referring to the same person," see Synman, 133. Cf. Achtemeier, *Nahum—Malachi*, 184.

9. "In spite of the preparation effected by the forerunner, the King's arrival will be unexpected." Verhoef, *Books of Haggai and Malachi*, 288.

10. Consistent with this, the designations of the Lord as $^{\,a}ser$-$\,'attem\ m^e ba qšîm$ ("whom you seek") and the messenger of the covenant as $^{\,a}ser$-$\,'attem\ h^a p\=e \d{s}îm$ ("in whom you delight") in Malachi 3:1 should be read as ironic. So Achtemeier, *Nahum—Malachi*, 184.

11. Snyman, *Malachi*, 128.

12. "Part of the duties of the priests was to cleanse and purify objects, and even people. What they were unable to do, Yahweh as the covenant angel to come, will do." Synman, 137.

13. Achtemeier, *Nahum—Malachi*, 186.

14. Charles Spurgeon, "The Lesson of the Almond Tree," Metropolitan Tabernacle, April 7, 1881.

15. Snyman, *Malachi*, 139.

16. Achtemeier, *Nahum—Malachi*, 185.

Chapter Seventy-Nine: Putting the Lord to the Test

1. Many scholars interpret Malachi 3:6, 7a as concluding the previous oracle. See, e.g., Elizabeth Achtemeier, *Nahum—Malachi* (Louisville: Westminster/John Knox, 1986), 186; S. D. (Fanie) Snyman, *Malachi*, Historical Commentary on the Old Testament (Leuven, Belgium: Peeters, 2015), 125–29; Karl William Weyde,

*Prophecy and Teaching* (Berlin: Walter de Gruyter, 2000), 315–24; Mignon R. Jacobs, *The Books of Haggai and Malachi*, New International Commentary on the Old Testament (Grand Rapids, MI: Eerdmans, 2017), 281–86; and Jonathan Gibson, *Covenant Continuity and Fidelity: A Study in Inner-Biblical Allusion and Exegesis in Malachi*, Library of Hebrew Studies/Old Testament Studies 65 (London: Bloomsbury T&T Clark, 2016), 184–85. On this controverted question of the function of 3:6, 7a as concluding the fourth or introducing the fifth oracle, Pieter A. Verhoef noted that "v. 6 introduces the central theme [of the fifth oracle] of the relationship between God and people." *The Books of Haggai and Malachi* (Grand Rapids, MI: Eerdmans, 1987), 298, cf. 298–300. See also Andrew E. Hill, *Malachi: A New Translation with Introduction and Commentary*, Anchor Bible 25D (New York: Doubleday, 1998), 291–94. Iain M. Duguid has made the compelling suggestion that verse 6 "looks both ways, concluding the preceding oracle as well as introducing this one." *Haggai, Zechariah, Malachi*, EP Study Commentary (Carlisle: Evangelical Press, 2010), 228. Similarly, Hill, *Malachi*, 292.

2. Achtemeier, *Nahum—Malachi*, 189.
3. Duguid, *Haggai, Zechariah, Malachi*, 231.
4. For similar instances, see Exodus 4:1–9; Judges 6:34–40.
5. According to Hill, Malachi, 295: "The suffixing form of *šnh* here conveys both the sense of the *indefinite perfective* ("I have not changed," so Verhoef [297]; Petersen, [212]) and *the instantaneous perfective* ("I do not change," so R. L. Smith [330] . . .")." Some translate *kî* as an asseverative; Bruce K. Waltke and Michael Patrick O'Connor, *An Introduction to Biblical Hebrew Syntax* (Winona Lake, IN: Eisenbrauns, 1990), 39.3.4; *Gesenius' Hebrew Grammar*, ed. E. Kautzsch, trans. A. E. Cowley, 2nd ed. (Oxford: Oxford University Press, 1910) §148.d. So Hill, *Malachi*, 294; and Verhoef, *Books of Haggai and Malachi*, 299.

6. "All that we consider in God is unchangeable, for his essence and his properties are the same, and therefore what is necessarily belonging to the essence of God belongs also to every perfection of the nature of God; none of them can receive an addition or diminution. The immutability of the divine counsel depends upon that of his essence. He is the Lord Jehovah; therefore he is true to his word." Stephen Charnock, *Discourses upon the Existence and Attributes of God* (1682), quoted in *ESV Church History Study Bible*, 1409.

7. "God cannot be more infinite, loving, or holy tomorrow than today. . . . For us, change might be for better or worse, but for a perfect God, change can only yield imperfection." Michael Horton, *The Christian Faith: A Systematic Theology for Pilgrims on the Way* (Grand Rapids, MI: Zondervan, 2011), 235. "But God who *is* cannot change, for every change would diminish his being." Herman Bavinck, *Reformed Dogmatics, Volume 2: God and Creation*, trans. John Vriend (Grand Rapids, MI: Baker, 2004), 154, cf. 158.

8. "If God were not immutable, he would not be God." Bavinck, *Reformed Dogmatics, Vol. 2*, 154.

9. See, e.g., Horton, *Christian Faith*, 236.

10. Hill's comments to this effect are correct (*Malachi*, 295). It should be noted, however, that metaphysical realities are clearly implied by the prophet's programmatic statement on the immutability of God relative to his covenantal pact with Israel. To be sure, Hill hints in this direction (322).

11. Though the translation of *wᵉ'attem bᵉnê-yaʿᵃqōḇ lō' ḵᵉlîṯem* as "and you, sons of Jacob, have not ceased" (i.e., "ceased to be sons of Jacob") is lexically and grammatically possible (so Joyce G. Baldwin, *Haggai, Zechariah, Malachi: An Introduction and Commentary*, Tyndale Old Testament Commentary [Downers Grove, IL: InterVarsity Press, 1972], 245), the conventional translation "you, O children of Jacob, are not consumed" is preferable as it "offers the more obvious sense of the Hebrew root *klh*, and it would carry with it an important assurance for those who preach the past traditions." Rex Mason, *Preaching the Tradition: Homily and Hermeneutics after the Exile* (Cambridge: Cambridge University Press, 1990), 252. Cf. Numbers 16:21, 45; 25:11; Deuteronomy 28:21; Zephaniah 1:18. See also Jacobs, *Books of Haggai and Malachi*, 284.

12. "The solemn assurance that the Lord had not changed presupposes a frame of mind which sincerely doubts the truth of this statement, in connection with either God's dispensing of his justice (2:17) or the profession of his love (1:2–5)." Verhoef, *Books of Haggai and Malachi*, 299.

13. Martin Luther, in *Luther's Works*, vol. 33 (Philadelphia: Fortress, 1957), 42.

14. For an excellent discussion of the Biblical doctrine of the immutability of God in the Protestant (Reformed) tradition, see Richard A. Muller, *Post-Reformation Reformed Dogmatics, Volume 3: The Divine Essence and Attributes* (Grand Rapids, MI: Baker, 2003), 308–20. Cf. Herman Bavinck, *Reformed Dogmatics, Volume 2: God and Creation* (Grand Rapids, MI: Baker, 2004), 153–59.

15. John Newton, "Amazing Grace," in *Olney Hymns* (1779).

16. Verhoef, *Book of Haggai and Malachi*, 300.

17. Despite numerous proposals for the particular generation in view with *lᵉmîmê 'ᵃḇōṯêḵem* ("from the days of your fathers," e.g., the patriarchs, the settlements period, preexilic, postexilic, etc.), Verhoef's interpretation that "the scope of this concept embraces the whole history of the covenant people" remains the most convincing (300).

18. Hebrew *haggôy kullô*. See Duguid, *Haggai, Zechariah, Malachi*, 230; and Verhoef, *Books of Haggai and Malachi*, 306.

19. Verhoef makes the insightful connection between the people's ignorance of the requirement of the Law and the priest's negligence in offering true instruction (Malachi 2:6, 8). *Books of Haggai and Malachi*, 303.

20. "[W]hen one has little, one is tempted to guard jealously one's meager stores." Achtemeier, *Nahum—Malachi*, 188.

21. Snyman, *Micah*, 145–46. For a thorough survey of the Biblical tithe law, see Andreas J. Köstenberger and David A. Croteau, "'Will a Man Rob God? (Malachi 3:8): A Study of Tithing in the Old and New Testaments," *Bulletin for Biblical Research* 16 (2006): 53–77.

22. For a detailed analysis of the theme of covenant curses being transformed to covenant blessings in Malachi 3:7–12, see Gibson, *Covenant Continuity and Fidelity*, 182–98.

23. Snyman, *Malachi*, 155. The Abrahamic promises (Genesis 12:3) sit clearly in the background of God's promises to the postexilic community in Malachi 3:12.

24. Dennis Johnson, *Him We Proclaim: Preaching Christ from All the Scriptures* (Phillipsburg, NJ: P&R, 2007), 202.

25. Duguid, *Haggai, Zechariah, Malachi*, 232–33.

26. "But it is not a tit-for-tat arrangement, not a vending machine concept of God, not a bargain by which Judah makes an investment and receives a reward in return. To find in this passage any such legalistic or automatic or materialistic understanding is a complete distortion of the covenant relation with our God." Achtemeier, *Nahum—Malachi*, 189.

## Chapter Eighty: When Faith Shall Be Sight

1. Elizabeth Achtemeier, *Nahum—Malachi* (Louisville: Westminster John Knox Press, 1986), 193.

2. Cf. 2 Samuel 24:4 and the parallel 1 Chronicles 21:4. With reference to Akkadian and Mishnaic Hebrew, Nahum M. Waldman has suggested the translation, "Your words have been too much for me." "Notes on Malachi 3:6, 3:13, and Psalm 42:11," *Journal of Biblical Literature* 93 (1974): 543–49, esp. 545–48. See also discussions by Karl William Weyde, *Prophecy and Teaching* (Berlin: Walter de Gruyter, 2000), 350–51; and Richard A. Taylor and E. Ray Clendenen, *Haggai, Malachi*, New American Commentary 21A (Nashville: Broadman & Holman, 2004), 435.

3. Rex Mason, *Preaching the Tradition: Homily and Hermeneutics after the Exile* (Cambridge: Cambridge University Press, 1990), 254.

4. Cf. Malachi 2:17. S. D. (Fanie) Snyman, however, observes a subtle difference between issues addressed in these two passages. *Malachi*, Historical Commentary on the Old Testament (Leuven, Belgium: Peeters, 2015), 164.

5. For a helpful discussion of the difficult expression *hālaknû qᵉdōrannît*, see Andrew E. Hill, *Malachi: A New Translation with Introduction and Commentary*, Anchor Bible 25D (New York: Doubleday, 1998), 333–34.

6. Achtemeier suggested that these witnesses for God also served as a jury in the court case, which, she observed, is "a notable fact, for it implies that only those who are faithful to God the King can see the situation as it really is." *Nahum—Malachi*, 194–95.

7. Many commentators regard *yir'ê yhwh* ("those who feared YHWH") as converts from the group who spoke harsh words against Yahweh identified in Malachi 3:13–15. See, e.g., John Calvin, *Commentaries on the Twelve Minor Prophets*, vol. 5, trans. John Owen (Grand Rapids, MI: Baker, 2003), 602; Snyman, *Malachi*, 166; Weyde, *Prophecy and Teaching*, 354–56; and Jonathan Gibson, *Covenant Continuity and Fidelity: A Study in Inner-Biblical Allusion and Exegesis in Malachi*, Library of Hebrew Studies/Old Testament Studies 65 (London: Bloomsbury T&T Clark, 2016), 203–5. I think the better reading is to see two groups: the larger community characterized by cynicism and doubt, and the community of faith within that larger community characterized by the fear of Yahweh. Space does not permit a full rehearsal of the issues involved. Readers should note, however, that the oft-mentioned repetition of the Hebrew *dābar* in verse 16 does not *necessarily* identify the subjects with the speakers of strong words in verse 13. The repetition could also serve contrastive purposes. Furthermore, *'āz* ("then") in verse 16 may be understood in the ordinary temporal sense that may refer to simultaneous (Taylor and Clendenen) or subsequent action (so Pieter A. Verhoef, *The Books of Haggai and Malachi* [Grand Rapids, MI: Eerdmans, 1987]), either of which establishes an antithesis between "those who feared the LORD" (3:16) and the "arrogant" and "evildoers"

(3:15) (Verhoef, 319). Hearing the prophet's invective against cynicism and unbelief that stirred up the conversation mentioned in verse 16 does not entail that those who so discussed amongst themselves were necessarily party to the cynicism. Some may have been, and some may not have been. As Taylor and Clendenen, *Haggai, Malachi*, 441–42 put it: "Whether at least some of these are ones who have repented in response to Malachi's preaching, as some commentators have suggested, is unclear from the text." Cf. Achtemeier, *Nahum—Malachi*, 193–94; Duguid, *Haggai, Zechariah, Malachi*, 235; Waldman, "Notes," 546. Rhetorically, the prophet establishes two groups—those who issue harsh words against YHWH and those who fear him. These two groups are intermingled in Malachi's day but will one day be distinguished eternally according to the book of remembrance.

8. This is not to suggest that the faithful could not struggle with the challenges presented by the prosperity of the wicked (cf. Psalm 73:3). This was no doubt a struggle for many of them, as it is for many of us today. True faith, however, brings God's people back to humility and trust in God's word and God's promises despite human reason and experience (Psalm 73:27, 28).

9. Snyman, *Malachi*, 167; Verhoef, *Books of Haggai and Malachi*, 321.

10. Snyman, *Malachi*, 167.

11. Hebrew *sᵉgullâ*. Cf. Exodus 19:5; Deuteronomy 7:6; 14:2; 26:18; Psalm 135:4 for instances where it refers to Israel's relationship to God. For the significance of this term, see Moshe Greenberg, "Hebrew Segulla: Akkadian Sikiltu," *Journal of the American Oriental Society* 71 (1951): 172–74. Moshe Weinfeld argued that the term carries covenantal connotation in both Ugaritic and Hebrew. *Deuteronomy and the Deuteronomic School* (Oxford: Oxford University Press, 1972), 226. For the intertextual and covenantal significance of *sᵉgullâ* in Malachi 3:17, especially its connection to the theme of sonship also present in 3:17, see Gibson, *Covenant Continuity and Fidelity*, 208–12.

12. "This is to be understood as a contracted simile, where everything that will happen on that day with the evil-doers can be described as burning, that is, judgment by Yahweh." Snyman, *Malachi*, 171.

13. Mignon R. Jacobs, *The Books of Haggai and Malachi*, New International Commentary on the Old Testament (Grand Rapids, MI: Eerdmans, 2017), 322; Weyde, *Prophecy and Teaching*, 372–74; Snyman, *Malachi*, 173. Cf. Psalm 84:11; Isaiah 60:19, 20.

14. Snyman, *Malachi*, 173.

15. For a discussion of the interpretive options for the expression *šemeš ṣᵉdāqâ* ("sun of righteousness"), see Snyman, 172–73. Snyman, 172–73, has observed, "Righteousness is likened to the sun, and not the sun to righteousness."

16. "Is it a coincidence that the same verb is used to describe the people's initial deliverance from Egypt? (Exod. 20:2; Deut. 5:6)." Snyman, 174.

17. Synman, 161.

18. For a detailed discussion of the issues surrounding the origin and intent of Malachi 4:4–6, as well as a defense of its originality to the book of Malachi, see Gibson, *Covenant Continuity and Fidelity*, 215–35.

19. Jacobs, *Books of Haggai and Malachi*, 333.

20. The view adopted here combines a number of interpretations that, to this author's mind, are not mutually exclusive. Just the opposite; each addresses an issue

faced by the postexilic community, and together they represent a fitting conclusion not only to the book of Malachi but to the prophetic corpus as a whole. Specifically the expression $w^eh\bar{e}\check{s}\hat{\imath}\underline{b}$ $l\bar{e}\underline{b}$-'ă$\underline{b}\hat{o}\underline{t}$ 'al-bānîm $w^el\bar{e}\underline{b}$ bānîm 'al-'ă$\underline{b}\hat{o}\underline{t}$om ("he will turn the hearts of fathers to their children and the hearts of children to their fathers") refers to 1) healing the societal disintegration that obtained among the postexilic community, including but not limited to the problem of apostate marriages (e.g., Beth Glazier-McDonald, *Malachi: The Divine Messenger*, Society of Biblical Literature Dissertation Series 98 [Atlanta: Scholars, 1987], 253–55; Snyman, *Malachi*, 191); 2) covenant renewal (i.e., reestablishing the fidelity of latter generations with that former generation with whom Yahweh covenanted at Horeb (e.g., Verhoef, *Books of Haggai and Malachi*, 342; Hill, *Malachi*, 388; Jacobs, *Books of Haggai and Malachi*, 333–34; similarly Calvin, *Commentaries on the Twelve Minor Prophets*, 630); and 3) reconciling God to his covenant people (see esp. Caryn A. Reeder, "Malachi 3:24 and the Eschatological Restoration of the 'Family,'" *Catholic Bible Quarterly* 69 (2007): 695–709; Elie Assis, "Moses, Elijah and the Messianic Hope," *Zeitschrift für die alttestamentliche Wissenschaft* (2011), 207–20; Achtemeier, *Nahum—Malachi*, 197). This view seems close to Iain M. Duguid, *Haggai, Zechariah, Malachi*, EP Study Commentary (Carlisle: Evangelical Press, 2010), 238.

21. Horatio Spafford, "It Is Well with My Soul," in Ira Sankey and Philip Bliss, *Gospel Hymns No. 2* (1876).

# Scripture Index

| Genesis | | 12:3 | 179, 262, 279, 319, |
|---|---|---|---|
| 1–2 | 69, 227 | | 370, 381, 603, 634, |
| 1:1 | 543 | | 690, 779, 875n5 (ch. |
| 1:2 | 137 | | 48), 913n23 |
| 1:3–5 | 747 | 12:7 | 179, 516 |
| 1:14–19 | 747 | 12:8 | 38 |
| 1:20–21 | 850n1 | 14:2 | 82 |
| 1:26 | 203, 782 | 14:8 | 82 |
| 1:26–27 | 910n22 | 15:1–6 | 14, 231 |
| 1:26–28 | 507 | 15:6 | 99, 107 |
| 1:26–31 | 209, 543 | 15:12 | 848n18 |
| 1:27 | 203 | 15:12–16 | 491, 516 |
| 1:28 | 628 | 15:12–21 | 700 |
| 2 | 910n22 | 15:13 | 466 |
| 2:10–14 | 345, 748 | 15:13–16 | 500 |
| 2:21 | 848n18 | 15:16 | 466 |
| 2:23–24 | 910n22 | 16:10 | 616 |
| 2:24 | 782, 788, 792 | 16:11b | 330 |
| 2:25 | 457, 788, 792 | 16:12 | 330 |
| 3–4 | 136 | 16:13 | 616 |
| 3:6 | 250 | 17:4–8 | 675 |
| 3:7 | 458, 781 | 17:5 | 330, 601 |
| 3:10 | 458 | 17:10 | 675 |
| 3:12 | 781 | 17:15 | 330 |
| 3:14 | 618 | 18:25 | 389 |
| 3:15 | 734, 782, 791, 814, 910n22 | 19:21 | 855n23 |
| | | 19:25 | 82, 593 |
| | | 21:33 | 193 |
| 3:20 | 601 | 22:8 | 732 |
| 3:21 | 458 | 22:12 | 872n6 |
| 4:8 | 872n6 | 22:14 | 732 |
| 4:10 | 508 | 22:16–18 | 642 |
| 9:4 | 695 | 25–36 | 240 |
| 10 | 899n20 | 25:19–26 | 87 |
| 11:4 | 354, 432 | 25:19–34 | 86 |
| 11:9 | 362 | 25:23 | 761 |
| 12:1–8 | 132 | 25:24–26 | 761 |
| 12:1–9 | 14, 83, 231, 497 | 25:26 | 601 |

917

| | | | |
|---|---|---|---|
| 26:1–5 | 231 | 3:13–17 | 124 |
| 26:23–25 | 193 | 4:1–9 | 912n4 |
| 26:24 | 885n14 | 4:22 | 78, 783 |
| 27:1–19 | 86 | 4:23 | 78, 783 |
| 27:1–40 | 86 | 5–14 | 833n8 |
| 27:24 | 837n11 | 5:1 | 415 |
| 27:29 | 902n18 | 5:2 | 415 |
| 27:41 | 86 | 5:18 | 346 |
| 28:1–5 | 86 | 6:7 | 338, 392 |
| 28:10–17 | 87, 193, 231 | 8:7 | 272 |
| 28:10–22 | 86, 185 | 8:8 | 272 |
| 28:11–19 | 38 | 9:13–35 | 583 |
| 29–30 | 86 | 10:13–19 | 849n13 |
| 31 | 86 | 11:4 | 842n8 (ch. 24) |
| 31:25 | 50 | 11:5 | 842n8 (ch. 24) |
| 31:36 | 858n12 | 12:2 | 842n8 (ch. 24) |
| 32:22–32 | 282, 810 | 12:5 | 907n7 |
| 32:28 | 86, 330 | 12:43–13:10 | 675 |
| 32:31 | 87 | 14 | 286, 380, 849n13 |
| 32:32 | 87 | 14:5 | 855n23 |
| 33:1–11 | 87 | 15 | 594, 849n13 |
| 34 | 51 | 15:1 | 594 |
| 35:1 | 87 | 15:1–18 | 285, 288 |
| 35:1–15 | 87 | 15:4 | 285, 594 |
| 35:2 | 87 | 15:5 | 285, 852n15 |
| 35:4 | 87 | 15:8 | 285 |
| 35:9–15 | 230 | 15:11 | 406 |
| 35:21 | 863n2 | 15:13–16 | 405 |
| 48:4 | 902n18 | 15:17 | 346 |
| 48:15 | 709 | 15:21 | 433 |
| 49:10 | 418, 902n18 | 15:23–26 | 731 |
| 49:11 | 699 | 16 | 96 |
| 50:19 | 210 | 16–18 | 124 |
| 50:20 | 210 | 17:1–7 | 96, 288 |
| | | 17:3 | 805 |
| *Exodus* | | 17:4 | 805 |
| book of | 415 | 17:7 | 805 |
| 1 | 61 | 17:12 | 893n2 |
| 1–15 | 123 | 18:13–27 | 862n5 |
| 1:7–10 | 14 | 19:4–6 | 32, 34 |
| 1:8–22 | 380 | 19:5 | 23, 40, 48, 79, 106, 124, 132, 169, 177, 179, 194, 234, 498, 915n11 |
| 1:22 | 418 | | |
| 2:2 | 524 | | |
| 2:3 | 524 | 19:6 | 23, 34, 40, 48, 79, 106, 124, 132, 169, 177, 179, 194, 234, 294, 498, 515–16 |
| 2:23–25 | 124, 231, 489 | | |
| 3:2 | 616 | | |
| 3:4 | 616 | | |

| | | | |
|---|---|---|---|
| 19:10–16 | 833n1 | 32:10 | 305 |
| 19:20ff | 345 | 32:11 | 896n3 |
| 20–24 | 124, 125 | 32:12 | 854n13 |
| 20–Deut. 34 | 497 | 32:14 | 298 |
| 20:1–17 | 13, 180 | 32:15 | 893n2 |
| 20:2 | 531, 915n16 | 32:20 | 902n7 |
| 20:3 | 13, 41, 58, 509, 531 | 32:26 | 776 |
| 20:3–6 | 526 | 32:26–28 | 776 |
| 20:4 | 58, 125 | 32:26–29 | 908n17 |
| 20:5 | 125 | 32:29 | 776 |
| 20:7 | 33, 835n7 (ch. 9) | 33:17 | 124 |
| 20:12–17 | 194 | 34 | 123, 125, 838n6 |
| 20:13 | 33 | 34:5–8 | 417 |
| 20:14 | 33 | 34:5–9 | 124 |
| 20:15 | 33 | 34:6 | 7, 13, 15, 22, 48, 53, 66, 82, 83, 123, 124, 125, 147, 183, 188, 216, 217, 305, 385, 489, 549 |
| 20:16 | 33 | | |
| 20:17 | 860n11 | | |
| 21:24 | 252 | | |
| 21:32 | 724 | | |
| 22:15 | 22 | 34:7 | 7, 13, 15, 22, 48, 53, 66, 82, 83, 123, 124, 125, 147, 183, 188, 194, 216, 217, 489, 491, 500 |
| 22:25–27 | 173 | | |
| 22:26 | 174 | | |
| 22:27 | 174 | | |
| 23:14–19 | 533 | | |
| 23:16 | 64 | 34:7a | 305 |
| 24:1–8 | 516 | 34:7b | 124 |
| 24:3 | 378, 784 | 34:29–35 | 350 |
| 24:7 | 723 | 35:35 | 627 |
| 24:8 | 700 | 38:23 | 627 |
| 25:19 | 893n2 | | |
| 25:31–40 | 649 | *Leviticus* | |
| 26 | 862n30 | 1:3 | 907n7 |
| 26:13 | 893n2 | 4:11 | 775 |
| 28 | 637, 752, 862n30 | 4:12 | 775 |
| 28:11 | 889n7 | 4:26 | 216 |
| 28:17 | 891n14 | 4:31 | 216 |
| 28:36 | 752 | 4:35 | 216 |
| 29:1 | 907n7 | 5:17 | 850n23 |
| 29:40 | 64 | 6:20 | 884n5 |
| 30:10 | 752 | 8:1–13 | 637 |
| 31:1–3 | 137 | 10 | 775 |
| 31:15 | 752 | 10:1–6 | 328 |
| 32 | 124, 125, 171 | 11:44 | 194, 498, 549 |
| 32–34 | 417 | 13:45 | 350 |
| 32:1–7 | 125 | 16:22 | 850n23 |
| 32:3 | 58 | 17:10–14 | 695 |
| 32:4 | 58 | 18:1–5 | 491 |

Scripture Index 919

| | | | |
|---|---|---|---|
| 18:4–5 | 867n12 | 5:11–28 | 731 |
| 18:28 | 852n21 | 5:11–31 | 285, 468 |
| 19:8 | 752 | 6:1–21 | 174 |
| 19:17 | 186, 203, 209, 212, 541, 543, 549 | 6:23–26 | 774 |
| | | 6:24–26 | 353, 563 |
| 19:18 | 7, 89, 106, 145, 170, 186, 203, 209, 212, 498, 541, 543, 549, 682 | 6:25 | 649 |
| | | 6:26 | 649 |
| | | 6:27 | 774 |
| | | 10:11 | 516 |
| | | 10:12 | 516 |
| 19:34 | 106 | 11:24 | 137 |
| 19:34–37 | 186, 203, 209, 212, 541, 543 | 11:24–29 | 138 |
| | | 11:25 | 137 |
| 20:22 | 288 | 11:29 | 137 |
| 22:20–25 | 907n7 | 11:31 | 849n13 |
| 23:13 | 64 | 12:1 | 230 |
| 23:33–43 | 64, 533, 569 | 12:6 | 350 |
| 23:33–44 | 232 | 12:7 | 885n14 |
| 23:36 | 534 | 12:8 | 885n14 |
| 24:17–21 | 252 | 13:27–29 | 466 |
| 24:19 | 626 | 13:31 | 466 |
| 24:20 | 626 | 14:8 | 466 |
| 25:23 | 234, 543, 860n13 | 14:9 | 466 |
| 25:23–28 | 334 | 14:11 | 205 |
| 25:23–34 | 543 | 14:12 | 205 |
| 25:35–38 | 173 | 14:18 | 850n23, 856n10 |
| 25:35–55 | 204 | 15:1–12 | 64 |
| 26 | 660, 749 | 16:21 | 913n11 |
| 26:1–13 | 543, 814 | 16:45 | 913n11 |
| 26:1–45 | 183 | 18:28 | 811 |
| 26:3 | 867n12 | 20:14–21 | 906n15 |
| 26:3–13 | 70 | 21:4 | 901n17 |
| 26:14–39 | 68, 73, 171, 179, 192, 220, 527 | 22–24 | 381 |
| | | 22:24 | 893n2 |
| 26:14–45 | 56, 69, 486 | 23:19 | 298, 396 |
| 26:16 | 867n8 | 24:15 | 350 |
| 26:19 | 33 | 24:16 | 350 |
| 26:20 | 33, 187 | 25 | 66, 776 |
| 26:25 | 187 | 25:1 | 381, 777 |
| 26:27 | 187 | 25:1–9 | 205 |
| 26:40–45 | 48 | 25:2 | 381, 777 |
| 26:40–46 | 129 | 25:3 | 381, 777 |
| 27:30 | 752, 811 | 25:7 | 777 |
| 27:32 | 752 | 25:8 | 777 |
| | | 25:11 | 913n11 |
| *Numbers* | | 25:11–13 | 777 |
| 3:5–13 | 908n17 | 25:13 | 778 |
| 3:18 | 908n17 | | |

Scripture Index 921

| | | | |
|---|---|---|---|
| 27:17 | 709 | 16:13–17 | 64, 232, 533, 534, 569 |
| 28:11–15 | 844n6 (ch. 28) | | |
| 29:12–39 | 569 | 16:16 | 223 |
| 29:12–40 | 533, 534 | 16:17 | 223 |
| 32:14 | 872n6 | 17:16 | 326 |
| | | 18:22 | 654 |
| *Deuteronomy* | | 19:9 | 867n12 |
| 1:9–18 | 862n5 | 20:14 | 904n6 |
| 1:17 | 862n5 | 21:18–21 | 736 |
| 2:1–8 | 240, 543 | 23:5 | 381 |
| 4:35–39 | 132 | 23:6 | 381 |
| 5 | 860n11 | 23:7 | 244 |
| 5:6 | 915n16 | 24:1–4 | 18, 783 |
| 5:8–10 | 132 | 24:12 | 174 |
| 5:21 | 333, 860n13 | 24:13 | 174 |
| 6:2 | 867n12 | 25:4 | 74 |
| 6:2–9 | 543 | 26:1–15 | 223 |
| 6:4 | 186, 749 | 26:14 | 65 |
| 6:4–6 | 203, 212 | 26:18 | 915n11 |
| 6:4–9 | 7, 23, 32, 41, 106, 123, 132, 145, 170, 526, 541, 549 | 27–28 | 56, 113 |
| | | 28 | 390, 660, 749, 868n13 |
| 6:5 | 186, 498 | 28:1–14 | 70, 74, 497, 543, 814 |
| 6:16 | 805, 806 | | |
| 7:3 | 783, 784 | 28:1–68 | 183 |
| 7:4 | 783, 784 | 28:11 | 390 |
| 7:6 | 15, 752, 915n11 | 28:12 | 390 |
| 7:6–11 | 104, 114 | 28:15 | 607, 664 |
| 7:6–26 | 177 | 28:15–19 | 21 |
| 7:9 | 124 | 28:15–68 | 68, 69, 73, 120, 171, 179, 192, 220, 486, 498, 527, 606, 867n10 |
| 7:10 | 124 | | |
| 7:23 | 594 | | |
| 8:1–10 | 97 | 28:18 | 908n14 |
| 8:3 | 227 | 28:19 | 194 |
| 8:6 | 867n12 | 28:21 | 913n11 |
| 8:11–20 | 97, 543 | 28:22 | 583, 867n8 |
| 10:16 | 681 | 28:23 | 33, 560 |
| 11:14 | 369 | 28:24 | 33 |
| 11:24 | 904n8 | 28:27 | 867n8 |
| 11:29 | 345 | 28:30 | 194 |
| 12:8–11a | 338 | 28:30–35 | 868n13 |
| 12:11 | 346 | 28:32 | 908n14 |
| 13:1–5 | 736 | 28:37 | 392, 868n13 |
| 14:2 | 915n11 | 28:38–40 | 390, 560 |
| 15:21 | 907n7 | 28:41 | 908n14 |
| 16:13–15 | 223, 224 | 28:45 | 607 |

| | | | |
|---|---|---|---|
| 28:53 | 908n14 | 24:3 | 14 |
| 28:55 | 908n14 | 24:19 | 870n10 |
| 28:57 | 908n14 | | |
| 28:59–61 | 867n8 | *Judges* | |
| 30:1 | 720 | book of | 195, 288, 698 |
| 30:1–10 | 48, 69, 114, 129, 183, 497, 498 | 2:1b–3 | 372 |
| | | 3:7–12 | 288 |
| 30:6 | 743 | 4:21 | 848n18 |
| 30:10 | 867n12 | 6:28 | 865n25 |
| 30:19–20 | 910n23 | 6:34 | 137 |
| 31:6 | 822 | 6:34–40 | 912n4 |
| 31:7 | 890n15 | 7 | 12 |
| 31:23 | 572 | 7:22 | 594, 750 |
| 32 | 866n10 | 8:24 | 904n6 |
| 32:1 | 377 | 10:16 | 901n17 |
| 32:4 | 497 | 10:17 | 50 |
| 32:9–11 | 783 | 11:30–40 | 384 |
| 32:14 | 184 | 12:7 | 50 |
| 32:21 | 262, 293 | 12:14 | 898n13 |
| 32:35 | 861n24 | 14:15 | 22 |
| 33:2–5 | 515 | 14:19 | 137 |
| 32:47 | 824 | 16:5 | 22 |
| 33:8–11 | 34 | 16:16 | 901n17 |
| 33:8ff | 908n17 | 16:20 | 42 |
| 33:10 | 883n1 (ch. 60) | 16:23–30 | 230 |
| 33:28 | 702 | 19 | 66 |
| 33:29 | 898n10 | 19:22–30 | 73 |
| | | | |
| *Joshua* | | *Ruth* | |
| 1:3 | 904n8 | 1:6 | 604 |
| 1:6 | 818 | 1:6–18 | 167 |
| 3:7–17 | 382 | 1:12 | 907n17 |
| 3:16 | 50 | | |
| 3:17 | 50 | *1 Samuel* | |
| 4:1–10 | 675 | 1:9–20 | 495 |
| 4:19 | 193 | 1:19 | 332 |
| 5:1–9 | 185 | 1:21–28 | 495 |
| 5:7–12 | 37 | 2:1–10 | 495 |
| 5:14 | 616 | 2:10 | 625 |
| 5:15 | 616 | 2:12–17 | 35 |
| 7:14 | 271 | 2:12–25 | 832n8 (ch. 4) |
| 7:15 | 271 | 7:15 | 185 |
| 8:2 | 904n6 | 7:16 | 185 |
| 10:1–15 | 516 | 8 | 392 |
| 14:2 | 335 | 8:5 | 725 |
| 15:59 | 325 | 11:14 | 37, 185 |
| 24:2 | 14 | 11:15 | 37, 185 |

Scripture Index   923

| | | | |
|---|---|---|---|
| 13:8–14 | 673 | *1 Kings* | |
| 14:4 | 893n2 | book of | 10, 391 |
| 14:20 | 750 | 3:16–28 | 800 |
| 14:42 | 271 | 3:26 | 82, 103, 124 |
| 15:10 | 846n3 (ch. 32) | 3:27 | 103, 124 |
| 15:22 | 681 | 6 | 346 |
| 15:29 | 298 | 6:11 | 846n3 (ch. 32) |
| 17:3 | 893n2 | 7:49 | 649 |
| 17:45 | 448 | 8:10 | 576 |
| 17:45ff | 431 | 8:11 | 576 |
| 17:46 | 448 | 8:41–43 | 132 |
| 20:5–6 | 225 | 8:56 | 339 |
| 20:26 | 225 | 10:2 | 891n14 |
| 22:1 | 327 | 10:26 | 326 |
| 22:2 | 327 | 10:28 | 326 |
| 23:26 | 893n2 | 11:1–5 | 785 |
| 25:25 | 601 | 11:1–12:24 | 10 |
| 26:10 | 848n20 | 11:3 | 861n24 |
| 26:12 | 848n18 | 11:7 | 785, 904n8 |
| | | 11:8 | 785 |
| *2 Samuel* | | 11:26–12:24 | 29 |
| 1:17–27 | 841n2 (ch. 24) | 11:26–12:33 | 155, 839n7 |
| 1:20 | 327 | 12:1–24 | 94 |
| 3:18 | 885n14 | 12:25–33 | 10, 34, 224 |
| 5:11 | 889n7 | 12:32–34 | 673 |
| 5:20 | 342 | 13:6 | 896n3 |
| 5:24 | 869n17 | 15:26 | 10 |
| 6:8 | 342 | 15:34 | 10 |
| 7:1 | 648 | 16:25 | 391 |
| 7:1–17 | 14 | 16:26 | 391 |
| 7:2 | 648 | 17–2 Kings 13 | 10 |
| 7:3 | 648 | 17:2–4 | 264 |
| 7:4 | 846n3 (ch. 32) | 17:5 | 264 |
| 7:4–17 | 418, 497, 591 | 17:8–24 | 293 |
| 7:5 | 885n14 | 17:9 | 253 |
| 7:5–7 | 562 | 18:18 | 183 |
| 7:8 | 885n14 | 18:20–40 | 420 |
| 7:11–16 | 232 | 18:27 | 870n23 |
| 7:12 | 365 | 18:46 | 853n9 |
| 7:13 | 365 | 19:2 | 391 |
| 7:16 | 652 | 19:9–18 | 79 |
| 7:19 | 232 | 19:10 | 817 |
| 8:11–14 | 234 | 19:14 | 393 |
| 12:13 | 771 | 19:15 | 57 |
| 12:22 | 854n13 | 19:16 | 57 |
| 14:13 | 872n6 | 19:18 | 817 |
| 18:13 | 245 | 20:20ff | 22 |
| 24:4 | 914n2 | | |

| | | | |
|---|---|---|---|
| 20:35 | 219 | 17:6 | 73 |
| 21 | 12 | 17:7–23 | 59 |
| 21:1–16 | 334 | 17:13 | 89, 549 |
| 21:1–24 | 391 | 17:14 | 89 |
| 22:8 | 869n19 | 17:24 | 523 |
| 22:23 | 863n13 | 17:24–41 | 836n1 (ch. 12) |
| 22:28 | 902n18 | 18–19 | 546 |
| | | 18:1–8 | 524 |
| *2 Kings* | | 18:13–17 | 242 |
| book of | 10, 524, 847n8 | 21 | 549 |
| 2:3–5 | 219 | 21:1 | 384 |
| 3:4 | 153 | 21:1–6 | 457 |
| 4:1 | 219 | 21:1–9 | 524 |
| 4:23 | 225 | 21:6 | 384 |
| 4:38 | 37 | 21:16 | 457 |
| 5:1–14 | 167, 293 | 21:17–26 | 549 |
| 8:9–15 | 293 | 22:6 | 627, 889n7 |
| 6:1 | 219 | 23:4–20 | 533 |
| 6:17 | 614 | 23:13 | 904n8 |
| 6:20–23 | 246 | 23:28–35 | 492 |
| 9–10 | 12 | 25:1 | 689 |
| 9:1 | 219 | 25:3 | 689 |
| 10:32 | 161 | 25:4 | 689 |
| 10:33 | 161 | 25:25 | 689 |
| 12:11 | 627 | | |
| 12:12 | 889n7 | *1 Chronicles* | |
| 13:4 | 896n3 | 14:1 | 889n7 |
| 13:7 | 161 | 15:1–3 | 346 |
| 14 | 847n8 | 16:40 | 333 |
| 14:23–27 | 192 | 17:4 | 885n14 |
| 14:24 | 9 | 21:4 | 914n2 |
| 14:24–26 | 261 | 22:8 | 674 |
| 14:24–29 | 9 | 22:9 | 674 |
| 14:25 | 213, 846n3 (ch. 32) | | |
| 14:25–28 | 212 | *2 Chronicles* | |
| 14:26ff | 847n7 | book of | 524 |
| 15:8–21 | 41 | 4:7 | 649 |
| 15:27–30 | 43 | 6:1–11 | 525 |
| 15:29 | 523 | 7:11–18 | 880n4 (ch. 54) |
| 15:29–31 | 72 | 7:14 | 527 |
| 16:3 | 384 | 11:5–12 | 153 |
| 16:5 | 43 | 18:7 | 869n19 |
| 16:6 | 43, 245 | 20:20 | 854n16 |
| 16:7 | 245 | 20:25 | 904n6 |
| 16:7–9 | 43 | 26:16 | 673 |
| 17:1–6 | 43, 59, 72, 523 | 26:19 | 673 |
| 17:1–23 | 36, 53 | 26:22 | 673 |
| 17:4 | 52 | | |

| | | | |
|---|---|---|---|
| 28:1–15 | 245 | 6:21 | 785 |
| 28:1–21 | 240, 845n3 | 9 | 782 |
| 28:5–15 | 246 | 10 | 782 |
| 28:17 | 245 | 10:1–17 | 854n17 |
| 30:1 | 526 | | |
| 30:2 | 526 | *Nehemiah* | |
| 33:12 | 896n3 | book of | 782 |
| 33:21 | 525 | 9:1–3 | 854n17 |
| 33:22 | 525 | 9:17 | 856n10 |
| 33:25 | 525 | 9:27 | 254 |
| 34–35 | 524 | 12:16 | 603 |
| 34:1 | 525 | 13:23–31 | 782 |
| 34:1–7 | 525, 526 | | |
| 34:3 | 525 | *Esther* | |
| 34:4 | 525 | book of | 821 |
| 34:6 | 526 | 3:13 | 904n6 |
| 34:7 | 526 | 6:1 | 821 |
| 34:8–13 | 526 | 6:2 | 821 |
| 34:8–28 | 526, 526 | 6:3 | 821 |
| 34:14 | 526 | 6:10 | 821 |
| 34:19 | 526 | 8:10 | 859n26 |
| 34:21 | 526, 527 | 8:11 | 904n6 |
| 34:22 | 527 | 8:14 | 859n26 |
| 34:23 | 527 | | |
| 34:25 | 527 | *Job* | |
| 34:26 | 527 | 3:8 | 851n1 |
| 34:27 | 527 | 4:13 | 848n18 |
| 34:28 | 527 | 5:1 | 904n10 |
| 34:29–35:27 | 527 | 9:8 | 858n11 |
| 34:30 | 527 | 15:15 | 904n10 |
| 34:31 | 527 | 16:10 | 364 |
| 34:32 | 527 | 19:25 | 904n8 |
| 34:33 | 527 | 20:15 | 852n21 |
| 35:1–19 | 528 | 24:1–4 | 901n17 |
| 35:20–24 | 528 | 26:12 | 849n13, 850n1 |
| 35:22 | 528 | 33:24 | 848n20 |
| 35:24 | 734 | 38 | 892n10 |
| 35:25 | 528 | 38:4 | 309 |
| | | 38:5 | 309 |
| *Ezra* | | 38:8–11 | 850n1 |
| book of | 782 | 39 | 892n10 |
| 1:2–4 | 557 | 39:19–25 | 900n11 |
| 3:12 | 883n9 | 39:20 | 900n11 |
| 4:1 | 836n1 (ch. 12) | 40:3–5 | 176 |
| 4:2 | 836n1 (ch. 12) | 40:5 | 634 |
| 4:4–5:5 | 557 | 41 | 850n1 |
| 6:2–5 | 557 | 42:1–6 | 176 |

*Psalms*

| | |
|---|---|
| book of | 346, 414, 551 |
| 1 | 212 |
| 1:1 | 820 |
| 1:1–6 | 838n13 |
| 1:2 | 820 |
| 1:3 | 105 |
| 2 | 145, 146, 626 |
| 2:1 | 145, 743 |
| 2:1–3 | 626 |
| 2:2 | 145, 743 |
| 2:4–6 | 666–67 |
| 2:6 | 626 |
| 2:7–12 | 327 |
| 2:12 | 551 |
| 3:7 | 364 |
| 4:3 | 349 |
| 5:3 | 333 |
| 7 | 414 |
| 7:1 | 551 |
| 9:12–13 | 540 |
| 10:1 | 877n8 |
| 10:10 | 897n20 |
| 10:17 | 540 |
| 13:1 | 489, 616 |
| 13:2 | 616 |
| 14:1 | 159 |
| 15:1 | 801 |
| 15:2–4 | 801 |
| 15:5 | 801 |
| 16:11 | 265, 816 |
| 17:8 | 106 |
| 18:4f | 851n6 |
| 18:46–48 | 433 |
| 19:7–9 | 488 |
| 19:12–14 | 21 |
| 20:7 | 326, 371 |
| 21:11 | 860n6 |
| 22:5 | 349 |
| 22:12 | 184 |
| 22:29 | 848n20 |
| 23 | 405, 709 |
| 23:1 | 720, 728 |
| 23:1–3 | 405 |
| 23:1–3a | 709 |
| 23:4 | 709, 722 |
| 23:5 | 710 |
| 23:6 | 665, 728 |
| 24:2 | 851n6 |
| 24:4–6 | 49 |
| 25:9 | 540 |
| 27:8 | 49 |
| 30:3 | 852n16 |
| 30:5 | 332 |
| 33:5 | 254 |
| 33:16 | 898n10 |
| 33:20 | 96 |
| 35:17 | 795, 796 |
| 36:7 | 106 |
| 37:1–4 | 500 |
| 37:11 | 540 |
| 38:11 | 245 |
| 42:3 | 870n23 |
| 44:23–24 | 877n8 |
| 46:1–3 | 363 |
| 46:4 | 623 |
| 46:5 | 332, 623 |
| 46:10 | 396 |
| 49:12 | 478 |
| 49:14 | 478 |
| 50:14 | 277 |
| 50:15 | 277 |
| 51 | 103, 771 |
| 51:16 | 386 |
| 51:17 | 386 |
| 51:17–19 | 837n2 |
| 56:13 | 837n2 |
| 59:16 | 332 |
| 60:3 | 342, 468, 852n14 |
| 68:5 | 894n16 |
| 69:9 | 418, 597, 778 |
| 69:32 | 540 |
| 70:5 | 97 |
| 71:1 | 551 |
| 71:20 | 852n16 |
| 72 | 899n18 |
| 72:7 | 899n18 |
| 72:8 | 899n18 |
| 73:3 | 795 |
| 73:3–9 | 575 |
| 73:4 | 795 |
| 73:5 | 795 |
| 73:6 | 444 |
| 73:3 | 915n8 |

| | | | |
|---|---|---|---|
| 73:12 | 444 | 103:14 | 675 |
| 73:13 | 444, 795 | 104:24–26 | 850n1 |
| 73:14 | 795 | 106:30 | 778 |
| 73:18 | 444 | 106:31 | 778 |
| 73:19 | 444 | 107:13 | 349 |
| 73:25 | 575, 633 | 107:42 | 824 |
| 73:26 | 575, 633 | 111 | 419 |
| 73:27 | 915n8 | 113 | 320 |
| 73:28 | 915n8 | 113:4–6 | 320 |
| 74:1 | 877n8 | 115:2 | 870n23 |
| 74:10 | 794 | 115:9–10 | 97 |
| 74:11 | 794, 877n8 | 119 | 419 |
| 74:12–14 | 850n1 | 121:1 | 320 |
| 75:4 | 625 | 121:1–2 | 97 |
| 75:5 | 625 | 124:1–3a | 595 |
| 75:8 | 467, 731, 852n14 | 124:8 | 97 |
| 76:6 | 848n18 | 125:1 | 624 |
| 78:47 | 583 | 125:2 | 624 |
| 78:70 | 885n14 | 130:6 | 332 |
| 79:5 | 489 | 131 | 802 |
| 80:1 | 709 | 132:10 | 885n14 |
| 80:12 | 877n8 | 135:4 | 915n11 |
| 84:2 | 773 | 135:7 | 849n13 |
| 84:11 | 915n13 | 145:7–13 | 254 |
| 86:15 | 856n10 | 145:8 | 856n10 |
| 87:1–3 | 346, 623 | 147:7 | 369 |
| 88:13 | 333 | 147:8 | 369 |
| 88:14 | 877n8 | 149:4 | 540 |
| 89:3 | 885n14 | | |
| 89:6 | 904n10 | *Proverbs* | |
| 89:9–10 | 850n1 | book of | 160 |
| 89:17 | 625 | 1:20 | 388 |
| 89:46 | 489 | 1:21 | 388 |
| 90:1 | 497 | 3:12 | 274 |
| 90:2 | 497, 498 | 5:3 | 71 |
| 90:3 | 129 | 5:5 | 848n20 |
| 91 | 414 | 16:18 | 242 |
| 91:2 | 551 | 16:33 | 271 |
| 93:3 | 851n6 | 18:18 | 897n20 |
| 93:3–6 | 851n6 | 26:3 | 388 |
| 94:12 | 274 | 26:28 | 71 |
| 95:5 | 849n13 | 30:15–33 | 160 |
| 95:7b–11 | 805 | | |
| 98 | 414 | *Isaiah* | |
| 103:1–5 | 180 | 1:1 | 241, 487, 857n3 |
| 103:8–10 | 305 | 1:2 | 378 |
| 103:12 | 431 | 1:10–20 | 186 |

| | | | |
|---|---|---|---|
| 1:12–13 | 225 | 18 | 546 |
| 1:13 | 836n3 (ch. 11) | 18:1–7 | 230, 544 |
| 2:1–4 | 905n16 | 18:4 | 510 |
| 2:2 | 634 | 18:7 | 510, 545 |
| 2:3 | 634 | 19:14 | 852n21 |
| 2:6–22 | 140, 176, 842n2 (ch. 25) | 20:1–6 | 11 |
| | | 20:2–4 | 859n24 |
| 2:7 | 859n26 | 20:3 | 858n19 |
| 2:12 | 253 | 20:4 | 858n19 |
| 2:12ff | 871n15 | 21:6–9 | 878n10 |
| 2:13 | 184 | 22:20–23 | 900n13 |
| 2:17–22 | 835n9 | 24:18 | 866n11 |
| 3:13 | 18, 902n18 | 26:4 | 370 |
| 4:2–6 | 130, 508 | 26:19 | 105 |
| 4:11–12 | 130 | 27 | 855n1 |
| 5:8 | 860n13 | 27:1 | 851n1 |
| 5:8–30 | 535 | 28–29 | 546 |
| 5:29–30 | 874n12 | 28:8 | 852n21 |
| 6:1–3 | 510 | 28:17 | 583 |
| 6:3 | 116 | 28:21 | 53 |
| 6:9 | 833n8 | 29:9–14 | 350 |
| 6:10 | 833n8 | 29:10 | 848n18 |
| 7 | 365, 371 | 29:13 | 276, 288 |
| 7:1 | 12, 160, 240, 245 | 30:1 | 455 |
| 7:1–9 | 43 | 31:1 | 455 |
| 7:2 | 160, 240, 245 | 32:1 | 254 |
| 7:9 | 455 | 34 | 243 |
| 7:11 | 455, 806 | 34:5–6 | 907n19 |
| 7:12 | 455 | 34:8–12 | 254 |
| 7:17 | 29, 455 | 35 | 553 |
| 7:17–25 | 43 | 36–37 | 546 |
| 7:18 | 712 | 36:1–21 | 242 |
| 8:3 | 12 | 37 | 253, 859n30 |
| 8:7 | 420, 435 | 37:8–13 | 242 |
| 8:8 | 420, 861n24 | 40:8 | 477, 607 |
| 9:1–7 | 29 | 40:19 | 889n7 |
| 9:6 | 366 | 40:21–23 | 510 |
| 10:2 | 904n6 | 40:27–31 | 227 |
| 10:5 | 294, 418, 619 | 40:31 | 500 |
| 10:5–12 | 835n11 | 41:8 | 885n14 |
| 10:5–34 | 253, 491 | 41:15 | 161 |
| 10:11 | 619 | 42:2 | 698 |
| 11:1–9 | 29, 147 | 42:3 | 698 |
| 13–24 | 855n1 | 43:1–3 | 567 |
| 14:7 | 888n13 | 43:2 | 286 |
| 14:18 | 877, 877n15 | 43:6 | 895n16 |
| 15–16 | 234 | 43:10 | 498 |

| | | | |
|---|---|---|---|
| 44:1 | 885n14 | *Jeremiah* | |
| 44:9–20 | 58, 132, 498, 509 | book of | 524 |
| 44:13 | 889n7 | 1:1 | 857n3 |
| 44:22 | 604 | 1:4 | 846n3 (ch. 32) |
| 44:27 | 851n6 | 1:17–19 | 89 |
| 45:22 | 537 | 2:9 | 18 |
| 45:23 | 537 | 2:10 | 275 |
| 49:12 | 895n16 | 2:11 | 275 |
| 49:19 | 499 | 3:16–18 | 28, 29 |
| 50:2 | 849n13 | 4:1–4 | 123 |
| 50:6 | 267, 364 | 5:3 | 896n6 |
| 50:7 | 267, 480 | 5:21 | 896n6 |
| 51:9 | 850n1 | 5:22 | 850n1 |
| 51:13 | 902n1 | 5:24 | 369 |
| 51:17 | 468, 731, 852n14 | 6:6 | 867n4 |
| 51:17–23 | 252 | 6:14 | 337, 464 |
| 51:22 | 469, 731, 852n14 | 7:1–8:3 | 231 |
| 52:14 | 458 | 7:23 | 631, 723 |
| 53:3 | 458 | 7:25 | 885n14 |
| 53:4–6 | 436 | 7:26 | 896n6 |
| 53:5 | 343, 610, 735 | 8:5 | 896n6 |
| 53:6 | 343 | 8:13 | 533 |
| 53:9 | 407 | 8:16 | 867n4 |
| 54:1–3 | 402 | 9:1–22 | 841n2 (ch. 24) |
| 55:8 | 307, 362 | 10 | 58, 498 |
| 55:9 | 307, 362, 655 | 10:1–16 | 498 |
| 55:11 | 299, 558, 609 | 10:3 | 889n7 |
| 55:12 | 602 | 11:10 | 896n6 |
| 55:13 | 602 | 11:14 | 216 |
| 56:1–8 | 130 | 13:3 | 264 |
| 56:9–12 | 404 | 13:5 | 264 |
| 59:6 | 860n6 | 14:11 | 216 |
| 60:1–3 | 759 | 16:1–4 | 11 |
| 60:4 | 895n16 | 17:1 | 896n6 |
| 60:19 | 915n13 | 17:9 | 724 |
| 60:20 | 915n13 | 17:23 | 896n6 |
| 61:1 | 540 | 17:24 | 867n4 |
| 61:8–9 | 910n23 | 18:7–10 | 854n23 |
| 63:1–6 | 907n19 | 18:8 | 883n1 (ch. 60) |
| 63:7–14 | 137 | 19:9 | 900n4 |
| 65–66 | 114, 130 | 20:7 | 22 |
| 65:15–27 | 2 | 21–45 | 517 |
| 65:17–25 | 23, 114, 485, 490, 508, 553 | 21:12 | 333 |
| | | 22 | 596 |
| | | 22:24 | 597, 886n15 |
| 66:17–23 | 551 | 22:25 | 597 |
| 66:24 | 206 | 23:1–4 | 404 |

| | | | |
|---|---|---|---|
| 23:1–8 | 29 | 51:38 | 874n13 |
| 23:3 | 710 | 51:39 | 877n15 |
| 23:4 | 710 | 51:44 | 499 |
| 23:5 | 643 | 52:6 | 689 |
| 23:9–40 | 171 | 52:7 | 689 |
| 23:40 | 861n24 | 52:12–15 | 689 |
| 25:9 | 885n14 | | |
| 25:15 | 852n14 | *Lamentations* | |
| 25:15–17 | 878n6 (ch. 52) | book of | 419 |
| 25:15–29 | 731 | 1 | 841n2 (ch. 24) |
| 25:15–38 | 243 | 1–4 | 253, 419 |
| 25:26 | 895n16 | 1:1 | 684 |
| 25:30 | 836n8 (ch. 10) | 1:19 | 867n4 |
| 26:1–6 | 528 | 2:2 | 499 |
| 26:11 | 528 | 2:5 | 499 |
| 26:16–18 | 352 | 2:12 | 867n4 |
| 26:17–19 | 528 | 2:16 | 499 |
| 26:19 | 896n3 | 2:20 | 495 |
| 27:1–11 | 243 | 3:33 | 53 |
| 27:1–15 | 240 | 3:58 | 869n8 |
| 27:6 | 885n14 | 4:21 | 240, 254, 878n6 (ch. 52) |
| 28:1 | 890n15 | | |
| 28:1–17 | 171 | 4:22 | 240, 253, 254 |
| 28:5 | 890n15 | | |
| 28:11 | 890n15 | *Ezekiel* | |
| 29:26 | 218 | 2:10 | 893n2 |
| 30:9 | 29 | 3:16 | 846n3 (ch. 32) |
| 31:31–34 | 23 | 3:22 | 264 |
| 32:35 | 95 | 3:23 | 264 |
| 32:38 | 685 | 4 | 848n22 |
| 33:21 | 908n16 | 4:3 | 867n4 |
| 36 | 528 | 5 | 848n22 |
| 39–52 | 253 | 5:2 | 867n4 |
| 39:2 | 689 | 7:15 | 867n4 |
| 41:1–3 | 689 | 7:26 | 883n1 (ch. 60) |
| 41:5 | 528 | 10 | 576 |
| 45:1–5 | 528 | 11:2 | 860n6 |
| 46–51 | 855n1 | 12:1–20 | 848n22 |
| 48:26 | 852n21 | 12:24 | 71 |
| 49:7–22 | 243 | 14:9 | 22 |
| 49:13 | 907n19 | 18:17 | 125 |
| 49:17 | 907n19 | 19:2–9 | 874n13 |
| 49:18 | 907n19 | 21:26 | 895n9 |
| 49:32–36 | 849n13 | 23:31–34 | 731 |
| 51:7 | 252 | 23:32 | 252 |
| 51:33 | 51 | 23:33 | 252 |
| 51:34 | 499 | 24:1 | 689 |

Scripture Index   931

| | | | |
|---|---|---|---|
| 24:2 | 689 | 8:24 | 897n20 |
| 24:15ff | 848n22 | 9:1–23 | 608 |
| 25–32 | 855n1 | 10:9 | 848n18 |
| 25:12–14 | 243 | | |
| 28:14 | 345 | *Hosea* | |
| 29:19 | 904n6 | book of | 7, 8, 77, 93, 96, 155 |
| 33:1–9 | 500 | 1 | 323 |
| 34:1–6 | 479 | 1–2 | 26 |
| 34:1–10 | 404 | 1–3 | 63, 101, 848n22 |
| 34:2–5 | 707 | 1–4 | 96 |
| 34:11 | 479 | 1–5 | 47 |
| 34:11–16 | 341, 710 | 1:1 | 8, 9, 15 |
| 34:16a | 479 | 1:1–11 | 880n6 (ch. 54) |
| 34:23 | 29 | 1:1–2:1 | 7, 831n2 (ch. 3), 832n9 (ch. 4), 839n1 (ch. 19), 839n7, 880n6 (ch. 54) |
| 34:24 | 29 | | |
| 34:28 | 759 | | |
| 34:29 | 759 | | |
| 35 | 240 | 1:2 | 831n2 (ch. 3) |
| 35:10 | 240 | 1:2–9 | 8, 11, 15, 27 |
| 35:15 | 763 | 1:2a | 11 |
| 36:20 | 179 | 1:2b | 11 |
| 37:1–14 | 48, 299 | 1:3 | 11, 12, 13 |
| 37:15–28 | 900n4 | 1:4 | 12, 24 |
| 37:24 | 29 | 1:4b | 12 |
| 37:25 | 29 | 1:5 | 12, 24 |
| 38:11 | 889n10 | 1:6 | 24, 67 |
| 38:17 | 885n14 | 1:6a | 12 |
| 38:21 | 885 | 1:6b | 12 |
| 44:19 | 884n5 | 1:7 | 13, 24, 253 |
| 45:7 | 893n2 | 1:8 | 13 |
| 47:1–12 | 147 | 1:9 | 13, 24 |
| 47:7 | 893n2 | 1:10–2:1 | 8, 13, 15 |
| | | 1:10a | 14 |
| *Daniel* | | 1:10b | 14 |
| 2:31–35 | 354 | 1:11 | 14, 15 |
| 2:44 | 354 | 2 | 64, 69, 78 |
| 2:45 | 354 | 2–3 | 78 |
| 4:28–33 | 176 | 2:1–13 | 48 |
| 4:28–37 | 167 | 2:2 | 18 |
| 4:34 | 441 | 2:2–5 | 18 |
| 4:34–37 | 176 | 2:2–23 | 17, 18, 26, 29, 880n6 (ch. 54) |
| 4:35 | 441 | | |
| 7:7 | 625 | 2:2–25 | 27 |
| 7:8 | 625 | 2:3 | 18, 19 |
| 7:14 | 356 | 2:4 | 18, 19 |
| 8:13 | 904n10 | 2:5 | 18, 19, 27 |
| 8:18 | 848n18 | 2:5–13 | 70 |

| | | | |
|---|---|---|---|
| 2:5a | 19 | 4:1–3 | 32, 35 |
| 2:5b | 19 | 4:1–6 | 60, 61 |
| 2:6 | 20 | 4:1–19 | 39 |
| 2:6–13 | 18, 20 | 4:1a | 32 |
| 2:7 | 20, 39 | 4:1b | 32 |
| 2:8 | 20, 21, 57 | 4:2 | 32, 33, 39 |
| 2:8–23 | 32 | 4:3 | 32, 33, 39, 533 |
| 2:9 | 20, 21 | 4:4 | 34 |
| 2:10 | 21 | 4:4–6 | 34, 56 |
| 2:10–13 | 20, 21 | 4:4–11 | 32, 34 |
| 2:11 | 21 | 4:4–19 | 39 |
| 2:13 | 21, 225 | 4:5 | 34 |
| 2:14 | 22 | 4:6 | 40 |
| 2:14–23 | 18, 22, 49, 104 | 4:6a | 34 |
| 2:15 | 22 | 4:6b | 34 |
| 2:16 | 22 | 4:7 | 34, 35 |
| 2:16–20 | 22 | 4:7–8 | 60 |
| 2:17 | 23 | 4:8 | 34, 35 |
| 2:18 | 23 | 4:8a | 35 |
| 2:19 | 23, 27 | 4:8b | 35 |
| 2:20 | 27 | 4:9 | 36 |
| 2:20a | 23 | 4:9–11 | 34 |
| 2:20b | 23 | 4:10 | 36 |
| 2:21 | 24 | 4:11 | 36 |
| 2:21–23 | 22, 130 | 4:12 | 32, 36 |
| 2:22 | 24 | 4:12–19 | 32, 36 |
| 2:23 | 24 | 4:12a | 37 |
| 3 | 25, 26, 39, 78, 132, 206, 832n2 (ch. 5), 835n1 (ch. 9), 880n4 (ch. 54) | 4:12b | 37 |
| | | 4:13 | 36, 37 |
| | | 4:14 | 36, 37, 174 |
| | | 4:15 | 36, 37, 67 |
| 3:1 | 26, 27, 831n2 (ch. 3) | 4:16 | 38 |
| 3:1–5 | 27, 104 | 4:16–19 | 36 |
| 3:1a | 26 | 4:17 | 38 |
| 3:1b | 27 | 4:18 | 38 |
| 3:2 | 26, 27 | 4:19 | 38 |
| 3:2–4 | 27 | 5 | 39, 48, 835n1 (ch. 9), 881n2 |
| 3:3 | 26, 27, 28 | | |
| 3:4 | 26, 28, 253, 255 | 5:1 | 39, 40, 43, 45, 77, 552, 862n4, 881n6 (ch. 57) |
| 3:5 | 26, 28, 29, 233, 253, 255, 841n1 (ch. 24), 880n1 (ch. 56) | | |
| | | 5:1–14 | 39 |
| 4 | 31, 32 | 5:1a | 39, 40 |
| 4–5 | 63 | 5:1b | 40 |
| 4–5:1 | 50 | 5:2 | 39, 40, 41, 45, 881n6 (ch. 57) |
| 4:1 | 32, 33, 34, 39, 41, 57, 86 | | |
| | | 5:3 | 41 |

| | | | |
|---|---|---|---|
| 5:3–7 | 40, 41, 45 | 6:11b | 834n5 (ch. 6) |
| 5:3–15 | 39 | 6:11b–7:1a | 51 |
| 5:4 | 41, 44, 47, 56 | 7 | 81 |
| 5:4–6 | 44 | 7:1 | 834n5 (ch. 6) |
| 5:4a | 41 | 7:1–10 | 50 |
| 5:4b–7 | 41 | 7:1b | 51 |
| 5:5 | 42 | 7:2 | 51 |
| 5:6 | 42, 87 | 7:3 | 51 |
| 5:7 | 42, 87 | 7:3–7 | 57 |
| 5:8 | 43, 55 | 7:3–10 | 52 |
| 5:8–14 | 48 | 7:4 | 51, 77 |
| 5:8–15 | 40, 43, 45 | 7:5 | 51 |
| 5:9 | 43 | 7:6 | 51 |
| 5:10 | 43, 880n9 | 7:7 | 51 |
| 5:11 | 44 | 7:7b | 51 |
| 5:12 | 44 | 7:8–10 | 51 |
| 5:13 | 44 | 7:8a | 51 |
| 5:14 | 44, 865n22 | 7:8b | 52 |
| 5:15 | 39, 44, 48, 841n1 (ch. 24), 880n1 (ch. 56) | 7:9 | 52 |
| 6 | 47, 81 | 7:10a | 52 |
| 6–7 | 47, 63 | 7:10b | 52 |
| 6:1 | 48 | 7:11 | 52 |
| 6:1–3 | 47, 48, 78 | 7:11–13 | 52 |
| 6:1a | 48 | 7:11–16 | 47, 50, 52, 80 |
| 6:1b | 48 | 7:11b | 64 |
| 6:1c | 48 | 7:12 | 52 |
| 6:2 | 49 | 7:13 | 52, 53 |
| 6:2b | 49 | 7:14–16 | 52, 102 |
| 6:3 | 49, 56 | 7:14a | 53 |
| 6:3b | 49 | 7:14b | 53 |
| 6:3c | 49 | 7:15 | 53 |
| 6:4 | 51, 77, 834n5 (ch. 6) | 7:16 | 53 |
| 6:4–6 | 52 | 8 | 55, 62, 63 |
| 6:4–11 | 50, 51 | 8:1 | 55, 56, 57, 59 |
| 6:4–7:10 | 47, 50 | 8:1–3 | 56, 59 |
| 6:4a | 50 | 8:1–10 | 60 |
| 6:4b | 50 | 8:2 | 55, 56 |
| 6:5 | 50 | 8:3 | 56 |
| 6:6 | 833n3 | 8:3a | 57 |
| 6:6a | 50 | 8:3b | 57 |
| 6:7 | 50, 56 | 8:4 | 57 |
| 6:7–7:2 | 52 | 8:4–6 | 57 |
| 6:8 | 50, 89 | 8:4–10 | 57 |
| 6:9 | 50 | 8:4a | 57 |
| 6:10 | 51 | 8:5 | 58, 72 |
| 6:11 | 51, 834n5 (ch. 6) | 8:6 | 58 |
| | | 8:7 | 55, 59, 197 |

Scripture Index 933

| | | | |
|---|---|---|---|
| 8:7–10 | 57, 59 | 9:17b | 68 |
| 8:7a | 59 | 10 | 69, 832n2 (ch. 5) |
| 8:8 | 59, 266, 499 | 10:1 | 69, 70, 77 |
| 8:8–10 | 59 | 10:1a | 70 |
| 8:9 | 59 | 10:1b | 70 |
| 8:10 | 59 | 10:2 | 69, 70, 72 |
| 8:11 | 60 | 10:2b | 71 |
| 8:11–14 | 59 | 10:3 | 72 |
| 8:12 | 55, 60 | 10:3–10 | 69, 70, 71 |
| 8:13 | 55, 60 | 10:3a | 72 |
| 8:13b | 60 | 10:3b | 72 |
| 8:14 | 55 | 10:4a | 72 |
| 8:14a | 61 | 10:4b | 72 |
| 8:14b | 61 | 10:5 | 72 |
| 9 | 63, 69, 70 | 10:5–15 | 87 |
| 9:1–6 | 63 | 10:6 | 72 |
| 9:1a | 64 | 10:6a | 72 |
| 9:1b | 64 | 10:7 | 73 |
| 9:2 | 64 | 10:8 | 73, 76 |
| 9:3 | 64, 80 | 10:8b | 73 |
| 9:4 | 64, 65 | 10:9 | 73 |
| 9:5 | 65 | 10:10a | 73 |
| 9:6a | 65 | 10:10b | 73 |
| 9:6b | 65 | 10:11 | 69 |
| 9:7 | 65, 68 | 10:11–15 | 70, 73 |
| 9:7–9 | 63 | 10:11a | 73 |
| 9:7–14 | 65 | 10:11b | 74 |
| 9:7a | 65 | 10:12 | 69, 70, 841n1 (ch. 24), 880n1 (ch. 56) |
| 9:7b | 65 | | |
| 9:7c | 65 | 10:12a | 74 |
| 9:8 | 66, 68 | 10:13–15 | 69, 74 |
| 9:9 | 66 | 10:13a | 74 |
| 9:10 | 66 | 10:13b | 74 |
| 9:10–17 | 63, 66 | 10:14a | 75 |
| 9:10a | 66 | 10:14b | 75 |
| 9:10b | 66 | 10:15b | 75 |
| 9:11a | 67 | 11 | 78 |
| 9:11b | 67 | 11–12 | 837n11 |
| 9:12a | 67 | 11:1 | 77, 78, 79, 80, 83 |
| 9:13–15 | 67 | 11:1–4 | 78, 80 |
| 9:13a | 67 | 11:1–9 | 129, 216 |
| 9:13b | 67 | 11:1–11 | 77, 83, 84, 86, 98, 101, 103 |
| 9:14 | 67 | | |
| 9:15 | 67 | 11:2 | 77, 79, 80, 83 |
| 9:16a | 67 | 11:3 | 79 |
| 9:16b | 67 | 11:3a | 79 |
| 9:17a | 68 | 11:3b | 79 |

Scripture Index    935

| | | | |
|---|---|---|---|
| 11:4 | 79 | 13:1–3 | 93, 94, 97 |
| 11:4a | 79 | 13:1a | 94 |
| 11:4b | 79 | 13:1b | 94 |
| 11:3–7 | 77 | 13:2a | 94 |
| 11:5 | 80, 83 | 13:2b | 94, 836n4 (ch. 12) |
| 11:5–7 | 78, 80, 81, 82 | 13:3 | 95 |
| 11:6 | 81 | 13:4 | 93, 95, 96, 99 |
| 11:7 | 81 | 13:4–6 | 95 |
| 11:8 | 82, 98 | 13:4–11 | 93, 95 |
| 11:8–10 | 78 | 13:5 | 93, 96 |
| 11:8–11 | 78, 82 | 13:6 | 96 |
| 11:8a | 82 | 13:6b | 96 |
| 11:8b | 82 | 13:7 | 96 |
| 11:9 | 98 | 13:8 | 96 |
| 11:9a | 82, 83 | 13:9 | 93, 96, 99 |
| 11:9b | 83 | 13:9–11 | 97 |
| 11:10 | 83 | 13:10 | 97 |
| 11:10a | 83 | 13:11 | 97 |
| 11:10b | 83 | 13:12 | 98 |
| 11:11 | 78, 83 | 13:12–16 | 93, 97 |
| 11:11a | 83 | 13:13 | 98 |
| 11:11b | 83 | 13:14 | 98, 99, 101 |
| 11:12 | 86 | 13:15 | 99, 105 |
| 11:12–12:1 | 86 | 13:16 | 99, 101 |
| 11:12–12:6 | 86 | 14 | 101 |
| 11:12–12:14 | 85 | 14:1 | 104, 107 |
| 12 | 90, 94 | 14:1–3 | 101, 102, 103, 104 |
| 12:1 | 86 | 14:1–9 | 839n1 (ch. 17) |
| 12:2 | 86 | 14:1b | 102 |
| 12:2–14 | 86 | 14:2 | 102, 104 |
| 12:3 | 86 | 14:2a | 102 |
| 12:3–6 | 90 | 14:2b | 102 |
| 12:4 | 86 | 14:3 | 102 |
| 12:4b | 87 | 14:3a | 102 |
| 12:5 | 87 | 14:3b | 102 |
| 12:6 | 87 | 14:3c | 103 |
| 12:7 | 88 | 14:4 | 102, 103, 104 |
| 12:7–9 | 88 | 14:4–7 | 837n3 |
| 12:8 | 88 | 14:5 | 105, 865n22 |
| 12:9 | 88 | 14:5–8 | 102, 105 |
| 12:10 | 89 | 14:5b | 105 |
| 12:10–14 | 89 | 14:5c | 105 |
| 12:11 | 67, 89, 90 | 14:6 | 105 |
| 12:12 | 90, 836n1 (ch. 11) | 14:7 | 105, 106 |
| 12:13 | 90 | 14:8 | 106, 837n3, 838n12 |
| 12:14 | 90 | 14:9 | 9, 102, 106 |
| 13 | 93, 101 | | |

*Joel*

| | | | |
|---|---|---|---|
| book of | 127, 137, 151 | 2:11 | 121, 122, 252, 897n20 |
| 1 | 111, 112, 115, 116, 117, 119, 147, 838n5, 839n1 (ch. 19) | 2:12 | 120, 122, 123, 126, 127, 135, 604 |
| 1:1–12 | 112, 113, 114, 143 | 2:12–14 | 122, 125, 127, 128, 129 |
| 1:1a | 112 | 2:12–17 | 120, 122, 143 |
| 1:1b | 112 | 2:13 | 123, 125, 127, 135, 856n10 |
| 1:2–20 | 127, 216 | 2:14 | 126 |
| 1:2–2:1 | 135 | 2:15 | 126 |
| 1:2a | 112 | 2:15–17 | 122, 126, 128, 135 |
| 1:2b | 112 | 2:16a | 126 |
| 1:3 | 112 | 2:16b | 126 |
| 1:4 | 112 | 2:17 | 126, 127, 870n23 |
| 1:5 | 113 | 2:18 | 127, 128, 129 |
| 1:8 | 113 | 2:18–26 | 143 |
| 1:9 | 113 | 2:18–27 | 127, 128, 135, 144, 839n3 (ch. 16) |
| 1:11 | 113 | 2:18–3:21 | 135 |
| 1:12 | 130 | 2:19 | 130 |
| 1:13 | 113, 115, 120, 122, 143 | 2:19–26 | 128, 129, 130, 131 |
| 1:14 | 113, 115, 120, 122, 143 | 2:20 | 130 |
| 1:15 | 113, 114, 116, 135, 143, 252 | 2:21 | 130 |
| | | 2:21–26 | 130 |
| 1:16 | 116 | 2:22 | 130 |
| 1:16–20 | 115 | 2:23 | 130, 131 |
| 1:17 | 116 | 2:23–26 | 130 |
| 1:17–20 | 143 | 2:24 | 131 |
| 1:18 | 113, 116 | 2:25 | 131 |
| 1:19 | 116, 123 | 2:26 | 131, 133 |
| 1:20 | 113, 116, 123 | 2:27 | 127, 128, 131, 132, 133, 135, 138, 143 |
| 2 | 120 | | |
| 2:1 | 120, 252 | 2:28 | 138, 139 |
| 2:1–11 | 122, 127, 143, 146 | 2:28–32 | 127, 132, 135, 136, 138, 143, 144, 839n3 (ch. 16) |
| 2:1–17 | 119, 120, 126, 135 | | |
| 2:2 | 121 | | |
| 2:2a | 120 | 2:29 | 138, 139 |
| 2:2b–11 | 120, 121 | 2:30 | 140 |
| 2:3 | 121 | 2:31 | 140, 252 |
| 2:4 | 121 | 2:32 | 141, 253 |
| 2:5 | 121 | 3 | 127, 135, 143, 151 |
| 2:7 | 121 | 3:1 | 144 |
| 2:7–9 | 121 | 3:1–8 | 143, 144 |
| 2:8 | 121 | 3:1–21 | 135 |
| 2:9 | 121 | 3:2 | 144, 146 |
| 2:10 | 121 | 3:2b | 144 |

## Scripture Index

| | | | |
|---|---|---|---|
| 3:2c | 144 | 1:6 | 162, 234, 239, 243, 251 |
| 3:3 | 144, 146 | | |
| 3:4–8 | 144, 846n14 | 1:6–8 | 160, 162, 181, 542 |
| 3:8 | 895n16 | 1:6–12 | 144 |
| 3:9 | 146 | 1:9 | 160, 163, 203, 234 |
| 3:9–12 | 146 | 1:10 | 160, 163 |
| 3:9–15 | 143, 145, 146 | 1:11 | 160, 164, 239, 243, 880n9 |
| 3:10 | 146 | | |
| 3:11 | 146 | 1:11a | 165 |
| 3:12 | 146 | 1:12 | 160, 164, 239, 243 |
| 3:13 | 51, 146 | 1:13 | 165, 166 |
| 3:13–15 | 146 | 1:13–15 | 160, 165 |
| 3:14 | 146, 252 | 2:1 | 166 |
| 3:16 | 143, 147, 151, 157, 180, 836n8 (ch. 10) | 2:1–3 | 160, 166 |
| | | 2:2 | 167 |
| 3:16–18 | 147 | 2:3 | 167 |
| 3:16–21 | 143, 146 | 2:4 | 170, 171, 172, 177 |
| 3:17 | 147 | 2:4–15 | 208 |
| 3:18 | 147 | 2:4–16 | 145, 159, 169, 179, 880n6 (ch. 54) |
| 3:19 | 147, 844n1 (ch. 30) | | |
| 3:19–21 | 147 | 2:4–4:13 | 203 |
| 3:20 | 147 | 2:5 | 170, 171, 172, 177 |
| 3:21 | 147 | 2:6 | 145, 155, 172, 182, 204, 208 |
| *Amos* | | 2:6–8 | 175 |
| book of | 153, 156, 213, 229, 239 | 2:6–12 | 172 |
| | | 2:6–16 | 177, 180, 212 |
| 1–2 | 61, 184, 215, 229, 865n26 | 2:7 | 145, 155, 174, 182, 204, 208, 225, 235 |
| 1–3 | 183 | 2:7a | 173 |
| 1:1 | 151, 152, 153, 154, 155, 170, 226, 229, 841n4 (ch. 24), 842n6 (ch. 24), 842n3 (ch. 25) | 2:7b | 174 |
| | | 2:8 | 174, 176, 235 |
| | | 2:9 | 174, 175, 233 |
| | | 2:9–11 | 178 |
| | | 2:10 | 174, 175, 179, 180, 233 |
| 1:2 | 151, 152, 156, 157, 159, 170, 180, 213, 836n8 (ch. 10), 842n4 (ch. 24), 842n6 (ch. 24), 842n3 (ch. 25) | 2:11 | 174, 175 |
| | | 2:11a | 174 |
| | | 2:12 | 174, 175, 178 |
| | | 2:13 | 175 |
| 1:2–2:8 | 901n7 | 2:13–16 | 175, 178 |
| 1:3 | 153, 160, 165 | 2:14 | 175 |
| 1:3–5 | 159, 160 | 2:15 | 175 |
| 1:3–2:3 | 159, 169, 170, 200 | 2:16 | 175 |
| 1:3–2:16 | 157, 177, 180, 230, 233 | 3 | 177, 178 |
| | | 3–4 | 157 |
| 1:3b | 161 | 3–6 | 215, 229 |

| | | | |
|---|---|---|---|
| 3:1 | 178, 184, 208, 225, 233 | 4:12 | 114, 184, 188 |
| 3:1a | 179 | 4:13 | 114, 184, 188, 203, 207, 233, 849n13, 858n11 |
| 3:1b | 179 | | |
| 3:2 | 178, 179 | 5 | 205 |
| 3:2b | 179 | 5–6 | 157 |
| 3:3 | 180 | 5:1 | 192, 195, 196, 225, 842n7 (ch. 24) |
| 3:3–8 | 178, 180 | | |
| 3:4 | 180 | 5:1–3 | 191, 192 |
| 3:6 | 180 | 5:1–15 | 842n7 (ch. 24) |
| 3:7 | 180, 181 | 5:1–17 | 191, 832n2 (ch. 5), 835n1 (ch. 9), 880n4 (ch. 54) |
| 3:8 | 157, 180, 181, 836n8 (ch. 10) | | |
| 3:9 | 178, 181, 182 | 5:2 | 192 |
| 3:9–15 | 178, 181 | 5:3 | 192 |
| 3:10 | 178, 181, 182 | 5:4 | 191, 192, 213, 223, 226, 844n8 (ch. 28) |
| 3:11 | 181 | | |
| 3:11–15 | 181 | 5:4–6 | 195, 229, 231, 235, 879n1 (ch. 54), 880n7, 880n1 (ch. 56) |
| 3:12 | 155, 182 | | |
| 3:13 | 225 | | |
| 3:13–15 | 235 | 5:4–13 | 191, 192 |
| 3:14 | 182 | 5:5 | 155, 193 |
| 3:15 | 155, 182 | 5:6 | 191, 193, 523, 526 |
| 4 | 183, 184, 841n4 (ch. 24), 842n6 (ch. 24), 842n3 (ch. 25) | 5:6a | vi |
| | | 5:7 | 193, 212 |
| | | 5:8 | 193, 203, 207 |
| 4:1 | 155, 184, 225 | 5:8–9 | 233 |
| 4:1–3 | 212 | 5:9 | 203, 207 |
| 4:1–5 | 183, 184, 186, 189 | 5:10 | 194, 196 |
| 4:2 | 185, 211 | 5:10–13 | 194 |
| 4:2a | 185 | 5:11 | 194, 196 |
| 4:2b | 185 | 5:12 | 194, 196, 204 |
| 4:3 | 185 | 5:13 | 194 |
| 4:4 | 67, 155, 185, 193, 201, 333 | 5:14 | 196, 880n1 (ch. 56) |
| | | 5:14–17 | 191, 195 |
| 4:5 | 67, 185, 201 | 5:14a | 212 |
| 4:6 | 114, 184, 187, 604 | 5:14b | 212 |
| 4:6–11 | 183, 186, 187, 188 | 5:15 | 196 |
| 4:6–12 | 233 | 5:15a | 196 |
| 4:6–13 | 114 | 5:15b | 196 |
| 4:7 | 114, 187 | 5:16 | 196, 842n7 (ch. 24) |
| 4:8 | 114, 187 | 5:17 | 196, 842n7 (ch. 24) |
| 4:8–11 | 184 | 5:18 | 200, 842n7 (ch. 24) |
| 4:9 | 187 | 5:18–20 | 114, 200, 252 |
| 4:9–11 | 114 | 5:18–24 | 156 |
| 4:10 | 187 | 5:18–27 | 199, 207, 210, 212, 842n7 (ch. 24) |
| 4:11 | 187, 188, 593, 639 | | |

| | | | |
|---|---|---|---|
| 5:19 | 200 | 7:1–3 | 216, 223 |
| 5:20 | 200 | 7:1–6 | 219, 231 |
| 5:21 | 201 | 7:1–9 | 215, 216 |
| 5:21–24 | 200, 201, 203, 204 | 7:1–9:10 | 157, 199 |
| 5:22 | 202 | 7:1a | 216 |
| 5:23 | 202 | 7:1b | 216 |
| 5:24 | 199, 202, 206 | 7:2 | 216 |
| 5:25 | 205 | 7:2a | 216, 843n6 (ch. 27) |
| 5:25–27 | 200, 205 | 7:2b | 216 |
| 5:26 | 205 | 7:3 | 216 |
| 5:27 | 205 | 7:3a | 216 |
| 6 | 207, 217 | 7:4 | 216 |
| 6:1 | 208, 210 | 7:4–6 | 216 |
| 6:1–3 | 207, 208 | 7:4b | 216 |
| 6:1–6 | 155 | 7:5 | 217 |
| 6:1–7 | 184, 216, 235 | 7:6 | 217 |
| 6:1–14 | 199 | 7:7 | 217, 843n7 (ch. 27) |
| 6:1b | 208 | 7:7–9 | 224 |
| 6:1c | 208 | 7:8 | 224, 229, 843n7 (ch. 27), 844n1 (ch. 28) |
| 6:2 | 208 | | |
| 6:3 | 208 | 7:8b | 217 |
| 6:4 | 155, 209, 211 | 7:9 | 217, 218 |
| 6:4–6a | 209 | 7:10 | 218 |
| 6:4–7 | 207, 208, 209 | 7:10–13 | 155, 156, 182, 193, 215, 218, 224 |
| 6:4a | 209 | | |
| 6:4b | 209 | 7:10–17 | 151, 152, 180, 226, 236, 841n4 (ch. 24), 842n6 (ch. 24), 842n3 (ch. 25), 843n9 (ch. 27) |
| 6:5a | 209 | | |
| 6:5b | 210 | | |
| 6:6 | 155 | | |
| 6:6a | 210 | | |
| 6:6b | 209, 210 | 7:11 | 218 |
| 6:6c | 210 | 7:12 | 156, 218 |
| 6:7 | 208, 209, 210 | 7:12–17 | 211 |
| 6:8 | 207, 211 | 7:12a | 218 |
| 6:8–10 | 211, 212 | 7:13 | 156, 185, 218 |
| 6:8–14 | 156 | 7:13a | 218 |
| 6:9 | 208, 211, 212 | 7:13b | 218 |
| 6:10 | 208, 211, 212 | 7:14 | 152, 153, 154, 219, 229 |
| 6:11 | 212 | | |
| 6:11–13 | 207 | 7:14–17 | 215, 219, 220 |
| 6:11–14 | 212 | 7:15 | 152, 153, 154, 156, 219 |
| 6:12 | 199, 212 | | |
| 6:12–14 | 212 | 7:16 | 155, 219, 227 |
| 6:13 | 211, 212 | 7:17 | 155, 156, 219, 220, 227, 904n6 |
| 6:14 | 208, 212, 213 | | |
| 7 | 215 | 8 | 223, 229, 842n5 (ch. 24) |
| 7–9 | 215, 229 | | |

| | | | |
|---|---|---|---|
| 8:1 | 223 | 9:11–15 | 157, 839n1 (ch. 17) |
| 8:1–3 | 223, 225 | 9:11a | 232 |
| 8:1a | 224 | 9:11b | 232 |
| 8:1b | 224 | 9:12 | 229, 233, 234, 235, 239, 243, 255 |
| 8:2 | 224, 229 | | |
| 8:2a | 224 | 9:13 | 236 |
| 8:2b | 224 | 9:13–15 | 229, 236 |
| 8:3 | 224 | 9:14 | 230, 236 |
| 8:4 | 225 | 9:15 | 236 |
| 8:4–6 | 225 | | |
| 8:4–10 | 223, 225 | *Obadiah* | |
| 8:5 | 155, 225 | book of | 239 |
| 8:6 | 225 | 1 | 239, 241 |
| 8:7 | 211, 225, 226 | 1–4 | 241, 242 |
| 8:7–10 | 227 | 1–11 | 239, 240, 880n2 (ch. 55) |
| 8:8 | 225, 226 | | |
| 8:9 | 225, 226 | 1b | 241 |
| 8:10 | 225, 226 | 2 | 249 |
| 8:10a | 226 | 2–4 | 241 |
| 8:10b | 226 | 2a | 241 |
| 8:11 | 227 | 2b | 241 |
| 8:11–14 | 223, 226 | 3 | 241, 249 |
| 8:12 | 227 | 4 | 239, 242, 249 |
| 8:12a | 227 | 5 | 243 |
| 8:12b | 227 | 5–9 | 241, 242, 249 |
| 8:13 | 227 | 6 | 241, 243 |
| 8:14 | 227, 228, 230 | 7 | 243, 845n10 |
| 8:14b | 228 | 8 | 239, 243 |
| 9 | 229, 844n1 (ch. 30) | 9 | 243, 845n11 |
| 9:1 | 230 | 10 | 240, 241, 244, 246, 249, 250, 845n4, 845n11 |
| 9:1–6 | 231 | | |
| 9:1–10 | 229 | | |
| 9:1–15 | 845n9 | 10b | 246 |
| 9:1a | 230 | 11 | 241, 244, 245, 246, 249, 250, 251, 763, 845n4 |
| 9:1b | 230 | | |
| 9:2 | 230 | | |
| 9:3 | 230 | 12 | 240, 250, 251, 846n4 |
| 9:4 | 230 | 12–14 | 249, 250, 252, 846n4 |
| 9:5 | 230, 233 | 12–16 | 241 |
| 9:6 | 230, 233 | 12–21 | 240, 244, 249 |
| 9:7 | 230, 233 | 13 | 250, 251 |
| 9:7–10 | 231 | 13a | 251 |
| 9:8 | 230 | 13b | 251 |
| 9:8–10 | 233 | 14 | 251 |
| 9:9 | 230, 231 | 15 | 252, 254, 255 |
| 9:10 | 231 | 15–18 | 252 |
| 9:11 | 229, 232 | 15–20 | 249, 251 |

Scripture Index 941

| | | | |
|---|---|---|---|
| 15–21 | 249 | 1:16 | 272, 277, 278, 287, 855n5 |
| 15b | 252 | | |
| 16 | 252, 852n14 | 1:17 | 259, 270, 282, 849n8 |
| 16b | 252 | 1:17–2:10 | 281 |
| 17 | 253, 846n8 | 2 | 263, 288, 852n20 |
| 17–20 | 241 | 2:1 | 259, 851n7 |
| 17b | 253 | 2:2 | 265, 274, 283, 308, 851n7 |
| 17c | 253 | | |
| 18 | 239, 253 | 2:2–6 | 282 |
| 19 | 252, 253, 254 | 2:2–9 | 282, 306, 308 |
| 20 | 252, 253, 254 | 2:3 | 283, 284, 285 |
| 21 | 240, 241, 249, 254 | 2:5 | 283, 284, 285, 852n15 |

*Jonah*

| | | | |
|---|---|---|---|
| | | 2:6 | 273, 283, 285, 286 |
| book of | 215, 259, 260, 262, 269, 276, 282, 292, 294, 303, 545, 846n2, 846n3 (ch. 32), 847n8, 848n20, 849n8, 850n22, 853n3, 855n4 | 2:6–10 | 286 |
| | | 2:6f | 848n20 |
| | | 2:7 | 286 |
| | | 2:7–9 | 745 |
| | | 2:8 | 287 |
| | | 2:9 | 282, 287, 291, 300, 308 |
| 1 | 260, 261, 273, 281, 288, 847n8, 853n6 | 2:10 | 259, 282, 288 |
| | | 3 | 288, 292, 293, 294, 299, 300, 303, 310, 853n6 |
| 1:1 | 264, 846n3 (ch. 32) | | |
| 1:1–2 | 260 | | |
| 1:1–6 | 259 | 3:1–4 | 292 |
| 1:2 | 260, 261, 264, 270, 292, 852n2 | 3:1–4:1 | 291 |
| | | 3:2 | 852n2 |
| 1:3 | 261, 264, 265, 274, 282, 292, 848n20, 849n8, 850n15, 853n6 | 3:3 | 292, 299, 853n9 |
| | | 3:4 | 292, 295, 299 |
| | | 3:5 | 287, 295, 296, 299 |
| 1:3–5 | 263 | 3:5–9 | 292, 295, 297 |
| 1:4 | 264 | 3:6 | 295 |
| 1:5 | 264, 265, 269, 272, 282, 848n20, 849n8 | 3:6–8 | 279 |
| | | 3:6–10 | 477 |
| 1:6 | 264, 266 | 3:8 | 295 |
| 1:7 | 270, 271 | 3:9 | 296, 856n13 |
| 1:7–16 | 269 | 3:10 | 292, 297, 303, 855n5 |
| 1:8 | 274 | 4 | 261, 288, 303, 308, 309, 310 |
| 1:8–15 | 274 | | |
| 1:9 | 274, 276, 294, 847n8, 852n20 | 4:1 | 293, 304, 310, 856n14 |
| 1:10 | 275 | 4:1–3 | 263, 308 |
| 1:12 | 279, 308 | 4:1–4 | 304 |
| 1:13 | 271, 278, 849n8 | 4:2 | 260, 287, 305, 308, 849n8, 852n20 |
| 1:14 | 278 | | |
| 1:15 | 272, 279 | 4:3 | 267, 287, 293, 304 |

| | | | |
|---|---|---|---|
| 4:4 | 304, 309 | 2:1 | 332, 335, 860n7, 861n16 |
| 4:5–10 | 308 | | |
| 4:6 | 288, 309, 849n8 | 2:1–5 | 332, 860n4 |
| 4:8 | 288, 304, 309, 310 | 2:1–11 | 343 |
| 4:9 | 309 | 2:1b | 332 |
| 4:10 | 857n23 | 2:2 | 333, 338, 860n7, 860n11, 861n16 |
| 4:11 | 260, 312, 480, 856n21, 856n23, 857n23 | 2:2a | 333 |
| | | 2:2b | 333 |
| | | 2:3 | 335, 861n16 |
| *Micah* | | 2:3–5 | 861n16 |
| book of | 318, 320, 388, 399, 400 | 2:4 | 335, 861n16, 861n17 |
| | | 2:5 | 335, 861n16 |
| 1 | 317, 318, 320, 376, 860n11 | 2:5–8 | 399 |
| | | 2:6 | 337, 857n2, 861n23 |
| 1:1 | 318, 864n4 | 2:6–11 | 337, 860n4 |
| 1:2 | 319, 376 | 2:6a | 861n23 |
| 1:2–4 | 857n9 | 2:7 | 861n23 |
| 1:2–5a | 319 | 2:7a | 861n23 |
| 1:3 | 320, 323, 858n11 | 2:7b | 861n23 |
| 1:3–5 | 857n7 | 2:8 | 338 |
| 1:4 | 320 | 2:9 | 338 |
| 1:5–7 | 857n9 | 2:10 | 338, 342, 405 |
| 1:5a | 321 | 2:11 | 339, 405 |
| 1:5b | 321, 858n13 | 2:12 | 340, 341, 343, 356, 533, 709–10, 861n27, 869n15 |
| 1:5b–7 | 321 | | |
| 1:6 | 322, 863n16 | | |
| 1:6b | 322 | 2:12–13 | 340, 869n17 |
| 1:6c | 322 | 2:13 | 341, 342, 343, 404, 861n27 |
| 1:7 | 322, 323, 860n11 | | |
| 1:7a | 323 | 3 | 346, 347, 350 |
| 1:7b | 323 | 3:1 | 347, 355, 376, 862n4 |
| 1:8 | 324, 329 | 3:1–3 | 720 |
| 1:8–16 | 324 | 3:1–4 | 347 |
| 1:9 | 324 | 3:1–12 | 347 |
| 1:9b | 324 | 3:1–4:7 | 345 |
| 1:10 | 324, 325, 327 | 3:2 | 347, 355, 862n7 |
| 1:10–16 | 857n5 | 3:3 | 347, 355, 862n7 |
| 1:11a | 325 | 3:4 | 348, 352 |
| 1:11b | 325 | 3:5 | 349, 355 |
| 1:12 | 325 | 3:5–7 | 863n13 |
| 1:12b | 327 | 3:5–8 | 349 |
| 1:13 | 325, 326 | 3:6 | 350 |
| 1:14 | 326 | 3:7 | 350, 352 |
| 1:15 | 327 | 3:8 | 138 |
| 1:16 | 328 | 3:9 | 351 |
| 2 | 331, 347, 860n11 | 3:9–12 | 351 |

## Scripture Index 943

| | | | |
|---|---|---|---|
| 3:10 | 351 | 6:1 | 18, 376, 377 |
| 3:11 | 351, 883n1 (ch. 60) | 6:1–8 | 375, 376, 857n2 |
| 3:12 | 351, 352, 353, 354, 356, 863n16 | 6:2 | 18, 377, 379 |
| | | 6:3 | 379 |
| 4 | 353 | 6:3–5 | 379 |
| 4:1 | 353, 354, 359 | 6:4 | 380 |
| 4:1–4 | 403, 905n16 | 6:5 | 380, 381, 385 |
| 4:1–7 | 353, 360, 368 | 6:6 | 383, 681 |
| 4:2 | 354, 359, 861n16 | 6:6–8 | 116, 383 |
| 4:2b–4 | 355 | 6:6–11 | 857n2 |
| 4:3 | 359 | 6:7 | 383, 384, 681 |
| 4:4 | 355 | 6:8 | 89, 319, 384, 385, 498, 681, 825, 867n22 |
| 4:5 | 359 | | |
| 4:6 | 356, 359 | 6:9 | 388 |
| 4:7 | 356, 359 | 6:9–16 | 387, 388 |
| 4:8 | 359, 864n3 | 6:9–7:7 | 387 |
| 4:8–5:6 | 368 | 6:9a | 388 |
| 4:8–5:15 | 359 | 6:10 | 389 |
| 4:9 | 360 | 6:11 | 389 |
| 4:9–13 | 364 | 6:12–16 | 489 |
| 4:10 | 360, 361, 362, 367 | 6:13 | 389, 390 |
| 4:10b | 361 | 6:13–15 | 868n13 |
| 4:11 | 360, 362, 858n18 | 6:14 | 391 |
| 4:11–13 | 362 | 6:15 | 391 |
| 4:12 | 362 | 6:16 | 391, 392, 867n13, 868n13 |
| 4:13 | 363, 363–64, 367 | | |
| 5 | 364 | 7:1 | 387, 393 |
| 5:1 | 360, 364, 858n18, 865n16 | 7:1–6 | 868n16 |
| | | 7:1–7 | 393, 867n1 |
| 5:1–6 | 364 | 7:2 | 393 |
| 5:2 | 364, 365, 367, 865n16 | 7:2–3 | 867n1 |
| 5:2–4 | 865n18 | 7:3a | 394 |
| 5:3 | 365 | 7:3b | 394 |
| 5:4 | 365, 366, 869n15 | 7:4 | 395 |
| 5:5 | 254, 366, 368, 865n18 | 7:5 | 393, 394 |
| 5:6 | 254, 367, 368 | 7:6 | 394, 867n1 |
| 5:7 | 368, 369 | 7:7 | 388, 395, 396, 868n16 |
| 5:7–9 | 368 | 7:7–20 | 869n17 |
| 5:8 | 369 | 7:8 | 399, 400, 408, 869n9 |
| 5:9 | 370 | 7:8–10 | 400, 402, 869n12 |
| 5:10 | 370, 371, 859n26 | 7:8–20 | 399, 867n1, 868n16, 868n6, 870n25 |
| 5:10–13 | 371 | | |
| 5:10–15 | 370 | 7:9 | 401, 402, 407 |
| 5:11 | 370, 371 | 7:9a | 869n9 |
| 5:13b | 371 | 7:10 | 400, 401, 402, 403, 407, 408, 858n18 |
| 5:15 | 371, 372 | | |
| 6 | 376–77, 378 | 7:11 | 402 |

| | | | |
|---|---|---|---|
| 7:11–13 | 402, 869n12 | 1:15 | 431 |
| 7:12 | 402, 403 | 1:15b | 432 |
| 7:13 | 403 | 2 | 413, 452 |
| 7:14 | 403, 404, 869n6 | 2:1 | 434 |
| 7:14–17 | 403, 869n18 | 2:2 | 434 |
| 7:15 | 404, 405, 869n6 | 2:3 | 440, 441, 873n2 |
| 7:16 | 404 | 2:3–13 | 439, 440 |
| 7:17 | 404, 405 | 2:4 | 441, 873n7 |
| 7:18 | 405, 406, 407, 408 | 2:5 | 441, 874n7 |
| 7:18–20 | 405, 408, 839n1 (ch. 17) | 2:6 | 442 |
| | | 2:7 | 443, 444 |
| 7:19 | 406, 409, 869n18 | 2:8a | 443 |
| 7:19–20 | 406 | 2:8b | 443 |
| 7:20 | 406 | 2:9 | 443 |
| | | 2:10 | 444 |
| *Nahum* | | 2:11 | 445 |
| book of | 474, 477, 545 | 2:11–13 | 413, 874n11 |
| 1 | 433, 452 | 2:12 | 445 |
| 1:1 | 241, 414 | 2:13 | 446, 447, 449 |
| 1:1–8 | 413, 419 | 3 | 413, 451, 454, 462 |
| 1:2 | 415, 416, 873n4 | 3:1 | 421, 452, 453 |
| 1:2–3a | 414 | 3:1–4 | 452, 875n6 (ch. 47) |
| 1:2–8 | 871n16 | 3:1–7 | 451 |
| 1:3 | 416, 417, 418, 419, 420, 421, 474 | 3:2a | 453 |
| | | 3:2b | 453 |
| 1:3–5 | 418 | 3:3–6 | 440 |
| 1:3b–5 | 419 | 3:3a | 453 |
| 1:4 | 419, 420 | 3:3b | 453 |
| 1:4–5 | 422 | 3:3c | 453 |
| 1:5 | 419 | 3:4 | 454 |
| 1:6 | 421 | 3:4–7 | 413 |
| 1:7 | 421, 422, 467, 474 | 3:4a | 454, 456 |
| 1:8 | 415, 416, 419, 420, 423, 424 | 3:5 | 456 |
| | | 3:5–7 | 452, 456 |
| 1:9 | 427, 428, 429, 436, 872n6 | 3:6 | 456 |
| | | 3:6a | 456 |
| 1:9–13 | 428 | 3:7 | 458, 459 |
| 1:9–2:2 | 427, 428 | 3:7–10 | 443 |
| 1:10 | 429, 871n2 | 3:8 | 462, 463, 545, 870n4 |
| 1:10a | 429 | 3:8–10 | 462 |
| 1:10b | 429 | 3:8–13 | 413, 461, 462 |
| 1:11 | 427, 429, 872n6 | 3:8a | 462 |
| 1:12 | 424, 430, 431, 436, 870n4, 876n1 | 3:9 | 463, 545 |
| | | 3:10 | 463 |
| 1:12b | 435 | 3:11 | 445, 464, 467, 468 |
| 1:13 | 424, 430, 431 | 3:11–13 | 445, 464 |
| 1:14 | 431 | 3:14 | 472, 476 |

Scripture Index 945

| | | | |
|---|---|---|---|
| 3:14–15a | 472 | 1:15 | 499 |
| 3:14–17 | 413 | 1:17 | 499 |
| 3:14–19 | 471 | 2:1 | 395, 500 |
| 3:15 | 473 | 2:2 | 501, 505 |
| 3:15a | 476 | 2:2–4 | 511 |
| 3:15b | 475 | 2:2–5 | 496, 501 |
| 3:15b–17 | 475, 476 | 2:2–20 | 501 |
| 3:16 | 475 | 2:3 | 501, 505, 517 |
| 3:16a | 475 | 2:3b | 517 |
| 3:17 | 476 | 2:4 | 486, 501, 502, 505, 506, 519, 523 |
| 3:18 | 477 | | |
| 3:18–19 | 477 | 2:4b | 517 |
| 3:18a | 477 | 2:5 | 501, 505 |
| 3:18b | 478 | 2:6 | 506 |
| 3:19 | 479, 480 | 2:6–8 | 506 |
| 3:19a | 478 | 2:6–20 | 486, 505, 514 |
| | | 2:7 | 506 |
| *Habakkuk* | | 2:8 | 506, 507 |
| book of | 485 | 2:9 | 506 |
| 1:1 | 487 | 2:9–11 | 506 |
| 1:1–11 | 485, 514, 878n4 (ch. 51) | 2:10 | 507 |
| | | 2:11 | 507 |
| | | 2:12 | 487 |
| 1:2 | 486, 489, 491 | 2:12–14 | 507 |
| 1:2–4 | 486, 489, 496 | 2:12a | 507 |
| 1:3 | 486, 490, 491, 846n3 (ch. 32) | 2:12b | 507 |
| | | 2:13a | 507 |
| 1:4 | 486, 490 | 2:13b | 507 |
| 1:5 | 491 | 2:14 | 508, 514, 520 |
| 1:5–11 | 486, 491, 496 | 2:15 | 508 |
| 1:6 | 491, 492, 506 | 2:15–17 | 508 |
| 1:7a | 492 | 2:16 | 252, 731 |
| 1:7b | 492 | 2:16a | 508 |
| 1:8 | 492 | 2:16b | 508 |
| 1:9 | 492 | 2:17 | 508 |
| 1:10 | 492 | 2:18 | 509 |
| 1:11 | 492 | 2:18a | 509 |
| 1:11a | 492 | 2:18b | 509 |
| 1:12 | 491, 496, 497, 515 | 2:18c | 509 |
| 1:12–2:1 | 486 | 2:19 | 487, 509 |
| 1:12–2:5 | 495, 514, 881n8 (ch. 57) | 2:20 | 487, 509, 510, 511 |
| | | 2:21 | 593 |
| 1:12a | 498 | 2:21–22 | 593 |
| 1:12b | 498 | 2:22 | 593 |
| 1:13 | 499, 515, 639 | 3 | 513, 592, 881n8 (ch. 57) |
| 1:13–16 | 499 | | |
| 1:13–2:1 | 496, 499 | 3:1 | 514 |
| 1:14 | 499 | 3:1–15 | 487 |

| | | | |
|---|---|---|---|
| 3:2 | 514 | 1:7–13 | 532, 534, 536, 540 |
| 3:3–5 | 515 | 1:8 | 531, 535, 542 |
| 3:3–15 | 514, 515 | 1:8–11 | 534, 535 |
| 3:3a | 515 | 1:9 | 535, 542 |
| 3:4 | 516 | 1:10 | 524, 535 |
| 3:5 | 516 | 1:11 | 535 |
| 3:6 | 516 | 1:12 | 66, 531, 534, 535, 536 |
| 3:6–15 | 515 | 1:13 | 534, 535, 536 |
| 3:7 | 516 | 1:14 | 531, 536 |
| 3:8 | 880n9 | 1:14–16 | 536 |
| 3:8–10 | 516 | 1:14–18 | 532, 536 |
| 3:9–13a | 593 | 1:14a | 536 |
| 3:11 | 516 | 1:14b | 536 |
| 3:12–15 | 516 | 1:15 | 536 |
| 3:13 | 322, 516 | 1:16 | 537 |
| 3:16 | 487, 517 | 1:17 | 536, 537 |
| 3:16–19 | 517 | 1:18 | 536, 913n11 |
| 3:16b | 517 | 2 | 537, 539, 835n1 (ch. 9), 880n4 (ch. 54) |
| 3:17 | 517, 518 | | |
| 3:17–19 | 396, 487, 514 | 2:1 | 540, 546, 547, 551, 553 |
| 3:18 | 517, 518, 868n16 | | |
| 3:19 | 517, 519, 520 | 2:1–3 | 539, 540, 541 |
| | | 2:1–5 | 835n1 (ch. 9) |
| *Zephaniah* | | 2:1–11 | 552 |
| 1 | 140, 491, 539 | 2:2 | 524, 540, 546, 553 |
| 1:1 | 523, 524, 877n2 (ch. 50), 880n1 (ch. 55), 881n1, 881n2, 881n4 (ch. 57) | 2:3 | 524, 532, 540, 541, 542, 543, 545, 546, 547, 549, 550, 551, 554, 841n1 (ch. 24) |
| 1:1–2 | 533, 537 | 2:3–11 | 551 |
| 1:2 | 524, 532, 533, 540, 551, 879n1 (ch. 54), 880n4 (ch. 55), 880n2 (ch. 56), 881n3 (ch. 56), 881n9 (ch. 57) | 2:3a | 546 |
| | | 2:3b | 546 |
| | | 2:4 | 542 |
| | | 2:4–7 | 541 |
| | | 2:4–11 | 539, 541 |
| 1:2–6 | 532, 534 | 2:4–15 | 546, 554 |
| 1:2–18 | 531, 532, 543, 547, 553, 832n2 (ch. 5), 880n1 (ch. 56) | 2:5 | 542, 547 |
| | | 2:6 | 542 |
| | | 2:7 | 540, 541, 542, 543, 546, 547, 549, 550, 551, 552, 554 |
| 1:3 | 524, 532, 533, 540 | | |
| 1:4 | 531, 532, 533 | | |
| 1:4–6 | 526, 533, 548 | 2:8 | 533 |
| 1:4–13 | 548 | 2:8–11 | 541, 542 |
| 1:5 | 531, 533 | 2:9 | 541, 543, 546, 547, 549, 550, 551, 552, 554 |
| 1:6 | 533, 540, 841n1 (ch. 24) | | |
| 1:7 | 532, 534 | 2:9b | 542, 543 |

Scripture Index 947

| | | | |
|---|---|---|---|
| 2:10 | 543 | 1:2–11 | 686 |
| 2:11 | 541, 543, 546 | 1:3 | 882n9 |
| 2:12 | 544 | 1:4 | 559, 562 |
| 2:12–15 | 539, 544, 546 | 1:4–6 | 605 |
| 2:13 | 545 | 1:5 | 560 |
| 2:13–15 | 528, 545, 548 | 1:6 | 560, 575 |
| 2:14 | 545 | 1:7 | 562, 589 |
| 2:15 | 545 | 1:8 | 562, 589 |
| 3 | 543, 547 | 1:9 | 560 |
| 3:1 | 547, 548, 549 | 1:10 | 560 |
| 3:1–5 | 547, 548 | 1:11 | 560 |
| 3:1–6 | 554 | 1:12 | 564, 565 |
| 3:2 | 548 | 1:12–15 | 564, 608, 640 |
| 3:3 | 548, 549 | 1:13 | 566 |
| 3:4 | 548, 549 | 1:14 | 564, 565 |
| 3:5 | 333, 548, 549 | 1:14b | 564 |
| 3:6 | 548, 550 | 1:15 | 564 |
| 3:6–8 | 550 | 1:15b | 883n1 (ch. 59) |
| 3:6–13 | 547, 550 | 1:15b–2:1a | 569 |
| 3:7 | 548, 550 | 1:15b–2:9 | 569, 591 |
| 3:8 | 550, 551, 554 | 2 | 580 |
| 3:9 | 550, 551 | 2:3 | 571, 576 |
| 3:9–13 | 554 | 2:3–5 | 570 |
| 3:9–20 | 839n1 (ch. 17) | 2:4 | 572, 589, 818 |
| 3:9a | 551 | 2:5 | 572, 577 |
| 3:9b | 551 | 2:6 | 574 |
| 3:10 | 550, 551 | 2:6–9 | 574 |
| 3:11 | 551, 552 | 2:7–9 | 671 |
| 3:11–13 | 550, 552 | 2:8 | 575 |
| 3:12 | 551, 841n1 (ch. 24) | 2:9 | 574, 575, 576, 577 |
| 3:13 | 551, 552 | 2:10 | 584, 590 |
| 3:14 | 552 | 2:10–13 | 580 |
| 3:14–17 | 552 | 2:10–19 | 579 |
| 3:14–20 | 2, 548, 552, 554 | 2:11 | 580 |
| 3:15 | 549, 552, 553 | 2:12 | 580, 884n5 |
| 3:16 | 553 | 2:13 | 581 |
| 3:17 | 553 | 2:14 | 582 |
| 3:18 | 553 | 2:15 | 584, 589, 884n11 |
| 3:18–20 | 552, 553 | 2:16 | 582, 583 |
| 3:19 | 553 | 2:17 | 582, 583 |
| 3:20 | 553 | 2:18 | 584, 884n11 |
| | | 2:19 | 584, 585, 884n11 |
| *Haggai* | | 2:20 | 590, 885n2 |
| book of | 215 | 2:20–21 | 590 |
| 1:1–11 | 558 | 2:20–23 | 589 |
| 1:1–15a | 557 | 2:21 | 589, 591, 595, 596, 885n2 |
| 1:2 | 558 | | |

| | | | |
|---|---|---|---|
| 2:22 | 589, 594, 885n2 | 2:6 | 631, 632 |
| 2:23 | 589, 595, 596, 597, 885n2, 886n15 | 2:6–9 | 631 |
| | | 2:6–13 | 631 |
| | | 2:7 | 632 |
| *Zechariah* | | 2:8 | 819, 889n14 |
| book of | 215, 602, 608, 640, 702, 719, 738 | 2:10 | 633 |
| | | 2:10–12 | 633 |
| 1–8 | 694, 697 | 2:11 | 633, 694 |
| 1:1 | 602, 603 | 2:13 | 634 |
| 1:1–6 | 601, 603 | 3 | 637 |
| 1:2 | 604, 887n18 | 3:1 | 638 |
| 1:2–3 | 603 | 3:1–5 | 638 |
| 1:3 | 604, 605 | 3:1–10 | 672 |
| 1:4 | 606 | 3:2 | 639 |
| 1:4–5 | 606, 887n18 | 3:3 | 638, 639 |
| 1:4–6a | 887n18 | 3:4a | 640 |
| 1:5 | 606 | 3:4b | 640 |
| 1:6 | 606, 608, 640 | 3:5a | 640 |
| 1:6a | 608 | 3:5b | 640 |
| 1:6b | 608 | 3:6 | 641 |
| 1:7 | 612, 615 | 3:6–10 | 641, 895n17 |
| 1:7–17 | 611 | 3:7 | 641 |
| 1:8 | 612, 613, 665 | 3:8 | 643 |
| 1:8–10 | 612 | 3:9 | 643, 644 |
| 1:9 | 614 | 3:10 | 644 |
| 1:10 | 614, 665 | 4 | 647 |
| 1:11 | 614, 665, 666, 888n13 | 4:1 | 648 |
| 1:12 | 615, 616, 666, 888n13 | 4:2 | 648, 649 |
| 1:13 | 618 | 4:3 | 648, 649 |
| 1:13–17 | 618 | 4:4 | 649 |
| 1:14 | 129, 618 | 4:5 | 649, 656 |
| 1:15 | 418, 618, 619, 625 | 4:6 | 650, 651 |
| 1:16 | 619, 694, 883n9, 889n8 | 4:7 | 650, 651, 652 |
| 1:17 | 620, 671 | 4:8 | 653, 846n3 (ch. 32) |
| 1:18 | 625 | 4:8–10a | 653 |
| 1:18–21 | 625 | 4:9 | 653 |
| 1:18–2:5 | 625 | 4:10 | 571, 595, 654, 656, 759 |
| 1:18–2:13 | 623 | | |
| 1:19 | 625, 626 | 4:10b–14 | 655 |
| 1:20 | 626, 889n8 | 4:11 | 656 |
| 1:21 | 625, 626, 627 | 4:12 | 656, 657 |
| 2:1 | 628 | 4:14 | 656 |
| 2:1–4 | 628 | 5 | 663 |
| 2:2 | 628 | 5:1 | 660 |
| 2:3 | 628 | 5:1–4 | 660 |
| 2:4 | 628 | 5:1–6:8 | 659 |
| 2:5 | 629, 630, 694, 883n9 | 5:2 | 660 |

| Reference | Page(s) |
|---|---|
| 5:3 | 660 |
| 5:3a | 661 |
| 5:3b | 661 |
| 5:5–10 | 662 |
| 5:6 | 662 |
| 5:7 | 662 |
| 5:8 | 662 |
| 5:9 | 662 |
| 5:10 | 663 |
| 5:11 | 663 |
| 6 | 676, 719 |
| 6:1 | 665 |
| 6:1–8 | 665 |
| 6:2 | 665 |
| 6:3 | 665 |
| 6:5 | 665, 666 |
| 6:7 | 666 |
| 6:8 | 666, 667, 668 |
| 6:9 | 669, 670 |
| 6:9–15 | 669 |
| 6:10 | 670 |
| 6:11 | 670, 672 |
| 6:11–13 | 672 |
| 6:12 | 672, 674 |
| 6:13 | 672, 673, 674 |
| 6:14 | 674 |
| 6:15 | 676, 677 |
| 7 | 680, 683, 688 |
| 7–8 | 679 |
| 7:1 | 680 |
| 7:2 | 680, 896n1 |
| 7:3 | 679, 680, 688, 689, 896n1 |
| 7:5 | 680 |
| 7:6 | 680 |
| 7:7–14 | 886n10 |
| 7:8–12 | 896n6 |
| 7:9 | 681, 688 |
| 7:10 | 681, 682, 688 |
| 7:11 | 682 |
| 7:12 | 682 |
| 7:13 | 682 |
| 8 | 683, 688 |
| 8:1–8 | 683 |
| 8:2 | 683 |
| 8:3 | 684 |
| 8:4 | 684 |
| 8:5 | 684 |
| 8:6 | 685 |
| 8:7 | 685, 690 |
| 8:8 | 685, 694 |
| 8:9 | 685, 686 |
| 8:9–13 | 685 |
| 8:10 | 686 |
| 8:11 | 686 |
| 8:12 | 686, 760 |
| 8:13 | 687, 691, 760 |
| 8:14 | 687, 688 |
| 8:14–17 | 687 |
| 8:15 | 687 |
| 8:16 | 688, 897n14 |
| 8:17 | 688, 897n14 |
| 8:18 | 688 |
| 8:19 | 688, 689 |
| 8:19–23 | 896n1 |
| 8:20 | 691 |
| 8:20–23 | 690 |
| 8:21 | 691, 841n1 (ch. 24) |
| 8:22 | 691, 694, 841n1 (ch. 24) |
| 8:23 | 691 |
| 9 | 693, 694, 697 |
| 9–14 | 693, 694, 905n21 |
| 9:1 | 694 |
| 9:1–8 | 694, 898n10 |
| 9:2 | 694 |
| 9:3 | 694 |
| 9:4 | 695 |
| 9:5 | 695 |
| 9:7 | 695 |
| 9:7a | 695 |
| 9:7b | 695, 696 |
| 9:8 | 696 |
| 9:9 | 576, 697, 698 |
| 9:9–13 | 697 |
| 9:9–10:12 | 233 |
| 9:9ff | 898n12 |
| 9:10 | 700, 703 |
| 9:10–13 | 699 |
| 9:10c | 899n18 |
| 9:11 | 700 |
| 9:12 | 700, 827 |
| 9:13 | 701 |
| 9:14 | 701 |

| | | | |
|---|---|---|---|
| 9:14–17 | 701 | 11:11 | 723 |
| 9:15 | 701, 702 | 11:12 | 724 |
| 9:16 | 702 | 11:13 | 724 |
| 9:17 | 702 | 11:14 | 724 |
| 10 | 705, 706, 719 | 11:15 | 725 |
| 10:1 | 706 | 11:15–17 | 725 |
| 10:1–5 | 708 | 11:16 | 725 |
| 10:2 | 706, 707, 708, 900n5 | 11:17 | 727 |
| 10:3 | 709, 710, 719, 737, 900n11 | 12 | 735 |
| | | 12–13 | 729 |
| 10:3–6 | 712 | 12:1 | 730 |
| 10:3a | 900n17 | 12:1–9 | 730 |
| 10:3b–5 | 900n17 | 12:2 | 730, 731, 732, 902n3 |
| 10:4 | 711 | 12:3 | 731 |
| 10:5 | 711 | 12:5 | 732 |
| 10:6 | 28, 712 | 12:6 | 731 |
| 10:6–10 | 712 | 12:8 | 732 |
| 10:6–12 | 712, 900n17 | 12:9 | 732 |
| 10:6a | 712, 900n15 | 12:10 | 733, 734, 735, 903n12 |
| 10:6b | 712 | 12:10–14 | 733 |
| 10:7 | 28 | 12:11 | 734 |
| 10:8 | 712 | 12:12 | 734 |
| 10:9 | 713 | 13 | 735, 737 |
| 10:10 | 713, 714 | 13:1 | 735 |
| 10:11 | 713 | 13:1–6 | 735 |
| 10:12 | 713, 714 | 13:2 | 736 |
| 10:12–13 | 901n6 | 13:2b | 736 |
| 10:14 | 712 | 13:3 | 736 |
| 10:15 | 712 | 13:4 | 736 |
| 11 | 404, 717, 719 | 13:5 | 736 |
| 11:1 | 718 | 13:6 | 736 |
| 11:1–6 | 719 | 13:7 | 737, 903n12 |
| 11:2 | 718 | 13:7–9 | 404, 737, 743, 903n12 |
| 11:4 | 719, 720 | 13:8 | 738 |
| 11:4–17 | 737, 900n4 | 13:9 | 738, 903n17 |
| 11:5 | 720, 721 | 13:9b | 738 |
| 11:6a | 721 | 13:9c | 739 |
| 11:6b | 721 | 14 | 741, 742, 904n4 |
| 11:7 | 722 | 14:1 | 742, 751 |
| 11:7–14 | 722 | 14:1–2 | 742 |
| 11:7–15 | 901n12 | 14:1–5 | 904n4 |
| 11:8a | 722 | 14:2 | 743, 744, 751 |
| 11:8b | 722 | 14:3 | 745, 746 |
| 11:9 | 900n4 | 14:3–5 | 745 |
| 11:9a | 723 | 14:4 | 745 |
| 11:9b | 723 | 14:5 | 745 |
| 11:10 | 723 | 14:6 | 747, 748 |

Scripture Index  951

| | | | |
|---|---|---|---|
| 14:6–11 | 746, 904n4 | 1:8b | 771 |
| 14:7 | 747, 748 | 1:9 | 771 |
| 14:8 | 748 | 1:10 | 772, 907n6 |
| 14:9 | 749, 754 | 1:11 | 779, 909n22 |
| 14:11 | 748 | 1:12 | 783 |
| 14:12 | 750 | 1:14 | 907n1 |
| 14:12–15 | 904n4 | 1:14–2:3 | 773 |
| 14:12–19 | 750, 894n18 | 1:14a | 773 |
| 14:13 | 750 | 2 | 787 |
| 14:14 | 751 | 2:1 | 774 |
| 14:14a | 750 | 2:1–9 | 34, 909n9 |
| 14:15 | 751 | 2:2 | 774 |
| 14:16 | 751, 905n21 | 2:3 | 775 |
| 14:16–21 | 904n4 | 2:4 | 776, 777, 908n17 |
| 14:17 | 751 | 2:4–6 | 776 |
| 14:18 | 751 | 2:5 | 776, 777, 778 |
| 14:19 | 751 | 2:6 | 777, 778, 908n19 |
| 14:20 | 752, 753 | 2:7 | 841n1 (ch. 24), 908n19 |
| 14:21 | 752 | | |
| 14:21a | 753 | 2:8 | 773, 778 |
| 14:21b | 753 | 2:9 | 773 |
| | | 2:10 | 782, 783 |
| *Malachi* | | 2:10–16 | 781, 909n9, 910n22, 911n4 |
| book of | 757, 774, 789, 817, 915n18, 916n20 | 2:11 | 784, 785, 788 |
| 1:1–5 | 757 | 2:11b | 783–84 |
| 1:2 | 67, 757, 758, 761, 772 | 2:12 | 784, 786, 791, 800–01 |
| 1:2–5 | 196, 234, 243, 254, 913n12 | 2:13 | 787 |
| | | 2:13–14 | 787 |
| 1:2b | 761, 764 | 2:14 | 788, 800–01 |
| 1:2b–3a | 760 | 2:14a | 787 |
| 1:3 | 67, 761, 764 | 2:14b | 788 |
| 1:3a | 761 | 2:15 | 789, 790 |
| 1:3b–5 | 763 | 2:16 | 788, 789 |
| 1:4 | 766 | 2:17 | 794, 800, 913n12, 914n4 |
| 1:4a | 764 | | |
| 1:4b | 764, 765 | 2:17–3:5 | 793 |
| 1:5 | 765, 766, 767 | 3 | 800 |
| 1:6 | 769, 826 | 3:1 | 796, 841n1 (ch. 24), 911n10 |
| 1:6–13 | 770 | | |
| 1:6–14 | 34, 911n4 | 3:2 | 801, 802 |
| 1:6–2:9 | 769 | 3:2a | 797, 798 |
| 1:6a | 770 | 3:2b | 798 |
| 1:6b | 771 | 3:2b–4 | 798 |
| 1:7 | 771 | 3:3 | 799 |
| 1:7a | 771 | 3:4 | 799, 810 |
| 1:8a | 771 | 3:5 | 800 |

| | | | |
|---|---|---|---|
| 3:6 | 298, 299, 396, 605, 807, 808, 809, 810, 911n1 (ch. 79) | 3:13–17 | 138 |
| | | 3:15 | 819 |
| | | 3:16 | 819 |
| 3:6–12 | 805 | 3:16b | 821 |
| 3:6a | 807 | 3:17 | 564 |
| 3:7 | 604, 809, 810, 811 | 4:1 | 138 |
| 3:7–9 | 810 | 4:1–4 | 227 |
| 3:7–12 | 913n22 | 4:6 | 806 |
| 3:7a | 911n1 (ch. 79) | 4:7 | 806 |
| 3:8a | 811 | 4:17 | 610 |
| 3:8b | 811 | 5:1ff | 345 |
| 3:8c | 811 | 5:3 | 541 |
| 3:9 | 774, 810 | 5:5 | 541, 544, 546 |
| 3:9a | 811 | 5:6 | 737 |
| 3:10 | 807, 813, 814 | 5:9 | 220 |
| 3:10–12 | 813 | 5:11 | 89, 513 |
| 3:11 | 774, 813, 814, 911n4 | 5:12 | 89, 513 |
| | | 5:13–20 | 178 |
| 3:12 | 814, 913n23 | 5:21–26 | 178 |
| 3:13 | 820, 914n7 | 5:31 | 792 |
| 3:13–15 | 914n7 | 5:32 | 792 |
| 3:13–17 | 818 | 5:43–48 | 146, 161 |
| 3:13–4:6 | 817 | 5:45 | 822 |
| 3:13a | 818 | 6:1–4 | 186 |
| 3:13b | 818 | 6:2 | 32 |
| 3:14 | 818, 819 | 6:10 | 116, 495, 615, 666, 668, 796, 827 |
| 3:15 | 823, 915n7 | | |
| 3:16 | 820, 823, 914n7 | 6:12 | 247 |
| 3:17 | 821, 827, 915n11 | 6:19–21 | 336 |
| 3:18 | 822 | 6:19–34 | 97 |
| 3:18–4:3 | 822 | 6:20 | 431 |
| 4:1 | 822 | 6:21 | 389 |
| 4:2a | 823 | 6:24 | 155, 203, 534 |
| 4:2b | 823 | 6:25–33 | 106 |
| 4:4 | 824 | 6:25–34 | 529, 546 |
| 4:4–6 | 824, 915n18 | 6:31–33 | 561 |
| 4:5 | 825, 826 | 6:33 | 39 |
| 4:6 | 825, 827 | 6:34 | 106 |
| | | 7:11 | 770 |
| *Matthew* | | 7:12 | 163 |
| 1:1–17 | 15, 29, 233 | 7:24–27 | 497 |
| 1:12 | 597 | 9:13 | 50 |
| 2:6 | 366 | 9:35–38 | 84 |
| 2:15 | 49, 80 | 10:29 | 273 |
| 2:16 | 366 | 11:1–6 | 15 |
| 2:16–18 | 726 | 11:9 | 826 |
| 3:7 | 418 | 11:10 | 826 |

Scripture Index   953

| | | | |
|---|---|---|---|
| 11:25 | 375 | 27:50–52 | 423 |
| 11:25–30 | 178, 375 | 28:16–20 | 136, 196 |
| 11:28 | 714 | 28:20 | 196, 517, 652 |
| 11:29 | 714 | | |
| 12:7 | 50 | *Mark* | |
| 12:28 | 255 | 1 | 586 |
| 12:38–41 | 260 | 1:4 | 826 |
| 12:39 | 296 | 1:4–11 | 311 |
| 12:39–41 | 267 | 1:9 | 617 |
| 12:40 | 289, 846n3 (ch. 32) | 1:9–11 | 617 |
| 12:41 | 276, 296 | 1:15 | 255 |
| 13:30 | 743, 822 | 1:40 | 586 |
| 15:21–28 | 495 | 1:41 | 586, 587 |
| 16:16–18 | 121 | 1:43–45 | 587 |
| 16:18 | 652, 668 | 2:9 | 407 |
| 16:24 | 690 | 2:17 | 263, 306 |
| 16:25 | 690 | 4:35–41 | 272 |
| 17:1–8 | 345 | 4:41 | 272 |
| 18:21–35 | 308 | 6:17–20 | 726 |
| 18:34 | 308 | 6:21–29 | 726 |
| 19:8 | 792 | 6:34 | 479, 727 |
| 19:9 | 792 | 6:39 | 728 |
| 19:16–30 | 97 | 6:40 | 728 |
| 20:1–16 | 123, 500 | 6:41–44 | 728 |
| 21:1–9 | 699 | 7:24–29 | 280 |
| 21:9 | 699 | 8:17–21 | 97 |
| 21:31 | 263, 306 | 10:9 | 792 |
| 21:32 | 306 | 10:17 | 679 |
| 22:21 | 773 | 10:17–22 | 84 |
| 23:13–36 | 351 | 10:18 | 679 |
| 24:1 | 212 | 10:27 | 650 |
| 24:2 | 212 | 10:35 | 469 |
| 24:29–31 | 667 | 10:37 | 469 |
| 25:23 | 596 | 10:38 | 286, 469, 617, 679 |
| 25:31–46 | 145, 178, 246 | 11:1–10 | 699 |
| 25:32 | 822 | 11:9 | 576 |
| 26:15 | 724 | 11:10 | 576 |
| 26:30 | 738 | 11:11 | 576 |
| 26:31 | 738 | 12:28–32 | 7, 23, 123, 145 |
| 26:32 | 738 | 12:28–34 | 89 |
| 26:33 | 738 | 15:34 | 352 |
| 26:52 | 74 | 15:38 | 657 |
| 26:69–75 | 738 | | |
| 27:5 | 724 | *Luke* | |
| 27:43 | 407 | 1:15 | 138 |
| 27:45 | 423 | 1:41 | 138 |
| 27:46 | 284, 566, 821 | 1:67 | 138 |

| | | | |
|---|---|---|---|
| 2:25 | 620 | 1:14 | 127, 563, 576, 586, 610, 633, 655 |
| 2:28–32 | 620 | | |
| 3:23–28 | 29, 233 | 2:13–17 | 418 |
| 3:27 | 597 | 2:17 | 597, 778 |
| 4:17–21 | 553 | 2:18–21 | 896n19 |
| 4:18 | 541 | 2:18–22 | 627 |
| 4:27 | 293 | 2:19 | 563, 607, 633 |
| 4:43 | 255 | 2:19–21 | 586 |
| 6:20 | 255, 541 | 2:21 | 597 |
| 6:24–26 | 210 | 3:9 | 679 |
| 6:31 | 163 | 3:10 | 679 |
| 6:46–49 | 255 | 3:14–17 | 44, 75 |
| 7:21 | 553 | 3:16 | 84 |
| 7:22 | 553 | 3:16–21 | 107 |
| 7:25 | 617 | 3:18 | 876n8 (ch. 49) |
| 7:36–50 | 277 | 3:30 | 826 |
| 9:51 | 267, 480 | 4:1–25 | 12 |
| 10:25–37 | 245 | 4:1–30 | 280 |
| 10:33 | 246 | 4:19–26 | 95 |
| 10:36 | 246 | 5:24 | 289 |
| 10:37 | 246 | 6:39 | 368 |
| 12:48 | 172, 178 | 6:68 | 519 |
| 13:34 | 564 | 6:69 | 519 |
| 15 | 297 | 8:21 | 189, 841n13 |
| 15:11–24 | 605 | 8:22 | 841n13 |
| 15:11–32 | 83, 304 | 9 | 356 |
| 15:17 | 562 | 9:35 | 356 |
| 15:20–24 | 490 | 10:1 | 727 |
| 15:25–32 | 310 | 10:8–11 | 357 |
| 16:31 | 137, 806 | 10:11 | 341, 479, 714 |
| 17:11–19 | 586 | 10:17 | 714 |
| 18:27 | 580, 685 | 10:27 | 727 |
| 19:29–38 | 699 | 10:28 | 13, 727 |
| 19:41–44 | 267, 329 | 10:29 | 13 |
| 22:18 | 255 | 11:25 | 431 |
| 22:20 | 24, 87, 469, 664, 700 | 11:26 | 431 |
| 22:31 | 617 | 12:24 | 362 |
| 22:32 | 617 | 12:25 | 362 |
| 22:42 | 286, 469 | 12:31 | 480 |
| 23:30 | 835n9 | 14:6 | 195, 509, 531, 586 |
| 23:34 | 267, 311, 617 | 14:12–31 | 138 |
| 23:41–43 | 122 | 14:15 | 531, 546 |
| 24:25–27 | 4 | 14:15–17 | 497 |
| 24:26 | 690 | 14:17 | 138 |
| | | 14:21 | 546 |
| *John* | | 14:27 | 577 |
| 1:1–18 | 44, 136 | 15:13 | 84 |
| 1:11 | 280 | | |

Scripture Index   955

| | | | |
|---|---|---|---|
| 16:33 | 8, 75, 144, 368, 517 | 13:22–36 | 235 |
| 16:33a | 485 | 15:1–12 | 235 |
| 16:33b | 485 | 15:1–21 | 157, 239 |
| 17:20–23 | 84 | 15:1–35 | 136, 243 |
| 17:26 | 84 | 15:11 | 235 |
| 18:36 | 255, 650 | 15:12–19 | 239 |
| 19:30 | 423 | 15:15–19 | 255 |
| 19:33 | 735 | 15:16 | 235 |
| 19:34 | 735 | 15:17 | 235 |
| 21:15–19 | 13 | 15:19–21 | 235 |
| | | 16:6–40 | 136 |
| *Acts* | | 16:25 | 633 |
| book of | 136, 139, 140 | 17:16–34 | 136 |
| 1:6 | 591, 680 | 18:24–19:40 | 179 |
| 1:6–11 | 141 | 20:17–38 | 179 |
| 1:8 | 235 | | |
| 1:11 | 595, 676, 702 | *Romans* | |
| 1:15 | 138 | 1:1–6 | 233 |
| 2 | 136, 139 | 1:3 | 15, 29 |
| 2:1–21 | 127 | 1:4 | 15, 29 |
| 2:14–36 | 140 | 1:16 | 139, 383, 691, 815 |
| 2:17 | 139 | 1:18–32 | 136, 195 |
| 2:22–32 | 141 | 2:28 | 743 |
| 2:23 | 280, 619 | 2:29 | 743 |
| 2:25–36 | 235 | 3:4 | 565 |
| 2:33 | 141 | 3:10 | 159 |
| 2:36 | 141 | 3:10–18 | 277 |
| 2:38 | 141 | 3:19 | 137 |
| 2:39 | 280 | 3:23 | 159, 169 |
| 2:40 | 141 | 5:1–11 | 184 |
| 2:42–47 | 141 | 5:8 | 267 |
| 4:12 | 509 | 5:10 | 311 |
| 4:25–27 | 235 | 6:15–23 | 502 |
| 5:17–42 | 513 | 6:16 | 61 |
| 5:41 | 235, 513 | 6:23 | 372, 447 |
| 5:42 | 235 | 8:9 | 139 |
| 8 | 311 | 8:20 | 575 |
| 8:3 | 312 | 8:21 | 575 |
| 8:12 | 235 | 8:26 | 617 |
| 8:26–40 | 545 | 8:28 | 189, 195, 763, 765, 802 |
| 9:1–18 | 312 | | |
| 9:1–19 | 123 | 8:29 | 195 |
| 9:28 | 235 | 8:31 | 449 |
| 10 | 136, 139 | 8:32 | 449, 816, 827 |
| 10:42 | 122, 235 | 8:37 | 449 |
| 10:43 | 122, 235 | 8:38 | 763 |
| 11:19–26 | 235 | 8:39 | 763 |

| | | | |
|---|---|---|---|
| 9–11 | 145 | 15:56 | 450 |
| 9:6 | 340, 743 | 15:57 | 450 |
| 9:7 | 743 | 16:2 | 816 |
| 9:11–13 | 762 | | |
| 9:14–16 | 308 | *2 Corinthians* | |
| 9:26 | 14 | book of | 178 |
| 10:14–17 | 434 | 2:14–16 | 370 |
| 10:15 | 873n14 | 4:16–18 | 629 |
| 11:30–32 | 895n19 | 5:10 | 11, 160, 189 |
| 11:33 | 312 | 5:16–21 | 550 |
| 11:36 | 312 | 5:17 | 603, 729 |
| 12:1 | 9, 184, 386, 500, 773, 815 | 5:17–21 | 206 |
| | | 5:21 | 386, 664, 766 |
| 12:2 | 9, 184 | 6:14 | 787 |
| 12:3–8 | 500 | 8:1 | 816 |
| 12:19 | 418 | 8:2 | 816 |
| 14:11 | 160 | 8:9 | 815 |
| 14:12 | 160, 189 | 9:7 | 816 |
| 16:20 | 472 | 10:3 | 711 |
| | | 10:5 | 711 |
| *1 Corinthians* | | 11:7–15 | 36 |
| book of | 178 | 12:10 | 733 |
| 1:18–31 | 66 | 13:14 | 136 |
| 1:20–31 | 300 | | |
| 1:27–29 | 654 | *Galatians* | |
| 1:31 | 566 | book of | 178 |
| 2:9 | 824 | 2:20 | 106, 178, 195 |
| 3:6 | 653 | 3:2 | 206 |
| 3:7 | 653 | 3:13 | 353 |
| 3:16 | 577 | 3:16 | 910n23 |
| 4:5 | 457 | 3:29 | 91 |
| 6:19 | 620–21 | 4:4 | 267 |
| 7:15 | 792 | 5:16–26 | 196 |
| 7:39 | 787 | 5:22–26 | 106 |
| 10:1–6 | 153 | 6:7 | 53 |
| 10:1–13 | 76, 489 | 6:14 | 566 |
| 10:16 | 470 | | |
| 12 | 139, 180 | *Ephesians* | |
| 12:1–11 | 196, 500 | 1:3 | 502, 621, 816 |
| 15 | 99 | 1:3–14 | 22, 516 |
| 15:4 | 49 | 1:4 | 502, 767 |
| 15:20 | 750 | 1:6 | 343 |
| 15:50–58 | 99 | 1:13 | 139 |
| 15:54 | 450 | 1:13–14 | 139 |
| 15:54–56 | 289 | 1:14 | 139 |
| 15:55 | 450, 837n12 | 2:1 | 395, 729 |
| | | 2:1–3 | 94 |

| | | | |
|---|---|---|---|
| 2:1–10 | 48, 106, 206, 502, 834n17 | 4:13 | 388 |
| | | 5:17 | 115 |
| 2:5 | 49 | | |
| 2:6 | 49 | *2 Thessalonians* | |
| 2:8–10 | 195 | 1:3 | 145 |
| 2:9 | 566, 762 | 1:4 | 145 |
| 2:10 | 500 | 1:5–10 | 544 |
| 2:11–22 | 262 | 1:5–12 | 145 |
| 2:12 | 896n19 | 3:6–12 | 544 |
| 2:13 | 896n19 | | |
| 2:14 | 434 | *1 Timothy* | |
| 3:20 | 128 | 1:12–15 | 312 |
| 4:26 | 307, 448 | 2:2 | 544 |
| 5:22–33 | 23 | 5:17 | 36 |
| 5:25 | 782 | 5:24 | 116 |
| 5:25–33 | 787, 788 | 6:5 | 173 |
| 5:32 | 792 | 6:10 | 58, 173, 203 |
| 6:12 | 480, 627 | | |
| | | *2 Timothy* | |
| *Philippians* | | 1:5 | 495 |
| 1:6 | 762 | 2:13 | 762, 792 |
| 2:5–11 | 541 | 3:2–4 | 203 |
| 2:6–8 | 815 | 3:14–17 | 137 |
| 2:9–11 | 537, 749 | 3:16 | 488 |
| 2:10 | 459, 766 | 3:17 | 488 |
| 2:11 | 459, 766 | 4:2 | 2 |
| 2:12b | 566 | | |
| 2:13 | 566 | *Hebrews* | |
| 3:4b–9 | 640 | book of | 178 |
| 3:13 | 195 | 1:1 | 137, 497 |
| 3:14 | 195 | 1:2 | 137, 497 |
| 3:19 | 349 | 2:1–4 | 137 |
| 4:4–7 | 75 | 2:3 | 137 |
| 4:7 | 621 | 2:12 | 889n14 |
| 4:10–13 | 510 | 3:16–4:2 | 379 |
| 4:19 | 510 | 4:1–13 | 489 |
| 4:20 | 510 | 4:12 | 610 |
| | | 4:14 | 858n18 |
| *Colossians* | | 4:15 | 311 |
| 1:15–20 | 136 | 4:16 | 498 |
| 2:13 | 481 | 6:19 | 396 |
| 2:14 | 459, 481 | 7:9 | 799 |
| 2:15 | 368, 459, 598, 627 | 7:10 | 799 |
| 3:5 | 58 | 8:8–12 | 23 |
| | | 9:11 | 778 |
| *1 Thessalonians* | | 9:12 | 778 |
| 4:11 | 544 | 9:14 | 677 |
| 4:12 | 544 | | |

| | | | |
|---|---|---|---|
| 9:27 | 801 | 2:9 | 23, 32, 34, 40, 106, 132, 169, 177, 234, 498, 516 |
| 10:11–14 | 779 | | |
| 10:19–22 | 657 | | |
| 10:31 | 442 | 2:10 | 23, 32, 34, 40, 106, 132, 177, 234, 498 |
| 11 | 136, 233 | | |
| 11:1–31 | 502 | 3:7 | 789 |
| 11:6 | 502 | 4:12–15 | 503 |
| 11:10 | 329, 357, 592, 621, 747 | 5:6 | 209, 428 |
| | | 5:7 | 209 |
| 11:32–40 | 502 | | |
| 12:1 | 541 | *2 Peter* | |
| 12:2 | 447 | 1:16 | 8 |
| 12:3–11 | 56, 115, 121, 184, 189 | 1:16–18 | 8 |
| | | 1:16–21 | 112, 137 |
| 12:3–17 | 56, 81, 82 | 1:19 | 8, 9 |
| 12:6 | 274 | 1:19–21 | 153, 488 |
| 12:11 | 17 | 1:21 | 9 |
| 12:22–24 | 357 | 2:1–3 | 145 |
| 12:25–29 | 598 | 3:1–10 | 66 |
| 12:28 | 802–03 | 3:1–13 | 500 |
| 12:29 | 802–03 | 3:7 | 474 |
| 13:5 | 203, 567 | 3:9 | 490, 549, 721 |
| 13:8 | 396, 420, 809 | 3:11–13 | 66 |
| 13:20 | 715 | 3:13 | 475 |
| 13:21 | 715 | | |
| | | *1 John* | |
| *James* | | 1 | 123 |
| book of | 807 | 1:5–10 | 47 |
| 1:2–4 | 184, 513 | 1:9 | 68, 103, 178, 255 |
| 1:13–15 | 744 | 1:10 | 68, 103, 178, 255 |
| 1:16 | 209 | 2:16 | 242 |
| 1:17 | 69, 113, 209, 708, 807 | 4:7 | 7, 22, 104 |
| 1:27 | 683 | 4:8 | 7, 22, 104 |
| 2:1–7 | 186 | 4:10 | 762 |
| 2:14–26 | 502 | | |
| 2:26 | 206 | *Revelation* | |
| 4:6 | 242 | book of | 330, 403, 545, 667, 747 |
| *1 Peter* | | 1:7 | 735 |
| 1:6 | 503 | 2–3 | 121, 179, 184 |
| 1:10–12 | 137 | 2:1–7 | 19, 179 |
| 1:11 | 3 | 2:4 | 179, 206 |
| 2:4 | 597, 620 | 2:5 | 179, 206 |
| 2:5 | 577, 597, 677 | 2:17 | 330 |
| 2:6–8 | 329 | 5:9 | 145 |
| 2:7 | 370 | 5:10 | 145 |
| 2:8 | 370 | 6:10 | 489 |

| | | | |
|---|---|---|---|
| 6:16 | 835n9 | 20 | 252, 511 |
| 7:9 | 145 | 21:1 | 23, 621, 749 |
| 7:9–12 | 621 | 21:1–4 | 23 |
| 7:10 | 145 | 21:1–7 | 114, 254, 490, 508, 532, 553 |
| 11:15 | 697 | | |
| 12:11 | 145 | 21:1–8 | 255, 485 |
| 14:10 | 852n14 | 21:2 | 23, 621, 749, 862n30 |
| 16:19 | 878n6 (ch. 52) | 21:4 | 373, 436, 749 |
| 19:11 | 703 | 21:11 | 621 |
| 19:11–16 | 122, 145, 668 | 21:23–25 | 747, 749 |
| 19:16 | 508, 538 | 22:20 | 373 |

# General Index

Aaron, 328, 752, 891n12
Abihu, 328
Abraham, 14, 26, 38, 78, 95, 193, 230, 280, 330, 601, 690, 700, 732, 735; and the blessings of the nations, 132; God's covenant with, 87; God's promise to, 319, 370
Abram, 262; renaming of, 330, 601
Achtemeier, Elizabeth, 882n11, 899n20, 914n6
Ackroyd, Peter R., 889–80n14
Adam, 457–58, 743, 895–96n19
Adullam, 327
Ahab, 10, 334, 391, 537
Ahasuerus, 821
Ahaz, 9, 318, 365–66, 384, 864n4
Alabama, 62
Amalekites, 465
Amaziah, 156, 218–20, 226
"Amazing Grace" (Newton), 167
America/Americans, 58, 119, 156, 161–62, 172, 209, 210, 234, 534, 800; as a Christian nation, 61–62; culture of, 203; luxurious churches in, 71; sex-saturated society of, 58–59
Ammon, 160, 165–66, 542, 543, 544
Amon, 525
Amorites, 466
Amos (book/prophecies of), 152–53, 175, 177–78, 843n1, 843n7, 901n7; and Amaziah, 218–20; announcement of a famine descending on Israel, 226–28; attack of on Israel's vain hope, 200–1; on darkness descending on Israel, 225–26; on death coming to Israel, 223–24; denunciation of sin and announcing of the day of the Lord, 152; funeral song of (*qinah*), 192; love of for the Israelites, 215–16; pronouncement of woe on Samaria, 208–9; three major sections of, 229; on the unleashing of war because of Israel's non-repentance, 219–20; visions of, 215–18, 223–24
Amos (person), 61, 89, 152, 153, 240; as a farmer, 206; as a shepherd, 154
Andersen, Francis, 161, 491, 506, 862n7, 863–64n2, 867n1, 867–68n13
animals/birds, 33, 40, 50, 59, 113, 295–96, 889n2; bulls, 837n3; calves, 383, 823; eagles, 328; lions (including God as a lion), 151, 152, 213, 865n22; oxen, 212; rams, 383; snakes, 862n11; and the vulture circling over Israel, 56–57
Apollos, 179, 653
Apostle's Creed, 594
Aram/Arameans/Aramean kingdom, 90, 160, 161
Ashdod, 163, 696
Asherah, 525, 526
Asherim, the, 525
Ashkelon, 163, 696
Assurbanipal, 428, 429, 430, 453, 526, 870n4, 872n9, 876n1; library of, 444
Ashur-Dan II, 847n11
Assyria/Assyrians/Assyrian Empire, 13, 52, 61, 70, 75, 83, 101, 163, 164, 185, 230, 234, 240, 264, 323, 365, 366–67, 368, 413, 414, 422, 423–24, 429–32, 435, 440, 445, 463, 466, 471, 477–78, 523, 542, 545–46, 696, 701, 712, 713, 864n7, 873n19, 891n1; conquest of Israel by, 53, 71–72, 75, 93; demise/ruin of, 414–15, 417–18, 876n8; might of, 81; rise of the Neo-Assyrian Empire, 847n11; support of Hoshea by, 72
astral deities (of Egypt or Syria), 205

Auden, W. H., 317
Azal, 745

Baal/Baal worship, 64, 155, 525, 526, 531, 533, 707, 817; prostitutes, 65; worship of by Israelites, 10, 67
Baalism, 64
Babel, 432
Babylon/Babylonians, 13, 164, 232, 234, 240, 435, 440, 447, 476, 486, 506, 523, 557, 606, 631–33, 671, 682, 701, 712, 743, 798, 864n7, 873n19, 894n12; conquest of Judah by, 112; flood narratives, 272
Baldwin, Joyce G., 888n12
Barnabas, 235, 541
Bashan, 184, 871n15
Bavinck, Herman, 854n21
Beersheba, 193
Beeson, John Wesley, 186
Beeson, Ralph Waldo, 186
Belial, 429
Benjamin, tribe of, 185, 833n17
Beth-arbel, 75
Beth-aven, 37
Bethel, 38, 72, 185–86, 193, 680; idol worship at, 87
Beth ezel ("House of Withdrawal"), 325, 859n25
Beth-le-aphrah ("House of Dust"), 325
Bethlehem (Bethlehem Ephrathah), 364–65, 726, 863–64n2
Bezalel, 137
Bible, the, 112, 120, 122, 132, 142, 153, 188, 233, 244, 309, 348–49, 495, 545; connection of buildings to bodies in, 862n30; depiction of God's people as sheep in, 340–41; and the expression "latter days," 353; God's renaming of persons throughout, 329–30, 859n33; importance of mountains in, 345–47; names throughout reveal identities, 327. See also Hebrew language, debates concerning the translations of in the Bible
Boaz, 98, 785
Boda, Mark J., 885n10, 890–91n9, 901n8, 902n1

Boice, James M., 112
Browning, Elizabeth Barrett, 760
Bruce, F. F., 501, 519

Calneh, 208
Calvin, John, 207–8, 284, 298, 364, 486, 615, 850n22, 857–58n10, 860n11, 864n10
Canaan/Canaanites, 70, 79, 88, 89, 193, 372, 423, 466, 516, 750, 753, 784, 872n11
*Canterbury Tales* (Chaucer), 31–32
Caphtor, 844n1
Carmel, 151
Cathy, Truett, 225–26
Chaldeans, 486
Chaucer, Geoffrey, 31–32
Chesterton, G. K., 169
Christensen, Duane L., 446, 875n3
Christianity, 172, 182, 209, 233, 246, 573
Christians, 43, 58, 115, 117, 132, 136, 139, 167, 189, 200, 201, 202–3, 226, 263, 300, 367, 388, 420, 423, 424, 493, 519, 537–38, 594, 603, 645, 653, 655, 725, 793–94, 816, 865n16; difficulty in worshiping God, 433; liberal, 209; life of, 480–81; warning to, 294–95
*Christmas Carol, A* (Dickens), 192
Christophany, 888n18
Church, the (Christ's Church on earth), 19, 59, 186, 263, 349, 368, 396–97, 421, 424, 574, 621, 653, 711, 746, 792, 825; history of, 297; Paul's initial hatred of, 311–12; trials of, 744–45
comminties/community, 204, 793, 867n11, 869n9; agricultural communities, 63
Cook, Gregory, 873n17
Corinthians: terrible treatment of Paul by, 14
covenant, blood of, 899n19
covenant-breaking, 62, 124, 163–64
covenant curses, 353, 686
covenant with Levi, 908n17
covenant of peace, 777
covenant sanctions, 390–91

General Index   963

covenant of works, 891n12
Cush/Cushites, 463, 544–45
cynicism, 793
Cyrus the Great, 557

Dali, Salvador, 611
Damascus, 159, 160–62, 170, 173, 206
Darius, 584, 589–90, 602, 615
David, 26, 28, 78, 167, 171, 245, 342, 596, 601, 648, 653, 696, 698, 702, 710, 745, 854n13; booth of, 232–33; conquering of Edom by, 234; and the Davidic kingdom, 185; Davidic line of, 157, 365, 557; and the Davidic promise, 364; descendants of, 157; faith of, 448; God's promises to, 14–15; household of, 236, 732; lament over the death of Saul and Jonathan, 327
Day of Atonement, 644
"day of the Lord," 113–15, 152, 201, 536
death, 70; ransom from, 97–99
Deborah, 171
Delilah, 42
Dempster, Stephen, 319, 343, 860n7; on the expansion desolation from Zion to Jerusalem, 863n17
dew/rain, 369
Dickens, Charles, 192
Dinah, 51
discipline, 24, 53; forms of, 17–18; of God, 51, 81–82, 183–84, 274; for renewal, 20–21
divorce, 781–82, 788–89, 791–92
Duguid, Iain, 889–90n14, 893–94n8, 895n15, 899n20, 900n13, 903n12, 905n26, 911–12n1

Edom/Edomites, 147, 160, 164–65, 166, 167, 234, 240, 246, 515, 532, 763, 907n19; God's justice concerning, 251–54; Obadiah's announcement of God's decimation of its resources, 242–44; Obadiah's announcement of God's decree of destruction against, 240–42; remnant of, 233–36; slave-trading of, 239

Egypt, 32, 52, 60, 61, 78, 90, 147, 205, 272, 285, 326, 404, 405, 463, 486, 515, 523, 542, 546, 696, 713; the holy family's time in, 80; plagues of, 415
Ekron, 696
Elamites, 888n12
election, doctrine of, 762–63
Elijah, 10, 79, 89, 160, 293, 391, 393, 525, 537, 817–18, 825
Elisha, 10, 37, 79, 89, 160, 293, 614
Ephesus/Ephesians, 179, 206
Ephraim (as a name used for Israel), 51–52, 67, 83, 88, 701; and money, 88–89
Erickson, Amy, 299
Ervin, Sam, 53
Esau, 87, 90, 761, 764, 886n3
Estelle, Bryan, 277, 312, 849n9, 850n22
Esther, 821
ethics, Christian, 418
Eve, 250, 457–58
Ezekiel, 478–79, 603, 607, 669, 707, 710, 763, 885n10
Ezra (book of), 782
Ezra (person), 29

faith/faithfulness, 62, 95, 100, 105–6, 127, 142, 276, 286, 329, 372, 501, 517, 567, 596, 816, 839n1, 915n8; Biblical faith, 245; confession of, 274–75. See also God, faithfulness of
false prophets, 171, 210, 337, 339, 349–51, 399, 464, 606, 707, 736–37, 861n23, 862n11, 863n13
Faulkner, William, 837n6
Feast of Booths (or Tabernacles), 64, 65, 89, 341, 532–33, 534, 569–70, 752
fertility/fertility gods/fertility worship, 65, 67–68
Flavel, John, 690
forgiveness, 124, 126, 180, 216, 260, 264, 280, 288, 295, 296, 299, 306, 399, 401, 402, 406–7, 417, 469, 498, 551, 552, 609, 642–43, 665, 708, 713, 782, 826. See also God forgiveness of
Freedman, David Noel, 161, 862n7, 863–64n2, 867n1, 867–68n13

## General Index

Galatians, Paul's message to, 206
Garrett, Duane, 18, 208
Gaza, 159–60, 162–63, 167, 170, 173, 696
Gentiles/Gentile nations, 235, 259, 277–80, 294, 303, 319–20, 696, 743, 744, 895n16, 905n26; Gentile sinners, 260
Gibson, Jonathan, 906n10, 906n16, 910n14
Gideon, 12, 137
Gignilliat, Mark S., 865n22, 866n11
Gilead, 50, 161, 165
Gilgal, 37, 38, 89–90, 185–86, 193
"Glorious Things of Thee Are Spoken" (Newton), 397
God/Yahweh, 363–64, 376, 388, 392, 427–28, 433–34, 477, 587, 605–6, 752, 772–73, 852n16, 869n9, 912n7, 914n26; anger of, 244, 604, 806–7, 869n15, 872n12, 873nn16–17, 890n15, 900n17, 905n2; character of, 7, 82, 84, 124, 126, 184, 203–4, 216, 305, 486–87, 502–3, 795–96, 807–9; commands of to Israel (*see also* Ten Commandments), 338; commitment to God, 41–43; commitment of God to Israel, 104–5; compassion of, 131, 291, 300, 305, 308–13, 406, 723; covenant jealousy of, 131; creativity of, 77; as Creator God, 194, 585, 655; decision of concerning rebellious nations, 145–46; failure to seek God, 194–95; faithfulness of, 271, 279, 680, 761, 784; faithful prophets of, 180–81; forgiveness of, 124, 126, 195, 213, 288, 292, 293–94, 377, 449, 680, 786, 810; and the fruits of walking with God, 201–5; glory of, 131, 517, 620, 766; goodness of, 218, 456, 744; grace of, 66, 69, 101, 131, 141, 172, 179, 180, 261, 263, 270, 271, 276, 277, 288, 297, 306, 310, 343, 376, 385, 585, 607, 680, 695, 721, 723, 724, 744, 762, 786; grace of before Pentecost, 136–38; greatness of, 267, 297, 300, 310, 363, 469, 713, 766,
907n18; healing of, 104; holiness of, 510, 609, 776, 777, 778; immutability of, 854n21; indictment of Israel's people, 36–38; indictment of Israel's priests, 34–36; jealousy of, 416, 537; judgment of, 140–41, 143–45, 155–56, 175–76, 188, 204, 239, 294, 300, 311, 319–21, 343, 346, 368–69, 382, 395, 418, 443–45, 487, 594, 605, 695, 696, 735, 738, 827, 857n9, 915n12; justice of, 120–21, 131, 199, 251–54, 311, 346, 390, 442, 456, 796–97, 913n12; kingdom of, 249–50, 255, 420, 654, 665, 667, 711, 736; lawsuit of against Israel, 32–34, 39–40; as a lion, 152, 156–57, 213; love of for his people, 7–8, 13–15, 101–2, 132–33, 401–2, 906n12; majesty of, 405; mercy of, 82, 122–26, 143, 216, 260, 262, 267, 278–79, 297, 300, 303, 306, 309, 310, 311, 346, 407, 607, 695, 721, 735, 738, 744, 786; missionary heart of, 267; of the New and Old Testaments, 418–19; patience of, 38, 131, 548–50, 721–22; pity of, 131; power of, 80, 129–32, 270, 299, 321; presence of, 265, 270, 273, 566, 580, 607, 630, 657; promises/plans /purposes of, 14–15, 78, 127, 129–32, 148, 151, 157, 286, 297, 299, 562–64, 605, 634, 654–55, 674–75, 687–90, 746; providence of, 259; purity of, 798; redemption of Israel from slavery in Egypt, 32; as a refuge to his people, 146–47; relationship with Israel, 28, 41–42; repentance of, 297–301; as the restoring father, 82–84; righteousness of, 199, 254, 328, 351, 385, 458, 640–41, 676; as the ruler of history, 155–56; and the "seed of God," 790–91, 910n23; seeking, 40, 43–45, 192–97, 199, 539, 540–41; singing of, 552–53; sorrow of, 80; sovereignty of, 132, 239, 270, 280, 298, 440, 551, 761; there is no savior but, 95–97; universal scope of redemptive work of, 403; will of, 128; wrath of, 83, 321, 437, 440–43, 536, 605,

General Index    965

709, 751, 766. *See also* discipline, of God; God's mountain, renewal and glorification of; God's mountain, three verdicts concerning the ruin of
God's mountain, renewal and glorification of, 353–57; three verdicts concerning ruin, 347–49, 349–51, 351–53
Gog, 885n10
Goldingay, John, 394, 858n21
Goliath, 448
Gomer, 11–12, 19, 26, 70, 206; daughter of, 12–13; sad end to her life, 22; unfaithfulness of to Hosea, 13
Gomorrah, 187
*Gracious and Compassionate God, A* (Timmer), 270
Graham, Billy, 769
Great Commission, the, 485
Greece/Greeks, 144, 545
greed, 35–36
*Gulag Archipelago, The* (Solzhenitsyn), 331

Habakkuk (book/prophecies of), 485–87, 505–6, 513–14; on committing to rejoicing, 517–19; concerns of about Judah's wickedness, 489–91; on date rapists, 508; on faithfully recounting God's past deeds for present comfort, 515–16; on humbly asking God to renew his past great deeds, 514–15; on the Lord's solution to Judah's wickedness, 491–93; and the message he saw, 487–89; on the path away from woe, 509–11; on prayer committed to patience and service, 499–501; on prayer expecting to live by faith, 501–2; on wicked bankers, 506; on wicked builders, 506–7; on wicked city planners, 507–8; on the worshiper of idols, 509
Habakkuk (person), 152, 171, 396, 523, 639
Hafemann, Scott, 839n1
Hagar, 329
Haggai (book/prophecies of), 557–58, 569–70, 579–80; on God's gracious promise, 562–64; on God's sobering complaint, 558–62; on the hope of God's deliverance in the future,

590–93; on human action, 884–85n1; on the lessons from an inglorious temple, 570–74; on the power of impurity, 580–82; on the problem of impurity, 582–84; on the promises of a glorious future for Israel, 574–77; on the provision for the impure, 584–87; on remembering God's faithfulness, 593–95; on the response of God's people (Israel/Jerusalem) to God's complaint, 564–67; on the second temple, 883nn8–9, 884n4; on serving faithfully in the present, 595–98
Haggai (person), 215, 657, 671, 882n3
Hamath, 208
Hammurabi, 478
Hassler, Jon, 25
Hayman, May, 514
Hazael, 161
Hebrew language, debates concerning the translations of in the Bible, 836n3, 836n7, 843n7, 845nn10–1, 846n4, 846n8, 848n13, 853n9, 856n14, 856–57n23, 858nn11–13, 861–62n28, 866n6, 867n3, 867n8, 867–68n13, 868n16, 871n16, 875n3, 880n2, 881n3, 884n9, 888n10, 889n4, 890–91n9, 891n14, 893n2, 894n16, 896n1, 897n20, 898n10, 902n3, 904n6, 904n10, 906–7n17, 907n18, 909–10n11, 911n10, 912n5, 913n11, 914–15n7, 915n11; on the first two Hebrew words of Zephaniah, 880n4; and qinah meter, 841n2; on the translation of *dābār*, 882n9; on the translation "empty oaths," 835n7, 837n11, 837n13, 838nn11–13, 839n3; on the translation of "fruit" and "bulls," 837n3; on the translation "love," 833n3; on the translation of "nations," 844n6; on the translation "overflowed," 833n4; on the translation of *rādam*, 848n18; on the translation of *yārad*, 848n20; on the use of numerous pronouns in Nahum, 871n3, 872n6; on the word *dqr*, 903n12; on the word form *riv*, 843n4

Heidelberg Catechism, 675–76
Heldai, 670, 672
Helem, 674
Hen, 674
Herod the Great, 234, 366, 726, 727
Herodotus, 613
Hezekiah, 9, 318, 327, 526, 745, 859n30
Hilkiah, 526
Hill, Andrew, 905n1, 906–7n17, 909nn8–9, 910n23, 912n5, 912n10
Hitler, Adolf, 443, 471
Hittites, 465
Hobbes, Thomas, 557
Holy Spirit, the (Spirit of God), 9, 127, 136–38, 140, 154, 350, 488, 541, 573, 620, 733; pouring out of God's spirit on God's people, 138–39; power of, 157, 299, 351. See also Pentecost
Hosea (book/prophecies of), 8, 55, 175, 832–33n4, 833n17; calling of Israel to repentance, 73–75; God's charges against Israel, 57–59; God's indictment of Israel's sins, 18–20, 59–62; and God's lawsuit against Israel, 32–34; on Israel's corrupt heart and corrupt gifts, 70–71; on Israel's repentance, 102–3; prophecy concerning the days of punishment to come for Israel, 65–66; prophecy concerning feast days and harvest festivals, 63–66; prophecy that Israel will bear no fruit, 66–68; soul-searching words of concerning wisdom, 106–7
Hosea (person), 7–8, 89, 152, 488, 669; as carried by the Holy Spirit, 9; children of (No Mercy and Not My People), 19; God's calling of, 26; God's command to love again, 26–28; as an engaging writer, 63; family situation of, 29–30; lack of information concerning, 9; marriage of, 11–12; ministry of, 10–11; perseverance of, 75–76; symbolic acts of, 11. See also Gomer
Huldah, 152, 527, 528, 529
human trafficking, 144, 145

idolatry, 58, 206, 319, 372, 509, 695, 736; danger of, 464–67; deceptiveness of, 462–64; hope for idolaters, 467–70; unexpected results of, 59. See also Baal/Baal worship; Baalism
idols: at Samaria, 72; skillfully made idols, 94–95. See also Jacob, and the idols
Idumea, 234
Isaac, 193, 230, 735
Isaiah, 160, 171, 234, 240, 276, 288, 318, 366, 488
Ishmael, 329–30
Israel/Israelites, 28–29, 50, 137–38, 160, 169–70, 229–30, 232, 245, 246, 285, 435, 606, 724, 766–67, 810–13, 852n16, 861n14, 869n17; adulterous relationship with Nineveh, 873n17; conquest of Canaan, 423; and the end of God's patience concerning, 188–89; ending of their monarchy by Assyria, 40–41; faithlessness of in marriage, 782–84, 893–94n8; and the fruits of walking with God, 201–5; God's judgment of, 175–76; God's lawsuit against, 818–22; as God's privileged people, 178–80; God's verdict on Israel's sins, 181–82; and the golden calf, 305; living of under the lunar calendar, 225–26; mounting losses to Assyria, 71–75; plagues against sent by God, 187; postexilic community of, 565, 582–83, 633, 672, 681, 682, 695, 700, 711, 786, 794, 795, 838n2, 900n5, 915–16n20; prophets of, 427; release/deliverance of from slavery in Egypt, 79, 80–81, 96, 123–24; remnant of, 564; return of to God, 53–54; serving of Baal by, 22–23; sins of (greed, sexual immorality, irreverence), 172–75, 191, 390–91, 718; spiritual adultery of, 13; stubbornness of, 186–88; temple building of, 589–80; unfaithfulness of, 124–25; work of as the dew/lion among the nations, 865n22. See also Amos; God/Yahweh, indictment of Israel's people;

God/Yahweh, indictment of Israel's priests; God/Yahweh, redemption of Israel from slavery in Egypt; God/Yahweh, relationship with Israel; Habakkuk; Haggai; Hosea; Joel; Jonah; Malachi; Micah; Nahum; Obadiah; Zechariah; Zephaniah

Jacob (as Israel), 240, 244, 318, 330; remnant of, 368–70
Jacob (person), 38, 50, 601, 761–62, 763, 764, 886n3; dream of, 185; household of, 229–32; and the idols, 86–88
James, 136, 235, 285, 345, 496, 502, 541, 679
Janus, 569
Jebusites, 465
Jedaiah, 670, 672, 674
Jehoshaphat, 144
Jehozadek, 670
Jensen, Phillip, 154
Jephthah, 384
Jeremiah, 11, 27, 152, 171, 328–29, 485, 488, 528, 529, 607, 684, 859n31
Jeroboam I, 9–10, 34, 155
Jeroboam II, 9, 10, 40, 155, 261
Jerusalem, 170, 240, 245, 267, 278, 318, 325, 329, 346, 351–52, 389, 390, 395, 532, 548, 552, 671–72, 730, 744, 745, 751, 764, 839n1, 845n3, 862n4, 863–64n2; call of to assemble for war, 364; destruction of, 13; faithlessness of, 391–92; God's purposes for, 688–90; temple of, 647–50, 650–53, 676–77. *See also* Jerusalem, glorious future of
Jerusalem, glorious future of: enemies overthrown, 625–28; expansion of the population, 628–29; security and safety of, 629–31. *See also* Jerusalem, living in the light of Israel's glorious future
Jerusalem, living in the light of Israel's glorious future, 631; and the residents of Babylon, 631–33; and the residents of Israel, 633–34; and the whole earth, 634–35

Jesus Christ, 8, 11, 24, 29, 32, 74, 135–36, 140, 154, 158, 172, 178, 182, 186, 210, 213, 220, 235, 245–46, 255, 267, 274, 280, 286, 341, 372, 379, 382, 389, 407, 408–9, 423, 479–80, 502, 537–38, 701, 702–3, 715, 725, 738, 743, 766–67, 773, 778–79, 792, 816, 826–27, 850n24, 862n30, 895–96n19; compassion of, 480; death/crucifixion/suffering of, 27, 80, 311, 352–53, 368, 407, 420–21, 437, 458, 577, 597–98, 644, 657, 735; healing of the leper by, 586–87; as the incarnate Son of God, 566–67, 618; kingdom of, 235–36; meal of with Simon the Pharisee, 277; ministry of, 667; reflection of on God's character, 84; rejection of, 722–25; on responding to God's voice, 80; resurrection of, 80, 289, 425, 750; on serving God and money, 155; trusting in, 195; at the tomb of Lazarus, 311; weeping of over Jerusalem, 329; work of on earth, 19. *See also* Jesus Christ, disciples of; Jesus Christ, parables of; Sermon on the Mount
Jesus Christ, disciples of, 272, 273, 389, 738
Jesus Christ, parables of: parable of the rich king forgiving the debt of his servant, 308–9
Jews, 235, 259, 598, 717, 743, 744, 895–96n19; of the Dispersion/Diaspora, 403, 779, 909n22; Jewish sinners, 260
Jezebel, 334, 391, 537
Jezreel, 12, 24
Joel (book/prophecies of), 151; description of the locust on plague on Judah, 111–13, 143; on God's judgment, 119–20, 122; on invasion and God's army, 121–22; proclamation of concerning the "day of the Lord," 113–15; proclamation of concerning the day of prayer, 115–16
Joel (person), 139, 152
John (the apostle), 27, 136, 286, 345, 541, 679, 735
John the Baptist, 418, 727

Jonah (person and book of), 215, 480, 545, 846n2, 855n8, 847n10, 849n11, 852nn20–21, 853n6, 853n9, 855n5, 856n13; among the sailors on the stormy (cosmic) sea, 271–72, 850–51n1, 851–52n9; ascent to a new life, 286–89; confession of, 276–77, 850n15; descent into death because of his sin (entrance into Sheol), 282–84; desire of for death, 308, 855n7; and the disastrous consequences of his anger, 304–8; failed prophecy of, 854–55n23; flight from God to Joppa/Tarshish, 265, 304–5; God's commission to, 260–63; God's compassion toward, 308–313, 855–56n8; God's gracious pursuit of, 266–67; God's gracious pursuit of in the episode of the *qiqayon* plant, 309–10; historicity of, 846–47n3; hymn of thanksgiving, 289; judgment and deliverance from, 284–86; message, 854n14; obedience of, 292–93; portrait of God, 281–82, 855–56n8; prayer of from the belly of the fish, 282, 283, 288–89; prophetic purpose of, 855n4; recommissioning of, 293, 294; repentance (as a warning to Israel), 292–95; and the sailors' (as Gentiles/pagans) humble worship, 277–80; surprising response to God's commission, 263–66

Jonathan, 271

Joshua, 37, 185, 565, 566, 589, 639, 669, 670, 672, 673–74, 694, 706, 719; obedience of, 891n13

Josiah, 486, 523, 526, 528, 529, 531; and Zephaniah, 524, 670

Jotham, 9, 318

Judah, 9, 37–38, 47, 50, 51, 62, 74, 127, 155, 160, 171, 185, 208, 229–30, 232, 244, 245, 246, 250–51, 428, 429, 432–33, 523, 532, 541–44, 547, 655, 701, 712, 724, 730, 751, 833–34n5, 882n10; construction of fortified cities by, 61; God's solutions to Hudah's wickedness, 491–93; Habakkuk's concerns about their wickedness, 489–91; persistence of the spirit of Ahaz in, 365–66; sins of, 170–73. *See also* Joel (book/prophecies of), description of the locust on plague on Judah

Judas Iscariot, 724

Jude, 136

justice, 193, 202, 204, 306, 385, 825; restoration of, 205. *See also* God, justice of

Keller, Timothy, 304
Kidner, Derek, 73–74
King, Martin Luther, Jr., 204
kinship, 244–45
Kir, 844n1
Kiyyun, 205
Knox, D. B., 514
Knox, John, 514

Laban, 50
Lachish, 325–26, 328
Langewiesche, William, 269–70
Lazarus, 541
Leach, Robin, 184
Lee, R. G., 537
*Le Morte D'Arthur* (Malory), 897n1
Lessing, Doris, 331
"Letter from a Birmingham Jail" (King), 204–5
Levi, person of, 50
Levi (tribe/priests of), 35, 185; covenant with, 908n17
Leviathan, 850–51n1
Lewis, C. S., 693
*lex talionis* (the law of retribution), 335
Lloyd-Jones, Martyn, 42, 496–97, 516
Loane, Marcus, 514
Longman, Tremper, III, 871n3, 873n2
Lord Acton, 669, 894n1
Luther, Martin, 330, 375–76, 427, 448–49, 486, 641

Macintosh, A. A., 22, 41
Magonet, Jonathan, 849n8
Malachi (book/prophecies of), 757–58, 769–70, 793–94, 906n16, 911–12n1; on the condemnation of defiled worship,

773–76, 909n22; on the consuming fire to come, 800–803; on the cynic's complaint, 794–96; on defiled worship exposed, 770–73; on the demonstration of God's love, 760–63; on the God of justice, 796–97; on God's lawsuit against Israel, 818–22; on God's unchanging people, 810–13; on God's unchanging purpose, 813–16; on hope for the faithless, 789–92; on how Israel should live, 824–28; on Israel's faithlessness in marital life, 787–89; on Israel's faithlessness in marital union, 784–87; on Israel's faithlessness of in marriage, 782–84; on putting God to the test, 805–7; questioning of God's love in, 758–60; structure of the book, 905n1; on two fates awaiting Israel, 822–24; on the vindication of God's love, 763–67; on who can stand before the Lord, 797–98

Malachi (person), 234
Malory, Thomas, 897n1
Manasseh, 384, 457
Maraath, 325
Mareshah, 327
Mark, 272, 586–87, 728
Maroth, 325
marriage, 273, 909n6, 909n9; Christian marriage, 23; fidelity in, 789; intermarriage, 909n2; Israel's faithlessness of in marriage, 782–89. *See also* Solomon, marriages of to foreign women
Martha, 541
Mary, 541
Masoretes, 892n10
materialism, 10, 21
Mays, James Luther, 52, 64–65, 97, 351, 834n6
McComiskey, Thomas, 21, 71, 202
Medes, 440
Mencken, H. L., 793
menorah, the, 603, 657, 892n6, 892n17; super-menorah, 649, 655, 656
Merrill, Eugene H., 901n6
Mesopotamia, 157, 533, 872n11
Micah (book/prophecies of), 720, 859n32, 860n7, 860n11, 861n16, 861n23,
861n27, 862n5, 864n7, 867n1, 868–69n6; on the condemnation of oppressors, 332–37; on divine prosecution, 379–83; on divine provision, 362–64; of the fate of false gods and the failure of false hopes, 321–24; on the final judgment and deliverance of Israel, 370–73; final oracle of, 400–2; goal of the prophecies, 318–19; on God leading his people through danger to rest, 403–5; on hope in hopeless times, 393–97; on Jerusalem's verdict, 388–92; on the judgment/devastation of Samaria, 321–23; lament of, 387–88, 393, 867n2; on lies exposed, 337–39; opening oracle(s) of, 318, 328, 399–400; oracle of concerning national death, 360–62; oracle of the faithful king, 364–68; oracles of as a form of invitations to lament, 324–30; on the promised deliverance, 340–43; as "prophet of the poor," 860n4; redundancy of, 367; second oracle of, 318; on the transcendent judge and his universal judgment, 319–21

Micah (person), 171, 240, 318, 528, 857n2; challenges of his ministry, 319; Hebrew name of, 869n19; as a poet, 369
Midianites, 137
Mizpah, 40
Moab/Moabites, 160, 166–67, 234, 380, 390, 405, 542, 543, 544, 604, 777, 805, 784; deities of, 381
money, 21, 36, 88–89
Mordecai, 821
Moresheth-gath, 326–27, 328
Moses, 14, 26, 32, 68, 78, 132, 137, 167, 171, 172, 201, 205, 298, 305, 339, 391, 526, 606–7, 681, 752; Law of, 377–78, 594, 672, 726, 784, 785; and the Mosaic covenant, 262, 384, 558, 561, 660, 662, 673, 700, 720, 736, 784, 815, 900n4, 901–2n18; and the Mosaic Law, 637, 672, 772, 824, 909n8; revelation of God to, 417; and the Song of the Sea, 262, 346

Motyer, Alec, 155, 161
mountains, importance of in the Bible, 345–47
Mount Ebal, 345
Mount Gerizim, 345
Mount Moriah, 732
Mount of Olives, 745
Mount Sinai, 124, 345, 899n19; revelation of God to Moses at, 305, 660
Mount of Transfiguration, 8, 345
Mount Zion, 346–47, 352, 359–60, 368, 531, 623–24. *See also* God's mountain, renewal and glorification of; God's mountain, three verdicts concerning the ruin of:
*MS Estonia*, 269–70

Naaman, 293
Naboth, 12, 334, 391
Nadab, 328
Nahum (book/prophecies of), 873–74n7; on the certainty of Nineveh's destruction, 472–75; on the danger of idolatry, 464–67; dating of his prophecies, 876n1; on the deceptiveness of idolatry, 462–64; on the demise of Nineveh's shepherd, 477–81; on the failure of Nineveh's hopes, 475–77; final oracle of (restoring the glory of God's people), 434–37; on the God of refuge, 421–23; on the God of vengeance, 414–19; on the God of war, 419–21; on hope for idolaters, 467–70; on Nineveh's crimes and the consequences of, 452–56; opening hymn of, 414; poetry of, 440; on the power of God's wrath, 440–43; on removing the source of Judah's affliction, 428–31; song of (call to courage), 423–24; song of (call to hope), 424–25; on the tragic fate of Nineveh, 456–59; on the unassailable assurance of God's deliverance, 445–50; on the unspeakable sorrow of God's judgment, 443–45
Nahum (person of), 413–14, 486, 523; date of his ministry, 870n4
Nazirites, 175

Nebuchadnezzar, 167, 440, 743
Nehemiah (book of), 782
Nehemiah (person), 29, 630
"new covenant," the, 23, 861n16
New Testament, the, 29, 49, 136, 178, 182, 249–50, 401, 544, 620; New Testament churches, 139–40
Newton, John, 167, 397, 623
Niebuhr, Reinhold, 169
Nineveh/Ninevites, 261–62, 264, 278–79, 291–92, 303, 304, 306, 307, 413, 422, 428, 429, 435, 442–43, 464, 466–67, 548, 856n14, 871n21, 873n16; certainty of its destruction, 472–75; contrast of with Israel, 296–97; crimes of and the consequences of, 452–56; demise of, 477–81; failure of Nineveh's hopes, 475–77; repentance of, 295–97, 299, 854n15; tragic fate of, 456–59; transformation of, 299
Noah, 78
non-Christians, 210–11

Obadiah (book/prophecies of), 239, 240; announcement of God's decimation of Edom's resources, 242–44; announcement of God's decree of destruction against Edom, 241–42; comfort of offered to Judah, 249–50; on Edom's day of decision, 250–51; eight prohibitions/commands issued to Edom, 250–51; on God's justice concerning Edom, 251–54
Obadiah (person), 152, 239–40, 763
obedience, 62, 295, 525, 564–65, 567, 573–74, 596. *See also* Jonah, obedience of
Old Testament, 132, 153, 182, 216, 303, 401, 536, 543, 623, 717, 816, 849n10, 859n24, 859n33; importance of Old Testament religion, 886n8; Old Testament prophets, 140
Omri, 391
*Ozmandias* (Shelley), 461

Packer, J. I., 263
Parsagadae, 613, 630

Passover, 526
Paul, 27, 58, 61, 99–100, 136, 167, 195, 235, 343, 383, 386, 395, 405, 418, 434, 448, 459, 481, 488, 496, 502, 541, 565, 629, 640, 653, 767, 816; on Christ's resurrection, 289; command to the Philippians, 566; declaration of that all have sinned and fallen short of the glory of God, 159, 169; on the "double honor" of elders who labor in preaching, 36; hatred of the Christian Church, 311–12; on marriage, 787, 792; message to the Galatians, 206; as a Pharisee, 312; theology of, 486; warning to Timothy, 173
Pentecost, 127, 136, 138–39
Persia/Persians/Persian Empire, 234, 545, 573–73, 590, 596–97, 611, 613, 696, 795, 882n2, 911n4, 911n6
Peter (Simon Peter), 8–9, 13, 74, 136, 139, 140, 141, 234, 235, 345, 428, 488, 541, 620; denial of Jesus by, 167
Pharaoh, 78, 272, 366, 406, 407, 418, 735
Pharaoh Neco, 528
Pharisees, 277, 296–97, 301, 311, 312, 418, 773
Philistia/Philistines, 144, 544, 695–96, 702
Phineas, 776–78
Phoebe, 541
pornography, 89
prayer, 116, 127–28, 129–32; answered prayer, 132
Presbyterian Church, 883n6
pride, 239; of place, 891n1
*Prodigal God, The* (Keller), 304
prosopopoeia, 849n2
prostitution, 68, 89, 163, 323, 858nn20–21; temple prostitution, 65, 323
Protestant Reformation, the, 640

*qal wahomer* ("from the light to the heavy"), 770, 771
Qumran, 824

Rahab, 850–51n1
Rebekah, 761

Rehoboam, 153, 724
repentance, 47–48, 60, 102–3, 114, 167, 287, 319; essentials of, 126; high cost of refusing to repent, 52–54; refusal to repent, 50–52; true repentance, 48–49. *See also* God, repentance of; Jonah, repentance (as a warning to Israel); Nineveh/Ninevites, repentance of; Zechariah (book/prophecies of), and the portrait of repentance
Rephidim, 805–6
*Return of the King, The* (Tolkien), 693
rich/greedy persons, lifestyle of, 184–86
righteousness, 193, 202, 405, 640, 799; sowing of, 73–75. *See also* God, righteousness of
Roberts, J. J. M., 517
Robertson, O. Palmer, 430, 487
Robin Hood, 897n2
Rogland, Max, 887n18
Rome/Romans, 144
Ruth, 27, 98, 785
Ryle, J. C., 514

Sabbath, 225
Sabeans, 144
sacrifices/burnt offerings, 34, 35, 50, 51, 55, 60, 65, 90, 183, 185, 202, 203, 205, 277–78, 287, 332, 383, 534, 563, 577, 580, 583, 585, 590, 644, 673, 681, 753, 773, 775, 812, 842n8, 862n7, 908n11; corrupt sacrifices, 778; human sacrifices, 94–95; spiritual sacrifices, 620
salvation, 11, 172–73, 291, 295, 330, 335, 343, 382, 395, 430, 594, 852n16
Samaria, 13, 51, 73, 182, 207, 351, 858n19, 862n4, 867n4; aristocratic prominence of, 208–9; idols of, 72, 322-23; judgment upon, 321–23, 324; military might of, 211; plans that are the opposite of God's plans, 212–13; wealth of, 209–11
Samson, 42, 137
Samuel, 185
Sarah, 330
Sarai, renaming of, 330

Sargon II, 323
Satan, 145, 227, 421, 449, 472, 481, 509, 515, 617, 638, 766, 806
Saul (Paul), 123
Saul (king), 37, 681, 726
Scythians, 888n12
Sennacherib, 318, 859n23, 872n7
Sermon on the Mount, 195, 822
Shalman, 75
Shalmaneser V, 323
Shaphir, 325, 328
Shechem, 50–51
Shelley, Percy, 461
Sheol, 265, 266, 274, 283–84, 286, 308, 455, 478, 501, 806, 851n7, 851–52n9
shepherds, 366–67, 403–4
Sidon, 144, 694, 695, 696
Sikkuth, 205
Simeon, 51
Simeon, Charles, 56, 514, 518, 519
Simon, Uriel, 855n5
Simon the Pharisee, 277
*Simon's Night* (Hassler), 25
sin/sinners/wickedness, 60, 61, 125, 147, 167, 208, 263, 267, 299, 301, 332, 334–35, 379, 282, 391, 395, 457, 639, 702; God's judgment of, 116–17, 323–24; God's triumph over, 405–9; Israel's addiction to, 73; Jewish and Gentile sinners, 260; seriousness of, 786. *See also* Israel, sins of (greed, sexual immorality, irreverence); Judah, sins of
Sippar Cylinder, the, 647
slavery, 60–61, 144, 162–63, 173
Smith, G. A., 259
Snyman, S. D., 909n22, 910n14
Sodom, 187
Solomon, 9–10, 67, 155, 230, 326, 574, 648, 902n20; dedication prayer of, 339; marriages of to foreign women, 785–86
Solzhenitsyn, Aleksandr, 331, 336, 860n1
Song of the Sea, 285, 594
songs, 203
Spurgeon, Charles, 800
Stek, John, 846n3, 847n7, 855n4

Stuart, Douglas, 60–61, 295–96
suzerain vassal treaties, 866n7
Sweeney, Marvin, 551
Syria/Syrians, 240, 245, 246

Tabor, 40
Tarshish, 292
Tekoa, 153
Teman, 515
Ten Commandments, 33, 58, 172; the Tenth Commandment, 333
Thebes, 463, 464
theology/theologians, 287; Christian theologians' interpretation of Micah 5:2, 865n16; confused theology of the Galatians, 13; and divine condescension, 298–99; escapist theology, 200–1; orthodox theology, 275; of Paul, 486; Zion theology, 372
Tiemeyer, Lena-Sophia, 909–10n11
Timmer, Daniel, 270, 275, 856n13, 876n8, 876–77n14
Timothy, 173
Titus, 541
Tobijah, 670, 672, 674
Tobin, Richard, 439
Tolkien, J. R. R., 693
Torah, the, 278, 345, 384, 580, 911n4
trial by ordeal, 284–85; the river ordeal, 285
Trible, Phyllis, 305, 849n2, 849n11, 850n15
Trinity, the, 136
Tyre, 144, 160, 163–64, 167, 694, 695, 696

United States. *See* America/Americans
Ussishkin, David, 325–6
Uzziah, 9, 155, 673, 745

Verhoef, Pater, 907n1, 907n18
Vos, Geerhardus, 763

Waltke, Bruce, 366, 370, 860n4, 866n21, 867n3
Webb, Barry, 644
Wesley, John, 486
West, Don, 503

*Why Does God Allow War?* (Lloyd-Jones), 42
Wiccans, 883n6
Wolters, Al, 889n2, 893n1, 897n20, 899n22, 901n11
worship, 202, 204; improper worship of God, 10
Wright, Christopher, 859n31

Xerxes, 726
Xi Jinping, 462

Yates, Kyle, 213

Zaanan, 325
Zaraphath, 293
Zechariah (book/prophecies of), 601–3, 659–60, 669–70, 679–80, 693–94, 705–6, 717–19, 729–30, 741–42, 886n7, 889n3, 889n8, 889–90n14, 890n8, 893n20, 897n7; on the angel's lament, 616–18; on both a scattered and gathered people, 737–39; on the building of God's house, 650–53; on the cleansing of God's people, 735–37; on the coronation, 672–74; on the day of deliverance, 745–47; on the day of great trial, 742–45; on the day of holiness to the Lord, 752–54; on the day of new creation, 746–50; on the day of reckoning, 750–52; on death being the shepherd, 725–28; on the demands of the law, 680–83; on the deportation of idolaters, 662–65; on the Divine Warrior, 904n4; on God guiding his flock, 713–15; on God protecting his flock, 708–11; on God restoring his flock, 712–13; on God sustaining his people (providing for his flock), 655–57, 706–8; on God's final victory, 701–3; on God's provision for the high priest, 638–45; on God's return to the temple, 694–97; on the judgment of apostates, 660–62; on the Lord's gracious response, 618–21; and the meaning of the horsemen, 612–14; on the memorial, 674–76, 895n15; and the message of the horsemen, 614–15; on the newly fashioned crown, 670–72; night visions of, 637–38, 648–49, 660–61, 665–66, 667, 890n3, 892n8; on the outlines of a tragedy, 719–22; and the portrait of repentance, 608–10; on the rejection of the Good Shepherd, 722–25; on a repentant people, 732–35; sign-act of, 719, 724, 725–26, 901n12; on the strength of the people, 730–33; on the vindication of God's servants, 653–55. *See also* Jerusalem, glorious future of; Zechariah, on the grace of the gospel; Zechariah, on the Messiah coming for his people
Zechariah, on the grace of the gospel, 683; and the new blessing, 685–87; and the new city, 683–85; and the new life, 687–88; on the new people, 690–91; on the new season, 688–90
Zechariah, on the Messiah coming for his people, 697–98; on the character of the king, 698–99; on the mission of the king, 699–701
Zechariah (person), 215; surprising call of from God, 603–6
Zephaniah (book/prophecies of), 531–32, 547–48; on the basic steps to renewal, 525–26; on the end of the wicked, 536–37; on God's patience, 548–50; on God's renewal, 550–52; on God's singing, 552–53; on renewal in one's own time, 527–28; on renewal's rewards and limits, 526–27; on searching for the wicked, 534–36; on seeking the Lord, 540–41; on woe to distant lands, 544–46; on the woe coming to the neighboring lands of Judah, 541–44
Zephaniah (person), 171, 486, 523–24, 607; and Josiah, 524, 670
Zerubbabel, 29, 564, 565, 566, 589, 593, 596, 597, 628, 653, 654, 677, 694, 706, 885n2, 885n12
Zion, 147

# Index of Sermon Illustrations

*Accountability to God*
The abundance of spiritual helps—Bibles, Christian colleges, biblical resources, and churches—in the United States means few people can say they know nothing of Christianity and its claims, 172

*Anger toward God*
The author compares his young daughter's temper tantrums to Jonah's anger over the repentance of Nineveh, 304
Phyllis Trible: "Jonah accuses and condemns Yahweh for being Yahweh" (see full quote), 305–6

*Atonement*
Barry Webb: "What Zechariah has just seen done symbolically for Joshua the high priest will one day be done actually for the whole land . . . when the Messiah comes" (see full quote), 644
Gordon Wenham: "Whereas it was Phinehas' spear that pierced the sinners that made atonement for Israel, it was the nails and the spear that pierced Jesus that made atonement for the sins of the whole world," 778

*Betrothal*
Douglas Stuart: Betrothal "refers to the ancient Israelite practice of settling the marriage contractually" (see full quote), 27

*Biblical History*
The Bible is honest and open about our spiritual ancestors, unlike our common tendency to shield younger generations from knowledge of older generations' sins, 85
People tend to leave out unpleasant details of family history, but Hosea tells how Ephraim was crooked from the start, 89

*Christian Marriage*
Christian marriage seen as a covenant relationship, 23
Young people often see love as eternal and unending, failing to understand that it is a commitment made by choice, 26

*The Church*
John Newton wrote his great hymn "Glorious Things of Thee Are Spoken" by borrowing Scriptural language describing Jerusalem, but Israel often saw the city as less than glorious, 623–24

*Consummation*
Elizabeth Achtemeier: "The time is coming for the covenant people when all the earth will be quiet" (see full quote), 621
John Flavel: "It will doubtless be a part of our entertainment in heaven, to view with transporting delight how the designs and methods were laid to bring us hither," 690
Just as writers of secular literature love the theme of the rightful king returning to set things right, Zechariah proclaimed that Israel's King would come with righteousness, deliverance, and peace, 707

*Crying Out to God*
J. A. Motyer: "The humble cry out to the Lord (Ps. 10:17) and seek him (Ps. 69:32)" (see full quote), 540

*Discipline*
Discipline is compared to basketball and track practices, study of Greek and Hebrew, writing essays and lectures, and punishment from parents. The best forms of discipline are born from love, 17–18
A. A. Macintosh: Discipline "denotes both instruction and chastisement" (see full quote), 41
Martyn Lloyd-Jones: "What if war has come because we were not fit for peace" (see full quote), 42
James Luther Mays: "In their very search for help they fly into the real danger that threatens them," 52
Good human disciplinarians offered as a picture of God's good discipline, 183

*Exile*
James L. Mays: "When the celebrants end up in foreign lands, the cult will end" (see full quote), 64–65
The author compares the Assyrian treatment of exiled captives to Japanese forced marches of Allied soldiers in World War II and the United States' forced move of native American tribes, 81

*Faith in God*
F. F. Bruce: "As the sure-footed hind makes its way in rocky and precipitous places without slipping, so the prophet's faith empowers him to surmount his adversities" (see full quote), 519
Iain Duguid: "As we wait for the final shaking of the heavens and earth, our calling is to be faithful. . . . We are to be faithful in the little things" (see full quote), 598

The phrase "Hurry up and wait" is sometimes used humorously to describe life in the U.S. Army, but that is literally what God wanted postexilic Israel to do—through Haggai, he called them to work diligently to rebuild the temple and then wait faithfully, 589

*Family Troubles*
Difficulties in family life are often hardest on children, prompting adults to shield their children from unpleasant realities, 18

*Fatherhood of God*
The author compares Israel to the kind of foolish and heartless child no human parent wants, 78

*Forgetting God*
The author likens Martin Luther's final sermon—in which he rebuked the city of Eisleben for forgetting the gospel—to Micah's charge (In Mic. 6:1–8) that the people of Israel had forgotten God, 375–76
Martin Luther: "There is preaching every day, often many times every day, so that we soon grow weary of it" (see full quote), 376
Samuel Johnson: "Men more frequently need to be reminded than informed," 609

*God*
John Calvin: God uses "a mode of speaking that ought to be sufficiently known to us," 298
John Calvin: "Strictly speaking, no repentance can belong to God: and it ought not be ascribed to his secret and hidden counsel" (see full quote), 298

*God as Controller of Events*
The author compares the sudden sinking of the *MS Estonia* on the Baltic Sea in 1994 to the sudden chaos that came upon the ship carrying Jonah to Tarshish, 269

The author mentions his children's fascination with "Shark Week" to illustrate the common human fear of sea creatures, but he notes that Jonah shows that the sea and all it contains are under God's rule, 281

Stephen Dempster: "Any Israelite child would know that the curse was changed into a blessing in Balaam's mouth because of the intervention of Yahweh" (see full quote), 381

Charles Spurgeon: "The same sun which melts wax hardens clay," 800

*God's Care for His People*

David Garland: "The covenant people know a security that the idolaters can never experience" (see full quote), 510

Martyn Lloyd-Jones: "The Bible . . . plainly shows that my comfort and consolation lies in facts—the fact that God has done certain things and they have literally happened" (see full quote), 516

*God's Glory*

Bruce Waltke: God will "add even greater luster to his name in the last days when he hurls Israel's iniquities into the depths of the sea" (see full quote), 406

Elizabeth Achtemeier: "The God portrayed here is really God, different from all lesser imitations" (see full quote), 419

*God's Goodness*

Thomas Renz: "The goodness of YHWH . . . is affirmed here not over against his wrath but because of it" (see full quote), 422

*God's Immutability*

Martin Luther: "If God were not immutable, who can believe his promises?" 808

*God's Love and Compassion*

Just as Tim Keller showed in *The Prodigal God* that Jesus's parable of the prodigal son is primarily about not the father's love for the prodigal but for the older brother, so Jonah is primarily about not God's love for wicked Nineveh but for the hard-hearted prophet, 304

Bryan Estelle: "What we see in the final chapter [of *Jonah*] is God's pity not just on the weak and helpless but on the strong and the mighty" (see full quote), 312

Bruce Waltke: God "initiates the trial not to condemn Israel but to save them" (see full quote), 378

Mark Gignilliat: "The day of visitation yields to the day of restoration," 402

Geerhardus Vos: "The best proof that [God] will never cease to love us lies in that He never began," 763

*God's Omniscience*

The author recalls a song from his childhood that included the line "There's an all-seeing eye watching you" and notes that the people whom the prophet Zephaniah addressed needed to hear something like this line as a warning, 536

*God's Patience*

Tremper Longman III: "God's patience, not powerlessness, is responsible for the impression of divine inactivity in the face of evil," 417

*Gomer*

The author describes the prophet Hosea's wife as a party girl with many lovers, 21

*Good Works*

Martin Luther: "God doesn't need your good works, your neighbor does," 811

*Hell*

Hell is sometimes falsely depicted as a cool, hip place, like a popular nightclub, 73

The author compares the Civil War-era border war between his home state of Kansas and Missouri to the border war waged by Ammon, which resulted in brutalities to women and children, 166

*Human Dignity*
J. A. Motyer: Aram "had no liberty to treat people as if they were things" (see full quote), 161

*Human Pride*
Duane Garrett: Amos "speaks to the conceit of the aristocracy of Samaria, who think of themselves as the best people of the best country in the world," 208

*Idolatry*
Charles Simeon warned of the human tendency to claim to know God but trust in lesser things, 56
Americans engage in idolatry in numerous ways, most of which are attached to the love of money, 58–59
James L. Mays: "The development of cultic sanctuaries was simply turning part of the profit back into the business" (see full quote), 70
Many American churches are as spacious as shopping centers and as well-equipped as spas, 71
J. A. Motyer: "Money making and personal covetousness ruled all" (see full quote), 155
James Limburg: "When the motivation for worship is recognition by others and satisfaction for self, then that religion is rebellion, says the prophet," 186
In the author's view, the greater danger for the church in the United States is not a completely secular culture but people's preference for phony gods instead of the true God, 228
Daniel Timmer: "Their own gods . . . had failed to respond, or were unable to aid them" (see full quote), 270

James Luther Mays: "The 'nouveau riche' in Jerusalem had drawn prophet and priest into their own environment where money talked louder than God," 351
Elizabeth Achtemeier: "We take refuge in the petty powers of this world and 'do not look to the Holy one of Israel'" (see full quote), 455
Elizabeth Achtemeier: "The false gods of the tyrants and oppressors and military powers will be unable to save their people from the curse of the only true God," 509
John Calvin: "As then idols are dead things, it follows that they are most palpable impostures of Satan" (see full quote), 509

*Israel's Rejection of God*
Thomas McComiskey: "Israel did not acknowledge Yahweh as the source of her material blessing" (see full quote), 21
In a commercial, a father holds a young boy up so he can dunk a basketball; the child then exclaims, "I did it!," illustrating Israel's failure to acknowledge God's help, 79

*Judgment of Sin*
Charles Simeon: "Most assuredly the wrath of God shall follow and overtake sin" (see full quote), 56
Americans are prone to covet riches and power, failing to recognize that God judges sin, 117
The author tells of hearing of the Japanese invasion of Singapore in 1942 and likens it to an invasion of Israel prophesied by Joel, 121
Martin Luther King Jr.: "The judgment of God is upon the church as never before" (see full quote), 204–5
Kyle Yates: Amos "has reached the sad and somber conclusion that only destruction and captivity lie ahead," 213

Index of Sermon Illustrations  979

Johan Renkema: "When the nations are confronted with YHWH's [God's] judgment, the refugees in their midst are also in danger" (see full quote), 253

The author relates his experience of living in a state that practiced capital punishment, where news coverage of an execution often mentioned how long the prisoner had been on death row—it was often many years, but always the condemned man's time ran out, 215

W. H. Auden's poem "September 1, 1939" illustrates how human beings like to assure themselves that everything will be okay, much as the Israelites were doing before Micah's opening oracle bluntly told them that judgment was coming, 317

Stephen Dempster: "As the one from who all power is derived, [God] demands an accounting for how that power is used," 336

The author compares God's verdict against the Israelites in Micah 6:9–7:7 and the ensuing cry of anguish to a modern judge banging his gavel and so provoking a cry of pain, terror, and loss, 387

Klass Spronk: "The message of [God's] severe judgment is a comfort to those oppressed by evil powers" (see full quote), 424

O. Palmer Robertson: "The judgment of Nineveh must be viewed from the perspective of God's intent to show mercy to his people" (see full quote), 430

Klass Spronk: God humiliated Nineveh "to better represent her true nature than her former outward appearance of beauty," 457

Just as Jerusalem, Rome, Berlin, and Tokyo stand as examples of the tables being turned on oppressors, so the oppressive Babylon would itself be oppressed, Habakkuk warned, 508

Elmer Martens: The day of the Lord was a time when God "filled the whole horizon," 532

Famed Baptist preacher R. G. Lee often preached a sermon titled "Payday Someday" to teach that though God's judgment may be delayed, it will fall eventually, 537

Johnny Cash: "You can run on for a long time . . . sooner or later God'll cut you down," 537

Iain Duguid: God's "future intervention casts its shadow forward into the present," 596

Poet T. S. Eliot wrote, "This is the way the world ends, Not with a bang but a whimper," but the prophet Zechariah declared just the opposite: The world will end with a bang, 741

The expression "War is hell" is not literally true, but the scenes of warfare presented by the prophet Zechariah present a small glimpse of the eternal fate that awaits those outside of Christ, 744

*Justice*

James Boice: God's "love is not incompatible with justice," 180

Justice is an increasing topic of conversation in America as people long for an end to disparities and equal shares of the nation's financial pie, 202

Martin Luther King Jr.: "Injustice anywhere is a threat to justice everywhere," 204

Resistance to Jim Crow segregation laws in Alabama shows that a more just society is possible, 204–5

*Kingdoms of the World*

Waylon Bailey: "God saw [Babylon's] plan from a different perspective. Such a plan incurred guilt and thus promised sin's wages—death," 507

The Colossal Lion of Assyria at the British Museum was once a proud symbol of the Assyrian Empire, but Habakkuk did not hesitate to taunt the Assyrians with that very symbol (3:11), 445–46

The author cites the poem *Ozymandias* by Percy Shelley and comments by the president of the People's Republic of China as examples of the national pride, self-confidence, and self-reliance for which Nahum taunted Nineveh, 461–62

Almost every profession has an ultimate accomplishment—an Oscar, a Pulitzer Prize, a gold medal—but for a king in the ancient world, it was construction of a temple for his god, 647

*Lamentation*
The author recounts a funeral for a man from Cameroon—which was marked by loud cries of grief and other expressions of lamentation—as a picture of the opening words of Nahum 3, 451

*Materialism*
The author notes the pervasiveness of materialism in America and notes that God may use privation to cause people to return to him, 21

*Natural Disasters*
The author recalls 2011 as a year of disasters and describes the book of Joel as helpful in knowing how we should think about such events, 111

*Overcoming Doubts*
Martyn Lloyd-Jones: "We must . . . remind ourselves of those things of which we are absolutely certain, things which are entirely beyond doubt" (see full quote), 496–97

*Postexilic Israel*
The words that the philosopher Thomas Hobbes used to describe life in medieval Europe—"solitary, poor, nasty, brutish, and short"—could also be used to describe the existence of the Jewish people after their return from exile, 557

*Prayer*
Don West: Delayed or denied answers to prayer "are necessary ingredients in the struggle that each Christian assumes when he or she carries the shield of faith," 503

James Montgomery Boice: "What are the elements of faithful prayer? The first and most essential is humility" (see full quote), 514

Habakkuk teaches us to pray by demonstrating the faith of the many biblical and historical examples of mothers who prayed for their families, 495–96

*Predatory Priests*
The Pardoner in Chaucer's *Canterbury Tales* is a preacher who bilks the public, much like the predatory priests of Hosea's day, 31–32

Duane Garrett: "During a time of prosperity the number of people free to enter a religious vocation increases" (see full quote), 35

James Luther Mays: The "priests have changed the cult into a way for them to make a living" (see full quote), 35–36

*Presuming God's Help*
In Martyn Lloyd-Jones's book *Why Does God Allow War?*, he notes that at the time of World War II, British citizens asked why God had allowed Nazi Germany to oppress them. Though they had lived with no thought of God in good times, they expected his aid, 42

*Privileges and Responsibilities*
The author recalls his father giving his brother a stern lecture about responsibility when he was given the privilege of buying a .22-caliber rifle and then receiving a similar lecture when he received the privilege of driving, 177

The author tells of marking the anniversary of his call to preach God's Word as part of reflecting on God's goodness to him, 178

*Prophetic Warnings*
Public-safety warnings often go unheeded in America, much as prophetic warnings of judgment went largely unheeded in ancient Israel, 191–92
The author compares Amos's message to that of the Ghost of Christmas Yet to Come in Charles Dickens's *A Christmas Carol*, 192
The author compares Israel's failure to heed Amos's call for Israel to seek the Lord and live to the sadness that surrounds the funeral of a young person who commits suicide, 197
Amy Erickson: "The instant that Jonah's five-word prophecy leaves his mouth, 'the people of Nineveh believe in God'" (see full quote), 299
Stephen Dempster: "Micah . . . flatly contradicted false assurances of prosperity in the face of massive injustice" (see full quote), 318
The author recounts his freshman-year college roommate's very loud alarm clock to picture the "blaring alarm" of Micah 4:8 and what follows, 359
O. Palmer Robertson: Habakkuk "must be heard because he was the bearer of God's message, not because of what he was in himself," 487
The struggle of modern military veterans to describe their war experiences reflects Habakkuk's strain to capture the disorienting horror of warfare, 440
Nahum saw the Assyrian Empire in the same situation as Nazi Germany in April 1945—surrounded by enemies and on the verge of collapse, 471
The author notes that we tend to set our hopes on people and institutions—professors, politicians, preachers, and so forth—but Nahum warned Israel not to have confidence in things of this world, 476–77
J. A. Motyer: Those who heed God's warnings are "those at the bottom of life's heap, those who can be pushed around by the influential, by vested interests," 540
Just as the Roman god Janus supposedly had two faces, one for looking to the past and one to the future, Christians do well to heed the call of the prophet Haggai to both look back and look forward, 569
The author teaches his children to not always point out if something is wrong, deficient, inferior, or lacking, but the prophet Haggai did not hesitate to tell the postexilic Israelites that their temple was inferior to the temple of their forefathers, 570–71
Presbyterians are fond of looking back to the "good old days," but God instructed Israel to look to the past not because he wanted them to return there but so that they could learn something about the future, 574
Al Wolters: Zechariah 11 is "a chilling account of a God who shows no pity to his people" (see full quote), 719

*Prophets*
Martin Luther: "They have a queer way of talking . . . so that you cannot make head or tail of them or see what they are getting at" (see full quote), 427
The author tells of feeling a debt to Zephaniah because he did his dissertation on the book, launching his academic career, and believes all Christians owe a lot to the prophet, 554
Painter Salvador Dali said that surrealism seeks to destroy "what it considers to be shackles limiting our vision," and in a similar way, Zechariah's goal was to expand Israel's limited vision, 611

We have all sorts of rules about the right clothing for specific occasions, but Zechariah's fourth night vision—concerning Joshua the high priest—is all about wearing the wrong clothes for an occasion, 637–38

*Refusal to Repent*
The author likens Israel's failure to believe God would judge the nation to America's refusal to face the reality of death, 97–98

*Regeneration*
John Calvin: Christians may arise daily "by the power of God, who by his voice alone can restore us to life" (see full quote), 364
Modern people can transform their lives in countless ways, but the prophet Zechariah shows, only God can transform the human heart, 729–730

*Repentance*
Uriel Simon: "The reactions of the gentile sailors and the prophet of the Lord to the looming peril of death by drowning are poles apart" (see full quote), 278
Martin Luther: "It is certain, man must utterly despair of his own ability before he is able to receive the grace of God," 330
Aleksandr Solzhenitsyn: "There is nothing that so aids and assists the awakening of omniscience within us as insistent thoughts about one's own transgressions, errors, mistakes" (see full quote), 336
Martin Luther: "When our Lord and Master Jesus Christ said 'Repent' (Matthew 4:17), he willed the entire life of believers to be one of repentance," 610

*Restoration of Relationship*
Talk-show hosts might find Hosea's longing for Gomer pathetic or judge him to be codependent in a dysfunctional relationship, 20
In Jon Hassler's novel *Simon's Night*, the wife of the title character, Simon Shea, deserts him, but he never stops loving her, and they are eventually reconciled, 25

*Sabbath Observance*
Truett Cathy, founder of Chick-fil-A, explained that keeping restaurants closed on Sundays is a way to give employees rest, let them attend church if they wish, and contain costs; plus, he saw it as part of his family's Christian witness, 225–26

*Satan*
Martin Luther: "When the devil comes at night to worry me, this is what I say to him: 'Devil, I have to sleep now . . .'" (see full quote), 448–49

*Sinfulness*
The author relates the story of how the Watergate hearings seemed to bring daily revelations of wrongdoing in government and how Senator Sam Ervin quoted Galatians 6:7, 53
The author laments that despite the presence of numerous churches, Christian radio stations, and other evidences of Christianity, his home state is still a place of unbelief and sin, 61–62
The costs that sin demands from people's bodies and souls are easily seen: alcoholism, drug addiction, prostitution, oppression, and so on, 68
The people of Israel wanted to live as they wished with no consequences, much like Americans want healing from any and all diseases but refuse to practice disease prevention, 103–4
The author characterizes greed as a doorway to other sins, 172–73
The author likens the *Lifestyles of the Rich and Famous* television show to

Index of Sermon Illustrations 983

Amos's short tour of wealthy Israelites in Amos 4:1–5, 184
The author describes Ralph Waldo Beeson's gift to Samford University to found Beeson Divinity School as the antithesis of the Israelite greed Amos describes, 186
John Goldingay: "The single thing they're good at is doing what is bad" (see full quote), 394
Elizabeth Achtemeier: "Habakkuk's time is out of joint, as is every human era, because the world lives under slavery to sin rather than to the righteousness of God" (see full quote), 489
Just as Los Angeles is animated by the entertainment industry and Washington, D.C., is animated by politics, so ancient Nineveh was animated by violence, deceit, and theft, 452–53
People in Maine sometimes use the nonsensical phrase "You can't get there from here," but when it comes to human beings making their way to God, the phrase is literally true—they cannot escape their sinful state on their own, 579
King Midas needed to eat, but everything he touched became gold; in like manner, the Israelites needed to offer sacrifices to atone for sin, but everything they touched became unclean, 583
Elizabeth Achtemeier: "The leaders [of Israel] want a Messiah who can be bought. . . . In short, they want to run their own community" (see full quote), 724
Robert Robinson expressed the common Christian experience of wandering from God in his hymn "Come, Thou Fount of Every Blessing," which contains the line "Prone to wander, Lord, I feel it, prone to leave the God I love," a sentiment the Israelites understood and that motivated them to long for a shepherd, 705–6

Just as the National Holocaust Museum aims to help people remember what they might prefer to forget, Zechariah sought to remind the Israelites of their sinful and sordid past, 717–18
Elizabeth Achtemeier: "All our feeble claims to righteousness and faith, much less excuses for indifference and unbelief, will be unavailing" (see full quote), 801
Billy Graham said a person's checkbook reveals where his heart it, but it is really the actions indicated by expenses that show the heart's condition. That is why Malachi could tell the priests of Israel that their actions revealed that their hearts were far from God, 769–70

*Suffering of Christians*
Charles Simeon: "The Christian is not exempt from trials and troubles; yet is he far happier than any unregenerate man" (see full quote), 518

*Thankfulness*
J. A. Motyer: "The sense of prosperity, . . . joy and the reminder of belonging to the unique people of the Lord would have filled the minds of the worshipers" (see full quote), 224

*Trusting God*
J. J. M. Roberts: "Habakkuk is willing to cease from his complaints and to wait quietly for the vision's fulfillment" (see full quote), 517
May Hayman offered faithful service to the people of New Guinea in the face of danger until she was finally murdered by Japanese soldiers, 500
Just as reading Christian biographies and histories of Christian events can spark our hopes that past events will happen afresh in our day, Habakkuk noted that he had been told of what God had accomplished in the past, 514

Three couples known to the author lost daughters in their early years, but all three husbands and wives patiently endured and kept their Christian faith, just as Zephaniah called the Israelites to do, 552

*Trusting Self*
John Calvin: "Why is it that the great of this world, when they trust in their renown, in their might, in their munitions, in all the means they have to defend themselves with, act like they despise God" (see full quote), 207

*Truth Versus Falsehood*
Aleksandr Solzhenitsyn: "One word of truth outweighs the whole world" (see full quote), 331
Aleksandr Solzhenitsyn's *The Gulag Archipelago* exposed the truth about the Soviet Union, much as Micah's prophecies exposed the injustices of Israel, 331–32